TO THE STUDENT: Four helpful supplemental study aids for this textbook are available:

Student Guide by Dudley W. Curry and Frank H. Selto contains, for each chapter in this textbook, a detailed review of key ideas plus practice test questions and problems.

Working Papers by Dudley W. Curry provides partially filled in problem data and column headings for important in-text problems.

Practice Set (Chimes, Inc.) by Dudley W. Curry comprises a simulated case covering all the steps in the accounting cycle, tying together the fundamentals of bookkeeping and accounting, and including partially filled in working papers.

Spreadsheet Applications in Financial Accounting by Ali D. Payvandi and Wayne D. Robertson with revisions by Albert Fisher. This supplement leads students from a level of little or no experience in computers to a level where they can solve accounting problems using Lotus® 1-2-3®. It also includes a computer disk (for IBM PC computers and compatibles) that contains many partially completed problems and ample space for students to place all their assignments.

Introduction to
FINANCIAL
ACCOUNTING

PRENTICE-HALL SERIES IN ACCOUNTING

Charles T. Horngren, Consulting Editor

FOURTH EDITION

Introduction to Financial Accounting

Charles T. Horngren
Stanford University

Gary L. Sundem
University of Washington–Seattle

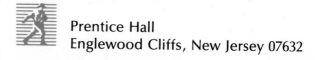
Prentice Hall
Englewood Cliffs, New Jersey 07632

Library of Congress Cataloging-in-Publication Data

Horngren, Charles T.
   Introduction to financial accounting/Charles T. Horngren, Gary
L. Sundem.—4th ed.
      p.   cm.—(Prentice Hall series in accounting)
   Includes bibliographical references.
   ISBN 0-13-476920-1
   1. Accounting.   I. Sundem, Gary L.   II. Title.
HF5635.H813   1990
657—dc20   89-22872
                                                              CIP

Editorial/production supervision: Eleanor Perz
Interior and cover design: Judith A. Matz-Coniglio
Cover photo: Miami, © Ed Taylor/FPG
Manufacturing buyer: Peter Havens

 © 1990, 1988, 1987, 1984, 1981 by Prentice-Hall, Inc.
A Division of Simon & Schuster
Englewood Cliffs, New Jersey 07632

Printed in the United States of America

10 9 8 7 6 5 4 3 2 1

ISBN 0-13-476920-1

Prentice-Hall International (UK) Limited, *London*
Prentice-Hall of Australia Pty. Limited, *Sydney*
Prentice-Hall Canada Inc., *Toronto*
Prentice-Hall Hispanoamericana, S.A., *Mexico*
Prentice-Hall of India Private Limited, *New Delhi*
Prentice-Hall of Japan, Inc., *Tokyo*
Simon & Schuster Asia Pte. Ltd., *Singapore*
Editora Prentice-Hall do Brasil, Ltda., *Rio de Janeiro*

To Professor Dudley W. Curry

Charles T. Horngren is the Edmund W. Littlefield Professor of Accounting at Stanford University. A graduate of Marquette University, he received his MBA from Harvard University and his Ph.D. from the University of Chicago. He is also the recipient of honorary doctorates from Marquette University and De Paul University.

A Certified Public Accountant, Horngren served on the Accounting Principles Board for six years, the Financial Accounting Standards Board Advisory Council for five years, the Council of the American Institute of Certified Public Accountants for three years, and as a trustee of the Financial Accounting Foundation for six years.

A member of the American Accounting Association, Horngren has been its President and its Director of Research. He received the Outstanding Accounting Educator Award in 1973, when the association initiated an annual series of such awards.

The California Certified Public Accountants Foundation gave Horngren its Faculty Excellence Award in 1975 and its Distinguished Professor Award in 1983. He is the first person to have received both awards.

In 1985 the American Institute of Certified Public Accountants presented its first Outstanding Educator Award to Horngren.

Professor Horngren is also a member of the National Association of Accountants, where he was on its research planning committee for three years. He was a member of the Board of Regents, Institute of Certified Management Accountants, which administers the Certified Management Accounting examinations.

Horngren is the co-author of three other books published by Prentice Hall: *Cost Accounting: A Managerial Emphasis, Sixth Edition,* 1987 (with George Foster); *Introduction to Management Accounting, Eighth Edition,* 1990 (with Gary L. Sundem); and *Accounting,* 1989 (with Walter T. Harrison, Jr.).

Charles T. Horngren is the Consulting Editor for the Prentice-Hall Series in Accounting.

Gary L. Sundem is Professor of Accounting at the University of Washington, Seattle. He received his B.A. degree from Carleton College and MBA and Ph.D. degrees from Stanford University.

Professor Sundem is currently Executive Director of the Commission on Accounting Education Change. He served as Editor of *The Accounting Review,* 1982–86. His other American Accounting Association positions have included membership on the Executive Committee, Chair of the Planning Committee for the Association's 1981 annual meeting, and Director of the AAA Doctoral Consortium.

A member of the National Association of Accountants, Sundem is past-president of the Seattle chapter. He has served on NAA's national Board of Directors, Committee on Academic Relations, and is currently on the Research committee.

Professor Sundem has numerous publications in accounting and finance journals, including *The Accounting Review, Journal of Accounting Research,* and *The Journal of Finance.* He received an award for the most notable contribution to accounting literature in 1978. He has made presentations at over 50 universities in the U.S. and abroad.

Sundem was chairman of the University of Washington's department of accounting in 1978–82 and 1988–89. He was selected as the Outstanding Accounting Educator by the Washington Society of CPAs in 1987. He has been a consultant to industry and government.

Contents

PREFACE xv

☐ PART TWO Major Elements of Basic Financial Statements

6 SALES REVENUE, CASH, AND ACCOUNTS RECEIVABLE 209

7 VALUING INVENTORIES AND MEASURING COST OF GOODS SOLD 255

8 LONG-LIVED ASSETS AND DEPRECIATION 317

9 LIABILITIES AND INTEREST 368

10 STOCKHOLDERS' EQUITY AND THE INCOME STATEMENT 438

11 STATEMENT OF CASH FLOWS 489

PART THREE Additional Elements of Financial Statements

12 INTERCORPORATE INVESTMENTS, INCLUDING CONSOLIDATIONS 532

13 INCOME TAXES, INCLUDING INTERPERIOD ALLOCATION 584

14 INTERNAL CONTROL 624

15 ANALYSIS OF FINANCIAL STATEMENTS 671

☐ PART FOUR The Contemporary Accounting Environment

16 FINANCIAL STATEMENTS: CONCEPTUAL FRAMEWORK AND INCOME MEASUREMENT 709

☐ PART ONE: Conceptual Framework of Accounting

Preface

Introduction to Financial Accounting is the first member of a matched pair of books that provides full coverage of the essentials of financial and managerial accounting. The second book is *Introduction to Management Accounting*. In combination, the pair can be used throughout two semesters or three quarters of introductory accounting.

Introduction to Financial Accounting is a textbook for introductory accounting courses that presuppose no prior knowledge of accounting. It deals with important topics that all students of management should study. Our goals have been to choose *relevant* subject matter and to present it *clearly* and *flexibly*. The book is oriented to the user of financial statements, but it gives ample attention to the needs of potential accounting practitioners.

Because financial accounting is so pervasive, an understanding of its uses and limitations is valuable whether the student eventually becomes a company president, a sales manager, a professional accountant, a hospital administrator, or a politician. In particular, knowledge of accounting for business is worthwhile because all of us relate to companies in one or more of the following ways: investors, managers, customers, creditors, government regulators, observers, or critics.

A philosopher once said, "You have to know what something *is* before you know what it *is used for*. When you know what it is used for, then you can decide what changes deserve serious thought." *Introduction to Financial Accounting* describes the most widely used accounting theory and practice. Emphasis is on *what accounting is* rather than *what it should be*. After all, beginning students must know what accounting today is really like before they can make judgments as to what changes in practice are desirable. Ample consideration is given to proposed changes in accounting throughout the book (especially in Chapter 16 on the conceptual framework), but the thrust is toward understanding generally accepted theory and practice.

This text stresses underlying concepts, but it makes them concrete with profuse illustrations, many taken from corporate annual reports. Moreover, accounting procedures such as transaction analysis, journalizing, and posting are given abundant consideration. For example, see the new sections on transaction analysis in Chapter 1. In this way, the reader obtains a thorough grasp of the fundamentals of accounting. The study of concepts develops understanding of procedures, and the study of procedures enriches understanding of concepts.

A major objective is to equip students with enough fundamental concepts and terminology so that they can comprehend a typical corporate annual report.

Flexibility has been a driving force in writing this book. Are you among the many instructors who favor solidifying the fundamentals by using lots of journal entries, T-accounts, work sheets, and special journals? Then see Chapters 3, 4, and 5, including its appendix, and the appendixes to Chapters 6, 11, and 14. Are you among the other instructors who favor downplaying the details and emphasizing concepts? Then consider skipping some of the material just cited, in whole or in part.

The flexibility of the book is illustrated by the heavy use of chapter appendixes. They give the instructor latitude in picking and choosing among various topics. In short, greater depth and breadth are available, depending on the preferences of the teacher. Moreover, parts of the bodies of some chapters can be omitted if desired. Prime candidates for exclusion can be found in Chapters 6–16. Examples are the following topics: any materials in Chapter 6, other than the valuation of accounts receivable, and the presentation of consolidated statements in Chapter 12.

A major feature is the use of the fundamental accounting equation as a central thread throughout the book for explaining new concepts and analyzing transactions. For example, consider the presentations in Chapter 9 on bonds, Chapter 11 on the statement of cash flows, Chapter 12 on intercompany investments, and Chapter 13 on interperiod income tax allocation. Such presentations give instructors immense latitude. They can use journal entries, or T-accounts, or the balance sheet equation format *exclusively*, if desired.

Additional features of this book include attempts to spark the reader's curiosity from the outset by:

1. Introducing financial statements of actual companies in Chapter 1.
2. Integrating a few financial ratios in an appendix to Chapter 2, a few more in Chapter 4, a few more in Chapter 6, and so on, rather than relegating all such matters of interpretation of financial statements to the rear of the book.
3. Introducing simple income tax aspects in Chapter 4 rather than later. Income taxes are not only important, they stimulate reader interest.
4. Providing a solid conceptual foundation in the first two chapters before covering the mechanics of journals, ledgers, and related procedural matters in Chapter 3.
5. Using a minimum of technical detail to introduce relatively complicated subjects and allowing chapter appendixes to examine the subjects in more depth. Examples are LIFO-FIFO in Chapter 7, compound interest in Chapter 9, and the statement of cash flows in Chapter 11.
6. Using published financial information as a basis for sections of assignment material in each chapter.
7. Presenting a set of learning objectives at the beginning of each chapter.

ALTERNATIVE WAYS OF USING THIS BOOK

Texts are fundamentally teaching instruments. Teaching is highly personal and heavily influenced by the backgrounds and interests of assorted students in miscellaneous settings. To satisfy this audience, a book must be a pliable tool, not a straitjacket.

In our opinion, the first eleven chapters provide the foundation for the field of financial accounting. These eleven chapters may be amplified by assigning other chapters in a variety of sequences that do not disrupt the readers' flow of thought. The most obvious candidates for insertion are:

☐   Chapters 1, 2, 3, 4, 5, 6, 7, 8, 9, 10, 11 and any of 12–16.

               ↑   ↑

             14*   11

             11   13

             16   16

* The appendix on special journals, which is needed as background for the practice set.

Chapter 14 deals with internal controls, cash, and special journals. The chapter appendix (special journals) may be assigned anytime after Chapter 5.

Chapter 11 may be assigned after Chapter 8 (or even after Chapter 5); it is placed as Chapter 11 because the statement of cash flows is an excellent vehicle for reviewing all the fundamentals of financial accounting.

ASSIGNMENT MATERIAL

As always, careful choices among the wide variety of assignment material in each chapter will slant the course toward various combinations of breadth and depth, theory and procedures, simplicity and complexity.

The assignment material contains sections called Understanding Published Financial Reports, which have exercises or problems that use information presented in actual corporate annual reports or news stories. In this way, some major points in the chapter will be underscored by "real world" illustrations. Most of the annual reports used are relatively recent. One complete annual report, that of House of Fabrics, Inc., is included as an appendix on pages 749–759. It is referred to in the last problem in each chapter. Using these problems will assure students that they can cope with real financial statements.

Special review assignment material is contained in Chapters 5 and 16. In addition, some assignments in Chapters 12–16 tend to crystallize previous work. The review assignment material for Chapter 16 is especially noteworthy. It uses corporate annual reports as a basis for review of all parts of the course. These cases or problems provide a splendid test of the student's overall comprehension. Their successful solution enhances a student's confidence enormously, especially because he or she is dealing with real companies' financial statements.

The front of the solutions manual contains several alternate detailed assignment schedules and ample additional suggestions to teachers regarding how best to use this book.

CHANGES IN THIS EDITION

Users of the third edition gave the assignment material high marks regarding quality, quantity, and range. They especially liked the references in the text and the assignment materials to actual companies. The fourth edition enhances the latter feature because it spurs student interest and enthusiasm.

We have devoted enormous attention to the assignment material for each chapter. The beginning of the Chapter 1 Assignment Material explains the format and the various ways of using the material. If they desire, instructors may select materials from the Understanding Published Financial Reports subgroups exclusively throughout a course and cover all the essentials of financial accounting. For example, instructors may assign relatively simple, straightforward homework in the Fundamental Assignment Material section by using only the subgroup called Understanding Published Financial Reports. These exercises demonstrate how a course in introductory accounting can stick to essentials even while using real-life numbers and organizations.

Of special note in this edition is Chapter 11, Statement of Cash Flows. This chapter provides an especially easy-to-learn explanation of the new required financial statement. In particular, the readers need not contend either with a long series of "things to do" or with awkward work sheets. Instead, the chapter employs the familiar balance sheet equation that threads throughout the entire book. Thus readers can quickly understand *why* as well as *how* the statement dovetails with balance sheets and income statements. A chapter appendix covers the T-account approach for those instructors who favor such a technique.

Another valuable feature of this edition is the series of House of Fabrics problems at the end of each chapter's assignment material. These problems directly link the chapter's subject matter to the actual financial statements of House of Fabrics, which are reproduced in the appendix at the end of the book. As students progress through the course, they will grow increasingly comfortable with the real-world report of a publicly-held company.

All chapters were thoroughly rewritten and updated. Consider the following examples of assorted changes and new features:

a. Expanded explanations of transaction analysis and the nature of paid-in capital in Chapter 1. New section on professional ethics.

b. More emphasis on real examples when presenting synonyms for net income and retained income in Chapter 2.

c. Introduction of accumulated depreciation and contra accounts in Chapter 3 instead of delaying until Chapter 5.

d. Improved summary of how typical adjusting entries are accounted for in Chapter 4.

e. New section on single-step and multiple-step income statements in Chapter 4, including a summary problem for review.

f. Reduction of length of Chapter 5. Expanded explanation of the declaration and payment of dividends and the role of the dividends declared account.

g. Deletion of all inventory discussions from Chapter 6, focusing instead on revenue, cash, and accounts receivable.

h. Consolidation of inventory sections previously in Chapters 6 and 7 into Chapter 7.

i. Shift of accelerated depreciation focus from sum-of-the-years'-digits to double-declining balance in Chapter 8, together with updating to MACRS.

j. Inclusion of effective-interest method of bond discount and premium in the body of Chapter 9 instead of in an appendix, with expanded illustrations of bonds issued at par, at a discount, and at a premium.

k. Improved comparison of common stock, preferred stock, and bonds in Chapter 10.

l. Statement of cash flows introduced in Chapter 11 instead of Chapter 15.

m. Incorporation of FASB Statement No. 94's requirements for consolidated statements in Chapter 12.

n. Tax discussion updated from ACRS to MACRS in Chapter 13, and coverage of the investment tax credit moved from the body of the chapter to an appendix. Deletion of discussion of the installment method and percentage of completion versus completed contract methods.

o. New Chapter 14 on internal control, covering much of the former Chapter 8, with greatly expanded use of examples.

p. New Chapter 15, expanding the coverage of financial statement analysis from Chapter 16 of the third edition. Extensive reorganization and rewriting, especially the section on financial ratios.

q. Combination of the third edition's Chapter 14 and Chapter 16, Part One, into Chapter 16. Streamlined discussion of the conceptual framework and briefer explanation of alternative measures of income. Additional section on accounting principles outside the United States.

SUPPLEMENTS FOR THE INSTRUCTOR

Solutions Manual—prepared by Horngren and Sundem, includes suggestions for how to tailor the text material to your course needs, solutions to all in-text assignment material and the practice set, and key amounts for students' use in checking their own solutions.

Instructor's Resource Outline—prepared by Jonathan Schiff, provides a complete teaching outline for the course with objectives, lecture discussions, problem and example selections, sources for additional materials, and a correlation of the *Solutions Manual* to the text.

Test Item File—prepared by James Barnhart, offers over 1500 true/false and multiple-choice questions, exercises, and problems with a wide range of rigor; available with *Prentice-Hall's Telephone Test Preparation Service*.

Transparencies of Solutions—features an increased number of transparencies of selected problems and key exhibits from the text. Free upon adoption.

Prentice-Hall's Telephone Test Preparation Service and Floppy Disk Testing Service—contact your local sales representative for further details.

SUPPLEMENTS FOR THE STUDENT

Student Guide—prepared by Dudley W. Curry and Frank H. Selto, gives a brief survey and a detailed summary of the text to assist study as well as a comprehensive set of self-test and practice exercises for each chapter with solutions.

Working Papers—prepared by Dudley W. Curry, provides partially filled in problem data and column headings for appropriate in-text problems.

Practice Set (Chimes Inc.)—prepared by Dudley W. Curry, comprises a simulated case covering all steps in the Accounting Cycle, tying together the fundamentals of bookkeeping and accounting, and including partially filled in working papers.

Spreadsheet Applications in Financial Accounting—prepared by Ali A. Peyvandi and Wayne D. Robertson and revised by Albert Fisher, this supplement leads students from a level of little or no experience in computers to a level where they can solve accounting problems using Lotus® 1-2-3®. This complete supplement also includes a computer disk (for IBM PC computers and compatibles) that contains many partially completed problems and ample space for students to place all their assignments.

ACKNOWLEDGMENTS

Introduction to Financial Accounting is dedicated to Dudley W. Curry, professor emeritus at Southern Methodist University, where he won several awards for outstanding teaching. His work on this book has earned our highest praise and deepest gratitude. He provided invaluable ideas and bountiful constructive criticism, and authored or co-authored the following supplementary aids: student guide, working papers, and the practice set.

This book has benefited greatly from the advice and critical evaluation of Frank H. Selto, who also has co-authored the student guide.

We appreciate the help of James Barnhart, who prepared an expanded test bank.

We are also especially grateful to Jonathan Schiff for his review of the manuscript and his preparation of Instructor's Resource Outlines.

Our appreciation extends to our present and former colleagues. The following professors supplied helpful comments and reviews of the previous edition or drafts of this edition: Elinor O. Boer, Linda J. Cantrell, Roger A. Chope, William P. Enderlein, David E. Hoffman, Graeme Rankine, Earl K. Stice, Leanna Stiefel, and Thomas L. Stober.

Elsie Young has our special appreciation for her cheerful and skillful typing and related help. Joseph Limacher has our gratitude for ably performing assorted editorial chores. Deborah S. Malestky deserves special recognition for her flawless typing of the solutions manual.

Finally, our thanks to Joe Heider, Eleanor Perz, Judy Matz-Coniglio, Marie Lines, and Jenny Sheehan at Prentice Hall.

Comments from users are welcome.

CHARLES T. HORNGREN
GARY L. SUNDEM

Introduction to
FINANCIAL
ACCOUNTING

CHAPTER 1

Entities and Balance Sheets

LEARNING OBJECTIVES

Learning objectives will be found at the beginning of each chapter. They specify some of the important knowledge and skills you should have after completing your study of the chapter and your solving of the assignment material.

1. Define and give an example of an **asset,** a **liability,** and **owner's equity,** which are the three major elements of a balance sheet

2. Define **accounting entity** and describe how we determine whether a transaction is a personal transaction or one that affects the accounting entity only

3. Define **transaction** and the role of reliability in accounting

4. Specify the direct effects of typical transactions on the balance sheet items of an entity

5. Explain the advantages and disadvantages of each form of business organization—proprietorships, partnerships, and corporations

6. Explain the roles of auditing and professional ethics with respect to financial statements

NATURE OF ACCOUNTING

Accounting is an important subject. This opinion is widely shared, as shown by eleven hundred responses to a questionnaire sent to professors and managers by the American Assembly of Collegiate Schools of Business. Here are the top three courses ranked in terms of how much time and effort should be spent by students on each one of them:

	RANKED BY MANAGERS	RANKED BY PROFESSORS
Accounting	1	2
Finance	2	3
Economics	3	1

☐ Decisions and Accounting

Do you make decisions that have a financial impact? Your answer is undoubtedly yes. Regardless of your roles in life (for example, manager, politician, investor, head of household, student), you will find a knowledge of accounting helpful. The major purpose of this book is to help you feel comfortable with financial information. Individuals who are uncomfortable are often severely handicapped in a variety of situations.

"Comfortable" means knowing the vocabulary and what financial statements mean and do not mean. Knowing what financial statements do *not* communicate is just as important as knowing what they do communicate. Accounting has been called the "language of business." It might better be called the "language of financial decisions." In any event, the degree of comfort being aimed at might be compared to living in a foreign country. The better you can speak the language, the more comfortable you will be; and you will be much more able to manage all aspects of living there than if you know no foreign words or only a few foreign words. You will be more likely to make intelligent decisions.

In brief, a beginning accounting student must learn a language. Accounting is the major means of communicating about the financial impact of an organization's activities. Learning includes becoming familiar with a vocabulary and developing an ability to construct, understand, and use financial statements.

☐ Applicability to Nonprofit Organizations

This book is aimed at a variety of readers, including students who aspire to become either managers or professional accountants. The major focus is on profit-seeking organizations. However, the fundamental ideas also apply to nonprofit (that is, not-for-profit) organizations. Moreover, all managers typically have personal investments in profit-seeking organizations or must interact with businesses in some way.

Managers and accountants in various settings such as hospitals, universities, and government agencies have much in common with their counterparts in profit-seeking organizations. There is money to be raised and spent. There are budgets to be prepared and control systems to be designed and implemented. There is an obligation to use resources wisely. If used intelligently, accounting contributes to efficient operations. The strengthening of the accounting system was a mandatory condition imposed by the federal government in saving New York City from bankruptcy in the 1970s.

The overlap of government and business is everywhere. Government administrators and politicians are much better equipped to deal inside and outside their organizations if they understand accounting. For example, a knowledge of accounting is crucial for decisions regarding research contracts, defense contracts, and loan guarantees. Keep in mind that decisions about loan guarantees have been made with respect to tiny businesses (for instance, through the Small Business Administration) as well as large businesses such as Lockheed and Chrysler.

☐ Scope of Accounting

Accounting is a broad subject. Do not confuse it with bookkeeping. Just as arithmetic is a small part of the broad discipline of mathematics, bookkeeping is a small part of the broad discipline of accounting. Accountants design their systems after considering the types of information desired by managers and other users. Bookkeepers and computers then perform the more routine tasks of following detailed procedures designed by accountants.

Managers, investors, and other interested groups usually want the answers to two important questions about an organization: How well did it do during a given period? and Where does the organization stand on a given day? The accountant answers these questions with two major financial statements—an income statement and a balance sheet. To obtain these statements, accountants analyze, record, quantify, accumulate, summarize, classify, report, and interpret the numerous events and their financial effects on the organization.

Accounting helps decision making by showing where and when money has been spent and commitments have been made, by evaluating performance, and by indicating the financial implications of choosing one plan versus another. Some type of accounting is an essential ingredient to the smooth functioning of almost all organizations, cultures, and economies.

Consider some fundamental relationships:

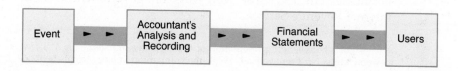

Here are some examples of users and the decisions they must make:

USERS	DECISIONS
Managers of organizations	Where to expand or reduce operations? How did subordinates perform? Whom to reward?
Lenders of money	Grant a loan? Which lending terms to specify?
Suppliers of goods and services	Extend credit? How much? How long?
Shareholders of organizations	Increase or reduce their investments?
Income tax authorities	Is taxable income measured properly?
U.S. Securities and Exchange Commission	Do the financial statements of a publicly held corporation conform to requirements of securities laws?

OVERALL ROLE OF ACCOUNTING

☐ Financial and Management Accounting

The financial statements discussed in this book are common to all areas of accounting. "Financial accounting" is often distinguished from "management accounting." The major distinction between them is their use by two different classes of decision makers. The field of **financial accounting** serves *external* decision makers, such as stockholders, suppliers, banks, and governmental agencies. **Management accounting** serves *internal* decision makers, such as top executives, department heads, college deans, hospital administrators, and people at other management levels *within* an organization.[1]

The more that managers know about accounting, the better they are able to plan and control their organization and its subunits. In dealing with both inside and outside parties, managers are handicapped if their comprehension of accounting is sketchy or confused. So the learning of accounting is almost always a wise investment, no matter what the manager's specialty. Moreover, managers' performance and rewards often hinge on how accounting measurements are made. Therefore managers have a natural self-interest in learning about accounting.

☐ Employers of Accountants

The accounting profession can be classified in many ways. A major classification is **public accounting** and **private accounting.** "Public" accountants are those whose services are offered to the general public on a fee basis. Such services include auditing, income taxes, and management consulting. "Private" accountants are all the rest. They consist of not only those individuals who work for businesses but also those who work for government agencies, including the Internal Revenue Service.

---

[1] For a book-length presentation of the field, see *Introduction to Management Accounting* (Englewood Cliffs, NJ: Prentice Hall, 1990), the companion volume to this textbook.

In the accompanying diagram, the long arrows indicate how accountants often move from public accounting firms to positions in business or government. Obviously, these movements can occur at any level or in any direction.

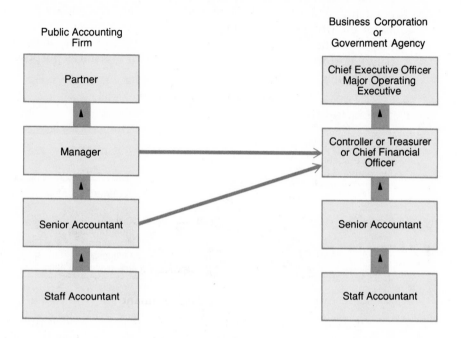

Accounting cuts across all management functions, including purchasing, manufacturing, wholesaling, retailing, and a variety of marketing and transportation activities. It provides an excellent opportunity for gaining broad knowledge. Senior accountants or controllers in a corporation are sometimes picked as production or marketing executives. Why? Because they may have impressed other executives as having acquired general management skills. A number of recent surveys have indicated that more chief executive officers began their careers in an accounting position than in marketing, production, engineering, or any other area.

THE BALANCE SHEET

The beginning of this chapter has provided a glimpse of the entire field of accounting. Basically, accounting provides information for a wide variety of decisions. At this point, we turn to what the accountant does. As you read on, you will become familiar with the underlying theory and concepts of accounting—gradually, chapter by chapter, rather than in one enormous gulp in Chapter 1. By working with concrete situations, you are more likely to get a solid grasp of the uses and limitations of accounting. The final chapter provides a review and knitting together of the various topics in this book.

Assets, Liabilities, and Owner's Equity

Suppose George Smith has had previous experience in the bicycle business but is now a salaried employee of a local company. He has decided to "go independent," that is, to quit his job and open a large bicycle shop. Smith has heard about the troubles of new businesses that lack money. So he invested plenty, $400,000. Then Smith, acting for the business (which is called Biwheels Company), borrowed $100,000 from a local bank for business purposes. An opening balance sheet of this new enterprise follows:

BIWHEELS COMPANY
Balance Sheet
December 31, 19X1[2]

ASSETS		LIABILITIES AND OWNER'S EQUITY	
Cash	$500,000	Liabilities (note payable)	$100,000
		Smith, capital	400,000
		Total liabilities	
Total assets	$500,000	and owner's equity	$500,000

Balance sheet is a widely used term. It is not as descriptive as its newer substitute terms: **statement of financial position** or **statement of financial condition**. But old terms die hard, so *balance sheet* will be used in this book. Besides, the term constantly reminds us of a powerful device, the accountant's balance sheet equation:

$$\text{Assets} = \text{Liabilities} + \text{Owner's equity}$$

Definitions of Major Balance Sheet Items

The **balance sheet** is a photograph of financial status at an instant of time. It has two counterbalancing sections, as the equation indicates. Key introductory definitions follow:

Assets are economic resources that are expected to benefit future cash inflows or help reduce future cash outflows. Examples are cash, inventories, and equipment.

Liabilities are economic obligations of the organization to outsiders. An example is a debt to a bank. The usual evidence of this debt is a promissory note that states the terms of payment. Accountants use **note payable** to describe the existence of such a promissory note.

Owner's equity is the residual interest in (that is, remaining claim against) the organization's assets after deducting liabilities. At the inception of a business,

---

[2] Throughout this book, years will usually be designated 19X1, 19X2, 19X3, etc.

the owner's equity is measured by the total amount invested by the owner. As illustrated by "Smith, capital," the accountant usually uses the term "capital" instead of "owner's equity" to designate an owner's investment in the business.

A mature business will have earned profits. As Chapter 2 will explain, the owner's equity will then consist of the total amounts invested by the owner (or owners) plus any cumulative profits retained in the business.

The right side of the balance sheet equation represents outsider and owner "claims against" the total assets shown on the left side. Many accountants prefer to think of the right side as "interests in" or "sources of" the total assets. The residual or "leftover" nature of owner's equity is often emphasized by reexpressing the balance sheet equation as follows:

$$\text{Owner's equity} = \text{Assets} - \text{Liabilities}$$

SOME GENERALLY ACCEPTED ACCOUNTING PRINCIPLES

☐ "Principles" Is a Misnomer

Many people think that accounting is an exact science, perhaps because of the tidy precision that financial statements seem to possess. However, accounting is more art than science. Financial statements are the result of a measurement process that rests on a set of principles.

Generally accepted accounting principles (GAAP) is a technical term that includes both broad concepts or guidelines and detailed practices. It includes all the conventions, rules, and procedures that together make up accepted accounting practice at a given time.

Accounting principles become "generally accepted" by agreement. Such agreement is not influenced solely by formal logical analysis. Experience, custom, usage, and practical necessity contribute to a set of principles. Accordingly, it might be preferable to call them conventions. Why? Because "principles" erroneously connotes that GAAP is the product of airtight logic. Nevertheless, accountants use "principles" rather than "conventions" to describe the entire framework that guides their work.

☐ The Entity Concept

The first basic concept or principle in accounting is the entity. An accounting **entity** is an organization or a section of an organization that stands apart from other organizations and individuals as a separate economic unit. The accounting draws sharp boundaries around each entity to avoid confusing its affairs with those of other entities. The entity concept is important because accounting usually focuses on how to measure the financial impact of events as they affect a particular organization.

An example of an entity is General Motors Corporation, an enormous entity that encompasses many smaller entities such as the Chevrolet Division and the Buick Division. In turn, Chevrolet encompasses many smaller entities such as a Michigan assembly plant and an Ohio assembly plant. Managers want accounting reports that are confined to their particular entities.

The key point here is that the entity concept helps the accountant relate events to a clearly defined area of accountability. For example, *business* entities should not be confused with *personal* entities. A purchase of groceries for merchandise inventory is an accounting transaction of a grocery store (the business entity), but the store owner's purchase of a diamond necklace with a personal check is a transaction of the owner (the personal entity).

☐ **Transactions and Reliability**

A **transaction** is any event that both affects the financial position of an entity and can be reliably recorded in money terms. The accounting process focuses on transactions as they affect an organization. As you know, many events may affect a company—including wars, elections, and general economic booms or depressions. However, the accountant recognizes only specified types of events as being worthy of formal recording as *accounting transactions*.

Consider an illustration. Suppose the president of Exxon is killed in an airplane crash, and the company carries no life insurance. The accountant would not record this event. Suppose further that an employee embezzles $1,000 in cash from Exxon, is discovered the same day, and the company carries no employee theft insurance. The accountant would record this event.

The death of the president may have considerably more economic or financial significance than the embezzlement. But the monetary effect is hard to measure in any objective way. The accountant is concerned about measuring the impact of events in some systematic, reliable manner.

Users want assurance that the numbers in the financial statements are not fabricated by management or by accountants. Consequently, accountants seek and prize reliability as one of their major strengths and regard it as an essential characteristic of measurement. **Reliability** is a quality of information that allows users to depend on it to represent the conditions or events that it purports to represent. More specifically, reliable data are accurate. Moreover, reliable data are supported by convincing evidence that can be verified by independent accountants. Without the reliability concept, accounting records might be based on whims and opinions open to dispute. Hence the accountant would record the financial impact of the Exxon embezzlement but would not record the unreliable financial impact of the Exxon president's death, wars, or elections.

TRANSACTIONS AND ENTITIES

☐ **Transaction Analysis**

We will now consider nine transactions and analyze each in terms of its effect on Biwheels Company. Transaction analysis is the nucleus of accounting.

Transaction 1, Initial Investment. The first Biwheels transaction was the investment by the owner on December 31, 19X1. Smith deposited $400,000 in a business bank account entitled Biwheels Company. The accounting equation is affected as follows: (최초로 투자한 것)

	ASSETS	=	LIABILITIES	+	OWNER'S EQUITY
	Cash				Smith, Capital
(1)	+400,000	=			+400,000
					(owner investment)

The first transaction increases both the assets, specifically Cash, and the owner's equity of the business, specifically Smith, Capital. Liabilities are unaffected. Why? Because Smith's business has as yet no obligation to an outside party arising from this transaction. A parenthetical note, "owner investment," is used to identify the reason for the transaction's effect on owner's equity.

The total amounts on the left side of the equation must always equal the total amounts on the right side.

Transaction 2, Loan From Bank. On January 2, 19X2, Smith borrows from a bank, signing a promissory note for $100,000. The $100,000 is added to the business's cash. The effect of this loan transaction on the accounting equation is:

	ASSETS	=	LIABILITIES	+	OWNER'S EQUITY
			Note		Smith,
	Cash		Payable		Capital
(1)	+400,000	=			+400,000
(2)	+100,000	=	+100,000		
Bal.	500,000		100,000		400,000
	500,000			500,000	

The loan increases the asset, Cash, and increases the liability, Note Payable, by the same amount, $100,000. After the transaction is completed, Biwheels has assets of $500,000, liabilities of $100,000, and owner's equity of $400,000.

The sums of the individual balances (abbreviated Bal.) on each side of the equation are equal. This equality must always exist.

Transaction 3, Acquire Inventory for Cash. On January 2, 19X2, Biwheels acquires bicycles from a manufacturer for $150,000 cash:

	ASSETS		= LIABILITIES +	OWNER'S EQUITY
	Cash	Merchandise Inventory	Note Payable	Smith, Capital
Bal.	500,000		= 100,000	400,000
(3)	− 150,000	+ 150,000	=	
Bal.	350,000	150,000	100,000	400,000
		500,000		500,000

The cash purchase of inventory increases one asset, Merchandise Inventory, and decreases another asset, Cash, by the same amount. The form of the assets changed because cash decreased and a new asset, the inventory of merchandise for sale, was recorded. But the total amount of assets is unchanged. Moreover, the right-side items are completely unchanged.

After any transaction has been completed, Biwheels can prepare a balance sheet. It would have the same heading except that the date would be January 2, 19X2:

ASSETS		LIABILITIES AND OWNER'S EQUITY	
Cash	$350,000	Liabilities	
Merchandise		(Note payable)	$100,000
inventory	150,000	Smith, capital	400,000
		Total liabilities	
Total assets	$500,000	and owner's equity	$500,000

From the start, note that after each transaction the total assets must always equal the total liabilities and owner's equity. That is, the equality of the balance sheet equation cannot (and should not) be destroyed by any transaction.

☐ Additional Illustrative Transactions

Exhibit 1–1 shows how a series of transactions may be analyzed using the balance sheet equation. The transactions are numbered for easy reference. Please examine how the first three transactions, which were discussed earlier, are analyzed in Exhibit 1–1.

Consider how each of the following additional transactions is analyzed:

4. Jan. 3. Biwheels buys bicycles for $10,000 from a manufacturer who is eager for business. Payment does not have to be made for thirty days.
5. Jan. 4. Biwheels acquires assorted store equipment for a total of $15,000. A cash down payment of $4,000 is made. The remaining balance must be paid in sixty days.
6. Jan. 5. Biwheels sells a store showcase to a business neighbor after Smith decides he dislikes it. Its selling price, $1,000, happens to be exactly equal to its cost. The neighbor agrees to pay within thirty days.

EXHIBIT 1–1 *(Place a clip on this page for easy reference.)*

BIWHEELS COMPANY
Analyis of Transactions for December 31, 19X1–January 12, 19X2 (in dollars)

DESCRIPTION OF TRANSACTION	Cash	+	Accounts Receivable	+	Merchandise Inventory	+	Store Equipment	=	Note Payable	+	Accounts Payable	+	Smith, Capital
(1) Initial investment	+400,000							=					+400,000
(2) Loan from bank	+100,000							=	+100,000				
(3) Acquire inventory for cash	−150,000				+150,000			=					
(4) Acquire Inventory on credit					+10,000			=			+10,000		
(5) Acquire store equipment for cash plus credit	−4,000						+15,000	=			+11,000		
(6) Sale of equipment			+1,000				−1,000	=					
(7) Return of inventory acquired on January 3					−800			=			−800		
(8) Payments to creditors	−4,000							=			−4,000		
(9) Collections from debtors	+700		−700					=					
Balance, January 12, 19X2	342,700	+	300	+	159,200	+	14,000	=	100,000	+	16,200	+	400,000

ASSETS = LIABILITIES + OWNER'S EQUITY

516,200 = 516,200

11

7. Jan. 6. Biwheels returns some inventory (which had been acquired on January 3 for $800) to the manufacturer for full credit (an $800 reduction of the amount that Biwheels owes the manufacturer).

8. Jan. 10. Biwheels pays $4,000 to the manufacturer described in transaction 4.

9. Jan. 12. Biwheels collects $700 of the $1,000 owed by the business neighbor for transaction 6.

—. Jan. 12. Smith remodels his home for $35,000, paying by check from his personal bank account.

To check your comprehension, use the format in Exhibit 1–1 to analyze each transaction. Try to do your own analysis of each transaction before looking at the entries shown for it in the exhibit. For example, you could cover the numerical entries with a sheet of paper or a ruler and then proceed through each transaction, one by one. Alternatively, before examining Exhibit 1–1, study the following explanations of transactions 4 through 9.

☐ Explanations of Transactions 4 Through 9

Transaction 4, Purchase on Credit. The vast bulk of purchases (and sales) throughout the world are conducted on a *credit* basis rather than on a *cash* basis. This "buy now, pay later" attitude is particularly prevalent in dealings among manufacturers, wholesalers, and retailers. Indeed, the extension of credit seems to be a major lubricant of the world's economies. Thus, unless evidence indicates that customers may not pay their debts, cash is not expected until a later date. Furthermore, an "authorized signature" of the buyer is usually sufficient; no formal promissory note is necessary. This practice is known as buying (or selling) on **open account;** the debt is shown on the buyer's balance sheet as an account payable. Thus an **account payable** is a liability that results from a purchase of goods or services on open account. As Exhibit 1–1 shows for this merchandise purchase on account, the inventory (asset) of Biwheels is increased and an account payable (liability) is created in an amount of $10,000. A detailed analysis follows:

	ASSETS		=	LIABILITIES		+	OWNER'S EQUITY
	Cash	Merchandise Inventory		Note Payable	Accounts Payable		Smith, Capital
Bal.	350,000	150,000	=	100,000			400,000
(4)		+ 10,000	=		+ 10,000		
Bal.	350,000	160,000		100,000	10,000		400,000
		510,000				510,000	

Transaction 5, Purchase for Cash Plus Credit. This is the first illustration of a *compound* effect in the sense that more than two balance sheet items are affected simultaneously. Store equipment is increased by the full amount of its cost regardless of whether payment is made in full now, in full later, or partially now and partially later. Therefore Biwheels' Store Equipment (asset) is increased by $15,000, Cash (asset) is decreased by $4,000, and Accounts Payable (liability) is increased by $11,000:

		ASSETS		=	LIABILITIES		+	OWNER'S EQUITY
	Cash	Merchandise Inventory	Store Equipment		Note Payable	Accounts Payable		Smith, Capital
Bal.	350,000	160,000		=	100,000	10,000		400,000
(5)	− 4,000		+15,000	=		+11,000		
Bal.	346,000	160,000	15,000		100,000	21,000		400,000
		521,000				521,000		

Transaction 6, Sale on Credit. This transaction is similar to a purchase on credit except that Biwheels is now the seller. Accounts Receivable (asset) of $1,000 is created and Store Equipment (asset) is decreased by $1,000. We are purposely avoiding transactions that result in profits or losses until the next chapter. Instead we are concentrating on elementary changes in the balance sheet equation:

			ASSETS		=	LIABILITIES		+	OWNER'S EQUITY
	Cash	Accounts Receivable	Merchandise Inventory	Store Equipment		Note Payable	Accounts Payable		Smith, Capital
Bal.	346,000		160,000	15,000	=	100,000	21,000		400,000
(6)		+1,000		− 1,000	=				
Bal.	346,000	1,000	160,000	14,000		100,000	21,000		400,000
			521,000				521,000		

This transaction affects assets only; liabilities and owner's equity are unchanged.

Transaction 7, Return of Inventory to Supplier. When a company returns merchandise to its suppliers for credit, its inventory is reduced and its liabilities are reduced. In this instance, the amount of the decrease on each side of the equation is $800:

			ASSETS		=	LIABILITIES		OWNER'S EQUITY
	Cash	Accounts Receivable	Merchandise Inventory	Store Equipment		Note Payable	Accounts Payable	Smith, Capital
Bal.	346,000	1,000	160,000	14,000	=	100,000	21,000	400,000
(7)			− 800		=		− 800	
Bal.	346,000	1,000	159,200	14,000		100,000	20,200	400,000
			520,200				520,200	

Transaction 8, Payments to Creditors. A *creditor* is one to whom money is owed. The manufacturer is an example of a creditor. These payments reduce Biwheels' assets (Cash) and its liabilities (Accounts Payable) by $4,000:

	ASSETS				=	LIABILITIES		+	OWNER'S EQUITY
	Cash	Accounts Receivable	Merchandise Inventory	Store Equipment		Note Payable	Accounts Payable		Smith, Capital
Bal.	346,000	1,000	159,200	14,000	=	100,000	20,200		400,000
(8)	− 4,000				=		− 4,000		
Bal.	342,000	1,000	159,200	14,000		100,000	16,200		400,000
	516,200							516,200	

Transaction 9, Collections from Debtors. A *debtor* is one who owes money. Here the business neighbor is the debtor and Biwheels is the creditor. These collections increase one of Biwheels' assets (Cash) and decrease another asset (Accounts Receivable) by $700:

	ASSETS				=	LIABILITIES		+	OWNER'S EQUITY
	Cash	Accounts Receivable	Merchandise Inventory	Store Equipment		Note Payable	Accounts Payable		Smith, Capital
Bal.	342,000	1,000	159,200	14,000	=	100,000	16,200		400,000
(9)	+ 700	− 700			=				
Bal.	342,700	300	159,200	14,000		100,000	16,200		400,000
	516,200							516,200	

Nonbusiness Transaction. Smith remodels his home for $35,000, paying by check from his personal bank account. This event is a nonbusiness transaction. The remodeling has no impact on Biwheels, and therefore the event is not recorded by the business. This event is a transaction of Smith's *personal* entity, not Smith's Biwheels *business* entity. Our focus is solely on the business entity. This transaction illustrates an application of the *entity concept*.

☐ The Account and Balance Sheets

An **account** is a summary of the changes in a particular asset or liability or owner's equity. As has just been explained, a cumulative total may be drawn at *any* date for each *account* in Exhibit 1–1. The following balance sheet uses the totals at the bottom of Exhibit 1–1. Observe that a balance sheet represents the financial impact of an accumulation of transactions to a specific point in time.

BIWHEELS COMPANY
Balance Sheet
January 12, 19X2

ASSETS		LIABILITIES AND OWNER'S EQUITY	
Cash	$342,700	Note payable	$100,000
Accounts receivable	300	Accounts payable	16,200
Merchandise		Total liabilities	$116,200
inventory	159,200	Smith, capital	400,000
Store equipment	14,000		
Total	$516,200	Total	$516,200

As we have illustrated, Biwheels could prepare a new balance sheet after each transaction. Obviously, such a practice would be awkward and unnecessary. Therefore balance sheets are usually produced once a month.

TYPES OF OWNERSHIP

☐ Proprietorships, Partnerships, and Corporations

Entities take many forms. Owners must decide whether their businesses should be organized as sole proprietorships, partnerships, or corporations. A **proprietorship** is a separate organization with a single owner. Most often the owner is also the manager. Therefore proprietorships tend to be small retail establishments and individual professional businesses such as those of dentists, physicians, and attorneys. From an *accounting* viewpoint, each proprietorship is an individual entity that is separate and distinct from the proprietor.

A **partnership** is a special form of organization that joins two or more individuals together as co-owners. Many retail establishments, as well as dentists, physicians, attorneys, and accountants, conduct their activities as partnerships. Indeed, partnerships can sometimes be gigantic. For instance, the largest independent accounting firms have more than one thousand partners. Again, from an *accounting* viewpoint, each partnership is an individual entity that is separate from the personal activities of each partner.

Corporations are organizations created by individual state laws. The owners are identified as stockholders or shareholders. Although large publicly owned corporations have thousands of stockholders, many states allow having only one stockholder; other states require at least two stockholders. Individuals form a corporation by applying to the state for approval of the company's *articles of incorporation*. When approved, the corporation becomes a *legal* entity, an "artificial person" that conducts its business completely apart from its owners. The corporation is also, of course, an *accounting* entity.

Advantages of Corporations

The corporate form of organization has many advantages. Perhaps its most notable feature is the **limited liability** of owners, which means that corporate creditors (such as banks or suppliers) ordinarily have claims against the corporate assets only. Therefore if a corporation drifts into financial trouble, its creditors cannot look for repayment beyond the corporate entity. That is, generally the owners' personal assets are not subject to the creditors' grasp. In contrast, the owners of proprietorships and partnerships typically have *unlimited liability*, which means that business creditors can look for repayment beyond the business entity's assets to the owners' personal assets. For example, if Biwheels were a partnership, *each* partner would bear a personal liability for full payment of the $100,000 bank loan.

Other advantages of the corporation include the ease of transfer of ownership, ease of raising ownership capital, and continuity of existence. The corporation usually issues **capital stock certificates** (often called simply **stock certificates**) as formal evidence of ownership shares. These shares may be sold and resold among present and potential owners. Moreover, ownership capital may be solicited from hundreds or thousands of potential stockholders. Indeed, AT&T has nearly 3 million stockholders. They own a total of over 1 billion shares of stock. Furthermore, the corporation has an indefinite life in the sense that it continues even if its ownership changes. In contrast, proprietorships and partnerships officially terminate upon the death or complete withdrawal by an owner.

The income tax effects of the form of ownership may vary significantly. For example, a corporation is taxed as a separate entity (as a corporation). But no income taxes are levied on a proprietorship (as a proprietorship) or on a partnership (as a partnership). Instead the income earned by proprietorships and partnerships is attributed to the owners as personal taxpayers. In short, the income tax laws regard corporations as being taxable entities, but proprietorships or partnerships as not being taxable entities. Whether the corporation provides tax advantages heavily depends on the personal tax situations of the owners. (See Chapter 13, Appendix B, for more discussion.)

Regardless of the economic and legal advantages or disadvantages of the corporate form, some small-business owners incorporate simply for prestige. That is, they feel more important if they can refer to "my corporation" and if they can refer to themselves as "chairman of the board" or "president" instead of "business owner" or "partner."

In terms of numbers of entities, there are fewer corporations than there are proprietorships or partnerships. However, the corporation has far more economic significance. Corporations conduct a sheer money volume of business that dwarfs the volume of other forms of organization. Moreover, almost every reader of this book interacts with, owes money to, or invests in corporations. For these reasons, this book emphasizes the corporate entity.

Financial Presentations of Owners' Equity

The basic accounting concepts that underlie the owners' equity are unchanged regardless of whether the organization is a proprietorship, a partnership, or a corporation. However, owners' equities for proprietorships and partnerships are often identified as **capital.** In contrast, owners' equity for a corporation is usually called **stockholders' equity** or **shareholders' equity.** Examine the possibilities for Biwheels that are shown in the accompanying table.

OWNER'S EQUITY FOR A PROPRIETORSHIP (Assume George Smith is the sole owner)	
George Smith, capital	$400,000
OWNERS' EQUITY FOR A PARTNERSHIP (Assume Smith has two partners)	
George Smith, capital	$320,000
Alex Handl, capital	40,000
Susan Eastman, capital	40,000
Total partners' capital	$400,000
OWNERS' EQUITY FOR A CORPORATION	
Stockholders' equity:	
Paid-in capital:	
Capital stock, 10,000 shares issued at par value of $10 per share	$100,000
Paid-in capital in excess of par value of capital stock	300,000
Total paid-in capital	$400,000

The presentations for the proprietorship and the partnership are self-explanatory. However, the corporation deserves comment. The capital investments in a corporation by its owners at the inception of business and subsequently are often called **paid-in capital.** In turn, as the table shows, paid-in capital is usually reported in two major parts.

☐ **Why Have Par Value?** 액면가

Stock certificates typically have some printed nominal dollar amount that is required by most states. This amount is determined by the board of directors and is usually called **par value** or **stated value.**

In our example, 10,000 shares have been issued for $40 per share. The par value is $10 per share, and the **paid-in capital in excess of par value** is $30 per share. As an outgrowth of these state laws, the total ownership claim of $400,000 arising from the investment is thus split between two equity claims, one for $100,000 "capital stock, at par" and one for $300,000 "paid-in capital in excess of par" or "additional paid-in capital."

The following formulas show the components of paid-in capital. The Biwheels numbers are used to make the relationships specific, assuming that Biwheels was organized as a corporation:

Total paid-in capital = Capital stock at par + Paid-in capital in excess of par
$400,000 = $100,000 + $300,000
Capital stock at par = Number of shares issued × Par value per share
$100,000 = 10,000 × $10
Paid-in capital in excess of par = Total paid-in capital − Common stock at par
$300,000 = $400,000 − $100,000
Total paid-in capital = Number of shares issued × Average issue price per share
$400,000 = 10,000 × $40

Originally, par or stated value was conceived as a measure of protection for creditors because it established the minimum legal liability of a stockholder. In this way, the creditors would be assured that the corporation would have at least a minimum amount of ownership capital ($10 for each share issued). Indeed, the stockholder had a commitment to invest at least $10 per share in the corporation.

☐ Illustrations of Paid-in Capital in Corporate Balance Sheets

In most states, it is illegal to issue shares unless their par value is fully paid in. As a result, the par or stated values are usually set far below the full market price of the shares upon issuance. For example, consider the following excerpts from recent actual corporate balance sheets.

Sun Microsystems, Inc.

Common stock, $.00067 par value, 125,000,000 shares authorized; issued and outstanding, 36,196,458 shares	$ 24,000
Additional paid-in capital	244,493,000
Total paid-in capital	$244,517,000

Above all, note the extremely small amount of par value in comparison with the additional paid-in capital. This illustrates the insignificance of "par value" in today's business world.

Also note the use of a frequently encountered term, "additional paid-in capital," as a short synonym for "paid-in capital in excess of par value of common stock."

Finally, the number of shares "authorized" is the maximum number that the company can issue as designated by the company's articles of incorporation.

Clark Equipment Company

This presentation does not split the paid-in capital into two lines. Inasmuch as par value is usually small and has little significance, this approach is praiseworthy.

In summary, both of the above corporate presentations can be described accurately with a simple term, *total paid-in capital* (which will be distinguished from other ownership equity arising from profitable operations). Par value has been described here, not because of its economic significance, but because it is so often actually reported on published balance sheets.

☐ Types of Capital Stock

The preceding excerpts use slightly different terms to describe capital stock: *common stock* and *capital stock common*. Sometimes there is more than one type of capital stock issued by a corporation (as explained in Chapter 10). But there is always **common stock,** which represents the "residual" ownership.

Common shareholders bear the most risk of all investors, but they are also entitled to unlimited rewards. In a few instances, the rewards become astronomical, as investors in the initial stock offerings of IBM, Apple Computer, and McDonald's will attest.

SOME ACTUAL BALANCE SHEETS

To become more familiar with the balance sheet and its equation, consider the following condensed excerpts from two actual recent financial reports. Some terms vary among organizations, but the essential balance sheet equation does not.

Delta Airlines, Inc. (in thousands)

ASSETS		LIABILITIES AND STOCKHOLDERS' EQUITY	
Cash	$ 822,791	Notes payable	$ 36,447
Accounts receivable	644,527	Accounts payable	1,355,483
Flight equipment	2,892,420	Other liabilities	2,147,602
Other equipment	673,815	Total liabilities	$3,539,532
Other assets	714,802	Stockholders' equity	2,208,823
		Total liabilities and	
Total assets	$5,748,355	stockholders' equity	$5,748,355

This balance sheet illustrates the prominence of flight equipment as a major amount of an airline's assets. Moreover, the total liabilities exceed the stockholders' equity, which is commonplace for airlines, but not for most publicly held industrial and service organizations. The other liabilities consist largely of long-term debt that usually arises in conjunction with the acquisition of long-term assets such as airplanes.

Nike, Inc. (in thousands)

ASSETS		LIABILITIES AND SHAREHOLDERS' EQUITY	
Cash	$ 75,357	Notes payable	$136,788
Accounts receivable	258,393	Accounts payable	50,288
Inventories	198,470	Other liabilities	110,245
Property, plant and		Total liabilities	$297,321
equipment	57,703	Shareholders' equity	411,774
Other assets	119,172	Total liabilities and	
Total assets	$709,095	shareholders' equity	$709,095

In contrast to Delta Airlines, Nike uses *shareholders'* equity instead of stockholders' equity. As you might expect, Nike has a significant amount of inventories; Delta's inventories are confined to a relatively insignificant amount of supplies classified as other assets.

Nike's total liabilities of $297,321 are easily exceeded by the shareholders' equity of $411,774. Some readers might expect the $57,703 of property, plant,and equipment to be much larger. However, Nike does not produce much of its own merchandise. Instead Nike contracts with various manufacturers to make goods in accordance with Nike's specifications.

Appendix A at the end of this book contains a complete set of the actual financial statements of House of Fabrics, Inc. As you proceed from chapter to chapter, you should examine the pertinent parts of the House of Fabrics actual financial statements. In this way, you will become increasingly comfortable with actual financial reports. For example, the general format and major items in the Fabrics balance sheet (p. 753) should be familiar by now. Details will gradually become understandable as each chapter explains the nature of the various major financial statements.

ROLE OF AUDITING

☐ Managers and Credibility

Financial statements are the ultimate responsibility of the managers who are entrusted with the resources under their command. In proprietorships, the owner is often also the top manager. In partnerships, top management may be shared.

In corporations, the ultimate responsibility is delegated by stockholders to the board of directors, as indicated in the following diagram:

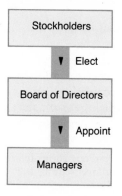

Frequently, the chairman of the board is also the top manager and the major shareholder. For example, for over thirty years Henry Ford II was the major stockholder, the chairman of the board, and the chief executive officer (CEO) of the Ford Motor Company. Nevertheless, ownership is often widely dispersed, the chairman also serves as a corporate officer, and the chief executive officer may be president.[3] Indeed, sometimes the chief executive officer is strictly a professional manager with no ownership position whatsoever.

Long ago stockholders and creditors such as banks wanted some third-party assurance about the reliability of the financial information being supplied by the managers. The public accounting profession arose to serve this function of adding credibility to financial reporting.

A **certified public accountant (CPA)** in the United States earns this designation by a combination of education, qualifying experience, and the passing of a $2\frac{1}{2}$-day written national examination. The examination is administered and graded by a national organization, the American Institute of Certified Public Accountants (AICPA). The institute is the principal professional association in the private sector that regulates the quality of the public accounting profession. Other English-speaking nations have similar arrangements but use the term *chartered accountant* (CA) instead of certified public accountant.

The CPA examination covers four major topical areas: auditing, accounting theory, business law, and accounting practice. The last is a series of accounting problems divided into two long parts covering a wide variety of topics, including income taxes, cost accounting, and accounting for nonprofit institutions.

Although the AICPA prepares and grades the CPA examination on a national basis, the individual states have their own regulations concerning the qualifications for taking and passing the examination and for earning the right

---

[3] Conference Board, *Who Is Top Management?* surveyed four hundred chief executives. In about 50% of the companies, the CEO is the chairman of the board of directors. In 30%, the CEO is the president of the corporation. In virtually all other companies, it is chairman, president, and CEO all rolled into one person.

to practice as a CPA. These regulations are determined and enforced by state boards of accountancy.[4]

Independent Auditor's Report

The financial statements of publicly held corporations and many other corporations are subject to independent audits by CPAs that form the basis for a professional accounting firm's opinion. The **independent opinion** typically includes key phrasing, as illustrated by the following opinion rendered by a large CPA firm, Arthur Andersen & Co., regarding Sara Lee Corporation:

☐ We conducted our audits in accordance with generally accepted auditing standards. Those standards require that we plan and perform the audit to obtain reasonable assurance about whether the financial statements are free of material misstatement. An audit includes examining, on a test basis, evidence supporting the amounts and disclosures in the financial statements. An audit also includes assessing the accounting principles used and significant estimates made by management, as well as evaluating the overall financial statement presentation. We believe that our audits provide a reasonable basis for our opinion.

In our opinion, the financial statements referred to above present fairly, in all material respects, the financial position of Sara Lee Corporation as of July 2, 1988, June 27, 1987 and June 28, 1986, and the results of their operations and their cash flows for the years then ended in conformity with generally accepted accounting principles.

Arthur Andersen & Co.
Chicago, Illinois,

This book will explore the meaning of such key phrases as "present fairly" and "generally accepted accounting principles." For now, reflect on the fact that the accounting firm must conduct an audit before it can render the above opinion. An **audit** is an in-depth examination that is made in accordance with generally accepted auditing standards (which have been developed primarily by the AICPA). This examination includes miscellaneous tests of the accounting records, internal control systems, and other auditing procedures as deemed necessary. The examination leads to the accountant's independent opinion. This opinion (sometimes called *certificate*) is the accountant's stamp of approval on *management's* financial statements.

Sizes of Accounting Firms

The sizes of accounting firms vary. There are small proprietorships, where auditing may represent as little as 10% or less of annual billings. *Billings* are the total amounts charged to clients for services rendered to them. The bulk of the

---

[4] The Certificate in Management Accounting (CMA) is the internal accountant's counterpart to the CPA. The major objective of the CMA is to establish management accounting as a distinct profession. Information can be obtained from the Institute of Certified Management Accountants, P.O. Box 405, Montvale, NJ, 07645–0405:

work of these firms is income taxes and "write-up" work (the actual bookkeeping services for clients who are not equipped to do their own accounting).

There are also a handful of gigantic firms that have over two thousand partners with offices located throughout the world. Such enormous firms are necessary because their clients are also enormous. For instance, a large CPA firm has reported that its annual audit of one client takes the equivalent of seventy-two accountants working a full year. Another client has three hundred separate corporate entities in forty foreign countries that must ultimately be consolidated into a set of overall financial statements.

Of the companies listed on the New York Stock Exchange, 97% are clients of these huge firms. These accounting firms have annual billings in excess of a billion dollars. As much as 70% of the billings is attributable to auditing services. The top partners in big accounting firms are compensated on about the same scale as their corporate counterparts.[5]

PROFESSIONAL ETHICS

Members of the American Institute of Certified Public Accountants must abide by a code of professional conduct. Surveys of public attitudes toward CPAs have consistently ranked the accounting profession as having high ethical standards. The code of professional conduct is especially concerned with integrity and independence. For example, independent auditors are forbidden to own shares of their client corporations. Moreover, the auditors must satisfy themselves that clients' financial statements are prepared in accordance with GAAP.

The emphasis on ethics extends beyond public accounting. For example, members of the National Association of Accountants are expected to abide by that organization's code of ethics for management accountants. All financial reports, whether to insiders or outsiders, are primarily the responsibility of operating managers. However, auditors and management accountants have professional responsibilities regarding competence, confidentiality, integrity, and objectivity. Professional accounting organizations have procedures for reviewing behavior alleged as not being consistent with codes of professional conduct.

SUMMARY

Financial statements are major sources of information for decision making by managers, creditors, and owners. Employers of accountants include profit-seeking and nonprofit organizations. Public accounting firms provide independent auditing services that add credibility to financial reports.

The balance sheet provides a photograph of the financial position of an organization at any instant. That is, it answers the basic question, Where are we?

---

[5] Huge accounting firms tend to receive more publicity than other firms. However, please remember that there are thousands of other able accounting firms, varying in size from sole practitioners to huge international partnerships.

The basic accounting equation is Assets = Liabilities + Owners' Equity. The amounts in the equation are affected by a host of transactions, which are events that require recording.

The entity is an extremely important accounting concept. Entities may take different forms, including proprietorships, partnerships, and corporations. There are also entities within entities. For example, the University of California contains various schools and departments within schools. The department is an accounting entity nested within the school, which is a larger entity nested within the university.

This chapter has introduced a conceptual framework of accounting that is by far the most widely followed throughout the world. Where do we go from here? Chapters 2 through 5 describe the framework more fully, emphasizing how income is measured and using the balance sheet equation as a primary tool for analysis. Then succeeding chapters probe various topics in more depth.

SUMMARY PROBLEMS FOR YOUR REVIEW

☐ **Problem One**

Review Exhibit 1–1 (p. 11). Analyze the following additional transactions of Biwheels Company. Begin with the balances shown for January 12, 19X2, in Exhibit 1–1. Prepare an ending balance sheet for Biwheels Company (say, on January 16 after these additional transactions).

    i. Biwheels pays $10,000 on the bank loan (ignore interest).
    ii. Smith buys furniture for his home for $5,000 using his family charge account at Macy's.
    iii. Biwheels buys merchandise inventory for $50,000. Half the amount is paid in cash, and half is owed on open account.
    iv. Biwheels collects $200 more from its business debtor.

☐ **Solution to Problem One**

See Exhibits 1–2 and 1–3. Note that transaction ii is ignored because it is wholly personal. However, visualize how Smith's personal balance sheet would be affected. His assets, Home Furniture, would rise by $5,000 and his liabilities, Accounts Payable, would also rise by $5,000.

☐ **Problem Two**

"If I purchase 100 shares of the outstanding stock of General Motors Corporation (or Biwheels Company), I invest my money directly in that corporation. General Motors must record that event." Do you agree? Explain.

☐ **Solution to Problem Two**

Money is invested directly in a corporation when the entity originally issues the stock. For example, 100,000 shares of stock may be issued at $80 per share, bringing in $8 million

EXHIBIT 1–2

BIWHEELS COMPANY
Analysis of Additional January Transactions

DESCRIPTION OF TRANSACTION	ASSETS				=	LIABILITIES + OWNER'S EQUITY		
	Cash	+ Accounts Receivable +	Merchandise Inventory +	Store Equipment =		Note Payable +	Accounts Payable +	Smith, Capital
Balance, January 12, 19X2	342,700 +	300 +	159,200 +	14,000 =		100,000 +	16,200 +	400,000
(i) Payment on bank loan	– 10,000				=	– 10,000		
(ii) Personal; no effect								
(iii) Acquire inventory, half for cash	– 25,000		+ 50,000		=		+25,000	
(iv) Collection of receivable	+ 200	–200			=			
Balance, January 16	307,900 +	100 +	209,200 +	14,000 =		90,000 +	41,200 +	400,000
			531,200		=		531,200	

EXHIBIT 1–3

BIWHEELS COMPANY
Balance Sheet
January 16, 19X2

ASSETS		LIABILITIES AND OWNER'S EQUITY	
		Liabilities:	
Cash	$307,900	Note payable	$ 90,000
Accounts receivable	100	Accounts payable	41,200
Merchandise inventory	209,200	Total liabilities	$131,200
Store equipment	14,000	Smith, capital	400,000
Total	$531,200	Total	$531,200

to the corporation. This is a transaction between the corporation and the stockholders. It affects the corporate financial position:

Cash	$8,000,000	Stockholders' equity	$8,000,000

In turn, 100 shares of that stock may be sold by an original stockholder (Dan Marino) to another individual (John Elway) for $130 per share. This is a private transaction; no cash is received by the corporation. Of course, the corporation records the fact that 100 shares originally owned by Marino are now owned by Elway, but the corporate financial position is unchanged. Accounting focuses on the business entity; the private dealings of the owners have no direct effect on the financial position of the entity and hence are unrecorded except for detailed records of the owners' identities.

In summary, Elway invests his money in the shares of the corporation when he buys them from Marino. However, individual dealings in shares already issued and held by stockholders have no direct effect on the financial position of the corporation.

☐ **Problem Three**

"The same individual can be an owner, an employee, and a creditor of a corporation." Do you agree? Explain.

☐ **Solution to Problem Three**

As a separate entity, the corporation enters contracts, hires employees, buys buildings, and conducts other business. In particular, note that the chairman of the board, the president, the other officers, and all the workers are employees of the corporation. Thus Katherine Graham could own some of the capital stock of a corporation and also be an employee. Moreover, money owed to employees for wages and salaries is a liability of a corporation. So the same person can simultaneously be an owner, an employee, and a creditor of a corporation. Similarly, consider an employee of a telephone company who is a stockholder of the company. She could be receiving telephone services from the same company and thus also be both a *customer* and a *debtor* of the company.

HIGHLIGHTS TO REMEMBER

A "Highlights to Remember" section is at the end of each chapter. These sections briefly recapitulate some key ideas, suggestions, comments, or terms that might otherwise be overlooked or misunderstood.

1. *Balance sheet* is a widely used term, but it is not as descriptive as its newer substitute terms: *statement of financial position* or *statement of financial condition*.
2. The entity concept is important because it helps the accountant relate transactions to a sharply defined area of accountability.
3. The transactions of a personal entity should not be mingled with those of a business entity.
4. The ownership equity of a corporation is usually called *stockholders' equity*. It initially takes the form of *common stock* at par or stated value plus *additional paid-in capital*.
5. The buyer of, say, 100 shares of stock almost always acquires the shares through the open marketplace. The seller of the 100 shares is some other shareholder, *not* the corporation itself. In other words, shares are issued en masse by a corporation at its inception and perhaps every few years thereafter. Once the shares are outstanding, the trading occurs between the individual shareholders and not between the corporation and any individual shareholder.

ACCOUNTING VOCABULARY

An "Accounting Vocabulary" section will immediately follow the "Highlights to Remember" section in each chapter. Vocabulary is an extremely important and often troublesome phase of the learning process. A fuzzy understanding of terms will hamper the learning of concepts and the ability to solve accounting problems.

Before proceeding to the assignment material or to the next chapter, be sure you understand the following words or terms. Their meaning is explained in the chapter and also in the glossary at the end of this book:

Account, p. 14
Accounts Payable, p. 12
Assets, p. 6
Audit, p. 22
Balance Sheet, p. 6
Capital, p. 17
Capital Stock Certificate, p. 16
Certified Public Accountant, p. 21
Common Stock, p. 19
Corporation, p. 15
Entity, p. 7
Financial Accounting, p. 4
GAAP, p. 7
Generally Accepted Accounting
   Principles, p. 7
Independent Opinion, p. 22
Liabilities, p. 6
Limited Liability, p. 16
Management Accounting, p. 4

Notes Payable, p. 6
Open Account, p. 12
Owner's Equity, p. 6
Paid-in Capital, p. 17
Paid-in Capital in Excess of Par
   Value, p. 17
Partnership, p. 15
Par Value, p. 17
Private Accounting, p. 4
Proprietorship, p. 15
Public Accounting, p. 4
Reliability, p. 8
Shareholders' Equity, p. 17
Stated Value, p. 17
Statement of Financial Condition, p. 6
Statement of Financial Position, p. 6
Stock Certificate, p. 16
Stockholders' Equity, p. 17
Transaction, p. 8

Formulate good habits now. Check your understanding of these words or terms as a routine part of your study. The habit of checking your accounting vocabulary, chapter by chapter, is a good investment of your time.

ASSIGNMENT MATERIAL

The assignment material for each chapter is usually divided as follows:

Fundamental assignment material
   General coverage
   Understanding published financial reports
Additional assignment material
   General coverage
   Understanding published financial reports

The *fundamental assignment material* consists of relatively straightforward material aimed at conveying the essential concepts and techniques of the particular chapter. These assignments provide a solid introduction to the major concepts of the chapter. They closely follow the chapter presentations with an absolute minimum of new twists.

The *additional assignment material* contains some problems that are specifically identified as substitutes for ones in the fundamental material, plus some problems that spur the reader to do some original thinking.

The *general coverage* subgroups contain the conventional types of textbook assignment materials.

The *understanding published financial reports* subgroups focus on real-life situations. This use of actual companies and news events enhances the student's interest in accounting. Indeed, the most elementary concepts can be learned just as easily by relating them to real companies rather than artificial companies.

The *understanding published financial reports* subgroups also underscore a major objective of this book: to increase the reader's ability to read, understand, and use published financial reports and news articles. In later chapters, this group provides a principal means of reviewing not only the immediate chapter but also the previous chapters. Thus the group is a major way of both testing the reader's cumulative grasp of the subject and enhancing self-confidence. In particular, note the House of Fabrics problem at the end of each chapter's assignment material.

FUNDAMENTAL ASSIGNMENT MATERIAL

☐ **General Coverage**

1–1. **ANALYSIS OF TRANSACTIONS.** (Alternates are 1–2, 1–3, 1–20, and 1–21.) Use the format of Exhibit 1–1 (p. 11) to analyze the following transactions for April of Perez Cleaners. Then prepare a balance sheet as of April 30, 19X1. Perez was founded on April 1.

   a. Issued 1,000 shares of $1 par common stock for cash, $40,000.
   b. Issued 1,500 shares of $1 par common stock for equipment, $60,000.
   c. Borrowed cash, signing a note payable for $30,000.
   d. Purchased equipment for cash, $20,000.
   e. Purchased office furniture on account, $10,000.
   f. Disbursed cash on account (to reduce the account payable), $4,000.
   g. Sold equipment on account at cost, $8,000.
   h. Discovered that the most prominent competitor in the area was bankrupt and was closing its doors on April 30.
   i. Collected cash on account, $3,000. See transaction g.

☐ **Understanding Published Financial Reports**

1–2. **ANALYSIS OF TRANSACTIONS.** (Alternates are 1–1, 1–3, 1–20, and 1–21.) H. J. Heinz Company is a well-known seller of catsup and other food products. Condensed items from a recent April 30 balance sheet follow (in thousands):

ASSETS		LIABILITIES AND STOCKHOLDERS' EQUITY	
Cash	$ 19,398	Notes payable	$ 189,742
Accounts receivable	333,463	Accounts payable	282,145
Inventories	708,389	Other liabilities	771,433
Property and		Stockholders' equity	1,230,454
other assets	1,412,524		
Total	$2,473,774	Total	$2,473,774

Required: | Use a format similar to Exhibit 1–1 (p. 11) to analyze the following transactions for the first two days of May. Then prepare a balance sheet as of May 2.
   1. Issued 1,000 shares of common stock to employees for cash, $18. (Dollar amounts are in thousands.)
   2. Issued 1,500 shares of common stock for the acquisition of special equipment from a supplier, $27.
   3. Borrowed cash, signing a note payable for $100.
   4. Purchased equipment for cash, $125.
   5. Purchased inventories on account, $90.
   6. Disbursed cash on account (to reduce the accounts payable), $354.
   7. Sold display equipment to retailer on account at cost, $14.
   8. Collected cash on account, $84.

1–3. **ANALYSIS OF TRANSACTIONS.** (Alternates are 1–1, 1–2, 1–20, and 1–21.) Nike, Inc., had the following condensed items in a recent May 31 balance sheet (in thousands):

ASSETS		LIABILITIES AND STOCKHOLDERS' EQUITY	
		Notes payable	$136,788
Cash	$ 75,357	Accounts payable	50,288
Accounts receivable	258,393	Other liabilities	110,245
Inventories	198,470	Total liabilities	$297,321
Equipment and other		Shareholders' equity	411,774
assets	176,875	Total liabilities and	
Total assets	$709,095	shareholders' equity	$709,095

Consider the following transactions that occurred during the first three days of June (in thousands of dollars):

1. Inventories were acquired for cash, $100.
2. Inventories were acquired on open account, $200.
3. Unsatisfactory shoes acquired on open account in March were returned for full credit, $40.
4. Equipment of $120 was acquired for a cash down payment of $30 plus a six-month promisory note of $90.
5. To encourage wider displays, special store equipment was sold on account to New York area stores for $400. The equipment had cost $400 in the preceding month.
6. Eddie Murphy produced, directed, and starred in a movie. As a favor to a Nike executive, he agreed to display Nike shoes in a basketball scene. No fee was paid by Nike.
7. Cash was disbursed on account (to reduce accounts payable), $170.
8. Collected cash on account, $180.
9. Borrowed cash from a bank, $500.
10. Sold additional common stock for cash to new investors, $900.
11. The president of the company sold 5,000 shares of his personal holdings of Nike stock through his stockbroker.

Required:

1. Using a format similar to Exhibit 1–1 (p. 11), prepare an analysis showing the effects of the June transactions on the financial position of Nike.
2. Prepare a balance sheet, June 3.

ADDITIONAL ASSIGNMENT MATERIAL

☐ General Coverage

1–4. Give three examples of decisions that are likely to be influenced by financial statements.
1–5. Give three examples of users of financial statements.
1–6. Briefly distinguish between *financial accounting* and *management accounting*.
1–7. Give four examples of accounting entities.
1–8. Give two synonyms for *balance sheet*.
1–9. Explain the difference between a *note payable* and an *account payable*.
1–10. Give two synonyms for *owner's equity*.
1–11. Explain the meaning of *limited liability*.
1–12. Why does this book emphasize the corporation rather than the proprietorship or the partnership?
1–13. "The idea of par value is insignificant." Explain.
1–14. Distinguish between CPA, CA, CMA, CEO, and AICPA.
1–15. **Describing Underlying Transactions.** (Alternate is 1–16.) CP Company, which was recently formed, is engaging in some preliminary transactions before beginning full-scale operations for retailing hand-held computers. The balances of each item in the company's accounting equation are given below for May 10 and for each of the next ten business

days. State briefly what you think took place on each of these ten days, assuming that only one transaction occurred each day.

	CASH	ACCOUNTS RECEIVABLE	COMPUTER INVENTORY	STORE FIXTURES	ACCOUNTS PAYABLE	OWNERS' EQUITY
May 10	$ 6,000	$4,000	$18,000	$ 3,000	$ 4,000	$27,000
11	11,000	4,000	18,000	3,000	4,000	32,000
12	11,000	4,000	18,000	7,000	4,000	36,000
15	8,000	4,000	21,000	7,000	4,000	36,000
16	8,000	4,000	26,000	7,000	9,000	36,000
17	11,000	1,000	26,000	7,000	9,000	36,000
18	6,000	1,000	26,000	14,000	11,000	36,000
19	3,000	1,000	26,000	14,000	8,000	36,000
22	3,000	1,000	25,500	14,000	7,500	36,000
23	4,000	5,000	25,500	9,000	7,500	36,000
24	1,000	5,000	25,500	9,000	7,500	33,000

1–16. DESCRIBING UNDERLYING TRANSACTIONS. (Alternate is 1–15.) The balances of each item in Cryptic Company's accounting equation are given below for August 31 and for each of the next eight business days. State briefly what you think took place on each of these eight days, assuming that only one transaction occurred each day.

		CASH	ACCOUNTS RECEIVABLE	LAND	EQUIPMENT	ACCOUNTS PAYABLE	OWNERS' EQUITY
Aug.	31	$3,000	$7,000	$ 9,000	$ 8,000	$ 6,000	$21,000
Sept.	1	4,000	6,000	9,000	8,000	6,000	21,000
	2	4,000	6,000	9,000	10,000	8,000	21,000
	3	1,000	6,000	9,000	10,000	8,000	18,000
	4	2,000	9,000	5,000	10,000	8,000	18,000
	5	2,000	9,000	10,000	10,000	8,000	23,000
	8	1,500	9,000	10,000	10,000	7,500	23,000
	9	1,000	9,000	10,000	13,000	10,000	23,000
	10	1,000	9,000	10,000	12,700	9,700	23,000

1–17. PREPARE BALANCE SHEET. (Alternate is 1–18.) Mohr Corporation's balance sheet at August 30, 19X1, contained only the following items (arranged here in random order):

Cash	$ 5,000	Accounts payable	$ 4,000
Notes payable	10,000	Furniture and fixtures	3,000
Merchandise inventory	40,000	Long-term debt payable	12,000
Paid-in capital	78,000	Building	20,000
Land	6,000	Notes receivable	2,000
Accounts receivable	13,000	Machinery and equipment	15,000

On August 31, 19X1, these transactions and events took place:

1. Purchased merchandise on account, $2,500.
2. Sold at cost for $1,000 cash some furniture that was not needed.
3. Issued additional capital stock for machinery and equipment valued at $12,000.
4. Purchased land for $25,000, of which $5,000 was paid in cash, the remaining being represented by a five-year note (long-term debt).
5. The building was valued by professional appraisers at $45,000.

Required: | Prepare in good form a balance sheet for August 31, 19X1, showing supporting computations for all new amounts.

1–18. **PREPARE BALANCE SHEET.** (Alternate is 1–17.) Cohen Corporation's balance sheet at June 29, 19X1, contained only the following items (arranged here in random order):

Paid-in capital	$198,000	Machinery and equipment	$ 20,000
Notes payable	20,000	Furniture and fixtures	8,000
Cash	8,000	Notes receivable	10,000
Accounts receivable	10,000	Accounts payable	12,000
Merchandise inventory	30,000	Building	230,000
Land	46,000	Long-term debt payable	132,000

On the following day, June 30, these transactions and events occurred:

1. Purchased machinery and equipment for $14,000, paying $3,000 in cash and signing a ninety-day note for the balance.
2. Paid $2,000 on accounts payable.
3. Sold on account some land that was not needed for $6,000, which was the Cohen Corporation's acquisition cost of the land.
4. The remaining land was valued at $250,000 by professional appraisers.
5. Issued capital stock as payment for $20,000 of the long-term debt, that is, debt due beyond one year.

Required: Prepare in good form a balance sheet for June 30, 19X1, showing supporting computations for all new amounts.

1–19. **PREPARE BALANCE SHEET.** Lisa Angelo is a realtor. She buys and sells properties on her own account, and she also earns commissions as a real estate agent for buyers and sellers. Her business was organized on November 24, 19X1, as a sole proprietorship. Angelo also owns her own personal residence. Consider the following on November 30, 19X1:

1. Angelo owes $100,000 on a mortgage on some undeveloped land, which was acquired by her business for a total price of $160,000.
2. Angelo had spent $15,000 cash for a Century 21 real estate franchise. Century 21 is a national affiliation of independent real estate brokers. This franchise is an asset.
3. Angelo owes $120,000 on a personal mortgage on her residence, which was acquired on November 20, 19X1, for a total price of $170,000.
4. Angelo owes $1,800 on a personal charge account with Bloomingdale's Department Store.
5. On November 28, Angelo hired David Goldstein as her first employee. He was to begin work on December 1. Angelo was pleased because Goldstein was one of the best real estate salesmen in the area. On November 29, Goldstein was killed in an automobile accident.
6. Business furniture of $17,000 was acquired on November 25 for $6,000 on open account plus $11,000 of business cash. On November 26, Angelo sold a $1,000 business chair for $1,000 to her next-door business neighbor on open account.
7. Angelo's balance at November 30 in her business checking account after all transactions was $14,500.

Required: Prepare a balance sheet as of November 30, 19X1, for Lisa Angelo, realtor.

1–20. **ANALYSIS OF TRANSACTIONS.** (Alternates are 1–1, 1–2, 1–3, and 1–21.) Consider the following January transactions:

1. Dart Corporation is formed on January 1, 19X1, by three persons, Granger, Gomez, and Chin. Dart will be a wholesale distributor of electronic games. Each of the three investors is issued 20,000 shares of common stock ($1 par value) for $10 cash per share. Use two stockholders' equity accounts: Capital Stock (at par) and Additional Paid-in Capital.
2. Merchandise inventory of $200,000 is acquired for cash.
3. Merchandise inventory of $80,000 is acquired on open account.
4. Unsatisfactory merchandise that cost $6,000 in transaction 3 is returned for full credit.
5. Equipment of $40,000 is acquired for a cash down payment of $10,000 plus a three-month promissory note of $30,000.

6. As a favor, Dart sells equipment of $4,000 to a business neighbor on open account. The equipment had cost $4,000.
7. Dart pays $20,000 on the account described in transaction 3.
8. Dart collects $2,000 from the business neighbor. See transaction 6.
9. Dart buys merchandise inventory of $100,000. One-fourth of the amount is paid in cash, and three-fourths is owed on open account.
10. Granger sells half of his common stock to Loring for $13 per share.

Required:
1. Using a format similar to Exhibit 1–1 (p. 11), prepare an analysis showing the effects of January transactions on the financial position of Dart Corporation.
2. Prepare a balance sheet, January 31, 19X1.

1–21. **ANALYSIS OF TRANSACTIONS.** (Alternates are 1–1, 1–2, 1–3, and 1–20.) You began a business as a wholesaler of gloves, scarves, and caps. The following events have occurred:

1. On March 1, 19X1, you invested $150,000 cash in your new sole proprietorship, which you call Arctic Products.
2. Acquired $20,000 inventory for cash.
3. Acquired $8,000 inventory on open account.
4. Acquired equipment for $15,000 in exchange for a $5,000 cash down payment and a $10,000 promissory note.
5. A large retail store, which you had hoped would be a big customer, discontinued operations.
6. You take gloves home for your family. The gloves were carried in Arctic's inventory at $600. (Regard this as a borrowing by you from Arctic Products.)
7. Gloves that cost $300 in transaction 2 were of the wrong style. You returned them and obtained a full cash refund.
8. Gloves that cost $800 in transaction 3 were of the wrong color. You returned them and obtained gloves of the correct color in exchange.
9. Caps that cost $500 in transaction 3 had an unacceptable quality. You returned them and obtained full credit on your account.
10. Paid $2,000 on promissory note.
11. You use your personal cash savings of $4,000 to acquire some equipment for Arctic. You consider this as an additional investment in your business.
12. Paid $3,000 on open account.
13. Two scarf manufacturers who are suppliers for Arctic announced a 7% rise in prices, effective in sixty days.
14. You use your personal cash savings of $1,000 to acquire a new TV set for your family.
15. You exchange equipment that cost $4,000 in transaction 4 with another wholesaler. However, the equipment received, which is almost new, is smaller and is worth only $1,500. Therefore the other wholesaler also agrees to pay you $500 in cash now and an additional $2,000 in cash in sixty days. (No gain or loss is recognized on this transaction.)

Required:
1. Using Exhibit 1–1 (p. 11) as a guide, prepare an analysis of Arctic's transactions for March. Confine your analysis to the effects on the financial position of Arctic Products.
2. Prepare a balance sheet for Arctic Products, March 31, 19X1.

1–22. **PERSONAL AND PROFESSIONAL ENTITIES.** J. Loreno, a recent graduate of a school of medicine, was penniless on December 25, 19X1.

1. On December 26, Loreno inherited an enormous sum of money.
2. On December 27, she placed $90,000 in a business checking account for her unincorporated practice of medicine.
3. On December 28, she purchased a home for a down payment of $100,000 plus a home mortgage payable of $300,000.

4. On December 28, Loreno agreed to rent a medical office. She provided a $1,000 cash damage deposit (from her business cash), which will be fully refundable when she vacates the premises. This deposit is a business asset. Rental payments are to be made in advance on the first business day of each month. (The first payment of $700 is not to be made until January 2, 19X2.)

5. On December 28, Loreno purchased medical equipment for $5,000 business cash plus an $11,000 promissory note due in ninety days.

6. On December 28, she also purchased medical supplies for $1,000 on open account.

7. On December 28, Loreno purchased medical office furniture for $4,000 of business cash.

8. On December 29, Loreno hired a medical assistant-receptionist for $380 per week. He was to report to work on January 2.

9. On December 30, Loreno lent $2,000 of business cash in return for a one-year note from G. Holden, a local candy store owner. Holden had indicated that she would spread the news about the new physician.

Required:

1. Use the format demonstrated in Exhibit 1–1 (p. 11) to analyze the transactions of J. Loreno, physician. To avoid crowding, put your numbers in thousands of dollars. Do not restrict yourself to the account titles in Exhibit 1–1.
2. Prepare a balance sheet as of December 31, 19X1.

☐ Understanding Published Financial Reports

1–23. BANK BALANCE SHEET. Consider the following balance sheet accounts of Bank of America:

ASSETS		LIABILITIES AND STOCKHOLDERS' EQUITY	
Cash	$ 7,649,266	Deposits	$ 94,047,703
U.S. government and		Other liabilities	18,513,288
other securities	15,911,503	Total liabilities	$112,560,991
Loans receivable	84,043,461	Stockholders' equity	5,118,511
Premises and equipment	2,367,152		
Other assets	7,708,120	Total liabilities and	
Total assets	$117,679,502	stockholders' equity	$117,679,502

This balance sheet illustrates how banks gather and use money. Over 70% of the total assets are in the form of investments in loans, and about 80% of the total liabilities and stockholders' equity are in the form of deposits, the major liability. That is, these financial institutions are in the business of raising funds from depositors and, in turn, lending those funds to businesses, homeowners, and others. The stockholders' equity is usually tiny in comparison with the deposits (only about 5% in this case).

Required:

1. What Bank of America accounts would be affected if you deposited $1,000?
2. Why are deposits listed as liabilities?
3. What accounts would be affected if the bank lends Joan Kessler $40,000 for home renovations?
4. What accounts would be affected if Isabel Garcia withdraws $5,000 from her savings account?

1-24. PRESENTING PAID-IN CAPITAL. Consider excerpts from two balance sheets:

Occidental Petroleum Corporation

Common shares, $.20 par value; authorized 100 million shares; issued 68,057,086 shares	$ 13,611,000
Additional paid-in capital	798,695,000

Clark Equipment

Capital stock common—$7.50 par value—outstanding 13,686,131 shares (includes capital in excess of par value)	$151,850,000

1. How would the presentation of Occidental's stockholders' equity accounts be affected if one million more shares were issued for $50 cash per share?
2. How would the presentation of Clark Equipment's stockholders' equity accounts be affected if one million more shares were issued for $50 cash per share? Be specific.

1-25. PRESENTING PAID-IN CAPITAL. (Alternate is 1–26.) Honeywell, Inc., maker of thermostats and a variety of complex control systems, presented the following in its balance sheet of January 1, 19XX:

Common stock—$1.50 par value, 47,422,792 shares issued and outstanding	?
Additional paid-in capital	675,700,000

What amount should be shown on the common stock line? What was the average price per share paid by the original investors for the Honeywell common stock? How do your answers compare with the $72 market price of the stock on January 2, 19XX? Comment briefly.

1-26. PRESENTING PAID-IN CAPITAL. (Alternate is 1–25.) The Procter & Gamble Company has many widely known products. Examples of brand names are Tide, Crest, Crisco, and Jif. The following items were presented in the balance sheet of June 30, 1988:

Common stock—$1 stated value, 169 million shares issued and outstanding	?
Additional paid-in capital (in millions of dollars)	463

1. What amount should be shown on the common stock line? (The term "stated value" is equivalent to "par value.")
2. What was the average price per share paid by the original investors for the Procter & Gamble common stock?
3. How do your answers compare with the $75 market price of the stock on July 1, 1988? Comment briefly.

1–27. PREPARE BALANCE SHEET. (Alternate is 1–28.) General Motors Corporation (GM) is the world's largest manufacturer of automobiles. GM's recent annual report included the following balance sheet items (in millions of dollars):

U.S. government and other securities	$ 8,100
Properties	19,402
Accounts payable	4,744
Inventories	7,360
Capital stock	788
Cash	?
Total stockholders' equity	?
Long-term debt	2,417
Total assets	52,145
Loans payable	3,086
Accounts receivable	7,358
Other assets	9,458
Additional stockholders' equity	23,426
Other liabilities	17,684

Required: Prepare a condensed balance sheet, including amounts for
1. Cash. What do you think of its relative size?
2. Total stockholders' equity.
3. Total liabilities.

1–28. PREPARE BALANCE SHEET. (Alternate is 1–27.) Procter & Gamble, Inc. has many popular products, including Tide, Jif, and Crest. Its balance sheet of June 30, 1988, contained the following (in millions):

Long-term debt payable	$ 2,462
Cash	(1)
Total shareholders' equity	(2)
Total liabilities	(3)
Accounts receivable	1,759
Common stock	169
Inventories	2,292
Accounts payable	1,835
Property, plant, and equipment	6,778
Additional shareholders' equity	6,168
Other assets	3,941
Other liabilities	4,186
Total assets	14,820

Required: Prepare a condensed balance sheet, including amounts for
1. Cash. What do you think of its relative size?
2. Total shareholders' equity.
3. Total liabilities.

1–29. HOUSE OF FABRICS ANNUAL REPORT. This and similar problems in succeeding chapters focus on the financial statements of an actual company. House of Fabrics, Inc., is the largest home-sewing/craft retailer in the United States. Its 672 company-owned stores located in forty-three states sell medium-priced fabrics, notions, crafts, and sewing machines. The stores are known either as House of Fabrics or as So-Fro Fabrics.

As each homework problem is solved, readers gradually strengthen their understanding of actual financial statements in their entirety.

Refer to the House of Fabrics balance sheet on page 753, and answer the following questions:

1. How much cash did House of Fabrics have on January 31, 1989?
2. What were total assets on January 31, 1989? January 31, 1988?
3. Write the company's accounting equation as of January 31, 1989, by filling in the dollar amounts:

Assets = Liabilities + Stockholders' equity

CHAPTER 2

The Income Statement: The Accrual Basis

LEARNING
OBJECTIVES

After studying this chapter, you should be able to

1. Define and explain **revenues, expenses, net income, dividends,** and **retained income**
2. Distinguish between **dividends** and **expense, unexpired costs** and **expired costs,** and the **cash** and **accrual** bases of accounting
3. Use the expanded balance sheet equation for analyzing some typical transactions of an entity and for constructing a set of financial statements
4. Explain the basic accounting concepts described in this chapter: **accounting time period, recognition, matching** and **cost recovery,** and **stable monetary unit**
5. Compute and explain four popular ratios relating to the earnings, dividends, and market prices of the common stock of corporations (Appendix 2)

What is income? How is it measured? These questions have been the subject of perpetual debate among accountants, economists, managers, investors, politicians, and others. We now consider income-producing activities and how the accountant portrays them.

THE RUDIMENTS OF INCOME

☐ Various Meanings

Almost all of us have a reason for learning about how accountants measure income. For example, we want to know how we are doing as individuals, as corporations, as hospitals, or as universities. Even nonprofit institutions use a concept of income as a way of determining how much they can afford to spend to accomplish their objectives. Investors use a concept of income to measure their successes and failures and to compare the performance of their existing and potential holdings. Indeed, income is the primary way of evaluating the economic performance of people, corporations, other entities, and economies as a whole.

At first glance, income seems like a straightforward concept. Most persons think of income as being what is reported on individual tax returns. However, individuals who have filed any but the simplest income tax returns will quickly testify that the concept of taxable income frequently drives calm, intelligent, honest taxpayers to the brink of madness. The problems of measuring income are seldom simple.

The general ideal of income has been expressed in several ways, including a net increase in "wealth" or "capital" or "general purchasing power" or "financial resources" or "command over goods and services." Most people may agree with such abstract descriptions, but fierce arguments have occurred regarding how to measure the income of a *specific* individual or entity for a *specific* time period.

Politicians may assail an industry or company for ill-gotten profits; in turn, executives will complain that the accounting measurements of income are faulty. These disputes will never be fully resolved. Still, accountants are usually in the center of the arguments. Most controversies in accounting deal with how income should be measured. The issues are usually vital in the minds of the disputants, whose livelihood or measures of accomplishment are frequently affected. Examples of these parties include managers, tax collectors, hospital administrators, economists, and attorneys.

This chapter *introduces* the subject of income measurement. Income will then receive ample attention throughout the rest of this book.

☐ Operating Cycle

Most organizations exist to satisfy a desire for some type of goods or services. Whether they are profit seeking or not, they typically follow a similar, somewhat rhythmic, pattern of economic activity. An **operating cycle** (also called a *cash cycle* or *earnings cycle*) is the time span during which cash is used to acquire goods and services, which in turn are sold to customers, who in turn pay for their purchases with cash. Consider the following example. A retail business usually engages in some version of the operating cycle in order to earn profits:

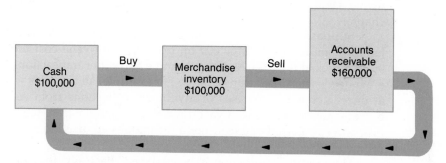

The box for Accounts Receivable (amounts owed to the business by customers) is larger than the other two boxes because the objective is to sell goods at a price higher than the acquisition cost. Retailers and nearly all other businesses buy goods and services and perform acts (such as placing them in a convenient location or changing their form) that merit selling prices that yield an expected profit. The total amount of profit earned during a particular period depends on the excess of selling prices over costs of the goods and additional expenses and on the speed of the operating cycle.

☐ The Accounting Time Period

The lone way to be certain of how successfully a business has performed is to close its doors, sell all its assets, pay all liabilities, and return any leftover cash to the owner. However, owners, managers, and others want periodic reports on how well an entity has performed. The accountant's measurements of income are a major means for evaluating progress during the accounting time period.

The calendar year is the most popular time span for measuring income. However, about 40% of large companies use a **fiscal year,** which is the year established for accounting purposes that ends on some date other than December 31. The fiscal year-end date is often the low point in annual business activity. For example, retailers like J. C. Penney use a fiscal year ending on January 31. Why? Because Christmas sales and post-Christmas sales are over, and inventories, which are at their lowest point of the year, can be counted more easily and valued with greater accuracy.

Users of financial statements want to know how well the business is doing each month, each quarter, and each half-year. Therefore, companies prepare financial statements for **interim periods,** which are the time spans established for accounting purposes that are less than a year.

We now extend the Biwheels illustration presented in Chapter 1. Exhibit 2–1 is a direct reproduction of Exhibit 1–1 (p. 11). It summarizes the nine transactions of Chapter 1. However, a corporate organization is assumed instead of a sole proprietorship. That is, the owner's equity account is no longer George Smith, Capital. In Exhibit 2–1, it is stockholders' equity. Shortly, stockholders' equity will have two parts, paid-in capital and retained income. Paid-in capital denotes the amount of capital paid in by the shareholders. **Retained income** is additional owner's equity generated by profits. It is discussed more completely later in this chapter.

Suppose a tenth transaction is a summary of sales for the entire month of January amounting to $160,000 on open account. The cost to Biwheels of the inventory sold is $100,000. Note that this and other transactions illustrated here are indeed *summarized* transactions. For example, all the sales will not take place at once, nor will purchases of inventory, collections from customers, or disbursements to suppliers. A vast number of repetitive transactions occur in practice, and specialized data-collection techniques are used to measure their effects on the entity.

How should transaction 10 be analyzed? Basically, this transaction has two phases, a *revenue phase* (10a) and an *expense phase* (10b) (dollar signs omitted):

	ASSETS		=	LIABILITIES	+	STOCKHOLDERS' EQUITY
	Accounts Receivable	Merchandise Inventory				Retained Income
(10a) Sales on open account	+160,000		=			+160,000 (sales revenues)
(10b) Cost of merchandise inventory sold		−100,000	=			−100,000 (cost of goods sold expenses)

Transaction 10a illustrates the accounting for revenues. **Revenues** are generally gross increases in owners' equity arising from gross increases in assets from the delivery of goods or services to customers.

Transaction 10b illustrates the accounting for expenses. **Expenses** are decreases in owners' equity that relate to the delivery of goods or services to customers.

Transactions 10a and 10b also illustrate the fundamental meaning of **profits** or **earnings,** or **income** which can simply be defined as the excess of revenues over expenses.

Transaction 10 is also analyzed in Exhibit 2–2, which merely continues Exhibit 2–1.

As the Retained Income column in Exhibit 2–2 shows, increases in revenues increase stockholders' equity. In contrast, increases in expenses decrease stockholders' equity. So expenses are negative stockholders' equity accounts.

EXHIBIT 2-1

BIWHEELS COMPANY

Analysis of Transactions for December 31, 19X1–January 12, 19X2 (in dollars)

DESCRIPTION OF TRANSACTION	ASSETS				=	LIABILITIES + OWNERS' EQUITY		
	Cash +	Accounts Receivable +	Merchandise Inventory +	Store Equipment =		Note Payable +	Accounts Payable +	Stockholders' Equity
(1) Initial investment	+400,000				=			+400,000
(2) Loan from bank	+100,000				=	+100,000		
(3) Acquire inventory for cash	−150,000		+150,000		=			
(4) Acquire inventory on credit			+10,000		=		+10,000	
(5) Acquire store equipment for cash plus credit	− 4,000			+15,000 =			+11,000	
(6) Sales of equipment		+1,000		− 1,000 =				
(7) Return of inventory acquired on January 3			− 800		=		− 800	
(8) Payments to creditors	− 4,000				=		− 4,000	
(9) Collections from debtors	+ 700	− 700			=			
Balance, January 12, 19X2	342,700 +	300 +	159,200 +	14,000 =		100,000 +	16,200 +	400,000
	516,200				=			516,200

41

EXHIBIT 2–2 *(Place a clip on this page for easy reference.)*

BIWHEELS COMPANY
Analysis of Transactions for January 19X2 (in dollars)

DESCRIPTION OF TRANSACTION	ASSETS					=	LIABILITIES + OWNERS' EQUITY			
							Liabilities		Stockholders' Equity	
	Cash	+ Accounts Receivable	+ Merchandise Inventory	+ Prepaid Rent	+ Store Equipment	=	Note Payable	+ Accounts Payable	+ Paid-in Capital	+ Retained Income
(1)–(9) Balance, January 12, 19X2	342,700	+ 300	+ 159,200	+	+ 14,000	=	100,000	+ 16,200	+ 400,000	
(10a) Sales on open account (inflow of assets)		+ 160,000				=				+ 160,000 (sales revenue)
(10b) Cost of merchandise inventory sold (outflow of assets)			– 100,000			=				– 100,000 (increase cost of goods sold expense)
(11) Pay rent in advance	– 6,000			+ 6,000		=				
(12) Recognize expiration of rental services				– 2,000		=				– 2,000 (increase rent expense)
(13) Recognize expiration of equipment services (depreciation)					– 100	=				– 100 (increase depreciation expense)
Balance, January 31, 19X2	336,700	+ 160,300	+ 59,200	+ 4,000	+ 13,900	=	100,000	+ 16,200	+ 400,000	+ 57,900
			574,100						574,100	

42

The relationships just depicted can also be illustrated as follows:

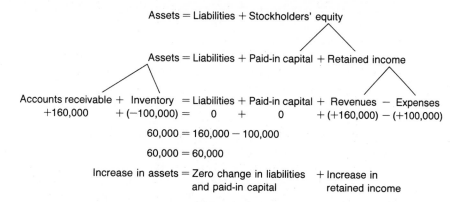

Assets = Liabilities + Stockholders' equity

Assets = Liabilities + Paid-in capital + Retained income

Accounts receivable + Inventory = Liabilities + Paid-in capital + Revenues − Expenses
+160,000 + (−100,000) = 0 + 0 + (+160,000) − (+100,000)

60,000 = 160,000 − 100,000

60,000 = 60,000

Increase in assets = Zero change in liabilities + Increase in
and paid-in capital retained income

Transaction 10 is the $160,000 sale on open account of inventory that had cost $100,000. Two things happen simultaneously: an inflow of assets in the form of accounts receivable (10a) in exchange for an outflow of assets in the form of merchandise inventory (10b). Liabilities are completely unaffected, so owners' equity rises by $160,000 (sales revenues) − $100,000 (cost of goods sold expense), or $60,000.

Recognition

Transactions 3 and 4 in Exhibit 2–1 were purchases of merchandise inventory. They were steps toward the ultimate goal–the earning of profit. But by themselves purchases earn no profit; remember that owner's equity was unaffected by the inventory acquisitions in transactions 3 and 4. Ponder the operating cycle. No profit is recognized until a sale is actually made to customers.

Accountants use several measurement concepts or conventions. A major convention is **recognition** of revenues, which is a test for determining whether revenues should be recorded in the financial statements of a given period. To be recognized, revenues must ordinarily meet two criteria:

1. Be *earned*. For revenues to be earned, the goods or services must be fully rendered. The usual evidence is full delivery to customers.
2. Be *realized*. Revenues are realized when cash or claims to cash are received in exchange for goods or services. The usual evidence is a market transaction whereby the buyer pays or promises to pay cash and the seller delivers merchandise or services. If cash is not received directly, the eventual collectibility of cash must be reasonably assured.

Matching and Cost Recovery

Another measurement concept or convention is *matching*, a favorite buzzword in accounting. **Matching** is the assignment of revenues and expenses to a particular time period for which a measurement of net income is desired. For any given time period, expenses are (1) identified, (2) measured, and (3) linked with the revenues earned. To match means to subtract the expenses from the revenues and thus compute the period's net income (or net loss).

There is a natural link between revenues and some expenses. Examples of such expenses are cost of goods sold or sales commissions. If there are no revenues, there are no cost of goods sold or sales commissions.

Many expenses relate more easily to the given time period than to revenues. For instance, rent expense occurs regardless of the level of sales in a particular month. The matching concept directs that rent and other expenses such as advertising and utilities be identified as expenses of that month's operations.

The heart of recognizing expense in the accounts is the **cost recovery** concept. That is, assets such as inventories are carried forward as assets because their costs are expected to be recovered in the form of cash inflows (or reduced cash outflows) in future periods. At the end of each period, the accountant (especially the outside auditor at the end of each year) carefully examines the evidence to determine whether these assets—these prepaid costs—should be carried forward to future periods or written off as an expense of the current period.

☐ **Prepaid Rent and Rent Expense, Transactions 11 and 12**

To focus on the matching concept, assume that there are only two expenses other than the cost of goods sold: rent expense and depreciation expense. (Interest expense on the bank loan will be considered separately in a later chapter.)

Transaction 11 is the payment of store rent of $6,000 covering January, February, and March of 19X2. Rent is $2,000 per month, payable quarterly in advance. (For simplicity regarding the dates in Chapter 1, assume that this initial payment was made on January 16, although rent is commonly paid at the start of the rental period.)

The rent disbursement acquires the right to use store facilities for the next three months. The $6,000 measures the *future* benefit from these services, so the asset *Prepaid Rent* is created (see Exhibit 2–2). Assets are defined as economic resources. They are not confined to tangible items that you can see or touch, such as cash or inventory. Assets also include the intangible legal rights to future services, such as the use of facilities.

Transaction 11's effect on the balance sheet equation is analyzed below. Transaction 12's effect is also analyzed; it is explained immediately.

	ASSETS		= LIABILITIES +	STOCKHOLDERS' EQUITY
	Cash	Prepaid Rent		Retained Income
(11) Pay rent in advance	−6,000	+6,000	=	
(12) Recognize rent expense		−2,000	=	−2,000 (increase rent expense)

Transaction 12 recognizes that one-third of the rental services has expired, so the asset is reduced and stockholders' equity is also reduced by $2,000 as rent expense for January. This recognition of rent *expense* means that $2,000 of the asset, Prepaid Rent, has been "used up" in the conduct of operations during January.

Prepaid rent of $4,000 is carried forward as an asset as of January 31 because the accountant was virtually certain that it represented a future benefit. Why? Because without the prepayment, cash outflows of $2,000 each would have to be made for February and March. So the presence of the prepayment is a benefit in the sense that future cash outflows will be reduced by $4,000. Furthermore, future revenues (sales) are expected to be high enough to ensure the recovery of the $4,000.

☐ Depreciation Expenses, Transaction 13

Transaction 13 recognizes that store equipment is really a bundle of services that will have a useful life beyond one year. **Depreciation** is the systematic allocation of the acquisition cost of plant and equipment to the expense accounts of the particular periods that benefit from the use of the assets. Depreciation applies to physical assets such as buildings, equipment, furniture, and fixtures owned by the entity. Land is not subject to depreciation.

The same matching and cost recovery concepts underlie the accounting for equipment and for prepaid rent. In both cases, the business purchases an asset that gradually wears out or is used up. As the asset is being used, more and more of its original cost is transferred from an asset account to an expense account. The sole difference between equipment and prepaid rent is the length of time taken before the asset loses its usefulness. Buildings, equipment, and furniture remain useful for many years; prepaid expenses usually expire within a year.

Consider the Biwheels equipment. A portion of the original cost of $14,000 becomes depreciation expense in each month of the equipment's useful life, say, 140 months. Applying the matching concept, depreciation expense would be $14,000 ÷ 140 months, or $100 per month:

	ASSETS	= LIABILITIES +	STOCKHOLDERS' EQUITY
	Store Equipment		Retained Income
(13) Recognize depreciation expense	− 100	=	− 100 (increase depreciation expense)

More will be said about depreciation in Chapter 3. But no matter how much is said, the general concept of expense should be clear by now. The purchases and uses of goods and services (for example, inventories, rent, equipment) ordinarily consist of two basic steps: (a) the *acquisition* of the *assets* (transactions 3, 4, 5, and 11) and (b) the *expiration* of the assets as *expenses* (transactions 10b, 12, and 13). When these assets expire, the total assets and owners' equity are decreased. When sales to customers bring new assets to the business, its total assets and owners' equity are increased. Expense accounts are basically deductions from stockholders' equity. Similarly, revenue accounts are basically additions to stockholders' equity.

The Income Statement

Exhibits 2–1 and 2–2 are important because they provide an overview of the entire accounting process. We have already seen how a balance sheet may be prepared through the use of such exhibits. Similarly, an income statement may be prepared by analyzing the *changes* in owners' equity, as Exhibit 2–3 demonstrates. An **income statement** is a report of all revenues and expenses pertaining to a specific time period. The term *net income* is the world-famous "bottom line"— the remainder after *all* expenses (including income taxes, which are illustrated later) have been deducted from revenue.

EXHIBIT 2–3

BIWHEELS COMPANY
Income Statement
For the Month Ended January 31, 19X2

Sales (revenues)		$160,000
Deduct expenses:		
Cost of goods sold	$100,000	
Rent	2,000	
Depreciation	100	
Total expenses		102,100
Net income		$ 57,900

Relationship Between Balance Sheet and Income Statement

The income statement measures the operating performance of the corporation by relating its accomplishments (revenues from customers) and its efforts (cost of goods sold and other expenses). It measures performance for *a span of time*, whether it be a month, a quarter, or longer. Therefore the income statement must always indicate the exact period covered. The above example was for the month ended January 31, 19X2. Recall that the balance sheet shows the financial position at an *instant of time*, and therefore the balance sheet must always indicate the exact date.

The income statement is the major link between two balance sheets:

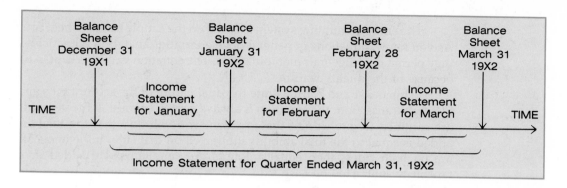

Remember that the balance sheet provides a snapshot, a photograph at an *instant* of time; in contrast, the income statement provides a moving picture for a *span* of time.

As Exhibit 2–2 shows, the accountant records increases (revenues of $160,000) and decreases (expenses of $102,100) in owners' equity. At the end of a given period, these items are summarized and explained in the form of an income statement, as Exhibit 2–3 illustrates. The net income ($57,900) is then added to Retained Income, which appears in the balance sheet as an element of owners' equity and which, for successful companies, often accumulates to vast amounts over many years as the major part of the shareholders' residual claim against total assets.

☐ Analytical Power of the Balance Sheet Equation

As you study Exhibits 2–1 and 2–2, the following points should clarify the way in which accountants use the fundamental balance sheet equation as their framework for analyzing and reporting the effects of transactions:

$$\text{Assets (A)} = \text{Liabilities (L)} + \text{Stockholders' equity (SE)} \tag{1}$$

SE equals the original ownership claim plus the increase in ownership claim due to profitable operations. That is, SE equals the claim arising from paid-in capital plus the claim arising from retained income. Therefore

$$\text{Assets} = \text{Liabilities} + \text{Paid-in capital} + \text{Retained income} \tag{2}$$

But, in our illustration, Retained Income equals Revenue minus Expenses. Therefore

$$\text{Assets} = \text{Liabilities} + \text{Paid-in capital} + \text{Revenue} - \text{Expenses} \tag{3}$$

Revenue and expense accounts are nothing more than subdivisions of stockholders' equity—temporary stockholders' equity accounts, as it were. Their purpose is to summarize the volume of sales and the various expenses so that management is kept informed of the reasons for the numerous increases and decreases in stockholders' equity in the course of ordinary operations. In this way comparisons can be made, standards or goals can be set, and control can be better exercised.

The entire accounting system is based on the simple balance sheet equation. As you know, equations in general have enormous analytical potential because they permit dual algebraic manipulations. The equation is always kept in balance because of the duality feature.

Exhibits 2–1 and 2–2 illustrate the dual nature of the accountant's analysis. For each transaction, the equation is always kept in balance. If the items affected are confined to one side of the equation, you will find that the total amount added is equal to the total amount subtracted on that side. If the items affected are on both sides, then equal amounts are simultaneously added or simultaneously subtracted on each side.

The striking feature of the balance sheet equation is its universal applicability. No transaction has ever been conceived, no matter how simple or complex, that cannot be analyzed via the equation. The top technical partners in the world's largest professional accounting firms, when confronted with the most intricate transactions of multinational companies, will inevitably discuss and think about their analyses in terms of the balance sheet equation and its major components: assets, liabilities, and owners' equity (including the explanations of changes in owners' equity that must often take the form of revenues and expenses).

☐ **Measurement of Expenses: Assets Expire** 만효되다.

Transactions 10b, 12, and 13 recognize the cost of merchandise sold and the expiration of services acquired. They demonstrate how assets can be viewed as bundles of economic services awaiting future use or expiration. It is helpful to think of assets, other than cash and receivables, as prepaid or stored costs (for example, inventories or equipment) that are carried forward to future periods rather than immediately charged against revenue:

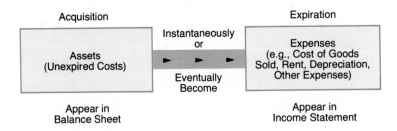

Expenses are decreases in owners' equity because of used-up assets. Thus assets are unexpired costs held back from the expense stream and carried in the balance sheet to await expiration in future periods.

The analysis of the inventory, rent, and depreciation transactions in Exhibit 2–2 maintains this distinction of acquisition and expiration. The unexpired costs of inventory, prepaid rent, and equipment are assets until they are used up and become expenses.

Services are often acquired and used almost instantaneously. Examples are advertising services, miscellaneous supplies, and sales salaries and commissions. Conceptually, these costs should, at least momentarily, be viewed as assets upon acquisition before being written off as expenses. For example, suppose there was an extra transaction in Exhibit 2–2 whereby newspaper advertising was acquired for $1,000 cash. To abide by the acquisition-expiration sequence, the transaction could be analyzed in two phases:

	ASSETS			= LIABILITIES +	STOCKHOLDERS' EQUITY	
TRANSACTION	Cash	Other + Assets +	Prepaid Advertising =		Paid-in Capital +	Retained Income
Phase (a) Prepay for advertising	−1,000		+1,000 =			
Phase (b) Use up advertising			−1,000 =			−1,000 (advertising expense)

As a matter of practice, however, many services are acquired and used up so quickly that accountants do not bother recording an asset such as Prepaid Advertising or Prepaid Rent for them. Instead a shortcut is usually taken when goods and services are to be routinely consumed in the period of their purchase:

TRANSACTION	Cash	+ Other Assets = Liabilities +	Paid-in Capital +	Retained Income
Phases (a) and (b) together	−1,000	=		−1,000 (advertising expense)

Making the entry in two steps instead of one is cumbersome from a practical bookkeeping viewpoint. However, the two steps underscore a *crucial concept*. We want an orderly way of thinking about what the manager does. The manager acquires goods and services, not expenses per se. These goods and services become expenses as they are used in obtaining revenue.

Some of the most difficult issues in accounting center on *when* an unexpired cost expires and becomes an expense. For example, some accountants believe that research and development costs should be accounted for as unexpired costs (and shown on balance sheets among the assets as "Deferred Research and Development Costs") and written off to expense in some systematic manner over a period of years. But the regulators of financial accounting in the United States have ruled that such costs have vague future benefits that are difficult to measure reliably and thus have required writing them off as expenses immediately. In cases such as this, research costs are not found on balance sheets.

ACCRUAL BASIS AND CASH BASIS OF ACCOUNTING

☐ Efforts and Accomplishments

The process of determining income and financial position is anchored to the accrual basis of accounting, as distinguished from the cash basis. The **accrual basis** recognizes the impact of transactions on the financial statements in the time periods when revenues and expenses occur. That is, revenue is recorded as it is *earned* (the recognition concept) and expenses are recorded as they are *incurred* (the matching concept)—not necessarily when cash changes hands.

In contrast, the **cash basis** of accounting recognizes the impact of transactions on the financial statements only when cash is received or disbursed. The accrual basis is required under GAAP; the cash basis does not accord with GAAP.

Compare the accrual basis with the cash basis. Transaction 10a in Exhibit 2–2, page 42, shows an example of the accrual basis. Sales revenue of $160,000 is recognized when sales are made on credit, not when cash is received. Similarly, transactions 10b, 12, and 13 (for cost of goods sold, rent, and depreciation) show that expenses are recognized as efforts are expended or services used to obtain the revenue (regardless of when cash is disbursed). Therefore income is often affected by measurements of noncash resources and obligations. The accrual basis is the principal conceptual framework for relating accomplishments (revenues) with efforts (expenses).

If the *cash basis* of accounting were used instead of the accrual basis, *revenue and expense recognition would depend solely on the timing of various cash receipts and disbursements.* Our Biwheels example for January would show zero revenue because no cash was collected from customers. Similarly, rent expense would be $6,000 (the cash disbursed for rent) rather than the $2,000 rent applicable to January. A cash measurement of net income or net loss is obviously ridiculous in this case, and it could mislead those unacquainted with the fundamentals of accounting.

Ponder the rent example. Under the cash basis, January must bear expenses for the entire quarter's rent of $6,000 merely because cash outflows occurred then. In contrast, the accrual basis measures performance more sharply by allocating the rental expense to the operations of the three months that *benefited from the use* of the facilities. In this way, the economic performance of each month will be comparable. Most accountants maintain that it is nonsense to say that January's rent expense was $6,000 and February's and March's were zero.

☐ Pause for Reflection

Our illustrations have shown that the accrual basis provides more accurate and complete accounting than the cash basis. The more complete the accounting, the better equipped the decision makers are to reach conclusions about an organization's financial performance and position. Four concepts or conventions highlighted in the accrual basis are the accounting time period, recognition, matching, and cost recovery.

If you have never studied accounting before, or if you studied it long ago, do not proceed further until you have solved the following problem. There are no shortcuts. Pushing a pencil is an absolute necessity for becoming comfortable with accounting concepts. The cost-benefit test will easily be met; your gain in knowledge will exceed your investment of time.

Please do the work on your own. In particular, do not ask for help from professional accountants or advanced accounting students if they introduce any new terms beyond those already covered. For example, the technical terms *debits*, *credits*, and *ledger accounts* will only confuse, not clarify, at this stage. Instead, scrutinize Exhibits 2–1 and 2–2. Note how each transaction affects the balance sheet equation. Then solve the review problem that follows.

SUMMARY PROBLEM FOR YOUR REVIEW

☐ **Problem One**

Biwheels' transactions for January were analyzed in Exhibits 2–1 and 2–2, pages 41–42. The balance sheet, January 31, 19X2, is:

BIWHEELS COMPANY
Balance Sheet
January 31, 19X2

ASSETS		LIABILITIES AND STOCKHOLDERS' EQUITY		
		Liabilities:		
Cash	$336,700	Note payable		$100,000
Accounts receivable	160,300	Accounts payable		16,200
Merchandise		Total liabilities		$116,200
inventory	59,200	Stockholder's equity:		
Prepaid rent	4,000	Paid-in capital	$400,000	
Store equipment	13,900	Retained income	57,900	
		Total stockholders' equity		457,900
		Total liabilities and		
Total assets	$574,100	stockholders' equity		$574,100

The following series of transactions occurred during February:

(14) Collection of accounts receivable, $130,000.
(15) Payments of accounts payable, $15,000.
(16) Acquisitions of inventory on open account, $80,000, and for cash, $10,000.
(17) Merchandise carried in inventory at a cost of $110,000 was sold on open account for $125,000 and for cash for $51,000.
(18) Recognition of rent expense for February.
(19) Recognition of depreciation expense for February.

Required:
1. Prepare an analysis of transactions, employing the equation approach demonstrated in Exhibit 2–2.
2. Prepare a balance sheet as of February 28, 19X2, and an income statement for the month of February.

1. *Analysis of transactions.* The answer is in Exhibit 2–4. All transactions are straightforward extensions or repetitions of the January transactions.

2. *Preparation of financial statements.* Exhibits 2–5 and 2–6 contain the balance sheet and the income statement, which have been described earlier.

DIVIDENDS AND RETAINED INCOME
이익배당

□ **Dividends Are Not Expenses**

Extending our Biwheels illustration, we now assume an additional transaction in February. On February 28, cash dividends of $50,000 are declared by the board of directors and disbursed to stockholders. The accountant would analyze this transaction (20) as follows:

	ASSETS =	LIABILITIES +	STOCKHOLDERS' EQUITY
	Cash		Retained Income
(20) Declaration and payment of cash dividends	− 50,000 =		− 50,000 (dividends)

As transaction 20 shows, cash dividends are not expenses like rent and depreciation. They should not be deducted from revenues because dividends are not directly related to the generation of sales or the conduct of operations. Generally, **dividends** are distributions of cash to stockholders that reduce retained income. The ability to pay dividends is fundamentally caused by profitable operations. Retained income increases as profits accumulate, and it decreases as dividends occur.

The entire right-hand side of the balance sheet can be thought of as claims against the total assets. The liabilities are the claims of creditors. The stockholders' equity represents the residual claims of owners arising out of their initial investment (paid-in capital) and subsequent profitable operations (retained income).

As a successful company grows, the Retained Income account can soar enormously if dividends are not paid. It can easily be the largest stockholders' equity account. Its balance is the cumulative, lifetime earnings of the company less its cumulative, lifetime losses and dividends.

□ **Statement of Retained Income**

Exhibit 2–7 shows a new financial statement, the **statement of retained income.** The statement merely lists the beginning balance (in this case, January 31), followed by a description of any major changes (in this case, net income and dividends), and the ending balance (February 28).

EXHIBIT 2–4

BIWHEELS COMPANY
Analysis of Transactions for February 19X2 (in dollars)

DESCRIPTION OF TRANSACTION		ASSETS					=	LIABILITIES + OWNERS' EQUITY			
								Liabilities		Stockholders' Equity	
	Cash +	Accounts Receivable +	Merchandise Inventory +	Prepaid Rent +	Store Equipment	=	Notes Payable +	Accounts Payable +	Paid-in Capital +	Retained Income
Balance, January 31, 19X2	336,700 +	160,300 +	59,200 +	4,000 +	13,900	=	100,000 +	16,200 +	400,000 +	57,900
(14) Collection of accounts receivable	+130,000	−130,000				=				
(15) Payments of accounts payable	−15,000					=		−15,000		
(16) Acquisitions of Inventory on open account and for cash	−10,000		+90,000			=		+80,000		
(17a) Sales on open account and for cash	+51,000	+125,000				=				+176,000 (increase sales revenue)
(17b) Cost of inventory sold			−110,000			=				−110,000 (increase cost of goods sold expense)
(18) Recognize expiration of rental services				−2,000		=				−2,000 (increase rent expense)
(19) Recognize expiration of equipment services (depreciation)					−100	=				−100 (increase depreciation expense)
Balance, February 28, 19X2	492,700 +	155,300 +	39,200 +	2,000 +	13,800	=	100,000 +	81,200 +	400,000 +	121,800
	703,000						703,000			

EXHIBIT 2–5

BIWHEELS COMPANY
Balance Sheet February 28, 19X2

ASSETS			LIABILITIES AND STOCKHOLDERS' EQUITY		
			Liabilities:		
Cash	$492,700		Notes payable	$100,000	
Accounts receivable	155,300		Accounts payable	81,200	$181,200
Merchandise					
inventory	39,200		Stockholders' equity:		
Prepaid rent	2,000		Paid-in capital	$400,000	
Store equipment	13,800		Retained income	121,800	521,800
Total	$703,000		Total		$703,000

EXHIBIT 2–6

BIWHEELS COMPANY
Income Statement
For the Month Ended February 28, 19X2

Sales		$176,000
Deduct expenses:		
Cost of goods sold	$110,000	
Rent	2,000	
Depreciation	100	112,100
Net income		$ 63,900

EXHIBIT 2–7

BIWHEELS COMPANY
Statement of Retained Income
For the Month Ended February 28, 19X2

Retained income, January 31, 19X2	$ 57,900
Net income for February	63,900
Total	$121,800
Dividends declared (ᅟ)	50,000
Retained income, February 28, 19X2	$ 71,800

Frequently, the statement of retained income is added on to the bottom of the income statement. If so, the combined statements are called a *statement of income and retained income*. For example, Exhibits 2–6 and 2–7 could be combined and retitled and would appear as shown in Exhibit 2–8.

Note how Exhibits 2–6 and 2–7 are anchored to the balance sheet equation:

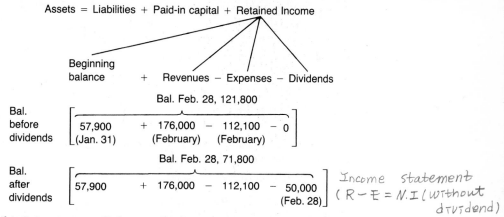

Assets = Liabilities + Paid-in capital + Retained Income

Beginning balance + Revenues − Expenses − Dividends

Bal. Feb. 28, 121,800

Bal. before dividends	57,900 (Jan. 31)	+ 176,000 (February)	− 112,100 (February)	− 0

Bal. Feb. 28, 71,800

Bal. after dividends	57,900	+ 176,000	− 112,100	− 50,000 (Feb. 28)

Income statement
(R−E = N.I (without dividend)

Exhibit 2-8 presents all the numbers contained in the second set of brackets and concludes with the $71,800 ending balance of retained income. *Retained Income St (R−E = N.I − dividend)*

☐ Customs of Presentation

Exhibits 2–7 and 2–8 illustrate some customs that accountants follow when they prepare all their financial statements. To save space and unnecessary repetition, accountants often place a subtotal on the right side of the final number in a column, as is illustrated by the $112,100 in Exhibit 2–8. Under this arrangement, the expenses caption is used only once. As an alternative, accountants sometimes use the caption twice, as a first line to describe the classification and then on a separate additional final line to describe the subtotal of the classification. In our example, the final line would be: Total expenses $112,100.

EXHIBIT 2–8

BIWHEELS COMPANY
Statement of Income and Retained Income
For the Month Ended February 28, 19X2

Sales		$176,000
Deduct expenses:		
Cost of goods sold	$110,000	
Rent	2,000	
Depreciation	100	112,100
Net income		$ 63,900*
Retained income, January 31, 19X2		57,900
Total		$121,800
Dividends declared		50,000
Retained income, February 28, 19X2		$ 71,800

* Note how the income statement ends here. The $63,900 simultaneously becomes the initial item on the statement of retained income portion of this combined statement.

Dollar signs are customarily used at the beginning and end of each column of dollar amounts and for each subtotal or total within the column. However, many accountants will use a dollar sign only with the beginning number in a column and with the final number in the same column. For example, these accountants would not use a dollar sign with the $63,900 and the $121,800 in Exhibit 2–8. Double-underscores (double rulings) are typically used to denote final numbers.

Retained Income and Cash

Retained income is not a pot of cash that is awaiting distribution to stockholders. Consider the following illustration:

Step 1. Assume an opening balance sheet of:

Cash	$100	Paid-in capital	$100

Step 2. Purchase inventory for $50 cash. The balance sheet now reads:

Cash	$ 50	Paid-in capital	$100
Inventory	50		
Total assets	$100		

Steps 1 and 2 demonstrate a fundamental point. Owners' equity is an undivided claim against the total assets (in the aggregate). For example, half the shareholders do not have a specific claim on cash, and the other half do not have a specific claim on inventory. Instead all the shareholders have an undivided claim against (or, if you prefer, an undivided interest in) all the assets.

Step 3. Now sell the inventory for $80 cash, which produces a retained income of $80 − $50 = $30:

Cash	$130	Paid-in capital	$100
		Retained income	30
		Total owners' equity	$130

At this stage, the retained income might be reflected by a $30 increase in cash. But the $30 in retained income connotes only a *general* claim against *total assets*. This can be clarified by the transaction that follows.

Step 4. Purchase inventory and equipment, in the amounts of $60 and $50, respectively. Now:

Cash	$ 20	Paid-in capital	$100
Inventory	60	Retained income	30
Equipment	50		
Total assets	$130	Total owners' equity	$130

Where is the $30 in retained income reflected? Is it reflected in Cash, in Inventory, or in Equipment? The answer is indeterminate. This example helps to explain the nature of the Retained Income account. It is a *claim*, not a pot of gold. Retained income is increased by profitable operations, but the cash inflow from sales is an increment in assets (see Step 3). When the cash inflow takes place, management will use the cash, most often to buy more inventory or equipment (Step 4). Retained income (and also paid-in capital) is a *general* claim against, or *undivided* interest in, *total* assets, *not* a specific claim against cash or against any other particular asset. Do not confuse the assets themselves with the claims against the assets.

Misconceptions About Dividends

As previously stated, dividends are distributions of assets that reduce ownership claims. The cash assets that are distributed typically arose from profitable operations. Thus dividends or withdrawals are often spoken of as "distributions of profits" or "distributions of retained income." Dividends are often erroneously described as being "paid out of retained income." In reality, cash dividends are distributions of assets that reduce a portion of the ownership claim. The distribution is made possible by profitable operations.

The amount of cash dividends declared by the board of directors of a company depends on many factors. For example, the amount of a dividend often is some fraction of net income, but dividends are not necessarily tied to current net income. Although profitable operations and the existence of a balance in Retained Income are generally essential, dividend policy is also influenced by the company's cash position and future needs for cash to pay debts or to purchase additional assets. Dividends are also influenced by whether the company is committed to a stable dividend policy or to a policy that normally ties dividends to fluctuations in net income. Under a stable policy, dividends may be paid consistently even if a company encounters a few years of little or no net income. (More is said about dividends in Chapter 10.)

The existence of retained income enables a board of directors to *declare* a dividend. The existence of cash enables the corporation to *pay* the dividend. Cash and Retained Income are two entirely separate accounts sharing no necessary relationship.

Incidentally, the terms liquidation and *to liquidate* are often encountered in the world of accounting. Depending on the specific situation, **liquidation** means payment of a debt, or the conversion of assets into cash, or the complete sale of assets and settlement of claims when an entity is terminated. Thus an entity is sometimes described as being "highly liquid" when it has a vast amount of cash in relation to its other assets or its debts. Then liabilities are more likely to be paid, that is, liquidated.

Steps in Paying Dividends

As shown earlier, the effect of the declaration and payment of a dividend is as follows:

	ASSETS	=	LIABILITIES	+	STOCKHOLDERS' EQUITY
	Cash				Retained Income
(20) Declaration and payment of cash dividends	− 50,000	=			− 50,000 (dividends)

Entry 20 combined the declaration and payment into a single transaction as if everything had occurred on the same day. However, corporations usually approach dividend matters in steps. The board of directors declares a dividend on one date (declaration date) payable to stockholders of record as of a second date (record date) and actually pays the dividend on a third date (payment date).

The *Wall Street Journal* lists dividends as follows:

COMPANY	PERIOD	AMT.	PAYABLE DATE	RECORD DATE
Colgate-Palmolive Co.	Q*	$.34	5–15	4–25
Dow Chemical Co.	Q	.45	4–30	3–31

* Q indicates that the dividend is typically declared quarterly.

Such dividend actions entail two accounting transactions. First, the *declaration* affects the corporation's financial position because the shareholders also become creditors for the amount (only) of the legally declared dividend. Second, the resulting liability is reduced only when the cash is disbursed. Consequently, entry 20 would be subdivided into two phases:

	ASSETS	=	LIABILITIES	+	STOCKHOLDERS' EQUITY
	Cash	=	Dividends Payable	+	Retained Income
(20a) Date of declaration		=	+ 50,000		− 50,000 (dividends)
(20b) Date of payment	− 50,000	=	− 50,000		
The net effect is eventually the same as in 20 above	− 50,000	=	0		− 50,000

Although the ultimate effect is the same as that shown originally in transaction 20, a balance sheet prepared *between* the date of declaration and the date of payment must show dividends payable as a *liability*. Note too that although a corporation may be expected to pay dividends, no legal liability occurs until a board of directors formally declares a dividend.

SYNONYMS AND THE REAL WORLD

Unfortunately for the new student of accounting, various organizations do not use identical terms to describe the same concept or account. Instead there are a multitude of synonyms. These terms are not introduced here to confuse you. Our major objective here is to acquaint you with the real world of accounting vocabulary. In this way, you will not be surprised when a company's financial statement uses a term that may differ from the term you learned initially.

The terms *income, earnings,* and *profits* are often used interchangeably. Indeed, many companies will use net *income* on their income statements but will refer to retained income as retained *earnings.* As Exhibit 2–9 shows, Anheuser-Busch, H. J. Heinz, and Colgate-Palmolive are examples. In short, retained income is frequently called **retained earnings** or **reinvested earnings**.

The term *earnings* is becoming increasingly popular because it has a preferable image. *Earnings* apparently implies compensation for honest toil, whereas *income* or *profit* evidently inspires cartoonists to portray managers as greedy, evil-looking individuals.

The income statement is frequently called the **statement of income, statement of operations, results of operations, or statement of earnings.** Other terms sometimes encountered are the **operating statement** and **statement of revenues and expenses.** For many years, the most popular name for this statement was statement of profit and loss, often termed the **P & L statement.** Such a label is justifiably fading into oblivion. After all, the ultimate result is either a profit *or* a loss.

The terms **revenues, sales,** and **sales revenues** are synonyms.

The term **cost of sales** is a synonym for **cost of goods sold.** For example, La-Z-Boy Chair Company uses cost of sales, not cost of goods sold. Both terms mean the entity's original acquisition cost of the inventory that was sold to customers during the reporting period.

EXHIBIT 2–9

SOME SYNONYMS IN ACCOUNTING

TERM INITIALLY USED IN THIS BOOK	EXAMPLES OF SYNONYMS	EXAMPLE OF COMPANIES
1. Net income		Anheuser-Busch, H. J. Heinz, Colgate-Palmolive
	Net earnings	General Mills, Chrysler, Johnson & Johnson
	Profit	Caterpillar
2. Retained income		General Motors
	Retained earnings	Anheuser-Busch, H. J. Heinz, Colgate-Palmolive
	Reinvested earnings	Scott Paper, Coca-Cola
	Earnings retained for use in the business	Ford Motor
	Profit employed in the business	Caterpillar

Fortunately, some accounting terms have no synonyms. Examples are *expenses* and *dividends*.

NONPROFIT ORGANIZATIONS

The examples in this chapter have focused on profit-seeking organizations, but balance sheets and income statements are also used by not-for-profit organizations. For example, hospitals and universities have income statements, although they are called statements of *revenue* and *expense*. The "bottom line" is frequently called "excess of revenue over expense" or "net financial result" rather than "net income."

The basic concepts of assets, liabilities, revenue, expense, and operating statements are applicable to all organizations, whether they be utilities, symphony orchestras, private, public, American, Asian, and so forth. However, some nonprofit organizations have been slow to adopt some ideas that are widely used in progressive companies. For example, in many governmental organizations the accrual basis of accounting has not yet supplanted the cash basis. This has hampered the evaluation of the performance of such organizations. A recent annual report of the New York Metropolitan Museum of Art stated: "As the Museum's financial operations have begun to resemble in complexity those of a corporation, it has become necessary to make certain changes in our accounting . . . operating results are reported on an accrual rather than the previously followed cash basis. Thus, revenue and expenses are recorded in the proper time period."

An article in *Forbes* commented:

☐ Shoddy, misleading accounting has not been the cause of our cities' problems but it has prevented us from finding solutions. Or even looking for solutions until it's too late. Chicago's schools, for example, suddenly found themselves unable to pay their teachers. Had the books been kept like any decent corporation's, that could never have happened. The most basic difference is in the common use of cash accounting rather than the accrual method that nearly all businesses use.

MORE ON GENERALLY ACCEPTED ACCOUNTING PRINCIPLES (GAAP)

This section continues our study of accounting principles. So far in this chapter, the accrual basis and the concepts of recognition, matching, and cost recovery have been discussed.

☐ Stable Monetary Unit

The monetary unit (called the dollar in the United States, Canada, Australia, New Zealand, and elsewhere) is the principal means for measuring assets and equities. It is the common denominator for quantifying the effects of a wide variety of transactions. Accountants record, classify, summarize, and report in terms of the monetary unit.

Such measurement assumes that the principal counter, the dollar, is an unchanging yardstick. Yet we all know that a 1990 dollar does not have the same purchasing power as a 1980 or 1970 dollar. Therefore accounting statements that include different dollars must be interpreted and compared with full consciousness of the limitations of the basic measurement unit.

□ FASB, APB, and SEC

Every technical area seems to have regulatory bodies or professional associations whose names are often abbreviated. Accounting is no exception.

American generally accepted accounting principles have been most heavily influenced by the **Financial Accounting Standards Board (FASB)** and its predecessor body, the **Accounting Principles Board (APB)**. The FASB consists of seven qualified individuals who work full time. The board is supported by a large staff and an annual $12 million budget.

The FASB is an independent creature of the private sector and is financially supported by various professional accounting associations (such as the leading organization of auditors, the American Institute of Certified Public Accountants, also known as the **AICPA**).

The FASB was established in 1973 as the replacement for the APB. The APB consisted of a group of eighteen accountants (mostly partners in large accounting firms) who worked part time. The APB issued a series of thirty-one *Opinions* during 1962–73, many of which are still the "accounting law of the land." Many of these **APB Opinions** and **FASB Statements** will be referred to in succeeding chapters of this book.

The U.S. Congress has designated the **Securities and Exchange Commission (SEC)** as holding the ultimate responsibility for authorizing the generally accepted accounting principles for companies whose stock is held by the general investing public. However, the SEC has informally delegated much rule-making power to the FASB. This public sector–private sector authority relationship can be sketched as follows:

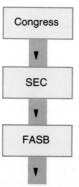

Issues pronouncements on various accounting issues. These pronouncements govern the preparation of typical financial statements.

Reconsider the three-tiered structure above. Note that Congress can overrule both the SEC and the FASB, and the SEC can overrule the FASB. Such undermining of the FASB occurs rarely, but pressure is exerted on all three tiers by corporations if they think an impending pronouncement is "wrong." Hence the setting of accounting principles is a complex process involving heavy interactions among the affected parties: public regulators (Congress and SEC), private regulators (FASB), companies, the public accounting profession, representatives of investors, and other interested groups.

In sum, the public body (the SEC) has informally delegated much rule-making power regarding accounting theory and practice to the private bodies (the APB and FASB). These boards have rendered a series of pronouncements on various accounting issues. Certified public accountants issue opinions concerning the fairness of corporate financial statements prepared for external use. These auditors must see that corporate statements do not depart from these pronouncements.

SUMMARY

An underlying structure of concepts, techniques, and conventions provides a basis for accounting practice. This structure is typically referred to as a set of generally accepted accounting principles (GAAP). This chapter has focused on how accountants measure income (the excess of revenue over expense) on the accrual basis. The essence of the accrual basis is the so-called matching process whereby revenues and expenses are assigned to a particular period for which a measurement of income is desired.

Revenues (accomplishments) are assigned to the period in which they are *recognized* (earned). Expenses (efforts) are assigned to a period in which the pertinent goods and services are either *used* or appear to have no future benefit. The *cost recovery* concept helps determine whether resources such as inventories, prepayments, and equipment should be carried forward to future periods as assets or written off to the current period as expenses.

SUMMARY PROBLEM FOR YOUR REVIEW

☐ **Problem Two** (The first problem appeared earlier in the chapter, page 51).

The following are samples of the interpretations and remarks frequently encountered with regard to financial statements. Do you agree or disagree with these observations? Explain fully.
1. "Sales show the cash coming in from customers, and the various expenses show the cash going out for goods and services. The difference is net income."
2. Consider the following June 30, 1988, accounts of Delta, a leading U.S. airline:

Common stock, par value $3.00 per share, 49,101,271 shares outstanding	$ 147,304,000
Additional paid-in capital	505,553,000
Retained earnings	1,555,966,000
Total stockholders' equity	$2,208,823,000

A shareholder commented, "Why can't that big airline pay higher wages and dividends too? It can use its hundreds of millions of dollars of retained earnings to do so."

3. "The total Delta stockholders' equity measures the amount that the shareholders would get today if the corporation were liquidated."

☐ Solution to Problem Two

1. Cash receipts and disbursements are not the fundamental basis for the accounting recognition of revenues and expenses. Credit, not cash, lubricates the economy. Therefore, if services or goods have been delivered to a customer, a legal claim to cash in the form of a receivable is deemed sufficient justification for recognizing revenue. Similarly, if services or goods have been used up, a legal obligation in the form of a payable is justification for recognizing expense.

This approach to the measurement of net income is known as the accrual method. Revenue is recognized as it is (a) earned by goods or services rendered and (b) realized. Expenses are recognized when goods or services are used up in the obtaining of revenue (or when such goods or services cannot justifiably be carried forward as an asset because they have no potential future benefit). The expenses and losses are deducted from the revenue, and the result of this matching process is net income, the net increase in stockholders' equity from the conduct of operations.

2. As the chapter indicated, retained earnings is not cash. It is a stockholders' equity account that represents the accumulated increase in ownership claims due to profitable operations. This claim or interest may be partially liquidated by the payment of cash dividends, but a growing company will reinvest cash in sustaining the added investments in receivables, inventories, plant, equipment, and other assets so necessary for expansion. As a result, the ownership claims measured by retained earnings may become "permanent" in the sense that, as a practical matter, they will never be liquidated as long as the company remains a going concern.

This linking of retained earnings and cash is only one example of fallacious interpretation. As a general rule, there is no direct relationship between the individual items on the two sides of the balance sheet. For example, Delta's cash was less than $823 million on the balance sheet date when its retained earnings exceeded $1.5 billion.

3. Stockholders' equity is a difference, the excess of assets over liabilities. If the assets were carried in the accounting records at their liquidating value today, and the liabilities were carried at the exact amounts needed for their extinguishment, the remark would be true. But such valuations would be coincidental because assets are customarily carried at *historical cost* expressed in an unchanging monetary unit. Intervening changes in markets and general price levels in inflationary times may mean that the assets are woefully understated. Investors may make a critical error if they think that balance sheets indicate current values.

Furthermore, the "market values" for publicly owned shares are usually determined by daily trading conducted in the financial marketplaces such as the New York Stock Exchange. These values are affected by numerous factors, including the *expectations* of (a) price appreciation and (b) cash flows in the form of dividends. The focus is on the future; the present and the past are examined as clues to what may be forthcoming. Therefore the present stockholders' equity is usually of only incidental concern.

For example, the above stockholders' equity was $2,208,823,000 ÷ 49,101,271 shares, or $45 per share. During that year, a year of low profits, Delta's market price per common share fluctuated between $32 and $60.

HIGHLIGHTS TO REMEMBER

1. Other than cash and receivables, assets may be regarded as unexpired, prepaid, or stored costs (for example, inventory or equipment) that are carried forward to future periods rather than being immediately offset against revenue as expenses of the current period.

2. Revenues and expenses are components of stockholders' equity. Revenues increase stockholders' equity; expenses decrease stockholders' equity.

3. Dividends are not expenses.

4. Among the synonyms for *income statement* are *statement of income*, *statement of earnings*, *results of operations*, *statement of operations*, *statement of revenues and expenses*, and *profit and loss statement*.

5. *Income, earnings*, and *profits* are synonyms.

6. *Cost of goods sold* and *cost of sales* are synonyms.

7. If you have had little or no exposure to accounting, you should at least solve the "Summary Problems for Your Review" before proceeding to the next chapter. To read about basic accounting concepts is not enough. Work some problems too—the more, the better. Cramming at the end of a few more chapters is definitely not recommended. Accounting is a cumulative subject. The foundation is laid in these initial four chapters.

8. In accrual accounting, an expense is seldom accompanied by an immediate cash disbursement. That is, *expense* should not be confused with the term *cash disbursement*.

9. In accrual accounting, revenue is seldom accompanied by an immediate cash receipt. That is, *revenue* should not be confused with the term *cash receipt*.

ACCOUNTING VOCABULARY

Accounting Principles Board (APB), p. 61
Accrual Basis, p. 50
AICPA, p. 61
APB Opinions, p. 61
Cash Basis, p. 50
Cost of Goods Sold, p. 59
Cost of Sales, p. 59
Cost Recovery, p. 44
Depreciation, p. 45
Dividends, p. 52
Earnings, p. 40
Expense, p. 40
Financial Accounting Standards Board (FASB), p. 61
FASB Statements, p. 61
Fiscal Year, p. 39
Income, p. 40
Income Statement, p. 46
Interim Periods, p. 39
Liquidation, p. 57

Matching, p. 43
Operating Cycle, p. 39
Operating Statement, p. 59
Profits, p. 40
P & L Statement, p. 59
Recognition, p. 43
Reinvested Earnings, p. 59
Results of Operations, p. 59
Retained Earnings, p. 59
Retained Income, p. 40
Revenue, p. 40
Sales, p. 59
Sales Revenues, p. 59
Securities and Exchange Commission (SEC), p. 61
Statement of Earnings, p. 59
Statement of Operations, p. 59
Statement of Retained Income, p. 52
Statement of Revenues and Expenses, p. 59

APPENDIX 2: FOUR POPULAR FINANCIAL RATIOS

To underscore how financial statements are used, this book will gradually introduce you to various financial ratios. Because stock market prices are quoted on a per-share basis, many ratios are expressed per share (and after income taxes).

A financial ratio is computed by dividing one number by another. For a set of complex financial statements, literally hundreds of ratios can be computed if desired. Every analyst has a set of favorite ratios, but one is so popular that it dwarfs all others: earnings per share of common stock (EPS).

In its *Statement on Objectives*, the Financial Accounting Standards Board, which is described in this chapter, stressed that the main focus of financial reporting is on earnings. The income statement and its accompanying earnings per share are paramount to many users of financial reports, so accounting authorities have specified how various items therein must be displayed.

The accounting regulators have promulgated the requirement that EPS data appear on the face of the income statement of publicly held corporations. This is the only instance where a financial ratio is required as a part of the body of financial statements.

☐ Earnings Per Share (EPS)

When the owners' equity is relatively simple, the computation of EPS is straightforward. For example, consider a recent annual report of PepsiCo Corporation, the well-known beverage and food company. The bottom of its income statement showed:

Net income	$212,547,000
Net income per share of common stock	$2.25

The earnings per share (called *net income per share* by PepsiCo) was calculated as follows:

$$\text{EPS} = \frac{\text{Net income}}{\text{Average number of shares outstanding}}$$

$$\text{EPS} = \frac{\$212,547,000}{94,462,222} = \$2.25$$

The PepsiCo's computation is relatively simple because the company has only one type of capital stock, little fluctuation of shares outstanding throughout the year, and no unusual items affecting the computation of net income. EPS calculations can become more difficult when the last complications arise. See Chapter 10 for further discussion.

☐ Price-Earnings Ratio (P-E)

Another popular ratio is the price-earnings (P-E) ratio:

$$\text{P-E} = \frac{\text{Market price per share of common stock}}{\text{Earnings per share of common stock}}$$

The numerator is typically today's market price; the denominator, the EPS for the most recent twelve months. Thus the P-E ratio varies throughout a given year, depending on the fluctuations in the stock price. For example, PepsiCo's P-E ratio would be:

	USING HIGHEST MARKET PRICE DURING FOURTH QUARTER	USING LOWEST MARKET PRICE DURING FOURTH QUARTER
P-E =	$\frac{\$38}{\$2.25}$	$\frac{\$34}{\$2.25}$
P-E =	16.9	15.1

P-E ratios are rarely carried out to any decimal places when published in the business press. The P-E ratio is sometimes called the *earnings multiple*. It measures how much the investing public is willing to pay for the company's prospects for earnings. Note especially that the P-E ratio is a consensus of the marketplace. This earnings multiplier may differ considerably for two companies within the same industry. It may also change for the same company through the years. Glamour stocks often have astronomical ratios. In general, a high P-E ratio indicates that investors predict that the company's net income will grow at a fast rate.

☐ Dividend-Yield Ratio

Individual investors are usually interested in the profitability of their personal investments in common stock. That profitability takes two forms: cash dividends and market-price appreciation of the stock. Two popular ratios are the *dividend-yield ratio* (the current dividend per share divided by the current market price of the stock) and the price-earnings ratio (just discussed). The *dividend-yield ratio* (or *dividend-yield percentage*), also simply called *dividend yield*, is computed as follows:

$$\text{Dividend yield} = \frac{\text{Common dividends per share}}{\text{Market price per share}}$$

PepsiCo would show:

	USING HIGHEST MARKET PRICE DURING FOURTH QUARTER	USING LOWEST MARKET PRICE DURING FOURTH QUARTER
Dividend yield =	$\dfrac{\$1.665}{\$38}$	$\dfrac{\$1.665}{\$34}$
Dividend yield =	4.4%	4.9%

When published in the business press, dividend yields are ordinarily carried to one decimal place. Dividend ratios may be of particular importance to those investors in common stock who seek regular cash returns on their investments. For example, an investor who favored high current returns would not buy stock in growth companies. Growth companies have conservative dividend policies because they are using most of their profit-generated resources to help finance expansion of their operations.

Market prices at which stocks are traded in organized marketplaces, such as the New York Stock Exchange, are quoted in the daily newspapers. The dividend yields are also published, as measured by annual disbursements based on the last quarterly dividends.

Consider the following stock quotations for PepsiCo regarding trading on a particular day:

| 52 WEEKS | | | | YLD. | P-E | SALES | | | | NET |
HIGH	LOW	STOCK	DIV.	%	RATIO	100s	HIGH	LOW	CLOSE	CHG.
75⅜	40⅝	PepsiCo	1.78	2.5	12	4,622	71¼	70	70½	−1½

Reading from left to right, the highest price at which PepsiCo common stock was traded in the preceding fifty-two weeks was $75.375 per share; the lowest price, $40.625. The current dividend rate for twelve months is $1.78 per share, producing a yield of 2.5% based on the day's closing price of the stock. The P-E ratio is 12, also based on the closing price. Total sales for the day were 462,200 shares. The highest price at which the stock was traded was $71.25 per share; the lowest, $70. The closing price was that of the last trade for the day, $70.50, which was $1.50 lower than the preceding day's last trade.

Keep in mind that transactions in publicly traded stock are between *individual investors* in the stock, not between the *corporation* and the individuals. Thus a "typical trade" results in the selling of, say, 100 shares of PepsiCo stock held by Ms. Johnson in Minneapolis to Ms. Davis in Atlanta for $7,050 cash. Both of these parties would ordinarily transact the trade through their respective stockbrokers, who represent individual shareholders. PepsiCo Corporation would not be directly affected by the trade except that its records of shareholders would show the 100 shares now held by Davis and not held by Johnson.

□ **Dividend-Payout Ratio**

Although not routinely published, the dividend-payout ratio also receives much attention from analysts. Consider McDonald's, the well-known fast-food chain. The formula for its payout computation is given below, followed by McDonald' ratio, using figures from a recent annual report:

$$\text{Dividend-payout ratio} = \frac{\text{Common dividends per share}}{\text{Earnings per share}}$$

$$\text{Dividend-payout ratio} = \frac{\$.76}{\$4.39} = 17.3\%$$

Clearly, McDonald's fits into the category of a low-payment company. As long as McDonald's continues its worldwide expansion, a minimal payout can be anticipated. In contrast, companies without exceptional growth tend to pay a higher percentage of their earnings as dividends. Public utilities will ordinarily have a payout ratio of 60% to 70%. For instance, Pacific Gas and Electric Company paid dividends amounting to 62.4% of 1988 earnings.

Financial ratios are also covered in Chapters 4, 6, 7, 9, 10, and especially 15.

FUNDAMENTAL ASSIGNMENT MATERIAL

□ **General Coverage**

2–1. **BALANCE SHEET EQUATION.** (Alternates are 2–4 and 2–5.) For each of the following independent cases, compute the amounts (in thousands) for the items indicated by letters, and show your supporting computations:

	CASE		
	1	2	3
Revenues	$130	$ K	$310
Expenses	110	170	270
Dividends declared	–0–	5	Q
Additional investment by stockholders	–0–	30	35
Net income	E	20	P
Retained income:			
Beginning of year	30	60	100
End of year	D	J	110
Paid-in capital:			
Beginning of year	15	10	N
End of year	C	H	85
Total assets:			
Beginning of year	85	F	L
End of year	95	280	M
Total liabilities:			
Beginning of year	A	90	105
End of year	B	G	95

2–2. **ANALYSIS OF TRANSACTIONS, PREPARATION OF STATEMENTS.** (Alternates are 2–6, 2–8, 2–28, and 2–35.) The Boone Company was incorporated on April 1, 19X2. Boone had ten holders of common stock. Ella Boone, who was the president and chief executive officer, held 51% of the shares. The company rented space in chain discount stores and specialized in selling ladies' shoes. Boone's first location was in a store that was part of Century Market Centers, Inc.

The following events occurred during April:

1. The company was incorporated. Common stockholders invested $100,000 cash.
2. Purchased merchandise inventory for cash, $45,000.
3. Purchased merchandise inventory on open account, $25,000.
4. Merchandise carried in inventory at a cost of $37,000 was sold for cash for $25,000 and on open account for $65,000, a grand total of $90,000. Boone (not Century) carries and collects these accounts receivable.
5. Collection of the above accounts receivable, $15,000.
6. Payments of accounts payable $18,000. See transaction 3.
7. Special display equipment and fixtures were acquired on April 1 for $36,000. Their expected useful life was thirty-six months. This equipment was removable. Boone paid $12,000 as a down payment and signed a promissory note for $24,000. Also see transaction 11.
8. On April 1, Boone signed a rental agreement with Century. The agreement called for a flat $2,000 per month, payable quarterly in advance. Therefore Boone paid $6,000 cash on April 1.
9. The rental agreement also called for a payment of 10% of all sales. This payment was in addition to the flat $2,000 per month. In this way, Century would share in any success of the venture and be compensated for general services such as cleaning and utilities. This payment was to be made in cash on the last day of each month as soon as the sales for the month had been tabulated. Therefore Boone made the payment on April 30.
10. Wages, salaries, and sales commissions were all paid for in cash for all earnings by employees. The amount was $39,000.
11. Depreciation expense of $1,000 was recognized ($36,000 ÷ 36 months). See transaction 7.
12. The expiration of an appropriate amount of prepaid rental services was recognized. See transaction 8.

Required:
1. Prepare an analysis of Boone Company's transactions, employing the equation approach demonstrated in Exhibit 2–2 (p. 42). Show all amounts in thousands.
2. Prepare a balance sheet as of April 30, 19X2, and an income statement for the month of April. Ignore income taxes.
3. Given these sparse facts, analyze Boone's performance for April and its financial position as of April 30, 19X2.

2–3. COMPARISON OF CASH BASIS VERSUS ACCRUAL BASIS. Refer to the preceding problem. If Boone measured income on a cash basis, what revenue would be reported for April? Which basis (accrual or cash) provides a better measure of revenue? Why?

2–4. BALANCE SHEET EQUATION. (Alternates are 2–1 and 2–5.) Reebok International's actual terminology and actual data (in millions of dollars) follow for a recent fiscal year:

Cost and expenses	B
Net income	$ 165
Dividends	22
Additional investments by stockholders	145
Assets, beginning of period	440
Assets, end of period	E
Liabilities, beginning of period	A
Liabilities, end of period	283
Paid-in capital, beginning of period	120
Paid-in capital, end of period	D
Retained earnings, beginning of period	178
Retained earnings, end of period	C
Revenues	1,399

Required: ▎ Find the unknowns (in millions), showing computations to support your answers.

2–5. BALANCE SHEET EQUATION. (Alternates are 2–1 and 2–4). Ralston Purina's actual terminology and actual data for its 1988 fiscal year follow (in millions);

Assets, beginning of period	$3,864
Assets, end of period	4,044
Liabilities, beginning of period	A
Liabilities, end of period	E
Paid-in capital, beginning of period	292
Paid-in capital, end of period	D
Retained earnings, beginning of period	670
Retained earnings, end of period	C
Sales and other revenues	5,876
Cost of sales, and all other expenses	5,488
Net earnings	B
Dividends	83
Additional investment by stockholders	8

Required: ▎ Find the unknowns (in thousands), showing computations to support your answers.

2–6. ANALYSIS OF TRANSACTIONS, PREPARATION OF STATEMENTS. (Alternates are 2–2, 2–8, 2–28, and 2–35.) Ohio Mattress Company manufactures and sells Sealy-brand bedding. The company's actual condensed balance sheet data for a recent December 31 follow (in millions):

Cash	$ 9	Accounts payable	$ 2
Accounts receivable	8	Other liabilities	7
Inventories	7	Paid-in capital	6
Prepaid expenses	1	Retained earnings	30
Property, plant, and equipment	20		
Total	$45	Total	$45

The following summarizes some major transactions during January (in millions):

1. Mattresses carried in inventory at a cost of $3 were sold for cash of $2 and on open account of $5, a grand total of $7.
2. Acquired inventory on account, $5.

3. Collected receivables, $3.
4. On January 2, used $3 cash to prepay some rent and insurance for the entire year.
5. Payments on accounts payable (for inventories), $2.
6. Paid selling and administrative expenses in cash, $1.
7. The $1 of prepaid expenses, December 31, for rent and insurance expired in January.
8. Depreciation expense of $1 was recognized for January.

Required:
1. Prepare an analysis of Ohio's transactions, employing the equation approach demonstrated in Exhibit 2–2 (p. 42). Show all amounts in millions. (For simplicity, only a few major transactions are illustrated here.)
2. Prepare a statement of earnings for the month ended January 31 and a balance sheet, January 31. Ignore income taxes.

2–7. **CASH BASIS VERSUS ACCRUAL BASIS.** Refer to the preceding problem.
If Ohio Mattress measured income on the cash basis, what revenue would be reported for January? Which basis (accrual or cash) provides a better measure of revenue? Why?

2–8. **ANALYSIS OF TRANSACTIONS, PREPARATION OF STATEMENTS.** (Alternates are 2–2, 2–6, 2–28, and 2–35.) Wm. Wrigley Jr. Company manufactures and sells chewing gum. The company's actual condensed balance sheet data for a recent December 31 follow (in millions):

Cash	$ 99	Accounts payable	$ 44
Receivables	61	Dividends payable	5
Inventories	82	Other liabilities	75
Prepaid expenses	11	Paid-in capital	20
Property, plant, and equipment	154	Retained earnings	263
Total	$407	Total	$407

The following summarizes some major transactions during January (in millions):

1. Gum carried in inventory at a cost of $30 was sold for cash of $20 and on open account of $42, a grand total of $62.
2. Collection of receivables, $50.
3. Depreciation expense of $3 was recognized.
4. Selling and administrative expenses of $24 were paid in cash.
5. Prepaid expenses of $1 expired in January. These included fire insurance premiums paid in the previous year that applied to future months. The expiration increases selling and administrative expense.
6. The December 31 liability for dividends was paid in cash on January 25.
7. On January 30, the company declared a $2 dividend, which will be paid on February 25.

Required:
1. Prepare an analysis of Wrigley's transactions, employing the equation approach demonstrated in Exhibit 2–2 (p. 42). Show all amounts in millions. (For simplicity, only a few major transactions are illustrated here.)
2. Prepare a statement of earnings and also a statement of retained earnings for the month ended January 31. Also prepare a balance sheet, January 31. Ignore income taxes.

2–9. **CASH BASIS VERSUS ACCRUAL BASIS.** Refer to the preceding problem. If Wrigley measured income on the cash basis, what revenue would be reported for January? Which basis (accrual or cash) provides a better measure of revenue? Why?

ADDITIONAL ASSIGNMENT MATERIAL

☐ General Coverage

2–10. What are the two tests of recognition of revenue?

2–11. "Expenses are assets that have been used up." Explain.

2–12. "The manager acquires goods and services, not expenses per se." Explain.

2–13. Give two synonyms for *income statement*.

2–14. Give two synonyms for *net income*.

2–15. "Expenses are negative stockholders' equity accounts." Explain.

2–16. "The term *earnings* is becoming increasingly popular because it has a preferable image." Explain.

2–17. "Cash dividends are not expenses." Explain.

2–18. Give two synonyms for *retained income*.

2–19. "Retained income is not a pot of gold." Explain.

2–20. What is the meaning of a *general claim*?

2–21. What are the major defects of the cash basis?

2–22. "The heart of recognizing expense is the cost recovery concept." Explain.

2–23. "Changes in the purchasing power of the dollar hurt the credibility of financial statements." Do you agree? Explain.

2–24. Distinguish between GAAP, FASB, and APB.

2–25. "The SEC has informally delegated much rule-making power to the FASB." Explain.

2–26. Synonyms and Antonyms. Consider the following terms: (1) unexpired costs, (2) reinvested earnings, (3) expenses, (4) net earnings, (5) prepaid expenses, (6) stored costs, (7) statement of earnings, (8) used-up costs, (9) net profits, (10) net income, (11) revenues, (12) retained income, (13) sales, (14) statement of financial condition, (15) statement of income, (16) statement of financial position, (17) retained earnings, (18) statement of operations, (19) cost of goods sold, (20) undistributed earnings, and (21) cost of sales.

Required: Group the items that have similar meanings. Name the groups. Answer by indicating the numbered items that belong in each group.

2–27. Fundamental Revenue and Expense. Boswell Corporation was formed on June 1, 19X2, when some stockholders invested $90,000 in cash in the company. During the first week of June, $85,000 cash was spent for merchandise inventory (sportswear). During the remainder of the month, total sales reached $105,000, of which $60,000 was on open account. The cost of the inventory sold was $56,000. For simplicity, assume that no other transactions occurred except that on June 28 Boswell Corporation acquired $25,000 additional inventory on open account.

Required: 1. Using the balance sheet equation approach demonstrated in Exhibit 2–2 (p. 42), analyze all transactions for June. Show all amounts in thousands.
2. Prepare a balance sheet, June 30, 19X2.
3. Prepare two income statements for June, side by side. The first should use the accrual basis of accounting, and the second the cash basis. Which basis provides a more informative measure of economic performance? Why?

2–28. Accounting for Prepayments. (Alternates are 2–2, 2–6, 2–8, and 2–35.) The Brighten Company, a wholesale distributor of home appliances, began business on July 1, 19X2. The following summarized transactions occurred during July:

1. Brighten's stockholders contributed $200,000 in cash in exchange for their common stock.
2. On July 1, Brighten signed a one-year lease on a warehouse, paying $60,000 cash in advance for occupancy of twelve months.

3. On July 1, Brighten acquired warehouse equipment for $100,000. A cash down payment of $40,000 was made and a note payable was signed for the balance.
4. On July 1, Brighten paid $24,000 cash for a two-year insurance policy covering fire, casualty, and related risks.
5. Brighten acquired assorted merchandise for $35,000 cash.
6. Brighten acquired assorted merchandise for $190,000 on open account.
7. Total sales were $200,000, of which $30,000 were for cash.
8. Cost of inventory sold was $160,000.
9. Rent expense was recognized for the month of July.
10. Depreciation expense of $2,000 was recognized for the month.
11. Insurance expense was recognized for the month.
12. Collected $30,000 from credit customers.
13. Disbursed $75,000 to trade creditors.

For simplicity, ignore all other possible expenses.

Required:
1. Using the balance sheet equation format demonstrated in Exhibit 2–2 (p. 42), prepare an analysis of each transaction. Show all amounts in thousands. What do transactions 8–11 illustrate about the theory of assets and expenses? (Use a Prepaid Insurance account, which is not illustrated in Exhibit 2–2.)
2. Prepare an income statement for July on the accrual basis.
3. Prepare a balance sheet, July 31, 19X2.

2–29. **COMPARISON OF CASH BASIS VERSUS ACCRUAL BASIS.** Refer to the preceding problem. If Brighten Company measured income on the cash basis, what revenue would be reported for July? Which basis (accrual or cash) provides a better measure of revenue? Why?

2–30. **NATURE OF RETAINED INCOME.** This is an exercise on the relationships between assets, liabilities, and ownership equities. The numbers are small, but the underlying concepts are large.

1. Assume an opening balance sheet of:

Cash	$1,000	Paid-in capital	$1,000

2. Purchase inventory for $600 cash. Prepare a balance sheet. A heading is unnecessary in this and subsequent requirements.
3. Sell the entire inventory for $850 cash. Prepare a balance sheet. Where is the retained income in terms of relationships within the balance sheet? That is, what is the meaning of the retained income? Explain in your own words.
4. Buy inventory for $400 cash and equipment for $700 cash. Prepare a balance sheet. Where is the retained income in terms of relationships within the balance sheet? That is, what is the meaning of the retained income? Explain in your own words.
5. Buy inventory for $300 on open account. Prepare a balance sheet. Where is the retained income and account payable in terms of the relationships within the balance sheet? That is, what is the meaning of the account payable and the retained income? Explain in your own words.

2–31. **ASSET ACQUISITION AND EXPIRATION.** The Constance Company had the following transactions:

a. Paid $12,000 cash for rent for the next six months.
b. Paid $2,000 for stationery and wrapping supplies.
c. Paid $3,000 cash for an advertisement in the *Wall Street Journal*.
d. Paid $10,000 cash for a training program for employees.

Required:
1. To see the theory of asset acquisition–asset expiration, for each transaction show the effects on the balance sheet equation in two phases: acquisition and expiration at the end of the month of acquisition. Show all amounts in thousands.
2. For the same transactions, show how a shortcut analysis of each transaction is

conducted when goods or services are to be routinely consumed (or substantially consumed) in the period of their purchase. Show all amounts in thousands.

2–32. **FIND UNKNOWNS.** The following data pertain to the Davis Corporation. Total assets at January 1, 19X1, were $100,000; at December 31, 19X1, $124,000. During 19X1, sales were $204,000, cash dividends were $4,000, and operating expenses (exclusive of cost of goods sold) were $50,000. Total liabilities at December 31, 19X1, were $55,000; at January 1, 19X1, $40,000. There was no additional capital paid in during 19X1.

Required: | (These need not be computed in any particular order.)
1. Net income for 19X1
2. Cost of goods sold for 19X1
3. Stockholders' equity, January 1, 19X1

2–33. **INCOME STATEMENT.** A statement of an automobile dealer follows:

ADAMS TOYOTA, INC.
Statement of Profit and Loss
December 31, 19X3

Revenues:		
Sales	$1,000,000	
Increase in market value of land and building	200,000	$1,200,000
Deduct expenses:		
Advertising	$ 100,000	
Sales commissions	50,000	
Utilities	20,000	
Wages	150,000	
Dividends	100,000	
Cost of cars purchased	700,000	1,120,000
Net profit		$ 80,000

Required: | List and describe any shortcomings of this statement.

2–34. **PREPARE FINANCIAL STATEMENTS.** The Francini Corporation does not use the services of a professional accountant. However, at the end of its second year of operations, 19X2, the company's financial statements were prepared by its office manager. Listed below in random order are the items appearing in these statements:

Accounts receivable	$ 27,700	Office supplies inventory	$ 2,000
Paid-in capital	100,000	Notes payable	7,000
Trucks	33,700	Merchandise inventory	61,000
Cost of goods sold	151,000	Accounts payable	14,000
Salary expense	76,000	Notes receivable	2,500
Unexpired insurance	1,800	Utilities expenses	5,000
Rent expense	19,500	Net income	4,200
Sales	265,000	Retained income:	
Advertising expense	9,300	January 1, 19X2	8,000
Cash	4,500	December 31, 19X2	12,200

You are satisfied that the statements in which these items appear are correct except for several matters that the office manager overlooked. The following information should have been entered on the books and reflected in the financial statements:

a. The amount shown for rent expense includes $1,500 that is actually prepaid for the first month in 19X3.

b. Of the amount shown for unexpired insurance, only $600 is prepaid for periods after 19X2.

c. Depreciation of trucks for 19X2 is $4,800.

d. About $1,200 of the office supplies in the inventory shown above was actually issued and used during 19X2 operations.

e. Cash dividends of $3,000 were declared in December 19X2 by the board of directors. These dividends are to be distributed in February 19X3.

Required:

Prepare in good form the following corrected financial statements, ignoring income taxes:

1. Income statement for 19X2
2. Statement of retained income for 19X2
3. Balance sheet at December 31, 19X2

It is not necessary to prepare a columnar analysis to show the transaction effects on each of the elements of the accounting equation.

2–35. **TRANSACTION ANALYSIS AND FINANCIAL STATEMENTS.** (Alternates are 2–2, 2–6, 2–8, and 2–28.) Consider the following balance sheet of a wholesaler of lighting fixtures:

BALZER LIGHTING COMPANY
Balance Sheet
December 31, 19X1

ASSETS		LIABILITIES AND STOCKHOLDERS' EQUITY		
		Liabilities:		
Cash	$ 100,000	Accounts payable		$ 700,000
Accounts receivable	400,000	Stockholders' equity:		
Merchandise inventory	790,000	Paid-in capital	$150,000	
Prepaid rent	40,000	Retained income	570,000	
Equipment	90,000	Total stockholders'		
		equity		720,000
Total	$1,420,000	Total		$1,420,000

The following is a summary of transactions that occurred during 19X2:

a. Acquisitions of inventory on open account, $1 million.

b. Sales on open account, $1.4 million; and for cash, $100,000.

c. Merchandise carried in inventory at a cost of $1.1 million was sold as described in b.

d. The warehouse twelve-month lease expired on September 1, 19X2. However, the lease was immediately renewed at a rate of $84,000 for the next twelve-month period. The entire rent was paid in cash in advance.

e. Depreciation expense for 19X2 for the warehouse equipment was $20,000.

f. Collections on accounts receivable, $1.25 million.

g. Wages for 19X2 were paid in full in cash, $200,000.

h. Miscellaneous expenses for 19X2 were paid in full in cash, $80,000.

i. Payments on accounts payable, $900,000.

j. Cash dividends for 19X2 were paid in full in December, $100,000.

Required:

1. Prepare an analysis of transactions, employing the equation approach demonstrated in Exhibit 2–2 (p. 42). Show the amounts in thousands of dollars.
2. Prepare a balance sheet, statement of income, and statement of retained income. Also prepare a combined statement of income and retained income.
3. Reconsider transaction j. Suppose the dividends were declared on December 15, payable on January 31, 19X3, to shareholders of record on January 20. Indicate which accounts and financial statements in requirement 2 would be changed and by how much. Be complete and specific.

2–36. SPECIAL MEANINGS OF TERMS. A news story described the disappointing sales of a new model car, the Nova. An auto dealer said: "Even if the Nova is a little slow to move out of dealerships, it is more of a plus than a minus. . . . We're now selling 14 more cars per month than before. That's revenue. That's the bottom line."

Required: | Is the dealer confused about accounting terms? Explain.

2–37. TWO SIDES OF A TRANSACTION. For each of the following transactions, show the effects on the entities involved. As was illustrated in the chapter, use the $A = L + OE$ equation to demonstrate the effects. Also name each amount affected, show the dollar amount, and indicate whether the effects are increases or decreases.

Illustration. The Massachusetts General Hospital collects $1,000 from the Blue Cross Health Care Plan.

Entity	Cash	A Receivables	Trucks	=	L Payables	+ OE
Hospital	+1,000	−1,000		=		
Blue Cross	−1,000			=	−1,000	

1. Borrowing of $100,000 on a home mortgage from Fidelity Savings by Evan Porteus.
2. Payment of $10,000 principal on the above mortgage. Ignore interest.
3. Purchase of a two-year subscription to *Time* magazine for $80 cash by Charles Bonini.
4. Purchase of trucks by the U.S. Postal Service for $10 million cash from the U.S. General Services Administration. The trucks were carried in the accounts at $10 million by the Services Administration.
5. Purchase for $100,000 cash of U.S. government bonds by Lockheed Corporation.
6. Cash deposits of $10 on the returnable bottles sold by Safeway Stores to a retail customer, Herbert Simon.
7. Collections on open account of $100 by Sears store from a retail customer, Kenneth Arrow.
8. Purchase of traveler's checks of $1,000 from American Express Company by Michael Harrison.
9. Cash deposit of $500 in a checking account in Bank of America by David Kreps.
10. Purchase of a United Airlines "super-saver" airline ticket for $500 cash by Robert Wilson on June 15. The trip will be taken on September 10.

2–38. TRAVELER'S CHECKS. The American Express Company has $24 billion of traveler's checks outstanding on December 31, 1989. Each May, Citibank of New York conducts a special sale of its traveler's checks whereby up to $5,000 of its checks can be purchased for a flat fee of $2 instead of the usual commission percentage.

Required: | When a company issues $1,000 of its traveler's checks, how are its assets and liabilities affected? Describe how profits might be made in the traveler's checks business.

2–39. EARNINGS AND DIVIDEND RATIOS. Study Appendix 2. Procter & Gamble's brand names include Tide, Crest, Jif, and Prell. The company's 1988 annual report showed earnings of $1,020 million. Cash dividends per share were $2.75. Procter & Gamble had 167,300,000 average number of common shares outstanding. No other type of stock was outstanding. The market price of the stock at the end of the year was $75 per share.

Required: | Compute (1) earnings per share, (2) price-earnings ratio, (3) dividend yield, and (4) dividend-payout ratio.

2–40. EARNINGS AND DIVIDEND RATIOS. Study Appendix 2. Chevron Corporation is one of the largest oil companies in the world. The company's revenue in 1988 was $30 billion. Net income was $306,826,000. EPS was $6.30. The company's common stock is the only type of shares outstanding.

Required:

1. Compute the average number of common shares outstanding during the year.
2. The dividend-payout ratio was 19%. What was the amount of dividends per share?
3. The average market price of the stock for the year was $53 per share. Compute (a) dividend yield and (b) price-earnings ratio.

2–41. **FINANCIAL RATIOS.** Study Appendix 2. Following is a list of several well-known companies and selected financial data included in a letter sent by a stock brokerage firm to some of its clients:

	PER-SHARE DATA			RATIOS AND PERCENTAGES		
COMPANY	Price	Earnings	Dividends	Price-Earnings	Dividend Yield	Dividend-Payout
Bethlehem Steel	$22	$1.80	$—	$—	—%	90%
B. F. Goodrich	20	—	1.56	—	—	80
Gulf & Western	—	2.75	0.75	5.5	—	—
Inland Steel	22	—	2.00	22.0	9.1	—
Texaco	30	6.50	—	—	10.0	—
U.S. Steel	24	3.50	2.00	—	—	—
Wells Fargo	—	—	1.92	—	8.3	36

The missing figures for this schedule can be computed from the data given.

Required:

1. Compute the missing figures and identify the company with
   a. The highest dividend yield
   b. The highest dividend-payout percentage
   c. The lowest market price relative to earnings
2. Assume that you know nothing about any of these companies other than the data given and the computations you have made from the data. Which company would you choose as
   a. The most attractive investment? Why?
   b. The least attractive investment? Why?

2–42. **NONPROFIT OPERATING STATEMENT.** Examine the accompanying statement of the Stanford Faculty Club. Identify the Stanford classifications and terms that would not be used by a profit-seeking hotel and restaurant. Suggest terms that the profit-seeking entity would use instead.

STANFORD FACULTY CLUB

Statement of Income and Expenses
For Fiscal Year 1988–89

Food Service:
Sales		$545,128	
Expenses:			
Food	$287,088		
Labor	272,849		
Operating costs	30,535	590,472	
Deficit			$(45,344)
Bar:			
Sales		$ 90,549	
Expenses:			
Cost of liquor	$ 29,302		
Labor	5,591		
Operating costs	6,125	41,018	
Surplus			49,531

(continued from preceding page)

Hotel:

Sales	$ 33,771	
Expenses	23,803	
Surplus		9,968
Surplus from operations		$ 14,155
General income (members' dues, room fees, etc.)		95,546
General administration and operating expenses		(134,347)
Deficit before university subsidy		$ (24,646)
University subsidy		30,000
Net surplus after university subsidy		$ 5,354

2–43. NET INCOME AND RETAINED EARNINGS. John Wiley & Sons, Inc., is a book publisher. Like most companies, Wiley heavily condenses the data in its annual report. Wiley's data (in thousands) in a recent annual report included interest expense, $2,810; cash dividends, $4,510; income before income taxes, $8,652; net sales, $198,119; cost of sales, $85,092; retained earnings at the beginning of year, $59,996; provision for income taxes, $1,547; and operating and administrative expenses, $101,565.

Required:
>   Wiley presents a single "statement of income and retained earnings." Using the above data, reconstruct Wiley's statement for the year. Regarding the presentation of income taxes, include the following: income before income taxes, provision for income taxes, and net income.

2–44. NET INCOME AND RETAINED INCOME. McDonald's Corporation is a well-known fast-foods restaurant company. The following data are from a recent annual report (in thousands):

MCDONALD'S CORPORATION

Retained earnings, end of year	$3,396,046	Dividends paid	$ 93,572
Revenues	4,893,538	General, administrative, and selling expenses	525,126
Interest expense	203,099	Depreciation	278,906
Income tax expense	362,300	Retained earnings, beginning of year	2,893,156
Food and paper expense	1,297,796	Other operating expenses	696,990
Wages and salaries	799,741		
Rent	133,118		

Required:
>   1. Prepare the following for the year:
>   a. Income statement. The final three lines of the income statement were labeled as income before provision for income taxes, provision for income taxes, and net income.
>   b. Statement of retained income.
>   2. Comment briefly on the relative size of the cash dividend.

2–45. EARNINGS STATEMENT, RETAINED EARNINGS. The Procter & Gamble Company has many well-known products. Examples are Tide, Crest, Jif, and Prell. The following is an exact reproduction of the terms and amounts in the financial statements contained in its 1988 annual report (in millions):

Net sales and other income	$19,491	Retained earnings at	
Cash	50	beginning of year	5,170
Interest expense	321	Cost of products sold	11,880
Income taxes	610	Dividends to shareholders	502
Accounts payable—Trade	1,494	Marketing, administrative,	
		and other expenses	5,660

Required: Choose the relevant data and prepare (1) the income statement for the year and (2) the statement of retained income for the year. The final three lines of the income statement were labeled as earnings before income taxes, income taxes, and net earnings.

2–46. **CLASSIC CASE OF THE PRESIDENT'S WEALTH.** This is a classic case in accounting. From the *Chicago Tribune*, August 20, 1964:

☐ Accountants acting on President Johnson's orders today reported his family wealth totaled $3,484,098.

☐ The statement of capital, arrived at through conservative procedures of evaluation, contrasted with a recent estimate published by *Life* magazine, which put the total at 14 million dollars.

☐ The family fortune, which is held in trust while the Johnsons are in the White House, was set forth in terms of book values. The figures represent original cost rather than current market values on what the holdings would be worth if sold now.

☐ Announced by the White House press office, but turned over to reporters by a national accounting firm at their Washington branch office, the financial statement apparently was intended to still a flow of quasi-official and unofficial estimates of the Johnson fortune. . . .

ASSETS

Cash	$ 132,547
Bonds	398,540
Interest in Texas Broadcasting Corp.	2,543,838
Ranch properties and other real estate	525,791
Other assets, including insurance policies	82,054
Total assets	$3,682,770

LIABILITIES AND CAPITAL

Note payable on real estate holding, 5 percent due 1971	$ 150,000
Accounts payable, accrued interest, and income taxes	48,672
Total liabilities	$ 198,672
Capital	$3,484,098

☐ The report apportions the capital among the family, with $378,081 credited to the President; $2,126,298 to his wife Claudia T., who uses the name Lady Bird; $490,141 to their daughter Lynda Bird; and $489,578 to their daughter Luci Baines.

☐ The statement said the family holdings—under the names of the President, his wife, and his two daughters, Lynda Bird and Luci Baines—had increased from $737,730 on January 1, 1954, a year after Johnson became Democratic leader of the Senate, to $3,484,098 on July 31 this year, a gain of $2,746,368. . . .

☐ A covering letter addressed to Johnson said the statement was made "in conformity with generally accepted accounting principles applied on a consistent basis."

☐ By far the largest part of the fortune was listed as the Johnsons' interest in the Texas Broadcasting Corporation, carried on the books as worth $2,543,838.

□ The accountants stated that this valuation was arrived at on the basis of the cost of the stock when the Johnsons bought control of the debt-ridden radio station between 1943 and 1947, plus accumulated earnings ploughed back as equity, less 25 percent capital gains tax.[1]

Editorial, *Chicago Tribune*, August 22, 1964:

□ An accounting firm acting on Mr. Johnson's instructions and employing what it termed "generally accepted auditing standards" has released a statement putting the current worth of the Lyndon Johnson family at a little less than 3½ million dollars. . . .

□ Dean Burch, chairman of the Republican National Committee, has remarked that the method used to list the Johnson assets was comparable to placing the value of Manhattan Island at $24, the price at which it was purchased from the Indians. The Johnson accounting firm conceded that its report was "not intended to indicate the values that might be realized if the investment were sold."

□ In fact, it would be interesting to observe the response of the Johnson family if a syndicate of investors were to offer to take Texas Broadcasting off the family's hands at double the publicly reported worth of the operation. . . .

EXHIBIT 2–10

Perry, Chambliss, Sheppard and Thompson
Certified Public Accountants
Americus, Georgia

JAMES EARL CARTER, JR. AND ROSALYNN CARTER
STATEMENT OF ASSETS AND LIABILITIES
DECEMBER 31, 1977
(UNAUDITED)

ASSETS

	Cost Basis	Estimated Current Value
Cash	$204,979.04	$204,979.04
Cash Value of Life Insurance	45,506.88	45,506.88
U.S. Savings Bonds, Series E	1,425.00	1,550.94
Loan Receivable	50,000.00	50,000.00
Overpayment of 1977 Income Taxes	51,121.27	51,121.27
Personal Assets Trust—Note 3	151,097.87	557,717.11
Residence, Plains, Georgia	45,000.00	54,090.00
Lot in Plains, Georgia	1,100.00	3,155.00
Automobile	4,550.75	2,737.50
Total Assets	$554,780.81	$970,857.74

---

[1] You need not be concerned about the details of this method of accounting until you study Chapter 12. In brief, when an investor holds a large enough stake in a corporation, such investment is accounted for at its acquisition cost plus the investor's pro rata share of the investee's net income (or net loss) minus the investor's share of dividends. For example, suppose the Texas Broadcasting Corporation earned $500,000 in a given year and that Johnson owned 20% of the corporation. In this situation, the Johnson financial statements would show an increase in Interest in Texas Broadcasting Corp. of $100,000 less the $25,000 income tax that would become payable upon disposition of the investment. (Today's accountants would prefer to increase the Investment account by the full $100,000 and the liabilities by $25,000. See the Carter financial statements.)

Miscellaneous Accounts Payable, Estimated	$ 1,500.00	$ 1,500.00
Provision for Possible Income Taxes on		
Unrealized Asset Appreciation—Note 4	–0–	174,000.00
Total Liabilities	$ 1,500.00	$175,500.00
Excess of Assets Over Liabilities (Capital)	$553,280.81	$795,357.74

NOTE 1: Estimated market values of real estate are 100% of the fair market values as determined by county tax assessors except as to certain assets held in the personal assets trust, which are stated at book value.

NOTE 2: This statement excludes campaign fund assets and liabilities.

NOTE 3: The interest in Carter's Warehouse partnership, the capital stock of Carter's Farms, Inc., the remainder interest in certain real estate and securities and a commercial lot in Plains, Georgia, were transferred to a personal assets trust in January, 1977. The primary purpose of the trust is to isolate the President from those of his assets which are most likely to be affected by actions of the federal government. The President was responsible as a general partner for obligations of the partnership before his partnership interest was transferred to the trust. The transfer to the trust did not affect such responsibility.

NOTE 4: If the market values of the assets were realized, income taxes would be payable at an uncertain rate. A provision for such income taxes has been made at rates in effect for 1977.

NOTE 5: The amounts in the accompanying statements are based principally upon the accrual basis method of accounting.

Required:

1. Evaluate the criticisms, making special reference to fundamental accounting concepts or "principles."
2. The financial statements of President and Mrs. Carter are shown in Exhibit 2–10. Do you prefer the approach taken by the Carter statements as compared with the Johnson statements? Explain.
3. The Carter statements in Exhibit 2–10 indicate that the Carter residence cost $45,000. Its estimated current value is shown as $54,090. Which number do you believe is more precise or accurate? More pertinent or relevant? Which number, $45,000 or $54,090, would be used by a business in its statement of assets?
4. Have the Carters earned income of $54,090 − $45,000 on their residence?
5. Suppose you were asked tomorrow to prepare your family's (or your individual) statement of assets and liabilities. Could you do it? How would you measure your wealth?

2–47. **HOUSE OF FABRICS ANNUAL REPORT.** Refer to the financial statements of the actual company, House of Fabrics, on pages 752–759, and answer the following questions:

1. What was the amount of sales for the 1989 fiscal year? The net income?
2. What was the total amount of cash dividends for the 1989 fiscal year?
3. What was the title of the financial statement that contained the dividend amount? Did it differ from the title you expected? Explain.

The Recording Process: Journals and Ledgers

LEARNING
OBJECTIVES

After studying this chapter, you should be able to

1. Analyze transactions in the form of debits and credits and with the help of a general ledger
2. Prepare journal entries and post them to the general ledger
3. Check the accuracy of your work by preparing a trial balance
4. Use a trial balance to prepare an income statement
5. Explain the meaning of **going concern, materiality,** and **cost-benefit**

Chapters 1 and 2 concentrated on the accountant's *overall conceptual approach* to reporting on the economic activities of an organization. This chapter introduces the actual data-processing framework used in practice for recording and accumulating the financial effects of voluminous transactions. We concentrate on *specific procedures and techniques* instead of new accounting concepts.

DOUBLE-ENTRY SYSTEM AND LEDGER ACCOUNTS

☐ The Account

To begin, consider how the accountant would record the Biwheels transactions that were introduced in Chapter 1. Recall their effects on the elements of the balance sheet equation:

	A		=	L	+	SE
	Cash	Merchandise Inventory		Note Payable		Paid-in Capital
(1) Initial investment by owners	+400,000		=			+400,000
(2) Loan from bank	+100,000		=	+100,000		
(3) Acquire inventory for cash	−150,000	+150,000	=			

This balance sheet equation approach emphasizes the concepts, but it can obviously become unwieldy if there are many accounts and numerous transactions. You can readily see that changes in the balance sheet equation can occur many times daily. In large businesses, such as a department store, hundreds or thousands of repetitive transactions occur hourly. In practice, *ledgers* must be used to keep track of how these multitudes of transactions affect each particular asset, liability, revenue, and expense account. A **ledger** contains a group of related accounts kept up to date in a systematic manner. The ledger may be in the form of a bound record book, a loose-leaf set of pages, a set of machine account cards, or some kind of electronic storage element such as magnetic tape or disk. When you hear reference to "keeping the books" or "auditing the books," the word *books* refers to the ledger.

The ledger accounts used here are simplified versions of those used in practice. They are called **T-accounts** because they take the form of the capital letter T. The vertical line in the T divides the account into its left and right sides. The account title is on the horizontal line. For example, consider the format of the Cash account:

	Cash	
Left side		Right side
Increases		Decreases

The above transactions would be shown in T-accounts as follows:

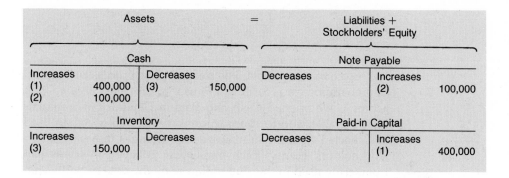

| | Assets | | = | | Liabilities + Stockholders' Equity |

Cash				Note Payable	
Increases		Decreases		Decreases	Increases
(1)	400,000	(3)	150,000		(2)	100,000
(2)	100,000				

Inventory				Paid-in Capital	
Increases		Decreases		Decreases	Increases
(3)	150,000				(1)	400,000

The above entries were made in accordance with the rules of a **double-entry system**, so named because at least two accounts are always affected by each transaction.

Asset accounts have left-side balances. They are increased by entries on the left side and decreased by entries on the right side. Liabilities and owners' equity accounts have right-side balances. They are increased by entries on the right side and decreased by entries on the left side.

Consider each entry:

1. Transaction: Initial investment by owners, $400,000 cash.
    Analysis: The asset **Cash** is increased.
              The stockholders' equity **Paid-in Capital** is increased.
    Entry:

Cash			Paid-in Capital	
(1)	400,000		(1)	400,000

2. Transaction: Loan from bank, $100,000.
    Analysis: The asset **Cash** is increased.
              The liability **Note Payable** is increased.
    Entry:

Cash			Note Payable	
(1)	400,000		(2)	100,000
(2)	100,000			

3. Transaction: Acquired inventory for cash, $150,000.

Analysis: The asset **Cash** is decreased.
The asset **Merchandise Inventory** is increased.

Entry:

Cash

(1)	400,000	(3)	150,000
(2)	100,000		

Merchandise Inventory

(3)	150,000	

Accounts are created as needed. The process of writing a new T-account in preparation for recording a transaction is called _opening the account._ For transaction 1, we opened Cash and Paid-in Capital. For transaction 2, we opened Note Payable, and for transaction 3 we opened Merchandise Inventory.

Each T-account summarizes the changes in a particular asset, liability, or stockholders' equity. Each transaction is keyed in some way, such as by the numbering used in this illustration or by the date or both. This keying helps the rechecking (auditing) process by aiding the tracing of transactions to original sources. A **balance** is the difference between the total left-side and right-side amounts in an account at any particular time. Accounts exist to keep an up-to-date summary of the changes in specific assets and equities. Financial statements can be prepared at any instant if the accounts are up to date. The necessary information is tabulated in the accounts. For example, the balance sheet after the first three transactions would contain the following accounts:

ASSETS		LIABILITIES + OWNERS' EQUITY	
Cash	$350,000	Liabilities:	
Merchandise		Note payable	$100,000
Inventory	150,000	Stockholders' equity:	
		Paid-in capital	400,000
Total	$500,000	Total	$500,000

The Strange Debit-Credit Language

You have just seen that the double-entry system features entries on left sides or right sides of each account. Accountants use special words, **debit** and **credit,** to denote how to analyze a transaction. For instance, suppose a CPA were asked how to analyze and record transaction 1. She would say, "That's easy. Debit Cash and credit Paid-in Capital." By so doing, she enters $400,000 on the _left_ side of Cash and $400,000 on the _right_ side of Paid-in Capital. In short, _debit_ means left and _credit_ means _right_. The word **charge** is often used instead of _debit_, but no single word is used as a synonym for _credit_.

Beginners in the study of accounting are frequently confused by the words *debit* and *credit*. Perhaps the best way to minimize confusion is to ask what words would be used as substitutes? *Left* would be used instead of debit, and *right* would be used instead of credit.

The words *debit* and *credit* have a Latin origin. They were used centuries ago when double-entry bookkeeping was introduced by Pacioli, an Italian monk. Even though *left* and *right* are more descriptive words, *debit* and *credit* are too deeply entrenched to avoid.

Debit and *credit* are used as verbs, adjectives, and nouns. "Debit $1,000 to cash and credit $1,000 to accounts receivable" are examples of uses as verbs, meaning that $1,000 should be placed on the left side of the Cash account and on the right side of the Accounts Receivable account. Similarly, if "a debit is made to cash" or "cash has a debit balance of $12,000," the word *debit* is a noun or an adjective that describes the status of a particular account. Thus *debit* and *credit* are short words packed with meaning.

In our everyday conversation, we sometimes use the words *debit* and *credit* in a general sense that may completely diverge from their technical accounting uses. For instance, we may give praise by saying, "She deserves plenty of credit for her good deed," or we may give criticism by saying, "That misplay is a debit on his ledger." When you study accounting, forget these general uses and misues of the words. Merely think right or left—that is, right side or left side.

Consider how the words *debit* and *credit* appear on your bank statement or your Visa or MasterCard statement of your account. For example, a *credit balance* in your checking account means that the bank owes you money. That is, a right-side (credit) balance in the *bank's* record of your account indicates a liability of the bank to you.

USING THE JOURNAL AND THE LEDGER

☐ Steps in Recording

To emphasize analysis (an activity of the brain rather than of the pen or computer), the effects of transactions 1, 2, and 3 were entered directly in the ledger. In actual practice, the accountant uses other records in addition to ledger accounts. The steps in recording are:

1. The recording steps begin when the transaction is substantiated by **source documents.** These are supporting original records of any transaction; they are memorandums of what happened. Examples of source documents include sales slips or invoices, check stubs, purchase orders, receiving reports, cash receipt slips, minutes of the board of directors, and other authorizing memorandums.

2. An analysis of the transaction is placed in a **book of original entry,** which is a formal chronological record of the effects of the entity's transactions on the balances in pertinent accounts. The most common example of a book of original entry is the **general journal.**

EXHIBIT 3–1

Journal Entries

GENERAL JOURNAL

Date	Entry No.	Accounts and Explanation	Post Ref.	Debit	Credit
19X1					
12/31	1	Cash	100	400,000	
		Paid-in capital	300		400,000
		Capital stock issued to Smith			
12/31	2	Cash	100	100,000	
		Note payable	202		100,000
		Borrowed at 9% interest on a			
		one-year note.			
19X2					
1/2	3	Merchandise inventory	130	150,000	
		Cash	100		150,000
		Acquired inventory for cash.			

GENERAL LEDGER

Cash   Account No. 100

Date	Explanation	Journ. Ref.	Debit	Date	Explanation	Journ. Ref.	Credit
19X1				19X2			
12/31	(often blank because			1/2		3	150,000
	the explanation is						
	already in the journal)	1	400,000				
12/31		2	100,000				

Merchandise Inventory   Account No. 130

Date	Explanation	Journ. Ref.	Debit	Date	Explanation	Journ. Ref.	Credit
19X2							
1/2		3	150,000				

EXHIBIT 3–1   (continued)

Note Payable   Account No. 202

Date	Explanation	Journ. Ref.	Debit	Date	Explanation	Journ. Ref.	Credit
				19X1			
				12/31		2	100,000

Paid-in Capital   Account No. 300

Date	Explanation	Journ. Ref.	Debit	Date	Explanation	Journ. Ref.	Credit
				19X1			
				12/31		1	400,000

The Journal Entry

A **journal entry** is an analysis of the effects of a transaction on the accounts, usually accompanied by an explanation. The accounts to be debited and credited are identified. For example, the top part of Exhibit 3–1 shows how the opening three entries for Biwheels would be "journalized."

The conventional form of the general journal includes the following:

1. The date and number of the entry are placed near the left margin.
2. In the space for the description, the title of the account or accounts to be *debited* (charged) are placed flush left. The title of the account or accounts to be *credited* are indented in a consistent way, but only for two or three letter spaces.
3. The amounts are placed in the debit-credit *money columns*. No dollar signs are used.
4. The journal entry is not complete without the narrative explanation, which is sometimes brief and sometimes exhaustive. The length of the explanation depends on the complexity of the transaction and how extensively the details are to be carried in supporting files of documents.
5. The explanation is often placed flush left and aligned with the debit entry, although practice varies. The important point is consistency so that all explanations will be vertically aligned.
6. To avoid a blurry mess, a space is skipped between each journal entry.

Posting to the Ledger

Posting is the transferring of amounts from the journal to the appropriate accounts in the ledger. To demonstrate, consider entry 3 for Biwheels. Exhibit 3–1 shows how the credit to cash is posted.

The sample of the general ledger in Exhibit 3–1 is in the form of elaborate T-accounts; that is, debits are on the left side and credits are on the right side.

Note how cross-referencing occurs. The date is traced to the ledger, and the journal entry number is placed in the reference column. The completion of the posting is signified by inserting the account number in the reference column of the journal. (A blank reference column for an entry in the journal would indicate that the entry has not yet been posted to the ledger account.) The process of numbering or otherwise specifically identifying each journal entry and each posting is known as the **keying of entries.** This helps auditing and finding and correcting errors. Always key your entries.

☐ Running Balance Column

Exhibit 3–2 shows a popular account format that provides a running balance. There are three money columns: debit, credit, and balance. The running balance feature is easily achieved by electronic computers or accounting machines.

Above all, note that the same postings to Cash (or any other pertinent accounts) are made regardless of the account format used: T-account (Exhibit 3–1) or running balance (Exhibit 3–2).

☐ Chart of Accounts

Organizations have a **chart of accounts,** which is normally a numbered or coded list describing all account titles. These numbers are used as references, as Exhibit 3–1 demonstrates. Each account described in the journal should have an identifying number in the Post Ref. column. The following is the chart of accounts for Biwheels:

ACCOUNT NUMBER		ACCOUNT NUMBER	
100	Cash	202	Note payable
120	Accounts receivable	203	Accounts payable
		300	Paid-in capital
130	Merchandise inventory	400	Retained income
		500	Sales
140	Prepaid rent	600	Cost of goods sold
170	Store equipment	601	Rent expense
170A	Accumulated depreciation, store equipment (explained later)	602	Depreciation expense

Although an outsider may not know what the code means, accounting employees become so familiar with the code that they think, talk, and write in terms of account numbers instead of account names. Thus an outside auditor may find entry 3, the acquisition of Merchandise Inventory (Account #130) for Cash (Account #100), journalized as follows:

19X2		MONEY COLUMNS	
		dr.	cr.
Jan. 2	#130	150,000	
	#100		150,000

This journal entry is the employee's shorthand. Its brevity and lack of explanation would hamper any outsider's understanding of the transaction, but the entry's meaning would be clear to anyone within the organization.

EXHIBIT 3–2

Ledger Account with Running Balance Column

Cash   Account No. 100

Date	Explanation	Journ. Ref.	Debit	Credit	Balance
19X1					
12/31	(often blank because the explanation is	1	400,000		400,000
12/31	already in the journal)	2	100,000		500,000
19X2					
1/2		3		150,000	350,000

ADDITIONAL TRANSACTIONS

As we have seen, the transaction is analyzed mentally, then journalized, and then posted to the ledger. Therefore we now prepare journal entries for transactions 4 through 13 as a continuation of the journal entries 1 through 3 already appearing in Exhibit 3–1.

4. Transaction: Acquired inventory on credit, $10,000.
Analysis: The asset **Merchandise Inventory** is increased.
The liability **Accounts Payable** is increased.
Entry: In the journal (explanation omitted):

Merchandise inventory	10,000	
Accounts payable		10,000

Post to the ledger (postings are indicated by circled amounts):

Merchandise Inventory*		Accounts Payable	
(3)	150,000		
(4)	10,000	(4)	10,000

* Also often called Inventory of Merchandise, or if it is the only type of inventory account, it is simply called Inventory.

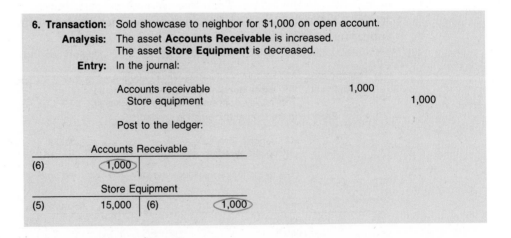

5. Transaction: Acquired store equipment for $4,000 cash plus $11,000 trade credit.
Analysis: The asset **Cash** is decreased.
The asset **Store Equipment** is increased.
The liability **Accounts Payable** is increased.
Entry: In the journal:

Store equipment	15,000	
Cash		4,000
Accounts payable		11,000

Post to the ledger:

	Cash				Accounts Payable	
(1)	400,000	(3)	150,000		(4)	10,000
(2)	100,000	(5)	4,000		(5)	11,000

	Store Equipment	
(5)	15,000	

Entry 5 is called a **compound entry,** which means that more than two accounts are affected by a single entry. In contrast, a **simple entry** affects only two accounts. Whether simple or compound, as entry 5 shows, the net effect is *always* to keep the accounting equation in balance:

$$\text{Assets} = \text{Liabilities} + \text{Stockholders' equity}$$
$$+15,000 - 4,000 = +11,000$$

A helpful hint: When analyzing a transaction, initially pinpoint the effects (if any) on cash. Did cash increase or decrease? Then think of the effects on other accounts. In this way, you get off to the right start. Usually, it is much easier to identify the effects of a transaction on cash than to identify the effects on other accounts.

6. Transaction: Sold showcase to neighbor for $1,000 on open account.
Analysis: The asset **Accounts Receivable** is increased.
The asset **Store Equipment** is decreased.
Entry: In the journal:

Accounts receivable	1,000	
Store equipment		1,000

Post to the ledger:

	Accounts Receivable	
(6)	1,000	

	Store Equipment		
(5)	15,000	(6)	1,000

One asset goes up, but another asset goes down. No liability or owners' equity account is affected.

7. Transaction: Returned inventory to supplier for full credit, $800.

Analysis: The asset **Merchandise Inventory** is decreased.
The liability **Accounts Payable** is decreased.

Entry: In the journal:

Accounts payable	800	
Merchandise inventory		800

Post to the ledger:

Merchandise Inventory					Accounts Payable			
(3)	150,000	(7)	800	(7)	800	(4)	10,000
(4)	10,000					(5)	11,000

---

8. Transaction: Paid cash to creditors, $4,000.

Analysis: The asset **Cash** is decreased.
The liability **Accounts Payable** is decreased.

Entry: In the journal:

Accounts payable	4,000	
Cash		4,000

Post to the ledger:

Cash					Accounts Payable			
(1)	400,000	(3)	150,000	(7)	800	(4)	10,000
(2)	100,000	(5)	4,000	(8)	4,000	(5)	11,000
		(8)	4,000				

---

9. Transaction: Collected cash from debtors, $700.

Analysis: The asset **Cash** is increased.
The asset **Accounts Receivable** is decreased.

Entry: In the journal:

Cash	700	
Accounts receivable		700

Post to the ledger:

Cash			
(1)	400,000	(3)	150,000
(2)	100,000	(5)	4,000
(9)	700	(8)	4,000

Accounts Receivable			
(6)	1,000	(9)	700

REVENUE AND EXPENSE TRANSACTIONS

Revenue and expense transactions deserve special attention because their relation to the balance sheet equation is less obvious. Focus on the equation:

Assets = Liabilities + Stockholders' equity   (1)

Assets = Liabilities + Paid-in capital + Retained income   (2)

If we ignore dividends at this stage, Retained Income is merely the accumulated revenue less expenses. Therefore the T-accounts can be grouped as follows:

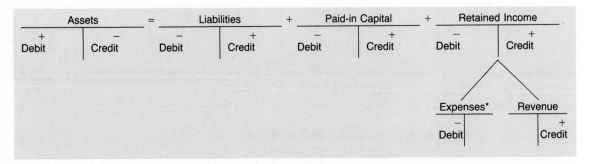

Be careful here. Although entries on the left side of this account *increase* expenses, their effect on the balance sheet equation is to *decrease* Retained Income. The negative sign denotes this decrease in Stockholders' Equity.

Revenue and expense accounts are really "little" stockholders' equity accounts. *That is, they are primarily a part of stockholders' equity.* Their *net* effects are periodically summarized as one number, net income, which increases retained income (or net loss, which decreases retained income).

Retained income is a balance sheet account, whereas revenue and expense accounts record the *changes* between balance sheet dates in the stockholders' equity attributable to operations. Thus these revenues and expenses are shown in the income statement.

Consider each entry in detail:

10a. Transaction:	Sales on credit, $160,000.
Analysis:	The asset **Accounts Receivable** is increased. The stockholders' equity **Sales** is increased.
Entry:	In the journal:

Accounts receivable	160,000	
Sales		160,000

Post to the ledger:

Accounts Receivable			Sales	
(6)	1,000	(9) 700		(10a) 160,000
(10a)	160,000			

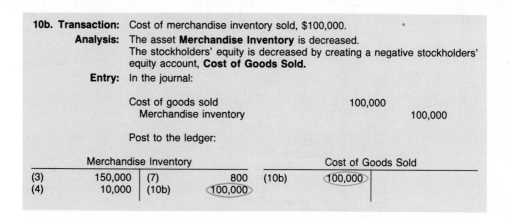

10b. Transaction: Cost of merchandise inventory sold, $100,000.
Analysis: The asset **Merchandise Inventory** is decreased.
The stockholders' equity is decreased by creating a negative stockholders' equity account, **Cost of Goods Sold.**
Entry: In the journal:

Cost of goods sold	100,000	
Merchandise inventory		100,000

Post to the ledger:

Merchandise Inventory				Cost of Goods Sold		
(3)	150,000	(7)	800	(10b)	100,000	
(4)	10,000	(10b)	100,000			

Before proceeding, reflect on the logic. Expenses *decrease* stockholders' equity. They are offsets to the normal right-side balances of stockholders' equity accounts. Therefore *increases* in expenses are *decreases* in stockholders' equity. For Cost of Goods Sold of $100,000, the following logic applies:

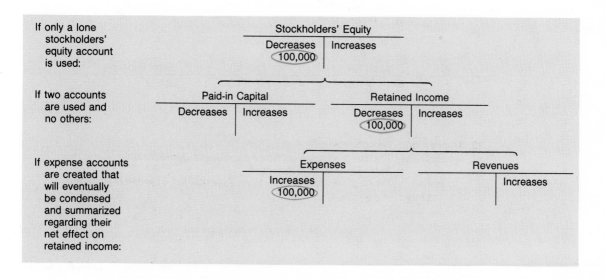

There is no contradiction here. Expenses are negative stockholders' equity accounts. An *increase* in a negative account (such as increasing Cost of Goods Sold by $100,000) has the ultimate effect of *decreasing* stockholders' equity.

11. Transaction: Paid rent for three months in advance, $6,000.

    Analysis: The asset **Cash** is decreased.
                 The asset **Prepaid Rent** is increased.

    Entry: In the journal:

Prepaid rent	6,000	
Cash		6,000

Post to the ledger:

	Cash		
(1)	400,000	(3)	150,000
(2)	100,000	(5)	4,000
(9)	700	(8)	4,000
		(11)	6,000

	Prepaid Rent	
(11)	6,000	

---

12. Transaction: Recognized expiration of rental services, $2,000.

    Analysis: The asset **Prepaid Rent** is decreased.
                 The negative stockholders' equity **Rent Expense** is increased.

    Entry: In the journal:

Rent expense	2,000	
Prepaid rent		2,000

Post to the ledger:

	Prepaid Rent				Rent Expense	
(11)	6,000	(12)	2,000	(12)	2,000	

---

13. Transaction: Recognized depreciation, $100.

    Analysis: The asset-reduction account **Accumulated Depreciation, Store Equipment** is increased.
                 The negative stockholders' equity **Depreciation Expense** is increased.

    Entry: In the journal:

Depreciation expense	100	
Accumulated depreciation, store equipment		100

Post to the ledger:

	Accumulated Depreciation, Store Equipment				Depreciation Expense	
		(13)	100	(13)	100	

Exhibit 3–3 shows the formal journal entries for transactions 4 through 13. The Posting Reference (Post. Ref.) column used the numbers from the chart of accounts, which are also shown on each account in the ledger.

Transaction 13 introduced *accumulated depreciation*, which was described as an *asset-reduction* account in our illustrative analysis and corresponding journal

EXHIBIT 3–3

Journal

Date	Entry No.	Accounts and Explanation	Post Ref.	Debit	Credit
19X2	4	Merchandise inventory	130	10,000	
		Accounts payable	203		10,000
		Acquired inventory on credit.			
	5	Store equipment	170	15,000	
		Cash	100		4,000
		Accounts payable	203		11,000
		Acquired store equipment for cash plus credit. (This is an example of a *compound journal entry*, whereby more than two accounts are affected by the same transaction.)			
	6	Accounts receivable	120	1,000	
		Store equipment	170		1,000
		Sold store equipment to business neighbor.			
	7	Accounts payable	203	800	
		Merchandise inventory	130		800
		Returned some inventory to supplier.			
	8	Accounts payable	203	4,000	
		Cash	100		4,000
		Payments to creditors.			
	9	Cash	100	700	
		Accounts receivable	120		700
		Collections from debtors.			
	10a	Accounts receivable	120	160,000	
		Sales	500		160,000
		Sales to customers on credit.			
	10b	Cost of goods sold	600	100,000	
		Merchandise inventory	130		100,000
		To record the cost of inventory sold.			
	11	Prepaid rent	140	6,000	
		Cash	100		6,000
		Payment of rent in advance.			
	12	Rent expense	601	2,000	
		Prepaid rent	140		2,000
		Recognize expiration of rental service.			
	13	Depreciation expense	602	100	
		Accumulated depreciation, store equipment	170A		100
		Recognize depreciation for January.			

entry. A more popular term is **contra asset.** As used by accountants, *contra* means an offset to, deduction from, or reduction of a companion or an associated amount. Therefore a **contra account** is a separate but related account that offsets a companion account. A contra account has two distinguishing features: (1) it always has a companion account, and (2) it has the opposite balance of the companion account. In our illustration, the relationships on January 31, 19X2, are:

Asset:	Store equipment	$14,000
Contra asset:	Accumulated depreciation, equipment	100
Net asset:	Book value	$13,900

The **book value** or **net book value** or **carrying amount** or **carrying value** is defined as the balance of an account shown on the books, net of any contra accounts. In our example, the book value is $13,900, the original acquisition cost less the contra account for accumulated depreciation.

The balance sheet distinguishes between the store equipment's original cost and its accumulated depreciation. As the name implies, **accumulated depreciation** (sometimes called **allowance for depreciation**) is the cumulative sum of all depreciation recognized since the date of acquisition of the particular assets described. Published balance sheets routinely report both the original cost and accumulated depreciation.

ACCUMULATED DEPRECIATION IS CONTRA ACCOUNT

Why is there an Accumulated Depreciation account? Why not reduce Store Equipment directly for $100? Conceptually, a direct reduction is indeed justified. However, accountants have traditionally preserved the original cost in the original asset account throughout the asset's useful life. Accountants can then readily refer to that account to learn the asset's initial cost. Such information may be sought for reports to management, government regulators, and tax authorities. Moreover the original $14,000 cost is the height of accuracy; it is a reliable, objective number. In contrast, the Accumulated Depreciation is an *estimate*, the result of a calculation whose accuracy depends heavily on the accountant's less reliable prediction of an asset's useful life.

DEBITS = CREDITS

Recall the balance sheet equation:

$$A = L + \text{Stockholders' equity} \tag{1}$$

$$A = L + \text{Paid-in capital} + \text{Retained income} \tag{2}$$

$$A = L + \text{Paid-in capital} + (\text{Revenues} - \text{Expenses} - \text{Dividends}) \qquad (3)$$

$$\text{transposing: } A + \text{Expenses} + \text{Dividends} = L + \text{Paid-in capital} + \text{Revenues} \qquad (4)$$

Finally,

$$\text{Left} = \text{Right}$$
$$\text{Debit} = \text{Credit}$$

Debit means one thing and one thing only— "left side" (not "bad," "something coming," etc.). *Credit* means one thing and one thing only—"right side" (not "good," "something owed," etc.).

The accountant usually employs technical terms. For example, if you asked an accountant what entry to make for transaction 10b, the answer would be, "I would debit (or charge) Cost of Goods Sold for $100,000; and I would credit Merchandise Inventory for $100,000." Note that the total dollar amount of the debits (entries on the left side of the account(s) affected) will *always* equal the total dollar amount of the credits (entries on the right side of the accounts affected) because the whole accounting system is based on an equation. The symmetry and power of this analytical debit-credit technique is indeed impressive.

Assets are traditionally carried as left-side balances. Why do assets and expenses both carry debit balances? They carry left-side balances for different reasons. *Expenses* are temporary stockholders' equity accounts; they are negative equity accounts. Decreases in stockholders' equity are entered on the left side of the accounts because they offset the normal (i.e., right-side) stockholders' equity balances. Because expenses decrease stockholders' equity, they are carried as left-side balances.

Debits are often abbreviated as *dr.*, and credits are often abbreviated as *cr.*

Exhibit 3–4 presents the rules of debit and credit and the normal balances of various accounts. As the exhibit emphasizes, revenues increase owners' equity; hence they are recorded as credits. Because expenses decrease owners' equity, they are recorded as debits.

Professional accountants frequently think about complicated transactions in terms of how they would be analyzed in a journal or in T-accounts. That is, accountants use these bookkeeping devices as models of the organization. Accountants often ask one another, "How would you journalize that transaction?" or "How would the T-accounts be affected?" In short, accountants have found that they can think straighter if they force themselves to visualize the transaction in terms of the balance sheet equation and debits and credits.

GENERAL LEDGER AND TRIAL BALANCE

□ General Ledger and Presenting of Balances

The **general ledger** is the record that contains the group of accounts that supports the amounts shown in the major financial statements. Exhibit 3-5 shows the Biwheels general ledger in T-account form. Pause and examine the postings in

EXHIBIT 3–4

Rules of Debit and Credit and Normal Balances of Accounts

Rules of Debit and Credit

	ASSETS		=		LIABILITIES		+		OWNERS' EQUITY	

Assets		=	Liabilities		+	Paid-in Capital	
+	−		−	+		−	+
Increase	Decrease		Decrease	Increase		Decrease	Increase
Debit	Credit		Debit	Credit		Debit	Credit
Left	Right		Left	Right		Left	Right

Revenues	
−	+
Decrease	Increase
Debit	Credit
Left	Right

Expenses	
−*	+
Increase	Decrease
Debit	Credit
Left	Right

* There is a negative sign here because increases in expenses decrease owners' equity

Normal Balances

Assets	Debit	
Liabilities		Credit
Owners' equity (overall)		Credit
Paid-in capital		Credit
Revenues		Credit
Expenses	Debit	

the general ledger. (It is customary *not* to use dollar signs in either the journal or the ledger. Note too that negative numbers are never used in the journal or the ledger.)

The account balance may be kept as a running balance, or it may be updated from time to time as desired. There are many acceptable techniques for updating. Accountants' preferences vary. The double horizontal lines in Exhibit 3–5 mean that all postings above the double lines are summarized as a single balance immediately below the double lines. Therefore all amounts above the double underscores should be ignored for purposes of computing the next updated balance. (Many accountants prefer to use single horizontal lines instead of the double lines used in this book.)

The accounts without double underscores in Exhibit 3–5 contain a lone number. This number automatically serves also as the ending balance. For example, the Note Payable entry of $100,000 also serves as the ending balance for trial balance purposes.

EXHIBIT 3–5

General Ledger of Biwheels Company

Transactions contained in this illustration:

1. Initial investment
2. Loan from bank
3. Acquired merchandise inventory for cash
4. Acquired merchandise inventory on credit
5. Acquired store equipment for cash plus credit
6. Sales of equipment on credit
7. Return of merchandise inventory for credit

8. Payments to creditors
9. Collections from debtors
10a. Sales on credit
10b. Cost of merchandise inventory sold
11. Pay rent in advance
12. Recognize expiration of rental services
13. Recognize depreciation

ASSETS
(Increases on left, decreases on right)

LIABILITIES AND STOCKHOLDERS' EQUITY
(Decreases on left, increases on right)

Cash — Account No. 100

(1)	400,000	(3)	150,000
(2)	100,000	(5)	4,000
(9)	700	(8)	4,000
		(11)	6,000

1/31 Bal. 336,700

Note Payable 202

		(2)	100,000

Paid-in Capital 300

		(1)	400,000

Accounts Receivable 120

(6)	1,000	(9)	700
(10a)	160,000		

1/31 Bal 160,300

Accounts Payable 203

(7)	800	(4)	10,000
(8)	4,000	(5)	11,000

1/31 Bal. 16,200

Retained Income 400

	1/31 Bal.
	57,900*

Expense and Revenue Accounts

Merchandise Inventory 130

(3)	150,000	(7)	800
(4)	10,000	(10b)	100,000

3/31 Bal. 59,200

Cost of Goods Sold 600

(10b)	100,000

Sales 500

		(10a)	160,000

Prepaid Rent 140

(11)	6,000	(12)	2,000

1/31 Bal 4,000

Rent Expense 601

(12)	2,000

* The details of the revenue and expense accounts appear in the income statement. Their net effect is then transferred to a single account, Retained Income, in the balance sheet. The procedures for accomplishing this transfer, called closing the books, are explained in Chapter 5.

Store Equipment 170

(5)	15,000	(6)	1,000

1/31 Bal 14,000

Depreciation Expense 602

(13)	100

Accumulated Depreciation, Store Equipment 170A

		(13)	100

Note: An ending balance is shown on the side of the account with the larger total.

☐ Trial Balance

A **trial balance** is a list of all accounts with their balances. Its purpose is twofold: (a) to help check on accuracy of posting by proving whether the total debits equal the total credits, and (b) to establish a convenient summary of balances in all accounts for the preparation of formal financial statements.

A trial balance may be taken at any time the accounts are up to date, for example, on January 2, 19X2, after the first three transactions of Biwheels:

BIWHEELS COMPANY
Trial Balance
January 2, 19X2

	BALANCE	
ACCOUNT TITLES	Debit	Credit
Cash	$350,000	
Merchandise Inventory	150,000	
Note payable		$100,000
Paid-in capital		400,000
Total	$500,000	$500,000

Obviously, the trial balance becomes more detailed (and more essential) when there are many more accounts. The word "trial" was well chosen; the list is prepared as a *test* or *check* before proceeding further.

Exhibit 3–6 is the trial balance of the general ledger of Exhibit 3–5. In particular, note that Retained Income has no balance here. Instead all the revenue and expense accounts are listed. As Exhibit 3–5 indicates, when the formal balance sheet is prepared, the retained income would summarize the net effect of the revenue and expense accounts on stockholders' equity.

The trial balance assures the accountant that the debits and credits are equal. It is also the springboard for the preparation of the balance sheet and the income statement. The income statement accounts are summarized later as a single number, net income, which then becomes Retained Income in the formal balance sheet.

The trial balance helps alert the accountant to possible errors. However, a trial balance may balance even when there are recording errors. For example, a $10,000 cash receipt on account may erroneously be recorded as $1,000. Then both Cash and Accounts Receivable would be in error by offsetting amounts of $9,000. Another example would be the recording of a $10,000 cash receipt on account as a credit to Sales rather than as a reduction of Accounts Receivable. Sales would be overstated and Accounts Receivable overstated by $10,000. Nevertheless, the trial balance would still show total debits equal to total credits.

EXHIBIT 3–6

BIWHEELS COMPANY
Trial Balance
January 31, 19X2

	DEBITS	CREDITS
Cash	$336,700	
Accounts receivable	160,300	
Merchandise inventory	59,200	
Prepaid rent	4,000	
Store equipment	14,000	
Accumulated depreciation, store equipment		$ 100
Note payable		100,000
Accounts payable		16,200
✓Paid-in capital		400,000
Retained income*		—
Sales		160,000
Cost of goods sold	100,000	
Rent expense	2,000	
Depreciation expense	100	
Total	$676,300	$676,300

*Of course, if a Retained Income balance existed at the start of the accounting period, it would appear here. However, in our example Retained Income was zero at the start of the period.

SUBSIDIARY LEDGERS

The general ledger is usually supported by various **subsidiary ledgers,** which provide details for several accounts in the general ledger. For instance, an accounts receivable subsidiary ledger (which is illustrated in Chapter 6) would contain a separate account for each credit customer. The accounts receivable balance that appears in the Sears balance sheet is in a single account in the Sears general ledger. However, that lone balance is buttressed by detailed individual accounts receivable with millions of credit customers. You can readily visualize how some accounts in general ledgers might have subsidiary ledgers, which in turn are supported by sub-subsidiary ledgers, and so on. Thus a subsidiary accounts receivable ledger might be subdivided alphabetically into Customers A–D, E–H, and so forth, or by customer account numbers.

DATA PROCESSING AND COMPUTERS

Data processing is a general term that usually means the totality of the procedures used to record, analyze, store, and report on chosen activities. An accounting system is a data-processing system. For instructional ease, most introductory accounting textbooks (including this one) focus on manual (pen and ink) methods of data processing. Of course, almost all organizations use mechanical aids (for example, a simple cash register) and electronic aids (for example, massive computer systems for billing telephone services).

The physical forms of journals and ledgers have changed signficantly. The data may be kept on tape or disks or some other form of computer record. Nevertheless, whatever their form, journals and ledgers remain as the backbone of accounting systems.

Entries in journals and ledgers by pen or pencil are efficient ways to learn the accounting cycle. However, each transaction can be journalized by entering the appropriate account numbers and amounts into a computer. The computer then does the posting to the ledger. If managers desire, they can have a new balance sheet each day.

The microcomputer has enabled small organizations to process data more efficiently than ever. When you check out at a pharmacy or clothing store, the cash register often does more than just record a sale. It may also record a decrease in inventory. It may activate an order to a supplier if the inventory level is low. If a sale is on credit, the machine may check a customer's credit limit, update the accounts receivable, and eventually prepare monthly statements for mailing to the customer.

The magnitude of the data-processing task is illustrated by the Amoco Oil Company, which changed its method of recording credit sales. A new "transaction recorder" device records the carbon-copy impressions of every transaction on a one-inch-deep line on special log sheets inside the recorder. The sheets are scanned by the Amoco computer, and the data are later reproduced on the customer's monthly statement of account.

With the old system, Amoco had received 650,000 separate sales slips daily. Each slip was being handled fourteen times. The new system reduces the incoming paper load by 90% and eliminates all but one handling.

MORE ON GENERALLY ACCEPTED ACCOUNTING PRINCIPLES (GAAP)

Basic concepts of accounting theory are too vast to consume in one gulp, so they are being introduced gradually as we proceed. Previous chapters discussed some basic concepts of accounting, such as entity, recognition, matching and cost recovery, and stable monetary unit. We now consider three other major ideas that are part of the body of generally accepted accounting principles: going concern, materiality, and cost-benefit.

☐ Continuity or the Going Concern Convention

The **continuity** or **going concern convention** is the assumption that in all ordinary situations an entity persists indefinitely. This notion implies that existing *resources*, such as plant assets, *will be used* to fulfill the general purposes of a continuing entity *rather than sold* in tomorrow's real estate or equipment markets. It also implies that existing liabilities will be paid at maturity in an orderly manner.

Suppose some old specialized equipment has a depreciated cost (that is, original cost less accumulated depreciation) of $10,000, a replacement cost of $12,000, and a realizable value of $7,000 on the used-equipment market. The continuity convention is often cited as the justification for adhering to acquisition cost (or acquisition cost less depreciation, $10,000 in this example) as the primary basis for valuing assets such as inventories, land, buildings, and equipment. Some critics of these accounting practices believe that such valuations are not as informative as their replacement cost ($12,000) or their realizable values upon liquidation ($7,000). Defenders of using $10,000 as an appropriate asset valuation argue that a going concern will generally use the asset as originally intended. Therefore the recorded cost (the acquisition cost less depreciation) is the preferable basis for accountability and evaluation of performance. Hence other values are not germane because replacement or disposal will not occur en masse as of the balance sheet date.

The opposite view of this going concern or continuity convention is an immediate-liquidation assumption whereby all items on a balance sheet are valued at the amounts appropriate if the entity were to be liquidated in piecemeal fashion within a few days or months. This liquidation approach to valuation is usually used only when the entity is in severe, near-bankrupt straits.

☐ Materiality

Because accounting is a practical art, the practitioner often tempers accounting reports by applying judgments about materiality. The **materiality convention** is a characteristic attaching to a statement, fact, or item that, if omitted or misstated, would tend to mislead the user of the financial statements under consideration.

Many outlays that should theoretically be recorded as assets are immediately written off as expenses because of their lack of significance. For example, many corporations have a rule that requires the immediate write-off to expense of all outlays under a specified minimum of, say, $100, regardless of the useful life of the asset acquired. In such a case, coat hangers may be acquired and may last indefinitely, but they may never appear in the balance sheet as assets. The resulting $100 understatement of assets and stockholders' equity would be too trivial to worry about.

When is an item material? There will probably never be a universal clear-cut answer. What is trivial to General Motors may be material to Joe's Tavern. A working rule is that an item is material if its proper accounting would probably affect the decision of a knowledgeable user. In sum, materiality is an important convention. But it is difficult to use anything other than prudent judgment to tell whether an item is material.

☐ Cost-Benefit

Accounting systems vary in complexity from the minimum crude records kept to satisfy governmental authorities to the sophisticated budgeting and feedback schemes that are at the heart of management planning and controlling. The **cost-benefit criterion** means that as a system is changed, its expected additional benefits should exceed its expected additional costs. Often the benefits are difficult to measure, but this criterion at least implicitly underlies the decisions about the design of accounting systems. Sometimes the reluctance to adopt suggestions for new ways of measuring financial position and performance is because of inertia. More often it is because the apparent benefits do not exceed the obvious costs of gathering and interpreting the information.

☐ Room for Judgment

Accounting is commonly misunderstood as being a precise discipline that produces exact measurements of a company's financial position and performance. As a result, many individuals regard accountants as little more than mechanical tabulators who grind out financial reports after processing an imposing amount of detail in accordance with stringent predetermined rules. Although accountants take methodical steps with masses of data, their rules of measurement allow much room for judgment. Managers and accountants who exercise this judgment have more influence on financial reporting than is commonly believed. These judgments are guided by the basic concepts, techniques, and conventions called generally accepted accounting principles (GAAP). Examples of the latter include the basic concepts just discussed. Their meaning will become clearer as these concepts are applied in future chapters.

SUMMARY

The accountant's recording process concentrates on the journal and the general ledger. The journal provides a chronological record of transactions, whereas the general ledger provides a dated summary of the effects of the transactions on all accounts, account by account.

Accounting can be learned without journals. The general ledger is really the major backup for financial statements. Nevertheless, the journal entry is a convenient, simple way of presenting an analysis of a transaction. Consequently, journal entries are popular teaching devices and provide an easy basis for discussion among students, teachers, and professional accountants.

SUMMARY PROBLEMS FOR YOUR REVIEW

☐ Problem One

Do you agree with the following statements? Explain.

1. To charge an account means to credit it.
2. One person's debit is another person's credit.
3. A charge account may be credited.

4. My credit is my most valuable asset.
5. She has more credits than debits.
6. When I give credit, I debit my customers' account.

Solution to Problem One

Remember that in accounting, *debit* means left side and *credit* means right side.

1. No. *Charge* and *debit* and *left side* are synonyms.
2. Yes, in certain situations. The clearest example is probably the sale of merchandise on open account. The buyer's account payable would have a credit (right) balance, and the seller's account receivable would have a debit (left) balance.
3. Yes. When collections are received, Accounts Receivable are credited (right).
4. It depends. In technical accounting terms, asset balances are debits, not credits. Of course, the word *credit* also has some general, nontechnical meanings. As used in this statement, "my credit" refers to "my ability to borrow," not which side of a balance sheet is affected. "My ability to borrow" may indeed be a valuable right, but the accountant does not recognize that ability (as such) as an asset to be measured and reported in the balance sheet. When borrowing occurs, the borrower's assets are increased (debited, increased on the left side) and the liabilities are increased (credited, increased on the right side).
5. No. From a technical accounting standpoint, the total debits (left) must always equal the total credits (right). As used here in a general sense, the statement could be translated: She has more positive characteristics than negative.
6. Yes. Accounts Receivable is debited (left). "Give credit" in this context means that the corresponding account payable on the customer's accounting records will be increased (credited, right).

Problem Two

The trial balance of Perez Used Auto Co. on March 31, 19X1, follows:

ACCOUNT TITLE	BALANCE	
	Debit	Credit
Cash	$ 10,000	
Accounts receivable	20,000	
Automobile inventory	100,000	
Accounts payable		$ 3,000
Notes payable		70,000
Perez, owner's equity		57,000
Total	$130,000	$130,000

The Perez business entity is not incorporated; it is a proprietorship. The account used here is Perez, Owner's Equity; in practice, it is often called Perez, Capital.

Perez rented operating space and equipment on a month-to-month basis. During April, the business had the following summarized transactions:

a. Perez invested an additional $20,000 cash in the business.
b. Collected $10,000 on accounts receivable.
c. Paid $2,000 on accounts payable.

d. Sold autos for $120,000 cash.

e. Cost of autos sold was $70,000.

f. Replenished inventory for $60,000 cash.

g. Paid rent expense in cash, $14,000.

h. Paid utilities in cash, $1,000.

i. Paid selling expense in cash, $30,000.

j. Paid interest expense in cash, $1,000.

EXHIBIT 3–7

PEREZ USED AUTO CO.
General Journal

ENTRY	ACCOUNTS AND EXPLANATION	POST REF.*	DEBIT	CREDIT
a.	Cash	✓	20,000	
	Perez, owner's equity	✓		20,000
	Investment in business by Perez.			
b.	Cash	✓	10,000	
	Accounts receivable	✓		10,000
	Collected cash on accounts.			
c.	Accounts payable	✓	2,000	
	Cash	✓		2,000
	Disbursed cash on accounts owed to others.			
d.	Cash	✓	120,000	
	Sales	✓		120,000
	Sales for cash.			
e.	Cost of goods sold	✓	70,000	
	Automobile inventory	✓		70,000
	Cost of inventory that was sold to customers.			
f.	Automobile inventory	✓	60,000	
	Cash	✓		60,000
	Replenished inventory.			
g.	Rent expense	✓	14,000	
	Cash	✓		14,000
	Paid April rent.			
h.	Utilities expense	✓	1,000	
	Cash	✓		1,000
	Paid April utilities.			
i.	Selling expense	✓	30,000	
	Cash	✓		30,000
	Paid April selling expenses.			
j.	Interest expense	✓	1,000	
	Cash	✓		1,000
	Paid April interest expense.			

* Ordinarily, account numbers are used to denote specific posting references. Otherwise check marks are used.

EXHIBIT 3–8

PEREZ USED AUTO CO.
General Ledger

Cash

Bal.*	10,000	(c)	2,000
(a)	20,000	(f)	60,000
(b)	10,000	(g)	14,000
(d)	120,000	(h)	1,000
	160,000	(i)	30,000
		(j)	1,000
			108,000†
Bal.	52,000		

Accounts Receivable

Bal.*	20,000	(b)	10,000
Bal.	10,000		

Automobile Inventory

Bal.*	100,000	(e)	70,000
(f)	60,000		
Bal.	90,000		

Accounts Payable

(c)	2,000	Bal.*	3,000
		Bal.	1,000

Notes Payable

		Bal.*	70,000

Cost of Goods Sold

(e)	70,000		

Selling Expense

(i)	30,000		

Utilities Expense

(h)	1,000		

Perez, Owner's Equity

		Bal.*	57,000
		(a)	20,000
		Bal.	77,000

Sales

		(d)	120,000

Rent Expense

(g)	14,000		

Interest Expense

(j)	1,000		

* Balances denoted with an asterisk are as of March 31; balances without asterisks are as of April 30. Lone numbers in any accounts also serve as ending balances.
† Subtotals are included in the Cash account. They are not an essential part of T-accounts. However, when an account contains many postings, subtotals ease the checking of arithmetic.

EXHIBIT 3–9

PEREZ USED AUTO CO.
Trial Balance
April 30, 19X1

ACCOUNT TITLE	BALANCE Debit	BALANCE Credit
Cash	$ 52,000	
Accounts receivable	10,000	
Automobile inventory	90,000	
Accounts payable		$ 1,000
Notes payable		70,000
Perez, owner's equity		77,000
Sales		120,000
Cost of goods sold	70,000	
Rent expense	14,000	
Utilities expense	1,000	
Selling expense	30,000	
Interest expense	1,000	
Total	$268,000	$268,000

EXHIBIT 3-10

PEREZ USED AUTO CO.
Income Statement
For the Month Ended April 30, 19X1

Sales		$120,000
Deduct expenses:		
Cost of goods sold	$70,000	
Rent expense	14,000	
Utilities expense	1,000	
Selling expense	30,000	
Interest expense	1,000	116,000
Net income		$ 4,000

Required:
1. Open the following T-accounts in the general ledger: cash, accounts receivable, automobile inventory, accounts payable, notes payable, Perez, owner's equity, sales, cost of goods sold, rent expense, utilities expense, selling expense, and interest expense. Enter the March 31 balances in the appropriate accounts.
2. Journalize transactions *a–j* and post the entries to the ledger. Key entries by transaction letter.
3. Prepare the trial balance at April 30, 19X1.
4. Prepare an income statement for April. Ignore income taxes.

☐ Solution to Problem Two

The solutions to requirements 1 through 4 are in Exhibits 3–7 through 3–10. The opening balances are placed in the appropriate accounts in Exhibit 3–8; the journal entries are prepared in Exhibit 3–7 and posted to the ledger in Exhibit 3–8; a trial balance is prepared in Exhibit 3–9; and the income statement is shown in Exhibit 3–10.

☐ Problem Three

A recent annual report of Scott Paper Company showed (in millions):

Plant assets, at cost	$4,689.3	
Accumulated depreciation	1,933.7	$2,755.6

Required:
1. Open T-accounts for (a) Plant Assets; (b) Accumulated Depreciation, Plant Assets; and (c) Depreciation Expense. Enter the above amounts therein.
2. Assume that a month ensues. No additional plant assets were acquired, but depreciation expense of $100 million was incurred. Prepare the journal entry and post to the T-accounts.
3. Show how Scott Paper would present its plant assets accounts in its balance sheet after the journal entry in requirement 2.

Solution to Problem Three

1.

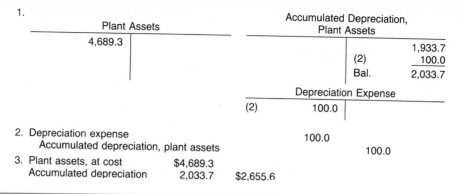

Plant Assets	
4,689.3	

Accumulated Depreciation, Plant Assets	
	1,933.7
	(2) 100.0
	Bal. 2,033.7

Depreciation Expense	
(2) 100.0	

2. Depreciation expense 100.0
      Accumulated depreciation, plant assets 100.0

3. Plant assets, at cost $4,689.3
      Accumulated depreciation 2,033.7 $2,655.6

HIGHLIGHTS TO REMEMBER

1. Concentrate on relating journals and ledgers to changes in the balance sheet equation.

2. Students tend to be puzzled by the fact that both assets and expenses normally have debit balances. Expenses have debit balances because they are reductions in stockholders' equity. In other words, expenses are a negative component of stockholders' equity.

3. There is no shortcut to learning debits and credits. Learning occurs by solving homework problems. Whether such homework is satisfying depends largely on your approach. Before you prepare journal entries, think hard about the relationships between the accounts. The mechanics of the journal and the ledger then become much easier to understand.

4. All accountants, including your authors, will testify that fewer aspects of accounting are more maddening than trial balances that fail to balance. Such failures are inevitably the result of some careless or rushed journalizing or posting. Use deliberate care. Avoid shortcuts. Much more time is invested in trying to find an error after it has been made than is invested in exercising care in the first place. Moreover, trying to find one's error is seldom fun.

ACCOUNTING VOCABULARY

Accumulated Depreciation, p. 96
Allowance for Depreciation, p. 96
Balance, p. 84
Book of Original Entry, p. 85
Book Value, p. 96
Carrying Amount, p. 96
Carrying Value, p. 96
Charge, p. 84
Chart of Accounts, p. 88
Compound Entry, p. 90
Continuity Convention, p. 102
Contra Account, p. 96
Contra Asset, p. 96
Cost-Benefit Criterion, p. 103
Credit, p. 84
Data Processing, p. 101

Debit, p. 84
Double-Entry System, p. 83
General Journal, p. 85
General Ledger, p. 97
Going Concern Convention, p. 102
Journal Entry, p. 87
Keying of Entries, p. 88
Ledger, p. 82
Materiality Convention, p. 103
Net Book Value, p. 96
Posting, p. 87
Simple Entry, p. 90
Source Document, p. 88
Subsidiary Ledger, p. 101
T-account, p. 82
Trial Balance, p. 100

FUNDAMENTAL ASSIGNMENT MATERIAL

General Coverage

3–1. JOURNAL, LEDGER, TRIAL BALANCE.   (Alternates are 3–2, 3–3, and 3–29 through 3–34.) The trial balance of O'Leary and Goldstein's Appliance Co. on December 31, 19X1, follows:

ACCOUNT TITLE	BALANCE Debit	BALANCE Credit
Cash	$ 20,000	
Accounts receivable	30,000	
Merchandise inventory	120,000	
Accounts payable		$ 35,000
Notes payable		80,000
Paid-in capital		29,000
Retained income		26,000
Total	$170,000	$170,000

Operating space and equipment are rented on a month-to-month basis. A summary of January transactions follows:

a. Paid $18,000 on accounts payable.
b. Collected $23,000 on accounts receivable.
c. Sold appliances for $70,000 cash and $40,000 on open account.
d. Cost of appliances sold was $60,000.
e. Replenished inventory for $63,000 on open account.
f. Paid selling expense in cash, $30,000.
g. Paid rent expense in cash, $5,000.
h. Paid interest expense in cash, $1,000.

Required:
1. Open the appropriate T-accounts in the general ledger. In addition to the seven accounts listed in the trial balance of December 31, open accounts for Sales, Cost of Goods Sold, Selling Expense, Rent Expense, and Interest Expense. Enter the December 31 balances in the accounts.
2. Journalize transactions a–h. Post the entries to the ledger, keying by transaction letter.
3. Prepare a trial balance, January 31, 19X2.

☐ **Understanding Published Financial Reports**

3–2. **TRANSACTION ANALYSIS, TRIAL BALANCE.** (Alternates are 3–1, 3–3, and 3–29 through 3–34.) McDonald's Corporation is a well-known fast-foods restaurant company. Examine the accompanying condensed trial balance, which is based on McDonald's annual report and actual terminology.

McDONALD'S CORPORATION
Trial Balance
December 31, 19X8
(in millions)

Cash	$ 40	
Accounts and notes receivable	76	
Inventories	23	
Prepaid expenses	37	
Property and equipment, net	3,490	
Other assets	226	
Accumulated depreciation		$ 993
Notes and accounts payable		141
Other liabilities		1,388
Paid-in capital		81
Retained earnings		1,289
Total	$3,892	$3,892

Consider the following assumed partial summary of transactions for 19X9 (in millions):

a. Revenues in cash, company-owned restaurants, $2,000.
b. Revenues, on open account from franchised restaurants, $600. Set up a separate revenue account for these sales.
c. Inventories acquired on open account, $727.
d. Cost of the inventories sold, $720.
e. Depreciation, $226. (Debit Depreciation Expense.)
f. Paid rents and insurance premiums in cash in advance, $42. (Debit Prepaid Expenses.)
g. Prepaid expenses expired, $37. (Debit Operating Expenses.)
h. Paid other liabilities, $148.
i. Cash collections on receivables, $590.
j. Cash disbursements on notes and accounts payable, $747.
k. Interest expense in cash, $100.
l. Other expenses in cash, mostly payroll and advertising, $1,510. (Debit Operating Expenses.)

Required:

1. Record the transactions in the journal.
2. Enter beginning balances in T-accounts. Post the journal entries to the T-accounts. Key your entries with the transaction letters used here.
3. Prepare a trial balance, December 31, 19X9

3-3. **TRANSACTION ANALYSIS, TRIAL BALANCE.** (Alternates are 3–1, 3–2, and 3–29 through 3–34.) Kellogg Company's major product line is ready-to-eat breakfast cereals. Examine the accompanying condensed trial balance, which is based on Kellogg's annual report and actual terminology.

KELLOGG COMPANY
Trial Balance
December 31, 19X8
(in millions)

Cash	$ 163.7	
Accounts receivable	158.9	
Inventories	231.2	
Prepaid expenses	28.4	
Property and equipment	958.4	
Other assets	38.5	
Accumulated depreciation		$ 300.0
Accounts payable		104.5
Other liabilities		364.3
Paid-in capital		48.7
Retained earnings		761.6
Total	$1,579.1	$1,579.1

Consider the following assumed partial summary of transactions for 19X9 (in millions):

a. Acquired inventories for $1,600 on open account.
b. Sold inventories that cost $1,500 for $2,400 on open account.
c. Collected $2,300 on open account.
d. Disbursed $1,550 on open accounts payable.
e. Paid cash of $300 for advertising expenses. (Debit Operating Expenses.)
f. Paid rents and insurance premiums in cash in advance, $20. (Debit Prepaid Expenses.)
g. Prepaid expenses expired, $18. (Debit Operating Expenses.)
h. Other liabilities paid in cash, $110.
i. Interest expense of $13 was paid in cash. (Debit Interest Expense.)
j. Depreciation of $50 was recognized. (Debit Operating Expenses.)

Required:
1. Record the transactions in the journal.
2. Enter beginning balances in T-accounts. Post the journal entries to the T-accounts. Key your entries with the transaction letters used here.
3. Prepare a trial balance, December 31, 19X9.

ADDITIONAL ASSIGNMENT MATERIAL

☐ **General Coverage**

3–4. "Double entry means that amounts are shown in the journal and the ledger." Do you agree? Explain.

3–5. "Increases in cash and stockholders' equity are shown on the right side of their respective accounts." Do you agree? Explain.

3–6. "Revenue and expense accounts are really little stockholders' equity accounts." Explain.

3–7. "Accumulated depreciation is the total depreciation expense for the year." Do you agree? Explain.

3–8. "*Debit* and *credit* are used as verbs, adjectives, or nouns." Give examples of how *debit* may be used in these three meanings.

3–9. "A trial balance assumes that the amounts in the financial statements are correct." Do you agree? Explain.

3–10. Give two examples of subsidiary ledgers.

3–11. "There can be no more than two subsidiary ledgers. Otherwise the double-entry system cannot be maintained." Do you agree? Explain.

3–12. Name three source documents for transactions.

3–13. "The ledger is the major book of original entry because it is more essential than the journal." Do you agree? Explain.

3–14. "This idea implies that existing equipment will be *used* rather than *sold* in tomorrow's equipment markets." What is the name of this idea?

3–15. Give two synonyms for *book value*.

3–16. "What is trivial to General Motors may be significant to Joe's Tavern." What idea is being described?

3–17. DEBITS AND CREDITS. For each of the following accounts, indicate whether it normally possesses a debit or a credit balance. Use *DR* or *CR*:

1. Accounts receivable
2. Supplies expense
3. Supplies inventory
4. Retained income
5. Depreciation expense
6. Dividends payable
7. Paid-in capital
8. Subscription revenue
9. Sales
10. Accounts payable

3–18. DEBITS AND CREDITS. Determine for the following transactions whether the account *named in parentheses* is to be debited or credited.

1. Paid Johnson Associates $3,000 owed them (Accounts Payable).
2. Bought merchandise on account (Merchandise Inventory), $2,000.
3. Received cash from customers on accounts due (Accounts Receivable), $1,000.
4. Bought merchandise on open account (Accounts Payable), $5,000.
5. Borrowed money from a bank (Notes Payable), $10,000.
6. Sold merchandise (Merchandise Inventory), $1,000.

3–19. DEBITS AND CREDITS. For the following transactions, indicate whether the accounts in *parentheses* are to be debited or credited. Use *DR* or *CR*:

1. A three-year fire insurance policy was acquired (Prepaid Expenses).
2. Wages were paid to employees (Wages Expense).
3. A newsstand sold magazines (Sales Revenue).

4. Merchandise was sold on credit (Accounts Receivable).
5. Dividends were declared and paid in cash (Retained Income).
6. A county government received property taxes (Tax Revenue).

3–20. **TRUE OR FALSE.** Use T or F to indicate whether each of the following statements is true or false:

1. Cash collections of accounts receivable should be recorded as debits to Cash and credits to Accounts Receivable. *T*
2. Credit purchases of equipment should be debited to Equipment and charged to Accounts Payable. *T*
3. Repayments of bank loans should be charged to Notes Payable and credited to Cash. *T*
4. Asset debits should be on the left and liability debits should be on the right. *F*
5. Inventory purchases on account should be credited to Accounts Payable and debited to an expense account. *F*
6. In general, entries on the right side of asset accounts represent decreases in the account balances. *T*
7. Increases in liability and revenue accounts should be recorded on the left side of the accounts. *F*
8. Decreases in retained income are recorded as debits. *T*
9. In general, all credit entries are recorded on the right side of accounts and represent decreases in the account balances. *F*
10. Both increases in assets and decreases in liabilities are recorded on the debit sides of accounts. *T*
11. In some cases, increases in account balances are recorded on the right sides of accounts. *T*

3–21. **MATCHING TRANSACTIONS OF ACCOUNTS.** Listed here are a series of accounts that are numbered for identification. Accompanying this problem are columns in which you are to write the identification numbers of the accounts affected by the transactions described. The same account may be used in several answers. Answer all; omit none.

1. Cash
2. Accounts receivable
3. Inventory
4. Equipment
5. Accumulated depreciation, equipment
6. Prepaid insurance
7. Accounts payable
8. Notes payable
9. Paid-in capital
10. Retained earnings
11. Sales
12. Cost of goods sold
13. Operating expenses

	DEBIT	CREDIT
(a) Purchased new equipment for cash plus a short-term note.	4	1,8
(b) Paid cash for salaries and wages for work done during the current fiscal period.	_____	_____
(c) Made sales on credit. Inventory is accounted for as each sale is made.	_____	_____
(d) Collected cash from customers on account.	_____	_____
(e) Paid some old trade bills with cash.	_____	_____
(f) Purchased three-year insurance policy on credit.	_____	_____
(g) Sold for cash some old equipment at cost.	_____	_____
(h) Paid off note owed to bank.	_____	_____
(i) Paid cash for inventory that arrived today.	_____	_____
(j) Bought regular merchandise on credit.	_____	_____
(k) In order to secure additonal funds, 400 new shares of common stock were sold for cash.	_____	_____
(l) Some insurance premiums have expired.	_____	_____
(m) Paid cash for ad in today's *Chicago Tribune*.	_____	_____
(n) Recorded the entry for depreciation on equipment for the current fiscal period.	_____	_____

3–22. **JOURNALIZING AND POSTING.** (Alternate is 3–23.) Prepare journal entries and post to T-accounts for the following transactions of Maria Delgado's Gourmet Foods Company:

a. Collections on accounts, $6,000.
b. Cash sales, $12,000.
c. Paid cash for wages, $3,000.
d. Acquired inventory on open account, $5,000.
e. Paid cash for janitorial services, $400.

3–23. **JOURNALIZING AND POSTING.** (Alternate is 3–22) Prepare journal entries and post to T-accounts for the following transactions of Chris Olsen, Realtor:

a. Acquired office supplies of $1,000 on open account. Use a Supplies Inventory account.
b. Sold a house and collected a $10,000 commission on the sale. Use a Commissions Revenue account.
c. Paid cash of $700 to a local newspaper for current advertisements.
d. Paid $800 for a previous credit purchase of a desk.
e. Recorded office supplies used of $200.

3–24. **RECONSTRUCT JOURNAL ENTRIES.** (Alternate is 3–25.) Reconstruct the journal entries (omit explanations) that resulted in the postings to the following T-accounts of a consulting firm:

Cash				Equipment				Revenue from Fees		
(a)	60,000	(b)	1,000	(c)	15,000				(d)	80,000
		(c)	5,000							

Accounts Receivable			Note Payable			
(d)	80,000				(c)	10,000

Supplies Inventory				Paid-in Capital			Supplies Used		
(b)	1,000	(e)	300			(a)	60,000	(e)	300

3–25. **RECONSTRUCT JOURNAL ENTRIES.** (Alternate is 3–24.) Reconstruct the journal entries (omit explanations) that resulted in the postings to the following T-accounts:

Cash				Accounts Payable				Paid-in Capital		
(a)	50,000	(e)	30,000	(e)	30,000	(b)	90,000		(a)	50,000

Accounts Receivable		
(c)	100,000	

Inventory				Cost of Goods Sold			Sales		
(b)	90,000	(d)	55,000	(d)	55,000			(c)	100,000

3–26. **ACCOUNT NUMBERS, JOURNAL, LEDGER, TRIAL BALANCE.** Journalize and post the entries required by the following transactions. Prepare a trial balance, January 31, 19X3. Ignore interest. Use dates, posting references, and the following account numbers:

Cash	100	Note payable	130
Accounts receivable	101	Paid-in capital	140
Equipment	111	Retained income	150
Accumulated depreciation,		Revenues	200
equipment	111A	Expenses	300–301, etc.
Accounts payable	120		

January 1, 19X3. The Dryden Laundry and Cleaning Company was formed with $100,000 cash upon the issuance of common stock.

January 2. Equipment was acquired for $75,000. A cash down payment of $25,000 was made. In addition, a note for $50,000 was signed.

January 3. Sales on credit to a local hotel, $1,200.

January 3. Supplies acquired (and used) on open account, $200.

January 3. Wages paid in cash, $600.

January 31. Depreciation expense for January, $1,000.

3–27. ACCOUNT NUMBERS, T-ACCOUNTS, AND TRANSACTION ANALYSIS. Consider the following (in thousands):

ASTORIA STATIONERY SUPPLIERS
Trial Balance
December 31, 19X5

ACCOUNT NUMBER	ACCOUNT TITLES	BALANCE Debit	BALANCE Credit
10	Cash	$ 50	
20	Accounts receivable	110	
21	Note receivable	100	
30	Inventory	120	
40	Prepaid insurance	12	
70	Equipment	120	
70A	Accumulated depreciation, equipment		$ 30
80	Accounts payable		130
100	Paid-in capital		60
110	Retained income		172
130	Sales		900
150	Cost of goods sold	500	
160	Wages expense	200	
170	Miscellaneous expense	80	
		$1,292	$1,292

The following information had not been considered before preparing the trial balance:

1. The note receivable is a 12% note signed by a major customer. It is a three-month note dated November 1, 19X5. Interest earned during November and December was collected at 4 P.M. on December 31. The interest rate is 12% per year.
2. The Prepaid Insurance account reflects a one-year fire insurance policy acquired for cash on August 1, 19X5.
3. Depreciation for 19X5 was $15,000.
4. Wages of $11,000 were paid in cash at 5 P.M. on December 31.

Required:

1. Enter the December 31 balances in a general ledger. Number the accounts. Allow room for additional T-accounts.
2. Prepare the journal entries prompted by the additional information. Show amounts in thousands.
3. Post the journal entries to the ledger. Key your postings. Create logical new account numbers as necessary.
4. Prepare a new trial balance, December 31, 19X5.

3–28. **TRIAL BALANCE ERRORS.** Consider the accompanying Angelio trial balance (in thousands of dollars):

ANGELIO AUTO PARTS STORE
Trial Balance
For the Year Ended December 31, 19X7

Cash	$ 10	
Equipment	28	
Accumulated depreciation, equipment	10	
Accounts payable	42	
Accounts receivable	15	
Prepaid insurance	1	
Prepaid rent		$ 4
Inventory	129	
Paid-in capital		12
Retained income		5
Cost of goods sold	600	
Wages expense	100	
Miscellaneous expenses	80	
Advertising expense		30
Sales		888
Note payable	40	
	$1,055	$939

Required: | List and describe all the errors in the above trial balance. Be specific. Based on the available data, prepare a corrected trial balance.

3–29. **JOURNAL, LEDGER, AND TRIAL BALANCE.** (Alternates are 3–1, 3–2, 3–3, and 3–30 through 3–34.) Shoeware Unlimited is a retailer. The entity's balance sheet had the following balances on March 31, 19X1:

Cash	$ 42,000	
Accounts receivable	90,000	
Inventory	10,000	
Prepaid rent	2,000	
Accounts payable		$ 25,000
Paid-in capital		100,000
Retained income		19,000
	$144,000	$144,000

Following is a summary of the transactions that occurred during April:

   a. Collections of accounts receivable, $88,000.
   b. Payments of accounts payable, $24,000.
   c. Acquisitions of inventory on open account, $80,000.
   d. Merchandise carried in inventory at a cost of $70,000 was sold on open account for $86,000.
   e. Recognition of rent expense for April, $1,000.
   f. Wages paid in cash for April, $8,000.
   g. Cash dividends declared and disbursed to stockholders on April 29, $18,000.

Required: | **1.** Prepare journal entries (in thousands of dollars).
2. Enter beginning balances in T-accounts. Post the journal entries to T-accounts. Use the transaction letters to key your postings.
3. Prepare a trial balance, April 30, 19X1.

3–30. FINANCIAL STATEMENTS. (Alternates are 3–1, 3–2, 3–3, 3–29, and 3–31 through 3–34.) Refer to the preceding problem. Prepare a balance sheet as of April 30, 19X1, and an income statement for the month of April. Prepare a statement of retained income. Prepare the income statement first.

3–31. JOURNAL, LEDGER, TRIAL BALANCE. (Alternates are 3–1, 3–2, 3–3, 3–29, 3–30, 3–32, 3–33, and 3–34.) Joan Jensen owned and managed a corporation that operated as a retail gift store. The accompanying trial balance existed on March 1, 19X2, the beginning of a fiscal year.

JENSEN GIFT STORE
Trial Balance
March 1, 19X2

Cash	$ 2,300	
Accounts receivable	25,000	
Merchandise inventory	78,000	
Prepaid rent	4,000	
Store Equipment	20,000	
Accumulated depreciation,		
store equipment		$ 5,000
Accounts payable		45,000
Paid-in capital		30,000
Retained income		49,300
	$129,300	$129,300

Summarized transactions for March were:

1. Acquisitions of merchandise inventory on account, $49,000.
2. Sales for cash, $39,300.
3. Payments to creditors, $34,000.
4. Sales on account, $38,000.
5. Advertising in newspapers, paid in cash, $3,000.
6. Cost of goods sold, $40,000.
7. Collections on account, $29,000.
8. Miscellaneous expenses paid in cash, $8,000.
9. Wages paid in cash, $9,000.
10. Entry for rent expense (Rent was paid quarterly in advance, $6,000 per quarter. Payments were due on February, 1, May 1, August 1, and November 1.)
11. Depreciation of store equipment, $250.

Required:
1. Enter the March 1 balances in a general ledger.
2. Prepare journal entries for each transaction.
3. Post the journal entries to the ledger. Key your postings.
4. Prepare a trial balance, March 31, 19X2.

3–32. JOURNAL, LEDGER, TRIAL BALANCE. (Alternates 3–1, 3–2, 3–3, 3–29, 3–30, 3–31, 3–33, and 3–34.) Three women who had been college classmates have decided to pool a variety of work experiences by opening a women's clothing store. The business has been incorporated as Sartorial Choice, Inc. The following transactions occurred during April:

1. On April 1, 19X1, each woman invested $11,000 in cash in exchange for 1,000 shares of stock each.
2. The corporation quickly acquired $50,000 in inventory, half of which had to be paid for in cash. The other half was acquired on open accounts that were payable after thirty days.
3. A store was rented for $500 monthly. A lease was signed for one year on April 1. The first two months' rent were paid in advance. Other payments were to be made on the second of each month. An entry was also made for April rent expense. Make two entries, 3a and 3b.
4. Advertising during April was purchased on open account for $3,000 from a newspaper owned

by one of the stockholders. Additional advertising services of $6,000 were acquired for cash. Make two entries, 4a and 4b.

5. Sales were $65,000. The average markup above the cost of the merchandise was two-thirds of cost (not two-thirds of sales revenue). Eighty percent of the sales were on open account. make two entries, 5a and 5b.

6. Wages and salaries incurred in April and paid in cash amounted to $11,000.

7. Miscellaneous services paid for in cash were $1,410.

8. On April 1, fixtures and equipment were purchased for $6,000 with a down payment of $1,000 plus a $5,000 note payable in one year.

9. See transaction 8 and pay interest of $40 on April 30.

10. See transaction 8 and make the April 30 entry for depreciation expense of $100.

Required:

1. Journalize all transactions for April.
2. Post the entries to the ledger, keying your postings by transaction number.
3. Prepare a trial balance, April 30, 19X1.

3–33. **JOURNALIZING, POSTING, TRIAL BALANCE.** (Alternates are 3–1, 3–2, 3–3, 3–29 through 3–32, and 3–34.) Reynolds Nursery Company, a retailer of garden supplies and equipment, had the accompanying balance sheet accounts, December 31, 19X3:

ASSETS			LIABILITIES AND STOCKHOLDERS' EQUITY	
Cash		$ 20,000	Accounts payable*	$110,000
Accounts receivable		40,000	Paid-in capital	50,000
Inventory		150,000	Retained income	90,000
Prepaid rent		4,000		
Store equipment	$ 48,000			
Less: Accumulated				
depreciation	12,000	36,000		
Total		$250,000	Total	$250,000

* For merchandise only.

Following is a summary of transactions that occurred during 19X4:

a. Purchases of merchandise inventory on open account, $500,000.

b. Sales, all on credit, $800,000.

c. Cost of merchandise sold to customers, $440,000.

d. On June 1, 19X4, borrowed $80,000 from a supplier. The note is payable at the end of 19X8. Interest is payable yearly on December 31 at a rate of 15% per annum.

e. Disbursed $23,000 for the rent of the store. Add to Prepaid Rent.

f. Disbursed $165,000 for wages through November.

g. Disbursed $76,000 for miscellaneous expenses such as utilities, advertising, and legal help. (Combined here to save space. Debit Miscellaneous expenses.)

h. On July 1, 19X4, lent $20,000 to the office manager. He signed a note that will mature on July 1, 19X5, together with interest at 10% per annum. Interest for 19X4 is due on December 31, 19X4.

i. Collections on accounts receivable, $690,000.

j. Payments on accounts payable, $480,000.
The following entries were made at December 31, 19X4:

k. Previous rent payments applicable to 19X5 amounted to $3,000.

l. Depreciation for 19X4 was $6,000.

m. Wages earned by employees during December were paid on December 31, $5,000.

n. Interest on the loan from the supplier was disbursed.

o. Interest on the loan made to the office manager was received.

Required:

1. Prepare journal entries in thousands of dollars.
2. Post the entries to the ledger, keying your postings by transaction letter.
3. Prepare a trial balance, December 31, 19X4.

3–34. **TRANSACTION ANALYSIS, TRIAL BALANCE.** (Alternates are 3–1, 3–2, 3–3, and 3–29 through 3–33.) Television Repair Service, Incorporated, had the accompanying trial balance on January 1, 19X2.

TELEVISION REPAIR SERVICE, INC.
Trial Balance
January 1, 19X2

Cash	$ 4,000	
Accounts receivable	5,000	
Parts inventory	2,000	
Prepaid rent	2,000	
Trucks	25,000	
Equipment	8,000	
Accumulated depreciation, trucks		$10,000
Accumulated depreciation, equipment		5,000
Accounts payable		1,800
Paid-in capital		17,000
Retained income		12,200
Total	$46,000	$46,000

During January, the following summarized transactions occurred:

Jan. 2 Collected accounts receivable, $3,000.
   3 Rendered services to customers for cash, $2,200 ($700 collected for parts, $1,500 for labor). Use two accounts, Parts Revenue and Labor Revenue.
   3 Cost of parts used for services rendered, $300.
   7 Paid legal expenses, $400 cash.
   9 Acquired parts on open account, $900.
  11 Paid cash for wages, $1,100.
  13 Paid cash for truck repairs, $500.
  15 Paid cash for utilities, $300.
  19 Billed hotel for services, $4,000 ($1,200 for parts and $2,800 for labor).
  19 Cost of parts used for services rendered, $500.
  24 Paid cash for wages, $1,300.
  27 Paid cash on accounts payable, $1,400.
  31 Rent expense for January, $1,000 (credit Prepaid Rent).
  31 Depreciation for January: trucks, $600; equipment, $200.
  31 Paid cash to local gas station for gasoline for trucks for January, $300.
  31 Paid cash for wages, $900.

Required:
1. Enter the January 1 balances in T-accounts. Leave room for additional accounts.
2. Record the transactions in the journal.
3. Post the journal entries to the T-accounts. Key your entries by date. (Note how keying by date is not as precise as by transaction number or letter. Why? Because there is usually more than one transaction on any given date.)
4. Prepare a trial balance, January 31, 19X2.

☐ **Understanding Published Financial Reports**

3–35. **RECONSTRUCTING JOURNAL ENTRIES, POSTING.** H. J. Heinz Company has many food products, including catsup. Ore-Ida, Star-Kist, and Weight Watchers brands. The Heinz annual report at the end of this 1989 fiscal year included the following balance sheet items (in thousands):

Cash	$ 47,894
Receivables	491,903
Prepaid expenses	122,511
Land	42,198
Accounts payable	397,075

Consider the following assumed transactions that occurred immediately subsequent to the balance sheet date. Dollars are in thousands:

a. Collections from customers	$110,000
b. Purchase of land for cash	2,000
c. Purchase of insurance policies on account	1,200
d. Disbursements to trade creditors	95,000

Required:
1. Enter the five account balances in T-accounts.
2. Journalize each transaction.
3. Post the journal entries to T-accounts. Key each posting by transaction letter.

3–36. **RECONSTRUCTING JOURNAL ENTRIES, POSTING.** (Alternate is 3–37.) Procter & Gamble has many popular products, including Tide, Crest, and Jif. A partial income statement from its annual report for the 1990 fiscal year showed the following actual numbers, nomenclature, and format (in millions):

Income:	
Net sales	$19,336
Interest and other income	155
	19,491
Costs and expenses:	
Cost of products sold	11,880
Marketing, administrative, and other expenses	5,660
Interest expense	321
	17,861
Earnings before income taxes	$ 1,630

Required:
1. Prepare five summary journal entries for the given data. Omit explanations. For simplicity, assume that all transactions (except for cost of products sold) were for cash.
2. Post to a ledger for all affected accounts. Key your postings by transaction letter.
3. The company uses *income* as a heading for the first part of its income statement. Suggest a more descriptive term. Why is it more descriptive?

3–37. **RECONSTRUCTING JOURNAL ENTRIES, POSTING.** (Alternate is 3–36.) General Mills, Inc., has many popular products, including Cheerios and Wheaties. A partial income statement from its annual report for the 1990 fiscal year showed the following actual numbers, nomenclature, and format (in millions):

Sales		$5,179
Cost and expenses:		
Cost of sales, exclusive of items below	$2,848	
Selling, general and administrative expenses	1,711	
Depreciation expenses	140	
Interest expense	38	
Total costs and expenses		4,737
Earnings before income taxes		$ 442

Required: 1. Prepare five summary journal entries for the given data. Omit explanations. For simplicity, assume that all transactions (except for cost of sales) were for cash.
2. Post to a ledger for all affected accounts. Key your postings by transaction letter.

3–38. **HOUSE OF FABRICS ANNUAL REPORT.** This problem helps to develop skill in recording transactions by using an actual company's account titles. Refer to the financial statements of House of Fabrics (pp. 752–759). Note the following items from the income statement for the 1989 fiscal year (in millions):

Sales		$338
Cost of sales	$154	
Store and operating expenses	133	
Warehouse and administrative expenses	29	
Interest expense	3	319
Income before income taxes		$ 19

Required: 1. Prepare five summary journal entries for the given data. Use the House of Fabrics account titles. Omit explanations. For simplicity, assume that all transactions (except for cost of sales) were for cash.
2. Post to a ledger for all affected accounts. Key your postings by transaction letter.

CHAPTER 4

Accounting Adjustments and Financial Statement Preparation

After studying this chapter, you should be able to

1. Make adjustments for the expiration of unexpired costs, the realization (earning) of unearned revenues, the accrual of unrecorded expenses, and the accrual of unrecorded revenues

2. Prepare an elementary classified balance sheet and explain the major relationships therein

3. Show the major differences between single-step and multiple-step income statements

4. Distinguish between common terms used to describe items in the income statement

This chapter covers three major topics: (1) accounting adjustments, (2) classified balance sheets, and (3) various formats of the income statement.

ADJUSTMENTS TO THE ACCOUNTS

The preceding chapter demonstrated the various steps in recording:

These steps have a final aim: financial statements prepared on the accrual basis of accounting.

Focus on the trial-balance step. This chapter underscores the necessity of having a complete, accurate trial balance before the financial statements are prepared. Therefore the final steps are divided further as follows:

The arguments on behalf of the accrual basis instead of the cash basis of accounting are in Chapter 2 (p. 50). In short, the accrual basis provides more precise measures of economic performance (income statement) and financial position (balance sheet). To obtain satisfactory precision, the accountant uses **adjustments** at the end of each reporting period. *Adjustments* (also called **adjusting entries,** *adjusting the books*, and *adjusting the accounts*) can be defined as the key final process (before the computation of ending account balances) of assigning the financial effects of transactions to the appropriate time periods. Thus adjustments are made at periodic intervals, that is, when the financial statements are about to be prepared.

Earlier a *transaction* was defined as any event that both affects the financial position of an entity and can be reliably recorded in money terms. Note that this definition is *not* confined to market transactions, which are actual exchanges of goods and services between the entity and another party. For instance, the losses of assets from fire or theft are also transactions even though no market exchange occurs.

Adjustments are a special category of transactions. The principal adjustments can be classified into four types:

I. Expiration of unexpired costs
II. Realization (earning) of unearned revenues
III. Accrual of unrecorded expenses
IV. Accrual of unrecorded revenues

As we will see, all of these adjustments have an important common characteristic. They record implicit transactions, in contrast to explicit transactions. **Explicit transactions** are events such as cash receipts and disbursements, credit purchases, and credit sales that trigger nearly all day-to-day routine entries. Entries for such transactions are supported by explicit evidence, usually in the form of miscellaneous source documents (for example, sales slips, purchase invoices, employee payroll checks).

On the other hand, **implicit transactions** are events (like the passage of time) that are temporarily ignored in day-to-day recording procedures and are recognized via end-of-period adjustments. For example, adjustments for depreciation expense and expiration of prepaid rent are prepared from special schedules or memorandums.

Adjustments provide a more complete and accurate measure of efforts, accomplishments, and financial position. They are an essential part of accrual accounting because they improve the matching of revenues and expenses. In contrast, a strictly defined cash basis of accounting uses no adjustments.

I. EXPIRATION OF UNEXPIRED COSTS

Assets frequently expire because of the passage of time. This type of adjustment was illustrated in the preceding chapter by the recognition of monthly depreciation expense and rent expense. Because we have already described this important adjustment, we will not dwell on it here. Other examples of adjusting for asset expirations include the write-offs to expense of such assets as Office Supplies Inventory, Advertising Supplies Inventory, and Prepaid Fire Insurance.

II. REALIZATION (EARNING) OF UNEARNED REVENUES

Sometimes it is easier to see how accountants analyze transactions by visualizing the financial positions of both parties to a contract. Recall the Biwheels' January advance payment of $6,000 for three months' rent. Compare the financial impact on Biwheels Company with the impact on the owner of the property, who received the rental payment:

	OWNER OF PROPERTY (LANDLORD, LESSOR)				BIWHEELS COMPANY (TENANT, LESSEE)		
	A	= L +		SE	A	= L +	SE
		Unearned Rent		Rent		Prepaid	Rent
	Cash	Revenue		Revenue	Cash	Rent	Expense
(a) Explicit transaction (advance payment of three months' rent)	+6,000 =	+6,000			−6,000	+6,000 =	
(b) January adjustment (for one month's rent)	=	−2,000		+2,000		−2,000 =	−2,000
(c) February adjustment (for one month's rent)	=	−2,000		+2,000		−2,000 =	−2,000
(d) March adjustment (for one month's rent)	=	−2,000		+2,000		−2,000 =	−2,000

The adjusting journal entries for (a) and (b) follow:

OWNER (LANDLORD)			TENANT (BIWHEELS CO.)		
(a) Cash	6,000		Prepaid rent	6,000	
Unearned rent revenue		6,000	Cash		6,000
(b) Unearned rent revenue	2,000		Rent expense	2,000	
Rent revenue		2,000	Prepaid rent		2,000

Entries for (c) and (d) would be the same as for (b).

You are already familiar with the Biwheels analysis. The $2,000 monthly entries for Biwheels are examples of the first type of adjustments, the expiration of unexpired costs.

Study the transactions from the viewpoint of the owner of the rental property. Transaction *a* recognizes **unearned revenue,** which is revenue received or recorded before it is earned. Unearned revenue is also called **deferred revenue** or **deferred credit,** which is a *liability* because the lessor is obligated to deliver the rental services (or to refund the money if the services are not delivered). Sometimes this account is called Rent Collected in Advance, but it is an unearned revenue type of liability account no matter what its label. That is, it is revenue collected in advance that has not been earned as yet.

Adjustments I and II (p. 124) are really mirror images of each other. If one party to a contract has a prepaid expense, the other has an unearned revenue. A similar analysis could be conducted for, say, a three-year fire insurance policy or a three-year magazine subscription. The buyer recognizes a prepaid expense (asset) and uses adjustments to spread the initial cost to expense over the useful life of the services. In turn, the seller, such as a magazine publisher, must initially recognize its liability, Unearned Subscription Revenue. For example, the publisher of *Time* magazine showed a balance of over $250 million as of December 31, 1989, calling it Unearned Portion of Paid Subscriptions. The unearned revenue is then systematically recognized as *earned* revenue when magazines are delivered throughout the life of the subscription. The following diagrams show that explicit cash transactions in such situations are initially recognized as balance sheet items and are later transformed into income statement items via periodic adjustments:

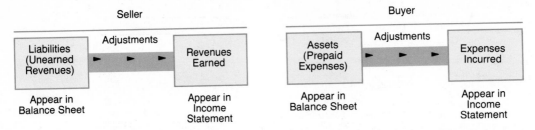

Other examples of unearned revenues are advances from customers who have paid for goods or services to be delivered at a future date. For instance, airlines often require advance payments for special-fare tickets. Northwest Airlines showed a recent balance of $263 million in an account labeled Air Traffic Liability, which is an unearned revenue account.

Unearned revenue is sometimes called **unearned income** or **deferred income,** but revenue is a more accurate description than income because the latter is, strictly speaking, a difference or "what's left over" after deducting appropriate expenses from revenue. When unearned revenue becomes earned, the expenses matched with the revenue are also recognized. Income is only the amount by which the earned revenue exceeds the related cost of goods or services delivered to customers.

III. ACCRUAL OF UNRECORDED EXPENSES

Accrue means the accumulation of a receivable or payable during a given period even though no explicit transaction occurs. Examples of accruals are the wages of employees for partial payroll periods and the interest on borrowed money before the interest payment date. The receivables or payables grow as the clock ticks or as some services are continuously acquired and used, so they are said to accrue (accumulate).

It is awkward and unnecessary to make hourly, daily, or even weekly formal recordings in the account for many accruals. Consequently, adjustments are made to bring each expense (and corresponding liability) account up to date just before the formal financial statements are prepared.

☐ **Accounting for Payment of Wages**

Consider wages. Most companies pay their employees at predetermined times. Here is a sample calendar for January:

Suppose Biwheels pays its employees each Friday for services rendered during that week. For example, wages paid on January 26 would be compensation for the week ended January 26. The cumulative total wages paid on the Fridays during January were $20,000, or $5,000 per five-day workweek, or $1,000 per day. Although day-to-day and week-to-week procedures may differ from entity to entity, a popular way to account for wages expense is the shortcut procedure described in Chapter 2 for goods and services that are routinely consumed in the period of their purchase:

	ASSETS (A)	=	LIABILITIES (L)	+	STOCKHOLDERS' EQUITY (SE)
	Cash				Wages Expense
(a) Routine entries for explicit transactions	−20,000	=			−20,000

Accounting for Accrual of Wages

In addition to the $20,000 already paid, Biwheels owes $3,000 for employee services rendered during the last three days of January. The employees will not be paid for these services until Friday, February 2. No matter how simple or complex a set of accounting procedures may be in a particular entity, periodic adjustments ensure that the financial statements adhere to accrual accounting. The tabulation below repeats entry a for convenience and then adds entry b:

	A	=	L	+	SE
	Cash		Accrued Wages Payable		Wages Expense
(a) Routine entries for explicit transactions	−20,000	=			−20,000
(b) Adjustment for implicit transaction, the accrual of unrecorded wages		=	+3,000		−3,000
Total effects	−20,000	=	+3,000		−23,000

The journal entries (a) and (b) would be:

(a)	Wages expense	20,000	
	Cash		20,000
(b)	Wages expense	3,000	
	Accrued wages payable		3,000

Entry *b* is the first example in this book of the impact of the analytical shortcut that bypasses the asset account and produces an expense that is offset by an increase in a liability.[1]

Accrual of Interest

Other examples of accrued expenses include sales commissions, property taxes, income taxes, and interest on borrowed money. Interest is rent paid for the use of money, just as rent is paid for the use of buildings or automobiles. The interest accumulates (accrues) as time unfolds, regardless of when the actual cash for interest is paid.

Incidentally, distinguish between the return *on* investment (for example, interest on a loan) and the return *of* investment (for example, *principal* of a loan). For example, suppose a loan of $100 is payable at the end of one year at 12% interest. The total payment of $112 would consist of the return *on* investment (interest) of $12 plus the return *of* investment (principal) of $100.

Recall that Biwheels borrowed $100,000 on December 31, 19X1. Assume that the principal and interest on the one-year loan are payable on December 31, 19X2. The interest rate is 9%. (Unless stated otherwise, quoted interest rates typically imply an interest rate *per year*.)

Ponder the theory of asset acquisition and expiration as applied to a bank loan. As of January 31, Biwheels has had the benefit of a $100,000 bank loan for one month. Biwheels owes the bank for these services (the use of money); the amount is $\frac{1}{12} \times .09 \times \$100,000 = \$750$. These money services of $750 have been acquired *and* used up (just like employee services) because Biwheels has had the loan for one month. Therefore the shortcut approach is usually taken; the adjustment is recorded in a fashion similar to the adjustment for accrued wages:

A =	L	+	SE
	Accrued Interest Payable		Interest Expense
Adjustment for January interest not yet recorded	= +750		−750

The adjusting journal entry is:

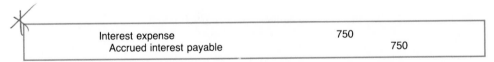

Interest expense	750	
Accrued interest payable		750

---

[1] Conceptually, entries *a* and *b* could each be subdivided into the asset acquisition–asset expiration sequence, but this two-step sequence is not generally used in practice for such expenses that represent the immediate consumption of services.

IV. ACCRUAL OF UNRECORDED REVENUES

The accrual of unrecorded revenues is the mirror image of the accrual of un-recorded expenses. The adjustments show the realization of revenues that have been earned but not yet shown in the accounts. Consider the bank that has lent the money to Biwheels. As of January 31, the bank has earned $750 on the loan. The following tabulation shows the mirror-image effect:

	BANK, AS A LENDER			BIWHEELS, AS A BORROWER		
	A	= L +	SE	A =	L	+	SE
	Accrued Interest Receivable		Interest Revenue		Accrued Interest Payable	Interest Expense
January interest	+750	=	+750	=	+750	−750

The adjusting journal entries are:

LENDER			BORROWER		
Accrued interest receivable	750		Interest expense	750	
Interest revenue		750	Accrued interest payable		750

Other examples of accrued revenues and receivables include "unbilled" fees. For example, attorneys, public accountants, physicians, and advertising agencies may earn hourly fees during a particular month but not send out bills to their clients until the completion of an entire contract or engagement. Under the accrual basis of accounting, such earnings should be attributed to the month when earned rather than later. Suppose an attorney had rendered $10,000 of services during January that would not be billed until March 31. Before the attorney's financial statements could be prepared for January, an adjustment for previously unrecorded revenues would be necessary:

	A	= L +	SE
	Accrued (Unbilled) Fees Receivable		Fee Revenue
Adjustment for fees earned	+10,000	=	+10,000

The adjusting journal entry would be:

Accrued (unbilled) fees receivable	10,000	
Fee revenue		10,000

THE ADJUSTING PROCESS IN PERSPECTIVE

Each adjusting entry affects at least one income statement account—a revenue or an expense. The other side of the entry is a balance sheet account—an asset or a liability. No adjusting entry debits or credits cash. Why? Because cash transactions are routinely recorded at other times. The end-of-period adjustment process is reserved for the noncash transactions that must be recognized by the accrual basis of accounting. Exhibit 4–1 summarizes the major adjusting entries.

EXHIBIT 4–1
Summary of Adjusting Entries

ADJUSTING ENTRY	TYPE OF ACCOUNT DEBITED	TYPE OF ACCOUNT CREDITED
I Expiration of unexpired costs	Expense	Prepaid Expense, Accumulated Depreciation
II Realization (earning) of unearned revenues	Unearned Revenue	Revenue
III Accrual of unrecorded expenses	Expense	Payable
IV Accrual of unrecorded revenues	Receivable	Revenue

CASH LEADS AND LAGS

Cash flows (that is, cash receipts and disbursements) may lead or lag the recognition of revenue and expense. Recall that the first two types of adjustments were usually made *subsequent* to the cash flows. For example, the cash received or disbursed for rent had an *initial* impact on the balance sheet. The adjustment process was used to show the *later* impact on the income statements.

The third and fourth types of adjustments are made *before* the related cash flows. The income statement is affected *before* the cash receipts and disbursements occur.

The accompanying diagrams underscore the basic differences between the cash basis and the accrual basis of accounting:

I. Expiration of Unexpired Costs. Entails computing the portion of an asset used up as expense in the current reporting period:

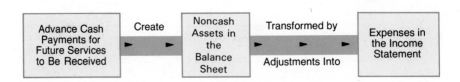

II. Realization (Earning) of Unearned Revenues. Entails computing the portion of advance payment previously received that has been earned (realized) in the current reporting period by performing a service or delivering goods to a customer:

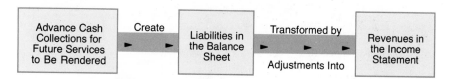

III. Accrual of Unrecorded Expenses. Entails computing the amount owed for goods and services rendered for the entity by outside parties such as suppliers and employees. Therefore the entity has an expense not previously recognized and a liability in the form of a legal obligation to pay:

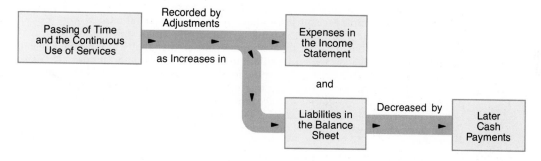

IV. Accrual of Unrecorded Revenues. Entails computing the amount owed by customers or clients for goods and services rendered by the entity. Therefore the entity has revenue not previously recognized and an asset in the form of a legal right to collect:

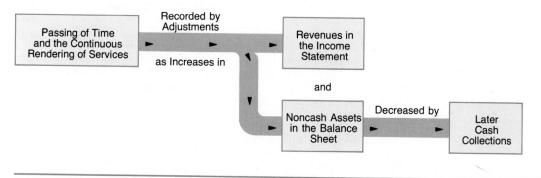

SUMMARY PROBLEM FOR YOUR REVIEW

☐ **Problem One**

Chan Co. is a retailer of stereo equipment. Chan has been in business one month. The company's unadjusted trial balance, January 31, 19X2, has the following accounts:

Cash	$ 71,700	
Accounts receivable	160,300	
Note receivable	40,000	
Merchandise inventory	250,200	
Prepaid rent	15,000	
Store equipment	114,900	
Note payable		$100,000
Accounts payable		117,100
Unearned rent revenue		3,000
Paid-in capital		400,000
Sales		160,000
Cost of goods sold	100,000	
Wages expense	28,000	
Total	$780,100	$780,100

Consider the following adjustments on January 31:

a. January depreciation, $1,000.

b. On January 2, rent of $15,000 was paid in advance for the first quarter of 19X2, as shown by the debit balance in the Prepaid Rent account. Adjust for January rent.

c. Wages earned by employees during January but not paid as of January 31 were $3,750.

d. Chan borrowed $100,000 from the bank on January 1. This explicit transaction was recorded when the business began, as shown by the credit balance in the Note Payable account. The principal and 9% interest are to be paid one year later (January 1, 19X3). However, an adjustment is necessary now for the interest expense of $750 for January.

e. On January 1, a cash loan of $40,000 was made to a local supplier, as shown by the debit balance in the Note Receivable account. The promissory note stated that the loan is to be repaid one year later (January 1, 19X3), together with interest at 12% per annum. On January 31, an adjustment is needed to recognize the interest earned on the note receivable.

f. On January 15, a nearby corporation paid $3,000 cash to Chan Co. as an advance rental for Chan's storage space and equipment to be used temporarily from January 15 to April 15 (three months). This $3,000 is the credit balance in the Unearned Revenue account. On January 31, an adjustment is needed to recognize the rent revenue earned for one-half month.

g. Adjustment. Income tax expense was accrued on January income at a rate of 50% of income before taxes. (Income taxes are discussed later in this chapter, but prepare the adjustment now. Debit Income Tax Expense for $11,200 and credit Accrued Income Taxes Payable.)

Required:

1. Enter the trial-balance amounts in the general ledger. Set up the new asset account, Accrued Interest Receivable, and the new asset-reduction account, the contra account, Accumulated Depreciation, Store Equipment. Set up the following new liability accounts: Accrued Wages Payable, Accrued Interest Payable, and Accrued Income Taxes Payable. Set up the following new expense and revenue accounts: Depreciation Expense, Rent Expense, Interest Expense, Interest Revenue, Rent Revenue, and Income Tax Expense.

2. Journalize adjustments a–g and post the entries to the ledger. Key entries by transaction letter.

3. Prepare an adjusted trial balance as of January 31, 19X2.

☐ **Solution to Problem One**

The solutions to requirements 1 through 3 are in Exhibits 4–2 (p. 133), 4–3 (p. 134), and 4–4 (p. 135), respectively. Accountants often refer to the final trial balance, Exhibit 4–4, as the adjusted trial balance. Why? Because all the necessary adjustments have been made, and the trial balance provides the data directly for the formal financial statements.

EXHIBIT 4–2

CHAN CO.
Journal Entries

(a) Depreciation expense	1,000	
Accumulated depreciation, store equipment		1,000
Depreciation for January.		
(b) Rent expense	5,000	
Prepaid rent		5,000
Rent expense for January.		
(c) Wages expense	3,750	
Accrued wages payable		3,750
Wages earned but not paid.		
(d) Interest expense	750	
Accrued interest payable		750
Interest for January.		
(e) Accrued interest receivable	400	
Interest revenue		400
Interest earned for January:		
12% × $40,000 × $\frac{1}{12}$ = $400.		
(f) Unearned rent revenue	500	
Rent revenue		500
Rent earned for January. Rent per month is		
$3,000 ÷ 3 = $1,000; for one-half month, $500.		
(g) Income tax expense	11,200	
Accrued income taxes payable		11,200
Income tax on January income.		

CLASSIFIED BALANCE SHEET

☐ **Current Assets and Liabilities**

There are now enough items to justify the preparation of a **classified balance sheet** for Chan Co., as in Exhibit 4–5. A balance sheet is *classified* when its items are grouped into various subcategories. You can readily imagine many more categories than are shown in Exhibit 4–5. At this stage, concentrate on the *current assets* and *current liabilities*. **Current assets** are cash plus assets that are expected to be converted to cash or sold or consumed during the next twelve months or within the normal operating cycle if longer than a year. Similarly, **current liabilities** are those liabilities that fall due within the coming year or within the normal operating cycle if longer than a year. **Working capital** is the excess of current assets over current liabilities.

Exhibit 4–5 shows only one long-term asset, Store Equipment (and its related accumulated depreciation) and no long-term liabilities. However, most balance sheets contain several long-term assets and at least one type of long-term debt.

The stockholders' equity is now $400,000 plus January net income of $11,200, or $411,200. Of course, the $11,200 does not appear as a separate number in the trial balance. Instead the $11,200 is the net effect of all the balances in the revenue

EXHIBIT 4–3

CHAN CO.
General Ledger

ASSETS	LIABILITIES + STOCKHOLDERS' EQUITY
(Increases Left, Decreases Right)	(Decreases Left, Increases Right)

ASSETS

Cash		
Bal.	71,700	

Accounts Receivable		
Bal.	160,300	

Note Receivable		
Bal.	40,000	

Merchandise Inventory		
Bal.	250,200	

Prepaid Rent			
Bal.	15,000	(b)	5,000
Bal.	10,000		

Store Equipment		
Bal.	114,900	

Accumulated Depreciation, Store Equipment		
	(a)	1,000

Accrued Interest Receivable		
(e)	400	

LIABILITIES

Note Payable		
	Bal.	100,000

Accounts Payable		
	Bal.	117,100

Unearned Rent Revenue			
(f)	500	Bal.	3,000
		Bal.	2,500

Accrued Wages Payable		
	(c)	3,750

Accrued Interest Payable		
	(d)	750

Accrued Income Taxes Payable		
	(g)	11,200

STOCKHOLDERS' EQUITY

Paid-in Capital		
	Bal.	400,000

Sales		
	Bal.	160,000

Cost of Goods Sold		
Bal.	100,000	

Wages Expense		
Bal.	28,000	
(c)	3,750	
Bal.	31,750	

Depreciation Expense		
(a)	1,000	

Rent Expense		
(b)	5,000	

Interest Expense		
(d)	750	

Interest Revenue		
	(e)	400

Rent Revenue		
	(f)	500

Income Tax Expense		
(g)	11,200	

and expense accounts. The balance sheet condenses the $11,200 effect as retained income. (The next chapter will explain the journal entries necessary to achieve this effect.)

☐ **Current Ratio**

Users of balance sheets often worry about **solvency determination**. This is the assessment of an entity's ability to meet its financial obligations as they become

EXHIBIT 4–4

CHAN CO.
Adjusted Trial Balance
January 31, 19X2

ACCOUNT TITLE	BALANCE Debit	BALANCE Credit	
Cash	$ 71,700		
Accounts receivable	160,300		
Note receivable	40,000		
Merchandise inventory	250,200		
Prepaid rent	10,000		
Store equipment	114,900		
Accumulated depreciation, store equipment		$ 1,000	Balance
Accrued interest receivable	400		Sheet
Note payable		100,000	Exhibit 4–5
Accounts payable		117,100	
Unearned rent revenue		2,500	
Accrued wages payable		3,750	
Accrued interest payable		750	
Accrued income taxes payable		11,200	
Paid-in capital		400,000	
Sales		160,000	
Cost of goods sold	100,000		
Wages expense	31,750		
Depreciation expense	1,000		Income
Rent expene	5,000		Statement,
Interest expense	750		Exhibit 4–7
Interest revenue		400	
Rent revenue		500	
Income tax expense	11,200		
Total	$797,200	$797,200	

due. Classifications of current assets and current liabilities can help assess solvency.

The **current ratio** (also called the **working capital ratio**) is widely used as a part of solvency determination. Chan's current ratio is

$$\text{Current ratio} = \frac{\text{Current assets}}{\text{Current liabilities}} = \frac{\$532,600}{\$235,300} = 2.3$$

Other things being equal, the higher the current ratio, the more assurance the creditor has about being paid in full and on time. Short-term creditors might use the current ratio to help gauge whether Chan is in a good position to pay current debts on time. The analyst will compare these measures through time and with similar companies and will make judgments accordingly.

In particular, the creditors look at the level of cash. However, ratios and similar measures have limitations, so creditors usually want some budget (prediction) of cash receipts and disbursements. For instance, does Chan have plenty of cash in relation to short-term liabilities? Whether cash is too high or too low really depends on the predictions of operating requirements over the

EXHIBIT 4–5

CHAN CO.
Balance Sheet
January 31, 19X2

ASSETS			LIABILITIES AND OWNERS' EQUITY		
Current assets:			Current liabilities:		
Cash		$ 71,700	Note payable	$100,000	
Accounts receivable		160,300	Accounts payable	117,100	
Note receivable		40,000	Unearned rent		
Accrued interest			revenue	2,500	
receivable		400	Accrued wages		
Merchandise			payable	3,750	
inventory		250,200	Accrued interest		
Prepaid rent		10,000	payable	750	
Total current			Accrued income		
assets		$532,600	taxes payable	11,200	
			Total current		
			liabilities		$235,300
Long-term asset:			Stockholders' equity:		
Store equipment	$114,900		Paid-in capital	$400,000	
Accumulated			Retained income	11,200	411,200
depreciation	1,000	113,900			
Total		$646,500	Total		$646,500

coming months. Intelligent cash management would call for trying to invest any temporary excess cash to generate additional income.

Formats of Balance Sheets

The particular form and detail of financial statements vary among companies. Consider the exact reproduction of the balance sheet of Hawaiian Airlines as shown in Exhibit 4–6. The format, indentations, and classifications are those actually presented. Note that no separate captions are used for noncurrent items. Many accountants would prefer to use captions such as *long-term assets* and *long-term liabilities*, respectively, to parallel the captions for *current assets* and *current liabilities*. Other accountants prefer not to use such captions when there are only one or two items within a specific class.

The Current Portion of Long-Term Debt is that part due within the coming year. The Air Traffic Liability is unearned revenue. It represents airfares collected in advance from customers for services to be rendered. Note that the current liabilities exceed the current assets. Many airlines have continuing difficulties in generating enough cash to meet their obligations.

Exhibit 4–6 presents a classified balance sheet in the **report format** (assets at top) in contrast to the **account format** (assets at left) that has previously been illustrated (Exhibit 4–5). Either format is acceptable. A recent survey of six hundred companies indicated that 56% use the account format and 44% use the report format.

More is said about classifications and the analysis of the balance sheet in succeeding chapters, especially Chapter 15.

EXHIBIT 4-6

HAWAIIAN AIRLINES, INC.
Condensed Balance Sheet (in thousands)
March 31, 1989

ASSETS

Current Assets:	
Cash	$ 23,628
Accounts receivable	28,908
Inventories	6,427
Prepaid expenses and other current assets	188
Total current assets	59,151
Property and Equipment—less accumulated depreciation of $49,511	88,448
Other Assets	12,209
Total	$159,808

LIABILITIES AND STOCKHOLDERS' EQUITY

Current Liabilities:	
Current portion of long-term debt	$ 14,522
Notes payable	12,000
Accounts payable	37,616
Accrued liabilities	15,413
Air traffic liability	20,715
Total current liabilities	100,266
Long-Term Debt	39,356
Other Liabilities	24,424
Stockholders' Equity (Deficiency):	
Common stock	6,007
Capital in excess of par value	4,834
Retained earnings (deficit)	(15,079)
Total stockholders' equity	(4,238)
Total	$159,808

INCOME STATEMENT

We now continue the discussion of the income statement.

☐ Single- and Multiple-Step Statements

Most investors are vitally concerned about the company's ability to produce long-run earnings and dividends. In this regard, income statements are much more important than balance sheets.

Given the Chan Co. adjusted trial balance presented in Exhibit 4-4 (p. 135), consider the income statement shown in Exhibit 4-7, Part A. The statement there is called a **single-step income statement** because it merely groups all revenues together (sales plus interest and rent revenues) and then lists and deducts all expenses together without drawing any intermediate subtotals.

Another major form of income statement is the **multiple-step** statement. It contains one or more subtotals that often highlight significant relationships. For example, Exhibit 4-7, Part B, shows a *gross profit* figure. Gross profit is defined

EXHIBIT 4–7, Part A

Single-Step Income Statement

CHAN CO.
Income Statement
For the Month Ended January 31, 19X2

Sales	$160,000	
Rent revenue	500	
Interest revenue	400	
Total sales and other revenues		$160,900
Expenses:		
Cost of goods sold	$100,000	
Wages	31,750	
Depreciation	1,000	
Rent	5,000	
Interest	750	
Income taxes	11,200	
Total expenses		149,700
Net income		$ 11,200

EXHIBIT 4–7, Part B

Multiple-Step Income Statement

CHAN CO.
Income Statement
For the Month Ended January 31, 19X2

Sales		$160,000
Cost of goods sold		100,000
Gross profit		$ 60,000
Operating expenses:		
Wages	$ 31,750	
Depreciation	1,000	
Rent	5,000	37,750
Operating income		$ 22,250
Other revenue and expense:		
Rent revenue	$ 500	
Interest revenue	400	
Total other revenue	$ 900	
Deduct: Interest expense	750	150
Income before income taxes		$ 22,400
Income taxes (at 50%)		11,200
Net income		$ 11,200

as the excess of sales revenue over the cost of the inventory that was sold. It is also called **gross margin.**

    The next section of the multiple-step statement usually contains a group of recurring expenses that are often labeled as operating expenses because they pertain to the firm's routine, ongoing operations. Examples are wages, rent, depreciation, and various other expenses such as telephone, heat, and advertising. These operating expenses are deducted from the gross profit to obtain **operating income,** which is also called **operating profit.** Of course, cost of goods sold could also be viewed as an operating expense because it is also deducted from sales revenue to obtain "operating income." However, because of its size and importance, it is usually deducted separately from sales revenue, as shown here.

The next grouping is usually called *other revenue and expense* (or *other income* or *other expense* or *nonoperating items* or some similar catchall title). These are not directly related to the mainstream of a firm's operations. The revenues are usually minor in relation to the revenues shown at the top of the income statement. The expenses are also minor, with one likely exception, interest expense.

Accountants have usually regarded interest revenue and interest expense as "other" items because they arise from lending and borrowing money—activities that are distinct from the ordinary selling of goods or services. Because interest revenue and expense appear in a separate category, comparisons of operating income between years and between companies can easily be made. Some companies make heavy use of debt, which causes high interest expenses, whereas other companies incur little debt and low interest expenses.

Profitability Evaluation Ratios

In its ultimate sense, **profitability evaluation** is the assessment of the likelihood of a particular rate of return on an investment. Comparisons through time and within and among industries are used as a basis for predictions and decisions. Consider three of the most popular ratios for measuring profitability:

1. A multiple-step statement is often useful to a retailer in choosing a pricing strategy and in judging its results. Of particular interest is the **gross profit percentage,** or **gross margin percentage,** which is defined as gross profit divided by sales. The Chan gross profit percentage for January was

$$\text{Gross profit percentage} = \text{Gross profit} \div \text{Sales}$$
$$= \$60,000 \div \$160,000$$
$$= 37.5\%$$

These relationships can also be presented as follows:

	AMOUNT	PERCENTAGE
Sales	$160,000	100.0%
Cost of goods sold	100,000	62.5
Gross profit	$ 60,000	37.5%

2. Obviously, the ratios of various expenses to sales will be carefully followed by managers from month to month. Users of financial statements are particularly concerned about the relationship of net income, the famous "bottom line," to two basic amounts. One of these is the sales figure:

$$\text{Return on sales} = \text{Net income} \div \text{Sales}$$
$$= \$11,200 \div \$160,000$$
$$= 7\%$$

3. Another basic amount with which net income is often compared is invested capital (as measured by average stockholders' equity). This ratio is widely regarded as the ultimate measure of overall accomplishment:

Return on stockholders' equity = Net income ÷ Average stockholders' equity
= $11,200 ÷ ½ (January 1 balance, $400,000 + January 31
balance, $411,200)
= $11,200 ÷ $405,600
= 2.8% (for one month)

These ratios are being introduced at this early stage because they are so widely encountered. The 37.5% gross profit is relatively low as compared with the usual 40% to 45% for the retail stereo industry. However, Chan has maintained excellent expense control because its 7% return on sales and its 33.6% return on stockholders' equity (an annual rate of 2.8 × 12 = 33.6%) are higher than the 6% and 18% annual returns usually earned by the industry.[2]

Statistical studies have shown that *profitability evaluation ratios* have higher power than *solvency determination ratios* (such as the current ratio) for predicting performance regarding *both* income and solvency.[3]

Later chapters study the uses and limitations of these and other ratios. For example, Chapter 6 explores the analytical role of gross profit percentages, and Chapter 15 reviews the most widely used ratios.

☐ **Accrual of Income Taxes**

Income taxes are worldwide, although rates and details differ from country to country and state to state. Corporations in the United States are subject to federal and state corporate income taxes. Tax rates are progressive; taxable income over $75,000 is taxed at the maximum rate. The rates are changed almost yearly by either the U.S. Congress or the state legislatures or both. For many corporations, the federal-plus-state income tax rates hover around 40%.

Various labels are used for income taxes on the income statement: *income tax expense, provision for income taxes,* and just plain *income taxes* are found most frequently. About 85% of publicly held companies show federal income taxes as a separate last item just before net income. In contrast, the other 15% list federal income taxes along with other operating expenses such as wages. A recent IBM annual report contains the format adopted by the vast majority of companies:

Earnings before income taxes	$5,092,414,000
Provision for income taxes	2,373,000,000
Net earnings	$2,719,414,000

---

[2] Of course, returns on investments in partnerships are also computed. Consider this letter from the managing partner of the Fresno Ramada Inn: "In the Annual Report that was recently mailed, we found a typographical error in the discussion of operations which referred to a return of '$375,000 per $1,000 Partnership Capital Unit.' The Motel is a good investment, but not that good. It should have read '$375.00 per $1,000 Partnership Capital Units.' We apologize for the error."

[3] For an excellent presentation of the modern thinking in this area, see George Foster, *Financial Statement Analysis*, 2d ed. (Englewood Cliffs, NJ: Prentice Hall, 1986).

Income tax expenses are accrued each month (not just once a year) as pretax income is generated. **Pretax income** is a popular synonym for income before income taxes. The amount of the accrual for income taxes obviously depends on the amount of pretax income.

ILLUSTRATIONS OF INCOME STATEMENTS

This section demonstrates how various entities may use assorted terminology and formats for their individual statements of income. Note throughout that extremely condensed income statement information is provided in published reports (as opposed to the detail that is shown for internal users). The income statements below cover a recent year. To save space, the separate lines indicating the years are omitted; however, the particular titles of the statements are shown.

☐ Multiple-Step (Heinz)

The H. J. Heinz income statement uses a *multiple-step* format, as do 44% of corporate external reports. The multiple-step format has subtotals to highlight significant relationships. In addition to net income, the format also presents two key measures of performance, gross profit and operating income. The Heinz statement follows:

H. J. HEINZ CO.
Statement of Income (in thousands)

Sales		$5,244,230
Cost of products sold		3,174,159
Gross profit		2,070,071
Operating expenses		1,382,058
Operating Income		688,013
Interest income	$(39,850)	
Interest expense	73,995	
Other expense, net	31,295	65,440
Income before income taxes		622,573
Provision for income taxes		236,559
Net Income		$ 386,014

Accountants use the label *net* to denote that some amounts have been deducted in computing the final result. In a statement of income, the term *net* is not ordinarily used to describe any subtotals of income that precede the final net income number. For example, the Heinz statement shows "*income* before income taxes," not "*net income* before income taxes."

☐ Single-Step (Wm. Wrigley)

Wm. Wrigley Jr. Company, maker of chewing gum, uses a *single-step* format for its income statement, as do 56% of corporate external reports:

WM. WRIGLEY JR. COMPANY
Statement of Earnings (in thousands)

Revenues:	
Net sales	$781,059
Investment income	7,835
Total revenues	788,894
Costs and expenses:	
Cost of sales	338,081
Selling, distribution, and general administrative	327,199
Interest	606
Total costs and expenses	665,886
Earnings before income taxes	123,008
Income taxes	52,863
Net earnings	$ 70,145

In general, a single-step income statement merely groups all revenues together and all expenses together without drawing subtotals within revenue and expense categories.

Although Wrigley uses a single-step income statement, note where income taxes appear. Most companies follow this practice of showing income taxes as a separate item immediately above net income (regardless of the grouping of the other items on the income statement).

As Wrigley shows, the term "costs and expenses" is sometimes found instead of just "expenses." "Expenses" would be an adequate description. Why? Because the "costs" listed on the income statement are "expired costs," such as "cost of sales," and thus are really expenses of the current period.

The appendix to Chapter 10 contains additional explanations of income statements, including coverage of how to present the impacts of extraordinary gains and losses and effects of discontinued operations.

SUMMARY

At the end of each accounting period, adjustments must be made so that financial statements can be presented on a full-fledged accrual basis. The major adjustments are for (1) the expiration of unexpired costs, (2) the realization (earning) of unearned revenues, (3) the accrual of unrecorded expenses, and (4) the accrual of unrecorded revenues.

Classified balance sheets divide various items into subcategories. For example, assets and liabilities are separated into current and long-term.

Income statements often appear in single-step, condensed form in published annual reports and in multiple-step, detailed form in the reports used within an organization.

SUMMARY PROBLEM FOR YOUR REVIEW

The first problem appeared earlier in the chapter, page 131.

Problem Two

Johnson & Johnson (maker of Tylenol, Band-Aids, and other products) uses a statement of earnings and retained earnings, as follows:

JOHNSON & JOHNSON
Statement of Earnings and Retained Earnings
(Dollars in millions except per share figures)

Sales to customers	$8,012
Cost of products sold	2,958
Selling, distribution and administrative expenses	3,228
Research expense	617
Interest income	(95)
Interest expense	116
Other (income) expense, net	(5)
	6,819
Earnings before provision for taxes on income	1,193
Provision for taxes on income	360
Net earnings	833
Retained earnings at beginning of period	3,585
Cash dividends paid	(278)
Retained earnings at end of period	$4,140
Net earnings per share	$ 4.83

Required:

1. Is this a single-step or a multiple-step statement of earnings? Explain your answer.
2. What term would Wm. Wrigley Jr. use as a label for the line having the $6,819 figure? (Refer to the Wrigley income statement on page 142.)
3. Suggest an alternative term for interest *income*.
4. Compute the gross profit.
5. What is the amount of the famous "bottom line" that is so often referred to by managers?
6. Compute the average number of common shares outstanding during the year.

Solution to Problem Two

1. As is often the case, Johnson & Johnson uses a hybrid of single-step and multiple-step income statements. However, it is closer to a single-step than a multiple-step statement. A pure-bred single-step statement would place interest income and other income with sales to obtain total revenues.

2. Wrigley would use "total costs and expenses" to describe the $6,819 figure.

3. Interest *revenue* is preferable to interest *income*.

4.
Sales to customers	$8,012	100%
Cost of products sold	2,958	37
Gross profit	$5,054	63%

5. The bottom line in total is net earnings of $833 million. The bottom line per average common share outstanding is $4.83.

6. As the appendix to Chapter 2 explains, net earnings per share is required to be shown on the face of the income statement.

$$\text{Earnings per share (EPS)} = \frac{\text{Net earnings}}{\text{Average number of common shares outstanding}}$$

$$\$4.83 = \frac{\$833,000,000}{\text{Average shares}}$$

Average shares = $833,000,000 ÷ $4.83
Average shares = 172,463,760 shares

HIGHLIGHTS TO REMEMBER

1. Frequently, accounting adjustments are clarified when they are seen as mirror images by looking at both sides of the adjustment simultaneously. For example, (a) the expiration of unexpired costs (the tenant's rent expense) is accompanied by (b) the earning of unearned revenues (the landlord's rent revenue).

2. Similarly, (a) the accrual of unrecorded expenses (a borrower's interest expense) is accompanied by (b) the accrual of unrecorded revenues (a lender's interest revenue).

3. Income tax expense is usually accrued monthly (based on pretax income for the month), regardless of when cash is disbursed. Income tax expense usually appears just before the net income line on the income statement.

ACCOUNTING VOCABULARY

Account Format, p. 136
Accrue, p. 126
Adjusting Entries, p. 123
Adjustments, p. 123
Classified Balance Sheet, p. 133
Current Assets, p. 133
Current Liabilities, p. 133
Current Ratio, p. 135
Deferred Credit, p. 125
Deferred Income, p. 126
Deferred Revenue, p. 125
Explicit Transactions, p. 124
Gross Margin, p. 138
Gross Margin Percentage, p. 139
Gross Profit, p. 137

Gross Profit Percentage, p. 139
Implicit Transactions, p. 124
Multiple-Step Income Statement, p. 137
Operating Income, p. 139
Operating Profit, p. 139
Pretax Income, p. 141
Profitability Evaluation, p. 139
Report Format, p. 136
Single-Step Income Statement, p. 137
Solvency Determination, p. 134
Unearned Income, p. 126
Unearned Revenue, p. 125
Working Capital, p. 133
Working Capital Ratio, p. 135

FUNDAMENTAL ASSIGNMENT MATERIAL

☐ **General Coverage**

4–1. **ADJUSTING ENTRIES.** (Alternates are 4–3, 4–4, and 4–27.) Anna Ferrari, certified public accountant, had the following transactions (among others) during 19X2:

a. For accurate measurement of performance and position, Ferrari uses the accrual basis of accounting. On August 1, Ferrari acquired office supplies for $2,000. Office Supplies Inventory was increased and Cash was decreased by $2,000 on Ferrari's books. On December 31, Ferrari's inventory was $900.

b. On September 1, a client gave Ferrari a retainer fee of $48,000 cash for monthly services to be rendered over the following twelve months. Ferrari increased Cash and Unearned Fee Revenue.

c. Ferrari accepted a $10,000 note receivable from a client on October 1 for tax services. The note plus interest of 12% per year were due in six months. Ferrari increased Note Receivable and Fee Revenue for $10,000.

d. As of December 31, Ferrari had not recorded $500 of unpaid wages earned by her secretary during late December.

Required: For the year ended December 31, 19X2, prepare all adjustments called for by the above transactions. Assume that appropriate entries were routinely made for the explicit transactions described above. However, no adjustments have been made before December 31. For each adjustment, prepare an analysis in the same format used when the adjustment process was explained in the chapter. Also prepare the adjusting journal entry.

4–2. MULTIPLE–STEP INCOME STATEMENT.   (Alternate is 4–5). From the following data, prepare a multiple-step income statement for the Ferrin Company for the fiscal year ended May 31, 19X5 (in thousands except for percentage). *Hint*: see page 138.

Sales	$990	Cost of goods sold	$550
Interest expense	72	Depreciation	30
Rent expense	50	Rent revenue	10
Interest revenue	12	Wages	200
Income tax rate	40%		

☐ Understanding Published Financial Reports

4–3. FOUR MAJOR ADJUSTMENTS.   (Alternates are 4–1, 4–4, and 4–27.) The Goodyear Tire and Rubber Company included the following items in its January 31, 1989, balance sheet (in millions):

Prepaid expenses (a current asset)	$ 98
Domestic and foreign taxes (a current liability)	325

Required: Analyze the impact of the following transactions on the financial position of Goodyear. Prepare your analysis in the same format used when the adjustment process was explained in the chapter. Also show adjusting journal entries.

1. On January 31, an adjustment of $1 million was made for the rentals of various retail outlets that had originally increased Prepaid Expenses but had expired.
2. During December 1988, Goodyear sold tires for $2 million cash to Consolidated Freightways, but delivery was not made until January 28. Unearned Revenue had been increased in December. No other adjustments had been made since. Prepare the adjustment on January 31.
3. Goodyear had lent cash to several of its independent retail dealers. As of January 31, the dealers owed $2 million of interest that had been unrecorded.
4. On January 31, Goodyear increased its accrual of federal income taxes by $17 million.

4–4. FOUR MAJOR ADJUSTMENTS.   (Alternates are 4–1, 4–3, and 4–27.) Delta Airlines had the following items in its balance sheet, June 30, 1988, the end of the fiscal year:

Maintenance and operating supplies	$ 52,413,000
Prepaid expenses and other current assets	131,507,000
Air traffic liability	504,083,000
Accrued income taxes	107,041,000

A footnote stated: "Passenger ticket sales are recorded as revenue when the transportation is used. The value of unused tickets is included in current liabilities in the financial statements." The title of this current liability is Air Traffic Liability.

The income statement included:

Passenger revenues	$6,443,111,000
Income taxes provided	180,851,000

Required: Analyze the impact of the following assumed transactions on the financial position of Delta. Prepare your analysis in the same format used when the adjustment process was explained in the chapter. Also show adjusting journal entries.

1. Rented a sales office in a Bank of America office building for one year, beginning June 1, 1988, for $12,000 cash.
2. On June 30, 1988, an adjustment was made for the rent in requirement 1.
3. Sold two charter flights to Texas Instruments for $100,000 each. Cash of $200,000 was received in advance on May 20, 1988. The flights were for transporting marketing personnel to two business conventions in New York.
4. As the financial statements were being prepared on June 30, accountants for both Delta and Texas Instruments independently noted that the first charter flight had occurred in late June. The second would occur in early August. An adjustment was made on June 30.
5. Delta had lent $2 million to Boeing. Interest of $160,000 was accrued on June 30.
6. Additional federal income taxes of $100,000 were accrued on June 30.

4–5. **Budweiser Financial Statements.** (Alternate is 4–2.) Anheuser-Busch (maker of Budweiser beer) is the largest beer producer in the United States. Some actual financial data and nomenclature from its 1989 annual report were (in millions):

Anheuser-Busch, Inc.

Interest expense	$ 73	Cash dividends declared	?
Sales	8,258	Net income	$ 615
Gross profit	2,948	Retained earnings:	
Operating income	1,129	Beginning of year	2,472
Marketing, administrative,		End of year	2,918
and research expenses	?	Provision for income taxes	
Cost of products sold	?	(income tax expense)	441

Required:
1. Prepare a combined multiple-step statement of income and retained earnings for the year ended December 31, 1989. *Hint:* see page 138.
2. Compute the percentage of gross profit on sales and the percentage of net income on sales.
3. The average stockholders' equity for the year was $2,603 million. What was the percentage of net income on average stockholders' equity?

ADDITIONAL ASSIGNMENT MATERIAL

☐ **General Coverage**

4–6. Give two synonyms for *deferred revenue*.

4–7. Give two examples of an explicit transaction.

4–8. Give two examples of an implicit transaction.

4–9. Explain the difference between *incur* and *accrue*.

4–10. "Accountants often use routine shortcuts when they record expenses." Explain, giving an illustration.

4–11. Distinguish between the return *on* investment and the return *of* investment.

4–12. "The accrual of previously unrecorded revenues is the mirror image of the accrual of previously unrecorded expenses." Explain, using an illustration.

4–13. Explain the difference between a *single-step* and a *multiple-step* income statement.

4–14. Why does interest expense appear below operating income on a multiple-step income statement?

4–15. Name three popular ratios for measuring profitability.

4–16. Give a popular synonym for *income before income taxes*.

4–17. Give a synonym for *income tax expense*.

4–18. Explain why income tax expense is usually the final deduction on both single-step and multiple-step income statements.

4–19. The term "costs and expenses" is sometimes found instead of just "expenses" on the income statement. "Expenses" would be an adequate description. Why?

4–20. **TRUE OR FALSE.** Use *T* or *F* to indicate whether each of the following statements is true or false.

    1. Retained Earnings should be accounted for as a current asset item.
    2. Cash should be classified as a stockholders' equity item.
    3. Machinery used in the business should be recorded as a noncurrent asset item.
    4. The cash balance is the best evidence of stockholders' equity.
    5. From a single balance sheet you can find stockholders' equity for a period of time but not for a specific day.
    6. It is not possible to determine change in the condition of a business from a single balance sheet.

4–21. **TENANT AND LANDLORD.** The Veinott Company, a retail hardware store, pays quarterly rent on its store at the beginning of each quarter. The rent per quarter is $9,000. The owner of the building in which the store is located is the Rouse Corporation.

Required: | Using the balance sheet equation format, analyze the effects of the following on the tenant's and the landlord's financial position:

    1. Veinott pays $12,000 rent on July 1.
    2. Adjustment for July.
    3. Adjustment for August.
    4. Adjustment for September. Also prepare the journal entry.

4–22. **CUSTOMER AND AIRLINE.** The Levitz Furniture Company decided to hold a managers' meeting in Hawaii in February. To take advantage of special fares, Levitz purchased airline tickets in advance from United Airlines at a total cost of $90,000. These were acquired on December 1 for cash.

Required: | Using the balance sheet equation format, analyze the impact of the December payment and the February travel on the financial position of both Levitz and United. Also prepare journal entries for February.

4–23. **ACCRUALS OF WAGES.** Consider the following calendar:

APRIL						
S	M	T	W	T	F	S
		1	2	3	4	5
6	7	8	9	10	11	12
13	14	15	16	17	18	19
20	21	22	23	24	25	26
27	28	29	30			

    The Ace Department Store commenced business on April 1. It is open every day except Sunday. Its total payroll for all employees is $10,000 per day. Payments are made each Tuesday for the preceding week's work through Saturday.

Required: | Using the balance sheet equation format, analyze the financial impact on Ace of the following:

    1. Disbursements for wages on April 8, 15, 22, and 29.
    2. Adjustment for wages on April 30. Also prepare the journal entry.

4–24. **PLACEMENT OF INTEREST IN INCOME STATEMENT.** Two companies have the following balance sheets as of December 31, 19X2:

COMPANY A

Cash	$100,000	Note payable*	$200,000
Other assets	300,000	Stockholders' equity	200,000
Total	$400,000	Total	$400,000

* 12% interest.

COMPANY B

Cash	$100,000	Stockholders' equity	$400,000
Other assets	300,000		
Total	$400,000		

In 19X3, each company had sales of $900,000 and expenses (excluding interest) of $800,000. Ignore income taxes.

Required: | Did each company earn the same net income? The same operating income? Explain, showing computations of operating income and net income.

4–25. **IDENTIFICATION OF TRANSACTIONS.** Correlation Corporation's financial position is represented by the nine balances shown on the first line of the following schedule (in thousands of dollars). Assume that a single transaction took place for each of the following lines, and describe what you think happened, using one short sentence for each line.

	CASH	ACCOUNTS RECEIVABLE	INVEN-TORY	EQUIP-MENT	ACCOUNTS PAYABLE	ACCRUED WAGES PAYABLE	UNEARNED RENT REVENUE	PAID-IN CAPITAL	RETAINED INCOME
Bal.	14	32	54	0	29	0	0	50	21
(1)	24	32	54	0	29	0	0	60	21
(2)	24	32	54	20	29	0	0	80	21
(3)	24	32	66	20	41	0	0	80	21
(4a)	24	47	66	20	41	0	0	80	36
(4b)	24	47	58	20	41	0	0	80	28
(5)	30	41	58	20	41	0	0	80	28
(6)	10	41	58	20	21	0	0	80	28
(7)	14	41	58	20	21	0	4	80	28
(8)	14	41	58	20	21	2	4	80	26
(9)	14	41	58	19	21	2	4	80	25
(10)	14	41	58	19	21	2	3	80	26

4–26. **EFFECTS ON BALANCE SHEET EQUATION.** Following is a list of effects of accounting transactions on the basic accounting equation: Assets equal Liabilities plus Stockholders' Equity.

    a. Increase in assets, increase in liabilities
    b. Increase in assets, decrease in liabilities
    c. Increase in assets, increase in stockholders' equity
    d. Increase in assets, decrease in assets
    e. Decrease in assets, decrease in liabilities
    f. Increase in liabilities, decrease in stockholders' equity
    g. Decrease in assets, increase in liabilities
    h. Decrease in liabilities, increase in stockholders' equity
    i. Decrease in assets, decrease in stockholders' equity
    j. None of these

Which of the foregoing relationships defines the accounting effect of each of the following?

1. The adjusting entry to recognize periodic depreciation.
2. The adjusting entry to record accrued salaries.
3. The adjusting entry to record accrued interest receivable.
4. The collection of interest previously accrued.
5. The settlement of an account payable by the issuance of a note payable.
6. The earning of income previously collected. Unearned Revenue was increased when collection was made in advance.
7. The recognition of an expense that had been paid for previously. A "prepaid" account was increased upon payment.

4–27. **FOUR MAJOR ADJUSTMENTS.** (Alternates are 4–1, 4–3, and 4–4.) Anita Cavaretta, an attorney, had the following transactions (among others) during 19X2, her initial year in practicing law:

a. On August 1, Cavaretta leased office space for one year. The landlord (lessor) insisted on full payment in advance. Prepaid Rent was increased and Cash was decreased by $18,000 on Cavaretta's books. Similarly, the landlord increased Cash and increased Unearned Rent Revenue.

b. On October 1, Cavaretta received a retainer fee of $24,000 cash for services to be rendered to her client, a local trucking company, over the succeeding twelve months. Cavaretta increased Cash and Unearned Fee Revenue. The trucking company increased Prepaid Expenses and decreased Cash.

c. As of December 31, Cavaretta had not recorded $300 of unpaid wages earned by her secretary during late December.

d. During November and December, Cavaretta rendered services to another client, a utility company. She had intended to bill the company for $3,200 services through December 31, but she decided to delay formal billing until late January when the case would probably be settled.

Required:

1. For the year ended December 31, 19X2, prepare all adjustments called for by the above transactions. Assume that appropriate entries were routinely made for the explicit transactions described above. However, no adjustments have been made before December 31. For each adjustment, prepare an analysis in the same format used when the adjustment process was explained in the chapter. Prepare two adjustments for each transaction, one for Cavaretta and one for the other party to the transaction. In part c, assume that the secretary uses the accrual basis for his personal entity.

2. For each transaction, prepare the journal entries for Anita Cavaretta *and* the other entities involved.

4–28. **ACCOUNTING FOR DUES.** (Alternate is 4–29.) The Vasquez Athletic Club provided the following data from its comparative balance sheets:

	DECEMBER 31	
	19X2	19X1
Dues receivable	$30,000	$25,000
Unearned dues revenue	—	10,000

The income statement for 19X2, which was prepared on the accrual basis, showed dues revenue earned of $240,000.

Required:

Prepare journal entries and post to T-accounts for the following:

1. Billing of $25,000 of dues in 19X1. Billing occurs after dues have been earned. However, dues collected in advance are not billed.

2. Collections of $10,000 of unearned dues in advance during the final week of 19X1.
3. Billing of dues revenue during 19X2.
4. Collection of dues receivable in 19X2.
5. Earning of dues collected in advance.

4–29. **ACCOUNTING FOR SUBSCRIPTIONS.** (Alternate is 4–28.) A magazine company collects subscriptions in advance of delivery of its magazines. However, many magazines are delivered to magazine distributors (for newsstand sales), and these distributors are billed and pay later. The subscription revenue earned for the month of December on the accrual basis was $210,000. Other pertinent data were:

	DECEMBER	
	31	1
Unearned subscription revenue	$170,000	$120,000
Subscriptions receivable	7,000	9,000

Required:

Reconstruct the entries for December. Prepare journal entries and post to T-accounts for the following:

1. Collections of unearned subscription revenue of $120,000 prior to December 1.
2. Billing of subscriptions receivable (a) of $9,000 prior to December 1, and (b) of $80,000 during December. (Credit Revenue Earned.)
3. Collections of cash during December and any other entries that are indicated by the given data.

4–30. **FINANCIAL STATEMENTS AND ADJUSTMENTS.** Calloway Distributors, Inc., has just completed its third year of business, 19X3. A set of financial statements was prepared by the principal stockholder's eldest child, a college student who is beginning the third week of an accounting course. Following is a list (in no systematic order) of the items appearing in the student's balance sheet, income statement, and statement of retained income:

Accounts receivable	$175,100	Advertising expense	$ 98,300
Note receivable	36,000	Merchandise inventory	201,900
Cash	87,300	Cost of goods sold	590,000
Paid-in capital	600,000	Unearned rent revenue	4,800
Building	300,000	Insurance expense	2,500
Accumulated depreciation,		Unexpired insurance	2,300
building	20,000	Accounts payable	52,500
Land	169,200	Interest expense	600
Sales	936,800	Telephone expense	2,900
Salary expense	124,300	Notes payable	20,000
Retained income:		Net income	110,500
December 31, 19X2	164,000	Miscellaneous expense	4,400
December 31, 19X3	274,500	Maintenance expense	3,300

Assume that the statements in which these items appear are current and complete except for the following matters not taken into consideration by the student:

a. Salaries of $5,200 have been earned by employees for the last half of December 19X3. Payment by the company will be made on the next payday, January 2, 19X4.
b. Interest at 10% per annum on the note receivable has accrued for two months and is expected to be collected by the company when the note is due on January 31, 19X4.
c. Part of the building owned by the company was rented to a tenant on November 1, 19X3, for six months, payable in advance. This rent was collected in cash and is represented by the item labeled Unearned Rent Revenue.
d. Depreciation on the building for 19X3 is $6,100.
e. Cash dividends of $60,000 were declared in December 19X3, payable in January 19X4.
f. Income tax at 40% applies to 19X3, all of which is to be paid in the early part of 19X4.

Prepare the following corrected financial statements:

1. Multiple-step income statement for 19X3.
2. Statement of retained income for 19X3.
3. Classified balance sheet at December 31, 19X3. (Show appropriate support for the dollar amounts you compute.)

4–31. MIRROR SIDE OF ADJUSTMENTS. Problem 4–1 described some Ferrari adjustments. Repeat the requirement for each adjustment as it would be made by the client in transactions *b* and *c* and by the secretary in transaction *d*. For our purposes here, assume that the secretary keeps personal books on the accrual basis.

☐ Understanding Published Financial Reports

4–32. MIRROR SIDE OF ADJUSTMENTS. Problem 4–3 described some Goodyear adjustments. Repeat the requirements for each adjustment as it would be made by (1) landlords, (2) Consolidated Freightways, (3) retail dealers, and (4) U.S. government.

4–33. MIRROR SIDE OF ADJUSTMENTS. Problem 4–4 described some Delta Airlines adjustments. Repeat the requirements for each adjustment as it would be made by (1) Bank of America, (2) Bank of America, (3) Texas Instruments, (4) Texas Instruments, (5) Boeing, and (6) U.S. government.

4–34. EFFECTS OF INTEREST ON LENDERS AND BORROWERS. Sears lent Riegal Paint Manufacturing Company $900,000 on March 1, 19X1. The loan plus interest of 12% is payable on March 1, 19X2.

Required:
1. Using the balance sheet equation format, prepare an analysis of the impact of the transactions on both Sears's and Riegal's financial position on March 1, 19X1. Show the summary adjustment on December 31, 19X1, for the period March 1–December 31.
2. Prepare adjusting journal entries for Sears and Riegal.

4–35. ACCRUED VACATION PAY. Delta Airlines had the following as a current liability on its balance sheet, June 30, 1988:

Accrued vaction pay	$118,344

Under the accrual basis of accounting, vacation pay is ordinarily accrued throughout the year as workers are regularly paid. For example, suppose a Delta baggage handler earns $600 per week for fifty weeks and also gets paid $1,200 for two weeks' vacation. Accrual accounting requires that the obligation for the $1,200 be recognized as it is earned rather than when the payment is disbursed. Thus, in each of the fifty weeks Delta would recognize a wage expense (or vacation pay expense) of $1,200 \div 50 = $24.

Required:
1. Prepare the weekly Delta adjusting journal entry called for by the $24 example.
2. Prepare the entry for the $1,200 payment of vacation pay.

4–36. JOURNAL ENTRIES AND POSTING. Nike, Inc., has many well-known products, including footwear. The company's balance sheet included (in thousands):

	MAY 31	
	1988	1987
Prepaid expenses	$12,793	$6,717
Income taxes payable	8,617	8,309

During the fiscal year ended May 31, 1988, $90,000,000 cash was disbursed and charged to Prepaid Expenses. Similarly, $64,192,000 was disbursed for income taxes and charged to Income Taxes Payable.

Required: 1. Assume that the Prepaid Expenses account relates to outlays for miscellaneous operating expenses (for example, supplies, insurance, and short-term rentals). Prepare summary journal entries for (a) the disbursements and (b) the expenses for fiscal 1988. Post the entries to the T-accounts.
2. Assume that there were no other accounts related to income taxes. Prepare summary journal entries for (a) the disbursements and (b) the expenses for fiscal 1988. Post the entries to T-accounts.

4–37. **ADVANCE SERVICE CONTRACTS.** Savin Corporation, a manufacturer in the office copier industry, showed the following balance sheet accounts.

	APRIL 30	
	19X2	19X1
Deferred income, principally service contracts (Note 1)	$6,354,893	$4,062,580

Note 1 stated: "The Company bills customers in advance for service contracts. Advance service contract billings are deferred and reflected in income ratably over the term of the contract."

Required: 1. Prepare summary journal entries for the creation in 19X1 and subsequent earning in 19X2 of the deferred income of $4,062,580. Use the following accounts: Accounts Receivable, Deferred Income, and Income from Service Contracts.
2. Post the journal entries to T-accounts.
3. A one-year service contract was billed to the Mount Sinai Hospital on January 1, 19X2, for $1,200. The full amount was collected on February 15. Prepare all pertinent journal entries through February 28, 19X2. ("Ratably" means an equal amount per month.)

4–38. **JOURNAL ENTRIES AND ADJUSTMENTS.** Portland General Electric Company is a public utility in Oregon. An annual report included the following footnote:

☐ Revenues—Revenues have been recorded as customers' meters were read, principally on a cycle basis throughout each month. This resulted in revenue being earned but not billed at the end of an accounting period. The changes in unbilled revenues from year to year were generally not significant. Due to the accelerating increase in rate levels and costs, the disparity between billed revenues and costs increased significantly. Accordingly, effective January 1 of this year, the Company changed to a method of accounting to accrue the amount of estimated unbilled revenues for services provided to the month end to more closely match revenues and costs.

The income statements showed:

	19X2	19X1
Operating revenues	$303,678,000	$253,073,000
Operating income	83,239,000	73,127,000

The balance sheet showed as part of current assets (amounts in thousands):

	DECEMBER 31	
	19X2	19X1
Receivables, customer accounts	$22,477,000	$19,176,000
Estimated unbilled revenues	20,209,000	—

Required:

1. Prepare the adjusting journal entry for (a) the unbilled revenues at the end of 19X2 and (b) the eventual billing and collection of the unbilled revenues. Ignore income taxes.
2. Which of the accounts shown above would have been affected if the company had not adopted the new policy? Give the name of each account and the amount of the effect. Ignore income taxes.

4–39. **POSTAL SERVICE ACCOUNTING.** The U.S. Postal Service is a separate federal entity created by the Postal Reform Act. The Postal Service financial statements are audited by an independent accounting firm. Its current liabilities for a given year included:

Prepaid permit mail and box rentals	$329,355,000
Estimated prepaid postage—Note 1	770,000,000

Note 1 stated: "Estimated prepaid postage represents the estimated revenue collected prior to the end of the year for which services will be subsequently rendered."

The Postal Service's statement of operations showed "operating revenue" of $19,133,041,000.

The current assets included "Receivables, U.S. Government," of $126,890,000.

Required:

1. Provide alternative descriptions for the two accounts.
2. A large retailer, Sears, has rented boxes in thousands of post offices to accelerate receipts from customers. Suppose $1 million of those rentals that were prepaid by Sears had expired as of September 30. Journalize a $1 million adjustment for expired rentals on the accounts of the Postal Service and Sears.
3. Many mail-order retailers prepay postage. In addition, millions of citizens buy rolls of postage stamps for later use. Note 1 describes how the Postal Service recognizes such prepayments. Suppose in a given year that Sears used $2 million of its prepaid postage that had not been adjusted for. Journalize a $2 million adjustment on the accounts of the Postal Service and Sears.
4. The Postal Service's statement of operations included the following as a separate addition to its operating revenue:

Operating appropriations (for revenue forgone for certain classes of mail)	$789,108,000

A footnote stated that the Postal Reform Act authorizes "to be appropriated each year a sum determined by the Postal Service to be equal to revenue forgone by it in providing certain mail services to the U.S. Government at free or reduced rates." Journalize the effects on the accounts of the Postal Service of an adjustment as of September 30 that increases appropriations by $20 million. Also journalize the effects on the accounts of the U.S. government. For simplicity, assume that no cash had changed hands as yet regarding these appropriations.

4–40. **MULTIPLE-STEP INCOME STATEMENT.** Kimberly-Clark Corporation has many well-known products, including Kleenex and Huggies. Its 1989 annual report contained the following data and actual terms (in millions):

Cost of products sold	$3,066	Advertising, promotion	
Research expense	111	and selling expense	$675
Interest expense	86	Provision for income taxes	
Interest income	34	(income tax expense)	231
Gross profit	1,819	Distribution expense	181
		General expense	266

Required: Prepare a multiple-step statement of income.

4-41. SINGLE-STEP INCOME STATEMENT. A. T. Cross Company's best-known products are writing instruments such as ball-point pens. The Cross 1989 annual report contained the following items:

Interest income	$ 3,547,805	Selling, general and	
Cost of goods sold	95,310,453	administrative expenses	$50,673,147
Provision for income taxes		Retained earnings at end	
(income tax expense)	15,955,000	of year	97,507,271
Sales	187,269,821	Cash dividends	23,365,460

Required:

1. Prepare a combined single-step statement of income and retained earnings for the year.
2. Compute the percentage of gross profit on sales and the percentage of net income on sales.
3. The average stockholders' equity for the year was about $145 million. What was the percentage of net income on average stockholders' equity?

4-42. FOOD COMPANY FINANCIAL STATEMENTS. CPC International has annual sales that rank the company among the hundred largest U.S.-based industrial corporations and the ten largest food companies. Branded grocery products make up 58% of the company's sales: Hellmann's, Best Foods, Skippy, Mazola, Karo, and so forth. An annual report included the data shown below (in millions of dollars). Unless otherwise specified, the balance sheet amounts are the balances at the end of the year.

Net sales	$4,343	Cash	$ 30
Long-term debt	282	Cost of sales	3,112
Plants and properties	1,182	Financing costs	99
Selling, administrative		Accounts payable	184
and general expenses	495	Loans and notes payable	205
Inventories:		Temporary investments	
Beginning of year	636	(a current asset)	51
End of year	560	Provision for income taxes	146
Marketing and other expenses	273	Cash dividends declared	92
Retained earnings at		Prepaid expenses	15
beginning of year	950	Other assets	151
Notes and accounts receivable	473	Income taxes payable	85
Accrued expenses payable	210	Other noncurrent liabilities	238
Dividends payable	23		
Paid-in capital	159		

Required:

1. Prepare a combined multiple-step statement of income and retained earnings.
2. Prepare a classified balance sheet.
3. The average stockholders' equity for the year was about $1,171 million. What was the percentage of net income on average stockholders' equity?
4. Compute (a) gross profit percentage and (b) percentage of net income to sales.
5. Optional: Why might stockholders want to invest in a company with such a consistently low percentage of net income to sales?

4-43. PROFESSIONAL FOOTBALL INCOME. Examine the accompanying condensed income statement of the Green Bay Packers Inc. for a recent year.

Income:		
Regular season:		
Net receipts from home games	$ 3,223,803	
Out-of-town games	2,288,967	
Television and radio programs	14,322,244	$19,835,014
Preseason:		
Net receipts from preseason games	1,356,751	
Television and radio programs	355,032	1,711,783
Miscellaneous:		
Club allocation of league receipts	784,988	
Other income	511,516	1,296,504
Total income		22,843,301
Expenses:		
Salaries and other season expenses	16,243,729	
Training expense	725,079	
Overhead expense	4,744,336	
Severance pay	656,250	22,369,394
Income from operations		473,907
Interest income		1,203,281
Income before taxes		1,677,188
Provision for income taxes		167,000
Net income		$ 1,510,188

Required:
1. Do you agree with the choice of terms in this statement? If not, suggest where a preferable label should be used.
2. Is this a single-step income statement? If not, which items would you shift to prepare a single-step statement?
3. Identify the major factors that affect the Packers' net income.

4-44. HOUSE OF FABRICS ANNUAL REPORT. This problem uses some actual company's accounts to develop skill in preparing adjusting journal entries. Refer to the financial statements of House of Fabrics (pp. 752–759). Note the following balance sheet items:

	JANUARY 31	
	1989	1988
Prepaid expenses	$ 4,510,000	$ 4,127,000
Accrued liabilities	10,111,000	10,168,000

During the 1989 fiscal year, $24,100,000 cash was disbursed and charged to Prepaid Expenses. Similarly, $19,600,000 was distributed to reduce accrued liabilities.

Required:
1. Assume that the Prepaid Expenses account relates to outlays for miscellaneous operating expenses (for example, supplies, insurance, and short-term rentals). Prepare summary journal entries for (a) the disbursements and (b) the expenses (for our purposes, here debit Miscellaneous Operating Expenses) for fiscal 1989. Post the entries to the T-accounts.
2. Assume that the Accrued Liabilities account relates to obligations for store, operating, and interest expenses. Prepare summary journal entries for (a) the disbursements and (b) the expenses (debit Store, Operating and Interest Expenses) for fiscal 1989. Post the entries to the T-accounts.

Accounting Cycle: Recording and Formal Presentation

After studying this chapter, you should be able to

1. Explain the accounting cycle
2. Analyze and journalize transactions that relate to the adjustments of the preceding period
3. Prepare closing entries for pertinent accounts
4. Correct erroneous entries and describe how errors affect accounts
5. Use T-accounts to aid the discovery of unknown amounts
6. Use a work sheet to prepare adjustments, financial statements, and closing entries (Appendix 5A)
7. Prepare adjustments when alternative recording methods are used for the related originating transactions (Appendix 5B)

This chapter begins with a set of financial statements. It then shows in detail how this set—the accountant's and the manager's formal financial reports—has been produced. Thus our focus is on the final output of the accounting cycle and on the recording process rather than solely on the recording process.

Our illustrative company is the Oxley Company, a retailer of nursery products for lawns and gardens. To keep the data manageable for instructional purposes, many simplifying assumptions are made. Nevertheless, this illustration provides an opportunity to review the previous chapters, to see how assorted concepts tie together, to visualize the magnitude of the accounting information system, and to learn more about the techniques of recording and accumulating data.

COMPARATIVE FINANCIAL STATEMENTS

Exhibits 5–1, 5–2, and 5–3 display Oxley's balance sheet, income statement, and statement of retained income, respectively. These exhibits contain **comparative financial statements,** which present data for two or more reporting periods. The columnar format is usually favored. Note too that the most recent data are usually shown first; in a series of years, for instance, the oldest data would appear last. Publicly held corporations generally present comparative income statements for three years and balance sheets for two dates.

THE ACCOUNTING CYCLE

☐ Various Steps Taken

The **accounting cycle** is the several-stage process by which accountants produce an entity's financial statements for a specific period of time. Pause and study Exhibit 5–4, which shows the principal steps.

The steps in the accounting cycle can be enumerated more fully than shown in Exhibit 5–4. For example, the accountant frequently uses a work sheet (explained in Appendix 5A, pp. 182–187) to cope with the task of preparing the formal financial statements. Moreover, the cycle shown here is for a year, but it could occur monthly, quarterly, or for any other period as desired.

Consider the Oxley balance sheet for December 31, 19X1, as the start of our illustration of the accounting cycle. The following Oxley transactions, which are condensed here, occurred during 19X2 (amounts are in thousands):

a. Acquired merchandise inventory on account, $359.
b. Delivered merchandise to customers who had previously paid $5 in full in advance.

EXHIBIT 5–1   *(Place a clip on this page for easy reference.)*

OXLEY COMPANY
Balance Sheet (in thousands)

		DECEMBER 31	
ASSETS		19X2	19X1
Current assets:			
Cash		$150	$ 57
Accounts receivable		95	70
Accrued interest receivable		15	15
Inventory of merchandise		20	60
Prepaid rent		10	—
Total current assets		$290	$202
Long-term assets*			
Long-term note receivable		288	288

	DECEMBER 31	
	19X2	19X1
Equipment, at original cost	$200	$200
Deduct: Accumulated depreciation	120	80

		19X2	19X1
Equipment, net		80	120
Total asets		$658	$610

LIABILITIES AND STOCKHOLDERS' EQUITY

		19X2	19X1
Current liabilities:			
Accounts payable		$ 90	$ 65
Accrued wages payable		24	10
Accrued income taxes payable		16	12
Accrued interest payable		9	9
Unearned sales revenue		—	5
Note payable, current portion		80	—
Total current liabilities		$219	$101
Long-term note payable		40	120
Total liabilities		$259	$221
Stockholders' equity:			
Paid-in capital†		$102	$102
Retained income		297	287
Total stockholders' equity		$399	$389
Total liabilities and stockholders' equity		$658	$610

* This caption is frequently omitted. Instead the long-term note receivable, the equipment, and other categories are merely listed as separate items following the current assets.

† Details are often shown in a supplementary statement or in footnotes. In this case, there are 200,000 common shares outstanding: $.25 par per share, or 200,000 × $.25 = $50,000. Additional paid-in capital is $52,000, the total being $102,000 shown here.

EXHIBIT 5–2

OXLEY COMPANY
Statement of Income
(in thousands except earnings per share)

	FOR THE YEAR ENDED DECEMBER 31, 19X2		FOR THE YEAR ENDED DECEMBER 31, 19X1	
Sales		$999		$800
Cost of goods sold		399		336
Gross profit (or gross margin)		$600		$464
Operating expenses:				
Wages	$214		$150	
Rent	120		120	
Miscellaneous	100		50	
Depreciation	40	474	40	360
Operating income (or operating profit)		$126		$104
Other revenue and expense:				
Interest revenue	$ 36		$ 36	
Deduct: Interest expense	12	24	12	24
Income before income taxes		$150		$128
Income tax expense		60		48
Net income		$ 90		$ 80
Earnings per common share*		$ .45		$ .40

* Dividends per share, $.40 and $.20, respectively. For publicly held companies, there is a requirement to show earnings per share on the face of the income statement, but it is not necessary to show dividends per share. Calculations of earnings per share: $90,000 ÷ 200,000 = $.45, and $80,000 ÷ 200,000 = $.40.

EXHIBIT 5–3

OXLEY COMPANY
Statement of Retained Income
(in thousands)

	FOR THE YEAR ENDED DECEMBER 31	
	19X2	19X1
Retained income, beginning of year	$287	$247
Add: Net income	90	80
Total	$377	$327
Deduct: Dividends declared	80	40
Retained income, end of year	$297	$287

   c. Sales of merchandise (all on account and excluding transaction *b*) during 19X2 were $994.

   d. The cost of merchandise sold (including that in transaction *b*) during 19X2 was $399.

   e. Cash collected on account was $969.

   f. The note receivable was from a key industrial customer. The $288 principal is payable on August 1, 19X4. Interest of 12.5% per annum is collected each August 1 (to be computed).

EXHIBIT 5–4

Steps in Accounting Cycle

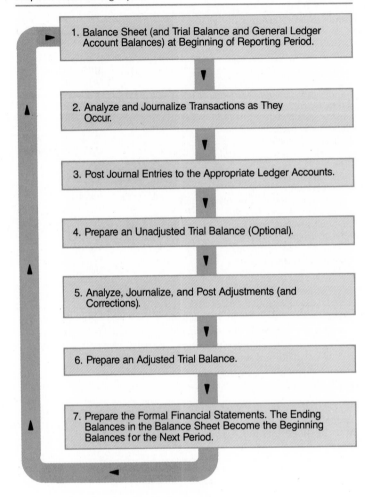

Cash was disbursed as follows for

g. Accounts payable, $334.

h. Wages, $200, including the $10 accrued in December 31, 19X1.

i. Income taxes, $56, including the $12 accrued on December 31, 19X1.

j. Interest on note payable, including the $9 accrued on December 31, 19X1. Interest of 10% per annum on the $120 principal is paid each March 31 (to be computed).

k. Rent, $130 for 13 months, which was debited to Prepaid Rent.

l. Miscellaneous expenses, $100.

m. Dividends, $80. A separate account called Dividends Declared was created. For simplicity, assume that declaration and payment occurred on the same day.

No interim statements were prepared, so no adjusting entries were made until December 31, 19X2, when the following were recognized:

n. Accrual of interest receivable (to be computed).

o. The disbursements for rent included $10 paid on December 31, 19X2, pertaining to the month of January 19X3.

p. Accrual of wages payable, $24.

q. Accrual of interest payable (to be computed).

r. Depreciation for 19X2, $40.

s. Two-thirds of the principal of the note payable is transferred to Note Payable, Current Portion, because two-thirds is due March 31, 19X3. The other third is payable on March 31, 19X5.

t. Accrual of income taxes payable. The total income tax expense for 19X2 is 40% of the income before income taxes (to be computed).

Required:

I. Prepare a general ledger in T-account form, entering the account balances of December 31, 19X1. Provide space for additional accounts.

II. Analyze and journalize all transactions for 19X2, including the year-end adjustments.

III. Post the entries in II to the T-accounts.

IV. Prepare an adjusted trial balance as of December 31, 19X2. If it fails to balance, check to see that all items were posted to the correct sides of the accounts.

V. Prepare a multiple-step income statement for 19X2.

VI. Prepare a statement of retained income for 19X2.

VII. Prepare a comparative classified balance sheet for December 31, 19X1 and 19X2.

VIII. Journalize and post the entries necessary to "close the books" for 19X2.

You are *urged* to try to solve requirements I–IV on your own before examining the solution. The general ledger (Parts I and III) is illustrated in Exhibit 5–6. The general journal (Part II) is illustrated in Exhibit 5–5. Note how the accounts are numbered. Posting and journalizing are keyed to facilitate cross-checking. The trial balance (Part IV) is illustrated in Exhibit 5–7.

Parts V through VII were illustrated in the preceding sections of this chapter: Exhibits 5–1, 5–2, and 5–3. Part VIII is described in the section entitled "Closing the Accounts."

☐ **Detailed Explanation of Parts I, II, and III**

Parts I, II, and III are covered in their entirety in Exhibits 5–5 and 5–6. Therefore many readers will find the following detailed step-by-step explanation (on pages 166–172) unnecessary. However, other readers prefer this transaction-by-transaction analysis. Why? Because it strengthens understanding by reviewing some fundamental concepts and procedures.

EXHIBIT 5–5

Journal Entries

Date	Entry No.	Accounts and Explanation	Post. Ref.	Debit	Credit
				(in thousands of dollars)	
19X2					
Dates are varied and are not entered in this illustration, except for Dec. 31	a	Inventory of merchandise	130	359	
		Accounts payable	200		359
		Acquired inventory on account			
	b	Unearned sales revenue	237	5	
		Sales	320		5
		Delivery of merchandise to customers who had paid in advance			
	c	Accounts receivable	110	994	
		Sales	320		994
		Sales on account			
	d	Cost of goods sold	340	399	
		Inventory of merchandise	130		399
		To record the cost of inventory sold			
	e	Cash	100	969	
		Accounts receivable	110		969
		Collections from customers			
	f	Cash	100	36	
		Accrued interest receivable	111		15
		Interest revenue	330		21
		Collection of interest (12.5% of $288 = $36)			
	g	Accounts payable	200	334	
		Cash	100		334
		Payments to creditors			
	h	Accrued wages payable	210	10	
		Wages expense	350	190	
		Cash	100		200
		Payments of wages			
	i	Accrued income taxes payable	220	12	
		Income tax expense	395	44	
		Cash	100		56
		Payments of income taxes			
	j	Accrued interest payable	230	9	
		Interest expense	380	3	
		Cash	100		12
		Payment of interest (10% of $120)			
	k	Prepaid rent	140	130	
		Cash	100		130
		Disbursements for rent			

EXHIBIT 5–5   (continued)

Date	Entry No.	Accounts and Explanation	Post. Ref.	Debit	Credit
				(in thousands of dollars)	
19X2					
	l	Miscellaneous expenses	364	100	
		Cash	100		100
		Disbursements for miscellaneous expense items such as utilities, repairs, etc.			
	m	Dividends declared	310A	80	
		Cash	100		80
		Declaration and payment of dividends			
		Year-End Adjusting Entries			
Dec. 31	n	Accrued interest receivable	111	15	
		Interest revenue	330		15
		Accrual of interest for five months at 12.5% on $288: (12.5%) ($288) (5/12) = $15			
Dec. 31	o	Rent expense	360	120	
		Prepaid rent	140		120
		To record 19X2 rent expense at $10 per month. (Note that this leaves a $10 debit balance in Prepaid Rent for January, 19X3.)			
Dec. 31	p	Wages expense	350	24	
		Accrued wages payable	210		24
		To recognize wages accrued but unpaid at December 31, 19X2			
Dec. 31	q	Interest expense	380	9	
		Accrued interest payable	230		9
		Accrual of interest for nine months at 10% on $120: (10%) ($120) (9/12) = 9			
Dec. 31	r	Depreciation expense	370	40	
		Accumulated depreciation, equipment	170A		40
		To record depreciation for 19X2.			
Dec. 31	s	Long-term note payable	280	80	
		Note payable, current	240		80
		To reclassify $80 as a current liability			
Dec. 31	t	Income tax expense	395	16	
		Accrued income tax payable	220		16
		To record the income tax expense, which is 40% of the income before income taxes, or .40 × $150 = $60. (Of this amount, $44 has already been paid and charged to expense in entry i, leaving $16 of expense accrued but not paid.)			

EXHIBIT 5-6

GENERAL LEDGER OF OXLEY COMPANY

ASSETS
(Increases Left, Decreases Right)

Cash — Account No. 100

Bal.*	57	(g)	334
(e)	969	(h)	200
(f)	36	(i)	56
		(j)	12
		(k)	130
		(l)	100
		(m)	80
	1,062		912
†	150		

Accounts Receivable — 110

*	70	(e)	969
(c)	994		
†	95		

Accrued Interest Receivable — 111

*	15	(f)	15
(n)	15		
†	15		

LIABILITIES + STOCKHOLDERS' EQUITY
(Decreases Left, Increases Right)

Accounts Payable — 200

(g)	334	*	65
		(a)	359
		†	90

Accrued Wages Payable — 210

(h)	10	*	10
		(p)	24
		†	24

Accrued Income Taxes Payable — 220

(i)	12	*	12
		(t)	16
		†	16

Accrued Interest Payable — 230

(j)	9	*	9
		(q)	9
		†	9

Unearned Sales Revenue — 237

(b)	5	*	5
		†	0

Note Payable, Current Portion — 240

		*	80
		(s)	80
		†	80

Long-Term Note Payable — 280

(s)	80	*	120
		†	40

Dividends Declared — 310A

(m)	80

Paid-In Capital — 300

		*	102
		†	102

Retained Income — 310

		*	287

Inventory of Merchandise 130

* 60	(d) 399
(a) 359	
† 20	

Cost of Goods Sold 340

(d) 399	

Wages Expense 350

(h) 190	
(p) 24	

Sales 320

	(b) 5
	(c) 994

Prepaid Rent 140

(k) 130	(o) 120
† 10	

Rent Expense 360

(o) 120	

Miscellaneous Expense 364

(l) 100	

Long-Term Note Receivable 160

* 288	
† 288	

Interest Expense 380

(j) 3	
(q) 9	

Interest Revenue 330

	(f) 21
	(n) 15

Equipment 170

* 200	
† 200	

Accumulated Depreciation, Equipment 170A

	* 80
	(r) 40
	† 120

Depreciation Expense 370

(r) 40	

Income Tax Expense 395

(l) 44	
(t) 16	

* All amounts denoted with an asterisk are balances, December 31, 19X1.
† Balances drawn and carried forward to below the double underlines, December 31, 19X2.

165

EXHIBIT 5–7

OXLEY COMPANY
Adjusted Trial Balance
December 31, 19X2 (in thousands)

Cash	$ 150	
Accounts receivable	95	
Accrued interest receivable	15	
Inventory of merchandise	20	
Prepaid rent	10	
Long-term note receivable	288	
Equipment	200	
Accumulated depreciation, equipment		$ 120
Accounts payable		90
Accrued wages payable		24
Accrued income taxes payable		16
Accrued interest payable		9
Note payable, current portion		80
Long-term note payable		40
Paid-in capital		102
Retained income, December 31, 19X1		287
Dividends declared	80	
Sales		999
Interest revenue		36
Cost of goods sold	399	
Wages expense	214	
Rent expense	120	
Miscellaneous expense	100	
Depreciation expense	40	
Interest expense	12	
Income tax expense	60	
	$1,803	$1,803

DETAILED ANALYSIS OF TRANSACTIONS

a. Transaction: Acquired merchandise inventory on account, $359.

Analysis: The asset **Inventory of Merchandise** is increased.
The liability **Accounts Payable** is increased.

Entry: In the journal (explanation omitted):

Inventory of merchandise	359	
Accounts payable		359

Post to the ledger (postings are indicated by the circled amounts):

Inventory of Merchandise*			Accounts Payable	
Bal.	60		Bal.	65
(a)	⃝359		(a)	⃝359

* Also often called Merchandise Inventory, or if it is the only type of inventory account, it is
simply called Inventory.

b. Transaction: Delivered merchandise to customers who had previously paid $5.

     Analysis: The liability **Unearned Sales Revenue** is decreased.
               The stockholders' equity **Sales** is increased.

        Entry: In the journal:

Unearned sales revenue	5	
Sales		5

Post to the ledger:

Unearned Sales Revenue		Sales	
(b) 5	Bal. 5		(b) 5

c. Transaction: Sales of merchandise on account, $994.

     Analysis: The asset **Accounts Receivable** is increased.
               The stockholders' equity **Sales** is increased.

        Entry: In the journal:

Accounts receivable	994	
Sales		994

Post to the ledger:

Accounts Receivable		Sales	
Bal. 70			(b) 5
(c) 994			(c) 994

d. Transaction: The cost of merchandise sold, $399.

     Analysis: The Asset **Inventory of Merchandise** is decreased.
               The negative stockholders' equity **Cost of Goods Sold** is increased.

               Recall that all expense accounts are reductions in stockholders' equity; thus expense accounts can properly be regarded as negative stockholders' equity.

        Entry: In the journal:

Cost of goods sold	399	
Inventory of merchandise		399

Post to the ledger:

Inventory of Merchandise		Cost of Goods Sold	
Bal. 60	(d) 399	(d) 399	
(a) 359			

e. Transaction: Cash collected on account from customers, $969.

     Analysis: The asset **Cash** is increased.
               The asset **Accounts Receivable** is decreased.

        Entry: In the journal:

Cash	969	
Accounts receivable		969

Post to the ledger:

Cash		Accounts Receivable	
Bal. 57		Bal. 70	(e) 969
(e) 969		(c) 994	

f. Transaction: Collection of interest on August 1, 12.5% of $288 = $36.

Analysis: The asset **Cash** is increased.
The asset **Accrued Interest Receivable** is decreased.
The stockholders' equity **Interest Revenue** is increased.
Interest revenue earned is $36 ÷ 12 = $3 per month. Seven months × $3 = $21. The $15 decrease in Accrued Interest Receivable pertains to revenue earned during the preceding year.

Entry: In the journal:

Cash	36	
Accrued interest receivable		15
Interest revenue		21

Post to the ledger:

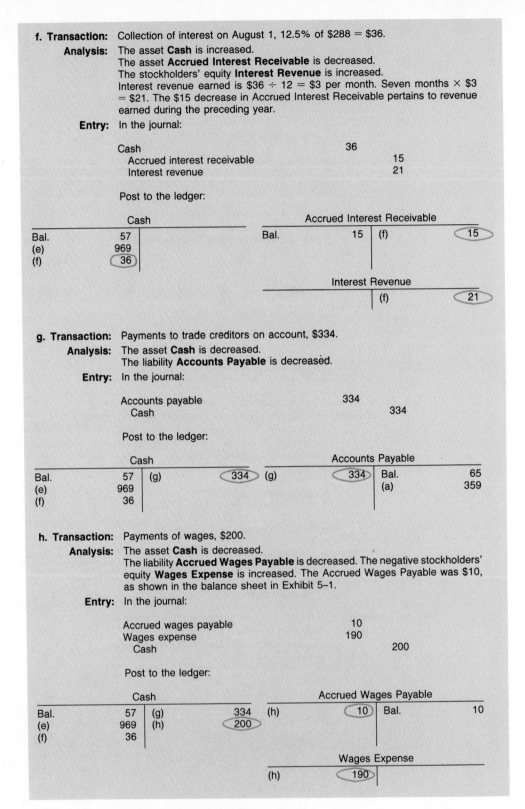

Cash				Accrued Interest Receivable			
Bal.	57			Bal.	15	(f)	15
(e)	969						
(f)	36						

Interest Revenue		
	(f)	21

g. Transaction: Payments to trade creditors on account, $334.

Analysis: The asset **Cash** is decreased.
The liability **Accounts Payable** is decreased.

Entry: In the journal:

Accounts payable	334	
Cash		334

Post to the ledger:

Cash				Accounts Payable			
Bal.	57	(g)	334	(g)	334	Bal.	65
(e)	969					(a)	359
(f)	36						

h. Transaction: Payments of wages, $200.

Analysis: The asset **Cash** is decreased.
The liability **Accrued Wages Payable** is decreased. The negative stockholders' equity **Wages Expense** is increased. The Accrued Wages Payable was $10, as shown in the balance sheet in Exhibit 5–1.

Entry: In the journal:

Accrued wages payable	10	
Wages expense	190	
Cash		200

Post to the ledger:

Cash				Accrued Wages Payable			
Bal.	57	(g)	334	(h)	10	Bal.	10
(e)	969	(h)	200				
(f)	36						

Wages Expense		
(h)	190	

i. Transaction: Payments of income taxes, $56.

  Analysis: The asset **Cash** is decreased.
The liability **Accrued Income Taxes Payable** is decreased.
The negative stockholders' equity **Income Tax Expense** is increased. The payable was $12, as shown in the balance sheet in Exhibit 5–1.

  Entry: In the journal:

Accrued income taxes payable	12	
Income tax expense	44	
Cash		56

Post to the ledger:

Cash					Accrued Income Taxes Payable		
Bal.	57	(g)	334	(i)	12	Bal.	12
(e)	969	(h)	200				
(f)	36	(i)	56				

		Income Tax Expense	
(i)		44	

j. Transaction: Payment of interest on March 31, 10% of $120 = $12.

  Analysis: The asset **Cash** is decreased.
The liability **Accrued Interest Payable** is decreased. The negative stock-holders' equity **Interest Expense** is increased. Interest expense is $12 ÷ 12 = $1 per month; three months × $1 = $3. The $9 decrease in Accrued Interest Payable pertains to interest expense during the preceding year.

  Entry: In the journal:

Accrued interest payable	9	
Interest expense	3	
Cash		12

Post to the ledger:

Cash					Accrued Interest Payable		
Bal.	57	(g)	334	(j)	9	Bal.	9
(e)	969	(h)	200				
(f)	36	(i)	56				
		(j)	12				

		Interest Expense	
(j)		3	

k. Transaction: Payment of rent, $130.

  Analysis: The asset **Cash** is decreased.
The asset **Prepaid Rent** is increased.

  Entry: In the journal:

Prepaid rent	130	
Cash		130

Post to the ledger:

Cash					Prepaid Rent	
Bal.	57	(g)	334	(k)	130	
(e)	969	(h)	200			
(f)	36	(i)	56			
		(j)	12			
		(k)	130			

l. Transaction: Payment of miscellaneous expenses, $100.

Analysis: The asset **Cash** is decreased.
The negative stockholders' equity **Miscellaneous Expense** is increased.

Entry: In the journal:

Miscellaneous expense	100	
Cash		100

Post to the ledger:

Cash				Miscellaneous Expense	
Bal.	57	(g)	334	(l)	100
(e)	969	(h)	200		
(f)	36	(i)	56		
		(j)	12		
		(k)	130		
		(l)	100		

m. Transaction: Dividends declared and paid, $80.

Analysis: The asset **Cash** is decreased.
The negative stockholders' equity **Dividends Declared** (an offsetting account to Retained Income) is increased.

Entry: In the journal:

Dividends declared	80	
Cash		80

Post to the ledger:

Cash				Dividends Declared	
Bal.	57	(g)	334	(m)	80
(e)	969	(h)	200		
(f)	36	(i)	56		
		(j)	12		
		(k)	130		
		(l)	100		
		(m)	80		

n. Transaction: Accrual of interest receivable for 5 months × $3 = $15.

Analysis: The asset **Accrued Interest Receivable** is increased.
The stockholders' equity **Interest Revenue** is increased.

Entry: In the journal:

Accrued interest receivable	15	
Interest revenue		15

Post to the ledger:

Accrued Interest Receivable				Interest Revenue	
Bal.	15	(f)	15	(f)	21
(n)	15			(n)	15

o. Transaction: Recognition of rent expense.

Analysis: All prepaid rent has expired except for $10 for the month of January 19X3.
The asset **Prepaid Rent** is decreased.
The negative stockholders' equity **Rent Expense** is increased.

Entry: In the journal:

| Rent expense | 120 | |
| Prepaid rent | | 120 |

Post to the ledger:

Prepaid Rent			Rent Expense	
(k)	130	(o)	120	(o)	120

p. Transaction: Accrual of wages payable, $24.

Analysis: The liability **Accrued Wages Payable** is increased.
The negative stockholders' equity **Wages Expense** is increased.

Entry: In the journal:

| Wages expense | 24 | |
| Accrued wages payable | | 24 |

Post to the ledger:

Accrued Wages Payable			Wages Expense	
(h)	190	Bal.	10	(h)	190
		(p)	24	(p)	24

q. Transaction: Accrual of interest payable for 9 months × $1 = $9.

Analysis: The liability **Accrued Interest Payable** is increased.
The negative stockholders' equity **Interest Expense** is increased.

Entry: In the journal:

| Interest expense | 9 | |
| Accrued interest payable | | 9 |

Post to the ledger:

Accrued Interest Payable			Interest Expense	
(j)	9	Bal.	9	(j)	3
		(q)	9	(q)	9

r. Transaction: Depreciation, $40.

Analysis: The asset reduction account **Accumulated Depreciation, Equipment** is increased.
The negative stockholders' equity **Depreciation Expense** is increased.

Entry: In the journal:

| Depreciation expense | 40 | |
| Accumulated depreciation, equipment | | 40 |

Accumulated Depreciation, Equipment			Depreciation Expense	
	Bal.	80	(r)	40
	(r)	40		

s. Transaction: Reclassification of note payable ⅔ × $120 = $80.

Analysis: The liability **Long-term Note Payable** is decreased.
The liability **Note Payable, Current** portion is increased.

Entry: In the journal:

| Long-term note payable | 80 | |
| Note payable, current | | 80 |

Post to the ledger:

Long-term Note Payable				Note Payable, Current	
(s)	80	Bal.	120	(s)	80

t. Transaction: Income tax expense for the year. Income before taxes must be computed and then 40% thereof recognized as expense (.40 × $150 = $60). Moreover, the accrued liability must be accurate. Therefore, because $44 has already been paid for the current year and charged to expense (see Transaction i), the amount remaining ($60 − $44 = $16) must be charged to expense.

Analysis: The liability **Accrued Income Taxes Payable** is increased.
The negative stockholders' equity **Income Tax Expense** is increased.

Entry: In the journal:

Income tax expense	16	
Accrued income taxes payable		16

Accrued Income Taxes Payable				Income Tax Expense	
(i)	12	Bal.	12	(i)	44
		(t)	16	(t)	16

AFTERMATH OF ADJUSTMENTS

Entries for interest, wages, income taxes, and other accruals (for example, see f, h, i, and j) have a common theme: Beware of the transactions that relate to the adjustments of the preceding period. The explicit subsequent transaction involves a cash inflow or outflow. Part of each cash flow in this example relates to the accrual made at the end of 19X1. Why be concerned? Because failure to remember the accruals may result in double-counting of expenses (or revenues). A common error, for instance, would be to recognize the entire $12,000 disbursement for interest in entry j as an expense of 19X2, whereas $9,000 was already recognized as an expense in 19X1 and is properly charged in entry j to the liability account *Accrued Interest Payable*.

DIVIDENDS DECLARED

A corporation must declare a dividend before paying it. The board of directors alone has the authority to declare a dividend. The corporation has no obligation to pay a dividend unless the board declares one; however, when declared, the dividend becomes a legal liability of the corporation.

The overall approach to accounting for cash dividends was explained in Chapter 2, page 52. As shown there, some companies reduce Retained Income directly when their board of directors declares dividends. However, as shown in transaction m in Exhibits 5–5 and 5–6, other companies prefer to use a separate "temporary" stockholders' equity account (Dividends Declared or simply Dividends) to compile the cumulative amounts of the dividends for a given year. Publicly held companies generally declare dividends quarterly.

Oxley's transaction *m* summarized the overall effect of $80,000 dividend payments throughout the year. In the real world, $20,000 would have been declared and paid quarterly. The declaration is usually made on one date, and the payment follows declaration by a few weeks. Oxley would have made the following entries for the first quarter, specific dates assumed:

February 10	Dividends declared	20	
	Dividends payable		20
	To record quarterly declaration of dividends.		
February 27	Dividends payable	20	
	Cash		20
	To record payment of dividends.		

Dividends Payable is a current liability. If a balance sheet is prepared between the date of declaration and the date of payment, Dividends Payable will be listed with the other current liabilities.

Consider another example. The journal entry for the quarterly dividend recently declared by Chrysler Corporation would be:

Dividends declared	55,304,238	
Dividends payable		55,304,238
To record declaration of $.25 per share dividend on 221,216,951 shares.		

The Dividends Declared account will have a normal left-side balance. It represents a reduction in Retained Income and stockholders' equity.

CLOSING THE ACCOUNTS

☐ **Transferring and Summarizing**

Accountants often use the term **closing the books** to refer to the final step taken at the end of a *given* year to facilitate the recording of the *next* year's transactions. The step is called *closing,* but *transferring and summarizing* or *clearing* are better labels. Why? Because all balances in the "temporary" stockholders' equity accounts are summarized and transferred to a "permanent" stockholders' equity account, Retained Income. **Closing entries** transfer the revenues, expenses, and dividends balances from their respective accounts to the retained income account.

When the closing entries are completed, the current revenue, expense, and dividends accounts have zero balances. Closing is a clerical procedure. It is devoid of any new accounting theory. Its main purpose is to set the revenue and expense meters back to zero so that those accounts can be used afresh in the new year. For instance, without the closing process the sales account of a business like Shell Oil would continue to cumulate revenue, so that the balance would be the sum of many years of sales rather than only one year of sales.

Exhibit 5–8 shows the general effects of the closing (transferring) process, using numbers from our illustration. How does the debit-credit process accomplish this summarizing and transferring?

Step 1. An Income Summary account, which has a life of one day (or an instant), is often created. As Exhibit 5–8 indicates, the Income Summary account is a convenience. However, it is not absolutely necessary; many accountants prefer to accomplish the entire closing process by a single (massive) compound entry to Retained Income.

EXHIBIT 5–8

General Effects of Closing the Accounts (Data are from Exhibit 5–6, p. 164)

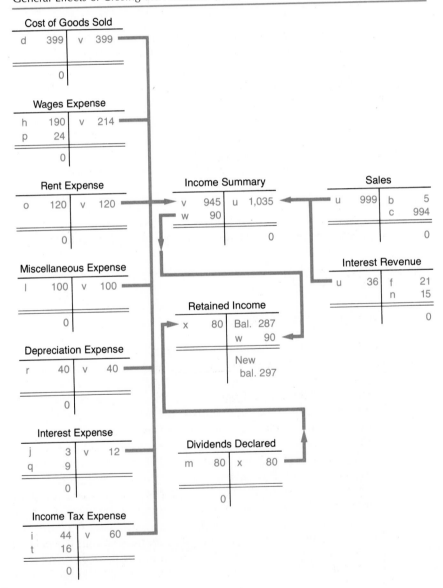

Step 2. The credit balances of the revenue accounts are debited in entry *u* in Exhibit 5–8. The balances in Sales and Interest Revenue are now zero. They have been "closed." Their meters are back to zero, but their amounts have not vanished. Instead the amounts now rest in aggregate form as a credit in Income Summary.

Step 3. The debit balances of the expense accounts are credited, as shown in entry *v*. Their individual amounts also now reside in aggregate form as a debit in Income Summary.

Step 4. The net income is computed and transferred from Income Summary to its "permanent" home, Retained Income, as shown in entry *w*.

Step 5. The Dividends Declared account is then closed directly to Retained Income, as shown in entry *x*. Note that the Income Summary account is *not* used for closing the Dividends account. Why? Because dividends are not expenses and do not affect net income.

At the end of Step 5, the Retained Income account has been brought up to date. The books (the journal and ledger) are now ready for a new year. Exhibit 5–8 presents zero balances for all affected accounts except for Retained Income. In practice, these zero balances are not specifically shown. They appear in Exhibit 5–8 and in the following detailed explanations to emphasize the fundamental purpose of the closing process—setting the revenue and expense meters back to zero.

☐ Detailed Explanation of Closing

The following entries and explanations provide a more detailed description of the closing process that has been summarized in Exhibit 5–8:

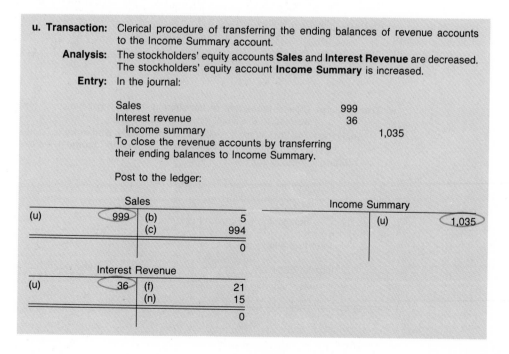

u. Transaction: Clerical procedure of transferring the ending balances of revenue accounts to the Income Summary account.

Analysis: The stockholders' equity accounts **Sales** and **Interest Revenue** are decreased. The stockholders' equity account **Income Summary** is increased.

Entry: In the journal:

Sales	999	
Interest revenue	36	
Income summary		1,035

To close the revenue accounts by transferring their ending balances to Income Summary.

Post to the ledger:

Sales					Income Summary		
(u)	999	(b)	5			(u)	1,035
		(c)	994				
			0				

Interest Revenue			
(u)	36	(f)	21
		(n)	15
			0

v. Transaction: Clerical procedure of transferring the ending balances of expense accounts to the Income Summary account.

Analysis: The negative stockholders' equity accounts **Cost of Goods Sold, Wages Expense**, etc., are decreased. The stockholders' equity account **Income Summary** is decreased.

Entry: In the journal:

Income summary	945	
Cost of goods sold		399
Wages expense		214
Rent expense		120
Miscellaneous expense		100
Depreciation expense		40
Interest expense		12
Income tax expense		60

To close the expense accounts by transferring their ending balances to Income Summary.

Post to the ledger:

Cost of Goods Sold				Income Summary			
(d)	399	(v)	399	(v)	945	(u)	1,035
	0						

Rent Expense				Wages Expense			
(o)	120	(v)	120	(h)	190	(v)	214
				(p)	24		
	0				0		

Depreciation Expense				Miscellaneous Expense			
(r)	40	(v)	40	(l)	100	(v)	100
	0				0		

Interest Expense				Income Tax Expense			
(j)	3	(v)	12	(i)	44	(v)	60
(q)	9			(t)	16		
	0				0		

w. Transaction: Clerical procedure of transferring the ending balance of Income Summary account to the Retained Income account.

Analysis: The stockholders' equity account **Income Summary** is decreased.
The stockholders' equity account **Retained Income** is increased.

Entry: In the journal:

Income summary	90	
Retained income		90

To close Income Summary by transferring net income to Retained Income.

Post to the ledger:

Income Summary				Retained Income			
(v)	945	(u)	1,035			Bal.	287
(w)	90					(w)	90
			0				

x. Transaction: Clerical procedure of transferring the ending balance of Dividends Declared to the Retained Income account.

Analysis: The negative stockholders' equity account **Dividends Declared** is decreased. The stockholders' equity account **Retained Income** is decreased.

Entry: In the journal:

Retained Income	80	
Dividends declared		80
To close Dividends Declared by transferring the ending balance to Retained Income.		

Post to the ledger:

Dividends Declared				Retained Income		
(m) 80	(x) 80	(x)	80	Bal.	287
				(w)	90
0				Bal.	297

Terminology of Types of Accounts

Accounts that are subjected to periodic closing are frequently called **temporary** (also called **nominal**) accounts, as distinguished from **permanent** (also called **real**) accounts. The temporary (nominal) accounts are the revenues, expenses, and dividends declared. They are all really subparts of ownership equity. They are created to provide a detailed explanation for the changes in retained income from period to period. They are the ingredients of the income statement and the statement of retained income.

In contrast, the permanent (real) accounts are the balance sheet accounts. The word *permanent* may be misleading. After all, the balances of permanent (real) accounts fluctuate. Moreover, some permanent accounts come and go. For example, unearned sales revenue appears on Oxley's balance sheet of December 31, 19X1, but not December 31, 19X2.

COMPUTERS AND THE ACCOUNTING CYCLE

Professionally prepared computer programs (called *software*) can do all the steps in the accounting cycle except generate the numbers for initial journal entries and for many adjusting entries.

The details of computer systems are beyond the scope of this book. However, their presence has made many time-honored manual accounting methods obsolete. For example, the entire "closing the books" process, including the use of Income Summary accounts, becomes obsolete when computers merely remove the old balances in revenue and expense accounts and automatically transfer the resulting net income to a Retained Income account. Furthermore, an ordinary journal is unnecessary if a computer can indefinitely store the effects of accounting transactions in its memory and print an analysis of any transaction upon command.

So-called spreadsheet computer programs are widely used. They provide accountants with a trial balance on an "electronic" work sheet. Any adjustments or corrections are entered into a computer, which automatically changes the trial balance and the resulting financial statements. As you can imagine, accountants save considerable time. For a short description of an electronic work sheet, see page 186.

EFFECTS OF ERRORS

☐ Incorrect Journal Entries

When a journal entry contains an error, the entry can be erased and corrected— if the error is discovered immediately. Some accountants prefer to draw a line through the incorrect entry and thus preserve a record of all journal entries. After the incorrect entry has been crossed out, the accountant can make the correct entry.

However, if the error is detected later, typically after posting to ledger accounts, the accountant makes a *correcting entry*, as distinguished from a correct entry. Consider the following examples:

1. A repair expense was erroneously debited to Equipment on December 27. The error is discovered on December 31:

ERRONEOUS ENTRY, 12/27			CORRECTING ENTRY, 12/31		
Equipment	500		Repair expense	500	
Cash		500	Equipment		500

The correcting entry shows a credit to Equipment to cancel or offset the erroneous debit to Equipment. Moreover, the entry debits Repair Expense correctly.

2. A collection on account was erroneously credited to Sales on November 2. The error is discovered on November 28:

ERRONEOUS ENTRY, 11/2			CORRECTING ENTRY, 11/28		
Cash	3,000		Sales	3,000	
Sales		3,000	Accounts receivable		3,000

The debit to Sales in the correcting entry offsets the incorrect credit to Sales in the erroneous entry. The credit to Accounts Receivable in the correcting entry places the collected amount where it belongs.

☐ Some Errors Counterbalanced

Accountants' errors affect a variety of items, including revenues and expenses for a given period. Some errors are counterbalanced by offsetting errors in the ordinary bookkeeping process in the next period. Such errors misstate net income in both periods; they also affect the balance sheet of the first period but not the second.

Consider the failure to make an adjustment for accrued wages at the end of 19X1:

	Incorrect Entry			Correct Entry		
12/31/X1	Omit adjustment for accrued wages payable			Wages expense Accrued wages payable	1,000	1,000

During 19X2	Wages expense
	    Cash
	Entry on payroll date.
		1,000	1,000	Accrued wages payable
				    Cash
				Entry on payroll date.
					1,000	1,000

The effects of this counterbalancing error would (a) for the first year, over-state pretax income and understate year-end liabilities by $1,000 and (b) for the second year, understate income by $1,000 and have no effect on year-end lia-bilities. The *total* of the incorrect pretax incomes for the two years would be identical with the *total* of the correct pretax incomes for the two years. The retained income balance at the end of the second year would be correct on a pretax basis.

☐ **Some Errors Not Counterbalanced**

Accountants' errors that are undetected affect a variety of accounts. As we have just seen, some errors may be counterbalanced in the ordinary course of the next period's transactions. However, other errors may not be counterbalanced in the ordinary bookkeeping process. Until specific correcting entries are made, all subsequent balance sheets will be in error.

For example, overlooking a depreciation expense of $2,000 in *one year only* (a) would overstate pretax income, assets, and retained income by $2,000 in that year, and (b) would continue to overstate assets and retained earnings on suc-cessive balance sheets for the life of the fixed asset. But observe that pretax income for each subsequent year would not be affected unless the same error is committed again.

INCOMPLETE RECORDS

Accountants must sometimes construct financial statements from incomplete data. For example, documents may be stolen, destroyed, or lost. Moreover, many instructors believe that students reinforce their understanding of underlying concepts by solving problems that contain a variety of disorganized and frag-mentary data.

T-accounts help organize an accountant's thinking and aid the discovery of unknown amounts. For example, suppose the proprietor of a local sports shop asks you to prepare an income statement for 19X2. She provides the following accurate but incomplete information:

List of customers who owe money:	
December 31, 19X1	$ 4,000
December 31, 19X2	6,000
Cash receipts from customers during 19X2, appropriately credited to customers' accounts	280,000

You want to compute revenue (sales) on the accrual basis. Assume that all sales were made on account. Shortcuts may be available, but the following steps demonstrate a general approach to the reconstruction of incomplete accounts:

Step 1: Enter all known items into the key T-account. Knowledge of the usual components of such an account is essential. Let S equal sales on account:

Accounts Receivable			
Bal. 12/31/X1	4,000	Collections	280,000
Sales	S		
Total debits	(4,000 + S)	Total credits	280,000
Bal. 12/31/X2	6,000		

Step 2: Find the unknown. Simple arithmetic will often suffice; however, the following solution illustrates the algebraic nature of the relationships in an asset T-account:

$$\text{Total debits} - \text{Total credits} = \text{Balance}$$
$$(4{,}000 + S) - 280{,}000 = 6{,}000$$
$$S = 6{,}000 + 280{,}000 - 4{,}000$$
$$S = 282{,}000$$

Obviously, the analyses become more complicated if more entries have affected a particular account. Nevertheless, the key idea is to fill in the account with all known debits, credits, and balances. Then solve for the unknown.

SUMMARY

Comparative and classified financial statements help readers detect changes in key account balances and ratios.

The accounting cycle refers to the recording process that leads from the beginning to the ending financial statements. Closing the accounts is a clerical procedure that aids the periodic compilation of revenues and expenses and the start of a new accounting cycle.

The steps in the accounting cycle can be enumerated in different ways. For example:

1. Begin with the general ledger balances at the start of the reporting period.
2. Analyze and journalize transactions as they occur.

3. Post journal entries to the appropriate ledger accounts.

4. Prepare an unadjusted trial balance (optional).

5. Analyze, journalize, and post adjustments and corrections.

6. Prepare an adjusted trial balance.

7. Prepare the formal financial statements.

8. Prepare closing journal entries and post them so that the ledger is ready for the new accounting cycle.

SUMMARY PROBLEMS FOR YOUR REVIEW

☐ Problem One

Review the transactions for the Oxley Company during 19X2. Suppose wages expense accrued but unpaid at the end of 19X2 were $34 instead of $24. What numbers would be changed on the income statement for 19X2 and on the balance sheet, December 31, 19X2? What would be the new numbers? The financial statements are on pages 158–159.

☐ Solution to Problem One

	FOR THE YEAR ENDED DECEMBER 31, 19X2	
INCOME STATEMENT ACCOUNTS	As in Exhibit 5–2	Revised
Wages expense	$214	$224
Income before income taxes	150	140
Income tax expense (at 40%)	60	56
Net income	90	84
	DECEMBER 31, 19X2	
BALANCE SHEET ACCOUNTS	As in Exhibit 5–1	Revised
Accrued wages payable	$ 24	$ 34
Accrued income taxes payable	16	12
Retained income	297	291

Note the effects on the year-end balance sheet. Retained income would be decreased by $6, and total liabilities would be increased by a net of $6. Accrued wages increase by $10, but accrued income taxes decrease by $4 (40% of the $10 decrease in income before taxes).

☐ Problem Two

The balance sheet of Holiday Inns showed Accrued Interest of $18,558,000 under current liabilities at the beginning of a recent year. Interest payments of $98 million were disbursed during the year. Prepare the journal entry that summarizes those disbursements.

Accrued interest	18,558,000	
Interest expense	79,442,000	
Cash		98,000,000
To record disbursements for interest; interest expense is $98,000,000 less $18,558,000, or $79,442,000.		

The nomenclature used here illustrates why beginners in accounting should be alert to how the account description is used by a particular entity. That is, the term *Accrued Interest* is basically unclear. Does it mean *receivable or payable*? The answer is obvious in the annual report of Holiday Inns because the account is classified as a current liability. But some other company may use the same term, *Accrued Interest*, to describe a receivable. Hence, for clarity this textbook generally uses *accrued interest receivable* or *accrued interest payable* rather than *accrued interest* alone.

HIGHLIGHTS TO REMEMBER

1. Beginners in accounting often err by ignoring the effects on the current period of adjustments that were made at the end of the preceding period.
2. T-accounts help organize thinking and aid in the discovery of unknown amounts. The key idea is to fill in the related accounts with all known debits, credits, and balances. Then solve for the unknown amounts.

ACCOUNTING VOCABULARY

Accounting Cycle, p. 157
Closing Entries, p. 173
Closing the Books, p. 173
Comparative Financial Statements, p. 157
Nominal Accounts, p. 177
Permanent Accounts, p. 177

Real Accounts, p. 177
Reversing Entries, p. 189
Temporary Accounts, p. 177
Working Paper, p. 182
Work Sheet, p. 182

APPENDIX 5A: THE WORK SHEET

Purpose of Work Sheet

The body of this chapter described the rudiments of the accounting cycle. This appendix explores the cycle in more detail by explaining a favorite tool of the accountant. The **work sheet** (also called a **working paper**) is a columnar approach to moving from a trial balance to the finished financial statements. It provides an orderly means for (a) preparing adjusting entries, (b) computing net income, (c) preparing the formal financial statements, and (d) closing the books.

Although a work sheet is not essential to obtaining financial statements, it is a valuable informal device for bringing everything together in a single place, especially when there are numerous accounts and year-end adjustments. It helps assure the accountant that potential errors and overlooked adjustments will be discovered.

For learning purposes, the work sheet is usually prepared with a pencil. However, as already mentioned, accountants typically use the electronic spreadsheets for work sheets, as discussed at the end of this appendix.

☐ Steps in Preparation

Because the work sheet is an informal tool, there is no unique way of preparing it. However, a typical work sheet is illustrated in Exhibit 5–9. A step-by-step description of its preparation follows.

1. In the body of the chapter we focused on an adjusted trial balance, which was prepared *after* the adjusting entries had been made. Frequently, however, the accountant initially prepares an "unadjusted" trial balance as the first pair of columns in the work sheet. Then adjustments are entered in the second pair of columns. This provides a systematic and convenient way of reviewing the unadjusted trial balance together with the adjustments to make sure that nothing is overlooked.

The numbers in the first pair of columns come from the balances in the general ledger in Exhibit 5–6 *after* the last entry for the period's transactions (entry *m*) but *before* the first entry for the end-of-period adjustments (entry *n*). This preparation of the unadjusted trial balance provides a check on the general accuracy of the ledger *before* adjustments are entered. Thus it provides an early chance to catch errors. The frequent use of self-checks as detailed work proceeds may seem unnecessary. Nevertheless, as students and practicing accountants will testify, time is inevitably saved in doing the complete job. Few accounting tasks are more maddening than trying to trace an error discovered at a final stage back through a maze of interrelated journal entries and ledgers.

Concentrate on the first pair of columns, the Unadjusted Trial Balance. Many accounts are listed in their appropriate locations even though they have zero balances (for example, Accrued Wages Payable). Why? Because through experience the accountant knows that such accounts are almost always affected by the adjustment process. Listing all the accounts can help avoid overlooking required adjustments. However, inasmuch as the work sheet is an informal document, some accountants prefer first to list only the accounts with balances and later to list the additional accounts (below the $1,699 total in this illustration) when adjustments are made.

2. The second pair of columns is used for preparing the adjusting entries *n* through *t*. These columns are also totaled as a check on accuracy.

3. After the adjustments have been made, the third pair of columns represents the net effects of the first pair plus the second pair. That is, the unadjusted trial balance plus the adjustments equals the adjusted trial balance. Note how check after check is built into the work sheet.

4. The fourth pair of columns provides an income statement; the fifth pair, a statement of retained income; the sixth pair, a balance sheet. By tracing the numbers in those columns to the formal statements in Exhibits 5–1, 5–2, and 5–3 (pp. 158–159), you can readily see how a work sheet can aid the preparation of the formal statements, especially when there are numerous accounts and adjustments.

The Income Statement columns are sometimes used as the primary place for computing income before taxes and (in simple cases) the income tax expense for the year. That is why the subtotals are drawn as shown. When the net income has finally been computed, the amount is transferred to the fifth pair of columns for the statement of retained income. Again, as in every pair, the columns are totaled to check accuracy.

The Income Statement and the Retained Income columns often guide the preparation of closing entries. Note how the Income Statement columns contain all the details necessary for the closing process; indeed, you can visualize the pair as a detailed Income Summary T-account used for closing. Similarly, the Retained Income columns can be visualized as the Retained Income T-account.

The final step is to move the ending balance of Retained Income from the fifth pair of columns to the sixth pair, the Balance Sheet columns.

EXHIBIT 5–9

OXLEY COMPANY
Work Sheet
For the Year Ended December 31, 19X2

Account Titles (in thousands of dollars)	Unadjusted Trial Balance Debit	Credit	Adjustments Debit	Credit	Adjusted Trial Balance Debit	Credit	Income Statement Debit	Credit	Statement of Retained Income Debit	Credit	Balance Sheet Debit	Credit
Cash	150				150						150	
Accounts receivable	95				95						95	
Accrued interest receivable			(n) 15		15						15	
Inventory of merchandise	20				20						20	
Prepaid rent	130			(o) 120	10						10	
Long-term note receivable	288				288						288	
Equipment	200				200						200	
Accumulated depreciation, equipment		80		(R) 40		120						120
Accounts payable		90				90						90
Accrued wages payable				(p) 24		24						24
Accrued income taxes payable				(t) 16		16						16
Accrued interest payable				(q) 9		9						9
Note payable—current portion				(s) 80		80						80
Long-term note payable		120	(s) 80			40						40
Paid-in capital		102				102						102
Retained income, December 31, 19X1		287				287				287		
Dividends declared	80				80				80			
Sales		999				999		999				
Interest revenue		21		(n) 15		36		36				
Cost of goods sold	399				399		399					
Wages expense	190		(p) 24		214		214					
Rent expense			(o) 120		120		120					
Miscellaneous expense	100				100		100					
Depreciation expense			(R) 40		40		40					
Interest expense	3		(q) 9		12		12					
	1699	1699					885	1035				
Income tax expense	44		(t) 16		60		60					
			304	304	1803	1803						
Net income							90			90		
							1035	1035	80	377	778	297
Retained income, December 31, 19X2									297			297
									377	377	778	778

(n) Accrual of interest receivable, $15   (o) Rent expense, $120   (p) Accrual of wages, $24   (q) Accrual of interest payable, $9   (r) Depreciation expense, $40
(s) Reclassification of note, $80   (t) Income tax expense, .40 × $150 income before income taxes = $60. Adjustment for accrued portion is $16.

The detailed sequence for the fourth, fifth, and sixth pairs of columns follows:

a. Add each of the two Income Statement columns and calculate the difference, as follows:

Credit column total (revenues)	$1,035
Debit column total (expenses)	885
Income before income taxes	$ 150

b. Compute the income tax expense, which is .40 × $150 = $60. Extend the $60 on the Income Tax Expense line as a debit in the Income Statement columns. Net income amounts to $150 − $60 = $90.

c. Add "net income" to the list of account titles. Place the $90 amount in the Income Statement debit column and in the Statement of Retained Income credit column. Note that this is akin to the closing journal entry that transfers net income from the Income Statement Summary to Retained Income.

d. Add each of the two Income Statement columns to see that the totals are equal.

e. Add the two Statement of Retained Income columns and calculate the difference, as follows:

Credit column total (beginning balance of retained income plus net income for the period)	$377
Debit column total (dividends declared)	80
Retained earnings balance, December 31, 19X2	$297

f. Add "retained income, December 31, 19X2," to the list of account titles. Place the $297 amount in the Statement of Retained Income debit column and in the Balance Sheet credit column.

g. Add each of the two Statement of Retained Income columns to see that the totals are equal.

h. Add each of the two Balance Sheet columns to see that the totals are equal. When they are equal, the accountant is ready to prepare the formal statements. When they are not equal, the accountant seldom smiles. He or she faces the labors of rechecking the preceding steps in reverse order.

☐ Flexibility of Uses

Ponder the work sheet in its entirety. It is a clever means of summarizing masses of interrelated data. Obviously, the work sheet in Exhibit 5–9 is tiny in comparison with some work sheets used to prepare the financial statements of huge corporations that have many subdivisions. Work sheets are flexible. Many more sets of columns may be added. On the other hand, Exhibit 5–9 could be cut to six columns instead of twelve by using parentheses instead of separate columns for the credits.

Accountants often use the work sheet as the principal means of preparing monthly and quarterly financial statements. Adjustments may be necessary for preparing these interim statements, but the accountant may not wish to enter adjustments formally in the journal and ledger each month. For example, suppose the work sheet in Exhibit 5–9 were for the month of January 19X2. Adjustments might be entered on the work sheet in the same manner, but no adjusting entries would be made in the journals and ledgers. In this way, formal interim financial statements can be prepared without the books being cluttered by the elaborate adjusting and closing entries.

☐ Detailed Accounting Cycle

The body of this chapter described the major steps of the accounting cycle. The appendix described the work sheet. Earlier chapters described other features of the cycle. The detailed steps of the accounting cycle when a work sheet is used are summarized below.

1. Begin with the balance sheet (and general ledger balances) at the start of the reporting period.
2. Analyze and journalize transactions as they occur.
3. Post journal entries to the appropriate ledger accounts.
4. Prepare an unadjusted trial balance on a work sheet.
5. Complete the work sheet.
6. Prepare the formal financial statements.
7. Using the work sheet as a guide:
   a. Journalize and post the adjusting entries.
   b. Journalize and post the closing entries.
8. Use the ledger to prepare an after-closing, or postclosing, trial balance. This serves as a double-check to ensure that the ledger is ready for the new accounting cycle. The balances in the after-closing trial balance (which is not shown here) should be identical to those in the Balance Sheet columns of the work sheet.

☐ Electronic Spreadsheet

The general procedure for electronic spreadsheets as applied to the accountant's typical work sheet follows:

1. List the accounts.
2. Enter the trial balance amount of each account as shown in the first two amount columns of Exhibit 5–9, page 184.
3. Enter the adjustment amounts. The adjustment amount for Accrued Interest Receivable belongs in line 3, column 3.
4. Write the equation to calculate each income statement amount. For example, Interest Revenue's final credit balance is $36, as follows:

Trial balance amount, a credit	$21
− Debit adjustments	0
+ Credit adjustments	15
= Income statement amount, a credit	$36

The spreadsheet is programmed to place $36 on line 19 in columns 6 and 8 of the work sheet.

5. Write the equation to calculate each balance sheet amount. For example, Prepaid Rent's final debit balance is:

Trial balance amount, a debit	$130
+ Debit adjustments	0
− Credit adjustments	−120
= Balance sheet amount, a debit	$ 10

The spreadsheet is programmed to place $10 on line 5 in columns 5 and 11 of the work sheet.

Major advantages of the electronic spreadsheet include the following:

1. The format is stored and can be used repeatedly. This avoids laborious writing of column heads and account titles.
2. Revisions of the basic format are easy.
3. Mathematical computations and placements of each account are achieved via computer. Speed and accuracy are maximized. Drudgery is minimized.
4. "What if" analysis is easily conducted. For example, suppose a manager desired to know the effects of various contemplated expense or revenue transactions on the income statement and balance sheet. Electronic spreadsheets can answer such questions instantly.

APPENDIX 5B: VARIETY IN DATA PROCESSING AND JOURNALIZING

This appendix stresses that there are many appropriate data-processing paths to the same objectives. The focus should be on the final product, not on whether one path is theoretically better than other paths. For example, should we use manual or computer methods? Should we use one pattern of journal entries or another? The answers to the questions of data-processing alternatives are inherently tied to the *overall* costs and benefits of the possible competing systems in a *specific* organization. What is good for General Motors is probably not good for Sophia's Pizza House, and vice versa.

☐ Variety in Recording Assets

Oxley Company's entries for rent (see entries *k* and *o* reproduced below from our chapter illustration) exemplify how accountants might adopt different patterns for journalizing:

ENTRY	AS IN CHAPTER: ALL ASSET NOW; RECOGNIZE EXPENSE LATER		FIRST ALTERNATIVE: FORESEE ULTIMATE EFFECTS NOW; NO ADJUSTMENT LATER			SECOND ALTERNATIVE: ALL EXPENSE NOW; RECOGNIZE ASSET LATER		
k Cash payment	Prepaid rent Cash	130 	 130	Rent expense Prepaid rent Cash	120 10 	 130	Rent expense Cash	130 	 130
o End-of-period adjustment	Rent expense Prepaid rent	120 	 120	No entry			Prepaid rent Rent expense	10 	 10

Is one choice better than another? All produce the same final account balances. However, from a strict theory point of view, the first-column method is superior because of its straightforward recognition that all acquisitions of goods and services are assets that expire and become expenses later. Under the first-column method, entry *k* regards all acquisitions as assets, and entry *o* writes off the prepayments that have expired. Good theory often also makes good practice. For example, it is often easier to review asset accounts to determine what should be expensed than it is to review expense accounts to determine what should not have been expensed.

The alternative in the middle column foresees the fact that Prepaid Rent will be $10 at the end of the year and anticipates the year-end adjustment in compound fashion, as entry *k* indicates. In practice, this pattern of entries is seldom found because it requires too much analytical time when each cash disbursement occurs.

The alternative in the third column is the direct opposite of the first column and is frequently encountered in practice. The pattern is to record as expenses such items as rent (or insurance premiums or office supplies) when cash is disbursed (or when a liability such as accounts payable is created) upon their acquisition, as entry *k* illustrates. Adjustments such as entry *o* are made at the end of the reporting period to reduce the expenses that would otherwise be overstated and to increase the assets for the appropriate amount of prepayments.

From an economical data-processing point of view, any of the three alternatives might be acceptable. The accountant should choose the one that is easiest to record. By far the most important point here is that any of the alternatives, properly applied, will lead to the same answers—the correct expense and the correct ending asset balance.

☐ Variety in Recording Liabilities

As in the recording of assets, many varieties of the recording of liabilities are acceptable, provided that they result in the proper ending balances for the expense and liability accounts for any particular time in question. Consider the entries for income taxes:

ENTRY	AS IN CHAPTER: PAY OLD LIABILITY AND RECOGNIZE EXPENSE; RECOGNIZE MORE EXPENSE LATER			FIRST ALTERNATIVE: PAY LIABILITY NOW; RECOGNIZE EXPENSE LATER			SECOND ALTERNATIVE RECOGNIZE EXPENSE NOW; ADJUST TO GET CORRECT BALANCES LATER		
i Cash payment	Accrued income taxes payable	12		Accrued income taxes payable	56		Income tax expense	56	
	Income tax expense	44		Cash		56	Cash		56
	Cash		56						
t End-of-period adjustment	Income tax expense	16		Income tax expense	60		Income tax expense	4	
	Accrued income taxes payable		16	Accrued income taxes payable		60	Accrued income taxes payable		4

The chapter entries *i* and *t* followed the most theoretically defensible position. Entry *i* recognized that $12 of the $56 disbursement pertained to the liability carried over from the preceding period. Entry *t* recognized that the year-end liability arising from the current period was $16.

In contrast, the alternatives in the other two columns are often found. In the middle column, the pattern results in a *temporary* debit balance in Accrued Income Taxes Payable, which normally has a credit balance. The U.S. government does not want to wait until after the end of the year to get its income taxes. Interim payments of estimated income taxes must be made and are frequently debited to the liability account (entry *i*) even before any income tax expense is computed and credited to the liability account (entry *t*). The accrued liability account will now show the same $16 balance as in the preceding method: $12 - $56 + $60 = $16.

The alternative in the third column contrasts sharply with that of the middle column, but the final account balances are the same. As entry *i* indicates, all disbursements are regarded as expenses. At year-end (entry *t*), the accrued liability account is adjusted so that an accurate amount is shown: $12 + $4 = $16.

☐ Temporarily Incorrect Balances

The major lesson of this appendix deserves emphasis. For sensible reasons governing day-to-day recording procedures, accountants may routinely debit expense for the *full amount* (or credit revenue or credit asset or debit liability accounts) when cash changes hands. This may result in temporarily incorrect balances in a number of accounts throughout a reporting period. However, the accountant is aware that such a condition is commonplace. Consequently, many adjustments become necessary for legitimate data-processing reasons. Their aim is to achieve the correct balances for the reporting period.

The justification for such "full amount" approaches centers on costs and benefits. On a day-to-day basis, an accountant or a clerk or a computer does not have to be concerned with remembering whether routine cash flows really affect past accruals. Instead all receipts or disbursements are handled in *identical fashion* throughout the year. To the extent that such routines (used by, say, a computer or a lower-level clerk) cause temporary errors in accruals, the year-end adjustments (prepared by, say, a higher-level accountant) produce the necessary corrections.

☐ Reversing Entries

Reversing entries are sometimes used to cope with the proper accounting for accruals. As the name implies, *reversing entries* switch back all debits and credits made in a related preceding adjusting entry. To illustrate their effect, compare the pattern of journal entries illustrated in the chapter with the pattern of reversing entries that would be employed, as shown in Exhibit 5–10. The adjustments (and the closing entries, not shown) would be identical whether reversing entries are used or not. The differences occur only for the routine journalizing during the following year, 19X3, as Exhibit 5–10 demonstrates.

Some accountants favor using reversing entries because they or their clerks or their computers do not have to be concerned with whether a later routine cash disbusement (or receipt) applies to any accrued liabilities (or assets) that were recognized at the end of the preceding period. So reversing entries are creatures of practical data processing. They have no theoretical merit, and their use is diminishing.

FUNDAMENTAL ASSIGNMENT MATERIAL

☐ General Coverage

5–1. **EFFECTS OF ADJUSTMENTS OF PRECEDING PERIOD.** (Alternates are 5–3, 5–4, and 5–42.) The Verdi Company had the following balances as of December 31, 19X1:

Accrued interest receivable	$130,000
Accrued wages payable	190,000
Unearned sales revenue	100,000

During early 19X2, cash was collected for interest of $220,000. Cash was disbursed for wages of $900,000. Total sales of $700,000 included $100,000 of deliveries to all customers who had made advance payments during 19X1.

Required: Set up T-accounts and prepare the journal entries for the 19X2 transactions described. Post to the T-accounts.

5–2. **CLOSING ENTRIES.** (Alternates are 5–5, 5–6, 5–25, and 5–26.) After posting the following balances to T-accounts, journalize and post the entries required to close the books (in thousands):

Retained income		Wages expense	$300
(before closing entries)	$210	Miscellaneous	
Sales	900	expenses	35
Interest revenue	20	Income tax expense	20
Cost of goods sold	500	Dividends declared	30

What is the balance in Retained Income after closing entries?

EXHIBIT 5–10

Reversing Entries

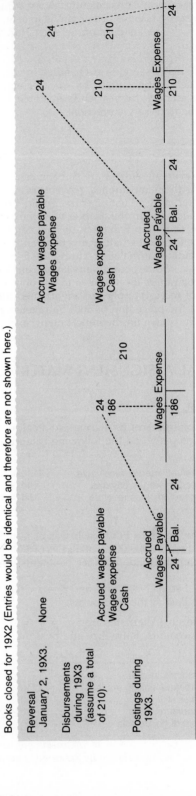

WITHOUT REVERSING ENTRIES:
THE PATTERN ILLUSTRATED IN CHAPTER

WITH REVERSING ENTRIES

Adjustment, December 31, 19X2 Entry p as in chapter.

Wages expense ... 24
   Accrued wages payable ... 24

Wages expense ... 24
   Accrued wages payable ... 24

Books closed for 19X2 (Entries would be identical and therefore are not shown here.)

Reversal January 2, 19X3.

None

Accrued wages payable ... 24
   Wages expense ... 24

Disbursements during 19X3 (assume a total of 210).

Accrued wages payable ... 24
Wages expense ... 186
   Cash ... 210

Wages expense ... 210
   Cash ... 210

Postings during 19X3.

Accrued Wages Payable
24 | Bal. 24

Wages Expense
186 | 186

Accrued Wages Payable
24 | Bal. 24

Wages Expense
210 | 210   24

5–3. EFFECTS OF ADJUSTMENTS OF PRECEDING PERIOD. (Alternates are 5–1, 5–4, and 5–42.) The New York Times Company showed the following actual balances and descriptions in its balance sheet, January 1, 1989:

Current liabilities:	
Payrolls	$55,040,000
Unexpired subscriptions	48,609,000

The company also showed Interest Receivable of $440,000.

During early 1989, assume the following: $842,000 was collected for interest; cash of $98,054,000 was disbursed for payrolls; and deliveries of $33,621,000 were made of the company's publications that had been subscribed to and fully collected before 1989.

Required: Set up T-accounts and prepare the journal entries for the 1989 transactions. Post to the T-accounts.

5–4. EFFECTS OF ADJUSTMENTS OF PRECEDING PERIOD. (Alternates are 5–1, 5–3, and 5–42.) The Times Mirror Company engages principally in publishing, notably the *Los Angeles Times*, *Newsday*, *Sporting News*, *Golf*, and *Popular Science*. Its annual report included the following balances, January 1, 1989:

Interest receivable	$ 3,210,000
Employees' compensation payable	73,624,000
Unearned income	55,140,000

Assume that during early 1989, cash of $4,841,000 was collected for interest. Cash of $99,417,000 was disbursed for employees' compensation. Deliveries of $28,162,000 were made of magazines and newspapers that had been subscribed to and fully collected before 1989.

Required: Set up T-accounts and prepare the journal entries for the 1989 transactions. Post to the T-accounts.

5–5. CLOSING ENTRIES. (Alternates are 5–2, 5–6, 5–25, and 5–26.) Albertson's, Inc., is a prominent supermarket chain located in the southern and western United States. The actual balances and descriptions that follow pertain to a recent year and are in millions of dollars:

Sales		Federal and state taxes on	
and other revenue	$3,489	income	$ 40
Cost of sales	2,719	Cash dividends	13
Operating and		Retained earnings, beginning	
administrative expenses	682	of year	191

Required: After posting the balances to T-accounts, journalize and post the entries required to close the books. What is the balance in Retained Earnings after closing entries?

5–6. CLOSING ENTRIES. (Alternates are 5–2, 5–5, 5–25, and 5–26.) Hershey Foods Corporation has many well-known products, including Hershey's and Reese's candies. The accompanying actual balances and descriptions pertain to a recent year and are in millions of dollars.

Retained earnings, beginning of year	$ 395	Selling, administrative, and general expenses	$268
Net sales	1,451	Interest expense	13
Cost of sales	1,016	Provision for income taxes	75
		Cash dividends	26

Required: After posting the balances to T-accounts, journalize and post the entries required to close the books. What is the balance in Retained Earnings after closing entries?

ADDITIONAL ASSIGNMENT MATERIAL

☐ General Coverage

5–7. How many years are usually covered by the comparative income statements of publicly held corporations?

5–8. "It's a several-stage process by which accountants produce an entity's financial statements for a specific period of time." What is the term that describes the process?

5–9. What is the purpose of a Dividends Declared account?

5–10. "A corporation has no obligation to pay a dividend on its common stock." Do you agree? Explain.

5–11. A company declared a dividend of $100,000. Using a Dividends Declared account, prepare a journal entry for the transaction.

5–12. "Cash dividends that are payable are a part of stockholders' equity." Do you agree? Explain.

5–13. "Dividends Declared has a normal left-side balance. It represents a reduction in Retained Income and stockholders' equity." Do you agree? Explain.

5–14. "Closing is a clerical procedure. It is devoid of any new accounting theory." Do you agree? Explain.

5–15. "Net assets are always equal to stockholders' equity." Do you agree? Explain.

5–16. "Closing the books might better be called clearing the nominal accounts." Do you agree? Explain.

5–17. "The word *permanent* to describe real accounts is misleading." Explain.

5–18. Appendix 5A. Why are work sheets used?

5–19. Appendix 5B. "Variety in recording accounting transactions is unacceptable diversity." Do you agree? Explain.

5–20. Appendix 5B. "Liabilities can have temporary debit balances." Explain.

5–21. Appendix 5B. "Reversing entries are designed for the correction of errors." Do you agree? Explain.

5–22. JOURNALIZE, POST, AND PREPARE TRIAL BALANCE. Consider the accompanying Ijiri trial balance.

IJIRI ENGINEERING CONSULTANTS, INC.
Trial Balance
June 28, 19X5
(in thousands)

	DEBIT	CREDIT
Cash	$ 20	
Accounts receivable	110	
Unbilled client receivables	—	
Prepaid trade association dues	6	
Prepaid insurance	3	
Equipment	59	
Accumulated depreciation, equipment		$ 8
Accounts payable		16
Note payable		80
Accrued interest payable (on note)		5
Dividends payable		10
Accrued wages payable		—
Accrued income taxes payable		—
Unearned fee revenue		—
Paid-in capital		50
Retained income		20
Dividends declared	10	
Fee revenue		840
Rent expense	24	
Wages expense	400	
Depreciation expense	—	
Miscellaneous expenses	362	
Interest expense	5	
Income tax expense	30	
Total	$1,029	$1,029

The following additional information pertains to June 29 and 30, which is the end of Ijiri's fiscal year (amounts in thousands):

 a. Billed clients for $15.
 b. Paid the liability for dividends.
 c. Unbilled revenue as of June 30, based on time logged on various client projects, was $60. (Debit Unbilled Client Receivables.)
 d. Half the prepaid association dues had expired. (Debit Miscellaneous Expenses.)
 e. Wages incurred but unpaid, $9.
 f. One-third of the prepaid insurance had expired. (Debit Miscellaneous Expenses.)
 g. The note is payable on July 31. It is a 15%, seven-month note. Principal and interest are payable at maturity.
 h. Depreciation expense for the fiscal year is $10.
 i. Received $14 cash advance from a client for services to be rendered after June 30.
 j. Income tax rate was 35%.

Required:
1. After posting the above balances to T-accounts, analyze and journalize all entries arising from the above information.
2. Post the journal entries to T-accounts. Use check marks as posting references in the journal.
3. Prepare an adjusted trial balance, June 30, 19X5.

5–23. ADJUSTMENTS AND CLOSING. Consider the accompanying Neilsen trial balance.

NEILSEN COMPANY
Unadjusted Trial Balance
December 31, 19X2
(in thousands of dollars)

	DEBIT	CREDIT
Cash	$ 19	
Accounts receivable	100	
Notes receivable	50	
Merchandise inventory	120	
Prepaid rent	12	
Equipment	90	
Accumulated depreciation, equipment		$ 20
Accounts payable		130
Paid-in capital		100
Retained income		66
Sales		880
Cost of goods sold	460	
Wages expense	200	
Miscellaneous expenses	120	
Income tax expense	25	
Total	$1,196	$1,196

The following additional information is not reflected in the trial balance (amounts are in thousands):

a. Interest accrued on notes receivable, $5.
b. Depreciation, $10.
c. Wages accrued but unpaid, $6.
d. Utilities accrued but unpaid, $4 (charge Miscellaneous Expenses).
e. Rent expired, $5.
f. Dividend declared but unpaid, $12. Use a Dividends Declared account, which is really just an offset to Retained Income.
g. A cash receipt of $2 from a credit customer was credited erroneously to Accounts Payable, so a correction must be made.
h. Additional income tax expense must be accrued. The income tax rate is 40% of pretax income. Compute the additional tax after computing the effects of the above adjustments to revenue and expense accounts.

Required:
1. After posting the above balances to T-accounts, analyze and journalize all entries arising from the descriptions in *a* through *h* above. Use new accounts as necessary.
2. Post your journal entries to T-accounts. Use check marks as posting references in the journal.
3. Prepare an adjusted trial balance, December 31, 19X2. Allow space for four columns, placing your numbers for this requirement in the first pair of columns.
4. Prepare and post the closing journal entries to T-accounts. Key the entries as *i, j,* etc.
5. Prepare a postclosing trial balance by placing the appropriate numbers in the second pair of columns in your answer to requirement 3 above.

5–24. PREPARE FINANCIAL STATEMENTS. Consider the accompanying Maxmart trial balance.

MAXMART RETAILERS, INC.
Adjusted Trial Balance
December 31, 19X5
(in thousands)

	DEBIT	CREDIT
Accounts payable		$ 70
Accounts receivable	$ 90	
Accrued income taxes payable		10
Accrued interest payable (due annually)		4
Accrued wages payable		20
Accumulated depreciation, building		70
Accumulated depreciation, equipment		47
Building	120	
Cash	48	
Cost of goods sold	498	
Dividends declared	11	
Equipment	60	
Income tax expense	20	
Interest expense	6	
Inventory	120	
Long-term note payable (due in 19X8)		50
Other operating expenses	110	
Paid-in capital		110
Prepaid insurance	2	
Retained income		34
Sales		970
Wages expense	300	
Total	$1,385	$1,385

Required:
1. Prepare a multiple-step income statement.
2. Prepare a statement of retained income.
3. Prepare a classified balance sheet.
4. Compute the working capital and the current ratio.

5–25. **CLOSING ENTRIES.** (Alternates are 5–2, 5–5, 5–6, and 5–26.) Maxmart Retailers, Inc., had the following accounts included in an adjusted trial balance, December 31, 19X5 (in thousands):

Cost of goods sold	$498	Interest		Sales	$970
Dividends declared	11	expense	$ 6	Wages	
Income tax expense	20	Other		expense	300
		operating		Retained	
		expenses	110	income	34

Required:
After posting the above balances to T-accounts, journalize and post the entries to close the books. What is the balance in Retained Income after closing?

5–26. **CLOSING ENTRIES.** (Alternates are 5–2, 5–5, 5–6, and 5–25.) Ijiri Engineering Consultants, Inc., had the following accounts included in an adjusted trial balance, June 30, 19X5 (in thousands):

Retained income	$ 20	Rent expense	$ 24	Miscellaneous	
Dividends		Wages expense	409	expenses	$366
declared	10	Depreciation		Interest expense	6
Fee revenue	915	expense	10	Income tax	
				expense	35

After posting the above balances to T-accounts, journalize and post the entries necessary to close the books. Number your entries as 1, 2, etc.

What is the balance in Retained Income after closing?

5–27. **CLOSING THE ACCOUNTS.** The following accounts show their final balances before closing and their closing entries (in thousands). Prepare the closing journal entries that were evidently made.

Cost of Goods Sold			Dividends Declared			Other Revenues	
500	500		70	70		40	40

Income Summary			Sales			Retained Income	
840	940		900	900		70	500
100							100

Other Expenses	
340	340

What is the balance in Retained Income after closing?

5–28. **WORK SHEET.** Appendix 5A. An unadjusted trial balance for Hartman Sporting Goods is on the accompanying work sheet. The following additional information is available.

   a. Wages earned but unpaid, $2,000.
   b. Adjustment for prepaid rent. Rent was paid quarterly in advance, $9,000 per quarter. Payments were due on January 1, April 1, July 1, and October 1.
   c. The store equipment originally cost $16,800 on February 1, 19X1. It is being depreciated on a straight-line basis over seven years with zero expected terminal value.
   d. The note payable is based on a one-year loan of $20,000. The note is dated November 1, 19X1. Principal plus 15% interest is payable at maturity.
   e. Income taxes are to be accrued. The applicable income tax rate is 30%.

Required: | Enter the adjustments and complete the work sheet.

5–29. **WORK SHEET.** Appendix 5A. Refer to Problem 5–22. Prepare a complete work sheet, including pairs of columns for unadjusted trial balance, adjustments and other entries, adjusted trial balance, income statement, statement of retained income, and balance sheet for Ijiri Engineering Consultants, Inc.

5–30. **WORK SHEET.** Study Appendix 5A. Refer to Problem 5–23. Prepare a complete work sheet, including pairs of columns for unadjusted trial balance, adjustments and other entries, adjusted trial balance, income statement, statement of retained income, and balance sheet for Neilsen Company. If you did not solve Problem 5–23, prepare closing journal entries now.

5–31. **ALTERNATIVE ANALYSES OF TRANSACTIONS.** (Alternate is 5–32.) Study Appendix 5B. Consider the following balances, December 31, 19X1:

Accrued interest receivable	$10,000
Prepaid rent	6,000
Accrued wages payable	16,000

During 19X2, $30,000 cash was received for interest for one year on a long-term note of $200,000. Interest was due yearly on September 1. In addition, half the principal of the note was paid on September 1, 19X2.

During 19X2, cash disbursements of $39,000 were made for rent. The rent was

EXHIBIT FOR ASSIGNMENT 5-28

HARTMAN SPORTING GOODS
Work Sheet
For the Month Ended February 28, 19X2

Account Title	Unadjusted Trial Balance		Adjustments		Adjusted Trial Balance		Income Statement		Statement of Retained Income		Balance Sheet	
	Debit	Credit	Debit	Credit	Debit	Credit	Debit	Credit	Debit	Credit	Debit	Credit
Cash	26800											
Accounts receivable	36600											
Merchandise inventory	110000											
Prepaid rent	6000											
Store equipment	16800											
Accumulated depreciation, equip.		2400										
Accounts payable		62000										
Note payable		20000										
Accrued interest payable		750										
Paid-in capital		50000										
Retained income		45150										
Sales		70200										
Cost of goods sold	50000											
Advertising expense	4000											
Wages expense	11000											
Miscellaneous expenses	10000											
	270600	270600										

197

payable $9,000 quarterly in advance on March 1, June 1, September 1, and December 1. The rent was raised to $12,000 quarterly beginning December 1, 19X2.

During 19X2, $800,000 was disbursed for wages. The ending balance of accrued wages payable, December 31, 19X2, was $26,000.

Required: | In responding to the requirement for journal entries, use the following format:

EXPLANATION OF ENTRY	REQUIREMENT 1			REQUIREMENT 2		
	(in thousands of dollars)					
Summary cash receipts or disbursements	Journal entry			Journal entry		
End-of-period adjustments	Journal entry			Journal entry		
Example: Paid insurance of $40,000	Prepaid insurance Cash	40	40	Insurance expense Cash	40	40
Adjustment so that ending balance of prepaid insurance is $30,000	Insurance expense Prepaid insurance	10	10	Prepaid insurance Cash	30	30

Required: |

1. Assume that the accounting system provides for the appropriate portions of the above cash collections and cash disbursements to be applied to any balances of accruals and prepayments carried over from the preceding period. Given the above data, prepare summary journal entries, including the adjusting entries, for 19X2. Post the entries to T-accounts. Do not prepare the entry for the repayment of the principal on the note.

2. Assume that the accounting system regards all the above cash collections and cash disbursements as revenues or expenses. Adjustments are then made at the end of each year to recognize the appropriate accruals and prepayments. Given the above data, prepare summary journal entries, including the adjusting entries for 19X2. Post the entries to T-accounts.

3. Which set of data-processing procedures do you prefer, those in requirement 1 or those in requirement 2? Explain.

5–32. **ATERNATIVE ANALYSES OF TRANSACTIONS.** (Alternate is 5–31.) Study Appendix 5B. Consider the following balances, December 31, 19X1 (in thousands of dollars):

Accrued interest receivable	$16
Prepaid fire insurance	3
Accrued wages payable	8

The accounting system provides for cash collections of interest to be credited first to any existing accrued interest receivable carried over from the preceding period. Cash collections for interest during 19X2 were $24. Label this as entry *f*.

The accounting system for wages is to debit any existing accrued payables first and debit any remainder of the disbursement to expense. Cash disbursements for wages during 19X2 were $193. Label this as entry *i*.

Prepayments of expenses are routinely debited to asset accounts. A cash disbursement for a three-year insurance policy, effective September 1, 19X2, was $36. Label this as entry *l*.

Required: |

1. Prepare T-accounts for Accrued Interest Receivable, Interest Revenue, Prepaid Fire Insurance, Insurance Expense, Accrued Wages Payable, and Wages Expense. Post the opening balances therein, December 31, 19X1. Journalize and post the above

entries *f*, *i*, and *l* to the appropriate accounts. (At the same time, you may wish to use a Cash T-account to complete the postings. However, the Cash T-account is not required for purposes of this problem.)

2. The following correct balances were applicable at the end of 19X2:

Accrued interest receivable	$ 8
Prepaid fire insurance	?
Accrued wages payable	15

Journalize and post the adjusting entries, December 31, 19X2. Label them as *o*, *p*, and *s*. Assume that the prepaid insurance of December 31, 19X1, expired during 19X2.

3. Assume the same data as in requirements 1 and 2. However, suppose the following summarized journal entries had been made during 19X2:

ENTRY	ACCOUNTS AND EXPLANATION	POST REF.	DEBIT (in thousands of dollars)	CREDIT (in thousands of dollars)
f	Cash	✓	24	
	Interest revenue	✓		24
	Collection of interest.			
i	Wages expense	✓	193	
	Cash	✓		193
	Payments of wages.			
l	Insurance expense	✓	36	
	Cash	✓		36
	Payment of insurance.			

Given the above entries *f*, *i*, and *l*, prepare the adjusting journal entries *o*, *p*, and *s*, December 31, 19X2. Post the entries to a new set of T-accounts having the same opening balances given in the first paragraph of this problem. How do the ending balances in the accounts affected by the adjustments compare with the ending balances in the same accounts in requirement 2?

4. Which set of data-processing procedures do you prefer for interest, wages, and insurance, those in requirements 1 and 2 or those in requirement 3? Explain.

SPECIAL REVIEW MATERIAL

The problems in this special collection cover Chapters 1 through 5 in their entirety, with particular emphasis on relating the cash and accrual bases. Problem 5–33 is the most comprehensive.

5–33. ACCOUNTING CYCLE. This is a comprehensive review of Chapters 1 through 5. Ruiz Lumber, a retail corporation, had the following postclosing trial balance, December 31, 19X1 (in thousands of dollars):

ACCOUNT NUMBER	NAME OF ACCOUNT	DR.	CR.
10	Cash	21	
20	Accounts receivable	100	
34	Notes receivable, current	100	
35	Accrued interest receivable	16	
40	Merchandise inventory	160	
52	Prepaid fire insurance	3	
62	Notes receivable, long-term	100	
74	Equipment	110	
74A	Accumulated depreciation, equipment		66
100	Accounts payable		90
111	Accrued wages payable		8
123	Accrued income taxes payable		4
137	Unearned sales revenue		10
200	Paid-in capital		110
230	Retained income		322
		610	610

The following summarized transactions (in thousands of dollars) occurred during 19X2:

a. Merchandise inventory purchased on open account was $520.

b. Total sales were $890, of which 80% were on credit.

c. The sales in *b* were exclusive of the deliveries of goods to customers who had paid in advance as of December 31, 19X1. All of those goods ordered in advance were indeed delivered during 19X2.

d. The cost of goods sold for 19X2, including those in *c*, was $440.

e. Collections from credit customers were $682.

f. The notes receivable are from a major supplier of lumber. Interest for twelve months on all notes was collected on May 1. The rate is 12% per annum. The accounting system provides for cash collections of interest to be credited first to any existing accrued interest receivable carried over from the preceding period.

g. The principal of the current notes receivable was collected on May 1, 19X2. The principal of the remaining notes is payable on May 1, 19X3 (see entry *q*). Transaction *t* also affects cash receipts.

Cash disbursements were:

h. To trade creditors, $500.

i. To employees for wages, $193. The accounting system for wages is to debit any existing accrued payables first and debit any remainder of a disbursement to expense.

j. For miscellaneous expenses such as store rents, advertising, utilities, and supplies, which were all paid in cash, $189. (These items are combined here to reduce the detailed recording of items that are basically accounted for alike.)

k. For new equipment acquired on July 1, 19X2, $74.

l. To the insurance company for a new three-year fire insurance policy effective September 1, 19X2, $36 (rates had increased). Prepayments of expenses are routinely debited to asset accounts.

m. To the federal and state governments for income taxes, $19. Income tax expense was debited for $15 of the $19. (For your general information, most businesses must pay income taxes regularly throughout the year.)

n. The board of directors declared cash dividends of $26 on December 15 to stockholders of record, January 5, and to be paid on January 21, 19X3. (Note that this is not a cash disbursement until payment has been made.) Debit Dividends Declared, which is really just an offset to Retained Income.

The following adjustments were made on December 31, 19X2:

    o. For interest on notes receivable.

    p. For insurance. The prepaid insurance of December 31, 19X1, had expired too.

    q. For reclassification of the notes receivable.

    r. For depreciation. Depreciation expense for 19X2 was $30.

    s. Wages earned but unpaid, December 31, 19X2, $15.

    t. As of December 31, 19X2, customers had made a total of $7 in advance cash payments for "layaway" plans and for merchandise not yet in stock. These payments were exclusive of any other transactions described above. This is an explicit transaction rather than an adjustment. (Recall that in Chapter 4 adjustments were described as relating to *implicit* transactions.)

    u. Total income tax expense for 19X2 is $20, computed as 40% of pretax income of $50. (Note that part of the 19X2 tax expense has already been recorded and paid, as indicated in transaction *m*.)

Required:

    1. After posting the opening balances to T-accounts, analyze and journalize all transactions, including adjustments, for 19X2.

    2. Post all journal entries to T-accounts. Be painstaking as you post. Use the given account numbers as posting references. For accounts not in the trial balance of December 31, 19X1, use check marks as posting references instead.

    3. Prepare a trial balance, December 31, 19X2.

    4. Prepare a multiple-step income statement for 19X2.

    5. Prepare a statement of retained income for 19X2.

    6. Prepare classified comparative balance sheets for December 31, 19X1 and 19X2. Classify the prepaid insurance, December 31, 19X2, as a current asset even though a portion thereof might justifiably be classified as a long-term asset.

    7. Journalize and post the entries necessary to "close the books" for 19X2.

5–34. WORK SHEET. Study Appendix 5A. Refer to the preceding problem. Examine the accompanying unadjusted trial balance that includes the results of transactions *a* through *n* (and also *t*) (in thousands).

Required:

    1. Prepare a twelve-column work sheet, using the unadjusted trial balance as the first pair of columns. Add pairs of columns for adjustments, adjusted trial balance, income statement, statement of retained income, and balance sheet. When entering the unadjusted trial balance on the work sheet, allow space for new accounts as follows: two spaces after Accounts Receivable, two spaces after Accounts Payable, and three spaces between Miscellaneous Expenses and Income Tax Expense.

    2. Enter the adjustments for transactions *o* through *u*. The effects of transaction *t* are already contained in the unadjusted trial balance.

    3. Complete the work sheet. Check the accuracy of your work by comparing the work sheet results with the formal financial statements prepared in the solution to Problem 5–33.

ACCOUNT TITLE	DEBIT	CREDIT
Cash	$ 1	
Accounts receivable	130	
Merchandise inventory	240	
Prepaid fire insurance	39	
Notes receivable, long-term portion	100	
Equipment	184	
Accumulated depreciation, equipment		$ 66
Accounts payable		110
Dividends payable		26
Unearned sales revenue		7
Paid-in capital		110
Retained income		322
Dividends declared	26	
Sales		900
Interest revenue		8
Cost of goods sold	440	
Wages expense	185	
Miscellaneous expense	189	
Income tax expense	15	
Total	$1,549	$1,549

5–35. **EFFECTS OF ERROR.** The bookkeeper of a certain firm, the Lark Co., included the cost of a new motor truck, purchased on December 30 for $16,000 to be paid in January, as an operating expense instead of as an addition to the proper asset account. What was the effect of this error ("no effect," "overstated," or "understated"?—use symbols *n*, *o*, or *u*, respectively) on:

1. Operating expenses for the year ended December 31 _____
2. Profit from operations for the year _____
3. Retained earnings as of December 31 after
   the books are closed _____
4. Total assets as of December 31 _____
5. Total liabilities as of December 31 _____

5–36. **EFFECTS OF ERRORS.** What will be the effect—understated (*u*), overstated (*o*), or no effect (*n*)—upon the income of the present and future periods if:

	PERIOD 19X1	19X2
1. Revenue for services rendered has been earned, but the unbilled amounts have not been recognized at the end of 19X1.	_____	_____
2. Prepaid items like rent have been paid (in late 19X1) through half of 19X2 but not adjusted at the end of 19X1. The payments have been debited to Prepaid Rent. They were written off in mid-19X2.	_____	_____
3. Accrued wages payable have not been recognized at the end of 19X1.	_____	_____
4. Revenue has been collected in advance, but earned amounts have not been recognized at the end of 19X1. Instead all revenue was recognized as earned in 19X2.	_____	_____

In all cases assume that amounts carried over into 19X2 would affect 19X2 operations via the routine accounting entries of 19X2.

5-37. EFFECTS OF ERRORS. Assume a going concern and analyze the effect of the following errors on the net profit figures for 19X1 and 19X2. Choose one of three answers: understated (*u*), overstated (*o*), or no effect (*n*). Problem *a* has been answered as an illustration.

    a. EXAMPLE: Failure to adjust at end of 19X1 for sales salaries accrued. 19X1: *o*; 19X2: *u*. (*Explanation*: In 19X1, expenses would be understated and profits overstated. This error would carry forward so that expenses in 19X2 would be overstated and profits understated.)

    b. Omission of Depreciation on Office Machines in 19X1 only. Correct depreciation was taken in 19X2.

    c. Machinery, cost price $500, bought in 19X1, was not entered in the books until paid for in 19X2. Ignore depreciation; answer in terms of the specific error described.

    d. Failure to adjust for the following at end of 19X2: Physical count of office supplies on hand, $100. Office Supplies, an asset account, was charged for purchases of supplies and had an unadjusted balance of $300.

    e. Three months' rent, collected in advance in December 19X1, for the first quarter of 19X2 was credited directly to Rent Earned in 19X1. No adjustment was made for the unearned rent at the end of 19X1.

    f. Failure to adjust at end of 19X1 for interest earned but not received on notes receivable.

5-38. EFFECTS OF ADJUSTMENTS AND CORRECTIONS. (Appendix 5B is helpful regarding some items.) Listed below are a series of accounts which are numbered for identification. All accounts needed to answer the parts of this question are included. Prepare an answer sheet with columns in which you are to write the identification numbers of the accounts affected by your answers. The same account may be used in several answers.

1. Cash	15. Notes payable
2. Accounts receivable	16. Accrued wages and salaries payable
3. Notes receivable	17. Accrued interest payable
4. Inventory	18. Unearned subscription revenue
5. Accrued interest receivable	19. Capital stock
6. Accrued rent receivable	20. Sales
7. Fuel on hand	21. Fuel expense
8. Unexpired rent	22. Salaries and wages
9. Unexpired insurance	23. Insurance expense
10. Unexpired repairs and maintenance	24. Repairs and maintenance expense
11. Land	25. Rent expense
12. Buildings	26. Rent revenue
13. Machinery and equipment	27. Subscription revenue
14. Accounts payable	28. Interest revenue
	29. Interest expense

Required:

Prepare any necessary adjusting or correcting entries called for by the following situations, *which were discovered at the end of the calendar year*. With respect to each situation, assume that no entries have been made regarding the situation other than those specifically described (i.e., no monthly adjustments have been made during the year). *Consider each situation separately*. These transactions were not necessarily conducted by one business firm. Amounts are in thousands of dollars. *Illustration*: Purchased new equipment for $100 cash, plus a $300 short-term note. The bookkeeper failed to record the transaction. The answer would appear as follows:

	ACCOUNT		AMOUNT	
	Debit	Credit	Debit	Credit
Illustration	13	1 & 15	400	100 & 300
a.	—	——	—	——
b.	—	——	—	——
c.	—	——	—	——
etc.	—	——	—	——

a. A $300 purchase of equipment on December 5 was erroneously debited to Accounts Payable. The credit was correctly made to Cash.

b. A business made several purchases of fuel oil. Some purchases ($800) were debited to Fuel Expense, while others ($1,100) wre charged to an asset account. An oil gauge revealed $400 of fuel on hand at the end of the year. There was no fuel on hand at the beginning of the year.

c. On April 1, a business took out a fire insurance policy. The policy was for two years and the premium paid was $400. It was debited to Insurance Expense on April 1.

d. On December 1, $400 was paid in advance to the landlord for four months' rent. The tenant debited Unexpired Rent for $400 on December 1. What adjustment is necessary on December 31 on the tenant's books?

e. Machinery is repaired and maintained by an outside maintenance company on an annual fee basis, payable in advance. The $240 fee was paid in advance on September 1 and charged to Repairs and Maintenance Expense. What adjustment is necessary on December 31?

f. On November 16, $800 of machinery was purchased. $200 cash was paid down and a ninety-day, 5% note payable was signed for the balance. The November 16 transaction was properly recorded. Prepare the adjustment for the interest.

g. A publisher sells subscriptions to magazines. Customers pay in advance. Receipts are originally credited to Unearned Subscription Revenue. On August 1, many one-year subscriptions were collected and recorded, amounting to $12,000.

h. On December 30, certain merchandise was purchased for $1,000 on open account. The bookkeeper debited Machinery and Equipment and credited Accounts Payable for $1,000. Prepare a correcting entry.

i. A 120-day, 7%, $7,500 cash loan was made to a customer on November 1. The November 1 transaction was recorded correctly.

5–39. **MEASURING INCOME ON CASH AND ACCRUAL BASES.** Following are the summarized transactions of Dr. Cristina Faragher, a dentist, for 19X7, her first year in practice:

1. Acquired equipment and furniture for $50,000. Depreciation expense for 19X7 is $10,000.
2. Fees collected, $80,000. These fees included $2,000 paid in advance by some patients on December 31, 19X7.
3. Rent is paid at the rate of $500 monthly, payable on the twenty-fifth of each month for the following month. Total disbursements during 19X7 for rent were $6,500.
4. Fees billed but uncollected, December 31, 19X7, $15,000.
5. Utilities expense paid in cash, $600. Additional utility bills unpaid at December 31, 19X7, $100.
6. Salaries expense of dental assistant and secretary, $16,000 paid in cash. In addition, $1,000 was earned but unpaid on December 31, 19X7.

Dr. Faragher may elect either the cash basis or accrual basis of measuring income for income tax purposes, provided that she uses it consistently in subsequent years. Under either alternative, depreciation expense must be recognized rather than the original cost of $50,000 being regarded as a lump-sum expense in the first year.

Required:
1. Prepare a comparative income statement on both the cash and accrual bases, using one column for each basis.
2. Which basis do you prefer as a measure of Dr. Faragher's performance? Why? What is the justification for the government's allowing the use of the cash basis for income tax purposes?

5–40. **ACCRUAL BASIS OF ACCOUNTING.** Maria Galvez runs a small consulting-engineering firm that specializes in designing and overseeing the installation of environmental-control systems. However, even though she is the president, she has had no formal training in management. She has been in business one year and has prepared the following income statement for her fiscal year ended June 30, 19X4:

GALVEZ CONSULTING ENGINEERS, INC.
Income Statement
For the Year Ended June 30, 19X4

Fees collected in cash		$500,000
Expenses paid in cash except for depreciation:		
Rent	$ 12,500	
Utilities	10,000	
Wages	200,000	
President's salary	46,000	
Office supplies	14,000	
Travel	40,000	
Miscellaneous	80,000	
Depreciation	10,000	412,500
Operating income		$ 87,500

Galvez realized that the entire $50,000 cost of the equipment acquired on July 1, 19X3, should not be an expense of one year. She predicted a useful life of five years, a terminal value of zero, and deducted $10,000 as depreciation for the first year.

Galvez is thinking about future needs for her expanding business. For example, although she now uses rented space in an office building, she is considering buying a small building. She showed her income statement to a local banker, who reacted: "Maria, this statement may suffice for filing income tax forms, but the bank will not consider any long-term financing until it receives a balance sheet and income statement prepared on the accrual basis of accounting. Moreover, the statements must be subjected to an audit by an independent certified public accountant."

As a CPA, you are asked to audit her records and fulfill the bank's request. The following data have been gathered:

1. On July 1, 19X3, Galvez invested $25,000 cash, and two friends each invested $2,000 cash in the firm in return for capital stock.
2. Galvez acquired $50,000 of equipment on July 1, 19X3. A down payment of $20,000 cash was made. A $30,000 two-year note bearing an annual interest rate of 15% was signed. Principal plus interest were both payable at maturity.
3. On June 30, 19X4, clients owed Galvez $95,000 on open accounts.
4. Salaries are paid on the fifteenth of every month. As business expanded throughout the fiscal year, additional employees were added. The total payroll paid on June 15, 19X4, including the president's monthly salary of $4,000, was $40,000.
5. Rent was paid in advance on the fifteenth of every month. An initial payment of $1,500 covered July 1, 19X3–August 15, 19X3. Payments of $1,000 monthly were paid beginning August 15, 19X3.
6. Office Supplies on hand on June 30, 19X4, were $5,000.
7. On April 1, 19X4, a local oil refinery gave Galvez a retainer fee of $60,000 cash in exchange for twelve months of consulting services beginning at that date.

Required:
1. Using the accrual basis of accounting, prepare an income statement for the fiscal year. Submit supporting computations properly labeled.
2. Prepare a balance sheet, dated June 30, 19X4. Assume that the cash balance is $106,500.

5–41. **RECONSTRUCT THE CASH ACCOUNT.** Refer to the preceding problem. Show a summary analysis of the cash receipts and disbursements that proves that the ending cash balance is indeed $106,500. Label your analysis fully.

5–42. JOURNAL ENTRIES. (Alternates are 5–1, 5–3, and 5–4.) Delta Air Lines, Inc., had the following three actual balance sheet items in its 1989 annual report (in thousands):

Maintenance and operating supplies	$131,507
Air traffic liability	504,083
Accrued income tax	107,041

A footnote stated: "Passenger ticket sales are recorded as revenue when the transportation is provided. The value of unused tickets is included in current liabilities." Therefore air traffic liability is an unearned revenue account.

Required: Set up T-accounts and prepare journal entries and postings for the following transactions that occurred subsequent to the date of the balance sheet in the 1989 annual report. All numbers are in thousands.

1. Use of $80,000 of maintenance and operating supplies.
2. Sales of $900,000 of tickets in advance of air travel. (Debit Cash.)
3. Revenues of $4,440,000, including $1,100,000 of transportation provided for passengers who paid in advance.
4. Additional accruals of income tax payable, $180,000.
5. Payments of income taxes, $217,041.

Indicate the balances in Maintenance and Operating Supplies, Air Traffic Liability, and Accrued Income Tax after posting for the five transactions.

5–43. JOURNAL ENTRIES. Cincinnati Bell, Inc., has provided communications services, mainly telephone services, in parts of Ohio, Kentucky, and Indiana. Its total operating revenues for a recent year were $275,733,000. Its balance sheets showed:

	END OF YEAR	BEGINNING OF YEAR
Advance billing and customers' deposits	$4,941,000	$4,085,000

To save space, annual reports often combine accounts. In this instance, Advance Billing is really one account, an unearned revenue account. For example, customers typically are billed for their basic monthly phone charges in advance of the service rendered.

Customers' Deposits is another account. For example, a new customer may be required to make a security deposit of $300. When the customer terminates the service, the deposit is usually returned in cash.

Required: Post all entries to three T-accounts. (Use Cash, Advance Billing and Customers' Deposits, and Operating Revenues.)

1. Prepare a summary journal entry to show how the $4,085,000 was initially recorded.
2. (a) During the year, additional amounts of advance billings and deposits amounted to $14 million. (b) Moreover, $2 million of customers' deposits was returned in cash to customers. Prepare summary journal entries for these events.
3. At the end of the year, prepare any necessary adjusting journal entry to obtain the balance given for the year.

5–44. FINANCIAL STATEMENTS. NL Industries, Inc., has widespread operations in petroleum services to the oil industry and in the manufacture of chemicals. A recent annual report included the items listed below (in millions of dollars). The balance sheet items included here are the amounts at December 31, unless otherwise indicated.

Property, plant, and equipment, original cost	$1,362
Accumulated depreciation	466
Net sales	2,536
Interest expense	65
Bank loans payable	32
Retained earnings, beginning of year	762
Common stock	50
Cost of goods sold	1,469
Provision for income taxes	194
Income taxes payable	108
Long-term debt	499
Additional paid-in capital	145
Selling, general, and administrative expenses	492
Dividends declared	59
Inventories	394
Prepaid expenses	12
Accounts payable	119
Accounts receivable	460
Accrued liabilities	209
Other liabilities (noncurrent)	117
Cash and equivalents	27
Other assets (noncurrent)	509

Required:

1. Prepare a combined multiple-step statement of income and retained earnings.
2. Prepare the classified balance sheet as of the end of the year.
3. Compute the working capital and the current ratio.

5–45. **SUMMARIZED CORPORATE ANNUAL REPORT.** Inspect an annual report of a publicly held corporation. (Your instructor will give more specific instructions regarding how to obtain access to such reports at your school.) Read the report. The report will contain many details not covered in your study to date. Nevertheless, you will see the general picture portrayed by the balance sheet, income statement, and other statements. Complete the following:

1. Name of company
2. Location of corporate headquarters
3. Principal products or services
4. Main geographic area of activity
5. Name and title of chief executive officer (CEO)
6. Ending date of latest operating year reported
7. Indicate the terms (if any) used instead of (a) balance sheet, (b) income statement, (c) retained income, (d) stockholders' equity, (e) revenues, (f) expenses
8. Total assets
9. Total liabilities
10. Total stockholders' equity
11. Total revenues (you may need to compute this)
12. Total expenses (you may need to compute this)
13. Net income (see above and subtract item 12 from item 11, then check the result with reported net income)
14. Total cash dividends declared
15. Earnings per share of common stock (EPS)
16. Annual dividends per share of common stock
17. Market in which stock is traded (see *Wall Street Journal* or local newspapers)
18. Latest market price of common (see *Wall Street Journal* or local newspapers)
19. Price-earnings ratio (compute or see *Wall Street Journal* or local newspapers)
20. Dividend yield (compute or see *Wall Street Journal* or local newspapers)

21. Dividend-payout ratio (you may need to compute this)
22. Name of independent public accountants
23. Did they certify that all amounts were correct? If not, what did they say? (Do not simply copy the actual wording; be brief.)
24. Total number of shareholders*
25. Total number of employees*
26. Total number of shares of common stock outstanding
27. Common stockholders' equity per share* (book value per share)
28. Comparative statistics (financial and operating data) were reported for how many years?
29. Give very briefly your general impression of this report (for example, quality, scope, usefulness, format, readability, interest to you, etc.)

5–46. **HOUSE OF FABRICS ANNUAL REPORT.** Refer to the financial statements of House of Fabrics (pp. 752–759). This problem will familiarize you with some of the accounts of this actual company.

Required:

1. Which balance sheet format does the House of Fabrics use, the account format or the report format?
2. Name the company's largest current asset and current liability.
3. How much were total current assets and total current liabilities at January 31, 1989? What is the current ratio at January 31, 1989?
4. What was the original cost of the "Property" assets at January 31, 1989? What was the book value of the "Property" assets at January 31, 1989?
5. What is a more descriptive term for the "Paid-in Capital" account used by House of Fabrics?

---

* May not be reported by the corporation. If not reported, write "not available."

Sales Revenue, Cash, and Accounts Receivable

After studying this chapter, you should be able to

1. Compute gross profit rates and explain why they are important to managers and shareholders
2. Determine the proper time to record a particular revenue item on the income statement
4. Explain why cash is important and how it is managed
5. Explain how accounts receivable are valued via the specific write-off method and the allowance method of accounting for uncollectible accounts
6. Reconcile the cash balance in an organization's books with that shown by the bank (Appendix 6A)
7. Explain popular ways to estimate bad debt expense under the allowance method: (a) percentage of sales, (b) aging of accounts, and (c) percentage of ending accounts receivable (Appendix 6B)

TOPICAL COVERAGE OF TWO CHAPTERS

Accounting is commonly misunderstood as being a precise discipline that produces exact measurements of a company's financial position and performance. As a result, many individuals regard accountants as little more than mechanical tabulators who grind out financial reports after processing an imposing amount of detail in accordance with stringent predetermined rules. However, although accountants do take methodical steps with masses of data, their rules of measurement allow much room for judgment. Managers and accountants who exercise this judgment have more influence on financial reporting than is commonly believed.

The measurements of *sales revenue* and *cost of goods sold* are important areas affected by choices among accounting alternatives. This and the next chapter are a two-part package. Together they explain the calculation and meaning of *gross profit*, that is, sales revenue minus cost of goods sold. This chapter considers

1. Why gross profit is an important measure
2. When revenue should be recognized
3. What effects merchandise returns, allowances, and cash discounts have on revenue
4. How to account for credit sales and accounts receivable

The next chapter explains the measurement of cost of goods sold. It compares different methods of valuing inventories and discusses the impact of market prices on accounting for inventories.

IMPORTANCE OF GROSS PROFIT

Managers and investors are intensely interested in *gross profit*, or *gross margin*, and in its changes. Gross profit must exceed all operating expenses to produce a net income.

The approach here pertains to any entity that sells goods. However, we focus mostly on retailers and wholesalers. The accounting becomes more complicated for manufacturers because they use three major types of inventories: materials, work in process, and finished goods. Such coverage is beyond the scope of this discussion.[1]

---

[1] For a discussion of inventories in a manufacturing company, see *Introduction to Management Accounting*, the companion to this textbook.

Gross Profit Percentage

Gross profit is often expressed as a percentage of sales. Consider a typical Safeway grocery store:

	AMOUNT	PERCENTAGE
Sales	$1,000,000	100%
Cost of goods sold (also called cost of sales)	800,000	80
Gross profit (also called gross margin)	$ 200,000	20%

The gross profit percentage is 20%. Investors and managers closely watch this percentage. It provides clues about the causes of changes in profit, as we shall see in the next sections.

Reports to Shareholders

Investors are often concerned about gross profits. Consider an example based on a quarterly report to shareholders of Superscope, Inc., a real-life manufacturer and distributor of stereophonic equipment that encountered rocky times. The following condensed income statement was presented for a three-month period (thousands omitted):

	CURRENT YEAR	PREVIOUS YEAR
Net sales	$40,000	$40,200
Costs and expenses:		
Cost of sales	33,100	28,200
Selling, general and administrative	11,200	9,900
Interest	2,000	1,200
Income (loss) before income tax provision (benefit)	(6,300)	900
Income tax provision (benefit)	(3,000)	200
Net income (loss)	$ (3,300)	$ 700

Although the statement does not show the amount of gross profit, the gross profit percentages can readily be computed as ($40,000 − $33,100) ÷ $40,000 = 17% and ($40,200 − $28,200) ÷ $40,200 = 30%. To show how seriously these percentages are considered, the chairman's letter to shareholders began as follows:

☐ I shall attempt herein to provide you with a candid analysis of the Company's present condition, the steps we have instituted to overcome current adversities, and the potential which we believe can, in due course, be realized by the Company's realistic and positive determination to regain profitability.

☐ In the second quarter the Company's gross profit margins decreased to 17% compared to 30% in the corresponding quarter of a year ago. For the first six months gross profit margins were 22%, down from 31% for the corresponding period of a year ago.

☐ Essentially, the gross profits and consequential operating losses in the second quarter, as reflected in the condensed financial statements appearing in this report, resulted from lower than anticipated sales volume and from the following second quarter factors: liquidation of our entire citizens band inventory; increases in dealer cash discounts and sales incentive expenses; gross margin reductions resulting from sales of slow moving models at less than normal prices; and markdown of slow moving inventory on hand to a realistic net realizable market value.

☐ **Gross Profit Tests**

Auditors, including those from the Internal Revenue Service (IRS), use the gross profit percentage to help satisfy themselves about the accuracy of records. For example, the IRS compiles gross profit percentages by types of retail establishment. If a company shows an unusually low percentage compared with similar companies, IRS auditors may suspect that the taxpayer has failed to record all cash sales. Similarly, managers watch changes in gross profit percentages to judge operating profitability and to monitor how well employee theft and shoplifting are being controlled.

Suppose an internal revenue agent, a manager, or an outside auditor had gathered the following data for a particular jewelry company for the past three years (in millions):

	19X3	19X2	19X1
Net sales	$350	$300	$300
Cost of goods sold	210	150	150
Gross profit	$140	$150	$150
Gross profit percentage	40%	50%	50%

This illustrates a **gross profit test** whereby the percentages are compared to detect any phenomenon worth investigating. Obviously, the decline in the percentage might be attributable to many factors. Possible explanations include the following:

1. Competition has intensified, resulting in intensive price wars that reduced selling prices.
2. The mix of goods sold has shifted so that, for instance, the $350 million of sales in 19X3 is composed of relatively more products bearing lower gross margins (e.g., more costume jewelry bearing low margins and less diamond jewelry bearing high margins).
3. Shoplifting or embezzling has soared out of control. For example, a manager may be pocketing and not recording cash sales of $70 million. After all, sales in 19X3 would have been $210 × 2 = $420 million if the past 50% margin had been maintained.[2]

---

[2] Gross profit tests are applied in retailing to help control inventory shortages. This *retail method* of inventory control is explained in Chapter 14.

RECOGNITION OF REVENUE

Chapter 2 (p. 43) described the principles that determine when revenue is recognized in the financial statements. Under *cash-basis accounting*, accountants recognize revenue when cash is collected for sales of goods and services. Under *accrual-basis accounting*, however, recognition of revenue requires a two-pronged test: (1) goods or services must be delivered to the customers (that is, the revenue is *earned*); and (2) cash or an asset virtually assured of being converted into cash must be received (that is, the revenue is *realized*).

Most revenue is recognized at the point of sale.[3] Suppose you buy a record at a local record store. Both revenue recognition tests are generally met at the time of purchase. You receive the merchandise and the store receives cash, a check, or a credit card slip. Because both checks and credit card slips are readily converted to cash, the store can recognize revenue at the point of sale regardless of which of these three methods of payment you use.

Sometimes both revenue recognition tests are not met at the same time. In such cases, revenue is generally recognized only when both tests are met. Consider magazine subscriptions. The *realization* test is met when the publisher receives cash. However, revenues are not *earned* until magazines are delivered; therefore revenue recognition is delayed until the point of delivery.

Sometimes accountants must exercise judgment in deciding when the recognition criteria are met. For example, accounting for long-term contracts might require such judgment. Suppose Lockheed signs a $40 million contract with the U.S. government to produce a part for the space shuttle. The contract is signed and work begins on January 2, 19X1. The completion date is December 31, 19X4. Payment will be made upon delivery of the part. Lockheed expects to complete one-fourth of the project each year. When should the $40 million of revenue be recorded on the income statement?

The most common answer is that one-fourth of the revenue is *earned* each year, so $10 million of the revenue should be recognized annually. However, if final payment on the contract is uncertain, the *realization* test may not be met until the product is delivered and a bill is sent. In such a case, all revenues might be recognized at completion of the project. Generally, payments on contracts with the government or with major corporations are reasonably certain; therefore revenues on such contracts are recognized as the work is performed.

MEASUREMENT OF REVENUE

☐ **Cash and Credit Sales**

After deciding *when* revenue is to be recognized, the accountant must determine *how much* revenue to record. In other words, how should accountants measure revenue? Ordinarily, by approximating the "net realizable value" of the asset

---

[3] Because of the matching principle, described in Chapter 2 (p. 43), the cost of the items sold is reported in the same reporting period as the one in which revenue is recognized. The cost of goods sold is discussed in Chapter 7; we focus only on revenues in this chapter.

inflow from the customer. That is, the revenue is the present cash equivalent value of the asset received.

For cash sales, revenue is obviously equal to the cash received.

Cash	xxx	
Sales revenue		xxx

Notice that a cash sale increases revenue, an income statement account, and increases cash, a balance sheet account. The cash account is discussed later in this chapter, beginning on page 218.

A credit sale on open account is recorded much like a cash sale except that the balance sheet account *Accounts Receivable* is increased instead of cash:

Accounts receivable	xxx	
Sales revenue		xxx

However, the realizable value of a credit sale is often less than that of a cash sale. Why? Because some accounts receivable may never be collected. Adjustments for uncollectible accounts are discussed later in this chapter in the "Credit Sales and Accounts Receivable" section beginning on page 220.

☐ Merchandise Returns and Allowances

Suppose revenue is recognized at the point of sale, but later the customer decides to return the merchandise. He or she may be unhappy with the product for many reasons, including color, size, style, quality, and a simple changing of the mind. The supplier (vendor) calls these **sales returns;** the customer calls them **purchase returns.** Such merchandise returns are minor for manufacturers and wholesalers but are major for retail department stores. For instance, returns of 12% of gross sales are not abnormal for stores such as Marshall Field's or Macy's.

Or suppose that instead of returning the merchandise, the customer demands a reduction of the selling price (the original price previously agreed upon). For example, a customer may complain about finding scratches on a household appliance or about buying a toaster for $40 on Wednesday and seeing the same item for sale in the same store or elsewhere for $35 on Thursday. Such complaints are often settled by the seller's granting a **sales allowance,** which is essentially a reduction of the selling price. The buyer calls such a price reduction a **purchase allowance.**

Revenue must be decreased by the amount of the returns and allowances. But instead of directly reducing the revenue (or sales) account, managers of retail stores typically use a contra account, *Sales Returns and Allowances* (which combines both returns and allowances in a single account). Sales returns and allowances are deducted from sales to give net sales or net revenue. Managers use a contra account so they can watch changes in the level of returns and allowances. For instance, a change in the percentage of returns in fashion merchandise may give early signals about changes in customer tastes. Similarly, a buyer of fashion or fad merchandise may want to keep track of purchase returns to help assess the quality of products and services of various suppliers.

Consider an example of how to account for sales and sales returns and allowances. Suppose a J.C. Penney's Department Store has $900,000 gross sales on credit and $80,000 sales returns and allowances. The analysis of transactions would show:

	A	= L +	SE
Credit sales on open account	+900,000 [Increase Accounts Receivable]	=	+900,000 [Increase Sales]
Returns and allowances	−80,000 [Decrease Accounts Receivable]	=	−80,000 [Increase Sales Returns and Allowances]

The journal entries (without explanations) are:

Accounts receivable	900,000	
Sales		900,000
Sales returns and allowances	80,000	
Accounts receivable		80,000

The income statement would begin:

Gross sales	$900,000
Deduct: Sales returns and allowances	80,000
Net sales	$820,000

or

Sales, net of $80,000 returns and allowances	$820,000

☐ Discounts From Selling Prices

There are two major types of sales discounts: *trade* and *cash*. **Trade discounts** begin with some gross selling price and apply one or more reductions thereto in accordance with management policies. These discounts are price concessions or ways of quoting the actual prices that are charged to various customers. An example is a discount for large-volume purchases. The amount of revenue recognized from a sale should be the price to be received after deducting the discount.

In contrast to trade discounts, **cash discounts** are rewards for prompt payment. They are rarely given to retail customers, and their use is decreasing among manufacturers and wholesalers. Consider an example. A manufacturer sells toys to a retailer such as K Mart for $30,000. Terms are stated on the sales invoice as 2/10, n/60. This means that the retailer may remit $30,000 less a cash discount of .02 × $30,000, or $30,000 − $600 = $29,400, if payment is made within ten days after the invoice date. Otherwise the full $30,000 is due in sixty days.[4]

The cash discount is offered to entice prompt payment, which reduces the manufacturer's need to invest in Accounts Receivable. Early collection also reduces the risk of bad debts. On the other hand, the granting of favorable credit terms with attractive cash discounts is a way to compete with other sellers. That is, if one competitor grants such terms, other competitors tend to do likewise.

Should cash discounts be taken by purchasers? The answer is usually yes, but this depends on the relative costs of interest. Suppose K Mart decides not to pay for sixty days. It has the use of $29,400 for an extra fifty days (60 − 10) for an "interest" payment of $600. Based on a 365-day year, that is an effective interest rate of approximately:

$$\frac{\$600}{\$29,400} = \begin{array}{l} 2.04\% \text{ for 50 days, or 14.9\% for 365 days} \\ (\text{which is 2.04\% multiplied by 365} \div 50, \text{ or 7.3 periods of 50 days each}) \end{array}$$

Most well-managed companies, such as K Mart, can usually obtain funds for less than 14.9% per annum, so their accounting systems are designed to take advantage of all cash discounts automatically. However, some retailers pass up the discounts. Why? Because they have trouble getting loans or other financing at interest rates lower than the annual rates implied by the cash discount terms offered by their suppliers.

☐ Accounting for Cash Discounts

Cash discounts are essentially reductions of sales prices. The vast bulk of discounts offered are indeed taken. Consequently, a detailed income statement for management will often contain:

Gross sales		XXX
Deduct:		
Sales returns and allowances	X	
Cash discounts on sales	X	XXX
Net sales		XXX

---

[4] Terms may be quoted in various ways. For example:

n/30 means the full billed price is due on the thirtieth day after the invoice date.

1/5, n/30 means payment less a 1% cash discount must be made within five days of the invoice date; otherwise the full billed price is due in thirty days after the invoice date.

15 E.O.M. means the full price is due within fifteen days after the end of the month of sale. Thus, if the invoice is dated December 20, payment is due January 15.

In contrast, reports to shareholders offer highly summarized figures. For example, Nike simply shows "Revenues . . . $1,203,440,000" on its 1988 income statement.[5]

The important feature of the presentation is the fact that returns, allowances, and discounts are offsets to gross sales. Management may design an accounting system to use one account, Sales, or several accounts, as shown above. If only one account is used, all returns, allowances, and cash discounts would be direct decreases to the sales account. If a separate account is used for cash discounts on sales, the following analysis is made, using the numbers in our example:

	A	= L +	SE
1. Sell at terms of 2/10,n/60	+30,000 [Increase Accounts Receivable]	=	+30,000 [Increase Sales]
2. Either collect $29,400 ($30,000 less 2%)	+29,400 [Increase Cash] −30,000 [Decrease Accounts Receivable]	=	−600 [Increase Cash Discounts on Sales]
or collect $30,000	+30,000 [Increase Cash] −30,000 [Decrease Accounts Receivable]	=	(no effect)

The journal entries follow:

1.	Accounts receivable	30,000	
	Sales		30,000
2.	Cash	29,400	
	Cash discounts on sales	600	
	Accounts receivable		30,000
or			
	Cash	30,000	
	Accounts receivable		30,000

---

[5] In many countries outside the United States, the word *turnover* is used as a synonym for *sales*. For instance, in Denmark, Nike's performance would be described as a "turnover of $1,203,440,000."

□ Bank Cards

Many retailers accept bank cards such as VISA or MasterCard (or similar cards, such as American Express, Carte Blanche, or Diner's Club). Retailers do so for two major reasons: (a) to obtain credit customers who would otherwise shop elsewhere, and (b) to get cash immediately rather than wait for customers to pay in due course.

Retailers can deposit VISA slips in their bank accounts daily (just like cash). But this service costs money (usually from 1% to 3% of gross sales).[6] Thus sales of $10,000 could result in cash of only $10,000 − .03($10,000), or $10,000 − $300, or $9,700. The $300 amount could be separately tabulated for management control purposes:

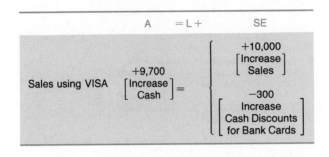

Cash	9,700	
Cash discounts for bank cards	300	
Sales		10,000

CASH

Revenue is generally accompanied by an increase in either cash or accounts receivable. This section discusses cash, and the next discusses accounts receivable.

Cash has the same meaning to organizations that it does to individuals. Cash encompasses all the items that are accepted for deposit by a bank, notably currency, coins, money orders, and checks. Banks do not accept postage stamps (which are really prepaid expenses) or notes receivable as cash. Indeed, although deposits are often credited to the accounts of bank customers on the date received, the bank may place a "hold" on a deposit until the check "clears" through the banking system. Therefore, if a check fails to clear because its writer has insufficient funds, its amount is deducted from the depositor's account.

Many companies combine cash and *cash equivalents* on their balance sheets.

---

[6] Large-volume retailers bear less cost as a percentage of sales. For example, J. C. Penney had an arrangement where it paid 4.3 cents per transaction plus 1.08% of the gross sales using bank cards.

Cash equivalents are highly liquid short-term investments that can easily be converted into cash with little delay. For example, the balance sheet of Nike, Inc., begins with "Cash and equivalents . . . $75,357,000." Nike describes its cash equivalents as "short-term, highly liquid investments with maturities of essentially three months or less." Examples of cash equivalents include money market funds and treasury bills.

☐ Compensating Balances

Sometimes the entire cash balance is not available for unrestricted use. Companies must frequently maintain **compensating balances,** which are required minimum cash balances on deposit with banks from which a company borrows money. The size of the minimum balance often depends on either the amount borrowed or the amount of credit available, or both.

To prevent any misleading information regarding cash, annual reports must disclose the state of any compensating balances. For example, a footnote in the annual report of North Carolina Natural Gas Corporation disclosed a requirement for a compensating balance "of 10% of the annual average loan outstanding."

☐ Management of Cash

Cash is usually a small portion of the total assets of a company. Yet, managers spend much time managing cash. Why? For many reasons. First, although the cash balance may be small at any one time, the flow of cash can be enormous. Weekly receipts and disbursements of cash may be many times as large as the cash balance. Second, because cash is the most liquid asset, it is enticing to thieves and embezzlers. Safeguards are necessary. Third, adequate cash is essential to the smooth functioning of operations. Managers must carefully plan for the acquisition and use of cash. Finally, cash itself does not earn income, so it is important not to hold excess cash.

Most organizations have detailed, well-specified procedures for receiving, recording, and disbursing cash. Cash is usually placed in a bank account, and the company's books are periodically reconciled with the bank's records. Appendix 6A shows how this is done. In addition, internal control procedures (discussed in Chapter 14) are set up to safeguard cash. Briefly, the major procedures include the following:

1. Those individuals in an organization who receive cash should not also disburse cash.
2. Those who handle cash should not have access to the accounting records.
3. All receipts of cash should be recorded and deposited. They should not be used directly to make payments.
4. Disbursements should be made by serially numbered checks only upon proper authorization by someone other than the person writing the check.
5. Bank accounts should be reconciled monthly.

Why are such controls necessary? Consider a person who handles cash and makes entries into the accounting records. That person could take cash and cover it up by making the following entry in the books:

Operating expenses	xxx	
Cash		xxx

Besides guarding against dishonest actions, the procedures help ensure accurate accounting records. Suppose a check is written but not recorded in the books. Without serially numbered checks, there would be no way of discovering the error before receiving a bank statement showing that the check was paid. But if checks are numbered, an unrecorded check can be identified, and such errors can be discovered early.

CREDIT SALES AND ACCOUNTS RECEIVABLE

Credit sales on open account create an increase in *accounts receivable*. An entity's **accounts receivable** (sometimes called **trade receivables** or simply **receivables**) are amounts owed to the entity by its customers as a result of delivering goods or services and of extending credit in the ordinary course of business. Accounts receivable should be distinguished from deposits, accruals, notes, and other assets not arising out of everyday sales. Moreover, the amounts included as accounts receivable should be collectible in accordance with the company's usual terms of sale.

☐ Uncollectible Accounts

Granting credit entails costs and benefits. One *cost* is the possibility that some credit customers will never pay. Another is the cost of administration and collection. The *benefit* is the boost in sales and profit that would otherwise be lost if credit were not extended. That is, many potential customers would not buy if credit were unavailable. The accountant often labels the major cost as "bad debt expenses" and the benefit as the additional gross profit on credit sales.

The extent of nonpayment of debts varies from industry to industry. It depends on the credit risks that managers are willing to accept. For instance, many small retail establishments will accept a higher level of risk than large stores such as Sears. Accompanying the risks are corresponding collection expenses.

The problem of uncollectible accounts is especially difficult in the health-care field. Some hospitals and physicians hire a collection agency for a fee based on collections attained, whereas others do not delegate this pursuit of delinquent debtors. For example, the Bayfront Medical Center of St. Petersburg, Florida, suffered bad debts equal to 21% of gross revenue. Management decided to collect its own delinquent accounts receivable instead of paying fees to a collection agency. The management problem here is also one of weighing costs and benefits.

Will the reduction in collection fee expense exceed the reduction in collections of revenue?

☐ Measuring Bad Debts: Specific Write-Off Method

The measurement of income becomes complicated because some debtors are either unable or unwilling to pay their debts. Such **"bad debts"** are also called "uncollectible accounts" or "doubtful accounts."

Suppose a retailer has credit sales of $100,000 (two hundred customers averaging $500 each) during 19X1. Collections during 19X1 were $60,000. The December 31, 19X1, accounts receivable of $40,000 includes the accounts of eighty different customers who have not yet paid for their 19X1 purchases:

CUSTOMER	AMOUNT OWED
1. Jones	$1,400
2. Smith	125
.	.
.	.
.	.
42. Montgomery	600
.	.
.	.
.	.
79. Weinberg	700
80. Porras	11
Total receivables	$40,000

The retailer knows from experience that 2% of sales is never collected. Therefore 2% × $100,000 = $2,000 of the 19X1 sales is expected to be uncollectible. However, the exact customer accounts that will not be collected are unknown at December 31, 19X1. (Of course, all $2,000 must be among the $40,000 of accounts receivable because the other $60,000 has already been collected.)

How should we account for this situation? There are two basic ways. First, consider the **specific write-off method,** which assumes that all sales are fully collectible until proved otherwise. Only when a specific customer account is identified as uncollectible is accounts receivable reduced. Because no specific customer's account is deemed to be uncollectible at the end of 19X1, the December 31, 19X1, balance sheet would show an asset:

Accounts receivable	$40,000

Now assume that during the second year, 19X2, the retailer identifies Jones and Montgomery as customers who are not expected to pay. When the chances of collection from specific customers become dim, the amounts in the *particular accounts* are written down and some sort of selling expense (frequently called *bad debts expense* or *uncollectible accounts expense*) is recognized:

Bad debts expense	2,000	
Accounts receivable, Jones		1,400
Accounts receivable, Montgomery		600

Effects of the specific write-off method on the balance sheet equation in 19X1 and 19X2 are (ignoring the collections of accounts receivable):

	A	= L +	SE
Specific Write-off Method			
19X1 Sales	+100,000 [Increase Accounts Receivable]	=	+100,000 [Increase Sales]
19X2 Write-off	−2,000 [Decrease Accounts Receivable]	=	−2,000 [Increase Bad Debts Expense]

The specific write-off method has justifiably been criticized because it fails to apply the matching principle of accrual accounting. The $2,000 bad debts expense in 19X2 is related to (or caused by) the $100,000 of 19X1 sales. Matching requires recognition of the bad debts expense at the same time as the related revenue, that is, in 19X1, not 19X2. The specific write-off method produces two wrongs. First, 19X1 income is overstated by $2,000 because no bad debts expense is charged. Second, 19X2 income is understated by $2,000. Why? Because 19X1's bad debts expense of $2,000 is charged in 19X2. Compare the specific write-off method with a correct matching of revenue and expense:

	Specific Write-off Method: Violates Matching		Matching Applied Correctly	
	19X1	19X2	19X1	19X2
Sales revenue	100,000	0	100,000	0
Bad debts expense	0	2,000	2,000	0

The principal arguments in favor of the specific write-off method are based on cost-benefit and materiality. The method is simple. Moreover, no great error in measurement occurs if amounts of bad debts are small or do not vary much from year to year.

☐ **Measuring Bad Debts: Allowance Method**

Most accountants oppose the specific write-off method because it violates the matching principle. But how can the bad debts expense be recognized in 19X1, before the specific uncollectible accounts are identified? By using the **allowance method,** which has two basic elements: (1) an *estimate* of the amount of sales that will ultimately be uncollectible, and (2) a *contra account*, usually called **al-**

lowance for doubtful accounts (or **allowance for uncollectible accounts, allowance for bad debts,** or **reserve for doubtful accounts**). The contra account is deducted from the accounts receivable, and it measures the amount of receivables estimated to be uncollectible from as yet unidentified customers. The effects of the allowance method on the balance sheet equation follow:

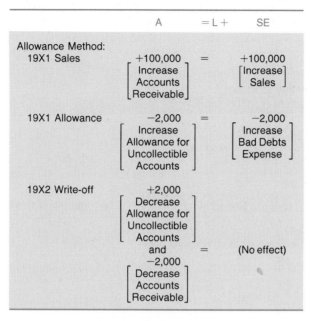

	A	= L +	SE
Allowance Method:			
19X1 Sales	+100,000 [Increase Accounts Receivable]	=	+100,000 [Increase Sales]
19X1 Allowance	−2,000 [Increase Allowance for Uncollectible Accounts]	=	−2,000 [Increase Bad Debts Expense]
19X2 Write-off	+2,000 [Decrease Allowance for Uncollectible Accounts] and −2,000 [Decrease Accounts Receivable]	=	(No effect)

The associated journal entries are:

19X1 Sales	Accounts receivable	100,000	
	Sales		100,000
19X1 Allowances	Bad debts expense	2,000	
	Allowance for uncollectible accounts		2,000
19X2 Write-offs	Allowance for uncollectible accounts	2,000	
	Accounts receivable, Jones		1,400
	Accounts receivable, Montgomery		600

The principal argument in favor of the allowance method is its superiority in measuring accrual accounting income in any given year. That is, the $2,000 of 19X1 sales that is estimated never to be collected should be recorded in 19X1, the same period as the one in which the $100,000 sales revenue is recognized.

The allowance method would result in the following presentation in the balance sheet, December 31, 19X1:[7]

---

[7] Banks call their "allowances" *loan loss reserves*, which are offset against their total loans receivable from customers. During the 1980s, a nationwide rash of bad loans caused much concern about the adequacy of these reserves.

Accounts receivable	$40,000
Less: Allowance for uncollectible accounts	2,000
Net accounts receivable	$38,000

Other formats for presenting the allowance method on balance sheets of actual companies include:

	1988	1987
NYNEX Corporation (in millions):		
Receivables (net of allowances of $145.8 and $111.8, respectively)	$2,510.4	$2,421.8
Pitney Bowes, Inc. (in thousands):		
Accounts receivable, less allowances:		
1987, $10,517; 1986, $10,730	$370,490	$365,740
Clean Harbors, Inc.:		
Accounts receivable, less reserves of $501,000 in 1988 and $282,000 in 1987	$17,188,316	$11,450,479
AT&T (in millions):		
Receivables less allowances of $466 and $484	$8,709	$8,038

□ Applying the Allowance Method

A contra asset account is created under the allowance method because of the inability to write down a specific customer's account at the time bad debts expense is recognized. In our example, at the end of 19X1 the retailer has $40,000 in Accounts Receivable. Based on past experience, a bad debts expense is recognized at a rate of 2% of total credit sales, or .02 × $100,000, or $2,000.

Visualize the relationship between the general ledger item *Accounts Receivable* and its supporting detail (which is a form of supporting ledger, called a *subsidiary ledger*) on December 31, 19X1. The sum of the balances of all the customer accounts in the subsidiary ledger must equal the accounts receivable balance in the general ledger:

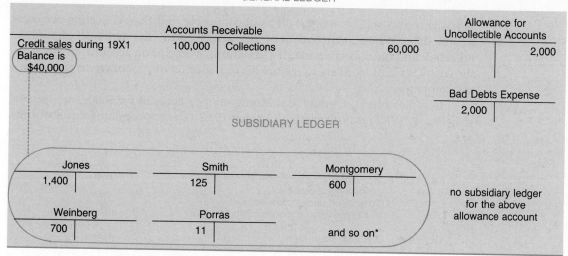

GENERAL LEDGER

* Total of these individual customer accounts must equal $40,000.

In 19X2, the Jones and Montgomery accounts become past due. After exhausting all practical means of collection, the retailer judges the accounts to be uncollectible. The following write-off entries would be made:

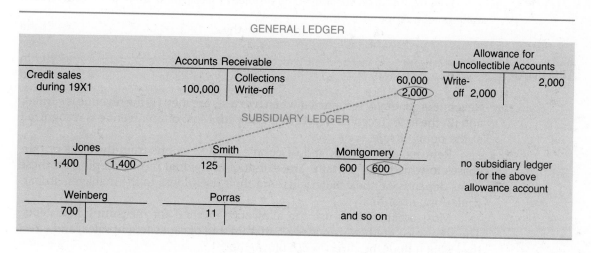

GENERAL LEDGER

Convince yourself that the ultimate write-off has no effect on total assets:

	BEFORE WRITE-OFF	AFTER WRITE-OFF
Accounts receivable	$40,000	$38,000
Allowance for uncollectible accounts	2,000	—
Book value (net realizable value)	$38,000	$38,000

□ Bad Debt Recoveries

A few accounts will be written off as uncollectible, but then collection occurs at a later date. When such **bad debt recoveries** occur, the write-off should be reversed, and the collection handled as a normal receipt on account. In this way, the customer is more likely to restore his or her otherwise poor credit rating with the company.

In our example, assume that Montgomery's account for $600 is written off in February 19X2 and collected in October 19X2. The appropriate journal entries are:

Feb. 19X2	Allowance for uncollectible accounts	600	
	Accounts receivable		600
	To write off uncollectible account		
	of Montgomery, a specific customer.		
Oct. 19X2	Accounts receivable	600	
	Allowance for uncollectible accounts		600
	To reverse February 19X2 write-off		
	of account of Montgomery.		
	Cash	600	
	Accounts receivable		600
	Collection on account		

For additional discussion of the problems of estimating bad debts and related matters, see Appendix 6B.

SUMMARY

Revenue is generally recognized when two tests are met: (1) the revenue is earned, and (2) the asset received in return is realized. Most often revenue is recognized at the point of sale.

Returns, allowances, and discounts are deductions from the sales or purchases to which they pertain. The extent of individual record keeping for these items depends on their materiality and their usefulness to the managers in particular organizations.

Most organizations use the allowance method for measuring bad debts. The allowance method provides a better linking of cause (credit sales) and effect (bad debts) than the direct write-off method.

SUMMARY PROBLEMS FOR YOUR REVIEW

□ Problem One

Hector Lopez, marketing manager for Fireplace Distributors, sold twelve woodstoves to Woodside Condominiums, Inc. The sales contract was signed on April 27, 19X1. The list price of each woodstove was $1,200, but a 5% quantity discount was allowed. The wood-stoves were to be delivered on May 10, and a cash discount of 2% of the amount owed was offered if payment was made by June 10. Fireplace Distributors delivered the wood-stoves as promised and received the proper payment on June 9.

Required:
1. In what month should the revenue be recognized? Explain.
2. Suppose Fireplace Distributors has a separate account titled "Cash Discounts on Sales." What journal entries would be made on June 9 when the cash payment is received?
3. Suppose Fireplace Distributors has another account titled "Sales Returns and Allowances." Suppose further that one of the woodstoves had a scratch, and Fireplace Distributors allowed Woodside to deduct $100 from the total amount due. What journal entries would be made on June 9 when the cash payment is received?

☐ Solution to Problem One

1. The revenue would be recognized in May. The key is whether the revenue is earned and the asset received is realized. The revenue is not earned until the merchandise is delivered; therefore revenue cannot be recognized in April. Provided that Woodside Condominiums has a good credit rating, the receipt of cash is reasonably ensured before the cash is actually received. Therefore recognition of revenue need not be delayed until June. On May 10 both revenue recognition tests are met, and the revenue would be recorded on May's income statement.

2. The original revenue recorded was 95% × (12 × $1,200) = $13,680, after deducting the 5% trade discount. The 2% cash discount is 2% × $13,680 = $273.60. Therefore the cash payment is $13,680 − $273.60 = $13,406.40:

Cash	13,406.40	
Cash discounts on sales	273.60	
Accounts receivable		13,680.00

3. The only difference from requirement 2 is a $100 smaller cash payment and a $100 debit to sales returns and allowances:

Cash	13,306.40	
Cash discounts on sales	273.60	
Sales returns and allowances	100.00	
Accounts receivable		13,680.00

☐ Problem Two

H. J. Heinz Company sells many popular food products, including its best selling Heinz ketchup. Its balance sheet showed the following (in thousands):

	May 1	
	1988	1987
Receivables:	499,405	455,306
Less allowance for doubtful accounts	7,502	9,021
	491,903	446,285

Required:

Suppose a large grocery chain that owed Heinz $2 million announced bankruptcy on May 2, 1988. Heinz decided that chances for collection were virtually zero. The account was immediately written off. Show the balances as of May 2, 1988, after the write-off. Explain the effect of the write-off on income for May 1988.

☐ Solution to Problem Two

Receivables ($449,405 − $2,000)	$497,405
Less allowance for doubtful accounts	5,502
	$491,903

Because Heinz has an account labeled allowance for doubtful accounts, it must use the allowance method. The write-off will not affect the *net* carrying amount of the receivables, which is still $491,903,000. Moreover, the income for May 1988 will be unaffected. Why? Because the estimated expense has already been recognized in prior periods. Under the allowance method, net assets and income are affected when the estimation process occurs, not when the write-off actually happens.

HIGHLIGHTS TO REMEMBER

1. Changes in gross profit can inform managers and investors about the profitability of a company's products.
2. The terms *net sales* and *net purchases* represent gross amounts less offsetting amounts for returns, allowances, and cash discounts.
3. The allowance method of accounting for bad debts recognizes an expense before the specific bad account is identified and written off.

ACCOUNTING VOCABULARY

Accounts Receivable, p. 220
Aging of Accounts, p. 235
Allowance for Bad Debts, p. 223
Allowance for Doubtful Accounts, p. 223
Allowance for Uncollectible Accounts, p. 223
Allowance Method, p. 222
Average Collection Period, p. 236
Bad Debt Recoveries, p. 226
Bad Debts, p. 221
Bank Reconciliation, p. 230
Cash Discounts, p. 216
Cash Equivalents, p. 219

Compensating Balances, p. 219
Gross Profit Test, p. 212
Imprest Basis, p. 233
Purchase Allowances, p. 214
Purchase Returns, p. 214
Receivables, p. 220
Reserve for Doubtful Accounts, p. 223
Sales Allowances, p. 214
Sales Returns, p. 214
Specific Write-off Method, p. 221
Trade Discounts, p. 215
Trade Receivables, p. 220

APPENDIX 6A: ACCOUNTING FOR CASH

This appendix describes how organizations account for cash. Most cash is kept in bank accounts. Therefore the focus is on understanding bank statements and transactions.

Exhibit 6–1 displays an actual bank statement. The overall format shows that the statement is basically one account among hundreds or thousands of the bank's deposits. Together, these accounts form the subsidiary ledger that supports the bank's general ledger account *Deposits*, a liability. The statement shows checks as debits and deposits as credits, which is consistent with the idea that this is the *bank's* statement of its deposit payable.

The supporting documents for the detailed checks on the statement are canceled checks; for additional deposits, deposit slips. Symbols are often used to denote other types of transactions. In Exhibit 6–1, the symbol *S* means subtotal (the previous balance brought forward), *A* means activity charge (the amount frequently depends on whether the average balance is above a specified minimum), and *OD* means overdraft (an overdrawn account, a negative checking account balance arising from the bank's paying a check even though the depositor had insufficient funds available at the instant the check was presented).

Banks do not like overdrafts. Overdrafts are permitted as an occasional courtesy by the bank. However, the depositor is rarely given more than a day or two to eliminate the overdraft by making an additional deposit. Moreover, the bank may levy a fee ($5 or $10) for each overdraft if the depositor is careless and overdraws his or her account more than once every year or two.

Banks often provide (for a fee plus interest) "automatic" loan privileges for valued depositors. This arrangement provides for short-term loans (from ten to thirty days or more) to ensure against overdrafts. That is, when a depositor has an insufficient balance to cover his or her checks, the bank credits the depositor's account with additional money (an "automatic" loan). In this way, overdrafts are avoided. Furthermore, the depositor avoids any embarrassment or risks of a bank's delaying payment of a check to await an additional deposit.

EXHIBIT 6–1

An Actual Bank Statement

Bank Statement

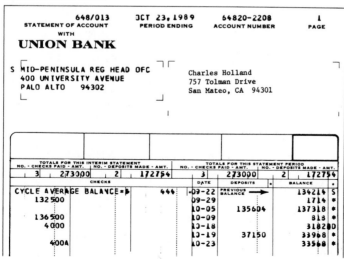

BANK RECONCILIATIONS

Exhibit 6–2 demonstrates how an independent check of cash balances works for any bank depositor (individual or entity). First, note how parallel records are kept. The balance on December 31 is an asset (Cash) on the depositor's books and a liability (Deposits) on the bank's books. The terms *debit* and *credit* are often used in banking. They refer to the entries in the bank's books. Banks *credit* the depositor's account for additional deposits and *debit* the account for checks cleared and canceled (paid) by the bank. Thus the $2,000 check drawn by the depositor on January 5 is paid on January 8 when it is presented to the bank for payment. The bank's journal entry would be:

Jan. 8	Deposits	2,000	
	Cash		2,000
	To debit the depositor's account		

A credit balance on the bank's books means that the bank owes money to the depositor. A monthly bank reconciliation is conducted by the depositor to make sure that all cash receipts and disbursements are accounted for. A **bank reconciliation** is an analysis

EXHIBIT 6–2

Comparative Cash Balance

Depositor's Records

Cash in Bank (receivable from bank)

		19X2	
12/31/X1 Bal.	11,000	1/5	2,000
19X2		1/15	3,000
1/10	4,000		
		1/19	5,000
1/24	6,000		
1/31	7,000	1/29	10,000
	28,000		20,000
1/31/X2 Bal.	8,000		

Bank's Records

Deposits (payable)

19X2			
1/8	2,000	12/31/X1 Bal.	11,000
1/20	3,000	19X2	
		1/11	4,000
1/28	5,000	1/26	6,000
1/31	20*		
	10,020		21,000
		1/31/X2 Bal.	10,980

Date	Depositor's General Journal	Debit	Credit
19X2			
1/5	Accounts payable	2,000	
	Cash		2,000
	Check No. 1.		
1/10	Cash	4,000	
	Accounts receivable		4,000
	Deposit slip No. 1.		
1/15	Income taxes payable	3,000	
	Cash		3,000
	Check No. 2.		
1/19	Accounts payable	5,000	
	Cash		5,000
	Check No. 3.		
1/24	Cash	6,000	
	Accounts receivable		6,000
	Deposit No. 2.		
1/29	Accounts payable	10,000	
	Cash		10,000
	Check No. 4.		
1/31	Cash	7,000	
	Accounts receivable		7,000
	Deposit No. 3.		

* Service charge for printing checks.

that explains any differences existing between the cash balance shown by the depositor and that shown by the bank. Bank reconciliations can take many formats, but the objective is unchanged: to explain all differences in a cash balance at a given date. Using the data in Exhibit 6–2:

Bank Reconciliation
January 31, 19X2

Balance per books (also called *balance per check register, register balance*)	$ 8,000
Deduct: Bank service charges for January not recorded (also include any other	
charges by the bank not yet deducted)*	20
Adjusted (corrected) balance per books	$ 7,980
Balance per bank (also called *bank statement balance, statement balance*)	$10,980
Add: Deposits not recorded by bank (also called *unrecorded deposits, deposits*	
in transit), deposit of 1/31	7,000
Total	$17,980
Deduct: Outstanding checks, check of 1/29	10,000
Adjusted (corrected) balance per bank	$ 7,980

* Note that new entries on the depositor's books are required for all additions and deductions made to achieve the adjusted balance per books.

As the bank reconciliation indicates, an adjustment is necessary on the books of the depositor:

Jan. 31	Bank service charge expense		20	
	Cash			20
	To record bank charges for printing checks.			

This popular format has two major sections. The first section begins with the balance per books (that is, the balance in the Cash T-account). Adjustments are made for items not entered on the *books* but already entered by the *bank*, such as deduction of the $20 service charge. No additions are shown in the illustrated section, but an example would be the bank's collection of a customer receivable on behalf of the company. The second section begins with the balance per bank. Adjustments are made for items not entered by the *bank* but already entered in the books. After adjustments, each section should end with identical adjusted cash balances. This is the amount that should appear as cash in bank on the depositor's balance sheet.

ILLUSTRATION OF VARIOUS BANK TRANSACTIONS

Each passing year brings us closer to so-called paperless banking. For example, many employees never see their payroll checks. Instead the employer deposits the "checks" in the employees' bank accounts. This is an example of an "automatic" deposit. If the employee forgets to add the amount to his or her check register, the bank's books would show a higher balance than the depositor's books.

Suppose an employee, Mary Phelan, has a personal bank account. Her employer deposits her weekly paycheck automatically each Friday. Her check register (checkbook) for March is summarized as follows:

Reconciled cash balance, March 1, 19X7			$1,000
Additions:			
Weekly payroll deposits:	March		
	2		500
	9		500
	16		500
	23		500
Deposit of check received for used car sold to brother-in-law	25		800
Deposit of check received as birthday gift from parents	31		100
Subtotal			$3,900
Deductions:			
Checks written #291–#303	1–23	$3,000	
Check #304	27	60	
Check #305	30	80	
Check #306	31	430	3,570
Cash in bank, March 31, 19X7			$ 330

Her bank statement is summarized in Exhibit 6–3. Note the code at the bottom of the exhibit, which explains the transactions on the bank's books. The brother-in-law's $800 check "bounced"; that is, when the bank presented the check for payment, his bank refused to honor it. Mary's bank then reversed the $800 deposit of March 25 by charging it back to her on March 28. This led to an overdraft of $60. By prearrangement with Mary, the bank automatically lends sufficient amounts (in multiples of $100) to ensure that her balance is never less than $100. Therefore a loan of $200 was made.

Exhibit 6–4 shows a bank reconciliation of the discrepancies between the bank's books and the depositor's books. Assume that the individual keeps a complete set of

EXHIBIT 6–3

Bank Statement of Deposit Account, Mary Phelan

CHECKS AND OTHER CHARGES		DEPOSITS	DATE	BALANCE
			3/1	1,000 BF
		500 AP	3/2	1,500
		500 AP	3/9	2,000
		500 AP	3/16	2,500
		500 AP	3/23	3,000
#291–#303 various dates in March. These would be shown by specific amounts, but are shown here as a total:	3,000		3/1–3/24	0
		800	3/25	800
#304	60		3/27	740
	800 NSF		3/28	60 OD
		200 AL	3/28	140
		500 AP	3/30	640
	20 MA		3/31	620

AL—automatic loan
AP—automatic deposit from employee payroll
BF—balance brought forward

MA—monthly activity charge
NSF—returned check
OD—overdraft

EXHIBIT 6–4

Mary Phelan's Bank Reconciliation
March 31, 19X7

Balance per books		$ 330
Additions:		
Unrecorded automatic deposit of weekly payroll, March 30	$500	
Unrecorded automatic loan by bank to cover overdraft	200	700
Subtotal		$1,030
Deductions:		
Brother-in-law's returned check, often called NSF check (for Not Sufficient Funds)	$800	
Monthly activity fees	20	820
Adjusted (corrected) balance per books		$ 210
Balance per bank		$ 620
Additions:		
Unrecorded deposit of March 31 (deposit in transit)		100
Subtotal		$ 720
Deductions:		
Outstanding checks:		
#305	$ 80	
#306	430	510
Adjusted (corrected) balance per bank		$ 210

personal books on the accrual basis. The bank reconciliation leads to the following compound journal entry by the depositor:

Receivable from brother-in-law	800	
Bank service charge expense	20	
Note payable to bank		200
Salary revenue		500
Cash in bank		120
To update and correct balances in various accounts as indicated by monthly bank reconciliation.		

The reconciliation pointed out entries that belonged on the depositor's books but had not yet been entered. After these transactions were recorded with the foregoing journal entry, the depositor's book balance differed from the bank's balance by $620 − $210 = $410. Why? Because two checks ($430 and $80) and one deposit ($100) had been recorded by the depositor but were still in transit to the bank.

PETTY CASH

Every organization desires to minimize red tape—for example, avoiding unjustifiably complicated procedures for minor disbursements. Consequently, petty cash funds are usually created and accounted for on an **imprest basis.** An imprest petty cash fund is initiated with a fixed amount of currency and coins. As the currency is used, petty cash receipts or vouchers are prepared to show the purposes of the disbursements. When the balance of currency gets low, the fund is restored to its original level by drawing and cashing a single check for the exact amount of the needed cash replenishment. The following are typical journal entries:

Petty cash	100	
Cash in bank		100
To set up a fund for miscellaneous		
minor office disbursements. (A check		
is drawn, cashed, and proceeds placed		
with some responsible person.)		
Postage	10	
Freight in	40	
Miscellaneous office expenses	35	
Cash in bank		85
To replenish the petty cash fund and		
record expenses paid therefrom.		

Examples of petty cash outlays include special post-office charges for certifying or insuring mail, collections by delivery personnel, and dinner money given to a secretary when working overtime.

Note that after inception the Petty Cash account iself is never directly charged or credited unless the $100 initial amount of the fund is increased or decreased. Further, the cash on hand plus the receipts (or vouchers) should always equal the $100 amount of the petty cash fund.

APPENDIX 6B: MORE ON ACCOUNTS RECEIVABLE AND BAD DEBTS

ESTIMATING UNCOLLECTIBLES

This chapter includes two sections on accounting for bad debts. The allowance method was cited as being more consistent with accrual accounting than the specific write-off method. We now explore the allowance method in more detail. To refresh your memory, please review the chapter presentation on pages 222–225 before proceeding here.

The net amount of Accounts Receivable is supposed to equal the net realizable value of the asset. Therefore, if the Allowance for Bad Debts is too high, the net asset is understated; if too low, the net asset is overstated. The general tendency is to be conservative, which means that the allowance is usually overstated. Therefore the net asset is generally understated.

Under the allowance method, there are three popular ways to estimate the bad debts expense for a particular year: (1) percentage of sales, (2) percentage of ending accounts receivable, and (3) aging of accounts. The percentage of sales method is used in the example on page 224. Based on past experience, bad debts expense is recognized at a percentage rate of total credit sales (or of total sales if the proportions of cash and credit sales are little changed through the years). This percentage may be altered from year to year, depending on the amount in the Allowance for Bad Debts that is carried over from one year to the next. Bad debts expense is debited and the allowance account is credited.

The main weakness of the percentage of sales method is that it ignores the most current information about receivables, the actual collection experience for the year. The other two methods incorporate this information by basing the allowance on the end-of-the-year accounts receivable balance rather than on the entire year's sales.

PERCENTAGE OF ENDING ACCOUNTS RECEIVABLE

Auditors of the Internal Revenue Service favor the percentage of ending accounts receivable method as a reasonable approach for applying the accrual method of accounting for bad debts. The additions to the Allowance for Bad Debts are calculated to achieve a desired balance in the Allowance account. Consider the following:

	ACCOUNTS RECEIVABLE AT END OF YEAR	BAD DEBT EXPERIENCE	
		Deemed Uncollectible and Written Off	Recoveries
19X1	$100,000	$ 3,800	$ 300
19X2	80,000	2,700	250
19X3	90,000	2,700	150
19X4	110,000	4,600	500
19X5	120,000	6,000	400
19X6	112,000	2,400	200
Six-year total	$612,000	$22,200	$1,800
Average (divide by 6)	$102,000	$ 3,700	$ 300

The 19X6 addition to the Allowance for Bad Debts would be computed as follows:

1. Determine the average net losses as a percentage of the average ending balance of Accounts Receivable: Average net bad debt losses would be $3,700 less $300 average recoveries, or $3,400. Divide $3,400 by $102,000 to obtain 3.333%.
2. Apply the percentage to the ending Accounts Receivable balance to determine the balance that should be in the Allowance account at the end of the year: 3.333% × $112,000 receivables at the end of 19X6 is $3,733.
3. Prepare an adjusting entry to bring the Allowance to the appropriate amount. Suppose the books show a $600 balance at the end of 19X6. Then the bad debts expense for 19X6 is $3,733 − $600, or $3,133. The journal entry would be:

Bad debts expense	3,133	
Allowance for bad debts		3,133
To bring the Allowance to the level justified by bad debt experience during the past six years.		

The *percentage of accounts receivable method* differs from the percentage of sales method in two ways: (1) the percentage is based on the ending accounts receivable balance rather than on sales, and (2) the dollar amount calculated is the appropriate *ending balance* in the allowance account, not the amount added to the account for the year.

AGING OF ACCOUNTS

Aging of accounts is an analysis of the elements of individual accounts receivable according to the time elapsed since the dates of billing. Aging is done for management control purposes as well as for financial reporting purposes. Like the percentage of ending accounts receivable method, the aging method estimates the appropriate *ending balance* in the allowance account. Computer technology facilitates the regular aging of accounts for credit managers. In this way, managers can easily detect the accounts that deserve follow-up for collection purposes. For example, the $112,000 balance in Accounts Receivable on December 31, 19X6, might be aged as follows:

NAME	TOTAL	1–30 DAYS	31–60 DAYS	61–90 DAYS	OVER 90 DAYS
Oxwall Tools	$ 20,000	$20,000			
Chicago Castings	10,000	10,000			
Estee	20,000	15,000	$ 5,000		
Sarasota Pipe	22,000		12,000	$10,000	
Ceilcote	4,000			3,000	$1,000
Other accounts (each detailed)	36,000	24,000	8,000	2,000	2,000
Total	$112,000	$69,000	$25,000	$15,000	$3,000
Bad debt percentages		0.1%	1%	5%	90%
Bad debt allowance to be provided	$ 3,769	$ 69	$ 250	$ 750	$2,700

Experience with the aging schedule may lead to its being used as the primary basis for estimating bad debts. The accounts with the oldest outstanding balances should have already been subject to extra collection efforts. As the tabulation indicates, the outlook for ultimate collection is less optimistic as the age of the account balance increases. Experience leads to the percentages illustrated. In this case, fully 90% of the balances older than ninety days are not expected to be collected.

The outside auditors examine the aging schedule to assess the net realizable value of the accounts. It is foolhardy to rely solely on some overall percentage. In particular, this year's proportion of the accounts receivable in the over-ninety-days category is compared with the proportion in previous years.

Auditors do not like surprises. Percentages based on past experience may not provide an appropriate allowance for bad debts when a big customer has suddenly slowed payments. For example, is Sarasota Pipe's $22,000 balance heading for the over-ninety-days category? Is Sarasota Pipe heading for bankruptcy? These are specific questions that the credit manager and the auditors should ask (rather than blindly using past percentages).

Another advantage of the aging schedule is that credit managers can make particular judgments about the quality of their customers. For instance, suppose Oxwall Tools bought plenty of merchandise but habitually was a "slow-pay" customer. Aging schedules always showed substantial balances in the 61–90 and over-ninety-days columns. Should the credit manager crack down on Oxwall? Many companies tolerate slow-paying customers (especially if they are big customers) as a way of competing. If so, the over-ninety-days schedule would have to be divided between those slow payers who are tolerated for legitimate competitive reasons and those who are likely deadbeats.

AVERAGE COLLECTION PERIOD

The average age of accounts receivable is a key financial ratio. It is often called the **average collection period** and is defined as follows:

$$\text{Average collection period} = \frac{\text{Average accounts receivable}}{\text{Sales on account}} \times 365$$

In our example, suppose sales on account (or credit sales) in 19X6 were $1 million:

$$\text{Average collection period} = \frac{\frac{1}{2}(\$120,000 + 112,000)}{\$1,000,000} \times 365$$

$$= 42.3 \text{ days}$$

Credit managers, bank loan officers, and auditors follow changes in this ratio and compare it with the entity's credit terms. Of course, the lengthening of collection periods is usually not a welcome signal, although it is sometimes the result of a deliberate loosening of credit terms in order to attract more sales.

Another way of computing the average collection period follows:

$$\text{One day's sales on account} = \frac{\text{Sales on account for the year}}{365 \text{ days}}$$
$$= \$1{,}000{,}000 \div 365$$
$$= \$2{,}740$$

$$\text{Average collection period} = \frac{\text{Average accounts receivable}}{\text{One day's sales on account}}$$
$$= \frac{\tfrac{1}{2}\,(\$120{,}000 + \$112{,}000)}{\$2{,}740}$$
$$= \$116{,}000 \div \$2{,}740$$
$$= 42.3 \text{ days}$$

FUNDAMENTAL ASSIGNMENT MATERIAL

☐ General Coverage

6–1 **GROSS PROFIT TEST.** (Alternates are 6–4 and 6–53.) Kramer Shoe Store had the following results for the past four years (in thousands):

	19X6	19X7	19X8	19X9
Sales revenues	$400	$450	$600	$700
Cost of goods sold	244	270	342	455
Gross profit	$156	$180	$258	$245

Ken Kramer is concerned about the drop in gross profit in 19X9 despite an increase in sales.

Required: I Apply a gross profit test. What are some possible causes of the change in gross profit?

6–2. **REVENUE RECOGNITION, CASH DISCOUNTS, AND RETURNS.** University Bookstore ordered 1,000 copies of an introductory economics textbook from Prentice Hall on July 17, 19X0. The books were delivered on August 12, at which time a bill was sent requesting payment of $30 per book. However, a 1.5% discount was allowed if Prentice Hall received payment by September 12. University Bookstore sent the proper payment, which was received by Prentice Hall on September 10. On December 18 University Bookstore returned 60 books to Prentice Hall for a full cash refund.

Required:
1. Prepare the journal entries (if any) for Prentice Hall on (a) July 17, (b) August 12, (c) September 10, and (d) December 18. Include appropriate explanations.
2. Suppose this was the only sales transaction in 19X0. Prepare the revenue section of Prentice Hall's income statement.

6–3. **UNCOLLECTIBLE ACCOUNTS.** (Alternates are 6–5 and 6–6.) During 19X2, the El Paso Hardware Store had credit sales of $500,000. The store manager expects that 2% of the credit sales will never be collected, although no accounts are written off until ten assorted steps have been taken to attain collection. The ten steps require a minimum of fourteen months.

Assume that during 19X3, specific customers are identified who are never expected to pay $10,000 that they owe from the sales of 19X2.

Required:	1. Show the impact on the balance sheet equation of the above transactions in 19X2 and 19X3 under (a) the specific write-off method and (b) the allowance method. Which method do you prefer? Why?
	2. Prepare journal entries for both methods. Omit explanations.

☐ **Understanding Published Financial Reports**

6–4. Gross Profit Test.   (Alternates are 6–1 and 6–53.) Lincoln Logs Ltd. is a leading producer of building packages for log homes. The company's actual income statements show:

	1988	1987	1986
Net sales	$18,647,079	$13,836,731	$9,453,813
Cost of sales	10,128,312	7,299,752	4,729,952
Gross profit	$ 8,518,767	$6,536,979	$4,723,861

Required: | Apply a gross profit test. What are some possible causes of the change in gross profit?

6–5. Uncollectible Accounts.   (Alternates are 6–3 and 6–6.) Intermec Corporation is the world's leading manufacturer of bar code data collection systems. Its balance sheet at the end of fiscal 1988 included the following data (in thousands):

Trade accounts receivable, net of allowances for doubtful accounts of $691	$24,309

Required:	1. The company uses the allowance method for accounting for bad debts. Suppose the company added $600,000 to the allowance during fiscal 1988. Write-offs of uncollectible accounts were $576,000. Show (a) the impact on the balance sheet equation of these transactions and (b) the journal entries.
	2. Suppose Intermec had used the specific write-off method for accounting for bad debts. Using the same information as in requirement 1, show (a) the impact on the balance sheet equation and (b) the journal entry.
	3. How would the Intermec balance sheet amounts shown above have been affected if the specific write-off method had been used up to that date? Be specific.

6–6. Uncollectible Accounts.   (Alternates are 6–3 and 6–5.) Exxon Corporation is the world's largest producer of oil and gas. Its balance sheet included the following actual presentation:

	DECEMBER 31	
	1986	1987
	(Millions of Dollars)	
Notes and accounts receivable, less estimated doubtful accounts	$6,784	$6,278

(Unlike most corporations, Exxon presents its most recent financial statement in the final column of a comparative presentation.)

Required: 1. Footnote 2 to Exxon's financial statements read: "Estimated doubtful notes and accounts receivable were $151 million at the end of 1986 and $164 million at the end of 1987." Suppose that during 1987 Exxon added $145 million to its allowance for estimated doubtful accounts. Write-offs of uncollectible accounts were $132 million. Show (a) the impact on the balance sheet equation of these transactions and (b) the journal entries.

2. Assume that Exxon had used the specific write-off method for accounting for bad debts. Using the same information as in requirement 1, show (a) the impact on the balance sheet equation and (b) the journal entry.

3. How would the Exxon balance sheet amounts have been affected if the specific write-off method had been used? Be specific.

ADDITIONAL ASSIGNMENT MATERIAL

☐ **General Coverage**

6–7. "A gross profit test is a computation of the minimum price permitted by federal law." Do you agree? Explain.

6–8. Suppose a company's gross profit declines. What are some possible causes for the decline?

6–9. Describe the two alternatives for the timing of revenue recognition on a $50 million long-term government contract with work spread evenly over five years. Which method do you prefer? Explain.

6–10. Why is the realizable value of a credit sale often less than that of a cash sale?

6–11. Distinguish between a *sales allowance* and a *purchase allowance*.

6–12. Distinguish between a *cash discount* and a *trade discount*.

6–13. "Trade discounts should not be recorded by the accountant." Do you agree? Explain.

6–14. "Retailers who accept VISA or MasterCharge are foolish because they do not receive the full price for merchandise they sell." Comment.

6–15. Describe and give two examples of *cash equivalents*.

6–16. "A compensating balance essentially increases the interest rate on money borrowed." Explain.

6–17. "Cash is only 3% of our total assets. Therefore we should not waste time designing systems to manage cash. We should use our time on matters that have a better chance of affecting our profits." Do you agree? Explain.

6–18. The El Camino Hospital uses the allowance method in accounting for bad debts. A journal entry was made for writing off the accounts of Jane Jensen, Eunice Belmont, and Samuel Maze:

Bad debts expense	14,321	
Accounts receivable		14,321

Do you agree with this entry? If not, show the correct entry and the correcting entry.

6–19. Distinguish between the allowance method and the specific write-off method for bad debts.

6–20. "The Allowance for Bad Debts account has no subsidiary ledger, but the Accounts Receivable account does." Explain.

6–21. Z Company received a $100 cash payment from a customer and immediately deposited the cash in a bank account. Z Company *debited* its Cash account, but the bank statement showed the deposit as a *credit*. Explain.

6–22. "The cash balance on a company's books should always equal the cash balance shown by its bank." Do you agree? Explain.

6–23. How can a credit balance arise in an Accounts Receivable subsidiary ledger? How should it be accounted for?

6–24. "Under the allowance method, there are three popular ways to estimate the bad debts expense for a particular year." Name the three.

6–25. What is meant by "aging of accounts"?

6–26. Describe why a write-off of a bad debt should be reversed if collection occurs at a later date.

6–27. What is the relationship between the average collection period and the average age of accounts receivable?

6–28. **GROSS PROFIT TEST AND THE IRS.** A local hardware store was purchased by a new owner in January 19X9. The financial statement submitted to the Internal Revenue Service for 19X9 included:

	19X9
Sales revenues	$480,000
Cost of goods sold	320,000
Gross profit	160,000
Operating expenses (detailed)	140,000
Taxable income	$ 20,000

A tax auditor was surprised at the low reported taxable income. He compared the 19X9 results with the statements submitted by the previous owner:

	19X6	19X7	19X8
Sales revenues	$370,000	$420,000	$480,000
Cost of goods sold	215,000	245,000	280,000
Gross profit	155,000	175,000	200,000
Operating expenses (detailed)	125,000	130,000	135,000
Taxable income	$ 30,000	$ 45,000	$ 65,000

Required: | Suppose you were the tax auditor. Apply a gross profit test. Based on the results of the gross profit test, what are some possible causes for the low taxable income?

6–29. **REVENUE RECOGNITION.** Mason Logging Company hired Gonzales Construction Co. to build a new bridge across the Gray River. The bridge would extend a logging road into a new stand of timber. The contract called for a payment of $6 million upon completion of the bridge. Work was begun in 19X0 and completed in 19X2. Total costs were:

19X0	$1 million
19X1	$2 million
19X2	$1 million
Total	$4 million

Required: | 1. Suppose the accountant for Gonzales Construction Co. judged that Mason Logging might not be able to pay the $6 million. Still, the chance of a $2 million profit makes the contract attractive enough to sign. How much revenue would you recognize each year?
2. Suppose Mason Logging is a subsidiary of a major wood-products company. Therefore receipt of payment on the contract is reasonably certain. How much revenue would you recognize each year?

6–30. **SALES RETURNS AND DISCOUNTS.** Alliance Hardware Wholesalers had gross sales of $800,000 during the month of February. Sales returns and allowances were $40,000. Cash discounts granted were $18,000.

Required: Prepare an analysis of the impact of these transactions on the balance sheet equation. Also show the journal entries. Prepare a detailed presentation of the revenue section of the income statement.

6–31. **GROSS AND NET SALES.** Bowen Company reported the following in 19X0 (in thousands):

Net sales	$380
Cash discounts on sales	8
Sales returns and allowances	17

Required:
1. Prepare the revenue section of Bowen's income statement.
2. Prepare journal entries for (a) initial revenue recognition for 19X0 sales, (b) sales returns and allowances, and (c) collection of accounts receivable. Assume that all sales were on credit and all accounts receivable for 19X0 sales were collected in 19X0. Omit explanations.

6–32. **CASH DISCOUNT TRANSACTIONS.** Video Equipment Wholesalers sells at terms of 2/10, n/30. It sold equipment to Phonic Retailers for $80,000 on open account on January 10. Payment (net of cash discount) was received on January 19. Using the equation framework, analyze the two transactions for Video. Also prepare journal entries.

6–33. **ENTRIES FOR CASH DISCOUNTS AND RETURNS ON SALES.** The Gateway Company is a wholesaler of furniture that sells on credit terms of 2/10, n/30. Consider the following transactions:

June 9 Sales on credit to Riordan Store, $10,000.
June 11 Sales on credit to Marty's Furniture, $12,000.
June 18 Collected from Riordan Store.
June 26 Accepted the return of furniture from Marty's Furniture, $1,000.
July 10 Collected from Marty's Furniture.
July 12 Riordan returned some defective furniture that she had acquired on June 9 for $500. Gateway issued a cash refund immediately.

Required: Prepare journal entries for these transactions. Omit explanations. Assume that the full appropriate amounts were exchanged.

6–34. **CREDIT TERMS, DISCOUNTS, AND ANNUAL INTEREST RATES.** As the struggling owner of a new restaurant, you suffer from a habitual shortage of cash. Yesterday the following invoices arrived:

VENDOR	FACE AMOUNT	TERMS
Val Produce	$ 600	n/30
Rose Exterminators	90	EOM
Top Meat Supply	500	n/5, EOM
John's Fisheries	1,000	1/10, n/30
Garcia Equipment	2,000	2/10, n/30

Required:
1. Write out the exact meaning of each of the terms.
2. You can borrow cash from the local bank on a ten-, twenty-, or thirty-day note bearing an annual interest rate of 16%. Should you borrow to take advantage of the cash discounts offered by the two vendors? Why? Show computations. For interest rate computations, assume a 360-day year.

6–35. **Accounting for Credit Cards.** The Moyer Shoe Store has extended credit to customers on open account. Its average experience for each of the past three years has been:

	CASH	CREDIT	TOTAL
Sales	$500,000	$200,000	$700,000
Bad debts expense	—	4,000	4,000
Administrative expense	—	2,000	2,000

Moyer is considering whether to accept bank cards (e.g., VISA, MasterCard). She has resisted because she does not want to bear the cost of the service, which would be 5% of gross sales.

The representative of VISA claims that the availability of bank cards would have increased overall sales by at least 10%. However, regardless of the level of sales, the new mix of the sales would be 50% bank card and 50% cash.

Required:
1. How would a bank card sale of $200 affect the accounting equation? Where would the discount appear on the income statement?
2. Should Moyer adopt the bank card if sales do not increase? Base your answer solely on the sparse facts given here.
3. Repeat requirement 2, but assume that total sales would increase 10%.

6–36. **Trade-ins versus Discounts.** Many states base their sales tax on gross sales less any discount. Trade-in allowances are not discounts, so they are not deducted from the sales price for sales tax purposes.

Suppose Sven Gustafson had decided to trade in his old car for a new one with a list price of $20,000. He will pay cash of $12,000 plus sales tax. If he had not traded in a car, the dealer would have offered a discount of 15% of the list price. The sales tax is 8%.

Required:
How much of the $8,000 price reduction should be called a discount? How much a trade in? Mr. Gustafson wants to pay as little sales tax as legally possible.

6–37. **Late Payment Fees.** Clark and Ketchum, a law firm, has been plagued by slow payments from clients. During 19X1, the firm instituted the following credit policy: 1/10, n/30, but add 2% of the invoice for each thirty days or part thereof after the due date.

Invoices dated September 30, 19X1, were billed to clients for $200,000. The appropriate amount of cash was collected for 10% of that amount within the first ten days. Another 60% was collected within the next twenty days. Of the remainder, 10% was paid within the following thirty days. No other payments had been received by December 31, the end of the fiscal year. (The "due date" was October 30.)

Required:
Prepare all the journal entries required by the above data. Ignore the question of bad debts; that is, assume that all receivables will ultimately be collected.

6–38. **Compensating Balances.** Pegasus Company borrowed $100,000 from First Bank at 8% interest. The loan agreement stated that a compensating balance of $20,000 must be kept in the Pegasus checking account at First Bank. The total Pegasus cash balance is $45,000.

Required:
1. How much usable cash did Pegasus Company receive for its $100,000 loan?
2. What was the real interest rate paid by Pegasus?
3. Prepare a footnote for the annual report of Pegasus Company explaining the compensating balance.

6–39. **Bad Debts.** Prepare all journal entries regarding the following data. Consider the following balances of a hospital, December 31, 19X1: Receivables from Patients, $200,000; and Allowance for Doubtful Receivables, $40,000. During 19X2, total billings to individual patients, excluding the billings to third-party payers such as Blue Cross and Medicare, were $3 million. Past experience indicated that 20% of such individual billings would ultimately be uncollectible. Write-offs of receivables during 19X2 were $580,000.

6–40. **Bad Debt Allowance.** Holtz Hardware Store had sales of $950,000 during 19X2, including $400,000 of sales on credit. Balances on December 31, 19X1, were: Accounts Receivable, $45,000; and Allowance for Bad Debts, $5,000. Data for 19X2: Collections on accounts receivable were $370,000. Bad debts expense was estimated at 2% of credit sales, as in previous years. Write-offs of bad debts during 19X2 were $9,000.

Required:
1. Prepare journal entries regarding the above information for 19X2.
2. Show the ending balances of the balance sheet accounts, December 31, 19X2.
3. Based on the given data, what questions seem worth raising with Ingrid Holtz, the president of the store?

6–41. **Bad Debt Recoveries.** (Alternate is 6–43.) Alamos Department Store has many accounts receivable. The Alamos balance sheet, December 31, 19X1, showed: Accounts Receivable, $900,000; and Allowance for Uncollectible Accounts, $36,000. In early 19X2, write-offs of customer accounts of $20,000 were made. In late 19X2, a customer, whose $3,000 debt had been written off earlier, won a $1 million sweepstakes cash prize. She immediately remitted $3,000 to Alamos. The store welcomed her money and her return to a high credit standing. Prepare the journal entries for the $20,000 write-off in early 19X2 and the $3,000 receipt in late 19X2.

6–42. **Subsidiary Ledger.** An appliance store makes credit sales of $900,000 in 19X4 to a thousand customers: Schumacher, $4,000; Cerruti, $7,000; Dougall, $5,000; others, $884,000. Total collections during 19X4 were $700,000 including $3,000 from Dougall, but nothing was collected from Schumacher or Cerruti. At the end of 19X4 an allowance for uncollectible accounts was provided of 5% of credit sales.

Required:
1. Set up appropriate general ledger accounts plus a subsidiary ledger for Accounts Receivable. The subsidiary ledger should consist of three individual accounts plus a fourth account called *Others*. Post the entries for 19X4. Prepare a statement of the ending balances of the individual accounts receivable to show that they reconcile with the general ledger account.
2. On March 24, 19X5, the Schumacher and Cerruti accounts are written off. Post the entries.

6–43. **Bad Debt Recoveries.** (Alternate is 6–41.) The Nordmark Department Store uses the allowance method for accounting for bad debts. Assume that on February 26, 19X1, G. Ramoy's account is written off in the amount of $900 after several attempts to collect from him. On September 26, 19X1, Ramoy, filled with remorse and cash, pays his debt in full.

Required:
1. Prepare the journal entry of February 26.
2. Show two ways to journalize the transaction of September 26.

6–44. **Bank Reconciliation.** (Alternate is 6–63.) Study Appendix 6A. The Good Samaritan Hospital has a bank account. Consider the following information:

a. Balances as of July 31: per books, $50,000; per bank statement, $28,880.
b. Cash receipts of July 31 amounting to $10,000 were recorded and then deposited in the bank's night depository. The bank did not include this deposit on its July statement.
c. The bank statement included service charges of $120.
d. Patients had given the hospital some bad checks amounting to $15,000. The bank marked them NSF and returned them with the bank statement after charging the hospital for the $15,000. The hospital had made no entry for these checks.
c. The hospital's outstanding checks amounted to $4,000.

Required:
1. Prepare a bank reconciliation as of July 31.
2. Prepare the hospital journal entries required by the given information.

6-45. STRAIGHTFORWARD BANK RECONCILIATION. Study Appendix 6A. The Village of Lewis has a checking account with the Blanton Bank. The Village cash balance on February 28, 19X1, was $30,000. The deposit balance on the bank's books on February 28, 19X1, was also $30,000. The following transactions occurred during March:

DATE	CHECK NUMBER	AMOUNT	EXPLANATION
3/1	492	$10,000	Payment of previously billed consulting fee
3/6	493	8,000	Payment of accounts payable
3/10		12,000	Collection of taxes receivable
3/14	494	14,000	Acquisition of equipment for cash
3/17		16,000	Collection of license fees receivable
3/28	495	9,000	Payment of accounts payable
3/30	496	21,000	Payment of interest on municipal bonds
3/31		24,000	Collection of taxes receivable

All cash receipts are deposited via a night depository system after the close of the municipal business day. Therefore the receipts are not recorded by the bank until the succeeding day.

On March 31, the bank charged the Village of Lewis $100 for miscellaneous bank services.

Required:

1. Prepare the journal entries on the bank's books for check 493 and the deposit of March 10.
2. Prepare the journal entries for all March transactions on the books of the Village of Lewis.
3. Post all transactions for March to T-accounts for the Village's Cash in Bank and the bank's Deposits account. Assume that only checks 492–494 have been presented to the bank in March, each taking four days to clear the bank's records.
4. Prepare a bank reconciliation for the Village of Lewis, March 31, 19X1. The final three Village of Lewis transactions of March had not affected the bank's records as of March 31. What adjusting entry in the books of the Village of Lewis is required on March 31?
5. What would be the cash balance shown on the balance sheet of the Village of Lewis on March 31, 19X1?

6-46. SEMICOMPLEX BANK RECONCILIATION. Study Appendix 6A. An employee, Lucy Riordan, has a personal bank account. Her employer deposits her weekly paycheck automatically each Friday. The employee's check register (checkbook) for October is summarized as follows:

Reconciled cash balance, September 30, 19X1			$100
Additions:			
Weekly payroll deposits:	October		
	3		800
	10		800
	17		800
	24		800
Deposit of check received for gambling debt	25		600
Deposit of check received as winner of cereal contest	31		400
Subtotal			$4,300
Deductions:			
Checks written #325–#339	1–23	$3,300	
Check #340	26	70	
Check #341	30	90	
Check #342	31	340	3,800
Cash in bank, October 31, 19X1			$ 500

The bank statement is summarized in Exhibit 6–5. Note the code at the bottom of the exhibit, which explains the transactions on the bank's books. The check deposited on October 25 bounced.

EXHIBIT 6–5

Bank Statement of Deposit Account, Lucy Riordan

CHECKS AND OTHER CHARGES	DEPOSITS	DATE	BALANCE
		9/30	100 BF
	800 AP	10/3	900
	800 AP	10/10	1,700
	800 AP	10/17	2,500
	800 AP	10/24	3,300
#325–#339 various dates in October. These would be shown by specific amounts but are shown here as a total: 3,300		10/24	0
	600	10/25	600
#340 70		10/27	530
600 NSF		10/28	80 OD
10 RC			
	200 AL	10/28	120
	800 AP	10/31	920
15 MA		10/31	905

AL—automatic loan*
AP—automatic deposit from employee payroll
BF—balance brought forward
MA—monthly activity charge

NSF—returned check
OD—overdraft
RC—returned check charge

* By prearrangement with Riordan, the bank automatically lends sufficient amounts (in multiples of $100) to ensure that her balance is never less than $100.

Required: 1. Prepare Riordan's bank reconciliation, October 31, 19X1.
2. Assume that Riordan keeps a personal set of books on the accrual basis. Prepare the compound journal entry called for by the bank reconciliation.

6–47. **PETTY CASH FUND.** (Alternate is 6–64.) Study Appendix 6A. On July 1, 19X7, the treasurer of Haynie Company established an imprest petty cash fund of $120 by writing a check on the company's regular bank account payable to "Cash." This check was cashed by the office receptionist, who became responsible for the fund. On July 30, there was cash of $13 in the fund along with petty cash "vouchers" (signed receipts for disbursements) as follows: airport limousine fares, $22; postage, $13; office supplies, $35; delivery charges for incoming merchandise, $17; and "supper money" for two secretaries who worked late, $20.

Required: 1. Prepare journal entries for (a) creation of the petty cash fund and (b) reimbursement of the fund on July 31 for the payments made from it.
2. Assume that the petty cash fund had been replenished on July 31. Where would its balance appear in the financial statements?
3. Suppose the cash balance in the fund had been only $8 instead of $13 just before its replenishment. Comment briefly.
4. Suppose that sometime in December 19X7 the treasurer decided to decrease the fund to $75. Prepare the journal entry for the transaction.

6–48. **AGING OF ACCOUNTS.** Study Appendix 6B. Consider the following analysis of Accounts Receivable, February 28, 19X1:

NAME OF CUSTOMER	TOTAL	REMARKS
Bing Nurseries	$ 12,000	50% over 90 days, 50% 61–90 days
Devon Landscaping	8,000	75% 31–60 days, 25% under 30 days
Shoven Garden Supply	10,000	60% 61–90 days, 40% 31–60 days
Bostick Tree Farm	16,000	all under 30 days
Vanguard Florists	4,000	25% 61–90 days, 75% 1–30 days
Other accounts (each detailed)	60,000	50% 1–30 days, 30% 31–60 days, 15% 61–90 days, 5% over 90 days
Total	$110,000	

Required: Prepare an aging schedule, classifying ages into four categories: 1–30 days, 31–60 days, 61–90 days, and over 90 days. Assume that the prospective bad debt percentages for each category are 0.2%, 0.8%, 10%, and 80%, respectively. What is the ending balance in the Allowance for Uncollectible Accounts?

6–49. **PERCENTAGE OF ENDING ACCOUNTS RECEIVABLE.** Study Appendix 6B. Consider the following data.

| | ACCOUNTS RECEIVABLE AT END OF YEAR | BAD DEBT EXPERIENCE | |
		Deemed Uncollectible and Written Off	Recoveries
19X1	$210,000	$ 8,000	$600
19X2	170,000	5,600	500
19X3	180,000	5,400	300
19X4	230,000	9,000	900
19X5	250,000	12,000	800
19X6	220,000	5,000	500

Required

The unadjusted balance in Allowance for Uncollectible Accounts at December 31, 19X6, is $500. Using the percentage of ending accounts receivable method, prepare an adjusting entry to bring the Allowance to the appropriate amount at December 31, 19X6.

6–50. **ESTIMATING ALLOWANCE FOR UNCOLLECTIBLE ACCOUNTS.** Study Appendix 6B. Fukahara Company has made an analysis of its sales and accounts receivable for the past five years. Assume that all accounts written off in a year relate to sales of the preceding year and were part of the accounts receivable at the end of that year. That is, no account is written off before the end of the year of the sale, and all accounts remaining unpaid are written off before the end of the year following the sale. The analysis showed:

	SALES	ENDING ACCOUNTS RECEIVABLE	BAD DEBTS WRITTEN OFF DURING THE YEAR
19X1	$650,000	$ 90,000	$12,000
19X2	750,000	97,000	12,500
19X3	750,000	103,000	14,000
19X4	850,000	110,000	16,500
19X5	850,000	110,000	17,000

The balance in Allowance for Uncollectible Accounts on December 31, 19X4, was $16,000.

Required:

1. Determine the bad debts expense for 19X5 and the balance of the Allowance for Uncollectible Accounts for December 31, 19X5, using the percentage of sales method.
2. Repeat requirement 1 using the percentage of ending accounts receivable method.

6–51. **PERCENTAGE OF SALES AND PERCENTAGE OF ENDING ACCOUNTS RECEIVABLE.** Study Appendix 6B. The Tartabull Company had credit sales of $3 million during 19X7. Most customers paid promptly (within 30 days), but a few took longer; an average of 1.2% of credit sales was never paid. On December 31, 19X7, accounts receivable were $200,000. The Allowance for Bad Debts account, before any recognition of 19X7 bad debts, had a $1,000 credit balance.

Tartabull produces and sells playground equipment and other outdoor children's toys. Most of the sales (about 80%) come in the period of March through August; the other 20% is spread almost evenly over the other six months. Over the last six years, an average of 15% of the December 31 accounts receivable has not been collected.

1. Suppose Tartabull Company uses the percentage of sales method to calculate an allowance for bad debts. Present the accounts receivable and allowance accounts as they should appear on the December 31, 19X7, balance sheet. Give the journal entry required to recognize the bad debts expense for 19X7.
2. Repeat requirement 1 except assume that the Tartabull Company uses the percentage of ending accounts receivable method.
3. Which method do you prefer? Why?

6–52. AVERAGE COLLECTION PERIOD. Study Appendix 6B. Consider the following:

	19X3	19X2	19X1
Sales	$4,000,000	$5,000,000	$4,800,000

	DECEMBER 31		
	19X3	19X2	19X1
Accounts receivable	$ 310,000	$ 450,000	$ 270,000

Eighty percent of the sales are on account.

Required: Compute the average collection period for the years 19X2 and 19X3. Comment on the results.

UNDERSTANDING PUBLISHED FINANCIAL REPORTS

6–53. GROSS PROFIT TEST. (Alternates are 6–1 and 6–4.) The Dow Chemical Company reported the following data (in millions):

	1987	1986	1985
Net Sales	$13,377	$11,113	$10,500
Cost of Sales	8,660	7,727	8,031

Required: Compute the gross profit and gross profit percentages for 1985, 1986, and 1987. Assess the changes in gross profit percentages over the three years. Give possible reasons for the changes.

6–54. BANK CARDS. VISA and MasterCard are used to pay for a large percentage of retail purchases. The financial arrangements are similar for both bank cards. A news story said:

☐ If a cardholder charges a pair of $60 shoes, for instance, the merchant deposits the sales draft with his bank, which immediately credits $60 less a small transaction fee (usually 2 percent of the sale) to the merchant's account. The bank that issued the customer his card then pays the shoe merchant's bank $60 less a 1.5 percent transaction fee, allowing the merchant's bank a .5 percent profit on the transaction.

Required: **1.** Prepare the journal entry for the sale by the merchant.
2. Prepare the journal entries for the merchant's bank regarding (a) the merchant's deposit and (b) the collection from the second bank.
3. Prepare the journal entry for the second bank (the bank that issued the credit card).

4. The national losses from bad debts for bank cards are about 1.8% of the total billings to cardholders. If so, how can the banks justify providing this service if their revenue from processing is typically 1.5% to 2.0%?

6–55. **ILLEGAL PAYMENT.** The Internal Revenue Code does not permit taxpayers to deduct bribes, kickbacks, and other illegal payments as business expenses.

A wholesaler violated state law by secretly selling liquor at a discount to certain retailers. The specific discounts were agreed upon before each sale and rebated at a later date. The IRS deemed them nondeductible business expenses. The wholesaler took the case to court.

Required: | As an attorney, what arguments would you submit in court on behalf of the wholesaler?

6–56. **RETURNABLE DIAMONDS.** Norton Company is the world's largest producer of abrasive products and a leading supplier of industrial diamond products. A recent annual report contained the following account that related to its sale of diamond bits for petroleum drilling and mining:

Unrealized gross earnings on returnable diamonds	$8,674,000

Required: |
1. Name the financial statement and the specific classification therein of the above account. Suppose the above unrealized amount related to $30 million of gross sales of the product. Show the effect of the sale on Norton's balance sheet equation. Also prepare the pertinent journal entry for the sale.
2. Suppose Norton Company sells diamond bits amounting to $100,000 to the Shell Oil Company. Later Shell receives a $14,000 credit for the unconsumed usable diamond content of the salvaged bits returned. Show the effect of the return on Norton's balance sheet equation. Also prepare the pertinent journal entry for the return.

6–57. **STUDENT LOANS.** The 1988 annual report of the University of Washington includes information about its receivables from student loans in a footnote to the financial statements (in thousands):

	1987		1988	
Student Loans:				
Federal programs	$30,905		$33,109	
Less—allowances	2,793	$28,112	2,378	$30,731
University funds	$ 4,748		$ 4,999	
Less—allowances	337	4,411	271	4,728
Total, net		$32,523		$35,459

Required: |
1. Compare the quality of the loans under federal programs with the quality of those using university funds. Compare the quality of the loans outstanding at the end of 1988 with the quality of those outstanding at the end of 1987.
2. Using the balance sheet equation format, show which University of Washington accounts would be affected by new student tuition loans of $200,000 from university funds. Ignore allowances for bad debts.
3. Using the allowance method, show which accounts would be affected by an allowance for bad debts of an appropriate percentage of the $200,000. Choose a percentage. Also show the effects if a student loan of $1,600 is subsequently written off.

6–58. **HOSPITAL BAD DEBTS.** Hospital Corporation of America is a health-care company that operates over 350 hospitals and other medical facilities. A recent annual report showed the beginning of the company's income statement as follows (in thousands):

Operating revenues	$4,177,971
Less provision for contractual adjustments and doubtful accounts	679,327
Net revenues	$3,498,644

Required:
1. Prepare a reasonable footnote to accompany the above presentation. What do you think is the purpose of contractual allowances?
2. Prepare the summary journal entries for the $4,177,971 and the $679,327.

6-59. **DISCOUNTS AND DOUBTFUL ITEMS.** Scott Paper Company includes the following in its annual report (in millions):

	JANUARY 1	
	1988	1987
Customer receivables	$566.6	$475.1
Reserves for discounts and doubtful items	(29.4)	(24.4)
	$537.2	$450.7

Required:
1. What is the most common substitute term for *reserve* in the context of accounting for receivables?
2. Compute the ratio of the reserves for discounts and doubtful items to gross accounts receivable for each of the two dates. What are some possible reasons for the change in this ratio?
3. Assume that all discounts are cash discounts, not trade discounts. Why does the reserve for cash discounts exist? Prepare a journal entry to create a reserve for discounts of $5,409,000. Prepare the journal entry that would ordinarily reduce the reserve for discounts.

6-60. **RECONSTRUCTION OF TRANSACTIONS.** Consider the following actual account descriptions and balances of La-Z-Boy Chair Company, maker of the popular La-Z-Boy chairs and other furniture (in thousands):

	APRIL 28	
	1988	1987
Receivables, less allowances of $4,976 in 1988 and $3,118 in 1987 for doubtful accounts	$130,584	$113,834

Required: Suppose that for the fiscal year ended April 28, 1988, La-Z-Boy had a bad debts expense of $3,950,000. Compute the amount of bad debts written off during the year.

6-61. **NONPROFIT FINANCIAL REPORTS, BAD DEBTS.** Following is the condensed partial statement of SRI International, a nonprofit corporation that offers an array of consulting services:

SRI INTERNATIONAL
Statement of Revenue, Cost and Expenses for the Year Ended
December 31, 19X6

Project revenue	$113,878,000
Project costs	64,116,000
Excess of revenue over costs	$ 49,762,000
Expenses (detailed and including a separate line, Uncollectible Project Revenue, of $2,845)	48,278,000
Excess of revenue over costs and expenses from operations	$ 1,484,000

The balance sheet showed:

	DECEMBER 31	
	19X6	19X5
Receivables (less allowance for uncollectible accounts, $1,958,000, 19X6; and $518,000, 19X5)	21,514,000	20,068,000

A footnote stated:

☐ Project revenue comprises direct costs and related overhead and fees. Revenue is recorded as costs are incurred. Provision for uncollectible project revenue is based on past experience and review of receivables as to collectibility.

Required:

1. Are bad debts accounted for on the specific charge-off or allowance basis? Explain. Compare the collectibility of the accounts at the end of 19X5 and 19X6. Why might collectibility differ at the end of each year?
2. Examine the descriptions used by SRI International. What terms might be used instead by a profit-seeking enterprise?

6–62. **ALLOWANCE FOR CREDIT LOSSES.** BankAmerica Corp. included the following in the footnotes to its 1987 annual report:

The following is a summary of changes in the allowance for credit losses (in millions):

	1987	1986
Balance, beginning of year	$ 2,172	$ 1,584
Credit losses	(1,275)	(1,749)
Credit loss recoveries	432	330
Net credit losses	$ (843)	$(1,419)
Provision for credit losses	1,951	2,004
Other additions (deductions)	(17)	3
Balance, end of year	$ 3,263	$ 2,172

1. Terminology in bank financial statements sometimes differs slightly from that in statements of industrial companies. Explain what is meant by "allowance for credit losses," "provision for credit losses," and "credit losses" in the footnote.

2. Prepare the 1987 journal entries to record the writing off of specific credit losses, the recovery of previously written off credit losses, and the charge for credit losses against 1987 income. Omit explanations.

3. Suppose BankAmerica analyzed its loans at the end of 1987 and decided that an allowance for credit losses equal to the 1986 amount ($2,172 million) was sufficient. Compute the provision for credit losses that would be charged in 1987. In other words, instead of a provision for credit losses of $1,951 million, what provision would have been charged?

4. BankAmerica had a net loss of $955 million in 1987. Compute the net profit (loss) if the allowance for credit losses at the end of 1987 had been the same as at the end of 1986. Ignore income tax effects.

6–63. BANK RECONCILIATION. (Alternate is 6–44.) Study Appendix 6A. American Building Maintenance Industries is the largest janitorial service company in the world. Most of its twenty-five thousand employees clean structures such as the buildings of Bank of America. The company has many branch offices throughout the United States and elsewhere.

A Dallas branch office has a checking account with a local bank. The branch's cash balance per books was $5,000 on June 30; the bank statement showed a balance of $5,400. Other information follows:

a. The branch office had two checks outstanding at June 30: #704 for $400 and #706 for $300.

b. The bank had enclosed a branch customer's $2,000 check with the bank statement. It was marked NSF, and the bank had reduced the branch's balance accordingly.

c. The branch office had mailed a $1,200 deposit on June 29, but the June bank statement failed to show it.

d. The branch borrowed $3,000 from the bank on June 30. The bank had credited the branch's deposit account on that date. However, the branch had not recorded the transaction.

e. Miscellaneous bank service charges of $100 were on the bank statement. The branch had not recorded them.

Required: **1.** Prepare a bank reconciliation as of June 30. (The correct balance is $5,900.)

2. Prepare the American Building Maintenance Industries journal entries required by the given information.

6–64. IMPREST PETTY CASH. (Alternate is 6–47.) Study Appendix 6A. The Stanford Business School created an imprest petty cash fund of $150 on January 2.

During January the following outlays were made from petty cash:

Auto mileage at 20¢ per mile for secretary to deliver documents to alumni office in San Francisco, round trip 80 miles	$16.00
Dinner allowance for mail clerk working overtime	9.00
Postal charges for insuring mail	4.50
Payments to delivery personnel	22.40
Purchase of special posters	12.75
Total	$64.65

Required: Prepare journal entries for

1. Creation of the fund on January 2

2. Replenishment of the fund on January 31

3. Reduction of the fund from $150 to $100 on February 15

6–65. BANK SERVICE CHARGES. Study Appendix 6A. *U.S. News and World Report* contained the following story on the sudden increase in bank fees: "Many banks are experimenting with a new pricing system for checking services. Philadelphia's Girard, for example, gives each depositor a monthly credit based on the average account balance. Each time a check is written, the bank subtracts 30 cents from the credit allowance. If the credit is exhausted, Girard collects as a service fee the difference between the initial credit and the total check charge."

Suppose a Kinney Shoe Store had a checking account at Girard. Its average account balance in March was $1,000. On April 1, Girard credited the Kinney account with 2% of the $1,000 average balance. It then charged Kinney 30 cents for each of the 100 checks written during April.

Required:
1. Prepare the probable journal entries Girard made for these transactions.
2. Prepare the probable journal entries on Kinney's books for these transactions.

6–66. BANK VERSUS BOOK RECORDS. Study Appendix 6A. The Mead Corporation, primarily a forest products company, lists the following among its current assets and current liabilities (in millions):

	JANUARY 1	
	1988	1987
As part of current assets:		
Cash and temporary cash investments	$ 45.3	$ 18.6
As part of current liabilities:		
Accounts payable:		
Trade	201.8	206.1
Affiliated companies	68.8	160.4
Outstanding checks	62.5	23.3

It is unusual to find a liability account labeled "Outstanding Checks."

Required:
1. Most companies have checks outstanding at any balance sheet date. Why is it unusual to have a liability for outstanding checks?
2. Suppose you examined the "Cash and Temporary Cash Investments" account in Mead's general ledger. What balance would you find for January 1, 1988? For January 1, 1987?
3. Why do you suppose Mead reported outstanding checks as a liability?

6–67. BAD DEBTS AND CASINOS. Study Appendix 6B. Metro-Goldwyn-Mayer, Inc. (MGM), conducts extensive hotel and gaming operations. A footnote in a recent annual report showed (in thousands):

Metro-Goldwyn-Mayer, Inc.

Allowances for uncollectible gaming receivables are provided to reduce gaming receivables and revenues to amounts anticipated to be collected. Gaming receivables and the related allowances were as follows (in thousands):

	19X4	19X3
Gaming receivables	$6,949	$6,945
Allowances for uncollectibles	2,214	2,904
Receivables charged against allowances during period, net of recoveries	2,294	6,934

Required:

1. Prepare the ratios of allowances for uncollectibles to gaming receivables for both dates. (The footnote does not disclose the specific dates. However, the first two items apply to August 31, 19X4 and 19X3, respectively. The third item pertains to the fiscal years 19X4 and 19X3.
2. What other title could be used for "Receivables charged against allowances during period"?
3. How do you think these ratios compare with those of other industries? Would these ratios differ markedly among various casino companies? Why?

6–68. **BAD DEBT RECOVERIES.** See the preceding problem. Assume that bad debt recoveries by MGM during the year were $400,000. Prepare all summary journal entries affecting the Allowances for Uncollectibles for the fiscal year 19X4. Also show the Allowance T-account.

6–69. **ALLOWANCE AND PROVISION FOR DOUBTFUL ACCOUNTS.** Study Appendix 6B. Allied Stores is one of the country's largest retailing companies, owning department stores such as The Bon and Jordan Marsh and specialty stores such as Ann Taylor. It is a subsidiary of Campeau Corporation. The following footnote was in Allied's annual report:

Accounts Receivable—Customers

(in thousands)	JANUARY 2, 1988	JANUARY 3, 1987
Revolving credit accounts	$687,416	$671,157
Installment accounts	57,053	69,792
Other accounts	33,625	29,183
	778,094	770,132
Less allowance for doubtful accounts	12,193	14,111
	$765,901	$756,021

Suppose additional analysis revealed that sales made on credit were 65% of total sales and the provision for doubtful accounts for fiscal 1988 was .80% of credit sales, or $21.1 million.

Required:

1. Compute the amount of total sales for fiscal 1988.
2. Assume that there were no bad debt recoveries in fiscal 1988. Compute the amount of accounts receivable written off as uncollectible in fiscal 1988.

6–70. **HOUSE OF FABRICS ANNUAL REPORT.** Refer to the financial statements of House of Fabrics, pages 752–759.

Required:

1. Perform a gross profit test for 1987, 1988, and 1989. Does this test identify any reasons why an investor in House of Fabrics should be concerned? Explain.
2. Consider the amount of receivables on the 1989 balance sheet. Suppose this is the net amount of receivables, after deducting an allowance for bad debts of $320,000. Assume that 1.5% of credit sales is added to the allowance for bad debts, credit sales were 70% of total sales, and the balance in the Allowance for Bad Debts account at the beginning of fiscal 1989 was $300,000. Compute the amount of bad debts written off during fiscal 1989. (*Hint*: Use the T-account for the allowance for bad debts.)

Valuing Inventories and Measuring Cost of Goods Sold

This chapter describes how the cost of goods sold is measured. The key to calculating the cost of goods sold is accounting for inventory. This chapter explains how inventory records are kept and how different inventory valuation methods affect financial statements. It also describes how market prices affect the accounting for inventories and explains the relationship between gross profit and inventories.

INVENTORIES AND THE ACCRUAL BASIS

The presence of inventories underscores the desirability of accrual accounting. The mere purchase of inventory does not result in an expense on the income statement. Purchased merchandise is first listed as an asset (inventory) and only becomes an expense (cost of goods sold) when sold, as shown in Exhibit 7–1. The central idea is straightforward. Inventories on hand represent future benefits, and inventories no longer on hand should not be listed as assets.

There are two major steps in accounting for inventories. First, obtain a *physical count*. Second, obtain a *cost valuation*. The physical count is an imposing, time-consuming, and expensive process that sometimes requires a complete

EXHIBIT 7–1

Merchandising Company (Retailer or Wholesaler)

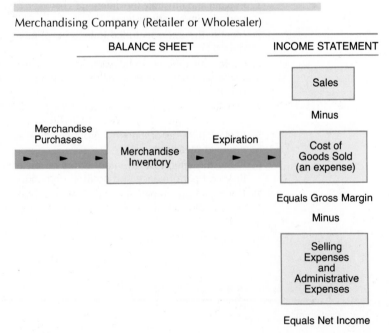

BALANCE SHEET	INCOME STATEMENT

Sales

Minus

Merchandise Purchases → → → Merchandise Inventory → Expiration → → → Cost of Goods Sold (an expense)

Equals Gross Margin

Minus

Selling Expenses and Administrative Expenses

Equals Net Income

stoppage of normal business. For instance, you have probably seen "closed for inventory taking" signs either in departments or in entire businesses. Frequently, the process is conducted on staggered dates and by resorting to statistical sampling procedures. In any case, the inventories in corporate annual reports are not based merely on accounting records alone. The external auditors must assure themselves that accurate up-to-date physical counting has occurred.

PERPETUAL AND PERIODIC INVENTORIES

This part of the chapter explains two methods of keeping inventory records: perpetual and periodic inventory systems. Later parts discuss the valuation of inventories.

□ General Comparison

There are two fundamental ways of keeping inventory records for merchandise: perpetual and periodic. The **perpetual inventory system** (which has been assumed in this textbook until now) keeps a running, continuous record that tracks inventories and the cost of goods sold on a day-to-day basis. Such a record helps managerial control and the preparation of interim financial statements. However, physical inventory counts should be taken at least once a year to check on the accuracy of the clerical records.

Previous chapters have described sales as two-phased transactions:

	A	= L +	SE
a. Sale	$+ \left(\begin{array}{c} \text{Increase} \\ \text{Accounts} \\ \text{Receivable} \end{array} \right)$	$= +$	$\left(\begin{array}{c} \text{Increase} \\ \text{Sales Revenue} \end{array} \right)$
b. Cost of inventory sold	$- \left(\begin{array}{c} \text{Decrease} \\ \text{Inventory} \end{array} \right)$	$= -$	$\left(\begin{array}{c} \text{Increase Cost} \\ \text{of Goods Sold} \end{array} \right)$

The journal entries are:

a.	Accounts receivable (or cash)	xxx	
	Sales revenue		xxx
b.	Cost of goods sold	xxx	
	Inventory		xxx

The second phase illustrates the perpetual inventory system, which simultaneously attributes a specific cost to the inventory delivered to customers in the first phase.

The **periodic inventory system,** on the other hand, does *not* involve a day-to-day record of inventories or of the cost of goods sold. Instead the cost of goods sold and an updated inventory balance are computed only at the end of an

EXHIBIT 7–2

Inventory Systems

PERIODIC SYSTEM		PERPETUAL SYSTEM	
Beginning inventories		Cost of goods sold (kept on a	
(by physical count)	xxx	day-to-day basis rather than	
Add: Purchases	xxx	being determined periodi-	
Cost of goods available for sale	xxx	cally)*	xxx
Less: Ending inventories			
(by physical count)	xxx		
Cost of goods sold	xxx		

* Such a condensed figure does not preclude the presentation of a supplementary schedule similar to that on the left.

accounting period, when a physical count of inventory is taken. The cost of the goods purchased is accumulated by recording the individual purchase transactions throughout any given reporting period, such as a year. The accountant computes the cost of goods sold by subtracting the ending inventories (determined by physical count) from the sum of the opening inventory and purchases. Exhibit 7–2 compares the perpetual and periodic inventory systems.

As Exhibit 7–2 implies, the cost of goods sold under the perpetual system is computed instantaneously as goods are sold, whereas under the periodic system, the computation is delayed:

$$\underbrace{\text{Beginning inventory} + \text{Purchases}}_{\text{Amount available for sale}} - \underbrace{\text{Ending inventory}}_{-\ \text{Amount left over}} = \underbrace{\text{Cost of good sold}}_{=\ \text{Amount sold}}$$

The periodic system computes cost of goods sold as a *residual amount*. First, the beginning inventory is added to the purchases to obtain the total cost of goods available for sale. Then the ending inventory is counted, and its cost is deducted from the cost of goods available for sale to obtain the cost of goods sold.

☐ Physical Inventory

Good inventory control procedures require a physical count of inventory at least annually in both periodic and perpetual inventory systems. Such a count is *necessary* for calculating the cost of goods sold in a periodic inventory system. However, it can be just as important in a perpetual system, providing a check on the accuracy of the inventory records. Suppose the physical count differs from the perpetual inventory amount. For example, the following result might be obtained:

Perpetual inventory record:	Part 1F68X	142 units @ $20	$2,840
Physical count:	Part 1F68X	125 units @ $20	$2,500

Seventeen units (142 units − 125 units) have disappeared without being charged as cost of goods sold. Accountants call this *inventory shrinkage,* and it is discussed in detail on pages 639–641 of Chapter 14. The journal entry to adjust inventory from $2,840 to $2,500 is:

Inventory shrinkage	340	
Merchandise inventory		340
To adjust the ending inventory		
to its balance per physical count.		

☐ Which to Choose?

Whether a perpetual or a periodic system is desirable depends on the relative costs and benefits of each. Perpetual systems are becoming more popular because they increase management's control over operations and because their data-processing costs have dropped substantially. Computers and optical scanning equipment have become more versatile and less costly.

Small businesses tend to favor the periodic inventory system. As businesses grow and become more complex, perpetual inventory systems are installed. Many unhappy surprises can be avoided if managers keep a closer watch on inventories than periodic systems ordinarily provide.

In summary, the perpetual system is more accurate but more costly. The periodic system is less accurate, especially for monthly or quarterly statements. It is less costly because there is no day-to-day processing regarding cost of goods sold. However, if theft or the accumulation of obsolete merchandise is likely, periodic systems often prove to be more expensive in the long run.

COST OF MERCHANDISE ACQUIRED

☐ Measuring Cost of Merchandise Acquired

The cost of merchandise acquired eventually becomes part of the cost of goods sold in the gross profit section of the income statement. What items constitute the cost of incoming merchandise? To be more specific, does cost include all or part of the following: invoice price, transportation charges, trade and cash discounts, cost of handling and placing in stock, storage, purchasing department, receiving department, and other indirect charges? In practice, accountants usually regard only the invoice price plus the directly identifiable transportation charges less any offsetting discounts as the cost of merchandise. The other costs are classified as administrative or operating expenses; they are placed below the gross profit line in an income statement.

The accounting for *purchase* returns, purchase allowances, and cash discounts on purchases is just the opposite of their sales counterparts. Using the periodic inventory system, suppose gross purchases were $960,000 and purchase returns and allowances were $75,000. The summary journal entries would be:

Purchases	960,000	
Accounts payable		960,000
Accounts payable	75,000	
Purchase returns and allowances		75,000

Suppose also that cash discounts of $5,000 were taken upon payment of the remaining $960,000 − $75,000 = $885,000 of payables. The summary journal entry would be:

Accounts payable	885,000	
Cash discounts on purchases		5,000
Cash		880,000

The accounts *Cash Discounts on Purchases* and *Purchase Returns and Allowances* are deducted from Purchases in calculating cost of goods sold.

☐ Inward Transportation

The major cost of transporting merchandise is typically the freight charges from the shipping point of the seller to the receiving point of the buyer. When the seller bears this cost, the terms are stated on the sales invoice as F.O.B. destination. When the buyer bears this cost, the terms are stated as F.O.B. shipping point. **F.O.B.** means "free on board."

In theory, any transportation costs borne by the buyer should be added to the cost of the inventory acquired. In practice, several different items are typically ordered and shipped simultaneously. Therefore it is often difficult to allocate freight costs among the items. In addition, management may want to compile freight costs separately to see how they compare with regard to periods and modes of transportation. Consequently, accountants frequently use a separate transportation cost account, labeled as Freight In, Transportation In, Inbound Transportation, or Inward Transportation.

Freight in (or **inward transportation**) appears in the purchases section of an income statement as an additional cost of the goods acquired during the period. On the other hand, **freight out** represents the costs borne by the *seller* and is shown as a "shipping expense," which is a form of selling expense. Thus Freight In affects the gross profit section of an income statement, but Freight Out does not and should therefore appear below the gross profit line. A detailed gross profit section is often arranged as follows (figures in thousands are assumed):

Gross sales
Deduct: Sales returns and allowances
       Cash discounts on sales
Net sales
Deduct: Cost of goods sold:
 Merchandise inventory, December 31, 19X1
 Purchases (gross)
  Deduct: Purchase returns and allowances $
        Cash discounts on purchases
  Net purchases
  Add: Inward transportation
 Total cost of merchandise acquired
 Cost of goods available for sale
 Deduct: Merchandise inventory,
      December 31, 19X2
 Cost of goods sold
Gross profit or gross margin

ACCOUNTING PROCEDURES FOR PERIODIC INVENTORY SYSTEMS

☐ Details of Cost of Goods Sold Section

Exhibit 7–3 provides a detailed cost of goods sold section of an income statement for 19X2. The balance in merchandise inventory at the beginning of 19X2 (December 31, 19X1) was $100,000. A summary of transactions for 19X2 follows:

a. Purchases	$990,000
b. Purchase returns and allowances	$ 80,000

Net purchases were therefore $990,000 less $80,000, or $910,000. The physical count of the ending inventory for 19X2 led to a cost valuation of $140,000. Note how these figures are used to compute the $870,000 cost of goods sold:

$$\begin{array}{c} \text{Beginning} \\ \text{inventory} \end{array} + \text{Net purchases} - \begin{array}{c} \text{Ending} \\ \text{inventory} \end{array} = \begin{array}{c} \text{Cost of} \\ \text{goods sold} \end{array}$$

$$\$100,000 + \$910,000 - \$140,000 = \$870,000$$

$$\underbrace{\qquad\qquad\qquad\qquad}$$

$$\begin{array}{c} \text{Cost of goods} \\ \text{available for sale} \end{array} - \begin{array}{c} \text{Cost of goods} \\ \text{left over} \end{array} = \begin{array}{c} \text{Cost of} \\ \text{goods sold} \end{array}$$

$$\$1,010,000 - \$140,000 = \$870,000$$

Exhibit 7–4 compares the balance sheet effects of the perpetual and periodic inventory systems. The analysis is confined to the relevant accounts. For simplicity, the opening balance sheet consists solely of Inventory and Accounts Payable; furthermore, no cash is paid on accounts throughout the year.

As Exhibit 7–4 shows, the perpetual system entails directly increasing the Inventory account by the $990,000 purchases and decreasing it by the $870,000 cost of goods sold. The Cost of Goods Sold account would be increased daily ross Profit Section of Income Statement for 19X2 (in thousands)

	PERPETUAL		PERIODIC	
Sales (assumed)		$1,570		$1,570
Deduct cost of goods sold:				
Merchandise inventory,				
December 31, 19X1			$ 100	
Add: Purchases			$990	
Deduct: Purchase returns and allowances			80	
Net purchases			910	
Cost of goods available for sale			$1,010	
Deduct: Merchandise Inventory,				
December 31, 19X2			140	
Cost of goods sold		870*		870
Gross profit or gross margin		$ 700		$ 700

* As Exhibit 7–4 shows, the records are kept so that no separate accounts exist for Purchases, Purchase Returns and Allowances, and similar accounts. Nevertheless, the Inventory account could be analyzed if desired to present the same details revealed on the right by the periodic method.

as sales are made. In a nutshell, these entries should be familiar. The only new aspect here is the accounting for the purchase returns, allowances, and cash discounts (if any). These directly reduce the Inventory account, as the $80,000 purchase return illustrates. The only closing entry at the end of the period is the transfer of cost of goods sold to Income Summary.

Before proceeding, reflect on the perpetual system in Exhibit 7–4.

The periodic system is called "periodic" because neither the Cost of Goods Sold account nor the Inventory account is computed on a daily basis. Moreover, Purchases and Purchase Returns and Allowances are accounted for separately, as entries *a* and *b* indicate. Entries *d*1 and *d*2 in Exhibit 7–4 show the eventual periodic calculation of cost of goods sold.

The periodic system may seem awkward when compared with the perpetual system. The beginning inventory and cost of goods sold are untouched until the end of the period. However, the periodic system avoids the costly process of calculating the cost of goods sold for each sale.

Entry *d*1 transfers the beginning inventory balance, purchases, and purchase returns and allowances, totaling $1,010,000, to cost of goods sold. This provides the cost of goods available for sale, the first step in calculating cost of goods sold.

Next, the ending inventory is physically counted and its cost is computed. Entry *d*2 recognizes the $140,000 ending inventory and reduces the $1,010,000 cost of goods available for sale by $140,000 to obtain a final cost of goods sold of $870,000. All of these details can be shown in the cost of goods sold section of the income statement. However, published income statements usually include only a single cost of goods sold number.

EXHIBIT 7–4

Comparative Analysis of Purchase Transactions (in thousands of dollars)

	A			=	L	+	SE
PERIODIC SYSTEM	Inventory	Purchases	Purchase Returns and Allowances		Accounts Payable		
Balance, 12/31/X1	+100			=	+100		
a. Gross purchases		+990		=	+990		
b. Returns and allowances			−80	=	−80		
c. As goods are sold (no entry)							
Closing the accounts at end of period:							
d1. Transfer to cost of goods sold	−100	−990	+80	=		−1,010	[Increase Cost of Goods Sold]
d2. Recognize ending inventory	+140			=		+140	[Decrease Cost of Goods Sold]
d3. Transfer cost of goods sold to income summary				=		+870	[Decrease Cost of Goods Sold]
						−870	[Decrease Income Summary]
Ending balances, 12/31/X2	+140	0	0	=	+1,010	−870	
PERPETUAL SYSTEM							
Balance, 12/31/X1	+100			=	+100		
a. Gross purchases	+990			=	+990		
b. Returns and allowances	−80			=	−80		
c. As goods are sold	−870			=		−870	[Increase Cost of Goods Sold]
Closing the accounts at end of period:							
d1. \ d2. / No entry							
d3. Transfer cost of goods sold to income summary				=		+870	[Decrease Cost of Goods Sold]
						−870	[Decrease Income Summary]
Ending balances, 12/31/X2	+140			=	+1,010	−870	

☐ Journal Entries

The journal entries for the perpetual and periodic records follow, using the foregoing data:

	PERPETUAL RECORDS			PERIODIC RECORDS		

a. Gross purchases:	Inventory
	   Accounts payable
		990	990	Purchases
				   Accounts payable
					990	990

b. Returns and allowances:	Accounts payable
	   Inventory
		80	80	Accounts payable
				   Purchase returns
				     and allowances
					80	80

c. As goods are sold:	Cost of goods sold Inventory	870	870	No entry		

d. At the end of the accounting period:	d1.
	d2. } No entry
				d1. Cost of goods sold
				    Purchase returns
				     and allowances
				    Purchases
				    Inventory
					1,010
					
					80
						
						990
						100

				d2. Inventory Cost of goods sold	140	140

The cost of goods sold would be closed to income summary under either method:

d3. Income summary	870	
Cost of goods sold		870

Exhibit 7–5 shows the postings of the above journal entries. Note that the periodic method produces the same final balances in Inventory and Income Summary as the perpetual method. However, as entries d1 and d2 demonstrate, the cost of goods sold is computed at the end of the year; consequently, the related journal entries and postings are made then.

PRINCIPAL INVENTORY VALUATION METHODS

Each period, accountants must divide the cost of beginning inventory and merchandise acquired between cost of goods sold and cost of items remaining in ending inventory. Under a perpetual system, this means assigning a cost to each item sold. Under a periodic system, it entails measuring the costs of the items remaining in ending inventory. Regardless of the inventory system, costs of individual items must be determined. Various inventory valuation methods accomplish this.

☐ Four Major Methods

If unit prices and costs did not fluctuate, all inventory methods would show identical results. But prices change, and these changes raise central issues re-

EXHIBIT 7–5

General Ledger

PERPETUAL INVENTORY	PERIODIC INVENTORY

PERPETUAL INVENTORY

Accounts Payable

(b)	80	*	100
		(a)	990

Inventory			
*	100	(b)	80
(a)	990	(c)	870

Cost of Goods Sold

(c)	870	(d3)	870

Income Summary

(d3)	870	

PERIODIC INVENTORY

Accounts Payable

(b)	80	*	100
		(a)	990

Inventory			
*	100	(d1)	100
(d2)	140		

Cost of Goods Sold

(d1)	1,010	(d2)	140
		(d3)	870

Income Summary

(d3)	870	

Purchases

(a)	990	(d1)	990

Purchase Returns
and Allowances

(d1)	80	(b)	80

* Balance in thousands of dollars, December 31, 19X1.

garding cost of goods sold (income measurement) and inventories (asset measurement). Four principal inventory methods have been generally accepted in the United States: specific identification, weighted average, FIFO, and LIFO. Each will be explained and compared.

As a preview of the remainder of this chapter, consider the following simple example of the choices facing management. A new vendor of a cola drink at the fairgrounds began the week with no inventory. He bought one can on Monday for 30 cents; a second can on Tuesday for 40 cents; and a third can on Wednesday for 56 cents. He then sold one can on Thursday for 90 cents. What was his gross profit? His ending inventory? Answer these questions in your own mind before reading on.

Panel I of Exhibit 7–6 provides a quick glimpse of the nature of the generally accepted methods. Their underlying assumptions will be explained shortly. As you can readily see, the vendor's choice of an inventory method can often significantly affect gross profit (and hence net income) and ending inventory valuation for balance sheet purposes.

1. SPECIFIC IDENTIFICATION (COLUMN 1). This method concentrates on the *physical* linking of the *particular* items sold. If the vendor reached for the Monday can instead of the Wednesday can, the *same inventory method* would show different results. Thus Panel I of Exhibit 7–6 indicates that gross profit for operations of Monday through Thursday could be 60¢, 50¢, or 34¢, depending on the particular can handed to the customer. Obviously, this method permits great latitude for measuring results in any given period. The next three methods do not trace the actual physical flow of goods except by coincidence.

EXHIBIT 7–6

Comparison of Inventory Methods for Cola Vendor (all monetary amounts are in cents)

	(1) SPECIFIC IDENTIFICATION			(2)	(3)	(4)
	(1A)	(1B)	(1C)	FIFO	LIFO	WEIGHTED AVERAGE
Panel I Income Statement for the Period Monday through Thursday						
Sales	90	90	90	90	90	90
Deduct cost of goods sold:						
1 30¢ (Monday) unit	30			30		
1 40¢ (Tuesday) unit		40				
1 56¢ (Wednesday) unit			56		56	
1 weighted-average unit [(30 + 40 + 56) ÷ 3 = 42]						42
Gross profit for Monday through Thursday	60	50	34	60	34	48
Thursday's ending inventory, 2 units:						
Monday unit @ 30¢		30	30		30	
Tuesday unit @ 40¢	40		40	40	40	
Wednesday unit @ 56¢	56	56		56		
Weighted-average units @ 42¢						84
Total ending inventory on Thursday	96	86	70	96	70	84
Panel II Income Statements for Friday Only and for Monday through Friday						
Sales, 2 units @ 90	180	180	180	180	180	180
Cost of goods sold (Thursday ending inventory from above)	96	86	70	96	70	84
Gross profit, Friday only	84	94	110	84	110	96
Gross profit, Monday through Thursday (from above)	60	50	34	60	34	48
Gross profit, Monday through Friday	144	144	144	144	144	144

2. FIRST-IN, FIRST-OUT (FIFO) (COLUMN 2). This method assumes that the stock acquired earliest is sold (used up) first. Thus the Monday unit is deemed to have been sold regardless of the actual physical unit delivered. In times of rising prices, FIFO usually shows the largest gross profit (60¢ in Panel I of Exhibit 7–6).

3. LAST-IN, FIRST-OUT (LIFO) (COLUMN 3). This method assumes that the stock acquired most recently is sold (used up) first. Thus the Wednesday unit is deemed to have been sold regardless of the actual physical unit delivered. In times of rising prices, LIFO generally shows the lowest gross profit (34¢ in Panel I of Exhibit 7–6).

4. WEIGHTED-AVERAGE COST (COLUMN 4). This method assumes that all items available for sale during the period are best represented by a weighted-average cost. Exhibit 7–6 shows the calculations. The weighted-average method usually produces a gross profit somewhere between that obtained under FIFO and LIFO (48¢ as compared with 60¢ and 34¢ in Panel I of Exhibit 7–6).

☐ Inventories and Matching

Panel I of Exhibit 7–6 indicates why theoretical and practical disputes can easily arise regarding the "best" inventory method. As Exhibit 7–7 demonstrates, the four inventory methods have four separate cost-flow assumptions. When identical goods are purchased at different times and at different prices, accountants face a "matching" problem. The choice of an inventory method is an attempt to adhere to the basic concept of matching and cost recovery, which was introduced in Chapter 2. The difficulty is not with "matching" as an *abstract* idea; instead disputes arise regarding how to *apply* it. Thus more than one inventory method has evolved, and the four methods illustrated in Exhibits 7–6 and 7–7

EXHIBIT 7–7

Diagram of Inventory Methods (Data are from Panel I, Exhibit 7–6; monetary amounts are in cents)

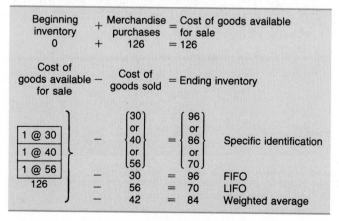

have all become accepted as part of the body of generally accepted accounting principles.

The Consistency Convention

Inventory methods have chainlike effects because the ending asset balance for one reporting period becomes the beginning asset balance for the succeeding reporting period. Suppose the vendor sells his remaining inventory on Friday and goes into a more attractive business. Panel II of Exhibit 7–6 shows that the *cumulative* gross profit over the life of an entity will be the same under all inventory methods. However, *individual* reporting periods can be dramatically affected. For example, income based on FIFO is higher than income based on LIFO for Monday through Thursday, but not for Friday only.

The major distinction among inventory methods is timing: *When* should the cost of inventories be released from being an asset to become an expense? The remainder of this chapter will explore the various suggested answers to this question.

As we proceed, keep in mind that a chosen inventory method must be used consistently from year to year. Although switches from one inventory method to another may occur occasionally (most notably from FIFO to LIFO), they are relatively rare events in the life of an entity. GAAP requires **consistency,** which has been defined by the FASB as "conformity from period to period with unchanging policies and procedures." Frequent switches in accounting method would hinder the comparison of a period's income with that of the preceding periods. However, changes to a preferred method of accounting are permitted if accompanied by disclosure of the effects of the change.

The differences between LIFO and FIFO can be substantial. Furthermore, a company does not necessarily use one inventory method for all its products. To illustrate, General Mills, maker of Wheaties, Cheerios, and other food products, reported the following inventories:

⚔ General Mills, Inc.

The components of year-end inventories are as follows (in millions):

	1988	1987
Valued at LIFO	$185.2	$151.5
Valued primarily at FIFO	238.3	237.1
Total Inventories	$423.5	$388.6

If the FIFO method of inventory accounting had been used in place of LIFO, inventories would have been $53.0 million and $51.5 million higher than reported for 1988 and 1987, respectively

LIFO is the most popular inventory method for large U.S. companies. About two-thirds of the companies use LIFO for at least some of their inventories. Over 60% use FIFO, and 40% use weighted average for a portion of their inventories. Less than 10% use any other method, including specific identification. Over half the companies use more than one inventory method.

☐ Specific Identification

An obvious way to account for inventory is through *specific identification* via physical observation or the labeling of items in stock with individual numbers or codes. Such an approach is easy and economically justifiable for relatively expensive merchandise like custom artwork, diamond jewelry, and automobiles. However, most organizations have vast segments of inventories that are too numerous and insufficiently valuable per unit to warrant such individualized attention.

As Exhibit 7–6 shows, specific identification requires the linkage of individual inventory items with the exact purchase costs of each unit. In the past, this tracing might have been simple if the item was a Cadillac or a Lincoln, but not if the item was a toothbrush or a jar of peanut butter.

Of course, in this computer age it is becoming economically feasible to track more and more inventory in this manner. Nevertheless, the computerized inventory systems are most often used to help management plan and control the *physical* levels of various inventories. These systems rarely attempt to use specific identification to trace individual *costs* to individual items such as boxes of cereal or jars of coffee. In sum, the specific identification method continues to be largely confined to expensive individualized merchandise.

To the extent that accountants and managers believe that sales and cost of goods sold should reflect the *physical flow* of goods, specific identification is the most attractive inventory method. Its major drawback in many cases is its expense. Moreover, many critics claim that income measurement's first concern should not be with *physical* flows but with the *economic* flows (to be explained momentarily).

Exhibit 7–6 also demonstrates how the specific identification method can measure three different gross profits with the same set of facts. Thus, unlike FIFO or LIFO, specific identification may permit management to manipulate income and inventory values by filling a sales order from a number of physically equivalent items bearing various inventory cost prices.

☐ FIFO, LIFO, Weighted Average

As briefly explained earlier, FIFO assumes for costing purposes that the units acquired latest are still on hand. The earliest costs are considered to be the cost of goods sold. In contrast, LIFO assumes that the units acquired earliest are still on hand. Thus the most recent, or last, inventory costs are considered to be the cost of goods sold. The attempt is to match the most current costs against current revenue (sales).

As Panel I of Exhibit 7–6 indicates, LIFO usually results in the reporting of less income than FIFO when prices are rising.[1] Why? Because the recent *higher* costs become the cost of goods sold. Suppose prices are falling. The most recent costs are then *lower*, so LIFO reports higher income than FIFO. As might be expected, the weighted-average method generally produces results that lie between the extremes of FIFO and LIFO.

Ponder the calculation of a *weighted* average. *Weighted* average should be used to give appropriate consideration to quantities. The average is computed by dividing the *total* cost of the beginning inventory plus purchases, by the *total* number of units in those two classes. Suppose our cola vendor had bought two cans rather than one on Monday at 30¢ each:

$$\text{Weighted average} = \text{Cost of goods available for sale} \div \text{Units available for sale}$$
$$\text{Weighted average} = [(2 \times 30¢) + (1 \times 40¢) + (1 \times 56¢)] \div 4$$
$$= 156¢ \div 4$$
$$= 39¢$$

☐ Essence of FIFO

Accountants and managers tend to develop strong feelings regarding the comparative merits of FIFO and LIFO. Adherents of FIFO maintain that it is the most practical way to describe what operating managers actually do. That is, most managers deliberately attempt to move their merchandise on a first-in, first-out basis. This approach avoids spoilage, obsolescence, and the like. Thus the inventory flow assumption underlying FIFO corresponds most closely to the actual physical flows of inventory items in most businesses. Furthermore, the asset balance for inventories is a close approximation of the "actual" dollars invested, because the inventory is carried at the most recent purchase prices paid. Such prices are not likely to differ much from current prices at the balance sheet date. Consequently, its proponents maintain that FIFO properly meets the objectives of both the income statement and the balance sheet.

☐ Essence of LIFO

Adherents of LIFO are usually critical of FIFO because of the latter's effects on income when prices are rising. They claim that FIFO-based income is deceiving in the sense that some of the corresponding increase in net assets is merely an "inventory profit." That is, an "inventory profit" is fictitious for a going concern because the amount of reported cost of goods sold is less than the amount required for replenishing the inventory. Consequently, it is not profit in the layperson's sense of the term; it does not indicate an amount that permits both replenishment of inventory and payment of dividends. For instance, consider our cola vendor:

	FIFO	LIFO
Sales, one unit on Thursday	90¢	90¢
Cost of goods sold	30	56
Gross profit	60¢	34¢

---

[1] An exception can occur when inventories are seriously depleted. See the gross profit for Friday only in Exhibit 7–6 and the section "LIFO Inventory Liquidations" on page 272.

The proponent of LIFO would claim that FIFO "overstates" profits (the "inventory profit") by 60¢ − 34¢ = 26¢. Suppose replacement prices stay at 56¢. The vendor will need 30¢ + 26¢ = 56¢, not merely the 30¢ reported as FIFO cost of goods sold, to replace the unit sold. In commenting on reporting profits in general, a *Newsweek* article said:

☐　But inventory profits also played a significant role. In an inflationary world, parts acquired for inventory tend to appreciate in value by the time they are used in the manufacturing process. The company then reflects the difference in its selling price— and takes an "inventory profit." It must restock at the new, higher cost, of course, but as long as the inflation continues, so does the inventory-profit process.

Advocates of LIFO also stress that in times of rising prices, there may be greater pressure from stockholders to pay unjustified higher cash dividends under FIFO than LIFO. In the above example, the payment of a cash dividend of 60¢ by a vendor using FIFO would result in his not having enough cash to replenish his inventory. He would have only 90¢ − 60¢ = 30¢. In contrast, LIFO would be more likely to conserve cash to the extent that less cash dividends would be paid if less income is reported. The vendor would have 90¢ − 34¢ = 56¢ available for replenishing inventory (if he paid a cash dividend of 34¢, ignoring the effects of other expenses).

☐　## Criticisms of LIFO

Critics of LIFO point to absurd balance sheet valuations. Under LIFO, older and older prices, and hence less-useful inventory values, are reported, especially if physical stocks grow through the years. In contrast, under FIFO, the balance sheet tends to contain current prices and values. LIFO companies can offset this criticism to some extent by disclosing FIFO inventory values in a footnote to the financial statement. For example, see the General Mills annual report footnote on page 268.

Another criticism of LIFO is that, unlike FIFO, it permits management to influence immediate net income by the *timing of purchases*. For instance, if prices are rising and a company desires, for income tax or other reasons, to report less income in a given year, managers may be inclined to buy a large amount of inventory near the end of the year, that is, to accelerate the replacement of inventory that would normally not occur until early in the next year.

Consider an example. Suppose in our illustration that acquisition prices had increased from 56¢ on Wednesday to 68¢ on Thursday, the day of the sale of the one unit. Suppose one more unit was acquired on Thursday for 68¢. How would net income be affected under FIFO? Under LIFO?

There would be no effect on cost of goods sold or gross profit under FIFO, although the balance sheet would show ending inventory as 68¢ higher. In contrast, LIFO would show a 12¢ higher cost of goods sold and a 12¢ lower gross profit:

	LIFO	
	As in Exhibit 7–6	If One More Unit Acquired
Sales	90¢	90¢
Cost of goods sold	56¢	68¢
Gross profit	34¢	22¢
Ending inventory:		
First layer, Monday	30¢	30¢
Second layer, Tuesday	40¢	40¢
Third layer, Wednesday		56¢
	70¢	126¢

Thus a 34¢ gross profit may be transformed into a 22¢ gross profit merely because of a change in the timing and amount of merchandise *acquired*, not because of any change in *sales*.

The second part of the above tabulation uses the word *layer*. As the term implies, a **LIFO layer** (also called **LIFO increment** or **LIFO pool**) is an identifiable addition to inventory. As a company grows, the LIFO layers tend to pile on one another as the years go by. Thus many LIFO companies will show inventories that may have ancient layers (going back to 1940 in some instances). The reported LIFO values may therefore be far below what FIFO values might otherwise show.

☐ **LIFO Inventory Liquidations**

The existence of old LIFO layers can cause problems if inventory decreases. Examine Exhibit 7–8. Suppose a company bought an inventory of 100 units at $10 per unit on December 31, 19X0. The company bought and sold 100 units each year, 19X1 through 19X4, at the purchase and selling prices shown. In 19X5 100 units were sold but none were purchased.

EXHIBIT 7–8

Effect of Inventory Liquidations under LIFO
(Purchases and sales of 100 units in 19X1–19X4. Purchases but no sales in 19X0; sales but no purchases in 19X5.)

YEAR	PURCHASE PRICE PER UNIT	SELLING PRICE PER UNIT	REVENUE	FIFO Cost of Goods Sold	FIFO Gross Profit	FIFO Ending Inventory	LIFO Cost of Goods Sold	LIFO Gross Profit	LIFO Ending Inventory
19X0	$10	—	—	—	—	$1,000	—	—	$1,000
19X1	12	$15	$1,500	$1,000	$ 500	1,200	$1,200	$ 300	1,000
19X2	14	17	1,700	1,200	500	1,400	1,400	300	1,000
19X3	16	19	1,900	1,400	500	1,600	1,600	300	1,000
19X4	18	21	2,100	1,600	500	1,800	1,800	300	1,000
19X5		23	2,300	1,800	500	0	1,000	1,300	0
Total			$9,500	$7,000	$2,500		$7,000	$2,500	

Compare the gross profit each year under LIFO with that under FIFO in Exhibit 7–8. As expected, LIFO gross profit is generally less than FIFO gross profit because prices were rising. But what happened in 19X5? The old 19X0 inventory became the cost of goods sold under LIFO because inventory was depleted. Consequently, gross profit under LIFO soared. In general, when the physical amount of inventory decreases, LIFO charges the cost of old LIFO layers as cost of goods sold, beginning with the most recent layers. If the inventory decrease is large enough, very old layers may be penetrated, resulting in ancient costs being recognized as cost of goods sold. This can create an unrealistically low cost of goods sold and high gross profit.

In general, prices have been rising throughout the world for many years. Companies that have been on LIFO for a number of years typically have many LIFO layers, some at unit prices that are relatively old and low. Occasionally, circumstances (such as a prolonged strike or the discontinuance of a segment of the business) call for the liquidation of some or all of the LIFO layers. This decrease in the physical levels of inventories would cause unusually low cost of goods sold, high income, and high income tax expense in comparison with FIFO. For example, LIFO inventory liquidations by CrownAmerica, Inc., a Georgia-based yarn mill and general warehousing company, increased its 1985 net income by over $300,000, from about $100,000 to over $400,000.

A company's **LIFO reserve,** which is generally defined as the difference between inventories valued at LIFO and what they would be under FIFO, measures the potential effects of inventory liquidations. For example, suppose our cola vendor uses LIFO (see column 3 of Exhibit 7–6, page 266). The LIFO reserve at the end of Thursday would be:

Inventory if it had been valued by FIFO	96¢
Inventory valued at LIFO	70¢
LIFO reserve	26¢

When inventory was completely liquidated on Friday, LIFO gross profit exceeded FIFO gross profit by 110¢ − 84¢ = 26¢, the amount of the LIFO reserve, as shown in Panel II of Exhibit 7–6.

Companies often disclose their LIFO reserve in a footnote. For example, the General Mills illustration on page 268 shows a LIFO reserve of $53.0 million in 1988 and $51.5 million in 1987.

☐ Importance of Income Taxes

The accounting literature is full of fancy theoretical arguments that support LIFO. For example, some accountants maintain that LIFO shows the "real" impact of inflation on cost of goods sold more clearly than FIFO. But there is one—and only one—dominant reason why more and more U.S. companies have adopted LIFO. *Income taxes!* LIFO is acceptable for income tax purposes. Furthermore, the Internal Revenue Code requires that if LIFO is used for income tax purposes, it must also be used for financial reporting purposes. If prices persistently rise, and if inventory quantities are maintained so that LIFO layers bearing "old" prices are not used up, current taxable income will be less under LIFO than FIFO. Consequently, income taxes will be postponed. Intelligent financial managers would therefore be tempted to adopt LIFO. Indeed, some observers maintain that executives are guilty of serious mismanagement by not adopting LIFO when FIFO produces significantly higher taxable income.

The *Wall Street Journal* reported that inflation jitters in 1989 were causing many small firms to change from FIFO to LIFO. As an example, Chicago Heights Steel Co. "recently boosted cash by 5% to 10% by lowering income taxes when it switched to LIFO" (April 27, 1989). When Becton, Dickinson and Company changed to LIFO, its annual report stated that its "change to the LIFO method . . . for both financial reporting and income tax purposes resulted in improved cash flow due to lower income taxes paid." Management often faces some significant choices between accounting methods. The impact of these choices on the cash position can be enormous.

Tyranny of Reported Earnings

The accrual accounting model has survived many tests through time. It is here to stay. Nevertheless, as useful as it is for evaluating performance, its limitations should never be overlooked. For example, net income (or earnings per share) is *only one* measure of performance. Even though this "bottom line" is important, it is sometimes overemphasized in the minds of management. It may lead to decisions that boost current reported net income but may not be in the best long-run interests of the stockholders. Thus managers may slash advertising, maintenance, and research expenses to bolster 19X0 earnings. But such "economy measures" can produce some unfavorable results: reduction in share of the customer market, poorer condition of equipment, and lack of new products, all of which may have devastating effects on earnings in 19X1, 19X2, and thereafter.

Similarly, managers may be reluctant to switch to LIFO from FIFO because reported income will be less. There is widespread but mistaken belief that the stock market can be fooled by the reported net income numbers. In the long run, the wealth of the shareholders is usually enhanced by decisions that postpone income tax disbursements even though reported net income may be lower. Intelligent investors have observed that FIFO results in higher taxes and less cash retained by the corporation. Investors who rely entirely on "earnings-per-share multiples" may be doing so at considerable risk.

The following table summarizes the choices faced by many top managers when prices are rising:

INVENTORY METHOD	ACTUAL CASH POSITION	REPORTED NET INCOME
FIFO	Lower	Higher
LIFO	Higher	Lower

As noted above, the dilemma should usually be resolved in favor of LIFO. The company would then be better able to meet the dividend expectations of stockholders or of other demands. Why? Because the company will have a better cash position despite lower reported net income.

Why do some companies continue to use FIFO? Some may be swayed by the cosmetic effect of higher reported earnings despite paying higher taxes. But more often it is because (1) they expect the cost of their inventory to fall, (2) they expect large fluctuations in amounts of physical inventory, or (3) inventories are so small that the choice makes little difference. Examples of industries where most companies use FIFO are baking, electronic equipment, and business equipment.

LOWER OF COST OR MARKET

☐ The Conservatism Convention

Conservatism has been a hallmark of accounting. In a technical sense, **conservatism** means selecting the method of measurement that yields the gloomiest immediate results. This attitude is reflected in such working rules as "Anticipate no gains, but provide for all possible losses," and "If in doubt, write it off."

Accountants have traditionally regarded the historical costs of acquiring an asset as the ceiling for its valuation. Assets may be written up only upon an exchange, but they may be written down without an exchange. For example, consider *lower-of-cost-or-market* procedures. Inventories are written down when replacement costs decline, but they are never written up when replacement costs increase.

Conservatism has been criticized as being inherently inconsistent. If replacement market prices are sufficiently objective and verifiable to justify write-downs, why aren't they just as valid for write-ups? Furthermore, the critics maintain, conservatism is not a fundamental concept. Accounting reports should try to present the most accurate picture feasible—neither too high nor too low. Accountants defend their attitude by saying that erring in the direction of conservatism would usually have less-severe economic consequences than erring in the direction of overstating assets and net income.

Conservatism that leads to understating net income in one period also creates an overstatement of net income in a future period. For example, if a $100 inventory is written down to $80, net income is reduced by $20 in the period of the write-down but *increased* by $20 in the period the inventory is sold.

☐ Role of Replacement Cost

A prime example of conservatism is the **lower-of-cost-or-market** method (LCM), which is the superimposition of a market-price test on an inventory cost method. That is, the current market price is compared with cost (derived by specific identification, FIFO, and so forth), and the lower of the two is selected as the basis for the valuation of goods at a specific inventory date. The annual report of ITT Corporation states: "Inventories are valued generally at the lower of cost (first-in, first-out) or market . . . counts of inventories are made at least ar nually."

Market generally means the *current replacement cost* or its equivalent. It ordinarily does *not* mean the ultimate selling price to customers. Consider the following facts. A company has 100 units in its ending FIFO inventory on December 31, 19X1. Its gross profit for 19X1 has been tentatively computed as follows:

Sales	$2,180
Cost of goods available for sale	$1,980
Ending inventory, at cost of 100 units	790
Cost of goods sold	$1,190
Gross profit	$ 990

There has been a sudden decline in market prices during the final week of December to $4 per unit. If the lower market price is indicative of lower ultimate sales prices, an inventory write-down of $790 − (100 × $4), or $390, is in order. The required journal entry (without explanation) is:

Loss on write-down of inventories	390	
Merchandise inventory		390

The loss on write-down of inventories increases cost of goods sold by $390. Therefore reported income for 19X1 would be lowered by $390:

	BEFORE $390 WRITE-DOWN	AFTER $390 WRITE-DOWN	DIFFERENCE
Sales	$2,180	$2,180	
Cost of goods available	$1,980	$1,980	
Ending inventory	790	400	−$390
Cost of goods sold	$1,190	$1,580	+$390
Gross profit	$ 990	$ 600	−$390

The theory states that of the $790 cost, $390 is considered to have expired during 19X1 because the cost cannot be justifiably carried forward to the future as an asset measure. Furthermore, the decision to purchase was made during 19X1, but unfortunate fluctuations occurred in the replacement market during the same period. These declines in prices caused the inventory to lose some value, some revenue-producing power. On the other hand, if *selling prices* also are not likely to fall, the revenue-producing power of the inventory will be maintained and no write-down would be justified.

In sum, if predicted selling prices will be *unaffected* by the fact that current replacement costs are below the carrying cost of the inventory, do nothing. If predicted selling prices will be lower, use replacement cost.

If a write-down occurs, the new $400 valuation is what is left of the original cost of the inventory. In other words, the new market price becomes, for accounting purposes, the remaining unexpired cost of the inventory. Thus, if replacement prices rise to $8 per unit in January 19X2, no restoration of the December write-down will be permitted. In short, the lower-of-cost-or-market method would regard the $4 cost as of December 31 as the "new cost" of the inventory. Historical cost is the ceiling for valuation under generally accepted accounting principles.

☐ Conservatism in Action

Compared with a strict cost method, the lower-of-cost-or-market method reports less net income in the period of decline in market value of the inventory and more net income in the period of sale. More generally, cumulative net income (the sum of all net income amounts from the inception of the firm to the present date) is never lower and is usually higher under the strict cost method. Exhibit 7–9 underscores this point. Suppose our example company goes out of business in early 19X2. That is, no more units are acquired. There are no sales in 19X2 except for the disposal of the inventory in question at $8 per unit (100 × $8 = $800). Neither combined gross profit nor combined net income for the two periods will be affected by the LCM method, as the bottom of Exhibit 7–9 reveals.

EXHIBIT 7–9

Effects of Lower-of-Cost-or-Market

	COST METHOD		LOWER-OF-COST-OR-MARKET METHOD	
	19X1	19X2	19X1	19X2
Sales	$2,180	$800	$2,180	$800
Cost of goods available	$1,980	$790	$1,980	$400
Ending inventory	790	—	400*	—
Cost of goods sold	$1,190	$790	$1,580	$400
Gross profit	$ 990	$ 10	$ 600	$400

Combined gross profit for two years:
　Cost method:
　　$990 + $10 = $1,000
　Lower-of-cost-or-market method:
　　$600 + $400 = $1,000

* The inventory is shown here after being written down by $390, from $790 to $400. For internal purposes, many accountants prefer to show the write-down separately, presenting a gross profit before write-down of inventory, the write-down, and a gross profit after write-down. The journal entry would be:

Loss on write-down of inventory	390	
Inventory		390
To write down inventory from $790 cost to $400 market value.		

This example shows that conservatism can be a double-edged sword in the sense that net income in a current year will be hurt by a write-down of inventory (or any asset) and in a future year will be helped by the amount of the write-down. As Exhibit 7–9 illustrates, 19X2 income is higher by the $390 write-down of 19X1.

A full-blown lower-of-cost-or-market method is rarely encountered in practice. Why? Because it is expensive to get the correct replacement costs of hundreds or thousands of different products in inventory. Still, auditors definitely feel that the costs of inventories should be fully recoverable from future revenues. Therefore auditors inevitably make market-price tests of a representative sample of the ending inventories. In particular, auditors want to write down the subclasses of inventory that are obsolete, shopworn, or otherwise of only nominal value.

GROSS PROFIT AND INVENTORIES

☐ Gross Profit Equations

A thorough understanding of the relationships among inventory, cost of goods sold, and gross profit aids managers, investors, and anyone else who wishes to assess a company's performance. Suppose a manager of a K Mart store wants to prepare a monthly income statement without incurring the expense of a physical inventory count. The manager can estimate gross profit (based on past experience) and calculate both cost of goods sold and ending inventory.

The conventional presentation of gross profit for a K Mart store (in thousands) is:

SYMBOL			
S	Net sales		$10,000 (100%)
	Deduct cost of goods sold:		
BI	Beginning inventory	$1,300	
P	Add net purchases	8,200	
CGA	Cost of goods available for sale	$9,500	
EI	Deduct ending inventory	2,300	
CGS	Cost of goods sold (also called cost of sales)		7,200
GP	Gross profit (also called gross margin and sometimes called gross profit margin)		$ 2,800 (28%)

The basic relationship can be stated algebraically:

$$\text{Net sales} - \text{Cost of goods sold} = \text{Gross profit}$$
$$S \quad - \quad CGS \quad = \quad GP$$

and

$$\text{Cost of goods sold} = \text{Beginning inventory} + \text{Net purchases} - \text{Ending inventory}$$
$$CGS \quad = \quad BI \quad + \quad P \quad - \quad EI$$

The ending inventory is customarily measured at the close of each reporting period. However, the actual amount of the ending inventory for monthly and quarterly financial statements frequently is not known because it is too costly to obtain a physical count. In such cases, the gross profit relationships are often used to estimate the ending inventory figure.

For example, in our illustration, assume that past sales have usually resulted in a gross profit percentage of 28%. (Unless otherwise stated, any gross profit percentage given is based on *net sales*, not cost.)[2] Then the accountant would estimate gross profit to be .28 × $10,000, or $2,800. Using the above equations, the ending inventory could have been estimated:

$$\text{S} - \text{CGS} = \text{GP}$$
$$\$10{,}000 - \text{CGS} = \$2{,}800$$
$$\text{CGS} = \$7{,}200$$

and

$$\text{CGS} = \text{BI} + \text{P} - \text{EI}$$
$$\$7{,}200 = \$1{,}300 + \$8{,}200 - \text{EI}$$
$$\text{EI} = \$1{,}300 + \$8{,}200 - \$7{,}200$$
$$\text{EI} = \$2{,}300$$

☐ Gross Profit Percentage and Turnover

Retailers often use a well-known strategy to increase profits. They lower prices and yet hope to increase their gross profits by selling their inventories more quickly, replenishing, selling again, and so forth. Managers speak of improving their **inventory turnover,** which is defined as cost of goods sold divided by the average inventory held during a given period. Average inventory is usually the sum of beginning inventory and ending inventory divided by 2. Using our assumed K Mart data, the average inventory would be ($1,300 + $2,300) ÷ 2 = $1,800. The inventory turnover would be computed as follows:

$$\text{Turnover} = \text{Cost of goods sold} \div \text{Average inventory}$$
$$= \$7{,}200 \div \$1{,}800 = 4$$

How could K Mart have improved its total gross profit? Maybe the store could not change the amount of its investment in inventory but could sell the inventory more quickly by cutting selling prices.

Suppose our data pertained to operations for January. Perhaps lowering prices by 10% could have resulted in selling inventory twice as quickly. This means that inventory costing $1,800 and sold for $2,500 would now be sold for $2,500 less 10%, or $2,250. The lower prices would cause a doubling of the physical quantity sold. Inventory turnover would increase from 4 to 8. Total gross profit for January would have been $3,600 instead of the given $2,800:

---

[2] As a general rule, when dealing with percentages in any situation, it is wise to ask, What is the base? That is, which item represents 100%? On an income statement, net sales is invariably the base.

	AMOUNT	%
Sales	$2,500 × 4 turnovers = $10,000	100%
Cost of goods sold	1,800 × 4 turnovers = 7,200	72
Gross profit	$ 700 × 4 turnovers = $ 2,800	28%
Sales	$2,250 × 8 turnovers = $18,000	100%
Cost of goods sold	1,800 × 8 turnovers = 14,400	80
Gross profit	$ 450 × 8 turnovers = $ 3,600	20%

As the above example demonstrates, all other things being equal, the quicker the turnover, the greater the total gross profit obtained. Each time the inventory is sold, it is said to have been turned over. Obviously, for any given investment in inventory, and a given rate of gross profit, the quicker the turnover, the higher the rate of return on investment. Again we see how accounting measurements can help in the evaluation of performance and in making decisions.

Inventory turnover varies greatly by industry. Consider the inventory turnover of three companies in different industries: (1) PACCAR, manufacturer of heavy-duty trucks such as Kenworth and Peterbilt, (2) US West, telecommunications company that provides telephone service to much of the western United States, and (3) The Good Guys, a specialty retailer of electronics products in northern California:

PACCAR:
$$\frac{\$2,423,539,000}{(\$192,609,000 + \$101,302,000) \div 2} = 16.5$$

US West:
$$\frac{\$8,445,300,000}{(\$205,600,000 + \$259,000,000) \div 2} = 36.4$$

The Good Guys:
$$\frac{\$120,239,000}{(\$13,772,000 + \$10,624,000) \div 2} = 9.9$$

SUMMARY

Perpetual inventory records may be kept for units only or for both units and dollars. Periodic inventory records are less detailed, although separate accounts are usually kept for purchases, purchase returns and allowances, and cash discounts on purchases. The journal entries for cost of goods sold in the periodic system are made at the end of the accounting period. Such entries in a perpetual system are made continuously.

Four major inventory methods are in use: specific identification, weighted average, FIFO, and LIFO. When prices are rising, less income is generally shown by LIFO than FIFO.

LIFO is popular in the United States because it offers income tax advantages that become most pronounced during times of steady or rising inventories combined with rising prices. Note that even when inventories are declining, *cumulative* taxable income is always less under LIFO than FIFO because the inventory valuation is less and the cumulative cost of goods sold is higher.

The lower-of-cost-or-market method requires a write-down of inventory to its replacement cost if purchase prices fall and selling prices are also likely to fall.

SUMMARY PROBLEMS FOR YOUR REVIEW

☐ **Problem One**

Examine Exhibit 7–10. The company uses the periodic inventory system. Using these facts, prepare a columnar comparison of income statements for the year ended December 31, 19X2. Compare the FIFO, LIFO, and weighted-average inventory methods. Assume that other expenses are $1,000. The income tax rate is 40%.

☐ **Solution to Problem One**

See Exhibit 7–11.

☐ **Problem Two**

"When prices are rising, FIFO results in fool's profits because more resources are needed to maintain operations than previously." Do you agree? Explain.

☐ **Solution to Problem Two**

The merit of this position depends on the concept of income favored. LIFO gives a better measure of "distributable" income than FIFO. Recall the cola example in the chapter (Exhibit 7–6, p. 266). The gross profit under FIFO was sixty cents and under LIFO was

EXHIBIT 7–10

Facts for Summary Problem One

	IN	OUT	BALANCE
December 31, 19X1			200 @ $5 = $1,000
January 25	170 @ $6 = $1,020		
January 29		150*	
May 28	190 @ $7 = $1,330		
June 7		230*	
November 20	150 @ $8 = $1,200		
December 15		100*	
Total	510 $3,550	480	
December 31, 19X2			230 @ ?

* Selling prices were $9, $11, and $13, respectively:

			Summary of costs to account for:
150 @ $ 9 = $1,350		Beginning inventory	$1,000
230 @ $11 = $2,530		Purchases	3,550
100 @ $13 = $1,300		Cost of goods available	
Total sales 480 $5,180		for sale	$4,550

EXHIBIT 7–11

Comparison of Inventory Methods
For the Year Ended December 31, 19X2

		FIFO		LIFO		WEIGHTED AVERAGE
Sales, 480 units			$5,180		$5,180	$5,180
Deduct cost of goods sold:						
Beginning inventory, 200 @ $5		$1,000		$1,000		$1,000
Purchases, 510 units (from Exhibit 7–10)*		3,550		3,550		3,550
Available for sale, 710 units†		$4,550		$4,550		$4,550
Ending inventory, 230 units:‡						
150 @ $8	$1,200					
80 @ $7	560	1,760				
or						
200 @ $5				$1,000		
30 @ $6				180	1,180	
or						
230 @ $6.408						1,474
Cost of goods sold, 480 units		——	2,790	——	3,370	3,076
Gross profit			$2,390		$1,810	$2,104
Other expenses			1,000		1,000	1,000
Income before income taxes			$1,390		$ 810	$1,104
Income taxes at 40%			556		324	442
Net income			$ 834		$ 486	662

* Always equal across all three methods.

† These amounts will not be equal in general across the three methods because beginning inventories will generally be different. They are equal here only because beginning inventories were assumed to be equal.

‡ Under FIFO, the ending inventory is composed of the last purchases plus the second-last purchases, and so forth, until the costs of 230 units are compiled. Under LIFO, the ending inventory is composed of the beginning inventory plus the earliest purchases of the current year until the costs of 230 units are compiled. Under weighted average, the ending inventory and cost of goods sold are accumulations based on a unit cost. The latter is the cost of goods available for sale divided by the number of units available for sale: $4,550 ÷ 710 = $6.408.

thirty-four cents. The 60¢ − 34¢ = 26¢ difference is a fool's profit because it must be reinvested to maintain the same inventory level as previously. Therefore the twenty-six cents cannot be distributed as a cash dividend without reducing the current level of operations.

☐ **Problem Three**

Fay's Drug Company operates about 155 super drugstores in the Northeast. Some results for fiscal 1988 were (in thousands):

Sales	$500,414
Cost of merchandise sold	$361,141
Net earnings	$ 5,942
Beginning merchandise inventory	$ 64,102
Ending merchandise inventory	$ 65,682

Required:
1. Calculate the 1988 gross profit and gross profit percentage for Fay's Drug Company.
2. Calculate the inventory turnover ratio.

3. What gross profit would have been reported if inventory turnover in 1988 had been 7, the gross profit percentage calculated in requirement 1 had been achieved, and the level of inventory was unchanged?

☐ Solution to Problem Three

1. Gross profit = Sales − Cost of merchandise sold
   = $500,414 − $361,141
   = $139,273
   Gross profit percentage = Gross profit ÷ Sales
   = $139,273 ÷ $500,414
   = 27.8%

2. Inventory turnover = Cost of merchandise sold ÷ Average merchandise inventory
   = $361,141 ÷ [($64,102 + $65,682) ÷ 2]
   = $361,141 ÷ $64,892
   = 5.6

3. Cost of merchandise sold = Inventory turnover × Average merchandise inventory
   = 7 × $64,892
   = $454,244
   Gross profit percentage = (Sales − Cost of merchandise sold) ÷ Sales
   27.8% = (S − $454,244) ÷ S
   .278 × S = S − $454,244
   S − (.278 × S) = $454,244
   S × (1 − .278) = $454,244
   S = $454,244 ÷ (1 − .278)
   S = $629,147
   Gross profit = Sales − Cost of merchandise sold
   = $629,147 − $454,244
   = $174,903

The increase in inventory turnover from 5.6 to 7 raised gross profit from $139,273 to $174,903.

HIGHLIGHTS TO REMEMBER

1. Ponder the contents of this chapter and the preceding chapter. Much of the space in these two chapters concentrated on decisions faced by accountants and managers. For example, what customer credit policies should be adopted? Should we use bank cards? Should we grant cash discounts? What gross profit percentage and inventory turnover strategies would be most appealing? What inventory method would be best for our company? Note too that investors often raise these same questions.
2. Gross profit percentages and inventory turnover are key financial ratios in many companies.
3. The mechanics of a periodic inventory system may seem cumbersome, but the aims are the same as those of the perpetual inventory system: to compute the proper cost of goods sold for the period in question and the proper ending inventory.
4. The following table summarizes differences between FIFO and LIFO:

INVENTORY METHOD	INCOME STATEMENT: MEASUREMENT OF COST OF GOODS SOLD	BALANCE SHEET: MEASUREMENT OF INVENTORY ASSET
FIFO	Distant from current replacement cost	Near current replacement cost
LIFO	Near current replacement cost	Distant from current replacement cost

ACCOUNTING VOCABULARY

Conservatism, p. 275
Consistency, p. 268
First-in, First-out (FIFO), p. 267
F.O.B., p. 260
Freight in, p. 260
Freight out, p. 260
Inventory Turnover, p. 279
Inward Transportation, p. 260
Last-in, First-out (LIFO), p. 267

LIFO Increment, p. 272
LIFO Layer, p. 272
LIFO Pool, p. 272
LIFO Reserve, p. 273
Lower-of-Cost-or-Market, p. 275
Periodic Inventory System, p. 257
Perpetual Inventory System, p. 257
Specific Identification, p. 265
Weighted-Average Cost, p. 267

APPENDIX 7A: EFFECTS OF INVENTORY ERRORS

The identification of inventory errors and their effects is a popular way (a) to test understanding and develop perspective regarding the nature and role of inventories in relation to income statements and balance sheets and (b) to show the interrelationships of financial statements for two or more reporting periods. Inventory errors can arise from many sources. Examples are wrong physical counts (possibly because goods that are in receiving or shipping areas instead of the inventory stockroom were omitted when physical counts were made) and clerical errors.

An undiscovered inventory error usually affects two reporting periods. It is counterbalanced by the ordinary accounting process in the next period. That is, the error affects income by identical offsetting amounts; it also affects the balance sheet at the end of the first period but not at the end of the second. For example, suppose ending inventory in 19X7 is understated by $10,000 because of errors in physical count. The year's cost of goods sold would be overstated, pretax income understated, assets understated, and retained income understated. For the moment, ignore income taxes:

	A	= L +	SE
	Inventory		Retained Income
Effects of error	$10,000 understated =		$10,000 understated because cost of goods sold is overstated and net income is understated

Again, thinking in terms of effects on the balance sheet equation is helpful. A useful generalization is: If ending inventory is understated, retained income is understated. Similarly, if ending inventory is overstated, retained income is overstated.

Now consider also the effects of income taxes, using a 40% tax rate:

	A	=	L	+	SE
			Income Tax		Retained
	Inventory		Liability		Income

Effects of error $10,000 understated = $4,000 understated + $6,000 understated*

* Cost of goods sold overstated	$10,000
Pretax income understated	$10,000
Income taxes understated	4,000
Net income, which is included in ending retained income, understated	$ 6,000

The above effects are not particularly easy to understand unless a complete illustration is studied. Consider the complete income statements (all numbers are in thousands and are assumed):

19X7	CORRECT REPORTING		INCORRECT REPORTING*		EFFECTS OF ERRORS
Sales		$980		$980	
Deduct: Cost of goods sold:					
Beginning inventory	$100		$100		
Purchases	500		500		
Cost of goods available for sale	$600		$600		
Deduct: Ending inventory	70		60		Understated by $10
Cost of goods sold		530		540	Overstated by $10
Gross profit		$450		$440	Understated by $10
Other expenses		250		250	
Income before income taxes		$200		$190	Understated by $10
Income tax expense at 40%		80		76	Understated by $4
Net income		$120		$114	Understated by $6
Ending balance sheet items:					
Inventory		$ 70		$ 60	Understated by $10
Retained income includes					
current net income of		120		114	Understated by $6
Income tax liability†		80		76	Understated by $4

* Because of error in ending inventory.

† For simplicity, assume that the entire income tax expense for the year will not be paid until the succeeding year. Therefore the ending liability will equal the income tax expense.

Think about the effects of the uncorrected error on the following year, 19X8. The beginning inventory will be $60,000 rather than the correct $70,000. Therefore *all* the errors in 19X7 will be offset by counterbalancing errors in 19X8. Thus the retained income at the end of 19X8 would show a cumulative effect of zero. This is because the net income in 19X7 would be understated by $6,000, but the net income in 19X8 would be overstated by $6,000.

The point not to overlook is that the ending inventory of one period is also the beginning inventory of the succeeding period. Assume that the operations during 19X8 are a duplication of those of 19X7 except that the ending inventory is correctly counted as $40,000. Note the role of the error in the beginning inventory:

19X8	CORRECT REPORTING		INCORRECT REPORTING*		EFFECTS OF ERRORS
Sales		$980		$980	
Deduct: Cost of goods sold:					
Beginning inventory	$ 70		$ 60		Understated by $10
Purchases	500		500		
Cost of goods available for sale	$570		$560		Understated by $10
Deduct: Ending inventory	40		40		
Cost of goods sold		530		520	Understated by $10
Gross profit		$450		$460	Overstated by $10
Other expenses		250		250	
Income before income taxes		$200		$210	Overstated by $10
Income tax expense at 40%		80		84	Overstated by $4
Net income		$120		$126	Overstated by $6
Ending balance sheet items:					
Inventory		$ 40		$ 40	Correct
Retained income includes:					
Net income of previous year		120		114	Counterbalanced and thus
Net income of current year		120		126	now correct
Income tax liability:					
End of previous year		80		76	Counterbalanced and thus
End of current year		80		84	now correct†

* Because of error in beginning inventory.

† The $84 really consists of the $4 that pertains to income of the previous year plus $80 that pertains to income of the current year.

APPENDIX 7B: ACCOUNTING CYCLE FOR PERIODIC AND PERPETUAL INVENTORIES

This appendix shows how accounting data are processed under both periodic and perpetual inventory systems. The data regarding inventories are the same as those used on pages 261–264 of the chapter—inventories: beginning, $100,000; ending, $140,000; purchases, $990,000; purchase returns and allowances, $80,000. This appendix adds more data and provides an overall review of the data-processing aspects of Chapters 5 through 7.

☐ **Problem**

Gomez Radio Stores sells radios and related equipment. Exhibit 7–12 shows how the Gomez unadjusted trial balances would appear under two different inventory systems as of December 31, 19X2 (in thousands of dollars).

Required:

1. Prepare two work sheets, one for the perpetual inventory system and one for the periodic inventory system. Enter the pertinent unadjusted trial balance in the first pair of columns for each work sheet. Enter the amounts in thousands of dollars.
2. The unadjusted trial balances given here are probably misnamed. A more descriptive title would be "partially adjusted" trial balances. We assume that all necessary entries (for example, depreciation) have already been made except for the three following (labeled j, k, and l for later reference):
   j. Bad debts expense should be recognized. Past experience indicates that a provision should be made of 1% of the year's credit sales of $1 million.

EXHIBIT 7–12

GOMEZ RADIO STORES
Unadjusted Trial Balance
December 31, 19X2

	PERPETUAL INVENTORY		PERIODIC INVENTORY	
	Debit	Credit	Debit	Credit
Cash	900		900	
Accounts receivable	180		180	
Allowance for uncollectible accounts				
Merchandise inventory	140*		100†	
Equipment	300		300	
Accumulated depreciation, equipment		100		100
Accounts payable		1,010		1,010
Accrued income taxes payable				
Paid-in capital		100		100
Retained income		110		110
Sales		1,640		1,640
Sales returns and allowances	70		70	
Cost of goods sold	870			
Purchases			990	
Purchase returns and allowances				80
Various expenses (summarized here)	500		500	
Bad debts expense				
Income tax expense				
	2,960	2,960	3,040	3,040

* Balance, December 31, 19X2.
† Balance, December 31, 19X1.

k. The cost of the ending inventory was $140,000.
l. Income tax expense was recognized at a rate of 30% of pretax income.
Enter any necessary entries in the adjustment columns. Then complete the work sheet. To show the flexibility of the work sheet, omit the columns for the adjusted trial balance.
3. Prepare formal income statements, using a format for the gross profit section that is similar to that of Exhibit 7–3.
4. Prepare the adjusting journal entries, using the work sheets as a guide. Show adjacent sets of entries for the perpetual and periodic systems.
5. Prepare the closing journal entries, using the work sheets as a guide. Show adjacent sets of entries for the perpetual and periodic systems.

The solutions to the above requirements are shown sequentially in Exhibits 7–13 through 7–16.

Periodic Inventory System on Work Sheet

The work sheet for the perpetual inventory system (Exhibit 7–13) has the same format as that introduced in Chapter 5. The general format for the periodic inventory system is similar except for the items shaded in Exhibits 7–13 and 7–14. The purpose of the differences is to include all details of cost of goods sold in the income statement. The work sheet for the periodic system (Exhibit 7–14) has two inventory lines rather than one and includes

EXHIBIT 7–13

GOMEZ RADIO STORES
Work Sheet (Perpetual Inventory System)
For the Year Ended December 31, 19X2 (in thousands of dollars)

Account Titles	Unadjusted Trial Balance Debit	Unadjusted Trial Balance Credit	Adjustments Debit	Adjustments Credit	Income Statement Debit	Income Statement Credit	Statement of Retained Income Debit	Statement of Retained Income Credit	Balance Sheet Debit	Balance Sheet Credit
Cash	900								900	
Accounts receivable	180								180	
Allowance for uncollectible accounts				(j) 10						10
Merchandise inventory	140								140	
Equipment	300								300	
Accumulated depreciation—equipment		100								100
Accounts payable		1010								1010
Accrued income taxes payable				(l) 57						57
Paid-in capital		100								100
Retained income		110						110		
Sales		1640				1640				
Sales returns and allowances	70				70					
Cost of goods sold	870				870					
Various expenses (summarized here)	500				500					
	2960	2960								
Bad debts expense			(j) 10		10					
Income tax expense			(l) 57		57					
			67	67						
					1450	1640				
Net income					133			133		
					1640	1640				
Retained income, December 31, 19X2							243			243
							243	243	1520	1520

j. Bad debts estimated, .01 × $1,000,000 = $10,000.   k. Not applicable.
l. Income tax expense, .30 ($1640 − $1450) = .30 × $190 income before income taxes, or $57.

EXHIBIT 7–14

GOMEZ RADIO STORES
Work Sheet (Periodic Inventory System)
For the Year Ended December 31, 19X2 (in thousands of dollars)

Account Titles	Unadjusted Trial Balance Debit	Unadjusted Trial Balance Credit	Adjustments Debit	Adjustments Credit	Income Statement Debit	Income Statement Credit	Statement of Retained Income Debit	Statement of Retained Income Credit	Balance Sheet Debit	Balance Sheet Credit
Cash	900								900	
Accounts receivable	180								180	
Allowance for uncollectible accounts				(j) 10						10
Merchandise inventory, December 31, 19X1	100				100					
Equipment	300								300	
Accumulated depreciation—equipment		100								100
Accounts payable		1010								1010
Accrued income taxes payable				(l) 57						57
Paid-in capital		100								100
Retained income		110						110		
Sales		1640				1640				
Sales returns and allowances	70				70					
Purchases	990				990					
Purchase returns and allowances		80				80				
Various expenses (summarized here)	500				500					
	3040	3040								
Bad debts expense			(j) 10		10					
Merchandise inventory, December 31, 19X2						140			140	
					1670	1860				
Income tax expense			(l) 57	57	57					
			67	67						
					1860	1860				
Net income					133			133		
							243	243		
Retained income, December 31, 19X2							243			243
							243	243	1520	1520

j. Bad debts estimated, .01 × $1,000,000 = $10,000.   k. See text for thorough explanation of how ending inventory is accounted for.
l. Income tax expense, .30 ($1,860 − $1,670) = .30 × $190 income before income taxes, or $57.

289

lines for purchases and purchase returns and allowances instead of a line for cost of goods sold. The beginning inventory (December 31, 19X1) remains untouched in the ledger throughout 19X2. It appears as a debit in the unadjusted trial balance, and it is also placed in the income statement debit column. Of course, in the formal income statement it is added to net purchases to obtain the cost of goods available for sale. (The *beginning* inventory does not belong in the section for the ending balance sheet.)

The ending inventory (December 31, 19X2) is not in the unadjusted trial balance. Mechanically, it can be placed on the work sheet in various ways. A popular way is shown in Exhibit 7–14 where the ending balance is a separate line item below the totals of the unadjusted trial balance.

The ending inventory amount is shown in two places: the income statement credit column and the balance sheet debit column. The $140,000 is a credit in the income statement section because it is deducted from the cost of goods available for sale to obtain the cost of goods sold. The $140,000 is a debit in the balance sheet section because it represents an asset on the ending balance sheet.

Entries in the income statement columns of the four shaded lines of Exhibit 7–14 provide the cost of goods sold: beginning inventory + purchases − purchase returns and allowances − ending inventory = $100,000 + $990,000 − $80,000 − $140,000 = $870,000.

Comparison of Journal Entries

The formal income statement is shown in Exhibit 7–15. Exhibit 7–16 represents the adjusting and closing journal entries in response to requirements 4 and 5. All entries are identical

EXHIBIT 7–15

GOMEZ RADIO STORES
Income Statement
For the Year Ended December 31, 19X2
(in thousands of dollars)

	PERPETUAL SYSTEM		PERIODIC SYSTEM	
Gross sales		$1,640		$1,640
Deduct: Sales returns and allowances		70		70
Net sales		$1,570		$1,570
Deduct: Cost of goods sold				
Merchandise inventory, December 31, 19X1			$ 100	
Gross purchases	$990			
Deduct: Purchase returns and allowances	80			
Net purchases			910	
Cost of goods available for sale			$1,010	
Deduct: Merchandise inventory, December 31, 19X2			140	
Cost of goods sold		870		870
Gross profit		$ 700		$ 700
Operating expenses:				
Bad debts expense	$ 10			$ 10
Various expenses	500			500
Total operating expenses		$ 510		$ 510
Income before income taxes		$ 190		$ 190
Income tax expense		57		57
Net income		$ 133		$ 133

EXHIBIT 7–16

GOMEZ RADIO STORES
Adjusting and Closing Journal Entries
For the Year Ended December 31, 19X2

	PERPETUAL INVENTORY SYSTEM		PERIODIC INVENTORY SYSTEM	
4. Adjusting journal entries:				
j. Bad debts:	Bad debts expense	10	Bad debts expense	10
	Allowance for uncollectible accounts	10	Allowance for uncollectible accounts	10
k. Ending inventory:	Not applicable		See closing entries below	
l. Income tax expense:	Income tax expense	57	Income tax expense	57
	Accrued income taxes payable	57	Accrued income taxes payable	57
5. Closing journal entries:				
m. Revenue accounts:	Sales	1,640	Sales	1,640
	Sales returns and allowances	70	Sales returns and allowances	70
	Income summary	1,570	Income summary	1,570
n. Expense accounts:			n1. Cost of goods sold	870
	Income summary	1,437	Purchase returns and	
	Cost of goods sold	870	allowances	80
	Various expenses	500	Merchandise inventory	140
	Bad debts expense	10	Purchases	990
	Income tax expense	57	Merchandise inventory	100
			n2. Income summary	1,437
			Cost of goods sold	870
			Various expenses	500
			Bad debts expense	10
			Income tax expense	57

for the perpetual and periodic systems except for summarizing the cost of goods sold (see entries *n1* and *n2*).

Under the perpetual system, the cost of goods sold is accumulated on a continuous basis throughout the year. As sales are made, Cost of Goods Sold is debited and Inventory is credited. Under the periodic system the cost of goods sold is computed at the end of the year. The closing entries highlight this aspect of the periodic method.

In practice, entries under the periodic system vary considerably. No matter what the entries, the ending inventory and the cost of goods sold must be $140 and $870, respectively. Many accountants would use one compound entry as entry *n*. Note how such an entry directly lists each entry in the income statement columns of the work sheet. There is no explicit listing of the cost of goods sold:

Income summary	1,437	
Merchandise inventory	140	
Purchase returns and allowances	80	
Merchandise inventory		100
Purchases		990
Various expenses		500
Bad debts expense		10
Income tax expense		57

☐ Record Keeping in Perpetual Inventory Systems

Exhibit 7–17 shows a perpetual (continuous) inventory record, using the same data as those employed in the first "Summary Problem" of this chapter. The FIFO method is illustrated, but similar details (applying different cost-flow assumptions) may be kept for average cost and LIFO methods. Such details may be kept on individual cards for each

EXHIBIT 7–17

Perpetual Inventory Card (or similar computer record)

Description	Hand calculator #4326A			Location	Shelf 42B		
Cost-Flow Assumption	FIFO			Maximum	250		
				Minimum	100		

	Units*				Dollars†		
Date	Purchased	Sold	Balance	Unit Cost	Purchased	Sold	Balance
19X1							
Dec. 31			200	5			1,000
19X2							
Jan. 25	170			6	1,020		
			{ 200	5			{ 1,000
			170	6			1,020
Jan. 29		150		5		750	
			{ 50	5			{ 250
			170	6			1,020
May 28	190			7	1,330		
			{ 50	5			{ 250
			170	6			1,020
			190	7			1,330
June 7		{ 50		5		{ 250	
		170		6		1,020	
		10		7		70	
			180	7			1,260
Nov. 20	150			8	1,200		
			{ 180	7			{ 1,260
			150	8			1,200
Dec. 15		100		7		700	
			{ 80	7			{ 560
			150	8			1,200

*Entries always the same regardless of cost-flow assumption in use. Many organizations confine their perpetual inventory system to quantities only.
†Entries differ, depending on cost-flow assumptions such as FIFO, specific identification, average cost, or LIFO.

item in stock, on computer tape, or on any record that supports the aggregate dollar amounts assigned to cost of goods sold and inventories.

Many perpetual inventory systems are confined to *units* only. Dollar amounts are determined only at year-end through some averaging process or some overall assumptions as to cost flow (such as LIFO) for the year. These systems are best described as combined perpetual-periodic inventory systems. For instance, a full-blown LIFO perpetual inventory system on a day-to-day basis is virtually unknown. Indeed, the LIFO results from using perpetual records would not always coincide exactly with the periodic records.[3]

FUNDAMENTAL ASSIGNMENT MATERIAL

☐ General Coverage

7–1. **DETAILED INCOME STATEMENT.** (Alternates are 7–4 and 7–5.) Following are accounts taken from the adjusted trial balance of the Gemello Building Supply Company, December 31, 19X5. The company uses the periodic inventory system. Prepare a detailed income statement for 19X5. All amounts are in thousands:

Sales salaries and		Freight in	$ 50
commissions	$160	Miscellaneous expenses	17
Inventory, December 31, 19X4	300	Sales	1,080
Allowance for bad debts	14	Bad debts expense	8
Rent expense, office space	10	Cash discounts on purchases	15
Gross purchases	500	Inventory, December 31, 19X5	325
Depreciation expense, office		Office salaries	60
equipment	2	Rent expense, selling space	90
Cash discounts on sales	10	Income tax expense	40
Advertising expense	40	Sales returns and allowances	50
Purchase returns and		Office supplies used	4
allowances	40	Depreciation expenses, trucks	
Delivery expense	20	and store fixtures	30

7–2. **COMPARISON OF INVENTORY METHODS.** (Alternates are 7–6 and 7–8.) The Eppler Co. is a wholesaler of hardware for commercial builders. The company uses a periodic inventory system. The data concerning Airvent Grill RD8 for the year 19X2 follow:

---

[3] For instance, in Exhibit 7–17, suppose the January 29 sale were 200 units instead of 150 units. A perpetual LIFO method would show:

	SOLD	BALANCE
Jan. 29	170 @ $6 = $1,020	170 @ $5 = $850
	30 @ $5 = 150	

Note that 30 units from the beginning inventory would be released as Cost of Goods Sold under perpetual LIFO, whereas periodic LIFO would wait until the end of the year and would assign no amounts from the beginning of the inventory to Cost of Goods Sold unless the physical inventory levels had declined *for the year as a whole*. In other words, interim declines in inventory wuld be ignored under the periodic LIFO approach.

	PURCHASES	SOLD	BALANCE
December 31, 19X1			110 @ $5 = $550
February 10, 19X2	80 @ $6 = $ 480		
April 14		60	
May 9	110 @ $7 = $ 770		
July 14		120	
October 21	100 @ $8 = $ 800		
November 12		80	
Total	290	$2,050	260
December 31, 19X2			140 @ ?

The sales during 19X2 were made at the following selling prices:

```
 60 @ $ 8 = $  480
120 @  10 =  1,200
 80 @  11 =    880
260          $2,560
```

Required:

1. Prepare a comparative statement of gross profit for the year ended December 31, 19X2, using FIFO, LIFO, and weighted-average inventory methods.
2. By how much would income taxes differ if Eppler used LIFO instead of FIFO for Airvent Grill RD8? Assume a 30% income tax rate.

For additional questions on these data, see Problems 7–3 and 7–48.

7–3. **EFFECTS OF LATE PURCHASES.** (Alternates are 7–7 and 7–9.) Refer to the preceding problem. Suppose 100 extra units had been acquired on December 30 for $8 each, a total of $800. How would net income and income taxes have been affected under FIFO? Under LIFO? Show a tabulated comparison.

☐ **Understanding Published Financial Reports**

7–4. **DETAILED INCOME STATEMENT.** (Alternates are 7–1 and 7–5.) The Ohio Mattress Co. makes Sealy mattresses. Its annual report had the following actual descriptions and data for the year ended November 30, 1987 (in thousands):

Net sales	$598,149
Cost of goods sold	381,013
Gross profit	217,136
Selling, general and administrative expenses	167,502
Operating profit	$ 49,634

Consider the following additional data, in thousands (inventories and allowances for doubtful accounts are actual; remaining data are assumed):

Inventory:		Allowances for doubtful accounts:	
November 30, 1987	$74,667	November 30, 1987	$ 3,834
November 30, 1986	34,411	November 30, 1986	871
Cash discounts on purchases	1,200	Advertising expense	6,000
Depreciation expense, office		Delivery expense	6,700
equipment	4,157	Cash discounts on sales	1,600
Bad debts expense	1,900	Inward transportation	2,590
Sales returns and allowances	3,200	Sales salaries and	
Miscellaneous general expenses	2,420	commissions	87,100
Purchase returns and allowances	2,800	Administrative salaries	45,425
Depreciation expense, trucks		Gross purchases	422,679
and selling space	13,800		

Required: l   Prepare a detailed multiple-step income statement that ends with operating profit.

7–5. DETAILED INCOME STATEMENT. (Alternates are 7–1 and 7–4.) Hartmarx Corporation is a clothing company with many retail outlets, including Country Miss and Kuppenheimer. The company's annual report contained the following actual data for the year ended November 30, 1987 (in thousands):

Net sales	$1,080,420
Cost of goods sold	634,433
Selling, administrative and occupancy expenses	373,942
Operating profit	72,045

The balance sheets included the following actual data (in thousands of dollars):

	NOVEMBER 30	
	1987	1986
Allowance for doubtful accounts	$ 8,463	$ 9,042
Inventories	325,356	298,117

Consider the following additional assumed data (in thousands of dollars):

Bad debts expense	$ 5,400	Freight in	$32,000
Gross purchases	657,672	Advertising expense	29,000
Cash discounts on sales	10,000	Sales returns and allowances	35,000
Sales salaries and compensation	180,000	Depreciation expense	26,000
Purchase returns and allowances	24,000	Cash discounts on purchases	4,000
Freight out	52,000	Rent expense	15,000
		Miscellaneous expenses	66,542

Required: | Prepare a detailed multiple-step income statement that ends with operating profit. You need not subclassify the selling, administrative, and occupancy expenses into three separate categories.

7–6. COMPARISON OF INVENTORY METHODS. (Alternates are 7–2 and 7–8.) Unisys Corporation is a producer of computer-based information systems. The following actual data and descriptions are from the company's fiscal 1987 annual report (in millions):

	DECEMBER 31	
	1987	1986
Inventories	$1,855.8	$1,951.9

A footnote states: "Inventories are valued at the lower of cost or market. Cost is determined principally on the first-in, first-out method."

The income statement for the fiscal year ended December 31, 1987, included (in millions):

Net revenue from sales, service, and rentals	$9,712.9
Cost of products sold, service, and rentals	5,639.1

Assume that Unisys used the periodic inventory system. Suppose a division of Unisys had the accompanying data regarding the use of its computer parts that it acquires and resells to customers for maintaining equipment (dollars are *not* in millions):

Data for Problem 7–6

	UNITS	TOTAL
Inventory (December 31, 1987)	100	$ 400
Purchase (February 20, 1988)	200	1,000
Sales, March 17 (at $9 per unit)	150	
Purchase (June 25, 1988)	140	840
Sales, November 7, 1988 (at $10 per unit)	160	

Required:

1. For these computer parts only, prepare a tabulation of the cost of goods sold section of the income statement for the year ended December 31, 1988. Support your computations. Round totals to the nearest dollar. Show your tabulation for four different inventory methods: (a) FIFO, (b) LIFO, (c) weighted-average, and (d) specific identification.

For requirement *d*, assume that the purchase of February 20 was identified with the sale of March 17. Also assume that the purchase of June 25 was identified with the sale of November 7; the additional units sold were identified with the beginning inventory.

2. By how much would income taxes differ if Unisys used (a) LIFO instead of FIFO for this inventory item? (b) LIFO instead of weighted-average? Assume a 40% tax rate.

7–7. **EFFECTS OF LATE PURCHASES.** (Alternates are 7–3 and 7–9.) Refer to the preceding problem. Suppose Unisys acquired 60 extra units @ $7 each on December 29, 1988, a total of $420. How would gross profit and income taxes be affected under FIFO? That is, compare FIFO results before and after the purchase of 60 extra units. Under LIFO? That is, compare LIFO results before and after the purchase of 60 extra units. Show computations and explain.

7–8. **COMPARISON OF INVENTORY METHODS.** (Alternates are 7–2 and 7–6.) Texas Instruments is a major producer of semiconductors and other electrical and electronic products. Semiconductors are especially vulnerable to price fluctuations. The following actual data and descriptions are from the company's annual report (in millions):

	DECEMBER 31	
	1987	1986
Inventories	$738.7	$609.5

Texas Instruments uses a variety of inventory methods, but for this problem assume that only FIFO is used.

Net sales for the fiscal year ended December 31, 1987, were $5,594.5 million. Cost of sales was $4,382.9 million.

Assume that Texas Instruments had the accompanying data regarding one of its semiconductors. Assume a periodic inventory system.

Data for Problem 7–8

	IN	OUT	BALANCE
December 31, 1986			80 @ $5 = 400
February 25, 1987	50 @ $6 = $ 300		
March 29		60* @ ?	
May 28	80 @ $7 = $ 560		
June 7		90* @ ?	
November 20	90 @ $8 = $ 720		
December 15		50* @ ?	
Total	220	$1,580	200
December 31, 1987		100 @ ?	

* Selling prices were $9, $11, and $13, respectively:

	60 @ $ 9 = $ 540
	90 @ 11 = 990
	50 @ 13 = 650
Total sales 200	$2,180

Summary of costs to account for:

Beginning inventory	$ 400
Purchases	1,580
Cost of goods available for sale	$1,980
Other expenses for this product	$ 500
Income tax rate, 40%	

Required:

1. Prepare a comparative income statement for the 1987 fiscal year for the product in question. Use the FIFO, LIFO, and weighted-average inventory methods.
2. By how much would income taxes have differed if Texas Instruments had used LIFO instead of FIFO for this product?
3. Suppose Texas Instruments had used the specific identification method. Compute the gross margin (or gross profit) if the ending inventory had consisted of (a) 90 units @ $8 and 10 units @ $7, and (b) 60 units @ $5 and 40 units @ $8.

7–9. EFFECTS OF LATE PURCHASES. (Alternates are 7–3 and 7–7.) Refer to the preceding problem. Suppose Texas Instruments had acquired 50 extra units @ $8 each on December 30, 1987, a total of $400. How would income before income taxes and income taxes have been affected under FIFO? That is, compare FIFO results before and after the purchase of 50 extra units. Under LIFO? That is, compare LIFO results before and after the purchase of 50 extra units. Show computations and explain.

ADDITIONAL ASSIGNMENT MATERIAL

☐ **General Coverage**

7–10. "There are two major steps in accounting for inventories." What are they?

7–11. Distinguish between *F.O.B. destination* and *F.O.B. shipping point*.

7–12. "Freight out should be classified as a direct offset to sales, not as an expense." Do you agree? Explain.

7–13. What are the two phases of a sales transaction?

7–14. Distinguish between the *perpetual* and *periodic* inventory systems.

7–15. "An advantage of the perpetual inventory system is that a physical count of inventory is unnecessary. The periodic method requires a physical count to compute cost of goods sold." Do you agree? Explain.

7–16. Name the four inventory methods that are generally accepted in the United States. Give a brief phrase describing each.

7–17. What is *consistency* and why is it an important accounting principle?

7–18. "An inventory profit is a fictitious profit." Do you agree? Explain.

7–19. LIFO produces absurd inventory valuations. Why?

7–20. "Purchases of inventory at the end of a fiscal period can have a direct effect on income under LIFO." Do you agree? Explain.

7–21. "There is a single dominant reason why more and more companies have adopted LIFO." What is the reason?

7–22. "Conservatism now is liberalism later." Do you agree? Explain.

7–23. "Conservatism always results in lower reported profits." Do you agree? Explain.

7–24. "Accountants have traditionally favored taking some losses but no gains before an asset is exchanged." What is this tradition or convention called?

7–25. What does *market* mean in inventory accounting?

7–26. "The lower-of-cost-or-market method is inherently inconsistent." Do you agree? Explain.

7–27. Express the gross profit section of the income statement as an equation.

7–28. Express the cost of goods sold section of the income statement as an equation.

7–29. "Gross profit percentages help the preparation of interim financial statements." Explain.

7–30. "Inventory errors are counterbalancing." Explain.

7–31. ENTRIES FOR PURCHASE TRANSACTIONS. The Zund Company is a Swiss wholesaler of small giftware. Its unit of currency is the Swiss franc (Sfr.). Zund uses a periodic inventory system. Prepare journal entries for the following summarized transactions (omit explanations):

> Aug. 2. Purchased merchandise, Sfr. 400,000, terms 2/10, n/45.
> Aug. 3. Paid cash for freight in, Sfr. 10,000.
> Aug. 7. Zund complained about some defects in the merchandise acquired on August 2. The supplier hand-delivered a credit memo granting an allowance of Sfr. 20,000.
> Aug. 11. Cash disbursement to settle purchase of August 2.

7–32. COST OF INVENTORY ACQUIRED. On July 5, Polanski Company purchased on account a shipment of sheet steel from Bethlehem Steel Co. The invoice price was $150,000, F.O.B. shipping point. Shipping cost from the steel mill to Polanski's plant was $12,000. When inspecting the shipment, the Polanski receiving clerk found several flaws in the steel. She informed Bethlehem's sales representative of the flaws, and after some negotiation, Bethlehem granted an allowance of $8,000.

To encourage prompt payment, Bethlehem grants a 2% cash discount to customers who pay their accounts within thirty days of billing. Polanski paid the proper amount on August 1.

Required:
1. Compute the total cost of the sheet steel acquired.
2. Prepare the journal entries for the transaction. Omit explanations.

7–33. ENTRIES FOR PERIODIC AND PERPETUAL SYSTEMS. Ronowski Co. has an inventory of $200,000, December 31, 19X1. Data for 19X2 follow:

Gross purchases	$900,000
Cost of goods sold	910,000
Inventory, December 31, 19X2	150,000
Purchase returns and allowances	40,000

Required: Using the data, prepare a comparative analysis of the entries for a perpetual and a periodic inventory system. Present your comparison as it affects the balance sheet equation. Also present comparative journal entries, including closing entries.

7–34. ENTRIES FOR PURCHASE TRANSACTIONS. Leuner Landscape Wholesalers uses a periodic inventory system. Prepare journal entries for the following summarized transactions for 19X2 (omit explanations). For simplicity, assume that the beginning and ending balances in accounts payable were zero.

1. Purchases (all using trade credit), $800,000.
2. Purchase returns and allowances, $60,000.
3. Freight in, $82,000 paid in cash.
4. Cash discounts on purchases, $10,000.

7–35. CLOSING ENTRIES, PERIODIC INVENTORY SYSTEM. Refer to the data in the preceding problem. Inventories were: December 31, 19X1, $81,000; December 31, 19X2, $110,000. Sales were $1,300,000. Prepare the closing journal entries, December 31, 19X2. Omit explanations.

7–36. CLOSING ENTRIES, PERIODIC INVENTORY SYSTEM. Consider the following data taken from the adjusted trial balance of the Howton Company, December 31, 19X3 (in millions):

Purchases	$100	Sales	$220
Sales returns and allowances	11	Purchase returns and	
Freight in	14	allowances	6
Cash discounts on purchases	1	Cash discounts on sales	8
Inventory (beginning of year)	20	Other expenses	80

Required: Prepare the closing journal entries. The ending inventory was $30 million. Show postings to T-accounts for Cost of Goods Sold, Income Summary, and Retained Income.

7–37. GROSS PROFIT SECTION. Given the following, prepare a detailed gross profit section for Goldstar Jewelry Wholesalers for the year ended December 31, 19X1 (in thousands):

Cash discounts on purchases	$ 7	Cash discounts on sales	$ 5
Sales returns and allowances	35	Purchase returns and	
Gross purchases	600	allowances	21
Merchandise inventory,		Merchandise inventory,	
December 31, 19X0	120	December 31, 19X1	152
Gross profit	360	Freight in	50

7–38. RECONSTRUCTION OF RECORDS. An earthquake caused heavy damage to the Fantasy Record Store on May 3, 19X1. All the merchandise was destroyed. Some accounting data are missing. In conjunction with an insurance investigation, you have been asked to estimate the cost of the inventory destroyed. The following data are available:

Cash discounts on purchases	$ 1,000	Inventory, December 31, 19X0	$17,000
Gross sales	112,000	Purchase returns and allowances	4,000
Sales returns and allowances	12,000	Inward transportation	2,000
Gross purchases	61,000	Gross profit percentage on net sales	45%

7–39. COST OF INVENTORY DESTROYED BY FIRE. L. Klein requires an estimate of the cost of merchandise lost by fire on March 9. Merchandise inventory on January 1 was $60,000. Purchases since January 1 were $190,000; freight in, $28,000; purchase returns and allowances, $10,000. Sales are made at a gross margin of 40% of *sales* and totaled $250,000 up to March 9. What was the cost of the merchandise destroyed?

7–40. INVENTORY SHORTAGE. An accounting clerk of the K. L. Company absconded with cash and a truck full of the entire electronic merchandise on May 14, 19X2. The following data have been compiled:

Beginning inventory, January 1	$ 60,000
Sales to May 14, 19X2	200,000
Average gross profit rate	35%
Purchases to May 14, 19X2	180,000

Required: | Compute the estimated cost of the missing merchandise.

7–41. FIRE LOSS. Country Day Gift Shop had a fire on March 24, 19X0. Its last physical inventory had been on January 31, 19X0, the close of its fiscal year. For the past three years, Country Day's gross profit percentage had been averaging 35%.

Purchases, February 1–March 24, 19X0	$ 80,000
Inventory, January 31, 19X0	65,000
Sales, February 1–March 24, 19X0	160,000

Required: | Estimate the cost of inventory, March 24, 19X0. Show your computations. The insurance company will use this estimate of historical cost as a basis for estimating the replacement cost (which is the usual basis for paying insurance claims).

7–42. DECISION ABOUT PRICING. Epstein Jewelers, Inc., a retail jewelry store, had gross profit of $440,000 on sales of $800,000 in 19X3. Average inventory was $360,000.

Required: | 1. Compute inventory turnover.
2. Epstein is considering whether to become a "discount" jeweler. For example, Epstein believes that a cut of 20% in average selling prices would have increased turnover to 1.5 times per year. Beginning and ending inventory would be unchanged. Suppose Epstein's beliefs are valid. Would the gross profit in 19X3 have improved? Show computations.

7–43. LIFO, FIFO, PURCHASE DECISIONS, AND EARNINGS PER SHARE. Suppose a company with one milion shares of common stock outstanding has had the following transactions during 19X1, its first year in business:

Sales:	1,000,000 units @ $5
Purchases:	800,000 units @ $2
	300,000 units @ $3

The current income tax rate is a flat 50%; the rate next year is expected to be 40%.

It is December 20, and as the president, you are trying to decide whether you should buy the 600,000 units you need for inventory now or early next year. The current price is $4 per unit. Prices on inventory are expected to remain stable; in any event, no decline in prices is anticipated.

You have not chosen an inventory method as yet, but you will pick either LIFO or FIFO.

Other expenses for the year will be $1.4 million.

Required:

1. Using LIFO, prepare a comparative income statement assuming the 600,000 units (a) are not purchased, (b) are purchased. The statement should end with reported earnings per share.
2. Repeat requirement 1, using FIFO.
3. Comment on the above results. Which method would you choose? Why? Be specific.
4. Suppose that in Year 2 the tax rate drops to 40%, prices remain stable, 1 million units are sold @ $5, enough units are purchased at $4 so that the ending inventory will be 700,000 units, and other expenses are reduced to $800,000:

   a. Prepare a comparative income statement for the second year showing the impact of each of the four alternatives on net income and earnings per share for the second year.
   b. Explain any differences in net income that you encounter among the four alternatives.
   c. Why is there a difference in ending inventory values under LIFO even though the same amount of physical inventory is in stock?
   d. What is the total cash outflow for income taxes for the two years together under the four alternatives?
   e. Would you change your answer in requirement 3 now that you have completed requirement 4? Why?

7–44. **GROSS PROFIT AND TURNOVER.** Retailers closely watch a number of financial ratios, including the gross profit (gross margin) percentage and inventory turnover. Suppose the results for furniture in a large department store in a given year were:

Sales	$2,000,000
Cost of goods sold	1,200,000
Gross profit	$ 800,000
Beginning inventory	$ 450,000
Ending inventory	350,000

Required:

1. Compute the gross profit percentage and the inventory turnover.
2. Suppose the retailer is able to reduce inventory to $300,000 throughout the succeeding year. What inventory turnover would have to be obtained to achieve the same total gross profit? Assume that the gross profit percentage is unchanged.
3. Suppose the retailer maintains inventory at the $300,000 level throughout the succeeding year. What gross profit percentage would have to be obtained to achieve the same total gross profit? Assume that the inventory turnover is unchanged.
4. Suppose the average inventory of $400,000 is maintained. Compute the total gross profit in the succeeding year if there is
   a. A 10% increase of the gross profit *percentage* (that is, 10% of the percentage, not an additional ten percentage points) and a 10% decrease of the inventory turnover;

or
b. A 10% decrease of the gross profit percentage and a 10% increase of the inventory turnover.
5. Why do retailers find the above types of ratios helpful?

7-45. LIFO AND FIFO. The inventory of the Snyder Gravel Company on June 30 shows 1,000 tons at $9 per ton. A physical inventory on July 31 shows a total of 1,200 tons on hand. Revenue from sales of gravel for July totals $44,000. The following purchases were made during July:

July 8	2,000 tons @ $10 per ton
July 13	500 tons @ $11 per ton
July 22	600 tons @ $12 per ton

Required:
1. Compute the inventory cost as of July 31, using (a) LIFO and (b) FIFO.
2. Compute the gross profit, using each method.

7-46. LOWER OF COST OR MARKET. (Alternate is 7-69.) Kriss Company uses the inventory method "cost or market, whichever is lower." There were no sales or purchases during the periods indicated, although selling prices generally fluctuated in the same directions as replacement costs. At what amount would you value merchandise on the dates listed below?

	INVOICE COST	REPLACEMENT COST
December 31, 19X1	$200,000	$170,000
April 30, 19X2	200,000	190,000
August 31, 19X2	200,000	220,000
December 31, 19X2	200,000	165,000

7-47. LIFO, FIFO, AND LOWER-OF-COST-OR-MARKET. Olivia Company began business on March 15, 19X0. The following are Olivia's purchases of inventory.

March 17	100 units @ $10	$1,000
April 19	50 units @ $12	600
May 14	70 units @ $13	910
Total		$2,510

On May 25, 100 units were sold, leaving inventory of 120 units. Olivia Company's accountant was preparing a balance sheet for June 1, at which time the replacement cost of the inventory was $12 per unit.

Required:
1. Suppose Olivia Company uses strict LIFO, without applying lower-of-cost-or-market. Compute the June 1 inventory amount.
2. Suppose Olivia Company uses lower-of-LIFO-cost-or-market. Compute the June 1 inventory amount.
3. Suppose Olivia Company uses strict FIFO, without applying lower-of-cost-or-market. Compute the June 1 inventory amount.
4. Suppose Olivia Company uses lower-of-FIFO-cost-or-market. Compute the June 1 inventory amount.

7–48. LOWER-OF-COST-OR-MARKET. Refer to Problem 7–2. Suppose the ending FIFO inventory is valued at $1,080 at FIFO cost and $560 at market (based on a sudden decline on December 31, 19X2, to $4 per unit, which leads to 140 units × $4 = $560). The lower market price is indicative of lower ultimate sales prices.

Suppose Eppler Co. goes out of business in 19X3. The 140 units are sold in January for $5 each.

Required:
1. Prepare a statement of gross profit for 19X2 and 19X3. Show the results under a strict FIFO cost method in the first two columns and under a lower-of-FIFO-cost-or-market method in the next two columns.
2. Suppose Eppler does not go out of business. Instead, replacement cost price rises in 19X3 to $9 per unit. Would this rise in price affect the inventory valuation of the 140 units? Explain.

7–49. LIFO, FIFO, CASH EFFECTS. In 19X2, Inverness Company had sales revenue of £360,000 for a line of woolen sweaters. The company uses a periodic inventory system. Pertinent data for 19X2 included:

Inventory, December 31, 19X1	14,000 units @ £6	£ 84,000
January purchases	20,000 units @ £7	140,000
July purchases	32,000 units @ £8	256,000
Sales for the year	30,000 units	

Required:
1. Prepare a statement of gross margin for 19X2. Use two columns, one assuming LIFO and one assuming FIFO.
2. Assume a 40% income tax rate. Suppose all transactions were for cash. Which inventory method would result in more cash for Inverness Company? By how much?

7–50. LIFO, FIFO, PRICES RISING AND FALLING. The Romero Company has a periodic inventory system. Inventory on December 31, 19X1, consisted of 10,000 units @ $10 = $100,000. Purchases during 19X2 were 13,000 units. Sales were 12,000 units for sales revenue of $20 per unit.

Required:
Prepare a four-column comparative statement of gross margin for 19X2:

1. Assume purchases were at $12 per unit. Assume FIFO and then LIFO.
2. Assume purchases were at $8 per unit. Assume FIFO and then LIFO.
3. Assume an income tax rate of 30%. Suppose all transactions were for cash. Which inventory method in requirement 1 would result in more cash for Romero Company? By how much?
4. Repeat requirement 3. Which inventory method in requirement 2 would result in more cash for Romero Company? By how much?

7–51. MULTIPLE CHOICE: COMPARISON OF INVENTORY METHODS. The Byron Corporation began business on January 1, 19X4. Information about its inventories under different valuation methods is shown below. Using this information, you are to choose the phrase that best answers each of the following questions. For each question, insert on an answer sheet *the letter that identifies the answer* you select.

			INVENTORY	
	LIFO Cost	FIFO Cost	Market	Lower of Specifically Identified Cost or Market
December 31, 19X4	$10,200	$10,000	$ 9,600	$ 8,900
December 31, 19X5	9,100	9,000	8,800	8,500
December 31, 19X6	10,300	11,000	12,000	10,900

1. The inventory basis that would show the *highest net income for 19X4* is (a) LIFO cost, (b) FIFO cost, (c) market, (d) lower-of-cost-or-market.
2. The inventory basis that would show the *highest net income for 19X5* is (a) LIFO cost, (b) FIFO cost, (c) market, (d) lower-of-cost-or-market.
3. The inventory basis that would show the *lowest net income for the three years combined* is (a) LIFO cost, (b) FIFO cost, (c) market, (d) lower-of-cost-or-market.
4. For the year 19X5, how much higher or lower would profits be on the *FIFO-cost basis* than on the *lower-of-cost-or-market basis*? (a) $400 higher, (b) $400 lower, (c) $600 higher, (d) $600 lower, (e) $1,000 higher, (f) $1,000 lower, (g) $1,400 higher, (h) $1,400 lower.
5. On the basis of the information given, it appears that *the movement of prices* for the items in the inventory was (a) up in 19X4 and down in 19X6, (b) up in both 19X4 and 19X6, (c) down in 19X4 and up in 19X6, (d) down in both 19X4 and 19X6.

7–52. **FIFO AND LIFO.** Two companies, the Lifo Company and the Fifo Company, are in the scrap metal warehousing business as arch competitors. They are about the same size and in 19X1 coincidentally encountered seemingly identical operating situations. Only their inventory accounting systems differed.

Their beginning inventory was 10,000 tons; it cost $50 per ton. During the year, each company purchased 50,000 tons at the following prices:

    ☐ 20,000 @ $70
    ☐ 30,000 @ $90

Each company sold 45,000 tons at average prices of $100 per ton. Other expenses in addition to cost of goods sold but excluding income taxes were $700,000. The income tax rate is 40%.

Required:
1. Compute net income for the year for both companies. Show your calculations.
2. As a manager, which method would you prefer? Why? Explain fully. Include your estimate of the overall effect of these events on the cash balances of each company, assuming that all transactions during 19X1 were direct receipts or disbursements of cash.

7–53. **EFFECTS OF LIFO AND FIFO.** (George H. Sorter, adapted.) The Cado Company is starting in business on December 31, 19X0. In each *half year*, from 19X1 through 19X4, it expects to purchase 1,000 units and sell 500 units for the amounts listed below. In 19X5, it expects to purchase no units and sell 4,000 units for the amount indicated in the following table:

	19X1	19X2	19X3	19X4	19X5
Purchases:					
First 6 months	$ 2,000	$ 4,000	$ 6,000	$ 6,000	0
Second 6 months	4,000	9,000	6,000	8,000	0
Total	$ 6,000	$13,000	$12,000	$14,000	0
Sales (at selling price)	$10,000	$10,000	$10,000	$10,000	$40,000

Assume that there are no costs or expenses other than those shown above. The tax rate is 40%, and taxes for each year are payable on December 31 of each year. Cado Company is trying to decide whether to use periodic FIFO or LIFO throughout the five-year period.

Required:
1. What was net income under FIFO for each of the five years? Under LIFO? Show calculations.
2. Explain briefly which method, LIFO or FIFO, seems more advantageous, and why.

7–54. **EFFECTS OF LIFO ON PURCHASE DECISIONS.** The Merlino Corporation is nearing the end of its first year in business. The following purchases of its single product have been made:

	UNITS	UNIT PRICE	TOTAL COST
January	1,000	$10	$10,000
March	1,000	10	10,000
May	1,000	11	11,000
July	1,000	13	13,000
September	1,000	14	14,000
November	1,000	15	15,000
	6,000		$73,000

Sales for the year will be 5,000 units for $120,000. Expenses other than cost of goods sold will be $20,000.

The president is undecided about whether to adopt FIFO or LIFO for income tax purposes. The company has ample storage space for up to 7,000 units of inventory. Inventory prices are expected to stay at $15 per unit for the next few months.

Required:

1. If the president decided to purchase 4,000 units @ $15 in December, what would be the net income before taxes, the income taxes, and the net income after taxes for the year under (a) FIFO and (b) LIFO? Income tax rates are 30% on the first $25,000 of net taxable income and 50% on the excess.
2. If the company sells its year-end inventory in Year 2 @ $24 per unit and goes out of business, what would be the net income before taxes, the income taxes, and the net income after taxes under (a) FIFO and (b) LIFO? Assume that other expenses in Year 2 are $20,000.
3. Repeat requirements 1 and 2, assuming that 4,000 units, @ $15, were not purchased until January of the second year. Generalize on the effect on net income of the timing of purchases under FIFO and LIFO.

7–55. **CHANGING QUANTITIES AND LIFO RESERVE.** Consider the following data for the year 19X2:

	UNITS	UNIT COST
Beginning inventory	2	*
Purchases:	3	24
	3	28
Ending inventory	2	†

* FIFO, $20; LIFO, $16.
† To be computed.

Required:

1. Prepare a comparative table computing the cost of goods sold, using columns for FIFO and LIFO. In a final column, show (a) the LIFO reserve at the beginning of the year and at the end of the year, and (b) how its *change* in amount explains the difference in cost of goods sold.
2. Repeat requirement 1 except assume that the ending inventory consisted of (a) 3 units, (b) 1 unit, (c) zero units.
3. In your own words, explain why, for a given year, the increase in the LIFO reserve measures the amount by which cost of goods sold is higher under LIFO than FIFO.

7–56. **STATEMENT OF GROSS PROFIT.** Junko's Lawn and Garden Supply began 19X1 with inventory of $180,000. Junko's 19X1 sales were $800,000, purchases of inventory totaled $640,000, and ending inventory was $220,000.

Required:

1. Prepare a statement of gross profit for 19X1.
2. What was Junko's inventory turnover?

7-57. Gross Margin Computations and Inventory Costs. On January 15, 19X4, R. Novikoff valued her inventory at cost, $18,000. Her statements are based on the calendar year, so you find it necessary to establish an inventory figure as of January 1, 19X4. You find that from January 2 to January 15, sales were $71,000; sales returns, $2,100; goods purchased and placed in stock, $54,000; goods removed from stock and returned to suppliers, $2,000; freight in, $500. Calculate the inventory cost as of January 1, assuming that goods are marked to sell at 30% above cost.

7-58. Inventory Errors. (Alternate is 7–59.) Study Appendix 7A. The following data are from the 19X1 income statement of the Snohomish Carpet Stores (in thousands):

Sales		$1,500
Deduct: Cost of goods sold:		
Beginning inventory	$ 420	
Purchases	690	
Cost of goods available for sale	$1,110	
Deduct: Ending inventory	370	
Cost of goods sold		740
Gross profit		$ 760
Other expenses		610
Income before income taxes		$ 150
Income tax expense at 40%		60
Net income		$ 90

The ending inventory was overstated by $40,000 because of errors in the physical count. The income tax rate was 40% in 19X1 and 19X2.

Required:

1. Which items in the income statement are incorrect? By how much? Use *O* for overstated, *U* for understated, and *N* for not affected. Complete the following tabulation:

	19X1	19X2
Beginning inventory	N	O $40
Ending inventory	?	?
Cost of goods sold	?	?
Gross margin	?	?
Income before income taxes	?	?
Income tax expense	?	?
Net income	?	?

2. What is the dollar effect of the inventory error on retained income at the end of 19X1? At the end of 19X2?

7-59. Inventory Errors, Three Years. (Alternate is 7–58.) Study Appendix 7A. The Rohm Company had the accompanying data for three successive years (in millions):

	19X3	19X2	19X1
Sales	$200	$160	$175
Deduct: Cost of goods sold:			
Beginning inventory	15	25	40
Purchases	135	100	90
Cost of goods available for sale	150	125	130
Ending inventory	30	15	25
Cost of goods sold	120	110	105
Gross profit	80	50	70
Other expenses	70	30	30
Income before income taxes	10	20	40
Income tax expense at 40%	4	8	16
Net income	$ 6	$ 12	$ 24

In early 19X4, a team of internal auditors discovered that the ending inventory for 19X1 had been overstated by $20 million. Furthermore, the ending inventory for 19X3 had been understated by $5 million. The ending inventory for December 31, 19X2, was correct.

Required:

1. Which items in the income statements are incorrect? By how much? Prepare a tabulation covering each of the three years.
2. Is the amount of retained income correct at the end of 19X1, 19X2, and 19X3? If it is erroneous, indicate the amount and whether it is overstated (*O*) or understated (*U*).

7–60. **WORK SHEETS FOR PERIODIC AND PERPETUAL INVENTORIES.** Study Appendix 7B. Adrian Company sells sporting goods. Exhibit 7–18 shows how the Adrian unadjusted trial balances would appear under two different inventory systems as of December 31, 19X2 (in thousands of dollars).

Required:

1. Prepare two work sheets, one for the perpetual inventory system and one for the periodic inventory system. Enter the pertinent unadjusted trial balance in the first set of columns for each work sheet. Enter the amounts in thousands of dollars.
2. The unadjusted trial balances given here are probably misnamed. A more descriptive title would be "partially adjusted" trial balances. Assume that all necessary adjustments (for example, depreciation) have already been entered except for (labeled *j, k,* and *l* for later reference):
   j. Bad debts expense should be recognized. Past experience indicates that a provision should be made of 2% of the year's credit sales of $1 million.
   k. The cost of the ending inventory was $500,000.
   l. Enter any necessary adjustments in the adjustment columns. Then complete the work sheet. To show the flexibility of the work sheet, omit the columns for the adjusted trial balance.
3. Prepare formal income statements in a format similar to that in Exhibit 7–3.
4. Prepare the adjusting journal entries, using the work sheets as a guide. Show adjacent sets of entries for the perpetual and periodic systems.
5. Prepare the closing journal entries, using the work sheets as a guide. Show adjacent sets of entries for the perpetual and periodic systems.

EXHIBIT 7–18

ADRIAN COMPANY
Unadjusted Trial Balance
December 31, 19X2
(in thousands of dollars)

	PERPETUAL INVENTORY		PERIODIC INVENTORY	
	Debit	Credit	Debit	Credit
Cash	200		200	
Accounts receivable	370		370	
Allowance for uncollectible accounts	·			
Merchandise inventory	500*		300†	
Equipment	400		400	
Accumulated depreciation, equipment		100		100
Accounts payable		400		400
Accrued income taxes payable				
Paid-in capital		100		100
Retained income		470		470
Sales		2,300		2,300
Sales returns and allowances	100		100	
Cost of goods sold	1,400			
Purchases			1,690	
Purchase returns and allowances				90
All other expenses (summarized here)	400		400	
Bad debts expense				
Income tax expenses				
	3,370	3,370	3,460	3,460

* Balance, December 31, 19X2.
† Balance, December 31, 19X1.

7–61. **RPETUAL INVENTORY RECORDS.** (Alternate is 7–70.) Study Appendix 7B. Empson Co. is a wholesaler of hardware for commercial builders. The company uses a perpetual inventory system and a FIFO cost-flow assumption. The data concerning Jansen Disposals for the year 19X2 follows:

	PURCHASED	SOLD	BALANCE
December 31, 19X1			110 @ $5 = $550
February 10, 19X2	80 @ $6 = $ 480		
April 14		60	
May 9	110 @ $7 = $ 770		
July 14		120	
October 21	100 @ $8 = $ 800		
November 12		90	
Total	290	$2,050	270

Required: I Prepare a perpetual inventory card. What is the ending balance in units and dollars?

7–62. **REVIEW OF CHAPTERS 1–7. ADJUSTING AND CORRECTING ENTRIES.** Examine the accompanying Unadjusted Trial Balance as of December 31, 19X2.

MANTLE CLOAK COMPANY
Unadjusted Trial Balance
December 31, 19X2

ACCOUNT
NUMBER

1. Cash	$ 5,000	
2. Note receivable	1,000	
3. Accounts receivable	10,300	
4. Allowance for bad debts		$ 300
5. Inventory balance, as of January 1, 19X2	20,000	
6. Unexpired insurance	600	
7. Office supplies on hand		
8. Unexpired rent		
9. Equipment	4,000	
10. Accumulated depreciation, equipment		500
11. Accounts payable		10,000
12. Long-term 5% mortgage payable		3,000
13. Accrued interest payable		
14. Accrued wages payable		
15. Mantle capital		18,500
16. Sales		120,000
17. Sales returns	1,000	
18. Cash discounts on sales	1,000	
19. Purchases	71,000	
20. Purchase returns		1,000
21. Wages	22,000	
22. Rent and heat	10,000	
23. Bad debts expense		
24. Other operating expenses	7,000	
25. Supplies expense	400	
26. Insurance expense		
27. Depreciation		
28. Interest expense		
	$153,300	$153,300

Required:

For each of the following items 1 through 12 prepare the necessary entries. Select only from the accounts listed in the Trial Balance. The same account may be used in several answers. Answer by using account *numbers* and indicating the dollar amounts of debits and credits. For example, item 1 would call for a debit to Cash (1) for $200, a debit to Equipment (9) for $300, and a credit to Mantle Capital (15) for $500. (*Note*: The accounts that carry no balances are listed in the table for your convenience in making adjustments. All accounts needed to answer the questions are included.)

1. On December 30, the owner invested $200 in cash plus equipment valued at $300. The bookkeeper has not recorded the transaction.
2. It is estimated that the Allowance for Bad Debts should be *increased* by an amount equal to 0.5% of 19X2 gross sales.
3. A correct entry was made, early in December, for $1,000 worth of goods sold to a customer on open account. The customer returned these goods on December 29. The bookkeeper has made no entry for the latter transaction, although a credit memo was issued, December 31.
4. Unexpired insurance was $450 on December 31, 19X2.
5. The interest on the mortgage is payable yearly on January 2. (Adjust for a *full year's* interest. Do not refine the arithmetic for one or two days' interest.)
6. There was a $1,000 payroll robbery on December 15. Wages had been debited for $1,000 and Cash credited for $1,000 for the original payroll. A substitute payroll

was made up on December 16, Wages again debited for $1,000, and Cash again credited for $1,000. However, the loss was covered by insurance. On December 20, the insurance company remitted $1,000, and the Mantle bookkeeper debited Cash and credited Sales.

7. The equipment cost is being allocated to operations on the basis of an estimated useful life of twenty years and no residual value.

8. Mantle withdrew $500 in cash on December 31. The bookkeeper has not recorded the transaction.

9. A $400 rental charge for January 19X3 was paid in cash to the DiMaggio Realty Company on December 31. The Mantle Company bookkeeper did not record the transaction.

10. Wages of salesclerks earned, but not paid, amount to $100.

11. A physical count of the office supplies revealed that there is a balance of $300 on hand as of December 31, 19X2.

12. On December 20, a customer paid the Mantle Company $980 for a $1,000 invoice, deducting a 2% discount. The bookkeeper made the appropriate entries. On December 30, Mr. Mantle discovered that the customer should have paid the full $1,000 because the discount period had expired on December 17. He sent the customer another invoice for the extra $20. The bookkeeper has not recorded the latter transaction.

□ **Understanding Published Financial Reports**

7–63. **Shipping Expenses and Discounts.** The 1987 income statement of Kimberly-Clark Corporation, maker of Kleenex, Huggies, and other products using absorbent fibers, shows the following gross profit (in millions):

Net sales	$4,884.7
Cost of products sold	3,065.9
Distribution expense	181.2
Gross profit	$1,637.6

Required:

1. Does the "Distribution expense" refer to freight in or freight out for Kimberly-Clark?
2. Suppose that on March 1, 1990. Kimberly-Clark bought $1 million of paper with terms 2/10, n/30, F.O.B. shipping point. Shipping costs were $42,000. The total amount due was paid on March 7. The paper was sold on credit for $1.3 million on March 25 with terms 2/20, n/30, F.O.B. destination. Shipping costs were $30,000, which was paid immediately. The customer paid on April 16. Prepare journal entries for these two transactions. Assume a perpetual inventory system.

7–64. **Reconstruction of Transactions.** Consider the following account balances of La-Z-Boy Chair Company, maker of the popular La-Z-Boy chairs and other furniture:

	APRIL 28	
	1988	1987
Inventories	$66,822	$45,475

Required:

The income statement for the fiscal year included the item "cost of sales" of $352,069,000. Compute the net cost of the acquisitions of inventory for the 1988 fiscal year.

7–65. RECONSTRUCTION OF TRANSACTIONS. Ralston Purina Company has many well-known products, including Purina Dog Chow, Ry-Krisp, and Jack in the Box restaurants. Consider the following account balances (in millions):

	SEPTEMBER 30	
	1988	1987
Inventories	$559.9	$577.6

Required:

The purchases of inventories during the 1988 fiscal year were $3,132.4 million. The income statement had an item "cost of products sold." Compute its amount.

7–66. CLASSIC SWITCH FROM LIFO TO FIFO. Effective January 1, 1970, Chrysler Corporation adopted the FIFO method for inventories previously valued by the LIFO method. The 1970 annual report stated: "This . . . makes the financial statements with respect to inventory valuation comparable with those of the other United States automobile manufacturers."

The *Wall Street Journal* reported:

☐ The change improved Chrysler's 1970 financial results several ways. Besides narrowing the 1970 loss by $20 million it improved Chrysler's working capital. The change also made the comparison with 1969 earnings look somewhat more favorable because, upon restatement, Chrysler's 1969 profit was raised only $10.2 million from the original figures.

☐ Finally, the change helped Chrysler's balance sheet by boosting inventories, and thus current assets, by $150 million at the end of 1970 over what they would have been under LIFO. As Chrysler's profit has collapsed over the last two years and its financial position tightened, auto analysts have eyed warily Chrysler's shrinking ratio of current assets to current liabilities.

☐ To get the improvements in its balance sheet and results, however, Chrysler paid a price. Roger Helder, vice president and comptroller, said Chrysler owed the government $53 million in tax savings it accumulated by using the LIFO method since it switched from FIFO in 1957. The major advantage of LIFO is that it holds down profit and thus tax liabilities. The other three major auto makers stayed on the FIFO method. Mr. Helder said Chrysler now has to pay back that $53 million to the government over 20 years, which will boost Chrysler's tax bills about $3 million a year.

Required:

Given the content of this text chapter, do you think the Chrysler decision to switch from LIFO to FIFO was beneficial to its stockholders? Explain, being as specific and using as many data as you can.

7–67. YEAR-END PURCHASES AND LIFO. A company engaged in the manufacture and sale of jewelry maintained an inventory of gold for use in its business. The company used LIFO for the gold content of its products.

On the final day of its fiscal year, the company bought 10,000 ounces of gold at $400 per ounce. Had the purchase not been made, the company would have penetrated its LIFO layers for 8,000 ounces of gold acquired at $260 per ounce.

The applicable income tax rate is 40%.

Required:

1. Compute the effect of the year-end purchase on the income taxes of the fiscal year.
2. On the second day of the next fiscal year, the company resold the 10,000 ounces of gold to its suppliers. What do you think the Internal Revenue Service should do if it discovers this resale? Explain.

7–68. ERODING THE LIFO BASE. Many companies on LIFO are occasionally faced with strikes or material shortages that necessitate a reduction in their normal inventory levels in order to satisfy current sales demands. A few years ago several large steel companies requested special legislative relief from the additional taxes that ensued from such events.

A news story stated:

☐ As steelworkers slowly streamed back to the mills this week, most steel companies began adding up the tremendous losses imposed by the longest strike in history. At a significant number of plants across the country, however, the worry wasn't losses but profits—"windfall" bookkeeping profits that for some companies may mean painful increases in corporate income taxes.

☐ These outfits have been caught in the backfire of a special mechanism for figuring up inventory costs on tax returns. It's known to accountants as LIFO, or last in, first out. Ironically, it's designed to slice the corporate tax bill in a time of rising prices.

☐ *Biggest Bite*—Most of the big steel companies—16 out of the top 20—as well as 40 percent of all steel warehousers, use LIFO accounting in figuring their taxes. But the tax squeeze from paper LIFO profits won't affect them all equally. It will put the biggest bite on warehousers that kept going during the strike—and as a result, the American Steel Warehouse Assn. may ask Congress for a special tax exemption on these paper profits. . . .

☐ Companies such as Ryerson and Castle have been caught because they have had to strip their shelves bare in order to satisfy customer demands during the strike. And they probably won't be able to rebuild their stocks by the time they close their books for tax purposes.

To see how this situation can happen, consider the following example. Suppose a company adopted LIFO in 1983. At December 31, 1988, its LIFO inventory consisted of three "layers":

From 1983:	100,000 units @ $1.00	$100,000
From 1985:	50,000 units @ 1.10	55,000
From 1987:	30,000 units @ 1.20	36,000
		$191,000

In 1989, prices rose enormously. Data follow:

Sales	500,0000 units @ $3.00 = $1,500,000
Purchases	340,000 units @ $2.00 = $ 680,000
Operating expenses	$ 500,000

A prolonged strike near the end of the year resulted in a severe depletion of the normal inventory stock of 180,000 units. The strike was settled on December 28, 1989. The company intended to replenish the inventory as soon as possible.

The applicable income tax rate is 60%.

Required:
1. Compute the income taxes for 1989.
2. Suppose the company had been able to meet the 500,000-unit demand out of current purchases. Compute the income taxes for 1989 under those circumstances.

7–69. **LOWER OF COST OR MARKET.** (Alternate is 7–46.) Polaroid Corporation's annual report stated: "Inventories are valued on a first-in, first-out basis at the lower of standard cost (which approximates actual cost) or market value." Assume that severe price competition in 1989 necessitated a write-down on December 31 for a class of camera inventories bearing a standard cost of $10 million. The appropriate valuation at market was deemed to be $7 million.

Suppose the product line had been terminated in early 1990 and the remaining inventory had been sold for $7 million.

Required:
1. Assume that sales of this line of camera for 1989 were $19 million and cost of goods sold was $15 million. Prepare a statement of gross margin for 1989 and 1990. Show the results under a strict FIFO cost method in the first two columns and under a lower-of-FIFO-cost-or-market method in the next two columns.
2. Assume that Polaroid did not discontinue the product line. Instead a new marketing campaign spurred market demand. Replacement cost of the cameras in the December 31 inventory was $9 million on January 31, 1990. What inventory valuation would be appropriate if the inventory of December 31, 1989, was still held on January 31, 1990?

7–70. PERPETUAL INVENTORY RECORDS. (Alternate is 7–61.) Study Appendix 7B. Control Data Corporation produces and sells computers, computer systems, and computer services. Its annual report showed inventories of $598.7 million on January 1, 1988. The company uses FIFO for much of its inventory.

Control Data uses a perpetual inventory system for many items, including parts sold in conjunction with servicing. Assume that the data concerning Part 431 for 1988 were:

	PURCHASED	SOLD	BALANCE
January 1, 1988			100 @ $4 = $400
March 4, 1988	90 @ $5 = $ 450		
May 19		60	
July 22	100 @ $6 = $ 600		
September 9		120	
October 15	80 @ $8 = $ 640		
December 5		40	
	270	$1,690	220

Required: Prepare a perpetual inventory card. What is the ending balance in units and dollars?

7–71. FIFO VERSUS LIFO NET INCOME. Maytag Corporation reported 1987 pretax income of $261,703,000. Footnotes to Maytag's financial statements read: "Inventories are stated at the lower of cost (last-in, first-out method) or market . . . If the first-in, first-out (FIFO) method of inventory accounting had been used, inventory would have been $65,000,000 and $60,800,000 higher than reported at December 31, 1987 and 1986, respectively."

Required:
1. Calculate the pretax income that Maytag would have reported if the FIFO inventory method had been used.
2. Suppose Maytag's income tax rate is 34%. What were Maytag's income taxes using LIFO? What would they have been if Maytag had used FIFO?

7–72. LIFO LIQUIDATION. Campbell Soup Company included the following footnote in its 1988 annual report:

☐ Liquidation of LIFO inventory quantities increased net earnings $1.7 million in 1988, $2.8 million in 1987, and $1.4 million in 1986. Inventories for which the LIFO method of determining cost is used represent approximately 68% of inventories in 1988 and 72% in 1987.

Required: 1. Suppose the income tax rate was 40% in each of the three years. What was the effect of the LIFO liquidations on the (before tax) operating income in each year? What was the effect on taxes?

2. How could Campbell Soup have avoided the extra taxes?

7-73. **EFFECT OF LIFO.** Georgia-Pacific, one of the world's largest forest products companies, reported 1988 operating income of $778 million. Part of Footnote 1 to the financial statements stated:

☐ The last-in, first-out (LIFO) method of inventory valuation is utilized for the majority of inventories at manufacturing facilities and the Corporation's manufactured inventories located at its building products distribution centers. The average cost method is used for all other inventories.

Inventories are valued at the lower of cost or market as follows (in millions):

	DECEMBER 31	
	1988	1987
Inventories	892	837

If LIFO inventories were valued at the lower of average cost or market, the inventories would have been $119 million and $112 million higher than those reported at December 31, 1988 and 1987, respectively.

Required: Suppose the weighted-average method had always been used for all inventories. Calculate Georgia-Pacific's operating income for 1988. By how much would the cumulative operating income for all years through 1988 differ from that reported? Would it be more or less than that reported?

7-74. **LIFO RESERVE.** Brunswick Corporation reported inventories of $383.8 million on its 1987 balance sheet. A footnote to the financial statements indicated that if "the FIFO method of inventory accounting had been used by the Company for inventories valued at LIFO, inventories would have been $63.7 million higher than reported."

Required: 1. Has the cost of Brunswick's inventory generally been increasing or decreasing? Explain.

2. Suppose Brunswick sold its entire inventory for $500 million in 1988 and did not replace it. Compute the gross profit from the sale of this inventory (a) as Brunswick would report it using LIFO and (b) as it would have been reported if Brunswick had always used FIFO instead of LIFO. Which inventory method creates higher 1988 gross profit? Explain.

7-75. **INVENTORY ERRORS.** (Alternate is 7-76.) Study Appendix 7A. Claire's Stores, Inc., operates over 560 specialty retail stores selling inexpensively priced fashion accessories. The accompanying actual data are from the company's annual report for the 1988 fiscal year:

Net sales	$103,404,000
Cost of sales, occupancy, and buying expenses	49,815,000
Gross profit	$53,589,000
Other expenses (detailed)	44,231,000
Income before income taxes	$ 9,358,000
Income taxes	3,658,000
Net income	$ 5,700,000

The inventories were $10,707,000 at the end of fiscal 1988 and $10,892,000 a year earlier. The applicable tax rate is 34% for both fiscal years, 1987 and 1988.

Required: **1.** Suppose the beginning inventory for fiscal 1988 had been overstated by $50,000 because of errors in physical counts. Which items in the financial statement would be incorrect? By how much? Use *O* for overstated, *U* for understated, and *N* for not affected.

	EFFECT ON FISCAL YEAR	
	1988	1987
Beginning inventory	O by $50,000	N
Ending inventory	?	?
Cost of sales	?	?
Gross profit	?	?
Income before taxes on income	?	?
Taxes on income	?	?
Net income	?	?

Required: **2.** What is the dollar effect of the inventory error on retained earnings at the end of fiscal 1987? 1988?

7–76. INVENTORY ERRORS. (Alternate is 7–75.) Study Appendix 7A. American Greetings is a large producer of greetings cards. The accompanying actual data are from the company's fiscal 1988 annual report (in thousands):

Net sales	$1,174,817
Cost of sales	533,590
Gross profit	$ 641,227

The applicable income tax rate was 41%. Balance sheet items included (in thousands):

	FEBRUARY 28	
	1988	1987
Inventories	$316,354	$282,515

Required: **1.** Suppose the inventory on February 28, 1987, had been understated by $2 million because of errors in physical counts. Which items in the financial statements would be incorrect? By how much? Use *O* for overstated, *U* for understated, and *N* for not affected.

	EFFECT ON YEAR	
	1988	1987
Beginning inventory	U by $2 million	N
Ending inventory	?	?
Cost of sales	?	?
Gross margin	?	?
Income taxes	?	?
Net income	?	?

Required: **2.** What is the dollar effect of the inventory error on retained earnings on February 28, 1987, and February 28, 1988?

7–77. **House of Fabrics Annual Report.** Refer to the financial statements of House of Fabrics, pages 752–759. Focus on the cost of sales and gross profit on the income statement, merchandise inventories on the balance sheet, and the "inventories" section of Note 1.

Required: **1.** Assume that House of Fabrics uses a periodic inventory system. Compute the amount of merchandise inventory purchased during fiscal 1989. (*Hint:* Use the inventory T-account.)

2. Suppose House of Fabrics had always used LIFO instead of FIFO and had LIFO reserves of $18 million and $16 million at January 31, 1989 and 1988, respectively. Compute (a) LIFO merchandise inventory at January 31, 1989 and 1988, respectively, and (b) fiscal 1989 gross profit under LIFO.

3. Compute the fiscal 1989 inventory turnover for House of Fabrics.

Long-Lived Assets and Depreciation

LEARNING OBJECTIVES After studying this chapter, you should be able to

1. Define and explain depreciation and show how it relates to income measurement, income taxes, and cash balances
2. Define, compute, and compare some typical depreciation methods
3. Contrast the accounting for repairs, maintenance, and improvements
4. Demonstrate how gains and losses on sales of fixed assets are computed and presented in financial statements
5. Define and explain depletion and amortization
6. Define *intangible assets* and explain how to account for them for both shareholder purposes and income tax purposes

Cost of goods sold and depreciation expense are the two most widely encountered and debated items on an income statement. Chapter 7 emphasized FIFO, LIFO, and other ways of computing cost of goods sold. This chapter emphasizes various ways of computing depreciation as well as similar items like depletion and amortization.

This chapter considers some major assets, such as land, buildings, equipment, natural resources, and patents. These resources are often described as **long-lived assets** because they are held for an extended time. A distinguishing feature of these assets is their underlying purpose: to facilitate the production and sale of goods or services to customers. That is, these assets by themselves are not available for sale in the ordinary course of business. Thus a delivery truck is a long-lived asset for nearly all companies; of course, a truck dealer would regard trucks as merchandise inventory.

GENERAL PERSPECTIVE

With the exception of land, the acquisition costs of all long-lived assets are typically charged to expense over a period of years in some systematic way. As Exhibit 8–1 shows, such expenses are called depreciation, depletion, or amortization, depending on the asset in question.

The word **amortization** is probably the most general in the sense that it means the systematic reduction of a lump-sum amount. Therefore there is nothing inherently wrong with using a single word such as *amortization* to describe the application of the *same fundamental idea* to various types of long-lived assets. However, it is customary to use three words, as shown in Exhibit 8–1.

How do you compute the acquisition cost of long-lived assets? How do you account for useful lives? Residual values? Gains or losses on disposition? Intervening changes in original estimates? This chapter explores these fundamental questions.

EXHIBIT 8–1

Summary of Accounting for Long-Lived Assets

	BALANCE SHEET	INCOME STATEMENT
Land		—
Buildings and equipment	——————→	Depreciation
Natural resources	——————→	Depletion
Intangible assets (for example, franchises or patents)	————→	Amortization

The major long-lived assets are often divided into tangible and intangible categories. **Examples** of tangible assets are land, natural resources, buildings, and equipment. **Tangible assets** are physical items that can be seen and touched. In contrast, **intangible assets** are rights or economic benefits that are not physical in nature. Examples are franchises, patents, trademarks, copyrights, and goodwill.

Tangible assets are often called **fixed assets** for brevity, but **plant assets** is more descriptive. Corporate annual reports generally use the following nomenclature, which is taken from the annual report of the American Telephone and Telegraph Company (AT&T):

AT&T COMPANY
Property, Plant, and Equipment:

	AT JANUARY 1,	
(in millions)	1988	1987
Land and improvements	$ 512	$ 499
Buildings and improvements	6,502	6,199
Machinery, electronic and other equipment	32,532	33,190
Total property, plant, and equipment	39,546	39,888
Less: Accumulated depreciation	18,685	18,810
Property, plant, and equipment—net	$20,861	$21,078

Shareholders' reports often contain summarized data, as shown by AT&T. However, in the accounting records, accumulated depreciation and amortization are kept in great detail for various categories of plant and equipment.

LAND

The acquisition cost of all long-lived assets is their cash-equivalent purchase price, including incidental costs.

The cost of land includes charges to the purchaser for the cost of land surveys, legal fees, title fees, realtors' commissions, transfer taxes, and even the demolition costs of old structures that might be torn down to get the land ready for its intended use.

Land such as plant sites or building sites is ordinarily accounted for as a separate item. Under historical-cost accounting, land is carried indefinitely at its original cost. As a result, if land is held for many years of persistent inflation, its carrying amount is likely to be far below its current realizable value.

Should land acquired and held since 1932 be placed on a 1990 balance sheet at cost expressed in 1932 dollars? Accountants do exactly that. For example, Weyerhaeuser lists 5.9 million acres of land at $125 million (only $21 per acre). Many critics of accounting point to such extreme examples as illustrations of why the basic historical-cost framework of accounting deserves drastic overhauling. They claim that some type of accounting for inflation should be mandatory. This worrisome problem of inflation is discussed in Chapter 16.

BUILDINGS AND EQUIPMENT

☐ Acquisition Cost

The cost of buildings, plant, and equipment should include all costs of acquisition and preparation for use. Consider the following example for some used packaging equipment:

Invoice price, gross	$100,000
Deduct 2% cash discount for payment within 30 days	2,000
Invoice price, net	$ 98,000
State sales tax at 8% of $98,000	7,840
Transportation costs	3,000
Installation costs	8,000
Repair costs prior to use	7,000
Total acquisition cost	$123,840

The $123,840 would be the total *capitalized cost* added to the Equipment account. A cost is described as being **capitalized** when it is added to an asset account, as distinguished from being "expensed" immediately. Note that ordinary repair costs are expensed if incurred *after* the equipment is placed in use.

Generally accepted accounting principles usually regard interest cost as an expense. However, FASB *Statement No. 34* specifies that interest on expenditures during an extended construction period should be added to the acquisition cost of the fixed asset under construction. Suppose a $2 million plant was constructed over two years. If no construction payments were made before the plant was completed, no interest would be capitalized. However, suppose $1 million was paid at the end of the first year, and $1 million at completion. Assume the interest rate on recent borrowing was 12%. Interest of $1,000,000 × .12 = $120,000 would be part of the capitalized cost of the plant.

☐ Basket Purchases

Frequently, more than one type of long-lived asset is acquired for a single overall outlay. For instance, suppose land and a building were acquired for $1 million. The acquisition of two or more types of assets for a lump-sum cost is sometimes called a **basket purchase.** How much of the $1 million should be allocated to each? Invariably, the cost is allocated in proportion to some estimate of their relative sales values as separate items. For example, an appraiser or a tax assessor might indicate that the market value of the land is $480,000 and of the building is $720,000. The cost would be allocated as follows:

	(1) MARKET VALUE	(2) WEIGHTING	(3) TOTAL COST TO ALLOCATE	(2) × (3) ALLOCATED COSTS
Land	$ 480,000	480/1,200 (or 40%)	$1,000,000	$ 400,000
Building	720,000	720/1,200 (or 60%)	$1,000,000	600,000
Total	$1,200,000			$1,000,000

This problem of allocating a basket purchase cost to the individual assets is often extremely important.[1] Why? Because the useful lives of various assets differ. Consequently, the reported income might be affected considerably. The higher the cost allocated to land, the lower the cost of the depreciable assets, the lower the depreciation expense, and the higher the subsequent reported income. In our example, suppose the building bore an $800,000 cost instead of the $600,000 cost above. Then straight-line depreciation based on a twenty-year useful life and zero residual value could be $800,000 ÷ 20, or $40,000, instead of $600,000 ÷ 20, or $30,000.

However, if managers want to reduce their income tax outflows in earlier years, they would tend to take advantage of any doubts (within the bounds of the law) about relative market values by loading as much cost as possible on depreciable assets rather than on land.

☐ Depreciation in General

Equipment and similar long-lived assets are initially recorded at *cost*. The major difficulties of measurement center on the choice of a pattern of depreciation—that is, the allocation of the original cost to the particular periods that benefit from the use of the assets.

In particular, note that accountants regard depreciation as a process of *allocating the acquisition cost* to the particular periods or products that are related to the use of the assets. Depreciation is frequently misunderstood. It is *not* a process of *valuation*. In everyday use, we might say that an auto depreciates in value, meaning a decrease in its current market value. But to an accountant, depreciation is *not* a technique for approximating current values such as replacement costs or resale values. It is simply *cost allocation*.

The amount of the acquisition cost to be allocated over the total useful life of the asset as depreciation is the **depreciable value**. It is the difference between the total acquisition cost and the predicted residual value. The **residual value** is the amount received from disposal of a long-lived asset at the end of its useful life. Synonyms for residual value are **terminal value, disposal value, salvage value,** and **scrap value.**

---

[1] The allocation of a lump-sum cost of a sports team, which includes player contracts, has been the subject of litigation between taxpayers and the Internal Revenue Service. Buyers want to allocate as much of the cost to player contracts as possible. Such contracts may be depreciated (amortized) for income tax purposes, but the sports franchise itself may not. (See problem 8–66 for an example.)

The depreciation allocation to each year may be made on the basis of either time or service. The prediction of useful life, which is a crucial factor in determining the yearly amount of depreciation, is influenced by predictions of physical wear and tear. However, the useful lives are almost always more heavily affected by economic and technological factors than by when equipment may physically wear out.

The following symbols and amounts will be used to compare various depreciation patterns:

	AMOUNTS FOR ILLUSTRATION
Let	
C = total acquisition cost on December 31, 19X7	$41,000
R = residual value	1,000
n = estimated useful life	4 years
D = amount of depreciation (or amortization) per unit of n	

Straight-Line Depreciation

Straight-line depreciation spreads the depreciable value evenly over the useful life of an asset. It is by far the most popular method for corporate reporting to shareholders. It is used by almost 95% of major companies for at least part of their fixed assets, and over 66% use it exclusively.

Exhibit 8–2 shows how the asset would be displayed in the balance sheet if a straight-line method of depreciation were used. The annual depreciation expense that would appear on the income statement would be:

$$D = \frac{\text{Acquisition cost} - \text{Residual value}}{\text{Years of useful life}}$$

$$= \frac{C - R}{n}$$

$$= \frac{\$41,000 - \$1,000}{4} = \$10,000 \text{ per year}$$

EXHIBIT 8–2

Straight-Line Depreciation Schedule*

	BALANCES AT END OF YEAR			
	1	2	3	4
Plant and equipment (at original acquisition cost)	41,000	$41,000	$41,000	$41,000
Less: Accumulated depreciation (the portion of original cost that has already been charged to operations as expense)	10,000	20,000	30,000	40,000
Net book value (the portion of original cost that will be charged to future operations as expense)	$31,000	$21,000	$11,000	$ 1,000

* Other patterns of depreciation are discussed later in this chapter.

The listing of depreciation amounts for each year of an asset's useful life is called a **depreciation schedule.**

☐ Depreciation Based on Units

When physical wear and tear is the dominating influence on the useful life of the asset, depreciation may be based on *units of service* or *units of production* rather than on the units of time (years) so commonly used. Depreciation based on units of service is called **unit depreciation.** Suppose the asset in our example were a large truck that would be kept for a useful life of two hundred thousand miles. Depreciation would then be computed on a mileage basis:

$$D = \frac{C - R}{n}$$
$$= \frac{\$41,000 - \$1,000}{200,000 \text{ miles}}$$
$$= \$.20 \text{ per mile}$$

For some assets, such as transportation equipment, this depreciation pattern may have more logical appeal than the straight-line method. However, the unit depreciation method is not widely used, probably for two major reasons:

1. Straight-line depreciation frequently produces approximately the same yearly depreciation amounts.
2. Straight-line depreciation entails less data-collection costs. The entire depreciation schedule can be set at the time of acquisition, and detailed records of units of service are not necessary.

The most commonly encountered example of unit depreciation relates to the use of mining equipment. Instead of writing such costs off on a time basis, the equipment costs are depreciated at a rate per ton of minerals extracted.

☐ Double-Declining-Balance Depreciation

Any pattern of depreciation that writes off depreciable costs more quickly than the ordinary straight-line method based on expected useful life is called **accelerated depreciation.**[2] The most popular form of accelerated depreciation is the **double-declining-balance (DDB)** method. DDB is computed as follows:

1. Compute a rate *(ignoring the residual value)* by dividing 100% by the years of useful life. This is the straight-line rate. Then double the rate.[3] In our example, the straight-line rate is 100% ÷ 4 years = 25%. The DDB rate would be 2 × 25%, or 50%.
2. To compute the depreciation for any year, multiply the beginning book value for the year by the DDB rate.

---

[2] Between 20% and 25% of major U.S. companies use accelerated depreciation for part of their fixed assets in reporting to shareholders.

[3] *Double*-declining-balance requires doubling the rate. Other declining-balance methods use other multiples. For instance, 150% declining-balance requires the straight-line rate to be multiplied by 1.5.

The DDB method can be illustrated as follows:

$$\text{DDB rate} = 2(100\% \div n)$$
$$\text{DDB rate, 4-year life} = 2(100\% \div 4) = 50\%$$
$$\text{DDB depreciation} = \text{DDB rate} \times \text{Beginning book value}$$

For year 1: $D = .50\ (\$41,000) = \$20,500$

For year 2: $D = .50\ (\$41,000 - \$20,500)$
$= .50\ (\$20,500) = \$10,250$

For year 3: $D = .50\ [\$41,000 - (\$20,500 + \$10,250)]$
$= .50\ (\$10,250) = \$5,125$

For year 4: $D = .50\ [\$41,000 - (\$20,500 + \$10,250 + \$5,125)]$
$= .50\ (\$5,125) = \$2,563$

Cumulative total = \$35,875

In this example, by coincidence the depreciation amount for each year happens to be half the preceding year's depreciation. However, this is a special case; it happens only with a four-year life. As the equations show, the basic approach is to apply the depreciation rate to the beginning book value.

☐ Sum-of-the-Years'-Digits Depreciation

Another method of accelerated depreciation is the **sum-of-the-years'-digits (SYD) method**. DuPont and Holly Sugar are among the few companies currently using SYD for reporting to stockholders. Sum of the digits is the total of the numbers representing the years of life; for example, assuming a four-year life, $1 + 2 + 3 + 4 = 10$. This sum becomes the denominator[4] in a key fraction as follows:

$$\text{SYD depreciation} = \text{Fraction} \times \text{Depreciable amount}$$

$$= \frac{\text{Number of remaining years of life}}{\text{Sum of digits}}(C - R)$$

For year 1: $D = \dfrac{4}{1 + 2 + 3 + 4}(\$41,000 - \$1,000)$
$D = 4/10\ (\$40,000) = \$16,000$

For year 2: $D = 3/10\ (\$40,000) = \$12,000$

For year 3: $D = 2/10\ (\$40,000) = \$\ 8,000$

For year 4: $D = 1/10\ (\$40,000) = \$\ 4,000$

SYD became popular mainly because of its use in tax reporting. Until 1954, U.S. companies used straight-line depreciation for their reports to shareholders and to the Internal Revenue Service (IRS). In 1954, the IRS began to allow accelerated depreciation, either SYD or DDB, for tax reporting. Even though companies were permitted to use different depreciation methods for reporting to shareholders and to income tax authorities, some companies used the same depreciation methods for reporting to all interested parties. Since 1980, when tax laws changed and SYD was no longer permitted for tax purposes, its use for reporting to shareholders has gradually declined.

---

[4] A general formula for the denominator is $S = \dfrac{n(n + 1)}{2}$ where S = sum of the digits and

n = useful life: $S = \dfrac{4(4 + 1)}{2} = 10$

☐ Comparing Depreciation Methods

Exhibit 8–3 compares the results of these three popular depreciation methods. Note that the DDB method will not write off the full depreciable cost of $40,000. When DDB is used for tax reporting, American income tax regulations permit the taxpayer to change to the straight-line method part way through the asset's depreciable life. Straight-line depreciation over the remaining useful life is applied to the remaining depreciable value, thereby fully writing off the depreciable value. The change comes when the next year's straight-line depreciation first exceeds the amount in the original DDB schedule.

Consider the DDB section of Exhibit 8–3, for example. The taxpayer could switch to the straight-line method at the beginning of the fourth year. The total accumulated depreciation for the first three years is $35,875. Because the maximum depreciation allowed for this asset over its four-year life is $40,000, the taxpayer would deduct $40,000 − $35,875, or $4,125, in the fourth year (rather than the $2,563 shown in Exhibit 8–3). In this way, the taxpayer obtains the complete depreciation deduction allowable.

Because different depreciation methods can be used for tax and shareholder reporting, it is important to recognize which reporting is at issue. The following table gives a summary:

WHEN ASSETS ACQUIRED	REPORTS TO SHAREHOLDERS	REPORTS TO INTERNAL REVENUE SERVICE
Before 1954	Straight-line	Straight-line
1954 to date:		
Most companies	Straight-line	Accelerated
Some companies (such as Dupont and Motorola)	Accelerated	Accelerated

Even for shareholder reporting alone, companies do not necessarily use the same depreciation policies for all types of depreciable assets. For example, consider the 1988 annual report of Kobe Steel, Ltd., a major Japanese company: "Buildings and structures in all locations and machinery and equipment located in Kakogawa Works, Kobe Works, Takasago Works, Mooka Plant and Chofu Plant are depreciated on the straight-line method and all other machinery and equipment are depreciated on the declining balance method over estimated useful lives."

☐ Modified Accelerated Cost Recovery System (MACRS)

Tax laws have greatly influenced depreciation methods. The tax laws pertaining to depreciation changed twice during the 1980s. For most fixed assets placed in service after December 31, 1980, and before December 31, 1986, the tax regulations require use of the Accelerated Cost Recovery System (ACRS). Assets acquired after December 31, 1986, use the Modified Accelerated Cost Recovery System

EXHIBIT 8–3

Depreciation: Three Popular Methods
(Assume equipment costs $41,000, four-year life, predicted residual value of $1,000)

	Straight-Line*		Sum-of-Years'-Digits (SYD)†		Declining Balance at Twice the Straight-Line Rate (DDB)‡	
	Annual Depreciation	Book Value	Annual Depreciation	Book Value	Annual Depreciation	Book Value
At acquisition		$41,000		$41,000		$41,000
Year						
1	$10,000	31,000	$16,000	25,000	$20,500	20,500
2	10,000	21,000	12,000	13,000	10,250	10,250
3	10,000	11,000	8,000	5,000	5,125	5,125
4	10,000	1,000	4,000	1,000	2,563	2,562
Total	$40,000		$40,000		$38,438	

Above the SYD and DDB columns: ACCELERATED DEPRECIATION

* Depreciation is the same each year, 25% of ($41,000 − $1,000).

† Sum of digits is $1 + 2 + 3 + 4 = 10$. Then $4/10 \times \$40,000$; $3/10 \times \$40,000$; etc.

‡ $100\% \div 4 = 25\%$. The double rate is 50%. Then 50% of $41,000; 50% of ($41,000 − $20,500); 50% of [$41,000 − ($20,500 + $10,250)]; etc. Unmodified, this method will never fully depreciate the existing book value. Therefore, in the later years of an asset's life, companies typically switch to a straight-line method. See the text for a fuller explanation.

(MACRS). Both ACRS and MACRS have assigned shorter useful lives to the assets than previously. In essence, for most assets MACRS approximates (*a*) *double-declining-balance* depreciation[5] (*b*) applied *over shorter lives*. In combination, *a* and *b* provide greater acceleration of depreciation than was allowed before 1981. (Taxpayers have the option of using straight-line depreciation.) For the most part, these shorter lives are not used for reporting to shareholders. See Chapter 13 for a fuller explanation.

The key word in depreciation schedules that differ from straight-line based on expected useful service life is *accelerated*. For example, whether declining-balance depreciation is 200%, 175%, or 150% of the straight-line rate, in the early years of an asset's service life there will be higher depreciation than with the straight-line method. Moreover, the use of a shorter useful life is also a form of accelerated depreciation. Carried to its extreme, an accelerated depreciation method would call for immediate total write-off in the year of acquisition.

INCOME TAX REPORTING AND SHAREHOLDER REPORTING

☐ Purposes and Income Taxes

Throughout this discussion of long-lived assets, please distinguish between reporting to stockholders and reporting to the income tax authorities. Reports to

---

[5] Some categories of assets use a 150% declining-balance method, and residential rental property and nonresidential real estate are depreciated using the straight-line method.

stockholders must abide by "generally accepted accounting principles (GAAP)." In contrast, reports to income tax authorities must abide by the income tax rules and regulations. These rules comply with GAAP in many respects, but they frequently diverge. Therefore there is nothing immoral or unethical about "keeping two sets of records." In fact, it is necessary.

Keep in mind that the income tax laws are patchworks that are often designed to give taxpayers special incentives for making investments. For example, tax authorities in some countries have permitted taxpayers to write off the full cost of new equipment as expense in the year acquired. Although such a total write-off may be permitted for income tax purposes, it is not permitted for shareholder-reporting purposes.

Major differences between GAAP and the U.S. tax laws are found in accounting for amortization and depreciation. For example, consider how the accounting for perpetual franchises, trademarks, and goodwill differs. Their acquisition costs must be amortized for shareholder reporting. However, the Internal Revenue Service will not allow amortization because such assets are deemed to have indefinite useful lives. Tax reporting and shareholder reporting are *required* to differ.

☐ Straight-Line or Accelerated Depreciation

The vast bulk of companies use straight-line depreciation for reporting to shareholders. Practical reasons for adopting straight-line depreciation are simplicity, convenience, and the reporting of higher earnings in early years than would be reported under accelerated depreciation. Managers tend not to choose accounting methods that hurt reported earnings in the early years of long-lived assets.

An additional reason given in support of straight-line depreciation is the assumption that depreciation is a function of time rather than of use. Therefore the "service potential" of the asset is assumed to decline by an equal amount each period; the total cost of the services consumed in any period is the same regardless of actual use. Further, suppose the benefit from using an asset is the same each period. The matching principle would require that the cost be spread equally to all periods.

For income-tax-reporting purposes, most corporations use *accelerated depreciation*. Why? To postpone payments of income taxes. Most of the same companies simultaneously use straight-line depreciation for shareholder reporting. Chapter 13 discusses the accounting problems that arise from such simultaneous reporting.

A few companies also use some form of accelerated depreciation for reporting to shareholders. For example, Texas Instruments Corporation states that "substantially all depreciation is computed by either the declining balance method . . . or the sum-of-the-years'-digits method." Among the reasons for using accelerated depreciation is conservatism. A more persuasive reason is that fixed assets are bundles of services or economic benefits that are used at a faster rate in early years. For example, suppose repair and maintenance expenses increase as an asset ages. If the service obtained is the same each year, the total cost should not increase across time. In essence, the asset is more responsible for the services in early years, and repairs and maintenance are relatively more responsible in later years. Hence depreciation expense should be higher in earlier years and lower in later years.

For simplicity, unless stated otherwise, throughout this chapter we assume that the company uses the same accounting for both income tax reporting and shareholder reporting.

DEPRECIATION AND GENERATION OF CASH

☐ Misunderstood Relationships

Depreciation is widely misunderstood. Depreciation is simply an allocation of the original cost of an asset to the periods in which the asset is used, nothing more and nothing less. Accumulated depreciation is a summation of the amounts of the original cost already written off to expense in prior periods. Thus accumulated depreciation is not a pile of cash waiting to be used to replace the assets.

For example, suppose a $40,000 machine is acquired early in 19X1 and is expected to be used through the end of 19X5, at which time the residual value will be zero. Each year, some of the services of the machine are used; depreciation expense recognizes this use. By the end of 19X5, the accumulated depreciation will be $40,000 because the entire original cost will have been charged as depreciation expense. Charging depreciation does nothing to set aside cash for replacement of the machine; it simply measures the consumption of some of the services of an asset. Accumulated depreciation shows the total amount consumed.

A major objective of this chapter is to pinpoint the relationships between depreciation expense, income tax expense, cash, and accumulated depreciation. Too often, these relationships are confused. For example, the business press frequently contains misleading quotations such as ". . . we're looking for financing $3.75 billion. Of that, about 60% will be recovered in depreciation and amortization." As another example, consider a *Business Week* news report concerning an airline company: "And with a hefty boost from depreciation and the sale of $6 million worth of property, its cash balance rose by $10 million in the year's first quarter." Also consider *Forbes*: "Now, by dragging out their depreciation schedules, firms may run the risk of repeating the errors of the automobile and steel industries, which found themselves hard pressed to replace assets because of years of underdepreciation."

☐ Depreciation Is Not Cash

Suppose Acme Service Company began business with cash and common stock equity of $100,000. On the same day, equipment was acquired for $40,000 cash. The equipment had an expected four-year life and zero predicted residual value. The first year's operations generated cash sales of $103,000 and cash operating expenses of $53,000. These relationships are depicted in Exhibit 8–4, using straight-line depreciation in Panel I and accelerated depreciation in Panel II. The

EXHIBIT 8–4

ACME SERVICE COMPANY
Analysis of Transactions
(in thousands of dollars)

	A			=	=	L	+	Paid-in Capital +	SE Retained Income
	Cash	+ Equipment	− Accumulated Depreciation			Liabilities	+		
Panel I. STRAIGHT-LINE DEPRECIATION									
Initial investment	+100			=				+100	
Acquisition	− 40	+40		=					
Cash sales	+103			=					+103 Sales
Cash operating expenses	− 53			=					− 53 Expense
Depreciation, year 1			−10	=					− 10 Expense
Bal. Dec. 31 before taxes	+110	+40	−10	=				+100	+ 40
Income taxes (40% of 40)	− 16			=					− 16 Expense
Bal. Dec. 31 after taxes	+ 94	+40	−10	=				+100	+ 24
Panel II. ACCELERATED DEPRECIATION									
Initial investment	+100			=				+100	
Acquisition	− 40	+40		=					
Cash sales	+103			=					+103 Sales
Cash operating expenses	− 53			=					− 53 Expense
Depreciation, year 1			−20	=					− 20 Expense
Bal. Dec. 31 before taxes	+110	+40	−20	=				+100	+ 30
Income taxes (40% of 30)	− 12			=					− 12 Expense
Bal. Dec. 31 after taxes	+ 98	+40	−20	=				+100	+ 18

form of accelerated depreciation assumed here is double-declining-balance. DDB depreciation for the first year is $2 \times 25\% \times \$40,000 = \$20,000$, compared with straight-line depreciation of $\frac{1}{4} \times \$40,000 = \$10,000$.

Focus first on the December 31 balances before taxes in Exhibit 8–4. A comparison of the before-tax amounts stresses the role of depreciation expense most vividly. At the end of the year, the cash balance before taxes is $110,000, regardless of the depreciation method used. Changes in the depreciation method affect only the accumulated depreciation and retained earnings accounts. The before-tax ending cash balances are completely unaffected. The same conclusions can be drawn from the before-tax balance sheet shown in the top half of Exhibit 8–5.

Consider next the effect of depreciation on the before-tax income statement. The relevant amounts are in the last column of Exhibit 8–4, but the first two columns of Exhibit 8–6 present the same numbers in a more useful format. The cash provided by operations before income taxes is $50,000, regardless of the depreciation method used. Pretax income under straight-line differs from that under accelerated depreciation only because of differences in the noncash depreciation expense. Examine the diagram in Exhibit 8–7. Only sales and cash operating expenses affect cash. Each extra dollar of depreciation reduces pretax income by a dollar but leaves the increase in cash unaffected.

Suppose depreciation were $40,000. Before reading on, compute the pretax income and increase in cash. You should have obtained pretax income of only $10,000. However, the increase in cash remains at $50,000, the sum of the pretax income and the depreciation expense.

EXHIBIT 8–5

ACME SERVICE COMPANY
Balance Sheet
December 31, 19X1
(in thousands)

ASSETS	STRAIGHT-LINE DEPRECIATION		ACCEL-ERATED DEPRECIATION		STOCK-HOLDERS' EQUITY	STRAIGHT-LINE DEPRECIATION	ACCEL-ERATED DEPRECIATION
BEFORE TAXES							
Cash		$110		$110			
Equipment	$40		$40		Paid-in		
Deduct:					capital	$100	$100
Accumulated					Retained		
depreciation	10	30	20	20	income	40	30
Total		$140		$130	Total	$140	$130
AFTER TAXES							
Cash		$ 94		$ 98			
Equipment	$40		$40		Paid-in		
Deduct:					capital	$100	$100
Accumulated					Retained		
depreciation	10	30	20	20	income	24	18
Total		$124		$118	Total	$124	$118

EXHIBIT 8–6

ACME SERVICE COMPANY
Income Statement
For the Year Ended December 31, 19X1
(in thousands)

	Before Taxes		After Taxes	
	STRAIGHT-LINE DEPRECIATION	ACCELERATED DEPRECIATION	STRAIGHT-LINE DEPRECIATION	ACCELERATED DEPRECIATION
Sales	$103	$103	$103	$103
Cash operating expenses	53	53	53	53
Cash provided by operations before income tax	50	50	50	50
Depreciation expense	10	20	10	20
Pretax income	40	30	40	30
Income tax expense (40%)	—	—	16	12
Net income	$ 40	$ 30	$ 24	$ 18
Supplementary analysis:				
Cash provided by operations before income tax	$ 50	$ 50	$ 50	$ 50
Income tax expense	—	—	16	12
Cash provided by operations*	$ 50	$ 50	$ 34	$ 38

* Sometimes called cash flow from operations or just cash flow. But it is usually simply called cash provided by operations, which is typically defined as cash collected on sales (a) less all operating expenses requiring cash and (b) less income taxes.

☐ Effects on Income Taxes

Now consider the after-tax portions of Exhibits 8–4, 8–5, and 8–6. Depreciation is a deductible noncash expense for income tax purposes. Hence the higher the depreciation allowed to be deducted in any given year, the lower the taxable income, and therefore the lower the cash disbursement for income taxes. In short, if depreciation expense is higher, more cash is conserved and kept for use in the business. From the first column of Exhibit 8–4 or the last two columns of Exhibit 8–6, you can see that Acme would pay $16,000 of income taxes using straight-line depreciation but only $12,000 using accelerated depreciation. Therefore, compared with the straight-line method, the accelerated method results in a higher cash balance *after* income tax ($98,000 instead of $94,000). At a 40% income tax rate, a $10,000 higher depreciation expense postpones $4,000 of income taxes.

Some strange results occur here. The reported net income is *lower* under accelerated than under straight-line depreciation, but the cash balance is *higher*. Thus, suppose managers were forced to choose one depreciation method for all purposes. Managers who are concerned about reported net income to shareholders may prefer straight-line to accelerated depreciation. This dilemma is not faced by managers in the United States, where straight-line depreciation is often used for shareholder purposes while accelerated depreciation is used for income

EXHIBIT 8–7

Depreciation, Pretax Income, and Cash

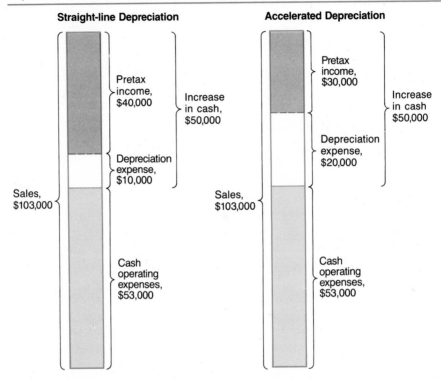

Each extra dollar of depreciation reduces pretax income by a dollar but leaves the increase in cash unchanged. If depreciation were $40,000, pretax income would be only $10,000, but the increase in cash would remain at $50,000.

tax purposes. You may recall from Chapter 7 that companies using the LIFO inventory method for tax purposes are also required to use LIFO for reporting to shareholders. Such is NOT the case with depreciation, where methods for tax and shareholder reporting are allowed to differ. See Chapter 13 for additional explanation.

Governments throughout the world have increasingly tolerated a wide variety of depreciation methods "to provide more cash for industrial expansion." The business press and financial analysts' reports are peppered with such phrasing as "cash provided by depreciation" or "funds generated by depreciation." Accountants quarrel with such phrasing because depreciation by itself is *not* a source of cash.

There is only one source of cash from operations: the cash provided through *sales to customers*. As our example shows, the effect of more depreciation on cash is *indirect*; it reduces income taxes by 40% of the extra depreciation of $10,000, or $4,000. Therefore accelerated depreciation keeps more cash in the business for a longer span of time because of the postponement of cash disbursements for income taxes.

Examine the account for accumulated depreciation. *No cash is there.* It is a deduction from an asset, regardless of whether income tax rates are zero, 20%, or 90%.

CHANGES IN DEPRECIATION ESTIMATES

Predictions of useful lives and residual values are invariably not accurate. If the inaccuracies are material, how should the affected accounts be adjusted? Consider the example of the $41,000 asset with a $1,000 residual value. Use the straight-line method. Suppose it is the beginning of Year 3. The firm's economists and engineers have altered their expectations; the asset's new expected useful life is five instead of four years. Moreover, the new expected residual value is $3,000 instead of $1,000:

	EXPECTATIONS.	
	Original	Revised
Cost	$41,000	$41,000
Useful life	4 years	5 years
Residual value	$ 1,000	$ 3,000
Straight-line depreciation per year:		
Old, $40,000 ÷ 4	$10,000	
New, as computed below		$ 6,000

These modifications to predictions are "changes in accounting estimates." They must be accounted for "prospectively" rather than "retroactively" in the sense that the records through Year 2 would not be adjusted. Instead the *remaining* depreciable amount would be written off over the new *remaining* useful life:

New book value at end of Year 2: $41,000 − 2 ($10,000) =	$21,000
Revised residual value	3,000
Revised depreciable amount	$18,000
Divide by remaining useful life in years, ÷3	
New straight-line depreciation per year	= $ 6,000

Critics of the foregoing "prospective" method assert that it misstates the yearly depreciation throughout the entire life of the asset. That is, depreciation in early years is overstated and in later years is understated. This can be illustrated by comparing the prospective method in our example with the retroactive method (which uses perfect hindsight):

YEAR	PROSPECTIVE METHOD	RETROACTIVE METHOD
1	$10,000	$ 7,600*
2	10,000	7,600
3	6,000	7,600
4	6,000	7,600
5	6,000	7,600
	$38,000	$38,000

* ($41,000 − $3,000) ÷ 5 = $7,600.

Applying the retroactive method would entail restating the accounts of prior periods, a procedure that many accountants oppose mainly on the grounds that the past accounting was as accurate as possible given the knowledge then existing. Although the retroactive way of adjusting the accounts has much logical appeal, Accounting Principles Board *Opinion No. 20* stated: "A change in estimate should not be accounted for by restating amounts reported in financial statements of prior periods."

DEPRECIATION FOR PARTS OF A YEAR

Assets are rarely acquired exactly at the start of a year or a month. To economize on recordkeeping, various simplifying assumptions are made about depreciation within the year. Each assumption must be reasonable and be consistently applied.[6]

For interim reporting, yearly depreciation is usually spread uniformly *within* a given fiscal year (an equal amount for each month), regardless of whether straight-line or accelerated depreciation is used to compute the total amount for the year. Moreover, depreciation for an asset acquired during a month is usually provided for the full month or not at all (depending on specific accounting policies, which vary among companies). For instance, suppose our $41,000 asset had been acquired on October 14, 19X1, and SYD depreciation was used. As Exhibit 8–3 (page 326) shows, the depreciation for Year 1 would be $16,000 and for Year 2 would be $12,000.

Assume that the company's fiscal year and calendar year are the same and that depreciation is to be included for the full month of October. The depreciation schedule could appear as follows (in thousands of dollars):

---

[6] For example, one of two methods might be used to determine when certain specified assets are placed in service:

1. *Half-year convention.* Treat all assets placed in service during the year as if they had been placed in service at the year's midpoint.
2. *Modified half-year convention.* Treat each asset placed in service during the first half of a tax year as if it had been placed in service on the first day of that tax year. Treat each asset placed in service during the last half of the tax year as if it had been placed in service on the first day of the *following* tax year.

ASSET YEAR	DEPRECIATION FOR 12-MONTH PERIODS	ALLOCATION TO EACH CALENDAR YEAR				
		19X1	19X2	19X3	19X4	19X5
1	4/10(40) = 16	4*	12†			
2	3/10(40) = 12		3*	9†		
3	2/10(40) = 8			2*	6†	
4	1/10(40) = 4				1*	3†
10	40	4	15	11	7	3

* 3/12 of column 2 (for example, 19X1: 16 ÷ 12 months = $1.33⅓ per month; 3 months, $1.33⅓ × 3 = $4).

† 9/12 of column 2 (for example, 19X2: 16 ÷ 12 months = $1.33⅓ per month; 9 months, $1.33⅓ × 9 = $12).

The monthly statements in October, November, and December, 19X1, would each have depreciation expense of $4,000 ÷ 3 = $1,333. In turn, the monthly statements of 19X2 would each have depreciation expense of $15,000 ÷ 12 = $1,250.

EXPENSES VERSUS EXPENDITURES

☐ Types of Expenditures

This section explores the accounting for expenditures. **Expenditures** are defined by accountants as the purchases of goods or services, whether for cash or credit. **Capital expenditures** are those expected to benefit more than the current accounting year. **Revenue expenditures** are those deemed to have a useful life no longer than the current accounting year. Capital expenditures generally add new fixed assets or increase the capacity, efficiency, useful life, or economy of operation of an existing fixed asset.

The terminology here is a good example of entrenched usage that does not provide particularly accurate descriptions of the classification intended. For example, a capital expenditure might better be called an *asset* expenditure. Similarly, a revenue expenditure might better be called an *expense* expenditure.

Every expenditure eventually becomes an expense. Revenue expenditures are matched with current revenues and therefore become expenses in the current period. Capital expenditures benefit *future* revenues. They are charged as expenses over future periods.

Sometimes the distinction between capital and revenue expenditures is subjective. Auditors from both the public accounting firms and the income tax authorities regularly investigate whether a given outlay is a capital expenditure or a revenue expenditure. That is, is a particular outlay for the engine repair or part properly classified as an asset or an expense? The public accountant (who tends to prefer conservatism) is usually on the alert for any tendencies to understate current expenses through the unjustified charging of a repair to an asset account. In contrast, the income tax auditor is looking for the unjustified charging to an expense account (which provides an immediate income tax deduction).

Wherever doubt exists, there is a general tendency in practice to charge an expense rather than an asset account for repairs, parts, and similar items. First, many of these outlays are minor, so the cost-benefit test of recordkeeping (the concept of materiality) justifies such action. For instance, many companies have a policy of charging to expense all outlays that are less than a specified minimum such as $100, $500, or $1,000. Second, there is the temptation of an immediate deduction for income tax purposes (if, indeed, the deductions are allowable as reasonable expenses).

☐ Repairs and Maintenance

Repairs and maintenance costs are necessary if a fixed asset is to continue in a specified operating condition. The costs of repairs and maintenance are usually compiled in the same account and are labeled as revenue expenditures because they are regarded as expenses of the current period.

Repairs are sometimes distinguished from *maintenance* as follows. *Repairs* include the occasional costs of restoring a fixed asset to its ordinary operating condition after breakdowns, accidents, or damage. *Maintenance* includes the routine recurring costs of oiling, polishing, painting, and adjusting.

Obviously, distinctions between repairs and maintenance are sometimes hard to draw. For example, is an engine tuneup a repair expense or a maintenance expense? Nobody loses much sleep over such matters, so one account typically contains both repairs and maintenance.

☐ Capital Improvements

An **improvement** (sometimes called a **betterment** or a **capital improvement**) is a capital expenditure that is intended to add to the future benefits from an existing fixed asset. How? By decreasing its operating cost, increasing its rate of output, or prolonging its useful life. An improvement differs from repairs and maintenance because the latter help ensure a specified level of benefits but do not enlarge the expected future benefits.

Examples of capital improvements or betterments include the rehabilitation of an apartment house that will allow increased rents and the rebuilding of a packaging machine that increases its speed or extends its useful life.

In Exhibit 8–2 (page 322), suppose that at the start of Year 3 a major overhaul costing $7,000 occurred. If this is judged to extend the useful life from four to five years, the required accounting would be:

1. Increase the book value of the asset (now $41,000 − $20,000 = $21,000) by $7,000. This is usually done by adding the $7,000 to Equipment.[7]

---

[7] A few accountants prefer to debit Accumulated Depreciation instead of Equipment. The theory is that a portion of past depreciation is being "reversed" or "made good" by the improvement or betterment. In any event, the effect of the improvement is to increase the net book value of the equipment and increase subsequent depreciation in identical amounts, regardless of whether the debit is made to Equipment or to Accumulated Depreciation. The major justification for debiting Accumulated Depreciation is that old machine parts have been replaced, but their original cost cannot be isolated.

2. Assume straight-line depreciation. Revise the depreciation schedule so that the new unexpired cost is spread over the remaining three years, as follows:

	ORIGINAL DEPRECIATION SCHEDULE		REVISED DEPRECIATION SCHEDULE	
	Year	Amount	Year	Amount
	1	$10,000	1	$10,000
	2	10,000	2	10,000
	3	10,000	3	9,000*
	4	10,000	4	9,000
			5	9,000
Accumulated depreciation		$40,000†		$47,000†

* New depreciable amount is ($41,000 − $20,000 + $7,000) − $1,000 residual value = $27,000. New depreciation expense is $27,000 divided by remaining useful life of 3 years, or $9,000 per year.

† Recapitulation:

	NET BOOK VALUE	
	Original	Revised
Original outlay	$41,000	$41,000
Major overhaul	—	7,000
Total	$41,000	$48,000
Accumulated depreciation	40,000	47,000
Residual value	$ 1,000	$ 1,000

GAINS AND LOSSES ON SALES OF FIXED ASSETS

Gains or losses on the disposal of property, plant, and equipment are inevitable. They are usually measured in a cash sale by the difference between the cash received and the net book value (net carrying amount) of the asset given up.[8]

☐ Income Statement Presentation

Gain on Sale of Equipment is usually shown as a separate item on an income statement as a part of "other income" or some similar category.

In single-step income statements, the gain is shown at the top along with other revenue items. For example:

---

[8] When an old asset is traded for a similar new asset, the new asset is valued at its cash-equivalent value for purposes of computing gain or loss. For example, consider the trade-in of a five-year-old truck for a new truck. The cash-equivalent value of the old truck is the difference between the cash cost of the new truck without the trade-in and the cash paid with the trade-in. The trading of assets can become complex. It is explained in advanced accounting texts. Also see Accounting Principles Board *Opinion No. 29*, "Accounting for Nonmonetary Transactions."

Revenue:
Sales of products	$xxx
Interest income (or interest revenue)	x
Other income: Gain on sale of equipment	x
Total sales and other income	$xxx

When a multiple-step income statement is used, the gain (or loss) is usually excluded from the computation of major profit categories such as gross profit or operating profit. Therefore the gain or loss appears in some type of "other income" or nonoperating income section in the lower part of the income statement.

In most instances, gains or losses on disposition of plant assets are not significant, so they are buried as a part of "other income" and are not separately identified. For example, W. R. Grace & Co. includes an item on its income statement immediately after sales labeled "Dividends, interest, and other income." American Telephone and Telegraph (AT&T) shows "Other income, net (Note D)" on a separate line after operating income in a recent annual report. Note D lists Gains (loss) on sale of fixed assets, $9.0 million, out of a total of $251.8 million of net other income.

☐ **Recording Gains and Losses**

Suppose the equipment in Exhibit 8–2 (p. 322) were sold at the end of Year 2 for $27,000. The sale would have the following effects:

	A		= L +	SE

+27,000 − 41,000 + 20,000 = +6,000

[Increase Cash] [Decrease Equipment] [Decrease Accumulated Depreciation] [Increase Gain on Sale of Equipment]

Note that the disposal of the equipment requires the removal of its carrying amount or book value, which appears in *two* accounts, not one. Therefore *both* the Accumulated Depreciation account and the Equipment account are affected when dispositions occur.

If the selling price were $17,000 rather than $27,000:

+17,000 − 41,000 + 20,000 = −4,000

[Increase Cash] [Decrease Equipment] [Decrease Accumulated Depreciation] [Increase Loss on Sale of Equipment]

EXHIBIT 8–8

Journal and Ledger Entries
Gain or Loss on Sale of Equipment
(in thousands of dollars)

Sale at $27,000:

				Cash		Equipment		Gain on Sale of Equipment	
Cash	27			27			41		6
Accumulated depreciation	20								
Equipment		41				Accumulated Depreciation, Equipment			
Gain on sale of equipment		6				20			

Sale at $17,000:

				Cash		Equipment		Loss on Sale of Equipment	
Cash	17			17			41	4	
Accumulated depreciation	20								
Loss on sale of equipment	4					Accumulated Depreciation, Equipment			
Equipment		41				20			

The T-account presentations and journal entries are in Exhibit 8–8. Note especially that the disposal of the equipment necessitates the removal of the original cost of the equipment *and* the accompanying accumulated depreciation. Of course, the net effect is to decrease the carrying amount of the equipment by $21,000.

AMORTIZATION OF LEASEHOLDS AND LEASEHOLD IMPROVEMENTS

Leaseholds and *leasehold improvements* are frequently classified with plant assets. A **leasehold** is the right to use a fixed asset (such as a building or some portion thereof) for a specified period of time beyond one year. A **leasehold improvement** incurred by a lessee (tenant) can take various forms. Examples are the installation of new fixtures, panels, walls, and air-conditioning equipment that are not permitted to be removed from the premises when a lease expires.

The costs of leases and leasehold improvements are written off in the same way as depreciation. However, the straight-line method is used almost exclusively, probably because accelerated methods have not been permitted for income tax purposes. Furthermore, these systematic write-offs are often described as amortization rather than as depreciation.

Sometimes the useful life of a *leasehold improvement* is expected to exceed the life of the lease. In such cases, amortization must be based on the shorter time span, the life of the lease. For more on leases, see Chapter 9, page 411.

DEPLETION

Natural resources such as minerals, oil, and timber are sometimes called *wasting assets*. **Depletion** is the gradual exhaustion of the original amounts of the resources acquired. Depletion differs from depreciation because the former focuses narrowly on a physical phenomenon and the latter focuses more broadly on any cause of the reduction of the economic value of a fixed asset, including physical wear and tear plus obsolescence.

The costs of natural resources are usually classified as fixed assets. However, the investment in natural resources can be likened to a lump-sum acquisition of massive quantities of inventories under the ground (iron ore) or over the ground (timber). Depletion expense is the measure of that portion of this "long-term inventory" that is used up in a particular period. For example, a coal mine may cost $20 million and originally contain an estimated one million tons. The depletion rate would be $20 per ton. If 100,000 tons were mined during the first year, the depletion would be 100,000 × $20, or $2 million for that year; if 150,000 tons were mined the second year, depletion would be 150,000 × $20, or $3 million; and so forth.

As the above example shows, depletion is measured on a units-of-production basis. The annual depletion may be accounted for as a direct reduction of the mining asset, or it may be accumulated in a separate account similar to accumulated depreciation.

Another example is timber. Boise Cascade Corporation, a large producer of forest products, describes its approach to depletion as follows:

☐ Timber and timberlands are shown at cost, less the cost of company timber harvested. Cost of company timber harvested and amortization of logging roads are determined on the basis of timber removals at rates based on the estimated volume of recoverable timber and are credited to the respective asset accounts.

The "cost of company timber harvested" is Boise Cascade's synonym for "depletion" of timber.

AMORTIZATION OF VARIOUS INTANGIBLE ASSETS

Intangible assets are a class of long-lived assets that are not physical in nature. They are rights to expected benefits deriving from their acquisition and continued possession. Examples of intangible assets are *patents, copyrights, franchises,* and *goodwill.*

Intangible assets are accounted for like plant and equipment. That is, the acquisition costs are capitalized as assets and are then amortized over estimated useful lives. Because of obsolescence, the *economic lives* of intangible assets tend to be shorter than their *legal lives.*

Patents are grants by the federal government to an inventor, bestowing (in the United States) the exclusive right for 17 years to produce and sell the invention. Suppose a company acquires such a patent from the inventor for $170,000. Suppose further that because of fast-changing technology, the *economic life* (the expected useful life) of the patent is only five years. The amortization would be $170,000 ÷ 5 = $34,000 per year, rather than $170,000 ÷ 17 = $10,000 per year.

The write-offs of intangible assets are usually made via direct reductions of the accounts in question. Thus accounts such as Accumulated Amortization of Patents are rarely found. Furthermore, the residual values of intangible assets are nearly always zero.

Copyrights are exclusive rights to reproduce and sell a book, musical composition, film, and similar items. These rights are issued (in the United States) by the federal government and provide protection to a company for 75 years. The original costs of obtaining copyrights from the government are nominal, but a company may pay a large sum to purchase an existing asset from the owner. For example, a publisher of paperback books will pay the author of a popular novel in excess of a million dollars for his or her copyright. The economic lives of such assets are usually no longer than two or three years, so amortization occurs accordingly.

Trademarks are distinctive identifications of a manufactured product or of a service taking the form of a name, a sign, a slogan, or an emblem. An example is an emblem for Coca-Cola. Trademarks, trade names, trade brands, secret formulas, and similar items are property rights with economic lives depending on their length of use. For stockholder-reporting purposes, their costs are amortized over their useful lives, but no longer than 40 years.

Franchises and **licenses** are privileges granted by a government, manufacturer, or distributor to sell a product or service in accordance with specified conditions. An example is the franchise of a baseball team or the franchise of a local owner of a Holiday Inn. The lengths of the franchises vary from one year to perpetuity. Again, the acquisition costs of franchises and licenses are amortized over their economic lives rather than their legal lives.

Goodwill, which is discussed in more detail in Chapter 11, is defined as the excess of the cost of an acquired company over the sum of the fair market values of its identifiable individual assets less the liabilities. For example, General Motors acquired Hughes Aircraft for $5 billion but could assign only $1 billion to various identifiable assets such as receivables, plant, and patents less liabilities assumed by GM; the remainder, $4 billion, is goodwill. Identifiable intangible assets, such as franchises and patents, may be acquired singly, but goodwill cannot be acquired separately from a related business. This excess of the purchase price over the fair market value is called "goodwill" or "purchased goodwill" or, more accurately, "excess of cost over fair value of net identifiable assets of businesses acquired."

The accounting for goodwill illustrates how an *exchange* transaction is a basic concept of accounting. After all, there are many owners who could obtain a premium price for their companies. *But such goodwill is never recorded.* Only the goodwill arising from an *actual acquisition* with arm's-length bargaining is shown as an asset on the purchaser's records.

For shareholder-reporting purposes, goodwill must be amortized, generally in a straight-line manner, over the periods benefited. The maximum amortization period is forty years. The minimum amortization period was not specified by the Accounting Principles Board (*Opinion No. 17*), but a lump-sum write-off on acquisition is forbidden.

HISTORICAL THRUST TOWARD CONSERVATISM

☐ Goodwill

The attitude of the regulatory bodies toward accounting for intangible assets has become increasingly conservative. For example, many managers and accountants insist that some intangible assets have unlimited lives. Indeed, before 1970, the amortization of goodwill, trademarks, and franchises with indefinite useful lives was not mandatory. But the Accounting Principles Board ruled in 1970 that the values of all intangible assets eventually disappear, and therefore such assets must be amortized. However, the new requirement for amortization was not imposed retroactively. Consequently, many companies *are* currently amortizing goodwill acquired after 1970 but *are not* amortizing goodwill acquired before that date. For example, American Brands, maker of Titleist golf balls, Master locks, and many other consumer products, states in its annual report: "Intangibles resulting from business acquisitions, comprising brands and trademarks and cost in excess of net assets of businesses acquired, are considered to have a continuing value over an indefinite period and are not being amortized, except for intangibles acquired after 1970, which are being amortized on a straight-line basis over 40 years."

☐ Research and Development

Before 1975, many companies regarded *research and development costs* as assets and amortized them over the years of expected benefit, usually three to six years. Such costs result from planned search or critical investigation aimed at obtaining new products or processes or significant improvements in existing products or processes. Since 1975, the Financial Accounting Standards Board (*Statement No. 2*) has required that all such costs be charged to expense when incurred. The FASB recognized that research and development costs may generate many long-term benefits, but the general high degree of uncertainty about the extent and measurement of future benefits led to conservative accounting in the form of immediate write-off.

An exception to the immediate expensing of all research and development costs is accounting for the costs of developing computer software to be sold or leased. Such costs should be expensed only until *the technological feasibility* of the product is established. Thereafter, software production costs should be capitalized and amortized based on anticipated revenue.

AMORTIZATION OF DEFERRED CHARGES

Sometimes prepaid expenses are lumped with **deferred charges** as a single amount, *prepaid expenses and deferred charges*, that appears on the balance sheet at the bottom of the current asset classification or at the bottom of all the assets as an "other asset." Deferred charges are like prepaid expenses, but they have longer-term benefits. For example, the costs of relocating a mass of employees to a different geographical area, or the costs of rearranging an assembly line, or the costs of developing new markets may be carried forward as deferred charges and written off as expense over a three- to five-year period. This procedure is often described as the amortization of deferred charges.

Another example of deferred charges is *organization costs*, which include certain types of expenditures made in forming a corporation: fees for legal and accounting services, promotional costs for the sale of corporate securities, and the printing costs of stock certificates. These costs theoretically benefit the corporation indefinitely, but they are usually amortized for both shareholder and tax purposes over five years (which happens to be the minimum span allowed by the Internal Revenue Service).

INTERNAL COSTS AND EXTERNAL COSTS

As we have seen, accountants tend to be extremely conservative about intangible assets and deferred charges, and most intangibles are swiftly amortized. The contrast between the accounting for tangible and intangible long-lived assets raises some provocative and knotty theoretical issues. Accountants are sometimes overly concerned with physical objects or contractual rights, tending to overlook the underlying reality of future economic benefits.

This preoccupation with physical evidence often results in the expensing of outlays that should be treated as assets. Thus expenditures for research, advertising, employee training, and the like are generally expensed, although it seems clear that in an economic sense such expenditures represent expected future benefits. The difficulty of measuring future benefits is the reason usually advanced for expensing these items. The Financial Accounting Standards Board requires that all *internal* research and development costs be written off to expense as incurred.

In summary, accounting practice for intangible assets is not consistent. An annual report of Omark Industries exemplifies this inconsistency: "Costs of internally developed patents, trademarks and formulas are charged to current operations. Costs of purchased patents, trademarks and formulas are amortized over their legal or economic lives."

CONFLICTS WITH INCOME TAX PURPOSES

As mentioned earlier in this chapter, accounting for shareholder purposes often coincides with but sometimes differs from accounting for income tax purposes. Tax and shareholder accounting for leaseholds, leasehold improvements, patents, and copyrights generally coincide. However, they differ for perpetual franchises, trademarks, and goodwill. The acquisition costs of such assets *must* be amortized for shareholder reporting but *must not* be amortized for income tax purposes; the Internal Revenue Service will not allow amortization because of the indefinite duration of their usefulness.

The following table recapitulates how accounting for two purposes can conflict:

TYPE OF INTANGIBLE ASSET	MAXIMUM USEFUL LIVES IN YEARS FOR MEASURING ANNUAL AMORTIZATION IN REPORTS*	
	To Shareholders	To Internal Revenue Service
Patents	17	Same as first column
Copyrights†	40	75
Sports player contracts	Length of contract	Same
Franchises and licenses	Length of contract	Same
	or	or
	40 if length is unlimited	No amortization permitted‡
Trademarks	40	No amortization permitted‡
Goodwill	40	No amortization permitted‡
Research and development	Full write-off as incurred	Same
Covenants not to compete§	Length of contract	Same

* These maximums are frequently far in excess of the economic lives. Thus patents and copyrights are often written off in two or three years because the related products have short lives.

† Assumed to be a company's copyright on works created by employees. Personal copyrights are for the life of the author plus 50 years.

‡ The Internal Revenue Service does not permit amortization of intangible assets with indefinite useful lives. Examples are franchises of unlimited duration such as a football franchise, goodwill, and trademarks.

§ For example, the seller of a pest control business promises not to open a competing business within one hundred miles for five years.

SUMMARY

Depreciation, depletion, and amortization are similar concepts, providing for systematic write-offs of the acquisition costs of long-lived assets over their useful lives. By itself, depreciation does not provide cash. Customers provide cash. However, depreciation is deductible for income tax purposes. Therefore the larger the depreciation in any given year, the greater the amount of cash from customers that may be kept by the business instead of being disbursed to the income tax authorities.

Accumulated depreciation is a deduction from an asset, not an increasing pile of cash for replacing assets.

Reporting to shareholders and reporting to income tax authorities sometimes diverge. Keeping two sets of records to satisfy these two purposes is necessary, not illegal or immoral.

Goodwill is never shown as an asset unless it was acquired through the purchase of another business.

SUMMARY PROBLEMS FOR YOUR REVIEW

☐ **Problem One**

"The net book value of plant assets is the amount that would be spent today for their replacement." Do you agree? Explain.

Solution to Problem One

Net book value of the plant assets is the result of deducting accumulated depreciation from original cost. It is a result of cost allocation, not valuation. This process does not attempt to reflect all the technological and economic events that may affect replacement value. Consequently, there is little assurance that net book value will approximate replacement cost.

Problem Two

"Accumulated depreciation provides cash for the replacement of fixed assets." Do you agree with this quotation from a business magazine? Explain.

Solution to Problem Two

Accumulated depreciation is a contra asset. It is the amount of the asset already used up and in no way represents a direct stockpile of cash for replacement.

Problem Three

Refer to Exhibit 8–3 (p. 326). Suppose the predicted residual value had been $5,000 instead of $1,000.

1. Compute depreciation for each of the first two years using straight-line, sum-of-the-years'-digits, and double-declining-balance methods.
2. Assume that DDB depreciation is used and that the equipment is sold for $20,000 cash at the end of the second year. Compute the gain or loss on the sale. Show the effects of the sale in T-accounts for the equipment and accumulated depreciation. Where and how would the sale appear in the income statement?

Solution to Problem Three

1.

	STRAIGHT-LINE DEPRECIATION $\frac{C-R^*}{n}$	SYD DEPRECIATION = FRACTION† × (C − R)	DDB DEPRECIATION = RATE‡ × (BEGINNING BOOK VALUE)
Year 1	$36,000/4 = $9,000	4/10 ($36,000) = $14,400	.50 ($41,000) = $20,500
Year 2	$36,000/4 = $9,000	3/10 ($36,000) = $10,800	.50 ($41,000 − $20,500) = $10,250

* C − R = $41,000 − $5,000 = $36,000.

† $\dfrac{\text{Number of remaining years of life}}{\text{Sum of digits}} = \dfrac{4}{1+2+3+4} = 4/10$ in Year 1 and 3/10 in Year 2.

‡ Rate = 2(100% ÷ n) = 2(100% ÷ 4) = 50%.

2.

Revenue	$20,000
Expense: net book value of equipment sold is $41,000 − (20,500 + $10,250), or $41,000 − $30,750 =	10,250
Gain on sale of equipment	$ 9,750

The effect of removing the book value is a $10,250 decrease in assets. Note that the effect of a *decrease* in Accumulated Depreciation (by itself) is an *increase* in assets:

Equipment			
Acquisition cost	41,000	Cost of equipment sold	41,000

Accumulated Depreciation, Equipment			
Accumulated on equipment sold	30,750	Depreciation for: Year 1 Year 2	20,500 10,250 30,750

The $9,750 gain is usually shown as a separate item on the income statement as Gain on Sale of Equipment or Gain on Disposal of Equipment.

Problem Four

Review the important chapter illustration in the section "Depreciation and Generation of Cash," pages 328–333. Suppose the equipment had been acquired for $80,000 instead of $40,000. The predicted residual value remains zero.

Required:
1. Prepare a revised Exhibit 8–6, which is on page 331. Assume an income tax rate of 40%; round all income tax computations to the nearest thousand.
2. Indicate all items affected by these changes. Also tabulate all differences between the final two columns in your revised exhibit as compared with Exhibit 8–6.

Solution to Problem Four

1. The revised income statements are in Exhibit 8–9.
2. The following comparisons of Exhibits 8–9 and 8–6 are noteworthy. *Sales, operating expenses, and cash provided by operations before income taxes are unaffected by the change in depreciation.* Because of higher depreciation, net income would be lower in all four columns of Exhibit 8–9 than in Exhibit 8–6. Comparison of the final two columns of the exhibits follows:

	AS SHOWN IN		
	EXHIBIT 8–9	EXHIBIT 8–6	DIFFERENCE
Straight-line depreciation	20	10	10 higher
Accelerated depreciation	40	20	20 higher
Income tax expense based on:			
Straight-line depreciation	12	16	4 lower
Accelerated depreciation	4	12	8 lower
Net income based on:			
Straight-line depreciation	18	24	6 lower
Accelerated depreciation	6	18	12 lower
Cash provided by operations based on:			
Straight-line depreciation	38	34	4 higher
Accelerated depreciation	46	38	8 higher

Especially noteworthy is the phenomenon that higher depreciation *decreases* net income but also decreases cash outflows for income taxes. As a result, cash provided by operations *increases*.

EXHIBIT 8–9

ACME SERVICE COMPANY
Income Statement
For the Year Ended December 31, 19X1
(in thousands)

	Before Taxes		After Taxes	
	STRAIGHT-LINE DEPRECIATION	ACCELERATED DEPRECIATION	STRAIGHT-LINE DEPRECIATION	ACCELERATED DEPRECIATION
Sales	$103	$103	$103	$103
Cash operating expenses	53	53	53	53
Cash provided by operations before income tax	50	50	50	50
Depreciation expense	20	40	20	40
Pretax income	30	10	30	10
Income tax expense (40%)	—	—	12	4
Net income	$ 30	$ 10	$ 18	$ 6
Supplementary analysis:				
Cash provided by operations before income tax	$ 50	$ 50	$ 50	$ 50
Income tax expense	—	—	12	4
Cash provided by operations	$ 50	$ 50	$ 38	$ 46

HIGHLIGHTS TO REMEMBER

1. This chapter contains an unusually high number of new terms. Check your understanding of the items in the next section, "Accounting Vocabulary."

2. Are you able to distinguish between the terms *expense* and *expenditure*? Consult the Glossary for definitions. Note that an expenditure may be a *capital expenditure*, whose amount becomes allocated as an expense in each of several years. In contrast, a *revenue expenditure* becomes an expense in the current accounting year.

3. Students of introductory accounting are often confused by the relationships of depreciation to cash. Students are also often confused by the idea that "generally accepted accounting principles" are aimed primarily at reporting to shareholders, not income tax authorities. A careful study of Problem Four of the "Summary Problems for Your Review" should reduce the confusion.

ACCOUNTING VOCABULARY

Accelerated Depreciation, p. 323
Amortization, p. 318
Basket Purchase, p. 320
Betterment, p. 336
Capital Expenditure, p. 335

Capital Improvement, p. 336
Capitalized, p. 320
Copyrights, p. 341
Deferred Charge, p. 342
Depletion, p. 340

FUNDAMENTAL ASSIGNMENT MATERIAL

☐ General Coverage

8–1. **JOURNAL ENTRIES FOR DEPRECIATION.** (Alternates are 8–6 and 8–7.) On January 1, 19X1, the Aquino Company acquired some assembly robots for $550,000 cash. The robots had an expected useful life of ten years and an expected terminal scrap value of $50,000. Straight-line depreciation was used.

Required:
1. Set up T-accounts and prepare the journal entries for the acquisition and for the first annual depreciation charge. Post to T-accounts.
2. Some of the robots with an original cost of $66,000 on January 1, 19X1, and an expected terminal scrap value of $6,000 were sold for $45,000 cash on December 31, 19X3. Prepare the journal entry for the sale.
3. Refer to requirement 2. Suppose the robots had been sold for $49,000 cash instead of $45,000. Prepare the journal entry for the sale.

8–2. **COMPARISON OF POPULAR DEPRECIATION METHODS.** (Alternates are 8–8, 8–9, and 8–36.) Kesler Company acquired a machine for $31,000 with an expected useful life of five years and a $1,000 expected residual value. Prepare a tabular comparison (similar to Exhibit 8–3, p. 326) of the annual depreciation and book value for each year under straight-line, sum-of-the-years'-digits, and double-declining-balance depreciation. (Note that this is a comparison of methods used for reporting to shareholders. Such methods may differ from those used for reporting to the income tax authorities.)

8–3. **DEPRECIATION, INCOME TAXES, AND CASH FLOW.** (Alternates are 8–10, 8–11, and 8–74.) Gonzales Co. had the following balances, among others, at the end of December 19X1: Cash, $200,000; Equipment, $400,000; Accumulated Depreciation, $100,000. Total revenues (all in cash) were $800,000. Cash operating expenses were $500,000. Straight-line depreciation expense was $50,000. If accelerated depreciation had been used, depreciation expense would have been $80,000.

Required:
1. Assume zero income taxes. Fill in the blanks in the accompanying table. Show the amounts in thousands.
2. Repeat requirement 1, but assume an income tax rate of 40%. Assume also that Gonzales uses the same depreciation method for reporting to shareholders and to income tax authorities.
3. Compare your answers to requirements 1 and 2. Does depreciation provide cash? Explain as precisely as possible.
4. Assume that Gonzales had used straight-line depreciation for reporting to shareholders and to income tax authorities. Indicate the change (increase or decrease and amount) in the following balances if Gonzales had used accelerated depreciation

instead of straight-line: Cash, Accumulated Depreciation, Operating Income, Income Tax Expense, and Retained Income.

5. Refer to requirement 1. Suppose depreciation were tripled under both straight-line and accelerated methods. How would cash be affected? Be specific.

Table for Problem 8–3
(amounts in thousands)

	1. ZERO INCOME TAXES		2. 40% INCOME TAXES	
	Straight-line Depreciation	Accelerated Depreciation	Straight-line Depreciation	Accelerated Depreciation
Revenues	$	$	$	$
Cash operating expenses				
Cash provided by operations be- fore income taxes				
Depreciation expense				
Operating income				
Income tax expense				
Net income	$	$	$	$
Supplementary analysis: Cash provided by operations be- fore income taxes				
Income tax expense	$	$	$	$
Net cash provided by operations	$	$	$	$

8–4. **DISPOSAL OF EQUIPMENT.** (Alternates are 8–12 and 8–13.) Kesler Company acquired equipment for $34,000 with an expected useful life of five years and a $4,000 expected residual value. Straight-line depreciation was used. The equipment was sold at the end of the fourth year for $17,000 cash.

Required:

1. Compute the gain or loss on the sale. Show the effects of the sale on the balance sheet equation, identifying all specific accounts by name. Where and how would the sale appear on the income statement?
2. (a) Show the journal entries and postings to T-accounts for the transaction in requirement 1. (b) Repeat 2a, assuming that the cash sales price was $6,000 instead of $17,000.

8–5. **VARIOUS INTANGIBLE ASSETS.** (Alternates are 8–14 and 8–15.) Consider the following:

1. On December 28, 19X8, Stiglitz Company purchased a patent for a calculator for $380,000. The patent has ten years of its legal life remaining. Technology changes fast, so Stiglitz expects the patent to be worthless in four years. What will be the amortization for 19X9?
2. On December 29, 19X1, a publisher acquires the copyright for a book by Robert Ludlum for $2 million. Most sales of this book are expected to take place during 19X2 and 19X3. What will be the amortization for 19X2?
3. On January 4, 19X1, Company X acquires Company Y for $45 million and can assign only $35 million to identifiable individual assets. What is the minimum amount of amortization of the goodwill for 19X1? Could the entire amount be written off in 19X1? Why?
4. In 19X1, Company C spent $15 million in its research department, which resulted in new valuable patents. In December 19X1, Company D paid $15 million to an outside inventor for some valuable new patents. How would the income statements for 19X1 for each company be affected? How would the balance sheets as of December 31, 19X1, be affected?

8–6. JOURNAL ENTRIES FOR DEPRECIATION. (Alternates are 8–1 and 8–7.) The Delta Air Lines balance sheet, January 1, 1989, included the following (in thousands):

Flight equipment owned	$4,624,630
Less: Accumulated depreciation	2,125,879
	$2,498,751
Ground property and equipment	$1,222,314
Less: Accumulated depreciation	548,499
	$ 673,815

Assume that on January 2, 1989, some new maintenance equipment was acquired for $848,000 cash. The equipment had an expected useful life of five years and an expected terminal scrap value of $48,000. Straight-line depreciation was used.

Required:

1. Prepare the journal entry that would be made annually for depreciation on the new equipment.
2. Suppose some of the equipment with an original cost of $214,000 on January 2, 1989, and an expected terminal scrap value of $14,000 was sold for $150,000 cash two years later. Prepare the journal entry for the sale.
3. Refer to requirement 2. Suppose the equipment had been sold for $120,000 cash instead of $150,000. Prepare the journal entry for the sale.

8–7. JOURNAL ENTRIES FOR DEPRECIATION. (Alternates are 8–1 and 8–6.) The Coca-Cola Company balance sheet, January 1, 1989, included the following:

Property, plant and equipment	$2,908,907,000
Less allowances for depreciation	1,149,832,000
	$1,759,075,000

Note that the company uses "allowances for" rather than "accumulated" depreciation. Assume that on January 2, 1989, some new bottling equipment was acquired for $880,000 cash. The equipment had an expected useful life of five years and an expected terminal scrap value of $80,000. Straight-line depreciation was used.

Required:

1. Prepare the journal entry that would be made annually for depreciation.
2. Suppose some of the equipment with an original cost of $55,000 on January 2, 1989, and an expected terminal scrap value of $5,000 was sold for $30,000 cash two years later. Prepare the journal entry for the sale.
3. Refer to requirement 2. Suppose the equipment had been sold for $45,000 cash instead of $30,000. Prepare the journal entry for the sale.

8–8. FUNDAMENTAL DEPRECIATION POLICIES. (Alternates are 8–2, 8–9, and 8–36.) The Mailing Services department of the Boeing Company acquired some new package-handling equipment for $200,000. The equipment's predicted useful life is eight years and predicted residual value is $24,000.

Required:

Prepare a depreciation schedule similar to Exhibit 8–3 (p. 326), comparing straight-line, sum-of-the-years'-digits, and double-declining-balance. Show all amounts in thousands of dollars (rounded to the nearest thousand). Limit the schedule to each of the first three years of useful life. Show the depreciation for each year and the book value at the end of each year. (Note that this is a comparison of methods used for reporting to shareholders. Such methods may differ from those used for reporting to the income tax authorities.)

8–9. POPULAR DEPRECIATION METHODS. (Alternates are 8–2, 8–8, and 8–36.) The annual report of Alaska Airlines contained the following footnote:

☐ PROPERTY, EQUIPMENT AND DEPRECIATION—Property and equipment are recorded at cost and depreciated using the straight-line method over their estimated useful lives, which are as follows:

Buildings	10–30 years
Flight equipment	10–18 years
Other equipment	3–15 years

Required: Consider a Boeing 727-100 airplane, which was acquired for $26 million on January 1, 19X1. Its useful life is ten years, and its expected residual value is $4 million. Prepare a tabular comparison of the annual depreciation and book value for each of the first three years of service life under straight-line, sum-of-the-years'-digits, and double-declining-balance depreciation. Show all amounts in thousands of dollars (rounded to the nearest thousand). (Note that this is a comparison of methods used for reporting to shareholders. Such methods may differ from those used for reporting to the income tax authorities.) *Hint:* See Exhibit 8–3, page 326.

8–10. DEPRECIATION, INCOME TAXES, AND CASH FLOW. (Alternates are 8–3, 8–11, and 8–74.) The 1988 annual report of Amgen, Inc., a major biotechnology company, listed the following property, plant, and equipment:

Property, plant, and equipment, at cost	$66,691,000
Less accumulated depreciation	11,925,000
Property, plant, and equipment, net	$54,766,000

The cash balance was $106,000.

Depreciation expense during 1988 was $4,120,000. The condensed income statement follows:

Revenues	$53,325,000
Expenses	51,251,000
Operating income	$ 2,074,000

For purposes of this problem, assume that all revenues and expenses, excluding depreciation, are for cash. Thus cash operating expenses were $51,251,000 − $4,120,000 = $47,131,000.

Required:
1. Amgen uses straight-line depreciation. Suppose accelerated depreciation for 1988 had been $5,120,000 instead of $4,120,000. Assume zero income taxes. Fill in the blanks in the accompanying table (in thousands of dollars).
2. Repeat requirement 1, but assume an income tax rate of 40%. Assume also that Amgen uses the same depreciation method for reporting to shareholders and to income tax authorities.

3. Compare your answers to requirements 1 and 2. Does depreciation provide cash? Explain as precisely as possible.
4. Assume that Amgen had used straight-line depreciation for reporting to shareholders and to income tax authorities. Indicate the change (increase or decrease and amount) in the following balances if Amgen had used accelerated depreciation instead of straight-line for 1988 only: Cash, Accumulated Depreciation, Operating Income, Income Tax Expenses, and Retained Income. What would be the new balances in Cash and Accumulated Depreciation?
5. Refer to requirement 1. Suppose depreciation were increased by an extra $300,000 under both straight-line and accelerated methods. How would cash be affected? Be specific.

Table for Problem 8–10
(amounts in thousands)

	1. ZERO INCOME TAXES		2. 40% INCOME TAXES	
	Straight-line Depreciation	Accelerated Depreciation	Straight-line Depreciation	Accelerated Depreciation
Revenues	$	$	$	$
Cash operating expenses				
Cash provided by operations before income taxes				
Depreciation expense				
Operating income				
Income tax expense				
Net income	$	$	$	$
Supplementary analysis:				
Cash provided by operations before income taxes				
Income tax expense	$	$	$	$
Net cash provided by operations	$	$	$	$

8–11. **DEPRECIATION, INCOME TAXES, AND CASH FLOW.** (Alternates are 8–3, 8–10, and 8–74.) Federal Express Corporation provides door-to-door overnight delivery of packages and documents throughout the United States. The company's 1988 annual report showed the following balances (in thousands):

Revenues	$3,882,817
Operating expenses	3,503,365
Operating income	$ 379,452

Federal Express had "depreciation and amortization" expense of $289,578,000 (included in operating expenses). The company's ending cash balance was $54,945,000.
Federal Express reported the property and equipment in the following way (in thousands):

Flight equipment	$1,301,978
Package handling and ground support equipment	755,585
Computer and electronic equipment	438,527
Other	853,019
	3,349,109
Less accumulated depreciation and amortization	1,117,234
Net property and equipment	$2,231,875

For purposes of this problem, assume that all revenues and expenses, excluding depreciation, are for cash.

Required:

1. Federal Express used straight-line depreciation and amortization. Suppose accelerated depreciation had been $389,578,000 instead of $289,578,000. Assume zero income taxes. Fill in the blanks in the accompanying table (in thousands of dollars).
2. Repeat requirement 1, but assume an income tax rate of 45%. Assume also that Federal Express uses the same depreciation method for reporting to shareholders and to income tax authorities.
3. Compare your answers to requirements 1 and 2. Does depreciation provide cash? Explain as precisely as possible.
4. Assume that Federal Express had used straight-line depreciation for reporting to shareholders and to income tax authorities. Indicate the change (increase or decrease and amount) in the following balances if Federal Express had used accelerated depreciation rather than straight-line: Cash, Accumulated Depreciation and Amortization, Operating Income, Income Tax Expense, and Retained Income. What would be the new balances in Cash and Accumulated Depreciation and Amortization?
5. Refer to requirement 1. Suppose depreciation were doubled under both straight-line and accelerated methods. How would cash be affected? Be specific.

Table for Problem 8–11
(amounts in thousands)

	1. ZERO INCOME TAXES		2. 45% INCOME TAXES	
	Straight-line Depreciation	Accelerated Depreciation	Straight-line Depreciation	Accelerated Depreciation
Revenues	$	$	$	$
Cash operating expenses				
Cash provided by operations before income taxes				
Depreciation expense				
Operating income				
Income tax expense				
Net income	$	$	$	$
Supplementary analysis:				
Cash provided by operations before income taxes				
Income tax expense	$	$	$	$
Net cash provided by operations	$	$	$	$

8-12. DISPOSAL OF EQUIPMENT. (Alternates are 8–4 and 8–13.) Alaska Airlines acquired a new Boeing 727-100 airplane for $24 million. Its expected residual value was $4 million. The company's annual report indicated that straight-line depreciation was used based on an estimated service life of ten years. In addition, the company stated: "The cost and related accumulated depreciation of assets sold or retired are removed from the appropriate accounts, and gain or loss, if any, is recognized in Other Income (Expense)."

Required: Show all amounts in millions of dollars.

1. Assume that the equipment is sold at the end of the sixth year for $13 million cash. Compute the gain or loss on the sale. Show the effects of the sale on the balance sheet equation, identifying all specific accounts by name. Where and how would the sale appear on the income statement?
2. (a) Show the journal entries and postings to T-accounts for the transaction in requirement 1. (b) Repeat 2a, assuming that the cash sales price was $7 million instead of $11 million.

8-13. DISPOSAL OF PROPERTY AND EQUIPMENT. (Alternates are 8–4 and 8–12.) Rockwell International is an advanced technology company operating primarily in aerospace and electronics. The company's annual report indicated that both accelerated and straight-line depreciation were used for its property and equipment. In addition, the annual report said: "When assets are sold or retired, accumulated depreciation is charged with the portion thereof applicable to such assets. The resulting gain or loss is recorded in income in the year of sale or retirement."

In 1987 Rockwell received $45.6 million for property and equipment that it sold.

Required:

1. Assume that the total property and equipment in question were originally acquired for $150 million, and the $45.6 million was received in cash. There was a gain of $8.5 million on the sale. Compute the accumulated depreciation on the property and equipment. Show the effects of the sale on the balance sheet equation, identifying all specific accounts by name.
2. For this requirement, round your entries to the nearest thousand dollars. (a) Show the journal entries and postings to T-accounts for the transaction in requirement 1. (b) Repeat 2a, assuming that the cash sales price was $35.6 million cash instead of $45.6 million.

8-14. VARIOUS INTANGIBLE ASSETS. (Alternates are 8–5 and 8–15.)

1. A recent annual report of Associated Hosts, owner and operator of many restaurants and hotels, including the Beverly Hillcrest Hotel, stated: "It is the company's policy to defer preopening costs during periods of construction of new units or remodeling of existing units and to amortize such costs over a period of 12 to 24 months commencing on the opening date."

   During the year, preopening costs of $582,000 were capitalized. The beginning-of-the-year asset balance for preopening costs was $779,000, and the end-of-the-year balance was $617,000. Compute the amortization for the year.
2. Philip Morris purchased General Foods for $5.6 billion. Philip Morris could assign only $1.7 billion to identifiable individual assets. What is the amount of goodwill created by the acquisition? What is the minimum amount of amortization in the first year?
3. (a) In 1989, DuPont spent over $1 billion in its research departments, and this resulted in valuable new patents. (b) Suppose that in December 1989, DuPont had paid $1 billion to various outside companies for the same new patents. How would the income statement for 1989 have been affected under a and b? The balance sheet, December 31, 1989?
4. On December 29, 1989, CBS Corporation purchased a patent on some broadcasting equipment for $900,000. The patent has sixteen years of its legal life remaining. Because technology moves rapidly, CBS expects the patent to be worthless at the end of three years. What is the amortization for 1990?

8–15. **VARIOUS INTANGIBLE ASSETS.** (Alternates are 8–5 and 8–14.) Consider the following:

1. (a) Dow Chemical Company's annual report indicated that research and development expenditures for the year were $670 million. How did this amount affect operating income, which was $2,292 million? (b) Suppose the entire $670 million arose from outlays for patents acquired from various outside parties on December 30. What would be the operating income for the year? (c) How would Dow's December 31 balance sheet be affected by *b*?

2. On December 30, 1989, American Telephone and Telegraph Company (AT&T) acquired new patents on some communications equipment for $10 million. Technology changes quickly. The equipment's useful life is expected to be five years rather than the seventeen-year life of the patent. What will be the amortization for 1990?

3. Hilton Hotels has an account classified under assets in its balance sheet called preopening costs. A footnote said that these costs "are charged to income over a three-year period after the opening date." Suppose expenditures for preopening costs in 1989 were $2,000,000 and the preopening costs account balance on December 31, 1989, was $1,840,000 and on December 31, 1988, was $2,390,000. What amount was amortized for 1989?

4. The Gannett Co., Inc., publisher of many newspapers, including *USA Today*, purchased radio stations KKBQ–AM and FM in Houston and WDAE–AM in Tampa for a total of $41 million. A footnote in the annual report stated that goodwill is "amortized over a period of 40 years." Assume that both purchases were made on January 2 and that Gannett could assign only $33 million to identifiable individual assets. What is the minimum amount of amortization of goodwill for the first year? Could the entire amount be written off immediately? Explain.

ADDITIONAL ASSIGNMENT MATERIAL

☐ General Coverage

8–16. Distinguish between *tangible* and *intangible* assets.

8–17. Distinguish between *amortization, depreciation,* and *depletion.*

8–18. "The cash discount on the purchase of equipment is income to the buyer during the year of acquisition." Do you agree? Explain.

8–19. "When an expenditure is capitalized, stockholders' equity is credited." Do you agree? Explain.

8–20. "Accumulated depreciation is a sum of cash being accumulated for the replacement of fixed assets." Do you agree? Explain.

8–21. "The accounting process of depreciation is allocation, not valuation." Explain.

8–22. "Keeping two sets of books is immoral." Do you agree? Explain.

8–23. "Most of the money we'll spend this year for replacing our equipment will be generated by depreciation." Do you agree? Explain.

8–24. Criticize: "Depreciation is the loss in value of a fixed asset over a given span of time."

8–25. "Accelerated depreciation saves cash but shows lower net income." Explain.

8–26. "Changes in accounting estimates should be reported prospectively rather than retroactively." Explain.

8–27. The manager of a division reported to the president of the company: "Now that our major capital improvements are finished, the division's expenses will be much lower." Is this really what he means to say? Explain.

8–28. "The gain on sale of equipment should be reported fully on the income statement." Explain what the complete reporting would include.

8–29. Name and describe four kinds of intangible assets.

8–30. Explain how goodwill is computed.

8–31. "Internally acquired patents are accounted for differently than externally acquired patents." Explain the difference.

8–32. "Goodwill may have nothing to do with the personality of the manager or employees." Do you agree? Explain.

8–33. "Accountants sometimes are too concerned with physical objects or contractual rights." Explain.

8–34. "Accounting for research and development is more conservative than it was before 1975." Explain.

8–35. Compare the choice between straight-line and accelerated depreciation with the choice between FIFO and LIFO. Give at least one similarity and one difference.

8–36. **FUNDAMENTAL DEPRECIATION APPROACHES.** (Alternates are 8–2, 8–8, and 8–9.) Consolidated Freightways acquired some new trucks for $1 million. Their predicted useful life is five years, and predicted residual value is $100,000.

Required: | Prepare a depreciation schedule similar to Exhibit 8–3, page 326, comparing straight-line, sum-of-the-years'-digits, and double-declining-balance.

8–37. **DEPRECIATION, INCOME TAXES, AND CASH FLOW.** (Alternate 8–57.) Fleck Company began business with cash and common stock equity of $150,000. The same day, December 31, 19X1, equipment was acquired for $50,000 cash. The equipment had an expected useful life of five years and a predicted residual value of $5,000. The first year's operations generated cash sales of $160,000 and cash operating expenses of $85,000.

Required: | 1. Prepare an analysis of transactions for December 31, 19X1, plus the year 19X2, using the balance sheet equation format as illustrated in Exhibit 8–4. Assume (a) straight-line depreciation and (b) sum-of-the-years'-digits depreciation. Assume zero income taxes. Exhibit 8–4 is on page 329.
2. Repeat requirement 1, but assume an income tax rate of 50% (to ease computations). Income taxes are paid in cash. The company uses the same depreciation method for reporting to shareholders and to income tax authorities.
3. Prepare columnar (a) income statements for 19X2 and (b) balance sheets as of December 31, 19X2, that compare the effects of the four alternatives covered in requirements 1 and 2. (*Hint*: See the illustration in the chapter, pp. 330–331.)
4. Compare your answers to requirements 1 and 2. Does depreciation provide cash? Explain as precisely as possible.
5. Refer to requirement 1. Suppose depreciation were tripled under straight-line and SYD methods. How would cash be affected? Be specific.

8–38. **COMPUTING ACQUISITION COSTS.** From the following data, calculate the cost to be added to the Land account and the Building account of Swedish Hospital.

On January 1, 19X9, the hospital acquired a twenty-acre parcel of land immediately adjacent to its existing facilities. The land included a warehouse, parking lots, and driveways. The hospital paid $500,000 cash and also gave a note for $2 million, payable at $200,000 per year plus interest of 13% on the outstanding balance.

The warehouse was demolished at a cash cost of $250,000 so that it could be replaced by a new hospital building. The construction of the building required a cash down payment of $2 million plus a mortgage note of $8 million. The mortgage was payable at $400,000 per year plus interest of 12% on the outstanding balance.

Prepare journal entries (without explanations) to record the above transactions.

8–39. **GOVERNMENT EQUIPMENT.** A tax agency of the state of Illinois acquired some used computer equipment. Installation costs were $8,000. Repair costs prior to use were $6,000. The purchasing manager's salary is $47,000 per annum. The invoice price was $400,000. The seller paid its salesman a commission of 4% and offered the buyer a cash discount of 2% if the invoice was paid within sixty days. Freight costs were $4,400. Repairs during the first year of use were $10,500. Compute the total capitalized cost to be added to the Equipment account. The seller was paid within sixty days.

8–40. **BASKET PURCHASE.** On February 21, 19X2, FastLube, an auto service chain, acquired an existing building and land for $840,000 from a local gas station that had failed. The tax assessor had placed an assessed valuation on January 1, 19X2, as follows:

Land	$220,000
Building	380,000
Total	$600,000

Required: | How much of the $840,000 purchase price should be attributed to the building? Why?

8–41. Basket Purchase of Sports Franchise. William Rooney has acquired the assets of the San Francisco football team, including the player contracts. The total cost is $12 million. The largest assets are the franchise and the contracts. For reporting to the IRS, the franchise has an indefinite useful life. The contracts have a five-year useful life. Other assets are relatively minor. The seller, Samuel Stefano, shows the following book values of the assets (in millions):

Player contracts	$3
Franchise	5
Total book value	$8

Required: | As Rooney, if you have complete discretion for tax purposes, how much of the $12 million price would you allocate to the contracts? Explain.

8–42. Simple Depreciation Computations. Compute the first three years of depreciation for the following assets:

    a. Conveyor, five-year useful life, $27,000 cost, straight-line method, $2,000 residual value.
    b. Truck, six-year useful life, $18,000 cost, DDB method, $1,000 residual value.
    c. Copy machine, four-year useful life, $6,000 cost, SYD method, $1,000 residual value.

8–43. Depreciation on a Group of Assets. Wilkening Company has just purchased the assets of a division of Sportsgear, Inc., for $3 million. Of the purchase price, $1.5 million was allocated to assets that will be depreciated on a straight-line basis over a useful life of six years (assume no residual value). Another $400,000 was for special production machinery that will be depreciated on a DDB basis over a useful life of five years. A total of $300,000 was for land. The remainder was goodwill, which Wilkening will amortize by the straight-line method over forty years.

Required: | Compute the total depreciation and amortization expense generated by the acquired assets for each of the first two years.

8–44. Units-of-Production Method. The Kelly Transport Company has many trucks that are kept for a useful life of 250,000 miles. Depreciation is computed on a mileage basis. Suppose a new truck is purchased for $81,000 cash. Its expected residual value is $6,000. Its mileage during Year 1 is 60,000 and during Year 2 is 90,000.

Required: | 1. What is the depreciation expense for each of the two years?
    2. Compute the gain or loss if the truck is sold for $45,500 at the end of Year 2.

8–45. MACRS versus Straight-Line. San Carlos Machinery bought special tooling equipment for $2 million. The useful life is five years, with no residual value. For tax purposes, MACRS specifies a three-year, DDB depreciation schedule. San Carlos uses the straight-line depreciation method for reporting to shareholders.

Required: | 1. Explain the two factors that account for the acceleration of depreciation for tax purposes.
    2. Compute the first year's depreciation (a) for shareholder reporting and (b) for tax purposes. (Ignore complications in the tax law that are not introduced in this chapter.)

8–46. **Units-of-Production, Straight-line, and DDB.** Newform Mining Company buys special drills for $325,000 each. Each drill can extract about 100,000 tons of ore, after which it has a $25,000 residual value. One such drill was bought in early January 19X1. Projected tonnage figures for the drill are 30,000 tons in 19X1, 50,000 tons in 19X2, and 20,000 tons in 19X3. Newform is considering units-of-production, straight-line, or double-declining-balance depreciation for the drill.

Required: | Compute depreciation for each year under each of the three methods.

8–47. **Depreciation for Parts of Year.** Ribiero Company acquired equipment on April 2, 19X1, for $140,000 cash. Its expected useful life was five years, and its expected residual value was $20,000. The sum-of-the-years'-digits method of depreciation was adopted. Prepare a schedule of depreciation for each calendar year of use. Show the total amount of depreciation for each calendar year affected.

8–48. **Repairs and Improvements.** Nakata Company acquired equipment for $88,000 with an expected useful life of five years and an $8,000 expected residual value. Straight-line depreciation was used. During its fourth year of service, expenditures related to the equipment were as follows:

1. Oiling and greasing, $180.
2. Replacing belts and hoses, $420.
3. Major overhaul during the final week of the year, including the replacement of an engine. The useful life of the equipment was extended from five to seven years. The cost was $18,000. The residual value is now expected to be $12,000 instead of $8,000.

Required: | Indicate in words how each of the three items would affect the income statement and the balance sheet. Prepare a tabulation that compares the original depreciation schedule with the revised depreciation schedule.

8–49. **Capital and Revenue Expenditures.** Consider the following transactions:

a. Paid janitorial wages.
b. Paid security guard wages.
c. Paid plumbers for repair of leaky faucets.
d. Acquired new air-conditioning system for the building.
e. Replaced smashed front door (not covered by insurance).
f. Paid travel expenses of sales personnel.
g. Acquired building for a down payment plus a mortgage payable.
h. Paid interest on building mortgage.
i. Paid principal on building mortgage.
j. Paid cash dividends.

Required: | Answer by letter:

1. Indicate which transactions are capital expenditures.
2. Indicate which transactions are revenue expenditures.

8–50. **Capital and Revenue Expenditures.** Consider each of the following transactions. For each one, indicate whether it is a capital expenditure (C) or a revenue expenditure (R).

a. Paid organization costs to incorporate a new company.
b. Paid a consultant to advise on marketing strategy.
c. Installed new lighting fixtures in a leased building.
d. Paid for routine maintenance on equipment.
e. Acquired a patent for $50,000.
f. Paid for overhaul of machinery that extends its useful life.
g. Developed a patentable product by paying for research and development.
h. Paid for a tune-up on one of the autos in the company's fleet.

8–51. **Depletion.** A zinc mine contains an estimated 600,000 tons of zinc ore. The mine cost $9 million. The tonnage mined during 19X4, the first year of operations, was 80,000 tons.

Required:

1. What was the depletion for 19X4?
2. Suppose that in January 19X5 it was discovered that the mine probably contained 130,000 more tons than originally estimated. What was the estimated depletion for 19X5, assuming that 40,000 tons were mined?

8–52. **LEASEHOLD IMPROVEMENTS.** A Burger King has a ten-year lease on space in a suburban shopping center. Near the end of the sixth year of the lease, the owner exercised his rights under the lease, removing walls and replacing floor coverings and lighting fixtures. The cost was $120,000. The useful life of the redesigned facilities was predicted to be twelve years.

Required: What accounts could be affected by the $120,000 outlay? What would be the annual amortization?

8–53. **CHANGES IN DEPRECIATION ESTIMATES.** Cascade Company acquired equipment for $50,000 with an expected useful life of five years and a $5,000 expected residual value. Straight-line depreciation was adopted. Suppose it is the end of Year 3. The company's engineers have altered their expectations; the equipment's new expected useful life is eight instead of five years. Furthermore, the expected residual value is $6,000 instead of $5,000.

Required:

1. Using the "prospective" method, compute the new annual straight-line depreciation.
2. Critics of the "prospective" method favor using the "retroactive" method instead. Prepare a table comparing annual depreciation throughout the eight-year life using the prospective method and the retroactive method. Which method do you favor? Why?

8–54. **GAIN OR LOSS ON SALES OF FIXED ASSETS.** J. N. Sykes Company purchased a delivery van in early 19X1 for $18,000. It was being depreciated on a straight-line basis over its useful life of five years. Estimated residual value was $3,000. The van was sold in early 19X3 after two years of depreciation had been recognized.

Required:

1. Suppose Sykes received $14,000 for the van. Compute the gain or loss on the sale. Prepare the journal entries for the sale of the van.
2. Suppose Sykes received $9,000 for the van. Compute the gain or loss on the sale. Prepare the journal entries for the sale of the van.

8–55. **NATURE OF RESEARCH COSTS.** Maria Gersteli, a distinguished scientist of international repute, had developed many successful drugs for a well-established pharmaceutical company. Having an entrepreneurial spirit, she persuaded the board of directors that she should resign her position as vice-president of research and launch a subsidiary company to produce and market some powerful new drugs for treating arthritis. However, she did not predict overnight success. Instead, she expected to gather a first-rate research team that might take three to five years to generate any marketable products. Furthermore, she admitted that the risks were so high that conceivably no commercial success might result. Nevertheless, she had little trouble obtaining an initial investment of $5 million. The Gersteli Pharmaceuticals Company was 80% owned by the parent and 20% by Maria.

Maria acquired a team of researchers and began operations. By the end of the first year of the life of the new subsidiary, $2 million had been expended on research activities, mostly for researchers' salaries, but also for related research costs.

No marketable products had been developed, but Maria and other top executives were extremely pleased about overall progress and were very optimistic about getting such products within the next three or four years.

Required: How would you account for the $2 million? Would you write it off as an expense in Year 1? Carry it indefinitely? Write it off systematically over three years or some longer span? Why? Explain, giving particular attention to the idea of an asset as an unexpired cost.

8–56. **MEANING OF BOOK VALUE.** Sanchez Company purchased an office building twenty years ago for $1 million, $200,000 of which was attributable to land. The mortgage has been fully paid. The current balance sheet follows:

Cash		$400,000	Stockholders'
Land		200,000	equity $750,000
Building at cost	$800,000		
Accumulated depreciation	650,000		
Net book value		150,000	
Total assets		$750,000	

The company is about to borrow $1.8 million on a first mortgage to modernize and expand the building. This amounts to 60% of the combined appraised value of the land and building before the modernization and expansion.

Required: Prepare a balance sheet after the loan is made and the building is expanded and modernized. Comment on its significance.

8–57. **DEPRECIATION, INCOME TAXES, AND CASH FLOW.** (Alternate is 8–37.) Mr. Kohl, president of the Rhone Transportation Company, had read a newspaper story that stated: "The Frankfurt Steel Company had a cash flow last year of 1,500,000 DM, consisting of 1,000,000 DM of net income plus 500,000 DM of depreciation. New plant facilities helped the cash flow, because depreciation was 25 percent higher than in the preceding year." "Cash flow" is frequently used as a synonym for "cash provided by operations," which, in turn, is cash revenue less cash operating expenses and income taxes. (DM stands for Deutschmark, the West German unit of currency.)

Kohl was encouraged by the quotation because the Rhone Company had just acquired a vast amount of new transportation equipment. These acquisitions had placed a severe financial strain on the company. Kohl was heartened because he thought that the added cash flow from the depreciation of the new equipment should ease the financial pressures on the company.

The income before income taxes of the Rhone Company last year (19X2) was 200,000 DM. Depreciation was 200,000 DM; it will also be 200,000 DM on the old equipment in 19X3.

Revenue in 19X2 was 1.9 million DM (all in cash), and operating expenses other than depreciation were 1.5 million DM (all in cash).

In 19X3, the new equipment is expected to help increase revenue by 1 million DM. However, operating expenses other than depreciation will increase by 800,000 DM.

Required:
1. Suppose depreciation on the new equipment for financial reporting purposes is 100,000 DM. What would be the "cash flow" from operations (cash provided by operations) for 19X3? Show computations. Ignore income taxes.
2. Repeat requirement 1, assuming that the depreciation on the new equipment is 50,000 DM. Ignore income taxes.
3. Assume an income tax rate of 40%. (a) Repeat requirement 1; (b) repeat requirement 2. Assume that the same amount of depreciation is shown for tax purposes and for financial reporting purposes.
4. In your own words, state as accurately as possible the effects on "cash flow" of depreciation. Comment on requirements 1, 2, and 3 above in order to bring out your points. This is a more important requirement than requirements 1, 2, and 3.

□ **Understanding Published Financial Reports**

8–58. **CLASSIC CASE FROM THE BUSINESS PRESS.** A news story regarding Chrysler Corporation stated:

□ Yet the $7.5 billion that John J. Riccardo, its money man, estimates the company will need to finance a recovery over the next five years is huge by any standard.

But, says Riccardo, "half is charged to the P&L [profit and loss] as incurred, so we're looking for $3.75 billion. Of that, about 60% will be recovered in depreciation and amortization. That leaves a balance of $1.5 billion over the five years, to be financed through earnings, borrowings, and divestitures. Over the period, that overall number is manageable.

Required:

Explain or comment on the following:

1. "Half is charged to the P&L as incurred, so we're looking for $3.75 billion."
2. "Of that, about 60% will be recovered in depreciation and amortization."

8–59. **BALANCE SHEET PRESENTATION.** Consider the presentation of the Procter & Gamble Company, whose brands include *Tide, Jif, Charmin, Folger's,* and *Crest* (in millions of dollars):

	JUNE 30	
	1988	1987
PROPERTY, PLANT, AND EQUIPMENT, at cost		
Buildings	$ 1,592	$1,464
Machinery and equipment	8,238	7,717
Land	179	185
Timberlands, less depletion	161	155
	10,170	9,521
Less accumulated depreciation	3,392	2,990
	$ 6,778	$6,531

Required:

Do any features of this presentation seem unusual? Explain.

8–60. **CAPITAL OR REVENUE EXPENDITURES.** Disputes sometimes arise between the taxpayer and the Internal Revenue Service regarding whether legal costs should be deductible as expenses in the year incurred (revenue expenditures) or be considered as capital expenditures because they relate to defending or perfecting title to business property.

Consider three examples from court cases:

☐ **EXAMPLE 1:** Several years after Rock set up his stone-quarrying business, Smalltown passed an ordinance banning it. Rock spent $1,000 to invalidate the ordinance.

☐ **EXAMPLE 2:** Now suppose Rock decided to expand his business. So he applied to Smalltown for a permit to build an additional crusher. It was denied because an ordinance prohibited the expansion of nonconforming uses, including quarrying. Rock sued to invalidate the ordinance and won after spending $2,000. He then built the crusher.

☐ **EXAMPLE 3:** Smalltown's zoning board established a restrictive building (setback) line across Rock's business property. The line lowered the property's value. Rock spent $3,000 trying unsuccessfully to challenge it.

Required:

Indicate whether each example should be deemed (a) a revenue expenditure or (b) a capital expenditure. Briefly explain your answer.

8–61. **RENTAL CARS.** A recent annual report of the Hertz rental car company contained the following footnote:

☐　　Depreciable assets—the provisions for depreciation and amortization are computed on a straight-line basis over the estimated useful lives of the respective assets. . . . Hertz follows the practice of charging maintenance and repairs, including the costs of minor replacements, to maintenance expense accounts. Costs of major replacement of units of property are charged to property and equipment accounts and depreciated. . . . Upon disposal of revenue earning equipment, depreciation expense is adjusted for the difference between the net proceeds from sale and the remaining book value.

Required:

1. Assume that some new cars are acquired on October 1, 1989, for $120 million. The useful life is one year. Expected residual values are $84 million. Prepare a summary journal entry for depreciation for 1989. The fiscal year ends on December 31.
2. Prepare a summary journal entry for depreciation for the first six months of 1990.
3. Assume that the automobiles are sold for $96 million cash on October 1, 1990. Prepare the journal entry for the sale. Automobiles are considered "revenue earning equipment."
4. What is the total depreciation expense for 1990? If the $96 million proceeds could exactly have been predicted when the cars were originally acquired, what would depreciation expense have been in 1989? In 1990? Explain.

8–62. **GAIN ON AIRPLANE CRASH.** In August 1988, a Delta Air Lines 727 crashed in Dallas. The crash resulted in a gain of $.11 per share for Delta. How could this happen? Consider the accounting for airplanes. Airlines insure their craft at market value, $6.5 million for Delta's 727. However, the planes' book values are often much less because of large accumulated depreciation amounts. The book value of Delta's 727 was only $962,000.

Required:

1. Suppose Delta received the insurance payment and immediately purchased another 727 for $6.5 million. Compute the effect of the crash on pretax income. Also compute the effect on Delta's total assets.
2. Do you think a casualty should generate a reported gain? Why?

8–63. **DISPOSAL OF EQUIPMENT.** *Airline Executive* reported on an airline as follows:

☐ Lufthansa's highly successful policy of rolling over entire fleets in roughly ten years— before the aircraft have outlived their usefulness—got started in a "spectacular" way when seven first-generation 747s were sold.

☐ The 747s were bought six to nine years earlier for $22–28 million each and sold for about the same price.

Required:

1. Assume an average original cost of $26 million each, an average original expected useful life of ten years, a $3.5 million expected residual value, and an average actual life of eight years before disposal. Use straight-line depreciation. Compute the total gain or loss on the sale of the seven planes.
2. Prepare a summary journal entry for the sale.

8–64. **BASKET PURCHASE AND INTANGIBLES.** A tax newsletter stated: "When a business is sold, part of the sales price may be allocated to a 'covenant not to compete' and another part to 'goodwill.' How this allocation is made can have important tax consequences to both the buyer and seller."

A large law firm, organized as a professional services corporation, purchased a successful local firm for $125,000. Only $25,000 was assigned to individual assets. The other $100,000 was for both a covenant not to compete for five years and goodwill. Suppose the buyer has legally supportable latitude concerning how to allocate this amount, as follows:

	ALLOCATION ONE	ALLOCATION TWO
Covenant	$ 65,000	$ 50,000
Goodwill	35,000	50,000
Total for two assets	$100,000	$100,000

Required:

1. For income tax purposes, which allocation would the buyer favor? Why?
2. For shareholder reporting purposes, which allocation would the buyer favor? Why?

8–65. **DEPRECIATION OF PROFESSIONAL SPORTS CONTRACTS.**   "Accounting Professor Says the Owners Lost $27 Million" read the headline on July 10, 1985. Major league baseball players and owners were engaged in contract negotiations. The owners claimed to have lost $43 million in 1984, and the Players Association maintained that the owners had made a profit of as much as $10 million. George Sorter, professor of accounting at New York University, fixed the loss at $27 million, primarily because he subtracted "initial roster depreciation" from the owners' figure. "That depreciation, an amount that arises when a team is sold and a portion of the purchase price that makes up player contracts is paid off [amortized] over several years, should not be treated as an operating expense," Sorter said. When a team is sold, an amount representing the value of current player contracts is put into an intangible asset account and amortized (or depreciated) over several years.

Required:

Explain why such an intangible asset account is created. Should this asset be amortized (or depreciated), thereby reducing income? Why would Professor Sorter eliminate this expense when assessing the financial operating performance of the major league teams?

8–66. **VALUATION OF INTANGIBLE ASSETS OF FOOTBALL TEAM.**   New owners acquired the Los Angeles Rams football team for $7.2 million. They valued the contracts of their forty players at a total of $3.5 million, the franchise at $3.6 million, and other assets at $100,000. For income tax purposes, the Rams amortized the $3.5 million over five years; therefore they took a tax deduction of $700,000 annually.

The Internal Revenue Service challenged the deductions. It maintained that only $300,000 of the $7.2 million purchase price was attributable to the player contracts, and that the $3.2 million of the $3.5 million in dispute should be attributed to the league franchise rights. Such franchise rights are regarded by the Internal Revenue Service as a valuable asset with an indefinite future life; therefore no amortization is permitted for tax-reporting purposes.

Suppose the operating income for each of the five years (before any amortization) was $1 million.

Required:

1. Consider the reporting to the Internal Revenue Service. Tabulate a comparison of annual operating income (after amortization) according to two approaches, (a) the Rams' and (b) the IRS's. What is the difference in annual operating income?
2. Consider the reporting to shareholders. Reports to shareholders by American companies do not have to adhere to the same basis used for income tax purposes. The Rams had been using a five-year life for player contracts and a forty-year life for the league franchise rights. Tabulate a comparison of operating income (after amortization) using (a) this initial approach and (b) the approach whereby only $300,000 would have been attributed to player contracts. What is the difference in annual operating income?
3. Comment on the results in requirements 1 and 2. Which alternative do you think provides the more informative report of operating results? Why?

8–67. **DEFERRED CHARGES.**   Simmons Airlines, Inc., is a Chicago-based regional carrier in the Midwest. Consider the following item under "Other assets" in its annual report:

	1987	1986
Deferred development costs, net of amortization (1987, $329,000; 1986, $285,000)	$385,000	$514,000

A footnote to the annual report stated: "Deferred development and preoperating costs: Costs related to the introduction of new types of aircraft are deferred and amortized over five years."

1. Suppose no new deferred development or preoperating costs were recorded during 1987. Calculate the amount of deferred development costs amortized during 1987.

2. Suppose Simmons received delivery of new Boeing 737s halfway through 1988 and incurred $42,000 of training costs associated with the introduction of the new aircraft. Show the journal entries for recording these costs (assume that payment was in cash) and for recognizing amortization at the end of the year.

8–68. ACQUISITION OF INTANGIBLE ASSETS. *Forbes* reported that CGA Computer Associates, a computer software marketer, had acquired another software company, Allen Services Corporation, for $19 million. CGA got only $1.2 million in net tangible assets.

The CGA president insisted that "the premium was justified because Allen had built up a huge inventory of software that was not reflected in the books. The reason: Spending on developing new software systems is treated as research and development and therefore written off immediately. In this case, CGA had to book $11.7 million of the $17.8 million discrepancy as software and the rest as goodwill."

The software would be amortized over its useful life, five years, because of the pace of developments in computers. Goodwill would be amortized over forty years.

Required: Compute the expenses for (1) amortization of software and (2) amortization of goodwill for the first complete year after the acquisition.

8–69. SOFTWARE DEVELOPMENT COSTS. Microsoft, Incorporated, is one of the largest producers of software for personal computers. In 1988 one of its divisions began working on some special business applications software for Apple MacIntosh computers. Suppose $400,000 had been spent on the project by the end of the year, but it was not yet clear whether the software was technologically feasible.

On about July 1, 1989, after spending another $200,000, management decided that the software was technologically feasible. During the second half of 1989, the division spent another $500,000 on this project. In December 1989 the product was announced, with deliveries to begin in March 1990. No research and development costs for the software were incurred after December 1990. Projected sales were: 1990, $400,000; 1991, $700,000; 1992, $600,000; 1993, $200,000; and 1994, $100,000.

Required:
1. Prepare journal entries to account for the research and development expenses for the software for 1988 and 1989. Assume that all expenditures were paid in cash.

2. Would any research and development expenses affect income in 1990? If so, prepare the appropriate journal entry. Actual 1990 sales were $400,000.

8–70. DEPRECIATION PRACTICES. The 1988 annual report of General Mills, maker of Wheaties, Cheerios, and Betty Crocker baking products, contained the following (in millions):

	1988	1987
Total land, buildings and equipment	$2,139.0	$1,939.1
Less accumulated depreciation	(762.6)	(689.6)
Net land, buildings and equipment	$1,376.4	$1,249.5

During 1988, depreciation expense was $137.3 million, and General Mills acquired land, buildings, and equipment worth $426.7 million. Assume that no gain or loss arose from the disposition of land, buildings, and equipment and that cash of $162.5 million was received from such disposals.

Required: Compute (1) the gross amount of assets written off (sold or retired), (2) the amount of accumulated depreciation written off, and (3) the book value of the assets written off. *Hint:* The use of T-accounts may help your analysis.

8–71. **RECONSTRUCTION OF PLANT ASSET TRANSACTIONS.** (J. Patell, adapted). The Ford Motor Company's balance sheets included (in millions of dollars):

 Ford Motor Company

	DECEMBER 31	
	1987	1986
Property:		
Land, plant and equipment, at cost (Note 7)	25,079.4	22,991.8
Less accumulated depreciation	14,567.4	13,187.2
Net land, plant and equipment	10,512.0	9,804.6
Unamortized special tools	3,521.5	3,396.1
Net property	14,033.5	13,200.7

The following additional information was available from the income statement for 1987 (in millions):

Depreciation	$1,814.2
Amortization of special tools	1,353.2

The account Unamortized Special Tools is increased by new investments in tools, dies, jigs, and fixtures necessary for new models and production processes. These investments are then amortized over various periods of two to four years. Hence the account is called "unamortized" because its amount will become amortized during future periods.

Required:

Hint: Analyze with the help of T-accounts.

1. There were no disposals of special tools during 1987. Compute the cost of new acquisitions of special tools.

2. Suppose the proceeds from the sales of land, plant, and equipment during 1987 were $92 million, and the loss on sale of land, plant, and equipment was $25 million. Compute the original cost *and* the accumulated depreciation of the land, plant, and equipment that was sold.

3. Compute the cost of the new acquisitions of land, plant, and equipment.

8–72. **CHANGE IN SERVICE LIFE.** An annual report of TWA contained the following footnote:

☐ Note 2. *Change in accounting estimate.* TWA extended the estimated useful lives of Boeing 727-100 aircraft from principally sixteen years to principally twenty years. As a result, depreciation and amortization expense was decreased by $9,000,000.

The TWA annual report also contained the following data: depreciation, $235,518,000; net income, $42,233,000.

The cost of the 727-100 aircraft subject to depreciation was $800 million. Residual values were predicted as 10% of acquisition cost.

Required: Assume a combined federal and state income tax rate of 46% throughout all parts of these requirements.

1. Was the effect of the change in estimated useful life a material difference? Explain, including computations.
2. The same year's annual report of Delta Air Lines contained the following footnote:

   Depreciation—Substantially all of the flight equipment is being depreciated on a straight-line basis to residual values (10% of cost) over a 10-year period from dates placed in service.

   The Delta annual report also contained the following data: depreciation, $220,979,000; net income, $146,474,000. Suppose Delta had used a twenty-year life instead of a ten-year life. Assume a 46% applicable income tax rate. Compute the new depreciation and net income.
3. Suppose TWA had used a ten-year life instead of a twenty-year life on its 727-100 equipment. Compute the new depreciation and net income. For purposes of this requirement, assume that the equipment cost $800 million and has been in service one year and that reported net income based on a twenty-year life was $42,233,000.

8–73. **AVERAGE AGE OF ASSETS.** NYNEX, owner of New England Telephone and New York Telephone, had the following on its January 1, 1989, balance sheet (in millions):

Total depreciable property, plant and equipment	$27,833.0
Less: accumulated depreciation	9,462.8
	$18,370.2

A footnote states that "all [depreciation] rates are calculated on a straight-line basis." Annual depreciation expense is approximately $2,150 million.

Required:
1. Estimate the average useful life of NYNEX's depreciable assets.
2. Estimate the average age of NYNEX's depreciable assets on January 1, 1989.

8–74. **HOUSE OF FABRICS ANNUAL REPORT.** (Alternates are 8–3, 8–10, and 8–11.) Refer to the financial statements of House of Fabrics, pages 749–759. House of Fabrics uses straight-line depreciation for all assets, as explained in Note 1, page 756. Depreciation and amortization expense was $6,286,000 in fiscal 1989. For purposes of this problem, assume that all revenues and expenses, except depreciation and amortization, are for cash. Therefore cash expenses for fiscal 1989 were $312,884,000.

Required:
1. Suppose House of Fabrics had used DDB instead of straight-line depreciation, and therefore depreciation and amortization expense was $8,286,000 instead of $6,286,000. Assume zero income taxes. Fill in the blanks in the accompanying table (in thousands of dollars).
2. Repeat requirement 1, but assume an income tax rate of 39.7%. Assume also that House of Fabrics uses the same depreciation method for reporting to shareholders and to the IRS.
3. Compare your answers to requirements 1 and 2. Does depreciation provide cash? Explain as precisely as possible.

House of Fabrics
(amounts in thousands)

	1. ZERO INCOME TAXES		2. 39.7% INCOME TAXES	
	Straight-line Depreciation	Accelerated Depreciation	Straight-line Depreciation	Accelerated Depreciation
Sales	$	$	$	$
Cash expenses				
Cash provided before income taxes				
Depreciation expense				
Income before income taxes				
Income taxes				
Net income	$	$	$	$
Supplementary analysis:				
Cash provided before income taxes				
Income taxes	$	$	$	$
Net cash provided	$	$	$	$

CHAPTER 9

Liabilities
and Interest

LEARNING
OBJECTIVES

After studying this chapter, you should be able to

1. Explain the nature and presentation of various liabilities, including payables, product warranties, and contingent liabilities

2. Make the accounting entries for bonds payable and describe their effects on financial statements

3. Compute effective-interest amortization and explain imputed interest

4. Explain compound interest and the use of present value tables (Appendix 9A)

5. Describe how to account for payroll (Appendix 9B)

6. Make the computations and accounting entries for leases and pensions (Appendix 9C)

This chapter discusses liabilities in more detail than in earlier presentations. The roles of interest and bonds are given particular attention.

An overview of liabilities is followed by sections on current liabilities and long-term liabilities. These sections are mainly descriptive. The next two sections, "Accounting for Bond Transactions" and "Non-Interest-Bearing Instruments," require thorough knowledge of compound interest fundamentals, which are presented in Appendix 9A. Additional appendixes present details on payroll accounting (Appendix 9B) and accounting for leases and pensions (Appendix 9C).

LIABILITIES IN PERSPECTIVE

The accounting literature contains many controversial discussions about when a resource qualifies as an asset, or an obligation as a liability. For introductory purposes, *liability* can be defined as a recognized obligation to pay money or to provide goods or services. Ordinarily, the obligation arises from some transaction with an "outside party" such as a supplier, a lending institution, or an employee. However, obligations also arise from the imposition of taxes or the loss of a lawsuit.

Current liabilities are obligations that fall due within the coming year or within the normal operating cycle if longer than a year. *Accounts payable* are amounts owed to suppliers who extended credit for purchases on open account. These open account purchases from trade creditors are ordinarily supported by signatures on purchase orders or similar business documents. *Notes payable* are backed by formal promissory notes held by a bank or business creditors.

As explained in earlier chapters, the accrual basis of accounting recognizes expenses as they pertain to the operations of a given time period regardless of when they are paid for in cash. A report to shareholders may combine liabilities for wages, salaries, commissions, interest, and similar items and show them as a single liability labeled as *accrued liabilities* or *accrued expenses payable*. However, each accrued expense liability is listed individually if its magnitude warrants a separate classification. For example, the liability for accrued income taxes payable is usually displayed separately.

Sometimes the adjective "accrued" is deleted, so that these liabilities are labeled simply as taxes payable, wages payable, and so on. Similarly, the term "accrued" may be used and "payable" deleted.

The real-life example of a presentation of liabilities, shown in Exhibit 9–1, is from the 1988 annual report of Mattel, Inc., maker of Barbie dolls, Hot Wheels, and other toys.

Long-term liabilities are obligations that fall due beyond one year from the balance sheet date. As the Mattel presentation illustrates, long-term debt is

EXHIBIT 9–1

MATTEL, INC.
Liabilities Section of Balance Sheet
(in thousands)

	DECEMBER 31	
	1988	1987
Current liabilities:		
Notes payable to foreign banks	$ 9,588	$105,670
Current portion of long-term liabilities	1,783	3,853
Accounts payable	73,853	68,255
Accrued liabilities	123,218	144,905
Income taxes payable	7,657	—
Total current liabilities	216,099	322,683
Long-term liabilities	283,898	284,852
Total liabilities	$499,997	$607,535

frequently payable in installments. The current portion is included as a part of current liabilities.

The journal entry for recognizing the current portion of long-term debt reclassifies a noncurrent liability as a current liability. Using the Mattel illustration (in thousands):

Long-term debt	1,783	
Current maturities of long-term debt		1,783

Conceptually, a liability is best measured as the amount of cash to be paid in the future discounted to the present time. The discounted amount is the sum that, if invested immediately, would provide enough cash, including interest, to pay off the obligation. This discounting, which is explained in Appendix 9A, is rarely done to measure current liabilities, but it is often done for obligations that are due beyond one year. Exceptions to the preceding sentence will be noted as various liabilities are discussed in more detail.

CURRENT LIABILITIES

Mattel lists five current liabilities in Exhibit 9–1: accounts payable, notes payable, accrued liabilities, income taxes payable, and current portion of long-term debt. Each will be described in this section. In addition, four other current liabilities will be discussed: sales taxes payable, product warranties, returnable deposits, and unearned revenue.

☐ Accounts Payable

As defined in Chapter 1 (page 12), *accounts payable* (or **trade accounts payable**) are obligations resulting from purchasing goods and services on credit. They are amounts owed to suppliers. Disbursements for accounts payable tend to be voluminous and repetitive. Therefore special data-processing and internal control systems are usually designed for these transactions. See Chapter 14, Appendix 14B, for a description of such a system.

Over 90% of major companies show accounts payable as a separate line under current liabilities on their balance sheet. However, a few combine accounts payable with accrued liabilities.

☐ Notes Payable

Obligations represented by a promissory note are called *notes payable*. A **promissory note** is a written promise to repay principal plus interest at specific future dates. Most notes are payable to banks. Some companies, such as Mattel, show the payee in the account title.

Only notes that are payable within the next year are shown as current liabilities; others are long-term liabilities. Some companies combine notes payable with other short-term obligations in a single account. For example, Chevron includes the current portion of long-term debt with notes payable in an account called *short-term debt*. Pfizer, a pharmaceutical company, calls a similar account *short-term borrowings*.

Notes payable often result from **lines of credit,** which are agreements with a bank to automatically provide short-term loans up to some preestablished maximum. Because of the seasonality of its business, Mattel has lines of credit totaling $335 million.

☐ Accrued Liabilities

The accrual process is described in Chapter 4, pages 126–129. Expenses that have been recognized on the income statement but not yet paid are *accrued liabilities*.

Employee-related liabilities account for a large part of most companies' accrued liabilities. In fact, a majority of companies have a separate current-liability account for such items, with a label such as *salaries, wages, payrolls, and commissions payable* or *compensation and benefits payable.*

Earlier chapters have described the payments to employees in an elementary way. Our implied assumption has been the condition that actually existed years ago when an employee earned, say, $100 per week and, in turn, received $100 in cash on payday. The bookkeeping problems for payroll were relatively straightforward. Only two parties were involved, the employer and the employee.

These days the complexities of payroll accounting are awesome. First, employers must *withhold* some employee earnings and pay them instead to the government, insurance companies, labor unions, charitable organizations, and so forth. For example, consider the withholding of income taxes and social security taxes (also called FICA taxes, for *Federal Insurance Compensation Act*). Assume a $100,000 monthly payroll and, for simplicity, assume that the only amounts withheld are $15,000 for income taxes and $7,000 for social security taxes. Three current liability accounts must be created:

Salaries and wages payable to employees	$ 78,000
Income tax withholding payable to the government	15,000
Social security withholding payable to the government	7,000
Total compensation liability	$100,000

Note that withholdings are not additional employer costs. They simply recognize that part of the wages and salaries are paid to third parties, not directly to employees.

The journal entry for this $100,000 payroll is:

Compensation expense	100,000	
Salaries and wages payable		78,000
Income tax withholding payable		15,000
Social security withholding payable		7,000

A second complication is the existence of payroll taxes and fringe benefits. These are employee-related costs *in addition* to salaries and wages. *Payroll taxes* are amounts paid to the government for items such as the employer's portion of social security, federal and state unemployment taxes, and workers' compensation taxes. *Fringe benefits* include employee pensions, life and health insurance, and vacation pay. Liabilities are accrued for each of these costs. If they have not yet been paid at the balance sheet date, they are included among the current liabilities.

More details on payroll accounting are in Appendix 9B, pages 408–411.

☐ Income Taxes Payable

A corporation must pay a tax on its earnings. (To review the basic accounting for income taxes, see transactions *i* (page 169) and *t* (page 172) in Chapter 5.) Like individuals, corporations pay income taxes throughout the year rather than paying a lump sum at the end of each year. Corporations make periodic installment payments based on their estimated tax for the year. Therefore the accrued liability for income taxes is generally much smaller than the annual income tax expense.

To illustrate, suppose a corporation has an estimated taxable income of $100 million for the calendar year 19X0. At a 40% tax rate, the company's estimated taxes for the year would be $40 million. Payments must be made as follows:

	APRIL 15	JUNE 15	SEPTEMBER 15	DECEMBER 15
Estimated taxes (in millions)	$10	$10	$10	$10

The final income tax return and payment date is March 15, 19X1. Suppose the actual taxable income is $110 million instead of the estimated $100 million. On March 15, the corporation must pay the $4 million additional tax on the additional $10 million of taxable income. The accrued liability on December 31, 19X0, would be:

Income taxes payable	$4,000,000

For simplicity, the illustration assumed equal quarterly payments. However, the estimated taxable income for a calendar year may change as the year unfolds. The corporation must change its quarterly payments accordingly. Although reasonably accurate estimates are typical, there will nearly always be a relatively small tax payment or refund due on March 15.

Current Portion of Long-Term Debt

A company's long-term debt often includes some payments due within a year. Such payments should be reclassified as current liabilities. For example, interest payments are often made semiannually. Therefore two interest payments would fall within the next year. Furthermore, at some time the repayment of the original amount borrowed will be less than a year away.

The journal entry for recognizing the current portion of long-term debt reclassifies a noncurrent liability as a current liability. Using the Mattel illustration in Exhibit 9–1, the reclassification journal entry for 1988 would be:

Long-term debt	1,783,000	
Current portion of long-term debt		1,783,000

Sales Taxes

When retailers collect sales taxes, they are agents of the state or local government. For example, suppose a 7% sales tax is levied on sales of $10,000. The total collected from the customer must be $10,000 + $700, or $10,700. The impact on the entity is:

	A	=	L	+	SE
	+10,700 [Increase Cash or Accounts Receivable]	=	+700 [Increase Sales Tax Payable]		+10,000 [Increase Sales]

The sales tax payable appears on the balance sheet as a liability until the taxes are paid to the government. The sales shown on the income statement would be $10,000, not $10,700.

When the sales taxes are paid at a later date:

	A	=	L	+ SE
	−700 [Decrease Cash]	=	−700 [Decrease Sales Tax Payable]	

The journal entries (without explanations) are:

Cash or accounts receivable	10,700	
Sales		10,000
Sales tax payable		700
Sales tax payable	700	
Cash		700

□ Product Warranties

Some liabilities are not measured with the same degree of certainty as the previous examples. A noteworthy example is the liability arising from product guarantees and warranties. If warranty obligations are material, they must be accrued when products are sold because the obligation arises then, not when the actual services are performed. General Motors describes its accounting as follows: "Provisions for estimated costs related to product warranties are made at the time the products are sold."

The estimated warranty expenses are typically based on past experience for replacing defective products or remedying the defects of products. Although the estimates should be close, they are bound to be inaccurate. Therefore any differences between the estimated and actual results are usually added to or subtracted from the current warranty expense account as additional information unfolds. The accounting entry at the time of sale is:

Warranty expense	600,000	
Liability for warranties (or some similar title)		600,000
To record the estimated liability for warranties arising from current sales. The provision is 3% of current sales of $20 million, or $600,000.		

When a warranty claim arises, an entry such as the following is made:

```
Liability for warranties                          1,000
     Cash, accounts payable, accrued
        wages payable, and similar
        accounts                                          1,000
     To record the acquisition of supplies,
     outside services, and employee
     services to satisfy claims for repairs.
```

If the estimate for warranty expense is accurate, the entries for all claims will total about $600,000.

☐ Returnable Deposits

Customers occasionally make money deposits that are to be returned in full, sometimes plus interest and sometimes not. Companies that receive these deposits view them as a form of payable, although the word "payable" may not be a part of their specific labeling.

The most notable deposits are those with banks and similar financial institutions. Savings deposits bear explicit interest, but many commercial checking deposits do not. Deposits take many forms. For instance, when American Express sells traveler's checks, it records "Traveler's Checks Outstanding," essentially an interest-free deposit.

Other examples of deposits include those for returnable containers such as soft-drink bottles, oil drums, or beer kegs. Moreover, many lessors (landlords) require damage deposits that are to be returned in full if specified conditions are met by their lessees (tenants).

The accounting entries by the recipients of deposits have the following basic pattern (numbers assumed in thousands of dollars):

	INTEREST BEARING		NON-INTEREST BEARING	
1. Deposit	Cash	100	Cash	100
	Deposits (payable)	100	Deposits (payable)	100
2. Interest recognized	Interest expense	9	No entry	
	Deposits	9		
3. Deposit returned	Deposits	109	Deposits	100
	Cash	109	Cash	100

The account "Deposits" is a liability of the company receiving the deposit. Ordinarily the recipient of the cash deposit may use the cash for investment purposes from the date of deposit to the date of its return to the depositor. For example, banks lend the cash to others to earn interest revenue.

☐ Unearned Revenue

Chapter 4 explained that revenue collected in advance was fundamentally a liability (usually a current liability). The seller either must deliver the product or service or is obligated to make a full refund. Examples include lease rentals, magazine subscriptions, insurance premiums, advance airline or theater ticket sales, and advance repair service contracts.

The accounting entries follow (in dollars):

Cash or accounts receivable	100,000	
Unearned sales revenue		100,000
To record advance collections from customers.		
Unearned sales revenue	100,000	
Sales		100,000
To record sales revenue when products are delivered to customers who paid in advance.		

Unearned revenues are also called *revenues collected in advance*. A more specific title may also be used. For example, Dow Jones & Company lists "Unexpired subscriptions," and Wang Laboratories shows "Unearned service revenue."[1]

LONG-TERM LIABILITIES

How do accountants measure the value of obligations that are not due for at least a year? Such measurement must recognize the "time value of money." A dollar to be paid (or received) in the future is not worth as much as a dollar today. For example, suppose a company owes $105, due in one year. It can put $100 in a savings account that pays 5% interest. In one year, the original $100 plus the $5 interest earned can be used to pay the $105 obligation. Satisfying the $105 obligation took only 100 of today's dollars. Therefore a current balance sheet should include an obligation of $100, not $105.

To understand the accounting for long-term liabilities, you need to understand the principles of *compound interest* and related terms such as *future value* and *present value*. If you do not already have a thorough understanding of these items, carefully study Appendix 9A before reading further. You can test your understanding by solving Summary Problems Four and Five on pages 407–408.

☐ Nature of Long-Term Liabilities

Long-term liabilities are recorded at the present value of all future payments, discounted at the market interest rate in effect when the liability was incurred.

---

[1] These advance collections are frequently referred to as *deferred credits*. Why? Because, as the second entry shows, the ultimate accounting entry is a "credit" to revenue, but such an entry has been deferred to a later accounting period.

EXHIBIT 9–2

Analysis of Car Loan

Year	(1) Beginning Liability	(2) Interest @ 10% (1) × .10	(3) End-of-Year Cash Payment	(4) Reduction of Principal (3) − (2)	(5) Ending Liability (1) − (4)
19X0	$10,000.00	$1,000.00	$3,154.71	$2,154.71	$7,845.29
19X1	7,845.29	784.53	3,154.71	2,370.18	5,475.11
19X2	5,475.11	547.51	3,154.71	2,607.20	2,867.91
19X3	2,867.91	286.79	3,154.71	2,867.92	−.01*

* Rounding error; should be 0.

Consider a loan for a new car. Michelle Young graduated from college and wishes to buy a $14,000 car on January 1, 19X0. She has only $4,000 cash. She borrows $10,000 at 10% interest, agreeing to pay $3,154.71 each December 31 from 19X0 through 19X3. (Normally payments would be made monthly, but for simplicity we assume annual payments.) The loan is illustrated in Exhibit 9–2.

Michelle's total payments are 4 × $3,154.71 = $12,618.84. However, the *present value* of the payments at 10% is only 3.1699 × $3,154.67 = $10,000. (The 3.1699 factor is from the 4-year row and 10% column of Table 3, page 406). What is the proper measure of her liability at January 1, 19X0? It is $10,000, the *present value* of the future payments, not the *total* of those payments.

Several types of obligations are classified as long-term liabilities. Notes and bonds are most common. Corporations issue notes when money is borrowed from a few sources. These issues are known as **private placements** because they are not held or traded among the general public. Instead the creditors are financial institutions such as insurance companies or pension funds. Private placements provide over half the capital borrowed by corporations in the United States.

Corporations have heavy demands for borrowed capital, so they often borrow from the general public by issuing bonds. **Bonds** are formal certificates of indebtedness that are typically accompanied by (1) a promise to pay interest in cash at a specified annual rate (often called the **nominal interest rate, contractual rate, coupon rate,** or **stated rate**) plus (2) a promise to pay the principal (often called the **face amount** or **par amount**) at a specific maturity date. The interest is usually paid every six months. Fundamentally, bonds are individual promissory notes issued to many lenders. Bonds are described in detail in the succeeding sections of this chapter.

Pension and lease obligations are also long-term liabilities. They have been controversial topics among accountants. The FASB has decided that both are appropriately listed as liabilities and has provided specific rules for their measurement. Pensions and leases are discussed in Appendix 9C.

Almost every company has a liability for deferred income taxes. This important liability is described in Chapter 13, pages 589–597. It is the prime example of a long-term liability that is not discounted. Accountants measure the total tax payments that have been deferred, not their present values.

☐ Mortgage Bonds and Debentures

A common type of bond is a **mortgage bond,** which is secured by the pledge of specific property. In case of default, the bondholders can sell the property to satisfy their claims. Moreover, the holders of mortgage bonds have a further unsecured claim on the corporation if the proceeds from the pledged property are insufficient.

If no lien exists against specific assets, the bond is called a **debenture.** The holders thereof have no special claims against the assets beyond their general claim against the *total* assets, a claim shared with other general creditors such as trade creditors. **Subordinated debentures** means that such bondholders are junior to the other general creditors in exercising claims against the total assets. If debentures were **unsubordinated,** the holders would have the same priority as holders of accounts payable.

The following simplified example should clarify these ideas. Suppose a company is liquidated. *Liquidation* means converting assets to cash and terminating outside claims. The company had a single asset, a building, that was sold for $110,000 cash. The balance sheet immediately after liquidation is:

ASSETS		EQUITIES	
Cash	$110,000	Accounts payable	$ 50,000
		First-mortgage bonds payable	80,000
		Subordinated debentures payable	40,000
		Total liabilities	$170,000
		Stockholders' equity (negative)	(60,000)
Total assets	$110,000	Total equities	$110,000

The mortgage bondholders would be paid in full ($80,000). The trade creditors would be paid the remaining $30,000 for their $50,000 claim ($.60 on the dollar). The other claimants would get nothing. If the debentures were *unsubordinated,* the $30,000 of cash remaining after paying $80,000 to the mortgage holders would be used to settle the $90,000 claims of the unsecured creditors as follows:

To trade creditors	$\frac{5}{9} \times \$30,000 =$	$16,667
To debenture holders	$\frac{4}{9} \times \$30,000 =$	13,333
Total cash distributed		$30,000

A *mortgage bond,* which has a specific lien on particular assets, is an inherently safer investment than the same company's *debentures,* which have no specific lien on any asset. However, the relative attractiveness of specific bonds depends *primarily* on the credit-worthiness of the issuer. Thus IBM can issue billions of dollars of debentures at relatively low interest rates when compared with the mortgage bonds that might be issued by real estate companies.

☐ Bond Provisions

Bonds typically have a par value of $1,000, but they are quoted in terms of *percentages of par*. Some bonds are traded on the New York Stock Exchange. A quotation for the Aluminum Company of America (Alcoa) follows:

DESCRIPTION	CURRENT YIELD	VOLUME	HIGH	LOW	CLOSE	NET CHANGE
Alcoa 9s95	8.9	5	101¾*	101½	101½	−½

* The price of one $1,000 bond is 101¾, or 1.0175 × $1,000 = $1,017.50.

Alcoa's bonds carrying a 9% coupon rate and maturing in 1995 traded at a high of $1,017.50 and closed at their low price of $1,015.00 (101½% of $1,000) at the end of the day. The **current yield,** based on the closing price, was 9/101.5, or 8.9%. Five bonds were traded, each having a face or par value of $1,000. The closing price was down one-half from that of the previous day. Therefore the preceding closing price must have been 101½ + ½ = 102, or $1,020 per bond.

An issue of bonds is usually accompanied by a **trust indenture** whereby the issuing corporation promises a *trustee* (usually a bank or trust company) that it will abide by stated provisions, often called **protective covenants** or simply **covenants.** The indenture is designed primarily to protect the safety of the bond-holders. The provisions pertain to payments of principal and interest, sales of pledged property, restrictions on dividends, and like matters. The trustee's major function is to represent the collective claims and concerns of the bondholders.

For example, MacMillan Bloedel, the large forest products company, in-dicated in a recent annual report that *"trust indentures* securing the company's debentures contain provisions limiting the amount of indebtedness the company can incur." Gordon Jewelry Corporation, a major jewelry company listed on the New York Stock Exchange, mentioned many constraints in its 1988 annual report: "The note agreement contains restrictive *covenants* regarding the nature of the business, liabilities, financial ratios, indebtedness, liens, investments, leases, company stock, mergers, and dispositions."

Bonds issued by American industrial corporations are normally **registered instruments,** which means that the interest and maturity payments are made to a specific owner. In contrast, bonds issued before 1983 by American governmental bodies such as municipalities are normally **unregistered** or **bearer instruments,** which means that the interest is paid to the individual who presents the interest *coupons* attached to the bond. Similarly, the principal is paid to the individual who presents the bond at the maturity date. Bearer instruments are like cash; they are more vulnerable to theft than are registered bonds.

☐ Callable, Sinking Fund, and Convertible Bonds

Some bonds are **callable,** which means that they are subject to redemption before maturity at the option of the issuer. The issuer typically provides for a prede-termined **call premium** (a redemption price in excess of par). The call premium declines as maturity comes closer. Thus a bond issued in 1975 with a 1995 maturity date may not be callable until 1990. Then it may be subject to call for an initial price in 1990 of 105 (105% of par), in 1991 of 104, in 1992 of 103, and so on. The call premium in 1990 would be $50 per $1,000 bond; $40 in 1991; $30 in 1992; and so on.

Sinking fund bonds are those with indentures that require the issuer to make annual payments into a sinking fund. A **sinking fund** is cash or securities segregated for meeting obligations on bonded debt. It is an asset that is usually classified as part of an asset category called "investments" or "other assets." This helps assure the bondholders that sufficient cash will be accumulated to repay the principal at maturity.

Convertible bonds are those bonds that may, at the holder's option, be exchanged for other securities. The conversion is usually for a predetermined number of common shares of the issuing company. Because of the conversion feature, convertible bondholders are willing to accept a lower interest rate than on a similar bond without the conversion privilege.

Most companies have an assortment of long-term debt, including a variety of bonds payable.[2] The body of the balance sheet usually summarizes such debt on one line. In contrast, the details in the footnotes can occupy an entire page.

ACCOUNTING FOR BOND TRANSACTIONS

☐ **Market Valuation of Bonds**

Bonds are typically sold through a syndicate (special group) of investment bankers called **underwriters.** That is, the syndicate buys the entire issue from the corporation, thus guaranteeing that the company will obtain all of its desired funds. In turn, the syndicate sells the bonds to the general investing public.

A company's board of directors sets the stated or nominal interest rate. The investment banker who manages the underwriting syndicate provides advice. The nominal rate is usually set as close to the current market rate as possible. Many factors affect this rate, notably general economic conditions, industry conditions, risks of the use of the proceeds, and specific features of the bonds (examples include callability, sinking fund, convertibility). On the day of issuance, the proceeds to the issuer may be above par or below par, depending on market conditions.[3] If above par, there is a **premium;** if below par, a **discount.** Therefore the **effective interest rate (market rate, real rate, yield rate, true rate)** frequently differs from the *nominal interest rate.* The interest paid in cash, usually semiannually, is determined by the nominal rate, not the effective rate.

---

[2] There are many types of bonds, too many to discuss exhaustively here. Textbooks on corporate finance contain detailed descriptions.

[3] The interest rate is often established at the last possible minute so that bonds may be issued exactly at par. The highest-quality corporate issues, such as IBM's notes and debentures, are usually priced as close as possible to their U.S. Treasury and corporate equivalents. A spread of one-quarter of one percent above the Treasuries in yield is a customary standard. Thus, if Treasuries of comparable maturities are yielding 10.50%, IBM's new issue would yield 10.75%.

EXHIBIT 9–3

Computation of Market Value of Bonds (in dollars)

	PRESENT VALUE FACTOR	TOTAL PRESENT VALUE	SKETCH OF CASH FLOWS				
			0	1	2	3	4
Valuation at 10% per year, or 5% per half-year:							
Principal, 4-period line, Table 2 .8227 × $1,000 = $822.70	.8227	822.70					1,000
Interest, 4-period line, Table 3 3.5460 × $50 = $177.30	3.5460	177.30		50	50	50	50
Total		1,000.00					
Valuation at 12% per year, or 6% per half-year:							
Principal	.7921	792.10					1,000
Interest	3.4651	173.25		50	50	50	50
Total		965.35					
Valuation at 8% per year, or 4% per half-year:							
Principal	.8548	854.80					1,000
Interest	3.6299	181.50		50	50	50	50
Total		1,036.30					

Note that bonds issued at a discount do not mean that the credit-worthiness of the issuer is especially bad, nor do bonds issued at a premium mean that credit-worthiness is especially good. Discounts and premiums are determined by market forces that fluctuate from day to day and by the choice of the nominal rate of interest, relative to the then-current market rate of interest for bonds of similar risk.

A typical bond consists of a promise to pay interest every six months until maturity and a promise to pay a lump sum at maturity. Suppose a two-year $1,000 bond is issued that bears a nominal interest rate of 10%. Consider how the investor would value the bond, using the tables on pages 404–406.

Exhibit 9–3 shows how the bond would be valued, using three different interest rates. Note the following about Exhibit 9–3:

1. The quoted bond rates imply a rate per annum, but the bond markets do not mean that rate literally. Thus a 10% bond really pays 5% interest each semiannual period. A two-year bond has four periods, a ten-year bond has twenty periods, and so on.
2. Consider the valuation using 10%. Uninformed investors think that the $1,000 liability represents the face amount and that the interest liability does not have any value when the bonds are issued. They are mistaken because the simple name "bonds payable" is deceptive. A more accurate statement of liability would be:

Present value of $1,000 to be paid at the end of two years, $1,000 × .8227	$ 822.70
Present value of $50 to be paid at the end of each of four semiannual periods, $50 × 3.5460	177.30
Total present value of liability	$1,000.00

3. The *higher* the effective (or market) rate of interest, the *lower* the present value.

4. If the market interest rate were 10%, proceeds from issuing the bond would be $1,000. We say such a bond is issued *at par*. If the market rate were 12%, proceeds would only be $965.35, and the bond would be issued at a *discount* of $1,000.00 − $965.35 = $34.65. Finally, if the market rate were 8%, proceeds to the issuer would be $1,036.30, and the bond would be issued at a *premium* of $1,036.30 − $1,000.00 = $36.30.

☐ Accounting for Bonds Issued at Par

Suppose that on December 31, 1989, a company issued 10,000 two-year, 10% debentures, at par. Therefore the proceeds were equal to the face amount of 10,000 × $1,000 = $10 million. Exhibit 9–4 shows how the issuer would account for the bonds throughout their life, assuming that they are held to maturity. Because the bonds were issued at par, the interest expense equals the amount of the interest payments, 5% × $10 million = $500,000 each six months. The interest expense and the cash payments for interest each totals $2,000,000 over the four semiannual periods. The journal entries for the issue follow:

1.	Cash	10,000,000	
	Bonds payable		10,000,000
	To record proceeds upon issuance of 10% bonds maturing on December 31, 1991.		
2.	Interest expense	500,000	
	Cash		500,000
	To record payment of interest each six-month period.		
3.	Bonds payable	10,000,000	
	Cash		10,000,000
	To record payment of maturity value of bonds and their retirement.		

The balance sheet at December 31, 1989, and December 31, 1990 (just after paying the semiannual interest) would show:

Bonds payable, 10% due December 31, 1991	$10,000,000

EXHIBIT 9–4

Analysis of Bond Transactions: Issued at Par
(in thousands of dollars)

	A	=	L	+	SE
			Bonds		Retained Income
	Cash		Payable		
Issuer's records					
1. Issuance	+10,000	=	+10,000		
2. Semiannual interest					⎡Increase⎤
(repeated twice a					⎢Interest⎥
year for two years)	− 500	=			− 500 ⎣Expense⎦
3. Maturity value					
(final payment)	−10,000	=	−10,000		
Bond-related					
totals	− 2,000		0		−2,000

Accounting for Bonds Issued at a Discount

Suppose the 10,000 bonds described in the preceding section were issued when annual market interest rates were 12%. Proceeds would be 10,000 × $965.35 = $9,653,500, which reflects an effective interest rate of 6% per semiannual period, as shown in Exhibit 9–3. Therefore a discount of $10,000,000 − $9,653,500 = $346,500 was recognized at issuance. The discount is the excess of the face amount over the proceeds. The company has use of only $9,653,500, not $10,000,000. The journal entry at issue is:

Cash	9,653,500	
Discount on bonds payable	346,500	
Bonds payable		10,000,000

The discount on bonds payable is a contra account. It is deducted from bonds payable. The bonds payable account always shows the face amount, and the difference between bonds payable and discount on bonds payable is the net carrying amount or net liability:

ISSUER'S BALANCE SHEET	DECEMBER 31, 1989
Bonds payable, 10% due December 31, 1991	$10,000,000
Deduct: Discount on bonds payable	346,500
Net liability	$ 9,653,500

For bonds issued at a discount, interest takes two forms, semiannual cash outlays of 5% × $10 million = $500,000 plus an extra lump-sum cash payment of $346,500 at maturity (total payment of $10,000,000 at maturity when only $9,653,500 was actually borrowed). The extra $346,500 is another cost of using the proceeds over the four semiannual periods. It should be spread over all four periods, not simply charged at maturity. The spreading of the discount over the life of the bonds is called **discount amortization.**

How much of the $346,500 should be amortized each semiannual period? A simple alternative is straight-line amortization:

Cash interest payment, .05 × $10,000,000	$500,000
Amortization of discount, $346,500 ÷ 4 periods	86,625
Total semiannual interest expense	$586,625

The discount is used as an adjustment of nominal interest to obtain the real interest. Notice that the amortization of bond discount increases the interest expense of the issuer. The following journal entry would be made each six months:

Interest expense	586,625	
Discount on bonds payable		86,625
Cash		500,000

The bond discount account decreases by $86,625 each period. Therefore the net bond liability increases. The balance sheet values just after each semiannual interest payment are:

ISSUER'S BALANCE SHEETS	12/31/89	6/30/90	12/31/90	6/30/91	12/31/91*
Bonds payable, 10% due 12/31/91	$10,000,000	$10,000,000	$10,000,000	$10,000,000	$10,000,000
Deduct: Discount on bonds payable	346,500	259,875	173,250	86,625	0
Net carrying amount	$ 9,653,500	$ 9,740,125	$ 9,826,750	$ 9,913,375	$10,000,000

* Before payment at maturity.

The straight-line amortization is simple, but it is conceptually flawed. Why? Because it implies a different effective interest rate each period:

FOR SIX MONTHS ENDED	BEGINNING NET CARRYING AMOUNT	INTEREST EXPENSE	IMPLIED INTEREST RATE*
6/30/90	$9,653,500	586,625	6.08%
12/31/90	9,740,125	586,625	6.02%
6/30/91	9,826,750	586,625	5.97%
12/31/91	9,913,375	586,625	5.92%

* $586,625 ÷ $9,653,500 = 6.08%; $586,625 ÷ $9,740,125 = 6.02%; etc.

An amortization method that uses a constant interest rate is **effective-interest amortization,** also called the **compound interest method.** The FASB requires its use for bond discounts and premiums. The key to effective-interest amortization is that each period bears an interest expense equal to the net liability (face amount less unamortized discount) multiplied by the market interest rate in effect when the bond was issued. The product is the *effective-interest amount.* The difference between the effective-interest amount and the nominal interest is the amount of discount amortized for the period.

Consider our example with a market rate of 12% (or 6% each semiannual period) when the bond was issued. The effective-interest amortization schedule is shown in Exhibit 9–5. Notice that the discount amortized is not the same amount each period, as in the straight-line method. However, the journal entries for amortization affect the same accounts, regardless of whether the straight-line or effective-interest method is used. For example, the journal entry on June 30, 1990, would be:

Bond interest expense (for effective interest)	579,207	
Discount on bonds payable (for amortization)		79,207
Cash (for nominal interest)		500,000
To record interest payment and bond amortization.		

Compare the amount of amortization over the four interest periods:

	METHOD OF AMORTIZATION	
Period	Effective-Interest (See Exhibit 9–5)	Straight-Line ($346,500 ÷ 4)
1	$ 79,207	$ 86,625
2	83,959	$ 86,625
3	88,997	$ 86,625
4	94,337	$ 86,625
Total	$346,500	$346,500

EXHIBIT 9–5

Effective-Interest Amortization of Bond Discount

For Six Months Ended	(1) Beginning Net Liability	(2) Effective Interest @ 6%*	(3) Nominal Interest @ 5%	(4) Discount Amortized (2) − (3)	ENDING LIABILITY		
					Face Amount	Unamortized Discount	Ending Net Liability
12/31/89	—	—	—	—	$10,000,000	$346,500	$ 9,653,500
6/30/90	$9,653,500	$579,207	$500,000	$79,207	$10,000,000	267,293†	9,732,707
12/31/90	9,732,707	583,959	500,000	83,959	$10,000,000	183,334	9,816,666
6/30/91	9,816,666	588,997	500,000	88,997	$10,000,000	94,337	9,905,663
12/31/91	9,905,663	594,337	500,000	94,337	$10,000,000	0	10,000,000

* To avoid rounding errors, an unrounded actual effective rate slightly under 6% was actually used.
† $346,500 − $79,207 = $267,293; $267,293 − $83,959 = $183,334; etc.

EXHIBIT 9–6

Effective-Interest Amortization of Bond Discount
Balance Sheet Equation: Discount Amortization
(rounded to thousands of dollars)

	A	=	L		+	SE
		Bonds	Discount on			
	Cash	Payable	Bonds Payable			Retained Income
Issuer's records:						
1. Issuance	+9,654	+10,000	−346 [Increase Discount]			
2. Semiannual interest Six months ended:						
6/30/90	−500		+79			−579 [Increase
12/31/90	−500		+84 [Decrease			−584 Interest
6/30/91	−500		+89 Discount]			−589 Expense]
12/31/91	−500		+94			−594
3. Maturity value (final payment)	−10,000	−10,000				
Bond-Related Totals	−2,346	0	0			−2,346

Journal entries: Discount Amortization
(without explanations)

1.	Cash		9,653,500	
	Discount on bonds payable		346,500	
	Bonds payable			10,000,000
2.	Interest expense		579,207	
	Discount on bonds payable			79,207
	Cash			500,000
	Interest expense		583,959	
	Discount on bonds payable			83,959
	Cash			500,000
	Interest expense		588,997	
	Discount on bonds payable			88,997
	Cash			500,000
	Interest expense		594,337	
	Discount on bonds payable			94,337
	Cash			500,000
3.	Bonds payable		10,000,000	
	Cash			10,000,000

Exhibit 9–6 shows the complete worksheet and journal entries for the effective-interest method of amortizing the bond discount. Be sure you understand this important exhibit before proceeding further.

☐ Accounting for Bonds Issued at a Premium

Accounting for bonds issued at a premium is not difficult after you have mastered bond discounts. The differences are:

1. The cash proceeds *exceed* the face amount.
2. The amount of the contra account "Premium on Bonds Payable" is *added to* the face amount to determine the net liability.
3. The amortization of bond premium *decreases* the interest expense.

To illustrate, suppose the 10,000 bonds described earlier were issued when annual market interest rates were 8% (and semiannual rates 4%). Proceeds would be 10,000 × $1,036.30 = $10,363,000, as shown in Exhibit 9–3. Exhibit 9–7 shows how the effective-interest method is applied to the bond premium. The key concept remains the same as for amortization of bond discount: The interest expense equals the net liability multiplied by the market interest rate in effect when the bond was issued. Balance sheets show that amortization of the bond premium reduces the net liability from $10,363,000 at issuance to the face value of $10,000,000 at maturity:

ISSUER'S BALANCE SHEETS	12/31/89	6/30/90	12/31/90	6/30/91	12/31/91*
Bonds payable, 10% due 12/31/91	$10,000,000	$10,000,000	$10,000,000	$10,000,000	$10,000,000
Add: Premium on bonds payable	363,000	277,517	188,615	96,157	0
Net carrying amount	$10,363,000	$10,277,517	$10,188,615	$10,096,157	$10,000,000

* Before payment at maturity.

Exhibit 9–8 shows the worksheet and journal entries for bond premiums.

☐ **Early Extinguishment**

Investors often dispose of bonds before maturity by selling them to other investors. Such a sale does not affect the issuer's books. However, the issuer may redeem *its own* bonds by purchases on the open market or by exercising its call

EXHIBIT 9–7

Effective-Interest Amortization of Bond Premium

For Six Months Ended	(1) Beginning Net Liability	(2) Effective Interest @ 4%*	(3) Nominal Interest @ 5%	(4) Premium Amortized (3) − (2)	ENDING LIABILITY Face Amount	Unamortized Premium	Ending Net Liability
12/31/89	—	—	—	—	$10,000,000	$363,000	$10,363,000
6/30/90	$10,363,000	$414,517	$500,000	$85,483	$10,000,000	277,517†	$10,277,517
12/31/90	10,277,517	411,098	500,000	88,902	$10,000,000	188,615	$10,188,615
6/30/91	10,188,615	407,542	500,000	92,458	$10,000,000	96,157	$10,096,157
12/31/91	10,096,157	403,843	500,000	96,157	$10,000,000	0	$10,000,000

* To avoid rounding errors, an unrounded actual effective rate slightly under 4% was actually used.
† $363,000 − $85,483 = $277,517; $277,517 − $88,902 = $188,615; etc.

EXHIBIT 9–8

Effective-Interest Amortization of Bond Premium
Balance Sheet Equation: Premium Amortization
(rounded to thousands of dollars)

	A	=	L	+	SE
	Cash	Bonds Payable	Premium on Bonds Payable		Retained Income
Issuer's records:					
1. Issuance	+10,363	+10,000	363 [Increase Premium]		
2. Semiannual interest Six months ended:					
6/30/90	−500		−85		−415 [Increase Interest Expense]
12/31/90	−500		−89 [Decrease Premium]		−411
6/30/91	−500		−92		−408
12/31/91	−500		−96		−404
3. Maturity value (final payment)	−10,000	−10,000			
Bond-Related Totals	−1,637	0	1*		−1,637

* Rounding error; should equal 0.

Journal entries: Premium Amortization
(without explanations)

1.	Cash	10,363,000	
	Premium on bonds payable		363,000
	Bonds payable		10,000,000
2.	Interest expense	414,517	
	Premium on bonds payable	85,483	
	Cash		500,000
	Interest expense	411,098	
	Premium on bonds payable	88,902	
	Cash		500,000
	Interest expense	407,542	
	Premium on bonds payable	92,458	
	Cash		500,000
	Interest expense	403,843	
	Premium on bonds payable	96,157	
	Cash		500,000
3.	Bonds payable	10,000,000	
	Cash		10,000,000

option. Gains or losses on these early extinguishments of debt are computed in the usual manner. That is, the difference between the cash paid and the net carrying amount of the bonds (face, less unamortized discount or plus unamortized premium) is the gain or loss.

Consider the bond issued at a discount and described in Exhibit 9–5, page 385. Suppose the issuer purchases all of its bonds on the open market for 96 on

December 31, 1990 (after all interest payments and amortization were recorded for 1990):

Carrying amount:		
Face or par value	$10,000,000	
Deduct: Unamortized discount on bonds*	183,334	$9,816,666
Cash required, 96% of $10,000,000		9,600,000
Difference, gain on early		
extinguishment of debt		$ 216,666

* See Exhibit 9–5, page 385. Of the original $346,500 discount, $79,207 + $83,959 = $163,166 has been amortized, leaving $183,334 of the discount unamortized.

Exhibit 9–9 presents an analysis of the transaction (rounded to thousands of dollars). The $216,666 gain on extinguishment of debt would be shown on an income statement below operating income as a separate classification called an extraordinary item.

The journal entry on December 31, 1990, is:

Bond payable	10,000,000	
Discount on bonds payable		183,334
Gain on early extinguishment of debt		216,666
Cash		9,600,000
To record open-market acquisition of		
entire issue of 10% bonds at 96.		

Bonds Sold between Interest Dates

Bond interest payments are typically made semiannually. Suppose the company in our example had its $10 million, 10% bonds printed and ready for issuance on December 31, 1989, but then market conditions delayed issuance of the bonds. On January 31, 1990, one month after the originally planned issuance date, the bonds were issued at par. The indenture requires the payment of $500,000 interest every six months, beginning June 30, 1990. Indeed, there may be interest coupons attached to the bonds that require such payment.

EXHIBIT 9–9

Analysis of Early Extinguishment of Debt on Issuer's Records
(in thousands of dollars)

	A	=	L	+	SE
	Cash	Bonds Payable	Discount on Bonds Payable		Retained Income
Redemption, December 31, 1990	−9,600	= −10,000	+183 [Decrease Discount]	+217	[Gain on Early Extinguishment]

When bonds are sold between interest dates, they command the market price *plus accrued interest*. Thus the market quotations you see for bonds *always* mean that the investor must pay an extra amount for any *unearned* interest to be received at the next interest payment date. In our example, the price to be paid is:

Market price of bonds at 100	$10,000,000
Accrued interest, .10 × $10,000,000 × $\frac{1}{12}$,	83,333
Market price plus accrued interest	$10,083,333

Note that the $500,000 interest payment due on June 30, 1990, is spread over the first six months of 1990 by the straight-line method, that is, with an equal amount to each month.

Exhibit 9–10 presents an analysis of these transactions (rounded to thousands of dollars). Note that the interest expense for the first half of 1990 is properly measured as $500,000 − $83,333 = $416,667, pertaining to only five months that the money was actually in use. The journal entries follow:

1/31/90	Cash	10,083,333	
	Bonds payable		10,000,000
	Accrued interest payable		83,333
6/30/90	Accrued interest payable	83,333	
	Interest expense	416,667	
	Cash		500,000

Obviously, the analysis of transactions can be made more complicated by combining the acquisitions of bonds between interest dates with discounts and premiums. However, these are mechanical details that do not involve any new accounting concepts.

EXHIBIT 9–10

Analysis of Bonds Sold between Interest Dates
(in thousands of dollars)

	A	=	L	+	SE	
	Cash		Bonds Payable	Accrued Interest Payable	Retained Income	
Issuance, 1/31/90	+ 10,083 =		+ 10,000	+ 83		
Interest payment, 6/30/90	− 500 =			− 83	− 417	⎡Increase⎤ Interest ⎣Expense⎦

NON-INTEREST-BEARING INSTRUMENTS

☐ Discounted Notes

Some notes and bonds do not bear explicit interest. Instead they contain a promise to pay a lump sum at a specified date. An example is *zero coupon bonds*. To call such notes *non-interest-bearing* is misleading. These instruments cannot be marketed at face value. The investor demands interest revenue. Therefore the investor pays less than the face value. The investor discounts the maturity value, using the market rate of interest for notes having similar terms and risks. The discount is amortized as interest over the life of the note.

Banks often discount both long-term and short-term notes when making loans. Consider a two-year, non-interest-bearing, $10,000 face-value note issued on December 31, 1989, when semiannual market interest rates were 5%. In exchange for a promise to pay $10,000 on December 31, 1991, the bank would provide the borrower with cash equal to the present value (PV) of the $10,000 payment:

☐ PV of $1.00 from Table 2, page 405, 5% column, 4-period row = .8277
☐ PV of $10,000 note = $10,000 × .8227 = $8,227

The note has no specific interest payments. However, there is **implicit interest** (or **imputed interest**), which is an interest expense that is not explicitly recognized in a loan agreement. The imputed interest amount is based on an **imputed interest rate,** which is the market rate that equates the proceeds with the present value of the loan payments.

In this example, the $10,000 payment on December 31, 1991, consists of $8,227 repayment of principal and $10,000 − $8,227 = $1,773 of imputed interest. At issue, the note would be shown on the balance sheet as follows:

Note payable, due December 31, 1991	$10,000
Deduct: Discount on note payable	1,773
Net liability	$8,227

Exhibit 9–11 shows how interest expense is recognized each semiannual period. Each amortization of discount decreases the discount account and increases the net carrying amount.

The appropriate journal entries follow:

12/31/89:	Cash	8,227	
	Discount on note payable	1,773	
	Note payable		10,000
6/30/90:	Interest expense	411	
	Discount on note payable		411
12/31/90:	Interest expense	432	
	Discount on note payable		432
6/30/91:	Interest expense	454	
	Discount on note payable		454
12/31/91:	Interest expense	476	
	Discount on note payable		476
	Note payable	10,000	
	Cash		10,000

CONTINGENT LIABILITIES

A **contingent liability** is *not* a liability. Instead it is a *potential* (possible) liability that depends on a *future* event arising out of a *past* transaction. Sometimes it has a definite amount. For instance, a company may guarantee the payment on a related company's note payable. This means that the guarantor will pay if, and only if, the primary borrower fails to pay. Such a note is the liability of the primary borrower, and the contingent liability of the guarantor.

More often, a contingent liability has an indefinite amount. A common example is a lawsuit. Many companies have lawsuits pending against them. These are possible obligations of indefinite amounts.

Some companies show contingent liabilities on the balance sheet. Most often they are listed after long-term liabilities but before stockholders' equity. Georgia-Pacific Corporation, the building products company, is an example (in millions):

EXHIBIT 9–11

Analysis of Transactions of Borrower, Discounted Notes

	A	=	L		+	SE
	Cash		Notes Payable	Discount on Notes Payable		Retained Income
Proceeds of loan	+8,227		+10,000	−1,773 [Increase Discount]		
Semiannual amortization						
Six months ended:						
6/30/1990				+411		−411 [Increase Interest Expense]
12/31/1990				+432 [Decrease Discount]		−432
6/30/1991				+454		−454
12/31/1991				+476		−476
Payment of note	−10,000		−10,000			
Bond-Related Totals	−1,773		0	0		−1,773

	1987	1986
Current liabilities	$ 996	$ 837
Other liabilities	2,194	1,712
Commitments and contingencies		
Stockholders' equity	2,680	2,452

In contrast, the Toro Company, maker of lawnmowers and other equipment, lists contingent liabilities after stockholders' equity (in thousands):

	1988	1987
Liabilities	$177,116	$159,473
Stockholders' equity	91,038	82,457
Commitments and contingencies liabilities (Notes 10 and 11)		

The presentations used by Georgia-Pacific and Toro are often called **short presentations.** That is, an item is described as being "short" when it is included in the body of a financial statement, but its amount (if any) is not shown on the face of the balance sheet. Inevitably, a short presentation is accompanied by an explanatory footnote. For example, Georgia-Pacific's footnote included:

☐ **Note 12. Commitments and Contingencies**

The Corporation is a party to various legal proceedings generally incidental to its business. Although the ultimate disposition of these proceedings is not presently determinable, management does not believe that adverse determinations in any or all of such proceedings would have a material adverse effect upon the financial condition of the Corporation.

Contingent liabilities do not have to be mentioned in the body of the balance sheet. Many companies merely reveal the contingencies in a footnote. Indeed, the International Business Machines Corporation, one of the world's most heavily sued corporations, revealed its contingent liabilities in a short supplementary note labeled as *litigation.*

The line between a contingent liability and a real liability is sometimes hard to draw. If an obligation is highly probable (likely to occur), it is no longer contingent even if its amount must be estimated. To illustrate, suppose that at the balance sheet date, a hospital has lost a court case for uninsured malpractice, but the amount of damages has not been set. A reasonable estimate is between $1.0 and $2.5 million. The hospital must recognize a loss and a liability for $1.0 million. Moreover, the possibility of an additional loss of $1.5 million must also be disclosed in a footnote.[4]

---

[4] At one point, the Manville Corporation's balance sheet showed stockholders' equity of $1.1 billion and *potential* liabilities of $2 billion from fifty-two thousand lawsuits regarding health damage from asbestos. Manville then successfully declared bankruptcy to protect itself from this contingent liability.

Although contingent liabilities are "iffy" and hard to measure, they are increasingly important in our litigation-happy society. As a result, fuller disclosure has occurred in corporate reports so investors can make informal judgments. Nevertheless, the investor often has little information that is concrete beyond a fair warning.

To recapitulate, there are definite liabilities of either definite amounts (accounts payable) or of estimated amounts (product warranties). There are also contingent liabilities of either definite amounts (guaranteeing a note) or estimated amounts (income tax dispute with IRS).

DEBT-TO-EQUITY RATIOS

Many ratios are used to measure the relative position of creditors and shareholders. For example, commonly encountered ratios include:

$$\text{Debt-to-equity ratio} = \frac{\text{Total liabilities}}{\text{Total shareholders' equity}}$$

$$\text{Long-term debt-to-equity ratio} = \frac{\text{Total long-term debt}}{\text{Total shareholders' equity}}$$

$$\text{Debt-to-total-assets ratio} = \frac{\text{Total liabilities}}{\text{Total assets}}$$

Standard & Poor's Corporation, a credit-rating company, reviews the ability of corporations to pay their debts. A review of Lear Siegler, an aerospace corporation, commented favorably on the company's "lowering of debt leverage from over 40% to a satisfactory 32%." In other words, the ratio of total debt to total stockholders' equity had fallen from .40 to .32.

The debt burden varies greatly from firm to firm and industry to industry. For example, retailing companies, utilities, and transportation companies tend to have debt of more than 60% of their assets. Computer companies and textile firms average debt of about 45% of assets.

Debt-to-equity ratios that were thought to be too high a few years ago are becoming commonplace today. The average debt-to-total-assets ratio for major U.S. industrial companies grew from about 35% in 1960 to nearly 60% in 1990.

Many high debt-to-equity ratios result from leveraged buyouts (LBOs). In an LBO, a buyer takes over a company by using money borrowed using the company's assets as collateral. For example, management might borrow against the firm's assets and use the proceeds to buy back all the outstanding stock.

The purchase of RJR Nabisco by Kohlberg Kravis Roberts was a $25 billion LBO. The resulting company had debt of $23 billion and equity of $7 billion for a debt-to-equity ratio of 23 to 7, or about 3.3 to 1. The debt-to-total-assets percentage was $23 \div 30 = 77\%$. Henry Kravis remarked that this debt-to-equity ratio was low compared with other LBOs: "We've rarely bought a company with a ratio that low. . . . It's usually 10 or 12 to 1. Others have gone as high as 25 to 1." (*Fortune*, January 2, 1989, p. 70.)

SUMMARY

A liability is a recognized obligation to pay money or to provide goods or services. It may have a definite or an estimated amount. A contingent liability is not a liability because it depends on a future event arising out of a past transaction.

Bond premium and bond discount are used as ways of adjusting nominal interest rates to market interest rates at issuance. Amortization is conducted so that interest expense is measured on an accrual basis throughout the life of the bonds. The effective-interest method is used for amortization.

For balance sheet presentations, discounts are subtractions from and premiums are additions to their related bonds or notes.

Appendix 9A discusses compound interest. Appendix 9B provides details on accounting for payroll. Appendix 9C discusses leases and pensions.

SUMMARY PROBLEMS FOR YOUR REVIEW

☐ Problem One

Suppose that on December 31, 1989, Exxon issued $12 million of ten-year, 10% debentures. Assume that the annual market interest rate at issuance was 10%.

Required:
1. Compute the proceeds from issuing the debentures.
2. Prepare an analysis of the following items: (a) issuance of the debentures; (b) the first two semiannual interest payments; and (c) the payment of the maturity value. Use the balance sheet equation (similar to Exhibit 9–4, p. 383). Round to the nearest thousand dollars.
3. Prepare journal entries for the items in requirement 2.

☐ Solution to Problem One

1. Because the market interest rate and the nominal rate are both 10%, the proceeds equal the face amount of $10 million. This can also be computed as the present value (PV) of the twenty $600,000 interest payments and the $10 million maturity value at 5% per semiannual period:

PV of interest payments: 12.4622 × $600,000	$ 7,477,320
PV of maturity value: .3769 × $12,000,000	4,522,800
Total proceeds (exceeds $12 million due to rounding error)	$12,000,120

2. See Exhibit 9–12.

EXHIBIT 9–12

Analysis of Exxon's Bond Transactions: Problem One
(rounded to thousands of dollars)

	A	=	L	+	SE
	Cash		Bonds Payable		Retained Income
Exxon's records:					
1. Issuance	12,000		12,000		
2. Semiannual interest					
Six months ended:					⎡Increase⎤
6/30/90	−600				−600 ⎢Interest⎥
12/31/90	−600				−600 ⎣Expense⎦
3. Maturity value					
(final payment)	−12,000		−12,000		
Bond-Related Totals*	−12,000		0		−12,000

* Totals after all 20 interest payments and payment at maturity.

3.	12/31/89:	Cash	12,000,000	
		Bonds payable		12,000,000
	6/30/90:	Interest expense	600,000	
		Cash		600,000
	12/31/90:	Interest expense	600,000	
		Cash		600,000
	12/31/99:	Bonds payable	12,000,000	
		Cash		12,000,000

☐ Problem Two

Suppose that on December 31, 1989, Exxon issued $12 million of ten-year, 10% debentures. Assume that the annual market interest rate at issuance was 14%.

Required:
1. Compute the proceeds from issuing the debentures.
2. Prepare an analysis of the following items: (a) issuance of the debentures; (b) the first two semiannual interest payments; and (c) the payment of the maturity value. Use the balance sheet equation (similar to Exhibit 9–6, p. 386). Round to the nearest thousand dollars.
3. Prepare journal entries for the items in requirement 2.

☐

1. Because the market interest rate exceeds the nominal rate, the proceeds will be less than the face amount. This can be computed as the present value (PV) of the twenty $600,000 interest payments and the $10 million maturity value at 7% per semiannual period:

PV of interest payments: 10.5940 × $600,000		$6,356,400	
PV of maturity value: .2584 × $12,000,000		3,100,800	
Total proceeds		$9,457,200	

2. See Exhibit 9–13.

3.	12/31/89:	Cash	9,457,200	
		Discount on bonds payable	2,542,800	
		Bonds payable		12,000,000
	6/30/90:	Interest expense	662,004	
		Discount on bonds payable		62,004
		Cash		600,000
	12/31/90:	Interest expense	666,344	
		Discount on bonds payable		66,344
		Cash		600,000
	12/31/99:	Bonds payable	12,000,000	
		Cash		12,000,000

☐ **Problem Three**

Suppose that on December 31, 1989, Exxon issued $12 million of ten-year, 10% debentures. Assume that the annual market interest rate at issuance was 6%.

Required:

1. Compute the proceeds from issuing the debentures.
2. Prepare an analysis of the following items: (a) issuance of the debentures; (b) the first two semiannual interest payments; and (c) the payment of the maturity value. Use the balance sheet equation (similar to Exhibit 9–8, p. 388). Round to the nearest thousand dollars.

EXHIBIT 9–13

Analysis of Exxon's Bond Transactions: Problem Two
(rounded to thousands of dollars)

	A	=	L		+	SE
	Cash		Bonds Payable	Discount on Bonds Payable		Retained Income
Exxon's records:						
1. Issuance	+9,457		+12,000	−2,543 [Increase Discount]		
2. Semiannual interest Six months ended:						
6/30/90	−600			+62 [Decrease Discount]		−662* [Increase Interest Expense]
12/31/90	−600			+66 [Decrease Discount]		−666 [Increase Interest Expense]
3. Maturity value (final payment)	−12,000		−12,000			
Bond-Related Totals†	−14,543		0	0		−14,543

* 7% × 9,457 = 662; 7% × (9,457 + 662) = 666
† Totals after payment at maturity and all 20 entries for discount amortization and interest payments are made.

3. Prepare journal entries for the items in requirement 2.

☐ **Solution to Problem Three**

1. Because the market interest rate is less than the nominal rate, the proceeds will exceed the face amount. This can be computed as the present value (PV) of the twenty $600,000 interest payments and the $10 million maturity value at 3% per semiannual period:

PV of interest payments: 14.8775 × $600,000	$ 8,926,500
PV of maturity value: .5537 × $12,000,000	6,644,400
Total proceeds	$15,570,900

2. See Exhibit 9–14.

3.

12/31/89:	Cash	15,570,900	
	Premium on bonds paya-ble		3,570,900
	Bonds payable		12,000,000
6/30/90:	Interest expense	467,127	
	Premium on bonds payable	132,873	
	Cash		600,000
12/31/90:	Interest expense	463,141	
	Premium on bonds payable	136,859	
	Cash		600,000
12/31/99:	Bonds payable	12,000,000	
	Cash		12,000,000

EXHIBIT 9–14

Analysis of Exxon's Bond Transactions: Problem Three
(rounded to thousands of dollars)

	A =	L		+	SE
	Cash	Bonds Payable	Premium on Bonds Payable		Retained Income
Exxon's records:					
1. Issuance	+15,571	+12,000	+3,571 [Increase Premium]		
2. Semiannual interest					[Increase Interest Expense]
Six months ended:					
6/30/90	−600		−133 [Decrease		−467
12/31/90	−600		−137 [Premium]		−463
3. Maturity value					
(final payment)	−12,000	−12,000			
Bond-Related Totals*	−8,429	0	0		−8,429

* Totals after payment at maturity and all 20 entries for premium amortization and interest payments are made.

HIGHLIGHTS TO REMEMBER

1. Organizations usually have three large, repetitive drains on cash: (a) to suppliers for goods and services, (b) to employees for labor services, and (c) to tax authorities.

2. *Debenture* is the name for the most popular type of long-term debt. A debenture is a general claim against total assets rather than a specific claim against particular assets.

3. Bonds usually have nominal interest rates that are stated on an annual basis. However, interest is generally paid semiannually, so the nominal rate should be halved when computing the actual cash disbursed for interest. For instance, a 10% debenture of $1,000 would ordinarily require an interest payment of .05 × $1,000, or $50, twice per year.

4. Periodic interest expense on bonds equals the beginning net liability (face amount less discount or plus premium) multiplied by the market interest rate in effect when the bond was issued.

5. Liabilities can be short-term or long-term. They can also be classified as follows:

DESCRIPTION	EXAMPLE
a. Definite liability of definite amount	Account payable for a repair
b. Definite liability of estimated amount	Liability for warranties

6. Contingent liabilities can have a definite amount (e.g., to pay a $1,000 note payable if a primary borrower fails to pay) or an indefinite amount (e.g., an income tax dispute). These amounts may be substantial, but they are not included in the total liabilities in a balance sheet. They are described in footnotes.

ACCOUNTING VOCABULARY

Bearer Instrument, p. 379
Bond, p. 377
Callable Bonds, p. 379
Call Premium, p. 379
Capital Lease, p. 412
Compound Interest, p. 400
Compound Interest Method, p. 385
Contingent Liability, p. 392
Contractual Rate, p. 377
Convertible Bonds, p. 380
Coupon Rate, p. 377
Covenant, p. 379
Current Yield, p. 379
Debenture, p. 378
Debt-to-Equity Ratio, p. 394
Debt-to-Total-Assets Ratio, p. 394
Discount Amortization, p. 384
Discount on Bonds, p. 380
Discount Rate, p. 402
Effective-Interest Amortization, p. 385
Effective Interest Rate, p. 380
Face Amount, p. 377
Future Value, p. 400
Implicit Interest, p. 391
Imputed Interest, p. 391
Imputed Interest Rate, p. 391
Interest, p. 400
Lease, p. 411
Line of Credit, p. 371

Long-Term Debt-to-Equity Ratio, p. 394
Long-Term Liabilities, p. 369
Market Interest Rate, p. 380
Mortgage Bond, p. 378
Nominal Rate, p. 377
Operating Lease, p. 412
Par Amount, p. 377
Premium on Bonds, p. 380
Present Value, p. 401
Principal, p. 400
Private Placement, p. 377
Promissory Note, p. 371
Protective Covenants, p. 379
Real Interest Rate, p. 380
Registered Instrument, p. 379
Short Presentation, p. 393
Simple Interest, p. 400
Sinking Fund, p. 380
Sinking Fund Bonds, p. 380
Stated Rate, p. 377
Subordinated Debentures, p. 378
Trade Accounts Payable, p. 371
True Interest Rate, p. 380
Trust Indenture, p. 379
Underwriters, p. 380
Unregistered Instrument, p. 379
Unsubordinated Debentures, p. 378
Yield Rate, p. 380

APPENDIX 9A: COMPOUND INTEREST, FUTURE VALUE, AND PRESENT VALUE

Interest is the cost of using money. It is the rental charge for cash, just as rental charges are often made for the use of automobiles or boats. Interest cost is often unimportant in the short run. The longer the time span and the higher the rate, the more significant the interest cost. Of course, for financial institutions, interest is a primary revenue and expense.

Contracts that bear interest have many forms, from simple short-term promissory notes to multimillion-dollar issues of long-term notes often called bonds. Commonly encountered terms include

- **Principal**—the amount invested, borrowed, or used on which interest accrues
- **Interest**—the rental charge for the use of principal

Simple interest is calculated by multiplying an interest rate by an unchanging principal amount. In contrast, **compound interest** is calculated by multiplying an interest rate by a principal amount that is changed each interest period by the previously accumulated (unpaid) interest. The accumulated interest is added to the principal to become the principal for the new period.

☐ Table 1: Future Value of $1

Consider an example. Suppose you deposited $10,000 in a financial institution that promised to pay 10% interest per annum. You let the amount accumulate for three years before withdrawing the full balance of the deposit. The amount accumulated in the account, including principal and interest, is called the **future value**. At *simple interest*, the future value of $10,000 at the end of three years is $13,000:

	PRINCIPAL	SIMPLE INTEREST	BALANCE, END OF YEAR
Year 1	$10,000	$10,000 × .10 = $1,000	$11,000
Year 2	10,000	10,000 × .10 = 1,000	12,000
Year 3	10,000	10,000 × .10 = 1,000	13,000

Compound interest provides interest on interest. That is, the principal changes from period to period. Interest in Year 1 is paid on $10,000: 10% × $10,000 = $1,000. If the interest is not withdrawn, the principal for Year 2 is $10,000 + .10 × $10,000 = 1.10 × $10,000 = $11,000. Interest in Year 2 is paid on the $11,000: 10% × $11,000 = $1,100. With no withdrawals, the principal becomes $11,000 + .10 × $11,000 = $(1.1)^2 × $10,000 = $12,100$. The future value of the deposit at the end of three years with compound interest would be $(1.10)^3 × $10,000 = 1.3310 × $10,000 = $13,310$:

	PRINCIPAL	COMPOUND INTEREST	BALANCE, END OF YEAR
Year 1	$10,000	$10,000 × .10 = $1,000	$11,000
Year 2	11,000	11,000 × .10 = 1,100	12,100
Year 3	12,100	12,100 × .10 = 1,210	13,310

Notice that the future value is $310 greater with compound interest than with simple interest. Why? Because the compound-interest amount includes interest paid on the interest earned in earlier years and which was not withdrawn.

The general formula for computing the future value (FV) of S dollars n years hence at interest rate i is[5]

$$FV = S \, (1 + i)^n$$

The "force" of compound interest can be staggering. For example, compare future values using simple interest with those using compound interest:

	FUTURE VALUES AT END OF		
	10 Years	20 Years	40 Years
Simple interest:			
$10,000 + 10 ($1,000) =	$20,000		
$10,000 + 20 ($1,000) =		$30,000	
$10,000 + 40 ($1,000) =			$ 50,000
Compound interest:			
$10,000 × (1.10)^{10} = $10,000 × 2.5937 = $25,937			
$10,000 × (1.10)^{20} = $10,000 × 6.7275 =		$67,275	
$10,000 × (1.10)^{40} = $10,000 × 45.2593 =			$452,593

Hand calculations of compound interest can quickly become burdensome. Therefore compound interest tables have been constructed to ease computations. (Indeed, many hand calculators and computer spreadsheets contain programs that provide speedy answers.) Table 1, page 404, shows the future values of $1 for various periods and interest rates. Notice that the three-year, 10% future value factor is 1.3310, the value used in our earlier example.

Suppose you want to know how much $800 will grow to if left in the bank for nine years at 8% interest. Multiply $800 by the factor from the 9-year row and 8% column of Table 1:

$800 × 1.9990 = $1,599.20

Table 2: Present Value of $1

Accountants use *present values* more often than future values. The **present value** is the value today of a future cash inflow or outflow. Table 2, page 405, provides factors that give the present value of a single, lump-sum cash flow to be received or paid at the *end* of a future period.[6]

Suppose you invest $1.00 today. As shown in the discussion of future values, the $1.00 will grow to $1.06 in one year at 6% interest; that is, $1 × 1.06 = $1.06. At the end of the second year its value is ($1 × 1.06) × 1.06 = $1 × (1.06)^2 = $1.124, and at the end of the third year it is $1 × (1.06)^3 = $1.1910. In general, $1.00 grows to $(1 + i)^n$ in n years at i% interest.

---

[5] Note that, in general, n refers to the number of periods the funds are invested. Periods can be years, months, days, or any other time period. However, the interest rate must be consistent with the time period. That is, if n refers to days, i must be expressed as x% per day.

[6] The factors in Tables 1, 2, and 3 are rounded to four decimal places. The examples in this text use these rounded factors. If you use tables with different rounding, or if you use a hand calculator or personal computer, your answers may differ from those given because of a small rounding error.

To determine the *present value*, you reverse this accumulation process. If $1.00 is to be received in one year, it is worth $1 ÷ 1.06 = $.9434 today. Suppose you invest $.9434 today. In one year you will have $.9434 × 1.06 = $1.00. Thus $.9434 is the *present value* of $1.00 a year hence at 6%. If the dollar will be received in two years, its present value is $1.00 ÷ (1.06)² = $.8900. If $.89 is invested today, it will grow to $1.00 at the end of two years. The general formula for the present value (*PV*) of an amount *S* to be received or paid in *n* periods at an interest rate of *i*% per period is

$$PV = \frac{S}{(1 + i)^n} = S \times \frac{1}{(1 + i)^n}$$

Table 2 gives factors for $1/(1 + i)^n$ (which is the present value of $1.00) at various interest rates (often called **discount rates**) over several different periods. Present values are also called *discounted* values, and the process of finding the present value is discounting. You can think of this as discounting (decreasing) the value of a future cash inflow or outflow. Why is the value discounted? Because the cash is to be received or paid in the future, not today.

Assume that a prominent city is issuing a three-year non-interest-bearing note payable that promises to pay a lump sum of $1,000 exactly three years from now. You desire a rate of return of exactly 6%, compounded annually. How much would you be willing to pay now for the three-year note? The situation is sketched as follows:

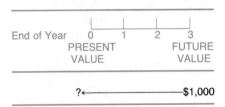

The factor in the Period 3 row and 6% column of Table 2 is .8396. The present value of the $1,000 payment is $1,000 × .8396 = $839.60. You would be willing to pay $839.60 for the $1,000 to be received in three years.

Suppose interest is compounded semiannually rather than annually. How much would you be willing to pay? The three years become six interest payment periods. The rate per period is half the annual rate, or 6% ÷ 2 = 3%. The factor in the Period 6 row and 3% column of Table 2 is .8375. You would be willing to pay $1,000 × .8375, or only $837.50 rather than $839.60.

As a further check on your understanding, review the earlier example of compound interest. Suppose the financial institution promised to pay $13,310 at the end of three years. How much would you be willing to deposit at time zero if you desired a 10% rate of return compounded annually? Using Table 2, the Period 3 row and the 10% column show a factor of .7513. Multiply this factor by the future amount and round to the nearest dollar:

$$PV = .7513 \times \$13,310 = \$10,000$$

A diagram of this computation follows:

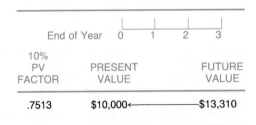

This illustrates the symmetry of future and present values. The 10%, 3-year future value of $10,000 is $13,310, and the 10%, 3-year present value of $13,310 is $10,000.

Pause for a moment. Use Table 2 to obtain the present values of

1. $1,600, @ 20%, at the end of 20 years
2. $8,300 @ 10%, at the end of 12 years
3. $8,000, @ 4%, at the end of 4 years

Answers:
1. $1,600 (.0261) = $41.76.
2. $8,300 (.3186) = $2,644.38
3. $8,000 (.8548) = $6,838.40

☐ **Table 3: Present Value of an Ordinary Annuity of $1**

An ordinary annuity is a series of equal cash flows to take place at the *end* of successive periods of equal length. Its present value is denoted PV_A. Assume that you buy a non-interest-bearing serial note from a municipality that promises to pay $1,000 at the end of *each* of three years. How much should you be willing to pay if you desire a rate of return of 6%, compounded annually?

You could solve this problem using Table 2. First, find the present value of each payment, and then add the present values as in Exhibit 9–15. You would be willing to pay $943.40 for the first payment, $890.00 for the second, and $839.60 for the third, a total of $2,673.00.

Since each cash payment is $1,000 with equal one-year periods between them, Table 3 provides a shortcut method. The present value in Exhibit 9–15 can be expressed as

$$PV_A = \$1,000 \times .9434 + \$1,000 \times .8900 + \$1,000 \times .8396$$
$$= \$1,000\,[.9434 + .8900 + .8396]$$
$$= \$1,000\,[2.6730]$$
$$= \$2,673.00$$

The three terms in brackets are the first three numbers from the 6% column of Table 2, and their sum is in the third row of the 6% column of Table 3: .9434 + .8900 + .8396 = 2.6730. Instead of adding the three present values and then multiplying, you simply multiply the cash payment by the PV factor from Table 3: 2.6730 × $1,000 = $2,673.

This shortcut is expecially valuable if the cash payments or receipts extend over many periods. Consider an annual cash payment of $1,000 for 20 years at 6%. The present value, calculated from Table 3, is $1,000 × 11.4699 = $11,469.90. To use Table 2 for this calculation, you would perform twenty multiplications and then add the twenty products.

EXHIBIT 9–15

	END OF YEAR 6% PV FACTOR	PRESENT VALUE	0	1	2	3
1st payment:	.9434	$ 943.40 ← $1,000				
2nd payment:	.8900	$ 890.00 ←———— $1,000				
3rd payment:	.8396	$ 839.60 ←———————— $1,000				
		$2,673.00				

TABLE 1 (Put a clip on this page for easy reference)

Future Value of $1

$$FV = 1(1 + i)^n$$

PERIODS	3%	4%	5%	6%	7%	8%	10%	12%	14%	16%	18%	20%	22%	24%	25%
1	1.0300	1.0400	1.0500	1.0600	1.0700	1.0800	1.1000	1.1200	1.1400	1.1600	1.1800	1.2000	1.2200	1.2400	1.2500
2	1.0609	1.0816	1.1025	1.1236	1.1449	1.1664	1.2100	1.2544	1.2996	1.3456	1.3924	1.4400	1.4884	1.5376	1.5625
3	1.0927	1.1249	1.1576	1.1910	1.2250	1.2597	1.3310	1.4049	1.0395	1.5609	1.6430	1.7280	1.8158	1.9066	1.9531
4	1.1255	1.1699	1.2155	1.2625	1.3108	1.3605	1.4641	1.5735	1.6890	1.8106	1.9388	2.0736	2.2153	2.3642	2.4414
5	1.1593	1.2167	1.2763	1.3382	1.4026	1.4693	1.6105	1.7623	1.9254	2.1003	2.2878	2.4883	2.7027	2.9316	3.0518
6	1.1941	1.2653	1.3401	1.4185	1.5007	1.5869	1.7716	1.9738	2.1950	2.4364	2.6996	2.9860	3.2973	3.6352	3.8147
7	1.2299	1.3159	1.4071	1.5036	1.6058	1.7138	1.9487	2.2107	2.5023	2.8262	3.1855	3.5832	4.0227	4.5077	4.7684
8	1.2668	1.3686	1.4775	1.5938	1.7182	1.8509	2.1436	2.4760	2.8526	3.2784	3.7589	4.2998	4.9077	5.5895	5.9605
9	1.3048	1.4233	1.5513	1.6895	1.8385	1.9990	2.3579	2.7731	3.2519	3.8030	4.4355	5.1598	5.9874	6.9310	7.4506
10	1.3439	1.4802	1.6289	1.7908	1.9672	2.1589	2.5937	3.1058	3.7072	4.4114	5.2338	6.1917	7.3046	8.5944	9.3132
11	1.3842	1.5395	1.7103	1.8983	2.1049	2.3316	2.8531	3.4785	4.2262	5.1173	6.1759	7.4301	8.9117	10.6571	11.6415
12	1.4258	1.6010	1.7959	2.0122	2.2522	2.5182	3.1384	3.8960	4.8179	5.9360	7.2876	8.9161	10.8722	13.2148	14.5519
13	1.4685	1.6651	1.8856	2.1329	2.4098	2.7196	3.4523	4.3635	5.4924	6.8858	8.5994	10.6993	13.2641	16.3863	18.1899
14	1.5126	1.7317	1.9799	2.2609	2.5785	2.9372	3.7975	4.8871	6.2613	7.9875	10.1472	12.8392	16.1822	20.3191	22.7374
15	1.5580	1.8009	2.0789	2.3966	2.7590	3.1772	4.1772	5.4736	7.1379	9.2655	11.9737	15.4070	19.7423	25.1956	28.4217
16	1.6047	1.8730	2.1829	2.5404	2.9522	3.4259	4.5950	6.1304	8.1372	10.7480	14.1290	18.4884	24.0856	31.2426	35.5271
17	1.6528	1.9479	2.2920	2.6928	3.1588	3.7000	5.0545	6.8660	9.2765	12.4677	16.6722	22.1861	29.3844	38.7408	44.4089
18	1.7024	2.0258	2.4066	2.8543	3.3799	3.9960	5.5599	7.6900	10.5752	14.4625	19.6733	26.6233	35.8490	48.0386	55.5112
19	1.7535	2.1068	2.5270	3.0256	3.6165	4.3157	6.1159	8.6128	12.0557	16.7765	23.2144	31.9480	43.7358	59.5679	69.3889
20	1.8061	2.1911	2.6533	3.2071	3.8697	4.6610	6.7275	9.6463	13.7435	19.4608	27.3930	38.3376	53.3576	73.8641	86.7362
21	1.8603	2.2788	2.7860	3.3996	4.1406	5.0338	7.4002	10.8038	15.6676	22.5745	32.3238	46.0051	65.0963	91.5915	108.4202
22	1.9161	2.3699	2.9253	3.6035	4.4304	5.4365	8.1403	12.1003	17.8610	26.1864	38.1421	55.2061	79.4175	113.5735	135.5253
23	1.9736	2.4647	3.0715	3.8197	4.7405	5.8715	8.9543	13.5523	20.3616	30.3762	45.0076	66.2474	96.8894	140.8312	169.4066
24	2.0328	2.5633	3.2251	4.0489	5.0724	6.3412	9.8497	15.1786	23.2122	35.2364	53.1090	79.4968	118.2050	174.6306	211.7582
25	2.0938	2.6658	3.3864	4.2919	5.4274	6.8485	10.8347	17.0001	26.4619	40.8742	62.6686	95.3962	144.2101	216.5420	264.6978
26	2.1566	2.7725	3.5557	4.5494	5.8074	7.3964	11.9182	19.0401	30.1666	47.4141	73.9490	114.4755	175.9364	268.5121	330.8722
27	2.2213	2.8834	3.7335	4.8223	6.2139	7.9881	13.1100	21.3249	34.3899	55.0004	87.2598	137.3706	214.6424	332.9550	413.5903
28	2.2879	2.9987	3.9201	5.1117	6.6488	8.6271	14.4210	23.8839	39.2045	63.8004	102.9666	164.8447	261.8637	412.8642	516.9879
29	2.3566	3.1187	4.1161	5.4184	7.1143	9.3173	15.8631	26.7499	44.6931	74.0085	121.5005	197.8136	319.4737	511.9516	646.2349
30	2.4273	3.2434	4.3219	5.7435	7.6123	10.0627	17.4494	29.9599	50.9502	85.8499	143.3706	237.3763	389.7579	634.8199	807.7936

TABLE 2

Present Value of $1

$$PV = \frac{1}{(1 + i)^n}$$

PERIODS	3%	4%	5%	6%	7%	8%	10%	12%	14%	16%	18%	20%	22%	24%	25%
1	.9709	.9615	.9524	.9434	.9346	.9259	.9091	.8929	.8772	.8621	.8475	.8333	.8197	.8065	.8000
2	.9426	.9246	.9070	.8900	.8734	.8573	.8264	.7972	.7695	.7432	.7182	.6944	.6719	.6504	.6400
3	.9151	.8890	.8638	.8396	.8163	.7938	.7513	.7118	.6750	.6407	.6086	.5787	.5507	.5245	.5120
4	.8885	.8548	.8227	.7921	.7629	.7350	.6830	.6355	.5921	.5523	.5158	.4823	.4514	.4230	.4096
5	.8626	.8219	.7835	.7473	.7130	.6806	.6209	.5674	.5194	.4761	.4371	.4019	.3700	.3411	.3277
6	.8375	.7903	.7462	.7050	.6663	.6302	.5645	.5066	.4556	.4104	.3704	.3349	.3033	.2751	.2621
7	.8131	.7599	.7107	.6651	.6227	.5835	.5132	.4523	.3996	.3538	.3139	.2791	.2486	.2218	.2097
8	.7894	.7307	.6768	.6274	.5820	.5403	.4665	.4039	.3506	.3050	.2660	.2326	.2038	.1789	.1678
9	.7664	.7026	.6446	.5919	.5439	.5002	.4241	.3606	.3075	.2630	.2255	.1938	.1670	.1443	.1342
10	.7441	.6756	.6139	.5584	.5083	.4632	.3855	.3220	.2697	.2267	.1911	.1615	.1369	.1164	.1074
11	.7224	.6496	.5847	.5268	.4751	.4289	.3505	.2875	.2366	.1954	.1619	.1346	.1122	.0938	.0859
12	.7014	.6246	.5568	.4970	.4440	.3971	.3186	.2567	.2076	.1685	.1372	.1122	.0920	.0757	.0687
13	.6810	.6006	.5303	.4688	.4150	.3677	.2897	.2292	.1821	.1452	.1163	.0935	.0754	.0610	.0550
14	.6611	.5775	.5051	.4423	.3878	.3405	.2633	.2046	.1597	.1252	.0985	.0779	.0618	.0492	.0440
15	.6419	.5553	.4810	.4173	.3624	.3152	.2394	.1827	.1401	.1079	.0835	.0649	.0507	.0397	.0352
16	.6232	.5339	.4581	.3936	.3387	.2919	.2176	.1631	.1229	.0930	.0708	.0541	.0415	.0320	.0281
17	.6050	.5134	.4363	.3714	.3166	.2703	.1978	.1456	.1078	.0802	.0600	.0451	.0340	.0258	.0225
18	.5874	.4936	.4155	.3503	.2959	.2502	.1799	.1300	.0946	.0691	.0508	.0376	.0279	.0208	.0180
19	.5703	.4746	.3957	.3305	.2765	.2317	.1635	.1161	.0829	.0596	.0431	.0313	.0229	.0168	.0144
20	.5537	.4564	.3769	.3118	.2584	.2145	.1486	.1037	.0728	.0514	.0365	.0261	.0187	.0135	.0115
21	.5375	.4388	.3589	.2942	.2415	.1987	.1351	.0926	.0638	.0443	.0309	.0217	.0154	.0109	.0092
22	.5219	.4220	.3418	.2775	.2257	.1839	.1228	.0826	.0560	.0382	.0262	.0181	.0126	.0088	.0074
23	.5067	.4057	.3256	.2618	.2109	.1703	.1117	.0738	.0491	.0329	.0222	.0151	.0103	.0071	.0059
24	.4919	.3901	.3101	.2470	.1971	.1577	.1015	.0659	.0431	.0284	.0188	.0126	.0085	.0057	.0047
25	.4776	.3751	.2953	.2330	.1842	.1460	.0923	.0588	.0378	.0245	.0160	.0105	.0069	.0046	.0038
26	.4637	.3607	.2812	.2198	.1722	.1352	.0839	.0525	.0331	.0211	.0135	.0087	.0057	.0037	.0030
27	.4502	.3468	.2678	.2074	.1609	.1252	.0763	.0469	.0291	.0182	.0115	.0073	.0047	.0030	.0024
28	.4371	.3335	.2551	.1956	.1504	.1159	.0693	.0419	.0255	.0157	.0097	.0061	.0038	.0024	.0019
29	.4243	.3207	.2429	.1846	.1406	.1073	.0630	.0374	.0224	.0135	.0082	.0051	.0031	.0020	.0015
30	.4120	.3083	.2314	.1741	.1314	.0994	.0573	.0334	.0196	.0116	.0070	.0042	.0026	.0016	.0012
40	.3066	.2083	.1420	.0972	.0668	.0460	.0221	.0107	.0053	.0026	.0013	.0007	.0004	.0002	.0001

TABLE 3

Present Value of Ordinary Annuity of $1

$$PV_A = \frac{1}{i}\left[1 - \frac{1}{(1+i)^n}\right]$$

PERIODS	3%	4%	5%	6%	7%	8%	10%	12%	14%	16%	18%	20%	22%	24%	25%
1	.9709	.9615	.9524	.9434	.9346	.9259	.9091	.8929	.8772	.8621	.8475	.8333	.8197	.8065	.8000
2	1.9135	1.8861	1.8594	1.8334	1.8080	1.7833	1.7355	1.6901	1.6467	1.6052	1.5656	1.5278	1.4915	1.4568	1.4400
3	2.8286	2.7751	2.7232	2.6730	2.6243	2.5771	2.4869	2.4018	2.3216	2.2459	2.1743	2.1065	2.0422	1.9813	1.9520
4	3.7171	3.6299	3.5460	3.4651	3.3872	3.3121	3.1699	3.0373	2.9137	2.7982	2.6901	2.5887	2.4936	2.4043	2.3616
5	4.5797	4.4518	4.3295	4.2124	4.1002	3.9927	3.7908	3.6048	3.4331	3.2743	3.1272	2.9906	2.8636	2.7454	2.6893
6	5.4172	5.2421	5.0757	4.9173	4.7665	4.6229	4.3553	4.1114	3.8887	3.6847	3.4976	3.3255	3.1669	3.0205	2.9514
7	6.2303	6.0021	5.7864	5.5824	5.3893	5.2064	4.8684	4.5638	4.2883	4.0386	3.8115	3.6046	3.4155	3.2423	3.1611
8	7.0197	6.7327	6.4632	6.2098	5.9713	5.7466	5.3349	4.9676	4.6389	4.3436	4.0776	3.8372	3.6193	3.4212	3.3289
9	7.7861	7.4353	7.1078	6.8017	6.5152	6.2469	5.7590	5.3282	4.9464	4.6065	4.3030	4.0310	3.7863	3.5655	3.4631
10	8.5302	8.1109	7.7217	7.3601	7.0236	6.7101	6.1446	5.6502	5.2161	4.8332	4.4941	4.1925	3.9232	3.6819	3.5705
11	9.2526	8.7605	8.3064	7.8869	7.4987	7.1390	6.4951	5.9377	5.4527	5.0286	4.6560	4.3271	4.0354	3.7757	3.6564
12	9.9540	9.3851	8.8633	8.3838	7.9427	7.5361	6.8137	6.1944	5.6603	5.1971	4.7932	4.4392	4.1274	3.8514	3.7251
13	10.6350	9.9856	9.3936	8.8527	8.3577	7.9038	7.1034	6.4235	5.8424	5.3423	4.9095	4.5327	4.2028	3.9124	3.7801
14	11.2961	10.5631	9.8986	9.2950	8.7455	8.2442	7.3667	6.6282	6.0021	5.4675	5.0081	4.6106	4.2646	3.9616	3.8241
15	11.9379	11.1184	10.3797	9.7122	9.1079	8.5595	7.6061	6.8109	6.1422	5.5755	5.0916	4.6755	4.3152	4.0013	3.8593
16	12.5611	11.6523	10.8378	10.1059	9.4466	8.8514	7.8237	6.9740	6.2651	5.6685	5.1624	4.7296	4.3567	4.0333	3.8874
17	13.1661	12.1657	11.2741	10.4773	9.7632	9.1216	8.0216	7.1196	6.3729	5.7487	5.2223	4.7746	4.3908	4.0591	3.9099
18	13.7535	12.6593	11.6896	10.8276	10.0591	9.3719	8.2014	7.2497	6.4674	5.8178	5.2732	4.8122	4.4187	4.0799	3.9279
19	14.3238	13.1339	12.0853	11.1581	10.3356	9.6036	8.3649	7.3658	6.5504	5.8775	5.3162	4.8435	4.4415	4.0967	3.9424
20	14.8775	13.5903	12.4622	11.4699	10.5940	9.8181	8.5136	7.4694	6.6231	5.9288	5.3527	4.8696	4.4603	4.1103	3.9539
21	15.4150	14.0292	12.8212	11.7641	10.8355	10.0168	8.6487	7.5620	6.6870	5.9731	5.3837	4.8913	4.4756	4.1212	3.9631
22	15.9369	14.4511	13.1630	12.0416	11.0612	10.2007	8.7715	7.6446	6.7429	6.0113	5.4099	4.9094	4.4882	4.1300	3.9705
23	16.4436	14.8568	13.4886	12.3034	11.2722	10.3711	8.8832	7.7184	6.7921	6.0442	5.4321	4.9245	4.4985	4.1371	3.9764
24	16.9355	15.2470	13.7986	12.5504	11.4693	10.5288	8.9847	7.7843	6.8351	6.0726	5.4509	4.9371	4.5070	4.1428	3.9811
25	17.4131	15.6221	14.0939	12.7834	11.6526	10.6748	9.0770	7.8431	6.8729	6.0971	5.4669	4.9476	4.5139	4.1474	3.9849
26	17.8768	15.9828	14.3752	13.0032	11.8258	10.8100	9.1609	7.8957	6.9061	6.1182	5.4804	4.9563	4.5196	4.1511	3.9879
27	18.3270	16.3296	14.6430	13.2105	11.9867	10.9352	9.2372	7.9426	6.9352	6.1364	5.4919	4.9636	4.5243	4.1542	3.9903
28	18.7641	16.6631	14.8981	13.4062	12.1371	11.0511	9.3066	7.9844	6.9607	6.1520	5.5016	4.9697	4.5281	4.1566	3.9923
29	19.1885	16.9837	15.1411	13.5907	12.2777	11.1584	9.3696	8.0218	6.9830	6.1656	5.5098	4.9747	4.5312	4.1585	3.9938
30	19.6004	17.2920	15.3725	13.7648	12.4090	11.2578	9.4269	8.0552	7.0027	6.1772	5.5168	4.9789	4.5338	4.1601	3.9950
40	23.1148	19.7928	17.1591	15.0463	13.3317	11.9246	9.7791	8.2438	7.1050	6.2335	5.5482	4.9966	4.5439	4.1659	3.9995

The factors in Table 3 can be calculated using the following general formula:

$$PV_A = \frac{1}{i}\left[1 - \frac{1}{(1 + i)^n}\right]$$

Applied to our illustration:

$$PV_A = \frac{1}{.06}(1 - .83962) = \frac{.16038}{.06} = 2.6730$$

Use Table 3 to obtain the present values of the following ordinary annuities:

1. $1,600 at 20% for 20 years
2. $8,300 at 10% for 12 years
3. $8,000 at 4% for 4 years

Answers:
1. $1,600 (4.8696) = $7,791.36
2. $8,300 (6.8137) = $56,553.71
3. $8,000 (3.6299) = $29,039.20

In particular, note that the higher the interest rate, the lower the present value. Why? Because, at a higher interest rate, you would need to invest less now to obtain the same future value.

SUMMARY PROBLEMS FOR YOUR REVIEW

Before proceeding to the next section, be sure to solve these review exercises.

☐ **Problem Four (Problems One through Three are in the body of the chapter.)**

Xerox Corporation plans to enter some new communications business. The company expects to accumulate sufficient cash from its new operations to pay a lump sum of $200 million to Prudential Insurance Company at the end of five years. Prudential will lend money on a promissory note now, will take no payments until the end of five years, and desires 12% interest compounded annually.

Required:
1. How much money will Prudential lend Xerox?
2. Prepare journal entries for Xerox at the inception of the loan and at the end of each of the first two years.

☐ **Solution to Problem Four**

The initial step in solving present value problems focuses on a basic question, Which table should I use? No computations should be made until you are convinced that you are using the correct table.

1. Use Table 2. The $200 million is a future amount. Its present value is

$$PV = \$200{,}000{,}000 \times \frac{1}{(1 + .12)^5}$$

The conversion factor, $1/(1 + .12)^5$, is in row 5 and the 12% column. It is .5674.

$$PV = \$200{,}000{,}000 \times .5674 = \$113{,}480{,}000$$

2.

Cash	113,480,000	
Long-term note payable		
(or long-term debt)		113,480,000
To record borrowing that is payable		
in a lump sum at the end of five		
years at 12% interest compounded		
annually.		
Interest expense	13,617,600	
Long-term note payable		13,617,600
To record interest expense and		
corresponding accumulation of		
principal at the end of the first year:		
.12 × $113,480,000 = $13,617,600		
Interest expense	15,251,712	
Long-term note payable		15,251,712
To record interest expense and		
corresponding accumulation of		
principal at the end of the second		
year: .12 × ($113,480,000		
+ $13,617,600).		

Reflect on the entries for interest. Note how the interest expense becomes larger if no interest payments are made from year to year. This mounting interest expense occurs because the unpaid interest is being added to the principal to form a new higher principal each year.

☐ **Problem Five**

Refer to the preceding problem. Suppose Xerox and Prudential agree on a 12% interest rate compounded annually. However, Xerox will pay a *total* of $200 million in the form of $40 million annual payments at the end of *each* of the next five years. How much money will Prudential lend Xerox?

☐ **Solution to Problem Five**

Use Table 3. The $40 million is a uniform periodic payment at the end of a series of years. Therefore it is an annuity. Its present value is:

$$PV_A = \text{Annual payment} \times \text{Present value factor}$$
$$= \$40 \text{ million} \times \text{Present value factor for 5 years at 12\%}$$
$$= \$40 \text{ million} \times 3.6048$$
$$= \$144,192,000$$

In particular, note that Prudential is willing to lend more than in Problem Four even though the interest rate is the same. Why? Because Prudential will get its money back more quickly.

APPENDIX 9B: ACCOUNTING FOR PAYROLL

This appendix discusses some details of payroll accounting. A complete analysis of payroll accounting is beyond the scope of this text. However, a description of three types of payroll transactions will illustrate the main ideas.

EXHIBIT 9–16·

Analysis of Transactions
(in thousands of dollars)

	A =		L		+	SE
	Cash	Accrued Wages Payable	Withheld Income Taxes Payable	Withheld Social Security Taxes Payable		Retained Income
1. Recognize liabilities	=	+78	+15	+7		−100 [Increase wages expense]
2. Pay cash to employees	−78 =	−78				
3. Pay cash to government	−22 =		−15	−7		

☐ Payroll Witholdings

In the United States, the employer must collect employees' ordinary income taxes and social security taxes. The latter tax provides government pensions and medical benefits to retired workers. It is also called the *Federal Insurance Contributions Act tax* (FICA tax).[7] The series of accounting entries to accomplish this collection service varies, but the basic pattern is shown in Exhibit 9–16. Assume that the wages expense subject to these tax withholdings is $100,000. All amounts earned were paid in cash, except for withholdings.

The journal entries to accompany Exhibit 9–16 would be:

1.	Wages expense	100	
	Accrued wages payable		78
	Withheld income taxes payable		15
	Withheld social security taxes payable		7
	To recognize liabilities arising from wages earned.		
2.	Accrued wages payable	78	
	Cash		78
	To pay employees.		
3.	Withheld income taxes payable	15	
	Withheld social security taxes payable	7	
	Cash		22
	To pay the government.		

The U.S. government is impatient. It wants its taxes quickly. The amount of tax withheld determines the frequency of payment. Large companies must pay eight times each month.

---

[7] The 1989 FICA rate for employees was 7.51% of the first $48,000 of earnings.

Many other withholdings from employees occur. They are accounted for in the same manner as withheld taxes. Examples are union dues, donations to community charities, hospitalization insurance, group life insurance, auto insurance, pension plans, and employee savings plans.

Above all, note that withholdings by themselves are not employer costs. They are merely those portions of the employees' gross earnings that are being diverted to third parties, primarily for the employees' convenience. Instead of an obligation to an employee, the company lists a liability to a third party.

Additional Employer Payroll Costs

The gross earnings of employees are only part of the payroll costs really borne. In addition to wages expense, the employer incurs other expenses that are based on the gross earnings of employees.

Governments levy special taxes on the *employer*, as distinguished from the *employee*. Examples are social security taxes, federal unemployment taxes, state unemployment taxes, and workers' accident compensation taxes. Together, these are often called *payroll taxes*. These tax rates change from year to year, generally in an upward direction. Together they average about 10% of the gross earnings of U.S. employees.

Employers also contribute to programs for employee pensions, health, life, and other insurance. Such programs are called *fringe benefits*, or simply *fringes*. These costs can easily exceed 30% of the gross earnings of U.S. employees.

The journal entries for these additional employer costs have the same basic pattern. The following numbers (in thousands) are typical for gross earnings of $100,000:

Employer payroll tax expenses (could be detailed)	10	
Employer pension expenses	15	
Employer health insurance expenses	5	
Employer payroll taxes payable		10
Employer pensions payable		15
Employer health insurance payable		5
To record various additional expenses related to gross earnings of employees.		
Employer payroll taxes payable	10	
Employer pensions payable	15	
Employer health insurance payable	5	
Cash		30
To record payments of various liabilities. (These individual disbursements occur at different times.)		

The above entries make heavy use of "employer" as part of the names for both expenses and liabilities. These names are often shortened by deleting "employer." Furthermore, many of the liabilities that have been shown in detail in these examples are combined if the amounts contributed by the employer plus the employees are to be paid to the same payee.

Accrual of Vacation Pay

There is often a time lag between incurrence and payment of various payroll fringe costs. A common illustration is payment for vacations. The liability for vacations really accrues from week to week as each employee accumulates a claim to vacation pay. Companies estimate total vacation expenses and spread them over a year. They cannot simply recognize such outlays as expenses when disbursements are made. Such a policy would violate the matching principle.

For example, suppose an employee receives wages of $1,000 per week and is entitled to a two-week vacation after one year. The $2,000 of vacation pay should be recognized as an expense of the fifty weeks worked, a cost of $2,000 ÷ 50 = $40 per week. An appropriate journal entry each week would be (ignoring withholdings and other fringe benefits):

Wages expense	1,040	
Accrued payroll		1,000
Accrued vacation pay		40
To recognize liabilities for wages earned including related vacation pay. Computation is based on liability for the year, or (2 weeks × $1,000)/(50 weeks × $1,000) = 4%. The accrual for vacation pay will accumulate to $40 × 50 = $2,000 at the end of fifty weeks. The $40 portion of wages expense might be accounted for in a separate account, such as Vacation Pay Expense.		
Accrued vacation pay	2,000	
Cash		2,000
The liability account for vacation pay is decreased as actual vacation payments occur.		

Liabilities for vacations and other compensated absences, such as sickness and disabilities, can become significant. Many companies specifically mention such items in their annual reports. For instance, J. C. Penney labels its liability as "Accrued Salaries, Vacations, Profit-sharing, and Bonuses." Adolph Coors calls it "Accrued Salaries and Vacations."

APPENDIX 9C: ACCOUNTING FOR LEASES AND PENSIONS

Lease and pension accounting is controversial. Some accountants maintain that lease and pension obligations are not sufficiently binding on companies to be included as liabilities. However, most accountants agree that they are liabilities, but many disagree about how to measure them. The FASB has issued detailed rules about the measurement of liabilities for leases and pensions. Even though companies must now comply with the rules, discussion about possible changes continues.

LEASES

Leasing is big business. Any asset imaginable, from television sets to jumbo aircraft to buildings, can be acquired via rental. *Euromoney* has pointed out that "leasing has now blossomed into the biggest single provider of fixed-rate finance for corporate America." A **lease** is a contract whereby an owner (lessor) grants the use of property to a second party (lessee) for rental payments. This appendix discusses leasing from the lessee's point of view.

In general, the legal form and economic substance of an exchange are straightforward and mutually reinforcing. For example, an ordinary sale of equipment passes title (legal form) of an asset to the purchaser, who subsequently bears the risk and rewards of ownership (economic substance). Generally, accountants do not record the asset and liability on the new owner's records unless legal title has passed.

Statement No. 13 of the Financial Accounting Standards Board (FASB) requires an exception to this rule for certain types of leases. The board asserted that many noncancelable leases are substantially equivalent to purchases. The lessee has full use of the asset and a legal obligation to make payments, the same as if money were borrowed and the asset purchased. Such leases should be recorded by the lessee as a leasehold *asset* and leasehold *liability* even though no legal title has passed. That is, legal passage of title (the form) is secondary; accountants should record the assumption of the risks and rewards of ownership by the lessee (economic substance).

☐ Operating and Capital Leases

Leases are divided into two major kinds: capital leases and operating leases. **Capital leases** are those that transfer substantially all the risks and benefits of ownership. They are equivalent to installment sale and purchase transactions. The asset must be recorded essentially as having been sold by the lessor and having been purchased by the lessee. All other leases are **operating leases.** Examples of the latter are telephones rented by the month and rooms rented by the day, week, or month. Operating leases are accounted for as ordinary rent expenses; no balance sheet accounts are affected by operating leases.

Consider a simple example to see how the accounting differs for operating and capital leases. Suppose B Company can acquire a truck (or a computer or a packaging machine) that has a useful life of four years and no residual value under either of the following conditions:

BUY OUTRIGHT	or	NONCANCELABLE LEASE
Cash outlays, $50,000		Rental of $16,462 per year, payable at the end of each of four years
Borrow $50,000 cash, four-year loan payable at maturity at 12% interest compounded annually		

There is no basic difference between buying outright or irrevocably leasing for four years.[8] B Company uses the asset for its entire useful life and must pay for repairs, property taxes, and other operating costs under either plan.

Most lease rentals are paid at the *start* of each payment period, but to ease our computations we assume that each payment will occur at the end of the year. To earn 12% per year, the lessor would consult Table 3, page 406. The 12% column and fourth-period row show a factor of 3.0373:

---

[8] Note the reason why a capital lease is regarded as no different from borrowing the cash and then buying an asset outright. The lessee bears the same risks and rewards as an owner. The difference is only in the form of financing. The management decision in this context is often expressed as, Should we buy or lease? But if you ponder the question more deeply, you will see that the question is better divided into two parts. First, regardless of the form of financing, Should we acquire the asset or not acquire it? If the answer is to acquire it, the second question is, Should we acquire it by leasing or by an outright purchase with borrowed money?

Let X = rental payment
$50,000 = PV of annuity of X per year for 4 years at 12%
$50,000 = 3.0373$X$
$X = $50,000 \div 3.0373$
$X = $16,462$ rental per year, as shown in the comparison above

The present value of the four $16,462 lease payments is

$$\$16{,}462 \times 3.0373 = \$50{,}000$$

From the lessee's perspective, both buying outright and leasing create a $50,000 obligation.

Before the passage of FASB *Statement No. 13* in 1976, the balance sheet of a company electing to lease the asset would have looked very different from that of a company that purchased the asset. Most companies used the operating lease method, with the following straightforward effect:

	A		=	L	+	SE
	Cash	Truck Leasehold		Lease Liability		Retained Income
Signing of lease	No entry					
Lease payment:						
Year 1	− 16,462		=			− 16,462 ⎡ Increase
Year 2	− 16,462		=			− 16,462 ⎢ Rent Expense
Year 3	− 16,462		=			− 16,462 ⎢
Year 4	− 16,462		=			− 16,462 ⎣
Cumulative totals	− 65,848		=			− 65,848

Each year the journal entry would be:

Rent expense	16,462	
Cash		16,462
To record lease payment.		

However, under today's accounting rules, such a lease must be accounted for as a *capital lease*. This means that both a leasehold asset and a lease liability must be placed on the balance sheet at the present value of future lease payments, $50,000 in this illustration. The signing of the lease would require the following journal entry:

Truck leasehold under capital lease	50,000	
Lease liability		50,000
To record the acquisition of an asset		
and its accompanying liability.		

At the end of each of the four years, the asset must be amortized. Straight-line amortization, which is used almost without exception, would be $50,000 \div 4 = $12,500 annually. In addition, the annual lease payment must be recorded. Each lease payment consists of interest expense plus an amount that reduces the outstanding liability. The effective-interest method is used, as Exhibit 9–17 demonstrates. Study the exhibit before proceeding.

Exhibit 9–18 uses the balance sheet equation to summarize the accounting for capital leases. The yearly journal entries for the leasehold expense would be:

EXHIBIT 9–17

Analytical Schedule of Lease Payments

End of Year	(1) Lease Liability at Beginning of Year	(2) Interest at 12% per Year	(3) (1) + (2) Accumulated Amount at End of Year	(4) Cash for Lease Payment	(5) (3) – (4) Lease Liability at End of Year	(6) SAME AS (2) Interest Expense	(7) (4) – (2) Reduction in Beginning Lease Liability
						Supplementary Analysis of Each Payment	
1	$50,000	$6,000	$56,000	$16,462	$39,538	$ 6,000	$10,462
2	39,538	4,745	44,283	16,462	27,821	4,745	11,717
3	27,821	3,339	31,160	16,462	14,698	3,339	13,123
4	14,698	1,764	16,462	16,462	0	1,764	14,698
						$15,848	$50,000

	Amortization of leasehold	12,500	
	Truck leasehold		12,500

The yearly journal entries for lease payments would be:

	YEAR 1		YEAR 2		YEAR 3		YEAR 4	
Interest expense	6,000		4,745		3,339		1,764	
Lease liability	10,462		11,717		13,123		14,698	
Cash		16,462		16,462		16,462		16,462

Leasehold assets and lease liabilities are illustrated by the following items from the annual report of Winn-Dixie Stores, Inc.:

WINN-DIXIE STORES, INC.
Balance Sheet (Selected Items)

	End of Fiscal Year	
	1988	1987
Assets:		
Leased Property under capital leases, less accumulated amortization of $29,504 ($37,255 in 1987)	$51,050	$65,561
Liabilities:		
Obligations under capital leases	$63,095	$78,046

EXHIBIT 9–18

Accounting for a Capital Lease

	A		= L +	SE
	Cash	Truck Leasehold	Lease Liability	Retained Income
Signing of lease		+50,000 =	+50,000	
Amortization of leasehold:*				
End of Year 1		−12,500* =		−12,500 ⎡ Increase
End of Year 2		−12,500 =		−12,500 ⎪ Amortization
End of Year 3		−12,500 =		−12,500 ⎪ of leasehold
End of Year 4		−12,500 =		−12,500 ⎣
Lease payments:†				
End of Year 1	−16,462		= −10,462	− 6,000 ⎡ Increase
End of Year 2	−16,462		= −11,717	− 4,745 ⎪ Interest
End of Year 3	−16,462		= −13,123	− 3,339 ⎣ Expense
End of Year 4	−16,462		= −14,698	− 1,764
Cumulative totals	−65,848	0	0	−65,848

* Straight-line amortization is followed in practice. A separate amount for Accumulated Amortization—Leasehold could be presented, but the Amortization is shown here as a direct reduction of Truck Leasehold.

† Exhibit 9–17 contains the analytical schedule of lease payments.

In addition, footnote disclosures are required for all significant leases, regardless of whether they are capital leases or operating leases. These footnotes reveal at least the minimum lease payments for the next five years, in the aggregate and year by year. Exhibit 9–19 shows the Winn-Dixie footnote for 1988.

EXHIBIT 9–19

WINN-DIXIE STORES, INC.
From Footnote on Leases

The following is an analysis of the leased property under capital leases by major category:

	ASSET BALANCES	
	1988	1987
Store facilities	$52,196	$ 53,070
Warehouses and manufacturing facilities	28,358	49,746
	80,554	102,816
Less: Accumulated amortization	29,504	37,255
	$51,050	$65,561

The following is a schedule by year of future minimum lease payments under capital and operating leases, together with the present value of the net minimum lease payments as of June 29, 1988:

	AMOUNTS IN THOUSANDS	
Fiscal Year	Capital	Operating
1989	$ 11,021	$ 153,190
1990	10,984	151,553
1991	11,151	149,945
1992	11,155	145,904
1993	10,667	142,633
Later years	129,165	1,347,576
Total minimum lease payments	184,143	$2,090,801
Less: Amount representing estimated taxes, maintenance and insurance costs included in total minimum lease payments	7,418	
Net minimum lease payments	176,725	
Less: Amount representing interest	111,541	
Present value of net minimum lease payments	$ 65,184	

Rental payments under operating leases including, where applicable, real estate taxes and other expenses are as follows:

	1988	1987
	Amounts in Thousands	
Minimum rentals	$143,757	$132,352
Contingent rentals	4,658	6,120
	$148,415	$138,472

☐ Differences in Income Statements

Exhibit 9–20 shows the major differences between the accounting for operating leases and the accounting for capital leases. The cumulative expenses are the same, $65,848, but the timing differs. In comparison with the operating-lease approach, the capital-lease approach tends to bunch heavier charges in the early years. The longer the lease, the more pronounced the differences will be in the early years. Therefore immediate reported income is hurt more under the capital-lease approach.

An operating lease affects the income statement as rent expense, which is the amount of the lease payment. A capital lease affects the income statement as amortization (of the asset) plus interest expense (on the liability). For each year of the lease, the difference in pretax income can be expressed as follows:

$$\begin{aligned} \text{Difference in pretax income} &= \text{Operating lease effect} - \text{Capital lease effect} \quad &(1) \\ &= \text{Lease payment} - (\text{Amortization} + \text{Interest}) \quad &(2) \\ &= (\text{Lease payment} - \text{Amortization}) - \text{Interest} \end{aligned}$$

The difference between the lease payment and amortization, $16,462 − $12,500 = $3,962, is the *average* interest included in the lease payment. Essentially, the operating lease method charges $3,962 of interest expense each year. In the early years of the lease, the capital lease charges more than $3,962 of interest, and in later years it charges less.

EXHIBIT 9–20

Comparison of Annual Expenses: Operating versus Capital Leases

OPERATING-LEASE METHOD	CAPITAL-LEASE METHOD			DIFFERENCE	
				(e)	(f)
			(d)	(a) − (d)	Difference in Ending
(a)	(b)	(c)	(b) + (c)	Difference	Balance,
Lease	Amortization	Interest	Total	in Pretax	Retained
Year	Payment*	of Asset†	Expense‡	Expense	Income	Income
1	$16,462	$12,500	$ 6,000	$18,500	$(2,038)	$(2,038)
2	16,462	12,500	4,745	17,245	(783)	(2,821)
3	16,462	12,500	3,339	15,839	623	(2,198)
4	16,462	12,500	1,764	14,264	2,198	—
Cumulative expenses	$65,848	$50,000	$15,848	$65,848	$ —	

* Rent expense for the year under the operating-lease method.
† $50,000 ÷ 4 = $12,500.
‡ From Exhibit 9–17.

The differences in income between operating and capital leases can be measured by the differences in interest:

	INTEREST INCLUDED IN OPERATING LEASE EXPENSE	INTEREST INCLUDED IN CAPITAL LEASE EXPENSE	DIFFERENCE
Year 1	$ 3,962	$ 6,000	$ −2,038
Year 2	3,962	4,745	−783
Year 3	3,962	3,339	623
Year 4	3,962	1,764	2,198
Total	$15,848	$15,848	$ 0

☐ Tests for Capital Leases

The capital-lease approach was adopted in 1976 after many years of controversy within the accounting profession regarding which leases deserve capitalization as balance sheet items. Until then, almost no leases were capitalized. Many companies were criticized for "invisible debt" or "off-balance sheet financing" in the sense that noncancelable leases existed but were not included as liabilities on the balance sheet.

A letter to the editor of *Business Week* shows the attitude that still persists among many managers:

☐ The fact is that capital leases do, indeed, have to be carried on a company's balance sheet as assets and liabilities, but operating leases do not. Operating leases are accounted for as expenses.

☐ Consequently operating leases provide considerably greater financial benefits. Companies will show a better return on assets and a lower debt-to-equity ratio. Asset turnover also will be higher. The lease payments are fully deductible.

Whether "considerably greater financial benefits" do in fact occur is a highly debatable, complex point. See Chapter 15, pages 690–692, for additional discussion.

A *capital lease* exists if *one* or more of the following conditions are met:

1. Title is transferred to the lessee by the end of the lease term.
2. A bargain purchase option is available to the lessee.
3. The lease term equals or exceeds 75% of the estimated economic life of the property.
4. At the start of the lease term, the present value of minimum lease payments is at least 90% of the excess of the property's fair value over any related investment tax credit retained by the lessor.

Criteria 3 and 4 are not applicable if the lease term begins during the final 25% of the property's economic life. A lease either meets one of these criteria or does not. Managers cannot choose to treat a given lease as either a capital lease or an operating lease. However, some managers seek to structure leases so that they do not meet any of the criteria and therefore are not shown on the balance sheet.

As you can readily visualize, accounting for leases can rapidly become enormously complicated.[9] For further discussion, see a textbook on intermediate or advanced accounting.

_____

[9] Consider the advertisement in the *Wall Street Journal* with big bold letters in black and white: FAS–13. (That refers to Financial Accounting Standards No. 13, although the ad found it unnecessary to say so.) The ad continues, "We specialize in leases and have developed a complete and easy-to-use system for lessees and lessors. All accounting, tax, disclosure and restatement schedules . . ."

☐ Liabilities for Pensions

In accounting for pensions, companies must recognize a liability to employees when the accumulated benefit obligation exceeds the fair value of the assets in a pension fund. Suppose a company's current pension expense is $100,000, $30,000 of which is paid in cash to a pension fund. The accounting for pensions has the following fundamental framework:

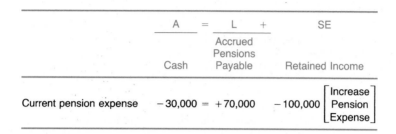

	A	=	L	+	SE
			Accrued Pensions		
	Cash		Payable		Retained Income
Current pension expense	− 30,000	=	+ 70,000		− 100,000 [Increase Pension Expense]

The journal entry would be:

Pension expense	100,000	
Cash		30,000
Accrued pensions payable		70,000
To record pension expense for the year.		

Accounting for pensions has been controversial. However, the debate is not overly concerned with what accounts should be affected. Rather, it is concerned with how to *measure* current expense and the long-term liability for pensions. This entails compound interest effects and fiery debates about what interest rates are applicable. The choice of an interest rate can have a telling impact on the present value of a liability. Pension liabilities are frequently substantial. FASB *Statements No. 87* and *88* provide detailed rules for many of the controversial measurement issues. For further discussion, see textbooks on intermediate and advanced accounting.

In addition to pensions, over half the major U.S. companies provide health care and life insurance benefits to retirees. Until now, no liability has been recognized for these obligations. However, the FASB has proposed that companies include the present value of the expected cost of these benefits as a liability. Such a requirement will probably be adopted in the near future.

SUMMARY PROBLEM FOR YOUR REVIEW

☐ Problem Six (Other review problems appeared earlier in the chapter.)

Exxon acquired computer equipment from IBM on a capital lease. There were annual lease payments of $60 million at the end of each of four years. The implicit interest rate was 14% compounded annually.

Required:
1. Compute the present value of the capital lease.
2. Prepare Exxon journal entries at the inception of the lease and for the first two years. Show computations.
3. For simplicity, the earlier presentation of leases ignored short-term and long-term classifications. Recast the initial journal entry in requirement 2 to make this distinction. Also prepare an entry at the end of Year 1 to reclassify the portion of long-term debt that has become current.

☐ Solution to Problem Six

1. PV_A = \$60,000,000 × Annuity factor for 4 years at 14%
   = \$60,000,000 × 2.9137
   = \$174,822,000

2.

Computer equipment leasehold	174,822,000	
Lease liability		174,822,000
To record capital lease.		
Terms are 4 years,		
annual payments of \$60 million,		
implicit interest of 14%.		

Entry for amortization of asset for each of first two years:

Amortization of computer equipment		
leasehold	43,705,500	
Computer equipment leasehold		43,705,500
To record straight-line amortization		
of \$174,822,000		
÷ 4 = \$43,705,500.		

Entries for reduction of liability:

Interest expense	24,475,080	
Lease liability	35,524,920	
Cash		60,000,000
Interest is .14 × \$174,822,000 = \$24,475,080.		
Principal reduction is \$60,000,000 − \$24,475,080 =		
\$35,524,920		
Interest expense	19,501,591	
Lease liability	40,498,409	
Cash		60,000,000
Interest is .14 (\$174,822,000 −\$35,524,920) or .14		
× \$139,297,080 = \$19,501,591.		
Principal reduction is \$60,000,000 − \$19,501,591 =		
\$40,498,409.		

3.

Computer equipment leasehold	174,822,000	
Lease liability, current		35,524,920
Lease liability, long-term		139,297,080
To record capital lease.		
Lease liability, long-term	40,498,409	
Lease liability, current		40,498,409
To reclassify current installment of long-term debt		
as short-term debt.		

FUNDAMENTAL ASSIGNMENT MATERIAL

☐ General Coverage

9–1. VARIOUS LIABILITIES. (Alternate is 9–8.)

1. A bank received a $24,000 savings deposit on August 1. On September 30, the bank recognized two months' interest thereon at an annual rate of 10%. On October 1, the depositor closed her account with the bank. Interest is payable from the date of deposit through the date before withdrawal. Prepare the bank's journal entries.

2. The Los Angeles Dodgers sold season tickets for $4 million cash in advance of the baseball season, which begins on April 10. These tickets are for eighty game dates.
   a. What is the effect on the balance sheet, March 31? Prepare the appropriate journal entry for the sale of the tickets.
   b. Assume that seventy game dates remain after April 30. What is the effect on the balance sheet, April 30? Prepare the related summary journal entry for April.

3. Zellner Corporation sells communications equipment. Experience has shown that warranty costs average 4% of sales. Sales for June were $10 million. Cash disbursements for rendering warranty service during June were $310,000. Prepare the journal entries for these transactions.

4. A wholesale distributor gets cash deposits for its returnable bottles. In July, the distributor received $160,000 cash and disbursed $120,000 for bottles returned. Prepare the journal entries for these transactions.

5. Contingencies are often shown "short" in the balance sheet. What is a "short" presentation?

6. A hospital has lost a lawsuit. Damages were set at $1 million. The hospital plans to appeal the decision to a higher court. The hospital's attorneys are 80% confident of a reversal of the lower court's decision. What liability, if any, should appear on the hospital's balance sheet?

9–2. BOND DISCOUNT TRANSACTIONS AND STRAIGHT-LINE AMORTIZATION. On December 31, 1989, Webster Company issued $20 million of ten-year, 12% debentures. Proceeds were $19.6 million.

Required: Show all amounts in thousands of dollars.

1. Using the balance sheet equation format, prepare an analysis of bond transactions. Assume straight-line amortization. Show entries for the issuer regarding (a) issuance, (b) one semiannual interest payment, and (c) payment of maturity value.
2. Show all the corresponding journal entries keyed as above.
3. Show how the bond-related accounts would appear on the balance sheets as of December 31, 1989, 1996, and 1998.

9–3. BONDS ISSUED AT PAR. (Alternate is 9–39.) On December 31, 1989, Cheung Computers issued $20 million of ten-year, 12% debentures at par.

Required:
1. Compute the proceeds from issuing the debentures.
2. Using the balance sheet equation format, prepare an analysis of this bond transaction.

Show entries for the issuer regarding (a) issuance, (b) the first semiannual interest payment, and (c) payment of maturity value.

3. Show all the corresponding journal entries keyed as in requirement 2.
4. Show how the bond-related accounts would appear on the balance sheet as of December 31, 1989, and June 30, 1990. Assume that the semiannual interest payment and amortization due on the balance sheet date have been recorded.

9–4. **Bonds Issued at a Discount.** (Alternates are 9–9, 9–40, and 9–64.) On December 31, 1989, Cheung Computers issued $20 million of ten-year, 12% debentures. The market interest rate at issuance was 14%.

Required:
1. Compute the proceeds from issuing the debentures.
2. Using the balance sheet equation format, prepare an analysis of this bond transaction. Show entries for the issuer regarding (a) issuance, (b) the first semiannual interest payment and discount amortization, and (c) payment of maturity value. Round all amounts to the nearest thousand.
3. Show all the corresponding journal entries keyed as in requirement 2.
4. Show how the bond-related accounts would appear on the balance sheet as of December 31, 1989, and June 30, 1990. Assume that the semiannual interest payment and amortization due on the balance sheet date have been recorded.

9–5. **Bonds Issued at a Premium.** (Alternates are 9–41 and 9–65.) On December 31, 1989, Cheung Computers issued $20 million of ten-year, 12% debentures. The market interest rate at issuance was 10%.

Required:
1. Compute the proceeds from issuing the debentures.
2. Using the balance sheet equation format, prepare an analysis of this bond transaction. Show entries for the issuer regarding (a) issuance, (b) the first semiannual interest payment and premium amortization, and (c) payment of maturity value. Round all amounts to the nearest thousand.
3. Show all the corresponding journal entries keyed as in requirement 2.
4. Show how the bond-related accounts would appear on the balance sheet as of December 31, 1989, and June 30, 1990. Assume that the semiannual interest payment and amortization due on the balance sheet date have been recorded.

9–6. **Early Extinguishment of Debt.** (Alternate is 9–10.) On December 31, 1989, Cheung Computers issued $20 million of ten-year, 12% debentures. The market interest rate at issuance was 14%. On December 31, 1990 (after all interest payments and amortization had been recorded for 1990), the company purchased all the debentures for $18.5 million. Throughout their life, the debentures had been held by a large insurance company.

Required:
Show all amounts in thousands of dollars. Round to the nearest thousand.

1. Compute the gain or loss on early extinguishment.
2. Using the balance sheet equation, present an analysis of the transaction on the issuer's books.
3. Show the appropriate journal entry.

9–7. **Non-Interest-Bearing Notes.** (Alternate is 9–11.) A college borrowed from a bank on a one-month note due on July 31, 19X0. The face value of the note was $200,000. However, the bank deducted its interest "in advance" at a monthly rate of 1% of the face value.

Required:
Show the effects on the borrower's records at inception and at the end of the month:

1. Using the balance sheet equation, prepare an analysis of transactions.
2. Prepare journal entries.

9–8. VARIOUS LIABILITIES. (Alternate is 9–1.)

1. Maytag Corporation sells electric appliances, including automatic washing machines. Experience in recent years has indicated that warranty costs average 3.1% of sales. Sales of washing machines for April were $3 million. Cash disbursements and obligations for warranty service on washing machines during April totaled $84,000. Prepare the journal entries prompted by these facts.

2. Pepsi-Cola Company of New York gets cash deposits for its returnable bottles. In June it received $100,000 cash and disbursed $91,000 for bottles returned. Prepare the journal entries regarding the receipts and returns of deposits.

3. Bank of America received a $2,000 savings deposit on April 1. On June 30, it recognized interest thereon at an annual rate of 5%. On July 1, the depositor closed her account with the bank. Prepare the necessary journal entries.

4. The Schubert Theater sold for $100,000 cash a "season's series" of tickets in advance of December 31 for four plays, each to be held in successive months beginning in January.
   a. What is the effect on the balance sheet, December 31? What is the appropriate journal entry for the sale of the tickets?
   b. What is the effect on the balance sheet, January 31? What is the related journal entry for January?

5. In its 1989 annual report, Alcoa shows "contingencies" short in the balance sheet just above the "stockholders' equity" section. What is a "short" presentation?

6. Suppose your local hospital has lost a lawsuit. Damages were set at $500,000. The hospital plans to appeal the decision to a higher court. The hospital's attorneys are 90% confident of a reversal of the lower court's decision. What liability, if any, should be shown on the hospital's balance sheet?

9–9. BOND DISCOUNT TRANSACTIONS. (Alternates are 9–4, 9–40, and 9–64.) On February 1, 1990, a large electric utility issued $200 million of twenty-year, 9% debentures. Proceeds were $182,382 million, implying a market interest rate of 10%.

Required: Show all amounts in thousands of dollars.

1. Using the balance sheet equation format, prepare an analysis of bond transactions. Assume effective-interest amortization. Show entries for the issuer regarding (a) issuance, (b) the first semiannual interest payment, and (c) payment of maturity value.
2. Show all the corresponding journal entries for (a), (b), and (c) in requirement 1.
3. Show how the bond-related accounts would appear on the balance sheets as of February 1, 1990 and 1991. Assume the February 1 interest payment and amortization of bond discount have been made.

9–10. EARLY EXTINGUISHMENT OF DEBT. (Alternate is 9–6.) On December 31, 1988, Texaco issued $10 million of ten-year, 12% debentures. The market interest rate at issuance was 12%. Suppose that on December 31, 1989 (after all interest payments and amortization had been recorded for 1989), the company purchased all the debentures for $9.8 million. The debentures had been held by a large insurance company throughout their life.

Required: Show all amounts in thousands of dollars.

1. Compute the gain or loss on early extinguishment.
2. Using the balance sheet equation, present an analysis of the transaction on the issuer's books.
3. Show the appropriate journal entry.

9–11. NON-INTEREST-BEARING NOTES. (Alternate is 9–7.) On July 31, 1989, St. Paul's Church borrowed money from a bank on a two-year note due on July 31, 1991. The face value of the note was $25,000. However, the bank deducted its interest "in advance" at a rate of 12% compounded annually.

Show the effects on the borrower's records. Show the effects at July 31, 1989, 1990, and 1991.

1. Using the balance sheet equation, prepare an analysis of transactions.
2. Prepare journal entries.

ADDITIONAL ASSIGNMENT MATERIAL

☐ **General Coverage**

9–12. Distinguish between *current liabilities* and *long-term liabilities*.

9–13. Name and briefly describe five items that are often classified as current liabilities.

9–14. "Withholding taxes really add to employer payroll costs." Do you agree? Explain.

9–15. "Product warranties expense should not be recognized until the actual services are performed. Until then you don't know which products might require warranty repairs." Do you agree? Explain.

9–16. Distinguish between a *mortgage bond* and a *debenture*. Which is safer?

9–17. Distinguish between *subordinated* and *unsubordinated* debentures.

9–18. "The face amount of a bond is what you can sell it for." Do you agree? Explain.

9–19. "Protective covenants protect the shareholders' interests in cases of liquidation of assets." Do you agree? Explain.

9–20. "The quoted bond interest rates imply a rate per annum, but the bond markets do not mean that rate literally." Explain.

9–21. Contrast *nominal* and *effective* interest rates for bonds.

9–22. "Discount *accumulation* is a better descriptive term than discount *amortization*." What would be the justification for making this assertion?

9–23. Distinguish between *straight-line* amortization and *effective-interest* amortization.

9–24. A company issued bonds with a nominal rate of 10%. At what market rates will the bonds be issued at a discount? At what market rates will they be issued at a premium?

9–25. What are the three main differences between accounting for a bond discount and accounting for a bond premium?

9–26. "A company that issues zero coupon bonds recognizes no interest expense until the bond matures." Do you agree? Explain.

9–27. "A contingent liability is a liability having an estimated amount." Do you agree? Explain.

9–28. "At the balance sheet date, a private high school has lost a court case for an uninsured football injury. The amount of damages has not been set. A reasonable estimate is between $800,000 and $2 million." How should this information be presented in the financial statements?

9–29. "Future value and present value are two sides of the same coin." Explain.

9–30. Distinguish between *employee* payroll taxes and *employer* payroll taxes.

9–31. Certain leases are essentially equivalent to purchases. A company must account for such leases as if the asset had been purchased. Explain.

9–32. "Because a company never knows how much it will have to pay for pensions, no pension liability is recognized. Pension obligations are simply explained in a footnote to the financial statements." Do you agree? Explain.

9–33. PAYROLL ACCOUNTING. Chavez, Inc., incurred payroll wages of $200,000 for the week ended May 17. Of the total payroll, amounts withheld for social security (FICA) and income taxes were $14,000 and $32,000, respectively. The employees were paid on May 29, and the government was paid on May 22.

Required:
1. Prepare journal entries to record the payroll on May 17.
2. Prepare journal entries for the payments on May 20 and May 22.

9–34. **INCOME TAX ESTIMATES.** Galleon Corporation has an estimated taxable income of $30 million for the calendar year 19X3. The applicable income tax rate is 40%. Ignore all other possible data regarding income taxes.

Required:
1. Compute the quarterly income tax payment.
2. Suppose pretax income is as follows for the first quarter: January, $4 million; February, $1 million; March, $3 million. Fill in the blanks:

	JANUARY	FEBRUARY	MARCH
Amount of income tax expense	?	?	?

3. Prepare the journal entry for January.
4. Prepare the journal entry for April 15.
5. What is the balance of Accrued Income Taxes Payable after the disbursement on April 15?

9–35. **SALES TAXES.** (Alternate is 9–62). The Riordan Store is in a mid-western state where the sales tax is 8%. Total sales for the month of April were $300,000, of which $250,000 was subject to sales tax.

Required:
1. Prepare a journal entry that summarizes sales (all in cash) for the month.
2. Prepare a journal entry regarding the disbursement for the sales tax.

9–36. **PRODUCT WARRANTIES.** During 19X9, the Magnan Company had sales of $1 million. The company estimates that the cost of servicing products under warranty will average 1.5% of sales.

Required:
1. Prepare journal entries for sales revenue and the related warranty expense for 19X9. Assume all sales are for cash.
2. The liability for warranties was $11,100 at the beginning of 19X9. Expenditures (all in cash) to satisfy warranty claims during 19X9 were $17,400, of which $4,500 was for products sold in 19X9. Prepare the journal entry for the warranty expenditures.
3. Compute the end-of-19X9 balance in the Liability for Warranties account.

9–37. **PRIORITIES OF CLAIMS.** Lustre Corporation is being liquidated. It has one major asset, an office building, which was converted into $18 million cash. The stockholders' equity has been wiped out by past losses. The following claims exist: accounts payable, $3 million; debentures payable, $5 million; first mortgage payable, $12 million.

Required:
1. Assume the debentures are unsubordinated. How much will each class of claimants receive?
2. If the debentures are subordinated, how much will each class of claimants receive? How much will each class receive if the cash proceeds from the sale of the building amount to only $13.5 million?

9–38. **ANALYSIS OF PRINCIPAL AND INTEREST.** (Alternate is 9–63.) Consider a bank loan of $720,000 to a church on August 31, 19X1. The loan bears interest at 10%. Principal and interest are due in one year. The church reports on a calendar-year basis.

Required:
1. Prepare an analysis of transactions, using the balance sheet equation. Indicate the entries for the church for August 31, 19X1, December 31, 19X1, and August 31, 19X2. Allocate interest within the year on a straight-line basis. Show all amounts in thousands of dollars.
2. Prepare all the corresponding journal entries keyed as above.

9–39. **BONDS ISSUED AT PAR.** (Alternate is 9–3.) On January 1, 1990, Sargent Electronics issued $1 million of five-year, 11% debentures at par.

Required:
1. Compute the proceeds from issuing the debentures.
2. Using the balance sheet equation format, prepare an analysis of this bond transaction. Show entries for the issuer regarding (a) issuance, (b) the first semiannual interest payment, and (c) payment of maturity value.
3. Show all the corresponding journal entries keyed as in requirement 2.
4. Show how the bond-related accounts would appear on the balance sheet as of January 1, 1990, and July 1, 1990. Assume that the semiannual interest payment and amortization due on the balance sheet date have been recorded.

9–40. **Bonds Issued at a Discount.** (Alternates are 9–4, 9–9, and 9–64.) On January 1, 1990, Sargent Electronics issued $1 million of five-year, 11% debentures. The market interest rate at issuance was 16%.

Required:
1. Compute the proceeds from issuing the debentures.
2. Using the balance sheet equation format, prepare an analysis of this bond transaction. Show entries for the issuer regarding (a) issuance, (b) the first semiannual interest payment, and (c) payment of maturity value. Round to the nearest thousand.
3. Show all the corresponding journal entries keyed as in requirement 2.
4. Show how the bond-related accounts would appear on the balance sheet as of January 1, 1990, and July 1, 1990. Assume that the semiannual interest payment and amortization due on the balance sheet date have been recorded.

9–41. **Bonds Issued at a Premium.** (Alternates are 9–5 and 9–65.) On January 1, 1990, Sargent Electronics issued $1 million of five-year, 11% debentures. The market interest rate at issuance was 8%.

Required:
1. Compute the proceeds from issuing the debentures.
2. Using the balance sheet equation format, prepare an analysis of this bond transaction. Show entries for the issuer regarding (a) issuance, (b) the first semiannual interest payment, and (c) payment of maturity value. Round to the nearest thousand.
3. Show all the corresponding journal entries keyed as in requirement 2.
4. Show how the bond-related accounts would appear on the balance sheet as of January 1, 1990, and July 1, 1990. Assume that the semiannual interest payment and amortization due on the balance sheet date have been recorded.

9–42. **Bonds Sold between Interest Dates.** On December 31, 1989, a company had some bonds printed and ready for issuance. But market conditions soured. The bonds were not issued until February 28, 1990, at par. The indenture requires payment of semiannual interest on December 31 and June 30. The face value of the bonds is $10 million. The interest rate is 12%.

Required:
1. Compute the total proceeds of the issue on February 28.
2. Prepare an analysis of transactions, using the balance sheet equation. Show amounts in thousands of dollars. Show the effects on the issuer's records on February 28 and June 30, 1990.
3. Prepare corresponding journal entries.

9–43. **Non-Interest-Bearing Note.** A sports club borrowed money from a bank on a six-month note due on September 30, 19X1. The face value of the note was $20,000. However, the bank deducted its interest in advance at an annual rate of 18% of face value.

Required:
1. Prepare journal entries for the sports club at the inception of the note, for one month's interest, and at maturity. Allocate interest to each of the six months on a straight-line basis.
2. What would be the liability after two months? How would it be presented on the club's balance sheet?

Special note: These problems are arranged to correspond with the sequence of topics covered in the appendixes.

9–44. EXERCISES IN COMPOUND INTEREST.

1. You deposit $5,000. How much will you have in four years at 8%, compounded annually? At 12%?
2. A savings and loan association offers depositors a lump-sum payment of $5,000 four years hence. If you desire an interest rate of 8% compounded annually, how much will you be willing to deposit? At an interest rate of 12%?
3. Repeat requirement 1, but assume that the interest rates are compounded semiannually.

9–45. EXERCISES IN COMPOUND INTEREST. A reliable friend has asked you for a loan. You are pondering various proposals for repayment.

1. Repayment of a lump sum of $40,000 four years hence. How much will you lend if your desired rate of return is (a) 10% compounded annually, (b) 20% compounded annually?
2. Repeat requirement 1, but assume that the interest rates are compounded semiannually.
3. Suppose the loan is to be paid in full by equal payments of $10,000 at the end of each of the next four years. How much will you lend if your desired rate of return is (a) 10% compounded annually, (b) 20% compounded annually?

9–46. COMPOUND INTEREST AND JOURNAL ENTRIES. Bruckner Company acquired equipment for a $250,000 promissory note, payable five years hence, non-interest-bearing, but having an implicit interest rate of 14% compounded annually. Prepare the journal entry for (1) the acquisition of the equipment and (2) interest expense for the first year.

9–47. COMPOUND INTEREST AND JOURNAL ENTRIES. A German company has bought some equipment on a contract entailing a DM 100,000 cash down payment and a DM 400,000 lump sum to be paid at the end of four years. The same equipment can be bought for DM 336,840 cash. DM refers to the German mark, a unit of currency.

Required:
1. Prepare the journal entry for the acquisition of the equipment.
2. Prepare journal entries at the end of each of the first two years. Ignore entries for depreciation.

9–48. COMPOUND INTEREST AND JOURNAL ENTRIES. A dry-cleaning company bought new presses for a $80,000 down payment and $100,000 to be paid at the end of each of four years. The applicable imputed interest rate is 10% on the unpaid balance. Prepare journal entries (1) for the acquisition and (2) at the end of the first year.

9–49. EXERCISES IN COMPOUND INTEREST.

a. It is your sixtieth birthday. You plan to work five more years before retiring. Then you want to take $10,000 for a Mediterranean cruise. What lump sum do you have to invest now in order to accumulte the $10,000? Assume that your minimum desired rate of return is
   (1) 6%, compounded annually
   (2) 10%, compounded annually
   (3) 20%, compounded annually
b. You want to spend $3,000 on a vacation at the end of each of the next five years. What lump sum do you have to invest now in order to take the five vacations? Assume that your minimum desired rate of return is
   (1) 6%, compounded annually
   (2) 10%, compounded annually
   (3) 20%, compounded annually
c. At age sixty, you find that your employer is moving to another location. You receive termination pay of $50,000. You have some savings and wonder whether to retire now.
   (1) If you invest the $50,000 now at 6%, compounded annually, how much money can you withdraw from your account each year so that at the end of five years there will be a zero balance?

(2) If you invest it at 10%?

d. At 16%, compounded annually, which of the following plans is more desirable in terms of present values? Show computations to support your answer.

	ANNUAL CASH INFLOWS	
Year	Mining	Farming
1	$100,000	$ 20,000
2	80,000	40,000
3	60,000	60,000
4	40,000	80,000
5	20,000	100,000
	$300,000	$300,000

9–50. BASIC RELATIONSHIPS IN INTEREST TABLES.

1. Suppose you borrow $15,000 now at 16% interest compounded annually. The borrowed amount plus interest will be repaid in a lump sum at the end of six years. How much must be repaid? Use Table 1 and basic equation: FV = Present amount × Future value factor.
2. Repeat requirement 1 using Table 2 and the basic equation: PV = Future amount × Present value factor.
3. Assume the same facts as in requirement 1 except that the loan will be repaid in equal installments at the end of each of six years. How much must be repaid each year? Use Table 3 and the basic equation: PV_A = Future annual amounts × Conversion factor.

9–51. DEFERRED ANNUITY EXERCISE. It is your thirty-fifth birthday. On your fortieth birthday, and on three successive birthdays thereafter, you intend to spend exactly $1,000 for a birthday celebration. What lump sum do you have to invest now in order to have the four celebrations? Assume that the money will earn interest, compounded annually, of 8%.

9–52. PRESENT VALUE AND SPORTS SALARIES. The *New York Times* reported that Jack Morris, a pitcher, signed a $4 million contract with the Detroit Tigers. His 1988 salary was $1,988,000, and his 1989 salary was $1,989,000. However, $1 million of his 1989 salary was paid in 1988. The *Times* reported that the advance payment increased the contract's value by about $50,000, pushing it over $4 million.

Assume that the contract was signed on December 1, 1987, that the 1988 and 1989 payments were both made on December 1 of the respective years, and that the appropriate discount rate was 10%.

Required:

1. What was the present value of the contract on the day it was signed?
2. What would have been the present value of the contract if the $1 million advance payment had been paid in 1989 instead of 1988?
3. How much present value (as of December 1, 1987) did Morris gain by receiving the $1 million payment in 1988 rather than in 1989?
4. Do you agree that the contract was worth more than $4 million? Explain.

9–53. DISCOUNTED PRESENT VALUE AND BONDS. On December 31, 19X1, a company issued a three-year $1,000 bond that bears a nominal interest rate of 12%, payable 6% semiannually. Compute the discounted present value of the principal and the interest as of December 31, 19X1, if the market rate of interest for such securities is 12%, 14%, and 10%, respectively. Show your computations, including a sketch of cash flows. Round to the nearest dollar.

9–54. DISCOUNTED PRESENT VALUE AND LEASES. Suppose Winn-Dixie Stores, Inc., signed a ten-year lease for a new store location. The lease calls for an immediate payment of $20,000 and annual payments of $15,000 at the end of each of the next nine years. Winn-Dixie expects to earn 16% interest, compounded annually, on its investments. What is the present value of the lease payments?

9–55. RETIREMENT OF BONDS. (J. Patell, adapted). This is a more difficult problem than others in this group.

On January 2, 1980, the Liverpool Financial Corporation sold a large issue of Series A $1,000 denomination bonds. The bonds had a stated coupon rate of 6% (annual), had a term to maturity of twenty years, and made semiannual coupon payments. Market conditions at the time were such that the bonds sold at their face value.

During the ensuing ten years, market interest rates fluctuated widely, and by January 2, 1990, the Liverpool bonds were trading at a price that provided an annual yield of 10%. Liverpool's management was considering purchasing the Series A bonds in the open market and retiring them; the necessary capital was to be raised by a new bond issue—the Series B bonds. Series B bonds were to be $1,000 denomination coupon (semiannual) bonds with a stated annual rate of 8% and a twenty-year term. Management felt that these bonds could be sold at a price yielding no more than 10%, especially if the Series A bonds were retired.

Required:
1. On January 2, 1990, at what price could Liverpool Financial purchase the Series A bonds? *Hint*: The applicable factors are 5% and 20 periods.
2. Show the journal entries necessary to record the following transactions:
   a. Issue of one Series B bond on January 2, 1990.
   b. Purchase and retirement of one Series A bond on January 2, 1990.
   c. The first coupon payment on a Series B bond on July 2, 1990. Liverpool uses the effective-interest method of accounting for bond premium and discount.
   d. The second coupon payment on a Series B bond on January 2, 1991.

9–56. ACCOUNTING FOR PAYROLL. For the week ended January 27, the Ehlo River Manufacturing Company had a total payroll of $176,000. Three items were withheld from employees' paychecks: (1) social security (FICA) tax of 7.1% of the payroll; (2) income taxes, which average 21% of the payroll; and (3) employees savings that are deposited in their Credit Union, which are $9,800. All three items were paid on January 30.

Required:
1. Use the balance sheet equation to analyze the transactions on January 27 and January 30.
2. Prepare journal entries for the recording of the items in requirement 1.
3. In addition to the payroll, Ehlo River pays (1) payroll taxes of 9% of the payroll, (2) health insurance premiums of $13,000, and (3) contributions to the employees' pension fund of $16,000. Prepare journal entries for the recognition of these additional expenses.

9–57. CAPITAL OR OPERATING LEASE. On December 31, 19X1, E Company has been offered an electronically controlled automatic lathe (a) outright for $100,000 cash or (b) on a noncancelable lease whereby rental payments would be made at the end of each year for three years. The lathe will become obsolete and worthless at the end of three years. The company can borrow $100,000 cash on a three-year loan payable at maturity at 16% compounded annually.

Required:
1. Compute the annual rental payment, assuming that the lessor desires a 16% rate of return per year.
2. If the lease were accounted for as an operating lease, what annual journal entry would be made?
3. The lease is a capital lease. Prepare an analytical schedule of each lease payment. Show the lease liability at the beginning of the year, interest, accumulated amount, lease payment, lease liability at end of year, and a supplementary breakdown of each payment into its interest and principal components.
4. Prepare an analysis of transactions, using the balance sheet equation format.
5. Prepare yearly journal entries.

9–58. CAPITAL LEASE. A company acquired packaging equipment on a capital lease. There were annual lease payments of $40 million at the end of each of three years. The implicit interest rate was 18% compounded annually.

1. Compute the present value of the capital lease. Use the appropriate table in this book (not a hand calculator).
2. Prepare journal entries at the inception of the lease and for each of the three years. Distinguish between the short-term and long-term classifications of the lease.

9–59. **COMPARISON OF OPERATING AND CAPITAL LEASE.** Refer to the preceding problem. Suppose the capital lease were regarded as an operating lease. Ignore income taxes. Fill in the blanks (prepare supporting computations):

	OPERATING LEASE	CAPITAL LEASE	DIFFERENCE
Total expenses:			
Year 1	?	?	?
Year 2	?	?	?
Two years together	?	?	?
End of year 1:			
Total assets	?	?	?
Total liabilities	?	?	?
Retained income	?	?	?
End of year 2:			
Total assets	?	?	?
Total liabilities	?	?	?
Retained income	?	?	?

9–60. **ACCOUNTING FOR PENSIONS.** A company's current pension expense is $800,000, $240,000 of which is paid in cash. Using the balance sheet equation format, show which accounts are affected by these data. Prepare the corresponding journal entry.

☐ Understanding Published Financial Reports

9–61. **TERMINOLOGY.** Consult Exhibit 9–1, page 370, the liabilities of Mattel. For each item therein, state at least one other way of describing the liability.

9–62. **SALES TAXES.** (Alternate is 9–35.) Most of the food sold in retail stores in California is not subject to sales taxes (for example, candy), but some items are (for example, soft drinks). Apparently, the candy lobbyists were more effective than soft drinks lobbyists when dealing with the state legislature. Most cash registers are designed to record taxable sales and nontaxable sales and automatically add the appropriate sales tax.

The sales for the past week in the local Safeway store were $130,000, $20,000 of which was taxable at a rate of 7%. Using the $A = L + SE$ equation, show the impact on the entity, both now and when the sales taxes are paid at a later date. Also prepare corresponding journal entries.

9–63. **ANALYSIS OF PRINCIPAL AND INTEREST.** (Alternate is 9–38.) A repertory theater borrowed $90,000 from Great Western Savings Bank on August 31, 19X1. The loan bears interest at 10%. Principal and interest are due in one year. The theater reports on a calendar-year basis. Interest is allocated to portions of a year on a straight-line basis.

Required: Show all amounts in thousands of dollars.

1. Using the balance sheet equation format, prepare an analysis of the transactions for the theater for August 31, 19X1, December 31, 19X1, and August 31, 19X2.
2. Prepare corresponding journal entries.

9–64. **BOND DISCOUNT TRANSACTIONS.** (Alternates are 9–4, 9–9, and 9–40.) Assume that on December 31, 1989, IBM issued $10 million of ten-year, 10% debentures. Proceeds were $7,881,000; therefore the market rate of interest was 14%.

Required:

1. Using the balance sheet equation format, prepare an analysis of transactions for IBM. Key your transactions as follows: (a) issuance, (b) first semiannual interest using effective-interest amortization of bond discount, and (c) payment of maturity value. Round all amounts to the nearest thousand.
2. Prepare corresponding journal entries keyed (a), (b), and (c) as in requirement 1.
3. Show how the bond-related accounts would appear on IBM's balance sheets as of December 31, 1989, and June 30, 1990. Assume that the semiannual interest payment and amortization have been recorded.

9–65. **BOND PREMIUM TRANSACTIONS.** (Alternates are 9–5 and 9–41.) Assume that on December 31, 1989, IBM issued $10 million of ten-year, 10% debentures. Proceeds were $11,359,000; therefore the market rate of interest was 8%.

Required:

1. Using the balance sheet equation format, prepare an analysis of transactions for IBM. Key your transactions as follows: (a) issuance, (b) first semiannual interest using effective-interest amortization of bond premium, and (c) payment of maturity value. Round all amounts to the nearest thousand.
2. Prepare corresponding journal entries keyed (a), (b), and (c) as in requirement 1.
3. Show how the bond-related accounts would appear on IBM's balance sheets as of December 31, 1989, and June 30, 1990. Assume that the semiannual interest payment and amortization have been recorded.

9–66. **BOND QUOTATIONS.** Following is a bond quotation for American Telephone and Telegraph Company:

DESCRIPTION	CURRENT YIELD	VOLUME	HIGH	LOW	CLOSE	NET CHANGE
AT&T 7s01	7.9	924	90	89	89	$+\frac{1}{4}$

Required:

1. How was the current yield of 7.9% calculated?
2. What price (in total dollars) would you have paid for one bond if you had bought it at a price halfway between its high and low for the day?
3. What was the closing price (in total dollars) for the bond on the preceding day?

9–67. **CONVERTIBLE BONDS.** K Mart has 6% convertible bonds that can each be exchanged for 28.169 shares of common stock. The price of the common stock is $48 per share, and quarterly dividends are $.37 per share.

Required:

1. What is the total market price of the common stock that a holder of one bond could obtain by converting the bond to common stock?
2. What amount of semiannual dividends would be received on the stock obtained in requirement 1?
3. What amount of semiannual interest does the holder of the bond receive on the bond?
4. Will the holder of a convertible bond always exchange it for common stock when the market value of the stock exceeds that of the bond? Explain.

9–68. **ZERO COUPON BONDS.** Since 1985, the U.S. Treasury has required issuers of "deep-discount" or "zero coupon" debt securities to use an effective-interest approach to amortization of discount rather than straight-line amortization. The Treasury claimed that the old law, which permitted straight-line amortization, resulted in overstatements of deductions in early years.

Required:

1. Assume that General Motors issues a ten-year zero coupon bond having a face amount of $20,000,000 to yield 10%. For simplicity, assume that the 10% yield is compounded annually. Prepare the journal entry for the issuer.

2. Prepare the journal entry for interest expense for the first full year and the second full year using (a) straight-line and (b) effective-interest amortization.
3. Assume an income tax rate of 40%. How much more income tax for the first year would the issuer have to pay because of applying effective-interest instead of straight-line amortization?

9–69. ZERO COUPON BONDS. American Medical International, Inc., operates over one hundred hospitals in the United States and abroad. The company included the following information on its balance sheet:

	August 31	
	1988	1987
Zero Coupon Guaranteed Bonds due 1997, $103 million face value	$32,950,000	$28,900,000

Assume that the bonds mature on May 15, 1997, and that none of the bonds were retired in fiscal 1988.

Required:
1. Assume that the bonds were issued on August 31, 1987. Prepare the journal entry at issuance.
2. Prepare the journal entry for recording interest expense on the bonds for fiscal 1988. Assume annual compounding of interest.
3. Compute the approximate effective rate of interest on the bonds. Round to the nearest whole percentage.
4. Prepare the journal entry for recording interest expense on the bonds for fiscal 1989.

9–70. DEBT-TO-EQUITY RATIOS. The total debt and stockholders' equity for four companies follows (in thousands):

	Total Debt		Stockholders' Equity	
	1988	1987	1988	1987
AT&T	$23,687,000	$24,936,000	$11,465,000	$14,455,000
NYNEX	15,942,600	13,809,300	9,419,500	9,196,500
Micron Technology	100,412	56,765	288,002	72,576
Amgen	29,291	12,850	163,544	83,959

The companies are described as follows:

□ AT&T provides long-distance phone service and is a large, well-established company.
□ NYNEX is a regional phone company that is diversifying into a variety of telecommunications and information systems areas.
□ Micron Technology is a fast-growing producer of memory products for electronic systems.
□ Amgen is a biotechnology company pioneering the development of products based on advances in recombinant DNA.

Required:
1. Compute debt-to-equity ratios for each company for 1987 and 1988.
2. Discuss the differences in the ratios across firms.
3. Discuss the changes in individual company ratios from 1987 to 1988.

9–71. REVIEW OF CHAPTERS 8 AND 9. Interpoint Corporation, based in Redmond, Washington, produces hybrid microcircuit products for the electronics industry. Sales in 1988 were over $15 million. The company's 1988 annual report contained the following:

INTERPOINT CORPORATION

	OCTOBER 31	
	1988	1987
Property, plant and equipment, at cost	$8,494,616	$8,130,862
Less accumulated depreciation	2,094,201	1,675,060
Net property, plant and equipment	$6,400,415	$6,455,802
Long-term debt due within one year	$ 470,362	$ 378,029
Long-term debt	4,226,130	4,271,198

Purchases of buildings, machinery, and equipment during 1988 were $466,730. Depreciation expense for 1988 was $519,155 million.

Proceeds from issuance of *Long-term debt* were $3,795,502 during 1988.

Required:

Show all amounts in millions of dollars. (The use of T-accounts should help your analysis.)

1. Compute the dollar amounts of
   a. Accumulated depreciation relating to properties and plants disposed of during 1988.
   b. Original acquisition cost of properties and plants disposed of during 1988.
2. Compute the dollar amounts of
   a. Long-term debt reductions
   b. The *net increase or decrease* in all long-term debt, including that due within one year.
3. What journal entry was probably made to obtain the ending balance in Long-term debt due within one year? Assume that the ending amount arose from a single journal entry.

9–72. REVIEW OF CHAPTERS 8 AND 9. (J. Patell, adapted) Here are excerpts from an annual report of Crane Company, a manufacturer of plumbing fixtures and related items.

From income statement (in thousands):

Depreciation	$23,178
Amortization of debt discount	779
Loss on disposal of property, plant and equipment	84

CRANE COMPANY
From Balance Sheets (in Thousands of Dollars)

	DECEMBER 31	
	19X4	19X3
Investments and Other Assets:		
Unamortized debt discount	$ 1,938	$ 2,717
Property, Plant and Equipment, at Cost:		
Land	$ 10,644	$ 10,751
Buildings and improvements	83,320	90,605
Machinery and equipment	303,063	314,732
	397,027	416,088
Less accumulated depreciation	269,078	269,896
	$127,949	$146,192
Long-Term Debt	$138,524	$202,232

Additional information (in thousands):

Additions to property, plant, and equipment during 19X4 amounted to $14,465. Reductions in long-term debt during 19X4 were $64,497.

Required:

(The use of T-accounts should help your analysis.) During 19X4, Crane's property, plant, and equipment accounts were affected by both purchases of new assets and disposals (sales) of old assets.

1. Determine the total original cost of the property, plant, and equipment sold by Crane during 19X4.
2. Determine the total dollar amount Crane received for the property, plant, and equipment that was sold during 19X4.

   In 19X4, as well as in the several previous years, Crane issued long-term bonds at a discount. Rather than showing the bond discount as a contra account to long-term debt, Crane has shown it on the asset side of the balance sheet under the heading "Investments and Other Assets." All reductions in debt occurred through the normal maturity of outstanding bonds. There were no early retirements.
3. Determine the face (or par) amount of the long-term debt issued during 19X4.
4. Determine the actual cash received by Crane for the bonds issued during 19X4.

9–73. **PAYROLL TAXES.** Sears, Roebuck had 1988 sales of over $50 billion. Only four U.S. companies had greater sales. Suppose a Sears store incurred gross wage expenses of $100,000 for the week ended March 31. Related obligations for withheld income taxes and social security taxes were $16,000 and $7,000, respectively. The employees were paid on April 2, and the government was paid on April 3.

Required:

Show all amounts in millions of dollars.

1. Prepare an analysis of the transactions, using the balance sheet equation format.
2. Prepare journal entries to accompany the analysis in requirement 1.
3. Assume that the Sears store has additional costs related to the above data, as follows (in thousands): vacation accruals, $5; pension obligations, $16; health insurance, $8; and employer payroll taxes, $11. Prepare journal entries to record (a) the liabilities and (b) the related cash disbursements.

9–74. **LEASES.** Study Appendix 9C. The following information appeared in a footnote to the annual report of Delta Air Lines, Incorporated:

□ At June 30, 1988, the company's minimum rental commitments under capital leases and noncancelable operating leases with initial or remaining terms of more than one year were:

	CAPITAL LEASES	OPERATING LEASES
	(In Thousands)	
1989	$ 30,017	$ 434,000
1990	30,027	477,000
1991	30,049	462,000
1992	22,117	452,000
1993	19,271	446,000
After 1993	141,071	6,575,000
Total minimum lease payment	$272,552	$8,846,000
Less: Amounts representing interest	$ 91,395	
Present value of future minimum capital lease payments	$181,157	

Required:

1. As of June 30, 1988, what was the present value of the minimum payments on operating leases for the fiscal years 1989 through 1991? Use an interest rate of 8% compounded annually. Assume that operating lease payments are made at the end of each fiscal year.
2. Suppose the minimum capital lease payments are made in equal amounts on September 30, December 31, March 31, and June 30 of each year. Compute the interest and principal to be paid on capital leases during the first half of fiscal 1989. Assume an interest rate of 8% per annum, compounded quarterly.
3. Prepare the journal entries for the lease payments in requirement 2 on September 30 and December 31, 1988.

9–75. **LEASES.** Study Appendix 9C. Consider footnote H from the 1988 annual report of American Telephone and Telegraph Company (AT&T):

□ Footnote H:

The Company leases land, buildings and equipment through contracts that expire in various years. Future minimum lease payments under capital and noncancelable operating leases at December 31, 1988 are as follows:

(DOLLARS IN MILLIONS)	CAPITAL LEASES	OPERATING LEASES
Minimum lease payments for year ending December 31,		
1989	$144	$ 521
1990	129	405
1991	96	300
1992	49	234
1993	42	176
Later years	120	835
Total minimum lease payments	580	$2,471
Less: Estimated executory cost	2	
Imputed interest	175	
Present value of net minimum lease payments	$403	

1. Footnote H contains the minimum future lease payments due under AT&T's capital and operating leases. Compute the net present value of the *operating* lease payments as of December 31, 1988. Use a 10% implicit interest rate. For ease of computation, assume that each payment is made on December 31 of the designated year (i.e., the first $521 million payment is made on December 31, 1989) and that the final payment, labeled "Later," is made on December 31, 1994.

2. Suppose AT&T were to capitalize the operating leases examined in requirement 1. Show the journal entries necessary to

   a. Capitalize the leases on January 1, 1989. Ignore any prior period adjustments and do not break the lease obligation into current and long-term portions.

   b. Record the first payment on December 31, 1989.

9–76. **EFFECT OF CAPITAL LEASES.** Study Appendix 9C. Deb Shops, Inc., a chain of specialty women's apparel stores, reported the following information about leases in its annual report (in thousands):

	JANUARY 31	
	1988	1987
Capital lease asset, gross	$1,982	$1,982
Less: Accumulated depreciation	562	463
Capital lease asset, net	$1,420	$1,519
Capital lease obligation	$2,040	$2,040

The only asset under a capital lease is a warehouse and office building. The building has an economic life of twenty years and is being depreciated on a straight-line basis. Deb Shops had operating income of $20,604,000 in fiscal 1988.

1. Calculate the depreciation on the warehouse and office building for the fiscal year ending January 31, 1988.

2. On what date was the building placed into service? (*Hint*: How long would it take to build up the accumulated depreciation shown?)

3. The implicit interest on the lease obligation is $4,860,000 at January 31, 1988. Compute the total minimum rental commitments under the capital lease.

4. The implicit interest rate is 14.7%. Compute the interest expense (to the nearest thousand dollars) on the capital lease obligation for fiscal 1988.

5. Compute the lease payment on the capital lease during fiscal 1988.

6. Suppose this building had met the requirements for an operating lease rather than a capital lease. Calculate the operating income for Deb Shops in fiscal 1988.

9–77. **EMPLOYEE RETIREMENT BENEFITS AND LIABILITIES.** Many companies provide health insurance and other benefits to retired employees at no cost (or very low cost) to the employee. Companies that provide pensions to retired employees must record the obligation as a liability, as described in Appendix 9C, pages 411–419. Currently, no liability is recorded for other retirement benefits.

The FASB has proposed that companies be required to recognize as a liability the obligation to provide such benefits and to accrue the expense for retiree benefits over the years an employee works for the company. *Business Week* estimated that such a requirement could cut the net income of some large U.S. corporations by 30% to 60%. The *Wall Street Journal* estimated that the liability for some large companies would be larger than their current stockholders' equity.

Is a promise to pay such benefits to retirees a liability of the company? Should an estimated amount be listed with the liabilities on the company's balance sheet?

9–78. **HOUSE OF FABRICS ANNUAL REPORT.** Refer to the financial statements of House of Fabrics, pages 749–759. Pay particular attention to the liabilities section of the balance sheet and footnotes 3, "Short-Term Borrowings," and 4, "Long-Term Debt."

Required:

1. The balance sheet shows short-term borrowings increasing from $17 million to $18 million during fiscal 1989. Is this $1 million increase a good measure of the added use of short-term debt during fiscal 1989? Explain. Include a computation of the interest paid on short-term debt in fiscal 1989 compared with the amount in fiscal 1988. (Hint: Focus on footnote 2, "Short-Term Borrowings.")
2. Assume that all payments of principal and interest on long-term debt proceed as expected in fiscal 1990 and that no new debt is issued. Prepare the journal entry to recognize the current portion of long-term debt on January 31, 1990.
3. Compute the following three ratios at January 31, 1989 and 1988:
   a. Total debt-to-equity ratio
   b. Total long-term debt-to-equity ratio
   c. Total debt-to-total assets ratio.
   Include deferred income taxes as a part of long-term debt. Explain the reasons for the changes in the ratios from fiscal 1988 to 1989.

Stockholders' Equity and the Income Statement

After studing this chapter, you should be able to

1. Explain the differences between the major types of bonds, stocks, and dividends
2. Compute and explain some additional financial ratios related to stockholders' equity
3. Account for stock dividends and stock splits and describe their financial effects
4. Explain the accounting for the repurchase of shares, including retirements and treasury stock
5. Explain the accounting for noncash exchanges and the conversion of securities
6. Explain the effects of extraordinary items and discontinued operations on the reporting of income (Appendix 10)

This chapter focuses on the most prominent type of accounting entity, the corporation. In terms of sheer numbers, there may be more sole proprietorships and partnerships than corporations. Nevertheless, there are over a million corporations in the United States. Corporations dominate economic activities in all respects. Look around you. Nearly all the products you use (food, books, gasoline, radios) and services (telephone, electricity) are being supplied by corporations. Moreover, you routinely interact with corporations on various levels, as customers, shareholders, employees, creditors, regulators, or in other capacities.

The highlights of the corporate form of ownership were covered in Chapter 1, pages 15–19. In addition, a separate section of Chapter 1 compared the sole proprietorship, partnership, and corporation. Please review this material before proceeding.

Corporations are creatures of the state. They are artificial persons created by law. They exist separately from their owners. As persons, corporations may enter into contracts, may sue, and may even marry (by affiliating with another corporation) and produce offspring (corporate subsidiaries). Corporations are also subject to taxation as separate entities.

SHAREHOLDERS' RIGHTS

Stockholders (or shareholders) are entitled to (a) vote, (b) share in corporate profits, (c) share residually in corporate assets upon liquidation, and (d) acquire more shares of subsequent issues of stock. The extent of the stockholders' powers is determined by the number and type of shares held.

Corporations hold annual meetings of shareholders, when votes are taken on important matters. For example, the shareholders elect the board of directors. They may also vote on changing employee bonus plans, choosing outside auditors, and similar matters. Large corporations make heavy use of the proxy system. A **corporate proxy** is a written authority granted by a shareholder to others (usually members of corporate management) to cast the shareholder's votes.

The ultimate power to manage a corporation almost always resides in the common shareholders. But shareholders of publicly owned corporations usually delegate that power via proxies to the top managers. The typical hierarchy is shown in the diagram at the top of the next page.

The modern large corporation frequently has a team of professional managers, from the chairman of the board downward. The top managers may have only a token number of shares. The chief executive officer (CEO) is frequently the chairman of the board rather than the president.

Chapter 2 described how stockholders share in corporate profits via divi-

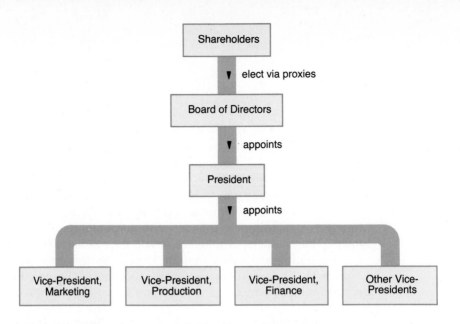

dends. Stockholders also generally have **preemptive rights,** which are the rights to acquire a pro-rata amount of any new issues of capital stock. The preemptive privilege gives the present shareholders the opportunity to purchase additional shares directly from the corporation before the shares can be sold to the general public. In this way, the shareholders are able to maintain their percentage ownership.

AUTHORIZED, ISSUED, AND OUTSTANDING STOCK

A useful illustration of authorized, issued, and outstanding stock is provided by Parker Hannifin Corporation, supplier of fluidpower products to the automotive, space, and marine industries. Consider the presentation in its balance sheet (in thousands of dollars):

| | JUNE 30 | |
SHAREHOLDER'S EQUITY	1988	1987
Common stock, $.50 par value, authorized 150,000,000 shares; issued: 48,713,564 shares in 1988 and 48,239,468 shares in 1987 at par value	24,357	24,120
Additional capital	154,351	146,791
Retained earnings	667,033	585,768
Total shareholders' equity	845,741	756,679

The state approves the articles of incorporation, which include authorization of the number and types of capital stock that can be issued. There are two main types of capital stock. All corporations have *common stock*. In addition, over 25% of the major U.S. corporations have preferred stock, which is described in the next section of this chapter.[1] Customarily, the articles authorize many more shares of each type than the company plans to issue immediately. In this way, if the corporation grows, it can proceed to issue additional shares without having to get the state's approval. Incidentally, such approval is usually a mere formality.

As Chapter 1 points out, par (or stated) value has no economic significance. Inevitably, as shown by the Parker Hannifin example of $.50 par value, par value per share is extremely small in relation to its market value upon issuance. The Parker Hannifin example has additional paid-in capital of over $154 million as compared with par value of about $24 million. It is generally illegal for a corporation to sell an original issue of its common stock below par. Common shareholders typically have limited liability, which means that creditors cannot enforce claims on individuals beyond their level of ownership if the corporation itself cannot pay its debts.

Avoid the frequent confusion between the words *authorized, issued,* and *outstanding.* Consider the common shares of Parker Hannifin on June 30, 1988:

	NUMBER OF SHARES
Authorized	150,000,000
Unissued	101,286,436
Issued and outstanding	48,713,564

Note that shares may be authorized (an upper limit) but unissued. They become issued when the company receives cash in exchange for the stock certificates. When stock is issued and held by stockholders, it is outstanding.

Many companies subsequently repurchase their own shares but do not retire them. Such shares are called **treasury stock.** They are no longer outstanding in the hands of stockholders. The details of treasury stock are explained later. For the time being, suppose Parker Hannifin had repurchased 500,000 of its own shares on the open market but had not retired them. The following nomenclature and tabulation would be appropriate:

	NUMBER OF SHARES
Authorized	150,000,000
Unissued	101,286,436
Issued	48,713,564
Deduct: Shares held in treasury	500,000
Total shares outstanding	48,213,564

---

[1] The use of preferred stock is declining. In the early 1980s, over 35% of the major U.S. companies had preferred stock, and by 1990 this had dropped to just over 25%.

PREFERRED STOCK

Preferred stocks are essentially a form of stockholders' equity, but they have characteristics of both bonds and common stock. They appeal to an investor who wants a higher rate of return than is offered by long-term debt and a lower risk than is offered by common stock.

As its name implies, **preferred stock** has a claim prior to common stock upon the earnings of a corporation and frequently upon the assets in the event of liquidation. At the same time, the preferred claims come after those of bondholders. The preferred stock usually appears in the top part of the stockholders' equity section of the balance sheet, not in a section with bonds payable, which are liabilities.

A typical example of preferred stock is that of Federal Paper Board, Inc. The first item under Stockholders' Equity in the company's balance sheet is:

	1987	1986
	(in thousands)	
Preferred stock—$1.20 cumulative, convertible, $1 par value (liquidation value at January 2, 1988— $2,080,980), authorized 1,900,000 shares; issued: 1987—104,049 shares; 1986—138,113 shares	$104	$138

☐ Comparison with Bonds and Common Stock

Like bonds, preferred shares typically have a specific return to investors. The return is called a dividend on preferred stock in contrast to interest on a bond. Federal Paper Board pays $1.20 per share annually. Sometimes the dividend is a percentage of the par value or stated value printed on the face of the certificate. For example, the New York Times Company has $100 par value preferred with a 5 ½% dividend rate. Such shares pay $5.50 annual dividends. Wurlitzer Company pays $2.00 per share based on an 8% rate and a $25 stated value. Common stock in contrast, has no predetermined rate of dividends.

A company is legally obligated to pay interest on bonds, but not dividends on preferred stock. Dividends on both preferred and common stock are declared by the board of directors. If resources to pay preferred dividends are unavailable, the board can omit the dividend declaration. However, holders of preferred shares have an advantage over holders of common shares. Ordinarily, corporations must declare dividends on preferred stock before any dividends can be declared on common stock. Therefore Federal Paper Board must pay $1.20 on each preferred share before any dividends are paid to common shareholders.

Because preferred dividends can be omitted, issuing preferred stock is less risky for a company than issuing bonds. But preferred stock is more risky than bonds to an investor. Why? Because preferred dividends are less assured than bond interest, and preferred claims come after bondholder claims in liquidation. Consequently, investors demand higher returns on preferred stock than on bonds.

Common stock is usually the most risky investment in a corporation. It is unattractive in dire times because common dividends have the lowest priority. However, it is attractive in prosperous times. Payments to bondholders and preferred stockholders are limited to their specified interest or dividends, but there is no limit to common stockholders' participation in earnings. Holders of common shares also generally have voting power in the management of the corporation, while bondholders and preferred shareholders do not.

☐ Cumulative Dividends

Preferred dividends are either *cumulative* or *noncumulative*. **Cumulative dividends** means that unpaid dividends for a particular period (usually quarterly or annually) accumulate as a claim upon future earnings, whereas *noncumulative dividends* do not accumulate. For example, if Federal Paper Board skips its $1.20 preferred dividend one year, it must pay $2.40 for each preferred share the next year before common dividends can be paid. The holders of cumulative preferred stock would receive all accumulated unpaid dividends (called **dividend arrearages**) before the holders of common shares receive anything. Moreover, in the event of liquidation, cumulative unpaid dividends must be paid before common stockholders receive any cash. However, the amount of dividends in arrears is not a liability. Why? Because *no* dividends are liabilities until declared. But dividends in arrears must be disclosed in a footnote to the balance sheet.

To illustrate these distinctions, consider a corporation with a stockholders' equity on January 1, 19X1, and a series of subsequent net incomes and dividends:

Preferred stock, no par, cumulative, $5 annual dividend per share:	
Issued and outstanding, 1,000,000 shares	$ 50,000,000
Common stock, no par, 5,000,000 shares	100,000,000
Retained income	400,000,000
Total stockholders' equity	$550,000,000

Despite the presence of a huge retained income, the board of directors is not legally obligated to declare dividends at any time. Dividends are paid out of assets, not stockholders' equity. Hence the amount of a dividend declaration depends on the availability of assets (usually cash) for distribution.

Dividends are generally limited by law to the unrestricted balance of retained income.[2] However, cash dividends are almost always limited primarily by the amount of available cash, not by the balance in retained income. Pursuing our illustration, consider the following data:

---

[2] Retained income may be restricted by, for example, protective debt covenants. See the section on retained income restrictions later in this chapter, pages 463–464.

| | NET INCOME | PREFERRED DIVIDENDS | | COMMON DIVIDENDS DECLARED | ENDING BALANCE, RETAINED INCOME |
		Declared	In Arrears		
19X1	$ (4,000,000)	—	$ 5,000,000	—	396,000,000
19X2	(4,000,000)	—	10,000,000	—	392,000,000
19X3	21,000,000	3,000,000	12,000,000	—	410,000,000
19X4	29,000,000	17,000,000	—	2,000,000	420,000,000
19X5	32,000,000	5,000,000	—	17,000,000	430,000,000

A partial payment of arrearages is illustrated in the year 19X3 in the tabulation. In 19X4, the remainder of the arrearages is paid ($12 million) plus the current dividend of $5 million.

Would you rather own cumulative or noncumulative preferred stock? In the above tabulation, a holder of noncumulative preferred stock would not be entitled to receive more than $5 million in any single year. Thus, despite three years of no dividends, the preferred dividend payment in 19X4 would have been only $5 million. Consequently, most buyers of preferred shares insist on cumulative status, and in actual practice such shares far outnumber the noncumulative type.

☐ Preferences as to Assets

In addition to the cumulative dividend feature, preferred stock usually has a **liquidating value,** which is a preference to receive assets in the event of corporate liquidation. The exact liquidating value is stated on the stock certificate; it is often the same as par value. As already mentioned, any dividends in arrears would also have preference ahead of common shareholders.

The liquidating value is typically indicated either in the body of the financial statement or in footnotes. For example, Federal Paper Board's preferred stock liquidation value is $20 per share ($2,080,980 ÷ 104,049 shares), although the par value is only $1 per share.

Consider an illustration of the liquidation of assets when short- and long-term debt, preferred stock, and common stock are all present. Recall the discussion of subordinated debentures in Chapter 9, page 378. Study Exhibit 10–1, which shows the distribution of cash for various levels of cash proceeds.

The cash available upon liquidation almost never coincides with the account balances for liabilities and stockholders' equity. The order of priorities is clearly displayed in Exhibit 10–1.

The common shareholders are frequently called the residual owners because they are last in line for cash distributions. Suppose there is bountiful cash because the proceeds exceeded the book values of the assets sold. For instance, assets listed at $1.0 million may have been sold for $1.5 million, as illustrated by the first distribution. Then the common shareholders benefit handsomely. However, if the cash proceeds are lower than the book value, the common shareholders may get as little as zero.

Because of their *limited liability,* stockholders are not subject to having their personal assets seized to satisfy corporate debts. In contrast, proprietors and partners have **unlimited liability** for the debts of their businesses.

EXHIBIT 10–1

Liquidation of Claims under Various Alternatives
(in thousands)

	Account Balances	ASSUMED TOTAL CASH PROCEEDS TO BE DISTRIBUTED						
		$1,500	$1,000	$500	$450	$350	$200	$100
Accounts payable	$ 100	$ 100	$ 100	$100	$100	$100	$100	$ 50*
Unsubordinated debentures	100	100	100	100	100	100	100	50*
Subordinated debentures	200	200	200	200	200	150		
Preferred stock ($100 par value and $120 liquidating value per share)	100	120	120	100	50			
Common stock and retained income	500	980	480					
Total liabilities and shareholders' equity	$1,000							
Total cash proceeds distributed		$1,500	$1,000	$500	$450	$350	$200	$100

* Ratio of 50:50 because each has a $100,000 claim.

Preferred shareholders in this example have a claim in liquidation of up to $120 per share plus dividends in arrears (if any), even though the corporation may originally have issued its stock for less ($100 per share in this example). Note how preferred shareholders rank lower in priority of claim than the holders of subordinated debentures. As Chapter 9 explained, holders of unsubordinated debt have a general claim against assets just like ordinary trade creditors. In contrast, the claims of holders of subordinated debt rank below those of all other creditors.

Like long-term debt, preferred stocks are frequently callable at the option of the corporation. The call price, which is often described as the **redemption price,** is typically 5% to 10% above the par value of the stock. It is frequently the same as the liquidating value.[3]

FINANCIAL RATIOS AND MEANING OF STOCKHOLDERS' EQUITY

Previous chapters described assorted financial ratios applicable to the subjects being discussed. For example, Chapter 2 introduced earnings-per-share and

---

[3] Two other features of preferred stock are sometimes encountered. First, a few preferred stocks have a *participation* feature, which means that preferred will share with common in dividends after both preferred and common have received dividends at the stated preferred rate. This specialized topic is discussed in intermediate accounting texts. Second, many preferred stocks have a *convertible* feature, which means that holders have the option of exchanging their shares for common shares at predetermined rates of exchange. For example, each share of Federal Paper Board's preferred stock can be exchanged for 2.51 shares of common stock. Convertibles are discussed later in this chapter.

price-earnings ratios. This section introduces two additional important ratios that relate to the stockholders' equity.

Consider the following data for Company Y:

| | DECEMBER 31 | |
	19X2	19X1
Stockholders' equity:		
$10 preferred stock, 100,000 shares, $100 par	$ 10,000,000	$ 10,000,000
Common stock, 5,000,000 shares, $1 par	5,000,000	5,000,000
Additional paid-in capital	35,000,000	35,000,000
Retained income	87,400,000	83,000,000
Total stockholders' equity	$137,400,000	$133,000,000
Net income	$11,000,000	
Preferred dividends @ $10 per share	1,000,000	
Net income available for common stock	$10,000,000	

The common stockholders received dividends of $1.12 per share during 19X2, or 5 million × $1.12 = $5,600,000.

The rate of return on common equity is naturally of great interest to common stockholders. The rate focuses on the ultimate profitability based on the book value of the common equity. To determine the numerator of the ratio, preferred dividends are subtracted from net income to obtain net income available for common stock. The denominator is the average of the beginning and ending *common* equity balances. Note that the *common* equity balance is the total stockholders' equity less the preferred stock at book value:[4]

$$\text{Rate of return on common equity} = \frac{\text{Net income} - \text{Preferred dividends}}{\text{Average common equity}}$$

$$= \frac{\$11,000,000 - \$1,000,000}{\frac{1}{2}[(\$133,000,00 - \$10,000,000) + (\$137,400,000 - \$10,000,000)]}$$

$$= \frac{\$10,000,000}{\frac{1}{2}(\$123,000,000 + \$127,400,000)}$$

$$= \frac{\$10,000,000}{\$125,200,000} = 8.0\%$$

Return on stockholders' equity varies considerably among companies and industries. For example, Coors's return on equity in 1988 was a paltry 4.4% compared with the beverage industry average of 21.8% and an average for all industries of 14.8%. In contrast, Coca-Cola's return was 33.1%.

---

[4] If the liquidating value of a company's preferred stock exceeds the book value, the liquidating value is deducted from the total stockholders' equity to determine the common equity balance.

Another often-quoted statistic is:

$$\text{Book value per share of common stock} = \frac{\text{Total stockholders' equity} - \text{Book value of preferred stock}}{\text{Number of common shares outstanding}}$$

$$= \frac{\$137{,}400{,}000 - \$10{,}000{,}000}{5{,}000{,}000} = \$25.48$$

Suppose the market value is $35. Note the low book value as compared with market value. The shareholders are paying for earning power rather than for the historical cost of assets. The usefulness of book value per share is highly questionable for most companies. Supposedly, if a stock's market price is below its book value, the stock is attractively priced. The trouble is that book values are based on balance sheet values, which show the historical cost of assets. The current value of those assets may differ greatly from their historical cost. Consequently, some companies may consistently have market prices in excess of book values, or vice versa. Book value may, however, be pertinent when companies have heavy investments in liquid assets and are contemplating liquidation. In these cases, book values probably approximate the market values of the assets.

The market value of common stock is sometimes less than its book value. This encourages takeovers of the corporation by other companies, particularly if the assets are relatively liquid. Sometimes the new owners sell assets that are valuable individually, even though the earning power of the entire firm has been weak.

ISSUANCE OF SHARES

Other than revenue and expense transactions, the typical transactions affecting stockholders' equity entail issuance of shares, distribution of dividends, and repurchase of shares. These items will now be discussed.

☐ Original Issue

Recall that Chapter 1 explains the accounting for the issuance of capital stock. The amount initially paid in by the shareholder is referred to as *paid-in capital*. A summary journal entry portrays the Parker Hannifin issuance of common shares for cash (amounts, in thousands, given on page 440):

12/31/89:	Cash	178,708	
	Common stock at par		24,357
	Additional paid-in capital on common stock		154,351
	To record the issuance of 48,713,564 shares of $.50 par value for an average price of $3.66854 per share.		

As already explained, for antiquated legal reasons the corporation may have two accounts for its common stock, one for par and one for additional paid-in capital. However, the economic substance of the issuance could be portrayed with one account, as indicated by the following journal entry (in thousands):

Cash	178,708	
Paid-in capital, common stock		178,708

Indeed, as you pursue your study of this chapter, keep in mind that distinguishing between the par or stated value, the additional paid-in capital, and retained income has little practical importance for ongoing corporations. To keep perspective, whenever feasible, think of stockholders' equity as a single amount.

The amounts in excess of par value are described in various ways in corporate balance sheets, but they all have substantially the same meaning. Examples are:

- Paid-in capital (Kelly Services, Inc.)
- Additional paid-in capital (Sara Lee Corporation)
- Capital in excess of par value of stock (Ford Motor Company)
- Capital surplus (Coca-Cola Company)
- Other paid-in capital (PanAm Corporation)

When more than one type of shares are outstanding, the additional paid-in capital may be identified accordingly. For example:

- Additional paid-in capital, preferred stock
- Additional paid-in capital, common stock

Such labels merely designate the *sources* of capital, not the *liquidation claims* of the particular classes of stockholders. Their importance relates to state laws and loan agreements that may restrict the power of corporations to declare dividends or repurchase shares.

EXCHANGES AND CONVERSIONS

Noncash Exchanges

Securities are sometimes issued for assets other than cash. For example, many assets or entire companies are acquired in exchange for the buyer's common stock. Such exchanges raise the question of the proper dollar value of the transaction to be recorded in both the buyer's and the seller's books. The proper amount is the "fair value" of either the securities or the exchanged assets, whichever is more objectively determinable. That amount should be used by both companies.

For example, suppose Company A acquires some equipment from Company B in exchange for 10,000 newly issued shares of A's common stock. The equipment was carried on B's books at the $200,000 original cost less accumulated depreciation of $50,000. Company A's stock is listed on the New York Stock Exchange; its current market price is $18 per share. Its par value is $1 per share. In this case, the market price of A's common stock would be regarded as a more objectively determinable fair value than the book value or the undepreciated cost of B's equipment. The accounts would be affected as follows:

	ASSETS		= LIABILITIES +	STOCKHOLDERS' EQUITY	
	Equipment			Common Stock	Additional Paid-in Capital
Issuance of stock by A	+180,000		=	+10,000	+170,000
	Investment in A Common Stock	Equipment	Accumulated Depreciation	Retained Income	
Disposal of equipment by B	+180,000	−200,000	+50,000 =	+30,000	$\begin{bmatrix} \text{gain on} \\ \text{disposal of} \\ \text{equipment} \end{bmatrix}$

The journal entries (without explanations) would be:

On issuer's books (A):	Equipment	180,000	
	Common stock		10,000
	Additional paid-in capital		170,000
On investor's books (B):	Investment in A common stock	180,000	
	Accumulated depreciation, equipment	50,000	
	Equipment		200,000
	Gain on disposal of equipment		30,000

☐ Convertible Securities

To make bonds and preferred stock more attractive, many companies add a conversion feature. Convertible bonds and convertible preferred stocks can be transformed into common shares at the option of the holder. They have widespread popularity.

When securities are exchanged pursuant to a conversion privilege, no gain or loss is recognized for tax purposes. Opinion is unsettled regarding whether gain or loss should be recognized for financial accounting purposes. Market quotations, when available, are an objective basis for computing gain or loss on a conversion; however, most accountants maintain that there is no actual realization of gain or loss—that a mere cost transfer has taken place. The form of the investment has been changed in accordance with a "deferred common stock" privilege that was obtained upon the purchase of the old asset. In this sense, all investments in convertible securities are made with the intention and ex-

EXHIBIT 10–2

Analysis of Convertible Preferred Stock

	ASSETS			= LIABILITIES +	STOCKHOLDERS' EQUITY			
	Cash	Investment in A Preferred	Investment in A Common		Preferred Stock	Additional Paid-In Capital, Preferred	Common Stock	Additional Paid-In Capital, Common
Company A's Books								
Issuance of preferred (19X1)	+160,000			=	+5,000	+155,000		
Conversion of preferred (19X8)				=	−5,000	−155,000	+10,000	+150,000
Company B's Books								
Acquisition of preferred (19X1)	−160,000	+160,000		=				
Conversion of preferred (19X8)		−160,000	+160,000	=				

pectation of their eventually being transformed into common stock. Therefore the conversion itself is a transaction of form rather than substance; no realization test has been met. The accounts are simply adjusted to reflect what would have been recorded if the common stock had been initially issued instead of the convertible preferred stock.

For example, suppose Company B had paid $160,000 for an investment in 5,000 shares of the $1 par value convertible preferred stock of Company A in 19X1. The preferred stock was converted into 10,000 shares of Company A common stock ($1 par value) in 19X8. The accounts would be affected as shown in Exhibit 10–2.

The journal entries would be as follows:

On issuer's books (A):	19X1	Cash	160,000	
		Preferred stock, convertible		5,000
		Additional paid-in capital, preferred		155,000
		To record issuance of 5,000 shares of $1 par preferred stock convertible into two common shares for one preferred share.		
	19X8	Preferred stock, convertible	5,000	
		Additional paid-in capital, preferred	155,000	
		Common stock		10,000
		Additional paid-in capital, common		150,000
		To record the conversion of 5,000 preferred shares to 10,000 common shares.		

On issuer's books (B):	19X1	Investment in Company A convertible preferred stock	160,000	
		Cash		160,000
		To record acquisition of 5,000 shares convertible into common at the rate of two common shares for one preferred.		
	19X8	Investment in Company A common stock	160,000	
		Investment in Company A preferred stock		160,000
		To record the conversion of 5,000 preferred shares for 10,000 common shares.		

The relation of convertible securities to earnings per share is discussed later in this chapter.

☐ Stock Splits

Many companies occasionally split their stock. A **stock split,** or split-up, refers to the issuance of additional shares for no payments by stockholders and under conditions indicating that the objective is to increase the number of outstanding shares for the purpose of *reducing their unit market price,* in order to bring the stock price down into a more popular range. This supposedly encourages wider distribution and a *higher total market value* for the same ownership interest. Corporate management naturally wants the stock to be as attractive as possible, easing the task of raising additional investment capital when needed. For a given ownership interest, the higher the total market value, the more capital can be raised by issuance of a specified number of additional shares.

Stock splits can be achieved by issuing new shares for old shares. Suppose Company A has the following stockholders' equity section:

	BEFORE 2-FOR-1 SPLIT	CHANGES	AFTER 2-FOR-1 SPLIT
Common stock, 100,000 shares @ $10 par	$ 1,000,000	−100,000 shares @ $10 par + 200,000 shares @ $5 par	$ 1,000,000
Additional paid-in capital	4,000,000		4,000,000
Total paid-in capital	$ 5,000,000		$ 5,000,000
Retained income	6,000,000		6,000,000
Stockholders' equity	$11,000,000		$11,000,000
Overall market value of stock @ assumed $150 per share	$15,000,000	@ assumed $80 per share	$16,000,000

The stock split has no effect on the reported amount of the total stockholders' equity. A person who previously owned 1,000 shares (a 1% interest) now owns 2,000 shares (still a 1% interest). Professor Willard Graham explained a stock split as being akin to taking a gallon of whiskey and pouring it into five individual bottles. The resulting packaging might attract a price for each fifth that would produce a higher total value than if the gallon were not split (less the amount spilled when pouring into the five bottles—that's the legal, printing, and clerical costs). Therefore Company A splits its stock with the hope[5] that the market value of the total ownership interest will increase from $15 million to, perhaps, $16 million because one share that previously sold for $150 will now be in the form of two shares that might sell for $80 each, or a total of $160.

The accounting for the stock split illustrated here would entrail no journal entry or change in the amounts of any accounts, as the above tabulation shows. However, there would be plenty of paper work. Each shareholder would have to exchange the $10 par certificates for the $5 par certificates, receiving two shares of the latter for one of the former. In sum, a stock split changes the evidence of ownership in form but not in substance.

DIVIDENDS

☐ Asset Dividends

Dividends are generally distributions of assets (almost always cash) to satisfy stockholders' claims arising from the generation of net income. The meaning of

---

[5] The myth is that a lower price will enhance total demand and total market value. But investors are not easily fooled by new wrappers placed on unchanged merchandise. Any increase in market value accompanying a stock split probably occurs because managers generally undertake stock splits when a company's prospects are bright.

dividends is explained in Chapter 2, page 52, so the details are not repeated here. Please reread that section now.

Recall that dividends must be *declared* by the board of directors. When dividends are declared, the shareholders simultaneously become creditors (with the same priorities as to assets as accounts payable) for the amount of the dividends. If a balance sheet is prepared between the date of declaration and the date of payment, the corporation must show a liability for dividends payable arising from the following journal entry (suppose the amount is $20,000):

Sept. 26	Retained income	20,000	
	Dividends payable		20,000
	To record the declaration of dividends to be paid on November 15 to shareholders of record as of October 25.		

No journal entry is necessary on October 25. An entry is made when the dividend is paid:

Nov. 15	Dividends payable	20,000	
	Cash		20,000
	To pay dividends declared on September 26 to shareholders of record as of October 25.		

☐ Amount Declared

The amount of cash dividends declared by a board of directors depends on many factors. The least important factor is the amount of retained income, except in cases where the company is on the brink of bankruptcy or where the company has just been incorporated. In either case, the wisdom of declaring dividends is highly questionable.

The more important factors that affect dividends include the stock market's expectations that have crystallized over a series of years, the current and predicted earnings, and the corporation's current cash position and financial plans regarding spending on plant assets and repayments of debts. Remember that payment of cash dividends requires *cash*. Large amounts of net income or retained income do not mean that the necessary cash is available.

Some corporations try to increase the attractiveness of their shares by maintaining a stable quarterly dividend payment on common shares (say, $1 per share each quarter). Others pay a predictable fraction of current earnings per share (say, 60% of whatever is earned in the current year). Some corporations also try to show steady growth in dividends by increasing the dividend per share each year. Sometimes an "extra" payment occurs at the end of an especially profitable year. General Motors has followed the latter practice.

If a company has maintained a series of uninterrupted dividends over a span of years, it will make every effort to continue such payments even in the face of net losses. Indeed, companies occasionally borrow money for the sole purpose of maintaining dividend payments.

☐ Small-Percentage Stock Dividends

Cash dividends are a straightforward means of rewarding the shareholder for investing in the corporation. In contrast, so-called stock dividends are often misunderstood. The term *stock dividends* is a misnomer because such dividends are totally different from cash dividends. A **stock dividend** is a distribution to stockholders of additional shares of the distributing company's stock; the stockholders make no additional investment in the corporation. The most frequently encountered type of stock dividend is the distribution of additional common stock to existing holders of outstanding common stock; usually anywhere from 1% to 10% of the number of common shares already outstanding are distributed.

In substance, stock dividends are not dividends at all, as the term is usually understood. Each shareholder's proportionate interest in the corporation is unchanged; the unit market price of each share tends to decline just enough to leave the total market value of the company unchanged. Reconsider our example of Company A (before the split). Suppose the market value of common shares is $150 at the time of issuance of the stock dividend. A common stock dividend of 2% would affect the stockholders' equity section as shown in the following table.

	BEFORE 2% STOCK DIVIDEND	CHANGES	AFTER 2% STOCK DIVIDEND
Common stock, 100,000 shares @ $10 par	$ 1,000,000	+(2,000 shares @ $10 par) = +20,000	$ 1,020,000
Additional paid-in capital	4,000,000	+[2,000 shares @ ($150 − $10)] = +280,000	4,280,000
Retained income	6,000,000	−(2,000 @ $150) = −300,000	5,700,000
Stockholders' equity	$11,000,000		$11,000,000
Overall market value of stock @ assumed $150 per share	$15,000,000	@ assumed $147.06 per share*	$15,000,000*
Total shares outstanding	100,000		102,000
Individual shareholder: Assumed ownership of shares	1,000		1,020
Percentage ownership interest	1%		Still 1%

* Many simultaneous events affect the level of stock prices, including expectations regarding the general economy, the industry, and the specific company. Thus the market price of the stock may move in either direction when the stock dividend is declared. Theory and complicated case studies indicate that a stock dividend should have zero effect on the total market value of the firm. Accordingly, the new market price per share should be $15,000,000 ÷ 102,000 shares = $147.06.

First, note that the individual shareholder receives no assets from the corporation. Moreover, the shareholder's fractional interest is unchanged; if the shareholders sell the dividend shares, their proportionate ownerhsip interest in the company will decrease.

Second, the company records the transaction by transferring the *market value* of the additional shares from retained income to common stock and additional "paid-in capital." The entry is often referred to as being a "capitalization of retained income." It is basically a signal to the shareholders that $300,000 of retained income is no longer available as part of their claim to future cash dividends.

Stock dividends are prime examples of have-your-cake-and-eat-it-too manipulations that in substance are meaningless but seemingly leave all interested parties happy. The company pays a "dividend" but gives up no assets. Some stockholders may think they are getting a dividend even though to realize it in cash they must sell a proportion of their predividend fractional interest in the company.

The stock dividend device is particularly effective where such a low percentage, such as 1% or 2%, of additional shares are issued that the effect on the market price is almost imperceptible. The recipient, who is not particularly concerned about the fractional ownership interest anyway, may hold 1,000 shares at a $150 market price before the dividend and 1,020 shares at close to the same $150 market price after the dividend. A favorable reaction may occur because it appears that the dividend increased the recipient's wealth by $20 \times \$150 = \$3,000$. But the recipient still owns the same percentage of the same company.

The major possible economic effect of a stock dividend is to signal increased cash dividends. Suppose the company in our example consistently paid cash dividends of $1 per share. Often this cash dividend level per share is maintained after a stock dividend. The recipient of the stock dividend can now expect a future annual cash dividend of $\$1 \times 1,020 = \$1,020$ rather than $\$1 \times 1,000 = \$1,000$.

Accounting for a stock dividend entails transferring an amount from retained income to common stock and additional paid-in capital. Some accountants think that the appropriate entry for a stock dividend is to transfer merely the par value of the additional shares, not the market value, from retained income to paid-in capital. Why? Because using market values compounds the false notion that the recipients are getting a dividend akin to a cash dividend. Nevertheless, the U.S. authoritative bodies require that market values be transferred. One major reason is that larger amounts of retained income are thus transferred to become a part of "permanent" stockholders' equity. This requirement helps put a brake on the practice of declaring a long series of stock dividends that may give a misleading appearance of greater profitability. In our example, the required journal entry would be:

Retained income	300,000	
Common stock		20,000
Additional paid-in capital		280,000
To record a 2% common stock dividend, resulting in the issuance of 2,000 shares. Retained income is reduced at the rate of the market value of $150 per share at date of issuance.		

☐ Large-Percentage Stock Dividends

The U.S. accounting authorities differentiate between the sizes of stock dividends. That is, the small-percentage dividends just described are really "stock dividends" and must be accounted for on the basis of the market prices of the shares. However, large-percentage dividends (typically those 20% or higher) must be accounted for differently.

The principal reason why large-percentage dividends require different accounting treatment is their effect on the market price of the shares. That is, a large percentage of additional shares issued as a stock dividend will materially reduce the market value per share. In large-percentage cases, the accounting authorities generally require capitalization of the par value of the shares issued. Such capitalization is usually achieved by transferring the par amount from Retained Income to the Common Stock (at par) account. However, the regulations are not ironclad. The amounts of large-percentage dividends are often shifted from additional paid-in capital instead of retained income.

Review the typical accounting for stock splits and stock dividends:

- ☐ Stock splits—no rearrangement of the amounts in paid-in capital and retained income
- ☐ Stock dividends—shift from retained income to paid-in capital:
  1. Small-percentage dividends—reduce retained income by market value of the additional shares issued
  2. Large-percentage dividends—reduce retained income or additional paid-in capital by only the par value of the additional shares issued

---

RELATION OF DIVIDENDS AND SPLITS

Companies typically use large-percentage stock dividends to accomplish exactly the same purpose as a stock split. That is, the companies want a material reduction in the market price of their shares. Therefore the use of large-percentage stock dividends is merely another way of obtaining the purpose of a stock split. For example, if the two-for-one split described earlier (see the section entitled "Stock Splits") were achieved through an equivalent 100% stock dividend, the total amount of stockholders' equity would be unaffected. However, its composition would change:

	BEFORE 100% STOCK DIVIDEND	CHANGES	AFTER 100% STOCK DIVIDEND
Common stock, 100,000 shares @ $10 par	$ 1,000,000	+(100,000 shares @ $10 par = $1,000,000)	$ 2,000,000
Additional paid-in capital	4,000,000		4,000,000
Total paid-in capital	$ 5,000,000		$ 6,000,000
		−$1,000,000 par value of "dividend"	
Retained income	6,000,000		5,000,000
Stockholders' equity	$11,000,000		$11,000,000

In substance, there is absolutely no difference between the 100% stock dividend and the 2-for-1 stock split. *In form*, the shareholder in this example has $10 par shares rather than $5 par shares. The 2-for-1 split requires no journal entry, but the stock dividend requires the following entry:

Retained income (or Additional paid-in capital)	1,000,000	
Common stock, at par		1,000,000

Be on the alert for the most apt description of this large-percentage dividend: "a stock split effected in the form of a stock dividend." This requires a decrease in Retained Income or Additional Paid-in Capital and an increase in Common Stock in the amount of only the *par value* (rather than the market value) of the additional shares. For example, Albertson's Inc., the grocery chain, issued 33,620,000 $1-par shares in a stock split described in the following footnote to its annual report:

☐ On August 31, 1987 the Board of Directors approved a two-for-one stock split, effected in the form of a stock dividend, payable October 5, 1987 to stockholders of record on September 18, 1987. Accordingly, January 28, 1988 balances reflect the split with an increase in common stock and a reduction in capital in excess of par value of $33,620,000. Stock option and per share data have also been retroactively adjusted to reflect the split.

Stock splits frequently occur in the form of a stock "dividend" instead of in the classical form described earlier. Why? The major reason is to save clerical costs and the bothering of shareholders. After all, the swapping of old $10-par certificates for new $5-par certificates is more expensive than the mere printing and mailing of additional $10-par certificates.

FRACTIONAL SHARES

Corporations ordinarily issue shares in whole units. However, some shareholders are entitled to stock dividends in amounts equal to fractional units. Consequently, corporations issue additional shares for whole units plus cash equal to the market value of the fractional amount.

An example will clarify the problem. Suppose a corporation issues a 3% stock dividend. A shareholder has 160 shares. The market value per share on the date of issuance is $40. Par value is $2. The shareholder would be entitled to $.03 \times 160 = 4.8$ shares. The company would issue 4 shares plus $.8($40) = $32 cash. The journal entry would be:

Retained income (4.8 × $40)	192	
Common stock, at par (4 × $2)		8
Additional paid-in capital (4 × $38)		152
Cash (.8 × $40)		32
To issue a stock dividend of 3%		
to a holder of 160 shares.		

INVESTOR'S ACCOUNTING

To crystallize understanding, consider the *investor's* entries for the transactions described so far. Suppose the investor is passive and takes no active voice in management. The investor buys 1,000 shares of the original issue of Company A (described earlier) for $50 per share:

Investment in common stock of Company A	50,000	
Cash		50,000
To record investment in 1,000 shares		
of an original issue of Company A		
common stock at $50 per share.		
The par value is $10 per share.		

The investor holds the shares indefinitely. Note that if Investor J sold the shares to Investor K at a subsequent price other than $50, a gain or loss would be recorded by J. K would carry the shares at whatever amount was paid to J. Meanwhile the stockholders' equity of Company A would be completely unaffected by this sale by one investor to another. The company's underlying shareholder records would simply be changed to delete J and add K as a shareholder.

The *investor* would proceed to record the transactions described earlier as follows:

a.	Stock split at 2 for 1:	No journal entry, but a memorandum would be made in the investment account to show that 2,000 shares are now held at a cost of $25 each instead of 1,000 shares at a cost of $50 each.		

b.	Cash dividends of $2 per share:	Cash	2,000	
		Dividend income		2,000
		To record cash dividends on Company A stock. If financial statements must be prepared between the declaration date and the payment date instead of this one entry, the two following entries would be made:		
	Date of declaration:	Dividends receivable	2,000	
		Dividend income		2,000
		To record dividends declared by Company A, and		
	Date of receipt:	Cash	2,000	
		Dividends receivable		2,000

c.	Stock dividends of 2%:	No journal entry, but a memorandum would be made in the investment account to show that (assuming the stock split in **a** had not occurred) 1,020 shares are now owned at an average cost of $50,000 ÷ 1,020, or $49.02 per share.		

d. Stock split in form of a 100% dividend	No journal entry, but a memorandum would be made in the investment account to show that (assuming the stock splits and stock dividends in **a** and **c** had not occurred) 2,000 shares are now owned at an average cost of $25 instead of 1,000 shares @ $50. Note that this memorandum has the same effect as the memorandum in **a** above.

REPURCHASE OF SHARES

☐ Contraction of Equity

Companies repurchase their own shares for two main purposes: (1) to permanently reduce shareholder claims, called retiring stock, and (2) to temporarily hold shares for later use, most often to be granted as part of employee bonus or stock purchase plans. Temporarily held shares are called *treasury stock* or *treasury shares*. By repurchasing shares, for whatever reason, a company liquidates some shareholders' claims:

Stockholders' equity	xxx	
Cash		xxx
Repurchase of outstanding shares.		

The purpose of the repurchase determines *which stockholders' equity accounts* are affected. Consider an illustration of Company B, whose stock has a market value of $15 per share:

Common stock, 1,000,000 shares at $1 par	$ 1,000,000
Additional paid-in capital	4,000,000
Total paid-in capital	$ 5,000,000
Retained income	6,000,000
Stockholders' equity	$11,000,000
Overall market value of stock @ assumed $15 per share	$15,000,000
Book value per share = $11,000,000 ÷ 1,000,000 = $11.	

☐ Retirement of Shares

Suppose the board of directors has decided that the $15 market value of its shares is "too low." Of course, the *book value per share of common stock* is only $11. Nevertheless, even though the market value exceeds the book value by $4 per share ($15 − $11), the board may think the market is too pessimistic regarding the company's shares. Because of inflation and other factors, it is not unusual to have the market value vastly exceed the book value.

The board might believe that the best use of corporate cash would be to purchase and retire a portion of the outstanding shares. In this way, the remaining shareholders would have the sole benefit of the predicted eventual increase in market value per share. (Of course, the board is usually more eager to retire its share if the market value is less than the book value, rather than the vice versa situation illustrated here.) It is not unusual for a firm to buy back its own shares. The *Economist* reported recently that "about 150 public companies in America have spent $50 billion on their own shares in the past 18 months." For example, IBM bought 19 million of its own shares in 1987 for about $3 billion.

Suppose the board of Company B purchases and retires 5% of its outstanding shares @ $15 for a total of 50,000 × $15, or $750,000 cash. The total stockholders' equity is reduced or contracted. The stock certificates would be canceled, and the shares would no longer be issued and outstanding:

	BEFORE REPURCHASE OF 5% OF OUTSTANDING SHARES	CHANGES BECAUSE OF RETIREMENT	AFTER REPURCHASE OF 5% OF OUTSTANDING SHARES
Common stock, 1,000,000 shares @ $1 par	$ 1,000,000	−(50,000 shares @ $1 par) = −$50,000	$ 950,000
Additional paid-in capital	4,000,000	−(50,000 shares @ $4) = −$200,000	3,800,000
Total paid-in capital	$ 5,000,000		$ 4,750,000
Retained income	6,000,000	−(50,000 @ $10*) = −$500,000	5,500,000
Stockholders' equity	$11,000,000		$10,250,000
Book value per common share:			
$11,000,000 ÷ 1,000,000	$11.00		
$10,250,000 ÷ 950,000			$10.79

* $15 − the $5 (or $1 + $4) originally paid in.

The journal entry would reverse the original average paid-in capital per share and would charge any additional amount to retained income. The additional $10 is sometimes described as being tantamount to a special cash dividend paid to the owners of the 50,000 retired shares:

Common stock	50,000	
Additional paid-in capital	200,000	
Retained income	500,000	
Cash		750,000
To record retirement of 50,000 shares of stock for $15 cash per share. The original paid-in capital was $5 per share, so the additional $10 per share is debited to Retained Income.		

Note how the book value per share of the outstanding shares has declined from $11.00 to $10.79. This phenomenon is called *dilution* of the common shareholders' equity. **Dilution** is usually defined as a reduction in shareholders' equity per share or earnings per share that arises from some changes among shareholders' proportionate interests. As a rule, boards of directors avoid dilution. However, the board sometimes favors deliberate dilution if expected future profits will more than compensate for a temporary undesirable reduction in book value per share.

☐ Treasury Stock

Suppose the board of directors in the foregoing example decided that the 50,000 repurchased shares would be held only temporarily and then resold. Perhaps the shares are needed for an employee stock purchase plan or for executive stock options. Such temporarily held shares are *treasury stock*. As in the retirement of shares, the repurchase is a *decrease in stockholders' equity*. Treasury stock is NOT an asset. It indicates a liquidation of the ownership claim of one or more stockholders. The shares had been issued previously but would no longer be outstanding:

Shares issued	1,000,000
Less: Treasury stock	50,000
Total shares outstanding	950,000

Cash dividends are not paid on shares held in the treasury; cash dividends are distributed only to the shares outstanding (in the hands of stockholders), and treasury stock is not outstanding.

In the foregoing example, the stockholders' equity section would be affected as follows:

	BEFORE REPURCHASE OF 5% OF OUTSTANDING SHARES	CHANGES BECAUSE OF TREASURY STOCK	AFTER REPURCHASE OF 5% OF OUTSTANDING SHARES
Common stock, 1,000,000 shares @ $1 par	$ 1,000,000		$ 1,000,000
Additional paid-in capital	4,000,000		4,000,000
Total paid-in capital	$ 5,000,000		$ 5,000,000
Retained income	6,000,000		6,000,000
Total	$11,000,000		$11,000,000
Deduct:			
Cost of treasury stock	—	−$750,000*	750,000
Stockholders' equity	$11,000,000		$10,250,000

The journal entry would be:

Treasury stock	750,000	
Cash		750,000
To record acquisition of 50,000 shares of common stock @ $15 (to be held as treasury stock).		

Like the retirement of shares, the purchase of treasury stock decreases stockholders' equity by $750,000. Unlike retirements, common stock at par value, additional paid-in capital and retained income remain untouched by treasury stock purchases. A separate treasury stock account is a deduction from total stockholders' equity on the balance sheet.

Remember that treasury stock is not an asset. A company's holding of shares in *another company* is an asset; its holding of *its own shares* is a negative element of stockholders' equity.

☐ Disposition of Treasury Stock

Treasury shares are often resold at a later date, perhaps in conjunction with an employee stock purchase plan. The sales price usually differs from the acquisition cost. Suppose the sales price is $18. The journal entry would be:

Cash	900,000	
Treasury stock		750,000
Additional paid-in capital		150,000
To record sale of treasury stock, 50,000 shares @ $18. Cost was $15 per share.		

Suppose the price is $13:

Cash	650,000	
Additional paid-in capital	100,000	
Treasury stock		750,000
To record sale of treasury stock, 50,000 shares @ $13. Cost was $15 per share.		

If the treasury shares are resold below their cost, accountants tend to debit (decrease) Additional Paid-in Capital for the difference, $2 per share in this case. Additional Paid-in Capital is sometimes divided into several separate accounts that identify different sources of capital. For example:

☐ Additional paid-in capital—preferred stock
☐ Additional paid-in capital—common stock
☐ Additional paid-in capital—treasury stock transactions

If such accounts are used, a consistent accounting treatment would call for debiting only Additional Paid-in Capital—Treasury Stock Transactions (and no other paid-in capital account) for the excess of the cost over the resale price of treasury shares. If there is no balance in such a paid-in capital account, the debit should be made to Retained Income.

Suppose 25,000 of the treasury shares in the foregoing example were sold for $17 and later the other 25,000 shares were sold for $12. The company had no previous sales of treasury stock. The journal entries would be:

Cash	425,000	
Treasury stock		375,000
Additional paid-in capital—treasury		
stock transactions		50,000
To record sale of treasury stock, 25,000		
shares @ $17. Cost was $15 per share.		

Cash	300,000	
Additional paid-in capital—treasury		
stock transactions	50,000	
Retained income	25,000	
Treasury stock		375,000
To record sale of treasury stock, 25,000		
shares @ $12. Cost was $15 per share.		

Although the specific accounting for transactions in the company's own stock may vary from company to company, one rule is paramount. Any differences between the acquisition costs and the resale proceeds of treasury stock must never be reported as losses, expenses, revenues, or gains in the income statement. Why? A corporation's own capital stock is part of its capital structure. It is *not* an asset of the corporation. Nor is stock intended to be treated like merchandise for sale to customers at a profit. Therefore changes in a corporation's capitalization should produce no gain or loss but should merely require direct adjustments to the owners' equity.

There is essentially no difference between unissued shares and treasury shares. In our example, a corporation can accomplish the same objective by (1) acquiring 50,000 shares, retiring them, and issuing 50,000 new shares, or (2) acquiring 50,000 shares and reselling them.

RETAINED INCOME RESTRICTIONS

Directors can make decisions that benefit shareholders but hurt creditors. For example, directors might pay such large dividends that payments of creditors' claims would be threatened. To protect creditors, dividend-declaring power is restricted by either state laws or contractual obligations or both. Moreover, boards of directors can voluntarily restrict their declarations of dividends.

States typically do not permit dividends if stockholders' equity is less than total paid-in capital. Therefore retained income must exceed the cost of treasury stock. If there is no treasury stock, retained income must be positive. A lack of this restriction could jeopardize the position of the creditors. For example, consider the following for a company (in millions):

	BEFORE DIVIDENDS	AFTER DIVIDEND PAYMENTS OF	
		$10	$4
Paid-in capital	$25	$25	$25
Retained income	10	—	6
Total	$35	$25	$31
Deduct:			
Cost of treasury stock	6	6	6
Stockholders' equity	$29	$19	$25

Without restricting retained income to a minimum of $6 million, the cost of the treasury stock, the corporation could pay a dividend of $10 million and thus reduce the stockholders' equity below the paid-in capital of $25 million. With the restriction, unrestricted retained income (and maximum legal payment of dividends) would be $10 − $6, or $4 million. The **restricted retained income** cannot be reduced by dividend declarations.

Most of the time, restrictions of retained income are disclosed by footnotes. Some companies show the restrictions in the stockholders' equity section. For example, consider the recent annual reports of two companies:[6]

Alatenn Resources:	
Retained earnings ($1,353,494 restricted as to cash dividends)	$18,233,000

H. F. Ahmanson & Company:	
Retained earnings:	
Restricted	$750,855
Unrestricted	48,962
Total retained earnings	$799,817

STOCK OPTIONS

Stock options are rights to purchase a corporation's capital stock. Various conditions are specified for the options, including times, prices, and amounts. Options are frequently given to corporate officers as a form of incentive compensation. Although options have assorted conditions, a typical form consists of granting executives the right to purchase shares (exercise the option) during some specified time in the *future* at *today's* market price (the exercise price, which is set at the date of grant).

---

[6] Restrictions of retained income are sometimes called **appropriated retained income** and sometimes *reserves*. The term *reserve* can be misleading. Accountants *never* use the word reserve to indicate cash set aside for a particular purpose; instead they call such assets a *fund*. The word **reserve** has one of three broad meanings in accounting: (a) restrictions of dividend declarations, (b) offset to an asset, and (c) estimate of a definite liability of indefinite or uncertain amount.

Suppose Company A granted its top executives options to purchase 60,000 shares of $1 par value common stock at $15 per share, the market price today (date of grant). The options can be exercised over a five-year span, beginning three years hence. Such options clearly are valuable rights. The executives can gain the benefits of price increases without bearing the risks of price declines. However, measurement of the value of options at the time of grant is difficult because executive options may not be sold to others. Therefore currently accepted accounting attributes zero value to most of them[7] as long as the exercise price is the same as the market price at the date of the grant. Thus the accounting approach is to make no entry at the time of grant. Subsequent financial statements must reveal (usually by a footnote) the number and type of options outstanding.[8]

Suppose all options are exercised three years hence. The journal entry would be as shown below.

Cash	900,000	
Common stock		60,000
Additional paid-in capital		840,000
To record issue of 60,000 shares upon exercise		
of options to acquire them @ $15 per share.		

Executives sometimes let their options lapse. For example, here the options will become worthless if the price of the common stock is no higher than $15 per share during the time they may be exercised. In such a case, no journal entry is made.

Many observers have severely criticized the above practice because no compensation (the value of the options) is ever recorded as salary expense. For example, if the options were required to be valued at the date of the grant at, say, $2 each,[9] or $120,000, the following entry would be logical but is not generally accepted:

Salary or bonus expense	120,000	
Additional paid-in capital		120,000
To record the value of 60,000 options issued to buy		
60,000 shares of common stock at $15 per share. The		
value of each option is $2.		

The $120,000 entry would be made regardless of whether the options are later exercised. The basic idea underlying the granting of options is to give key employees incentive to work harder on behalf of the corporation. Hence the $120,000 credit to Additional Paid-in Capital represents an additional stake in the corporation by these employees.

---

[7] There are many exceptions. See Accounting Principles Board *Opinion No. 25.*

[8] An example is provided by the 1988 annual report of Procter & Gamble: ". . . options have been granted to key employees to purchase common shares of the Company at the market value on the dates of the grants. Options for 4,539,512 shares were exercisable at June 30, 1988." Procter & Gamble has approximately 169 million common shares outstanding.

[9] Theorists in finance have developed models for valuing stock options that could be used to establish such values.

The importance of earnings per share (EPS) was illustrated in Chapter 2. When the capital structure is relatively simple, computations of EPS are straightforward. For example, consider the following calculation (figures assumed):

$$\frac{\text{Earnings per share}}{\text{of common stock}} = \frac{\text{Net income}}{\text{Weighted-average number of shares}\atop\text{outstanding during the period}}$$

$$= \frac{\$1,000,000}{800,000} = \$1.25$$

Computations of EPS are based on the weighted-average number of shares outstanding during a period. For example, suppose 750,000 shares were outstanding at the beginning of a calendar year, and 200,000 of additional shares were issue on October 1 (three months before the end of the year). The weighted average is based on the number of months that the shares were outstanding during the year. The basic computation is:

```
750,000 × weighting of 12/12 = 750,000
200,000 × weighting of 3/12  =  50,000
Weighted average             = 800,000    shares
```

However, if the capital structure includes preferred stock that is nonconvertible, the dividends on preferred stock applicable to the current period, whether or not paid, should be deducted in calculating earnings applicable to common stock (figures assumed):

$$\frac{\text{Earnings per share}}{\text{of common stock}^{10}} = \frac{\text{Net income} - \text{Preferred dividends}}{\text{Weighted-average number of shares}\atop\text{outstanding during the period}}$$

$$= \frac{\$1,000,000 - \$200,000}{800,000} = \$1.00$$

Historical summaries of EPS must be made comparable by adjusting for changes in capitalization structure (for example, stock splits and stock dividends).

PRIMARY AND FULLY DILUTED EPS

Accounting Principles Board *Opinion No. 15,* "Earnings per Share," stresses that the foregoing simple computations are inadequate when companies have convertible securities, stock options, or other financial instruments that can be ex-

---

[10] When preferred stock exists, the number of times that *preferred* dividends have been earned (net income ÷ preferred dividends, sometimes called earnings coverage) may be revealed in footnotes. Net income ÷ weighted-average preferred shares outstanding should *not* be called earnings per share of preferred stock.

changed for or converted to common shares. For example, suppose a firm has some convertible preferred stock in its capital structure:

5% convertible preferred stock, $100 par, each share convertible into 2 common shares	100,000 shares
Common stock	1,000,000 shares

The simple EPS computation follows:

Computation of earnings per share:	
Net income	$10,500,000
Preferred dividends	500,000
Net income to common stock	$10,000,000
Earnings per share of common stock:	
$10,000,000 ÷ 1,000,000 shares	$ 10.00

However, note how EPS would be affected if the preferred stock were converted, that is, exchanged into common stock. Dilution, a reduction in EPS, will occur. EPS can be calculated *as if* conversion had occurred at the beginning of the fiscal year:

Net income	$10,500,000
Preferred dividends	0
Net income to common stock	$10,500,000
Earnings per share of common stock—assuming conversion:	
$10,500,000 ÷ 1,200,000 shares	$ 8.75

The potential earnings dilution of common stock is $10.00 − $8.75 = $1.25 per share.

APB *Opinion No. 15* requires companies to divide securities that could cause dilution into two categories: (1) common stock equivalents[11] and (2) other sources of dilution. Common stock equivalents are securities whose major value is attributable to their being exchangeable for or convertible to common stock. There are complex rules, beyond the scope of this text, for identifying common stock equivalents. **Primary EPS** is the EPS calculated as if *common stock equivalents* that dilute EPS were converted. **Fully diluted EPS** is an EPS that includes assumed conversion of *all* potentially dilutive securities. Primary EPS is reported on the income statement. If primary and fully diluted EPS differ by more than 3%, both must be reported.

---

[11] All stock options and warrants and a few convertible securities have characteristics that qualify them as common stock equivalents. Complicated tests and assumptions are applied to determine the existence of common stock equivalents and how to measure their impact on EPS. These matters are described in APB *Opinion No. 15* and are covered in *Intermediate Accounting* textbooks.

Assume that the convertible preferred stock in our example is not a common stock equivalent. EPS would be presented as follows:

Primary earnings per common share (Note A)	$10.00
Fully diluted earnings per common share (Note B)	$ 8.75

Note A: Per share data are based on the average number of common shares outstanding during each year, after recognition of the dividend requirements on the 5% preferred stock.

Note B: Per share data based on the assumption that the outstanding preferred stock is converted into common shares at the beginning of the year, reflecting the 200,000 shares issuable on conversion and eliminating the preferred dividend requirements.

SUMMARY

Stockholders' equity is essentially a residual claim against (or interest in) the total assets of the entity. It can be very simple or enormously complex.

The composition of stockholders' equity is affected by a wide variety of transactions, including issuance of shares of various types, cash dividends, stock dividends, stock splits, retirement of shares, purchase and sale of treasury stock, exercise of stock options, and restrictions of retained income.

Earnings per share is the single number that gets the widest attention as a measure of the performance of publicly traded stocks. Its surface appeal is probably attributable to its deceptive simplicity. However, the difficulties of measuring net income plus the complexities of modern capitalization structures mean that both the numerator and the denominator are far from being simple computations.

Should an organization be formed as a corporation (the focus of this chapter), a partnership, or a sole proprietorship? The form of organization is heavily influenced by income taxes. See Appendix 13B for the discussion of this important topic.

SUMMARY PROBLEMS FOR YOUR REVIEW

☐ **Problem One**

From the following data, prepare a detailed statement of stockholders' equity for the Sample Corporation, December 31, 19X1:

Additional paid-in capital, preferred stock		$ 50,000
Additional paid-in capital, common stock		1,000,000
Retained income restricted as to dividends because of loan agreement		500,000
9% preferred stock, $50 par value, callable at $55, authorized 20,000 shares, issued and outstanding 12,000 shares		
Common stock, no par, stated value $2 per share, authorized 500,000 shares, issued 400,000 shares of which 25,000 shares are held in the treasury		
Dividends payable		90,000
Unrestricted retained income		1,500,000

The 25,000 shares of treasury stock cost $250,000.

Solution to Problem One

Dividends payable is a *liability*. It must therefore be excluded from a statement of stockholders' equity:

SAMPLE CORPORATION
Statement of Stockholders' Equity
December 31, 19X1

9% preferred stock, $50 par value, callable at $55, authorized 20,000 shares, issued and outstanding 12,000 shares		$ 600,000
Common stock, no par, stated value $2 per share, authorized 500,000 shares, issued 400,000 shares of which 25,000 shares are held in the treasury		800,000
Additional paid-in capital:		
Preferred	$ 50,000	
Common	1,000,000	1,050,000*
Retained income:		
Restricted	$ 500,000	
Unrestricted	1,500,000	2,000,000†
Subtotal		$4,450,000
Less: Cost of 25,000 shares of common stock reacquired and held in treasury		250,000
Total stockholders' equity		$4,200,000

* Many presentations would not show the detailed breakdown of additional paid-in capital into preferred and common portions.

† Many presentations would show the restrictions parenthetically, as follows:

Retained income ($500,000 restricted as to dividends because of loan agreement)	$2,000,000

Although not shown here, an additional $250,000 restriction in the amount of the cost of the treasury stock would be required by many state laws. This would reduce the unrestricted retained income from $1,500,000 to $1,250,000.

Problem Two

B Company splits its $10 par common stock 5 for 1. How will its balance sheet be affected? Its earnings per share?

Solution to Problem Two

The total amount of stockholders' equity would be unaffected, but there would be five times more outstanding shares than previously at $2 par rather than $10 par. Earnings per share would be one-fifth of that previously reported, assuming no change in total net income applicable to the common stock.

Problem Three

C Company distributes a 2% stock dividend on its 1 million outstanding $5 par common shares. Its stockholders' equity section before the dividend was:

Common stock, 1,000,000 shares @ $5 par	$ 5,000,000
Paid-in capital in excess of par	20,000,000
Retained income	75,000,000
Total stockholders' equity	$100,000,000

The common was selling on the open market for $150 per share when the dividend was distributed.

How will the stockholders' equity section be affected? If net income were $10.2 million next year, what would be the earnings per share before considering the effects of the stock dividend? After considering the effects of the stock dividend?

Solution to Problem Three

Stockholders' equity:

	BEFORE 2% STOCK DIVIDEND	CHANGES	AFTER 2% STOCK DIVIDEND
Common stock, 1,000,000 shares @ $5 par	$ 5,000,000	+ (20,000 @ $5)	$ 5,100,000
Paid-in capital	20,000,000	+ [20,000 @ ($150 − $5)]	22,900,000
Retained income	75,000,000	− (20,000 @ $150)	72,000,000
Total	$100,000,000		$100,000,000

Earnings per share before considering the effects of the stock dividend would be $10,200,000 ÷ 1,000,000, or $10.20. After the dividend: $10,200,000 ÷ 1,020,000, or $10. Note that the dividend has no effect on net income, the numerator of the earnings-per-share computation. But it does affect the denominator and causes a mild dilution which, in theory, should be reflected by a slight decline in the market price of the stock.

☐ Problem Four

Metro-Goldwyn-Mayer Film Co. declared and distributed a 3% stock dividend. The applicable market value per share was $7.75. The par value of the 966,000 additional shares issued was $1.00 each. The total cash paid to shareholders in lieu of issuing fractional shares was $70,000. Prepare the appropriate journal entry.

☐ Solution to Problem Four

Retained income	7,556,500	
Common stock, $1.00 par value		966,000
Capital in excess of par value		6,520,500
Cash		70,000

To record 3% stock dividend. Total shares issued were 966,000 at $7.75, a total market value of $7,486,500. In addition, cash of $70,000 was paid in lieu of issuing fractional shares. Total charge to retained earnings was $70,000 + (966,000 × $7.75) = $7,556,500. The account Capital in Excess of Par Value was the description actually used by MGM.

HIGHLIGHTS TO REMEMBER

1. A company may have plenty of retained income but almost no cash. The *practical ability* to pay dividends depends on the cash position and other requirements for cash, not the *legal ability* as often measured by balances in retained income.

2. At first glance, accounting for stockholders' equity may seem complex. However, do not be frightened by the many new labels and accounts. As you analyze each transaction, first ask yourself how the fundamental balance sheet equation is affected. For example, stock splits and stock dividends do not affect assets or liabilities (except for minor cash outlays in lieu of issuing fractional shares).

3. Treasury stock is usually carried at cost and is deducted from the total stockholders' equity. It is *issued* stock, but it has been repurchased by the company, so it is no longer *outstanding*.

4. Convertible preferred shares and convertible debentures are frequently used. When conversion occurs, additional common shares are issued in their place, using some predetermined ratio of exchange.

5. Become familiar with the basic computation of earnings per share of common stock. It is the only "financial ratio" that is in the body of publicly issued financial statements.

ACCOUNTING VOCABULARY

Appropriated Retained Income, p. 464
Book Value per Share of Common
   Stock, p. 447
Corporate Proxy, p. 439
Cumulative Dividends, p. 443
Dilution, p. 460
Dividend Arrearages, p. 443
Extraordinary Item, p. 473
Fully Diluted Earnings per Share, p. 467
Liquidating Value, p. 444
Preemptive Rights, p. 440

Preferred Stock, p. 442
Primary Earnings per Share, p. 467
Rate of Return on Common Equity,
   p. 446
Redemption Price, p. 445
Reserve, p. 464
Restricted Retained Income, p. 464
Stock Dividend, p. 454
Stock Option, p. 464
Stock Split, p. 451
Treasury Stock, p. 441
Unlimited Liability, p. 444

APPENDIX 10: A CLOSER LOOK AT THE INCOME STATEMENT

This appendix describes the characteristics of some special items that sometimes appear on income statements: gains or losses from (a) extraordinary items and (b) discontinued operations. Above all, note that the income tax effects of these items, as shown in Exhibit 10–3, are computed and shown separately, item by item.

The income statement that you are used to seeing ends as follows:

Income before income taxes	$50
Income taxes	20
Net income	$30

In contrast, the income statement in Exhibit 10–3 has a more elaborate ending. The $30 net income is relabeled as *income from continuing operations*, which is followed by the effects of *discontinued operations* and *extraordinary items* (net of their impact on income taxes).

EXTRAORDINARY ITEMS

The FASB and SEC insist that nearly all items of revenue, expense, gain, and loss recognized during the period be shown in the current income statement.[12] In contrast, in earlier years, some special or *extraordinary items* were shown in the Statement of Retained Income and never appeared as a part of the computation of net income or EPS for any year. Today they are listed in a special section of the income statement and are included in net income.

The regulators also insist that the following items should be *excluded* from the determination of net income under all circumstances:

a. Charges or credits resulting from transactions in the company's own capital stock
b. Transfers to and from accounts properly designated as appropriated retained earnings (such as general purpose contingency reserves or provisions for replacement costs of fixed assets)

Extraordinary items would affect net income but would be segregated as follows:

a. Income before extraordinary items
b. Extraordinary items (less applicable income tax)
c. Net income

In addition, EPS amounts *must* be reported for both *a* and *c* above, but most companies report EPS in a format that shows per share amounts for *a*, *b*, and *c*.

Many users of income statements have tried to distinguish between "normal" and "unusual" items affecting earnings. This distinction is supposed to assist in predicting future earnings; presumably, the unusual items will not be considered as heavily in any projections.

Through the years, the definition of extraordinary items has been narrowed considerably. Accounting Principles Board *Opinion No. 30* concluded that an event or transaction should be presumed to be an ordinary and usual activity of the reporting entity, and hence includable in income before extraordinary items, unless the evidence clearly

---

[12] There are three exceptions: (1) correction of errors, such as the failure to recognize depreciation in a previous period, (2) tax effects of preacquisition loss carryforwards of purchased subsidiaries, and (3) specified foreign currency translation adjustments.

EXHIBIT 10–3

Illustrated Partial Income Statement
(in millions, data assumed)

Income from continuing operations before income taxes		$ 50
Deduct applicable income taxes		20
Income from continuing operations		$ 30
Discontinued operations (Note _____):		
Income from operations of discontinued Division X (less applicable income taxes of $4)	$ 6	
Loss on disposal of Division X, including provision of $3 for operating losses during phase-out period (less applicable income taxes of $6)	(9)	(3)
Income before extraordinary items		$ 27
Add extraordinary items:		
Loss from earthquake (less applicable income taxes of $2)	(3)	
Gain from early extinguishment of debt (less applicable income taxes of $8)	12	9
Net income		$ 36
Per share amounts (in dollars), assuming 4 million shares of common stock outstanding:		
Income from continuing operations		$7.50
Loss on discontinued operations		(.75)
Income before extraordinary items		$6.75
Extraordinary items		2.25
Net income		$9.00

supports its classification as an extraordinary item as defined in *Opinion No. 30*. **Extraordinary items** result from events that must have both an *unusual nature* and an *infrequency of occurrence*.

The environment in which an entity operates is a primary consideration in determining whether some specific event is abnormal and significantly different from the ordinary activities of the entity. Moreover, extraordinary events cannot reasonably be expected to recur in the foreseeable future. Therefore write-downs of receivables and inventories are ordinary items, as are gains or losses on the sale or abandonment of fixed assets. The effects of a strike and many foreign currency revaluations are also ordinary items. In short, the burden of proof is on the reporting company to demonstrate that a special item is extraordinary. *Opinion No. 30* specifically states that casualties such as an earthquake or government expropriation or prohibition are examples of events that are likely to qualify as extraordinary items. Other examples of extraordinary items include gains or losses arising from governmental condemnation or early extinguishment of debt (except for purchases of debt to satisfy sinking fund requirements).

In an average year, fewer than 10% of major U.S. companies report an extraordinary item; fewer than 5% have an extraordinary item greater than 10% of their net income. Most of the extraordinary items arise from extinguishment of debt.

A tragic illustration of an extraordinary charge was caused by criminal tampering with Tylenol capsules. The manufacturer, Johnson & Johnson, reported the following on its income statement (in millions):

Earnings before extraordinary charge	$146.5
Extraordinary charge—costs associated with the withdrawal of TYLENOL capsules (less applicable tax relief of $50.0)	50.0
Net earnings	$ 96.5

Another example of an extraordinary item is described in a footnote to a recent annual report of the Toro Company:

☐ The company partially retired $3,725,000 of industrial bonds originally used to finance the Mason City, Iowa, facility. This retirement resulted in an after tax gain of $466,000 or $.08 per share and is reflected as an extraordinary item.

DISCONTINUED OPERATIONS

Opinion No. 30 states that the results of continuing operations should be reported separately from discontinued operations, although both must be reported on the income statement. Moreover, any gain or loss from the disposal of a segment of a business should be reported in conjunction with the related results of discontinued operations and not as an extraordinary item.

Exhibit 10–3 shows how discontinued operations should be reported. Amounts of income taxes applicable to the results of discontinued operations and the gain or loss from disposal of the segment should be disclosed on the face of the income statement or in related notes. Revenues applicable to the discontinued operations should be disclosed separately in the related notes.

In a two-year comparative income statement, the income or loss of the discontinued segment's operations during the first of the two years should be condensed and reclassified from continuing operations to discontinued operations. In this way, the income from continuing operations is placed on a comparable basis.

As a general rule, each item below income from continuing operations should be shown net of applicable income taxes. Moreover, separate and detailed disclosures are highly recommended.

Exhibit 10–3 shows how discontinued operations and extraordinary items should be presented separately on the income statement. The exhibit also shows how separate EPS figures must be displayed. You can readily visualize even more complicated presentations involving primary and fully diluted earnings per share.

The net income of a company can be greatly affected by the results of discontinued operations. Consider Whittaker Corporation, a technology and chemicals company. During 1987, the company completed a restructuring plan that entailed discontinuing the life sciences, metals, marine, and hydraulic material-handling businesses. The 1987 annual report separates the results of discontinued operations from the results of continuing operations as follows (in thousands):

	1987	1986	1985
Income (loss) from continuing operations	$12,689	$ 4,356	$(12,430)
Discontinued operations (Note 3):			
Income (loss) from discontinued operations	—	(9,302)	32,297
Gain on disposal of discontinued operations	23,926	—	—
Net income (loss)	$36,615	$(4,946)	$19,867

Notice that the results of discontinued operations had a major effect on net income for each of the three years. Footnote 3 provides more details about the discontinued operations and points out that the reported numbers are aftertax amounts. For example, footnote 3 states: "The net gain on disposal amounted to $23,926,000 (after applicable taxes of $14,394,000)."

Financial presentations such as those in Exhibit 10–3 and the Whittaker Corporation example are often criticized as being unnecessarily complex. However, the financial results of an entity are often produced by a variety of complicated forces. Consequently, the simplifying of innately complex data is not easy. Indeed, too much condensation and summarization may be undesirable.

FUNDAMENTAL ASSIGNMENT MATERIAL

☐ General Coverage

10–1. **STOCKHOLDERS' EQUITY SECTION.** (Alternate is 10–5.) The following are data for the Bianchi Corporation. Prepare a detailed stockholders' equity section as it would appear in the balance sheet at December 31, 19X3:

8% preferred stock, $40 par value, callable at $42, authorized 100,000 shares, issued and outstanding 80,000 shares	$3,200,000
Treasury stock, common (at cost)	8,000,000
Additional paid-in capital, common stock	9,000,000
Restricted retained earnings because of loan agreement	5,000,000
Dividends payable	64,000
Unrestricted retained income	7,000,000
Additional paid-in capital, preferred stock	1,000,000
Common stock, $5 par value per share, authorized 900,000 shares, issued 600,000 shares of which 30,000 are held in the treasury	3,000,000

10–2. **ISSUANCE, SPLITS, DIVIDENDS.** (Alternate is 10–6.)

1. Gomez Company issued 100,000 shares of common stock, $3 par, for $35 cash per share on December 31, 19X1. Prepare the journal entry.
2. Gomez Company had accumulated earnings of $5 million by December 31, 19X5. The board of directors declared a three-for-one stock split and immediately exchanged three $1 par shares for each share outstanding. Prepare the journal entry, if any. Present the stockholders' equity section of the balance sheet before and after the split.
3. Repeat requirement 2, but assume that instead of exchanging three shares for each share outstanding, two *additional* $3 par shares were issued for each share outstanding.
4. What journal entries would be made by the investor who bought 1,000 shares of Gomez Company common stock and held this investment throughout the time covered in requirements 1, 2, and 3?

10–3. **DIVIDENDS.** (Alternate is 10–7.)

1. Hahn Company issued 300,000 shares of common stock, $4 par, for $20 cash per share on December 31, 19X1. Prepare the journal entry.
2. Hahn Company declared and paid a cash dividend of $1 per share on December 31, 19X2. Prepare the journal entry. Assume that only the 300,000 shares from part 1 are outstanding.
3. Hahn Company had accumulated earnings of $7 million by December 31, 19X5. The market value of the common shares was $60 each. A common stock dividend of 3% was declared; the shares were issued on December 31, 19X5. Prepare the journal entry. Also present a tabulation that compares the stockholders' equity section before and after the declaration and issuance of the stock dividend. Also include at the bottom of the tabulation the effects on the overall market value of the stock, the total shares outstanding, and the number of shares and percentage ownership of an individual owner who originally bought 6,000 shares.
4. What journal entries would be made by the investor who bought 5,000 shares of Hahn Company common stock and held this investment throughout the time covered in requirements 1, 2, and 3?
5. Refer to requirement 4. Suppose the investor sold 160 shares for $58 each the day after receiving the stock dividend. Prepare the investor's journal entry for the sale of the shares.

10–4. TREASURY STOCK. (Alternate is 10–8.) Schmidt Company has the following:

Common stock, 2,000,000 shares @ $2 par	$ 4,000,000
Paid-in capital in excess of par	36,000,000
Total paid-in capital	$40,000,000
Retained income	18,000,000
Stockholders' equity	$58,000,000
Overall market value of stock @ assumed $40	$80,000,000

Book value per share = $58,000,000 ÷
2,000,000 = $29.

Required:
1. The company used cash to reacquire 100,000 shares for $40 each and held them in the treasury. Prepare the stockholders' equity section before and after the acquisition of treasury stock. Also prepare the journal entry.
2. All the treasury stock is sold for $50 per share. Prepare the journal entry.
3. All the treasury stock is sold for $30 per share. Prepare the journal entry.

☐ Understanding Published Financial Reports

10–5. SHAREHOLDERS' EQUITY SECTION. (Alternate is 10–1.) Consider the following data, which are from the body of the balance sheet of Johnstown American Companies, a real estate services company that manages income producing properties:

Retained earnings	$16,084,000
Convertible preferred shares: $10 par value, unlimited authorization,	
500,000 shares issued and outstanding	27,500,000
Common Shares held in treasury, 58,200 shares at cost	(444,000)
Capital in excess of par value	5,916,000
Common Shares: $1 par value, unlimited authorization, 8,492,673	
shares issued and outstanding	8,493,000

Required:
1. Johnstown American classified the above amounts as shareholders' equity. Prepare that section of the balance sheet.
2. Assume that $5 million of retained income was restricted as to payment of dividends because of loan agreements. Suppose the company wanted to indicate these restrictions in the body of the balance sheet rather than a footnote. Indicate specifically how your answer to requirement 1 would be changed.

10–6. ISSUANCE, SPLITS, DIVIDENDS. (Alternate is 10–2.) AT&T's 1988 annual report contained the following:

Common stock, par value $1.00 per share	$1,074,000,000

Required:
1. Suppose AT&T had originally issued 200,000 shares of common stock, $2 par, for $15 cash per share many years ago, say, on December 31, 19X1. Prepare the journal entry.

2. AT&T had accumulated earnings of $5 million by December 31, 19X5. The board of directors declared a two-for-one stock split and immediately exchanged two $1 par shares for each share outstanding. Prepare the journal entry, if any. Present the stockholders' equity section of the balance sheet before and after the split.

3. Repeat requirement 2, but assume that one additional $2 par share was issued by AT&T for each share outstanding (instead of exchanging shares).

4. What journal entries would be made by the investor who bought 2,000 shares of AT&T common stock and held this investment throughout the time covered in requirements 1, 2, and 3?

10–7. DIVIDENDS. (Alternate is 10–3.) John Fluke Manufacturing Company is a Seattle-based electronics company. Fluke pays both cash dividends and stock dividends. Consider the following assumed data:

1. The company issued 400,000 shares of common stock, $4 par, for $20 cash per share on March 31, 19X1. Prepare the journal entry.

2. The company declared and paid a cash dividend of $2 per share on March 31, 19X2. Prepare the journal entry.

3. The company had accumulated earnings of $9 million by March 31, 19X5. The market value of the common shares was $60 each. A common stock dividend of 5% was declared; the shares were issued on March 31, 19X5. Prepare the journal entry. Also present a tabulation that compares the stockholders' equity section before and after the declaration and issuance of the stock dividend. Also include at the bottom of the tabulation the effects on the overall market value of the stock, the total shares outstanding, and the number of shares and percentage ownership of an individual owner who originally bought 6,000 shares.

4. What journal entries would be made by the investor who bought 6,000 shares of the company common stock and held this investment throughout the time covered in requirements 1, 2, and 3?

5. Refer to requirement 4. Suppose the investor sold 180 shares for $58 each the day after receiving the stock dividend. Prepare the investor's journal entry for the sale of the shares.

10–8. TREASURY STOCK. (Alternate is 10–4.) Minnesota Mining and Manufacturing Company (3M) presented the following data in a recent annual report:

| | JANUARY 1 | |
| | 1989 | 1988 |
	(In millions)	
Stockholders' Equity:		
Common stock, without par value, 500,000,000 shares authorized, with 236,008,264 shares issued in 1989 and 1988	$ 296	$ 296
Reinvested earnings	5,786	5,147
Total	6,082	5,443
Less—Treasury stock, 11,675,399 shares at January 1, 1989, and 8,515,495 shares at January 1, 1988	568	383
Stockholders' Equity—Net	$5,514	$5,060

Required:

1. Suppose that on January 2, 1989, 3M used cash to reacquire 175,000 shares for $40 each and held them in the treasury. Prepare the stockholders' equity section after the acquisition of treasury stock. Also prepare the journal entry.

2. The 175,000 shares of treasury stock are sold for $50 per share. Prepare the journal entry.

3. The 175,000 shares of treasury stock are sold for $30 per share. Prepare the journal entry.

ADDITIONAL ASSIGNMENT MATERIAL

☐ **General Coverage**

10–9. In what ways are corporations "artificial persons"?

10–10. What is the purpose of preemptive rights?

10–11. Can a share of common stock be outstanding but not authorized or issued? Why?

10–12. In what way is preferred stock similar to debt? To common stock?

10–13. "Treasury stock is unissued stock." Do you agree? Explain.

10–14. "Cumulative dividends are liabilities that must be paid to preferred shareholders before any dividends are paid to common shareholders." Do you agree? Explain?

10–15. "The liquidating value of preferred stock is the amount of cash for which it can currently be exchanged." Do you agree? Explain.

10–16. "Common shareholders have limited liability." Explain.

10–17. "A common stock selling on the market far below its book value is an attractive buy." Do you agree? Explain.

10–18. What is the proper measure for an asset newly acquired through an exchange (e.g., an exchange of land for securities)? Explain.

10–19. What are convertible securities?

10–20. "The only real dividends are cash dividends." Do you agree? Explain.

10–21. "The term *stock dividends* is a misnomer." Why?

10–22. "A stock split can be achieved by means of a stock dividend." Do you agree? Explain.

10–23. "A 2% stock dividend increases every shareholder's fractional portion of the company by 2%." Do you agree? Explain.

10–24. "When a company retires shares, it must pay the stockholders an amount equal to the original par value and additional capital contributed for those shares plus the stockholders' fractional portion of retained earnings." Do you agree? Explain.

10–25. "Treasury stock is not an asset." Explain.

10–26. "Gains and losses are not possible from a corporation's acquiring or selling its own stock." Do you agree? Explain.

10–27. Restrictions on dividend-declaring power may be voluntary or involuntary. Give an example of each.

10–28. Why might a board of directors voluntarily restrict its dividend-declaring power?

10–29. "Earnings per share is net income divided by the number of common shares outstanding." Do you agree? Explain.

10–30. Explain the difference between *primary* and *fully diluted* earnings per share.

10–31. How may the distinction between contributed and accumulated capital be blurred by traditional accounting?

10–32. **Distinctions between Terms.** General Health Services, Inc., a hospital management company, had 5 million shares of common stock authorized on August 31, 19X8. Shares issued were 2,073,178. There were 22,000 shares held in the treasury. How many shares were issued and outstanding? How many shares were unissued? Label your computations.

10–33. **Cumulative Dividends.** In recent years, the Manzanita Company had severe cash flow problems. In 19X4, the company suspended payment of common stock dividends. In 19X5, it ceased payment on its $2 million of outstanding 8% cumulative preferred stock. No common or preferred dividends were paid in 19X5 or 19X6. In 19X7, Manzanita's board of directors decided that $520,000 was available for cash dividends. Compute the preferred stock dividend and the common stock dividend for 19X7.

10–34. **Cumulative Dividends.** Elton Corporation was founded on January 1, 19X1:

Preferred stock, no par, cumulative, $8 annual dividend per share:		
Issued and outstanding, 1,000,000 shares	$ 40,000,000	
Capital stock, no par, 6,000,000 shares	90,000,000	
Total stockholders' equity	$130,000,000	

The corporation's subsequent net incomes (losses) were:

19X1	$ (5,000,000)
19X2	(4,000,000)
19X3	14,000,000
19X4	30,000,000
19X5	12,000,000

Required: Assume that the board of directors declared dividends to the maximum extent permissible by law throughout the five years. Tabulate the annual dividend declarations on preferred and common shares. There is no treasury stock.

10–35. **PREFERENCES AS TO ASSETS.** The following are account balances of Discount Mart, Inc. (in thousands): common stock and retained income, $300; accounts payable, $300; preferred stock (5,000 shares; $20 par and $22 liquidating value per share), $100; subordinated debentures, $300; and unsubordinated debentures, $100. Prepare a table showing the distribution of the cash proceeds upon liquidation and dissolution of the corporation. Assume cash proceeds of (in thousands): $1,400; $1,000; $790; $500; $400; $200; and $100, respectively.

10–36. **FINANCIAL RATIOS AND STOCKHOLDERS' EQUITY.** Consider the following data for Prime Company:

	DECEMBER 31	
	19X2	19X1
Stockholders' equity:		
Preferred stock, 100,000 shares, $40 par, liquidation value $42	$ 4,000,000	$ 4,000,000
Common stock, 2,000,000 shares, $3 par	6,000,000	6,000,000
Additional paid-in capital	7,000,000	7,000,000
Retained income	3,000,000	1,400,000
Total stockholders' equity	$20,000,000	$18,400,000

Net income was $3 million for 19X2. The preferred stock is 10% cumulative. The regular annual dividend was declared on the preferred stock, and the common shareholders received dividends of $.50 per share. The market price of the common stock on December 31, 19X2, was $10.50 per share.

Required: Compute the following statistics for 19X2: rate of return on common equity, earnings per share of common stock, price-earnings ratio, dividend-payout ratio, dividend-yield ratio, and book value per share of common stock. (You may want to review pages 65–67.)

10–37. **BOOK VALUE AND RETURN ON EQUITY.** Auerbach Company had net income of $9 million in 19X8. The stockholders' equity section of its 19X8 annual report follows:

	19X8	19X7
Stockholders' Equity:		
9% Preferred stock, $100 par value, 200,000 shares authorized, 150,000 shares issued	$ 15,000,000	$ 15,000,000
Common stock, $1 par, 5,000,000 authorized, 2,000,000 and 1,800,000 issued	2,000,000	1,800,000
Additional paid-in capital	32,000,000	30,000,000
Retained earnings	69,000,000	65,000,000
Total stockholders' equity	$118,000,000	$111,800,000

Required:

1. Compute the book value per share of common stock at the end of 19X8.
2. Compute the rate of return on common equity for 19X8.
3. Compute the amount of cash dividends on common stock declared during 19X8. (*Hint*: Examine the retained earnings T-account.)

10–38. **ISSUANCE AND RETIREMENT OF SHARES, CASH DIVIDENDS.** On January 2, 19X1, Hopwood Investment Company began business by issuing 10,000 $1 par value shares for $100,000 cash. The cash was invested, and on December 26, 19X1, all investments were sold for $114,000 cash. Operating expenses for 19X1 were $2,000, all paid in cash. Therefore net income for 19X1 was $12,000. On December 27, the board of directors declared a $.70 per-share cash dividend, payable on January 15, 19X2, to owners of record on December 31, 19X1. On January 30, 19X2, the company bought and retired 1,000 of its own shares on the open market for $12 each.

Required:

1. Prepare journal entries for issuance of shares, declaration and payment of cash dividends, and retirement of shares.
2. Prepare a balance sheet as of December 31, 19X1.

10–39. **NONCASH EXCHANGES.** Suppose Company J acquires some equipment from Company K in exchange for issuance of 20,000 shares of J's common stock. The equipment was carried on K's books at the $300,000 original cost less accumulated depreciation of $120,000. Company J's stock is listed on the New York Stock Exchange; its current market value is $20 per share. Its par value is $1 per share.

Required:

1. Using the balance sheet equation, show the effects of the transaction on the accounts of Company J and Company K.
2. Show the journal entry on the books of Company J and Company K.

10–40. **CONVERTIBLE SECURITIES.** Suppose Company G had paid $300,000 to Company H for an investment in 10,000 shares of the $5 par value preferred stock of Company H. The preferred stock was later converted into 20,000 shares of Company H common stock ($1 par value).

Required:

1. Using the balance sheet equation, prepare an analysis of transactions of Company G and Company H.
2. Prepare the journal entries to accompany your analysis in requirement 1.

10–41. **STOCK DIVIDEND AND FRACTIONAL SHARES.** The Siegl Company declared and distributed a 2% stock dividend. The stockholders' equity before the dividend was:

Common stock, 5,000,000 shares, $2 par	$10,000,000
Additional paid-in capital	40,000,000
Retained earnings	25,000,000
Total stockholders' equity	$75,000,000

The market price of Siegl's shares was $20 when the stock dividend was distributed. Siegl paid cash of $20,000 in lieu of issuing fractional shares.

Required: 1. Prepare the journal entry for the declaration and distribution of the stock dividend.
2. Show the stockholders' equity section after the stock dividend.
3. How did the stock dividend affect total stockholders' equity? How did it affect the proportion of the company owned by each shareholder?

10–42. **STOCK SPLIT AND 100% STOCK DIVIDEND.** The Hamada Company wishes to double its number of shares outstanding. The company president asks the controller how a two-for-one stock split differs from a 100% stock dividend. Hamada has 100,000 shares ($1 par) outstanding at a market price of $60 per share.

The current stockholders' equity section is:

Common shares, 100,000 issued	
and outstanding	$ 100,000
Additional paid-in capital	2,400,000
Retained income	4,500,000

Required: 1. Prepare the journal entry for a two-for-one stock split.
2. Prepare the journal entry for a 100% stock dividend.
3. Explain the difference between a two-for-one stock split and a 100% stock dividend.

10–43. **RETIREMENT OF SHARES.** Safety Systems, Inc., has the following:

Common stock, 5,000,000 shares @ $1 par	$ 5,000,000
Paid-in capital in excess of par	40,000,000
Total paid-in capital	$ 45,000,000
Retained income	15,000,000
Stockholders' equity	$ 60,000,000
Overall market value of stock @ assumed $20	$100,000,000
Book value per share = $60,000,000 ÷ 5,000,000 = $12.	

Required: The company used cash to reacquire and retire 200,000 shares for $20 each. Prepare the stockholders' equity section before and after this retirement of shares. Also prepare the journal entry.

10–44. **EFFECTS OF TREASURY STOCK ON RETAINED INCOME.** Assume that T. Kim Company has retained income of $9 million, paid-in capital of $50 million, and cost of treasury stock of $5 million.

Required: 1. Tabulate the effects of dividend payments of (a) $9 million and (b) $4 million on retained income and total stockholders' equity.
2. Why do states forbid the payment of dividends if retained income does not exceed the cost of any treasury stock on hand? Explain, using the numbers from your answer to requirement 1.

10–45. **DISPOSITION OF TREASURY STOCK.** Visquel Company bought 10,000 of its own shares for $12 per share. The shares were held as treasury stock. This was the only time Visquel had ever purchased treasury stock.

Required: 1. Visquel sold 5,000 of the shares for $14 per share. Prepare the journal entry.
2. Visquel sold the remaining 5,000 shares later for $11 per share. Prepare the journal entry.
3. Repeat requirement 2 assuming the shares were sold for $9 instead of $11 per share.
4. Did you record gains or losses in requirements 1, 2, and 3? Explain.

10–46. **RESTRICTIONS OF DIVIDENDS.** Atlantic Aquaculture Company has total retained income of $60 million. It also has treasury stock that cost $12 million. The company also has loan agreements that restrict dividends in the amount of $18 million. State laws do not permit dividends if retained income does not exceed the cost of treasury stock on hand. Present at least two different ways of disclosing these facts on the balance sheet. Assume that formal journal entries have been made regarding all restrictions of dividends.

10–47. **STOCK OPTIONS.** Company Q granted its top executives options to purchase 10,000 shares of common stock (par $1) at $20 per share, the market price today. The options may be exercised over a four-year span, starting three years hence. Suppose all options are exercised three years hence, when the market value of the stock is $29 per share. Prepare the appropriate journal entry on the books of Company Q.

10–48. **EARNINGS PER SHARE.** Borens Company had 700,000 shares of common stock outstanding at the start of 19X1. There were 450,000 additional shares issued on April 30. Net income for 19X1 was $5.9 million. Throughout 19X1 there were 200,000 shares of 7% preferred stock, $100 par, outstanding. Compute the earnings per share of common stock.

10–49. **EARNINGS DILUTION.** (Alternate is 10–50.) G Company had 800,000 shares of common stock outstanding at the start of 19X1. On October 1, G Company issued 400,000 additional shares. Net income for 19X1 was $9.6 million. Throughout 19X1, there were 300,000 shares of 8% preferred stock, $100 par, outstanding. Each share was convertible into two shares of common stock.

Required: 1. Compute the primary earnings per share of common stock.
2. Compute the earnings per share of common stock, assuming full dilution.

10–50. **PRIMARY AND FULLY DILUTED EPS.** (Alternate is 10–49.) Goldwin Canvas Company has 100,000 shares of common stock. It also has two types of convertible preferred stock. Series A preferred stock is convertible into 10,000 shares of common stock, and it is a common stock equivalent. Series A preferred dividends are $80,000 per year. Series B preferred stock is convertible into 20,000 shares of common stock, and it is not a common stock equivalent. Series B preferred dividends are $120,000 per year. Net income in 19X0 was $1,550,000.

Required: 1. Calculate primary earnings per share.
2. Calculate fully diluted earnings per share.

10–51. **UNUSUAL ITEMS AND EPS.** Study Appendix 10. The Enrex Company has the following data pertaining to the year 19X2 (in millions): gain from early extinguishment of debt, $40; income from continuing operations before income taxes, $120; income from operations of discontinued Division B, $20; loss from government prohibition of saccharin, $10; and loss on disposal of Division B (including provision of $4 for operating losses during phase-out period), $25.
The applicable income tax rate for all items is 40%.

Required: Prepare a partial income statement that begins with income from continuing operations before income taxes. At the bottom, show all relevant earnings-per-share amounts. Assume that 10 million shares of common stock are outstanding.

□ **Understanding Published Financial Reports**

10–52. **DISTINCTIONS BETWEEN TERMS.** On January 1, 1989, McDonald's Corporation had 1.25 billion shares of common stock authorized. There were 207,578,189 shares issued, and 19,840,393 shares held as treasury stock. How many shares were issued and outstanding? How many shares were unissued? Label your computations.

10–53. DIVIDENDS AND CUMULATIVE PREFERRED STOCK. Commercial Decal, Inc., maker of ceramic decals and plastic foils, started fiscal 1988 with retained income of $2,463,951. Commercial Decal's balance sheet showed:

6% Cumulative Convertible Preferred Stock, par value $10 a share, authorized 200,000 shares; issued 52,136 shares	$ 521,360
Common stock, par value $.20 a share, authorized 2,000,000 shares, issued 1,322,850 shares	264,570
Additional paid-in capital	2,063,351
Retained income	2,463,951
Less: Treasury stock, at cost:	
Preferred stock, 11,528 shares	(80,249)
Common stock, 93,091 shares	(167,549)
Total stockholders' equity	$5,065,434

Required:

1. Suppose Commercial Decal had paid no dividends, preferred or common, in 1987. All preferred dividends had been paid through 1986. Management decided at the end of 1988 to pay $.05 per share common dividends. Calculate the preferred dividends that would be paid during 1988. Prepare journal entries for recording both preferred and common dividends. Assume that no preferred or common shares were issued or purchased during 1988.
2. Suppose 1988 net income was $200,000. Compute the ending balance in the Retained Income account.

10–54. ISSUE OF COMMON SHARES. Intermec Corporation, a leader in the field of bar code data collection, issued the following common shares during a recent year:

a. 780,000 shares through a public offering for net cash of $10,765,977, an average price of $13.80 per share.

b. 16,900 shares as part of an employee stock purchase plan; $218,093, or $12.90 per share, was received.

c. 88,283 shares for the exercise of stock options; $355,275, or $4.02 per share, was received.

The stockholders' equity section of Intermec's balance sheet at the beginning of the year was the following:

Common stock: authorized 10,000,000 shares with $.60 par value, issued and outstanding 4,510,908 shares	$ 2,706,545
Additional paid-in capital	4,603,092
Retained earnings	8,128,230
Total stockholders' equity	$15,437,867

Net income for the year was $4,008,991. No dividends were paid.

Required:

1. Prepare journal entries for the common stock issues in a, b, and c. Omit explanations.
2. Present the stockholders' equity section of the balance sheet at the end of the year.

10–55. REVERSE STOCK SPLIT. According to a news story, "The shareholders of QED approved a one-for-ten reverse split of QED's common stock." Accounting for a reverse stock split applies the same principles as accounting for a regular stock split. QED Exploration, Inc., is an oil development company operating in Texas and Louisiana. QED's stockholders' equity section before the reverse split included:

Common stock, authorized 30,000,000 shares, issued 23,530,000 shares	$ 287,637
Additional paid-in capital	3,437,547
Retained income	2,220,895
Less treasury stock, at cost, 1,017,500 shares	(305,250)
Total stockholders' equity	$5,640,829

Required: | Prepare QED's stockholders' equity section after the reverse stock split.

10–56. **MEANING OF STOCK SPLITS.** A letter of January 31 to shareholders of United Financial, a California savings and loan company, said:

☐ Once again, I want to take the opportunity of sending you some good news about recent developments at United Financial. Last week the board raised United's quarterly cash dividend 12½ percent and then declared a 5-for-4 stock split in the form of a 25 percent stock dividend. The additional shares will be distributed on March 15 to shareholders of record February 15.

On March 16, the board approved a merger between National Steel Corporation and United Financial. The agreement called for a cash payment of $33.60 on each outstanding United Financial share. The original National Steel offer (in early February) was $42 per share for the 5.8 million shares outstanding.

Required: | 1. As a recipient of the letter of January 31, you were annoyed by the five-for-four stock split. Prepare a letter to the chairman indicating the reasons for your displeasure.
2. A shareholder wrote to the chairman in early March: "I'm confused about the price per share, because of the recent stock split. I owned 100 shares and thought I'd receive $4,200. Now the price has dropped from $42.00 to $33.60." Prepare a response to the shareholder.

10–57. **STOCK DIVIDENDS.** The St. Regis Paper Company had 13.7 million shares of $5 par value common stock issued and outstanding when a 2% stock dividend was issued. The market value of the stock at the time was $36 per share.

Required: | Indicate what accounts would be affected by the issuance of the dividend and by how much.

10–58. **STOCK SPLIT.** The annual report of Dean Foods Company included the following in the statement of consolidated retained earnings:

Charge for stock split	$4,401,000

The balance sheets before and after the split showed:

	AFTER	BEFORE
Common stock $1 par value	$13,203,000	$8,802.000

Required: | Define *stock split*. What did Dean Foods do to achieve its stock split? Does this conflict with your definition? Explain fully.

10–59. **REPURCHASE OF SHARES AND BOOK VALUE PER SHARE.** Exxon recently announced that in the past year it had repurchased 46,553,000 of its own common shares for $2.34 billion. Suppose 800 million shares were outstanding before the purchase, and the shareholders' equity section of the balance sheet showed (in millions):

Common stock, $1 par, 800 million shares outstanding	$ 800
Additional paid-in capital	2,000
Retained earnings	32,300

Required:
1. Prepare the journal entry for the retirement of the 46,553,000 shares.
2. Compute the book value per share before the retirement.
3. Compute the book value per share after the retirement.

10–60. **TREASURY STOCK.** Ford Motor Company included the following in a footnote to a recent annual report:

☐ There were 850,666 shares of common stock of the company, with a cost of $37 million, included in Other Assets in the company's balance sheet. Such shares were acquired for various purposes.

Required: ǀ Comment on Ford's accounting for ownership of its own stock.

10–61. **SMALL STOCK DIVIDEND.** A news story stated:

☐ The Board of Directors of Wickes Companies Inc. today declared a 2½% stock dividend. . . . This is in lieu of the quarterly cash dividend, which had been 26¢ per share . . .

☐ The chairman said, "This dividend continues Wickes' 88-year record of uninterrupted dividend payments."

Required: ǀ Do you agree with the chairman? Explain.

10–62. **DIVIDEND REINVESTMENT PLANS.** Many corporations have automatic dividend reinvestment plans. The shareholder may elect not to receive his or her cash dividends. Instead an equivalent amount of cash is invested in additional stock (at the current market value) that is issued to the shareholder.

Holiday Inns, Inc., had the following data during a recent year:

Holiday Inns, Inc.

Common stock: authorized 120,000,000 shares; $1.50 par value; issued 34,786,931 shares	$ 52,180,396
Capital surplus	271,004,000
Retained earnings	710,909,000

Required:
1. Suppose Holiday Inns declared a cash dividend of $.14 per share. Holders of 10% of the company's shares decided to reinvest in the company under an automatic dividend reinvestment plan rather than accepting the cash. The market price of the shares upon issuance was $30 per share. Prepare the journal entry (or entries) for these transactions. There was no treasury stock.
2. A letter to the editor of *Business Week* commented:

□ Stockholders participating in dividend reinvestment programs pay taxes on dividends not really received.

□ If a company would refrain from paying dividends only to take them back as reinvestments, it would save paper-work, and the stockholder would save income tax.

Do you agree with the writer's remarks? Explain in detail.

10–63. EFFECTS ON STOCKHOLDERS' EQUITY. Indicate the effect (+, −, or 0) on *total* stockholders' equity of General Electric of each of the following:

1. Sale of 100 shares of General Electric by Jay Smith to Tom Jones
2. Operating loss for the period
3. Declaration of a stock dividend on common stock
4. Issuance of a stock dividend on common stock
5. Failing to declare a regular dividend on cumulative preferred stock
6. Declaration of a cash dividend
7. Payment of item 6
8. Purchase of ten shares of treasury stock for $1,000 cash
9. Sale of treasury stock, purchased in item 8, for $1,200
10. Sale of treasury stock, purchased in item 8, for $900

10–64. STOCK OPTIONS. AIM Telephones, Inc., is one of the top five independent telecommunications equipment suppliers in the country. Net income for fiscal 1988 was $1,018,000, and AIM paid no cash dividends. During fiscal 1988, AIM issued 538,522 new shares at an average price of $7.853 per share. In addition, executives exercised stock options for 99,813 shares at an average price of $2.304 per share. The stockholders' equity at the beginning of 1988 was:

Common stock, par value $.01 per share	$ 39,000
Capital in excess of par value	4,962,000
Retained earnings	1,182,000
Total stockholders' equity	$6,183,000

Required:
1. Prepare journal entries for (a) the newly issued shares and (b) the stock options that were exercised. Omit explanations. Round calculations to the nearest thousand dollars.
2. Prepare a statement of stockholders' equity at the end of fiscal 1988.
3. Suppose all the stock options were exercised when the stock price for AIM was $7.50 per share. How much did the executives gain from exercising the stock options?
4. How much compensation expense did AIM record when the options were granted? When they were exercised?

10–65. DILUTION. Micron Technology, Inc., based in Boise, Idaho, produces memory products for electronic systems. The company is a leading supplier of dynamic random access memory (DRAM) components. In fiscal 1988, Micron Technology reported primary earnings per share (EPS) of $3.38, fully diluted EPS of $3.25, and net income of $97,981,403. Suppose the company's only convertible security is preferred stock that is not a common stock equivalent. Micron Technology had 25,805,165 common shares outstanding at the beginning of the fiscal year. Suppose 4 million common shares were issued halfway through the year.

Required:
1. Compute Micron Technology's average common shares outstanding during the year.
2. Compute Micron Technology's preferred stock dividends for fiscal 1988. *Hint*: How was primary EPS of $3.38 computed?
3. Compute the number of common shares into which the preferred stock can be converted. *Hint*: How was fully diluted EPS of $3.25 computed?

10–66. **Cash Dividends, Stock Dividends, Stock Splits, and Stock Options.** In a recent annual report, SL Industries, a manufacturer of specialty industrial products in the electrical, metalworking, and plastics industries, disclosed the following facts affecting stockholders' equity:

    a. Cash dividends of $631,000 were declared and paid.

    b. A 6% stock dividend was declared and distributed to owners of 2,400,000 shares when the market price was $11.20 per share. Cash of $10,000 was issued in lieu of issuing fractional shares.

    c. A three-for-two stock split occurred after the stock dividend was distributed.

    d. Stock options for 2,000 common shares were exercised at an average exercise price of $11 per share. This occurred after the stock dividend and stock split.

    e. Net income for the year was $3,493,000.

The stockholders' equity at the beginning of the year was:

Common stock, $.20 par, 2,400,000 shares	$ 480,000
Capital in excess of par value	11,149,000
Retained earnings	11,192,000
Less: Treasury stock (160,000 shares) at cost	(3,817,000)
Total stockholders' equity	$19,004,000

Required:

    1. Prepare journal entries for all five items listed. Round all calculations (both dollars and number of shares) to the nearest thousand. Include any journal entries needed to close the books at the end of the year.

    2. Present the stockholders' equity section at the end of the year.

10–67. **Extraordinary Items.** Study Appendix 10. MCI Communications Corporation, the long-distance telephone company, included the following in a footnote to its 1988 annual report:

☐ $9\frac{1}{2}\%$ Subordinated Notes

The company purchased and retired $181 million in outstanding principal amount of these notes in 1988. . . . The recorded extraordinary loss on early retirement of these notes was $109 million, net of income tax benefit.

MCI paid $12 million in preferred dividends in 1988, and an average of 271.9 million common shares were outstanding during the year. Assume that the company has no potentially dilutive securities. Using the following condensed data for 1988, prepare an income statement, including amounts for earnings per share. The descriptions are those used by MCI. Amounts are in millions:

Income tax provision	$ 66
Total operating expenses	4,553
Net income	?
Revenues	5,137
Total other expenses	162
Extraordinary loss on early debt retirement, less applicable income tax benefit of $3	10
Income before income taxes and extraordinary item	?

10–68. **House of Fabrics Annual Report.** Study the stockholders' equity sec annual report (page 753), the Consolidated Statement of Stock and footnote 4, Capital Stock (page 757).

488

PART

1. Identify each transaction that affected stockholders' equity during fiscal 1989. Indicate which stockholders' equity account was affected and by how much. (Ignore the tax benefit related to stock options shown in the Consolidated Statement of Stockholders' Equity. It is beyond the scope of this text.)

2. House of Fabrics had 6,564,777 common shares outstanding at the beginning of fiscal 1989 and 6,596,745 at the end. Using net income and net income per share, determine the *weighted average* number of shares outstanding during 1989.

Statement of Cash Flows

After studying this chapter, you should be able to

1. Explain the concept of a statement of cash flows and how it relates to the income statement, retained income statement, and balance sheet

2. Identify those activities that affect cash, and classify them as operating, investing, or financing activities

3. Prepare a statement of cash flows using the direct method

4. Reconcile net income to net cash provided by operating activities

5. Explain the role of depreciation in the statement of cash flows

6. Show how some typical transactions affect income and cash differently and how such effects are represented on the statement of cash flows (Appendix 11A)

7. Use the T-account method to prepare a statement of cash flows (Appendix 11B)

The accrual basis of accounting is widely used as the primary means of presenting financial position (balance sheet) and performance in increasing net assets (income statement). But investors and managers are also concerned about performance in generating cash and an entity's ability to meet forthcoming obligations. Several large businesses have failed in the recent past because they did not produce enough cash to meet their obligations. Examples include W. T. Grant, People Express Airlines, and Penn Square Bank. This chapter shows how external reports focus on such questions as "If we have impressive earnings, why are we always scrambling for more cash?"

The chapter appendixes are highly recommended for anybody who wants a comprehensive review of all financial statements, particularly on how they are interlocked. (Few homework assignments are more enlightening than using balance sheets and income statements as a basis for preparing a statement of cash flows.) Appendix 11A considers items on the statement of cash flows in more detail, particularly with reference to material covered in specific chapters beyond Chapter 7. Appendix 11B presents a T-account approach to the construction of the statement of cash flows.

OVERVIEW OF STATEMENT OF CASH FLOWS

☐ Purposes of Statement

Rampant inflation in the late 1970s and early 1980s engendered many criticisms of the traditional accrual measures of income and financial position. One response has been a more intense focus on the effects of activities that affect cash. The FASB reacted to this change in focus by requiring the statement of cash flows as a basic financial statement. It replaced the previously required *statement of changes in financial position* which focused on changes in working capital instead of changes in cash.

Why did the FASB require a statement of cash flows? The statement has the following purposes:

1. It shows the relationship of net income to changes in cash balances. Cash balances can decline despite positive net income and vice versa.
2. It reports past cash flows as an aid to
   a. Predicting future cash flows
   b. Evaluating management's generation and use of cash
   c. Determining a company's ability to pay interest and dividends and to pay debts when they are due
3. It reveals commitments to assets that may restrict or expand future courses of action.

☐ Operating and Financial Management

Chapter 2 introduced the distinction between operating management and financial management. **Operating management** is largely concerned with the major day-to-day activities that generate revenues and expenses (that is, using a given set of resources). The major purpose of the income statement is to provide a detailed presentation of the results of operating management.

Financial management is largely concerned with where to get cash (*financing activities*) and how to use cash (*investing activities*) for the benefit of the entity. Examples of financial management include decisions regarding the issuance or retirement of long-term debt or additional capital stock, and deciding how to invest the capital raised. The statement of cash flows reports the results of financial management in addition to the results of operating management.

☐ Basic Concepts

A **statement of cash flows** reports the cash receipts and cash payments of an entity during a period. It explains the causes for the changes in cash by providing information about operating, financing, and investing activities. It explicitly shows information that readers of financial reports could otherwise obtain only by makeshift analysis and interpretation of published balance sheets and statements of income and retained income. The statement of cash flows must be presented as a basic financial statement in corporate annual reports. Exhibit 11–1 displays the statement for B Company. Later sections of the chapter will explain how to prepare and interpret the statement.

Balance sheets show the status of an entity at a day in time. In contrast, statements of cash flows, income statements, and statements of retained income cover periods of time; they provide the explanations of why the balance sheet items have changed. This linkage is depicted in the accompanying diagram:

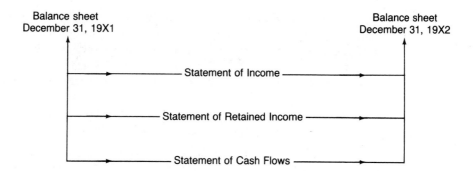

The statement of cash flows explains where cash came from during a period and where it was spent.

The statement of cash flows usually explains changes in cash and cash equivalents, both of which can quickly be used to meet obligations. As explained

EXHIBIT 11–1

B COMPANY
Statement of Cash Flows
For the Year Ended December 31, 19X2
(in thousands)

CASH FLOWS FROM OPERATING ACTIVITIES		
Cash collections from customers		$ 180
Cash payments:		
To suppliers	$ 72	
To employees	15	
For interest	4	
For taxes	20	
Total cash payments		(111)
Net cash provided by operating activities		$ 69
CASH FLOWS FROM INVESTING ACTIVITIES		
Purchases of fixed assets	$(287)	
Proceeds from sale of fixed assets	10	
Net cash used in investing activities		(277)
CASH FLOWS FROM FINANCING ACTIVITIES		
Proceeds from issue of long-term debt	$ 120	
Proceeds from issue of common stock	98	
Dividends paid	(19)	
Net cash provided by financing activities		199
Net decrease in cash		$ (9)
Cash, December 31, 19X1		25
Cash, December 31, 19X2		$ 16

in Chapter 6, *cash equivalents* are highly liquid short-term investments that can easily be converted into cash with little delay. Examples include money market funds and treasury bills. They are usually temporary investments of excess cash, and they can readily be converted into cash as obligations come due. Hereafter, when we refer to cash, we mean both cash and cash equivalents.

☐ Typical Activities Affecting Cash

The fundamental approach to the statement of cash flows is simple: (1) list the activities that increased cash (that is, cash inflows) and those that decreased cash (cash outflows), and (2) place each cash inflow and outflow into one of three categories according to the type of activity that caused it: *operating activities, investing activities,* and *financing activities.*

The following activities are those found most often in statements of cash flows:

OPERATING ACTIVITIES:

Cash Inflows	*Cash Outflows*
Collections from customers	Cash payments to suppliers
Interest and dividends collected	Cash payments to employees
Other operating receipts	Interest paid
	Taxes paid
	Other operating cash payments

INVESTING ACTIVITIES:

Cash Inflows	*Cash Outflows*
Sale of property, plant, and equipment	Purchase of property, plant, and equipment
Sale of securities that are not cash equivalents	Purchase of securities that are not cash equivalents
Receipt of loan repayments	Making loans

FINANCING ACTIVITIES:

Cash Inflows	*Cash Outflows*
Borrowing cash from creditors	Repayment of amounts borrowed
Issuing equity securities	Repurchase of equity shares (including the purchase of treasury stock)
	Payment of dividends

As the lists of activities indicate, cash flows from operating activities are generally the effects of transactions that affect the income statement (for example, sales and wages). Investing activities include (a) lending and collecting on loans and (b) acquiring and selling long-term assets. Financing activities include obtaining resources from creditors and owners and providing them with returns *of* their investments and owners with returns *on* their investments in the form of cash dividends.

Perhaps the most troublesome classifications are the receipts and payments of interest and the receipts of dividends. After all, these items are associated with investment and financing activities. After much debate, the FASB decided to include these items with cash flows from operating activities. Why? Mainly because they affect the computation of income. In contrast, payments of cash dividends are financing activities because they do not affect income.

☐ Focus of a Statement of Cash Flows

The basic ideas underlying the statement of cash flows are straightforward. Consider the illustration of the B Company. Exhibit 11–2 shows the company's condensed balance sheets and income statement.

Because the statement of cash flows explains the *causes* for the change in cash, the first step is to compute the amount of the change (which represents the net *effect*):

Cash, December 31, 19X1	$25,000
Cash, December 31, 19X2	16,000
Net decrease in cash	$ 9,000

EXHIBIT 11–2

B COMPANY
Statement of Income
For the Year Ended December 31, 19X2
(in thousands)

Sales		$200
Cost and Expenses:		
Cost of goods sold	$100	
Wages and salaries	36	
Depreciation	17	
Interest	4	
Total costs and expenses		$157
Income before income taxes		43
Income taxes		20
Net income		$ 23

B COMPANY
Balance Sheet
For the Years Ended December 31
(in thousands)

ASSETS	19X2	19X1	Increase (Decrease)	LIABILITIES AND STOCKHOLDERS' EQUITY	19X2	19X1	Increase (Decrease)
Current assets:				Current liabilities:			
				Accounts payable	$ 74	$ 6	$ 68
Cash	$ 16	$ 25	$ (9)	Wages and			
Accounts receivable	45	25	20	salaries payable	25	4	21
Inventory	100	60	40				
Total current assets	161	110	51	Total current liabilities	99	10	89
Fixed assets, gross	581	330	251	Long-term debt	125	5	120
Less accum. depreciation	(101)	(110)	9	Stockholders' equity	417	315	102
Net	480	220	260				
				Total liabilities and			
Total assets	$641	$330	$311	stockholders' equity	$641	$330	$311

Exhibit 11–1 illustrates how this information is often shown at the bottom of a statement of cash flows. The beginning cash balance is added to the net change to compute the ending cash balance. Another common practice is to place the beginning cash balance at the top of the statement and the ending cash balance at the bottom. However, there is no requirement that beginning and ending cash balances be shown explicitly in the statement of cash flows. Showing only the net change is sufficient.

When business expansion occurs, as in this case, and where there is a strong cash position at the outset, cash often declines. Why? Because cash is usually needed for investment in various business assets required for expansion, including investment in accounts receivable and inventories.

The statement in Exhibit 11–1 gives a direct picture of where cash came from and where it went. In this instance, the excess of cash outflows over cash inflows reduced cash by $9,000. Without the statement of cash flows, the readers of the annual report would have to conduct their own analyses of the beginning and ending balance sheets, the income statement, and the statement of retained income to get a grasp of the impact of financial management decisions.

Most important, this illustration demonstrates how a firm may simultaneously (a) have a significant amount of net income, as computed by accountants on the accrual basis, and yet (b) have a decline in cash that could become severe. Indeed, many growing businesses are desperate for cash even though reported net income zooms upward.

PREPARING A STATEMENT OF CASH FLOWS: THE DIRECT METHOD

☐ Changes in Balance Sheet Equation

Accountants use various techniques for preparing a statement of cash flows. We begin here with the balance sheet equation. Why? Because it provides the conceptual framework underlying all financial statements, including the statement of cash flows. The equation can be rearranged as follows:

Assets	= Liabilities +	Stockholders' equity
Cash + Noncash assets	= Liabilities + Paid-in capital + Retained income	
Cash	= Liabilities + Paid-in capital + Retained income − Noncash Assets	
Cash	= L + PC + RI − NCA	

Any change (Δ) in cash must be accompanied by a change in one or more items on the right side to keep the equation in balance:

$$\Delta\ Cash = \Delta\ L + \Delta\ PC + \Delta\ RI - \Delta\ NCA$$

Therefore:

Change in cash = Change in all noncash accounts

or

What happened to cash = Why it happened

The statement of cash flows focuses on the changes in the noncash accounts as a way of explaining how and why the level of cash has gone up or down during a given period. Thus the major changes in the accounts on the right side of the equation appear in the statement of cash flows as *causes* of the change in cash. The left side of the equation measures the net *effect* of the change in cash.

Consider the following summary of 19X2 transactions for B Company. Those involving cash have an asterisk (*):

1. Sales on credit, $200,000
*2. Collections on accounts receivable, $180,000
3. Recognition of cost of goods sold, $100,000
4. Purchases of inventory on account, $140,000
*5. Payments of trade accounts payable, $72,000

6. Recognition of wages expense, $36,000
*7. Payments of wages, $15,000
*8. Recognition of interest accrued and paid, $4,000
*9. Recognition and payment of income taxes, $20,000
10. Recognition of depreciation expense, $17,000
*11. Acquisition of fixed assets for cash, $287,000
*12. Sale of fixed assets at book value, $10,000
*13. Issuance of long-term debt, $120,000
*14. Issuance of common stock, $98,000
*15. Declaration and payment of dividends, $19,000

Exhibit 11–3 applies the balance sheet equation to the B Company data. We can see, step by step, how the statement of cash flows in Exhibit 11–1 is based on the same theoretical foundation that underlies the other financial statements.

When statements become complicated, accountants prefer to use work sheets or T-accounts to help their analysis. (See Appendix 11B for a description of the latter.) In any event, the totals in the above tabulation show that all transactions affecting cash have been accounted for. The $9,000 decrease in cash is explained by the changes in the noncash accounts. Each noncash account can be analyzed in detail if desired.

EXHIBIT 11–3

Conceptual Foundation: The Balance Sheet Equation
(in thousands of dollars)

	Δ Cash =	Δ L	$+\Delta$ PC	$+\Delta$ RI	$-\Delta$ NCA
Operating activities:					
1. Sales on credit	=			+200	$-(+200)$
*2. Cash collections from customers	+180 =				$-(-180)$
3. Cost of goods sold	=			−100	$-(-100)$
4. Inventory purchases on account	=	+140			$-(+140)$
*5. Payments to suppliers	− 72 =	− 72			
6. Wages and salaries expense	=	+ 36		− 36	
*7. Payments to employees	− 15 =	− 15			
*8. Interest expense paid	− 4 =			− 4	
*9. Income taxes paid	− 20 =			− 20	
Net cash provided by operating activities, a subtotal	69				
Expenses not requiring cash:					
10. Depreciation	=			− 17	$-(- 17)$
Net income, a subtotal				+ 23	
Investing activities:					
*11. Acquire fixed assets	−287 =				$-(+287)$
*12. Dispose of fixed assets	+ 10 =				$-(- 10)$
Financing activities:					
*13. Issue long-term debt	+120 =	+120			
*14. Issue common stock	+ 98 =		+98		
*15. Pay dividends	− 19 =			− 19	
Net changes	− 9 =	+209	+98	+ 4	$-(+320)$

Major Sections of Statement

The first major section in the statement of cash flows in Exhibit 11–1 (p. 492) is **cash flows from operating activities.** The section might also be called *cash flow from operations, cash provided by operations,* or, if operating activities decrease cash, *cash used for operations.*

Collections from sales to customers are almost always the major operating activity that increases cash. Correspondingly, disbursements for purchases of goods to be sold and operating expenses are almost always the major operating cash outflows. The excess of collections over disbursements is the net cash provided by operating activities. There are two ways to compute this amount: the *direct method* and the *indirect method.*

Because it shows operating cash receipts and payments in a way that is easier for investors to understand, the FASB favors the **direct method.** It is used in Exhibit 11–1: collections of $180,000 minus the $111,000 of operating disbursements equals net cash provided by operating activities, $69,000. The indirect method is explained later in this chapter.

The second and third major sections of the statement present examples of cash flows from investing activities ($277,000 outflow) and financing activities ($199,000 inflow), respectively.

Working from Income Statement Amounts to Cash Amounts

Many accountants build the statement of cash flows from the *changes* in balance sheet items, a few additional facts, and a familiarity with the typical causes of changes in cash. For instance, for convenience the $180,000 amount of cash collections from B Company customers for 19X2 was given in our example. However, most accounting systems do not provide such a balance. Therefore accountants often compute the collections by beginning with the sales revenue shown on the income statement (an amount calculated using the accrual basis) and adding (or deducting) the *change* in the accounts receivable balance. A detailed analysis of collections and other operating items follows.

a. B Company recognized $200,000 of revenue in 19X2, but because accounts receivable increased by $20,000, only $180,000 was collected from customers:

Sales	$200,000
+Beginning accounts receivable	25,000
Potential collections	$225,000
−Ending accounts receivable	45,000
Cash collections from customers	$180,000

or

Sales	$200,000
Decrease (increase) in accounts receivable	(20,000)
Cash collections from customers	$180,000

b. The difference between the $100,000 cost of goods sold and the $72,000 cash payment to suppliers is accounted for by changes in inventory *and* accounts payable. The $40,000 increase in inventory indicates that purchases exceeded the cost of goods sold by $40,000:

Ending inventory	$100,000
+Cost of goods sold	100,000
Inventory to account for	$200,000
−Beginning inventory	(60,000)
Purchases of inventory	$140,000

Although purchases were $140,000, payments to suppliers were only $72,000. Why? Because trade accounts payable increased by $68,000, from $6,000 to $74,000:

Beginning trade accounts payable	$ 6,000
+Purchases	140,000
Total amount to be paid	$146,000
−Ending trade accounts payable	(74,000)
Accounts paid in cash	$ 72,000

The effects of inventory and trade accounts payable can be combined as follows:

Cost of goods sold	$100,000
Increase (decrease) in inventory	40,000
Decrease (increase) in trade accounts payable	(68,000)
Payments to suppliers	$ 72,000

c. Cash payments to employees were only $15,000 because the wages and salaries expense of $36,000 was offset by a $21,000 increase in wages and salaries payable:

Beginning wages and salaries payable	$ 4,000
+Wages and salaries expense	36,000
Total to be paid	$40,000
−Ending wages and salaries payable	(25,000)
Cash payments to employees	$15,000

or

Wages and salaries expense	$36,000
Decrease (increase) in wages and salaries payable	(21,000)
Cash payments to employees	$15,000

EXHIBIT 11–4

Comparison of Net Income and Net Cash Provided
by Operating Activities

	INCOME STATEMENT	ADDITIONS (DEDUCTIONS)	CASH FLOWS STATEMENT
Sales	$ 200,000		
Increase in accounts receivable		$(20,000)	
Cash collections from customers			$180,000
Cost of goods sold	(100,000)		
Increase in inventory		(40,000)	
Increase in accounts payable		68,000	
Cash payments to suppliers			(72,000)
Wages and salaries expense	(36,000)		
Increase in wages and salaries payable		21,000	
Cash paid to employees			(15,000)
Interest: expense equals cash flow	(4,000)		(4,000)
Income taxes: expense equals cash flow	(20,000)		(20,000)
Depreciation: deducted in computing net income but not a cash outflow	(17,000)	17,000	
Net income	$ 23,000		
Total additions (deductions)		$ 46,000	
Net cash provided by operating activities			$ 69,000

d. Notice that both interest payable and income taxes payable were zero at the beginning and at the end of 19X2. Therefore the entire $4,000 interest expense and the $20,000 income tax expense were paid in cash in 19X2.

Exhibit 11–4 summarizes the differences between B Company's net income of $23,000 and net cash provided by operating activities of $69,000 in 19X2. Examine Exhibit 11–1 (p. 492) and confirm that the $69,000 cash inflow from operating activities is shown in the first section of the statement of cash flows.

☐ Computing Investing and Financing Cash Flows

If the necessary information regarding investing and financing cash flows is not directly available, accountants analyze *changes* in all balance sheet items *except* cash. The following rules pertain:

- ☐ *Increases in cash* (*cash inflows*)
    Increases in liabilities or stockholders' equity
    Decreases in noncash assets
- ☐ *Decreases in cash* (*cash outflows*)
    Decreases in liabilities or stockholders' equity
    Increases in noncash assets

Consider B Company's balance sheet (Exhibit 11–2, p. 494). All noncash *current* assets and *current* liabilities of B Company were affected only by operating activities. They were discussed in the previous section of the chapter. Three *noncurrent* accounts are now analyzed: (a) fixed assets, (b) long-term debt, and (c) stockholders' equity.

a. Fixed assets increased by $260,000 in 19X2. Three items usually explain changes in net fixed assets: (1) assets acquired, (2) asset dispositions, and (3) depreciation expense for the period. Therefore:

Increase in net plant assets = Acquisitions − Disposals − Depreciation expense

If no information were provided about B Company's asset disposals, the book value of disposals could be computed from the above equation:

$260,000 = $287,000 − Disposals − $17,000
Disposals = $287,000 − $17,000 − $260,000
Disposals = $10,000

B Company received exactly the book value for the assets sold. (Appendix 11A discusses disposals for more or less than book value.) If the amount of disposals were known, but either acquisitions or depreciation expense were unknown, the missing item could be determined by applying this same equation. Both asset acquisitions and asset disposals are *investing activities* that affect cash.

b. Long-term debt increased by $125,000 − $5,000 = $120,000. Long-term debt was issued, a *financing activity* that increased cash.

c. The $102,000 increase in stockholders' equity can be explained by three factors: (1) issuance of capital stock, (2) net income (or loss), and (3) dividends. Therefore:

Increase in stockholders' equity = New issuance + Net income − Dividends

Suppose data about the issuance of new capital stock had not been provided:

$102,000 = New issuance + $23,000 − $19,000
New issuance = $102,000 − $23,000 + $19,000
New issuance = $98,000, an inflow of cash

Both the issuance of new shares and the payment of cash dividends are *financing activities* that affect cash.

Reexamine Exhibit 11–1, p. 492. The asset acquisitions and disposals from paragraph **a** are listed with cash flows from investing activities, and the effects of debt and equity issues and dividend payments from paragraphs **b** and **c** are shown with cash flows from financing activities.

☐ Noncash Investing and Financing Activities

Major investment and financing activities that do not affect cash must be reported in a schedule that accompanies the statement of cash flows. For example, consider the acquisition of a $120,000 warehouse in exchange for the issuance of capital stock. The transaction would not be included in the body of the statement of cash flows. Why? Because cash was unaffected. But the transaction is almost identical with one in which capital stock is issued for cash of $120,000, which is immediately used to purchase the warehouse. Therefore such a transaction should be disclosed to readers of a statement of cash flows. Disclosure is made in a schedule that follows directly after the statement. B Company did not have such a transaction in 19X2. (See Appendix 11A for further discussion.)

Activities Affecting Cash

Exhibit 11–5 summarizes the effects of most major transactions on cash. It is worth studying to solidify your understanding of the conceptual underpinnings of the statement of cash flows. The zeros underscore the importance of distinguishing between those transactions that do or do not affect cash.

Cash Flow and Earnings

A focal point of the statement of cash flows is the net cash flow from operating activities. Frequently, this is called simply **cash flow.** The importance of cash

EXHIBIT 11–5

Analysis of Effects of Transactions on Cash

TYPE OF TRANSACTION	Δ Cash	=	Δ L	+ Δ PC	+ Δ RI	− Δ NCA
OPERATING ACTIVITIES:						
Sales of goods and services for cash	+	=			+	
Sales of goods and services on credit	0	=			+	−(+)
Receive dividends or interest	+	=			+	
Collection of accounts receivable	+	=				−(−)
Recognize cost of goods sold	0	=			−	−(−)
Purchase inventory for cash	−	=				−(+)
Purchase inventory on credit	0	=	+			−(+)
Pay trade accounts payable	−	=	−			
Accrue operating expenses	0	=	+		−	
Pay operating expenses	−	=	−			
Accrue taxes	0	=	+		−	
Pay taxes	−	=	−			
Accrue interest	0	=	+		−	
Pay interest	−	=	−			
Prepay expenses for cash	−	=				−(+)
Write off prepaid expenses	0	=			−	−(−)
Charge depreciation or amortization	0	=			−	−(−)
INVESTING ACTIVITIES:						
Purchase fixed assets for cash	−	=				−(+)
Purchase fixed assets by issuing debt	0	=	+			−(+)
Sell fixed assets at book value*	+	=				−(−)
Purchase securities that are not cash equivalents	−	=				−(+)
Sell securities that are not cash equivalents	+	=				−(−)
Make a loan	−	=				−(+)
FINANCING ACTIVITIES:						
Increase long-term or short-term debt	+	=	+			
Reduce long-term or short-term debt	−	=	−			
Sell common or preferred shares	+	=		+		
Repurchase and retire common or preferred shares	−	=		(−)		
Purchase treasury stock	−	=		(−)		
Pay dividends	−	=			−	
Convert debt to common stock	0	=	−	+		
Reclassify long-term debt to short-term debt	0	=	+,−			

* See Appendix 11A for sales at other than book value.

flow has been stressed by Harold Williams, the former chairman of the Securities and Exchange Commission, quoted in *Forbes*: "If I had to make a forced choice between having earnings information and having cash flow information, today I would take cash flow information." Fortunately, we do not have to make a choice. Cash flow and income both convey useful information about an entity.

Some companies used to stress a cash-flow-per-share figure and provide it in addition to the required earnings-per-share figure. Net income is an attempt to summarize management performance. Net cash flow from operating activities gives an incomplete picture of that performance. Why? Because it ignores noncash expenses that are just as important as cash expenses for judging overall company performance. Moreover, a reported cash-flow-per-share says nothing about the cash needed for replacement and expansion of facilities. Thus the entire per-share cash flow from operations may not be available for cash dividends. Because it gives an incomplete picture, a cash-flow-per-share figure can be quite misleading. Accordingly, the FASB has specifically prohibited the reporting of cash-flow-per-share amounts.

Both cash flow and accrual earnings data are useful. As Professor Loyd Heath said, "Asking which one is better, cash flow or earnings, is like asking which shoe is more useful, your right or your left?"

PREPARING A STATEMENT OF CASH FLOWS: THE INDIRECT METHOD

☐ **Reconciliation of Net Income to Net Cash Provided by Operations**

An alternative, and often convenient, way to compute cash flows from operating activities is the **indirect method.** The indirect method reconciles net income to the net cash provided by operating activities. It also shows the link between the income statement and the statement of cash flows.

The reconciliation begins with net income. Then additions or deductions are made for items that affect net income and net cash flow differently. Using the numbers in our B Company example, Exhibit 11–6 shows the reconciliation. The FASB requires such a reconciliation as a *supporting schedule* to the statement of cash flows prepared under the direct method. Net cash provided by operating activities exceeds net income by $46,000.

The FASB requires all preparers of a statement of cash flows to use either the direct or the indirect method. Furthermore, the reconciliation schedule must be included in some fashion under either the direct or the indirect method. The available alternatives can be related to Exhibit 11–1 (p. 492):

☐ *Direct Method* (favored by FASB)
   Exhibit 11–1 as the body. Include Exhibit 11–6 as a supporting schedule.
☐ *Indirect Method* (permitted by FASB)
   Alternative Format 1:
   Exhibit 11–1 as the body. However, replace the first section with a one-line item, net cash provided by operating activities. Include Exhibit 11–6 as a supporting schedule.

EXHIBIT 11–6

Supporting Schedule to Statement of Cash Flows
Reconciliation of Net Income to Net Cash Provided
by Operating Activities
(in thousands)

Net income		$23
Adjustments to reconcile net income to net cash		
provided by operating activities:		
Depreciation	$17	
Net increase in accounts receivable	(20)	
Net increase in inventory	(40)	
Net increase in accounts payable	68	
Net increase in wages and salaries payable	21	
Total additions and deductions		46
Net cash provided by operating activities		$69

Alternative Format 2:
Exhibit 11–1, except use Exhibit 11–6 in the body as the first section, cash flows from operating activities. Exhibit 11–7 (p. 505) illustrates this widely used method.

Consider the logic applied in the reconciliation in Exhibit 11–6:

1. Depreciation is added back to net income because it was deducted in the computation of net income. If the purpose is to calculate cash provided by operations, the depreciation of $17,000 should not have been subtracted. Why? Because it was not a cash expense this period. Since it *was* subtracted, it must now be added back to income to get cash from operations. The addback simply cancels the earlier deduction.

2. Increases in noncash current assets such as receivables and inventory result in less cash flow from operations. For instance, suppose the $20,000 increase in receivables was a result of credit sales made near the end of the year. The $20,000 sales figure would be included in the computation of net income, but the $20,000 would not have increased cash flow from operations. Therefore the reconciliation deducts the $20,000 from the net income to help pinpoint the effects on cash.

3. Increases in current liabilities such as accounts payable and wages payable result in more cash flow from operations. For instance, suppose the $21,000 increase in wages payable was attributable to wages earned near the end of the year, but not yet paid in cash. The $21,000 wages expense would be deducted in computing net income, but the $21,000 would not yet have decreased cash flow from operations. Therefore the reconciliation adds the $21,000 to net income to offset the deduction and thereby show the effect on cash.

The reconciliation's most common additions or deductions from net income are:

☐ Add decreases (or deduct increases) in accounts receivable
☐ Add decreases (or deduct increases) in inventories
☐ Add increases (or deduct decreases) in accounts payable

□ Add increases (or deduct decreases) in wages and salaries payable
□ Add increases (or deduct decreases) in unearned revenue

The general rules for reconciling for these items are:

□ Deduct increases in noncash current assets
□ Add decreases in noncash current assets
□ Add increases in current liabilities
□ Deduct decreases in current liabilities

A final step is to reconcile for amounts that are included in net income but represent investing or financing activities (in contrast to operating activities). Examples, which are explained in Appendix 11A, are:

□ Add loss (or deduct gain) from sale of fixed assets
□ Add loss (or deduct gain) on extinguishment of debt

□ Role of Depreciation

The most crucial aspect of a statement of cash flows is how depreciation and other expenses that do not require cash relate to the flow of cash. There is widespread misunderstanding of the role of depreciation in financial reporting, so let us examine this point in detail.

Accountants view depreciation as an allocation of historical cost to expense. Therefore depreciation expense does not entail a current outflow of cash. Consider again the comparison of B Company's net income and cash flows on page 499. Why is the $17,000 of depreciation added to net income to compute cash flow? Simply to cancel its deduction in calculating net income. Unfortunately, use of the indirect method may at first glance create an erroneous impression that depreciation is added because it, by itself, is a source of cash. If that were really true, a corporation could merely double or triple its bookkeeping entry for depreciation expense when cash was badly needed! What would happen? Cash provided by operations would be unaffected. Suppose depreciation for B Company is doubled:

	WITH DEPRECIATION OF $17,000	WITH DEPRECIATION OF $34,000
Sales	$200,000	$200,000
All expenses except depreciation (including income taxes)*	(160,000)	(160,000)
Depreciation	(17,000)	(34,000)
Net income	$ 23,000	$ 6,000
Nondepreciation adjustments†	29,000	29,000
Add depreciation	17,000	34,000
Net cash provided by operating activities	$ 69,000	$ 69,000

* $100,000 + $36,000 + $4,000 + $20,000 = $160,000
† $(20,000) + $(40,000) + $68,000 + $21,000 = $29,000

The doubling affects depreciation and net income, but it has no direct influence on cash provided by operations, which, of course, still amounts to $69,000. (For additional discussion, see Chapter 8, page 328, the section called "Depreciation and Generation of Cash." The effects of depreciation on income tax outflows are explained there.)

☐ Reconciliation Items

We have seen that net income rarely coincides with net cash provided by operating activities. Consequently, many necessary additions or deductions are commonly shown to reconcile net income to net cash provided by operating activities, as explained earlier for depreciation and changes in noncash current assets and current liabilities.

EXHIBIT 11–7

NIKE, Inc.
Statement of Cash Flows
For the Year Ended May 31, 1988
(in thousands)

Cash provided (used) by operations:	
Net income	$101,695
Income charges (credits) not affecting cash:	
Depreciation	14,020
Other	221
Changes in certain working capital components:	
Increase in inventory	(60,082)
Increase in accounts receivable	(64,187)
Increase in other current assets	(5,624)
Increase in accounts payable, accrued	
liabilities and income taxes payable	32,976
Cash provided by operations	19,019
Cash provided (used) by investing activities:	
Additions to property, plant and equipment	(25,513)
Disposals of property, plant and equipment	8,863
Acquisition of Cole Haan	(95,130)
Additions to other assets	(1,445)
Cash used by investing activities	(113,225)
Cash provided (used) by financing activities:	
Additions to long-term debt	12
Reductions in long-term debt including	
current portion	(11,693)
Increase in notes payable to banks	82,185
Proceeds from exercise of options	2,262
Issuance of common stock	5,813
Dividends—common and preferred	(14,904)
Purchase and retirement of common stock	(21,890)
Cash provided by financing activities	41,785
Effect of exchange rate changes on cash	911
Net decrease in cash and equivalents	(51,510)
Cash and equivalents, beginning of year	126,867
Cash and equivalents, end of year	$ 75,357

Some other additions and deductions are listed below. However, for our purposes in the body of this chapter, we need only be concerned with those already discussed. (Appendix 11A contains a fuller discussion of the contents of a statement of cash flows.) Chapter references are shown in parentheses for readers who want to study the nature of the items in more depth:

ADD CHARGES AGAINST INCOME (EXPENSES) NOT REQUIRING CASH	DEDUCT CREDITS TO INCOME (REVENUES) NOT PROVIDING CASH
Depreciation (Chapter 8)	Amortization of premium on bonds payable (Chapter 9)
Depletion (Chapter 8)	Extraordinary and nonoperating gains (Chapter 10)
Amortization of long-lived assets such as patents, copyrights, and goodwill (Chapter 8)	Equity in earnings of affiliated companies (Chapter 12)
Amortization of discount on bonds payable (Chapter 9)	
Extraordinary and nonoperating losses (Chapter 10)	
Income tax expense arising from deferred income taxes (Chapter 13)	

Exhibit 11–7 contains a statement of cash flows for Nike, Inc., maker of running shoes and other athletic clothing and equipment. Other publicly held corporations may include more details, but the general format of the statement of cash flows is similar to that shown. Note that Nike uses the indirect method in the body of the statement of cash flows to report the cash flows from operating activities. Many companies use this format.

Most of the items in Exhibit 11–7 have been discussed earlier in the chapter, but two deserve mention here. First, proceeds from exercise of options is *cash received* from issuance of shares to executives as part of a stock option compensation plan. Second, the effect of changes in the exchange rate on cash shows the impact of changes in the relative prices of foreign currencies on multinational operations. It is beyond the scope of this text.

SUMMARY

Statements of cash flows focus on the changes in cash and the activities that cause those changes. Where did cash go? How much change in cash was caused by operating activities? By investing activities? By financing activities?

Operating activities are a major source of cash inflows for most companies. The largest inflow is collections from customers; the largest outflows are generally for purchases of goods to be sold and operating expenses.

Investment activities usually create a net cash outflow. The activities include purchases and disposals of plant and equipment and long-term investments in other companies (including acquisition of subsidiaries).

Financing activities are often an important source of cash. Increases in debt and issuance of equity securities for cash provide cash inflows. Retirement of debt or equity and payment of dividends are cash outflows.

The statement of cash flows also directly explains why a company with high net income may nevertheless be unable to pay dividends because of the weight of other financial commitments to plant expansion or retirement of debt.

SUMMARY PROBLEM FOR YOUR REVIEW

☐ **Problem**

The Buretta Company has prepared the data in Exhibit 11–8.

In December 19X2, Buretta paid $54 million cash for a new building acquired to accommodate an expansion of operations. This was financed partly by a new issue of long-term debt for $40 million cash. During 19X2, the company also sold fixed assets for $5 million cash, which was equal to their book value. All sales and purchases of merchandise were on credit.

Because the net income of $4 million was the highest in the company's history, Mr. Buretta, the chairman of the board, was perplexed by the company's extremely low cash balance.

Required:

1. Prepare a statement of cash flows. Ignore income taxes. You may wish to use Exhibit 11–1 (p. 492) as a guide. Use the direct method for reporting cash flows from operating activities.
2. Prepare a supporting schedule that reconciles net income to net cash provided by operating activities.
3. What is revealed by the statement of cash flows? Does it help you reduce Mr. Buretta's puzzlement? Why?
4. Refer to requirement 1. Support your financial statement by using a form of the balance sheet equation. Step by step, show in equation form how each item in the statement of cash flows affects cash.

EXHIBIT 11–8

BURETTA CO.
Income Statement and Statement of Retained Earnings
For the Year Ended December 31, 19X2
(in millions)

Sales		$100
Less cost of goods sold:		
Inventory, December 31, 19X1	$ 15	
Purchases	104	
Cost of goods available for sale	$119	
Inventory, December 31, 19X2	46	73
Gross profit		$ 27
Less other expenses:		
General expenses	$ 8	
Depreciation	8	
Property taxes	4	
Interest expense	3	23
Net income		$ 4
Retained earnings, December 31, 19X1		7
Total		$ 11
Dividends		1
Retained earnings, December 31, 19X2		$ 10

EXHIBIT 11–8 (continued)

Trial Balances

	DECEMBER 31 (in millions)		INCREASE (DECREASE)
	19X2	19X1	
Debits			
Cash	$ 1	$20	$(19)
Accounts receivable	20	5	15
Inventory	46	15	31
Prepaid general expenses	4	2	2
Fixed assets, net	91	50	41
	$162	$92	$ 70
Credits			
Accounts payable for merchandise	$ 39	$14	$ 25
Accrued property tax payable	3	1	2
Long-term debt	40	—	40
Capital stock	70	70	—
Retained earnings	10	7	3
	$162	$92	$ 70

☐ Solution

1. See Exhibit 11–9. Cash flows from operating activities were computed as follows (in millions):

Sales	$100
Less increase in accounts receivable	(15)
Cash collections from customers	$ 85
Cost of goods sold	$ 73
Plus increase in inventory	31
Purchases	$104
Less increase in accounts payable	(25)
Cash paid to suppliers	$ 79
General expenses	$ 8
Plus increase in prepaid general expenses	2
Cash payment for general expenses	$ 10
Property taxes	$ 4
Less increase in accrued property tax payable	(2)
Cash paid for property taxes	$ 2
Cash paid for interest	$ 3

2. Exhibit 11–10 reconciles net income to net cash provided by operating activities.

EXHIBIT 11–9

BURETTA COMPANY
Statement of Cash Flows
For the Year Ended December 31, 19X2
(in millions)

CASH FLOWS FROM OPERATING ACTIVITIES:		
Cash collections from customers		$ 85
Cash payments:		
Cash paid to suppliers	$(79)	
General expenses	(10)	
Interest paid	(3)	
Property taxes	(2)	(94)
Net cash used by operating activities		$ (9)
CASH FLOWS FROM INVESTING ACTIVITIES:		
Purchase of fixed assets (building)	$(54)	
Proceeds from sale of fixed assets	5	
Net cash used by investing activities		(49)
CASH FLOWS FROM FINANCING ACTIVITIES:		
Long-term debt issued	$ 40	
Dividends paid	(1)	
Net cash provided by financing activities		39
Net decrease in cash		$(19)
Cash balance, December 31, 19X1		20
Cash balance, December 31, 19X2		$ 1

3. The statement of cash flows shows where cash has come from and where it has gone. Operations used $9 million of cash. Why? Exhibit 11–10 shows that large increases in accounts receivable ($15 million) and inventory ($31 million), plus a $2 million increase in prepaid expenses, used $48 million of cash. In contrast, only $39 million (that is, $4 + $8 + $25 + $2 million) was generated. Exhibit 11–9 explains the $9 million use of cash slightly differently; the $85 million of cash receipts and $94 million in disbursements are shown directly. Investing activities also consumed cash because $54 million was invested in a building, and only $5

EXHIBIT 11–10

SUPPORTING SCHEDULE TO STATEMENT OF CASH FLOWS
Reconciliation of Net Income to Net Cash Provided by Operating Activities
For the Year Ended December 31, 19X2
(in millions)

Net income (from income statement)	$ 4
Adjustments to reconcile net income to net cash provided by operating activities:	
Add: Depreciation, which was deducted in the computation of net income but does not decrease cash	8
Deduct: Increase in accounts receivable	(15)
Deduct: Increase in inventory	(31)
Deduct: Increase in prepaid general expenses	(2)
Add: Increase in accounts payable	25
Add: Increase in accrued property tax payable	2
Net cash provided by operating activities	$ (9)

million was received from sales of fixed assets. Financing activities generated $39 million cash, which was $19 million less than the $58 million used by operating and investing activities.

Mr. Buretta should no longer be puzzled. The statement of cash flows shows clearly that cash payments exceeded receipts by $19 million. However, he may still be concerned about the depletion of cash. Either operations must be changed so that they do not require so much cash, or investment must be curtailed, or more long-term debt or ownership equity must be raised. Otherwise Buretta Company would soon run out of cash.

4. Each item affects cash as follows:

	Δ Cash	=	ΔL	+ Δ PC	+ Δ RI	$- \Delta$ NCA
Sales		=			+100	$-(+100)$
Cash collections from customers	+85	=				$-(- 85)$
Cost of goods sold		=			-73	$-(- 73)$
Purchases		=		+104		$-(+104)$
Payments to suppliers	-79	=	$- 79$			
General expenses (excluding interest)		=		$+ 8$	$- 8$	
Payments for general expenses*	-10	=		$- 8$		$-(+ 2)$
Interest expense, paid in cash	$- 3$	=			$- 3$	
Property tax expense		=		$+ 4$	$- 4$	
Payments for property tax	$- 2$	=		$- 2$		
Net cash provided by operating activities, a subtotal	$- 9$					
Expenses not requiring cash:						
Depreciation		=			$- 8$	$-(- 8)$
Net income, a subtotal					$+ 4$	
Purchase of building	-54	=				$-(+ 54)$
Proceeds from sale of fixed assets	$+ 5$	=				$-(- 5)$
Issue long-term debt	$+40$	=	$+ 40$			
Dividends paid	$- 1$	=			$- 1$	
Net changes	-19	=	$+ 67$		$+ 3$	$-(+ 89)$

* Payments for general expenses include the $2 million increase in prepaid general expenses in addition to the $8 million expense for 19X2.

HIGHLIGHTS TO REMEMBER

1. The statement of cash flows is a required financial statement. It focuses on where cash came from and where it was spent.
2. The statement of cash flows focuses on cash and cash equivalents. It includes sections for the results of operating activities, investing activities, and financing activities.
3. The FASB favors reporting cash flows from operating activities using the direct method.
4. Both the direct and indirect methods use a schedule that reconciles net income to net cash provided by operating activities. It entails adjusting net income for noncash items. In the indirect method, the reconciliation may appear either in the body of the statement of cash flows or as a supporting schedule.

ACCOUNTING VOCABULARY

Cash Flow, p. 501
Cash Flows from Operating Activities, p. 497
Direct Method, p. 497

Financial Management, p. 491
Indirect Method, p. 502
Operating Management, p. 491
Statement of Cash Flows, p. 491

APPENDIX 11A: MORE ON THE STATEMENT OF CASH FLOWS

This appendix describes some common items that affect the statement of cash flows. One need not be familiar with these items to have a basic understanding of the statement. However, the items occur frequently in the statements of cash flows of major corporations. Some instructors may wish to assign some but not all of the following sections. Each section independently introduces an item for B Company that was not considered in the chapter. An additional item is introduced in Appendix 12C, "Equity Method Investments and the Statement of Cash Flows."

For purposes of this appendix, we will assume that B Company is concerned with preparing a supporting schedule that reconciles net income to net cash provided by operating activities. For simplicity, we will also assume that none of the changes introduced in this appendix affects income taxes.

☐ Gain or Loss on Disposal of Fixed Assets

In the chapter, the B Company sold fixed assets for their book value of $10,000. More often a fixed asset is sold for an amount that differs from its book value. Suppose the fixed assets sold by B Company for $10,000 had a book value of $6,000 (original cost = $36,000; accumulated depreciation = $30,000). Therefore net income would be $27,000, comprised of the $23,000 shown in Exhibit 11–2 (p. 494) plus a $4,000 gain on disposal of fixed assets. (Recall that we are assuming no tax effect.)

Consider first the disposal's effects on cash and income using the balance sheet equation:

$$\Delta \text{ Cash} = \Delta L + \Delta PC + \Delta RI - \Delta NCA$$
$$\text{Proceeds} = \qquad \text{Gain} - (-\text{Book value})$$
$$\$10,000 = \qquad \$4,000 - (-\$6,000)$$

The book value does not affect cash. The statement of cash flows again contains the following item under investing activities:

Proceeds from sale of fixed assets	$10,000

The body of the statement of cash flows, in the section "Cash flows from operating activities," would not include any gains (or losses) from the disposal of fixed assets. However, consider Exhibit 11–6, p. 503, which reconciles net income to net cash provided by operating activities. Net income of $27,000, which is the starting point of the reconciliation, already includes the $4,000 gain. To avoid double counting (that is, inflows of $4,000 in operating activities and $10,000 in investing activities), B Company must deduct from net income the $4,000 gain on disposal:

Net income	$27,000
Plus adjustments in Exhibit 11–6	46,000
Less gain on disposal of fixed assets	(4,000)
Net cash provided by operating activities	$69,000

Losses on the disposal of assets would be treated similarly except that they would be added back to net income. Suppose the book value of the fixed assets sold by B Company was $17,000, creating a $7,000 loss on disposal and net income of $16,000. The reconciliation would show:

Net income	$16,000
Plus adjustments in Exhibit 11–6	46,000
Plus loss on disposal of assets	7,000
Net cash provided by operating activities	$69,000

Losses and gains on disposal are essentially nonoperating items that are included in net income. As such, their effect must be removed from net income when it is reconciled to net cash flow provided by operating activities.

Gain or Loss on Extinguishment of Debt

Issuing and retiring debt are financing activities. Any gain or loss on extinguishment of debt must be removed from net income in a reconciliation schedule. Suppose B Company paid $37,000 to retire long-term debt with a book value of $34,000, a $3,000 loss on extinguishment of debt. Net income would be $23,000 − $3,000 = $20,000. The balance sheet equation would show:

$$\Delta \text{Cash} = \quad \Delta L \quad + \Delta PC + \Delta RI - \Delta NCA$$
$$-\text{Payment} = -\text{Book value} \qquad - \text{Loss}$$
$$-\$37,000 = -\$34,000 \qquad -\$3,000$$

The $3,000 loss would be added back to net income to determine net cash provided by operating activities:

Net income	$20,000
Plus adjustments in Exhibit 11–6	46,000
Plus loss on retirement of debt	7,000
Net cash provided by operating activities	$69,000

The entire *payment* for debt retirement would be listed among the financing activities:

Proceeds from issue of long-term debt	$120,000
Payment to retire long-term debt	(37,000)
Proceeds from issue of common stock	98,000
Dividends paid	(19,000)
Net cash provided by financing activities	$162,000

Investing and Financing Activities Not Involving Cash

Some investing and financing activities do not entail cash receipts or payments. Suppose B Company had the following such activities:

1. Acquired a $14,000 fixed asset by issuing common stock.
2. Acquired a small building by signing a mortgage payable for $97,000.
3. Long-term debt of $35,000 was converted to common stock.

These items affect the balance sheet equation as follows:

	Δ Cash = Δ L	+ ΔPC	+ ΔRI − ΔNCA
1.	0 =	+ Common stock	−(+ Fixed asset)
	0 =	+$14,000	−(+$14,000)
2.	0 = + Mortgage payable		−(+ Building, a fixed asset)
	0 = +$97,000		−(+$97,000)
3.	0 = − Long-term debt	+ Common stock	
	0 = − $35,000	+ $35,000	

None of these transactions affects cash, and therefore they do not belong in a statement of cash flows. On the other hand, each transaction is almost identical to one involving cash flows. For example, a company might accomplish the first by issuing common stock for $14,000 cash and immediately using the cash to purchase the fixed asset. Because of the similarities between these noncash transactions and ones involving cash, readers of statements of cash flows should be informed of such noncash activities. Therefore such items must be included in a separate schedule accompanying the statement of cash flows. B Company's schedule would be:

Schedule of noncash investing and financing activities:

Common stock issued to acquire fixed asset	$14,000
Mortgage payable for acquisition of building	$97,000
Common stock issued on conversion of long-term debt	$35,000

APPENDIX 11B: T-ACCOUNT APPROACH TO STATEMENT OF CASH FLOWS

Many statements of cash flow can be prepared by using the steps described in the body of the chapter. Work sheets or T-accounts are frequently a hindrance instead of a help. However, if the facts become complicated, a T-account approach deserves serious consideration. This appendix presents an overview of the T-account approach using the direct method to compute cash flows from operating activities.

The procedure focuses on the T-account for cash. We will use the data from the B Company illustration presented in the body of the chapter. For convenient reference, Exhibit 11–1 has been reproduced as Exhibit 11–11.

Exhibit 11–12 displays the entire T-account approach to the statement of cash flows. The following journal entries summarize B Company's transactions during 19X2. They are keyed to the entries in Exhibit 11–12:

1.	Sales on credit:		
	Accounts receivable	200	
	Sales		200
*2.	Collection of accounts receivable:		
	Cash	180	
	Accounts receivable		180
3.	Recognition of cost of goods sold:		
	Cost of goods sold	100	
	Inventory		100
4.	Purchases of inventory on credit:		
	Inventory	140	
	Trade accounts payable		140
*5.	Payments of trade accounts payable:		
	Trade accounts payable	72	
	Cash		72

6. Recognition of wages and salaries expense:		
Wages and salaries expense	36	
Wages and salaries payable		36
*7. Payment of wages and salaries:		
Wages and salaries payable	15	
Cash		15
*8. Recognition of interest accrued and paid:		
Interest expense	4	
Cash		4
*9. Recognition and payment of income taxes:		
Income tax expense	20	
Cash		20
10. Recognition of depreciation expense:		
Depreciation expense	17	
Fixed assets, net		17
*11. Acquisition of fixed assets for cash:		
Fixed assets, net	287	
Cash		287
*12. Sale of fixed assets at book value:		
Cash	10	
Fixed assets, net		10
*13. Issuance of long-term debt:		
Cash	120	
Long-term debt		120
*14. Issuance of common stock:		
Cash	98	
Stockholders' equity		98
*15. Declaration and payment of dividends:		
Dividends declared and paid	19	
Cash		19

The T-account approach displayed in Exhibit 11–12 is merely another way of applying the balance sheet equation described in the body of the chapter:

$$\Delta Cash = \begin{matrix}\Delta Current \\ liabilities\end{matrix} + \begin{matrix}\Delta Long\text{-}term \\ liabilities\end{matrix} + \begin{matrix}\Delta Stockholders' \\ equity\end{matrix} - \begin{matrix}\Delta Noncash\ current \\ assets\end{matrix} - \begin{matrix}\Delta Fixed\ assets, \\ net\end{matrix}$$

$$\Delta Cash = \begin{matrix}\Delta Accounts\ and \\ wages\ payable\end{matrix} + \begin{matrix}\Delta Long\text{-}term \\ debt\end{matrix} + \begin{matrix}\Delta Stockholders' \\ equity\end{matrix} - \begin{matrix}\Delta Accounts\ receivable \\ and\ inventory\end{matrix} - \begin{matrix}\Delta Fixed\ assets, \\ net\end{matrix}$$

9	68	120	102	20	260
	21			40	
	89			60	

$$-9 = 89 + 120 + 102 - 60 - 260$$
$$-9 = -9$$

Again, we focus on the *changes* in the noncash accounts to explain why cash *changed*.

The summarized transactions for 19X2 entered in the Cash account are the basis for the preparation of the formal statement of cash flows, as can be seen by comparing the cash account from Exhibit 11–12 with the statement of cash flows in Exhibit 11–11.

EXHIBIT 11–11

B COMPANY
Statement of Cash Flows
For the Year Ended December 31, 19X2
(in thousands)

CASH FLOWS FROM OPERATING ACTIVITIES

Cash collections from customers		$180
Cash payments:		
To suppliers	$ 72	
To employees	15	
For interest	4	
For taxes	20	
Total cash payments		(111)
Net cash provided by operating activities		$ 69

CASH FLOWS FROM INVESTING ACTIVITIES

Purchases of fixed assets	$(287)	
Proceeds from sale of fixed assets	10	
Net cash used in investing activities		(277)

CASH FLOWS FROM FINANCING ACTIVITIES

Proceeds from issue of long-term debt	$ 120	
Proceeds from issue of common stock	98	
Dividends paid	(19)	
Net cash provided by financing activities		199
Net decrease in cash		$ (9)
Cash, December 31, 19X1		25
Cash, December 31, 19X2		$ 16

EXHIBIT 11–12

B COMPANY
T-Account Approach Using Direct Method
Statement of Cash Flows
For the Year Ended December 31, 19X2
(in thousands)

Cash			
Bal. 12/31/X1	25		

Operating Activities

2. Collection of accounts receivable	180	5. Pay accounts payable	72
		7. Pay wages and salaries	15
		8. Pay interest	4
		9. Pay taxes	20

Investing Activities

12. Disposal of fixed assets	10	11. Acquisition of fixed assets	287

EXHIBIT 11–12 (continued)

Financing Activities

13. Issue long-term debt	120	15. Pay dividends	19
14. Issue common stock	98		
Total debits	408	Total credits	417
		Net decrease	9
Bal. 12/31/X2	16		

Accounts Receivable

Bal. 12/31/X1	25		
1. Sales	200	2. Collections	180
Net increase	20		
Bal. 12/31/X2	45		

Accounts Payable

		Bal. 12/31/X1	6
5. Payments	72	4. Purchases	140
		Net increase	68
		Bal. 12/31/X2	74

Inventory

Bal. 12/31/X1	60		
4. Purchases	140	2. Cost of goods sold	100
Net increase	40		
Bal. 12/31/X2	100		

Wages and Salaries Payable

		Bal. 12/31/X1	4
7. Payments	15	6. Accruals	36
		Net increase	21
		Bal. 12/31/X2	25

Fixed Assets, Net

Bal. 12/31/X1	220		
11. Acquisition	287	10. Depreciation	17
		12. Disposals	10
Net increase	260		
Bal. 12/31/X2	480		

Long-term Debt

		Bal. 12/31/X1	5
		13. New issue	120
		Bal. 12/31/X2	125

Stockholders' Equity

		Bal. 12/31/X1	315
3. Cost of goods sold	100	1. Sales	200
6. Wages	36	14. New issue	98
8. Interest	4		
9. Income taxes	20		
10. Depreciation	17		
15. Dividends	19		
Total debits	196	Total credits	298
		Net increase	102
		Bal. 12/31/X2	417

FUNDAMENTAL ASSIGNMENT MATERIAL

Special note: The following problems can be solved without reading beyond page 502, the end of "Preparing a Statement of Cash Flows: The Direct Method": 11–1, 11–3, 11–6, 11–8 through 11–21, 11–32 through 11–35, 11–39, 11–40, 11–42, 11–47, 11–54, 11–58, and 11–59.

☐ General Coverage

11–1. PREPARE A STATEMENT OF CASH FLOWS, DIRECT METHOD. (Alternate is 11–40.) Do-It-Yourself, Inc., is a chain of retail hardware stores. Its cash balance on December 31, 19X6, was $55 thousand, and net income for 19X7 was $464 thousand. Its 19X7 transactions affecting income or cash were (in thousands):

a. Sales of $1,650, all on credit. Cash collections from customers, $1,500.
b. The cost of items sold, $800. Purchases of inventory totaled $850; inventory and accounts payable were affected accordingly.
c. Cash payments on trade accounts payable, $825.
d. Salaries and wages: accrued, $190; paid in cash, $200.
e. Depreciation, $45.
f. Interest expense, all paid in cash, $11.
g. Other expenses, all paid in cash, $100.
h. Income taxes accrued, $40; income taxes paid in cash, $35.
i. Bought plant and facilities for $435 cash.
j. Issued long-term debt for $110 cash.
k. Paid cash dividends of $39.

Required: Prepare a statement of cash flows using the direct method for reporting cash flows from operating activities. Omit supporting schedules.

11–2. RECONCILE NET INCOME AND NET CASH PROVIDED BY OPERATING ACTIVITIES. (Alternate is 11–41.) Refer to Problem 11–1. Prepare a supporting schedule that reconciles net income to net cash provided by operating activities.

11–3. PREPARE STATEMENT OF CASH FLOWS FROM INCOME STATEMENT AND BALANCE SHEET. (Alternate is 11–42.) Spahn Company had the following income statement and balance sheet items (in thousands):

Income Statement for the Year Ended December 31, 19X8

Sales	$ 870
Cost of goods sold	(510)
Gross margin	$ 360
Operating expenses	(200)
Depreciation	(60)
Interest	(20)
Income before taxes	$ 80
Income taxes	(25)
Net income	$ 55
Cash dividends paid	(40)
Total increase in retained earnings	$ 15

Balance Sheets

| | DECEMBER 31 | | INCREASE (DECREASE) |
	19X8	19X7	
ASSETS			
Cash	$ 15	$ 60	$(45)
Accounts receivable	240	150	90
Inventories	450	350	100
Total current assets	$ 705	$560	$145
Fixed assets, gross	$ 890	$715	175
Accumulated depreciation	(570)	(550)	(20)
Fixed assets, net	$ 320	$165	$155
Total assets	$1,025	$725	$300
LIABILITIES AND STOCKHOLDERS' EQUITY			
Trade accounts payable	$ 520	$300	$220
Long-term debt	245	180	65
Stockholders' equity	260	245	15
Total liabilities and stockholders' equity	$1,025	$725	$300

During 19X8, Spahn purchased fixed assets for $415,000 cash and sold fixed assets for their book value of $200,000. Operating expenses, interest, and taxes were paid in cash. No long-term debt was retired.

Required: Prepare a statement of cash flows. Use the direct method for reporting cash flows from operating activities. Omit supporting schedules. Assume that the $200,000 of operating expenses were all paid in cash.

11–4. **Reconcile Net Income and Net Cash Provided by Operating Activities.** Refer to problem 11–3. Prepare a supporting schedule that reconciles net income to net cash provided by operating activities.

11–5. **Depreciation and Cash Flows.** (Alternate is 11–44.) Bates Company had sales of $910,000, all received in cash. Total operating expenses were $710,000. All except depreciation were paid in cash. Depreciation of $70,000 was included in the $710,000 of operating expenses. Ignore income taxes.

Required: 1. Compute net income and net cash provided by operating activities.
2. Assume that depreciation is tripled. Compute net income and net cash provided by operating activities.

☐ Understanding Published Financial Reports

11–6. **Statement of Cash Flows, Direct Method.** Interpoint, Inc. (formerly Integrated Circuits, Inc.) designs, manufactures, and markets hybrid microcircuit products for the electronics industry. The company's 1988 statement of cash flows contained the following items:

Interest received	$ 56,094
Proceeds from issuance of common stock for stock options	3,835
Cash received from customers	15,060,246
Payments on purchases of property, plant and equipment	(466,730)

Principal payments on long-term debt	(3,748,237)
Interest paid	(346,063)
Refund of federal income taxes received	52,338
Proceeds received on sale of property, plant and equipment	2,161
Proceeds from issuance of long-term debt	3,795,502
Income taxes paid	(26,736)
Cash paid to suppliers and employees	(13,825,903)
Payment of bond issuance costs	(124,042)
Cash at beginning of year	443,400

Required: Prepare Interpoint's statement of cash flows in proper format, using the direct method. Omit the schedule reconciling net income to net cash provided by operating activities.

11–7. **CASH PROVIDED BY OPERATIONS.** American Building Maintenance Industries, Inc., provides services throughout the United States. In 1988, net income was $7,100,000, depreciation and amortization expenses were $7,348,000, and dividends of $3,523,000 were paid. Among the changes in balance sheet accounts during 1988 were:

Accounts receivable	$9,063,000	increase
Inventories and supplies	431,000	decrease
Prepaid expenses	699,000	increase
Other current assets	40,000	increase
Income taxes payable	1,757,000	increase
Accounts payable	6,392,000	increase
Accrued liabilities	6,783,000	decrease
Long-term borrowings	4,822,000	increase

Required: Compute the net cash provided by operating activities.

11–8. **CASH FLOWS FROM INVESTING ACTIVITIES.** Liz Claiborne, Inc., designer of women's clothes, had the following items on its 1988 statement of cash flows (in thousands):

Purchases of investment instruments	(267,856)
Depreciation and amortization	12,548
Net cash paid for acquisitions	(2,170)
Disposals of investment instruments	160,195
Dividends paid	(15,313)
Purchases of property and equipment—net	(32,450)

Required: Prepare the section "Cash flows from investing activities" from Liz Claiborne's statement of cash flows. All items necessary are among those listed in this problem.

11–9. **CASH FLOWS FROM FINANCING ACTIVITIES.** McDonald's Corporation is the largest food service organization in the world. Its 1988 statement of cash flows included the following items (in thousands):

Property and equipment expenditures	$(1,321,261)
Repayment of notes payable and long-term debt	(540,608)
Treasury stock purchases	(126,026)
Issuance of notes payable and long-term debt	886,289
Other cash provided by financing activities	14,224
Depreciation and amortization	383,389
Common and preferred stock dividends	(102,516)

Required: Prepare the section "Cash flows from financing activities" from McDonald's statement of cash flows. All items necessary are among those listed in this problem.

ADDTITIONAL ASSIGNMENT MATERIAL

☐ **General Coverage**

11–10. "The statement of cash flows is an optional statement included by most companies in their annual reports." Do you agree? Explain.

11–11. What are the purposes of a statement of cash flows?

11–12. Distinguish between *operating management* and *financial management*.

11–13. Define *cash equivalents*.

11–14. What three types of activities are summarized in the statement of cash flows?

11–15. Name four major operating activities included in a statement of cash flows.

11–16. Name three major investing activities included in a statement of cash flows.

11–17. Name three major financing activities included in a statement of cash flows.

11–18. Where does interest received or paid appear on the statement of cash flows?

11–19. Why is there usually a difference between the cash collections from customers and sales revenue in a period's financial statements?

11–20. What are the two major ways of computing net cash provided by operating activities?

11–21. Demonstrate how the fundamental balance sheet equation can be recast to focus on cash.

11–22. The indirect method for reporting cash flows from operating activities can create an erroneous impression about noncash expenses (such as depreciation). What is the impression and why is it erroneous?

11–23. An investor's newsletter had the following item: "The company expects increased cash flow in 1990 because depreciation charges will be substantially greater than they were in 1991." Comment.

11–24. "Net losses mean drains on cash." Do you agree? Explain.

11–25. "Depreciation is an integral part of a statement of cash flows." Do you agree? Explain.

11–26. "Cash flow per share can be downright misleading." Why?

11–27. XYZ Company's only transaction in 19X1 was the sale of a fixed asset for cash of $20,000. The income statement included only "Gain on sale of fixed asset, $5,000." Correct the following statement of cash flows:

Cash flows from operating activities:	
Gain on sale of fixed asset	$ 5,000
Cash flows from investing activities:	
Proceeds from sale of fixed asset	20,000
Total increase in cash	$25,000

11–28. Why are noncash investing and financing activities listed on a separate schedule accompanying the statement of cash flows?

11–29. The Lawrence Company sold fixed assets with a book value of $5,000 and recorded a $4,000 gain. How should this be reported on a statement of cash flows?

11–30. A company acquired a fixed asset in exchange for common stock. Explain how this transaction should be shown, if at all, in the statement of cash flows. Why is your suggested treatment appropriate?

11–31. The T-account approach to preparing a statement of cash flows focuses on the T-account for cash. Why?

11–32. CASH RECEIVED FROM CUSTOMERS. Super Foods, Inc., had sales of $730,000 during 19X0, 80% of them on credit and 20% for cash. During the year, accounts receivable increased from $65,000 to $72,000, an increase of $7,000. What amount of cash was received from customers during 19X1?

11–33. CASH PAID TO SUPPLIERS. Cost of goods sold for Super Foods, Inc., during 19X0 was $445,000. Beginning inventory was $105,000 and ending inventory was $120,000. Beginning trade accounts payable were $24,000, and ending trade accounts payable were $49,000. What amount of cash was paid to suppliers?

11–34. CASH PAID TO EMPLOYEES. Super Foods, Inc., reported wage and salary expenses of $247,000 on its 19X1 income statement. It reported cash paid to employees of $215,000 on its statement of cash flows. The beginning balance of accrued wages and salaries payable was $18,000. What was the ending balance in accrued wages and salaries payable? Ignore payroll taxes.

11–35. SIMPLE CASH FLOWS FROM OPERATING ACTIVITIES. Ringwald and Associates provides accounting and consulting services. In 19X2, net income was $190,000 on revenues of $470,000 and expenses of $280,000. The only noncash expense was depreciation of $30,000. The company has no inventory. Accounts receivable increased by $8,000 during 19X2, and accounts payable and salaries payable were unchanged.

Required: Prepare a statement of cash flows from operating activities. Use the direct method. Omit supporting schedules.

11–36. NET INCOME AND CASH FLOW. Refer to problem 11–35. Prepare a schedule that reconciles net income to net cash flow from operating activities.

11–37. NET LOSS AND CASH FLOWS FROM OPERATING ACTIVITIES. The Perez Company had a net loss of $39,000 in 19X4. The following information is available:

Depreciation	$24,000
Decrease in accounts receivable	4,000
Increase in inventory	2,000
Increase in accounts payable	17,000
Increase in salaries and wages payable	5,000

Required: Present a schedule that reconciles net income (loss) to net cash provided by operating activities.

11–38. BOOK VALUE OF ASSETS DISPOSALS. The Motown Broadcasting Company reported net fixed assets of $47 million at December 31, 19X5 and $51 million at December 31, 19X6. During 19X6, the company purchased fixed assets for $10 million and had $3 million of depreciation. Compute the book value of the fixed assets disposals during 19X6.

11–39. FINANCING ACTIVITIES. During 19X3, the Bremen Shipping Company refinanced its long-term debt. It spent DM 175,000 to retire long-term debt due in 2 years and issued DM 200,000 of 15-year bonds at par. DM signifies deutsche mark, the West German monetary unit. It then bought and retired common shares for cash of DM 35,000. Interest expense for 19X3 was DM 22,000, of which DM 20,000 was paid in cash; the other DM 2,000 was still payable at the end of the year. Dividends declared and paid during the year were DM 13,000.

Required: Prepare a statement of cash flows from financing activities.

11–40. PREPARE A STATEMENT OF CASH FLOWS. (Alternate is 11–1.) Nakata Importers is a wholesaler of Asian goods. By the end of 19X0, the company's cash balance had dropped to $20 thousand, despite net income of $254 thousand in 19X0. Its transactions affecting income or cash in 19X0 were (in thousands):

a. Sales were $2,510, all on credit. Cash collections from customers were $2,413.

b. The cost of items sold was $1,599.

c. Inventory increased by $56.

d. Cash payments on trade accounts payable were $1,653.

e. Payments to employees were $305; accrued wages payable decreased by $24.

f. Other operating expenses, all paid in cash, were $94.

g. Interest expense, all paid in cash, was $26.

h. Income tax expense was $105; cash payments for income taxes were $108.

i. Depreciation was $151.

j. A warehouse was acquired for $540 cash.

k. Sold equipment for $37; original cost was $196, accumulated depreciation was $159.

l. Received $28 for issue of common stock.

m. Retired long-term debt for $25 cash.

n. Paid cash dividends of $88.

Required: | Prepare a statement of cash flows using the direct method for reporting cash flows from operating activities. Omit supporting schedules.

11–41. **RECONCILE NET INCOME AND NET CASH PROVIDED BY OPERATING ACTIVITIES.** (Alternate is 11–2.) Refer to problem 11–40. Prepare a supporting schedule to the statement of cash flows that reconciles net income to net cash provided by operating activities.

11–42. **PREPARE STATEMENT OF CASH FLOWS FROM INCOME STATEMENT AND BALANCE SHEET.** (Alternate is 11–3.) During 19X4, the Riley Software Company declared and paid cash dividends of $10 thousand. Late in the year, the company bought new personal computers for its staff for a cash cost of $125 thousand, financed partly by its first issue of long-term debt. Interest on the debt is payable annually. Several old computers were sold for cash equal to their aggregate book value of $5 thousand. Taxes are paid in cash as incurred. The following data are in thousands:

Income Statement
For the Year Ended December 31, 19X4

Sales		$316
Cost of sales		154
Gross margin		162
Salaries	$ 82	
Depreciation	40	
Cash operating expenses	15	
Interest	2	139
Income before taxes		23
Income taxes		8
Net income		$ 15

Balance Sheets

	DECEMBER 31		INCREASE (DECREASE)
	19X4	19X3	
ASSETS			
Cash and cash equivalents	$ 97	$ 5	$ 92
Accounts receivable	40	95	(55)
Inventories	57	62	(5)
Total current assets	194	162	32
Fixed assets, net	190	110	80
Total assets	$384	$272	$112

LIABILITIES AND STOCKHOLDERS' EQUITY			
Accounts payable	$ 21	$ 16	$ 5
Interest payable	2	—	2
Long-term debt	100	—	100
Paid-in capital	220	220	—
Retained income	41	36	5
Total liabilities and stockholders's equity	$384	$272	$112

Required: Prepare a statement of cash flows. Use the direct method for reporting cash flows from operating activities. Omit supporting schedules.

11–43. INDIRECT METHOD: RECONCILIATION SCHEDULE IN BODY OF STATEMENT. Refer to problem 11–42. Prepare a statement of cash flows that includes a reconciliation of net income to net cash provided by operating activities in the body of the statement.

11–44. DEPRECIATION AND CASH FLOWS. (Alternate is 11–5.) The following condensed income statement and reconciliation schedule are from the annual report of Hernandez Company (in millions):

Sales	$384
Expenses	364
Net income	$ 20

Reconcilation Schedule of Net Income to Net Cash Provided by Operating Activities

Net income	$ 20
Add noncash expenses:	
Depreciation	25
Deduct net increase in noncash operating working capital	(17)
Net cash provided by operating activities	$ 28

A shareholder has suggested that the company switch from straight-line to accelerated depreciation on its annual report to shareholders. He maintains that this will increase the cash flow provided by operating activities. According to his calculations, using accelerated methods would increase depreciation to $45 million, an increase of $20 million; net cash flow from operating activities would then be $48 million.

Required: 1. Suppose Hernandez Company adopts the accelerated depreciation method proposed. Compute net income and net cash flow from operating activities. Ignore income taxes.
2. Use your answer to requirement 1 to prepare a response to the shareholder.

11–45. CASH FLOWS, INDIRECT METHOD. The Chippewa Company has the following balance sheet data (in millions):

	DECEMBER 31				DECEMBER 31		
	19X7	19X6	CHANGE		19X7	19X6	CHANGE
Current assets:				Current liabilities			
Cash	$ 3	$ 10	$ (7)	(detailed)	$105	$ 30	$ 75
Receivables, net	60	30	30	Long-term debt	150	—	150
Inventories	100	50	50	Stockholders' equity	208	160	48
Total current assets	$163	$ 90	$ 73				
Plant assets (net of accumulated depreciation)	300	100	200				
				Total liabilities and stockholders' equity	$463	$190	$273
Total assets	$463	$190	$273				

Net income for 19X7 was $54 million. Net cash inflow from operating activities was $69 million. Cash dividends paid were $6 million. Depreciation was $20 million. Fixed assets were purchased for $230 million, $160 million of which was financed via the issuance of long-term debt outright for cash.

Dennis Lightfoot, the president and majority stockholder of Chippewa, was a superb operating executive. He was imaginative and aggressive in marketing and ingenious and creative in production. But he had little patience with financial matters. After examining the most recent balance sheet and income statement, he muttered, "We've enjoyed ten years of steady growth; 19X7 was our most profitable ever. Despite such profitability, we're in the worst cash position in our history. Just look at those current liabilities in relation to our available cash! This whole picture of the more you make, the poorer you get, just does not make sense. These statements must be cockeyed."

Required:

1. Prepare a statement of cash flows using the indirect method. Include a schedule reconciling net income to net cash provided by operating activities in the body of the statement.
2. Using the statement of cash flows and other information, write a short memorandum to Lightfoot, explaining why there is such a squeeze on cash.

11–46. **PREPARE STATEMENT OF CASH FLOWS.** The Friedlander Company has assembled the accompanying (a) balance sheets and (b) income statement and reconciliation of retained earnings for 19X9.

FRIEDLANDER CO.
Balance Sheets as of December 31
(in millions)

	19X9	19X8	CHANGE
Assets:			
Cash	$ 10	$ 25	$(15)
Accounts receivable	40	28	12
Inventory	70	50	20
Prepaid general expenses	4	3	1
Plant assets, net	202	150	52
	$326	$256	$ 70

Liabilities and Shareholders' Equity:			
Accounts payable for merchandise	$ 74	$ 60	$ 14
Accrued tax payable	3	2	1
Long-term debt	50	—	50
Capital stock	100	100	—
Retained earnings	99	94	5
	$326	$256	$ 70

FRIEDLANDER CO.
Income Statement and Reconciliation of Retained
Earnings
For the Year Ended December 31, 19X9
(in millions)

Sales		$250
Less cost of goods sold:		
Inventory, Dec. 31, 19X8	$ 50	
Purchases	160	
Cost of goods available for sale	$210	
Inventory, Dec. 31, 19X9	70	140
Gross profit		$110
Less other expenses:		
General expense	$ 51	
Depreciation	40	
Taxes	10	101
Net income		$ 9
Dividends		4
Net income of the period retained		$ 5
Retained earnings, Dec. 31, 19X8		94
Retained earnings, Dec. 31, 19X9		$ 99

On December 30, 19X9, Friedlander paid $98 million in cash to acquire a new plant to expand operations. This was partly financed by an issue of long-term debt for $50 million. Plant assets were sold for their book value of $6 million during 19X9. Because net income was $9 million, the highest in the company's history, Sidney Friedlander, the chief executive officer, was distressed by the company's extremely low cash balance.

Required:
1. Prepare a statement of cash flows using the direct method for reporting cash flows from operating activities. You may wish to use Exhibit 11–1, page 492, as a guide.
2. Prepare a schedule that reconciles net income to net cash provided by operating activities.
3. What is revealed by the statement of cash flows? Does it help you reduce Mr. Friedlander's distress? Why? Briefly explain to Mr. Friedlander why cash has decreased even though net income was $9 million.

11–47. **BALANCE SHEET EQUATION.** Refer to Problem 11–46, requirement 1. Support your financial statement by using a form of the balance sheet equation. Step by step, show in equation form how each item in the statement of cash flows affects cash.

11–48. **LOSS ON DISPOSAL OF EQUIPMENT.** Study Appendix 11A. The Heartland Insurance Company sold a computer. It had purchased the computer five years ago for $500,000, and accumulated depreciation at the time of sale was $350,000.

1. Suppose Heartland received $150,000 cash for the computer. How would the sale be shown on the statement of cash flows?
2. Suppose Heartland received $100,000 for the computer. How would the sale be shown on the statement of cash flows (including the schedule reconciling net income and net cash provided by operating activities)?

11–49. GAIN ON SALE OF EQUIPMENT. Study Appendix 11A. Langston Company developed the following preliminary condensed statement of cash flows (in thousands):

Cash Flows from Operating Activities:		
Net income	$ 621	
Add depreciation on fixed assets	350	
Deduct net increase in noncash operating		
working capital	(68)	
Cash provided by operations		$903
Cash Flows from Investing Activities:		
Acquisition of fixed assets	$(867)	
Proceeds from sale of fixed assets	120	
Cash used in investing activities		(747)
Cash Flows from Financing Activities:		
Issue capital stock		60
Net increase in cash		$216

The controller of Langston Company was concerned because cash had increased only $176,000, not the $216,000 shown on the preliminary statement of cash flows. Upon further inquiry, he learned that the increase in net fixed assets during the year was $437,000.

Required: Explain what was wrong with the preliminary statement of cash flows. Also, explain how to change the statement to show the correct $176,000 increase in cash.

11–50. NONCASH INVESTING AND FINANCING ACTIVITIES. Study Appendix 11A. The Aaron Amusement Company operates a chain of video-game arcades. Among Aaron's activities in 19X7 were:

1. Traded four old video games to another amusement company for one new "Flightime" game. The old games could have been sold for a total of $9,000 cash.
2. Paid off $50,000 of long-term debt by paying $30,000 cash and signing a $20,000 six-month note payable.
3. Issued debt for $75,000 cash, all of which was used to purchase new games for its Northwest arcade.
4. Purchased the building in which one of its arcades was located by assuming the $120,000 mortgage on the building and paying $15,000 cash.
5. Debtholders converted $66,000 of debt to common stock.
6. Refinanced debt by paying cash to buy back an old issue at its call price of $21,000, and issued new debt at a lower interest rate for $21,000.

Required: Prepare a schedule of noncash investing and financing activities to accompany a statement of cash flows.

11–51. COMPREHENSIVE STATEMENT OF CASH FLOWS. Study Appendix 11A. During the past 30 years, Cascade Toys, Inc. has grown from a single-location specialty toy store into a chain of stores selling a wide range of children's products. Its activities in 19X7 included the following:

a. Selected results for the year:

Net income	$ 679,000
Depreciation and amortization	615,000
Increase in inventory	72,000

Decrease in accounts receivable	13,000
Increase in accounts and wages payable	7,000
Increase in taxes payable	25,000
Interest expense	144,000
Increase in accrued interest payable	15,000
Sales	9,739,000
Cash dividends received from investments	159,000
Cash paid to suppliers and employees	8,074,000
Cash dividends paid	240,000
Cash paid for taxes	400,000

b. Purchased 40% of the stock of Kansas Toy Company for $3,846,000 cash.

c. Issued $1,906,000 in long-term debt; $850,000 of the proceeds was used to retire debt that became due in 19X7 and was listed on the books at $900,000.

d. Property, plant, and equipment were purchased for $1,986,000 cash, and property with a book value of $576,000 was sold for $500,000 cash.

e. A note payable was signed for the purchase of new equipment; the obligation was listed at $516,000.

f. Executives exercised stock options for 8,000 shares of common stock, paying cash of $166,000.

g. On December 30, 19X7, bought Sanchez Musical Instruments Company by issuing common stock with a market value of $297,000.

h. Issued common stock for $3,000,000 cash.

i. Withdrew $800,000 cash from a money market fund that was considered a cash equivalent.

j. Bought $249,000 of treasury stock to hold for future exercise of stock options.

k. Long-term debt of $960,000 was converted to common stock.

Required: Prepare a statement of cash flows for 19X7 using the direct method. Include a schedule that reconciles net income to net cash provided by operating activities. Also include a schedule of noncash investing and financing activities.

11–52. **T-Account Approach.** Study Appendix 11B. Refer to the facts concerning the Buretta Company's "Summary Problem for Your Review" in the chapter (p. 507). Prepare a set of T-accounts that supports the statement of cash flows shown in Exhibit 11–9 (p. 509). Use Exhibit 11–12 (pp. 515–516) as a guide. Key your postings by number.

11–53. **T-Account Approach.** Study Appendix 11B. Refer to the facts concerning the Friedlander Company in Problem 11–46. Prepare a set of T-accounts that supports the statement of cash flows. Use Exhibit 11–12 (pp. 515–516) as a guide. Key your postings by number.

☐ Understanding Published Financial Reports

11–54. **Identify Operating, Investing, and Financing Activities.** The items listed below were found on the 1988 statement of cash flows of the American Telephone and Telegraph Company (AT&T). For each item, indicate which section of the statement should contain the item—the operating, investing, or financing section. Also indicate whether AT&T uses the direct or indirect method for reporting cash flows from operating activities.

a. Proceeds from long-term debt issuance
b. Net income (loss)
c. Dividends paid
d. Capital expenditures net of proceeds from sale or disposal of property, plant, and equipment
e. Issuance of common shares
f. Retirements of long-term debt
g. Increase in investments—net
h. Decrease in short-term borrowing—net
i. Redemption of preferred shares
j. Depreciation

11–55. INTEREST EXPENSE. In 1988, Alcoa reported interest expense of $208.4 million on its income statement. Accrued interest, a current liability on the balance sheet, decreased from $57.9 million on December 31, 1987 to $33.6 million on December 31, 1988.

Required:
1. Describe how the transactions relating to interest would be shown in the body of the statement of cash flows. Assume that Alcoa uses the direct method for reporting cash flows from operating activities.
2. Describe how the transactions relating to interest would be shown on a supplementary schedule that reconciles net income to net cash provided by operating activities.

11–56. DISPOSITION OF PROPERTY. (Study Appendix 11A for requirements 2 and 3.) In a recent annual report, the Stanford University Bookstore reported acquisitions of fixed assets of $212,071, depreciation expense of $26,831, and an increase in net fixed assets (that is, gross fixed assets minus accumulated depreciation) of $180,079.

Required:
1. Suppose the Bookstore sold assets at their book value. Compute the proceeds from the sale of fixed assets. Where on the statement of cash flows would this amount appear?
2. The Bookstore actually had a gain of $142 on the sale of fixed assets. Compute the proceeds obtained from the sale. How would the body of the statement of cash flows show items related to the disposition of assets? How would the reconciliation of net income to net cash provided by operating activities be affected?
3. Suppose a loss of $142 (rather than a gain) had been obtained. How would your answer to requirement 2 change?

11–57. RECONCILIATION SCHEDULE. Knape & Vogt Manufacturing Company is a leader in home decor products for the do-it-yourself homeowner. The following data are from its 1988 statement of cash flows:

Depreciation of fixed assets	$2,629,514
Increase in accounts receivable	2,182,036
Increase in accounts payable	1,327,077
Net income	5,300,659
Amortization of intangible assets	347,041
Increase in inventories	3,955,308
Decrease in accrued liabilities	209,753
Increase in other current liabilities	128,974
Increase in prepaid expenses	241,265

Required: Prepare a schedule that reconciles net income to net cash provided by operating activities.

11–58. STATEMENT OF CASH FLOWS, DIRECT METHOD. MCI Communications Corporation had sales revenue of over $5 billion in 1988. On January 1, 1988, its cash and cash equivalents were $379 million. The following items are on the company's 1988 statement of cash flows (in millions):

Cash received from customers	$4,918
Retirement of debt	(272)
Interest paid, net	(178)
Cash outflow to purchase communications system	(796)
Purchase of treasury stock	(677)
Sales of marketable securities	158
Increase in long-term debt	241
Cash paid to suppliers and employees	(3,822)
Issuance of common stock for employee stock plans	33
Antitrust settlements received	11
Issuance of preferred stock	400
Acquisition of RCA Global Communications, Inc.	(130)

Required: Prepare a 1988 statement of cash flows for MCI using the direct method. Include the balance of cash and cash equivalents at December 31, 1988. The antitrust settlement is an operating item. Omit the schedule reconciling net income to net cash provided by operating activities and the schedule of noncash investing and financing activities.

11–59. **CASH FLOWS FROM INVESTING AND FINANCING ACTIVITIES.** Minnesota Mining and Manufacturing (3M) Company began 1988 with cash and cash equivalents of $432 million. Net cash provided by operating activities during 1988 was $1,656 million. The following items were listed under either investing or financing activities in the statement of cash flows (in millions):

Payments of dividends	$481
Issuances of common stock	96
Purchases of treasury stock	344
Net increase in short-term debt	98
Acquisition of businesses and investments	160
Capital expenditures	841
Disposals of property, plant and equipment	58
Repayments of long-term debt	65
Dividends received and other proceeds	39
Proceeds from long-term debt	34
Other cash flows from financing activities	51

Required: Compute (1) the cash flows from investing activities, (2) the cash flows from financing activities, and (3) the balance of cash and cash equivalents at the end of 1988.

11–60. **CASH FLOWS FROM OPERATING ACTIVITIES.** Boise Cascade Corporation, the forest products company with headquarters in Boise, Idaho, reported net income of over $180 million in 1987. The following data are from the company's income statement and balance sheet (in thousands):

	1987
Revenues:	
Sales	$3,829,120
Costs and expenses:	
Nondepreciation expenses (summarized)	(3,224,820)
Depreciation	(185,600)
Income from operations	418,700
Interest expense	(104,430)
Interest income	3,970
Income before income taxes	318,240
Income tax provision	135,250
Net income	$ 182,990

	DECEMBER 31		INCREASE
	1987	1986	(DECREASE)
Current assets:			
Cash	$ 11,157	$ 21,860	$(10,703)
Short-term investments	10,501	13,043	(2,542)
Receivables	359,012	359,743	(731)
Inventories	374,204	391,816	(17,612)
Other	70,399	74,323	(3,924)
Total current assets	$825,273	$860,785	$(35,512)

Current liabilities:			
Current portion of			
long-term debt	$ 47,434	$ 51,146	$ (3,712)
Income taxes payable	8,560	3,493	5,067
Notes payable	31,000	0	31,000
Accounts payable	254,161	265,928	(11,767)
Accrued liabilities:			
Compensation and benefits	94,903	91,422	3,481
Interest payable	29,746	32,865	(3,119)
Other	97,348	103,048	(5,700)
Total current liabilities	$563,152	$547,902	$ 15,250

You have determined that other current assets are all operating items, as are other accrued liabilities. Short-term investments are cash equivalents. Depreciation is the only noncash expense. Interest income is all in cash.

Required:
1. Prepare a statement of cash flows from operating activities. Use the direct method that begins with cash collections from customers.
2. Reconcile net income to net cash provided by operating activities. (*Hint*: The cash outflow for nondepreciation expense is an aggregation of more specific outflows. There is no way to break the total amount into its component parts.)

11–61. **PREPARE STATEMENT OF CASH FLOWS, INDIRECT METHOD.** The income statement and balance sheets in Exhibit 11–13 are from the 1988 annual report of Data I/O, a world leader in developing and marketing computer-aided engineering tools. (The statements are slightly modified to avoid items beyond the scope of this text.) Assume the following information about activities in 1988:

a. Depreciation on fixed assets was $3,427,000, which is included in operating expenses.
b. Fixed assets were sold for their book value of $2,186,000; fixed assets were acquired at a cost of $2,351,000.
c. Common stock was purchased for $16,064,000 and retired. Additional common stock was issued for stock options.
d. No notes payable were retired.

Required:
Prepare a 1988 statement of cash flows for Data I/O. Use the indirect method in the body of the statement for reporting cash flows from operating activities.

11–62. **T-ACCOUNT APPROACH.** Study Appendix 11B. Refer to the facts concerning Data I/O, problem 11–61. Prepare a set of T-accounts that supports the statement of cash flows. Use the direct method for computing net cash flow from operating activities. (This differs from the requirements of 11–61, which asked you to use the indirect method.) Key your postings by number. Use Exhibit 11–12 (pp. 515–516) as a guide. Assume that all sales are on open credit.

11–63. **HOUSE OF FABRICS ANNUAL REPORT.** Examine the statement of cash flows that is included with the annual report of House of Fabrics (page 754). Note that the cash flows from operating activities are reported using the indirect method.

Required:
1. Suppose House of Fabrics had used the direct method for reporting cash flows from operating activities. Compute three items: (a) cash collections from customers, (b) cash paid to suppliers, and (c) cash paid for all other operating activities.
2. Using information from the balance sheet and statement of cash flows, compute the original cost, accumulated depreciation, and book value of the assets disposed of during 1988. Note that because no proceeds from disposal of fixed assets are shown on the statement of cash flows, no cash was received for any asset disposals. *Hint*: Prepare T-accounts for *Property* and *Accumulated Depreciation and Amortization*.

EXHIBIT 11–13

DATA I/O
Income Statement
For the Year Ended December 31, 1988
(in thousands)

Net sales	$ 65,117
Cost of goods sold	(26,825)
	38,292
Operating expenses	(31,714)
Earnings before taxes on income	6,578
Taxes on income	1,973
Net earnings	$ 4,605

Balance Sheets
For the Years Ended December 31
(in thousands)

ASSETS	1988	1987	INCREASE (DECREASE)
Current Assets:			
Cash and cash equivalents	$ 20,344	$ 27,014	$ (6,670)
Trade accounts receivable, less allowance for doubtful accounts	14,811	13,796	1,015
Inventories	6,433	6,664	(231)
Prepaid operating expenses	1,317	4,602	(3,285)
Total current assets	42,905	52,076	(9,171)
Fixed assets, gross	34,608	38,091	(3,483)
Accumulated depreciation	(15,344)	(15,565)	221
Net fixed assets	19,264	22,526	(3,262)
Total assets	$ 62,169	$ 74,602	$(12,433)

LIABILITIES AND STOCKHOLDERS' EQUITY	1988	1987	INCREASE (DECREASE)
Current Liabilities:			
Trade accounts payable	$ 2,185	$ 3,173	$ (988)
Accrued operating expenses	9,084	10,004	(920)
Income taxes payable	1,600	1,160	440
Notes payable	1,052	974	78
Total current liabilities	13,921	15,311	(1,390)
Stockholders' equity:			
Common stock, authorized, 30,000,000 shares; issued and outstanding, 6,530,496 and 8,649,672 shares	17,647	33,295	(15,648)
Retained earnings	30,601	25,996	4,605
Total shareholders' equity	48,248	59,291	(11,043)
Total liabilities and stockholders' equity	$ 62,169	$ 74,602	$(12,433)

Intercorporate Investments, Including Consolidations

LEARNING
OBJECTIVES

After studying this chapter, you should be able to

1. Distinguish between accounting for short-term investments in debt securities and equity securities
2. Explain the basic approach to accounting for long-term investments in bonds
3. Contrast accounting for investments using the equity method and the cost method
4. Explain the basic ideas and methods used in the preparation of consolidated financial statements
5. Describe how goodwill arises and is accounted for
6. Explain the major features of segment reporting
7. Contrast the purchase method and the pooling-of-interests method of accounting for business combinations (Appendixes 12A and 12B)
8. Explain how equity-method investments affect the statement of cash flows (Appendix 12C)

Companies often invest in debt securities issued by governments or other corporations. They also invest in other corporations' equity securities. This chapter discusses the accounting for such investments.

The chapter begins with a discussion of short-term investments. It then examines accounting for intercorporate long-term investments in bonds and in equity securities. Consolidated statements, goodwill, and segment reporting are also covered. Pooling of interests is introduced in Appendix 12A and pursued in greater depth in Appendix 12B. The effects of equity investments on the statement of cash flows are covered in Appendix 12C.

Although this chapter covers much territory, it concentrates on underlying concepts rather than tedious details. Moveover, the topics can be studied separately. Consider the following convenient chunks: short-term investments, long-term investments in bonds, equity method for intercorporate investments, consolidated financial statements, accounting for goodwill, and segment reporting.

SHORT-TERM INVESTMENTS

Investments are classified on a balance sheet according to *purpose* or *intention*. An investment should be carried as a current asset if it is a short-term investment. All other investments are classified as noncurrent assets. The latter usually appear as either (1) a separate *investments* category between current assets and property, plant, and equipment or (2) a part of *other assets* below the plant assets category.

☐ Types of Securities

As its name implies, a **short-term investment** is a temporary investment of otherwise idle cash; the investment portfolio (total of securities owned) usually consists largely of notes and bonds with maturities of one year or less. Favorite investments are **certificates of deposit**, which are short-term obligations of banks, and **commercial paper**, which consists of short-term notes payable issued by large corporations with top credit ratings. The aim is usually the highest safety, so investments in stocks tend to be minor. The investments frequently are highly liquid (easily convertible into cash) and have stable prices.

Ordinarily, short-term investments are expected to be completely converted into cash within a year after the balance sheet date. But some companies hold part of their portfolio of investments beyond a twelve-month period. Nevertheless, these investments are still classified as current assets if management intends to convert them into cash *when needed*. The key point is that cash from the sale of the securities is immediately available at the option of management.

Some companies use the ill-chosen term *marketable securities* to describe their short-term investments. **Marketable securities** are any notes, bonds, or stocks that can readily be sold via public markets. Strictly speaking, marketable securities may be held as *either* short-term investments or long-term investments. Thus 100 shares of General Electric (GE) common stock may be held as a short-term investment by one company and another 100 shares of GE may be held as a long-term investment by a second company. Consequently, this book will not use the term *marketable securities* as a synonym for the more descriptive term *short-term investments*.

Short-Term Debt Securities

Balance sheets show short-term investments immediately after cash. Because short-term investments tend to be in *debt* securities such as highly stable notes and bonds with early maturities, most companies follow the reporting practice illustrated by Pacific Gas and Electric Company:

Short-term investments (at cost which approximates market)	$374,035,000

Some companies combine cash and short-term investments, as exemplified by the current asset section of Koppers Company, Inc.:

Cash, including short-term investments of $44,225,000	$57,777,000

Short-term investments in *debt securities* are usually carried at cost. What if their market values fall below cost? There is no requirement to write them down unless the decline is a substantial amount and is deemed to be "permanent."

Short-Term Equity Securities

When marketable *equity* securities (common and preferred stocks) are held as short-term investments, their balance sheet value must be the lower of the *aggregate* cost or current market value of the portfolio. The changes in the market value of the portfolio would affect the financial reporting. Suppose a portfolio cost $50 million, as follows (in millions of dollars):

	END OF PERIOD			
	1	2	3	4
Assumed market values	50	45	47	54
Balance Sheet Presentation:				
Short-term investments in equity securities, at cost	50	50	50	50
Contra asset account to reduce to lower of cost or market	0	5	3	0
Net short-term investments, lower of cost or market (balance sheet value)	50	45	47	50

	FOR PERIOD			
	1	2	3	4
Income Statement Presentation:				
Unrealized gain (loss) on portfolio of short-term investments in equity securities	0	(5)	2	3

The tabulation shows the results for four periods. Assume these are four quarters rather than four years. (The investments hardly qualify as short-term if they are held untouched for four years.) Current accounting rules require the write-down of the short-term investment to affect income in the period when the market falls below cost. If the market subsequently recovers, the net investment may be written up—but never above cost. Thus, even though the market value rises by $7 million in period 4, only $3 million will be shown as income for that period. Journal entries for periods 2, 3, and 4 follow:

2.	Unrealized loss on short-term investment portfolio	5	
	Allowance to reduce short-term investment		5
	To record unrealized loss on portfolio. (A more descriptive valuation account such as the one illustrated in the table could be used, but Allowance to Reduce Short-Term Investment is used here.)		
3.	Allowance to reduce short-term investment	2	
	Unrealized gain on short-term investment portfolio		2
	To record recovery of market value and restore previously recorded unrealized loss.		
4.	Allowance to reduce short-term investment	3	
	Unrealized gain on short-term investment portfolio		3
	To record recovery of market value and restore previously recorded unrealized loss. (The total unrealized gain was $7 million, but no write-ups above original cost are permissible.)		

The accounting for short-term debt securities and short-term equity securities is obviously inconsistent. Why? Because the lower-of-cost-or-market method must be routinely applied to equity securities but not to debt securities. This inconsistency is an excellent illustration of how accounting principles have developed in piecemeal fashion. Regulatory bodies seldom have the time to make pronouncements that envelop many similar items. For various reasons, including severe time pressures, the FASB chose to confine its pronouncement to certain marketable securities, excluding debt securities.

LONG-TERM INVESTMENTS IN BONDS

☐ Acquisition and Holding

Chapter 9 explained the fundamental approach to accounting for bonds payable. Recall that the issuer amortizes bond discounts and premiums as periodic adjustments of interest expense. Investors analyze bonds in a parallel fashion.

However, while the issuer typically keeps a separate account for unamortized discounts and premiums, investors do not (although they could if desired).

Consider the same illustration that was used for bonds issued at a discount in Chapter 9, pages 383–386, except that we now view the bond from the investor's viewpoint. Suppose an investor purchased 10,000 two-year, 10% debentures for $9,653,500 on December 31, 1989. The face value was 10,000 × $1,000 = $10 million, and therefore there was a discount on the bonds at issuance of $10,000,000 − $9,653,500 = $346,500. Despite the face value of $10 million, the amount invested (the principal amount) was only $9,653,500. Interest (rental payment for the $9,653,500) will take two forms, a semiannual cash receipt of 5% × $10,000,000 = $500,000 plus an extra lump-sum cash receipt of $346,500 (total of $10 million less repayment of principal of $9,635,500) at maturity.

The extra $346,500 to be paid at maturity relates to the use of the proceeds over the two years. Therefore, like the issuer, the investor amortizes the discount:

	6/30/90	12/31/90	6/30/91	12/31/91
Semiannual interest revenue:				
Cash interest payments, .05 × $10 million	$500,000	$500,000	$500,000	$500,000
Amortization of $346,500 discount*	79,207	83,959	88,997	94,337
Semi-annual revenue	$579,207	$583,959	$588,997	$594,337

* For the amortization schedule, see column 4 of Exhibit 9–5, page 385. Note that $79,207 + $83,959 + $88,997 + $94,337 = $346,500.

As the above tabulation shows, the discount is used as an adjustment of nominal interest to obtain the real interest. The amortization of a discount *increases* the interest revenue of investors. (Investor accounting for bonds issued at a premium is similar except that amortization of bond premium *decreases* the interest revenue of investors.)

Exhibit 12–1 shows how the investors would account for the bonds throughout their life, assuming that they are held to maturity. The top of the exhibit analyzes the balance sheet equation; the bottom shows the journal entries.

☐ Early Extinguishment of Investment

Consider another illustration of parallel recording. Suppose in our example that the issuer buys back all of its bonds on the open market for $9.6 million on December 31, 1990 (after all interest payments and amortization were recorded for 1990). The investor would be affected as follows:

Carrying amount:		
Face or par value	$10,000,000	
Deduct: Unamortized discount on bonds*	183,334	$9,816,666
Cash received		9,600,000
Difference, loss on sale		$ 216,666

* The remaining discount is $88,997 + $94,337 = $183,334, or $346,500 − $79,207 − $83,959 = $183,334.

EXHIBIT 12–1

Accounting for Bonds
Investor's Records

BALANCE SHEET EQUATION: (rounded to thousands of dollars)	A		= L +	SE
	Cash	Investment in Bonds		Retained Income
Issuer's records:				
1. Issuance	−9,654	+9,654 [Increase Investment]		
2. Semiannual interest				
Six months ended:				
6/30/90	+500	+79		+579 [Increase
12/31/90	+500	+84 [Increase		+584 Interest
6/30/91	+500	+89 Investment]		+589 Revenue]
12/31/91	+500	+94		+594
3. Maturity value (final payment)	+10,000	−10,000		
Bond-Related Totals	+2,346	0		+2,346

JOURNAL ENTRIES:
(without explanations)

1. Investment in bonds	9,653,500	
Cash		9,653,500
2. Cash	500,000	
Investment in bonds	79,207	
Interest revenue		579,207
Cash	500,000	
Investment in bonds	83,959	
Interest revenue		583,959
Cash	500,000	
Investment in bonds	88,997	
Interest revenue		588,997
Cash	500,000	
Investment in bonds	94,337	
Interest revenue		594,337
3. Cash	10,000,000	
Investment in bonds		10,000,000

The appropriate journal entry for the investor, December 31, 1990, would be:

Cash	9,600,000	
Loss on disposal of bonds	216,666	
Investment in bonds		9,816,666
To record the sale of bonds on the open market.		

Recall that this same extinguishment of debt was analyzed from the issuer's viewpoint in Chapter 9, pages 387–389. The issuer had a *gain* on extinguishment of debt of $216,666.

EQUITY METHOD FOR INTERCORPORATE INVESTMENTS

Equity securities were discussed from the issuer's point of view in Chapter 10. In this chapter we are concerned with the investor's records. Investments in the equity securities of one company by another company are accounted for in different ways, depending on the type of relationship between the "investor" and the "investee." For example, the ordinary stockholder who is a passive investor follows the **cost method** whereby the initial investment is recorded at cost and dividends are recorded as income when received.

Suppose an investor company exerts a "significant influence" over the operating and financial policies of an investee. Such influence can exist even when the investor holds 50% or less of the outstanding voting stock. In the United States, such an investor must use the **equity method**, which accounts for the investment at acquisition cost adjusted for the investor's share of dividends and earnings or losses of the investee subsequent to the date of investment. Accordingly, the carrying amount of the investment is increased by the investor's share of investee's earnings. The carrying amount is reduced by dividends received from the investee and by the investor's share of investee's losses. The equity method is generally used for a 20% through 50% interest, because such a level of ownership is regarded as a presumption that the investor has the ability to exert significant influence, whereas the cost method is generally used to account for interests of less than 20%. The treatment of an interest in excess of 50% is explained in the following section, "Consolidated Financial Statements."

Compare the cost and equity methods. Suppose Company A acquires 40% of the voting stock of Company B for $80 million. In Year 1, B has a net income of $30 million and pays cash dividends of $10 million. A's 40% shares of net income and dividends would be $12 million and $4 million, respectively. The balance sheet equation of A would be affected as follows:

| | EQUITY METHOD | | | | COST METHOD | | | |
| | Assets | | = Liab. and Stk. Eq. | | Assets | | = Liab. and Stk. Eq. | |
	Cash	Investments	Liab.	Stk. Eq.	Cash	Investments	Liab.	Stk. Eq.
1. Acquisition	−80	+80	=		−80	+80	=	
2. Net income of B		+12	=	+12	No entry and no effect			
3. Dividends from B	+4	−4	=		+4		=	+4
Effects for year	−76	+88	=	+12	−76	+80	=	+4

The investment account will have a net increase of $8 million for the year. The dividend will increase the cash account by $4 million. Investment revenue increases stockholders' equity by $12 million.

The investment account will be unaffected. The dividend will increase the cash amount by $4 million. Dividend revenue increases stockholders' equity by $4 million.

The following journal entries would accompany the above table:

EQUITY METHOD			COST METHOD		
1. Investment in B	80		1. Investment in B	80	
Cash		80	Cash		80
2. Investment in B	12		2. No entry		
Investment revenue*		12			
3. Cash	4		3. Cash	4	
Investment in B		4	Dividend revenue†		4

* Frequently called "equity in earnings of affiliated companies."
† Frequently called "dividend income."

Under the equity method, income is recognized by A as it is earned by B rather than when dividends are received. Cash dividends do not affect net income; they increase Cash and decrease the Investment balance. In a sense, A's claim on B grows by its share of B's net income. The dividend is a partial liquidation of A's "claim." The receipt of a dividend is similar to the collection of an account receivable. The revenue from a sale of merchandise on account is recognized when the receivable is created; to include the collection also as revenue would be double-counting. Similarly, it would be double-counting to include the $4 million of dividends as income after the $12 million of income is already recognized as it is earned.

The major justification for using the equity method instead of the cost method is that it more appropriately recognizes increases or decreases in the economic resources underlying the investments. Further, the cost method may allow management of the investor company to unduly influence its own reported net income. How? Under the cost method, the reported net income of the investor is directly affected by the dividend policies of the investee, over which the investor might have significant influence. Under the equity method, the investor's reported net income could not be influenced by the manipulation of the investee's dividend policies.

Sears, the world's largest retailer of general merchandise, holds ownership in several companies. For years Sears held a 23% interest in Roper Corporation, a manufacturer of household appliances. Sears used the equity method in accounting for the investment because an ownership interest in excess of 20% is presumed to be evidence of ability to exert significant influence.[1]

CONSOLIDATED FINANCIAL STATEMENTS

United States companies having substantial ownership of other companies must issue consolidated financial statements, which are explained in this section. A

---

[1] The equity method is generally attractive to investors because it requires the recognition of a pro-rata share of income as earned regardless of whether dividends are paid by the investee. Although the 20% ownership interest is the usual rule, significant influence must indeed exist before the equity method can be justified. For example, McLouth Steel owned nearly 20% of Jewell Coal & Coke Co. However, McLouth had so little practical control it was unable to get a director on Jewell's board, as the remainder of the company was closely held by the Thompson family. Therefore the equity method was inappropriate.

reader cannot hope to understand a corporate annual report without understanding the assumptions underlying consolidations. Consolidated financial statements have been required for many years in the United States. Moreover, many other countries have adopted such requirements in recent years.

A publicly held business is typically composed of two or more separate legal entities that constitute a single overall economic unit. This is almost always a parent-subsidiary relationship where one corporation (the **parent company**) owns more than 50% of the outstanding voting shares of another corporation (the **subsidiary**).

Why have subsidiaries? Why not have the corporation take the form of a single legal entity? The reasons include limiting the liabilities in a risky venture, saving income taxes, conforming with government regulations with respect to a part of the business, doing business in a foreign country, and expanding in an orderly way. For example, there are often tax advantages in acquiring the capital stock of a going concern rather than its individual assets.

Consolidated statements combine the financial positions and earnings reports of the parent company with those of various subsidiaries into an overall report as if they were a single entity. The aim is to give the readers a better perspective than could be obtained by their examining a large number of separate reports of individual companies.

□ **The Acquisition**

When parent and subsidiary financial statements are consolidated, double-counting of assets and equities must be avoided via "intercompany eliminations." Suppose Company P (Parent) acquired a 100% voting interest in S (Subsidiary) for $213 million cash paid to the former owners at the beginning of the year.[2] Their balance sheet accounts are analyzed in the equation form below. Investment in S is presented in the first column because it is a focal point in this chapter, not because it appears first in actual balance sheets. Figures in this and subsequent tables are in millions of dollars:

	ASSETS		= LIABILITIES +		STOCKHOLDERS' EQUITY
	Investment + in S	Cash and Other = Assets	Accounts Payable, etc.	+	Stockholders' Equity
P's accounts, Jan. 1:					
Before acquisition		650 =	200	+	450
Acquisition of S	+213	−213 =			
S's accounts, Jan. 1		400 =	187	+	213
Intercompany eliminations	−213	=			−213
Consolidated, Jan. 1	0 +	837 =	387	+	450

_____

[2] In this example, the purchase price equals the stockholders' equity of the acquired company. The preparation of consolidated statements in situations where these two amounts differ is discussed later in the section entitled "Accounting for Goodwill," pages 550–554.

Note that the $213 million is paid to the *former owners* of S as private investors. The $213 million is *not* an addition to the existing assets and stockholders' equity of S. *That is, the books of S are completely unaffected by P's initial investment and P's subsequent accounting thereof.* S is not dissolved; it lives on as a separate legal entity but with a new owner, P.

The following journal entry would occur:

	P BOOKS		S BOOKS
Investment in S	213		No entry
Cash		213	

Each legal entity has its individual set of books; the consolidated entity does not keep a separate set of books. Instead working papers are used to prepare the consolidated statements.

Suppose a consolidated balance sheet were prepared immediately after the acquisition. The consolidated statement shows the details of all assets and liabilities of both the parent and the subsidiary. The *Investment in S* account on P's books is the evidence of an ownership interest, which is held by P but is really composed of all the assets and liabilities of S. The consolidated statements cannot show both the evidence of interest *plus* the detailed underlying assets and liabilities. So this double-counting is avoided by eliminating the reciprocal evidence of ownership present in two places: (a) the Investment in S on P's books, and (b) the Stockholders' Equity on S's books.

In summary, if the $213 million elimination of the reciprocal accounts did not occur, there would be a double-counting in the consolidated statement:

ENTITY	TYPES OF RECORDS
P	Parent books
+ S	Subsidiary books
= Preliminary consolidated report	No separate books, but periodically P and S assets and liabilities are added together via work sheets
− E	"Eliminating entries" remove double-counting
= Consolidated report to investors	

On the work sheet for consolidating the balance sheet, the eliminating entry in journal format would be:

Stockholders' equity (on S books)	213	
Investment in S (on P books)		213

☐ After Acquisition

Long-term investments in equity securities, such as this investment in S, are carried in the *investor's* balance sheet by the equity method, the same method of accounting for an unconsolidated ownership interest of 20% through 50%, as previously described. Suppose S has a net income of $50 million for the year. If the parent company P were reporting alone, it would have to account for the net income of its subsidiary by increasing its Investment in S account and its Stockholders' Equity account (in the form of Retained Income) by 100% of $50 million.

The income statements for the year would contain (numbers in millions assumed):

	P	S	CONSOLIDATED
Sales	$900	$300	$1,200
Expenses	800	250	1,050
Operating income	$100	$ 50	$ 150
Pro-rata share (100%) of subsidiary net income	50	—	
Net income	$150	$ 50	

P's parent-company-only income statement would show its own sales and expenses plus its pro-rata share of S's net income (as the equity method requires). The journal entry on P's books would be:

Investment in S	50	
Invesment revenue*		50

* Or "equity in net income of subsidiary."

The eliminating entry on the work sheet used for consolidating the balance sheets would be for $213 + $50 = $263.

Reflect on the changes in P's accounts, S's accounts, and the consolidated accounts (in millions of dollars):

	ASSETS		= LIABILITIES +	STOCKHOLDERS' EQUITY
	Investment + in S	Cash and Other = Assets	Accounts Payable, + etc.	Stockholders' Equity
P's accounts:				
Beginning of year	213 +	437 =	200 +	450
Operating income		+100 =		+100*
Share of S income	+50	=		+50*
End of year	263 +	537 =	200 +	600
S's accounts:				
Beginning of year		400 =	187 +	213
Net income		+50 =		+50*
End of year		450 =	187 +	263
Intercompany eliminations	−263	=		−263
Consolidated, end of year	0 +	987 =	387 +	600

* Changes in the retained income portion of stockholders' equity.

Review at this point to see that consolidated statements are the summation of the individual accounts of two or more separate legal entities. They are prepared periodically via work sheets. The consolidated entity does not have a separate continuous set of books like the legal entities. Moreover, a consolidated income statement is merely the summation of the revenue and expenses of the separate legal entities being consolidated after eliminating double-counting.[3] The income statement for P shows a $150 million net income; for S, a $50 million net income; for consolidated, a $150 million net income.

☐ Minority Interests

A consolidated balance sheet often includes an account on the equities side called *Minority Interests in Subsidiaries,* or simply **Minority Interests**. The account shows the outside stockholders' interest, as opposed to the parent's interest, in a subsidiary corporation. It arises because the consolidated balance sheet is a combination of all the assets and liabilities of a subsidiary. If the parent owns, for example, 90% of the subsidiary stock, then outsiders to the consolidated group own the other 10%. The Minority Interest in Subsidiaries account is a measure of the outside stockholders' interest. The diagram that follows shows the area encompassed by the consolidated statements; it includes all the subsidiary assets, item by item. The creation of an account for minority interests, in effect, corrects this overstatement. The remainder after deducting minority interests is P's total ownership interest:

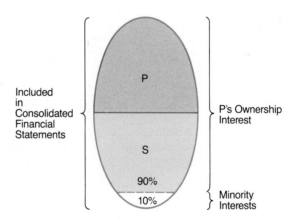

---

[3] An example of double-counting is sales by P to S (or by S to P). A consolidated income statement should not include the sale when P sells the item to S and again when S sells it to an outsider. Suppose P bought an item for $1,000 and sold it to S for $1,200. P recognized revenue of $1,200, cost of goods sold of $1,000, and income of $200. S recorded an inventory item of $1,200. In consolidation, this transaction must be eliminated. After adding together the individual accounts of P and S, you must deduct $1,200 from revenue, $1,000 from cost of goods sold, and $200 from inventory. This eliminates the $200 of income that P recognized and reduces inventory to the original $1,000 that P paid for the item.

The next table, using the basic figures of the previous example, shows the overall approach to a consolidated balance sheet immediately after the acquisition. P owns 90% of the stock of S for a cost of .90 × $213, or $192 million. The minority interest is 10%, or $21 million. (All dollar amounts are rounded to the nearest million.)

	ASSETS		= LIABILITIES +	STOCKHOLDERS' EQUITY	
	Investment + in S	Cash and Other = Assets	Accounts Payable, etc.	+ Minority + Interest	Stockholders' Equity
P's accounts, Jan. 1: Before acquisition		650 =	200	+	450
Acquisition of 90% of S	+192	−192 =			
S's accounts, Jan. 1:		400 =	187	+	213
Intercompany eliminations	−192	=		+21	−213
Consolidated, Jan. 1	0 +	858 =	387	+ 21 +	450

Again, suppose S has a net income of $50 million for the year. The same basic procedures are followed by P and by S regardless of whether S is 100% owned or 90% owned. However, the presence of a minority interest changes the *consolidated* income statement slightly, as follows:

	P	S	CONSOLIDATED
Sales	$900	$300	$1,200
Expenses	800	250	1,050
Operating income	$100	$ 50	$ 150
Pro-rata share (90%) of subsidiary net income	45	—	
Net income	$145	$ 50	
Minority interest (10%) in subsidiary's net income			5
Net income to consolidated entity			$ 145

Consolidated balance sheets at the end of the year would also be affected, as follows:

	ASSETS		=	LIABILITIES +		STOCKHOLDERS' EQUITY	
	Investment + in S	Cash and Other Assets	=	Accounts Payable, etc.	+ Minority Interest	+ Stockholders' Equity	
P's accounts:							
Beginning of year, before acquisition		650	=	200	+	450	
Acquisition	192	−192	=				
Operating income		+100	=			+100	
Share of S income	+45		=			+45	
End of year	237 +	558	=	200	+	595	
S's accounts:							
Beginning of year		400	=	187	+	213	
Net income		+50	=			+50	
End of year	+	450	=	187	+	263	
Intercompany eliminations	−237		=		+26*	−263	
Consolidated, end of year	0 +	1,008	=	387	+ 26 +	595	

* Beginning minority interest plus minority interest in net income: $21 + .10(50) = 21 + 5 = 26$.

As indicated in the table, the eliminating entry on the work sheet used for consolidating the balance sheet would be:

Stockholders' equity (on S books)	263	
Investment in S (on P books)		237
Minority interest (on consolidated statements)		26

Thus the minority interest can be regarded as identifying the interests of those shareholders who own the 10% of the *subsidiary* stockholders' equity that is not eliminated by consolidation.

☐ Perspective on Consolidated Statements

Exhibits 12–2 and 12–3 provide an overall look at how the balance sheet and income statement appear in corporate annual reports. The circled items ①, ②, and ③ in the exhibits deserve special mention:

① The headings indicate that these are *consolidated* financial statements.

② On balance sheets the minority interest typically appears just above the stockholders' equity section, as Exhibit 12–2 shows. On income statements, the minority interest in net income is deducted as if it were an expense of the consolidated entity, as Exhibit 12–3 demonstrates. It generally follows all other expenses. Note that minority interest is a claim of outside stockholders' interest in a *consolidated subsidiary* company. Note also that minority interests arise only in conjunction with *consolidated* financial statements.

EXHIBIT 12-2   *(Place a clip on this page for easy reference.)*

GOLIATH CORPORATION
① Consolidated Balance Sheets
As of December 31
(in millions of dollars)

ASSETS	19X3	19X2	CHANGE
Current assets:			
Cash	$ 90	$ 56	
Short-term investments in debt securities at cost (which approximates market value)	—	28	
Accounts receivable (less allowance for doubtful accounts of $2,000,000 and $2,100,000 at their respective dates)	91	95	
Inventories at average cost	120	130	
Total current assets	301	309	(8)
③ Investments in affiliated companies	10	9	1
Property, plant, and equipment:			
Land at original cost	50	39	11

Plant and equipment:	19X3	19X2	
Original cost	$255	$190	65
Accumulated depreciation	126	112	(14)

ASSETS	19X3	19X2	CHANGE
Net plant and equipment	129	78	
Total property, plant, and equipment	179	117	
Other assets:			
Franchises and trademarks	15	16	
Deferred charges and prepayments	3	4	
Total other assets	18	20	(2)
Total assets	$508	$455	53

LIAB. AND STK. EQUITY	19X3	19X2	CHANGE
Current liabilities:			
Accounts payable	$100	$ 84	
Notes payable	10	—	
Accrued expenses payable	32	22	
Accrued income taxes payable	34	38	
Total current liabilities	176	144	32
Long-term liabilities:			
First mortgage bonds, 5% interest, due Dec. 31, 19X6	25	25	
Subordinated debentures, 6% interest, due Dec. 31, 19X9	30	20	10
Total long-term liabilities	55	45	
Unearned income*	12	9.3	2.7
② Minority interest in consolidated subsidiaries	6	5.7	0.3
Total liabilities	249	204	
Stockholders' equity:			
Preferred stock, 100,000 shares, $30 par†	3	3	
Common stock, 1,000,000 shares, $1 par	1	1	
Paid-in capital in excess of par	55	55	
Retained income	200	192	8
Total stockholders' equity	259	251	
Total liab. and stk. equity	$508	$455	53

* Advances from customers on long-term contracts. Other examples are collections for rent and subscriptions, which often are classified as current liabilities.

† Dividend rate is $5 per share; each share is convertible into two shares of common stock. The shares were originally issued for $100. The excess over par is included in "paid-in capital in excess of par." Liquidating value is $100 per share.

EXHIBIT 12–3

GOLIATH CORPORATION
① Consolidated Income Statements
for the Year Ended December 31
(000's omitted)

	19X3	19X2
Net sales and other operating revenue	$507,000	$609,100
Cost of goods sold and operating expenses, exclusive of depreciation	468,750	554,550
Depreciation	14,000	11,000
Total operating expenses	482,750	565,550
Operating income	24,250	43,550
③ Equity in earnings of affiliates	1,000	900
Total income before interest expense and income taxes	25,250	44,450
Interest expense	2,450	2,450
Income before income taxes	22,800	42,000
Income taxes	12,000	21,900
Income before minority interests	10,800	20,100
② Minority interests in consolidated subsidiaries' net income	300	600
Net consolidated income to Goliath Corporation*	10,500	19,500
Preferred dividends	500	500
Net income to Goliath Corporation common stock	$ 10,000	$ 19,000
Earnings per share of common stock:		
On shares outstanding (1,000,000 shares)	$10.00†	$19.00
Assuming full dilution, reflecting conversion of all convertible securities (1,200,000 shares)	$ 8.75‡	$16.25

* This is the total figure in dollars that the accountant traditionally labels net income. It is reported accordingly in the financial press.
† This is the figure most widely quoted by the investment community: $10,000,000 ÷ 1,000,000 = $10.00, $19,000,000 ÷ 1,000,000 = $19.00.
‡ Computed, respectively: $10,500,000 ÷ 1,200,000 = $8.75; $19,500,000 ÷ 1,200,000 = $16.25.

③ As described earlier in the chapter, investments in equity securities that represent 20% to 50% ownership are usually accounted for under the equity method. These investments are frequently called Investments in **Affiliated Companies** or Investments in Associates. For example, see the items marked as ③ in Exhibits 12–2 and 12–3. General Motors would account for its 34% investment in Isuzu in this manner. Exhibit 12–2 shows how the Investment account in the balance sheet has risen by the pro-rata share of the current earnings of affiliates, the $1 million shown in the income statement in Exhibit 12–3.[4]

To help understand, consider the following hypothetical relationships that exist for Goliath Corporation, which for more realism could be viewed as a simplified version of General Motors.

---

[4] Appendix 12C and Problems 12–47 and 12–48 explore how investments carried by the equity method relate to the statement of cash flows.

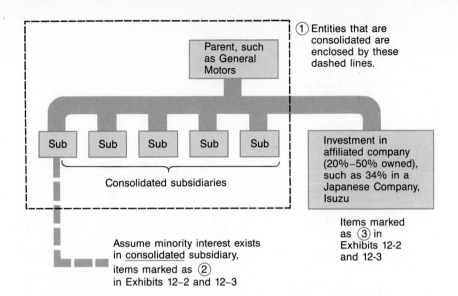

The FASB requires that all subsidiaries be consolidated. That is, *all* subsidiaries, regardless of whether they are finance companies, brokerage companies, insurance companies, or other types, are an integral part of the complete consolidated entity.

The FASB's major reason for requiring complete consolidation is to provide an overall picture of the economic entity. The FASB believes that excluding some subsidiaries from consolidation would result in the omission of significant amounts of assets, liabilities, revenues, and expenses.

There are exceptions to the general rule, but they are rare. A subsidiary shall not be consolidated if control is likely to be temporary or it does not rest with the majority owner. For example, a subsidiary could be in bankruptcy or operating under foreign exchange restrictions or other controls. In these cases, the subsidiaries are carried on the cost basis until control by the parent is resumed.

RECAPITULATION OF INVESTMENTS IN EQUITY SECURITIES

Exhibit 12–4 summarizes all the relationships depicted in the preceding exhibits. Take a few moments to review Exhibits 12–2 and 12–3 in conjunction with Exhibit 12–4. In particular, note that minority interests arise only in conjunction with *consolidated* subsidiaries. Why? Because consolidated balance sheets and income statements aggregate 100% of the detailed assets, liabilities, sales, and expenses of the subsidiary companies. Thus, if a minority interest were not recognized, the stockholders' equity and net income of the consolidated enterprise would be overstated.

In contrast, minority interests do not arise in connection with the accounting for investments in affiliated companies. Why? Because no detailed assets, liabilities, revenues, and expenses of the affiliated companies are included in the consolidated statements. The investor's interests in these companies have been recognized on a pro-rata basis only.

EXHIBIT 12–4

Summary of Equity Method and Consolidations

ITEM IN EXHIBITS 12–2 AND 12–3	PERCENTAGE OF OWNERSHIP	TYPE OF ACCOUNTING	BALANCE SHEET EFFECTS	INCOME STATEMENT EFFECTS	MAJOR JOURNAL ENTRIES
①	100%	Consolidation	Individual assets, individual liabilities added together	Individual revenues, individual expenses added together	None, except in work sheets for preparing consolidated statements; to eliminate reciprocal accounts, to avoid double-counting, and to recognize any goodwill or minority interests
②	Greater than 50% and less than 100%	Consolidation	Same as 1, but recognition given to minority interest in liability section	Same as 1, but recognition given to minority interest near bottom of statement when consolidated net income is computed	

③	20% to and including 50%	Equity method	Investment carried at cost plus pro-rata share of subsidiary earnings less dividends received	Equity in earnings of *affiliated* or *associated* companies shown on one line as addition to income	Investment xx
					  Equity in earnings xx
					To record earnings.
					
					Cash xx
					  Investment xx
					To record dividends received.

As we have seen, the accounting for investments *in voting stock* depends on the nature of the investment:

1. Investments that represent more than a 50% ownership interest are usually consolidated. A *subsidiary* is a corporation controlled by another corporation. The usual condition for control is ownership of a majority (more than 50%) of the outstanding voting stock.

2. **a.** The equity method is generally used for a 20% through 50% interest because such a level of ownership is regarded as a presumption that the owner has the ability to exert significant influence. Under the equity method, the cost at date of acquisition is adjusted for the investor's share of the earnings or losses of the investee subsequent to the date of investment. Dividends received from the investee reduce the carrying amount of the investment.

   b. Investments in corporate joint ventures should also be accounted for under the equity method. "Corporate joint ventures" are corporations owned and operated by a small group of businesses (the "joint venturers") as a separate business or project for the mutual benefit of the members of the group. Joint ventures are common in the petroleum and construction industries.

3. Marketable *equity* securities held as short-term investments are generally carried at the lower-of-cost-or-market value.[5] These investments are typically passive in the sense that the investor exerts no significant influence on the investee.

ACCOUNTING FOR GOODWILL

☐ Purchased Goodwill

The example on consolidated financial statements earlier in the chapter assumed that the acquisition cost of Company S by Company P was equal to the *book value* of Company S. However, the total purchase price paid by P often exceeds the book values of the assets acquired. In fact, the purchase price also often exceeds the sum of the fair market values (current values) of the identifiable individual assets less the liabilities. For example, Philip Morris paid $13 billion for Kraft, but only $2 billion was assigned to identifiable individual assets. Such excess of purchase price over fair market value is called *goodwill* or *purchased goodwill* or, more accurately, *excess of cost over fair value of net identifiable assets of businesses acquired*. Recall that Chapter 8 discusses goodwill on pages 341–342.

To see the impact of goodwill on the consolidated statements, refer to our initial example on consolidations, where there was an acquisition of a 100% interest in S by P for $213 million. Suppose the price were $40 million higher, or a total of $253 million cash. For simplicity, assume that the fair values of the

---

[5] FASB *Statement No. 12*, "Accounting for Certain Marketable Securities," requires that a portfolio of securities (rather than each security as an individual investment) should be stated at the lower of cost or market. If the investment is classified as a current asset, any write-down to market should affect current net income. If the investment is a noncurrent asset, the write-down should be recorded directly in the stockholders' equity section of the balance sheet as a separate valuation account and not as a component of the determination of net income.

individual assets of S are equal to their book values. The balance sheets immediately after the acquisition are:

	ASSETS		= LIABILITIES +		STOCKHOLDERS' EQUITY
	Investment + in S	Cash and Other Assets	Accounts Payable, etc.	+	Stockholders' Equity
P's accounts:					
Before acquisition		650 =	200	+	450
Acquisition	+253	−253 =			
S's accounts		400 =	187	+	213
Intercompany eliminations	−213	=			−213
Consolidated	40* +	797 =	387	+	450

* The $40 million "goodwill" would appear in the consolidated balance sheet as a separate intangible asset account. It is often shown as the final item in a listing of assets. It is usually amortized in a straight-line manner as an expense in the consolidated income statement over a span of no greater than forty years.

As indicated in the table, the eliminating entry on the work sheet for consolidating the balance sheet would be:

Stockholders' equity (on S books)	213	
Goodwill (on consolidated balance sheet)	40	
Investment in S (on P books)		253

☐ **Fair Values of Individual Assets**

If the book values of the individual assets of S are not equal to their fair values, the usual procedures are:

1. S continues as a going concern and keeps its accounts on the same basis as before.
2. P records its investment at its acquisition cost (the agreed purchase price).
3. For consolidated reporting purposes, the excess of the acquisition cost over the book values of S is identified with the individual assets, item by item. (In effect, they are revalued at the current market prices prevailing when P acquired S.) Any *remaining excess* that cannot be identified is labeled as purchased goodwill.

Suppose the fair value of the other assets of S (e.g., machinery and equipment) exceeded their book value by $30 million in our example. The balance sheets immediately after acquisition would be the same as above, with a single exception. The $40 million goodwill would now be only $10 million. The remaining $30 million would appear in the consolidated balance sheet as an integral part of the other assets. That is, the S equipment would be shown at $30 million higher in the consolidated balance sheet than the carrying amount on S's books. Similarly, the depreciation expense on the consolidated income statement would be higher. For instance, if the equipment had five years of useful life remaining, the straight-line depreciation would be $30 ÷ 5, or $6 million higher per year.

As in the preceding tabulation, the $10 million goodwill would appear in the consolidated balance sheet as a separate intangible asset account. The eliminating entry on the working papers for consolidating the balance sheet would be:

Stockholders' equity (on S books)	213	
Equipment (on consolidated balance sheet)	30	
Goodwill (on consolidated balance sheet)	10	
Investment in S (on P books)		253

☐ Goodwill and Abnormal Earnings

Goodwill is frequently misunderstood. The layperson often thinks of goodwill as being the friendly attitude of the neighborhood store manager. But goodwill can have many aspects. A purchaser may be willing to pay more than the current values of the individual assets received because the acquired company is able to generate abnormally high earnings. The causes of this excess earning power may be traceable to personalities, skills, locations, operating methods, and so forth. For example, a purchaser may be willing to pay extra because excess earnings can be forthcoming from

1. Saving in time and costs by purchasing a corporation having a share of the market in a type of business or in a geographical area where the acquiring corporation planned expansion
2. Excellent general management skills or a unique product line
3. Potential efficiency by combination, rearrangement, or elimination of duplicate facilities and administration

Of course, goodwill is originally generated internally. For example, a happy combination of advertising, research, management talent, and timing may give a particular company a dominant market position for which another company is willing to pay dearly. This ability to command a premium price for the total business is goodwill. Nevertheless, such goodwill should never be recorded by the selling company. Therefore the *only* goodwill generally recognized as an asset is that identified when one company is purchased by another. The consolidated company must then show in its financial statements the purchased goodwill.

As you might suspect, the final price paid by the purchaser of an ongoing business is the culmination of a bargaining process. Therefore the exact amount paid for goodwill is subject to the negotiations regarding the total purchase price. A popular logic for determining the maximum price follows.

Goodwill is fundamentally the price paid for "excess" or "abnormal" earning power. The following steps might be taken regarding the possible acquisition of Company M or Company N:

	ORDINARY COMPANY M	EXTRAORDINARY COMPANY N
1. Fair market value of identifiable assets, less liabilities	$800,000	$800,000
2. Normal annual earnings on net assets at 10%	80,000	80,000
3. Actual average annual earnings for past five years (including for Co. N an excess or abnormal return of $20,000)	80,000	100,000
4. Maximum price paid for normal annual earnings is ten times line 2	800,000	800,000
5. Maximum price paid for abnormal annual earnings (which are riskier and thus less valuable per dollar of expected earnings) is six times $20,000	—	120,000*
6. Maximum price a purchaser is willing to pay for the company (line 1 plus line 5)	800,000	920,000

* This is the most the purchaser is willing to pay for goodwill.

The above table uses a "capitalization rate" of 10% (earnings divided by .10 or earnings multiplied by 10) to arrive at a purchase price for a normal company. This normal rate varies by risk and by industry. For example, the normal rate for an oil exploration company will be higher (and the earnings multiplier lower) than for a retail food chain. Goodwill is attributed to the exceptional company, and the earnings multiplier paid for extra earnings (the abnormal layer) is less than the multiplier used for the basic earnings (the normal layer). The capitalization rate for the abnormal layer is $16\frac{2}{3}\%$ (earnings divided by .1667 or earnings multiplied by 6):

$20,000	Abnormal layer × 6 = $120,000
$80,000	Normal layer × 10 = 800,000
	Total purchase price $920,000

For shareholder reporting purposes, goodwill must be amortized by systematic charges in the income statement over the period estimated to be benefited. The maximum amortization period should not exceed forty years.[6] In our Company N example, a strong case could be made for amortization over six years or less.

Managers, investors, and accountants tend to be uncomfortable about the presence of goodwill on the balance sheet. Somehow it is regarded as an inferior asset even though management decided that it was valuable enough to warrant

---

[6] Before October 31, 1970, amortization was not required. Some companies still have large amounts of such goodwill purchased before 1970 that is not being amortized. For example, about a quarter of the $1.4 billion of intangible assets of American Brands, Inc., is not being amortized.

a total outlay in excess of the total current value of the individual assets. As a practical matter, many accountants feel that the income-producing factors of goodwill are unlikely to have a value in perpetuity even though expenditures may be aimed at maintaining their value. Nevertheless, the Accounting Principles Board did not permit the lump-sum write-off of goodwill upon acquisition.

SEGMENT REPORTING

The 1970s and 1980s can accurately be described as the years of fuller disclosure. The financial statements became thicker and more complex and were impressively adorned with detailed footnotes and supplementary information. Among the more controversial requirements was the issuance by the FASB in 1976 of *Statement No. 14*, "Financial Reporting for Segments of a Business Enterprise." Corporations must now disclose data about their operations in different industries and in foreign countries, their export sales, and their major customers.

The purpose of consolidated financial statements is to provide an overall view of an economic entity. However, consolidated data can hide some of the details that might be useful in predicting profitability, risk, and growth. The purpose of segment disclosures is to facilitate such prediction.

Exhibit 12–5 lists the four types of disclosures required by *Statement No. 14*. An *industry segment* is a product or service or a group of related products or services. Management has much discretion in defining industry segments. The nature of the product, the nature of the production process, and the markets or

EXHIBIT 12–5

Main Provisions of FASB Statement No. 14

TYPE OF DISCLOSURE	CRITERIA FOR DISCLOSURE	ITEMS TO BE DISCLOSED
1. Industry segment	a. Revenue at least 10% of company revenue, b. Profit at least 10% of company profit, or c. Assets at least 10% of company assets.	a. Segment revenue b. Segment profit c. Segment assets d. Other (e.g., segment depreciation and capital expenditures)
2. Geographic segment	a. Foreign operations contribute at least 10% of company's revenue, or b. Foreign operations use more than 10% of the company's assets	a. Segment revenue b. Segment profit c. Segment assets
3. Export disclosures	At least 10% of revenues from export sales	Export sales by geographic area
4. Major customers	Any customer providing more than 10% of company's revenue	Customer identity and amount of revenue

marketing methods should be considered in identifying a company's segments. Examples of industry segments include the following:

- ☐ American Express Company: travel-related services; international banking services; investment services; IDS financial services; insurance services
- ☐ Alcoa: aluminum processing; finished products

If an industry segment meets any one of the three criteria for disclosure in Exhibit 12–5, the segment's revenue, profit, assets, depreciation, and capital expenditures must be reported.

Companies with significant operations in foreign countries must separately disclose the results of operations by geographic area. For example, American Express Company reports revenue, profits, and assets for the United States, Europe, and Asia/Pacific. Even companies without foreign operations must disclose foreign *sales* by geographic area if such export sales are 10% or more of total revenues.

Finally, companies must report aggregate sales to any customer accounting for more than 10% of revenues. For example, Ball Corporation, maker of packaging materials, including metal beverage containers for brewers and soft drink companies, reports that 23% of its sales were to Anheuser-Busch and 20% were to various agencies of the United States government.

Exhibit 12–6 displays the segment information of American Brands, Inc., for two years (six years were included in the annual report). Examples of American Brands products include Carlton and Pall Mall cigarettes, Master locks, Wilson Jones office supplies, Jim Beam whiskey, Titleist golf balls, and Franklin life insurance.

SUMMARY

Nearly all corporate annual reports contain consolidated financial statements, as well as "investment" accounts of various sorts. Acquiring a fundamental understanding of accounting for intercorporate investments is therefore essential for intelligent use of financial reports.

Exhibits 12–2 and 12–3 summarize how to account for intercorporate investments. Note how the equity method is applied. The $1 million increase in the Investments account is attributable to the pro-rata share of the affiliated companies' net income shown in Exhibit 12–3. See pages 546 and 547.

Minority interests are also displayed in Exhibits 12–2 and 12–3. Consider the $300,000 increase (Exhibit 12–2) in Minority Interest in Consolidated Subsidiaries. It is attributable to the minority interests' share of the income of *consolidated* subsidiaries, as indicated in the income statement in Exhibit 12–3.

Even though consolidated statements are regarded as the heart of the financial report, companies must also disclose supplementary data regarding significant business segments.

EXHIBIT 12–6

AMERICAN BRANDS, INC. AND SUBSIDIARIES
Information on Business Segments
(in millions)

BUSINESS BY INDUSTRY SEGMENTS	1988	1987		1988	1987
Revenues			**Depreciation and amortization**		
Tobacco products	$ 7,018.6	$ 6,144.0	Tobacco products	$ 61.8	$ 55.0
Life insurance	923.4	923.7	Life insurance	11.0	10.2
Distilled spirits	758.7	599.4	Distilled spirits	23.4	16.9
Office products	883.2	516.3	Office products	44.5	20.9
Hardware and home			Hardware and home		
improvement products	437.2	165.3	improvement products	19.5	4.5
Specialty businesses	1,958.9	1,727.9	Specialty businesses	51.7	43.8
	$11,980.0	$10,076.6		$ 211.9	$ 151.3
Operating income			**Capital expenditures**		
Tobacco products	$ 826.0	$ 673.8	Tobacco products	$ 58.9	$ 83.8
Life insurance	192.3	179.4	Life insurance	8.6	34.5
Distilled spirits	100.4	68.3	Distilled spirits	16.1	6.2
Office products	26.6	25.2	Office products	47.5	24.2
Hardware and home			Hardware and home		
improvement products	63.8	39.6	improvement products	23.2	8.0
Specialty businesses	104.8	95.3	Specialty businesses	81.0	59.5
	$ 1,313.9	$ 1,081.6		$ 235.3	$ 216.2
Identifiable assets			**BUSINESS BY GEOGRAPHIC AREAS**	1988	1987
Tobacco products	$ 2,186.1	$ 2,235.5			
Life insurance	5,610.9	5,258.2			
Distilled spirits	822.2	875.7	**Revenues**		
Office products	1,537.9	1,177.0	United States	$ 4,459.7	$ 3,739.5
Hardware and home			Europe	7,378.5	6,250.9
improvement products	639.6	155.1	Other	141.8	86.2
Specialty businesses	1,115.4	1,010.6		$11,980.0	$10,076.6
	$11,912.1	$10,712.1			
			Operating income		
			United States	$ 831.7	$ 757.3
			Europe	457.5	315.0
			Other	24.7	9.3
				$ 1,313.9	$ 1,081.6
			Identifiable assets		
			United States	$ 9,014.9	$ 7,980.6
			Europe	2,739.1	2,615.1
			Other	158.1	116.4
				$11,912.1	$10,712.1

SUMMARY PROBLEMS FOR YOUR REVIEW

☐ **Problem One**

Dow Chemical's annual report used the following asset nomenclature and classifications
as of December 31 (in millions):

	$:
Marketable securities and interest-bearing deposits (at cost, which approximates market)	397
	:
Total Current Assets	5,752
Investments:	
Capital stock at cost plus equity in accumulated earnings of 20%–49% owned companies	1,064
Other investments	684
Noncurrent receivables	399
Total Investments	2,147
Plant Properties	13,502
Less—Accumulated depreciation	7,951
Net Plant Properties	5,551
Goodwill	485
Deferred Charges and Other Assets	421
TOTAL	$14,356

Dow also shows "Minority Interests in Subsidiary Companies" of $36 million among its liabilities.

Required:

1. Suppose "Marketable Securities" included a $24 million portfolio of equity securities. Their market values on the following March 31, June 30, and September 30 were $20, $23, and $28, respectively. Compute the following:
   (*a*) Carrying amount of the portfolio on each of the three dates
   (*b*) Unrealized gain (loss) on the portfolio for each of the three quarters
2. Suppose the $684 million of "Other Investments" included a $9 million investment in the debentures of an affiliate. The debentures had a par value of $10 million and a 10% nominal rate of interest, payable June 30 and December 31. Their market rate of interest when the investment was made was 12%. Prepare the Dow journal entry for the semiannual receipt of interest.
3. Suppose Dow's 20%–49% owned companies had net income of $200 million. Dow received cash dividends of $70 million from these companies. No other transactions occurred. Prepare the pertinent journal entries. Assume that on average Dow owns 40% of the companies.

☐ Solution to Problem One

1. Amounts are in millions.
   a. Lower of cost or market: $20, $23, and $24.
   b. $24 − $20 = $4 loss; $23 − $20 = $3 gain; $28 − $23 = $5 gain, but only $1 gain would appear on the income statement because the portfolio should not be written up above cost.
2.

Cash	500,000	
Other investments (in bonds)	40,000	
Interest revenue		540,000
Six months' interest earned is		
.5 × .12 × $9,000,000 = $540,000.		
Amortization is $540,000 − cash received		
of .5 × .10 × $10,000,000 = $540,000 − $500,000.		

3.

Investments in 20%–49% owned companies	80,000,000	
Investment revenue		80,000,000
To record 40% share of $200 million income.		
Cash	70,000,000	
Investments in 20%–49% owned companies		70,000,000
To record dividends received from 20%–49% owned companies.		

☐ Problem Two

1. Review the section on minority interests, pages 543–545. Suppose P buys 60% of the stock of S for a cost of .60 × $213, or $128 million. The total assets of P consist of this $128 million plus $522 million of other assets, a total of $650 million. The S assets and equities are unchanged from the amount given in the example on page 544. Prepare an analysis showing what amounts would appear in a consolidated balance sheet immediately after the acquisition.

2. Suppose S has a net income of $50 million for the year, and P has an operating income of $100 million. Other details are described in the example on page 544. Prepare an analysis showing what amounts would appear in a consolidated income statement and year-end balance sheet.

☐ Solution to Problem Two

1.

	ASSETS		= LIABILITIES +	STOCKHOLDERS' EQUITY	
	Investment in S	+ Cash and Other Assets =	Accounts Payable, etc.	Minority + Interest +	Stockholders' Equity
P's accounts, Jan. 1: Before acquisition		650 =	200	+	450
Acquisition of 60% of S	+128	−128 =			
S's accounts, Jan. 1		400 =	187	+	213
Intercompany eliminations	−128	=		+85	−213
Consolidated, Jan. 1	0 +	922 =	387	+ 85 +	450

2.

	P	S	CONSOLIDATED
Sales	$900	$300	$1,200
Expenses	800	250	1,050
Operating income	$100	$ 50	$ 150
Pro-rata share (60%) of unconsolidated subsidiary net income	30	—	
Net income	$130	$ 50	
Outside interest (40%) in consolidated subsidiary net income (minority interest in income)			20
Net income to consolidated entity			$ 130

| | ASSETS | | = LIABILITIES + | STOCKHOLDERS' EQUITY | |
	Investment in S +	Cash and Other Assets =	Accounts Payable, etc.	Minority Interest +	Stockholders' Equity
P's accounts:					
Beginning of year	128 +	522* =	200	+	450
Operating income		+100 =		+	+100
Share of S income	+ 30	=			+ 30
End of year	158 +	622 =	200	+	580
S's accounts:					
Beginning of year		400 =	187	+	213
Net income		+ 50 =			+ 50
End of year		450 =	187	+	263
Intercompany eliminations	−158	=		+105†	−263
Consolidated, end of year	0 +	1,072 =	387	+ 105 +	580

* 650 beginning of year − 128 for acquisition = 522.

† 85 beginning of year + .40 (50) = 85 + 20 = 105.

HIGHLIGHTS TO REMEMBER

1. Generally accepted accounting principles evolve in a patchwork way. Ponder the assortment of approaches to current assets:

TYPE OF CURRENT ASSET	APPLICATION OF LOWER OF COST OR MARKET
Investments in debt securities	Write down if "permanent" decline
Investments in equity securities	Write down and then write up recoveries, but not above original cost
Inventories	Write down, but do not write up any subsequent recoveries

2. The accounting for long-term investments in bonds is usually similar to the accounting on the issuer's books. That is, the investor's acquisition premium or discount is amortized over the remaining life of the bond.
3. Exhibit 12–4 (p. 549) summarizes the accounting for long-term investments in equity securities. Please review it before you try to solve any problems in these categories.

ACCOUNTING VOCABULARY

APPENDIX 12A: POOLING OF INTERESTS

☐ Nature of Pooling

The business combinations described in the body of the chapter were accounted for by using the *purchase method*, as contrasted with the *pooling-of-interests method*. The focus is on the acquired company. The **purchase method** accounts for a business combination on the basis of the *market prices* actually paid for the acquired company's assets. In contrast, the **pooling-of-interests method** is based on the *book values* of the acquired company's assets.

Both the purchase and the pooling methods are acceptable under the appropriate circumstances, but not as alternatives for the same business combination. Pooling is a uniting of ownership interests of two or more companies by the exchange of common stock. In theory, neither company *purchases* the other. The recorded assets and liabilities of the fused companies are carried forward at their book values by the combined corporation. The market values of both corporations are ignored on the grounds that no purchase has occurred; instead two going concerns have merely combined existing resources that are already being accounted for. To use pooling-of-interests accounting, the combination must completely adhere to a long list of restrictive conditions, including most importantly:

1. The acquirer must issue voting common shares (not cash) in exchange for substantially all (at least 90%) of the voting common shares of the acquired company.
2. The acquisition must occur in a single transaction.

Consider the way actual business combinations commonly occur:

1. The management of P and the management of S discuss the feasibility of P's acquiring S.
2. The *market value* of S as a going concern is established in a variety of ways, including the market values of securities, the appraisal values of individual assets, and negotiations between P and S. A final price is agreed upon.
3. P acquires S. The cash or stock issued by P is ultimately distributed to the individual shareholders of S, not to S itself. Thus, after the acquisition has been completed, S's assets, liabilities, and stockholders' equity are unchanged.
   (a) P may issue shares for cash and then use the cash to buy S. The acquisition would be accounted for as a *purchase*.
   (b) P may issue *the same number* of shares directly to S. If various conditions are met, the acquisition would be accounted for as a *pooling*.
   (c) Note especially that the owners of S would expect the *same total market value* for their shares sold to P, regardless of whether the transaction is accounted for as a purchase or a pooling. Also note that not all acquisitions by P's issuance of stock would necessarily be accounted for as a pooling. For example, P may fail to acquire at least 90% of the common shares of S. Or P may pay for S with half cash and half P shares. In either case, the transaction should be accounted for as a purchase.

☐ Illustration of Pooling

The basic data in the section "Purchased Goodwill," page 550, are reproduced at the top of Exhibit 12–7 for your reconsideration. Suppose P had issued stock for $253 million cash at the beginning of the year and then used the cash to acquire all the shares of S. This combination should be accounted for by using the purchase method.

EXHIBIT 12–7

Comparison of Purchase and Pooling for Business Combinations
(in millions of dollars)

	ASSETS		= LIABILITIES +		STOCKHOLDERS' EQUITY
	Investment in S +	Cash and Other Assets =	Accounts Payable, etc.	+	Stockholders' Equity
PURCHASE METHOD					
P's accounts:					
Before issuance of stock		397 =	200	+	197
Issuance of stock		+253 =			+253
Acquisition of S	+253	−253 =			
S's accounts		400 =	187	+	213
Intercompany eliminations	−213				−213
Consolidated	40* +	797 =	387	+	450
POOLING METHOD					
P's accounts:					
Before issuance of stock		397 =	200	+	197
Issuance of stock in acquisition of S	+213	=			+213
S's accounts		400 =	187	+	213
Intercompany eliminations	−213				−213
Consolidated	0 +	797 =	387	+	410

* Goodwill, as explained in the body of the chapter. See the section "Purchased Goodwill," page 550.

Instead of issuing its shares for $253 million cash, suppose P exchanges *the same number* of its shares for the shares of S. If all the conditions of pooling are met, the accounting would appear as shown in the bottom half of Exhibit 12–7.

The current value of Company S exceeds the recorded values by $40 million. Purchase accounting recognizes the fair values (current values) of the assets acquired, but pooling does not. Moreover, the future consolidated net income will be higher under pooling. Why? Because pooling has no $40 million goodwill to amortize as expense. Furthermore, net income is hurt doubly by the amortization of goodwill. Why? Because goodwill is not deductible for tax purposes. Assume a 40% income tax rate. Normally, a $10 expense would decrease net income by only $6 because the $10 reduction in pretax income will lower taxes by 40% × $10 = $4. In contrast, amortizing $10 of goodwill decreases net income by the full $10 because taxes are unaffected.

The magnitude of the difference between purchasing and pooling would become even more pronounced if S had several individual assets whose fair market values far exceeded book values. Examples are companies with large holdings of internally developed patents, copyrights, and trademarks. Under pooling, the combined company does not have to account for these market values either on its consolidated balance sheet or as a part of its expenses on future consolidated income statements.

☐ Criticisms of Pooling

Many critics maintain that pooling-of-interests accounting should be completely banned. Pooling is defective because it ignores the asset values on which the parties have traded and substitutes a wholly irrelevant figure—the amount on the seller's books. Such accounting also permits the reporting of erroneous profits upon subsequent disposition of such assets. If the assets had been acquired for cash, the buyer's cost would be the amount of the cash. Acquisition for stock should make no difference.

The accounting essence is the amount of consideration, not its nature. Payment in cash or stock can be a matter of form, not substance. Suppose the seller wants cash. The buyer can first sell stock and turn over the proceeds to the seller, or the seller can take stock and promptly sell the stock for cash.

Some say that the elimination of pooling would impede mergers and thus is not in the national interest. Others say that accounting does not exist to aid or discourage mergers, but to account for them fairly. Elimination of pooling would remove the confusion that comes from the coexistence of pooling and purchase accounting. Above all, the elimination of pooling would remove an aberration in historical-cost accounting that permits an acquisition to be accounted for on the basis of the seller's cost rather than the buyer's cost of the assets obtained in a bargained exchange.

APPENDIX 12B: MORE ON POOLING OF INTERESTS

Exhibit 12–7 does not provide a detailed illustration of the consolidation process for pooling. A detailed approach follows:

1. Sum the individual assets and liabilities of P and S, line by line.
2. Sum the individual retained incomes. By definition of pooling, the retained incomes are combined in this way.
3. Adjust common stock at par and additional paid-in capital accounts. This adjustment is usually small; it involves increasing one of the two accounts and decreasing the other by a like amount.

To illustrate, reconsider Exhibit 12–7. Suppose the following detailed stockholders' equity accounts had existed before the pooling of interests (in millions of dollars):

	P		S	
Common stock at par	8,000,000 shares @ $5 =	40	5,000,000 shares @ $4 =	20
Additional paid-in capital		87		140
Retained income		70		53
Total stockholders' equity		197		213

Assume that P pays $253 million to the owners of S, consisting of 4.6 million additional shares of P with a market value of $55 each (that is, 4.6 million × $55 = $253 million). In accounting for a pooling, the *number* of shares is pertinent, but their *value* is ignored.

In concept, a straightforward pooling would call for the following simple addition of all accounts (in millions of dollars):

	P	+	S	= CONSOLIDATED
Cash and other assets	397	+	400 =	797
Accounts payable	200	+	187 =	387
Common stock at par	40	+	20 =	60*
Additional paid-in capital	87	+	140 =	227*
Retained income	70	+	53 =	123
	397		400	797

* Total paid-in capital = 60 + 227 = 287.

Indeed, *in practice* the above addition does occur, including the noteworthy summing of retained incomes. However, a modest change in the Common Stock at Par and Additional Paid-in Capital accounts is necessary to show the appropriate par value for all the P shares:

	CONSOLIDATED	
Common stock at par	Old P, 8,000,000 shares @ $5 =	40
	New P, 4,600,000 shares @ $5 =	23
	New total	63*
Additional paid-in capital	Old P	87
	Old S	140
	Adjustment	(3)
	New total	224*

* Total paid-in capital = 63 + 224 = 287.

Compare the $63 million with the $60 million in the preceding tabulation; also compare the $224 million with the $227 million. The numbers differ only because the $23 million par value of the new P shares differs from the $20 million par value of the S shares. To bring the par value account up to the required $63 million, $3 million must be transferred from additional paid-in capital to common stock at par.

A consolidating journal entry (for the work sheet) may clarify the pooling transaction. The book values of S are added to P:

Cash and other assets	400	
Accounts payable		187
Common stock		23
Additional paid-in capital		137
Retained income		53

To issue 4,600,000 shares of P @ $5 par in a pooling of interests with S. S's retained income is added intact. The book value ($20 + $140) of S common stock and additional paid-in capital is also added, after recognizing that P's par value is different from S's. So instead of adding $20 + $140, the addition takes the form of $23 + $137.

Ponder the accounting for pooling. A "parent" is identified. The par value of P stock governs the new totals for common stock and for additional paid-in capital. The latter plays a residual role. That is, the new total for the par value of the consolidated company is the old P total of $40 plus the par value of the additional P shares issued of $23 = $63. But the total of $287 for both par and additional paid-in capital still holds. Consequently, the additional paid-in capital is a residual of $287 − $63 = $224. The consolidated balance sheet on the pooling basis would include the following:

ASSETS		LIABILITIES AND STOCKHOLDERS' EQUITY	
Cash and other assets	$797	Accounts payable	$387
		Common stock, 12,600,000 shares @ $5 par	63
		Additional paid-in capital	224
		Retained income	123
			$797

In contrast, the consolidated balance sheet on the purchase basis follows:

ASSETS		LIABILITIES AND STOCKHOLDERS' EQUITY	
Cash and other assets	$797	Accounts payable	$387
Goodwill	40	Common stock, 12,600,000 shares @ $5 par	63
	$837	Additional paid-in capital	317*
		Retained income	70
			$837

* Identified with the first 8,000,000 shares $ 87
  Identified with new 4,600,000 shares @ ($55 − $5) 230
                                                      $317

Compare the two consolidated balance sheets immediately after P acquires S:

	POOLING	PURCHASE COMPARED WITH POOLING
1. Assets	No goodwill No fair value of other assets	Higher because of goodwill and fair values of other assets such as property, plant, and equipment
2. Retained income	P and S added together	Lower because S retained income not added; the consolidated retained income equals P retained income
3. Common stock at par	Sum of all P shares	Same as pooling
4. Additional paid-in capital	Adjusted to accommodate changes in par values	Higher because new shares affect equity at market values at time of acquisition of S

How do income statements differ between purchasing and pooling? Consider the year of the acquisition. Pooling merely sums revenues and expenses as though both P and S were together throughout the year:

	POOLING	PURCHASE COMPARED WITH POOLING
Revenue and expenses	Added together for entire year regardless of when acquisition occurred during the year	Added together only for time span subsequent to date of acquisition
Goodwill amortization	No goodwill	Amortized for time span subsequent to acquisition
Depreciation expense	Based on old book values	Based on fair values at date of acquisition

A widespread criticism of pooling has been that a P company can "artificially" boost its net income by acquiring an S company late in a year. Under pooling, P can include the S income for the entire year in consolidated results. Under purchasing, P can include only the S income earned subsequent to the acquisition.

APPENDIX 12C: EQUITY METHOD AND THE STATEMENT OF CASH FLOWS

This appendix explains how investments in affiliated companies affect the statement of cash flows, which was introduced in Chapter 11.

☐ Equity in Earnings of Affiliated Companies

Suppose Chan Company has an investment in an affiliate, Bay Manufacturing. Chan uses the equity method to account for the investment, thereby recognizing its pro-rata share of Bay's net earnings. That is, if Bay makes a profit, Chan's Investment in Bay account and its Investment Revenue are increased regardless of whether Chan receives cash dividends from Bay. In turn, when Chan receives cash dividends from Bay, Chan's cash is increased, and its Investment in Bay account is decreased.

Assume that Chan had net income of $38,000 in 19X1 and its only noncash expense was $23,000 of depreciation. Chan's pro-rata share of Bay's 19X1 earnings was $13,000, and it received $10,000 in cash dividends from Bay. For simplicity, ignore tax effects and assume no changes in Chan's noncash current assets and current liabilities. Consider the reconciliation of net income and the net cash provided by operating activities, which appears in the statement of cash flows:

Net income		$38,000
Adjustments to reconcile net income to net cash provided by operating activities:		
Add: Depreciation	$23,000	
Deduct: Pro-rata share of earnings of affiliated company	(13,000)	
Add: Cash dividends received	10,000	
Total additions and deductions		20,000
Net cash provided by operating activities		$58,000

The reconciliation schedule deducts from Chan's net income the $13,000 noncash investment revenue. Why? Because net income includes the $13,000 share of Bay's earnings, which is not a cash flow. The statement then adds the $10,000 cash dividends received because it is a cash inflow to Chan. The net effect is a cash inflow $3,000 less than the $13,000 share of Bay's earnings that is included in Chan's net income.

☐ Noncash Investing and Financing Activities

Because Chan received only $10,000 in cash dividends when its share of Bay's net earnings was $13,000, Chan's investment in Bay increased by $3,000. This represents a $3,000 asset acquired by Chan without a cash payment:

$$\Delta \text{Cash} = \Delta L + \Delta PC + \Delta RI - \Delta NCA$$
$$\text{Dividends received} = \qquad + \text{Income} - (+\text{Asset})$$
$$\$10,000 = \qquad + \$13,000 - (+\$3,000)$$

Such an activity should be shown in the schedule of noncash investing and financing activities that accompanies a statement of cash flows:

Undistributed earnings in affiliated companies	$3,000

FUNDAMENTAL ASSIGNMENT MATERIAL

☐ General Coverage

12–1. COST METHOD OR EQUITY METHOD. (Alternates are 12–7 and 12–34.) Company G acquired 25% of the voting stock of Company H for $40 million cash. In Year 1, H had a net income of $36 million and paid a cash dividend of $20 million.

Required:

1. Using the equity and the cost methods, show the effects of the three transactions on the accounts of G. Use the balance sheet equation format. Also show the accompanying journal entries.
2. Which method, equity or cost, would G use to account for its investment in H? Explain.

12–2. CONSOLIDATED FINANCIAL STATEMENTS. (Alternate is 12–8.) Company P acquired a 100% voting interest in Company S for $100 million cash at the start of the year. Immediately before the business combination, each company had the following condensed balance sheet accounts (in millions):

	P	S
Cash and other assets	$500	$140
Accounts payable, etc.	$200	$ 40
Stockholders' equity	300	100
Total liab. & stk. eq.	$500	$140

Required:

1. Prepare a tabulation of the consolidated balance sheet accounts immediately after acquisition. Use the balance sheet equation format.
2. Suppose P and S have the following results for the year:

	P	S
Sales	$600	$200
Expenses	450	180

Prepare income statements for the year for P, S, and the consolidated entity. Assume that neither P nor S sold items to the other.

3. Present the effects of the operations for the year on P's accounts and on S's accounts, using the balance sheet equation. Also tabulate the consolidated balance sheet accounts at the end of the year. Assume that liabilities are unchanged.
4. Suppose S paid a cash dividend of $15 million. What accounts in requirement 3 would be affected and by how much?

12–3. MINORITY INTERESTS. This extends the preceding problem. However, this problem is self-contained because all the facts are reproduced below. Company P acquired an 80% voting interest in Company S for $80 million cash at the start of the year. Immediately before the business combination, each company had the following condensed balance sheet accounts (in millions):

	P	S
Cash and other assets	$500	$140
Accounts payable, etc.	$200	$ 40
Stockholders' equity	300	100
Total liab. & stk. eq.	$500	$140

Required:

1. Prepare a tabulation of the consolidated balance sheet accounts immediately after the acquisition. Use the balance sheet equation format.
2. Suppose P and S have the following results for the year:

	P	S
Sales	$600	$200
Expenses	450	180

Prepare income statements for the year for P, S, and the consolidated entity. Assume that neither P nor S sold items to the other.
3. Using the balance sheet equation format, present the effects of the operations for the year on P's accounts and S's accounts. Also tabulate consolidated balance sheet accounts at the end of the year. Assume that liabilities are unchanged.
4. Suppose S paid a cash dividend of $15 million. What accounts in requirement 3 would be affected and by how much?

12–4. **GOODWILL AND CONSOLIDATIONS.** This extends Problem 12–2. However, this problem is self-contained because all the facts are reproduced below. Company P acquired a 100% voting interest in Company S for $150 million cash at the start of the year. Immediately before the business combination, each company had the following condensed balance sheet accounts (in millions):

	P	S
Cash and other assets	$500	$140
Accounts payable, etc.	$200	$ 40
Stockholders' equity	300	100
Total liab. and stk. equity	$500	$140

Assume that the fair values of the individual assets of S were equal to their book values.

Required:

1. Prepare a tabulation of the consolidated balance sheet accounts immediately after the acquisition. Use the balance sheet equation format.
2. If goodwill is going to be amortized over forty years, how much was amortized for the first year? If over five years, how much was amortized for the first year?
3. Suppose the book values of the S individual assets are equal to their fair market values except for equipment. The net book value of equipment is $30 million and its fair market value is $50 million. The equipment has a remaining useful life of four years. Straight-line depreciation is used.
   a. Describe how the consolidated balance sheet accounts immediately after the acquisition would differ from those in requirement 1. Be specific as to accounts and amounts.
   b. By how much will consolidated income differ in comparison with the consolidated income that would be reported in requirement 2? Assume amortization of goodwill over a forty-year period.

12–5. SHORT-TERM INVESTMENT PORTFOLIO. (Alternate is 12–10.) The Jimenez Company has a portfolio of short-term investments consisting of common and preferred stocks. The portfolio cost $150 million on January 1. The market values of the portfolio were (in millions): March 31, $140; June 30, $128; September 30, $144; and December 31, $158.

Required:
1. Prepare a tabulation showing the balance sheet presentations and income statement presentations for interim reporting purposes.
2. Show the journal entries for quarters 1, 2, 3, and 4.

12–6. PREPARE CONSOLIDATED FINANCIAL STATEMENTS. From the following data, prepare a consolidated balance sheet and an income statement of the Schiff Corporation. All data are in millions and pertain to operations for 19X2 or to December 31, 19X2:

Paid-in capital in excess of par	$ 82
Interest expense	25
Retained income	218
Accrued income taxes payable	30
Cost of goods sold and operating expenses, exclusive of depreciation and amortization	700
Subordinated debentures, 11% interest, due December 31, 19X9	100
Minority interest in subsidiaries' net income	20
Goodwill	100
Net sales and other operating revenue	950
Investments in affiliated companies	100
Common stock, 10 million shares, $1 par	10
Depreciation and amortization	20
Accounts payable	200
Cash	50
First-mortgage bonds, 10% interest, due December 31, 19X8	80
Property, plant, and equipment, net	120
Preferred stock, 2 million shares, $50 par, dividend rate is $5 per share, each share is convertible into one share of common stock	100
Short-term investments at cost, which approximates current market	40
Income tax expense	90
Accounts receivable, net	100
Minority interest in subsidiaries	90
Inventories at average cost	400
Dividends declared and paid on preferred stock	10
Equity in earnings of affiliated companies	20

☐ **Understanding Published Financial Reports**

12–7. EQUITY METHOD. (Alternates are 12–1 and 12–34.) In 1989, Warner Communications, an entertainment conglomerate, purchased 100% of the voting stock of Lorimar Telepictures, a smaller movie studio. Suppose Warner had purchased only 20% of Lorimar for $127 million on January 2, 1989. Assume that during 1989 Lorimar had a net income of $50 million and paid cash dividends of $30 million.

Required:
Prepare a tabulation that compares the equity method and the cost method of accounting for Warner's investment in Lorimar. Show the effects on the balance sheet equation under each method. What is the year-end balance in the Investment in Lorimar account under the equity method? Under the cost method? Also show the accompanying journal entries.

12–8. CONSOLIDATED FINANCIAL STATEMENTS. (Alternate is 12–2.) Consider the purchase of boat maker Bayliner, Inc., by Brunswick Corporation. The purchase price was $400 million for a 100% interest.

Assume that the book value and the fair market value of Bayliner's net assets were $400 million. The balance sheet accounts immediately after the transaction were approximately (in millions):

	BRUNSWICK	BAYLINER
Investment in Bayliner	$ 400	—
Cash and other assets	1,000	$600
Total assets	$1,400	$600
Liabilities	800	200
Shareholders' equity	600	400
Total liab. & stk. eq.	$1,400	$600

Required:

1. Using the balance sheet equation format, prepare a tabulation of the consolidated balance sheet accounts immediately after the acquisition.
2. Suppose Bayliner had sales of $500 million and expenses of $400 million for the year. Brunswick had sales of $1,800 million and expenses of $1,300 million. Prepare income statements for Brunswick, for Bayliner, and for the consolidated company. Assume that neither Brunswick nor Bayliner sold items to the other.
3. Using the balance sheet equation, present the effects of the operations for the year on the accounts of Bayliner and Brunswick. Also tabulate the consolidated balance sheet accounts at the end of the year. Assume that liabilities are unchanged.
4. Suppose Bayliner paid a cash dividend of $10 million. What accounts in requirement 3 would be affected and by how much?

12–9. EQUITY INVESTMENTS. Phillips Petroleum Company's 1988 income statement reported equity in earnings of affiliated companies of $32 million. Its balance sheets included (in millions):

	DECEMBER 31	
	1988	1987
Investments in affiliated companies	$204	$203

A footnote indicated that retained earnings at December 31, 1988 "included $111 million relating to undistributed earnings of affiliated companies." Dividends of $41 million were received from affiliated companies in 1988.

Required:

1. Compute the amount of additional investment by Phillips in its affiliated companies during 1988. *Hint*: Use a T-account.
2. What is the total amount Phillips has invested in affiliated companies, exclusive of its share of undistributed earnings?
3. Phillips had 1988 income before taxes of $1,115 million. Compute the amount of income before taxes that Phillips would have reported (a) if the affiliated companies had been consolidated and (b) if the affiliated companies had been accounted for by the cost method.

12–10. MARKETABLE SECURITIES. (Alternate is 12–5.) On December 31, 1987, Pennzoil Company held a portfolio of marketable equity securities that cost $183,863,000 and had a market value of $159,127,000. Assume that the same portfolio was held until the end of the first quarter of 1988. The market value of the portfolio was $174,531,000 at January 31, $169,680,000 at February 29, and $188,432,000 at March 31.

Required: **1.** Prepare a tabulation showing the balance sheet presentation and income statement presentation for monthly reporting purposes.
2. Show the journal entries for January, February, and March.

ADDITIONAL ASSIGNMENT MATERIAL

☐ General Coverage

12–11. Why is *marketable securities* an ill-chosen term to describe short-term investments?

12–12. "The lower-of-cost-or-market rule is applied to investments in short-term securities." Do you agree? Explain.

12–13. Suppose an investor buys a $1,000 face value bond for $950, a discount of $50. Will amortization of the discount increase or decrease the investor's interest income? Explain.

12–14. What is the equity method?

12–15. "The equity method is usually used for long-term investments." Do you think this is appropriate? Explain.

12–16. Contrast the *cost* method with the *equity* method.

12–17. What criterion is used to determine whether a parent-subsidiary relationship exists?

12–18. Why have subsidiaries? Why not have the corporation take the form of a single legal entity?

12–19. Why does a consolidated balance sheet require "eliminating entries"?

12–20. What is a minority interest?

12–21. When is there justification for not consolidating subsidiaries in accounting reports?

12–22. Distinguish between *control of* a company and *significant influence over* a company.

12–23. What are joint ventures and how do companies account for them?

12–24. "Goodwill is the excess of purchase price over the book values of the individual assets acquired." Do you agree? Explain.

12–25. Why are segment disclosures required?

12–26. What four types of disclosures are required by FASB *Statement No. 14*, "Financial Reporting for Segments of a Business Enterprise"?

12–27. "If a company is acquired by an exchange of stock, pooling-of-interests accounting must be used." Do you agree? Explain.

12–28. "Pooling is an inferior accounting method." What major reason is usually offered for making such a comment?

12–29. "Pooling should be allowed because its elimination would impede business combinations and thus would not be in the national interest." What is the counterargument to this assertion?

12–30. Suppose P Company received $20,000 in cash dividends from Y Company, a 40%-owned affiliated company. Y Company's net income was $80,000. How will P's statement of cash flows show these items?

12–31. **BOND DISCOUNT TRANSACTIONS.**   (Alternate is 12–33.) On December 31, 1989, a company purchased $1 million of ten-year, 10% debentures for $885,295. The market interest rate was 12%.

Required: **1.** Using the balance sheet equation format, prepare an analysis of bond transactions. Assume effective-interest amortization. Show entries for the investor regarding (a) purchase, (b) the first semiannual interest payment, and (c) payment of maturity value.
2. Show the corresponding journal entries for (a), (b), and (c) above.

3. Show how the bond investment would appear on the balance sheets as of December 31, 1989, and June 30, 1990.

12–32. EARLY EXTINGUISHMENT OF INVESTMENT. On December 31, 1989, an insurance company purchased $10 million of ten-year, 10% debentures for $8,852,950. On December 31, 1990 (after all interest payments and amortization had been recorded for 1990), the insurance company sold all the debentures for $9 million. The market interest rate at issuance was 12%.

Required:
1. Compute the gain or loss on the sale for the insurance company (i.e., the investor).
2. Prepare the appropriate journal entries for the insurance company (i.e., the investor).

12–33. BOND PREMIUM TRANSACTIONS. (Alternate is 12–31.) On December 31, 1989, a company purchased $1 million of ten-year, 10% debentures for $1,135,915. The market interest rate was 8%.

Required:
1. Using the balance sheet equation format, prepare an analysis of transactions for the investor's records. Key your transactions as follows: (a) purchase, (b) the first semi-annual interest using effective-interest amortization of bond premium, and (c) payment of maturity value.
2. Prepare sample journal entries keyed as above.
3. Show how the bond-related accounts would appear on the balance sheets as of December 31, 1989, and June 30, 1990.

12–34. EQUITY METHOD. (Alternates are 12–1 and 12–7.) Company A acquired 30% of the voting stock of Company B for $90 million cash. In Year 1, B had a net income of $50 million and paid cash dividends of $30 million.

Required:
Prepare a tabulation that compares the equity method and the cost method of accounting for A's investment in B. Show the effects on the balance sheet equation under each method. What is the year-end balance in the Investment in B account under the equity method? Under the cost method?

12–35. CONSOLIDATED STATEMENTS. Consider the following for Kahane Company (the parent) as of December 31, 19X4:

	KAHANE	SUBSIDIARY*
Assets	$700,000	$200,000
Liabilities to creditors	$200,000	$ 80,000
Stockholders' equity	500,000	120,000
Total equities	$700,000	$200,000

* 60 percent owned by Kahane.

The $700,000 of assets of Kahane include a $72,000 investment in the subsidiary. The $72,000 includes Kahane's pro-rata share of the subsidiary's net income for 19X4. Kahane's sales were $990,000 and operating expenses were $922,000. These figures exclude any pro-rata share of the subsidiary's net income. The subsidiary's sales were $700,000 and operating expenses were $660,000. Prepare a consolidated income statement and a consolidated balance sheet.

12–36. CONSOLIDATED FINANCIAL STATEMENTS. Fresno Company (the parent) owns 100% of the common stock of Grand Company (the subsidiary), which was acquired at the start of 19X3. Their financial statements follow:

	FRESNO (PARENT)	GRAND (SUBSIDIARY)
INCOME STATEMENTS FOR 19X3		
Revenue and "other income"	$40,000,000	$10,000,000
Expenses	38,000,000	9,000,000
Net income	$ 2,000,000	$ 1,000,000
BALANCE SHEETS, DECEMBER 31, 19X3		
Assets	$10,000,000	$ 4,000,000
Liabilities to creditors	$ 4,500,000	$ 1,000,000
Stockholders' equity	5,500,000	3,000,000
Total liabilities and stk. equity	$10,000,000	$ 4,000,000

Required:

1. The subsidiary had enjoyed a fantastically profitable year in 19X3. The parent's income statement had been prepared by showing the parent's claim to the subsidiary's income as a part of the parent's "other income." On the other hand, the parent's balance sheet is really not completed. The $10 million of assets of the parent company includes a $2 million investment in the subsidiary and does *not* include the parent's claim to subsidiary's 19X3 net income.

   Prepare a consolidated income statement and a consolidated balance sheet. Use the balance sheet equation format for the latter.

2. Suppose Fresno Company owned 60% of the Grand Company. Liabilities to creditors are unchanged. The assets of the parent company include a $1.2 million investment in the subsidiary instead of $2.0 million. However, assume the total assets are $10.0 million. The balance sheet is really not completed because the investment account does not reflect the claim to the subsidiary's 19X3 net income. Similarly, the parent's revenue and other income is $39.6 million, not $40.0 million, but expenses remain at $38 million as in requirement 1.

   Prepare a consolidated income statement and a consolidated balance sheet. Use the balance sheet equation format for the latter.

12–37. **DETERMINATION OF GOODWILL.** Refer to the preceding problem, requirement 1. Suppose the investment in the subsidiary in requirement 1 was $2.8 million instead of the $2.0 million as stated. This would mean that the "other assets" would be $7.2 million instead of $8.0 million. Would the consolidated income differ? How? Be as specific as possible. Would the consolidated balance sheet differ? How? Be as specific as possible.

12–38. **PURCHASED GOODWILL.** Consider the following balance sheets (in millions of dollars):

	COMPANY X	COMPANY Y
Cash	150	20
Inventories	60	30
Plant assets, net	60	30
Total assets	270	80
Common stock and paid-in surplus	70	30
Retained income	200	50
Total liab. and stk. equity	270	80

X paid $120 million to Y stockholders for all their stock. The "fair value" of the plant assets of Y is $70 million. The fair value of cash and inventories is equal to their carrying amounts. X and Y continued to keep separate books.

1. Prepare a tabulation showing the balance sheets of X, of Y, Intercompany Elimi-nations, and Consolidated immediately after the acquisition.

2. Suppose that only $60 million rather than $70 million of the total purchase price of $120 million could logically be assigned to the plant assets. How would the con-solidated accounts be affected?

3. Refer to the facts in requirement 1. Suppose X had paid $144 million rather than $120 million. State how your tabulation in requirement 1 would change.

12–39. **AMORTIZATION AND DEPRECIATION.** Refer to the preceding problem, requirement 3. Suppose a year passes, and X and Y generate individual net incomes of $20 million and $13 million, respectively. The latter is after a deduction by Y of $6 million of straight-line depreciation. Compute the consolidated net income if goodwill is amortized (1) over forty years and (2) over ten years. Ignore income taxes.

12–40. **ALLOCATING TOTAL PURCHASE PRICE TO ASSETS.** Two entities had the following balance sheet accounts as of December 31, 19X1 (in millions):

	GREYMONT	PARADELT		GREYMONT	PARADELT
Cash and receivables	$ 30	$ 22	Current liabilities	$ 50	$ 20
Inventories	120	3	Common stock	100	10
Plant assets, net	150	95	Retained income	150	90
Total assets	$300	$120	Total liab. and stk. eq.	$300	$120
Net income for 19X1	$ 19	$ 4			

On January 4, 19X2, these entities combined. Greymont issued $180 million of its shares (at market value) in exchange for all the shares of Paradelt, a motion picture division of a large company. The inventory of films acquired through the combination had been fully amortized on Paradelt's books.

During 19X2, Paradelt received revenue of $21 million from the rental of films from its inventory. Greymont earned $20 million on its other operations (that is, excluding Paradelt) during 19X2. Paradelt broke even on its other operations (that is, excluding the film rental contracts) during 19X2.

Required:

1. Prepare a consolidated balance sheet for the combined company immediately after the combination on a purchase basis. Assume that $80 million of the purchase price was assigned to the inventory of films.

2. Prepare a comparison of Greymont's net income between 19X1 and 19X2 where the cost of the film inventories would be amortized on a straight-line basis over four years. What would be the net income for 19X2 if the $80 million were assigned to goodwill rather than to the inventory of films, and goodwill were amortized over forty years?

12–41. **CONSOLIDATED FINANCIAL STATEMENTS.** The Parent Company owns 90% of the common stock of Company S-1 and 60% of the common stock of Company S-2. The balances as of December 31, 19X4, in the condensed accounts follow:

	(IN THOUSANDS OF DOLLARS)		
	Parent	S-1	S-2
Sales	300,000	80,000	100,000
Investment in subsidiaries*	72,000	—	—
Other assets	128,000	90,000	20,000
Liabilities to creditors	100,000	20,000	5,000
Expenses	280,000	90,000	95,000
Stockholders' equity, including current net income	100,000	70,000	15,000

* Carried at equity in subsidiaries.

12–42. Preparing Individual Statements from Consolidated Statements and Other Information. Using the following, prepare *individual* balance sheets (in a balance sheet equation format) and income statements for P and S. P owns 60% of the stock of S and carries its investment at its underlying equity in Company S. All figures are expressed in millions of dollars:

Total minority interest	10
Consolidated assets	141
Minority interest in consolidated	
subsidiaries' net income	2
Consolidated liabilities	55
Consolidated sales	371
Consolidated expenses	360
Company P sales	301
Company P total assets	125

12–43. Equity Method, Consolidation, and Minority Interest. On January 2, 19X6, Gretzky Oil Company purchased 40% of Great Slave Lake Mining Company (GSLM) for $2 million cash. Before the acquisition, Gretzky had assets of $10 million and stockholders' equity of $8 million. GSLM had stockholders' equity of $5 million and liabilities of $1 million, and the fair values of its assets were equal to their book values.

GSLM reported 19X6 net income of $400,000 and declared and paid dividends of $200,000. Assume that Gretzky and GSLM had no sales to one another. Separate income statements for Gretzky and GSLM were as follows:

	GRETZKY	GSLM
Sales	$12,500,000	$4,400,000
Expenses	11,100,000	4,000,000
Operating income	$ 1,400,000	$ 400,000

Required: |

1. Prepare the journal entries for Gretzky Oil (a) to record the acquisition of GSLM and (b) to record its share of GSLM net income and dividends for 19X6.
2. Prepare Gretzky Oil's income statement for 19X6 and balance sheet as of December 31, 19X6.
3. Suppose Gretzky had purchased 60% of GSLM for $3 million. Using the balance sheet equation format, prepare a tabulation of the consolidated balance sheet immediately after acquisition. Prepare the journal entries for both Gretzky and GSLM to record the acquisition. Omit explanations.
4. Prepare a consolidated income statement for 19X6, using the facts of requirement 3.

12–44. Purchase or Pooling. Study Appendix 12A. Two companies had the following condensed balance sheet accounts at December 31, 19X1:

	P	S
Cash and other assets	$700	$220
Accounts payable, etc.	$300	$100
Stockholders' equity	400	120
Total liab. & stk. eq.	$700	$220

The fair value of the individual S assets is the same as their book values.

Required:
1. Company P issued stock for $180 million cash at the beginning of 19X2 and then immediately used the cash to acquire all the shares of Company S. Prepare a consolidated balance sheet after the acquisition of S by P.
2. Instead of issuing its shares for $180 million cash, suppose P exchanges the same number of its shares for the shares of S. Assume that all conditions of pooling are met. Prepare a consolidated balance sheet.
3. Which set of future consolidated income statements will show higher income, the ones resulting from purchasing or from pooling? Explain.

12–45. **PURCHASE AND POOLING.** Study Appendix 12A. The B Company and the Y Company have the following accounts at December 31, 19X1:

	B	Y
Net assets	$99,000,000	$27,000,000
Stockholders' equity	$99,000,000	$27,000,000
Net income for 19X1	$10,000,000	$10,000,000

On December 31, 19X1, B combined with Y by issuing stock with a market value of $72 million in exchange for the shares of Y. Assume that the book value and the current value of the individual assets of Y were equal.

Required:
1. Show the balance sheet accounts and net income for 19X1 for the combined companies as they would appear if the combination were accounted for as (a) a $72 million purchase with recognition of purchased goodwill and (b) a pooling.
2. Assume that the same net incomes of $10 million each are generated by the subparts of the combined entity in 19X2 (before considering amortization of goodwill). Show the net income for 19X2 for the combined companies if the business combination had been accounted for as (a) a purchase and (b) a pooling. Any goodwill amortized is to be written off on a straight-line basis over five years. Comment on the results.
3. Comment on the possible net incomes reported in 19X1 and 19X2.

12–46. **MORE ON POOLING OF INTERESTS.** Study Appendix 12B. Two companies had the following condensed balance sheet accounts at December 31, 19X1 (in millions):

	P	S
Cash and other assets	$700	$220
Accounts payable, etc.	$300	$100
Stockholders' equity:		
Common stock:		
4 million shares @ $4 par	16	
12 million shares @ $1 par		12
Additional paid-in capital	84	40
Retained income	300	68
Total stockholders' equity	$400	$120
Total liab. and stk. eq.	$700	$220

The fair values of the individual assets are the same as their book values.

Required:
1. Company P issued 5 million shares of stock @ $40 for $200 million cash at the beginning of 19X2 and then immediately used the cash to acquire all the shares of Company S. Prepare a consolidated balance sheet after the acquisition of S by P.

2. Instead of issuing its shares for $200 million cash, suppose P exchanges the same number of its shares for the shares of S. Assume that all conditions of pooling are met. Prepare a consolidated balance sheet.
3. List the major differences between the two consolidated balance sheets immediately after the acquisition.
4. Suppose the acquisition occurred on December 1, 19X2. All other information is unchanged. How will the income statements differ for 19X2? Respond by listing the major differences. No numerical differences are required.

12–47. **EQUITY METHOD AND CASH FLOWS.** Study Appendix 12C. The Sisly Company owns a 30% interest in the Rousseau Company. Sisly uses the equity method to account for the investment. During 19X6 Rousseau had net income of $100,000 and paid cash dividends of $60,000. Sisly's net income, including the effect of its investment in Rousseau, was $486,000.

Required:
1. In reconciling Sisly's net income with its net cash provided by operating activities, the net income must be adjusted for Sisly's pro-rata share of the net income of Rousseau. Compute the amount of the adjustment. Will it be added to or deducted from net income?
2. The dividends paid by Rousseau will affect the amounts Sisly lists under operating, investing, or financing activities. Which type(s) of activity will be affected? By how much? Will the amount(s) be cash inflows or cash outflows?

12–48. **INTERCORPORATE INVESTMENTS AND STATEMENTS OF CASH FLOW.** Study Appendix 12C. The 19X6 balance sheet of Fernandez Company contained the following three assets:

	19X6	19X5
Long-term investments in marketable securities	$ 166,000	$ 166,000
Investment in Hull Company, 43% owned	$ 981,000	$ 861,000
Investment in Gavilan Company, 25% owned	$1,145,000	$1,054,000

The marketable securities were shown at cost, and the equity method was used to account for both Hull Company and Gavilan Company. Results for 19X6 included:

	LONG-TERM MARKETABLE SECURITIES	HULL COMPANY	GAVILAN COMPANY
Fernandez Co. pro-rata share of net income	$21,000	$120,000	$91,000
Cash dividends received by Fernandez Co.	$14,000	$ 50,000	$ 0

Assume that Fernandez reported net income of $687,000 and depreciation of $129,000 in 19X6.

Required:
1. A schedule that reconciles net income to net cash provided by operating activities contained the following:

Net income	$687,000
Depreciation	129,000
Increase in noncash working capital	(16,000)

Given the available data, complete the reconciliation.
2. List the items and amounts related to these investments that would be shown in an accompanying schedule of noncash investing and financing activities.

12–49. MEANING OF ACCOUNT DESCRIPTIONS. The following account descriptions were found in two annual reports:

> ☐ **DuPont:** Minority interests in earnings of consolidated subsidiaries, Minority interests in consolidated subsidiaries
>
> ☐ **New York Times:** Investments in associated companies, Equity in earnings of associated companies

In your own words, explain what each type of account represents. Indicate whether the item appears on the balance sheet or the income statement.

12–50. CONSOLIDATIONS IN JAPAN. A few years ago, Japan's finance ministry issued a directive requiring the six hundred largest Japanese companies to produce consolidated financial statements. The previous practice had been to use parent-company-only statements. A story in *Business Week* said: "Financial observers hope that the move will help end the tradition-honored Japanese practice of 'window dressing' the parent company financial results by shoving losses onto hapless subsidiaries, whose red ink was seldom revealed. . . . When companies needed to show a bigger profit, they would sell their product to subsidiaries at an inflated price. . . . Or the parent company charged a higher rent to a subsidiary company using its building."

Required: | Could a parent company follow the quoted practices and achieve window dressing in its parent-only financial statements if it used the equity method of accounting for its intercorporate investments? The cost method? Explain.

12–51. EQUITY INVESTMENTS. Vishay Intertechnology, Inc., is a world leader in electronic and optical sensors, instruments used for stress measurement, and fixed resistors. Annual sales are over $300 million. In fiscal 1986, Vishay purchased 50% of Dale Company. Assume a lump-sum purchase for cash at the beginning of 1986. Dale's net income was $1,153,437, $2,061,698, and $3,133,677 for 1986, 1987, and 1988, respectively. Dale paid no dividends. At the end of 1988, Vishay's balance sheet showed an investment account having an equity in Dale of $45,025,272.

Required: | 1. Prepare Vishay's journal entry for the purchase of Dale.
2. Prepare journal entries to recognize Vishay's share of Dale's net income in 1986, 1987, and 1988. Omit explanations.
3. In 1989, Vishay purchased the remaining 50% of Dale. What method must Vishay use to account for its investment in Dale on its 1989 financial statements? How would Vishay's 1988 net income have been affected if this method had been used in 1988? (Assume a 50% ownership in 1988, but use the accounting method required in 1989.)

12–52. EFFECT OF TRANSACTIONS UNDER THE EQUITY METHOD. AT&T's balance sheet includes (in millions):

| | DECEMBER 31 | |
	1988	1987
Investments at equity	$670	$702

These affiliated companies were owned by AT&T in various proportions from 20% to 50%. Dividends received from these companies during 1988 totaled $27 million.

The income statement for 1988 included (in millions):

Equity in earnings of affiliates	$48

1. Did AT&T purchase more shares in affiliated companies during 1988 or sell off part of its holdings (in aggregate)? Give the dollar amount of the transaction, and label it as a purchase or sale. *Hint*: Use a T-account to aid your analysis.
2. Pretax loss in 1988 was $3,382 million. What would AT&T's 1988 pretax loss have been if it had accounted for its Investment in Affiliated Companies by the cost method?

12–53. **EQUITY IN LOSS OF AFFILIATED COMPANIES.** Amgen Inc., a major biotechnology company, develops products based on recombinant DNA and molecular biology. At the beginning of fiscal 1988, its investment in affiliated companies was $872,000. The 1988 income statement (summarized) showed:

Revenues	$53,325,000
Expenses	(50,202,000)
Equity in loss of affiliated companies	(1,049,000)
Income before income taxes	2,074,000
Provision for income taxes	349,000
Net income	$1,725,000

An additional $849,000 was invested in affiliated companies during fiscal 1988. The affiliated companies paid no dividends.

Required:

1. Compute the balance of the Investment in Affiliated Companies account at the end of fiscal 1988.
2. Suppose Amgen had used the cost method to account for its investment in affiliated companies. Compute 1988 income before income taxes.
3. Comment on the significance of the difference made by using the cost method instead of the equity method.

12–54. **JOINT VENTURE.** Nord Resources Corporation, headquartered in Dayton, Ohio, has mining operations throughout the world. It had 1988 pretax earnings of $16,254,000. The company uses joint ventures for many of its exploration activities. Its balance sheets included (in thousands):

	DECEMBER 31	
	1988	1987
Investments in joint ventures	$8,700	$3,359

In 1988, Nord received $2,875,000 in dividends from its joint ventures and invested an additional $156,000 in them.

Required:

1. What method does Nord use to account for investments in joint ventures?
2. Compute Nord's 1988 equity in earnings of joint ventures. *Hint*: Use a T-account.
3. How much 1988 pretax income would Nord have reported without the joint ventures?

12–55. **MINORITY INTERESTS.** The last portion of the 1988 income statement of Pfizer Inc., maker of health-care products, including pharmaceuticals, showed (in millions):

Income before provision for taxes and minority interests	$1,103.8
Provision for taxes on income	309.4
Income before minority interests	794.4
Minority interests	3.1
Net income	$ 791.3

Pfizer's balance sheets included the following summarized data (in millions):

	DECEMBER 31	
	1988	1987
Current liabilities	$2,344.3	$1,956.6
Non-current liabilities	967.0	1,061.4
Minority interests	?	22.2
Total liabilities	?	$3,040.2

Assume that minority shareholders neither increased nor decreased the number of shares they held during 1988 and that no dividends were paid to minority shareholders.

Required:
1. Compute Pfizer's minority interests and total liabilities at December 31, 1988.
2. Suppose a subsidiary of Pfizer paid $200,000 in cash dividends during 1988 to shareholders with minority interests. What amount of minority interests would be shown on Pfizer's December 31, 1988, balance sheet?

12–56. **MINORITY INTEREST.** The consolidated financial statements of Caesars World, Inc., include the accounts of Caesars New Jersey, Inc., an 86.6%-owned subsidiary. Assume that Caesars New Jersey is Caesars World's only consolidated subsidiary. Caesars World's 1987 income statement contained the following (in thousands):

Income before minority interest	$35,519
Minority interest in earnings of consolidated subsidiary	1,824
Net income	$33,695

Caesars World's account "Minority Interest in Consolidated Subsidiary" listed $14,114,000 at the beginning of 1987. Caesars New Jersey paid no dividends in 1987. Assume that Caesars World did not buy or sell any of its interest in Caesars New Jersey during 1987.

Required:
1. Compute the 1987 net income of Caesars New Jersey.
2. What proportion of Caesars World's $33,695,000 net income was contributed by Caesars New Jersey?
3. Compute Caesars World's balance in "Minority interest in consolidated subsidiary" at the end of 1987.
4. Comment on the reason for including a line for minority interest in the income statement and balance sheet of Caesars World.

12–57. **PURCHASE AND POOLING.** Study Appendix 12B. Suppose LTV Corporation acquired the common stock of Grumman in exchange for its own common stock. For purposes of this question, you are to assume the following:

☐ The acquisition occurred on the last day of the year.
☐ The market price of LTV stock at the time of acquisition was $22.50 per share.
☐ The market price of Grumman stock at the time of acquisition was $45.00 per share.
☐ The market value of Grumman's assets equals the book value of Grumman's assets.
☐ Any purchased goodwill is amortized over forty years on a straight-line basis.

The following data are from the financial reports of LTV and Grumman (in thousands):

	LTV	GRUMMAN
Net income for the year just ending	$127,893	$30,668

LTV shareholders' equity, end of the year:

Common stock (50¢ par value per share)	$ 17,896
Additional capital	501,038
Retained earnings	318,398
	$837,332

Grumman shareholders' equity, end of the year:

Preferred stock—$1.00 par value, authorized 10,000,000 shares	
Redeemable preferred stock—$2.80 cumulative preferred:	
redemption value $25 per share;	
outstanding 2,000,000 shares	$ 50,000
Non-redeemable preferred stock—$.80 convertible preferred:	
outstanding 14,216 shares	180
Common Stock—$1.00 par value, authorized 20,000,000 shares:	
outstanding 10,030,773 shares	
(net of 8,100 shares held in treasury)	82,607
Retained Earnings	183,594
	$316,381

Required:

Assume that the business combination occurred under each of the following scenarios:

1. LTV issued additional common stock for 100% of Grumman's outstanding common stock. Assume a pooling of interests.
2. LTV issued additional common stock for 80% of Grumman's outstanding common stock. Because at least 90% of the outstanding voting common shares was not acquired, the transaction would have been a purchase.

Compute for each of these two assumptions for a consolidated LTV–Grumman:
a. Retained earnings at the end of the year
b. Additional capital at the end of the year
c. Purchased goodwill at the end of the year
d. Net income for the year just ended

12–58. ACQUISITION OF RCA. The stockholders of RCA approved the sale of 100% of RCA's common stock to General Electric for $66.50 per share. Of the votes cast, over 90% were in favor of the $6.28 billion cash sale, the largest non-oil acquisition at the time. Assume that the $6.28 billion price was twice RCA's book value.

Required:

1. Suppose the fair market values of RCA's net assets totaled $6.28 billion. Prepare the journal entry or entries to record the acquisition on General Electric's books.
2. Suppose the fair market values of RCA's tangible assets were equal to their book values. Fair market value of identifiable intangible assets was $800 million; their useful life was eight years. None of the intangible assets appeared on RCA's balance sheet. Prepare the journal entry or entries to record the acquisition on General Electric's books.
3. Refer to requirement 2. Assume that the acquisition took place on January 2. Prepare the December 31 journal entry or entries to recognize the first year's amortization of goodwill and other intangible assets. Assume that goodwill is amortized as slowly as possible.

4. Assume that the acquisition occurred on July 1 and that RCA's net income for the year was $500 million. RCA's net income was earned at a constant rate per unit of time during the year. How much of that net income would appear in General Electric's consolidated net income for the year ended December 31?

12–59. **SEGMENT DISCLOSURES.** Rockwell International, a multi-industry advanced technology company, disclosed the business segment data in Exhibit 12–8. The only customer of the company that accounted for 10% or more of consolidated sales is the United States Government and its agencies. Such sales by business segment are as follows:

Sales to United States Government (in millions)

	1988	1987
Aerospace	$3,836	$4,986
Electronics	1,704	1,911
Other business segments	113	134
Total	$5,653	$7,031

Disclosures by geographic areas are as follows:

Sales, Operating Earnings, and Assets, by Geographic Area

GEOGRAPHIC AREA	SALES		OPERATING EARNINGS		IDENTIFIABLE ASSETS	
	1988	1987	1988	1987	1988	1987
United States	$ 9,986	$10,798	$ 966.4	$1,177.3	$6,342	$5,936
Europe	1,141	847	89.1	73.5	715	702
Canada	378	345	61.3	59.6	219	198
South America	192	48	54.4	15.4	147	169
Other	249	85	26.5	16.5	132	109
Total	$11,946	$12,123	$1,197.7	$1,342.3	$7,555	$7,114

Note: United States sales include export sales of $620 million in 1988 and $493 million in 1987.

Required:
1. Compute the percentage of Rockwell's 1987 and 1988 sales in each industry segment. Point out any significant changes from 1987 to 1988.
2. Compute the percentage of capital expenditures in each industry segment for 1988. In what industry segment did most investment take place?
3. Assume that none of Rockwell's foreign operations had any sales in the United States. What percentage of Rockwell's total 1988 sales were to customers outside the United States? Did foreign sales increase or decrease from 1987 to 1988 in total dollars? In percentage of total sales?
4. Does Rockwell rely heavily on sales to a single customer? What percentage of sales are to the largest customer? What industry segment depends most heavily on sales to a single customer?

12–60. **HOUSE OF FABRICS ANNUAL REPORT.** Examine the first item in *Note 1: Summary of Accounting Policies* in the House of Fabrics annual report (p. 756). House of Fabrics has no investments that are not consolidated subsidiaries. Suppose House of Fabrics purchased a fabric store in Minneapolis on January 30, 1989, for $400,000 cash. The store's balance sheet at the time of acquisition was:

EXHIBIT 12–8

ROCKWELL INTERNATIONAL

Business Segment Data
(in millions)

	SALES		EARNINGS		IDENTIFIABLE ASSETS		CAPITAL EXPENDITURES		PROVISION FOR DEPRECIATION AND AMORTIZATION	
	1988	1987	1988	1987	1988	1987	1988	1987	1988	1987
Aerospace	$ 3,971	$ 5,073	$ 492.6	$ 700.0	$1,646	$1,385	$105.9	$118.7	$114.2	$ 63.1
Electronics	4,522	4,342	377.9	367.0	3,843	3,810	319.0	315.6	231.9	211.5
Automotive	2,154	1,716	182.9	163.7	1,340	1,228	91.1	81.1	102.8	84.9
General Industries	1,299	992	144.3	111.6	726	691	39.1	36.4	73.5	71.0
Total	$11,946	$12,123	$1,197.7	$1,342.3	$7,555	$7,114	$555.1	$551.8	$522.4	$430.5

Cash	$ 60,000	Accounts payable	$ 50,000
Accounts receivable	90,000	Long-term debt	150,000
Inventories	150,000	Stockholders' equity	300,000
Property and equipment, net	200,000	Total liabilities and	
Total assets	$500,000	stockholders' equity	$500,000

The fair market values equal the book values for all items except for property and equipment, which has a fair market value of $250,000.

Required: Prepare a consolidated balance sheet for January 31, 1989, that combines the items from the House of Fabrics annual report with the newly purchased items. Assume that House of Fabrics had no sales to or purchases from the Minneapolis store before the acquisition. Use one line for all property, and do not include any details of that section on the balance sheet.

CHAPTER 13

Income Taxes, Including Interperiod Allocation

LEARNING
OBJECTIVES

After studying this chapter, you should be able to

1. Distinguish between tax credits and tax deductions
2. Demonstrate how the accounting for deferred income taxes affects the balance sheet and the measurement of net income
3. Explain why interperiod tax allocation has become generally accepted accounting
4. Contrast the financial statement effects of the two methods of accounting for tax credits associated with investments in business property: flow-through and deferral (Appendix 13A)
5. Distinguish between temporary differences and permanent differences in reporting revenues and expenses to stockholders and tax authorities (Appendix 13B)
6. Explain how operating losses are carried back and forward (Appendix 13B)
7. Compare and explain the major accounting and income tax distinctions between corporations, proprietorships, and partnerships (Appendix 13C)

The income tax is pervasive. Hence it has frequently been discussed in conjunction with various topics in preceding chapters. Obviously, an introductory book on financial accounting can only touch on some aspects of this huge, complex subject. Still, the subject of income taxes provides an excellent opportunity for reviewing financial statements as a whole.

Income tax returns filed with the Internal Revenue Service frequently differ from financial reports to shareholders and others. This chapter focuses on why these differences arise and how they are reconciled. The study of these differences accomplishes at least two important purposes. First, knowledge is gained about how to account for a prominent expense, income taxes. Second, understanding is enriched about fundamental ideas underlying the accrual accounting method in its entirety.

There are also three chapter appendixes. Appendix 13A discusses accounting for investment tax credits. Appendix 13B explores some income tax topics in more depth, including temporary differences, permanent differences, and operating losses. Appendix 13C describes differences between forms of business organization, emphasizing income tax aspects.

AN OVERVIEW OF INCOME TAXES

Throughout your study, remember that the income tax laws are designed as an arm of the fiscal policies of a government. For example, special tax incentives are created or changed to spur or discourage business investments and employment. Thus the taxable income reported on the income tax form may not necessarily coincide with the pretax income reported to shareholders and others.

Also remember that intelligent managers try to pay the least amount of income taxes at the latest possible time permitted within the law. This "least-latest" strategy often leads to situations where the accounting allowed in the income tax returns may not be acceptable in reports to others. For example, tax laws in some countries permit the entire cost of equipment to be deducted as an expense during the year of acquisition. However, for shareholder reporting, the accrual accounting method is required, which means that the equipment cost must be matched with the revenues generated by its use. This requires the equipment to be depreciated over its useful life.

The bulk of federal government revenue comes from income taxes collected from two types of taxpayers: individuals and corporations. In addition, all taxpayers are subject to a variety of other taxes, including state income and sales taxes, social security taxes (which are based on income), and local property taxes. We concentrate here on income taxes. Corporations pay graduated rates up to 34% of their pretax income to the federal government. However, to simplify our illustrations, we assume that a flat (nongraduated) tax rate applies. Many states also levy an income tax, the amount of which varies from state to state. Therefore the total income tax rate for many corporations is above the 34% federal rate.

TAX CREDITS AND TAX DEDUCTIONS

Income tax rates obviously affect a corporation's total tax bill. Moreover, laws affect a company's taxes by (a) permitting *deductions* of expenses and (b) granting *tax credits*.

Deductible items (or *tax deductions*) are expenses that can be subtracted from revenues to determine taxable income. Income taxes are determined by multiplying taxable income by the applicable tax rate. Most company expenses are *deductible*, although a few, such as amortization of goodwill, are not. Some expenses, such as business meals, are only partially deductible.

Tax laws also specify *when* an item should be deducted. For example, everyone agrees that the cost of equipment is deductible. However, there is considerable controversy over *when* the cost should be deducted. Companies prefer to have the deduction (and the related tax saving) sooner; the Internal Revenue Service (IRS) prefers to delay the deduction to speed up the collection of taxes.

Tax credits differ from deductible items; **tax credits** are direct reductions of the income tax itself. For instance, at a 40% tax rate, the tax effect of a $15,000 deductible expense would be a tax savings of only .40 × $15,000 = $6,000. In contrast, the tax effect of a $15,000 tax credit would be a tax savings of the full $15,000.

Tax credits have many forms, amounts, and labels. The government institutes new credits and removes old ones as fiscal and social policy objectives change. Tax credits are permanent reductions in taxes. They are not offset by higher taxes at a later date.

The most significant tax credit for many years was the *investment tax credit* (ITC). Since 1962, the ITC has been enacted, repealed, enacted, and repealed. The Internal Revenue Code of 1986 eliminated the ITC. However, when investment needs to be stimulated, the ITC may again be enacted.

The ITC allowed a tax credit equal to a percentage of the cost of business property (notably machinery and equipment) when it was placed in service. The percentage and other details were changed periodically. For many years, investments generated a tax credit equal to 10% of the cost of the depreciable assets. In addition, the total cost of the assets was *deductible* as depreciation expense. For example, when AT&T invested $1 million in switching equipment in a year with a 10% ITC, its taxes were decreased immediately by a tax credit of $100,000. Moreover, the full $1 million was deductible across the years as depreciation expense. (In some years, the tax law required the depreciable amount to be slightly reduced if the full investment tax credit was taken.) Accounting for investment tax credits is discussed in Appendix 13A.

Congress enacted the investment tax credit to encourage businesses to invest in property such as machinery and equipment. To encourage research and development, Congress created a *credit for increased research expenditures*. It provides a tax credit equal to 20% of the amount by which qualified research expenditures exceed the average research expenses for the past three years. For example, Upjohn Company, the pharmaceutical firm, spent an average of $318 million for research in 1985–87. Assume that all the company's research expenses qualify for the tax credit. The 1988 expense of $380 million created a tax credit of 20% × ($380 million − $318 million) = $12.4 million. The $12.4 million was deducted directly from Upjohn's 1988 tax bill.

Other recent tax credits have encouraged low-income housing, jobs for individuals in certain target groups (such as the handicapped), and use of alcohol fuels. Each credit is directed toward a specific social goal. The credit is kept only long enough to accomplish the goal. Therefore most tax credits have termination dates. For example, the alcohol fuels credit is available only until January 1, 1993, unless Congress passes a new law extending it.

MODIFIED ACCELERATED COST RECOVERY SYSTEM (MACRS)

We now shift our attention from *tax credits* to *tax deductions*, specifically deductions for depreciation. Depreciation for tax purposes is generally based on the **Modified Accelerated Cost Recovery System (MACRS)**. Depreciation deductions depend on arbitrary "recovery" periods instead of useful lives. As Exhibit 13–1 shows, property is classified by the number of years over which the acquisition cost is to be recovered through deductions. Estimates of future residual values are not required under MACRS. The entire acquisition cost is expensed over the recovery period.

The Internal Revenue Code specifies that three-, five-, seven-, and ten-year assets be depreciated using a double-declining-balance method (which is described on pages 323–324), switching to straight-line at a time that maximizes the depreciation allowance. A 150%-declining-balance method applies to fifteen- and twenty-year assets, and the straight-line method to 27.5- and 31.5-year assets. (A company can choose to use straight-line depreciation rather than the appropriate declining-balance method for any asset.)

EXHIBIT 13–1

Examples of Classifications in Modified Accelerated Cost
Recovery System (MACRS)

CLASS	EXAMPLES OF TYPES OF ASSETS
3-year	Special tools for several specific industries; tractor units for over-the-road.
5-year	Automobiles; trucks; research equipment; computers; airplanes; machinery and equipment in selected industries.
7-year	Office furniture; railroad track; machinery and equipment in a majority of industries.
10-year	Water transportation equipment (vessels, tugs, barges); machinery and equipment in selected industries.
15-year	Most land improvements; machinery and equipment in selected industries.
20-year	Farm buildings; electricity distribution (poles, cables, etc.); most electricity generation equipment.
27.5-year	Residential rental property.
31.5-year	Most nonresidential real property.

EXHIBIT 13–2

Examples of MACRS Depreciation
Percentages*

YEAR	3-YEAR PROPERTY	5-YEAR PROPERTY	7-YEAR PROPERTY
1	33%	20%	14%
2	45	32	24
3	15	19	18
4	7	12	13
5		12	9
6		5	9
7			9
8			4

* Rounded. For simplicity, these rounded percentages
will be used in the examples in this chapter.

The *half-year convention* should be used with the declining-balance methods. This calls for a half year of depreciation in the year an asset is acquired, regardless of the month of purchase. There is also a half year of depreciation in the year an asset is sold or retired from service.

The MACRS depreciation schedules for three-, five-, and seven-year assets are shown in Exhibit 13–2. For example, if an asset in the five-year property class is acquired any time in 1990 at a cost of $1,000, the 1990 depreciation deduction would be $200 (or 20% × $1,000). In 1991 the deduction would be 32% × $1,000, or $320. Notice that the schedule for a five-year asset extends into a sixth year because of the half-year convention.

The MACRS method provides *accelerated* depreciation by (a) using depreciation periods shorter than useful lives and (b) assigning higher depreciation percentages in the earlier years. Compare MACRS with straight-line and sum-of-the-year's-digits schedules. Suppose General Motors bought special tooling for the manufacture of Buicks. The acquisition cost was $100 million, the useful life was five years, and there was no residual value. This is a three-year asset for MACRS purposes. Depreciation under the three methods is the following (in millions):

YEAR	STRAIGHT-LINE	SUM-OF-THE-YEARS'-DIGITS	MACRS*
1	$ 20	$ 33.3	$ 33
2	20	26.7	45
3	20	20.0	15
4	20	13.3	7
5	20	6.7	
Total	$100	$100	

* Uses the rounded percentages as listed in Exhibit 13–2: 33% × 100 = $33;
45% × 100 = $45, etc.

Note that the total depreciation under all three methods is $100 million. The only difference is the *timing* of the depreciation.

In sum, for many assets, MACRS accelerates depreciation even faster than the sum-of-the-years'-digits method. Why? Because the recovery periods are shorter than useful lives.

DEFERRED FEDERAL INCOME TAXES

Most corporations try to take advantage of all the ways offered by governments to minimize immediate income tax disbursements. Hence MACRS depreciation methods are employed for reporting to the income tax authorities even though straight-line depreciation may be used for reporting to others. This section explores the meaning of the "deferred" income taxes that are engendered by using different measures of depreciation (and several other items) for tax purposes than are used for other purposes.

☐ A Matter of Timing

Accelerated methods of depreciation allow companies an opportunity to postpone disbursements for income taxes. Income tax payments are lower in the early years of the useful life of the asset and higher in the later years than they would be if straight-line depreciation were used for both tax and shareholder reporting purposes.

Differences in the timing of depreciation create what the FASB calls temporary differences. A **temporary difference** arises whenever the book value of an asset for shareholder reporting differs from the book value for tax reporting. Consider the $100 million asset from the preceding section. Assume that it is depreciated using MACRS for tax purposes and straight-line for shareholder reporting (in millions):

	SHAREHOLDER REPORTING			TAX REPORTING		
	Beginning Book Value	Depreciation Expense	Ending Book Value	Beginning Book Value	Depreciation Expense	Ending Book Value
Year 1	$100	$20	$80	$100	$33	$67
Year 2	80	20	60	67	45	22
Year 3	60	20	40	22	15	7
Year 4	40	20	20	7	7	0
Year 5	20	20	0	0	0	0

Examine the situation at the end of Year 2. Under shareholder reporting, the book value is $60 million, meaning that $40 million of depreciation expense has been charged and $60 million remains to be charged. For tax reporting, the book value is $22 million; $78 million of depreciation expense has been charged and $22 million remains. The difference in book values is a result of the different timing of depreciation expense. It is a *temporary* difference because higher depreciation in the early years for tax purposes will be offset by higher depreciation in later years for shareholder reporting. At the end of Year 5, both methods have charged $100 million of depreciation and have a zero book value.

Reporting Temporary Differences

How should these temporary differences affect shareholder reporting? After all, our main concern is with the reports to shareholders. An elaboration of our example should clarify the issues. Suppose B Company is begun on January 1, 19X1, with initial paid-in capital of $200 million cash. On January 2, 19X1, the company purchases a three-year MACRS asset for $100 million cash. The estimated useful life is five years, and the estimated residual value is zero. Although MACRS depreciation is used for tax reporting, the straight-line method is used for shareholder reporting purposes. Prospective annual income before depreciation and income taxes is $45 million. The income tax rate is 40% and is not expected to change over the life of the asset. Assume that all taxes are paid early in the next year after the income is earned.

Compare the MACRS depreciation used for tax purposes with the straight-line depreciation used for shareholder reporting (in millions):

	19X1	19X2	19X3	19X4	19X5	Total
MACRS depreciation*	$33	$45	$ 15	$ 7	$ 0	$100
Straight-line depreciation	20	20	20	20	20	100
Difference	$13	$25	$(5)	$(13)	$(20)	$ 0

* See Exhibit 13–2, page 588: 33% × $100 million = $33 million; 45% × $100 million = $45 million; etc.

Both methods charge $100 million of depreciation, but the *timing* of the charges differs.

Consider 19X1. The income tax return would show:[1]

Income before depreciation	$45,000,000
MACRS depreciation, 33% × $100,000,000	33,000,000
Taxable income	$12,000,000
Income tax to be paid:	
.40 × $12,000,000, or	$ 4,800,000

Now examine Exhibit 13–3, which shows the company's transactions as they would be prepared *for shareholder reporting*. Stop for a moment after transaction *d*. If straight-line depreciation is used for shareholder reporting purposes, should *income tax expense* be based on MACRS cost recovery or straight-line depreciation?

---

[1] Exhibits 13–3, 13–4, and 13–5 use MACRS percentages in effect for 1990. If the percentages change for later years, the specific numbers will be different but the general relationships will be the same.

EXHIBIT 13–3

Analysis of Transactions
for Shareholder Reporting
(in millions of dollars)

	A	=	L		+	SE	
			Income Tax	Deferred Tax		Paid-in	Retained
	Cash	Equipment	Payable	Liability		Capital	Income
a. Formation	+200		=			+200	
b. Acquisition of equipment	−100	+100	=				
c. Income before depreciation and taxes	+ 45		=				+45
d. Straight-line depreciation		− 20	=				−20
e1. Income tax expense—no deferral			=	+4.8			− 4.8
Bal. Dec. 31, 19X1, after e1	+145	+ 80	=	+4.8		+200	+20.2
e2. Income tax expense—deferral			=	+4.8	+5.2		−10
Bal. Dec. 31, 19X1, after e2 rather than e1	+145	+ 80	=	+4.8	+5.2	+200	+15

Notes:
e1. The 4.8 represents income taxes payable as calculated when using MACRS on the income tax return: $.40 \times 12$ taxable income = 4.8.
e2. The 10 represents the income tax that would be payable if straight-line depreciation had been used on the income tax return. Taxable income would be $45 - 20 = 25$; income tax expense would be $.40 \times 25 = 10$. The deferred income tax is $10 - 4.8 = 5.2$.

With *no deferral*, the income tax expense would be the amount of taxes actually payable to the government for the year, that is, taxes based on MACRS. With *deferral*, income tax expense is the amount of income taxes that would be payable if straight-line depreciation had been used for tax purposes.

Entry *e1* in Exhibit 13–3 shows what would happen if no deferral occurred. Many accountants believe that the income tax expense on the income statement to shareholders should be the actual amount paid or payable to the government for the year in question—no more, no less. Of course, this approach would show reported net income of $20.2 million, a happy combination based on *straight-line* depreciation and on tax payments geared to MACRS cost recovery. On the other hand, entry *e2* in Exhibit 13–3 shows the effects if deferral is recognized. (Computations for *e2* are in the footnotes to Exhibit 13–3.) Note that the income tax expense is now $10 million and net income is only $15 million. The $5.2 million balance in the Deferred Tax Liability at the end of the first year represents extra taxes that would have to be paid if straight-line depreciation were used in the tax returns as opposed to MACRS cost recovery.

Another summary of this illustration appears in Exhibit 13–4. The first column of the exhibit shows reporting of income to the government, which has already been discussed. The second column shows how reporting to shareholders would appear if no deferral were recognized. However, accountants have banned the no-deferral method in favor of the deferral method shown in entry *e2* in Exhibit 13–3 and in the third column of Exhibit 13–4.

EXHIBIT 13–4

Comparison of Reporting of Income

	YEAR 1* REPORTING		
	To Income Tax Authorities	No Deferral (Banned)	Deferral (Required)
Income before depreciation and income taxes	$45,000,000	$45,000,000	$45,000,000
Depreciation:			
MACRS cost recovery	33,000,000		
Straight-line		20,000,000	20,000,000
Pretax income	$12,000,000	$25,000,000	$25,000,000
Income tax expense:			
Paid or payable almost immediately	$ 4,800,000	$ 4,800,000	$ 4,800,000
Deferred	—	—	5,200,000†
Total income tax expense	$ 4,800,000	$ 4,800,000	$10,000,000‡
Net income	$ 7,200,000	$20,200,000	$15,000,000

* These comparisons are also displayed as part of Exhibit 13–5.

† The $5,200,000 deferred tax is the difference between the $10,000,000 total income tax expense and the $4,800,000 tax paid or payable almost immediately.

‡ Total income tax expense is 40% of the $25,000,000 income before income taxes, or $10,000,000.

☐ Interperiod Tax Allocation

Before considering the relative merits of deferral and no deferral, study all parts of Exhibit 13–5. This exhibit provides a comparison for five years. The first part is a tabulation of the reports made to the IRS on income tax returns. The second part shows reports made to shareholders. It displays, in turn, for five years (a) the banned no-deferral method and (b) the required deferral method.

Note in all the tabulations how the cumulative income tax paid is $50 million and the cumulative net income is $75 million. Furthermore, the comparison of tabulations *1* and *2a* clearly demonstrates how the favorable effect of lower taxes and higher net income in earlier years is offset by higher taxes and lower net income in later years. The FASB emphasized that temporary differences originate in one period and reverse, or "turn around," in one or more subsequent periods, as Exhibit 13–5 demonstrates.

As tabulation *2b* in Exhibit 13–5 shows, the FASB favored *deferral*, which in this context is also called **interperiod tax allocation**, or simply **tax allocation**. Method *2b* demonstrates that the effect for a particular asset would be to regard any reported income as if it were subject to the full current tax rate even though a more advantageous depreciation method were used for tax purposes. As Exhibit 13–5 shows, this results in a *smoothing effect* on income in these particular circumstances when the year-by-year effects are viewed over the five-year span.

In Years 1 and 2, the deferred tax liability builds. Income taxes paid are less than the income tax expense. In essence, the company pays only part of its income tax expense and recognizes an obligation to pay the remainder in later

EXHIBIT 13–5 (Place a clip on this page for easy reference.)

Comparison of Alternative Reporting Practices for Depreciation and Income Taxes
Facts: Purchase asset for $100 million; five-year life; 40% tax rate. Company uses MACRS for tax purposes but straight-line depreciation for financial reporting purposes.

1. REPORTING ON INCOME TAX RETURNS

YEAR	INCOME BEFORE DEPRECIATION AND TAXES	MACRS COST RECOVERY	TAXABLE INCOME	INCOME TAX PAID* @40%	NET INCOME
1	$ 45	.33 × $100 = $ 33	$ 12	$ 4.8	$ 7.2
2	45	.45 × $100 = 45	0	0.0	0.0
3	45	.15 × $100 = 15	30	12.0	18.0
4	45	.07 × $100 = 7	38	15.2	22.8
5	45		45	18.0	27.0
Cumulative	$225	$100	$125	$50.0	$75.0

2. REPORTING TO SHAREHOLDERS
a. Straight-line Depreciation and No Tax Deferral (Banned)

YEAR	INCOME BEFORE DEPRECIATION AND TAXES	STRAIGHT-LINE DEPRE-CIATION	PRETAX INCOME	INCOME TAX EXPENSE	NET INCOME	BALANCE SHEET EFFECT: DEFERRED TAX LIABILITY
1	$ 45	$ 20	$ 25	$ 4.8	$20.2	—
2	45	20	25	0.0	25.0	—
3	45	20	25	12.0	13.0	—
4	45	20	25	15.2	9.8	—
5	45	20	25	18.0	7.0	—
Cumulative	$225	$100	$125	$50.0	$75.0	—

b. Straight-Line Depreciation and Tax Deferral (Required)

YEAR	INCOME BEFORE DEPRECIATION AND TAXES	STRAIGHT-LINE DEPRE-CIATION	PRETAX INCOME	INCOME TAX EXPENSE Tax Paid	INCOME TAX EXPENSE Tax Deferred	INCOME TAX EXPENSE Total Tax Expense	NET INCOME	BALANCE SHEET EFFECT: DEFERRED TAX LIABILITY†
1	$ 45	$ 20	$ 25	$ 4.8	$ 5.2	$10	$15	$ 5.2
2	45	20	25	0.0	10.0	10	15	15.2
3	45	20	25	12.0	−2.0	10	15	13.2
4	45	20	25	15.2	−5.2	10	15	8.0
5	45	20	25	18.0	−8.0	10	15	0
Cumulative	$225	$100	$125	$50.0	0	$50	$75	—

* Or payable on that year's income.

† This would ordinarily appear in the liability section of the balance sheet as a separate item just above the shareholders' equity section.

years. In Years 3, 4, and 5 the company pays more income taxes than it charges as income tax expense. It is paying the taxes deferred from Years 1 and 2 in addition to the income tax expense incurred in Years 3, 4, and 5. This can be summarized as follows (in millions):

	INCOME TAX EXPENSE ON SHAREHOLDER REPORTS	INCOME TAX PAYMENT	INCOME TAX EXPENSE DEFERRED TO LATER YEARS*	PAYMENT OF INCOME TAX EXPENSE THAT WAS DEFERRED IN EARLIER YEARS†
	(1)	(2)	(3)	(4)
19X1	$10	$ 4.8	$ 5.2	—
19X2	10	0.0	10.0	—
19X3	10	12.8	—	$2.0
19X4	10	15.2	—	5.2
19X5	10	18.0	—	8.0

* (1) − (2) when (1) is greater than (2).

† (2) − (1) when (2) is greater than (1).

In Years 1 and 2, the total income tax expense on reports to shareholders is $20 million, but only $4.8 million is paid to the government. The other $15.2 million will be paid in Years 3, 4, and 5; therefore there is a liability of $15.2 million at the end of Year 2. The total income tax expense on shareholder reports in Years 3, 4, and 5 is $30 million, but $45.2 million ($12.0 million + $15.2 million + $18.0 million) is paid to the government. The extra $15.2 million is payment for the $15.2 million deferred in Years 1 and 2.

Another approach to computing the deferred tax liability is to focus directly on the difference between depreciation for tax and shareholder reporting. Exhibit 13–6 shows that in Year 1, tax depreciation exceeds shareholder depreciation by $13 million. Therefore taxable income on tax statements is $13 million less than pretax income on shareholder reports. Consequently, taxes paid (or payable) are .4 × $13 million = $5.2 million less than the taxes that would be due on the pretax income. Some time in the future the depreciation difference will reverse, and the $5.2 million of taxes will have to be paid. Therefore a deferred tax liability of $5.2 million is created. In Year 2, MACRS depreciation exceeds straight-line depreciation by $25 million. Therefore the taxes paid (or payable) are $10.0 million less than the taxes that would be due on the pretax income reported to shareholders, causing $10.0 million to be added to the deferred tax liability. In Years 3, 4, and 5, straight-line depreciation exceeds MACRS depreciation. Therefore the taxes paid (or payable) exceed the taxes on pretax income for shareholders,

EXHIBIT 13–6

Deferred Taxes Based Directly on Depreciation Differences
(in millions)

	STRAIGHT-LINE DEPRECIATION	MACRS DEPRECIATION	DIFFERENCE IN DEPRECIATION EXPENSE	TAX EFFECT @ 40%	DEFERRED TAX LIABILITY
Year 1	$20	$33	$ 13	$ 5.2	$ 5.2
Year 2	20	45	25	10.0	15.2
Year 3	20	15	(5)	(2.0)	13.2
Year 4	20	7	(13)	(5.2)	8.0
Year 5	20	0	(20)	(8.0)	0

EXHIBIT 13-7

Entries for Deferred Taxes

BALANCE SHEET EQUATION:				
A	=	L	+	SE
Cash	=	Deferred Tax Liability		+ Retained Income

19X1	−4.8 =	5.2	⎡ Increase	⎤	−10
19X2	0 =	10.0	⎣ Deferred Taxes ⎦		−10 ⎡ Income ⎤
19X3	−12.0 =	−2.0	⎡ Decrease ⎤		−10 ⎪ Tax ⎪
19X4	−15.2 =	−5.2	⎪ Deferred ⎪		−10 ⎣ Expense ⎦
19X5	−18.0 =	−8.0	⎣ Taxes ⎦		−10

JOURNAL ENTRIES (without explanations):

19X1	Income tax expense	10,000,000	
	Deferred tax liability		5,200,000
	Cash (or income taxes payable)		4,800,000
19X2	Income tax expense	10,000,000	
	Deferred tax liability		10,000,000
19X3	Income tax expense	10,000,000	
	Deferred tax liability	2,000,000	
	Cash (or income taxes payable)		12,000,000
19X4	Income tax expense	10,000,000	
	Deferred tax liability	5,200,000	
	Cash (or income taxes payable)		15,200,000
19X5	Income tax expense	10,000,000	
	Deferred tax liability	8,000,000	
	Cash (or income taxes payable)		18,000,000

so the deferred tax liability is reduced each year. By the end of Year 5, there is no remaining deferred tax liability.

Journal entries and the balance sheet equation for the income tax items in our example are shown in Exhibit 13–7.

Proponents of allocation maintain that the deferral method is necessary under the accrual method of accounting.[2] They believe that failure to allocate is tantamount to retrogressing to a cash basis of accounting. Therefore deferred income taxes should be recognized as a legitimate claim on the assets of the enterprise; the deferral is an obligation to the government that arises because the firm elects to postpone some income tax payments from the present to some future date.

☐ Growth of Deferred Taxes

For growing companies, deferred tax liability accounts are likely to accumulate to enormous amounts that will never diminish unless the company discontinues the replacement of old facilities used in its operations. For example, in Exhibit

---

[2] Many observers who maintain that deferred taxes are liabilities rightly state that the deferral should be measured by estimating the discounted present value of future payments. See Chapter 9, pages 401–403, for an explanation of discounted present value.

13–5, if the company spent $100 million each year for more plant assets, the additional deferrals in each of these years would more than offset the decline in deferrals in Years 3, 4, and 5 associated with the original $100 million outlay. Exhibit 13–8 summarizes this point.

The objectors to the deferral method point out that tax-allocation procedures should not apply to the recurring differences between taxable income and pretax accounting income in Exhibit 13–8 if there is a relatively stable or growing investment in depreciable assets. This results in an indefinite postponement of the additional tax, a mounting deferred tax liability account that may never be reduced, and a consequent understatement of net income. Note from Year 6 in Exhibit 13–8 that the deferred tax liability will never decline unless the company fails to maintain its $100 million annual expenditure each year.

The proponents of deferral reject the growing-firm argument as fallacious. The ever-increasing deferred tax liability is an example of a typical characteristic of growing companies that is also reflected in many other accounts. For example, accounts payable and liabilities for product warranties may also grow, but that is not justification for assuming that liabilties for these obligations are unnecessary.

EXHIBIT 13–8

Analysis of Growing Firm and Deferred Income Taxes
Facts: Same as in Exhibit 13–5 except that $100 million is spent each year for additional assets and income increases $45 million each year until leveling off in Year 6. In Year 6, the $100 million represents a replacement of the asset originally purchased in Year 1.

REPORTING FOR TAX PURPOSES

YEAR	INCOME BEFORE DEPRECIATION AND TAXES	MACRS COST RECOVERY	TAXABLE INCOME	INCOME TAX PAID	NET INCOME
1	$ 45	$33	$ 12	$ 4.8	$ 7.2
2	90	45 + 33 = 78	12	4.8	7.2
3	135	15 + 45 + 33 = 93	42	16.8	25.2
4	180	7 + 15 + 45 + 33 = 100	80	32.0	48.0
5	225	7 + 15 + 45 + 33 = 100	125	50.0	75.0
6	225	7 + 15 + 45 + 33 = 100	125	50.0	75.0

REPORTING TO SHAREHOLDERS
Straight-Line Depreciation and Tax Allocation

YEAR	INCOME BEFORE DEPRECIATION AND TAXES	STRAIGHT-LINE DEPRECIATION	PRETAX INCOME	INCOME TAX EXPENSE Tax Paid	INCOME TAX EXPENSE Tax Deferred	INCOME TAX EXPENSE Total Tax Expense	NET INCOME	BALANCE SHEET EFFECT: DEFERRED TAX LIABILITY
1	$ 45	$ 20	$ 25	$ 4.8	$ 5.2	$10	$15	$ 5.2
2	90	40	50	4.8	15.2	20	30	20.4
3	135	60	75	16.8	13.2	30	45	33.6
4	180	80	100	32.0	8.0	40	60	41.6
5	225	100	125	50.0	—	50	75	41.6
6	225	100	125	50.0	—	50	75	41.6

Whatever your reactions to these conflicting arguments, the FASB's accounting *requirements* are clear. Income tax expense on the income statement for shareholders is based on the revenue and expenses on that statement, not those on the tax statement. Therefore income tax expense seldom equals the taxes payable to the government for any given period. Deferred tax liabilities are found on the balance sheets of nearly every company.

WHY BOTHER WITH INTERPERIOD TAX ALLOCATION?

Many students, managers, and accountants are bewildered by the subject of deferred income taxes. Their general attitude can be described as a "cash-basis" attitude: "Why get complicated? Why don't we simply show as income tax expense and as income tax liability the actual amount payable in cash as computed on the company's income tax return?" The accounting regulators have rejected the cash-basis approach in favor of an "accrual-basis" approach. An extreme illustration may clarify why the concept of deferred income taxes is generally accepted. Until recently, companies in England were permitted to buy specified equipment and deduct its entire cost on their current income tax returns. Suppose an English company paid £10 million for equipment in early 19X0. (The British unit of currency is the pound, £.) The equipment has an expected useful life of ten years and no residual value. Compare the approaches if pretax income were £30 million before considering depreciation effects. Assume that the income tax rate is 60%:

	STOCKHOLDER REPORTING	
	"Cash Basis"	"Accrual Basis"
(In millions of British pounds)		
Income accounts for 19X0		
Pretax income before depreciation	30.0	30.0
Depreciation	10.0	1.0*
Pretax income	20.0	29.0
Income tax expense:		
Currently payable portion	12.0	12.0
Deferred portion	—	5.4
Total income tax expense	12.0	17.4†
Net income	8.0	11.6
Balance sheet accounts at end of 19X0:		
Assets:		
Equipment, net	0	9.0
Liabilities:		
Income tax payable	12.0	12.0
Deferred tax liability	—	5.4
Retained income (increase due to net income)	8.0	11.6

* Straight-line depreciation = £10 million ÷ 10 years = £1 million per year.
† .60 × 29 million = 17.4 million; 17.4 million less 12 million currently payable is the 5.4 million deferred portion.

EXHIBIT 13–9

NYNEX

The components of income tax expense are as follows:

(IN MILLIONS)	1988	1987
Federal:		
Current	$428.3	$618.6
Deferred—net	(18.4)	70.3
Deferred tax credits—net	(75.6)	(93.9)
	334.3	595.0
State and local:		
Current	10.3	66.1
Deferred—net	24.9	10.8
	35.2	76.9
Foreign	3.7	6.3
Total	$373.2	$678.2

Those who favor deferral essentially maintain that the underlying economic impact of taxes is measured more accurately via interperiod tax allocation. Unless tax allocation occurs, income, assets, and liabilities will be misstated. The most obvious faulty measurement is to show zero value for a one-year-old asset with a remaining useful life of nine years.

CLASSIFICATION ON FINANCIAL STATEMENTS

Most companies list only one line labeled "income taxes," or "provision for income taxes," on their income statements. They provide details about deferred taxes in a footnote. NYNEX, the telephone utility, is such a company. Its footnotes include the data shown in Exhibit 13–9. Deferred taxes are listed by the source of the deferrals.

Note that NYNEX uses the deferral method for its investment tax credits. (This method is explained in Appendix 13A.) Although the 1986 tax law repealed the investment tax credit, amortization of previously deferred credits will continue.

A few companies, such as La-Z-Boy Chair Company, list details on the face of the income statement:

Income before income taxes		$38,687,000
Provision for income taxes:		
Federal—current	$9,201,000	
—deferred	6,508,000	
State	1,619,000	
Total		17,328,000
Net income for the year		$21,359,000

A company's balance sheet should list the current portion of deferred taxes separately from the long-term portion. The balance sheet for NYNEX includes the following lines:

[listed with other current liabilities]	
Deferred tax liability	$126,400,000
[listed with long-term liabilities]	
Unamortized investment tax credits	$736,100,000
Deferred tax liability	$1,829,400,000

SUMMARY

Tax credits are granted by the federal government for various purposes. Such credits are direct reductions of the income tax itself. In contrast, deductible items reduce taxable income.

Deferred tax liabilities arise when the straight-line method of depreciation is used for shareholder reporting purposes and accelerated depreciation is used for income-tax reporting purposes. Deferral of income taxes is also often called interperiod tax allocation. Deferral is caused by other items besides depreciation. See Appendix 13B for additional discussion.

SUMMARY PROBLEMS FOR YOUR REVIEW

☐ Problem One

Kitsap Company bought a special-purpose tool for $200,000. The tool has a five-year economic life, is a three-year MACRS asset, and has no residual value. Kitsap uses straight-line depreciation in reports to shareholders and MACRS for tax purposes. The tax rate is 34%. For Years 1 through 5, compute the depreciation for tax purposes, the depreciation for shareholder reporting, and the deferred tax liability at the end of each year.

☐ Solution to Problem One

The format of Exhibit 13–6 on page 594 is helpful. Tax depreciation is in column (2), depreciation for shareholder reporting is in column (1), and the deferred tax liability is in column (5):

	(1) Straight-Line Depreciation	(2) MACRS Depreciation	(3) Difference in Depreciation Expense	(4) Tax Effect @34%	(5) Deferred Tax Liability
Year 1	$40,000	$66,000	$ 26,000	$ 8,840	$ 8,840
Year 2	$40,000	90,000	50,000	17,000	25,840
Year 3	$40,000	30,000	(10,000)	(3,400)	22,440
Year 4	$40,000	14,000	(26,000)	(8,840)	13,600
Year 5	$40,000	0	(40,000)	(13,600)	0

Examine Exhibit 13–8 on page 596. Suppose that $200 million was spent in Year 7 on additional three-year MACRS class assets with five-year useful lives and that income before depreciation and taxes reached $270 million. For Year 7, fill in all the columns in Exhibit 13–8.

□ **Solution to Problem Two**

For income tax authorities (in millions):

YEAR	INCOME BEFORE DEPRECIATION AND TAXES	MACRS COST RECOVERY	TAXABLE INCOME	INCOME TAX PAID	NET INCOME
7	$270	$7 + 15 + 45 + 66* = $133	$137	$54.8	$82.2

* .33 × 200 million = $66 million.

For shareholders (in millions):

YEAR	INCOME BEFORE DEPRECIATION AND TAXES	STRAIGHT-LINE DEPRECIATION	PRETAX INCOME	INCOME TAX EXPENSE Paid	INCOME TAX EXPENSE Deferred	INCOME TAX EXPENSE Total	NET INCOME	BALANCE SHEET EFFECT: DEFERRED TAX LIABILITY
7	$270	$120	$150	$54.8	$5.2	$60	$90	$46.8

Computations: 25 + 25 + 25 + 25 + 50 = 150; .40 × 150 = 60; 60 − 54.8 = 5.2; 41.6 + 5.2 = 46.8

HIGHLIGHTS TO REMEMBER

1. Income tax laws change frequently. Therefore beginners in accounting should not be overly concerned with the specific tax rates or deductions applicable to a particular year. Instead they should concentrate on how the general provisions of income tax laws affect reporting (a) to the government and (b) to the shareholders. Frequently, there are conflicts in reporting requirements between *a* and *b*.

2. Taxation is not a simple subject, nor is the reporting to shareholders by most corporations. In combination, the complexities multiply rapidly. In such circumstances, students should be especially concerned with the forest rather than the trees. For example, deferred tax liability accounts are creatures of reporting to shareholders; there are no deferred tax liability accounts when reporting to income tax authorities.

3. *Accelerated depreciation* is any depreciation method that writes off depreciable costs more quickly than the typical straight-line method. Acceleration takes various forms. The Modified Accelerated Cost Recovery System (MACRS) achieves acceleration primarily by shortening the lives of the write-off for depreciation and secondarily by writing off more cost in the early years of the recovery period than in the later years.

ACCOUNTING VOCABULARY

Deductible Items, p. 586
Deferral Method for ITC, 601
Flow-Through Method, 601
Interperiod Tax Allocation, 592
Modified Accelerated Cost
   Recovery System (MACRS), 587

Permanent Differences, 605
Tax Allocation, 592
Tax Credit, 586
Temporary Difference, 589

APPENDIX 13A: ACCOUNTING FOR INVESTMENT TAX CREDITS

For many years, the largest tax credit available to corporations was the investment tax credit (ITC). Although Congress eliminated the ITC for investments made after 1985, the ITC will probably be reenacted when Congress again wants to stimulate business investment. Furthermore, many companies that used the deferral method (to be explained shortly) still show deferred investment tax credit liabilities on their balance sheets. Why? Because the tax credit was spread over the lives of the related assets, and many of the assets have not yet reached the end of their lives. For example, consider NYNEX, the company that provides telephone services to the northeastern United States. On January 1, 1989, the unamortized investment tax credits were over $736 million. Amortization of these credits was averaging about $100 million each year.

☐ Illustration of Financial Reporting Methods

The cost of equipment that generated an ITC must be spread over future years as depreciation expense. The tax saving from the associated ITC is received in the year the investment is made. Should the financial statements for investors recognize the entire tax savings from such a tax credit as an increase in net income for the year of purchase (the **flow-through method**)? Or should the tax savings be spread over the useful life of the asset (**deferral method**)? What do you think? Both methods have been permitted, but controversy has raged on this issue for many years. In many industries (such as airlines and others that have heavy capital expenditures), the method chosen for the investment tax credit has had a material effect on reported net income. Keep in mind that the controversy concerns reports to shareholders, not reports to the income tax authorities.

To see the essence of the controversy regarding tax credits associated with investments in business property, consider the following problem:

☐   A company begins business on January 1, 19X1, with $500,000 cash raised by an issue of common stock. All of its transactions throughout 19X1 were for cash. On December 31, it had pretax income of $50,000. The income tax rate is 40%. No income taxes will be due before early 19X2. An investment in equipment of $150,000 cash was made on December 31, 19X1. The equipment has a five-year life and an expected residual value of zero.

EXHIBIT 13–10

Analysis of Transactions
(in thousands of dollars)

	A		=	L		+	SE	
	Cash	Equipment		Income Tax Payable	Deferred ITC Liability		Paid-in Capital	Retained Income
a. Formation	+500		=				+500	
b. Operations	+ 50		=					+ 50
c. Acquisition of equipment	−150	+150	=					
d. Income taxes			=	+20				− 20
Bal. Dec. 31, 19X1	+400	+150	=	+20			+500	+ 30
e1. Flow-through			=	−15				+ 15
Bal. Dec. 31, 19X1, after e1	+400	+150	=	+ 5			+500	+ 45
e2. Deferral								
Bal. Dec. 31, 19X1,			=	−15	+15			
after e2 rather than e1	+400	+150	=	+ 5	+15		+500	+ 30

Required:

1. Prepare an analysis of transactions using the A = L + SE format. Show the (a) effects of formation of the company, (b) effects of operating income on cash and retained income, (c) effects of acquisition of equipment, and (d) computation and effects of income taxes. Show the ending balances in all accounts, December 31, 19X1.

2. Suppose the company is eligible for a $15,000 tax credit because of its acquisition of equipment. Prepare an analysis of the flow-through effects. Label as e1. Also prepare an analysis of the deferral effects. Label as e2.
   Try to prepare your own solution before proceeding.

Exhibit 13–10 contains the complete analysis of transactions. Concentrate on items *a* through *d*. Note that the reporting to shareholders would show an income tax liability of $20,000 and an income tax expense of $20,000. If there is no tax credit available, the matter ends here. That is, there is basically nothing new in the analysis of transactions *a* through *d*.

☐ **Flow-Through**

The flow-through method is shown as *e1* in Exhibit 13–10. The journal entries would be:

d. Income tax expense	20,000	
Income tax payable		20,000
e1. Income tax payable	15,000	
Income tax expense		15,000

The proponents of the flow-through method claim that the entire amount of the tax credit is a selective reduction of income tax expense in the year in which taxes otherwise payable are reduced by the credit. It is not a determinant of cost of acquisition or use of the related assets. The majority of companies used this method.

Deferral

The deferral method is shown as *e2* in Exhibit 13–10. The journal entries would be:

d. Income tax expense	20,000	
Income tax payable		20,000
e2. Income tax payable	15,000	
Deferred ITC liability		15,000

Supporters of the deferral method are particularly critical of the idea that the amount spent for depreciable assets in a given year can directly affect net income; within constraints, the more the company *buys*, the more it earns. Such an implication conflicts with the generally accepted concept that net income is earned only by *using* assets to produce revenue from customers. The deferral method prevents current net income from being so significantly affected by unrelated management actions in buying depreciable assets.

Suppose 19X2 pretax income was again $50,000. However, no additional equipment is acquired. The journal entries for the deferral method would be:

d. Income tax expense	20,000	
Income tax payable		20,000
To recognize income tax owed to government.		
e2. Deferred ITC liability	3,000	
Income tax expense		3,000
Amortization for 19X2 of ITC liability $15,000 ÷ 5 years.		

EXHIBIT 13–11

Investment Tax Credit—Flow-Through and Deferral
(in thousands of dollars)

	19X1	19X2	19X3	19X4	19X5	19X6
ON STATEMENT TO TAX AUTHORITIES:						
Taxable income	$50	$50	$50	$50	$50	$50
Income taxes @ 40%	20	20	20	20	20	20
Deduct: Tax credit	15					
Income tax paid (or payable)	$ 5	$30	$30	$30	$30	$30
ON STATEMENT TO SHAREHOLDERS:						
Flow-through method:						
Pretax income	$50	$50	$50	$50	$50	$50
Deduct: Income tax expense	5	20	20	20	20	20
Net income	$45	$30	$30	$30	$30	$30
Deferral method:						
Pretax income	$50	$50	$50	$50	$50	$50
Deduct: Income tax expense	20	17	17	17	17	17
Net income	$30	$33	$33	$33	$33	$33

The amortization of the deferral spreads the $15,000 tax credit over the five years of useful life of the related equipment. (Remember that the equipment was acquired at the *end* of 19X1.) The effect will be to reduce income tax expense (by crediting the Income Tax Expense account) and hence increase reported net income by $3,000 for each of five years. Note that flow-through companies report considerably higher net income than deferral companies in the year a tax credit is granted. In contrast, deferral companies report slightly higher net income each year of the deferral period. Exhibit 13–11 summarizes flow-through and deferral methods for the five-year life of the equipment, assuming pretax income is $50,000 each year.

The advocates of deferral maintain that the amount of the tax credit is associated primarily with the use of the property qualifying for the credit. Deferral of the credit and its subsequent amortization associates the credit with the useful life of the related property. This matching is consistent with the objectives of income measurement on the accrual basis because it spreads a purchase discount over the useful life of the asset purchased.

APPENDIX 13B: TEMPORARY DIFFERENCES AND PERMANENT DIFFERENCES

This appendix covers temporary differences in more depth than in the body of the chapter. It also covers permanent differences and net operating losses.

☐ **Temporary Differences**

The body of this chapter describes how interperiod tax allocation accounts for temporary differences. Most temporary differences arise when expense or revenue items are recognized in one period for tax purposes and in another period for shareholder reporting. There are four major categories of such temporary differences:

1. *Expenses* are deducted in determining taxable income *earlier* than they are deducted in determining pretax income for shareholder-reporting purposes. The major example is accelerated depreciation. A similar example is the promotion cost that accompanies the opening of a new retail store. The cost may be deducted on the tax return, but it is deferred and amortized for financial reporting.

2. *Revenues* are included in taxable income *later* than they are included in pretax income for shareholder reporting. For instance, income tax laws sometimes permit persons who sell on installment plans to postpone some related income tax payments until the cash installments have actually been collected. Another example is the use of the percentage-of-completion method on long-term contracts for shareholder reporting together with the use of the completed contract method on some part of these contracts for income tax returns. Revenue and profits are recognized earlier under the percentage-of-completion method but are permitted to be shown later on income tax returns. Recent tax law changes have greatly limited the temporary differences arising from both installment sales and long-term contracts.

3. *Expenses* are deducted for income tax purposes *later* than they are deducted for shareholder reporting purposes. For instance, the estimated costs of product warranty contracts are not permitted to be deducted for tax purposes until the period paid or the period in which the liability becomes fixed. In contrast to the deferred income tax arising from accelerated depreciation, the deferred income tax arising from product warranty contracts is an *asset* rather than a liability. Automobile companies recognize estimated costs of product warranties as expenses when the related products are sold. However, no deductions are allowed on income tax returns until cash is disbursed to dealers as warranty service is rendered. Consider a concrete example. For simplicity, assume that a company stops offering warranty service on new sales at the start of Year 2 and that the first-year warranties are not paid in cash until the second year. The effects are (numbers assumed and in dollars):

	YEAR 1 REPORTING		YEAR 2 REPORTING	
	To Shareholders	On Income Tax Return	To Shareholders	On Income Tax Return
Income before warranty expenses	600,000	600,000	600,000	600,000
Warranty expenses estimated based on sales	100,000	—	—	100,000
Pretax income	500,000	600,000	600,000	500,000
Income tax expense @ 40%	200,000	240,000	240,000	200,000

The $40,000 difference in income taxes would be reported as a deferred tax asset.[3] Some accountants prefer to call the $40,000 a prepaid income tax.

The journal entries follow:

Year 1	Warranty expense	100,000	
	Estimated liability for warranties		100,000
	Income tax expense	200,000	
	Deferred tax asset	40,000	
	Income tax payable (or cash)		240,000
Year 2	Estimated liability for warranties	100,000	
	Cash		100,000
	Income tax expense	240,000	
	Deferred tax asset		40,000
	Income tax payable (or cash)		200,000

4. *Revenues* are included in income for tax purposes *earlier* than they are included in pretax income for shareholder purposes. For instance, some fees, dues, and service contracts are taxed when collected but are usually deferred as unearned revenue for financial reporting purposes. As in point 3 above, the deferred tax would be an *asset*.

☐ Permanent Differences

A **permanent difference** affects the computation of either pretax income as reported to shareholders or taxable income as reported to the government, but not both. Permanent differences will not "reverse," or "turn around," in subsequent periods. An example is nontaxable income: Interest received on municipal obligations is "permanently" exempt from tax. Other examples are nondeductible expenses: The costs of purchased goodwill and perpetual franchise rights are *not* deductible as expenses for income tax purposes but *must* be amortized for shareholder reporting purposes.

No interperiod income tax allocation (and therefore no deferred income tax liability) is appropriate in relation to these permanent differences. Consider an example (in dollars):

---

[3] FASB *Statement No. 96* places strict limitations on the recognition of deferred tax assets. Such details are beyond the scope of this text.

	REPORTING	
	To Shareholders	On Income Tax Return
No permanent difference		
Pretax income	120,000	120,000
Income taxes @ 40%	48,000	48,000
Permanent difference		
Income before amortization	120,000	120,000
Permanent difference is amortization of goodwill of $30,000	30,000	—
Pretax income	90,000	120,000
Income taxes	48,000	48,000

The income tax rate in reports to shareholders would be higher than the statutory rate of 40%; it would be $48,000 ÷ $90,000 = 53.3%. Because this condition is deemed a "permanent difference," no interperiod tax allocation would occur. The report to shareholders would indeed show a 53.3% rate, which would be explained by the fact that the amortization of goodwill is mandatory for shareholder reporting but forbidden for reporting to the income tax authorities.

In contrast, suppose the above company has a large portfolio of investments in tax-exempt municipal bonds and no purchased goodwill (in dollars):

	REPORTING	
	To Shareholders	On Income Tax Return
Permanent difference		
Income from all sources	120,000	120,000
Permanent difference is interest revenue on municipal obligations	—	30,000
Pretax income	120,000	90,000
Income taxes	36,000	36,000

The income tax rate in reports to shareholders would be lower than the statutory rate of 40%; it would be $36,000 ÷ $120,000 = 30%. No interperiod income tax allocation would be applicable.

☐ Net Operating Losses

Suppose a company reported a net operating loss (NOL) of $100,000 on its 19X4 income statement prepared for tax purposes. In other words, its tax deductions exceeded its taxable revenues by $100,000. The tax effects are as follows:

	NET OPERATING INCOME (LOSS)	19X4 CARRYBACK OR CARRYFORWARD	TAXABLE INCOME
19X1	$ 5,000	$ (5,000)	—
19X2	15,000	(15,000)	—
19X3	35,000	(35,000)	—
19X4	(100,000)	—	—
19X5	5,000	(5,000)	—
19X6	8,000	(8,000)	—
19X7	10,000	(10,000)	—
19X8	10,000	(10,000)	—
19X9	5,000	(5,000)	—
19X0	1,000	(1,000)	—
Next nine years combined	2,000	(2,000)	—
Used		(96,000)	
Unused and nondeductible		(4,000)	
Accounted for		$(100,000)	

The NOL can be used to reduce the taxable income of the three preceding or fifteen following years. The company receives a refund of taxes paid in 19X1, 19X2, and 19X3. In addition, the NOL reduces tax disbursements in future years. Any loss carry-forward unused after fifteen years becomes nondeductible.

NOL *carrybacks* result in tax refunds. They are recognized on the financial reports for shareholders in the period of the loss. The tax benefits from NOL *carryforwards* are usually deducted from the deferred tax liability. Why? Because the deferred income taxes will be paid only if the company is profitable, but such profitability will allow use of the NOL carryforward to reduce the amount of income taxes to be paid.

If the company has an insufficient amount of deferred income taxes, the remaining tax benefits of NOL carry forwards are not recognized until the tax benefits are actually received. Why? Such benefits cannot be anticipated because they depend on future profitability. Suppose a $100,000 NOL created a $40,000 tax benefit for a company with no deferred tax liability. The $40,000 benefit consists of a $25,000 tax refund for the preceding three years and a $15,000 potential reduction in future tax disbursements. The usual journal entry would be the following:

Income tax refund receivable	25,000	
Income tax benefit (a reduction of a loss)		25,000
Carryback of the tax effect of a net operation loss.		

The bottom of the income statement would show:

Pretax loss	$(100,000)
Add: Income tax benefit of operating loss carryback	25,000
Net loss	$ (75,000)

In addition, a footnote would disclose the existence of the $15,000 NOL tax benefit being carried forward.

APPENDIX 13C: PROPRIETORSHIPS AND PARTNERSHIPS

This appendix examines the fundamental distinctions between proprietorships, partnerships, and corporations. Particular attention is given to the role of income taxes in choosing the form of organization.

☐ Comparison of Transactions

Chapter 1 compares the three major types of ownership, so the details of such comparisons will not be repeated here. The fundamental accounting concepts that underlie the owner's equity are unchanged regardless of whether the organization is a corporation, a proprietorship, or a partnership. Furthermore, the typical business transactions such as sales, cost of goods sold, and operating expenses are accounted for exactly alike for all organizations.

Consider the following facts as a basis for illustrating the accounting for proprietorships and partnerships. On January 1, 19X1, Jane Smith invests $100,000 in a public accounting firm, Azure Accounting Services, as a sole proprietorship. Revenue of $460,000 and expenses of $270,000 apply to the year 19X1 (before considering any withdrawals or salaries for herself). Her withdrawals (called *drawings*) of cash were $10,000 monthly.

Similarly, Smith and Jones form a partnership that has identical operations during 19X1. Smith invests $60,000 and Jones invests $40,000. Although they can split the profits in any way they choose, their partnership agreement specifies 60% for Smith and 40% for Jones. Smith withdrew $6,000 monthly and Jones $4,000 monthly.

EXHIBIT 13–12

Analysis of Transactions for Proprietorship and Partnership
(in thousands of dollars)

	CASH AND OTHER ASSETS	=	LIABILITIES	+	OWNERS' EQUITY		
					Smith, Capital	Smith, Drawings	Income Summary
Proprietorship							
a. Initial investment	+100	=			+100		
b. Revenues	+460	=					+460
c. Expenses	−270	=					−270
d. Withdrawals	−120	=				−120	
e. Transfer of net income to capital		=			+70	+120	−190
Ending balances	+170	=			+170	0	0

	CASH AND OTHER ASSETS	=	LIABILITIES	+	Smith, Capital	Jones, Capital	Smith, Drawings	Jones, Drawings	Income Summary
Partnership									
a. Initial investment	+100	=			+60	+40			
b. Revenues	+460	=							+460
c. Expenses	−270	=							−270
d. Withdrawals	−120	=					−72	−48	
e. Transfer of net income to capital		=			+42	+28	+72	+48	−190
Ending balances	+170	=			+102	+68	0	0	0

Exhibit 13–12 shows how these transactions would affect the accounts. Transactions *a*, *b*, and *c* are the familiar investment, revenue, and expense transactions that are the same regardless of the form of organization. The net income for the year is $460,000 − $270,000 = $190,000.

The journal entries follow (in thousands of dollars). The Income Summary account obviously would not be used on a day-to-day basis. It is used here for convenience. Notice that the sum of Smith's drawings and her addition to capital ($72,000 + $42,000) are 60% of net income; Jones's are 40%.

	Smith			Smith and Jones		
a. Initial investment	Cash	100		Cash	100	
	Smith, capital		100	Smith, capital		60
				Jones, capital		40
b. Revenues	Cash	460		Cash	460	
	Income summary		460	Income summary		460
c. Expenses	Income summary	270		Income summary	270	
	Cash		270	Cash		270
d. Withdrawals	Smith, drawings	120		Smith, drawings	72	
	Cash		120	Jones, drawings	48	
				Cash		120
e. Transfers to capital	Income summary	190		Income summary	190	
	Smith, drawings		120	Smith, drawings		72
	Smith, capital		70	Jones, drawings		48
				Smith, capital		42
				Jones, capital		28

☐ Comparison with Corporations

From a legal and income tax standpoint, proprietorships and partnerships are not separate entities with limited liability and separate taxability. The owners have unlimited personal liability for all the debts of their businesses. Unlike the corporate entity, proprietorships and partnerships are not subject to income taxes as entities. Instead the entire net income (*before* withdrawals, which are regarded as similar to corporate dividends, *not* as expenses) is taxable as personal income of the owners. In particular, note that the income is fully taxable regardless of whether withdrawals are zero or any percentage of the entity's net income.

Exhibit 13–13 on page 611 compares the financial statements of the accounting firm under three forms of organization. Please read the footnote therein. The withdrawals in transaction *d* for proprietorships and partnerships are in lieu of the combination salaries-dividends paid by small corporations to their owner-managers. From a legal and income tax standpoint, an owner may be *both* an employee manager (one role) and a stockholder (a separate role). As an employee *manager*, the owner receives a salary; as an *owner*, he or she receives dividends.

How reasonable are the salaries of $72,000 and $48,000 shown in the corporate income statement? The Internal Revenue Service sometimes challenges such salary levels of closely held corporations. Why? Suppose one-third of the $120,000 could be established as being an unreasonable overpayment of salaries (given what these managers could command as salaried employees of other accounting firms). The $40,000 would be regarded as dividends. The salaries allowed by the IRS would therefore be only $48,000 and $32,000, respectively. Then the corporation would have to pay $8,000 more income taxes, $22,000 instead of $14,000. The entity would have $8,000 less cash, $156,000 (see Exhibit 13–13) minus $8,000 or $148,000. The corporate statements would be revised:

INCOME STATEMENT			STATEMENT OF RETAINED INCOME		BALANCE SHEET	
Revenues		$460	Retained income		Cash and other	
Expenses	$270		January 1, 19X1	$ 0	assets	$148
Salary expenses,			Net income	88	Capital stock	$100
$48 + $32	80	350	Total	$88	Retained income	48
Income before			Deduct dividends*	40	Total	$148
taxes		$110	Retained income,			
Income tax @ 20%		22	December 31, 19X1	$48		
Net income		$ 88				

* $120,000 total paid as "salaries," but one-third (or $40,000) disallowed by IRS and deemed to be dividends.

□ **Comparison of Results of Operations**

Consider a recent statement of income and partners' capital of Deloitte Haskins & Sells,[4] a public accounting firm with hundreds of partners.

DELOITTE HASKINS & SELLS (USA)
Statement of Earnings
(in millions of dollars)

Fees for professional services	$500
Operating expenses:	
Employee compensation and related benefits	228
Occupancy, including depreciation and amortization	41
Other	120
Total operating expenses	389
Earnings attributable to active partners	$111
Statement of Changes in Partners' Capital	
Balance at beginning of year	$118
Additions:	
Earnings attributable to active partners	111
Capital contributed by partners	4
Reductions:	
Distributions to active partners	104
Capital returned to partners who retired or resigned	13
Balance at end of year	$116

Note how the compensation of the partners is regarded as an allocation (or apportionment or distribution) of the income of the partnership, not as an operating expense. Under the corporate form, however, as the previous illustrations show, a "salary and bonus" expense would be deducted in the computation of the net income of a corporation.

---

[4] Deloitte Haskins & Sells recently merged with Touche Ross & Co. to form Deloitte & Touche.

EXHIBIT 13–13

AZURE ACCOUNTING SERVICES
Financial Statements
(in thousands of dollars)

SOLE PROPRIETORSHIP		PARTNERSHIP		CORPORATION	

INCOME STATEMENTS
FOR THE YEAR ENDED DECEMBER 31, 19X1

Revenues	$460	Revenues		$460	Revenues	$460
Expenses	270	Expenses		270	Expenses	$270
Net income	$190	Net income		$190	Salary expenses,*	
		Allocation of net			$72 + $48	120	390
		income:			Income before tax	70
		To Smith (60%)	$114		Income tax @ 20%	14
		To Jones (40%)	76	$190	Net income	$ 56*

STATEMENTS OF CAPITAL OR RETAINED INCOME
FOR THE YEAR ENDED DECEMBER 31, 19X1

			Smith	Jones		
Capital, January 1, 19X1	$100	Capital, January 1, 19X1	$ 60	$ 40	Retained income,	
Net income	190	Net income	114	76	January 1, 19X1	$ 0
Total	$290	Total	$174	$116	Net income	56
Drawings	120	Drawings	72	48	Retained income,	
Capital, December 31, 19X1	$170	Capital, December 31, 19X1	$102	$ 68	December 31, 19X1	$ 56

BALANCE SHEETS
DECEMBER 31, 19X1

Assets
(same for each entity)

Cash and other assets	$170	Cash and other assets	$170	Cash and other assets	$156*

Liabilities and Stockholders' Equity

Smith, capital	$170	Smith capital	$102	Capital stock	$100
		Jones, capital	68	Retained income	56*
		Total capital	$170	Stockholders' equity	$156*

* The corporate entity is subject to an income tax, assumed here to be 20% paid in cash. Furthermore, the withdrawals are assumed to be paid as executive salary expenses, which are deductible in computing the net income of the corporate entity.

Be on guard when you compare the income statements of incorporated and unincorporated businesses. To be strictly comparable, some "salaries" of the owner-managers of proprietorships and partnerships should be estimated as being equivalent to expenses.

For instance, suppose the drawings of Smith and Jones in our example were indeed reasonable approximations of the salaries they could earn in a comparable accounting firm. For comparison of their results with those of similar professional service *corporations*, their income statement would have to be revised as follows:

Revenues		$460
Expenses	$270	
Partner "salaries"	120	390
Operating income to be compared with the income before taxes of professional service corporations		$ 70

This approximation of partner "salaries" as an expense is highly desirable for routine internal reports to owner-managers. In this way, the partners can get a better measure of their overall compensation for their efforts. As managers, they wish to be compensated in an amount that they could earn for comparable work elsewhere. As owners, they wish a reasonable return on their ownership capital. If they fail to run an entity that can generate sufficient amounts of both types of rewards, the partners may take a variety of actions, including bringing in new partners or ceasing operations. In short, corporate and non-corporate income statements are not comparable unless approximations are made of partner or proprietor "salaries."

FUNDAMENTAL ASSIGNMENT MATERIAL

☐ General Coverage

13–1. TAX VERSUS SHAREHOLDER REPORTING OF DEPRECIATION. On January 2, 19X1, a wholesale company bought several forklifts for use in its warehouse. The total amount paid was $80,000. The forklifts have an eight-year useful life with a zero residual value. The forklifts qualify as five-year assets for MACRS purposes. The company uses straight-line depreciation for shareholder reporting and has a combined federal and state income tax rate of 40%.

Required: For years 19X1 through 19X8, compute (1) depreciation for shareholder reporting, (2) depreciation for tax purposes, and (3) the deferred tax liability at the end of each year.

13–2. DEFERRED INCOME TAXES. (Alternates are 13–4 and 13–6.) Ruiz Company began business on January 1, 19X7, with initial paid-in capital of $60 million cash. On January 2, 19X7, the company purchases an asset for $30 million cash with an estimated useful life of five years and an estimated scrap value of zero. MACRS depreciation is used for tax purposes. The asset has a MACRS recovery period of three years. However, *the straight-line method is used for shareholder reporting purposes.* Prospective annual income before depreciation and income taxes is $14.9 million. The income tax rate is 40%. Assume that all taxes are paid early in the next year after the income is earned.

Required:
1. Prepare an analysis of transactions for external reporting, using the balance sheet format. Show the effects of (a) formation, (b) acquisition, (c) income before depreciation and taxes, and (d) straight-line depreciation. Show the effects of (e1) no deferral and (e2) deferral of income taxes.
2. Prepare a three-column comparison of reporting of income for 19X7 (a) to income tax authorities, (b) to shareholders if no deferral is used, and (c) to shareholders if deferral is used.

13–3. TABULATION OF EFFECTS OF DEFERRAL. (Alternates are 13–5 and 13–7.) Refer to the data in the preceding problem. Prepare a five-year schedule like Exhibit 13–5 (p. 593) for each of the three reporting methods of the problem requirement 2. Show all amounts in millions of dollars.

13–4. DEFERRED INCOME TAXES. (Alternates are 13–2 and 13–6.) Monsanto Company produces chemicals and pharmaceuticals. The company's capital expenditures exceed $650 million annually. Suppose that on January 4, 1990, Monsanto purchased some special tools for the production of plastics. The acquisition cost was $10 million. The equipment's expected useful life is five years; expected residual value is zero. The MACRS class is three-year.

Assume that the combined state and federal income tax rate is 40%. No income tax payments will be due before early 1991. Assume that in 1990 Monsanto had pretax income of $650 million before considering depreciation related to this acquisition. For simplicity, assume also that this $650 million was the same for reporting to income tax authorities and to stockholders.

Regarding the $10 million acquisition, Monsanto uses straight-line depreciation for reporting to stockholders. However, the company uses the prescribed MACRS schedule for income tax purposes.

Required: **1.** Fill in the blanks in millions (based solely on the given data):

	1990 REPORTING	
	To Income Tax Authorities	To Stockholders
Pretax income as given	$650.0	$650.0
Depreciation:		
MACRS (3-year recovery basis)	?	?
Straight-line (5-year useful life)	?	?
Pretax income	?	?
Income tax expense:		
To be paid in early 1991	?	?
Deferred	?	?
Total income tax expense	?	?
Net income	$?	$?

2. Prepare the summary journal entry, December 31, 1990, for Monsanto's 1990 income taxes.

13–5. LONG-RUN EFFECTS OF DEFERRAL. (Alternates are 13–3 and 13–7).

1. Refer to the data in the preceding problem. Prepare a five-year schedule like Exhibit 13–5 (p. 593) for the two reporting methods of requirement 1. For each year, assume that income before the depreciation in question is $650 million and the income tax rate is 40%. Show all amounts in millions of dollars. Prepare only two schedules; omit the presentation similar to schedule 2(a) in Exhibit 13–5.

2. Prepare the journal entry for income tax expense for Year 5.

13–6. DEFERRED INCOME TAXES. (Alternates are 13–2 and 13–4.) Suppose that on January 5, 1990, American Airlines purchased some DC-10 aircraft for $400 million. The aircraft's expected useful life is ten years; expected residual value, zero.

Assume that the income tax rate is 40%. No income tax payments will be due before early 1991. Assume that in 1990 American had pretax income of $260 million before considering depreciation related to this acquisition. For simplicity, assume also that this $260 million was the same for reporting to income tax authorities and to stockholders.

Regarding the $400 million acquisition, American uses straight-line depreciation for reporting to stockholders. However, American uses the prescribed MACRS schedule for income tax purposes. Aircraft have a five-year recovery period.

1. Fill in the blanks in millions (based solely on the give data):

	1990 REPORTING	
	To Income Tax Authorities	To Stockholders
Pretax income as given	$260	$260
Depreciation:		
MACRS (5-year recovery basis)	?	?
Straight-line (10-year useful life)	?	?
Pretax income	?	?
Income tax expense:		
To be paid in early 1991	?	?
Deferred	?	?
Total income tax expense	?	?
Net income	$?	$?

2. Prepare the summary journal entry, December 31, 1990, for American's 1990 income taxes.

13–7. LONG-RUN EFFECTS OF DEFERRAL. (Alternates are 13–3 and 13–5.)

1. Refer to the data in the preceding problem. Prepare a seven-year schedule like Exhibit 13–5 (p. 593) for the two reporting methods in requirement 1. For each year, assume that the income before the depreciation in question is $260 million and the income tax rate is 40%. Show all amounts in millions of dollars. Do not continue the schedule beyond the seventh year; instead explain how the final three years would appear in a ten-year schedule. Prepare only two schedules; omit the presentation similar to schedule 2(a) in Exhibit 13–5.
2. Prepare the journal entry for income tax expense for Year 7.

ADDITIONAL ASSIGNMENT MATERIAL

☐ General Coverage

13–8. "Taxes are a fact of life, and they have little effect on business decisions." Do you agree? Explain.

13–9. "Tax credits are better than deductible items because they directly reduce taxes." Critically discuss this statement.

13–10. "Tax credits are deductible as expenses for income tax purposes." Do you agree? Explain.

13–11. Suppose a company's income tax rate is 40%. The company has a $100,000 expenditure that can either be a deductible item or receive a 25% tax credit. Which does the company prefer? Why?

13–12. "A five-year MACRS asset provides depreciation deductions over six years." Explain.

13–13. "MACRS results in an acceleration of income tax disbursements." Do you agree? Explain.

13–14. "Tax laws allow more depreciation than is allowed for reporting to shareholders." Do you agree? Explain.

13–15. Why do deferred federal income taxes arise?

13–16. "Deferred income taxes are also known as allocated income taxes." Do you agree? Explain.

13–17. In brief, why did the Financial Accounting Standards Board favor deferral of income taxes?

13–18. "Interperiod income tax allocation is the spreading of the year's income tax expense among the months within the year." Do you agree? Explain.

13–19. What are the two most widely used methods of accounting for the investment tax credit?

13–20. Which of the two methods of accounting for the investment tax credit will benefit reported current income the most?

13–21. Companies that use deferral of tax credits rather than flow-through show lower retained income. Why?

13–22. Give an example of a temporary difference where revenues are included in taxable income later than they are included in pretax income for stockholder reporting.

13–23. Give an example of a temporary difference where expenses are deducted from taxable income later than they are deducted for financial reporting purposes.

13–24. Give an example of a temporary difference where revenues are included in income for tax purposes earlier than they are for stockholder reporting purposes.

13–25. "Permanent differences are differences that persist beyond five years." Do you agree? Explain.

13–26. Give two examples of permanent differences.

13–27. "Operating losses are beneficial." Explain.

13–28. "Corporations are so different from proprietorships that completely different concepts of accounting apply to each." Do you agree? Explain.

13–29. **TAX CREDITS.**

1. Felix Company has sales of $900,000, tax-deductible expenses of $790,000, and an income tax rate of 40%. The company is also entitled to a tax credit of $9,000. Compute the company's taxable income and income tax to be paid.

2. Niles Company receives a tax credit for hiring handicapped workers. The credit is equal to 20% of the wages paid to the qualifying workers. In addition, the wages are deductible when computing taxable income. In 19X0, wages paid to qualifying handicapped workers were $150,000. Total tax-deductible expenses, including the $150,000 of wages, were $870,000. Sales revenues in 19X0 were $1.2 million. The income tax rate is 34%. Compute Niles Company's taxable income and the income tax to be paid for 19X0.

13–30. **RESEARCH TAX CREDIT.** An income tax credit is allowed for a company's research expenditures that exceed a base amount. The base amount is generally the average research expenditures for the past three years. Suppose the current rate for the credit is 25% of expenditures exceeding the base amount, and the income tax rate is 34%.

The Kwon Company had the following 19X0 income statement for tax purposes before considering research expenses:

Revenues	$250,000
Cost of goods sold	150,000
Gross margin	$100,000
General and administrative expenses (except for research expenses)	35,000
Pretax income (before research expenses)	$ 65,000

The Kwon Company incurred research expenses of $42,000 in 19X0, and research expenses for each of the past three years was $24,000. Assume that all expenses were paid in cash. The research tax credit was Kwon's only tax credit in 19X0.

Required:
1. Compute Kwon Company's taxable income for 19X0.
2. Compute the 19X0 income tax expense.
3. How much benefit did the Kwon Company receive from the 19X0 tax credit?
4. Suppose annual research expenses continue at $42,000 for 19X1, 19X2, and 19X3. Compute the research tax credit for each of the three years.

13–31. **MACRS RECOVERY PERIODS.** Consider the following business assets: (1) heavy-duty truck, (2) underground power transmission lines, (3) commercial building, and (4) electron microscope used in industrial research. What is the recovery period for each of these assets under the prescribed MACRS method?

13–32. **MACRS Depreciation.** Consider the following acquisitions of business assets on October 1, 1990: (1) office furniture, $4,000; (2) light truck, $16,000; and (3) tractor units for over-the-road, $60,000. For each asset, compute the depreciation for tax purposes for 1990 and 1991, as prescribed by MACRS.

13–33. **MACRS Depreciation.** In 1990, the Castillo Manufacturing Company acquired the following assets and immediately placed them into service:

1. Equipment with a seven-year MACRS life, a useful life of seventeen years, and a cost of $30 million
2. A desk-top computer that cost $8,000
3. An office desk that cost $2,000 but was sold sixteen months later

Required: | Compute the depreciation for tax purposes, under the prescribed MACRS method, in 1990 and 1991. Assume that all assets were acquired on March 1, 1990.

13–34. **Deferred Income Taxes.** Examine Exhibit 13–8. Suppose that in Year 7, $160 million was spent on three-year MACRS assets with five-year useful lives and that income before depreciation and taxes reached $270 million. For Year 7, fill in all the columns as shown in Exhibit 13–8, page 596.

13–35. **Growth of Deferred Taxes.** The facts are the same as in Problems 13–2. However, $30 million is spent *each year* for additional assets, and income increases $14.9 million each year until leveling off in Year 6. The $30 million spent in Year 6 represents a replacement of the asset originally acquired in Year 1.

Required: | Prepare two tabulations in millions of dollars. The first tabulation should display the effects of reporting for income tax purposes, assuming MACRS depreciation, including pretax income, income tax paid, and net income. The second tabulation should display the effects of reporting to stockholders, assuming straight-line depreciation and deferred income taxes. The second tabulation should include columns for pretax income, tax paid, tax deferred, total tax expense, net income, and the ending balance sheet effect on the Deferred Tax Liability.

13–36. **Comparison of Flow-Through and Deferral.** (Alternate is 13–52.) Study Appendix 13A. Jordan Shoe Corporation had $10 million of investment tax credits from acquisitions in late December 19X5.

Required: | 1. Compare the effects of two accounting methods by filling in the blanks (in millions of dollars):

	FLOW-THROUGH			DEFERRAL		
	A =	L +	SE	A =	L	+ SE
		Income Tax Payable	Retained Income		Income Tax Payable	Deferred ITC Liability	Retained Income
Effect on balances, 12/31/X5	0 =	−10	+10	0 =	−10	+10	
19X6 through 19X9 @ $1 per year		____	____	=	?	−4	?
Cumulative effect on balances, 12/31/X9	0 =	−10	+10	0 =	?	+6	?

2. Prepare the journal entries for all data in the table.

13–37. NET INCOME, FLOW-THROUGH, AND DEFERRAL OF ITC. Study Appendix 13A. Suppose Congress reenacted the investment tax credit, allowing a credit equal to 5% of the cost of certain machinery. Lutz Manufacturing bought an assembly robot for $450,000 on the first day of 19X1. Assume that both tax and shareholder reporting use straight-line depreciation over ten years. Income before depreciation on the new robot and before taxes was $140,000. The tax rate is 40%. Assume that the new robot qualifies for the investment tax credit.

Required:
1. Compute the taxes paid (or payable) to the government for 19X1.
2. Compute 19X1 net income reported to shareholders if the flow-through method is used for the investment tax credit.
3. Compute 19X1 net income reported to shareholders if the deferral method is used for the investment tax credit.

13–38. EFFECTS OF DEFERRAL AND FLOW-THROUGH. Study Appendix 13A. Landry Company began business on January 1, 19X1, with $1 million cash raised by an issue of common stock. All of its transactions throughout 19X1 were for cash. On December 31, it had income before income taxes of $300,000. The income tax rate is 35%. No income tax payments will be due before early 19X2. An investment in equipment of $240,000 cash was made on December 31, 19X1. The equipment has a ten-year life and an expected residual value of zero.

Required:
1. Prepare an analysis of transactions in thousands of dollars, using the A = L + SE format. Show the (a) effects of formation of the company, (b) effects on cash and retained income of income before income taxes, (c) effects of acquisition of equipment, and (d) computation and effects of income taxes. Show the ending balances in all accounts, December 31, 19X1.
2. Suppose the company were eligible for a 10% tax credit because of its acquisition of equipment. Prepare an analysis of the flow-through effects in thousands of dollars. Label as e1. Also prepare an analysis of the deferral effects. Label as e2.
3. Prepare journal entries, December 31, 19X1, for the income tax expense before considering the investment tax credit. Also prepare entries for the investment tax credit using (a) flow-through and (b) deferral.
4. Suppose 19X2 taxable income was again $300,000. However, no additional equipment was acquired. Prepare journal entries for the investment tax credit of 19X1 as it affects 19X2 using (a) flow-through and (b) deferral.

13–39. INVESTMENT CREDIT AND DEFERRED TAXES. Study Appendix 13A. Gulf Coast Electronics has used SYD depreciation for financial reporting and MACRS for tax purposes. It had also used the deferral method for the investment tax credit for financial reporting purposes. After enjoying steady growth in earnings for several years, the company encountered severe competition from foreign sources. This had a leveling effect on reported earnings per share.

In 19X8, the company invested over $60 million to update the equipment in one of its plants. The investment generated an investment tax credit of $3 million for 19X8. Management is seriously considering changing its method of reporting from that in requirement 2a to that in 2d below. Other data:

□ Useful life of the equipment, 15 years with no scrap value.
□ Net income before depreciation on new assets and income taxes and investment tax credit effects, $19 million.
□ If the investment credit is deferred, a full year of amortization is taken in 19X8.
□ Depreciation on new assets for 19X8:

Straight-line	$4,000,000
SYD	7,500,000
MACRS	9,000,000

Required: Show all total amounts in thousands of dollars.

1. Compute taxable income and the total income taxes for 19X8. The tax rate is 40%.
2. Suppose Gulf Coast Electronics has a simple capital structure with 10 million common shares outstanding and no preferred shares outstanding. For financial reporting purposes, compute net income and earnings per share where
   a. The company uses SYD depreciation and defers the investment credit
   b. The company uses SYD depreciation and "flows through" the investment credit
   c. The company uses straight-line depreciation and defers the investment credit
   d. The company uses straight-line depreciation and "flows through" the investment credit

13–40. **DEFERRED TAX ASSET.**   Study Appendix 13B. Matlock Toy Company introduced an electronic car in the middle of 19X0. Sales were $110,000 in 19X0, and the car was discontinued after the Christmas season. There were no sales in 19X1. The cars were sold with a one-year warranty, and Matlock estimated that warranty expenses would be $8,000. All warranty claims were made in 19X1, and they totaled exactly $8,000. Assume that both 19X0 and 19X1 pretax income before deducting warranty expenses was $100,000 for both tax and shareholder reporting, and the combined state and federal income tax rate is 40%.

Required:
1. Prepare journal entries for shareholder reporting to recognize both the warranty expense and income tax expense for 19X0.
2. Prepare journal entries relating to warranties and income tax expense for 19X1.

13–41. **NET OPERATING LOSSES.**   Study Appendix 13B. Bagley Company's tax deductions exceeded its taxable revenues by $450,000 in 19X5. Taxes paid each of the last five years were:

19X0	$40,000
19X1	10,000
19X2	20,000
19X3	50,000
19X4	10,000

The income tax rate is 40%, and Bagley has a deferred tax liability of $75,000.

Required:
1. Prepare the journal entry for 19X5 income taxes.
2. Prepare the bottom part of Bagley's 19X5 income statement, beginning with "Pretax loss . . . $(450,000)."

13–42. **OWNERS' EQUITY OF PROPRIETORS AND PARTNERS.**   Study Appendix 13C. On December 31, 19X1, Pamela Behling invested $500,000 in an architectural firm, Triangle Architectural Services, as a sole proprietorship. Revenue of $700,000 and expenses of $454,000 apply to the year 19X2 (before considering withdrawals or salary for herself). Her withdrawals (called *drawings*) of cash were $8,000 monthly.

Similarly, Behling and Miller formed a partnership that had identical operations during 19X1. Behling invested $300,000 and Miller invested $200,000. They decided to split the profits fifty-fifty even though their capital investments differed. Each withdrew $4,000 monthly.

Required:
1. Prepare an analysis of transactions for the proprietorship and partnership, using the balance sheet equation format. Use amounts in thousands.
2. Prepare summary journal entries for the proprietorship and the partnership.

13–43. **COMPARISON OF CORPORATIONS, PARTNERSHIPS, AND PROPRIETORSHIPS.**   Study Appendix 13C. Refer to the facts in the preceding problem. Also assume that a corporation existed that had exactly the same transactions as the partnership except: (a) the drawings were salaries, and (b) the corporation paid a combined state and federal income tax in cash of 40%.

Required: **1.** Prepare balance sheets, income statements, and statements of capital (or retained income) for each of the three entities.

2. Suppose the Internal Revenue Service established that the reasonable salary levels should be $43,000 each instead of $48,000. Prepare the revised corporate financial statements.

13-44. CHOOSING FORM OF ENTITY. Study Appendix 13C. Joan Lopez is subject to a marginal 40% income tax rate (combined state and federal). She is considering how to organize her wholly owned business. She anticipates the following average performance over the next few years: sales, $900,000; owner's salary, $80,000; other expenses, $720,000. Assume that the corporate income tax rate is 25%. Assume also that Lopez plans to withdraw an amount equal to all net income generated by the entity.

Required: **1.** Prepare a comparative income statement for the corporation and sole proprietorship.

2. Prepare an analysis of the cash available to the owner under each form of organization. Which form is more desirable (a) if the purpose is to maximize the cash available to the owner after personal income taxes and (b) if the purpose is to maximize the cash retention in the business? Explain.

☐ Understanding Published Financial Reports

13-45. TAX CREDITS AND TAX-EXEMPT INCOME. International Container Systems, Inc., makes cases for the transporting of bottles and cans of various products, such as soft drinks. The company's 1988 pretax income was $935,000. A footnote reported that normal state and federal income taxes would be 38.9% of taxable income. However, two items caused the actual rate on pretax income to differ from 38.9%: (1) tax-exempt income (possibly interest revenue from municipal bonds) totaled $25,000, and (2) the company received a research and development tax credit of $10,000.

Required: **1.** Compute the taxes paid or payable for 1988. Round to the nearest thousand.

2. Compute the actual income tax percentage on pretax income in 1988.

13-46. FUNDAMENTALS OF INCOME TAX ALLOCATION. Suppose the railroad division of Norfolk Southern Corporation purchases a group of highly specialized freight cars for $2.1 million. The cars have a ten-year life and no residual value. The company uses MACRS depreciation for tax purposes and straight-line depreciation for financial reporting purposes. The freight cars are seven-year MACRS property.

The income of this division before depreciation and taxes is $800,000. The applicable income tax rate is 30%.

Required: Show all amounts in thousands of dollars.

1. For the ten years, tabulate the details of how these facts would influence the Norfolk Southern reporting for tax purposes and for reporting to stockholders. *Hint:* See Exhibit 13-5 (p. 593).

2. How will the Deferred Tax Liability account be affected if capital expenditures are the same each year? If they grow each year?

13-47. MACRS DEPRECIATION. United Parcel Service (UPS) provides delivery of packages throughout the United States. Consider a light-duty van acquired for $20,000. Using the prescribed MACRS method, compute the depreciation deduction for tax purposes for each of six years.

13-48. MACRS AND DEFERRED TAXES. Emery Air Freight Corporation provides overnight delivery of packages throughout the United States. The company acquired new equipment to expand its "Dayton Superhub" as part of its goal to reach $1 billion of sales. Suppose the equipment was acquired for $10 million cash and installed on January 2, 1990. For shareholder reporting purposes, the equipment's useful life is ten years. There is zero expected residual value. However, for income tax purposes, assume that MACRS prescribes a five-year recovery period.

Show all dollar amounts in millions.

1. For simplicity, assume that this equipment is the only fixed asset subject to depreciation. Prepare a tabulation (similar to Exhibit 13–6, page 594) summarizing reporting to the Internal Revenue Service for the first six years. Assume that income before depreciation is $20 million and that the combined state and federal income tax rate if 40%.
2. Prepare a similar table summarizing reporting to shareholders. However, prepare a table for seven years. In the final column, show the balance sheet account Deferred Tax Liability at the end of each year. Assume straight-line depreciation.
3. Prepare the journal entry for Years 1 and 7 for income tax expense.

13–49. **RECONSTRUCT INCOME TAX TRANSACTIONS.** Lincoln Logs Ltd. sells easily assembled log home packages. Annual sales are nearly $20 million. Its fiscal 1988 income statement included a provision for income taxes of $565,000. A footnote disclosed the following:

☐ A summary of components of income taxes for the year ended January 31, 1988 is as follows:

Current expense:	
Federal	$375,000
State	121,250
	496,250
Deferred	68,750
	$565,000

The Lincoln Logs balance sheet included:

	JANUARY 31	
	1988	1987
Current liabilities:		
Accrued income taxes	$185,352	$ 0
Long-term liabilities:		
Deferred tax liability	$109,799	$41,049

Required:

1. Prepare summary journal entries for income tax transactions for 1988. Include entries for (1) income tax expense for the year and (2) cash disbursements for income taxes.
2. Present possible reasons for the increase in the Deferred Tax Liability account.

13–50. **DIFFERENCE IN DEPRECIATION FOR TAX AND SHAREHOLDER REPORTING.** International Paper Company is the world's largest producer of papers for food packaging and magazine printing. The company's 1988 depreciation on reports to shareholders was $446 million. A footnote stated that the use of MACRS depreciation for federal tax purposes and straight-line depreciation for shareholder reporting resulted in an increase of $111 million in the deferred tax liability in 1988. The federal income tax rate is 34%. The income statement reported (in millions):

Earnings before income taxes	$1,198
Provision for income taxes	444
Net earnings	$ 754

1. Compute the amount of depreciation reported on International Paper's income statement prepared for the Internal Revenue Service.
2. Other differences between shareholder and tax reporting caused a $95 million increase in the Deferred Tax Liability account. Prepare International Paper's summary journal entry to recognize income tax expense in 1988.

13–51. JOURNAL ENTRIES FOR INCOME TAXES. Brunswick Corporation makes recreation and leisure products, such as Bayliner boats, Mercury outboards, Zebco fishing reels, and Brunswick bowling products. In 1988, Brunswick paid cash of $129.7 million for income taxes. Income taxes payable were $18.6 million on December 31, 1987, and $15.9 million on December 31, 1988. Depreciation and amortization on the income statement prepared for shareholders was $147.9 million, and on the statement to tax authorities it was $179.1 million. Assume that depreciation and amortization provided the only differences between shareholder and tax reporting. The income tax rate was 34%.

Required: Prepare summary journal entries for recognition of income tax expense and for cash disbursements for income taxes in 1988.

13–52. COMPARISON OF FLOW-THROUGH AND DEFERRAL. (Alternate is 13–36.) Study Appendix 13A. Eastman Kodak had $5 million of investment tax credits from acquisitions in late December 1985, just before Congress eliminated the investment tax credit.

Required:

1. Compare the effects of two accounting methods by filling in the blanks (in millions of dollars):

	FLOW-THROUGH			DEFERRAL		
	A =	L +	SE	A =	L	+ SE
		Income Tax Payable	Retained Income		Income Tax Payable	Deferred Investment Tax Credits	Retained Income
Effect on balances, 12/31/85	0 =	?	?	0 =	−5	+5	
1986 through 1988 @ $1 per year				=	?	−3	?
Cumulative effect on balances, 12/31/88	0 =	−5	+5	0 =	?	+2	?

2. Prepare the journal entries for all data in the table.

13–53. INVESTMENT TAX CREDIT. Study Appendix 13A. Consolidated Edison Company of New York, the electric utility serving New York City and Westchester County, received investment tax credits totaling $37 million in 1985. The company's capital expenditures were $459 million. Net income after considering all expenses, including taxes, but before considering the investment tax credit, was $553 million. A footnote in Con Edison's annual report showed:

Investment tax credits deferred:	
Credits generated and utilized	$37,000,000
Less: Amortization	11,000,000
Total	$26,000,000

1. What method does Con Edison use to account for the investment tax credit?
2. Compute Con Edison's 1985 net income using the deferral method.
3. Compute Con Edison's 1985 net income using the flow-through method.

4. Suppose Congress had increased the investment tax credit to 40% of capital expenditures for 1985 only. Compute 1985 net income (a) under the deferral method and (b) under the flow-through method. Assume under the deferral method that none of the investment tax credit on 1985's investments is amortized in 1985. Which of the two methods do you prefer? Explain.

13–54. AMORTIZATION OF INVESTMENT TAX CREDIT. Study Appendix 13A. On December 31, 1985, General Telephone and Electronics (GTE) had deferred investment tax credits of $1,074 million and retained earnings of $2,941 million. No investment tax credits were available to GTE in 1986 or later years. Assume that GTE's income after tax but before considering amortization of the investment tax credit is $1 billion for each of 1986, 1987, and 1988. Also assume that 15% of the December 31, 1985, amount of deferred investment tax credits will be amortized in each of the next three years and that no dividends will be paid.

Required: **1.** Fill in the blanks in the following table (in millions, round to the nearest million):

	YEAR ENDED DECEMBER 31		
	1986	1987	1988
Income statement items:			
Income after tax but before amortization of ITC	$1,000	$1,000	$1,000
Amortization of ITC	?	?	?
Net income	?	?	?
Balance sheet items:			
Deferred investment tax credit	?	?	?
Retained earnings	?	?	?

2. Repeat requirement 1 except assume that GTE uses and has always used the flow-through method for the investment tax credit. (*Hint*: First compute the December 31, 1985, *retained earnings* balance *as if* GTE had been using the flow-through method.)
3. Assume that the entire $1,074 million of deferred investment tax credits is amortized in 1986, 1987, and 1988. Compute GTE's December 31, 1988, retained income under the conditions of requirement 1.
4. Assume that Congress does not reenact the investment tax credit. How long will GTE's financial statements be influenced by its accounting for the investment tax credit?

13–55. MEANING OF INCOME OF PARTNERSHIPS AND CORPORATIONS. Study Appendix 13C. Peat Marwick International, a large public accounting partnership, had the following income statement (in millions):

Fees earned for professional services		$586
Operating expenses:		
Employee compensation and fringe benefits	$282	
Occupancy and equipment rentals including depreciation and amortization	40	
Other expenses	97	419
Available for allocation		$167
Allocated to:		
Partners formal retirement plans	$ 5	
Retired partners	6	
Active partners for compensations, insurance and other fringe benefit costs, and return on capital	156	$167

1. Suppose Peat Marwick International were a corporation rather than a partnership. Recast its income statement as a corporation.

2. Note how the $156 million is described in the above statement. State some major differences regarding compensation between being a partner in a public accounting firm and being a top executive in a corporation.

13–56. COMPENSATION OF PARTNERS. Study Appendix 13C. The business press frequently cites the high compensation of partners of public accounting firms. Arthur Andersen & Co., a large public accounting firm, included the following format in an annual report:

Average earnings per partner		$203,312
Deduct:		
Return on capital at risk	$32,294	
Retirement, insurance, etc.	21,000	53,294
Average executive compensation		
equivalent per partner		$150,018

Required: What amount is subject to personal income tax currently for an average partner? For a comparable corporate executive? What reasoning would be used in formulating the above analysis?

13–57. HOUSE OF FABRICS ANNUAL REPORT. Examine the financial statements of House of Fabrics (pages 749–759), including Note 6 on page 758. Because FASB *Statement No. 96* had not been implemented for fiscal 1989, House of Fabrics labeled its Deferred Tax Liability account "Deferred Income Taxes."

Required: **1.** Prepare summary journal entries for (1) recognition of income tax expense and (2) cash disbursements for income taxes in fiscal 1989.

2. Compute the amount of depreciation and amortization charged on the company's income statement prepared for tax purposes. Assume that all deferred tax amounts relate to "the excess of tax over book depreciation." Note that the combined state and federal income tax rate in fiscal 1989 was 40%.

Internal Control

After studying this chapter, you should be able to

1. Describe the implications of the Foreign Corrupt Practices Act regarding internal accounting controls

2. Explain the role of the audit committee in a modern corporation

3. Describe and apply the checklist that may be used as a starting point for judging the effectiveness of an internal control system

4. Explain why managers sometimes seek to manipulate reported income

5. Describe the retail method of inventory control (Appendix 14A)

6. Describe and apply data-processing techniques using special journals (Appendix 14B)

Internal control was once regarded as a technical subject that belonged in advanced courses in accounting, particularly the course in auditing. But widespread disclosures of secret payments and embezzlements brought internal control to the forefront as a central responsibility of top management. A recent report in the *Wall Street Journal* estimated that so-called white-collar crime costs business $67 billion a year. This chapter explains internal control in general and illustrates its application to cash and inventories.

Chapter Appendix 14A provides more details about inventory control. Appendix 14B explores various ways of processing data, including special journals and subsidiary ledgers.

The problems of internal control extend to nonprofit organizations, which often suffer from defective systems. For example, an auditor's report regarding the U.S. Department of Energy listed many shortcomings of internal control. The auditors commented that the department "does not have an effective system of recording, managing, and disposing of government property."

Another example is a report by California's auditor general. In a 285-page report to the legislature, he reported that twenty-five of the thirty-six major state agencies each "had at least one weakness in the internal controls that apply to financial operations." The weaknesses created an unnecessary $24 million loss.

The problems of internal control are not confined to preventing theft. They are also concerned with adherence to management policies and procedures. Sometimes employees squander an organization's assets, not necessarily for direct personal gain, but to cover up their past mistakes. For example, an employee for Spectra-Physics shocked the top executives of that company, a pioneer manufacturer of lasers. The company lost $10 million in a series of unauthorized foreign exchange transactions when the employee, who was supposed to buy and sell small quantities of foreign currency, suddenly went overboard. The senior vice-president said that the employee with responsibility for trading in foreign exchange ended up with a small loss for the first quarter and did not disclose the facts. Instead he circumvented management controls and expanded his activities in an effort to wipe out the loss.

OVERVIEW OF INTERNAL CONTROL

☐ Importance of Accounting Systems

Regardless of an entity's size or type, and regardless of whether it is held privately or publicly, managers and accountants should be alert to the rudiments of accounting systems and controls. Accounting records are kept for a variety of purposes. A major purpose is to help managers operate their entities more efficiently and effectively. Any person who forms a business will soon discover that recordkeeping is absolutely essential. For instance, records of receivables and payables must be created for transactions with customers and creditors, and cash disbursements and receipts must be traced to the individual accounts. Even the simplest of organizations must have some records. The cost-benefit test is easily met. Unless orderly compilation occurs, intolerable chaos results. In short, an accounting system is a wise business investment.

The dictionary defines *system* as "an assemblage of objects united by some form of regular interaction or interdependence." The key word is *regular*. An **accounting system** is a set of records, procedures, and equipment that *routinely* deals with the events affecting the financial performance and position of the entity.

Chapters 3 and 4 provide an overview of the heart of the accounting system: source documents, journal entries, postings to ledgers, trial balances, adjustments, and financial reports. The focus of the system is on repetitive, voluminous transactions, which almost always fall into four categories:

1. Cash disbursements
2. Cash receipts
3. Purchases of goods and services, including employee payroll
4. Sales or other rendering of goods and services

The magnitude of the physical handling of records is often staggering. For example, consider the telephone company or the credit card companies. They must process *millions* of transactions daily. Without computers and photocopying equipment, most modern organizations would be forced to halt operations. Too often, systems are regarded as a necessary evil. But systems deserve a loftier status. Well-designed and well-run accounting systems are positive contributions to organizations and the economy.

Advances in computer technology continue to be awesome. The description of a specific accounting system is likely to be ancient history before it comes off the presses. Consequently, this chapter emphasizes the *general* features of accounting systems that persist regardless of specific computer programs and hardware. The purpose here is not to develop skills as a systems designer; the purpose is to develop an acquaintance with the scope and nature of accounting systems and controls. No manager or would-be manager can afford the risks of not having an awareness of the primary attributes of a suitable internal control system.

☐ Definition of Internal Control

Definitions of internal control vary considerably. In its broadest sense, **internal control** refers to both *administrative* control and *accounting* control:

1. *Administrative controls* include the plan of organization (for example, the formal organization chart concerning who reports to whom) and all methods and procedures that facilitate management planning and control of operations. Examples are de-

partmental budgeting procedures, reports on performance, and procedures for granting credit to customers.

2. *Accounting controls* include the methods and procedures for authorizing transactions, safeguarding assets, and ensuring the accuracy of the financial records. Good accounting controls help *maximize* efficiency; they help *minimize* waste, unintentional errors, and fraud.

This chapter focuses on **internal accounting controls**, as distinguished from internal administrative controls. The latter subject is covered in books on management accounting.

Management's Responsibility

Chapter 1 explains that outside auditors attest to the financial reports of an entity. However, management bears the *primary responsibility* for a company's financial statements. Today the annual reports of publicly held companies generally contain an explicit statement of management responsibility for its financial statements.

These **management reports** usually state that management is responsible for all audited and unaudited information in the annual report, include a statement on the adequacy of internal control. They include a description of the composition and duties of the audit committee as well as the duties of the independent auditor. These features are highlighted in color in Exhibit 14–1, the statement of McDonald's Corporation, operator of more than 10,500 restaurants in fifty countries.

EXHIBIT 14–1

McDonald's Corporation

MANAGEMENT'S REPORT

Management is responsible for the preparation and integrity of the consolidated financial statements and Financial Comments appearing in this annual report. The financial statements were prepared in accordance with generally accepted accounting principles and include certain amounts based on management's best estimates and judgments. Other financial information presented in the annual report is consistent with the financial statements.

The Company maintains a system of internal controls designed to provide reasonable assurance that assets are safeguarded and that transactions are executed as authorized and are recorded and reported properly. This system of controls is based upon written policies and procedures, appropriate divisions of responsibility and authority, careful selection and training of personnel and a comprehensive internal audit program. The Company's policies and procedures prescribe that the Company and all employees are to maintain the highest ethical standards and that its business practices throughout the world are to be conducted in a manner which is above reproach.

Arthur Young & Company, independent public accountants, has examined the Company's financial statements and their opinion is presented herein.

The Board of Directors has an Audit Committee composed entirely of outside Directors. Arthur Young & Company has direct access to the Audit Committee and they periodically meet with the Committee to discuss accounting, auditing and financial reporting matters.

U.S. companies must obey the **Foreign Corrupt Practices Act**. The title is misleading because the act's provisions pertain to the internal control systems of all publicly held companies, *even if they do no business outside the United States*. The act contains not only specific prohibitions against bribery and other corrupt practices but also requirements (a) for maintaining accounting records in reasonable detail and accuracy and (b) for maintaining an appropriate system of internal accounting controls. In general, as a part of intelligent management practices, most organizations already abide by these requirements. However, these responsibilities have now been explicitly codified as part of a federal law.

Public reporting on the adequacy of internal control is an explicit responsibility of management under the act. Consequently, management in general, not just accountants, focus on systems of internal control. Boards of directors assure themselves of compliance with the act and with SEC requirements by (a) obtaining documentation of the internal control system and (b) compiling written evidence of management's evaluation and ongoing review of the system. The biggest impact of the act has been the mandatory documentation of evaluation of internal control *by management* rather than only by auditors.[1]

The documentation should systematically refer to (a) management's cost-benefit choices regarding the system and (b) management's evaluation of how well the system is working. Documentation includes memos, minutes of meetings discussing internal control concepts with all affected individuals, written statements of compliance, flow charts, procedures manuals, and the like. Moreover, there should be a written program for ongoing review and evaluation of the system. Finally, there should be letters from independent auditors stating that they found no material weaknesses in internal control during their audit, or that necessary improvements have been made.

The act specifies that internal accounting controls are supposed to provide reasonable assurance concerning

1. *Authorization*. Transactions are executed in accordance with management's general or specific intentions.
2. *Recording*. All authorized transactions are recorded in the correct amounts, periods, and accounts. No fictitious transactions are recorded.
3. *Safeguarding*. Precautions and procedures appropriately restrict access to assets.
4. *Reconciliation*. Records are compared with other independently kept records and physical counts. Such comparisons help ensure that other control objectives are attained.
5. *Valuation*. Recorded amounts are periodically reviewed for impairment of values and necessary write-downs.

The first three general objectives—authorization, recording, and safeguarding—relate to establishing the system of accountability and are aimed at *prevention*

---

[1] These requirements were extended to managers in the public sector by the Federal Managers' Financial Integrity Act. Briefly, the act requires each executive agency to establish a system of internal accounting and administrative control that meets prescribed standards and to report annually, based on an evaluation conducted in accordance with established guidelines, to the president, Congress, and the public on the extent to which the agency's systems comply with the standards.

of errors and irregularities. The final two objectives—reconciliation and valuation—are aimed at *detection* of errors and irregularities.

A sixth objective of an internal control system should be added: *promoting operating efficiency*. Although the act is not particularly concerned with efficiency, management should recognize that an internal control system's purpose is as much a positive one (promoting efficiency) as a negative one (preventing errors and fraud).

THE AUDIT COMMITTEE

The first objective of internal accounting control is *authorization*; transactions should be executed in accordance with management's intentions. Moreover, management bears primary responsibility for the entity's financial statements. This authority and responsibility extends upward to the board of directors. Most boards have an **audit committee**, which oversees the accounting controls, financial statements, and financial affairs of the corporation. Indeed, such committees are required of companies whose shares are listed on the New York Stock Exchange. The primary responsibility of the audit committee is fiscal vigilance.

Audit committees are typically composed of three or more "outside" board members. Not being everyday employees of the company, they are usually considered to be more independent than the "inside" directors, who, as employees, also serve as part of the corporation's management.[2] The committee represents the full board and provides personal contact and communication among the board, the external auditors, the internal auditors, the financial executives, and the operating executives. These relationships are depicted in Exhibit 14–2.

Exhibit 14–2 shows only one of many possible arrangements. Above all, note how the audit committee serves as the main pipeline to the board of directors, especially for individuals responsible for the accounting function. In Exhibit 14–2, the internal audit manager is directly responsible (solid line) to the accounting executives, who, in turn, are directly responsible to both the audit committee and the executive vice-president. The dashed lines indicate that the audit committee should communicate with and gather information directly from the external auditors and the internal auditors.

These relationships are evolving. For example, the internal auditing department sometimes is directly responsible to the executive vice-president, or to the president, or to the audit committee itself. Many observers believe that the internal audit department should be totally independent of the financial officers.

The audit committee meets at least twice annually. The first meeting is typically to review the annual external audit plan; the second, to review the audited financial statements before their publication. Additional meetings may be held (a) to consider the retention or replacement of the independent external

---

[2] Mobil Corporation, the large oil company, has a typical board composition. Of eighteen directors, eight are also members of management and ten are "outside" directors. Five of the outside directors form the audit committee.

EXHIBIT 14–2

Typical Corporate Organization Chart

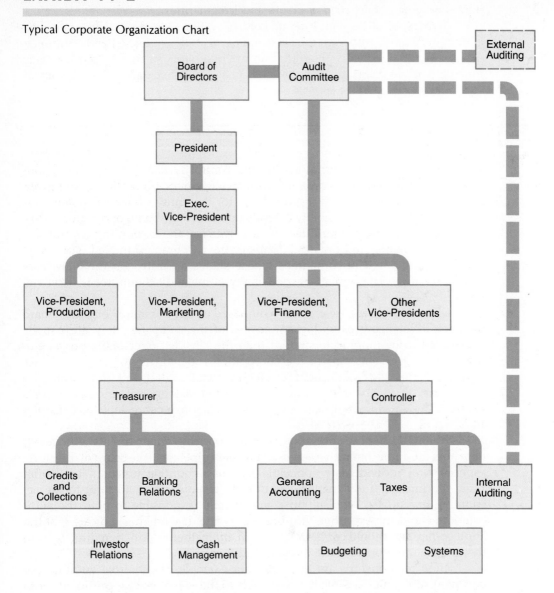

auditors; (b) to review the company's accounting system, particularly the internal controls; and (c) to review any special matters raised by internal audits.

As a minimum, meetings should be attended by the chief financial officer and a representative of the independent auditing firm. At least once a year, the committee should discuss with the independent auditors their evaluation of corporate management (without the presence of the latter). Similarly, the committee should obtain management's evaluation of the independent auditors.

Many companies include an audit committee report in their annual report. Merck & Co., the large pharmaceutical firm, included the report shown in Exhibit 14–3.

EXHIBIT 14–3

MERCK & CO.
Audit Committee's Report

The Audit Committee of the Board of Directors is comprised of five outside directors. The members of the Committee are: Lloyd C. Elam, M.D., Chairman, Frank T. Cary, Marian S. Heiskell, John K. McKinley, and Paul G. Rogers. The Committee held four meetings during 1988.

The Audit Committee meets with the independent public accountants, management, and internal auditors to assure that all are carrying out their respective responsibilities. The Audit Committee reviews the performance of the independent public accountants prior to recommending their appointment and meets with them, without management present, to discuss the scope and results of their audit work, including the adequacy of internal controls and the quality of financial reporting. Both the independent public accountants and the internal auditors have full access to the Audit Committee.

CHECKLIST OF INTERNAL CONTROL

All good systems of internal control have certain features in common. These features can be termed a *checklist of internal control*, which may be used to appraise any specific procedures for cash, purchases, sales, payroll, and the like. This checklist is sometimes called *principles* or *rules* or *concepts* or *characteristics* or *features* or *elements*. The following checklist summarizes the guidance that is found in much of the systems and auditing literature.[3]

☐ 1. Reliable Personnel with Clear Responsibilities

The most important element of successful control is personnel. Incompetent or dishonest individuals can undermine a system, no matter how well it meets the other items on the checklist. Procedures to hire, train, motivate, and supervise employees are essential. Individuals obviously must be given authority, responsibility, and duties commensurate with their abilities, interests, experience, and reliability. Yet many employers use low-cost talent that may prove exceedingly expensive in the long run, not only because of fraud but because of poor productivity.

Reliability begins at the top of the organization. The entire system deserves surveillance by operating management to see if it is working as prescribed and if changes are warranted. In addition, appropriate overseeing and appraisal of employees are essential. The most streamlined accounting system is deficient if its prescribed procedures are not being conscientiously followed.

Responsibility means tracking actions as far down in the organization as is feasible, so that results can be related to individuals. It means having salesclerks sign sales slips, inspectors initial packing slips, and workers sign time cards and

---

[3] For an expanded discussion, see Alvin Arens and James Loebbecke, *Auditing*, 4th ed. (Englewood Cliffs, NJ: Prentice Hall, 1988), Chap. 9.

requisitions. Grocery stores often assign each cashier a separate money tray; therefore shortages can easily be traced to the person responsible. The psychological impact of fixing responsibility tends to promote care and efficiency. Employees often perform better when they must explain deviations from required procedures.

The possibility of employee theft is distasteful to most managers, but it must be taken seriously. The National Mass Retailing Institute estimates that retailers lose about 2% of sales to theft and mistakes. Shoplifting accounts for part of this, but employee theft causes much larger losses than shoplifting. The institute estimates than an average retail store loses $10 per shift per clerk. Convenience stores and fast-food restaurants are especially vulnerable to employee theft. Such businesses need to be especially concerned with internal control systems.

□ 2. Separation of Duties

The separation of duties not only helps ensure accurate compilation of data but also limits the chances for fraud that would require the collusion of two or more persons. This extremely important and often neglected element can be subdivided into four parts:

a. *Separation of operational responsibility from recordkeeping responsibility.* The entire accounting function should be divorced from operating departments so that objective, independent records may be kept either by other operating people or by clerks. For example, product inspectors, not machine operators, should count units produced; inventory records clerks or computers, not material handlers, should keep perpetual inventory records. Why? Because those keeping the records should have nothing to gain by falsifying the records. A material handler should not be able to steal materials and cover up the theft by recording the issue of the materials to production.

b. *Separation of the custody of assets from accounting.* This practice reduces temptation and fraud. For example, the bookkeeper should not handle cash, and the cashier should not have access to ledger accounts such as the individual records of customers. A person with both accounting and cash-handling duties could pocket cash that is received and make a false entry in the accounting records.

In a computer system, a person with custody of assets should not have access to programming or any input records. Similarly, an individual who handles programming or input records should not have access to tempting assets. In a classic example, a programmer in a bank rounded transactions to the next lower cent rather than the nearest cent and had the computer put the fraction of a cent into his account. For example, a customer amount of $10.057 became $10.05, and the programmer's account received $.007. With millions of transactions, the programmer's account became very large.

c. *Separation of the authorization of transactions from the custody of related assets.* To the extent feasible, persons who authorize transactions should not have control over the related asset. For instance, the same individual should not authorize the payment of a supplier's invoice and also sign the check in payment of the bill. Nor should an individual who handles cash receipts have the authority to indicate which accounts receivable should be written off as uncollectible.

The latter separation of powers prevents such embezzlement as the following: A bookkeeper opens the mail, removes a $1,000 check from a customer, and somehow cashes it. To hide the theft, the bookkeeper prepares the following journal entry:

Allowance for bad debts	1,000	
Accounts receivable		1,000
To write off an amount owed by a customer.		

d. *Separation of duties within the accounting function.* An employee should not be able to record a transaction from its origin to its ultimate posting in a ledger. Independent performance of various phases will help ensure control over errors. Even a small company should have some separation of duties. For example, if there is only one bookkeeper who writes checks and keeps the accounting records, the owner can at least sign the checks and reconcile the monthly bank statement.

A main goal of the separation of duties is to make sure that one person, acting alone, cannot defraud the company. It is much more difficult, although certainly not impossible, for two or more employees to collude in a fraud. This is why movie theaters have a cashier selling tickets and an usher taking them. The cashier takes in cash, the usher keeps the ticket stubs, and the cash is compared with the number of stubs. But suppose they do collude. The ticket seller pockets the cash and issues a fake ticket. The usher accepts the fake ticket and allows entry. Separation of duties alone will not prevent such theft.

☐ 3. Proper Authorization

The Foreign Corrupt Practices Act has stressed proper authorization. Authorization can be either *general* or *specific*. General authorization is usually found in writing. It often sets definite limits on what price to pay (whether to fly economy or first class), on what price to receive (whether to offer a sales discount), on what credit limits to grant to customers, and so forth. There may also be complete prohibitions (against paying extra fees or bribes or overtime premiums).

Specific authorization usually means that a superior manager must permit (typically in writing) any particular deviations from the limits set by general authorization. For example, the plant manager, rather than the lathe supervisor, may have to approve any overtime. Another example is the need for approval from the board of directors regarding expenditures for capital assets in excess of a specific limit.

☐ 4. Adequate Documents

Documents and records vary considerably, from source documents such as sales invoices and purchase orders to journals and ledgers. Immediate, complete, and tamper-proof recording is the aim. It is encouraged by having all source documents prenumbered and accounted for, by using devices such as cash registers and locked compartments in invoice-writing machines, and by designing forms for ease of recording. Special journals, described in Appendix 14B, aid the accurate and efficient recording of transactions.

Immediate recording is especially important for handling cash sales. Devices used to ensure immediate recording include cash registers with loud bells and compiling tapes, private detectives, guaranteeing "rewards" to customers if they are not offered a receipt at the time of sale, and forcing clerks to make change by pricing items at $1.99, $2.99, and $3.99 rather than at $2, $3, and $4.[4] Cash sales receipts should be prenumbered to discourage theft by cashiers. Without prenumbered receipts, a cashier could destroy the business's copy of the receipt and pocket the cash. With prenumbered receipts, missing receipts can be identified and must be explained by the cashier. Therefore, when a store clerk makes a mistake on a receipt, it is marked "void" and kept, not destroyed.

☐ 5. Proper Procedures

Most organizations have *procedures manuals*, which specify the flow of documents and provide information and instructions to facilitate adequate recordkeeping.

Routine and automatic checks are major ways of attaining proper procedures. In a phrase, this means doing things "by the numbers." Just as manufacturing activities tend to be made more efficient by the division and specialization of repetitive activities, so can recordkeeping activities be made less costly and more accurate. Repetitive procedures may be prescribed for nonmanufacturing activities such as order taking, order filling, collating, and inspecting. The use of general routines permits specialization of effort, division of duties, and automatic checks on previous steps in the routine.

☐ 6. Physical Safeguards

Obviously, losses of cash, inventories, and records are minimized by safes, locks, guards, and limited access. For example, many companies (such as Boeing and Hewlett-Packard) require all visitors to sign a register and wear a name tag. Often employees will also wear name tags that are coded to show the facilities to which they have access. Doors to research areas or computer rooms often may be opened only with special keys or by use of a specific code.

Sometimes small businesses are especially vulnerable to theft of physical assets. For example, retail stores use alarm systems, guard dogs, security guards, special lighting, and many other safeguards to protect their property.

☐ 7. Bonding, Vacations, and Rotation of Duties

Key people may be subject to excessive temptation; top executives, branch managers, and individuals who handle cash or inventories should have understudies, be forced to take vacations, and be bonded.

Why rotate employees and force them to take vacations? First, it ensures that at least two employees know how to do each job so that an absence due to illness or a sudden resignation does not create major problems. Second, having another employee periodically perform their duties discourages employees from engaging in fraudulent activities that might be discovered when someone else has access to their records.

---

[4] Historically, such pricing was originally adopted to force clerks to make change as well as for its psychological impact on potential customers.

Rotation of duties is illustrated by the common practice of having employees such as receivables and payables clerks periodically exchange duties. Or a receivables clerk may handle accounts from A to C for three months and then be rotated to accounts M to P for three months, and so forth.

Incidentally, the act of bonding, that is, buying insurance against embezzlement, is not a substitute for vacations, rotation of duties, and similar precautions. Insurance companies will pay only when a loss is proved; establishing proof is often difficult and costly in itself.

☐ 8. Independent Check

All phases of the system should be subjected to periodic review by outsiders (for example, by independent public accountants) and by internal auditors who do not ordinarily have contact with the operation under review.

Auditors have a degree of objectivity that allows them to spot weaknesses overlooked by managers immersed in day-to-day operations. External auditors focus on the accounting records and the financial statements prepared from those records. It is too costly for auditors to examine all transactions, so they inspect a sample of the transactions. By first evaluating the system of internal control and testing the extent to which it is being followed, the auditor decides on the likelihood of undetected errors. If internal controls are weak, there is a greater probability of significant errors in the accounting records. Then the auditor chooses a larger sample to provide reasonable assurance that existing errors will be found. If internal controls are strong, the auditor can use a smaller sample to develop confidence in the accuracy of the accounting records.

Internal auditors are company employees, usually members of the controller's department. They focus on assessing adherence to the company's policies and procedures. Internal auditors help design control systems by pointing out internal control weaknesses, and they assess the degree of compliance with the existing systems. Their main goal is to enhance efficiency of operations by promoting adherence to both administrative and accounting controls.

The idea of an independent check extends beyond the work performed by professional auditors. For example, bank statements should be reconciled with book balances. The bank provides an independent record of cash. Furthermore, the monthly bank reconciliations should be conducted by some clerk other than the cash, receivables, or payables clerks. Other examples of independent checks include monthly statements sent to credit customers and physical counts of inventory to check against perpetual records.

☐ 9. Cost-Benefit Analysis

Highly complex systems tend to strangle people in red tape, so that the system impedes rather than promotes efficiency. Besides, there is "a cost of keeping the costs" that sometimes gets out of hand. Investments in more costly systems must be compared with the expected benefits. Unfortunately, such benefits are difficult to measure. It is much easier to relate new lathes or production methods to cost savings in manufacturing than a new computer to cost savings in the form of facilitating new attacks on problems of inventory control, production scheduling, and research. Yet hardheaded efforts, as are used in making other business decisions, must be made to measure alternative costs of various accounting systems. For example, the accounting firm of Peat Marwick completed a study of office automation for a client. After examining the jobs of 2,600 white-collar workers, Peat Marwick quantified a cost-benefit relationship: "A single investment of $10 million would result in a productivity savings equal to $8.4 million every year."

The relationship of costs to benefits sometimes leads to using sampling procedures. Although many companies implement more complex procedures to improve internal control, a few have taken a reverse course. They have decided that the increased costs of additional scrutiny are not worth the expected savings from catching mistakes or crooks. For example, an aerospace manufacturer routinely pays the invoice amounts without checking supporting documentation except on a random-sampling basis. An aluminum company sends out a blank check with its purchase orders, and then the supplier fills out the check and deposits it.

No framework for internal control is perfect in the sense that it can prevent some shrewd individual from "beating the system" either by outright embezzlement or by producing inaccurate records. The task is not total prevention of fraud, nor is it implementation of operating perfection; rather, the task is the designing of a *cost-effective* tool that will help achieve efficient operations and reduce temptation.

EFFECTS OF COMPUTERS ON INTERNAL CONTROL

☐ Computers Change the Control Environment

The computer has allowed relatively inexpensive processing of huge volumes of accounting data. Even most small companies use computers for some of their data processing. However, internal control over computerized operations has sometimes been weak. Consider an error that a human might make once a month. Such an error would be repeated thousands of times a day if contained in a computer program for processing vast quantities of data. Further, errors that would be obvious by scanning journal entries could be undetected because data are invisible, stored on tape or disks. Input and output data are transmitted over phone lines. Without appropriate security, anyone with a telephone and computer knowledge could read and possibly change a company's records. Thus the installation of internal control systems must accompany computerization.

Computers are amazingly accurate. The focus of internal control is not *computer* errors. Invariably, the computer has done exactly what it was told (or programmed) to do. Errors usually result because someone entered the wrong data, ran the wrong program, or asked for the wrong output.

The nine items in the checklist on pages 631–636 apply to both computer and manual systems. However, computers change the focus of internal control in two ways:

1. The computer can be used to accomplish some traditional internal control functions more efficiently.
2. Additional controls must be put in place to ensure the accuracy and reliability of computer-processed data.

☐ Types of Controls for Computer Systems

Controls for a computer system are divided into two types: *application controls* and *general controls.* The applications category includes *input*, *processing*, and *output controls.* The greatest source of errors in computerized systems is the data input. Both the original recording (for example, a sales slip) and the transcription of the data to computer-readable form (for example, key-punching cards or direct entry from a remote terminal) are sources of error. **Input controls** can help guard against the entry of false or erroneous data. Such controls include using standardized forms and verifying data input. Accountants also program the computer to verify that all required data are included on each input document, flag key numbers outside a range of reasonableness, and conduct other such checks. Use of optical scanning equipment can also limit data-recording errors.

Processing controls start with the design and programming of the system, including complete documentation. They also include normal separation and rotation of duties. For example, programmers should not be allowed to operate the computers. A computer consultant commented that he had immense stealing opportunities when he ran computer operations for a large bank: "I alone designed the dividend-payment operation, wrote the program for it, and ran the job on the machine. The operation was so big that it had a mistake tolerance of nearly $100,000. I could have paid at least half that much to myself, in small checks, and the money wouldn't even have been missed."

Processing controls can also be programmed into the computer. For example, files of data can be labeled so that only certain programs can read them or change (or update) the data.

Output controls check output against input, possibly by random manual processing of data. Output controls should also ensure that only authorized persons receive the reports. Computers often generate literally tons of printed output. A paper shredder can be an important control tool to safeguard privileged information.

General controls focus on the organization and operation of the data-processing activity. Good internal control requires well-defined procedures for developing, testing, and approving new systems and programs or changing old ones. Access to equipment and files should be restricted. But most important, as in any system, manual or computerized, are personnel controls. Hiring reliable personnel and keeping temptation from their doorsteps through commonsense controls are important goals of any internal control system.

EXAMPLES OF INTERNAL CONTROL

This section discusses specific internal control considerations for cash and inventories. More general coverage of accounting for cash is in Chapter 6 (pages

218–220) and Appendix 6A (pages 228–234). Accounting for inventories is in Chapter 7.

☐ Control of Cash

Cash is almost always the most enticing asset for potential thieves and embezzlers. Therefore internal controls are far more elaborate for cash than for, say, the paper clips and desks on the premises. We have already referred to various aspects of the control of cash. The following points are especially noteworthy:

1. As previously mentioned, the function of receiving cash should be separated from the function of disbursing cash. Moreover, individuals who handle cash or checks should not have access to the accounting records.

2. All receipts should be deposited intact each day. That is, none of the currency and checks received each day should be used directly for any other purposes. For example, sales in retail establishments are recorded in a cash register. A supervisor compares the locked cash register tape with the actual cash in the register drawer. Then the cash receipts are deposited, and the tape is forwarded to the accounting department as a basis for accounting entries. If cash from the till is sometimes used to pay suppliers, there is a serious internal control weakness.

3. All major disbursements should be made by serially numbered checks. Gaps should be investigated. The *Wall Street Journal* cited an example of good controls used poorly: "A bookkeeping assistant [was] under strict orders to note every missing number. . . . But no one checked to see how many were missing or why."

4. Bank accounts should be reconciled monthly. (This recommendation also applies to personal banking accounts.) It is surprising how many businesses (some of substantial size) do not reconcile their bank accounts regularly.

Control of cash requires procedures for handling both checks and currency. To control checks, many organizations use check protectors that perforate or otherwise establish an unalterable amount on the face of each check. Dual signatures are frequently required.

Currency is probably the most alluring form of cash. Businesses that handle much currency, such as gambling establishments, restaurants, and bars, are particularly subject to theft and false reporting. For example, many owners of small retail outlets do not record all of their cash receipts, a procedure known as *skimming*. Why? To save income taxes.

A recent news story reported: "Federal undercover agents in New York City opened an attack on the underground economy, which spawns billions of dollars yearly in untaxed income through off-the-books transactions." According to the affidavits, the establishments searched by the agents grossed more than $5.0 million while reporting on their tax returns only $3.6 million.

As explained in Chapter 6, a principal investigative weapon of the taxing authorities is the gross profit test. The agents know what gross profits a restaurant should generate for any specific level of revenues. However, restaurant owners are aware of this test; they may limit their cheating accordingly.

Comparing reported results with averages is not foolproof. An exclusive clothing store in San Francisco paid a percentage of sales for rent. Reported sales for a recent year were $11.2 million; an independent audit later disclosed actual sales of $20.5 million. The lessor always compared sales per square foot of floor space with those of similar stores. No clue to any impropriety arose. In fact, the lessor termed the reported sales per square foot "extraordinary" and the actual results as "unheard of."

☐ Internal Control of Inventories

In many organizations, inventories are more easily accessible than cash. Therefore they become a favorite target for thieves.

Retail merchants must contend with a major operating problem that is often called inventory shrinkage, a polite term for shoplifting by customers and embezzling by employees. More broadly defined, **inventory shrinkage** is the difference between (a) the value of inventory that would occur if there were no pilferage, misclassifications, breakage, and clerical errors and (b) the value of inventory when it is physically counted. Different types of companies have various levels of inventory shrinkage. Consider the following footnote from a recent annual report of Associated Dry Goods, one of the largest operators of department and discount stores in the country: "Physical inventories are taken twice each year. Department store inventory shrinkage at retail, as a percent to retail sales, was 2.4% this year compared with 2.1% last year. Discount store inventory shrinkage as a percent to retail sales was .4% and .3%, respectively." Some department stores have suffered shrinkage losses of 4% to 5% of their sales volume. Compare this with the typical net profit margin of 5% to 6%.

A management consultant firm has demonstrated how widespread shoplifting has become. The firm concentrated on a midtown New York department store. Five hundred shoppers, picked at random, were followed from the moment they entered the store to the time they departed. Forty-two shoppers, or one out of every twelve, took something. They stole $300 worth of merchandise, an average of $7.15 each. Similar experiments were conducted in Boston (1 of 20 shoplifted), Philadelphia (1 of 10), and again in New York (1 of 12).

Experts on controlling inventory shrinkage generally agree that the best deterrent is an alert employee at the point of sale. But other means are also used. Retail stores have gone so far as to use tiny sensitized tags on merchandise; if not detached or neutralized by a salesclerk, these miniature transmitters trip an alarm as the culprit begins to leave the store. Many libraries use a similar system to safeguard their books. Macy's in New York has continuous surveillance with over fifty television cameras. Retailers must also scrutinize their own personnel, because they account for at least 30% to 40% of inventory shortages.

Some stores have hired actors to pose as shoplifters, who are then subjected to fake, calm arrests. If potential thieves see the arrests, they may be deterred. Such ploys have helped reduce thefts by employees at major retail chains.

The problem of stealing is not confined to profit-seeking entities. According to the student newspaper at Northwestern University, $14,000 worth of silverware, glasses, and china was stolen from the university dining halls annually.

That amounts to $4.71 for every regular customer. Signs were posted at the end of each school term requesting the return of "borrowed" goods, but they have had little success. The food service director commented: "Two years ago, we put up really nice signs and set out boxes for returns. Kids saw the boxes and stole them for packing."

The imposing magnitude of retail inventory shrinkage demonstrates how management objectives may differ among industries. For example, consider the grocery business, where the net income percentage on sales hovers around 1%. You can readily see why a prime responsibility of the store manager is to control inventory shrinkage rather than boost gross sales volume. The trade-off is clear: If the operating profit on sales is 2%, to offset a $1,000 increase in shrinkage requires a $50,000 boost in gross sales.

☐   **Shrinkage in Perpetual and Periodic Inventory Systems**

Measuring inventory shrinkage is straightforward for companies using a perpetual inventory system. Shrinkage is simply the difference between the cost of the inventory identified by a physical count and the clerical inventory balance. Consider the following example:

Sales	$100,000
Cost of goods sold (perpetual inventory system)	$ 80,000
Beginning inventory	$ 15,000
Purchases	$ 85,000
Ending inventory, per clerical records	$ 20,000
Ending inventory, per physical count	$ 18,000

Shrinkage is $20,000 − $18,000 = $2,000. The journal entries under a perpetual inventory system would be:

Inventory shrinkage	2,000	
Inventory		2,000
To adjust ending inventory to its		
balance per physical count.		

Cost of goods sold	2,000	
Inventory shrinkage		2,000
To close inventory shrinkage to		
cost of goods sold.		

The total cost of goods sold would be $80,000 + $2,000 = $82,000.

By definition, a periodic inventory system has no clerical balance of the inventory account. Inventory shrinkage is automatically included in cost of goods sold. Why? Because beginning inventory plus purchases less ending inventory measures all inventory that has flowed out, whether it went to customers, shoplifters, or embezzlers or was simply lost or broken. Our example would show:

Beginning inventory	$ 15,000
Plus: Purchases	85,000
Goods available for sale	$100,000
Less: Ending inventory, per physical count	18,000
Cost of goods sold	$ 82,000

To assess shrinkage, we need some way to *estimate* what the ending inventory *should be*. The difference between this *estimate* and the physical count is inventory shrinkage. Appendix 14A describes how these estimates are made. No journal entries are necessary.

MANIPULATION OF REPORTED INCOME

Most organizations are managed honestly. Nevertheless, there will always be sinners. A recent news story commented: "The accounting tricks used in recent cases don't appear to be new, but the pattern of scheming is. In the accounting scandals of the early to mid 1970s, employees or executives bled money from operations for their own use. In many of the recent cases, however, employees apparently committed the improprieties under pressure to meet growth goals set by management."

Although many managers may not be directly lured by cash or inventories, they may nevertheless attempt to manipulate financial results. Why? Because bonuses, salary raises, and promotions are frequently affected by reported sales or income. For example, the achieving of a budgeted net income for a specific quarter or year may mean a tidy bonus.

Examples of manipulation of profits appear periodically. For instance, during the 1970s several executives of H. J. Heinz Company felt that they were under pressure to produce smooth earnings growth from quarter to quarter. These executives would prepay for advertising services near the end of a highly profitable quarter, charging the outlay to expense. They would then obtain the actual advertising services in the next quarter. In effect, such manipulation hurts the current quarter's profits by overstating its expenses and helps the subsequent quarter's profits by understating its expenses.

In a highly publicized case in the mid-1980s, E. F. Hutton, a securities brokerage firm, pleaded guilty to two thousand counts of fraud for writing checks for more than it had in its checking accounts. *Business Week* indicated that "Hutton's top management put in place incentives to encourage mid-level employees to boost cash-management income but neglected to set up systems to monitor the overdrafting of checking accounts."

In 1989, the manipulation of earnings at Boston Company was disclosed. This banking subsidiary of Shearson Lehman Hutton Inc. is a leader in administering pension funds, mutual funds, and trusts. Earnings for 1988 were inflated by $30 million, primarily by the improper deferral of expenses. The disclosure was followed by the firing of Boston Company's president and the resignation of its chief financial officer and senior vice-president. *Business Week* (February 6, 1989) reported that "some clients and Shearson insiders believe Boston Co. felt impelled by Shearson to produce extraordinary results at a time when most other units of Shearson were struggling."

Another common example of manipulation is the unjustifiable recognition of revenue. For example, a news story stated: "Datapoint, a computer maker, recently disclosed that much of its success was based on apparently phantom sales and earnings. Five marketing executives, three of them vice presidents, have resigned."

Undue pressures for profits not only induce the making of phony sales but also tempt marketing executives to sell to marginal customers who never pay.

The best protection against such manipulations is paying attention to these points in the checklist of internal control: (1) reliable personnel, (2) separation of duties, (3) proper authorization, and (4) independent check. Regarding the last, auditors typically conduct sales and purchase "cutoff" tests to see that revenues and expenses are indeed attributed to the correct reporting periods.

Above all, to ensure adequate control, a "control consciousness" must become embedded in the managers throughout the organization. Such consciousness must come from the top down. Unless top managers provide clear messages and examples of proper behavior, subordinates will be unlikely to take their responsibilities for control seriously. A *Business Week* editorial commented: "Middle management in a lot of companies is under excruciating pressure to meet profit goals that are too tough. There may be more indictments unless top management takes a more realistic view of its business."

SUMMARY

The following general characteristics form a checklist that can be used as a starting point for judging the effectiveness of internal control:

1. Reliable personnel with clear responsibilities
2. Separation of duties
3. Proper authorization
4. Adequate documents
5. Proper procedures
6. Physical safeguards
7. Bonding, vacations, and rotation of duties
8. Independent check
9. Cost-benefit analysis

This checklist is equally applicable to both computer and manual systems.

There are many well-established means of obtaining internal control over key assets such as cash and inventories. Independent check is especially popular, as is evidenced by bank reconciliations and surprise counts of inventories.

SUMMARY PROBLEMS FOR YOUR REVIEW

☐ **Problem One**

Identify the internal control weakness in each of the following situations:

a. Mike Reynolds performs all purchasing functions for Bayside Marine. He orders merchandise, oversees its delivery, and approves invoices for payment.

b. The Winthrop Mudhens, a minor league baseball team, is struggling financially. To save costs, and because all seating is general admission, the team has eliminated ticket takers. The ticket seller simply lets fans go through the gate when they pay the admission fee.

c. Cash and checks received by mail from customers who purchased items on open account are opened by an accounts receivable clerk, who deposits the cash and checks in the bank and prepares the appropriate accounting journal entry.

d. Ruth Ann Kilstrom is a trusted and dedicated employee. In fact, she is so dedicated that she has not taken a vacation in five years. Her boss appreciates her dedication because no one could do her job if she were gone.

e. Employees in Wing Point Grocery do a variety of jobs. When business is slack, they stock shelves and perform other necessary tasks. When the checkout stands are busy, everyone is expected to help with checkouts by manning whatever checkout stand is available. Each employee works at an average of four different checkout stands in an average shift, and every checkout stand is manned by an average of six different persons each day.

Solution to Problem One

a. A single person should not perform all these functions. Reynolds could order fictitious merchandise, record its delivery, and authorize payment to his own (or a confederate's) account.

b. There is no control against the ticket seller's letting friends in free or pocketing cash without issuing a ticket, simply letting the fan go through the gate.

c. The accounts receivable clerk performs too many functions. The clerk could keep cash (or forge an endorsement of a check) and make a false entry in the accounts, such as writing off the account as a bad debt.

d. There are at least two problems with Kilstrom's dedication. First, because no one else could do her job, the company would be in dire straits if something happened to her or if she resigned suddenly. Second, she has too great an opportunity to perpetrate a fraud without anyone discovering it. If someone replaced her periodically, he or she would be in a position to possibly discover any fraud.

e. Responsibility is not well defined. If a shortage of cash occurs at any checkout stand, it will be impossible to identify the employee responsible.

Problem Two

A news story reported:

☐ A federal grand jury indicted seven former Cenco Inc. officials, accusing them of an inventory overstatement scheme that led the concern to report about $25 million in false profits. The indictment charged that the overstatement was accomplished by increasing the number of products shown on inventory tabulating cards and making up new cards. The inflation of inventory lessened the reported cost of sales and thereby resulted in a greater reported profit figure.

Given this description, were any assets stolen? What is the major feature in the chapter checklist of internal control that is aimed at preventing such dishonesty? Indicate how such dishonest acts could be accomplished and how the dishonest officials might have expected to benefit from these acts.

Solution to Problem Two

Assets in the form of inventories were probably not stolen. Recall the section "Effects of Inventory Errors" in Appendix 7A, page 284; overstatement of ending inventory also causes overstatement of net income in the current period. Major motives were job security (by means of a display of higher net income) and greed (by means of management bonuses and raises in future salaries). Indeed, the manager who began the scheme was hired on a four-year contract with Cenco, giving him a modest annual base salary of $40,000 plus a bonus that added 1% to his salary for every 1% increase in the Cenco Medical Health (CMH) Group's net income. Net profits soared during the life of the manager's contract. The manager reaped total compensation far in excess of his base salary.

Two subordinate managers had no incentive bonus plans, but they played along with the inventory scheme to please their boss. A variety of ways were used to overstate inventories. For example, three boxes of gauze pads would become twenty-three. The auditors were fooled with the help of fake invoices and lies. The scheme was uncovered when a subordinate informed the company treasurer. Three executives were given prison terms ranging from one to three years.

The major feature that should prevent such dishonesty is *separation of duties*. Collusion makes dishonest acts harder to accomplish. Nevertheless, as the Cenco case illustrates, separation of duties is not enough to detect fictitious inventories.

Reliable personnel with clear responsibilities is an additional feature on the checklist that is illustrated by this case. Personnel must not only be competent and honest but also be adequately instructed and supervised. The lack of top-management surveillance undoubtedly contributed to this unfortunate situation. Immediate supervisors should know enough about underlying operations so that they can sense any significant unauthorized conduct.

Independent check is another feature that helps. That is why outside auditors conduct their own physical counts.

HIGHLIGHTS TO REMEMBER

1. Managers at all levels have a major responsibility for the success of a given control system. If managers do not insist on accurate documents, separation of duties, independent checks, and so on, trouble is inevitable.

2. In the United States there is a federal law that explicitly places the ultimate responsibility for the adequacy of internal controls of publicly held companies on top management, including the audit committee of the board of directors.

3. Retail merchandise is particularly subject to theft by both customers and employees. Systems help control the level of inventory shrinkage, but managers bear the primary responsibility for safeguarding assets.

4. Pressures for profits sometimes cause managers to manipulate records so that their performance will look better than it really is.

5. How elaborate should internal control systems be? The answer depends on the specific organization's problems. The design ultimately depends on weighing the costs of the system against the potential benefits in the form of more efficiency and less theft.

6. Accountants and managers should recognize that the role of an internal control system is as much a positive one (enhancing efficiency) as a negative one (reducing errors and fraud).

ACCOUNTING VOCABULARY

APPENDIX 14A: INVENTORY CONTROL VIA RETAIL METHOD, COST RATIOS, AND CUTOFFS

RETAIL METHOD OF INVENTORY CONTROL

A popular inventory method, known as the **retail inventory method**, or simply **retail method**, is often used as a control device. Its role in obtaining an inventory valuation (at cost) for financial statement purposes will be discussed in the next section; for now, concentrate on its internal control characteristics. Following is a general version of how food stores use the retail method to control grocery inventories at the store level. All merchandise is accounted for at *retail prices* as follows:

		RETAIL PRICES
	Inventory, January 5 (by surprise count by branch auditors)	$ 15,000
	Purchases (shipments to store from branch warehouse)	101,000
	Additional retail price changes:	
	Markups (from initial retail prices)	2,000
	Markdowns (from initial retail prices)	(5,000)
(1)	Total merchandise to account for	$113,000
	Sales (per cash-register records)	$100,000
	Allowable shrinkage (shoplifting, breakage, etc., usually a predetermined percentage of sales)	1,000
(2)	Total deductions	$101,000
(1) − (2)	Inventory, February 11, should be	$ 12,000
	Inventory, February 11, by physical count	11,100
	Excess shrinkage	$ 900

The total merchandise to account for is $113,000. What happens to it? Most is sold, some disappears as shrinkage, and some remains in ending inventory. Cash-register tabulations indicate sales of $100,000. If there were absolutely no shrinkage, the ending inventory at retail should be $113,000 − $100,000 = $13,000. But suppose an allowable "normal" shrinkage is 1% of sales, or $1,000. Therefore the expected inventory is $13,000 − $1,000 = $12,000.

The actual physical count provides a retail valuation of $11,100. Thus the total shrinkage is $1,900, consisting of $1,000 of allowable shrinkage plus $900 of excess shrinkage ($12,000 − $11,100 = $900).

If the inventory shrinkage is not within predetermined limits, the manager usually bears prime responsibility. There are worrisome behavioral implications here. For utmost accuracy, the retail method requires the prompt application of the directed changes in retail prices that are ordered by the branch managers. For example, to help ensure a good performance regarding control of shrinkage, store managers may be inclined to delay the entering of markdowns on price tags and may be inclined to overstate the retail prices of merchandise if possible. The branch manager usually relies on other means, such as surprise spot checks, to ensure that markup and markdown directives are being followed.

Computerized checkout systems also help to control inventory shrinkage. Such a system records each individual item that is sold, allowing a store to keep an item-by-item perpetual inventory. Such a system pinpoints the items that are disappearing, and additional control measures can be applied to these items.

ROLE OF COST RATIOS AND GROSS PROFIT PERCENTAGES

Inventories carried at retail values provide a satisfactory basis for internal control. However, inventories in financial statements are reported at cost. Therefore the retail values of inventories must be converted to costs. This is accomplished by approximations, using the ratio of cost to retail value based on an average. Consider the data in our illustration:

		RETAIL PRICES	COST
	Inventory, January 5 (by surprise count by branch auditors)	$ 15,000	$12,300
	Purchases (shipments to store from branch warehouse)	101,000	78,100
	Additional retail price changes:		
	Markups (from initial retail prices)	2,000	
	Markdowns (from initial retail prices)	(5,000)	
(1)	Total merchandise to account for	$113,000	$90,400
	Ratio of cost to retail value		80%
	Sales (per cash-register records)	$100,000	$80,000
	Allowable shrinkage (shoplifting, breakage, etc., usually a predetermined percentage of sales)	1,000	800
(2)	Total deductions	$101,000	$80,800
(1) − (2)	Inventory, February 11, should be	$ 12,000	$ 9,600
	Inventory, February 11, by physical count	11,100	8,880
	Excess shrinkage	$ 900	$ 720

The line denoted as (1) provides the basis for a ratio of cost to retail value:

$$\$90,400 \div \$113,000 = .80$$

This critical ratio[5] is then used to develop the key subsequent amounts at cost:

	RETAIL PRICES	AVERAGE RATIO OF COST TO RETAIL VALUE	COST
Allowable shrinkage	$ 1,000 ×	.80	= $ 800
Inventory, by physical count	11,100 ×	.80	= 8,880
Excess shrinkage	900 ×	.80	= 720

These amounts can be used in an income statement for a company with a periodic inventory system:

Sales		$100,000
Cost of sales:		
Beginning inventory per physical count	$12,300	
Purchases	78,100	
Available for sale	$90,400	
Ending inventory per physical count	8,800	
Cost of sales (including $800 allowable shrinkage and $720 excess shrinkage)		81,520
Gross margin (after inventory shrinkage)		$ 18,480

This approach is used over and over again as periods unfold. The ending inventory of $8,880 becomes the beginning inventory of the next reporting period. Purchases are then added at cost, a new ratio of cost to retail value is developed, and shrinkage and ending inventory values are approximated:

1. Compute the goods available for sale at retail value and cost.
2. Compute the ratio of cost to retail value.
3. Count the ending inventory and value it at retail value.
4. Convert the retail value of the ending inventory to cost by using the ratio of cost to retail value.

The *cost* of shrinkage, which can be divided into allowable and excess components, is approximated by using the ratio of cost to retail value.

Note that the ratio of cost to retail value is the complement of the gross profit ratio. In this illustration, the gross profit percentage is $100\% - 80\% = 20\%$. Thus the gross profit percentage or its related ratio of cost to retail value is a key element of internal control.

---

[5] Both markdowns and markups are included in this illustrative computation. Many retailers prefer to exclude markdowns because a lower cost ratio is developed:

$90,400 ÷ ($113,000 + $5,000 Markdowns) = .7661

This ratio would provide a "more conservative" ending inventory. Advocates of this approach say that it yields a better approximation of the lower-of-cost-or-market method.

CUTOFF ERRORS, CONSIGNMENTS, AND INVENTORY VALUATION

The accrual basis of accounting should include the physical counting and careful valuation of inventory at least once yearly. Auditors routinely search for **cutoff errors**, which are failures to record transactions in the correct time period. For example, assume a periodic inventory system. Suppose a physical inventory is conducted on December 31. Inventory purchases of $100,000 arrive in the receiving room during the afternoon of December 31. The acquisition is included in Purchases and Accounts Payable but excluded from the ending inventory valuation. Such an error would overstate cost of goods sold and understate gross profit. On the other hand, if the acquisition were not recorded until January 2, the error would understate the ending inventory and Accounts Payable as of December 31. However, cost of goods sold and gross profit would be correct because Purchases and the ending inventory would be understated by the same amount.

The general approach to recording purchases and sales is keyed to the legal transfer of ownership. Some major points follow:

1. Ownership typically changes hands when the goods are delivered by the seller to the purchaser. These terms are usually F.O.B. destination. If the terms are F.O.B. shipping point, ownership passes to the purchaser when the goods are delivered to the transportation company.
2. Sometimes goods are shipped on **consignment**. These are goods shipped for future sale, title remaining with the shipper (consignor), for which the receiver (consignee), upon his or her acceptance, is accountable. Even though such goods are physically elsewhere, they are part of the consignor's inventory until sold. For example, a manufacturer of bicycles might ship 20 units on consignment to a new retailer. Under such terms, the bicycles are included in the manufacturer's inventory and excluded from the retailer's inventory.

Auditors are especially careful about cutoff tests because the pressure for profits sometimes causes managers to postpone the recording of bona fide purchases of goods and services. Similarly, the same managers may deliberately include sales *orders* near year-end (rather than bona fide completed sales) in revenues. For example, consider the case of Datapoint, a maker of small computers and telecommunications equipment. A news story reported: "Datapoint's hard-pressed sales force was still logging orders that might not hold up after shipment." In the wake of an accounting scandal, Datapoint's president declared a three-week "amnesty period" during which scheduled shipments could be taken off the books, no questions asked.

A similar news story referred to difficulties at McCormick & Co., a firm best known for its spices: "The investigation also found that improprieties included the company's accounting for sales. In a longstanding practice, the company recorded as sales goods that had been selected and prepared for shipment rather than waiting until after they had been shipped as is the customary accounting practice."

APPENDIX 14B: PROCESSING DATA USING SPECIAL JOURNALS

Elsewhere in this textbook, the only book of original entry is a general journal. This appendix describes the use of special journals in addition to a general journal. This material is important to anyone who wants to know the details about how an accounting system processes data.

Chapters 4 and 5 use the general journal as the basic step in data processing. However, in all but the smallest accounting systems, **special journals** (or procedures akin to special journals) are used in addition to the general journal:

IN OTHER CHAPTERS	IN THIS APPENDIX
1. Transaction	1. Transaction
2. Source documents (invoices, receiving reports, checks, etc.)	2. Source documents
3. General journal	3. Sales journal (for credit sales) Cash receipts journal Purchases journal (for credit purchases of inventory) Cash disbursements journal General journal (for all other transactions)
4. General ledger	4. General and subsidiary ledgers[6]

Every accounting system has a general journal, whether kept in pen and ink or on computer tape or disk. But a general journal is not an efficient device for recording numerous repetitive transactions. How would you enjoy using a general journal to debit Accounts Receivable and credit Sales for each credit sale made in a department store on a Saturday? Moreover, how would you like to post each journal entry to the general ledger accounts for accounts receivable and sales? Not only would the work be long, tedious, and dull, but it would be outrageously expensive.

More than 90% of most companies' transactions are recorded in one of the four special journals listed. As we will see, all entries in these journals have common features, thereby allowing speed, efficiency, and economy of data processing. The same basic ideas apply to both manual and computerized systems.

SALES JOURNAL

The sales journal in Exhibit 14–4 is probably better called a *credit sales journal* because it includes only credit sales, cash sales being recorded in the cash receipts journal. If a general journal were used for these five credit sales transactions, five separate entries debiting Accounts Receivable and crediting Sales would be required. In addition, five separate postings would be made to these accounts in the general ledger. Obviously, if five thousand sales occurred in June, journalizing and posting each individual transaction would become oppressive.

Consider the details in Exhibit 14–4. As each sale is entered, the accountant debits the *subsidiary* ledger account for the particular customer. The invoice reference provides a trail to any underlying details of the sale. A check mark is put in the Post column as each amount is posted to the individual subsidiary accounts.

The general ledger accounts, Accounts Receivable and Sales, are not written out as entries are being made in the sales journal. The dollar amount is entered once, not twice, for each sale. Postings to the general ledger are made only periodically, usually at the end of the month. The $6,400 total is posted to two accounts and has the same effect as if the following general journal entry were made:

	POST	AMOUNTS	
Accounts receivable	4	6,400	
Sales	88		6,400

Of course, the direct posting from the sales journal eliminates having the above general journal entry.

---

[6] Chapter 6 illustrates a subsidiary ledger for accounts receivable on pages 224–225.

EXHIBIT 14–4

Sales Journal and Postings

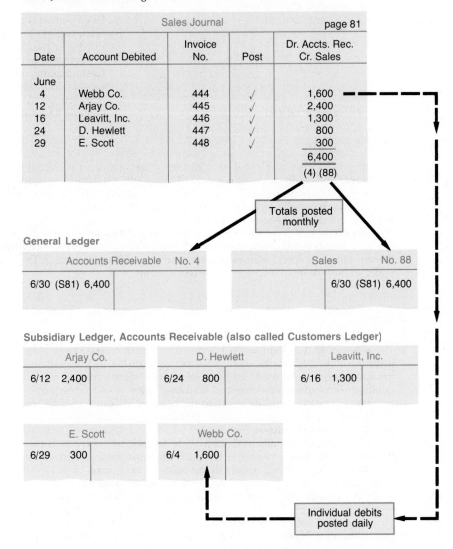

As explained in Chapter 6, the sum of the balances in the subsidiary ledger must agree with the Accounts Receivable account in the general ledger. When there is a subsidiary ledger, its corresponding summary account in the general ledger is often called a controlling account. The existence of a subsidiary ledger for a particular general ledger account is often denoted by adding the word *control* to the latter's title—for example, Accounts Receivable Control.

The sales journal (and other special journals) are being described here to help you visualize various ways of gathering data for posting to ledgers. However, these special journals have been abandoned as being completely unnecessary in many mechanical and computerized systems. For example, copies of all credit sales slips can be accumulated and summarized once a month and posted to ledgers without being journalized at all:

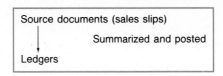

Source documents (sales slips)

Summarized and posted

Ledgers

CASH RECEIPTS JOURNAL

Special journals may have a single money column, as in the sales journal just illustrated, or they may have several columns, as Exhibit 14–5 demonstrates. The number of columns depends on the frequency of transactions affecting particular accounts. Moreover, as the cash receipts journal in Exhibit 14–5 shows, the most frequently affected columns might be placed at the far right—regardless of whether the amounts therein are debits or credits. The important point about debits and credits is that they are ultimately entered on the correct sides of the *ledger* accounts, even though the format of some special *journals* seems to put debits on the right.

Cash sales and collections on accounts receivable are generally the two most common types of cash receipts, so special columns are formed for Cash, Sales, and Accounts Receivable. The amounts of the cash sales are entered in the Cash and Sales columns. The amounts of the collections on accounts are entered in the Cash and Accounts Receivable columns. This specialized approach replaces the need for countless repetitions of the following familiar entries that would otherwise have to be made in the general journal:

Cash	xx	
Sales		xx
Cash	xx	
Accounts receivable		xx

Infrequent cash receipts, such as those illustrated for the bank loan and the sale of common stock, are entered in the Cash and the Other Accounts columns.

The columns are totaled at the end of each month to make sure that the total debits equal the total credits: 13,000 + 3,700 + 7,500 = 24,200. Then the totals of each column are posted to the indicated accounts in the general ledger. Of course, the Other Accounts total is not posted. Instead the individual amounts therein are posted to the relevant individual general ledger accounts. The numbers 54 and 70 are placed in the Post column as evidence that the postings have been made. The illustrated general ledger accounts now contain postings from the cash receipts journal and those made previously from the sales journal.

The only subsidiary ledger in this illustration is for Accounts Receivable. The postings from the cash receipts journal are made in the same manner as those from the sales journal. A principal internal control feature is illustrated by the monthly schedule of the individual customer balances. The sum should agree with the general ledger balance, June 30:

Arjay Co.	$2,400
E. Scott	300
Balance, subsidiary ledger	$2,700
Balance, Accounts Receivable in general ledger	$2,700

EXHIBIT 14–5

Cash Receipts Journal and Postings

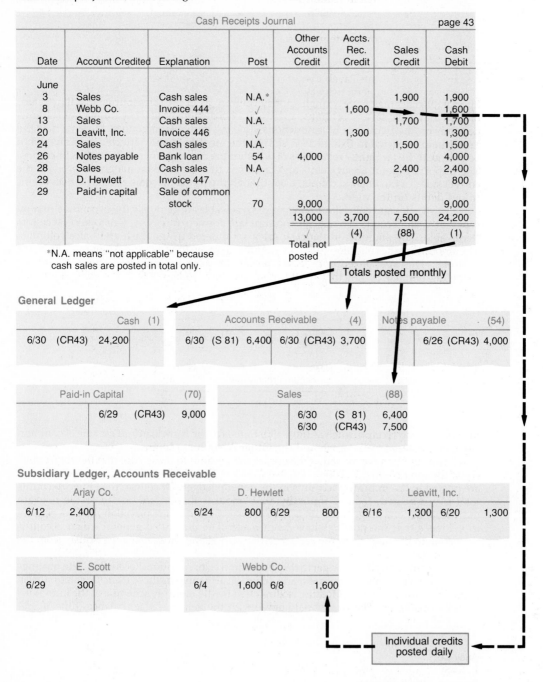

	Cash Receipts Journal						page 43
				Other Accounts Credit	Accts. Rec. Credit	Sales Credit	Cash Debit
Date	Account Credited	Explanation	Post				
June							
3	Sales	Cash sales	N.A.*			1,900	1,900
8	Webb Co.	Invoice 444	✓		1,600		1,600
13	Sales	Cash sales	N.A.			1,700	1,700
20	Leavitt, Inc.	Invoice 446	✓		1,300		1,300
24	Sales	Cash sales	N.A.			1,500	1,500
26	Notes payable	Bank loan	54	4,000			4,000
28	Sales	Cash sales	N.A.			2,400	2,400
29	D. Hewlett	Invoice 447	✓		800		800
29	Paid-in capital	Sale of common stock	70	9,000			9,000
				13,000	3,700	7,500	24,200
				✓ Total not posted	(4)	(88)	(1)

*N.A. means "not applicable" because cash sales are posted in total only.

Totals posted monthly

General Ledger

	Cash	(1)	
6/30	(CR43)	24,200	

	Accounts Receivable		(4)
6/30 (S 81) 6,400	6/30 (CR43) 3,700

	Notes payable		(54)
	6/26 (CR43) 4,000

	Paid-in Capital		(70)
	6/29 (CR43) 9,000

	Sales		(88)
	6/30 (S 81) 6,400
	6/30 (CR43) 7,500

Subsidiary Ledger, Accounts Receivable

	Arjay Co.	
6/12	2,400	

	D. Hewlett	
6/24	800	6/29 800

	Leavitt, Inc.	
6/16	1,300	6/20 1,300

	E. Scott	
6/29	300	

	Webb Co.	
6/4	1,600	6/8 1,600

Individual credits posted daily

PURCHASES JOURNAL

The purchases journal in Exhibit 14–6 is the mirror image of the sales journal except that the amounts and individuals differ. The purchases journal is better called a *credit merchandise purchases journal* because cash purchases are recorded in the cash disbursements journal. A perpetual inventory system is assumed, although the subsidiary ledger (composed of stock cards for individual inventory items) is not shown here. If a general journal were used for these five credit purchase transactions, five separate entries debiting Inventory and crediting Accounts Payable would be required. Moreover, five separate postings would be made to these general ledger accounts. (Under a periodic inventory system, the debits would be made to the Purchases account instead of Merchandise Inventory.)

EXHIBIT 14–6

Purchases Journal and Postings

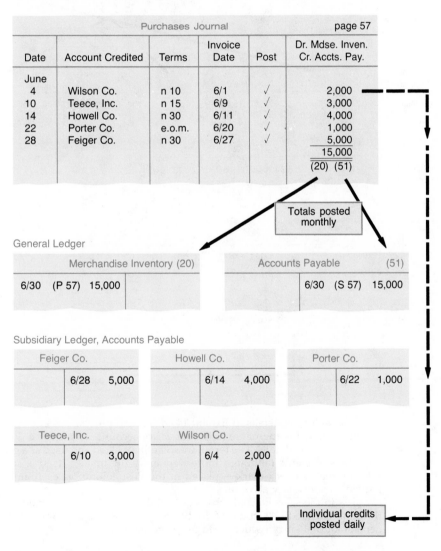

EXHIBIT 14–7

Cash Disbursements Journal and Postings

					Cash Disbursements Journal			page 67
					Other	Accts.	Mdse.	
	Check				Accounts	Payable	Inven.	Cash
Date	No.	Payee	Account Debited	Post	Debit	Debit	Debit	Credit
June								
6	322	Simpson Co.	Inventory	✓*			1,000	1,000
12	323	Wilson Co.	Wilson Co.	✓		2,000		2,000
15	324	IRS	Income taxes payable	55	4,000			4,000
19	325	Reese, Inc.	Inventory	✓			400	400
23	326	Teece, Inc.	Teece, Inc.	✓		3,000		3,000
26	327	Fixit Co.	Repair expense	94	200			200
28	328	Porter Co.	Porter Co.	✓		1,000		1,000
					4,200	6,000	1,400	11,600
					✓	(51)	(20)	(1)
					Total not posted			

*Posted to subsidiary accounts for Merchandise Inventory,
 but this subsidiary ledger is not illustrated here.

Totals posted monthly

General Ledger

Cash	(1)
6/30 (CR43) 24,200	6/30 (CD67) 11,600

Merchandise Inventory (20)	
6/30 (P 57) 15,000	
6/30 (CD67) 1,400	

Accounts Payable	(51)
6/30 (CD67) 6,000	6/30 (S57) 15,000

Income Taxes Payable	(55)
6/15 (CD67) 4,000	

Repair Expense	(94)
6/26 (CD67) 200	

Subsidiary Ledger, Accounts Payable

Feiger Co.	
	6/28 5,000

Howell Co.	
	6/14 4,000

Porter Co.	
6/28 1,000	6/22 1,000

Teece, Inc.	
6/23 3,000	6/10 3,000

Wilson Co.	
6/12 2,000	6/4 2,000

Individual debits
posted daily

Consider the details in Exhibit 14–6. As each purchase is entered, the name of the account credited is the name of the *subsidiary* account. The invoice date provides a trail to the underlying details. The terms are sometimes listed and used as a guide to scheduling cash disbursements (although more frequently the invoice itself is so used). As in the sales journal, a check mark is placed in the Post column as each amount is put in the individual subsidiary accounts.

As in the sales journal, postings to the general ledger are made only at the end of the month. The $15,000 total is "double posted" and has the same effect as the following general journal entry (which need no longer be made):

	POST	AMOUNTS	
Merchandise inventory	20	15,000	
Accounts payable	51		15,000

CASH DISBURSEMENTS JOURNAL

The cash disbursements journal is often called a *check register* or a *cash payments journal*. Like its counterpart, the cash receipts journal, the cash disbursements journal usually has multiple columns. As Exhibit 14–7 shows, special columns are formed for Cash, Merchandise Inventory, and Accounts Payable. The amounts of the cash purchases are entered in the Cash and Merchandise Inventory columns. The amounts of the payments on accounts are entered in the Cash and Accounts Payable columns. Thus countless repetitions of the following familiar general journal entries are avoided:

Merchandise inventory	xx	
Cash		xx
Accounts payable	xx	
Cash		xx

Payments on accounts payable are made so that suppliers receive the checks on the appropriate due dates. For instance, the Porter Co. terms are e.o.m., which means payment is due at the end of the month of the invoice. Therefore a check is sent on June 28 to allow two days for mail delivery.

Infrequent cash disbursements, such as those illustrated for income taxes and repairs, are entered in the columns *Cash* and *Other Accounts*.

Each column is totaled (accountants say *footed*) and the column totals are cross-added (*cross-footed*) to make sure that the total debits equal the total credits: 4,200 + 6,000 + 1,400 = 11,600. Then the totals of each column are posted to the indicated accounts in the general ledger. The total for Other Accounts is not posted. Instead the individual amounts are posted to the relevant individual general ledger accounts, as shown by numbers 55 and 94 in the Post column. The general ledger now has all postings from the pertinent special journals.

The postings from the cash disbursements journal to the subsidiary accounts payable ledger are made in the same way as from the purchases journal. For control purposes, a monthly schedule of the individual accounts payable balances should be compared with the general ledger balance. As of June 30:

Feiger Co.	$5,000
Howell Co.	4,000
Balance, subsidiary ledger	$9,000
Balance, Accounts Payable in general ledger	$9,000

OTHER JOURNALS, INCLUDING VOUCHER REGISTER

As indicated earlier, the general journal exists for all organizations. As a minimum, general journal entries are made for closing entries and for adjusting entries such as depreciation and various accruals.

The four special journals here come in a variety of shapes, sizes, names, and formats and are processed by manual, mechanical, or computerized means. Moreover, additional special journals are frequently justified, particularly in accounting for payroll. Other special journals include those for (a) sales returns and allowances and (b) purchase returns and allowances.

Some companies employ a **voucher system** for controlling cash disbursements. This system is too detailed for thorough coverage here, but a brief description follows.

1. A **voucher** is a form to which purchase orders, receiving reports, and invoices are often attached. The voucher is formal verification of a transaction and authority to prepare journal entries and to write and release a check. Sometimes this formal authority is called a **disbursement voucher.** Indeed, sometimes a copy of the disbursement voucher becomes the formal check itself (called a *voucher check*).

2. These vouchers are listed in a **voucher register**, which is similar to Exhibit 14–7 except that the Check No. column would be replaced by a Voucher No. and the Cash column would be replaced by a Vouchers Payable column.

3. A simple **check register** would be created and would appear as follows:

	Check Register		
Date	Check No.	Payee	Dr. Vouchers Payable Cr. Cash

FUNDAMENTAL ASSIGNMENT MATERIAL

☐ General Coverage

14–1. **MANAGEMENT'S RESPONSIBILITY FOR INTERNAL CONTROLS.** The Gerberding Company has always tried to prepare informative annual reports. A few years ago, Harold Gerberding, president, heard about the Foreign Corrupt Practices Act, but he assumed that it did not affect his company. After all, not only did Gerberding Company refrain from corrupt foreign practices but the company had no foreign operations or export sales.

Required: Explain how the Foreign Corrupt Practices Act affects a company such as Gerberding. How does it affect Gerberding's annual report?

14–2. **EMBEZZLEMENT AND CHECKLIST OF INTERNAL CONTROL.** (Alternate is 14–27.) Cranium Products Company manufactures a variety of sports headgear, which it sells to hundreds of distributors and retailers.

A company "cash clerk" processes all cash received in the mail (mostly checks from customers on account). He opens the mail, sending to the accounting department all accompanying letters and remittance advices that show the amounts received from each customer or other source. The letters and remittance advices are used by the accounting department for appropriate entries in the accounts. The cash clerk sends the currency and checks to another employee, who makes daily bank deposits but has no access to the accounting records. The monthly bank statements are reconciled by the accounting department, which has no access to cash or checks.

The sales manager has the authority for granting credit to customers for sales returns and allowances, and the credit manager has the authority for deciding when uncollectible accounts should be written off. However, a recent audit revealed that the cash clerk has forged the signatures of the sales manager and the credit manager to some forms authorizing sales allowances and bad debt write-offs for certain accounts. These forms were then sent to the accounting department, which entered them on the books and routinely posted them to customers' accounts.

Required:

1. How could the cash clerk have used these forgeries to cover an embezzlement by him? Assume there was no collusion with other employees. Be specific.
2. See the chapter checklist of internal control. Identify the items that would be relevant to such an embezzlement, and describe briefly any different procedures that should have been followed by Cranium Products.

14–3. **INTERNAL CONTROL WEAKNESSES.** (Alternate is 14–26.) Identify the internal control weaknesses in each of the following situations:

a. Rodney Williams was hired by D. A. Hills to work in the accounting department of Hills Electronics and Appliances during summer vacation. Williams is a football star at the local university, and providing the summer job is one way that Hills supports the team. After a week of training, Williams is assigned the task of opening the mail containing checks from customers, recording the payment in the books, and preparing the bank deposit slip.

b. Jim Sanchez is the manager of a local franchise of a major twenty-four-hour convenience store. Sanchez is pleased that he had been able to keep labor costs well below the average for such stores. He generally operates with only one clerk in the store. He has not granted a pay increase in four years. He loses a lot of clerks, but he can always find someone to replace them.

c. Martha McGuire operates a Shell service station. She has observed that it takes much extra time for attendants to walk from the gas pumps to the inside cash register after each sale. To save time, McGuire has placed a locked cash box next to the pumps and has given each attendant a key. Cash and credit card slips are placed in the cash box, and at the end of the day the amounts are counted and entered in total into the cash register.

d. Lazlo Perconte trusts his employees. The former manager in his position purchased fidelity bonds on all the employees who handle cash. Perconte decided that such bonds showed a lack of trust, so he ceased purchasing them. Besides, the money saved helped Perconte meet his budget for the year.

☐ Understanding Published Financial Reports

14–4. **USE OF CREDIT CARDS.** A business-school student used a VISA card for a variety of purchases. When checking his monthly bill, he compared his original copy with a duplicate copy for a gasoline purchase made at a local discount-store shopping center. The original copy showed a purchase of $14.25; the duplicate had been raised to $16.25.

Required: Who obtained the extra $2? How can the system be improved to prevent such thievery?

14–5. **OVERSTATEMENTS OF RESULTS.** Saxon Industries, Inc., sold office copiers before undergoing bankruptcy proceedings.

Forbes reported that Saxon's inventory had been overstated by at least $100 million out of a reported total inventory of $120 million. A news story reported that possible motives included "inflating earnings or increasing the company's borrowing capacity."

Regarding the manipulations, *Forbes* referred to the Saxon inventory methods as "not LIFO or FIFO but Presto!"

Required:

1. How does overstating inventory enhance reported results? Be specific.
2. How are such overstatements accomplished? Prevented? Be specific.

ADDITIONAL ASSIGNMENT MATERIAL

☐ General Coverage

14–6. Into what four categories can the most repetitive, voluminous transactions in most organizations be divided?

14–7. Distinguish between *internal accounting control* and *internal administrative control.*

14–8. "The primary responsibility for internal controls rests with the outside auditors." Do you agree? Explain.

14–9. "The Foreign Corrupt Practices Act governs the acts of multinational companies." Do you agree? Explain.

14–10. What are the two major ways of ensuring compliance with the Foreign Corrupt Practices Act regarding internal control systems?

14–11. Give three examples of documentation of an internal accounting control system.

14–12. Name five objectives of the Foreign Corrupt Practices Act with respect to internal accounting controls.

14–13. What is the primary responsibility of the audit committee?

14–14. Prepare a checklist of the most important factors to consider in judging an internal control system.

14–15. "The most important element of successful control is personnel." Explain.

14–16. What is the essential idea of separation of duties?

14–17. Authorization can be general or specific. Give an example of each.

14–18. "The words *internal control* are commonly misunderstood. They are thought to refer to those facets of the accounting system that are supposed to help prevent embezzling." Do you agree? Why?

14–19. "Internal control systems have both negative and positive objectives." Do you agree? Explain.

14–20. Internal control of a computerized system consists of applications controls and general controls. What are the three types of applications controls?

14–21. Briefly describe how a bottler of soda water might compile data regarding control of breakage of bottles at the plant, where normal breakage can be expected.

14–22. The branch manager of a national retail grocery chain has stated: "My managers are judged more heavily on the basis of their merchandise-shrinkage control than on their overall sales volume." Why? Explain.

14–23. "Business operations would be a hopeless tangle without the paper work that is often regarded with disdain." Explain.

14–24. "Our managers know they are expected to meet budgeted profit targets. We do not take excuses. Good managers find a way to make budget." Discuss the possible consequences of this policy.

14–25. Pressure for profits extends beyond managers in profit-seeking companies. A 1986 news story reported: "The profit motive, even in nonprofit hospitals, is steadily eroding the traditional concern to provide care to the medically indigent." Why does the profit motive affect even nonprofit organizations?

14–26. **INTERNAL CONTROL WEAKNESSES.** (Alternate is 14–3.) Identify the internal control weaknesses in each of the following situations, and indicate what change or changes you would recommend to eliminate the weaknesses:

    a. The internal audit staff of Aerospace, Inc., reports to the controller. However, internal audits are undertaken only when a department manager requests one, and audit reports are confidential documents prepared exclusively for the manager. Internal auditors are not allowed to talk to the external auditors.

    b. The president of Jackson State Bank, a small-town midwestern bank, wants to expand the size of his bank. He hired Alice Howell to begin a foreign-loan department. Howell had previously worked in the international department of a New York City bank. The president told her to consult with him on any large loans, but he never specified exactly what was meant by "large." At the end of Howell's first year, the president was surprised and pleased by her results. Although she had made several loans larger than any made by other sections of the bank and had not consulted with him on any of them, the president hesitated to say anything because her financial results were so good. He certainly did not want to upset the person most responsible for the bank's excellent growth in earnings.

    c. Michael Grant is in charge of purchasing and receiving watches for Blumberg, Inc., a chain of jewelry stores. Grant places orders, fills out receiving documents when the watches are delivered, and authorizes payment to suppliers. According to Blumberg's procedures manual, Grant's activities should be reviewed by a purchasing supervisor. But to save money, the supervisor was not replaced when she resigned three years ago. No one seems to miss the supervisor.

14–27. EMBEZZLEMENT OF CASH RECEIPTS. (Alternate is 14–2.) Leboe Company is a small wholesaler of exercise equipment. It has only a few employees.

    The owner of Leboe Company, who is also its president and general manager, makes daily deposits of customers' checks in the company bank account and writes all checks issued by the company. The president also reconciles the monthly bank statement with the books when the bank statement is received in the mail.

    The assistant to Leboe Company's president renders secretarial services, which include taking dictation, typing letters, and processing all mail, both incoming and outgoing. Each day the assistant opens the incoming mail and gives the president the checks received from customers. The vouchers attached to the checks are separated by the assistant and sent to the bookkeeper, along with any other remittance advices that have been enclosed with the checks.

    The bookkeeper makes prompt entries to credit customers' accounts for their remittances. From these accounts, the bookkeeper prepares monthly statements for mailing to customers.

    Other employees include marketing and warehouse personnel.

Required:

For the thefts described below, explain briefly how each could have been concealed and what precautions you would recommend for forestalling the theft and its concealment:

1. The president's assistant takes some customers' checks, forges the company's endorsements, deposits the checks in a personal bank account, and destroys the check vouchers and any other remittance advices that have accompanied these checks.
2. The same action is taken as above, except that the vouchers and other remittance advices are sent intact to the bookkeeper.

14–28. APPRAISAL OF PAYROLL SYSTEM. (CPA, adapted.) The Coastal Savings and Loan Company has one hundred branch loan offices. Each office has a manager and four or five subordinates who are employed by the manager. Branch managers prepare the weekly payroll, including their own salaries, and pay their employees from cash on hand. The employee signs the payroll sheet, signifying receipt of his or her salary. Hours worked by hourly personnel are inserted in the payroll sheet from time cards prepared by the employees and approved by the manager.

    The weekly payroll sheets are sent to the home office along with other accounting statements and reports. The home office compiles employee earnings records and prepares all federal and state salary reports from the weekly payroll sheets.

    Salaries are established by home-office job-evaluation schedules. Salary adjustments, promotions, and transfers of full-time employees are approved by a home-office salary committee, based on the recommendations of branch managers and area supervisors. Branch managers advise the salary committee of new full-time employees and of terminations. Part-time and temporary employees are hired without referral to the salary committee.

Required:

Based on your review of the payroll system, how might payroll funds be embezzled?

14–29. **MULTIPLE CHOICE.** (CPA, adapted.) Choose the best answer for each of the four questions that follow:

1. Which of the following internal control procedures would be *most* likely to prevent the concealment of a cash shortage resulting from the improper write-off of a trade account receivable?

    a. Write-offs must be authorized by company field sales employees who are in a position to determine the financial standing of the customers.

    b. Write-offs must be approved by a responsible officer after review of credit department recommendations and supporting evidence.

    c. Write-offs must be supported by an aging schedule showing that only receivables overdue several months have been written off.

    d. Write-offs must be approved by the cashier who is in a position to know if the receivables have, in fact, been collected.

2. Which of the following is an effective internal accounting control over accounts receivable?

    a. The billing function should be assigned to persons other than those responsible for maintaining accounts receivable subsidiary records.

    b. Only persons who handle cash receipts should be responsible for the preparation of documents that reduce accounts receivable balances.

    c. Responsibility for approval of the write-off of uncollectible accounts receivable should be assigned to the cashier.

    d. Balances in the subsidiary accounts ledger should be reconciled to the general ledger control account once a year, preferably at year-end.

3. Internal control over cash receipts is weakened when an employee who receives customer mail receipts also

    a. Prepares bank deposit slips for all mail receipts

    b. Maintains a petty cash fund

    c. Prepares initial cash receipts records

    d. Records credits to individual accounts receivable

4. Which of the following activities would be *least* likely to strengthen a company's internal control?

    a. Carefully selecting and training employees

    b. Separating accounting from other financial operations

    c. Maintaining insurance for fire and theft

    d. Fixing responsibility for the performance of employee duties

14–30. **FILM PROCESSING.** (W. Crum.) Write not over one page about the possible areas where internal controls should be instituted in the business described briefly below. Keep in mind the size of the business and do not suggest controls of a type impossible to set up in a firm of this sort. Make any reasonable assumptions about management duties and policies not expressly set forth below.

You have a film-developing service in Glendale, with ten employees driving their own cars six days a week to contact about forty places each, where film is left to be picked up and developed. Routes cover all parts of Los Angeles. Drivers bring film in one day and return the processed film the second or third day later. Stores pay the driver for his charges made on film picked up at their store, less a percentage for their work as an agency. The driver then turns this cash in to the Glendale office, where all film is developed and books are kept. Six to ten employees work at the office in Glendale, depending on the volume of work. You run the office and have one full-time accounting-clerical employee. Route drivers are paid monthly by mile of route covered.

14–31. **ASSIGNMENT OF DUTIES.** The Cyclometric Corporation is a distributor of several popular lines of drawing and measuring instruments. It purchases merchandise from several suppliers and sells to hundreds of retail stores. Here is a *partial list* of the company's necessary office routines:

1. Verifying and comparing related purchase documents: purchase orders, purchase invoices, receiving reports, etc.

2. Preparing vouchers for cash disbursements and attaching supporting purchase documents

3. Signing above vouchers to authorize payment (after examining vouchers with attached documents)

4. Preparing checks for above
5. Signing checks (for examining voucher authorization and supporting documents)
6. Mailing checks
7. Daily sorting of incoming mail into items that contain money and items that do not
8. Distributing the above mail: money to cashier, reports of money received to accounting department, and remainder to various appropriate offices
9. Making daily bank deposits
10. Reconciling monthly bank statements

The company's chief financial officer has decided that no more than five different people will handle all of these routines, including himself as necessary.

Required: Prepare a chart to show how these operations should be assigned to the five employees, including the chief financial officer. Use a line for each of the numbered routines and a column for each employee: Financial Officer, A, B, C, D. Place a check mark for each line in one or more of the columns. Observe the rules of the textbook checklist for internal control, especially separation of duties.

14–32. INTERNAL CONTROL. The Matsuhita Company keeps careful control over its inventory. An important factor in its internal control is *separation of duties*. The purchasing personnel are not authorized to sign for the receipt of physical inventories, and those in charge of inventory records do not perform the regular count of the physical inventory.

Required: Briefly describe an irregularity that would probably be discovered or prevented by each of the two separations of duties described.

14–33. MULTIPLE CHOICE; DISCOVERING IRREGULARITIES. In questions 1 through 4, you are given a well-recognized procedure of internal control. You are to identify the irregularity *that will be discovered or prevented by each procedure*. Write the numbers 1 through 4 on your answer sheet. Then place the letter of your chosen answer next to your numbers.

1. The general-ledger control account and the subsidiary ledger of Accounts Receivable are reconciled monthly. The two bookkeepers are independent.
   a. When friends purchase merchandise, the salesclerk allows them an employee discount by using an employee name on the sales slip and deducting the discount on the slip. This is against company policy.
   b. The Accounts Receivable subsidiary-ledger bookkeeper charges a sale to Mr. Smith instead of Mr. Smithe (that is, the wrong customer). The error is due to misreading the sales slip.
   c. The Accounts Receivable subsidiary-ledger bookkeeper charges a customer with $72 instead of $74, the correct amount. The error is due to misreading the sales slip. The credit-sales summary for the day has the correct amount of $74.
   d. The employee opening mail abstracts funds without making a record of their receipt. Customer accounts are not credited with their payments.
   e. The general-ledger bookkeeper takes funds and covers the loss by charging "Miscellaneous General Expenses."
2. Both cash and credit customers are educated to expect a sales ticket. Tickets are serially numbered. All numbers are accounted for daily.
   a. Customers complain that goods ordered are not received.
   b. Customers complain that their monthly bills contain items that have already been paid.
   c. Some customers have the correct change for the merchandise purchased. They pay and do not wait for a sales ticket.
   d. Customers complain that they are billed for goods they did not purchase.
   e. Salesclerks destroy duplicate sales tickets for the amount of cash stolen.
3. The storekeeper should sign a receipt for goods received from the receiving and inspection room, and no payment should be made without the storekeeper's signature.
   a. Employees send through purchase requisitions for materials for personal use. After the materials are received and receiving reports have been issued, employees take the merchandise for personal use.

b. Employees send through fictitious invoices and receive payment.

c. Invoices are paid twice.

d. Materials are withdrawn from the storeroom for personal use rather than for business purposes.

e. The storekeeper takes materials and charges them to company use.

4. At a movie theater box office, all tickets are prenumbered. At the end of each day, the beginning ticket number is subtracted from the ending number to give the number of tickets sold. Cash is counted and compared with the number of tickets sold.

a. Tickets from a previous day are discovered in the ticket taker's stub box despite the fact that tickets are stamped "Good on Date of Purchase Only."

b. The ticket taker admits his friends without a ticket.

c. The manager gives theater passes for personal expenses. This is against company policy.

d. The box office gives too much change.

e. A test check of customers entering the theater does not reconcile with ticket sales.

14–34. **INVENTORY SHRINKAGE.** José Chavez, owner of Handy Hardware Company, was concerned about his control of inventory. In December 19X9, he installed a computerized perpetual inventory system. In April, his accountant brought him the following information for the first three months of 19X9:

Sales	$350,000
Cost of goods sold	295,000
Beginning inventory (per physical count)	50,000
Merchandise purchases	325,000

Chavez had asked his public accounting firm to conduct a physical count of inventory on April 1. The CPAs reported inventory of $45,000.

Required:

1. Compute the ending inventory shown in the books by the new perpetual inventory system.

2. Provide the journal entry to reconcile the book inventory with the physical count. What is the corrected cost of goods sold for the first three months of 19X9?

3. Do your calculations point out areas about which Chavez should be concerned? Why?

14–35. **RETAIL METHOD AND INVENTORY SHRINKAGE.** Study Appendix 14A. The following figures pertain to the Zenith Gift Store for the two-month period November and December, 19X8:

Sales	$170,000	Purchases (at sales price)	$ 80,000
Additional markups	10,000	Inventory at November 1, 19X8:	
Markdowns	25,000	At cost price	93,000
Purchases (at cost price)	42,000	At selling price	160,000

Required:

1. What should the inventory amount to at December 31, 19X8, at retail price using the conventional retail inventory method?

2. Suppose the allowable shrinkage is 2% of sales. The physical inventory at retail prices at December 31 amounts to $50,000. What is the excess inventory shrinkage?

14–36. **COST TO RETAIL VALUE.** Study Appendix 14A. Refer to the preceding problem. Compute the ratio of cost to retail value. Compute the cost value of the ending inventory for inclusion in the financial statements.

14–37. **RETAIL METHOD AND INVENTORY SHRINKAGE.** (Suggested by W. Crum.) Study Appendix 14A. The following data are for a lawn and garden department in a large Sears store at retail selling prices:

Net sales	$1,900,000	Transfers in from other branches	$26,000
Discounts granted to		Transfers out to other branches	8,000
employees, churches, etc.	23,500	Additional markups	14,000
Beginning inventory	900,000	Markdowns	79,000
Net purchases	2,068,000		

Required:

1. What should be the ending inventory at retail prices using the conventional retail inventory method and assuming no allowances for losses (shrinkage)?
2. Suppose the estimated shrinkage is 1% of sales. What should be the ending inventory at retail prices? Suppose the cost ratio is 62%—that is, the *cost* of the ending inventory is approximated at 62% of retail price. What should be the ending inventory at cost? Again, assume 1% shrinkage.
3. The actual ending physical inventory at retail is $950,000. What is the total shrinkage at retail? At cost? Prepare a section of the income statement through gross profit on sales. Assume that beginning inventory at cost was $580,000 and that applicable net purchases (including transfer effects) at cost were $1,280,000.

14–38. **CONTROL OF RETAIL SHOE INVENTORY.** Study Appendix 14A. The Park Central Store of Youth Shoes, Inc., reported an ending inventory of shoes that seemed significantly smaller than usual despite no apparent deviations from the usual amounts of beginning inventory, purchases, and sales. Employee theft was suspected. Reported data included:

Beginning inventory:		Purchases:	
At cost prices	$ 55,000	At cost prices	$110,000
At retail prices	110,000	At retail prices	210,000
Sales	200,000	Markdowns	25,000
Additional markups	5,000	Ending physical inventory, retail	98,700

The company's auditing department discovered that the supplementary merchandise records showed an arithmetically incorrect total for purchases at retail prices. The correct total is $220,000.

Required:

1. Use the uncorrected data and assume that the allowable inventory shrinkage is 0.5% of sales. Compute the apparent inventory shortage.
2. Compute the apparent inventory shortage by using the corrected figure for purchases at retail prices.
3. Assume that the arithmetical error in determining the total purchases at retail prices had been deliberately committed to conceal a merchandise theft of an equal amount. Using a ratio of cost to retail value of 55%, compute the estimated cost of the inventory that may have been stolen.
4. See the chapter checklist of internal control. Briefly explain what precautions should be used to forestall such a theft and its concealment by employees.

14–39. **SPECIAL JOURNALS.** (Alternate is 14–40.) Study Appendix 14B. The London Trading Company uses a sales journal (journal page 42), a purchase journal (page 74), a cash receipts journal (page 63), a cash disbursements journal (page 81), and a general journal (page 19). It has a general ledger and subsidiary ledgers for accounts receivable and accounts payable. For simplicity, only a few transactions of each kind are illustrated in the accompanying list of transactions. Moreover, the beginning balances of the pertinent accounts are not given, nor are they necessary for the purposes of this problem. The currency is British pounds, £.

The numbers of some pertinent accounts are:

Cash	No. 10				
Accounts receivable	30				
Allowance for bad debts	32				
Merchandise inventory	50				
Accounts payable	70				
Notes payable	75				
Property taxes payable	77				
Paid-in capital	80				
Sales	90				
Advertising expense	97				
Bad debts expense	99				

Consider the following list of transactions.

List of Transactions for Problem 14–39

JULY	DESCRIPTION	INVOICE DATE	INVOICE NO.	TERMS	CHECK NO.	AMOUNT
2	Cash sales	—	—	—	—	£ 2,000
3	Credit sales to Martin	—	319	n30	—	1,400
5	Purchase of merchandise from Riggs	7/3	—	n30	—	2,200
6	Cash purchase of merchandise from Krueger	—	—	—	42	1,100
8	Collection of Invoice 319	—	—	—	—	1,400
10	Credit sale to Ramos	—	320	n30	—	2,800
11	Purchase of merchandise from Ryan	7/10	—	n10	—	2,900
12	Payment of Riggs invoice	—	—	—	43	2,200
13	Cash sales	—	—	—	—	1,900
14	Purchase of merchandise from Gates	7/12	—	n15	—	3,000
15	Payment of City of Hyde property taxes (set up previously as a payable)	—	—	—	44	3,200
16	Credit sale to Haynes	—	321	n30	—	1,800
18	Cash purchase of merchandise from Saucedo	—	—	—	45	500
19	Payment of Ryan invoice	—	—	—	46	2,900
20	Collection of Invoice 321	—	—	—	—	1,800
21	Purchase of merchandise from Goldman	7/19	—	n15	—	1,100
23	Credit sale to Lenz	—	322	n30	—	900
24	Cash sales	—	—	—	—	2,000
25	Advertising for cash to Tribune	—	—	—	47	700
26	Borrowed from bank, 60-day loan	—	—	—	—	5,000
27	Purchase of merchandise from Hunter	7/26	—	n30	—	3,800
28	Cash sales	—	—	—	—	2,500
28	Payment of Gates invoice	—	—	—	48	3,000
29	Credit sale to Holford	—	323	n30	—	600
31	Sale of additional common stock for cash	—	—	—	—	10,000
31	Addition to allowance for uncollectible accounts	—	—	—	—	100

Required:

1. Journalize the transactions for July, using the appropriate journals.
2. Post the effects of the transactions to the general and subsidiary ledgers (exclude the subsidiary ledger for merchandise inventory). Show posting details such as dates and account numbers.
3. Prepare a listing of subsidiary ledger balances. Make sure that their totals agree with the related general ledger accounts.
4. Suppose a voucher system were employed by the London Trading Company. Describe in detail how the special journals in requirement 1 would be affected.

14–40. **SPECIAL JOURNALS.** (Alternate is 14–39.) Study Appendix 14B. Quality Company, a wholesaler of luggage, uses a general journal and four special journals with current page numbers and amount columns as shown below:

☐ General journal (page 6): two columns, debit and credit
☐ Sales journal (page 15): single amount column
☐ Purchases journal (page 18): single amount column
☐ Cash receipts journal (page 25): debit columns for Cash and for Sales Discounts; credit columns for Sales, Accounts Receivable, and Other Accounts
☐ Cash payments journal (page 44): credit columns for Cash and for Purchase Discounts; debit columns for Purchases, Accounts Payable, and Other Accounts

The general-ledger accounts needed for this problem are shown below with their account numbers and June 1, 19X1, balances, if any:

Cash (10)	$ 3,000	
Accounts receivable (25)	18,000	
Office supplies (40)	2,000	
Office equipment (44)	21,000	
Accounts payable (84)		$12,000
Notes payable (88)		
Sales (142)		
Sales returns and allowances (143)		
Sales discounts (144)		
Purchases (162)		
Purchase returns and allowances (163)		
Purchase discounts (164)		
All other accounts (300)	46,000	78,000
Total	$90,000	$90,000

The subsidiary ledger accounts needed and their June 1 balances, if any, are:

ACCOUNTS RECEIVABLE:

Briggs Co.
Davey & Ramos
Maxson's Inc.
Sterne Bros. $18,000 debit balance

ACCOUNTS PAYABLE:

Crown Corp.
Langley Co.
Stanley Co.
Towne, Inc.
Village Stores, Inc., $12,000 credit balance

Quality Company uses the periodic inventory system, not the perpetual inventory system. All merchandise bought is debited to the Purchases account. The cost of goods sold is determined only at the end of the period when the physical inventory is measured (not required in this problem).

1. Set up journals and ledgers, entering beginning account balances, if any.
2. Enter the transactions described below in the appropriate journals.
3. Post amounts from all journals to T-accounts, showing details: dates, account numbers, and posting references.
4. Take a trial balance of the general ledger at June 30.
5. Prepare schedules of the two subsidiary ledgers to prove their agreement with the controlling accounts at June 30.

Transactions:

June	3	Issued check number 361 to Rothe Co. for cash purchase of merchandise, $2,400.
	4	Cash sales of merchandise, $1,800.
	5	Purchased merchandise from Crown Corp., $6,000; terms 1/15, n/30.
	6	Sold merchandise to Briggs Co., $9,000; terms 2/10, n/30; invoice number 1063.
	7	Purchased office supplies from Xenox Co. for cash, $300. Check number 362.
	8	Purchased merchandise from Towne, Inc., $7,500; terms 1/10, n/30.
	10	Sold merchandise to Davey & Ramos, $12,000; terms 2/10, n/30; invoice number 1064.
	*12	Purchased office equipment from Langley Co., $5,400; terms n/30.
	14	Received cash to settle Briggs Co. invoice 1063, less 2% cash discount. (Use only one line for this entry in the cash receipts journal.)
	15	Sold merchandise to Maxson's Inc., $15,000; terms 2/10, n/30; invoice number 1065.
	17	Issued check number 363 to Crown Corp. to pay for June 5 purchase less 1% cash discount. (Use only one line for this entry in the cash payments journal.)
	20	Purchased merchandise from Stanley Co., $5,400; terms 2/10, n/30.
	21	Borrowed $18,000 for ninety days from Park Bank at 15% interest to be paid at due date of note.
	*24	Issued credit memo number 88 for $600 to Davey & Ramos for unsatisfactory merchandise sold June 10.
	*28	Received cash memo number 1004 for $900 from Towne, Inc., for unsatisfactory merchandise purchased June 8.

* These transactions are to be entered in the general journal. Be sure to post the debit and credit amounts for receivables and payables to the subsidiary ledger accounts as well as to the related controlling accounts.

☐ Understanding Published Financial Reports

14–41. STATE AND COUNTY FAIRS. Nonprofit entities take various forms. For example, state and county fairs are usually important sources of revenue because the state gets a percentage of the bets made on horse races. In past years, the carnivals would bid for the rights to appear at the fair. The winner would be willing to pay the fairs a higher percentage of some measure of its revenue generated from rides, games, and food booths.

Required: What types of major internal control problems arise from such percentage revenue agreements? Which item or items of the chapter checklist of internal control seem most critical in these cases?

14–42. AUDIT COMMITTEE ROLE. In a recent court decision, an American corporation was required to delegate certain responsibilities to its audit committee, management being required to

1. Consult with its independent auditors before deciding any significant or material accounting question or policy
2. Retain independent auditors to perform quarterly reviews of all financial statements prior to public issuance
3. Conduct internal audits, with personnel reporting directly to the audit committee (internal auditors must report to the audit committee quarterly)

4. Retain or dismiss independent and internal auditors
5. Consult with the independent auditors on their quarterly reviews of financial statements
6. Review all monthly corporate and division financial statements and the auditor's management letter
7. Receive quarterly reports from independent auditors on internal control deficiencies
8. Review and approve all reports to shareholders and the SEC before dissemination

The court also ruled that the audit committee must be composed of at least three outside directors who have no business dealings with the firm other than directors' fees and expense reimbursements.

Required:

a. Prepare a partial corporation organization chart to depict these requirements. Use boxes only for Audit Committee, Independent Auditors, Internal Auditing, Finance Vice-President, and Board of Directors. Connect the appropriate boxes with lines: solid lines for direct responsiblity, dashed lines for information and communications. Place numbers on these lines to correspond to the eight items specified by the court decision.

b. Identify the main elements of the chapter checklist of internal control that seem most relevant to this system design.

14–43. APPRAISAL OF INTERNAL CONTROL SYSTEM. From the *San Francisco Chronicle*:

☐ The flap over missing ferry fares was peacefully—and openly—resolved at a meeting of the Golden Gate Bridge District finance committee yesterday.

☐ Only a week ago, the subject was a matter of furious dispute in which bridge manager Dale W. Luehring was twice called a liar and there were prospects of a closed meeting on personnel matters.

☐ But yesterday, after a week of investigation, the meeting turned out to be public after all, and attorney Thomas M. Jenkins revealed the full total of stolen ferry tickets equaled $26.20.

☐ The controversy began when auditor Gordon Dahlgren complained that there was an auditing "problem" and that he had not been informed when four children swiped $13.75 worth of tickets February 28. Committee chairman Ben K. Lerer, of San Francisco, ordered a full investigation.

☐ Jenkins said the situation was complicated because children under 5 have been allowed to ride the ferry without a ticket, but after May 1 everyone will have to have a ticket, allowing for a closer audit.

☐ Secondly, Jenkins explained, the "vault" in which tickets are deposited was proved insecure (resulting in two thefts totaling $26.20 worth of tickets) but has been replaced.

☐ In the future, it was decided, all thefts of cash or tickets must be reported immediately to the California Highway Patrol or the local police, the bridge lieutenant on duty, the general manager, the security officer, the auditor-controller, and the transit manager.

☐ In addition, employees must make a full written report within 24 hours to the president of the district board, the chairman of the finance-auditing committee, the auditor controller, the attorney, the bus transit manager, the water transit manager, the toll captain, and the chief of administration and security.

Required:

What is your reaction to the new system? Explain, giving particular attention to applicable criteria for appraising an internal control system.

14–44. CASINO SKIMMING. An article in the *Wall Street Journal* reported that about $7 million in quarters disappeared from the slot machines of four casinos of Argent Corporation in an 18-month period. The coins weighed nearly 150 tons, and the odds against such a payout to players of the slot machines is one in 3,875,000,000,000,000,000,000,000,000,000,000,000,000,-

000,000,000,000,000—an extremely unlikely event, to say the least. The disappearance was part of the biggest known skim operation ever. *Skimming* is taking a portion of gambling revenues before they can be counted for tax purposes.

Internal control is especially important in casinos. Meters in the slot machines record the winnings paid to customers. Coins are taken immediately to the slot counting room when machines are emptied. In the counting rooms coins are weighed, and a portion is returned to the change booths.

Required: | What items in the chapter checklist of internal control seem especially important regarding slot machine operations? How could the money from slot machine operations have been stolen in such large amounts?

14–45. DISHONESTY AND GAMBLING. A news article reported about Ruth Mishkin, a trusted employee of the Communications Group, a public relations firm in Boca Raton, Florida. She had worked nine years for the company. Her bosses had put her in charge of paying bills, balancing bank accounts, and handling other cash management chores.

When Mishkin took a sick leave, the company discovered that she had been taking company funds for years. In all, the 60-year-old widow allegedly stole about $320,000 to feed a gambling habit. The president of the company was quoted as saying, "We thought she was just playing cards with the girls."

Incidents such as this highlight weaknesses in internal controls, and preventive steps are often taken only after a crime has been committed.

Required: | What internal controls would have deterred Mishkin from the thievery? What internal controls would have helped the Communications Group to detect the theft at an earlier date?

14–46. EMPLOYEE DISHONESTY. Consider the following newspaper reports of dishonesty:

   a. At a small manufacturer, supervisors had access to time cards and gave out W-2 forms each year. The supervisors pocketed $80,000 a year in the paychecks for phantom workers.
   b. A manager at a busy branch office of a copying service had a receipt book of his own. Jobs of $200 and $300 were common. The manager stole cash by simply giving customers a receipt from his book instead of one of the company's numbered forms.
   c. A purchasing agent received tiny kickbacks on buttons, zippers, and other trims used at a successful dress company. The agent got rich, and the company was overcharged $10 million.

Required: | Specify what control or controls would have helped avoid each of the listed situations.

14–47. CHEATING ON INVENTORIES. The *Wall Street Journal* reported: "Cheating on inventories is a common way for small business to chisel on their income taxes. . . . A New York garment maker, for example, evades a sizable amount of income tax by undervaluing his firm's inventory by 20 percent on his tax return. He hides about $500,000 out of a $2.5 million inventory."

The news story concluded: "When it's time to borrow, business owners generally want profits and assets to look fat." The garment maker uses a different fiscal period for financial statements to his bank: "After writing down the inventory as of Dec. 31, he writes it up six months later when the fiscal year ends. In this way, he underpays the IRS and impresses his banker. Some describe that kind of inventory accounting as WIFL—Whatever I Feel Like."

Required: | 1. At a 34% income tax rate, what amount of federal income taxes would the owner evade according to the news story?
2. Consider the next year. By how much would the ending inventory have to be understated to evade the same amount of income taxes?

Use the following table and fill in the blanks:

	HONEST REPORTING		DISHONEST REPORTING	
	(in dollars)			
	First Year	Second Year	First Year	Second Year
Beginning inventory	3,000,000	?	3,000,000	?
Purchases	10,000,000	10,000,000	10,000,000	10,000,000
Available for sale	13,000,000	?	13,000,000	?
Ending inventory	2,500,000	2,500,000	2,000,000	?
Cost of goods sold	10,500,000	?	11,000,000	?
Income tax savings @ 34%*	3,570,000	?	?	?
Income tax savings for two years together		?		?

* This is the income tax effect of only the cost of goods sold. To shorten and simplify the analysis, sales and operating expenses are assumed to be the same each year.

14–48. **RETAIL METHOD AND INVENTORY SHRINKAGE.** Study Appendix 14A. Safeway Stores is a large food chain. Its 1989 sales exceeded $20 billion. Safeway uses the retail method of inventory control for many parts of its operations. Suppose the following data pertain to the grocery department of one of its stores for a given period (at retail prices):

Beginning inventory	$210,000	Sales	$1,040,000
Markups	30,000	Purchases	1,010,000
Markdowns	50,000		

Required:
1. Using the retail inventory method, compute the retail value of the ending inventory (in accordance with the given data).
2. Suppose the allowable shrinkage is 1% of sales. The physical inventory at retail prices at December 31 amounts to $142,000. Compute the excess shrinkage.
3. Consider the following additional data (at cost): beginning inventory, $150,000; purchases, $690,000. Compute the ratio of cost to retail value. Compute the cost value of the ending inventory for inclusion in the financial statements.

14–49. **PRESSURE FOR PROFITS.** The *Wall Street Journal* stated that "Datapoint Corp. reported its first quarterly loss in nearly a decade, partly reflecting the reversal of about $15 million in revenue generated in previous quarters by questionable sales practices." Datapoint is a maker of small computer systems and telecommunications equipment.

The news report stated that Datapoint was trying to explain the unusually high rate of product returns in recent months, and this led to an investigation of the sales practices of its domestic marketing division. Current and former Datapoint employees asserted that certain marketing officials were determined to continue a string of record profit that had lasted 39 quarters. The officials resorted to increasingly questionable practices of recording revenue. Their methods eventually backfired.

The practices included shipping computer equipment to customers who had not met Datapoint's credit requirements, executives using their own money to pay warehousing fees so that distributors would accept shipments they did not have room for, and, in one instance, shipping to an imaginary customer "just to get a shipment out the door and revenue logged."

Required: On what specific items on the checklist of internal control should Datapoint concentrate to prevent a recurrence of these questionable marketing practices?

14–50. MANIPULATION OF PROFITS. Throughout the decade, H. J. Heinz Company had a publicly stated objective: to seek an increase in earnings at a steady and consistent rate. For example, a Heinz annual report said: ". . . the annual compound growth rate has been 11.7% for the past 10 years and 14.0% for the past five years, which is consistent with the company's financial objectives for a compound growth rate in earnings per share of 10% to 12% per year."

Shortly after issuing that annual report, Heinz disclosed that several managers had engaged in "profit-switching" practices for the past seven years. These practices resulted in the improper transfer of $16.4 million in pretax income to the most recent fiscal year. A news story reported that "the intent of the practices was to smooth out earnings increases to create the appearance of consistent, orderly growth."

For your information, "profit-switching" and "improper transfer" refer to keeping records so that profits that appropriately belong in one reporting period are actually reported in a different reporting period.

Required: | Given this description, were any assets stolen by management? Identify at least one way to falsely defer profit to a future period. What feature in the chapter checklist of internal control is aimed at preventing the practice you describe?

14–51. COOKING THE BOOKS. In *The Accounting Wars* (Macmillan, 1985), author Mark Stevens presents a chapter on "Book Cooking, Number Juggling, and Other Tricks of the Trade." He quotes Glen Perry, a former chief accountant of the SEC's Enforcement Division: "Companies play games with their financial reports for any number of reasons, the most common being the intense pressure on corporate management to produce an unbroken stream of increasing earnings reports." Stevens then lists Perry's "terrible ten of accounting frauds—ploys used to misrepresent corporate financial statements":

1. Recognition of revenues before they are realized
2. Recognition of rentals to customers as sales
3. Inclusion of fictitious amounts in inventories
4. Improper cutoffs at year-end
5. Improper application of LIFO
6. Creation of fraudulent year-end transactions to boost earnings
7. Failure to recognize losses through write-offs and allowances
8. Inconsistent accounting practices without disclosures
9. Capitalization or improper deferral of expenses
10. Inclusion of unusual gains in operating income

Required: | Suppose you were a division manager in a major corporation. Briefly explain how you could use each of the ten methods to manipulate income. Be specific.

14–52. HOUSE OF FABRICS ANNUAL REPORT. Study Appendix 14A for requirement 2. Examine the 1989 amounts for cost of sales from the income statement and merchandise inventories from the balance sheet of House of Fabrics (pages 752–753).

Required: | 1. Suppose House of Fabrics uses a perpetual inventory system and the balance in merchandise inventories at the end of fiscal 1989 was $132,170,000 before taking a physical count. Compute the amount of inventory shrinkage, and prepare the journal entries to recognize the shrinkage and close it to cost of sales.
2. Suppose House of Fabrics uses a periodic inventory system and the retail method of inventory control. Purchases of merchandise during fiscal 1989 totaled $150,350,000. The ratio of cost to retail value was .45, and normal shrinkage is 1% of sales. Compute (a) the cost of sales before shrinkage, (b) the allowable shrinkage, (c) the excess shrinkage, and (d) the total cost of sales including all shrinkage.

Analysis of Financial Statements

After studying this chapter, you should be able to

1. Explain how financial statement analysis helps investors and creditors assess a company's performance and prospects
2. Use trend analysis and common-size statements to evaluate a company
3. Compute and interpret a variety of popular financial ratios
4. Identify the major implications that "efficient" stock markets have for accounting

The ultimate objective of financial statments is to provide information to investors, creditors, managers, suppliers, customers—anyone who wants to know about a company's financial position or prospects. For financial statements to be useful, decision makers must be able to extract relevant information from the vast amount of data contained in the statements. Using financial statements to assess a company's position and prospects is called **financial statement analysis.**

Earlier chapters have included some illustrations of how financial statements are used to evaluate the position and performance of an entity. This chapter will review the methods introduced earlier and will discuss additional ways to analyze financial statements. It contains the most popular techniques of financial statement analysis.

SOURCES OF INFORMATION ABOUT COMPANIES

Financial statement analysis focuses on techniques used by analysts external to the organization being analyzed, although managers use many of the same methods. These analysts rely on publicly available information, that is, information that is published. A major source of such information is the annual report. In addition to the financial statements (income statement, balance sheet, statement of cash flows, and statement of stockholders' equity), annual reports usually contain

1. Footnotes to the financial statements
2. A summary of the accounting principles used
3. Management's discussion and analysis of the financial results
4. The auditor's report
5. Comparative financial data for a series of years
6. Much narrative information about the company

Although analysts can learn much from the various parts of an annual report, we will focus most of our attention on the financial statements themselves.

Companies also prepare reports for the Securities and Exchange Commission (SEC). Form 10-K presents financial statement data in a standard format and is generally more comprehensive than the financial statements published in annual reports. Form 10-Q includes quarterly financial statements, so it provides more timely information than the annual reports, although the reports are less complete. Other SEC reports are required for certain specified events and for issuance of common shares or debt.

Both annual reports and SEC reports are issued well after the events being reported have occurred. More timely information is often available from company press releases and articles in the business press. The *Wall Street Journal*, *Business*

Week, *Forbes*, *Fortune*, and *Barron's* are among the more popular publications. Services such as Moody's Investors Services and Standard and Poor's Industrial Surveys also provide useful information. In addition, stockbrokers prepare company analyses for their clients, and private investment services and newsletters supply information to their subscribers.

Heavy financial commitments, whether by investors purchasing many shares of the common stock of a company or by banks making large loans to a new customer, are preceded by thorough investigations. These investigations use information from many sources. When the amounts being invested are significant, investors and creditors often ask for a set of budgeted financial statements. A *budget*, or **pro forma statement**, is a carefully formulated expression of predicted results. Major creditors expect the budget to include a schedule of the amounts and timings of cash repayments.

Most investors and creditors are not able to request specific information from companies. For example, the typical trade creditor cannot afford the time or resources for a thorough investigation of every customer. Instead, such creditors rely on published information and reports from credit agencies such as Dun & Bradstreet.

Because of the wide range of information available, financial statement analysis is only one method used by financial analysts. Nevertheless, the techniques presented in this chapter will be important to anyone who wants to gain a thorough understanding of a company's position and prospects.

OBJECTIVE OF FINANCIAL STATEMENT ANALYSIS

Investors purchase capital stock expecting to receive dividends and an increase in the value of the stock. Creditors make loans with the expectation of receiving interest and eventual repayment. However, both investors and creditors bear the risk that they will not receive their expected returns. They use financial statement analysis to (1) predict the amount of expected returns and (2) assess the risks associated with those returns.

Because creditors generally have specific fixed amounts to be received and have the first claim on assets, they are most concerned with assessing short-term liquidity and long-term solvency. **Short-term liquidity** is an organization's ability to meet current payments as they become due. **Long-term solvency** is the ability to generate enough cash to repay long-term debts as they mature.

In contrast, investors are more concerned with profitability, dividends, and future security prices. Why? Because dividend payments depend on profitable operations, and stock price appreciation depends on the market's assessment of the company's prospects. However, creditors also assess profitability. Why? Because profitable operations are the prime source of cash to repay loans.

How can financial statement analysis help creditors and investors? After all, financial statements report on past results and current position, but creditors and investors want to predict future returns and their risks. Financial statement analysis is useful because past performance is often a good indicator of future performance, and current position is the base on which future performance must be built. For example, trends in past sales, operating expenses, and net income may continue. Furthermore, evaluation of management's past performance gives clues to its ability to generate future returns. Finally, the assets a company owns, the liabilities it must pay, its amount of receivables and inventories, its cash balance, and other indicators of current position all affect its future prospects.

METHODS OF FINANCIAL STATEMENT ANALYSIS

This section discusses three methods used to analyze financial statement data: trend analysis, common-size statements, and financial ratios.

☐ Trend Analysis

Financial statements contain both the current year's and the previous year's amounts. In addition, annual reports must include the amounts of key financial items for at least the last five years. Many companies include ten years of data. Using these data, financial analysts can examine in detail the changes in the past year and can examine longer-term trends in several important items.

Consider the balance sheets and income statements of Oxley Company in Exhibits 15–1 and 15–2. The amounts are identical to the financial statements introduced in Chapter 5 in the Oxley Company illustration. (Recall that Oxley is a retailer of lawn and garden products.) However, two columns have been added to aid the comparison of 19X2 results with those of 19X1. The first new column shows the amount of the change in each item from 19X1 to 19X2, and the second shows the percentage change. The percentage change is computed as follows:

$$\text{Percentage change 19X1 to 19X2} = \left(\frac{\text{Amount of change}}{\text{19X1 amount}}\right) \times 100$$

The first year, 19X1 in this case, is the *base year*. The percentage change shows the percentage by which the current-year amount exceeds or falls short of the base-year amount. For example, Oxley's accounts receivables increased from $70,000 at the end of 19X1 to $95,000 at the end of 19X2, an increase of 35.7%:

$$\text{Percentage change} = \left(\frac{\$95,000 - \$70,000}{\$70,000}\right) \times 100 = 35.7\%$$

Notice that each percentage change is independent of the others. Unlike the amounts of change, the percentage changes cannot be added or subtracted to obtain subtotals.

Changes must be interpreted carefully. Both the amount and the percentage changes should be examined. For example, the amount of the sales increase, $199,000, seems much larger than the increase in operating income, $22,000. But the base for sales is much larger, so the percentage increase is only slightly larger, 24.9% to 21.2%. However, examination of percentage changes alone can also be misleading. For instance, the 140% increase in accrued wages payable seems to dominate the percentage increases. But the increase is only $14,000, a relatively small amount in the overall picture.

What would an analyst conclude from Oxley Company's changes from 19X1

EXHIBIT 15–1   (Place a clip on this page for easy reference)

OXLEY COMPANY
Balance Sheet (in thousands)

ASSETS	DECEMBER 31 19X2	DECEMBER 31 19X1	INCREASE (DECREASE) Amount	INCREASE (DECREASE) Percentage
Current assets:				
Cash	$150	$ 57	$ 93	163.2%
Accounts receivable	95	70	25	35.7
Accrued interest receivable	15	15	0	0.0
Inventory of merchandise	20	60	(40)	(66.7)
Prepaid rent	10	—	10	*
Total current assets	$290	$202	$ 88	43.6
Long-term assets:				
Long-term note receivable	288	288	0	0.0
Equipment, less accumulated depreciation of $120 and $80	80	120	(40)	(33.3)
Total assets	$658	$610	$ 48	7.9%
LIABILITIES AND STOCKHOLDERS' EQUITY				
Current liabilities:				
Accounts payable	$ 90	$ 65	$ 25	38.5%
Accrued wages payable	24	10	14	140.0
Accrued income taxes payable	16	12	4	33.0
Accrued interest payable	9	9	0	0.0
Unearned sales revenue	—	5	(5)	(100.0)
Note payable—current portion	80	—	80	*
Total current liabilities	$219	$101	$118	116.8
Long-term note payable	40	120	(80)	(66.7)
Total liabilities	$259	$221	$38	17.2
Stockholders' equity:				
Paid-in capital[†]	$102	$102	$ 0	0.0
Retained income	297	287	10	3.5
Total stockholders' equity	$399	$389	$ 10	2.6
Total liabilities and stockholders' equity	$658	$610	$ 48	7.9%

* When the base-year amount is zero, no percentage change can be computed.
† Details are often shown in a supplementary statement or in footnotes. In this case, there are 200,000 common shares outstanding, $.25 par per share, or 200,000 × $.25 = $50,000. Additional paid-in capital is $52,000.

to 19X2? Consider Exhibit 15–2, the income statement. The sales increase, 24.9%, is larger than the increase in cost of goods sold, 18.8%, causing a 29.3% increase in gross profit. That is the good news. The bad news is that operating expenses increased by 31.7%. There would be special concern because huge increases in only two items, wages and miscellaneous expenses, caused the entire increase. In addition, income tax expense increased by a larger percentage than pretax income (25.0% to 17.2%), meaning that the effective tax rate must have increased. In total, the nearly 25% increase in sales led to only a 12.5% increase in net income.

Consider next the balance sheet, Exhibit 15–1. Total assets increased by 7.9%, a relatively small change. But the composition of the assets changed con-

EXHIBIT 15–2

OXLEY COMPANY
Statement of Income
(in thousands except earnings per share)

	FOR THE YEAR ENDED DECEMBER 31, 19X2	FOR THE YEAR ENDED DECEMBER 31, 19X1	INCREASE (DECREASE) Amount	INCREASE (DECREASE) Percentage
Sales	$ 999	$ 800	$199	24.9%
Cost of goods sold	399	336	63	18.8
Gross profit (or gross margin)	$ 600	$ 464	$136	29.3
Operating expenses:				
Wages	$ 214	$ 150	$ 64	42.7
Rent	120	120	0	0.0
Miscellaneous	100	50	50	100.0
Depreciation	40	40	0	0.0
Total operating expenses	$ 474	$ 360	$114	31.7
Operating income (or operating profit)	$126	$104	$ 22	21.2
Other revenue and expense:				
Interest revenue	36	36	0	0.0
Deduct: Interest expense	(12)	(12)	0	0.0
Income before income taxes	$ 150	$ 128	$ 22	17.2
Income tax expense	60	48	12	25.0
Net income	$ 90	$ 80	$ 10	12.5
Earnings per common share*	$ .45	$ .40	$ .05	12.5%

* Dividends per share, $.40 and $.20, respectively. For publicly held companies, there is a requirement to show earnings per share on the face of the income statement, but it is not necessary to show dividends per share. Calculation of earnings per share: $90,000 ÷ 200,000 = $.45, and $80,000 ÷ 200,000 = $.40.

siderably, with current assets increasing by 43.6% while long-term assets decreased by 33.3%. Within the current assets, cash and accounts receivable had substantial increases, and inventories plummeted. Total liabilities increased by 17.2%, but most significant is the 116.8% increase in current liabilities and 66.7% decrease in long-term liabilities. This change is attributable primarily to $80,000 of the note payable becoming due within the next year, thereby qualifying as a current liability. The $88,000 increase in current assets is less than the $118,000 increase in current liabilities, resulting in a deterioration in the working capital position.

Financial analysts often examine changes over a series of years, not just the current year's changes. Exhibit 15–3 shows a five-year summary of key items for Oxley Company. Percentage changes could be computed for each year, using the earlier year as the base year. For example, percentage changes in sales are:

19X2
$$\left(\frac{\$999 - \$800}{\$800}\right) \times 100 = 24.9\%$$

19X1
$$\left(\frac{\$800 - \$765}{\$765}\right) \times 100 = 4.6\%$$

19X0
$$\left(\frac{\$765 - \$790}{\$790}\right) \times 100 = (3.2\%)$$

19Y9
$$\left(\frac{\$790 - \$694}{\$694}\right) \times 100 = 13.8\%$$

EXHIBIT 15–3

OXLEY COMPANY
Five-Year Financial Summary
(in thousands, except per share amounts)

| | FOR THE YEAR ENDED DECEMBER 31 | | | | |
	19X2	19X1	19X0	19Y9	19Y8
Income Statement Data:					
Sales	$999	$800	$765	$790	$694
Gross profit	600	464	448	460	410
Operating income	126	104	85	91	78
Net income	90	80	62	66	56
Earnings per share	.45	.40	.31	.33	.28
Dividends per share	.40	.20	.20	.20	.15
Balance Sheet Data:					
Total assets	$658	$610	$590	$585	$566
Total liabilities	259	221	241	258	265
Stockholders' equity	399	389	349	327	301

Analysts might use the average percentage growth in sales, (24.9% + 4.6% − 3.2% + 13.8%) ÷ 4 = 10.0%, instead of the most recent increase to predict future increases. Furthermore, the reasons for the decline in sales in 19X0 might be explored so that if similar conditions are forecast, the predictions of sales can be adjusted accordingly.

☐ Common-Size Statements

To aid comparisons with previous years and especially to aid the general comparison of companies that differ in size, income statements and balance sheets are often analyzed by percentage relationships, called **component percentages**. The resulting statements are called **common-size statements**. Consider Oxley Company's common-size statements in Exhibit 15–4. It is difficult to compare Oxley's $290,000 of current assets with another company's $480,000 if the other company is larger. But suppose the other company has total assets of $1 million. Oxley's 44% current asset *percentage* (shown in Exhibit 15–4) can be directly compared with the other company's $480,000 ÷ $1,000,000 = 48%.

The income statement percentages are usually based on sales = 100%. Oxley seems very profitable, but such percentages have more meaning when compared with the budgeted performance for the current year, 19X2 (not shown here). The gross margin rate seems high; Oxley may be vulnerable to price competition. The behavior of each expense in relation to changes in total revenue is often revealing. That is, which expenses go up or down as sales fluctuate? For example, during these two years, rent, depreciation, and interest have been fixed in total but have decreased in relation to sales. In contrast, the wages have increased in total and as a percentage of sales. The latter is not a welcome sign.

EXHIBIT 15–4

OXLEY COMPANY
Common-Size Statements
(in thousands except percentages)

	FOR THE YEAR ENDED DECEMBER 31			
	19X2		19X1	
Statement of Income				
Sales	$999*	100%	$800	100%
Cost of goods sold	399	40	336	42
Gross profit (or gross margin)	$600	60%	$464	58%
Wages	$214	21%	$150	19%
Rent	120	12	120	15
Miscellaneous	100	10	50	6
Depreciation	40	4	40	5
Operating expenses	$474	47%	$360	45%
Operating income	$126	13%	$104	13%
Other revenue and expense	24	2	24	3
Pretax income	$150	15%	$128	16%
Income tax expense	60	6	48	6
Net income	$ 90	9%	$ 80	10%

	DECEMBER 31			
	19X2		19X1	
Balance Sheet				
Current assets	$290	44%	$202	33%
Long-term note receivable	288	44	288	47
Equipment, net	80	12	120	20
Total assets	$658	100%	$610	100%
Current liabilities	$219	33%	$101	16%
Long-term note	40	6	120	20
Total liabilities	$259	39%	$221	36%
Stockholders' equity	399	61	389	64
Total liab. and stk. eq.	$658	100%	$610	100%
Working capital	$ 71		$101	

* Note the use of dollar signs in columns of numbers. Frequently, they are used at the top and bottom only and not for every subtotal. Their use by companies depends on the preference of management.

Exhibit 15–4 indicates that wages in 19X1 were $150 ÷ $800 = 19% of sales, whereas wages in 19X2 were $214 ÷ $999 = 21% of sales.

The balance sheet percentages are usually based on total assets = 100%. See Exhibit 15–4. The most notable feature of the balance sheet percentages is that both current assets and current liabilities are more prominent at the end of 19X2. Moreover, the working capital has declined largely because $80,000 of the long-term debt has become a current liability (because it is now less than one year from maturity). Some careful planning for 19X3 should provide for the orderly payment of this $80,000 and the probable increase of inventory levels.

☐ Management's Discussion and Analysis

Both trends and component percentages are generally discussed in a required section of annual reports called **management's discussion and analysis** (often called MD&A). This section concentrates on explaining the major changes in the income statement and the major changes in liquidity and capital resources. The space most companies devote to the section in annual reports has increased dramatically in recent years. For example, a recent McDonald's Corporation annual report has a twelve-page MD&A section.

Exhibit 15–5 contains excerpts from management's discussion and analysis in the annual report of American Greetings Corporation, the largest publicly held producer of greeting cards in the United States. The report is typical of the items discussed, but it has less detail than many such reports.

☐ Financial Ratios

The cornerstone of financial statement analysis is the computation and interpretation of ratios. Ratios are fractions that show the relationship of the numerator to the denominator. For example, the ratio "return on sales" is net income (the numerator) divided by sales (the denominator). Oxley Company's return on sales is $90,000 ÷ $999,000 = .09, which can also be expressed as 9%. For every $1 of sales, Oxley made net income of $.09.

Exhibit 15–6 shows some of the most popular ratios.[1] Many of these ratios have been introduced in earlier chapters, as indicated in the second column. (A dash in the column means that the ratio is being introduced in this chapter for the first time.) The ratios will be discussed in detail in the next section.

Evaluation of a financial ratio requires a comparison. There are three main types of comparisons: (1) with a company's own historical ratios (called **time-series comparisons**), (2) with general rules of thumb or **bench marks**, and (3) with ratios of other companies or with industry averages (called **cross-sectional comparisons**).

Much can be learned by examining the *time-series trend* of a company's ratios. That is why annual reports typically contain a table of comparative statistics for five or ten years. For example, some of the items listed in the annual report of Albertson's (the 497-store grocery chain) are:

	1989	1988	1987	1986	1985
Earnings as a percent of sales	2.40%	2.14%	1.86%	1.68%	1.68%
Earnings per share	$ 2.44	$ 1.88	$1.50	$1.28	$1.21
Book value per share	$11.96	$10.02	$8.90	$7.80	$6.87

Broad *rules of thumb* often serve as bench marks for comparison. For instance, the most quoted bench mark is a current ratio of 2 to 1. Others are described in *Key Business Ratios* by Dun & Bradstreet, a financial services firm. For example:

---

[1] For more details, see George Foster, *Financial Statement Analysis*, 2d ed. (Englewood Cliffs, NJ: Prentice Hall, 1986).

□ *Fixed assets to tangible net worth.* Ordinarily this relationship should not exceed 100% for a manufacturer and 75% for a wholesaler or retailer.

□ *Current debt to tangible net worth.* Ordinarily a business begins to pile up trouble when this relationship exceeds 80%.

Obviously, such bench marks are only general guides. More specific comparisons come from examining ratios of similar companies or from industry

EXHIBIT 15–5

AMERICAN GREETINGS CORPORATION
Excerpts from Management Discussion and Analysis

RESULTS OF OPERATIONS

Total revenue increased 6.5% in 1988 after increasing 8.7% in 1987. Net sales accounted for substantially all of this increase as other income increased only moderately. Net greeting card sales in dollars increased 3% in 1988 and 7% in 1987, but unit sales showed a decline of 3% in 1988 versus a 2% increase in 1987.

Other income increased moderately in 1988 by 2.9% versus 1.1% in 1987. Licensing income totaled $16.5 million in 1988, compared to $18.3 million in 1987 and $17.6 million in 1986.

Material, labor and other production costs were 44.5% of total revenue in 1988 versus 41.9% in 1987 and 40.2% in 1986. Increased sales volume in lower margin product categories and greater than normal inventory adjustments accounted for most of this increase.

Selling, distribution and marketing expenses were 32.2% of total revenue in 1988 and 30.3% in 1987 and 29.8% in 1986. This increase is primarily a result of increased costs associated with revenues not meeting expectations and costs associated with competition for market share.

Administrative and general expenses increased slightly to 13.0% of total revenue in 1988 versus 12.9% in 1987 and 12.7% in 1986.

Reflecting the Corporation's increased level of capital spending through 1988, depreciation expense increased $5.1 million compared to a $5.6 million increase in 1987, and increased as a percent of total revenue from 2.3% in 1986 to 2.6% in 1987 to 2.8% in 1988.

Interest expense increased $7.9 million in 1988 and $5.8 million in 1987 as increased levels of borrowing were required to fund capital expenditures and working capital requirements and, in 1987, acquisitions and treasury stock purchases.

The 1988 effective tax rate of 41.0% reflects the impact of lower US federal tax rates resulting from the Tax Reform Act of 1986.

CHANGES IN FINANCIAL POSITION

Cash provided from operations after changes in working capital was $110.4 million in 1988. This compares to $62.1 million in 1987 and $25.0 million in 1986.

Accounts receivable as a percent of prior twelve months' net sales decreased to 23.7% in 1988 compared to 25.8% in 1987 and 23.8% in 1986. Inventories, measured on the same basis, increased to 26.9% in 1988 from 25.6% in 1987 and 24.8% in 1986. The major reason for the decrease in accounts receivable and the increase in inventories in 1988 was the consolidation of several new subsidiaries.

In March 1988, the Corporation issued $100 million of five year notes to refinance short-term obligations. Accordingly, $93.9 million of short-term obligations were classified as long-term debt as of February 29, 1988. The reduction in long-term debt reflects the current maturity of the $50 million of notes due December, 1988.

As a result of the Corporation's higher borrowing levels at year-end 1988, the ratio of total debt to total capitalization (equity plus short and long-term debt) increased to 38.8% in 1988 from 34.1% in 1987 and 25.8% in 1986.

The Corporation invested $96.7 million in property, plant and equipment in 1988 ($68.7 million in 1987 and $61.8 million in 1986). Capital expenditures are expected to decrease significantly in 1989.

Dividend payments to shareholders were $21.2 million in 1988 which is comparable to 1987 and up from $19.9 million in 1986.

Shareholders' equity increased to $538.7 million at February 29, 1988 or $16.75 per share ($16.32 in 1987 and $15.01 in 1986).

EXHIBIT 15–6

Some Typical Financial Ratios

TYPICAL NAME OF RATIO	INTRODUCED IN CHAPTER	NUMERATOR	DENOMINATOR	USING APPROPRIATE OXLEY NUMBERS APPLIED TO DECEMBER 31 OF YEAR 19X2	USING APPROPRIATE OXLEY NUMBERS APPLIED TO DECEMBER 31 OF YEAR 19X1
Short-term liquidity ratios:					
Current ratio	4	Current assets	Current liabilities	$290 \div 219 = 1.3$	$202 \div 101 = 2.0$
Quick ratio	—	Cash + marketable securities + receivables	Current liabilities	$(150 + 0 + 95) \div 219 = 1.1$	$(57 + 0 + 70) \div 101 = 1.3$
Average collection period in days	6	Average accounts receivable × 365	Sales	$[½(95 + 70) \times 365] \div 999 = 30$†	Unknown*
Inventory turnover	7	Cost of goods sold	Average inventory at cost	$399 \div ½(20 + 60) = 10$	Unknown*
Long-term solvency ratios:					
Total debt to total assets	9	Total liabilities	Total assets	$259 \div 658 = 39.4\%$	$221 \div 610 = 36.2\%$
Total debt to equity	9	Total liabilities	Stockholders' equity	$259 \div 399 = 64.9\%$	$221 \div 389 = 56.8\%$
Interest coverage	—	Income before interest and taxes	Interest expense	$(150 + 12) \div 12 = 13.5$	$(128 + 12) \div 12 = 11.7$
Profitability ratios:					
Return on stockholders' equity	4,10	Net income	Average stockholders' equity	$90 \div ½(399 + 389) = 22.8\%$	Unknown*
Gross profit rate or percentage	4	Gross profit or gross margin	Sales	$600 \div 999 = 60\%$	$464 \div 800 = 58\%$
Return on sales	4	Net income	Sales	$90 \div 999 = 9\%$	$80 \div 800 = 10\%$
Asset turnover	—	Sales	Average total assets	$999 \div ½(658 + 610) = 1.6$	Unknown*
Pretax return on assets	—	Operating income	Average total assets	$126 \div ½(658 + 610) = 19.9\%$	Unknown*
Earnings per share	2,10	Net income less dividends on preferred stock, if any	Average common shares outstanding	$90 \div 200 = \$.45$	$80 \div 200 = \$.40$
Market price and dividend ratios:					
Price-earnings	2	Market price of common share (assume $4 and $3)	Earnings per share	$4 \div .45 = 8.9$	$3 \div .40 = 7.5$
Dividend-yield	2	Dividends per common share	Market price of common share (assume $4 and $3)	$.40 \div 4 = 10.0\%$	$.20 \div 3 = 6.7\%$
Dividend-payout	2	Dividends per common share	Earnings per share	$.40 \div .45 = 89\%$	$.20 \div .40 = 50\%$

* Insufficient data available because the *beginning* balance sheet balances for 19X1 are not provided. Without them, the *average* investment in receivables, inventory, total assets, or stockholders' equity during 19X1 cannot be computed.

† This may be easier to see as follows: Average receivables = ½(95 + 70) = 82.5. Average receivables as a percentage of annual sales = 82.5 ÷ 999 = 8.25%. Average collection period = 8.25% × 365 days = 30 days.

averages. Dun & Bradstreet also informs its subscribers of the credit-worthiness of thousands of individual companies. In addition, the firm regularly compiles many ratios of the companies it monitors. Consider the ratios for Oxley Company in Exhibit 15–6 in relation to the industry statistics. For example, some of the 1988 Dun-Bradstreet ratios for 1,646 retail nurseries and garden stores showed:

	CURRENT RATIO	QUICK RATIO	AVERAGE COLLECTION PERIOD	TOTAL DEBT TO STOCK-HOLDERS' EQUITY	NET INCOME ON SALES	NET INCOME ON STOCK-HOLDERS' EQUITY
	(Times)	(Times)	(Days)	(Percent)	(Percent)	(Percent)
1,646 companies:						
Upper quartile*	4.6	1.5	4.8	30.7	7.8	38.0
Median	2.1	0.6	10.2	87.7	3.1	14.2
Lower quartile	1.3	0.2	21.5	211.2	0.6	2.8
Oxley†	1.3	1.1	30	64.9	9.0	22.8

* The individual ratios are ranked from best to worst. The middle figure is the median. The figure halfway between the median and the best is the upper quartile. Similarly, the figure halfway between the median and the worst is the lower quartile.
† Ratios are from Exhibit 15–6. Please consult that exhibit for an explanation of the components of each ratio.

DISCUSSION OF INDIVIDUAL RATIOS

The ratios in Exhibit 15–6 are grouped into four categories, according to their most common use. This section discusses each of the categories. A later section will provide more details about using some of the ratios for evaluating operating and financial management.

☐ **Short-Term Liquidity Ratios**

Questions concerning liquidity focus on whether there are sufficient current assets to satisfy current liabilities as they become due. One measure is simply the amount of working capital (i.e., current assets less current liabilities). Oxley's working capital decreased by $30,000 from $202,000 − $101,000 = $101,000 in 19X1 to $290,000 − $219,000 = $71,000 in 19X2.

The most commonly used liquidity ratio is the current ratio. The higher the current ratio, the more assurance the short-term creditor usually has about being paid in full and on time. As Exhibit 15–6 shows, Oxley's current ratio of 1.3 has declined from 2.0 and is unimpressive in relation to the industry median of 2.1, which is shown above.

The quick ratio measures *very* short-term liquidity. The numerator includes only those current assets that can quickly be turned into cash. Oxley's quick ratio has also declined in 19X2, from 1.3 to 1.1, but is still greater than the industry median of 0.6.

Liquidity is also affected by how soon accounts receivable will be collected and how soon inventory will be sold. The average collection period and inventory turnover are closely watched signals. Deteriorations through time in these ratios can help alert investors and creditors to problem areas. For example, a decrease in inventory turnover may suggest slower-moving (or even unsalable) merchandise or a worsening coordination of the buying and selling functions. An increase in the average collection period of receivables may indicate increasing acceptance of poor credit risks or less-energetic collection efforts. Whether the inventory turnover of 10 and the average collection period of 30 days are "fast" or "slow" depends on past performance and the performance of similar companies. Inventory turnover is not available from Dun & Bradstreet on an industry comparable basis. The average collection period for Oxley is nearly three times as long as the industry median of 10.2 days.

Many analysts use sales *on account* in the denominator of the average collection period. This focuses attention on how long it takes to collect credit accounts, in contrast to how long it takes to receive payment on sales in general. A company with many cash sales may have a short average collection period for total sales, even though there may be long delays in receiving payments for items sold on credit. Suppose half of Oxley's sales were for cash (including bank cards) and only half on open credit. The average collection period for *credit sales* would be

$$\frac{(1/2)(95 + 70) \times 365}{(1/2)(999)} = 60 \text{ days}$$

To compare this with industry averages, the averages must also be adjusted for credit sales. Suppose only one-fourth of the sales in retail nurseries are on credit. The industry median collection period for credit accounts would be 10.2 ÷ (1/4) = 40.8 days.

Long-Term Solvency Ratios

Ratios of debt to assets and debt to equity are used for solvency evaluation. Although the focus is on the ability to repay long-term creditors, both creditors and shareholders watch these ratios to judge the degree of risk of insolvency and of stability of profits. Typically, companies with heavy debt in relation to ownership capital are in greater danger of suffering net losses or even insolvency when business conditions sour. Why? Because revenues and many expenses decline, but interest expenses and maturity dates do not change. Oxley's debt-to-equity ratio of 64.9% is below the industry median of 87.7%, reflecting above average stability of profits and less than average risk or uncertainty concerning the company's ability to pay its debts on time.

Another solvency measure is the interest coverage ratio. It shows how much danger there is that operations will not generate operating income (before interest expense) at least as large as the company's interest expense. A common rule of thumb is that interest coverage should be at least five times. Oxley's ratio of 13.5 comfortably exceeds this bench mark. The interest coverage ratio is discussed in more detail on page 690.

☐ Profitability Ratios

The owners of a company have one primary profitability measure, return on stockholders' equity. This ratio was introduced in Chapter 4 (p. 140) and discussed in more detail in Chapter 10 (p. 446). It measures the returns to shareholders in relation to the amount of capital they have invested. Oxley's return of 22.8% is above the industry median of 14.2% shown on page 682 and is well above the 1988 economywide average of 15.0%.

Each of the next four ratios measures a particular aspect of profitability. They measure specific types of operating success. Improvements in any one of the ratios will lead to increased profitability, provided they are not offset by a decline in another.

Consider the return on sales. Oxley's ratio has declined from 10% to 9%, but it is still significantly greater than the industry median of 3.1%. Comparisons with similar companies are important in judging the return on sales, because the ratio varies greatly across industries. For example, the 1988 average return on sales in the chemical industry was 9.0% and in food retailing it was 1.1%. Despite its low return on sales, the food-retailing industry had an average return on equity of 32.0% compared with the chemical industry's average of 21.5%.

Asset turnover and return on assets are measures of how efficiently a company is using its assets. They are indicators of operating performance, and they are discussed later in the chapter on page 685.

Earnings per share (EPS) is the best known of all financial ratios. It is a popular form of the "bottom line," the measure of earnings available to the holder of a share of common stock. It was discussed in both Chapter 2 (p. 65) and Chapter 10 (p. 466). Oxley's EPS of $.45 is compared with market price per share and dividends per share in the next section.

☐ Market Price and Dividend Ratios

Investors are particularly concerned with the market price of common shares. Both earnings and dividends are related to share price. The price-earnings (P/E) ratio shows how market participants value $1 of a company's earnings. A high P/E means that investors generally expect earnings to grow faster than average, and a low P/E indicates small expected earnings growth. In 1989, the average economywide P/E ratio was 12, but some companies such as Microsoft, the computer software company, and Merck, the pharmaceutical firm, had P/E ratios over 20. In contrast, Ford and Chrysler had P/E ratios of 5. Oxley's P/E of 8.9 is above last year's 7.5, but it is below the economywide average. Apparently, investors think Oxley has below-average growth potential.

Oxley doubled its dividend per share in 19X2, increasing the dividend yield to 10.0%. Therefore an investor who buys $1,000 of Oxley common stock will receive annual cash dividends of 10% × $1,000 = $100 if dividend rates do not change. Oxley is paying out 89% of earnings, as shown by the dividend-payout ratio. The high payout ratio may be one reason for the low projected growth; Oxley is not reinvesting much of its earnings.

Financial ratios can be used to judge both the operating performance and the financial performance of management. Recall that *operating management* is concerned primarily with the day-to-day activities that generate revenues and expenses. *Financial management* is concerned with where to get cash and how to use cash for the benefit of the entity.

Operating Performance

An important measure of overall accomplishment is the rate of return on invested capital:

$$\text{Rate of return on investment} = \frac{\text{Income}}{\text{Invested capital}} \tag{1}$$

On the surface, this measure is straightforward, but its ingredients may differ according to the purpose it is to serve. What is *invested capital*, the denominator of the ratio? What income figure is appropriate?

The measurement of *operating* performance (i.e., how profitably assets are employed) should not be influenced by the management's *financial* decisions (i.e., how assets are obtained). Operating performance is best measured by **pretax operating rate of return on total assets**:

$$\frac{\text{Pretax operating rate}}{\text{of return on total assets}} = \frac{\text{Operating income}}{\text{Average total assets available}} \tag{2}$$

The right side of Equation 2 consists, in turn, of two important ratios:

$$\frac{\text{Operating income}}{\text{Average total assets available}} = \frac{\text{Operating income}}{\text{Sales}} \times \frac{\text{Sales}}{\substack{\text{Average total} \\ \text{assets available}}} \tag{3}$$

Using Exhibits 15–1 and 15–2, pages 675–676, we can compute the following 19X2 results for Oxley Company:

$$\frac{\$126}{\frac{1}{2}\,(\$658 + \$610)} = \frac{\$126}{\$999} \times \frac{\$999}{\$634}$$

These relationships are displayed in a boxed format in Exhibit 15–7.

The right-side terms in Equation 3 are often called the **operating income percentage on sales** and the **total asset turnover**, respectively. Equation 3 may be reexpressed:

$$\frac{\text{Pretax operating rate}}{\text{of return on total assets}} = \text{Operating income percentage on sales} \times \text{Total asset turnover} \tag{4}$$
$$19.9\% = 12.6\% \times 1.576 \text{ times}$$

If ratios are used to evaluate operating performance, they should exclude extraordinary items which are regarded as nonrecurring items that do not reflect normal performance.

A scrutiny of Equation 4 shows that there are two basic factors in profit making: operating margin percentage and turnover. An improvement in either will, by itself, increase the rate of return on total assets.

EXHIBIT 15–7

Major Ingredients of Return on Total Assets

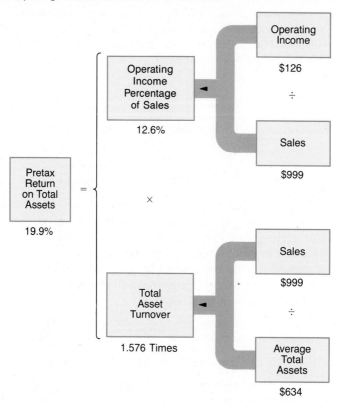

The ratios used can also be computed on the basis of figures after taxes. However, the peculiarities of the income tax laws may sometimes distort results— for example, the tax rate may change, or losses carried back or forward might eliminate the tax in certain years.

☐ Financial Performance

A major aspect of financial performance is achieving an appropriate balance of debt and equity financing. Debt surrounds us. Governments issue debt securities of all kinds for many purposes. Businesses do likewise. Individuals have small loans (on refrigerators) and big loans (on homes).

Business borrowing takes many forms. Short-term debt is usually created through trade credit (accounts payable) and bank credit (notes payable due within one year). This financing should ordinarily be for investments in current assets. Many entities have edged into deep financial water by using short-term debt for long-term investments (for example, plant and equipment) and then not having the cash when due. A notable example is the city of New York, which was unable to pay its debt during the 1970s.

Long-term investments should be financed by long-term capital: debt or stock. Debt is often a more attractive vehicle than common stock because (1) interest payments are deductible for income tax purposes but dividends are not, and (2) the ownership rights to voting and profits are kept by the present shareholders.

Trading on the Equity

Most companies have two basic types of long-term financing: long-term debt and stockholders' equity. The total of long-term financing is often called the **capitalization, capitalization structure**, or simply **capital structure** of a corporation. Suppose a company has long-term debt (in the form of bonds payable) and common stock as its capital structure. This means that common shareholders enjoy the benefits of all income in excess of interest on the bonds.

Trading on the equity, which is also referred to as using **financial leverage**, or **debt leverage**, generally means using borrowed money at fixed interest rates with the objective of enhancing the rate of return on common shareholders' equity. There are costs and benefits to shareholders from trading on the equity. The costs are interest payments and increased risk, and the benefits are the larger returns to the common shareholders—as long as overall income is sufficiently large.

Examine Exhibit 15–8. The computation in column 7 is based on the following formula for **return on total assets**:

$$\text{Rate of return on total assets} = \frac{\text{Income before interest expense}}{\text{Average total assets}}$$

$$= \frac{\$16,000}{\$80,000} = 20\%$$

EXHIBIT 15–8

Trading on the Equity
Effects of Debt on Rates of Return
(in thousands of dollars)

	(1)	(2)	(3)	(4)	(5) 10% of (2)	(6) (4) − (5)	(7) (4) ÷ (1)	(8) (6) ÷ (3)
							Return on	
	Average Assets	Average Bonds Payable	Average Stockholders' Equity	Income Before Interest	10% Interest	Net Income*	Assets	Stockholders' Equity
Year 1								
Co. A	$80,000	$30,000	$50,000	$16,000	$3,000	$13,000	20%	26%
Co. B	80,000	—	80,000	16,000	—	16,000	20	20
Year 2								
Co. A	80,000	30,000	50,000	8,000	3,000	5,000	10	10
Co. B	80,000	—	80,000	8,000	—	8,000	10	10
Year 3								
Co. A	80,000	30,000	50,000	4,000	3,000	1,000	5	2
Co. B	80,000	—	80,000	4,000	—	4,000	5	5

* Income taxes are ignored in this illustration (to highlight the major point).

The computation in column 8 is based on the following formula for **rate of return on stockholders' equity**:

$$\text{Rate of return on stockholders' equity} = \frac{\text{Net income}}{\text{Average stockholders' equity}}$$

$$= \frac{\$13,000}{\$50,000} = 26\%$$

The numerator in the latter formula is the net income that results after the deduction of all expenses, including interest expense. Interest expense is the return to the lenders, whereas net income is the return to the owners who provided the stockholders' equity.

Exhibit 15–8 shows how borrowing can be a two-edged sword. In Year 1, Company A paid 10% for the use of $30 million, which in turn earned 20%. This method of financing benefited the shareholders handsomely, resulting in an ultimate return on equity of 26%, compared with the 20% earned by debt-free Company B.

In Year 3, the picture is reversed. When a company is unable to earn at least the interest rate on the money borrowed, the return on equity will be lower than for the debt-free company. If earnings are low enough that the interest and principal payments on debt cannot be made, a company may be forced into bankruptcy. The possibility of bankruptcy increases the risk to the common stockholders as well as to debtholders.

Real estate promoters are examples of heavy traders on the equity. They use layers of mortgage debt and a minimum amount of owners' equity, and they enjoy extremely high returns on equity as long as revenues are ample. They are also prime candidates for bankruptcy when revenues decrease.

Obviously, the more stable the income, the less dangerous it is to trade on the equity (or, as it is often called, to use **leveraging** or **gearing**). Therefore regulated utilities such as electric, gas, and telephone companies tend to have a much heavier proportion of debt than manufacturers of computers or steel. The *prudent* use of debt is part of intelligent financial management. **Managers** who brag about having no long-term debt may not be obtaining the maximum returns on equity through the years. On the other hand, too much debt can cause financial disaster when operations become unprofitable (as the owners of Braniff common stock will attest).

☐ **Income Tax Effects**

Because interest payments are deductible as an expense for income tax purposes but dividends are not, if all other things are equal, the use of debt is less costly to the corporation than equity. Suppose additional capital of $10 million is going to be raised by a company either through long-term debt or through preferred stock. The latter is discussed in Chapter 10, pages 442–445. The typical preferred stock is a part of shareholders' equity, and the dividend thereon is not deductible for income tax purposes. Moreover, the rate of preferred dividends is usually higher than the rate of interest because the preferred stockholders have a greater risk due to their lower-priority claim on the total assets of a company. Assume that an interest rate of 10% for debt and a preferred dividend rate of 11% are applicable. The income tax rate is 40%. Compare the effects of obtaining additional capital by these two methods shown in the accompanying table.

	$10 MILLION LONG-TERM DEBT	$10 MILLION PREFERRED STOCK
Income before interest expense (assumed)	$5,000,000	$5,000,000
Interest expense at 10% of long-term debt	1,000,000	—
Income before income taxes	$4,000,000	$5,000,000
Income tax expense at 40%	1,600,000	2,000,000
Net income	$2,400,000	$3,000,000
Dividends to preferred shareholders at 11%	—	1,100,000
Net income less dividends	$2,400,000	$1,900,000
Pretax cost of capital raised	10%	11%
After-tax cost of capital raised:		
$600,000* ÷ $10,000,000	6%	
$1,100,000 ÷ $10,000,000		11%

* Interest expense	$1,000,000
Income tax savings because of interest deduction:	
.40 × $1,000,000	400,000
Interest expense after tax savings	$ 600,000

Two points deserve emphasis:

1. Interest is tax deductible, so its after-tax cost can be considerably less than dividends on preferred stock. In other words, *net income attributable to common shareholders* can be substantially higher if debt is used.

2. Interest is an expense, whereas preferred dividends are not. Therefore *net income* is higher if preferred shares are used. Note that trading on the equity can benefit the common stockholders by the issuance of either long-term debt securities or preferred stock, provided that the after-tax earnings on the additional assets acquired exceed the after-tax costs of obtaining the funds: in this case, 11% for the preferred stock but only 6% for the long-term debt.

Measuring Safety

Investors in debt securities want assurance that future operations will easily provide cash sufficient to make the scheduled payments of interest and principal. Corporate borrowers have a natural concern for the degree of risk they assume by trading on the equity through borrowing. Thus both lenders and borrowers may have a somewhat mutual aversion to excessive risks from debt, although lenders understandably tend to have the stronger aversion to risk.

Debt securities often have protective provisions, such as mortgage liens on real estate or restrictions on dividend payments to holders of common stock. However, these provisions are of minor importance compared with prospective earnings. Bondholders would like to avoid the trouble, costs, and inconvenience of foreclosure or bankruptcy litigation; they would rather receive a steady stream of interest and repayments of principal.

Debt-to-equity ratios are popular measures of risks. But they do not focus on the major concern of the holders of long-term debt: the ability to meet debt obligations on schedule. A ratio that focuses on interest-paying ability is **interest coverage** (sometimes called **times interest earned**). For example, in the above table, interest coverage is:

$$\text{Interest coverage} = \frac{\text{Income before interest expense and income taxes}}{\text{Interest expense}}$$

$$= \frac{\$5,000,000}{\$1,000,000} = 5.0 \text{ times}$$

The equation is self-explanatory. A rule of thumb for adequate safety of an industrial bond is that all interest charges should be earned at least five times in the poorest year in a span of seven to ten years that might be under review. The numerator does not deduct income taxes because interest expense is deductible for income tax purposes. In effect, income taxes, as a periodic "claim" on earnings, have a lower priority than interest. For instance, if the numerator were only $1 million, interest would be paid, leaving a net taxable income of zero. This tax-deductibility feature is a major reason why bonds are used so much more widely than preferred stock.

Regarding interest coverage, a recent news story stated:

The implications of the nuclear plant accident in Pennsylvania won't easily be sorted out by investors and promise to be an uncertainty of long duration. Even without this development, however, the operating climate for the utility industry doesn't provide much comfort for electric utility investors. Among other things, such investors will have to renew their vigilance about the investment quality of stocks in the group. There's some evidence of erosion recently in one key financial measure—*the ratio of income before interest expense to interest expense.*

EFFICIENT MARKETS AND INVESTOR DECISIONS

Much recent research in accounting and finance has concentrated on whether the stock markets are "efficient." An **efficient capital market** is one in which market prices "fully reflect" all information available to the public. Therefore searching for "underpriced" securities in such a market would be fruitless unless an investor has information that is not generally available. If the real-world markets are indeed efficient, a relatively inactive portfolio approach would be an appropriate investment strategy for most investors. The hallmarks of the approach are risk control, high diversification, and low turnover of securities. The role of accounting information would mainly be in identifying the different degrees of risk among various stocks so that investors can maintain desired levels of risk and diversification.

Research in finance and accounting during the past twenty years has reinforced the idea that financial ratios and other data such as reported earnings provide inputs to predictions of such economic phenomena as financial failure or earnings growth. Furthermore, many ratios are used simultaneously rather than one at a time for such predictions. Above all, the research showed that accounting reports are only one source of information and that in the aggregate the market is not fooled by companies that choose the least-conservative accounting policies. In sum, the market as a whole sees through any attempts by companies to gain favor through the choice of accounting policies that tend to boost immediate income. Thus there is evidence that the stock markets may indeed be "efficient," at least in their reflection of most accounting data.[2]

Suppose you are the chief executive officer of Company A. Reported earnings are $4 per share and the stock price is $40. You are contemplating changing your method of depreciation for investor-reporting purposes from accelerated to straight-line. Your competitors use straight-line. You think the Company A stock price unjustifiably suffers in comparison with other companies in the same industry.

If straight-line depreciation is adopted by Company A, reported earnings will be $5 instead of $4 per share. Would the stock price rise accordingly from $40 to $50? No, the empirical research on these issues indicates that the stock price would remain at $40 (all other things equal).

The chief executive's beliefs as shown in the above example are shared by many managers, who essentially adhere to an extremely narrow view of the role of an income statement. Such a "bottom-line" mentality is slowly, surely, and sensibly falling into disrepute. At the risk of unfair exaggeration, the view is summarized as:

1. The income statement is the sole (or at least the primary) source of information about a company.
2. Lenders and shareholders invest in a company because of its reported earnings. For instance, the higher the reported earnings per share, the higher the stock price, and the easier it is to raise capital.

Basically, these arguments assume that investors can be misled by how reported earnings are measured. But there is considerable evidence that securities markets are not fooled with respect to accounting changes that are devoid of economic substance (that have no effect on cash flows). Why? Because the change generally reveals no new information, so no significant change in stock price is likely.

Remember that the market is efficient only with respect to *publicly available* information. Therefore significant accounting issues deal with the disclosure of new information, not the format for reporting already available data. William Beaver has commented on the implications of market efficiency for accounting regulators:

☐ Many reporting issues are trivial and do not warrant an expenditure of FASB resources. The properties of such issues are twofold: (1) There is essentially no difference in cost to the firm of reporting either method. (2) There is essentially no cost to statement users in adjusting from one method to the other. In such cases, there is a simple solution. Report one method, with sufficient footnote disclosure to permit adjustment to the other, and let the market interpret implications of the data for security prices.

☐ The FASB should shift its resources to those controversies where there is nontrivial

---

[2] The stock market crash of October 1987 and other reported "anomalies" prevent unqualified endorsement of stock market efficiency. However, the evidence that stock prices efficiently reflect *accounting data* is quite strong.

additional cost to the firms or to investors in order to obtain certain types of information (for example, replacement cost accounting for depreciable assets). Whether such information should be a required part of reporting standards is a substantive issue.[3]

Be aware also that accounting statements are not the only source of financial information about companies. Some alternative sources were listed earlier in the chapter on pages 672–673. If accounting reports are to be useful, they must have some advantage over alternative sources in disclosing new information. Financial statement information may be more directly related to the item of interest, and it may be more reliable, lower-cost, or more timely than information from alternative sources.

The research described above concentrates on the effects of accounting on investors in the aggregate. Individual investors vary in how they analyze financial statements. One by one, individual users must either incur the costs of conducting careful analyses or delegate that chore to professional analysts. In any event, intelligent analysis cannot be accomplished without an understanding of the assumptions and limitations of financial statements, including the presence of various alternative accounting methods.

SUMMARY

Financial statements are one important source of information about companies. Creditors and investors use financial statement analysis to assess a company's position and prospects. Trend analysis, common-size statements, and financial ratios are used to analyze financial statements.

Financial ratios are the heart of financial statement analysis. They are used as a basis of evaluation, comparison, and prediction. The rate of return on invested capital is a popular means of comparing operating performance. Trading on the equity (that is, using leverage) is an important part of financial management.

Financial statements are only one of many sources of information about a company. Market efficiency implies that accounting regulators should focus on issues of disclosure, not format.

SUMMARY PROBLEM FOR YOUR REVIEW

☐ **Problem**

Exhibit 15–9 contains a condensed income statement and balance sheet for Gannett Company, Inc., the nation's largest newspaper group with eighty-eight dailies, including *USA Today*.

---

[3] William H. Beaver, "What Should Be the FASB's Objectives?" *Journal of Accountancy*, Vol. 136, p. 52.

Required: **1.** Compute the following ratios: (a) current ratio, (b) quick ratio, (c) average collection period, (d) total debt to stockholders' equity, (e) return on sales, and (f) return on stockholders' equity.

2. Dun & Bradstreet ratios for newspaper companies are:

	CURRENT RATIO	QUICK RATIO	AVERAGE COLLECTION PERIOD	TOTAL DEBT TO STOCKHOLDERS' EQUITY	NET INCOME ON SALES	NET INCOME ON STOCKHOLDERS' EQUITY
Upper quartile	5.5	3.8	30.3	19.1	9.6	29.3
Median	2.5	1.8	39.1	53.8	5.0	14.5
Lower quartile	1.3	1.0	54.9	123.6	1.7	4.6

Using only the ratios in requirement 1, assess Gannett Company's liquidity, solvency, and profitability.

EXHIBIT 15–9

Gannett Company, Inc.
(in thousands)

INCOME STATEMENT   FOR THE YEAR ENDED December 25, 1988

Revenues	$ 3,314,485
Operating expenses	(2,626,760)
Operating income	687,725
Interest expense	(88,557)
Interest and other income	8,292
Income before income taxes	607,460
Provision for income taxes	(243,000)
Net income	$ 364,460

BALANCE SHEETS

	FOR THE YEAR ENDED	
	December 25, 1988	December 27, 1987
Assets		
Current assets:		
Cash and marketable securities	$ 48,677	$ 26,899
Receivables	458,822	439,837
Inventories	84,214	64,719
Prepaid expenses	73,318	69,765
Total current assets	665,031	601,220
Property plant and equipment, net	1,377,432	1,311,625
Intangible and other assets	1,750,357	1,597,414
Total assets	$ 3,792,820	$3,510,259
Liabilities and Shareholders' Equity		
Total current liabilties	$ 500,835	$ 474,775
Long-term liabilties	1,505,544	1,426,090
Total liabilities	2,006,379	1,900,865
Total shareholders' equity	1,786,441	1,609,394
Total liabilities and shareholders' equity	$ 3,792,820	$3,510,259

1. a. Current ratio $= \dfrac{665,031}{500,835} = 1.3$

   b. Quick ratio $= \dfrac{48,677 + 458,822}{500,835} = 1.0$

   c. Average collection period $= \dfrac{(1/2)(458,822 + 439,837) \times 365}{3,314,485} = 49.4$

   d. Total debt to stockholders' equity $= \dfrac{2,006,379}{1,786,441} = 112.3\%$

   e. Return on sales $= \dfrac{364,460}{3,314,485} = 11.0\%$

   f. Return on stockholders' equity $= \dfrac{364,460}{(1/2)(1,609,394 + 1,786,441)} = 21.5\%$

2. Gannett's liquidity ratios are all close to the lower quartile value for the newspaper industry. Therefore about 75% of the newspaper companies have better ratios than Gannett's. The company's debt-to-equity ratio is only slightly better than the industry's lower quartile value, indicating below-average solvency. Because of lower-than-average liquidity and solvency ratios, the risk of default to creditors is likely to be greater for Gannett than for the average newspaper company. That is the bad news.

     The good news is that the two profitability ratios are better than the industry medians. The return on sales is especially high, well into the top quartile. The return on stockholders' equity is not in the top quartile but is significantly above the industry median.

     In general, Gannett seems to be more profitable and more risky than the average newspaper company.

HIGHLIGHTS TO REMEMBER

1. Avoid too heavy an emphasis on one financial ratio. A thorough understanding of a company's position and prospects requires examination of a large set of ratios.

2. Exhibit 15–6 deserves your review. The ratios are categorized by the type of decision they most commonly influence. However, their information is often useful for other decisions as well. For example, analysis of profitability ratios is important for solvency determinations.

3. Recent research has indicated that capital markets are "efficient" in the sense that investors in the aggregate are not fooled by companies that try to look good by choosing less-conservative accounting policies. Accounting is a major source of information, but it is not the sole source.

ACCOUNTING VOCABULARY

Asset Turnover, p. 685
Bench Mark, p. 679
Capital Structure, p. 687
Capitalization, p. 687
Capitalization Structure, p. 687
Common-Size Statements, p. 677
Component Percentages, p. 677
Cross-Sectional Comparisons, p. 679
Debt Leverage, p. 687
Efficient Capital Markets, p. 690
Financial Leverage, p. 687
Financial Statement Analysis, p. 672
Gearing, p. 688

Interest Coverage, p. 690
Leveraging, p. 688
Long-Term Solvency, p. 673
Management's Discussion and Analysis
  (MD&A), p. 679
Operating Income Percentage
  on Sales, p. 685
Pretax Operating Rate of Return
  on Total Assets, p. 685
Pro Forma Statement, p. 673
Rate of Return on Stockholders'
  Equity, p. 688
Return on Total Assets, p. 687

FUNDAMENTAL ASSIGNMENT MATERIAL

☐ **General Coverage**

15–1. **COMMON-SIZE STATEMENTS.**   J-Mart and Bullseye are both discount store chains. Condensed income statements and balance sheets for the two companies are shown in Exhibit 15–10. Amounts are in thousands.

EXHIBIT 15–10

Financial Statements for J-Mart and Bullseye

**Income Statements for the Year
Ended December 31, 19X9**

	J-MART	BULLSEYE
Sales	$ 875,600	$491,750
Cost of sales	582,360	301,910
Gross profit	293,240	189,840
Operating expenses	174,130	147,160
Operating income	119,110	42,680
Other revenue (expense)	(21,930)	6,270
Pretax income	97,180	48,950
Income tax expense	38,870	19,580
Net income	$ 58,310	$ 29,370

Balance Sheets

	J-MART		BULLSEYE	
	December 31		December 31	
	19X9	19X8	19X9	19X8
Assets				
Current assets				
Cash	$ 12,100	$ 10,700	$ 8,200	$ 6,900
Marketable securities	5,300	5,300	4,100	3,800
Accounts receivable	36,700	40,100	21,300	20,500
Inventories	155,600	149,400	105,100	106,600
Prepaid expenses	17,100	16,900	8,800	8,400
Total current assets	226,800	222,400	147,500	146,200
Property and equipment, net	461,800	452,300	287,600	273,500
Other assets	14,700	13,900	28,600	27,100
Total assets	$ 703,300	$688,600	$463,700	$446,800
Liabilities and Stockholders' Equity				
Liabilities				
Current liabilities (summarized)	$ 91,600	$ 93,700	$ 61,300	$ 58,800
Long-term debt	156,700	156,700	21,000	21,000
Total liabilities	248,300	250,400	82,300	79,800
Stockholder's equity	455,000	438,200	381,400	367,000
Total liabilities and stockholders' equity	$ 703,300	$688,600	$463,700	$446,800

1. Prepare common-size statements for J-Mart and Bullseye for 19X9.
2. Compare the financial performance for 19X9 and financial position at the end of 19X9 for J-Mart with the performance and position of Bullseye. Use only the statements prepared in requirement 1.

15–2. FINANCIAL RATIOS. (Alternate is 15–4.) This problem uses the same data as 15–1, but it can be solved independently. J-Mart and Bullseye are both discount store chains. Condensed income statements and balance sheets for the two companies are shown in Exhibit 15–10. Amounts are in thousands.

Additional information:

☐ Cash dividends per share: J-Mart, $2.00; Bullseye, $1.50
☐ Market price per share: J-Mart, $30; Bullseye, $40
☐ Average shares outstanding for 19X9: J-Mart, 15 million; Bullseye, 7 million

Required:

1. Compute the following ratios for both companies for 19X9: (a) current, (b) quick, (c) average collection period, (d) inventory turnover, (e) total debt to total assets, (f) total debt to total equity, (g) return on stockholders' equity, (h) gross profit rate, (i) return on sales, (j) asset turnover, (k) pretax return on assets, (l) earnings per share, (m) price-earnings, (n) dividend yield, and (o) dividend payout.
2. Compare the liquidity, solvency, profitability, and market price and dividend ratios of J-Mart with those of Bullseye.

☐ **Understanding Published Financial Reports**

15–3. TREND ANALYSIS. Merck & Co., the pharmaceutical company, is the seventh largest U.S. firm when ranked by total market value of common shares. Two recent income statements and balance sheets are in Exhibit 15–11.

Required:

1. Prepare an income statement and balance sheet for Merck & Co. that has two columns, one showing the amount of change between 1987 and 1988 and the other showing the percentage change.
2. Identify and discuss the most significant changes between 1987 and 1988.

15–4. FINANCIAL RATIOS. (Alternate is 15–2). Merck & Co. is the largest company in the health-care industry in the United States. Two recent income statements and balance sheets are in Exhibit 15–11. Additional 1988 data are:

☐ Cash dividends, $1.28 per share
☐ Market price per share, $65
☐ Average common shares outstanding, 395,640,000

Required:

Compute the following ratios for Merck & Co. for 1988: (a) current, (b) quick, (c) average collection period, (d) total debt to total assets, (e) total debt to total equity, (f) return on stockholders' equity, (g) return on sales, (h) asset turnover, (i) pretax return on assets, (j) earnings per share, (k) price-earnings, (l) dividend yield, and (m) dividend payout. Total debt includes current liabilities, long-term debt, and deferred income taxes and noncurrent liabilities.

ADDITIONAL ASSIGNMENT MATERIAL

☐ **General Coverage**

15–5. Why do decision makers use financial statement analysis?

15–6. In addition to the basic financial statements, what information is usually presented in a company's annual report?

EXHIBIT 15–11

MERCK & CO., INC.
(in millions)

Income Statement for Years Ended December 31

	1988	1987
Sales	$5,939.5	$5,061.3
Costs and Expenses:		
Materials and production	1,526.1	1,444.3
Marketing and administrative	1,877.8	1,682.1
Research and development	668.8	565.7
Other (income) expense, net	(4.2)	(36.0)
	4,068.5	3,656.1
Income Before Taxes	1,871.0	1,405.2
Taxes on Income	664.2	498.8
Net Income	$1,206.8	$ 906.4

Balance Sheets as of December 31

	1988	1987
ASSETS		
Current Assets:		
Cash and cash equivalents	$ 854.0	$ 408.0
Short-term investments	696.0	740.2
Accounts receivable	1,022.8	1,076.5
Inventories	657.7	659.6
Prepaid expenses and taxes	158.8	122.6
Total current assets	3,389.3	3,006.9
Property, Plant, and Equipment, at cost	3,590.5	3,337.3
Less allowance for depreciation	1,519.8	1,389.3
	2,070.7	1,948.0
Investments	402.9	458.7
Other Assets	264.6	266.4
Total assets	$6,127.5	$5,680.0
LIABILITIES AND STOCKHOLDERS' EQUITY		
Current Liabilities:		
Accounts payable and accrued liabilities	$ 832.9	$ 910.3
Loans payable	458.8	850.8
Income taxes payable	470.5	342.2
Dividends payable	146.8	105.3
Total current liabilities	1,909.0	2,208.6
Long-Term Debt	142.8	167.4
Deferred Income Taxes and Noncurrent Liabilities	676.2	652.2
Minority Interests	543.7	535.1
Total liabilities	3,271.7	3,563.3
Stockholders' Equity		
Common stock, 900,000,000 shares authorized, 455,524,308 shares issued	145.4	151.6
Retained earnings	4,580.3	3,919.8
	4,725.7	4,071.4
Less treasury stock, at cost	1,869.9	1,954.7
Total stockholders' equity	2,855.8	2,116.7
Total liabilities and stockholders' equity	$6,127.5	$5,680.0

15–7. Give three sources of information for investors besides accounting information.

15–8. "Financial statements report on *history*. Therefore they are not useful to creditors and investors who want to predict *future* returns and risk." Do you agree? Explain.

15–9. How do common-size statements aid comparisons with other companies?

15–10. What information is presented in the "management's discussion and analysis" (MD&A) section of annual reports?

15–11. Name three types of comparisons that are useful in evaluating financial ratios.

15–12. "Ratios are mechanical and incomplete." Explain.

15–13. Ratios are often grouped into four categories. What are the categories?

15–14. What two measures of operating performance are combined to give the pretax return on total assets?

15–15. "Trading on the equity means exchanging bonds for stock." Do you agree? Explain.

15–16. "Borrowing is a two-edged sword." Do you agree? Explain.

15–17. Why are companies with heavy debt in relation to ownership capital in greater danger when business conditions sour?

15–18. "The tax law discriminates against preferred stock and in favor of debt." Explain.

15–19. "An efficient capital market is one where securities are traded through stockbrokers." Do you agree? Explain.

15–20. Suppose the president of your company wanted to switch depreciation methods to increase reported net income: "Our stock price is 10% below what I think it should be; changing the depreciation method will increase income by 10%, thus getting our share price up to its proper level." How would you respond?

15–21. Evaluate the following quotation from *Forbes*: "If IBM had been forced to expense [the software development cost of] $785 million, its earnings would have been cut by 72 cents a share. With IBM selling at 14 times earnings, expensing the costs might have knocked over $10 off IBM's share price."

15–22. **TREND ANALYSIS AND COMMON-SIZE STATEMENTS.** Jason Company furnished the following condensed data (in thousands):

	DECEMBER 31		
	19X3	19X2	19X1
Cash	$ 25	$ 20	$ 15
Accounts receivable	90	70	50
Merchandise inventory	85	75	65
Prepaid expenses	10	10	10
Land	30	30	30
Building	70	75	80
Equipment	60	50	40
Total assets	$370	$330	$290
Accounts payable	$ 50	$ 40	$ 30
Taxes payable	20	15	10
Accrued expenses payable	15	10	5
Long-term debt	45	45	45
Paid-in capital	150	150	150
Retained income	90	70	50
Total liab. and stk. eq.	$370	$330	$290

	YEAR ENDED DECEMBER 31	
	19X3	19X2
Sales (all on credit)	$ 800	$ 750
Cost of goods sold	(440)	(420)
Operating expenses	(300)	(285)
Pretax income	60	45
Income taxes	(20)	(15)
Net income	$ 40	$ 30

Required:

1. Prepare a trend analysis for Jason's income statement and balance sheet that compares 19X3 with 19X2.
2. Prepare common-size income statements for 19X3 and 19X2 and balance sheets for December 31, 19X3 and December 31, 19X2 for Jason Company.
3. Comment on Jason Company's performance and position for 19X3 compared with 19X2.

15–23. FINANCIAL RATIOS. Consider the data for Jason Company in the preceding problem.

Required:

1. Compute the following ratios for each of the last two years, 19X2 and 19X3:
   a. Current ratio
   b. Gross profit rate
   c. Percentage of net income to sales
   d. Ratio of total debt to stockholders' equity
   e. Inventory turnover
   f. Percentage of net income to stockholders' equity
   g. Average collection period for accounts receivable
2. For each of the following items, indicate whether the change from 19X2 to 19X3 for Jason Company seems to be favorable or unfavorable, and identify the ratios you computed above that most directly support your answer. The first item below is given as an example.
   a. Gross margin: favorable, b
   b. Return to owners
   c. Ability to pay current debts on time
   d. Collectibility of receivables
   e. Risks of insolvency
   f. Salability of merchandise
   g. Return on sales
   h. Operating success
   i. Overall accomplishment
   j. Future stability of profits
   k. Coordination of buying and selling functions
   l. Screening of risks in granting credit to customers

15–24. FINANCIAL RATIOS. Examine the accompanying financial statements of Diaz Lumber. Dun & Bradstreet compiles many ratios of the companies it monitors. For instance, some of its ratios for 2,471 lumber and other building materials dealers were:

	CURRENT RATIO	QUICK RATIO	AVERAGE COLLECTION PERIOD	NET INCOME ON SALES	NET INCOME ON STOCK-HOLDERS' EQUITY	TOTAL DEBT TO STOCK-HOLDERS' EQUITY
	(Times)	(Times)	(Days)	(Percent)	(Percent)	(Percent)
For 2,471 companies:						
Upper quartile*	5.3	2.2	21.2	5.2	22.1	24.7
Median	2.8	1.2	33.2	2.6	10.6	66.6
Lower quartile	1.7	0.6	47.8	0.9	3.2	160.6

* See pages 680–681 for a description of the quartiles and how the various ratios are compiled.

DIAZ LUMBER
Income Statement
For the Year Ended December 31, 19X2
(in thousands)

Sales, including $188 of cash sales		$900
Cost of goods sold		440
Gross profit (or gross margin)		$460
Operating expenses:		
Wages	$200	
Miscellaneous	189	
Insurance	7	
Depreciation	30	
Total operating expenses		426
Operating income (or operating profit)		$ 34
Other revenue: interest		16
Income before income taxes		$ 50
Income tax expense		20
Net income		$ 30

Required:

1. Present Diaz Lumber's ratios for 19X2 as the final line of the above tabulation of Dun & Bradstreet ratios. Comment on Diaz's ratios in relation to those of similar companies.
2. Compute the following for Diaz:
   a. Inventory turnover
   b. Gross profit percentage of sales
   Add any comments to those made in requirement 1.

DIAZ LUMBER
Statement of Retained Income
For the Year Ended December 31, 19X2

Retained income, December 31, 19X1	$322
Add: Net income for 19X2	30
Total	$352
Deduct: Dividends declared	26
Retained income, December 31, 19X2	$326

DIAZ LUMBER
Balance Sheets

	DECEMBER 31	
ASSETS	19X2	19X1
Current assets:		
Cash	$ 1	$ 21
Accounts receivable	130	100
Note receivable–current portion	100	100
Accrued interest receivable	8	16
Merchandise inventory	240	160
Prepaid fire insurance	32	3
Total current assets	$511	$400
Long-term assets:		
Note receivable—long-term portion	—	100

	DECEMBER 31			
	19X2	19X1		
Equipment, at original cost	$184	$110		
Accumulated depreciation	96	66		
Equipment, net			88	44
Total assets			$599	$544

LIABILITIES AND STOCKHOLDERS' EQUITY

	19X2	19X1
Current liabilities:		
Accounts payable	$110	$ 90
Accrued wages payable	15	8
Accrued income taxes payable	5	4
Dividends payable	26	—
Deferred sales revenue	7	10
Total current liabilities	$163	$112
Stockholders' equity:		
Paid-in capital	$110	$110
Retained income	326	322
Total stockholders' equity	$436	$432
Total liabilities and stockholders' equity	$599	$544

15–25. RATE-OF-RETURN COMPUTATIONS.

1. Tokyo Company reported a 4% operating margin on sales, an 8% pretax operating return on total assets, and ¥2 billion of total assets. Compute (a) operating income, (b) total sales, and (c) total asset turnover.

2. Glasgow Corporation reported £600 million of sales, £32 million of operating income, and a total asset turnover of 4 times. Compute (a) total assets, (b) operating margin percentage on sales, and (c) pretax operating return on total assets.

15–26. EPS AND TIMES-INTEREST-EARNED COMPUTATIONS. Far East Shipping Co. has outstanding 400,000 shares of common stock, $4 million of 8% preferred stock, and $8 million of 10% bonds payable. Its income tax rate is 40%.

1. Assume the company has $6 million of income before interest and taxes. Compute (a) EPS and (b) number of times bond interest has been earned.

2. Assume $4 million of income before interest and taxes, and make the same computations.

15–27. COMMON STOCK RATIOS AND BOOK VALUE. You may wish to review Chapter 10. The Ramos Corporation has outstanding 500,000 shares of 8% preferred stock with a $100 par value and 10.5 million shares of common stock of $1 par value. The current market price of the common is $24, and the latest annual dividend rate is $2 per share. Common treasury stock consists of 500,000 shares costing $7.5 million. The company has $150 million of additional paid-in capital, $15 million of retained income, and a $12 million bond sinking fund. Net income for the current year is $20 million.

Required:
1. Total stockholders' equity
2. Common price-earnings ratio
3. Common dividend-yield percentage
4. Common dividend-payout percentage
5. Book value per share of common

15–28. TRADING ON THE EQUITY. Able Company has assets of $250 million, bonds payable of $100 million, and stockholders' equity of $150 million. The bonds bear interest at 10% per annum. Baker Company, which is in the same industry, has assets of $250 million and stockholders' equity of $250 million. Prepare a comparative tabulation of Able Company and Baker Company for each of three years. Show income before interest, interest, net income, return on assets, and return on stockholders' equity. The income before interest for both companies was: Year 1, $25 million; Year 2, $12.5 million; and Year 3, $37.5 million. Ignore income taxes. Show all monetary amounts in millions of dollars. Comment on the results.

15–29. USING DEBT OR EQUITY. The Hogan Corporation is trying to decide whether to raise additional capital of $15 million through a new issue of 12% long-term debt or of 9% preferred stock. The income tax rate is 40%. Compute net income less dividends for these alternatives, assuming that income before interest expense and taxes is $6 million. Show all dollar amounts in thousands. What is the after-tax cost of capital for debt and for preferred stock expressed in percentages? Comment on the comparison. Compute times interest earned for the first year.

15–30. COMPUTATION OF FINANCIAL RATIOS. You are given the financial statements of the Maxim Co.

THE MAXIM CO.
Balance Sheets
(in thousands of dollars)

	DECEMBER 31	
	19X2	19X1
Assets		
Current assets:		
Cash	$ 1,000	$ 1,000
Short-term investments		1,000
Receivables, net	5,000	4,000
Inventories at cost	12,000	9,000
Prepayments	1,000	1,000
Total current assets	$19,000	$16,000
Plant and equipment, net	22,000	23,000
Total assets	$41,000	$39,000

THE MAXIM CO. (continued)
Balance Sheets
(in thousands of dollars)

	DECEMBER 31	
	19X2	19X1
Liabilities and Stockholders' Equity		
Current liabilities:		
Accounts payable	$10,000	$ 6,000
Accrued expenses payable	500	500
Income taxes payable	1,500	1,500
Total current liabilities	$12,000	$ 8,000
8% bonds payable	$10,000	$10,000
Stockholders' equity:		
Preferred stock, 12%, par value		
$100 per share	$ 5,000	$ 5,000
Common stock, $10 par value	8,000	8,000
Premium on common stock	4,000	4,000
Unappropriated retained earnings	1,000	3,000
Reserve for plant expansion	1,000	1,000
Total stockholders' equity	$19,000	$21,000
Total liab. and stk. eq.	$41,000	$39,000

THE MAXIM CO.
Statement of Income and Reconciliation of Retained Earnings
For the Year Ended December 31, 19X2
(in thousands of dollars)

Sales (all on credit)		$44,000
Cost of goods sold		32,000
Gross profit on sales		$12,000
Other operating expenses:		
Selling expenses	$5,000	
Administrative expenses	2,000	
Depreciation	1,000	8,000
Operating income		$ 4,000
Interest expense		800
Income before income taxes		$ 3,200
Income taxes at 40%		1,280
Net income		$ 1,920
Dividends on preferred stock		600
Net income for common stockholders		$ 1,320
Dividends on common stock		3,320
Net income retained		$ (2,000)
Unappropriated retained earnings, December 31, 19X1		3,000
Unappropriated retained earnings, December 31, 19X2		$ 1,000

Required: Compute the following for the 19X2 financial statements:

1. Pretax return on total assets.
2. Divide your answer to requirement 1 into two components: operating income percentage of sales and total asset turnover.

3. After-tax rate of return on total assets. Be sure to add the *after-tax* interest expense to net income.
4. Rate of return on total stockholders' equity. Did the preferred and common stockholders benefit from the existence of debt? Explain fully.
5. Rate of return on *common* stockholders' equity. This ratio is the amount of net income available for the common stockholders divided by total stockholders' equity less the par value of preferred stock. Did the common stockholders benefit from the existence of preferred stock? Explain fully.

☐ Understanding Published Financial Statements

15–31. COMMON-SIZE STATEMENTS. Exhibit 15–12 contains the income statement and balance sheets of Minnesota Mining and Manufacturing Company (3M), a multinational company with sales over $6 billion in the United States and over $4 billion abroad.

Required:
1. Prepare common-size statements for 3M for 1987 and 1988.
2. Comment on the changes in component percentages from 1987 to 1988.

15–32. LIQUIDITY RATIOS. Exhibit 15–12 contains the income statement and balance sheets of Minnesota Mining and Manufacturing Company (3M), maker of Scotch brand tapes.

EXHIBIT 15–12

MINNESOTA MINING AND MANUFACTURING COMPANY
(in millions)

Income Statement for the Year Ended December 31

	1988	1987
Net Sales	$10,581	$9,429
Operating Expenses:		
Cost of goods sold	6,105	5,513
Selling, general and administrative expenses	2,593	2,338
Total	8,698	7,851
Operating Income	1,883	1,578
Other Income and Expense:		
Interest expense	95	95
Investment and other income—net	(94)	(82)
Total	1	13
Income Before Income Taxes	1,882	1,565
Provision for Income Taxes	728	647
Net Income	$ 1,154	$ 918

Balance Sheet as of December 31

	1988	1987
ASSETS		
Current Assets:		
Cash and cash equivalents	$ 522	$ 432
Other securities	375	274
Accounts receivable—net	1,727	1,615
Inventories	1,831	1,770
Other current assets	286	252
Total current assets	4,741	4,343
Investments	720	586
Property, Plant and Equipment—net	3,073	2,932
Other Assets	388	365
Total	$ 8,922	$8,226

EXHIBIT 15–12   (continued)

LIABILITIES AND STOCKHOLDERS' EQUITY
Current Liabilities:

Accounts payable	$ 572	$ 586
Payrolls	295	284
Income taxes	299	277
Short-term debt	347	264
Other current liabilities	858	693
Total current liabilities	2,371	2,104
Deferred Tax Liability	264	312
Other Liabilities	367	315
Long-Term Debt	406	435
Stockholders' Equity—net	5,514	5,060
Total	$ 8,922	$8,226

Required:

1. Compute the following ratios for 1988: (a) current, (b) quick, (c) average collection period, and (d) inventory turnover.
2. Assess 3M's liquidity compared with the following industry averages:

Current ratio	2.7 times
Quick ratio	1.3 times
Average collection period	45.1 days
Inventory turnover	6.3 times

15–33. SOLVENCY RATIOS.   Exhibit 15–12 contains the income statement and balance sheets of Minnesota Mining and Manufacturing Company (3M), a diversified manufacturing company with operations in the United States and fifty-one other countries.

Required:

1. Compute the following ratios for 1988: (a) total debt to total assets and (b) total debt to total equity.
2. Assess 3M's solvency compared with the following industry averages:

Total debt to total assets	42.1%
Total debt to total equity	72.5%

15–34. PROFITABILITY RATIOS.   Exhibit 15–12 contains the income statement and balance sheets of Minnesota Mining and Manufacturing Company (3M), a technology company with over one hundred technologies, including more than twenty that have been added in the last five years. An average of 226.9 million common shares were outstanding during 1988.

Required:

1. Compute the following ratios for 1988: (a) return on stockholders' equity, (b) gross profit rate, (c) return on sales, (d) asset turnover, (e) pretax return on assets, and (f) earnings per share.
2. Assess 3M's profitability in 1988 compared with the following industry averages:

Return on stockholders' equity	14.7%
Gross profit rate	33.2%
Return on sales	5.7%
Asset turnover	1.51 times
Pretax return on assets	11.3%
Earnings per share	3.66

15–35. MARKET PRICE AND DIVIDEND RATIOS.   Exhibit 15–12 contains the income statement and balance sheets of Minnesota Mining and Manufacturing Company (3M), a leader in bringing new technologically based products to the market. In 1988, 3M paid cash dividends of $2.12 per share, an average of 226.9 million common shares were outstanding, and the market price was $68 per share.

Required:
1. Compute the following ratios for 1988: (a) price-earnings, (b) dividend yield, and (c) dividend payout.
2. Assess 3M's market price and dividend ratios compared with the following industry averages:

Price earnings	12.1
Dividend yield	2.6%
Dividend payout	31%

15–36. INCOME RATIOS AND ASSET TURNOVER.   The following data are from the 1988 annual report of McDonald's Corporation, operator of over ten thousand McDonald's restaurants in fifty countries:

Rate of return on stockholders' equity	16.85%
Operating income percentage on sales	23.07%
Total asset turnover	.7353
Average total assets	$7,570 million
Income tax rate	38.34%
Income tax expense	401 million

Required:
1. Complete the following condensed income statement. Round to the nearest million.

Sales	$?
Operating expenses	?
Operating income	$?
Interest expense (net)	?
Pretax income	$?
Income tax expense	?
Net income	$?

2. Compute the following:
   a. Pretax operating rate of return on total assets
   b. Rate of return on sales
   c. Average stockholders' equity

15–37. INCOME RATIOS AND ASSET TURNOVER.   Tribune Company, publisher of the *Chicago Tribune* and owner of the Chicago Cubs baseball team, included the following data in its 1988 annual report to stockholders:

Net income	$ 210,406,000
Total assets:	
Beginning of year	2,758,395,000
End of year	2,941,582,000
Net income as a percent of:	
Total revenue	9.0%
Average stockholders' equity	18.4%

Required: Using only the above data, compute

1. Net income percentage of average assets
2. Total revenues
3. Average stockholders' equity
4. Asset turnover, using two different approaches

15–38. **FINANCIAL RATIOS.** Skyline Corporation produces manufactured housing and recreational vehicles at thirty-five facilities throughout the United States. The company's income statement and balance sheet for the fiscal year ended May 31, 1988, are shown (slightly condensed) in Exhibit 15–13.

Required:
1. Prepare a common-size income statement, that is, one showing component percentages.
2. Compute the following ratios:
   a. Current ratio
   b. Inventory turnover (1987 inventory was $7,828,000)
   c. Total debt to equity
   d. Gross profit rate
   e. Return on stockholders' equity (1987 stockholders' equity was $133,259,000)
   f. Price-earnings ratio (the market price was $14 per share)
   g. Dividend-payout ratio
3. What additional information would help you interpret the percentages and ratios you calculated?

15–39. **DEBT VERSUS PREFERRED STOCK.** Southwestern Bell Corporation provides telephone services to Arkansas, Kansas, Missouri, Oklahoma, and Texas. In 1988, the company had income before taxes and interest of $2,008.0 million. Interest expense was $597.9 million on long-term debt of $5,259.9 million, for an effective interest rate of 11.368%. The company has no preferred stock outstanding, although 10 million shares are authorized.

Suppose $4,000 million of preferred stock with a dividend rate of 12% had been issued instead of $4,000 million of the long-term debt. The remaining debt had the same effective interest rate of 11.368%. Assume that the income tax rate is 34%.

Required: Compute net income and net income attributable to common shareholders under (a) the current situation with $5,259.9 million of long-term debt and no preferred stock, and (b) the assumed situation with $4,000 million of preferred stock and $1,259.9 million of long-term debt.

15–40. **HOUSE OF FABRICS ANNUAL REPORT.** Refer to the income statement and balance sheet of House of Fabrics on pages 752–753. The following additional information is available:

Balances at the end of fiscal 1987:

Accounts receivable	$ 3,674,000
Inventories	111,698,000
Total assets	158,040,000
Stockholders' equity	85,287,000

Market price per share:

Fiscal 1989	$18
Fiscal 1988	14

Required:
1. Compute the following financial ratios for fiscal 1988 and 1989: (a) current, (b) quick, (c) average collection period, (d) inventory turnover, (e) total debt to total assets,

Chapter 15 Analysis of Financial Statements **707**

(f) total debt to total equity, (g) interest coverage, (h) return on stockholders' equity, (i) gross profit rate, (j) return on sales, (k) asset turnover, (l) pretax return on assets, (m) earnings per share, (n) price-earnings, (o) dividend yield, and (p) dividend payout.

2. Compare the liquidity, solvency, profitability, and market price and dividend ratios for 1989 with those for 1988.

EXHIBIT 15–13

SKYLINE CORPORATION
Consolidated Statement of Earnings
For the year ended May 31, 1988
(in thousands except per share)

Sales	$322,866
Cost of sales	269,750
Gross profit	53,116
Selling and administrative expenses	39,947
Operating earnings	13,169
Interest income	6,722
Gain on sale of property, plant and equipment	1,486
Earnings before income taxes	21,377
Provision for income taxes	8,307
Net earnings	$ 13,070
Net earnings per share	$ 1.17
Dividends per share	$ .48

Consolidated Balance Sheet
May 31, 1988
(in thousands)

Assets:	
Current assets:	
Cash	$ 5,565
Treasury bills	95,403
Accounts receivable	23,688
Inventories	8,951
Other	1,677
Total current assets	135,284
Property, plant and equipment, net	25,982
Other assets	1,820
	$163,086
Liabilities and Shareholders' Equity:	
Current liabilities:	
Accounts payable, trade	$ 9,204
Accrued liabilities	12,367
Total current liabilities	21,571
Long-term liabilities	570
Stockholders' equity:	
Common stock	312
Additional paid-in capital	4,928
Retained earnings	135,705
Total shareholders' equity	140,945
	$163,086

Financial Statements: Conceptual Framework and Income Measurement

After studying this chapter, you should be able to

1. Describe the FASB's conceptual framework
2. Identify the qualities that make information valuable
3. Explain how identical companies can report different net incomes because of their choice of accounting methods
4. Describe the major differences between financial capital and physical capital
5. Explain and illustrate four different ways of measuring income: (a) historical cost/nominal dollars, (b) current cost/nominal dollars, (c) historical cost/constant dollars, and (d) current cost/constant dollars

This book has intentionally introduced conceptual elements throughout the earlier chapters. Part One of this chapter provides an overview of the conceptual framework of accounting. It gathers some of the concepts introduced earlier and adds others to give a more complete framework. It also briefly compares and contrasts the concepts of generally accepted accounting principles (GAAP) in the United States with those in other countries.

Part Two focuses on income measurement. First, variations of methods of measuring income within GAAP are explored. Then alternatives to the traditional income measurement methods are discussed.

PART ONE: Conceptual Framework of Accounting

For years, accountants have sought a conceptual framework. But they still have a patchwork of generally accepted accounting principles (GAAP) that has slowly evolved over many years of accounting practice and regulatory effort. As a result, various accounting rules seem inconsistent within any single framework. For example, the lower-of-cost-or-market basis is applied differently to inventories, to short-term investments, and to long-term investments.

FASB'S CONCEPTUAL FRAMEWORK

Between 1978 and 1984, the FASB issued four *Statements of Financial Accounting Concepts* (SFACs) relating to business enterprises.[1] Exhibit 16–1 summarizes the highlights of these SFACs. The statements provide the conceptual framework used by the FASB.

The principal task of the FASB is **accounting policy making**, which is choosing the accounting measurement and disclosure methods required for financial reporting. Some persons may refer to the board's function as rule making, standard setting, or regulation of financial reporting. Whatever its role is called, the board is a policy-making body that must exercise judgment instead of being able to rely on objective criteria for its decisions. The conceptual framework aids the exercise of judgment; it does not provide solutions to all the reporting issues faced by the FASB.

---

[1] The FASB has also issued two statements on a conceptual framework for nonbusiness organizations. The statements apply to "most human service organizations, churches, foundations, and some other organizations, such as those private nonprofit hospitals and nonprofit schools that receive a significant portion of their financial resources from sources other than the sale of goods and services." See *Concepts Statement No. 4*, "Objectives of Financial Reporting by Nonbusiness Organizations" (Stamford, Conn.: FASB, 1980); and *Concepts Statement No. 6*, "Elements of Financial Statements" (Stamford, Conn.: FASB, 1985).

EXHIBIT 16–1

Statements of Financial Accounting Concepts for Business Enterprises

STATEMENT	HIGHLIGHTS
SFAC No. 1, Objectives of Financial Reporting by Business Enterprises	• Accounting should provide information useful for making economic decisions • Focuses on external users, e.g., creditors and investors • Information should aid the prediction of cash flows • Earnings based on accrual accounting provide a better measure of performance than do cash receipts and disbursements
SFAC No. 2, Qualitative Characteristics of Accounting Information	• Examines the characteristics that make accounting information useful • Usefulness is evaluated in relation to the purposes to be served • Different information is useful for different decisions • Hierarchy of desirable characteristics, with decision usefulness at the top • Both relevance and reliability are necessary for information to be useful • Relevance requires timeliness and either predictive or feedback value • Reliable information must have representational faithfulness and be verifiable and neutral • Comparability and consistency aid usefulness • To be useful, information must be material, that is, reported amounts must be large enough to make a difference in decisions • Benefits from using information should exceed its cost
SFAC No. 3, Elements of Financial Statements of Business Enterprises	• Defines the ten building blocks that comprise financial statements: (1) assets, (2) liabilities, (3) equity, (4) investments by owners, (5) distributions to owners, (6) comprehensive income, (7) revenues, (8) expenses, (9) gains, and (10) losses.
SFAC No. 5, Recognition and Measurement in Financial Statements of Business Enterprises	• Specifies what information should be included in financial statements and when • All components of financial statements are important, not just a single "bottom-line" number • A statement of financial position provides information about assets, liabilities, and equity; it does not show the market value of the entity • Earnings measures periodic performance; comprehensive income recognizes all effects on equity except investments by or distributions to owners • Financial statements are based on the concept of financial capital maintenance • Measurement is and will continue to be based on nominal units of money • Revenue is recognized when it is earned and realized (or realizable) • Information based on current prices, if reliable and more relevant than alternative information, should be reported if costs involved are not too high

Accounting policy making is complex. Progress will continue to come in fits and starts. It will always be considered as too fast by some critics and too slow by others. Most people favor "improvements" in accounting—the quicker the better. But one person's improvement is often another person's impairment. Resolving these trade-offs is the nucleus of policy making.

Above all, students, accountants, managers, and others should recognize that the process of setting accounting standards is not confined to the development of a conceptual framework and its application to specific issues via exercises in impeccable logic and fact gathering. The process also includes the gaining of general acceptance and support. A major role of the conceptual framework is ultimately to enhance the likelihood that proposed statements will be generally accepted. The more plausible the logic and the more compelling the facts, the greater the chance of winning the support of diverse interests.

CHOOSING AMONG REPORTING ALTERNATIVES

The FASB must make difficult decisions about reporting requirements. For example, should reporting of income tax expense include deferred taxes? How should the expense for pensions and the associated pension liability be measured? Should liabilities be shown at historical cost or current market value? The list could go on and on. The FASB has issued over one hundred standards in less than twenty years, and there is no sign of slowing down. How does the FASB decide that one level of disclosure or one measurement method is acceptable and another is not?

The overriding criterion for choosing reporting alternatives is cost/benefit. Accounting should help decision making. This is a benefit. But accounting information is a commodity, an economic good. It will not be sought unless its benefits exceed its costs. A policy-making body such as the FASB must do its best to issue its pronouncements so that their perceived benefits exceed their perceived costs for the whole of society. The costs and benefits are widely diffused and fall unevenly throughout the economy. Therefore the FASB's task of assessment is complex and subjective. Nevertheless, the board should never lose sight of the fundamental cost-benefit test.

The costs of providing information include the costs of data collecting and processing, costs of auditing, costs of educating preparers and users of financial information, and costs of lost competitive advantages or increased labor union pressures. The costs to users of information include those passed on by the providers plus the costs of education, analysis, and interpretation.

The benefits of accounting information surely exist, but they are harder to pinpoint than the costs. Better individual decisions lead to greater personal welfare. Furthermore, a highly developed economy depends on accounting to help obtain the efficient and equitable allocation of resources. In reality, then, resolving the cost/benefit trade-offs of financial reporting is very difficult.

An important concept in judging costs and benefits is materiality. Information is *material* when its inclusion or correct presentation would probably change the judgment of a reasonable person. Determining whether an item is material is a pervasive problem that is usually resolved by professional judgment on a case-by-case basis. The FASB should not get bogged down in issues whose effect is likely to be immaterial.

The FASB has identified a hierarchy of characteristics of information that lead to increased benefits. These are shown in Exhibit 16–2. Foremost is decision usefulness. Without usefulness there would be no benefits. The rest of the items specify what characteristics make information useful.

EXHIBIT 16–2

Qualities That Increase the Value of Information

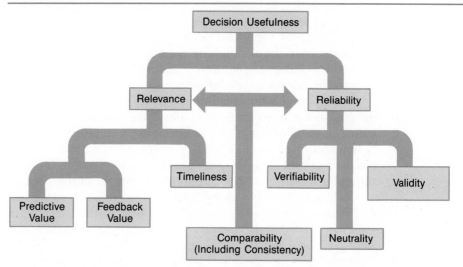

Source: Adapted from *Qualitative Characteristics of Accounting Information* (Stamford, Conn.: FASB, 1980), p. 15.

☐ Relevance, Reliability, and Comparability

Relevance and *reliability* are qualities that make accounting useful for decision making. **Relevance** is defined as the capability of information to make a difference to the decision maker. **Reliability** is defined as the quality of information that allows users to depend on it to represent the conditions or events that it purports to represent. The accounting literature is filled with arguments about the trade-offs between relevance and reliability. Consider the balance sheet value of Weyerhaeuser Company's timberlands, which are recorded at original cost. Most land was purchased more than fifty years ago. The historical cost is reliable, but not very relevant. In contrast, the current value of the land is more relevant, but estimates of value are subjective. The prevailing view is that such current market value estimates are not sufficiently reliable to be included in the accounting records, even though they are more relevant.

Reliability is enhanced by *verifiability* (or *objectivity*), *neutrality*, and *validity*. **Verifiability** means that there would be a high extent of consensus among independent measurers of an item. For example, the amount paid for assets is highly verifiable, but the predicted cost to replace the assets usually is not.

Validity means a correspondence between the accounting numbers and the resources or events those numbers purport to represent.[2] Consider goodwill, which represents excess earning power when a group of assets is acquired (i.e., excess of cost over the fair market value of the assets acquired). Suppose such

---

[2] The FASB calls validity **"representational faithfulness"** in SFAC No. 3.

earning power disappears before the goodwill is completely amortized. The amount of goodwill on the balance sheet would no longer be a valid measure of excess earning power.

Neutrality, or *freedom from bias*, means choosing accounting policies without attempting to achieve purposes other than measuring economic impact. In other words, financial reporting rules should not be used to achieve social policy objectives, nor should they be used to give an advantage to certain types of companies. For example, depreciation methods should not be chosen to encourage or discourage investment.

Tampering with accounting policies (standards or principles) to promote national goals is a dangerous path. First, research has demonstrated that accounting measurements per se are unlikely to affect investors' decisions if the timing and amounts of the underlying cash flows are unaffected. Therefore such tampering is not likely to achieve its objectives. Second, the credibility of financial reporting would quickly erode to the detriment of the public interest.

The quality of neutrality underscores a fundamental approach taken by the FASB. Arguments about accounting issues should concentrate on how measurements and disclosure can improve the communication of economic phenomena. These issues should be resolved, however imperfectly, by determining how economic information is best disseminated in light of the costs and benefits for society as a whole.

The final items affecting usefulness are *comparability* and *consistency*. Information is more useful if it can be compared with similar information about other companies or with similar information for other reporting periods. For example, financial results for two companies are hard to compare if one uses FIFO and the other uses LIFO. Furthermore, identifying trends for a single company is difficult if accounting methods are continually changed. Therefore consistency in applying accounting methods over a span of time is desirable.

☐ Time for Review

Exhibit 16–3 on pages 716–717 recaps key concepts covered in this chapter and elsewhere in the text. A concrete example of each is provided, as is a listing of the chapters in the text that contain the main discussions or examples of the individual concepts. This entire tabulation should be a convenient guide for recalling and comparing some major ingredients of accounting's conceptual framework.

Accounting theory (as expressed by a conceptual framework) and practice are intertwined and indivisible. There is some inclination, especially among students and young practitioners, to view accounting theory as chiefly an ivory tower endeavor that should be given only secondary recognition in everyday practice. This inclination probably arises from confusion of the word *practice* and the word *practical*, as if practice means something practical and theory means something merely abstract. This false distinction confuses the basic function of accounting theory, which is to establish the broad guidelines and methods that should govern the use of the discipline of accounting in a given situation. In other words, without underlying theory, practice becomes more chaotic, less satisfying, and harder to understand.

Lessons from History

Until the early 1930s, when the Securities and Exchange Commission was created by Congress, accounting practices in the United States evolved in accordance with the best professional judgment of CPAs and managers. Then private and public regulators entered the picture. To refresh your memory, see pages 61–62 for a description of the relationships among the Securities and Exchange Commission, the private regulatory bodies, and other interested groups such as managers, auditors, and investors. The Accounting Principles Board was the senior private regulatory body from 1959 to 1973, when it was succeeded by the FASB.

All regulatory bodies have been criticized for using piecemeal approaches, solving one accounting issue at a time. Again and again, critics have cited a need for a conceptual framework.

As we saw earlier, the FASB worked on constructing a conceptual framework for over ten years. Meanwhile the board also had to contend with an unending stream of specific accounting controversies that demanded immediate attention. Is there a lesson here? Why has the piecemeal approach persisted? The answer lies in a careful look at the policy-making process.

The term *generally accepted* is a key part of the familiar term *generally accepted accounting principles*. The policy-making process is much more complicated than having some intelligent, experienced regulators apply logic and evidence to an issue and then promulgate rules that are subsequently followed by the affected parties. The use of logic and evidence is absolutely necessary, but it is insufficient. When the FASB considers a financial accounting standard, assorted interested parties present arguments to support their favored choices. The standards issued are often compromises among the contending interests; therefore the standards are not necessarily products of airtight logic.

The FASB's task has been described as being not only technical but also political or educational. When the term *political* is used in this context, it means the ways of convincing interested persons about the wisdom of the board's decisions. In short, the FASB must tackle the task of obtaining general acceptance, particularly general acceptance by the SEC and Congress.

Future Role of Government

The FASB is a private-sector institution that has the general backing of the SEC. The SEC is an agency of the federal government created by the Securities Acts of 1933 and 1934. It is empowered to ensure "full and fair" disclosures by corporations. The SEC has the ultimate legal authority over most financial reporting to investors. On several occasions, the SEC has taken an active role in the setting of accounting standards. For instance, it put pressure on the FASB toward wider use of "current-cost" accounting.

The FASB is very conscious that its pronouncements need the support of the SEC. So the board and the SEC are in constant touch. In turn, Congress maintains oversight of the SEC. If Congress becomes sufficiently unhappy with progress in the setting of financial accounting standards, it could specifically require that the role of the FASB be dampened or eliminated.

EXHIBIT 16–3

Frequently Encountered Terminology in Conceptual Frameworks of Accounting

TERM	SHORT DESCRIPTION	EXAMPLE	CHAPTERS IN THIS TEXT*
Cost and benefits	Accounting information is an economic good. It should be gathered as long as its benefits exceed its costs.	Decisions must be improved sufficiently to justify recording current values in addition to historical costs.	Mainly in 3, 8, 14
Relevance	Capability of information to make a difference to the decision maker	Report of cash in bank is essential to determine how much money to borrow.	3, 16
Reliability	Dependability of information as representing what it purports to represent	The cost of the land was $1 million 1983 dollars.	1, 16
Verifiability (objectivity)	Characteristic of information that results in its reproducibility by a consensus of independent measurers.	Cash has high verifiability, accounts receivable less, inventories less, depreciable assets less, and so on.	3, 1, 16
Validity (representational faithfulness)	Correspondence between numbers and effects portrayed.	The historical cost/constant dollar cost of the land described above may be $1.2 million 1990 dollars, but the $1.2 million does not represent the current cost or market value of the land.	16
Consistency	Applying the same accounting methods over a series of reporting periods.	Use of FIFO inventory over a series of years, not FIFO for two years, LIFO for three, and so on.	6
Neutrality (evenhandedness)	Choosing accounting policies on the basis of quantifying without bias, that is, without purposes other than measuring economic impact.	An example of lack of neutrality may clarify: choosing the flow-through method in accounting for the investment tax credit for purposes of achieving national goals of encouraging capital expenditures.†	13
Materiality	An item is material if the judgment of a reasonable person would have been changed or influenced by its omission or misstatement.	Accounting policy to charge all capital expenditures of under $1,000 to expense regardless of useful life of the asset.	3

Term	Description	
Conservatism	Way of dealing with uncertainties and is intended to avoid recognition of income on the basis of inadequate evidence but to require recognition of losses when assets have been impaired or liabilities incurred. In short, when in doubt, write it off.	Charging all research and development costs to expense as incurred. Applying lower-of-cost-or-market methods to asset valuation.	6, 8, 12
Continuity (going concern)	Assumption that entity will continue indefinitely or at least will not be liquidated in the near future.	Letterhead stationery: supplies or rubbish, depending on going concern assumption. This assumption is frequently cited as a major justification for adhering to historical cost (less depreciation, if any) for valuing inventories, land, buildings, equipment, and similar assets.	3
Entity	The unit of accountability.	A parent corporation, a subsidiary, a retail store.	1,12
Accrual accounting	Record financial effects in the periods affected regardless of when cash is received or paid.	Recognition of receivables and payables.	2, 3, 4
Recognition	Formally recording or incorporating an item in accounts and financial statements. An element may be recognized (recorded) or unrecognized (unrecorded).	Recognition requires revenues to be earned and realized. Increases or decreases in the value of land may be earned but unrealized. Advance payments on subscriptions may be realized but not earned.	1, 2, 4, 6
Matching and cost recovery	Matching is relating revenues and expenses to a particular period. Combined or simultaneous recognition of revenues and expenses is the direct criterion for establishing a matching. However, other expenses are indirectly matched with revenues if their recovery from future revenues is not easily demonstrable.	Sales commission expenses are "matched" directly against related sales. Sales salaries, costs of heating, and depreciation on equipment are "matched" indirectly against current revenues because their benefits are considered to be exhausted in the current period.	2, 4, 6,16

* Many of these criteria or basic ideas underlie this entire textbook.

† See Appendix 13A for discussion of the investment tax credit. Suppose flow-through is chosen because it is deemed to be the best possible measure of the economic impact on the enterprise. Then neutrality exists if flow-through is chosen.

What looms ahead? Probably more government exercise of authority through the SEC. Although both the SEC and the FASB have been exceedingly active in recent years, congressional committees and others have stated that more activity is warranted. Despite the increasing activist role of the public sector, it is nevertheless highly likely that during the next ten years the FASB will continue to be the major single influence on changes in financial accounting standards.

ACCOUNTING STANDARDS THROUGHOUT THE WORLD

This text has focused on the principles of accounting that are generally accepted in the United States. However, the conceptual framework and reporting standards used in the United States differ from those used in many other countries.

Although this section will highlight differences in accounting principles, it is important to note that most of the methods of accounting are consistent throughout the world. Double-entry bookkeeping, the accrual accounting system, and the basic financial statements are used worldwide. Therefore differences in financial reporting, although significant, are of less magnitude than the similarities.

In Chapter 13, we emphasized that in the United States the methods used for reporting to tax authorities differ from the methods used for reporting to shareholders. In contrast, tax reporting and shareholder reporting are identical in many countries. For example, France has a "Plan Compatible" that specifies a National Uniform Chart of Accounts that is used for both tax returns and reporting to shareholders. West German financial reporting is also determined primarily by tax laws. If accounting records are not kept according to strict tax laws, the tax authorities can reject the records as a basis for taxation.

In some countries, tax laws have a major influence on shareholder reporting even if tax and shareholder reports are not required to be identical. In Japan, for example, certain principles are allowed for tax purposes only if they are also used for shareholder reporting. When such principles provide tax advantages, there is a large incentive for companies to use them for reporting to shareholders.

A significant difference among countries is the extent to which financial statements account for inflation. In the 1980s, the FASB experimented with requiring supplementary disclosure of inflation-adjusted numbers, but no requirement for such supplementary disclosure is now in place in the United States. In contrast, many countries have full or partial adjustments for inflation as part of their reporting method for reporting to both shareholders and tax authorities. For example, Brazil, which has experienced persistent double- and triple-digit inflation rates, requires all statements to be adjusted for changes in the general price level in the manner described later in this chapter. Such inflation-adjusted statements are used for both tax and shareholder reporting. Argentina requires dual reporting. Companies must include two columns in financial statements, one for traditional historical-cost numbers and one for general price-level-adjusted numbers.

The Netherlands has been a leader in the application of current replacement-cost measurements to financial accounts, although it has no formal requirement mandating either historical cost or replacement cost. In 1978, France instituted a partial inflation adjustment, using replacement cost for fixed assets. Similarly, Sweden allows (but does not require) the revaluation of certain property, plant, and equipment.

Not surprisingly, countries that have experienced the lowest inflation rates have been the slowest to recognize inflation in their accounting statements. Japan has no recognition of inflation, and West Germany has recommended supplementary disclosures, but few companies have responded.

Other differences in financial reporting include the following:[3]

1. France deducts no provision for uncollectible accounts from accounts receivable.
2. Switzerland excludes manufacturing overhead from the cost of manufactured inventory.
3. The Netherlands uses the equity method for all (even less than 20%-owned) long-term investments.
4. Several countries, including Japan, West Germany, and Sweden, use the cost method for all long-term investments with less than 50% ownership.
5. Goodwill is not amortized in West Germany; most companies in the United Kingdom and Switzerland do not amortize any intangible assets, including goodwill.
6. Sweden and Switzerland do not recognize deferred taxes.
7. Only a few countries, including the United States and Canada, require capitalization of long-term leases.

This sample of differences is not exhaustive. Its purpose is to emphasize that all of the principles and methods used in the United States and presented in this textbook are not universally accepted and used.

The growing globalization of business enterprises and capital markets is creating much interest in common, worldwide accounting standards. There are probably too many cultural, social, and political differences to expect complete worldwide standardization of financial reporting in the near future. However, the number of differences is decreasing. Cooperation among accountants has been fostered by the International Federation of Accountants (IFAC), an organization of approximately one hundred accountancy bodies from more than seventy-five countries.

International standards are being formulated and published by the International Accounting Standards Committee (IASC). Many professional accounting groups and national stock exchanges support the work of IASC. Although adherence to its standards is voluntary, IASC is influencing the standards used in many countries.

☐ PART TWO: **Variations in Income Measurement**

The measurement of income is easily the most controversial subject in accounting. The remainder of this chapter focuses on different methods of measuring income. First, the impact of different allowable methods of measuring traditional, historical-cost income is presented. Then alternative measures, which are designed to account for inflation, are introduced.

---

[3] From F. Choi and V. Bavishi, "Diversity of Multinational Accounting," *Financial Executive*, Vol. 50, No. 8, pp. 46–49.

The most popular approach to income measurement is commonly labeled the historical-cost method. It has been described at length in this book. However, the label "historical cost" does not completely define the way income is measured. Disputes often occur in applying the historical-cost method. The majority of these disputes center on timing. For example, when are revenues realized? When do the costs of assets become expenses?

Nearly every way of applying the historical-cost approach to income measurement has supporters and critics. However, the crudest approach, that of matching cash disbursements against cash receipts in a given period, has generally been rejected in favor of the accrual basis that was discussed in Chapter 2. To illustrate, nearly all "cash-basis" income measurement systems have at least been modified to provide for depreciation. After all, depreciation is central to an accrual basis. All variations in the concepts of income discussed below have the accrual basis as an anchor.

☐ Revenue Recognition

The timing of income is influenced most by the *recognition* principle. This book discusses revenue recognition in Chapters 2 and 6. It is a major feature of accrual accounting because it determines when revenues and the associated (matched) costs will be recorded. Thus it specifies when income will be reported.

To be recorded, revenue must ordinarily be *earned* and *realized*. When does this occur? Generally, revenue is recorded when goods or services are *delivered* to customers, even though delivery is only one of a series of events related to the sale. For most businesses, delivery is the occasion that validates a legal claim against the customer for goods or services rendered. Accountants maintain that although the importance of purchasing, production, and distribution may differ from business to business, revenue is generally regarded as an indivisible totality. In this sense, revenue cannot be allocated in bits and pieces to individual business functions such as purchasing inventory, obtaining orders, manufacturing products, delivering goods, and collecting cash.

There are two major exceptions to the notion that delivery triggers the recording of revenue. First, long-run construction contracts often necessitate a *percentage-of-completion method*. For example, the builder of an ocean liner may portray performance better by spreading prospective revenues, related costs, and resulting net income over the life of the contract in proportion to the work accomplished. Otherwise all the net income would appear in one chunk upon completion of the project, as if it had been earned on a single day.

Second, in exceptionally rare cases, revenue is recorded in proportion to cash collections under long-run installment contracts. An illustration is the retail sales of undeveloped lots. These receivables are collectible over an extended period of time, and there is no reliable basis for estimating the degree of collectibility.

Under the percentage-of-completion method, revenue is recognized before delivery takes place; under the installment method, revenue is recognized well after the delivery.

Uncertainty about the collectibility of receivables does not always delay the recording of revenue. Many accountants regard the revenue as realized but provide an ample allowance for uncollectible accounts. For example, a hospital can recognize revenue on the accrual basis as its services are delivered. However, its bad debts expense (which is conceptually an offset of gross revenue because it represents revenue never to be received) is a much higher percentage of revenue than in, for example, retail food stores.

☐ Impact of Alternative Timing of Expenses

In addition to timing differences caused by revenue recognition, generally accepted accounting principles allow accountants to choose when to recognize certain expenses. Comparing two companies can be difficult if each chooses a different method for recognizing major expenses. To achieve comparability, analysts often reconstruct a company's financial statements to place them on a basis consistent with other companies in the same industry.

Suppose two companies, M and N, began business in the same industry in 19X1. Each company would have had the following for 19X1, depending on the accounting method chosen (in millions):

		DIFFERENCE
Beginning inventory	$ 0	
Purchases	270,000	
Ending inventory, if FIFO is used	110,000	
Ending inventory, if LIFO is used	70,000	40,000
Depreciation, if accelerated is used	20,000	
Depreciation, if straight-line is used	10,000	10,000
Product introduction costs, original total amount	30,000	
Product introduction costs, amortized amount	10,000	20,000
Revenue	400,000	
Other expenses	100,000	
Common shares outstanding	10,000	
Income tax rate	40%	

For income-tax reporting purposes, the top management of M and N have both used accelerated (MACRS) depreciation and the immediate write-off of all product introduction costs. For all other items, assume that the same method would be used for tax purposes and stockholder reporting purposes.

For stockholder reporting purposes, the choice of accounting policies can have a dramatic effect on net income and earnings per share. Assume that M takes one extreme stance; N, the other extreme. As Exhibit 16–4 shows, the choices of LIFO, accelerated depreciation (assumed equal to MACRS depreciation), and immediate write-off of product introduction costs will result in M's earnings per share of $3.00. In contrast, N's earnings per share would be $7.20.

EXHIBIT 16–4

Stockholder Reporting
Possible Income Statements
For the Year Ended December 31, 19X1
(in thousands of dollars, except earnings per share)

	(1) M Company	(2) FIFO	(3) Straight Line	(4) Amortization	(5) N Company
		INDIVIDUAL EFFECTS			
Revenue	400				400
Expenses:					
Cost of goods sold	200	40			160
Depreciation	20		10		10
Product introduction costs	30			20	10
Other expenses	100				100
Total expenses	350				280
Income before income taxes	50				120
Income taxes:					
Currently payable	20*	16			36†
Deferred	—		4	8	12‡
Total income tax expense	20				48
Net income reported	30	24	6	12	72
Earnings per share on 10,000 shares	3.00	2.40	.60	1.20	7.20

* Income tax per the tax return would be .40 × $50 = $20.
† Same as for M Company except that FIFO would boost the current income tax per the tax return by .4 × $40 = $16. Therefore the total would be $20 + $16 = $36.
‡ Additional income tax expense equal to the deferred tax liability must be reported as the result of showing $10 less depreciation expense and $20 less amortization expense, a total of $30 multiplied by the tax rate of 40% = $12.

Many managers regard the maximizing of immediate reported earnings per share as a worthy objective. They tend to choose the accounting policies like those favored by N Company. Others tend to be more conservative and tend to choose the M Company policies. The point here is that similar operations may be portrayed differently in income statements. Note that all the data are the same as far as the underlying cash flows are concerned, with one exception: A company that used FIFO for stockholder reporting cannot use LIFO for tax purposes. Therefore N Company's current payments for income taxes are $16 million larger than M Company's.

Perhaps accounting measurements will eventually become better standardized and identical operations will be reported in more nearly identical figures. In the meantime, accountants and corporate executives should view increased disclosure and amplified description as the most pressing requirements in financial reporting. These requirements must be met if investors are to have sufficient data for making their own comparisons between companies.

Statement of Accounting Policies

As Exhibit 16–4 shows, there are a variety of generally accepted accounting practices. Information about the accounting principles, practices, procedures, or policies (words like these are used loosely) is essential for the intelligent analysis of financial statements. APB *Opinion No. 22* requires reporting companies to include a description of all significant accounting policies as an integral part of the financial report. The disclosure usually appears as a separate Summary of Significant Accounting Policies preceding the footnotes of financial statements.

Exhibit 16–5 displays a typical summary, that of Procter & Gamble Company. A reader can quickly obtain a general understanding of the financial statements by reading Exhibit 16–5. The Procter & Gamble summary of accounting policies mentions many items covered in earlier chapters: consolidated statements, LIFO, goodwill, depreciation methods, and income taxes.

EXHIBIT 16–5

THE PROCTER & GAMBLE COMPANY
Summary of Significant Accounting Policies

PRINCIPLES OF CONSOLIDATION: The financial statements include the accounts of The Procter & Gamble Company and its majority-owned subsidiaries. Investments in 20% to 50% owned affiliates in which significant management control is exercised are included at original cost adjusted for the change in equity since acquisition. Other investments in affiliates are carried at cost.

MARKETABLE SECURITIES: Substantially all of the marketable securities are government and corporate debt instruments which are carried at cost which approximates market.

INVENTORY VALUATION: Inventories are valued at the lower of cost or market. Cost for inventories in the United States is primarily determined by the last-in, first-out method. Cost is determined by the average cost method for substantially all of the remaining inventories.

GOODWILL: The excess of the purchase price over the value ascribed to net assets of businesses acquired after October 31, 1970 is amortized on a straight-line basis over forty years. Goodwill arising prior to that date is not amortized.

DEPRECIATION: For financial accounting purposes, depreciation is calculated on a straight-line basis over the estimated useful lives of the properties.

INCOME TAXES: Provision is made for the income tax effects of all transactions in the consolidated statement of earnings, including those for which actual tax payment or tax relief is deferred to future years. These deferrals result primarily from the use of shorter equipment lives and accelerated methods of depreciation for tax purposes.

OTHER EXPENSES: Advertising and research and development costs are charged against earnings in the year incurred.

INFLATION AND INCOME MEASUREMENT

Complaints about Historical Cost

Accountants traditionally have maintained that net income is a return *on* the capital invested by shareholders. Suppose an amount equal to the net income of a period is returned to the shareholders as dividends. In the absence of inflation, such a payment leaves the shareholders' invested capital at the end of the period equal to the beginning capital. However, when prices change, this relationship between income and capital is altered. In times of generally rising prices, paying dividends equal to net income, as conventionally measured, usually amounts to paying out some capital itself as well as the return on capital.

A pet theme of politicians and others often is the "unconscionable" or "obscene" profits reported by American companies. In turn, many business executives insist that our traditional historical-cost basis for measuring income produces misleading results, especially during a time of rising prices. Some managers have complained that the reported profits for most years in the past two decades have been so badly overstated that income taxes have been unfairly levied. In many cases, invested capital, rather than earned income, has been taxed.

The industries with huge investments in plant and equipment claim that their profits are badly misstated by generally accepted accounting principles. For instance, consider NYNEX, a company that emerged from the breakup of the Bell System. NYNEX recently reported net income of $1,095 million, which would have been a net loss of $82 million if depreciation had been adjusted for inflation.

The soaring inflation of the late 1970s in the United States raised many questions about the usefulness of traditional historical-cost financial statements. The FASB responded by issuing *Statement No. 33*, "Financial Reporting and Changing Prices." The statement required no changes in the primary financial statements. However, it required large companies to include supplementary inflation-adjusted schedules in their annual reports.

Statement No. 33 was experimental, and its requirements were in place for eight years. In 1987 inflation had subsided, and the FASB decided that inflation-adjusted disclosures would no longer be required. Although U.S. companies do not need to report inflation-adjusted numbers, a basic knowledge about reporting the effects of changing prices is useful for at least four reasons: (1) High inflation is still present in many countries, and most accounting reports in those countries report the effects of inflation; (2) if history is any indication, higher inflation rates will return to the United States sooner or later, and when they do, users of financial statements will again become concerned with inflation-adjusted statements; (3) the cumulative effect of even a 2% or 3% rate is substantial; and (4) understanding the limitations of traditional financial statements is enhanced by knowing how inflation affects (or does not affect) such financial statements.

☐ Income or Capital

Before presenting alternatives to historical-cost accounting, we first concentrate on various concepts of income and capital. At first glance, the concept of income seems straightforward. Income is increase in wealth. But what is wealth? It is capital. But what is capital? An endless chain of similar questions can be constructed. The heart of the issue is the distinction between invested capital and income. The time-honored interpretation is that invested capital is a *financial* concept (rather than a *physical* concept). The focus is on the potential profitability of the money invested, no matter what types of inventory, equipment, or other resources have been acquired.

Financial resources (capital) are invested with the expectation of an eventual return *of* that capital together with additional amounts representing the return *on* that capital. Controversies have arisen regarding whether the financial resources generated by the invested capital qualify as returns *of* or *on* capital.

The Financial Accounting Standards Board distinguished between financial and physical capital maintenance concepts in *Statement No. 33*, "Financial Reporting and Changing Prices":

☐ Capital is maintained when revenues are at least equal to all costs and expenses. The appropriate measurement of costs and expenses depends on the concept of capital maintenance adopted.

Consider an example where a company begins with owners' investment (capital) of $1,000, which is used immediately to purchase inventory. The inventory is sold a year later for $1,500. The cost of replacing the inventory has risen to $1,200.

	FINANCIAL CAPITAL MAINTENANCE	PHYSICAL CAPITAL MAINTENANCE
Sales	$1,500	$1,500
Cost of goods sold	1,000	1,200
Income	$ 500	$ 300

Most accountants and managers believe that income emerges after financial resources are recovered, a concept called **financial capital maintenance**. Because the $1,000 capital has been recovered, $500 is the measure of income.

On the other hand, some accountants believe that income emerges only after recovering an amount that allows physical operating capability to be maintained, called **physical capital maintenance**. Because $1,200 is the current cost of inventory (cost of maintaining physical capability) at the date of sale, $300 is the measure of income.

MEASUREMENT ALTERNATIVES UNDER CHANGING PRICES

Study the four definitions in this paragraph; they are critical to understanding inflation accounting. **Nominal dollars** are dollar measurements that are not restated for fluctuations in the general purchasing power of the monetary unit, whereas **constant dollars** are nominal dollars restated in terms of current purchasing power. The **historical cost** of an asset is the amount originally paid to acquire it; the **current cost** of an asset is generally the cost to replace it. Traditional accounting uses *nominal* (rather than constant) dollars and *historical* (rather than current) costs. Such accounting has almost exclusively dominated financial reporting in the United States throughout this century. Using historical costs implies maintenance of *financial* capital; current costs imply *physical* capital maintenance.

Two approaches, which can be applied separately or in combination, address problems caused by inflation: (1) constant-dollar disclosures account for *general* changes in the purchasing power of the dollar, and (2) current-cost disclosures account for changes in *specific* prices. The two approaches create the following four alternatives for measuring income:

	Historical Cost	Current Cost
Nominal Dollars	1 Historical cost/ nominal dollars	2 Current cost/ nominal dollars
Constant Dollars	3 Historical cost/ constant dollars	4 Current cost/ constant dollars

The G Company situation described next is used to compare various concepts of income and capital. The four basic methods of income measurement are presented. G Company has the following comparative balance sheets at December 31 (based on historical costs in nominal dollars):

	19X1	19X2
Cash	$ 0	$10,500
Inventory, 400 and 100 units, respectively	8,000	2,000
Total assets	$8,000	$12,500
Original paid-in capital	$8,000	$ 8,000
Retained income	—	4,500
Stockholders' equity	$8,000	$12,500

The company had acquired all 400 units of inventory at $20 per unit (total of $8,000) on December 31, 19X1, and had held the units until December 31, 19X2. Three hundred units were sold for $35 per unit (total of $10,500 cash) on December 31, 19X2. The replacement cost of the inventory at that date was $30 per unit. The general-price-level index was 100 on December 31, 19X1, and 110 on December 31, 19X2. Assume that these are the only transactions. Ignore income taxes.

☐ Historical Cost/Nominal Dollars

Exhibit 16–6 is the basis for the explanations that follow in the next several pages. The first set of financial statements in Exhibit 16–6 shows the time-honored method that uses historical cost/nominal dollars (Method 1). Basically, this method measures invested capital in nominal dollars. It is the most popular approach to income measurement and is commonly called the historical-cost method. Operating income (equals net income in this case) is the excess of realized revenue ($10,500 in 19X2) over the "not restated" historical costs of assets used in obtaining that revenue. As we have already seen, when the conventional

EXHIBIT 16–6 *(Put a clip on this page for easy reference)*

Four Major Methods to Measure Income and Capital
(in dollars)

	NOMINAL DOLLARS*				CONSTANT DOLLARS*			
	(METHOD 1)		(METHOD 2)		(METHOD 3)		(METHOD 4)	
	Historical Cost		Current Cost		Historical Cost		Current Cost	
Balance sheets as of December 31	19X1	19X2	19X1	19X2	19X1	19X2	19X1	19X2
Cash	—	10,500	—	10,500	—	10,500	—	10,500
Inventory, 400 and 100 units, respectively	8,000	2,000[b]	8,000	3,000[c]	8,800[e]	2,200[e]	8,800[e]	3,000[c]
Total assets	8,000	12,500	8,000	13,500	8,800	12,700	8,800[e]	13,500[c]
Original paid-in capital	8,000	8,000	8,000	8,000	8,800[f]	8,800[f]	8,800[f]	8,800[f]
Retained income (confined to income from continuing operations)		4,500		1,500		3,900		1,500
Revaluation equity (accumulated holding gains)				4,000				3,200
Total liab. & stk. eq.	8,000	12,500	8,000	13,500	8,800	12,700	8,800[e]	13,500[c]
Income Statements for 19X2								
Sales, 300 units @ $35		10,500		10,500		10,500		10,500
Cost of goods sold, 300 units		6,000[b]		9,000[c]		6,600[e]		9,000[c]
Income from continuing operations (to retained income)		4,500		1,500		3,900		1,500
Holding gains:[a]								
On 300 units sold				3,000[d]				2,400[g]
On 100 units unsold				1,000[d]				800[g]
Total holding gains[a] (to revaluation equity)				4,000				3,200

* Nominal dollars are not restated for a general price index, whereas constant dollars are restated.
[a] Many advocates of this current-cost method favor showing these gains in a completely separate statement of holding gains rather than as a part of the income statement. Others favor including some or all of these gains as a part of income for the year.
[b] 100 × $20,   [c] 100 × $30,   [d] 300 × ($30 − $20),   [e] 110/100 × $8,000,   [f] 110/100 × $8,000.
   300 × $20.   300 × $30.   100 × ($30 − $20).   110/100 × $2,000,
                                           110/100 × $6,000.
[g] $9,000 − restated cost of $6,600 = $2,400 $3,000 − restated cost of $2,200 = $800
   or   or
   300 × ($30 − 110% of $20) = $2,400.   100 × ($30 − 110% of $20) = $800.

accrual basis of accounting is used, an exchange transaction is ordinarily necessary before revenues (and resulting incomes) are recognized. Thus no income generally appears until the asset is sold; intervening price fluctuations are ignored.

☐ Current Cost/Nominal Dollars

The second set of financial statements in Exhibit 16–6 illustrates a **current-cost method** that has especially strong advocates in the United Kingdom and Australia

(Method 2). This method uses current cost/nominal dollars. In general, the current cost of an asset is the cost to replace it. The focus is on income from continuing operations. This model emphasizes that operating income should be "distributable" income. That is, G Company could pay dividends in an amount of only $1,500, leaving enough assets to allow for replacement of the inventory that has just been sold.

Critics of the historical-cost approach claim that the $4,500 measure of income from continuing operations is misleading because it inaccurately reflects (it overstates) the net increment in distributable assets. If a $4,500 dividend were paid, the company would be less able to continue operations at the same level as before. The $3,000 difference between the two operating incomes ($4,500 − $1,500 = $3,000) is frequently referred to as an "inventory profit" or an "inflated profit." Why? Because $9,000 instead of $6,000 is now necessary to replace the 300 units sold (300 × the increase in price from $20 to $30 equals the $3,000 difference).

☐ Holding Gains and Physical Capital

The current-cost method stresses a separation between *income from continuing operations*, which is defined as the excess of revenue over the current costs of the assets consumed in obtaining that revenue, and **holding gains** (or **losses**), which are increases (or decreases) in the replacement costs of the assets held during the current period. Accountants differ sharply on how to account for holding gains. The "correct" accounting depends on distinctions between capital and income. That is, income cannot occur until invested capital is "recovered" or "maintained." The issue of capital versus income is concretely illustrated in Exhibit 16–6. The advocates of a physical concept of capital maintenance claim that *all* holding gains (both those gains related to the units sold and the gains related to the units unsold) should be excluded from income and become a part of revalued capital, called **revaluation equity**. That is, for a going concern no income can result unless the physical capital devoted to operations during the current period can be replaced.

For simplicity, income taxes are ignored in Exhibit 16–6. The historical cost/nominal dollar method (Method 1) is the only acceptable method for reporting on income tax returns in English-speaking countries. Many managers of heavy industries such as steel and aluminum claim that their capital is being taxed under the historical-cost/nominal-dollar method. These managers maintain that taxes should be levied only on *income from continuing operations*, as computed under the current-cost/nominal-dollar method (Method 2).

☐ Historical Cost/Constant Dollars

Method 3 of Exhibit 16–6 shows the results of applying general index numbers to historical costs. Essentially, the income measurements in each year are restated in terms of *constant dollars* (possessing the same general purchasing power of the current year) instead of the *nominal dollars* (possessing different general purchasing power of various years).

The fundamental reasoning underlying the Method 3 approach goes to the heart of the measurement theory itself. Additions or subtractions must use a *common measuring unit*, be it dollars, francs, meters, ounces, or any chosen measure.

Consider the objections to Method 1. Deducting 6,000 19X1 dollars from 10,500 19X2 dollars to obtain $4,500 is akin to deducting 60 *centimeters* from 105 *meters* and calling the result 45. Grade-school tests are marked wrong when such nonsensical arithmetic is discovered, but accountants have been paid well for years for performing similar arithmetic.

Method 3, historical cost/constant dollars, shows how to remedy the foregoing objections. General indexes may be used to restate the amounts of historical-cost/nominal-dollar Method 1. Examples of such indexes are the Gross National Product Implicit Price Deflator and the Consumer Price Index for All Urban Consumers (CPI). Anyone who has lived long enough to be able to read this book is aware that the purchasing power of the dollar is unstable. Index numbers are used to gauge the relationship between current conditions and some norm or base condition (which is assigned the index number of 100). For our purpose, a **general price index** compares the average price of a group of goods and services at one date with the average price of a similar group at another date. A price index is an average. It does not measure the behavior of the individual component prices. Some individual prices may move in one direction and some in another. The general consumer price level may soar while the prices of eggs and chickens decline.

Do not confuse *general* indexes, which are used in constant-dollar accounting, with *specific* indexes. The two have entirely different purposes. Sometimes **specific price indexes** are used as a means of approximating the *current costs* of particular assets or types of assets. That is, companies have found specialized indexes to be good enough to get approximations of current costs. This avoids the hiring of professional appraisers or the employing of other expensive means of valuation. For example, Inland Steel has used the Engineering News Record Construction Cost Index to value most of its property, plant, and equipment for purposes of using the current-cost method.

☐ Maintaining Invested Capital

The historical-cost/constant-dollar approach (Method 3) is *not* a fundamental departure from historical costs. Instead it maintains that all historical costs to be matched against revenue should be restated on some constant-dollar basis so that all revenues and all expenses can be expressed in dollars of the same (usually current) purchasing power. The restated figures *are historical costs* expressed in constant dollars via the use of a general price index.

The *current* dollar is typically employed because users of financial statements tend to think in such terms instead of in terms of old dollars with significantly different purchasing power. The original units in inventory would be updated on each year's balance sheet along with their effect on stockholders' equity. For example, the December 31, 19X1, balance sheet would be restated for comparative purposes on December 31, 19X2:

	NOT RESTATED COST	MULTIPLIER	RESTATED COST
Inventory	$8,000	110/100	$8,800
Original paid-in capital	8,000	110/100	8,800

To extend the illustration, suppose all the inventory was held for two full years. The general price index rose from 110 to 132 during 19X3. The December 31, 19X2, balance sheet items would be restated for comparative purposes on December 31, 19X3:

	RESTATED COST 12/31/X2	MULTIPLIER	RESTATED COST 12/31/X3
Inventory	$8,800	132/110	$10,560*
Original paid-in capital	8,800	132/110	10,560*

* The same result could be tied to the year of acquisition:
Inventory $8,000 × 132/100 = $10,560
Original paid-in capital $8,000 × 132/100 = $10,560

The restated amount is just that—a restatement of original *cost* in terms of current dollars—not a gain in any sense. Therefore this approach should *not* be labeled as an adoption of "current-cost" accounting. Using this approach, if the specific current cost of the inventory goes up or down, the restated cost is unaffected.

The restated historical-cost approach harmonizes with the concept of *maintaining the general purchasing power* of the invested capital (a *financial* concept of capital maintenance) in total rather than maintaining "specific invested capital," item by item. More will be said about this distinction after we examine Method 4.

☐ Current Cost/Constant Dollars

Method 4 of Exhibit 16–6 shows the results of applying general index numbers to current costs. As the footnotes of the exhibit explain in more detail, the nominal gains reported under Method 2 are adjusted so that only gains in constant dollars are reported. For example, suppose you buy 100 units on December 31, 19X1 for $2,000 cash. If the current replacement cost of your inventory at December 31, 19X2 is $3,000 but the general price index has risen from 100 to 110, your nominal gain is $1,000, but your "real" gain in constant dollars in 19X2 is only $800: the $3,000 current cost minus the restated historical cost of $2,000 × 1.10 = $2,200.

Suppose the 100 units are held throughout 19X3. The general price index rises from 110 to 132. The replacement cost rises from $30 to $34, a nominal holding gain for 19X3 of $4 \times 100 = \$400$. However, the current-cost/constant-dollar approach (Method 4) would report a real holding loss:

Current cost, restated, December 31, 19X2:	
$3,000 \times 132/110$	$3,600
Current cost, December 31, 19X3, 100 $\times$ $34	3,400
Holding loss	$ 200

Many theorists disagree on the relative merits of historical-cost approaches versus miscellaneous versions of current-cost approaches to income measurement. But there is general agreement among the theorists that restatements in constant dollars would be an improvement (ignoring practical barriers), because otherwise income includes illusory gains caused by using an unstable measuring unit.

SUMMARY

Accountants have sought a conceptual framework for years, but financial accounting standards are still largely set on a piecemeal basis. The entire standard-setting process is complex. It involves far more than technical aspects because the gaining of general acceptance is a political task.

Accounting standards vary from country to country. Attempts at international standards are progressing, but significant differences are likely to persist.

The assortment of alternatives among generally accepted accounting principles means that managers and accountants have some latitude in selecting the accounting policies of a specific entity. Publicly held companies must publish a statement of their accounting policies as a part of their annual financial reports.

The matching of historical costs with revenue is the generally accepted means of measuring net income. However, this method is often criticized in times of high inflation. Some critics suggest using general price indexes to adjust historical costs so that all expenses are measured in current dollars of the same purchasing power. Such adjustments do not represent a departure from historical cost. A more fundamental change is to base net income computations on some version of current costs. Proponents claim that such a measure is a better gauge of the distinctions between income (the return *on* capital) and capital maintenance (the return *of* capital).

SUMMARY PROBLEMS FOR YOUR REVIEW

☐ **Problem One**

In 1970, a parcel of land, call it parcel 1, was purchased for $1,200. An identical parcel, 2, was purchased today for $3,600. The general-price-level index has risen from 100 in 1970 to 300 now. Fill in the blanks in the table below.

PARCEL	(1) HISTORICAL COST MEASURED IN 1970 PURCHASING POWER	(2) HISTORICAL COST MEASURED IN CURRENT PURCHASING POWER	(3) HISTORICAL COST AS ORIGINALLY MEASURED
1			
2	———	———	———
Total	═══	═══	═══

1. Compare the figures in the three columns. Which total presents a nonsense result. Why?
2. Does the write-up of parcel 1 in column 2 result in a gain? Why?
3. Assume that these parcels are the only assets of the business. There are no liabilities. Prepare a balance sheet for each of the three columns.

☐ Solution to Problem One

PARCEL	(1) HISTORICAL COST MEASURED IN 1970 PURCHASING POWER	(2) HISTORICAL COST MEASURED IN CURRENT PURCHASING POWER	(3) HISTORICAL COST AS ORIGINALLY MEASURED
1	$1,200	$3,600	$1,200
2	1,200	3,600	3,600
Total	$2,400	$7,200	$4,800

1. The addition in column 3 produces a nonsense result. In contrast, the other sums are the results of applying a standard unit of measure. The computations in columns 1 and 2 are illustrations of a restatement of historical cost in terms of a common dollar, a standard unit of measure. Such computations have frequently been called adjustments for changes in the general price level. Whether the restatement is made using the 1970 dollar or the current dollar is a matter of personal preference; columns 1 and 2 yield equivalent results. Restatement in terms of the current dollar (column 2) is most popular because the current dollar has more meaning than the old dollar to the reader of the financial statements.

2. The mere restatement of identical assets in terms of different but equivalent measuring units cannot be regarded as a gain. Expressing parcel 1 as $1,200 in column 1 and $3,600 in column 2 is like expressing parcel 1 in terms of, say, either 1,200 square yards or $9 \times 1,200 = 10,800$ square feet. Surely, the "write-up" from 1,200 square yards to 10,800 square feet is not a gain; it is merely another way of measuring the same asset. The 1,200 square yards and the 10,800 square feet are equivalent; they are different ways of describing the same asset. That is basically what general-price-level accounting is all about. It says you cannot measure one plot of land in square yards and another in square feet and add them together before converting to some common measure. Unfortunately, column 3 fails to perform such a conversion before adding the two parcels together; hence the total is internally inconsistent.

3. The balance sheets would be:

	(1)	(2)	(3)
Land	$2,400	$7,200	$4,800
Paid-in capital	$2,400	$7,200	$4,800

Note that (1) is expressed in 1970 dollars, (2) is in current dollars, and (3) is a mixture of 1970 and current dollars.

☐ Problem Two

Reexamine Exhibit 16–6, page 727. Suppose the replacement cost at December 31, 19X2, had been $25 instead of $30. Suppose also that the general price index has been 120 instead of 110. All other facts are unchanged. Use four columns to prepare balance sheets as of December 31, 19X2 (only) and income statements for 19X2 under the four concepts shown in Exhibit 16–6.

☐ Solution to Problem Two

The solution is in Exhibit 16–7. In particular, compare Methods 2 and 4. The current cost of inventory items has risen 25% during a period when the general level has risen 20%.

Note too that the historical cost/constant dollar concept restates the old historical-cost amounts in 19X2 dollars rather than 19X1 dollars by multiplying the old dollars by 120/100.

EXHIBIT 16–7

Solution Exhibit for Summary Problem Two for Your Review

	NOMINAL DOLLARS		CONSTANT DOLLARS	
	(METHOD 1) Historical Cost[a]	(METHOD 2) Current Cost	(METHOD 3) Historical Cost	(METHOD 4) Current Cost
Balance sheets, December 31, 19X2				
Cash	10,500	10,500	10,500	10,500
Inventory, 100 units	2,000	2,500[b]	2,400[d]	2,500[b]
Total assets	12,500	13,000	12,900	13,000
Original paid-in capital	8,000	8,000	9,600[e]	9,600[e]
Retained income (confined to income from continuing operations)	4,500	3,000	3,300	3,000
Revaluation equity (accumulated hold-ing gains)	—	2,000	—	400
Total stockholders' equity	12,500	13,000	12,900	13,000
Income statements for 19X2				
Sales, 300 units @ $35	10,500	10,500	10,500	10,500
Cost of goods sold, 300 units	6,000	7,500[b]	7,200[d]	7,500
Income from continuing operations	4,500	3,000	3,300	3,000
Holding gains (losses):				
On 300 units sold		1,500[c]		300[f]
On 100 units unsold		500[c]		100[f]
Total holding gains		2,000		400

[a] All numbers are the same as in Exhibit 16–6, page 727.
[b] 100 × $25   [c] 300 × ($25 − $20)   [d] 120/100 × $2,000   [e] 120/100 × $8,000
   300 × $25   100 × ($25 − $20)   120/100 × $6,000
[f] $7,500 − restated cost of $7,200 = $300
   $2,500 − restated cost of $2,400 = $100

HIGHLIGHTS TO REMEMBER

1. Avoid the temptation to dismiss a conceptual framework as being mere theory having no practical importance. A conceptual framework aids communication among all interested parties. Practice becomes less chaotic and easier to understand.

2. Exhibit 16–3, pages 716–717, deserves your review. It provides a convenient summary of key concepts used throughout this book.

3. Adjustments to financial statements for the effects of changing prices can focus on *general* price changes (constant instead of nominal dollars) or *specific* price changes (current instead of historical costs). Furthermore, both adjustments can be applied together.

4. The historical-cost/constant-dollar method is *not* concerned with current-cost concepts of income, whatever their strengths and weaknesses.

5. The current-cost methods for measuring income from operations are based on *physical* rather than *financial* concepts of maintenance of invested capital.

6. Write-ups of nonmonetary assets (inventory in this example) under the historical-cost/constant-dollar method do *not* result in the recognition of gains. They are restatements of *costs* in dollars of equivalent purchasing power.

ACCOUNTING VOCABULARY

Accounting Policy Making, p. 710
Constant Dollars, 725
Current Cost, 725
Current-Cost Method, 727
Financial Capital Maintenance, 725
General Price Index, 729
Historical Cost, 725
Holding Gains (or Losses), 728
Neutrality, 714

Nominal Dollars, 725
Physical Capital Maintenance, 725
Relevance, 713
Reliability, 713
Representational Faithfulness, 713
Revaluation Equity, 728
Specific Price Index, 729
Validity, 713
Verifiability, 713

FUNDAMENTAL ASSIGNMENT MATERIAL

Special note. Problems 16–43 and 16–44 provide a general review of the whole book. They can be solved without necessarily studying the material in this chapter. These problems focus on material from actual companies and on coverage of more than one accounting topic simultaneously.

☐ **General Coverage**

16–1. **EFFECTS OF VARIOUS ACCOUNTING METHODS ON NET INCOME.** (Alternate is 16–4). You are the manager of Nemo Company, a profitable new company that has high potential growth. It is nearing the end of your first year in business and you must make some decisions regarding accounting policies for financial reporting to stockholders. Your controller and your certified public accountant have gathered the following information (all figures in thousands except tax rate):

Revenue	$40,000
Beginning inventory	0
Purchases	21,000
Ending inventory—if LIFO is used	6,000
Ending inventory—if FIFO is used	8,000
Depreciation—if straight-line is used	1,500
Depreciation—if double-declining-balance is used	3,000
Store-opening costs	4,000
Store-opening costs (amortized amount)	800
Other expenses	5,000
Income tax rate	40%
Common shares outstanding	2,000

Double-declining-balance depreciation will be used for tax purposes regardless of the method chosen for reporting to stockholders. For all other items, assume that the same method is used for tax purposes and for financial reporting purposes.

Required:

1. Prepare a columnar income statement. In column 1 show the results using LIFO, double-declining-balance depreciation, and direct write-off of store-opening costs. Show earnings per share as well as net income. In successive columns, show the separate effects on net income and earnings per share of substituting the alternative methods: column 2, FIFO inventory; column 3, straight-line depreciation; column 4, amortization of store-opening costs. In column 5, show the total results of choosing all the alternative methods (columns 2 through 4). Note that in columns 2 through 4 only single changes in column 1 should be shown; that is, column 3 does not show the effects of columns 2 and 3 together, nor does column 4 show the effects of columns 2, 3, and 4 together.
2. As the manager, which accounting policies would you adopt? Why?

16–2. **FOUR VERSIONS OF INCOME AND CAPITAL.** (Alternate is 16–35.) Z Company has the following comparative balance sheets as of December 31 (based on historical costs in nominal dollars):

	19X4	19X5
Cash	$ —	$4,500
Inventory, 50 and 20 units, respectively	5,000	2,000
Total assets	$5,000	$6,500
Paid-in capital	$5,000	$5,000
Retained income	—	1,500
Stockholders' equity	$5,000	$6,500

The general-price-level index was 140 on December 31, 19X4, and 161 on December 31, 19X5. The company had acquired fifty units of inventory on December 31, 19X4, for $100 each and had held them throughout 19X5. Thirty units were sold on December 31, 19X5, for $150 cash each. The replacement cost of the inventory at that date was $120 per unit. Assume that these are the only transactions. Ignore income taxes.

Required:

Use four sets of columns to prepare comparative balance sheets as of December 31, 19X4, and 19X5, and income statements for 19X5 under (1) historical cost/nominal dollars, (2) current cost/nominal dollars, (3) historical cost/constant dollars, and (4) current cost/constant dollars.

16–3. CHARACTERISTICS OF INFORMATION.   International Paper Company shows the following under long-term assets in its balance sheet (in millions):

Timberlands	$772

A footnote described the timberlands as 6.5 million acres that are "stated at cost, less accumulated depletion." The average cost of the timberlands was $111 per acre. Suppose the current market price is estimated to be between $300 and $600 per acre, providing a best estimate of total market value of $450 × 6.5 million = $2,925 million.

Required:
1. Which measure, the $772 million or $2,925 million, is more relevant? What characteristics make it relevant?
2. Which measure is more reliable? What characteristics make it reliable?
3. If you were an investor considering the purchase of common stock in International Paper, which measure would be most valuable to you? Explain.

16–4. EFFECTS OF VARIOUS ACCOUNTING METHODS ON INCOME.   (Alternate is 16–1.) General Electric had the following data in its 1988 annual report (in millions of dollars except for earnings per share):

Total revenues	$50,089
Cost of goods and services sold	28,831
Depreciation, depletion and amortization	2,266
Other expenses (summarized here)	14,271
Total expenses	45,368
Earnings before income taxes	4,721
Provision for income taxes	1,335
Net earnings	$ 3,386
Net earnings per share (in dollars)	$ 3.75

Inventories on December 31, 1988, were $6,486 million and on December 31, 1987, were $6,265 million. If FIFO had been used instead of LIFO, the FIFO inventories would have been higher by $2,226 million at December 31, 1988, and $2,076 million at December 31, 1987.

The company stated that most depreciation is computed by accelerated methods, primarily sum-of-the-years'-digits.

General Electric's marginal 1988 income tax rate was 34%.

Required:
Suppose General Electric has used straight-line depreciation for reporting to shareholders, resulting in depreciation, depletion, and amortization expense of $1,766 million rather than $2,266 million in 1988. Also suppose the company had used FIFO instead of LIFO. Recast all the above data for 1988, including the amount earned per common share. Show supporting computations.

16–5. REPORTING ON CHANGING PRICES.   Transamerica Corporation, a large diversified company, reported operating income of $151 million on sales of $5,399 million. After adjusting for changes in specific prices (current costs), operating income was $107 million. Three other amounts reported were related to holding gains (in millions):

Effect of increase in general price level	$64
Excess of increase in specific prices over increase in general price level	$23
Increase in specific prices of inventories and property and equipment held during the year	$87

Required:
1. Identify the holding gain under the current-cost/nominal-dollars method.
2. Idenfity the holding gain under the current-cost/constant-dollars method.
3. Explain why the holding gain in requirement 1 differs from that in requirement 2.

ADDITIONAL ASSIGNMENT MATERIAL

☐ **General Coverage**

16–6. What are the major objectives of financial reporting as chosen by the FASB?

16–7. "Now that the FASB has a conceptual framework, accounting policy making is simply a matter of mechanistically applying the framework to issues that arise." Do you agree? Explain.

16–8. What is the fundamental cost-benefit test in accounting policy making?

16–9. Name three types of costs of producing accounting information.

16–10. "It is better to be roughly right than precisely wrong." Interpret this statement in light of the qualitative characteristics of accounting.

16–11. "The ability of a dozen independent accountants to apply the same measurement methods and obtain the same result is an example of validity." Do you agree? Explain.

16–12. "Neutrality underscores a fundamental approach that should be taken by the FASB." Describe the approach.

16–13. "Accounting theory is unimportant because it is impractical." Do you agree? Explain.

16–14. "Accounting policy making is a political endeavor." Do you agree? Explain.

16–15. "Accounting policies differ so much from country to country that accountants trained in one country have difficulty practicing in another, even if there is no language barrier." Do you agree? Explain.

16–16. Why have high inflation rates influenced accounting policies in many countries?

16–17. Do you expect common, world-wide accounting standards within the next decade? Explain.

16–18. "Recognition of revenue occurs at the time of delivery of a good or service." Do you agree? Explain.

16–19. What is a statement of accounting policies?

16–20. "The FASB no longer requires reporting of inflation-adjusted data in annual reports. Therefore there is no reason to study inflation-adjusted financial statements." Do you agree? Explain.

16–21. Distinguish between the *physical* and the *financial* concepts of maintenance of invested capital.

16–22. "The choice among accounting measures of income is often expressed as either historical-cost accounting or general-price-level accounting or current-cost accounting." Do you agree? Explain.

16–23. Explain how net income is measured under the current-cost approach.

16–24. What is the common meaning of *current cost*?

16–25. Explain what a general price index represents.

16–26. Distinguish between *general* indexes and *specific* indexes.

16–27. "Specific indexes are used in nominal-dollar accounting but not in constant-dollar accounting." Do you agree? Explain.

16–28. "All holding gains should be excluded from income." What is the major logic behind this statement?

16–29. STATEMENTS OF FINANCIAL ACCOUNTING CONCEPTS. Using *your own words*, describe the basic contents of *Statement of Financial Accounting Concepts* Numbers 1, 2, 3, and 5. Use only *one sentence* for each statement. Make each sentence as informative as possible.

16–30. COSTS AND BENEFITS OF INFORMATION. The FASB has proposed that companies include a liability for postretirement benefits on their balance sheets. Postretirement benefits are items such as health insurance that are provided to retired employees. (Pensions are excluded because a liability for pensions is already required.) Many companies have argued against such a requirement. They maintain that the costs would exceed the benefits.

Required:
1. Discuss the potential costs and benefits of mandatory reporting of a liability for postretirement benefits on companies' balance sheets.
2. Assess the relevance and reliability of measuring and reporting such a liability.

16–31. TIMING OF RECOGNITION OF REVENUE. Massive Enterprises, a huge conglomerate company, has recently acquired the Galaxy Publishing Company.

The president of Massive, Martin Mass, is surprised that the Galaxy income statement assumes that an equal proportion of the revenue is earned with the publication of every issue of the company's magazines: "The critical event in the process of earning revenue in the magazine business is the cash sale of the subscription. Therefore, why can't most of the revenue be recognized in the period of sale?"

Required:
Discuss the propriety of timing the recognition of revenue in relation to (1) the cash sale of the subscription, (2) the publication of magazines every month, (3) both events—by recognizing a portion of the revenue with the cash sale of the magazine subscription and a portion of the revenue with the publication of the magazine every month.

16–32. CONTRACTOR ACCOUNTING. Reynaldo Company contracted to build a large river bridge for New York City. The board of directors is about to meet to decide whether to adopt the completed-contract or the percentage-of-completion method of accounting. Reynaldo began business on January 1, 19X4. Construction activity for the year ended December 31, 19X4, revealed (in millions):

Total contract price	$84
Billings through December 31, 19X4	35
Cash collections	28
Contract costs incurred	42
Estimated additional costs to complete the contract	14

Any work remaining to be done is expected to be completed in 19X5.

Required:
Prepare a schedule computing the amount of revenue and income that would be reported for 19X4 under
a. The completed-contract method
b. The percentage-of-completion method (based on estimated costs)

Ignore selling and other expenses as well as income taxes.

The percentage-of-completion method recognizes income based on incurred costs to date divided by these known costs plus the estimated future costs to complete the contract.

The percentage-of-completion method computes an applicable percentage as follows:

$$\text{Percentage of completion} = \frac{\text{Costs incurred to date}}{\left(\begin{array}{c}\text{Costs incurred} \\ \text{to date}\end{array}\right) + \left(\begin{array}{c}\text{Estimated additional} \\ \text{costs to complete}\end{array}\right)}$$

The percentage is applied to the total contract price to determine the recognized revenue for the period.

16–33. **EFFECTS OF TRANSACTIONS ON FINANCIAL STATEMENTS.** For each of the following numbered items, select the lettered transaction that indicates its effect on the corporation's financial statements. If a transaction has more than one effect, list all applicable letters. Assume that the total current assets exceed the total current liabilities both before and after every transaction described.

NUMBERED TRANSACTIONS

1. Collection of account receivable.
2. Sale on account at a gross profit.
3. Payment of trade account payable.
4. Purchase of inventory on open account.
5. Issuance of additional common shares as a stock dividend.
6. Sale for cash of a factory building at a selling price that substantially exceeds the book value.
7. The destruction of a building by fire. Insurance proceeds, collected immediately, slightly exceed book value.
8. The appropriation of retained earnings as a reserve for contingencies.
9. Issue of new shares in a three-for-one split of common stock.

LETTERED EFFECTS

a. Increases current ratio.
b. Decreases current ratio.
c. Increases working capital.
d. Decreases working capital.
e. Increases the book value per share of common stock.
f. Decreases the book value per share of common stock.
g. Increases total retained earnings.
h. Decreases total retained earnings.
i. Increases total stockholders' equity.
j. Decreases total stockholders' equity.
k. None of the above.

16–34. **MEANING OF GENERAL INDEX APPLICATIONS AND CHOICE OF BASE YEAR.** Mears Company acquired land in mid-1970 for $3 million. In mid-1990 it acquired a substantially identical parcel of land for $6 million. The general-price-level index annual averages were:

1990—210.0   1980—100.0   1970—60.0

Required:
1. In four columns, show the computations of the total cost of the two parcels of land expressed in (a) costs as traditionally recorded, (b) dollars of 1990 purchasing power, (c) 1980 purchasing power, and (d) 1970 purchasing power.
2. Explain the meaning of the figures that you computed in requirement 1.

16–35. **CONCEPTS OF INCOME.** (Alternate is 16–2.) Suppose you are in the business of investing in land and holding it for resale. On December 31, 19X2, a parcel of land has a historical cost of $100,000 and a current value (measured via use of a specific price index) of $300,000; the general price level had doubled since the land was acquired. Suppose also that the land is sold on December 31, 19X3, for $360,000. The general price level rose by 5% during 19X3.

Required:
1. Prepare a tabulation of income from continuing operations and holding gains for 19X3, using the four methods illustrated in Exhibit 16–6.
2. In your own words, explain the meaning of the results, giving special attention to what income represents.

16–36. **DEPRECIATION AND PRICE-LEVEL ADJUSTMENTS.** The Moore Company purchased a computer for $400,000. This computer has an expected life of four years and an expected residual value of zero. Straight-line depreciation is used. The general price index is 150 at the date of acquisition; it increases 30 points annually during the next three years. The results follow:

YEAR	PRICE-LEVEL INDEX	HISTORICAL-COST/ NOMINAL-DOLLAR DEPRECIATION	MULTIPLIER	HISTORICAL-COST/ CONSTANT-DOLLAR DEPRECIATION AS RECORDED
1	150	$100,000	$\dfrac{150}{150}$	$100,000
2	180	100,000	$\dfrac{180}{150}$	120,000
3	210	100,000	$\dfrac{210}{150}$	140,000
4	240	100,000	$\dfrac{240}{150}$	160,000
		$400,000		

Required:

1. Convert the figures in the last column so that they are expressed in terms of fourth-year dollars. For example, the $120,000 second-year dollars would have to be restated by multiplying by 240/180.
2. Suppose in requirement 1 that revenue easily exceeds expenses for each year and that cash equal to the annual depreciation charge was invested in a non-interest-bearing cash account. If amounts equal to the unadjusted depreciation charge were invested each year, would sufficient cash have accumulated to equal the general purchasing power of $400,000 invested in the asset four years ago? If not, what is the extent of the total financial deficiency measured in terms of fourth-year dollars?
3. Suppose in requirement 2 that amounts equal to the constant-dollar depreciation for each year were used. What is the extent of the total financial deficiency?
4. Suppose in requirement 3 that the amounts were invested each year in assets that increased in value at the same rate as the increase in the general price level. What is the extent of the total financial deficiency?

☐ Understanding Published Financial Reports

16–37. **RECOGNITION CRITERIA.** *Fortune* reported on a recent Supreme Court decision related to accrual accounting. The Internal Revenue Service (IRS) and several casinos disagreed on when to recognize revenue and expenses for progressive slot machines. These slot machines have no limit to the payoff. They pay a lucky winner the money others have put into the machine since the last payoff (less the house takeout, of course). The longer since the last win, the larger the jackpot. Progressive slots pay off on average every four and one-half months.

Suppose that on December 31, 1989, Harrah's Casino has a progressive slot machine that had not paid off recently. In fact, $1.2 million had been placed in the machine since its last payoff on February 13, 1989. Assume that the house's takeout is 5%.

The IRS regarded the $1.2 million as revenue but allowed no expense until a payoff occurred. The casinos argued that an expense equal to 95% of the revenue will eventually be incurred, and accrual accounting would require recognition of the expense at the same time as the revenue is recorded.

Required:

1. How much revenue should Harrah's recognize in 1989 from the machine? Explain fully.
2. How much expense should Harrah's recognize in 1989 from the machine? Explain fully.
3. The IRS argued that no expense should be recognized until a payoff to the winner had been made. What do you suppose was the basis for their argument?

4. Suppose you are a gambler who uses accrual accounting. How would you account for $100 placed into the progressive slot machine described above? Is this consistent with your answers to requirements 1 and 2? Why or why not?

16–38. NATURE OF CAPITAL, INCOME, REVENUE. (M. Wolfson, adapted.) Here is a letter written by the financial vice-president of Acurex Corporation, a manufacturer of energy, environmental, and agriculture equipment:

Dear Professor:

☐ We are engaged in a somewhat unusual government contract with the Department of Energy as a demonstration, or "showcase," program. We are designing and constructing a fuel delivery system for industrial boilers in which we will cost-share 35% of the total cost with the government. In return, we are awarded immediate title to all the equipment involved, including the government's 65% portion.

☐ It seems to me that there is some real logic in reflecting the government's gift of 65% of total cost in current earnings, subject only to a test of net realizable value. I'd appreciate your thoughts.

Sincerely,

The company's net income the previous year was $1,007,000.

Required:

Suppose the cost of the fuel delivery system is $1.2 million. This consists of about $600,000 in "hard assets" (equipment, etc.) and about $600,000 in designing costs. Via journal entries, show at least two ways in which the government contract could be reflected in Acurex's books, assuming the costs are all incurred prior to the end of the year. What is the effect of your two ways on the year's pretax income?

16–39. JAPANESE ANNUAL REPORTS. Kobe Steel, Ltd., is one of the world's top twenty producers of iron and steel products and is also one of the most diversified corporations in Japan. The company's annual sales are over $8 billion at current exchange rates.

Kobe Steel maintains its records and prepares it financial statements in accordance with generally accepted accounting principles and practices in Japan. Selected parts of Kobe Steel's "Summary of Significant Accounting Policies" are reproduced below:

☐ 2. SUMMARY OF SIGNIFICANT ACCOUNTING POLICIES

Reporting Entity
The non-consolidated financial statements report only the accounts of the Company.

Allowance for Doubtful Receivables
The allowance for doubtful receivables is provided in amounts sufficient to cover possible losses on collection. It is determined by adding the uncollectible amounts individually estimated for doubtful receivables to a maximum amount permitted for tax purposes which is calculated collectively.

Marketable Securities and Investment Securities
Listed equity securities, both in marketable securities and investment securities, except for certain equity securities of subsidiaries and affiliates in which the Company's ownership equals or exceeds 25 percent, are stated at the lower of moving average cost or market value. Other securities, including investments in subsidiaries and affiliates, are stated at moving average cost. If significant impairment of value is deemed permanent, cost has been appropriately reduced.

Inventories
Inventories are valued at cost, as determined by the following methods:
Two main works of the Iron & Steel Division and four main plants of the Aluminum & Copper Division
.... Last-in, first-out method

Finished goods and work in process in the Machinery Division
.... Identification method

Others .... Weighted average method

Depreciation

Buildings and structures in all locations and machinery and equipment located in Kakogawa Works, Kobe Works, Takasago Works, Mooka Plant and Chofu Plant are depreciated on the straight-line method and all other machinery and equipment are depreciated on the declining balance method over estimated useful lives.

Long-term Construction Contracts

Sales and the related costs of certain long-term (over one year) construction contracts are recognized by the percentage of completion method.

Research and Development Expenses

Expenses for development of new products and research and application for new technologies, which are expected to contribute to future sales, are deferred and amortized over a five-year period.

Income Taxes

Income taxes are based on taxable income and charged to income on the taxes payable method. Deferred income taxes relating to timing differences between financial accounting and tax reporting purposes are not recognized.

Required: Identify the accounting policies used by Kobe Steel that would not be generally accepted in the United States.

16–40. **REVENUES IN CONSTANT DOLLARS.** Alcoa, the aluminum company, reported the following total revenues (in millions):

	1988	1987	1986	1985	1984
Historical basis	$9,795	$7,767	$6,431	$6,599	$7,136
In average 1988 dollars	9,795	8,088	6,941	7,255	?

The average Consumer Price Index was 118.3 in 1988 and 103.9 in 1984.

Required: Compute the following:

1. Total revenues for 1984 in average 1988 dollars. Round to the nearest million.
2. Percentage increase in revenues between 1984 and 1988 on a historical cost basis.
3. Percentage increase in revenues between 1984 and 1988 in average 1988 dollars.
4. Average Consumer Price Index for 1986.

16–41. **EFFECTS OF GENERAL VERSUS SPECIFIC PRICE CHANGES.** The following data are from the annual reports of Gannett Co., owner of 120 newspapers; Zayre Corporation, operator of 290 discount stores; and Goodyear Tire and Rubber Company:

(in millions)	GANNETT	ZAYRE	GOODYEAR
Increase in specific prices of assets held during the year*	$45.8	$ 24.9	$ (4.7)
Less effect of increase in general price level	37.5	55.5	252.0
Excess of increase in specific prices over increase in the general price level†	$ 8.3	$(30.6)	$(256.7)

* Holding gain using current-cost/nominal-dollars method.
† Holding gain using current-cost/constant-dollars method.

Required: Compare and contrast the relationship between changes in the general price level and changes in the prices of the specific assets of each of the three companies.

EXHIBIT 16–8

B. F. SAUL REAL ESTATE INVESTMENT TRUST
Condensed Consolidated Statement of Operations Adjusted for Changing Prices (in thousands)
Year Ended September 30, 1985

	FINANCIAL STATEMENTS (HISTORICAL COST)	ADJUSTED FOR GENERAL INFLATION (CONSTANT DOLLAR)	ADJUSTED FOR CHANGES IN SPECIFIC PRICES (CURRENT COST)
Total income	$ 65,337	$ 65,337	$ 65,337
Expenses:			
Direct operating expenses	39,437	39,437	39,437
Interest and debt expense	39,717	39,717	39,717
Interest capitalized	(9,147)	(9,147)	(9,147)
Depreciation	7,180	8,154	8,784
Advisory fee	2,480	2,480	2,480
General and administrative	792	792	792
Total expenses	80,459	81,433	82,063
Operating loss	(15,122)	(16,096)	(16,726)
Reduction of property inflation values to lower recoverable amounts		(2,478)	
Equity in earnings of savings and loan	932	932	932
Provision for income taxes	(75)	(75)	(75)
Loss from continuing operations	$(14,265)	$(17,717)	$(15,869)
Increase in specific prices of income-pro-ducing properties held during the year*			$ 9,181
Less effect of increase in the general price level			1,661
Excess of increase in specific prices over increase in the general price level			$ 7,520

* At September 30, 1985, current cost of income-producing properties, net of accumulated depreciation, was $241,197,000.

16–42. **FASB Format and Constant-Dollar Disclosures.** B. F. Saul Real Estate Investment Trust is a company with investments in income-producing properties, primarily shopping centers. The company's 1985 financial statement included some inflation-adjusted data that are no longer required.

Examine the comparative income statements for B. F. Saul in Exhibit 16–8.

Required: Recast the bottom of the income statements (beginning with loss from continuing operations) in the four-method format of Exhibit 16–6 (p. 727). Use the descriptive terms as shown in Exhibit 16–6. Note that total holding gains cannot be subdivided.

16–43. **Comprehensive Review: Reconstruct Transactions.** Burlington Coat Factory is a major independent "off-price" apparel chain with over 130 stores in thirty-seven states. The company's balance sheet and statement of cash flows are on this page and the next.

Required: Compute amounts to replace each of the question marks in Burlington Coat Factory's balance sheet.

BURLINGTON COAT FACTORY
Consolidated Balance Sheets
(all amounts in thousands)

	OCTOBER 29, 1988	OCTOBER 31, 1987
ASSETS		
Current Assets:		
Cash and cash equivalents	$?	$ 13,769
Accounts receivable, less provisions for losses	?	5,363
Merchandise inventories	?	196,500
Prepaid and other current assets	4,451	3,418
Total Current Assets	285,411	219,050
Property and equipment net of accumulated		
depreciation and amortization of $22,895 and $16,052, respectively	?	70,241
Restricted bond fund	1,761	1,082
Other assets	1,604	1,458
Total Assets	?	$292,551
LIABILITIES AND STOCKHOLDERS' EQUITY		
Current Liabilities:		
Notes payable	$ 30,900	$ 0
Accounts payable	?	107,682
Other current liabilities	20,259	14,056
Current maturities of long term debt	685	739
Total Current Liabilities	?	122,477
Long term debt	?	15,950
Other liabilities	283	—
Deferred income taxes	3,173	3,294
Total Liabilities	?	141,721
Stockholders' Equity:		
Common stock, par value $1; authorized 50,000,000 shares;		
11,762,000 shares issued and outstanding at October 29, 1988,		
11,761,000 shares issued and outstanding at October 31, 1987	?	11,761
Capital in excess of par value	?	43,845
Retained earnings	?	95,224
Total Stockholders' Equity	?	150,830
Total Liabilities and Stockholders' Equity	$?	$292,551

BURLINGTON COAT FACTORY
Consolidated Statements of Cash Flows
(all amounts in thousands)

YEAR ENDED	OCTOBER 29, 1988	OCTOBER 31, 1987
Operating Activities:		
Net income	$ 21,709	$ 20,262
Adjustments to reconcile net income to net cash provided by operating activities:		
Depreciation and amortization	6,889	4,865
Provision for losses on accounts receivable	183	192
Provision for deferred income taxes	(121)	813
Loss (gain) on sale of equipment	64	(13)
Other	93	75
Changes in operating assets and liabilities:		
Accounts receivable	(3,232)	(2,063)
Inventory	(62,147)	(47,649)
Prepaids and others	(1,033)	2,133
Accounts payable	24,505	24,685
Other current liabilities	6,203	(1,222)
Net cash (used) provided by operating activities	(6,887)	2,078
Investing Activities:		
Acquisition of property and equipment	(23,443)	(40,095)
Restricted funds additions	(79)	(367)
Restricted funds drawdown	120	9,067
Net additions to deposit on leases	(239)	(587)
Net cash used in investing activities	(23,641)	(31,982)
Financing Activities:		
Net proceeds from revolving lines of credit	30,900	—
Principal payments on long term debt	(739)	(1,088)
Proceeds from long term debt	200	3,866
Proceeds from issuance of common stock	16	508
Other	283	16
Net cash provided by financing activities	30,660	3,302
Increase (decrease) in cash and cash equivalents	132	(26,602)

16–44. **Comprehensive Review: Reconstruct Transactions.** American Software, Inc., develops, markets, and supports business applications software, primarily for IBM mainframe computers. The company's income statement, balance sheet, and statement of cash flows are in the accompanying financial statements. Some items on the statements have question marks. American Software's effective tax rate for 1988 was 37.984808%, and all assets disposed of had zero book value.

Required:

1. Compute the original purchase price of property and equipment disposed of during fiscal 1988. (*Hint*: Prepare T-accounts for (a) property and equipment, at cost, and (b) accumulated depreciation and amortization. Enter the balances and transaction amounts that are known. A key to computing the unknown entries to the accounts is that all assets disposed of had zero book value.)

2. Fill in the correct amounts for all question marks in the statements. (*Hint*: Begin with either net earnings or earnings before income taxes on the income statement. Also note that property and equipment, at cost, can be computed from the data developed in requirement 1.)

3. A footnote to American Software's financial statements follows:

Revenue Recognition

- [ ] Upon entering into a licensing agreement for proprietary software, the Company recognizes eighty percent (80%) of the licensing fee upon delivery of the software documentation (system and user manuals), ten percent (10%) upon delivery of the software (computer tapes with source code), and ten percent (10%) upon installation; this is conditioned upon at least fifty percent (50%) of the licensing fee being billable within 45 days and installation contemplated within 180 days of execution of the licensing agreement. Otherwise, the Company recognizes income on proprietary software as billed. Revenue related to custom programming, maintenance, and education is recognized as the related services are performed.

The April 30, 1988, balance sheet shows $3,794,486 of deferred revenue (a better name is *unearned revenue*). What is the most likely explanation for the existence of deferred revenue?

AMERICAN SOFTWARE, INC.
Consolidated Statement of Earnings

Revenues	$?
Cost and expenses:	
Salaries, commissions, and benefits	18,129,562
Other selling, general and administrative	?
Total cost and expenses	40,234,266
Other income:	
Interest income	2,214,512
Other	497,509
Earnings before income taxes	?
Income taxes	6,330,000
Net earnings	$?
Earnings per common share	$?
Weighted average number of common shares outstanding	10,366,729

AMERICAN SOFTWARE, INC.
Consolidated Balance Sheets

	APRIL 30,	
	1988	1987
Assets		
Current assets:		
Cash	$ 193,353	$ 586,620
Investments, at cost (approximate market)	43,582,848	36,822,019
Trade accounts receivable, net	?	12,083,836
Other	2,700,619	4,313,934
Total current assets	?	53,806,409
Property and equipment:		
At cost	?	16,576,838
Less accumulated depreciation and amortization	7,176,719	5,154,098
Net property and equipment	?	11,422,740
Other assets	?	2,701,033
	?	$67,930,182

Liabilities and Shareholders' Equity

Current liabilities:		
Accounts payable	$ 4,095,393	$ 3,650,944
Deferred income taxes	2,887,978	3,653,978
Deferred revenue	3,794,486	2,815,120
Other current liabilities	7,405,558	5,518,971
Total current liabilities	18,183,415	15,639,013
Deferred tax liability	3,419,782	2,243,782
Shareholders' equity:		
Common stock, $.10 par value	1,014,862	1,044,587
Additional paid-in capital	20,184,365	20,905,047
Retained earnings	34,071,194	28,097,753
Total shareholders' equity	55,270,421	50,047,387
	$76,873,618	$67,930,182

AMERICAN SOFTWARE, INC.
Consolidated Statement of Cash Flows

	Year Ended April 30, 1988
Cash Flows From Operating Activities:	
Net earnings	$?
Adjustments to reconcile net earnings to net cash provided by operating activities:	
Depreciation and amortization of property and equipment	2,046,012
Depreciation and amortization of other assets	318,796
Compensatory stock options	85,112
Deferred taxes	1,176,000
Increase in investments	(1,760,829)
Increase in trade accounts receivable	(2,279,721)
Decrease in other current assets	1,613,315
Increase in accounts payable	444,449
Decrease in deferred taxes	(766,000)
Increase in deferred revenue	976,366
Increase in other current liabilities	1,886,587
Net cash provided by operating activities	?
Cash Flows From Investing Activities:	
Additions to property and equipment	(1,193,233)
Increase in other assets	(3,081,043)
Net cash used by investing activities	(4,274,276)
Cash Flows from Financing Activities:	
Proceeds from stock options	232,777
Retirement of common stock	(3,169,063)
Dividends declared	(2,260,349)
Net cash used for financing activities	(5,196,635)
Net decrease in cash	$?

16-45. **HOUSE OF FABRICS ANNUAL REPORT.** Examine the income statement of House of Fabrics (p. 752). The cost of sales is based on the FIFO inventory method. The store and operating expenses include $6,286,000 of depreciation and amortization, which is computed using the straight-line method.

Suppose House of Fabrics had switched to LIFO and accelerated depreciation at the beginning of fiscal 1989. Prior-year results were not restated. Therefore balance sheet amounts for January 31, 1988, were unaffected by the change. As a result of the change, the ending inventory amount at January 31, 1989, was $127,735,000 instead of $129,735,000, and depreciation and amortization charged during fiscal 1989 was $7,077,000 instead of $6,286,000. For requirements 1 and 2, assume that the changes were made for shareholder reporting only; no change was made in tax statements.

<table>
<tr><td>Required:</td><td>

1. Compute the revised fiscal 1989 income before income taxes.
2. The effective tax rate is 39.7%. Compute the revised fiscal 1989 provision for income taxes, net income, and net income per share for House of Fabrics.
3. House of Fabrics uses accelerated depreciation for tax purposes and straight-line for shareholder reporting. However, FIFO is used for both tax and shareholder reporting. Suppose that in addition to switching to LIFO and accelerated depreciation for shareholder reporting, House of Fabrics switched to LIFO for tax reporting. What would be the effect of the change in tax reporting on the income taxes shown on the income statement for shareholder reporting? What would be the effect on the taxes currently payable and the deferred taxes? (Note that of the $7,479,000 income tax expense, $7,165,000 is currently payable and $314,000 was deferred.)

</td></tr>
</table>

Annual Report for House of Fabrics, Inc.

This section contains the annual financial report for House of Fabrics for the fiscal year ended January 31, 1989.* This information is used in the last problem in the assignment materials for each chapter.

The Company

House of Fabrics, Inc. is the largest home sewing/craft retailer in the United States with 658 Company-owned stores located in 43 states selling medium-priced fabrics, notions, crafts and sewing machines.

The Company began opening super stores in 1984, which have 12,000–15,000 square feet, as compared to traditional mall stores which have approximately 4,200 square feet. The Company has 269 super stores and 389 traditional mall stores.

In the fiscal year ended January 31, 1989 approximately 48% of the Company's sales was comprised of fabrics, sold by the yard and used principally for clothing, home decorating and crafts. Sewing notions represented 31% of the Company's sales, crafts represented 11% and sewing machines and related accessories represented 10%.

Fabric and notion sales have been the primary business of the Company since its incorporation in 1946. Sewing machine sales commenced in 1980 when the company became a dealer for the sale of Singer sewing machines and related accessories, which complement the basic fabric and notion business. The Company currently operates 382 full-line sewing machine departments in its stores. In 1981 the Company began opening full-line craft departments in its stores and currently has 576 such departments.

All of the Company's stores located west of the Rocky Mountains are operated under the name "House of Fabrics." Most of its stores in the other states are operated under the name "So-Fro Fabrics." The Company operates all of its stores in leased premises, principally in neighborhood and regional shopping centers, and does not engage in any franchising activity. The Company purchases finished goods directly from mills and manufacturers, and has facilities in South Carolina for processing and warehousing merchandise for distribution to its stores.

---

* We are grateful to House of Fabrics for granting permission to reproduce their financial statements from their 1989 annual report.

Years ended January 31,	1989	1988	1987	1986	1985¹
Summary of Operations					
Sales	$338,010,000	$322,480,000	$316,366,000	$286,743,000	$278,256,000
Gross profit	$183,787,000	$172,104,000	$160,114,000	$150,591,000	$144,530,000
Interest expense	$ 3,473,000	$ 2,236,000	$ 2,807,000	$ 1,656,000	$ 1,281,000
Income taxes	$ 7,479,000	$ 8,767,000	$ 6,444,000	$ 3,771,000	$ 10,473,000
Net income	$ 11,361,000	$ 10,501,000	$ 6,191,000	$ 4,257,000[b]	$ 11,332,000
Net income per share[a]	$1.69	$1.58	$.94	$.64[b]	$1.71
Cash dividends					
per share	$ .48	$ .48	$.48	$.48	$ .40
Return on average					
stockholders' equity	11.7%	11.8%	7.4%	5.2%	14.9%
Year-End Position					
Assets	$180,215,000	$184,624,000	$158,040,000	$157,945,000	$126,010,000
Long-term debt	$ 11,900,000	$ 11,736,000	$ 12,085,000	$ 3,394,000	$ 2,300,000
Stockholders' equity	$101,236,000	$ 92,718,000	$ 85,287,000	$ 82,094,000	$ 80,720,000
Stockholders' equity					
per share	$15.35	$14.12	$13.01	$12.56	$12.43
Number of stores	658	672	707	730[c]	698[c]

(a) Based on average shares and equivalents outstanding.
(b) Net income and net income per share were $6,357,000 and $.96, respectively, before the provision for loss on sale and disposition of assets.
(c) Excludes Craft Showcase stores

Management's Discussion and Analysis of Operations and Financial Condition

Operations

House of Fabrics achieved record sales and earnings in the fiscal year ended January 31, 1989, despite declines in sewing machine sales and profits, which lowered overall corporate profits by 21 cents per share.

Sales for the year totaled $338,010,000 compared to $322,480,000 in the preceding year and $316,366,000 in 1987. Net income in fiscal 1989 was $11,361,000 compared to $10,501,000 in fiscal 1988 and $6,191,000 in fiscal 1987.

During fiscal 1989, the number of stores decreased from 672 to 658, reflecting a planned reduction. The Company opened 55 new super stores, and closed 69 traditional mall location stores. The long-term strategy of converting from mall store locations to super stores had a favorable impact on sales and earnings for the fiscal year just ended. As marginal mall units are closed, the Company is left with stronger mall stores, while at the same time increasing the number of larger, more efficient super stores.

The addition of 55 new super stores, in addition to a 3% increase in store-for-store sales, increased overall sales for the year. This increase, however, was somewhat offset by the closing of 69 traditional stores. The overall sales increase in 1989 over 1988 was approximately 5%. Last year sales increased 2% over 1987 as a result of opening 62 super stores partially offset by closing 97 traditional stores and a slight decline in store-for-store sales.

In fiscal 1989, cost of sales as a percentage of sales decreased to 45.6% from 46.6% in 1988 and 49.4% in 1987. The decrease in 1989 over 1988 came from emphasis on improved margins. The decrease in 1988 over 1987 came from emphasis on improved markup and a decrease in promotional markdowns.

The Company experienced increases in all operating expenses in 1989 over 1988, especially rent and payroll expense. Store and operating expenses as a percentage of sales in 1989 increased to 39.3% compared to 38.0% in 1988 and 37.2% in 1987 primarily due to increases in rent and payroll expenses. Rent increased $4.0 million due to an increase in the number of mall store lease renewals and the addition of more super stores during 1989. Payroll expense in 1989 increased $4.4 million over 1988 as a result of opening more super stores and changes in various states minimum wage laws. The increase in expenses in 1988 and 1987 is primarily attributable to increases in rent expense which resulted from opening more super stores during 1988 and an increase in mall store lease renewals. Warehouse and administrative expenses as a percentage of sales in 1989 declined to 8.4% from 8.7% in 1988 and 8.6% in 1987.

The Company had $3,473,000 of net interest expense in fiscal 1989 compared to $2,236,000 in 1988 and $2,807,000 in 1987. The increase in net interest expense in 1989 over 1988 is directly related to higher average outstanding borrowings due to higher average inventory levels throughout most of the year. The decrease in interest expense in 1988 compared to 1987 is the result of lower average outstanding borrowing associated with lower average inventory levels.

The effective income tax rates for 1989, 1988 and 1987 were 40%, 46% and 51%, respectively. The difference between 1989 and 1988 and 1987 is due to the change in the statutory Federal income tax rates.

Financial Condition

Cash requirements of the Company are met by funds generated from operations, use of short-term debt provided by lines of credit as described in Note 2 of the Financial Statements, and in fiscal 1987 from long-term debt as described in Note 3 to the Financial Statements. During fiscal 1989, short-term borrowings ranged from $18,000,000 to $56,000,000 with an average borrowing level of approximately $33,000,000. This compares with fiscal 1988 borrowings which ranged from $9,000,000 to $24,000,000 with an average borrowing level of $17,000,000 and with fiscal 1987 borrowings which ranged from $18,000,000 to $39,000,000 with an average borrowing level of $28,000,000. Increased borrowing levels in 1989 over 1988 were due to higher average inventory levels during most of 1989. Decreased borrowing levels in 1988 compared to 1987 were due to lower average inventory levels and more internally generated funds. In June 1986, the Company obtained a three-year $10,000,000 unsecured loan from a bank at a fixed interest rate of 8.6% with interest payable quarterly and the entire principal balance due at maturity in May 1989. The maturity of this loan has been extended to May 1990.

Working capital at fiscal 1989 was $76,011,000, up from $67,955,000 at fiscal 1988 and from $61,815,000 at fiscal 1987. The increase in 1988 over 1987 was due to a decrease of $13.7 million in accounts payable partially offset by a $3.9 million decrease in inventories and a $2.5 million decrease in receivables. The Company anticipates no shortage of working capital during the upcoming 1990 fiscal year.

The Company's January 31, 1989 ending inventory of $129,735,000 decreased from 1988 levels of $133,608,000. During the current year, the average was $140,112,000 compared to $118,683,000 in the prior year. During fiscal 1989, the Company expended $8,117,000 on new stores and expansions and improvements to existing locations. This is compared to $9,538,000 in 1988 and $8,666,000 in 1987. The Company will continue to open and acquire new store locations and remodel existing locations whenever the projected rate of return is acceptable and will finance capital expenditures primarily with funds generated from operations. However, the Company will also consider using long-term financing when favorable market conditions prevail.

The percentage of long-term debt to total equity decreased to 11.8% in fiscal 1989 compared to 12.7% in fiscal 1988. The decrease was a result of higher equity of the Company. The Company believes that it continues to be in sound financial condition and has a strong capital structure.

For the years ended January 31,	1989	1988	1987
Sales	$338,010,000	$322,480,000	$316,366,000
Expenses:			
Cost of sales	154,223,000	150,376,000	156,252,000
Store and operating	132,938,000	122,596,000	117,563,000
Warehouse and administrative	28,536,000	28,004,000	27,109,000
Interest	3,473,000	2,236,000	2,807,000
Total	319,170,000	303,212,000	303,731,000
Income before income taxes	18,840,000	19,268,000	12,635,000
Income taxes	7,479,000	8,767,000	6,444,000
Net income	$ 11,361,000	$ 10,501,000	$ 6,191,000
Net income per share	$1.69	$1.58	$.94

See notes to financial statements.

January 31,	1989	1988
Assets Current assets:		
Cash	$ 1,217,000	$ 571,000
Receivables	3,427,000	5,932,000
Merchandise inventories	129,735,000	133,608,000
Prepaid expenses and other current assets	4,510,000	4,127,000
Total current assets	138,889,000	144,238,000
Property:		
Land	589,000	589,000
Buildings	6,624,000	6,443,000
Furniture and fixtures	42,430,000	40,016,000
Leasehold improvements	28,070,000	27,564,000
Total	77,713,000	74,612,000
Less accumulated depreciation and amortization	37,372,000	34,906,000
Property—net	40,341,000	39,706,000
Other assets	985,000	680,000
Total	$180,215,000	$184,624,000
Liabilities Current liabilites:		
Accounts payable	$ 34,433,000	$ 48,129,000
Notes payable to banks	18,000,000	17,000,000
Accrued liabilities	10,111,000	10,168,000
Income taxes payable	—	637,000
Current portion of long-term debt	334,000	349,000
Total current liabilities	62,878,000	76,283,000
Deferred income taxes	4,201,000	3,887,000
Long-term debt	11,900,000	11,736,000
Equity Stockholders' equity:		
Preferred stock, $.10 par value; authorized 1,000,000 shares; outstanding, none		
Common stock, $.10 par value; authorized 14,000,000 shares; outstanding 6,596,745 shares in 1989 and 6,564,777 shares in 1988	660,000	656,000
Paid-in capital	14,803,000	14,488,000
Retained earnings	85,773,000	77,574,000
Total stockholders' equity	101,236,000	92,718,000
Total	$180,215,000	$184,624,000

See notes to financial statements.

✂

For the years ended January 31,	1989	1988	1987
Cash Flows from Operating Activities			
Net income	$11,361,000	$10,501,000	$6,191,000
Adjustments to reconcile net income to net cash provided by operating activities:			
Depreciation and amortization	6,286,000	5,954,000	5,844,000
Loss on disposal of fixed assets	1,196,000	980,000	920,000
Deferred taxes	314,000	467,000	2,723,000
Other assets	(305,000)	958,000	(1,121,000)
Changes in other working capital components:			
Receivables	2,505,000	(2,258,000)	(2,285,000)
Inventories	3,873,000	(21,910,000)	320,000
Prepaid expenses and other current assets	157,000	(965,000)	(212,000)
Accounts payable and accrued liabilities	(13,813,000)	18,650,000	(7,243,000)
Income taxes payable	(637,000)	587,000	(950,000)
Total adjustments	(424,000)	2,463,000	(2,004,000)
Net cash provided by operating activities	10,937,000	12,964,000	4,187,000
Cash Flows Used for Investing Activity			
Capital expenditures	(8,117,000)	(9,538,000)	(8,666,000)
Cash Flows from Financing Activities			
Proceeds from issuance of long term debt	—	—	10,000,000
Reduction in long term debt	(331,000)	(314,000)	(2,309,000)
Payment of dividends	(3,162,000)	(3,151,000)	(3,147,000)
Proceeds from exercise of stock options	319,000	81,000	149,000
Change in net borrowings under lines of credit agreements	1,000,000	—	(1,000,000)
Net cash (used for) provided by financing activities	(2,174,000)	(3,384,000)	3,693,000
Net Increase (Decrease) in Cash	646,000	42,000	(786,000)
Cash at Beginning of Year	571,000	529,000	1,315,000
Cash at End of Year	$ 1,217,000	$ 571,000	$ 529,000

Supplemental Disclosures of Cash Flow Information

✂

Cash Paid During the Year for			
Interest	$3,565,000	$2,442,000	$2,441,000
Income taxes	$8,339,000	$7,850,000	$4,970,000

See notes to financial statements.

For the years ended January 31,	Common Stock	Paid-in Capital	Retained Earnings
Balance, January 31, 1986	$654,000	$14,260,000	$67,180,000
Exercise of stock options	2,000	147,000	—
Net income	—	—	6,191,000
Cash dividends — $.48 per share	—	—	(3,147,000)
Balance, January 31, 1987	$656,000	$14,407,000	$70,224,000
Exercise of stock options	—	76,000	—
Tax benefit related to stock options	—	5,000	—
Net income	—	—	10,501,000
Cash dividends — $.48 per share	—	—	(3,151,000)
Balance, January 31, 1988	$656,000	$14,488,000	$77,574,000
Exercise of stock options	4,000	310,000	—
Tax benefit related to stock options	—	5,000	—
Net income	—	—	11,361,000
Cash dividends — $.48 per share	—	—	(3,162,000)
Balance, January 31, 1989	$660,000	$14,803,000	$85,773,000

See notes to financial statements.

Note 1: Summary of Accounting Policies

Principles of Consolidation — *The consolidated financial statements include the accounts of all subsidiaries, all of which are wholly-owned. Intercompany accounts and transactions are eliminated.*

Inventories — *Merchandise inventories are stated on the basis of the lower of cost or market, cost being determined on the first-in, first-out method and market generally considered to be current replacement cost. Store inventories are counted on a cycle basis throughout the year, and markdowns are taken currently on out-of-season and discontinued merchandise.*

Property — *Property is stated at cost less accumulated depreciation and amortization. Depreciation is computed using the straight-line method at rates based upon the estimated lives of the assets. Leasehold improvements are amortized over the estimated physical life of the property or over the term of the lease, whichever is shorter.*

Net Income Per Share — *Net income per share is computed based on the weighted average number of shares of common stock and equivalents outstanding during the year: 6,732,047 in 1989, 6,656,719 in 1988 and 6,605,744 in 1987.*

Note 2: Short-Term Borrowings

The Company has agreements for unsecured lines of credit totaling $59,000,000 with several commercial banks. Short-term borrowings under the agreements consist of demand or 90-day notes. The Company's agreement with each bank has no compensating balances requirement. The daily weighted average of borrowings outstanding during the years ended January 31, 1989 and 1988 were approximately $33,000,000 and $17,000,000, and the interest rates averaged approximately 7.7% and 7.4%, respectively. The maximum outstanding borrowings at any point in time during fiscal 1989 and 1988 were $56,000,000 and $24,000,000, respectively. The borrowings under these lines of credit at January 31, 1989 and 1988 were $18,000,000 and $17,000,000, respectively.

Note 3: Long-Term Debt

Long-term debt at January 31, 1989 and 1988 consisted of the following:

	1989	1988
6% to 7% first mortgage industrial revenue bonds payable in annual amounts ranging from $125,000 to $230,000	$ 1,455,000	$ 1,760,000
8.6% note payable to bank, due at maturity in May, 1990	10,000,000	10,000,000
Other notes payable due in annual amounts of approximately $104,000 with maturities of up to 7 years	779,000	325,000
	12,234,000	12,085,000
Less current portion	334,000	349,000
Total long-term debt	$11,900,000	$11,736,000

The industrial revenue bonds are repayable in the form of rent on the facilities leased, which have been accounted for as purchases and are being depreciated over their useful lives. One bond matured in fiscal 1989 and the remaining two bonds mature in fiscal 1992 and 1998. The capitalized assets which are pledged with respect to these bonds have an original cost of $4,544,000 and a net book value of $1,713,000 at January 31, 1989. Aggregate payments of principal and interest in future periods are $1,843,000. Notes payable to others relate to the acquisition of a small retail fabric chain in fiscal 1986, and a fabric store in fiscal 1989 for which the Company paid $374,000 in cash and assumed $540,000 in liabilities. The note payable to bank was obtained in June, 1986 and is unsecured, with interest payments due quarterly and the entire payable balance due at maturity in May, 1990. This note provides, among other things, for a limitation on the payment of cash dividends. At January 31, 1989, there was approximately $4,568,000 available for additional dividends.

Maturities of long-term debt for the succeeding five fiscal years are as follows: 1990, $334,000 (included in current liabilities); 1991, $10,339,000; 1992, $344,000; 1993, $229,000; 1994, $229,000, and thereafter $635,000.

Note 4: Capital Stock

The Company has two stock option plans which provide for the granting of 1,250,000 options to officers and key employees. The incentive stock option plan provides for the granting of 750,000 options. During fiscal 1988, holders of these options elected to exchange 231,000 of these incentive stock options for non-qualified stock options that have an exercise price of $12.00 There were 3,150 incentive stock options outstanding at January 31, 1989. These options expire five to ten years from the date of the grant.

During fiscal year 1988, the Company authorized a new stock option plan consisting of 500,000 non-qualified stock options. The options granted allow employees to purchase shares of the Company's common stock for the market value on the date of grant. Generally, the stock options become exercisable in three equal installments commencing one year after date of grant. These options expire ten years from the date of grant.

At January 31, 1989, there were 437,042 options outstanding under both of these plans and 434,104 were available for future grant. Changes in stock options for the years ended January 31, 1989 and 1988 are summarized below:

	1989	1988
Outstanding, beginning of year	467,160	256,710
Granted ($12.00 to $18.13 per share)	8,000	226,750
Exercised ($4.10 to $12.00 per share)	(31,968)	(7,800)
Cancelled ($12.00 per share)	(6,150)	(8,500)
Outstanding January 31, ($4.10 to $18.13 per share)	437,042	467,160
Exercisable January 31, ($4.10 to $12.00 per share)	247,975	154,742

Note 5: Commitments

Total rental expense for the years ended January 31, 1989, 1988, and 1987 was $35,362,000, $31,337,000 and $28,703,000, respectively. Contingent rentals based on sales are not significant. Most of the store leases require the Company to pay real estate taxes and certain other expenses, and some contain renewal options for various periods. Minimum future rentals under operating leases in effect at January 31, 1989 are summarized as follows:

1990	$29,968,000
1991	$27,581,000
1992	$25,127,000
1993	$23,007,000
1994	$20,618,000
1995-2009	$75,518,000

In fiscal 1987, the Company entered into consulting and non-competition agreements with certain former officers. The Company purchased, at less than market value, 98,110 stock options previously granted and agreed to make monthly payments to the former officers over periods not exceeding five years. Related costs of $476,000, $674,000 and $417,000 were recognized in 1989, 1988 and 1987 respectively, and a minimum of $887,000 will be recognized in those future periods during which consulting services will be received.

Note 6: Income Taxes

The provision for income taxes includes deferred amounts of $314,000, $467,000 and $2,723,000 in 1989, 1988 and 1987, respectively. These amounts relate primarily to the excess tax over book depreciation.

The effective income tax rates for 1989, 1988 and 1987 were 40%, 46% and 51%, respectively. The difference between the effective income tax rates and the statutory income tax rates is due primarily to state income and franchise taxes (net of Federal benefits).

In December 1987, the Financial Accounting Standards Board issued Statement No. 96 "Accounting for Income Taxes." The Statement is required to be adopted by the Company no later than the fiscal year ending January 31, 1991. The Company expects that the adjustment required, if any, in the year the Statement is adopted, will not be material to the Consolidated Financial Statements.

Note 7: Quarterly Financial Data for the Years Ended January 31, 1989, 1988 and 1987 (Unaudited)

				Three Months Ended
	April 30	July 31	October 31	January 31
1989				
Sales	$74,985,000	$71,975,000	$90,227,000	$100,823,000
Gross profit	$42,170,000	$39,844,000	$49,930,000	$ 51,843,000
Net income	$ 2,002,000	$ 454,000	$ 4,180,000	$ 4,725,000
Net income per share	$.30	$.07	$.62	$.70
1988				
Sales	$73,535,000	$69,712,000	$87,291,000	$ 91,942,000
Gross profit	$39,540,000	$37,150,000	$46,560,000	$ 48,854,000
Net income	$ 1,757,000	$ 404,000	$ 4,006,000	$ 4,334,000
Net income per share	$.27	$.06	$.61	$.64
1987				
Sales	$71,178,000	$69,341,000	$86,183,000	$ 89,664,000
Gross profit	$37,493,000	$36,158,000	$43,389,000	$ 43,074,000
Net income	$ 1,201,000	$ 115,000	$ 2,622,000	$ 2,253,000
Net income per share	$.18	$.02	$.40	$.34

To the Stockholders and Board of Directors of House of Fabrics, Inc. *We have audited the accompanying consolidated balance sheets of House of Fabrics, Inc. and subsidiaries as of January 31, 1989 and 1988 and the related consolidated statements of income, stockholders' equity and cash flows for each of the three years in the period ended January 31, 1989. These financial statements are the responsibility of the Company's management. Our responsibility is to express an opinion on these financial statements based on our audits.*

We conducted our audits in accordance with generally accepted auditing standards. Those standards require that we plan and perform the audit to obtain reasonable assurance about whether the financial statements are free of material misstatement. An audit includes examining, on a test basis, evidence supporting the amounts and disclosures in the financial statements. An audit also includes assessing the accounting principles used and significant estimates made by management, as well as evaluating the overall financial statement presentation. We believe that our audits provide a reasonable basis for our opinion.

In our opinion, the consolidated financial statements referred to above present fairly, in all material respects, the financial position of House of Fabrics, Inc. and subsidiaries as of January 31, 1989 and 1988 and the results of their operations and their cash flows for each of the three years in the period ended January 31, 1989 in conformity with generally accepted accounting principles.

Deloitte Haskins & Sells

Deloitte Haskins & Sells

Los Angeles, California
March 23, 1989

Recommended Readings

The following readings are suggested as an aid to those readers who want to pursue some topics in more depth than is possible in this book. Of course, many of the chapters have footnotes containing suggested readings on a particular topic. Therefore the specific chapters should be consulted for additional references.

There is a hazard in compiling a group of recommended readings. Inevitably, some worthwhile books or periodicals are overlooked. Moreover, such a list cannot include books published subsequent to the compilation here.

Professional journals are typically available in university libraries. The *Journal of Accountancy* emphasizes financial accounting and is directed at the practicing CPA. *Accounting Horizons* stresses current, practice-oriented articles in all areas of accounting. *Management Accounting* focuses on management accounting. The *Harvard Business Review* and *Fortune*, which are aimed at general managers, contain many articles on planning and control.

The Accounting Review and the *Journal of Accounting Research* cover all phases of accounting at a more theoretical level than the preceding publications.

The *Opinions* of the Accounting Principles Board are available from the American Institute of CPAs, 1211 Avenue of the Americas, New York, NY 10036. The institute also has a series of research studies on a variety of topics. The pronouncements of the Financial Accounting Standards Board are available from the board's office, 401 Merritt 7, P.O. Box 5116, Norwalk, CT 06865–5116.

The Financial Executives Institute, 10 Madison Avenue, P.O. Box 1938, Morristown, NJ 07960, and the National Association of Accountants, 10 Paragon Drive, P.O. Box 433, Montvale, NJ 07645–0433, have long lists of accounting research publications.

Books on elementary financial accounting are available from almost all major publishers. The next steps in the study of financial accounting are in books entitled *Intermediate Accounting* and then *Advanced Accounting*, which are available from Dryden Press, Richard D. Irwin, Inc., McGraw-Hill Book Co., Prentice Hall, Inc., South-Western Publishing Co., Wiley-Hamilton, and other publishers.

For the analysis and interpretation of financial statements, especially in relationship to the market prices of stocks and bonds, see W. H. Beaver, *Financial Reporting: An Accounting Revolution*, second edition, and G. Foster, *Financial Statement Analysis*, second edition, both published by Prentice Hall, Inc.

There are many books on elementary management accounting. Also, many books entitled *Cost Accounting* stress a management approach. For examples, see C. T. Horngren and G. L. Sundem, *Introduction to Management Accounting*, the companion to this book. Also see *Cost Accounting: A Managerial Emphasis* by C. T. Horngren and G. Foster. Both are published by Prentice Hall, Inc.

Glossary

The italicized words within the definitions or explanations are also described in this glossary.

ACCELERATED DEPRECIATION (p. 323). Any *depreciation* method that writes off depreciable costs more quickly than the ordinary *straight-line method* based on expected useful life.

ACCOUNT (p. 14). Detailed summary of the changes in a particular *asset, liability,* or *owners' equity.*

ACCOUNT FORMAT (p. 136). A classified *balance sheet* with the *assets* at the left.

ACCOUNTANT'S OPINION (p. 22). See *independent opinion.*

ACCOUNTING CYCLE (p. 157). The several-stage process by which accountants produce an *entity's* financial statements for a specific period of time.

ACCOUNTING EVENT (p. 8). See *transaction.*

ACCOUNTING POLICY MAKING (p. 710). Choosing the accounting measurement and disclosure methods required for financial reporting.

ACCOUNTING PRINCIPLES BOARD (APB) (p. 61). The top private-sector regulatory body, which existed from 1959 to 1973, when it was succeeded by the *Financial Accounting Standards Board.*

ACCOUNTING SYSTEM (p. 626). A set of records, procedures, and equipment that routinely deal with the events affecting the financial performance and position of the *entity.*

ACCOUNTING TRANSACTION (p. 8). See *transaction.*

ACCOUNTS PAYABLE (p. 12). A *liability* that results from a purchase of goods or services on *open account.*

ACCOUNTS RECEIVABLE (p. 220). Amounts owed to an *entity* by customers as a result of delivering goods or services and extending credit in the ordinary course of business.

ACCRUAL BASIS (p. 50). Recognizes the impact of *transactions* on the financial statements in the time periods when *revenues* and *expenses* occur.

ACCRUE (p. 126). Accumulation of a receivable or payable during a given period even though no explicit *transaction* occurs.

ACCUMULATED DEPRECIATION (p. 96). The cumulative sum of all *depreciation* recognized since the date of acquisition of the particular *assets* described.

ADDITIONAL PAID-IN CAPITAL (p. 17). See *paid-in capital in excess of par value.*

ADJUSTING ENTRIES (p. 123). See *adjustments.*

ADJUSTMENTS (p. 123). The key final process (before the computation of ending account *balances*) of assigning the financial effects of *transactions* to the appropriate time periods.

AFFILIATED COMPANY (p. 547). A company that has 20% to 50% of its voting shares owned by another company.

AGING OF ACCOUNTS (p. 235). An analysis of the elements of individual *accounts receivable* according to the time elapsed after the dates of billing.

AICPA (p. 61). American Institute of Certified Public Accountants, the leading organization of the auditors of corporate financial reports.

ALLOWANCE FOR BAD DEBTS (p. 223). See *allowance for doubtful accounts*.

ALLOWANCE FOR DEPRECIATION (p. 96). See *accumulated depreciation*.

ALLOWANCE FOR DOUBTFUL ACCOUNTS (p. 223). A contra asset account that offsets total receivables by an estimated amount that will probably not be collected.

ALLOWANCE FOR UNCOLLECTIBLE ACCOUNTS (p. 223). See *allowance for doubtful accounts*.

ALLOWANCE METHOD (p. 222). This method of accounting for *bad debt* losses makes use of estimates and the presence of a *contra asset account, allowance for doubtful accounts*.

AMORTIZATION (p. 318). The systematic reduction of a lump-sum amount.

APB (p. 61). See *Accounting Principles Board*.

APB OPINIONS (p. 61). A series of thirty-one Opinions of the *Accounting Principles Board* issued during 1962–73, many of which are still "the accounting law of the land."

APPROPRIATED RETAINED INCOME (p. 464). Restrictions of *retained income* earmarked on the books of *account* and in financial statements for some specific or general purpose.

ARREARAGES (p. 443). See *dividend arrearages*.

ASSETS (p. 6). Economic resources that are expected to benefit future cash inflows or help reduce future cash outflows.

ASSET TURNOVER (p. 685). See *total asset turnover*.

AUDIT (p. 22). An examination that is made in accordance with generally accepted auditing standards. Its aim is to give credibility to financial statements.

AUDIT COMMITTEE (p. 629). A committee of the board of directors that oversees the *internal accounting controls*, financial statements, and financial affairs of the *corporation*.

AUDITOR'S REPORT (p. 22). See *independent opinion*.

AVERAGE COLLECTION PERIOD (p. 236). Average *accounts receivable* divided by sales on account.

BAD DEBT RECOVERIES (p. 226). *Accounts receivable* that were written off as uncollectible but then collected at a later date.

BAD DEBTS (p. 221). Receivables determined to be uncollectible because debtors are unable or unwilling to pay their debts.

BALANCE (p. 84). The difference between the total left-side and right-side amounts in an *account* at any particular time.

BALANCE SHEET (p. 6). A photograph of financial position at an instant of time.

BALANCE SHEET EQUATION (p. 6). *Assets = Liabilities + Owners' Equity.*

BANK RECONCILIATION (p. 230). An analysis that explains any differences existing between the cash balance shown by the depositor and that shown by the bank.

BASKET PURCHASE (p. 320). The acquisition of two or more types of *assets* for a lump-sum cost.

BEARER INSTRUMENT (p. 379). See *unregistered instrument*.

BENCH MARK (p. 679). General rules of thumb specifying appropriate levels for financial ratios.

BETTERMENT (p. 336). See *improvement*.

BONDS (p. 377). Formal certificates of indebtedness that are typically accompanied by (1) a promise to pay interest in cash at a specified annual rate plus (2) a promise to pay the principal at a specific maturity date.

BOOK OF ORIGINAL ENTRY (p. 85). A formal chronological record (usually called a *journal*) of the effects of the *entity's transactions* on the *balances* in pertinent *accounts*.

BOOK VALUE (p. 96). The *balance* of an *account* shown on the books, net of any *contra accounts*. For example, the book value of equipment is its acquisition cost minus *accumulated depreciation*.

BOOK VALUE PER SHARE OF COMMON STOCK (p. 459). *Stockholders' equity* attributable to *common stock* divided by the number of shares outstanding.

CALLABLE BONDS (p. 379). *Bonds* subject to redemption before maturity at the option of the issuer.

CALL PREMIUM (p. 379). A redemption price in excess of *par*.

CAPITAL (p. 17). In accounting, this word is too general by itself. In most cases, capital implies *owners' equity*. However, see *capitalization*. Money generated by *long-term debt* is also often called capital. *Owners' equities* of *proprietorships* and *partnerships* are often identified as capital.

CAPITAL EXPENDITURE (p. 335). An acquisition with long-term effects intended to benefit more than the current *fiscal year*.

CAPITAL IMPROVEMENT (p. 336). See *improvement*.

CAPITALIZATION (p. 687). *Owners' equity* plus *long-term debt*.

CAPITALIZATION STRUCTURE (p. 687). Same as *capitalization*.

CAPITALIZED (p. 320). A cost that is added to an asset, as distinguished from being expensed immediately.

CAPITAL LEASE (p. 412). A *lease* that transfers substantially all the risks and benefits of ownership. Such leases are equivalent to installment sales.

CAPITAL MAINTENANCE (p. 725). See *financial capital maintenance* and *physical capital maintenance*.

CAPITAL STOCK CERTIFICATE (p. 16). See *stock certificate*.

CAPITAL STRUCTURE (p. 687). Same as *capitalization*.

CARRYING AMOUNT (p. 96). Same as *book value*.

CARRYING VALUE (p. 96). Same as *book value*.

CASH BASIS (p. 50). Recognizes the impact of *transactions* on the financial statements only when cash is received or disbursed.

CASH DISCOUNTS (p. 216). Reductions of invoice prices awarded for prompt payment.

CASH EQUIVALENTS (p. 219). Highly liquid short-term investments that can easily be converted into cash with little delay.

CASH FLOW (p. 501). Usually refers to net cash provided by operating activities.

CASH FLOWS FROM OPERATING ACTIVITIES (p. 497). The first major section of the *statement of cash flows*.

CERTIFICATE (p. 22). See *independent opinion*.

CERTIFICATE OF DEPOSIT (p. 533). Short-term obligations of banks.

CERTIFIED PUBLIC ACCOUNTANT (p. 21). In the U.S., an accountant earns this designation by a combination of education, qualifying experience, and the passing of a two and one-half day written national examination.

CHARGE (p. 84). A word often used instead of *debit*.

CHART OF ACCOUNTS (p. 88). A list of all *account* titles of an *entity* together with some numbering or coding thereof.

CHECK REGISTER (p. 656). A cash disbursements journal used in a *voucher system*. Also is used as a synonym for cash disbursements journal.

CLASSIFIED BALANCE SHEET (p. 135). A *statement of financial position* with its items grouped into various subcategories.

CLOSING ENTRIES (p. 173). Entries that transfer the *revenues, expenses,* and *dividends* balances from their respective accounts to the *retained income* account.

CLOSING THE BOOKS (p. 173). The final step taken at the end of a given year to facilitate the recording of the next year's *transactions*.

COMMERCIAL PAPER (p. 533). Short-term *notes payable* issued by large *corporations* with top credit ratings.

COMMON-SIZE STATEMENTS (p. 677). Financial statements expressed in *component percentages*.

COMMON STOCK (p. 19). Stock representing the class of owners having a "residual" ownership of a *corporation*.

COMPARATIVE FINANCIAL STATEMENTS (p. 159). Statements that present data for two or more reporting periods.

COMPENSATING BALANCES (p. 219). Required minimum cash *balances* on deposit of the money borrowed from banks.

COMPONENT PERCENTAGES (p. 677). Analysis and presentation of financial statements in percentage form to aid comparability.

COMPOUND ENTRY (p. 90). A single accounting entry that affects more than two *accounts*.

COMPOUND INTEREST (p. 400). For any period, *interest* rate multiplied by a *principal* amount that is changed each interest period by the previous unpaid interest. The unpaid interest is added to the principal to become the principal for the new period.

COMPOUND INTEREST METHOD (p. 385). See *effective-interest amortization*.

CONSERVATISM (p. 275). Selecting the method of measurement that yields the gloomiest immediate financial results.

CONSIGNMENT (p. 648). Goods shipped for future sale, title remaining with the shipper (consignor), for which the receiver (consignee), upon his acceptance, is accountable. The goods are part of the consignor's inventory until sold.

CONSISTENCY (p. 268). Conformity from period to period with unchanging policies and procedures.

CONSOLIDATED STATEMENTS (p. 540). Combinations of the financial positions and *earnings* reports of the *parent company* with those of various *subsidiaries* into an overall report as a single *entity*.

CONSTANT DOLLARS (p. 725). Those monetary units restated so as to represent the same general purchasing power.

CONTINGENT LIABILITY (p. 392). A potential *liability* that depends on a future event arising out of a past *transaction*.

CONTINUITY CONVENTION (p. 102). The assumption that in all ordinary situations an *entity* persists indefinitely.

CONTRA ACCOUNT (p. 96). A separate but related *account* that offsets a companion account. Examples are *accumulated depreciation* and *allowance for doubtful accounts*.

CONTRA ASSET (p. 96). A *contra account* that offsets an *asset*.

CONTRACTUAL RATE (p. 377). See *nominal interest rate*.

CONVERTIBLE BONDS (p. 380). *Bonds* that may, at the holder's option, be exchanged for other securities.

COPYRIGHTS (p. 341). Exclusive rights conveyed by federal statute to reproduce and sell a book, design, pamphlet, drawing, or other creations, and to forbid the publication of excerpts or other imitations.

CORPORATE PROXY (p. 439). A written authority granted by individual shareholders to others to cast the shareholders' vote.

CORPORATION (p. 15). An organization that is an "artificial being" created by individual state laws.

COST-BENEFIT CRITERION (p. 103). As a system is changed, its expected additional benefits should exceed its expected additional *costs*.

COST METHOD FOR INVESTMENTS (p. 538). The method whereby the initial investment is recorded at cost and *dividends* received are recorded as *revenues*.

COST OF GOODS SOLD (p. 59). Beginning inventory plus purchases minus ending inventory.

COST OF SALES (p. 59). See *cost of goods sold*.

COST RECOVERY (p. 44). The concept that helps determine whether resources such as *inventories*, prepayments, and equipment should be carried forward to future periods as *assets* or written off to the current period as *expenses*.

COUPON INTEREST RATE (p. 377). See *nominal interest rate*.

COVENANT (p. 379). A provision stated in a *bond*, usually to protect the bondholders' interests.

CREDIT (p. 84). In accounting, this word means one thing and one thing only—"right," as distinguished from "left." It typically refers to an entry in an *account* or the *balance* of an account.

CROSS-SECTIONAL COMPARISON (p. 679). Comparison of a company's financial ratios with the ratios of other companies or with industry averages.

CUMULATIVE DIVIDENDS (p. 443). Undeclared *dividends* on *preferred stock* for a particular period that accumulate as a claim upon past and future *earnings*.

CURRENT ASSETS (p. 135). Cash plus *assets* that are expected to be converted to cash or sold or consumed during the next twelve months or as a part of the normal *operating cycle*.

CURRENT COST (p. 725). Generally, the cost to replace an asset.

CURRENT-COST/CONSTANT-DOLLAR METHOD (p. 730). An overall method of accounting that is based on *current costs* and monetary units restated to represent uniform purchasing power.

CURRENT-COST METHOD (p. 727). A measurement method using current costs and nominal dollars.

CURRENT-COST/NOMINAL-DOLLAR METHOD (p. 727). An overall method of accounting that is based on *current costs* and monetary units not restated for fluctuations in the general purchasing power of the monetary unit.

CURRENT LIABILITIES (p. 135). *Liabilities* that fall due within the coming year or within the normal *operating cycle* if longer than a year.

CURRENT RATIO (p. 135). *Current assets* divided by *current liabilities*.

CURRENT YIELD (p. 379). Usually refers to current *interest* payments divided by the market price of a *bond*. Also see *dividend-yield ratio*.

CUTOFF ERROR (p. 648). Failure to record *transactions* in the correct time period.

DATA PROCESSING (p. 101). The totality of the procedures used to record, analyze, store, and report on chosen activities.

DEBENTURE (p. 378). A debt security with a general claim against all *assets* rather than a specific claim against particular assets.

DEBIT (p. 84). In accounting, this word means one thing and one thing only—"left." It typically refers to an entry in an *account* or the *balance* of an account.

DEBT LEVERAGE (p. 687). See *trading on the equity*.

DEBT-TO-EQUITY RATIO (p. 394). Total *liabilities* divided by total *stockholders' equity*.

DEBT-TO-TOTAL-ASSETS RATIO (p. 394). Total *liabilities* divided by total *assets*.

DEDUCTIBLE ITEMS (p. 586). *Expenses* that may be subtracted from *revenues* to determine taxable *income*.

DEFERRAL METHOD (p. 601). A method of accounting for *tax credits* associated with business investments whereby the tax savings are spread over the useful life of the *asset*.

DEFERRED CHARGE (p. 342). An *expenditure* not recognized as a cost of operations of the period in which incurred but carried forward to be written off in one or more future periods.

DEFERRED CREDIT (p. 125). Often used as a synonym for *unearned revenue*. In its bookkeeping application, the term refers to an amount that is classified as a *liability* that will eventually be transferred as a *credit* to *revenue* or a *credit* to *expense*.

DEFERRED INCOME (p. 126). See *unearned revenue*.

DEFERRED REVENUE (p. 125). See *unearned revenue*.

DEPLETION (p. 340). Gradual exhaustion of the original amounts of natural resources acquired.

DEPRECIABLE VALUE (p. 321). The difference between the total acquisition cost of plant and equipment and the predicted *residual value* at the end of useful life.

DEPRECIATION (p. 45). The systematic allocation of the acquisition cost of plant and equipment to the *expense* accounts of the particular periods that benefit from the use of the *assets*.

DEPRECIATION SCHEDULE (p. 323). The listing of depreciation amounts for each year of an asset's useful life.

DILUTION (p. 460). Reduction in *stockholders' equity* per share or *earnings per share* that arises from some changes among shareholders' proportional interests.

DIRECT METHOD (p. 497). In a *statement of cash flows*, the method that calculates net cash provided by operating activities as collections minus operating disbursements.

DISBURSEMENT VOUCHER (p. 656). See *voucher*.

DISCOUNT AMORTIZATION (p. 384). The spreading of *bond discount* over the life of the bonds as *expense*.

DISCOUNT ON BONDS (p. 380). The excess of *face amount* over the proceeds upon issuance.

DISCOUNT RATE (p. 402). The interest rate used in determining *present value*.

DISPOSAL VALUE (p. 321). See *residual value*. This term also has a second, more general, meaning: the expected net cash value from sale of an *asset* at any given date.

DIVIDEND ARREARAGES (p. 443). Accumulated unpaid *dividends* on *preferred stock*.

DIVIDEND-PAYOUT RATIO (p. 67). Common *dividends* per share divided by common *earnings per share*.

DIVIDENDS (p. 52). Distributions of cash (or other *assets*) to stockholders that reduce *retained income*. See also *stock dividend*.

DIVIDEND-YIELD RATIO (p. 66). Common *dividends* per share divided by the market price per share of *common stock*.

DOUBLE-DECLINING-BALANCE DEPRECIATION (DDB) (p. 323). A form of *accelerated depreciation* that results in first-year *depreciation* being twice the amount of *straight-line depreciation* when zero *residual value* is assumed.

DOUBLE-ENTRY SYSTEM (p. 83). The method usually followed for recording *transactions*, whereby at least two *accounts* are always affected by each transaction.

EARNINGS (p. 40). The excess of *revenues* over *expenses*.

EARNINGS DILUTION (p. 460). See *dilution*.

EARNINGS PER SHARE (EPS) (p. 65). Net income divided by the number of common shares outstanding. However, where *preferred stock* exists, the preferred *dividends* must be deducted in order to compute the net income applicable to *common stock*. See also *primary EPS* and *fully diluted EPS*.

EFFECTIVE-INTEREST AMORTIZATION (p. 385). A method for amortizing *discount* (or *premium*) *on bonds* that uses a constant interest rate.

EFFECTIVE INTEREST RATE (p. 380). The market rate on the day of issuance of a *bond*. It is the rate of yield to maturity, as contrasted with the *coupon interest rate*. Thus, if the issuance price is greater than the *face amount* of the bond, the effective rate is lower than the *coupon rate*.

EFFICIENT CAPITAL MARKET (p. 690). One in which market prices "fully reflect" all information available at a given time.

ENTITY (p. 7). An organization or a section of an organization that stands apart from other organizations and individuals as a separate economic unit.

EQUITY METHOD (p. 538). Accounting for an investment at acquisition cost adjusted for the investor's share of *dividends* and *earnings* or losses of the investee subsequent to the date of investment.

EXPENDITURE (p. 335). Cash or other resources paid, or to be paid, for an *asset* purchased or service acquired.

EXPENSES (p. 40). Decreases in *owners' equity* that relate to the delivery of goods or services to customers.

EXPLICIT TRANSACTIONS (p. 124). Events such as cash receipts and disbursements, credit purchases, and credit sales that trigger nearly all day-to-day routine entries.

EXTRAORDINARY ITEM (p. 473). An extremely unusual and infrequent *expense* or *revenue* that is shown together with its income tax effects separately from *income* from continuing operations on an *income statement*. Examples are losses from earthquakes and gains or losses on the retirement of *bonds*.

FACE AMOUNT (p. 377). The *principal* as indicated on the certificates of *bonds* or other debt instruments.

FASB (p. 61). *Financial Accounting Standards Board.*

FASB STATEMENTS (p. 61). Official rules and regulations regarding external financial reporting issued in a numbered series by the *Financial Accounting Standards Board.*

FIFO (p. 267). See *first-in, first-out.*

FINANCIAL ACCOUNTING (p. 4). Serves external decision makers, such as stockholders, suppliers, banks, and government agencies. Distinguish from *management accounting.*

FINANCIAL ACCOUNTING STANDARDS BOARD (FASB) (p. 61). The primary regulatory body over accounting principles and practices. It is an independent creature of the private sector.

FINANCIAL CAPITAL MAINTENANCE (p. 725). The quantity of financial resources (usually *historical costs*), as distinguished from physical resources of operating capability, to be recovered before *income* emerges.

FINANCIAL LEVERAGE (p. 687). See *trading on the equity.*

FINANCIAL MANAGEMENT (p. 491). Is mainly concerned with where to get cash and how to use cash for the benefit of the *entity* (that is, obtaining and investing the needed *capital*). Compare with *operating management.*

FINANCIAL STATEMENT ANALYSIS (p. 672). Using financial statements to assess a company's position and prospects.

FIRST-IN, FIRST-OUT (FIFO) (p. 267). This method of accounting for inventory assumes that the units acquired earliest are used or sold first.

FISCAL PERIOD (p. 39). See *fiscal year.*

FISCAL YEAR (p. 39). The year established for accounting purposes that ends on some date other than December 31.

FIXED ASSETS (p. 319). Tangible *assets* or physical items that can be seen and touched, often called property, plant, and equipment or plant assets.

FLOW-THROUGH METHOD (p. 601). A method of accounting for *tax credits* associated with the purchase of business investments whereby the entire tax savings increases the net income for the year of purchase.

F.O.B. (p. 260). "Free on board," meaning the buyer bears the cost of shipping from the F.O.B. point specified by the seller to the receiving point of the buyer.

FOREIGN CORRUPT PRACTICES ACT (p. 628). A federal law that requires adequate *internal controls*, among other requirements.

FRANCHISE (p. 341). A privilege granted by a government, manufacturer, or distributor to sell a product or service in accordance with specific conditions.

FREIGHT IN (p. 260). An additional cost of the goods acquired during the period, which is often shown in the purchases section of an *income statement.*

FREIGHT OUT (p. 260). The transportation costs borne by the seller of merchandise and often shown as a "shipping expense."

FULLY DILUTED EARNINGS PER SHARE (p. 467). An *earnings-per-share* figure on *common stock* that assumes that all outstanding *convertible securities* and *stock options* are exchanged for common stock at the beginning of the period.

FUTURE VALUE (p. 400). The amount accumulated, including *principal* and *interest.*

GAAP (p. 7). See *generally accepted accounting principles.*

GEARING (p. 688). See *trading on the equity.*

GENERAL CONTROLS (p. 637). *Internal accounting controls* that focus on the organization and operation of the data-processing activity.

GENERAL JOURNAL (p. 85). A *book of original entry.*

General Ledger (p. 97). The record that contains the group of *accounts* that supports the amounts shown in the major financial statement.

General Price Index (p. 729). An index that compares the average price of a group of goods and services at one date with the average price of a similar group at another date.

Generally Accepted Accounting Principles (GAAP) (p. 7). A technical term including both broad concepts or guidelines and detailed practices. It includes all conventions, rules, and procedures that together make up accepted accounting practice at a given time.

Going Concern Convention (p. 102). See *continuity convention*.

Goodwill (p. 341). The excess of the cost of an acquired company over the sum of the fair market value of its identifiable individual *assets* less the *liabilities*.

Gross Margin (p. 138). Synonym for *gross profit*.

Gross Margin Percentage (p. 139). Same as *gross profit percentage*.

Gross Profit (p. 137). The difference between sales *revenue* and the cost of inventories sold.

Gross Profit Percentage (p. 139). *Gross profit* divided by sales.

Gross Profit Test (p. 212). The comparing of *gross profit percentages* to detect any phenomenon worth investigating.

Historical Cost (p. 725). The amount originally paid to acquire an *asset*.

Historical-Cost/Constant-Dollar Method (p. 728). An overall method of accounting that is based on *historical costs* restated in monetary units representing uniform purchasing power.

Historical-Cost/Nominal-Dollar Method (p. 726). An overall method of accounting that is based on *historical costs* not restated for fluctuations in the general purchasing power of the monetary unit.

Holding Gains (or Losses) (p. 728). Increases (or decreases) in the *replacement cost* (or other appropriate measure of current value) of the *assets* held during the current period.

Implicit Interest (p. 391). An *interest* expense that is not explicitly recognized in a loan agreement.

Implicit Transactions (p. 124). Events (like the passage of time) that are temporarily ignored in day-to-day recording procedures and are recognized via end-of-period *adjustments*.

Imprest Basis (p. 233). A method for accounting for a particular amount of cash, usually petty cash.

Improvement (p. 336). A *capital expenditure* that is intended to add to the future benefits from an existing *fixed asset*.

Imputed Interest (p. 391). See *implicit interest*.

Imputed Interest Rate (p. 391). The market *interest* rate that equates the proceeds from a loan with the present value of the loan payments.

Income (p. 40). The excess of *revenues* over *expenses*.

Income Statement (p. 46). A report of all *revenues* and *expenses* pertaining to a specific time period.

Indenture (p. 379). See *trust indenture*.

Independent Opinion (p. 22). The accountant's stamp of approval on management's financial statements, based on the findings of an *audit*.

Indirect Method (p. 502). In a *statement of cash flows*, the method that reconciles net income to net cash provided by operating activities.

Input Controls (p. 637). *Internal accounting controls* that help guard against the entry of false or erroneous data.

Intangible Assets (p. 319). Rights or economic benefits that are not physical in nature. Examples are *franchises, patents, trademarks, copyrights,* and *goodwill*.

INTEREST (p. 400). The cost of using money; the rental charge for cash.

INTEREST COVERAGE (p. 690). *Income* before *interest expense* and income taxes divided by interest expense.

INTERIM PERIODS (p. 39). The time spans established for accounting purposes that are less than a year.

INTERNAL ACCOUNTING CONTROL (p. 627). Methods and procedures that are mainly concerned with the authorization of *transactions*, safeguarding of *assets*, and accuracy of the financial records.

INTERNAL CONTROL (p. 626). Refers to both internal administrative control and *internal accounting control*.

INTERPERIOD TAX ALLOCATION (p. 592). A method that measures reported income as if it were subject to the full current tax rate even though a more advantageous accounting method was used for tax purposes.

INVENTORY SHRINKAGE (p. 639). Difference between (a) the value of inventory that would occur if there were no pilferage, misclassifications, breakage, and clerical errors and (b) the value of inventory when it is physically counted.

INVENTORY TURNOVER (p. 279). The *cost of goods sold* divided by the average inventory at cost.

INWARD TRANSPORTATION (p. 260). See *freight in*.

JOURNAL ENTRY (p. 87). An analysis in a journal of the effect of a *transaction* on the *accounts*, usually accompanied by an explanation.

KEYING OF ENTRIES (p. 88). The process of numbering or otherwise specifically identifying each *journal entry* and each *posting*.

LAST-IN, FIRST-OUT (LIFO) (p. 267). This inventory method assumes that the units acquired most recently are used or sold first.

LEASE (p. 411). A contract whereby an owner (lessor) grants the use of property to a second party (lessee) for rental payments.

LEASEHOLD (p. 339). The right to use a *fixed asset* for a specified period of time, typically beyond one year.

LEASEHOLD IMPROVEMENTS (p. 339). *Fixed assets* acquired by a lessee, such as installation of new fixtures, panels, and walls that may not be removed from the premises when a lease expires.

LEDGER (p. 82). Group of related *accounts* kept up to date in a systematic manner.

LEVERAGING (p. 688). See *trading on the equity*.

LIABILITIES (p. 6). Obligations of the organization to outsiders (nonowners). Probable future sacrifices of economic benefits stemming from present legal, equitable, or constructive obligations of a particular enterprise to transfer *assets* or provide services to other entities in the future as a result of past *transactions* or events affecting the enterprise.

LICENSES (p. 341). Privileges granted by a government, manufacturer, or distributor to sell a product or services in accordance with specified conditions.

LIFO (p. 267). See *last-in, first-out*.

LIFO INCREMENT (p. 272). See *LIFO layer*.

LIFO LAYER (p. 272). A separately identifiable additional segment of *LIFO* inventory.

LIFO POOL (p. 272). See *LIFO layer*.

LIFO RESERVE (p. 273). The difference between a company's inventory valued at *LIFO* and what it would be under *FIFO*.

LIMITED LIABILITY (p. 16). Corporate creditors ordinarily have claims against the corporate *assets* only. Therefore the stockholders as individuals do not have liability beyond their original investment in the *corporation*.

LINE OF CREDIT (p. 371). An agreement with a bank to automatically provide short-term loans up to some preestablished maximum.

LIQUIDATING VALUE (p. 444). A measure of the preference as to *assets* of various claims against a *corporation* that is facing *liquidation*, that is, the sale of all the *entity's assets*.

LIQUIDATION (p. 57). Payment of a debt, or the conversion of *assets* into cash, or the complete sale of assets and settlement of claims when the *entity* is terminated.

LIQUIDITY (p. 673). See *short-term liquidity*.

LONG-LIVED ASSETS (p. 318). Resources that are held for an extended time, such as land, buildings, equipment, natural resources, and *patents*.

LONG-TERM DEBT (p. 369). See *long-term liabilities*.

LONG-TERM DEBT TO EQUITY RATIO (p. 394). Total *long-term debt* divided by total *stockholders' equity*.

LONG-TERM LIABILITIES (p. 369). Obligations that fall due beyond one year from the balance sheet date.

LONG-TERM SOLVENCY (p. 673). An organization's ability to generate enough cash to repay *long-term debts* as they mature.

LOWER OF COST OR MARKET (p. 275). The superimposition of a market-price test on an inventory cost method.

MACRS (p. 587). See *Modified Accelerated Cost Recovery System*.

MANAGEMENT ACCOUNTING (p. 4). Services internal decision makers (i.e., executives and managers within an organization), as distinguished from *financial accounting*.

MANAGEMENT REPORTS (p. 627). Explicit statements in annual reports concerning management's responsibilities for its financial statements.

MANAGEMENT'S DISCUSSION AND ANALYSIS (MD&A) (p. 679). A required section of annual reports that concentrates on explaining the major changes in the income statement and the major changes in liquidity and capital resources.

MARKETABLE SECURITIES (p. 534). Any notes, *bonds*, or stocks that can readily be sold via public markets. The term is often used as a synonym for *short-term investments*.

MARKET INTEREST RATE (p. 380). See *effective interest rate*.

MATCHING (p. 43). The essence of the *accrual basis* whereby *revenue* and *expenses* are assigned to a particular period for which a measurement of *income* is desired.

MATCHING AND COST RECOVERY (p. 44). The procedure of accrual accounting whereby *expenses* either are directly attributed to related *revenues* (*matching*) of a given period or are otherwise regarded as costs that will not be recovered from revenue in future periods. In short, cost recovery is the justification for carrying *unexpired costs* as *assets* rather than writing them off as expenses. Also see *cost recovery* and *matching*.

MATERIALITY (p. 103). See *materiality convention*.

MATERIALITY CONVENTION (p. 103). The characteristic attaching to a statement, fact, or item that, if omitted or misstated, would tend to mislead the user of the financial statements under consideration.

MINORITY INTERESTS (p. 543). The outside shareholders' interests, as opposed to the *parent's* interests, in a *subsidiary* corporation.

MODIFIED ACCELERATED COST RECOVERY SYSTEM (p. 587). The basis for computing depreciation for tax purposes in the United States. It is based on arbitrary "recovery" periods instead of useful lives.

MORTGAGE BOND (p. 378). A form of *long-term debt* that is secured by the pledge of specific property.

MULTIPLE-STEP INCOME STATEMENT (p. 137). An *income statement* that contains one or more subtotals that often highlight significant relationships.

NET BOOK VALUE (p. 96). Same as *book value*. Most often, *book value* is used rather than *net book value*.

NET WORKING CAPITAL (p. 135). See *working capital*.

NET WORTH (p. 6). See *owners' equity*.

NEUTRALITY (p. 714). Choosing accounting policies without attempting to achieve purposes other than measuring economic impact; freedom from bias.

NOMINAL ACCOUNTS (p. 177). Those *accounts* subject to periodic closing, such as *revenues* and *expenses*, frequently called *temporary accounts*.

NOMINAL DOLLARS (p. 725). Those dollars that are not restated for fluctuations in the general purchasing power of the monetary unit.

NOMINAL INTEREST RATE (p. 377). A contractual rate of *interest* paid on *bonds*.

NOTES PAYABLE (p. 6). Promissory notes that are evidence of a debt and state the terms of payment.

OBJECTIVITY (p. 102). Accuracy supported by convincing evidence that can be verified by independent accountants.

OPEN ACCOUNT (p. 12). Buying or selling on credit, usually by just an "authorized signature" of the buyer.

OPERATING CYCLE (p. 39). The time span during which cash is used to acquire goods and services, which in turn are sold to customers, who in turn pay for their purchases with cash.

OPERATING INCOME (p. 139). See *operating profit*.

OPERATING INCOME PERCENTAGE ON SALES (p. 685). *Operating income* divided by sales.

OPERATING LEASE (p. 412). A *lease* that should be accounted for by the lessee as ordinary rent *expenses*; no related property or *liabilities* are presented in the body of the lessee's *balance sheet*.

OPERATING MANAGEMENT (p. 491). Is mainly concerned with the major day-to-day activities that generate sales *revenue* (that is, using a given set of resources). Compare with *financial management*.

OPERATING PROFIT (p. 139). *Revenues* from operations minus all operating expenses, including *cost of goods sold*.

OPERATING STATEMENT (p. 59). See *income statement*.

OPINION (p. 22). See *independent opinion*.

OUTPUT CONTROLS (p. 637). *Internal accounting controls* that check output against input and ensure that only authorized persons receive reports.

OWNERS' EQUITY (p. 6). Residual interest in (that is, remaining claim against) the organization's *assets* after deducting *liabilities*. Obligations of the *entity* to the owners. The interest of stockholders or other owners in the assets of an enterprise; at any time it is the cumulative net result of past *transactions* and other events and circumstances affecting the enterprise.

PAID-IN CAPITAL (p. 17). The *owners' equity* measured by the total amounts invested at the inception of a business and subsequently.

PAID-IN CAPITAL IN EXCESS OF PAR VALUE (p. 17). Amount of *paid-in capital* that is greater than the *par value* of issued shares of stock.

PAR AMOUNT (p. 377). See *face amount*.

PAR VALUE (p. 17). The value printed on the face of the security certificate.

PARENT COMPANY (p. 540). A company owning more than 50% of the voting shares of another company, called the *subsidiary* company.

PARTNERSHIP (p. 15). A special form of organization that joins two or more individuals together as co-owners.

PATENTS (p. 340). Grants by the federal government to inventors, giving them the exclusive right to produce and sell their inventions for a period of seventeen years.

PERIODIC INVENTORY SYSTEM (p. 257). The method used where the *cost of goods sold* is computed periodically by relying solely on physical counts and not keeping day-to-day records of units sold or on hand.

PERMANENT ACCOUNTS (p. 177). See *real accounts*.

PERMANENT DIFFERENCES (p. 605). Differences between *pretax income* as reported to shareholders and taxable income as reported to the government that will not "reverse," or "turn around," in subsequent periods.

PERPETUAL INVENTORY SYSTEM (p. 257). A system that keeps a running, continuous record that tracks inventories and the *cost of goods sold* on a day-to-day basis.

PHYSICAL CAPITAL MAINTENANCE (p. 725). *Income* emerges only after recovering an amount that allows physical operating capability to be maintained.

P. & L. STATEMENT (p. 59). A synonym for *statement of profit and loss*. See *income statement*.

PLANT ASSETS (p. 319). See *fixed assets*.

POOLING-OF-INTEREST METHOD (p. 560). A way of accounting for the combination of two *corporations* based on the *book values* of the acquired company's *net assets*, as distinguished from the *purchase method*.

POSTING (p. 87). To record an amount in a *ledger*. The amount is usually transferred from a journal.

PREEMPTIVE RIGHTS (p. 440). The rights to acquire a pro-rata amount of any new issues of capital stock.

PREFERRED STOCK (p. 442). Stock that has some priority over other shares regarding *dividends* or the distribution of *assets* upon *liquidation*.

PREMIUM ON BONDS (p. 380). The excess of the proceeds over the *face amount*.

PRESENT VALUE (p. 401). The value today of a future cash inflow or outflow.

PRETAX INCOME (p. 141). Income reported for accounting purposes before deduction for income tax.

PRETAX OPERATING RATE OF RETURN ON TOTAL ASSETS (p. 685). *Operating income* divided by average total *assets* available.

PRICE-EARNINGS RATIO (p. 65). The market price per share of *common stock* divided by the *earnings per share* of common stock.

PRIMARY EARNINGS PER SHARE (p. 467). EPS calculated as if all *common stock* equivalents that dilute EPS were converted to common stock.

PRINCIPAL (p. 400). The amount invested, borrowed, or used on which *interest accrues*.

PRIVATE ACCOUNTING (p. 4). The fields of accounting where individuals work for businesses and government agencies, including the Internal Revenue Service. Compare with *public accounting*.

PRIVATE PLACEMENT (p. 377). A process whereby notes are issued by *corporations* when money is borrowed from a few sources, not from the general public.

PROCESSING CONTROLS (p. 637). *Internal accounting controls* relating to the design, programming, and operation of the system. Such controls include separation of duties.

PROFITABILITY EVALUATION (p. 139). The assessment of the likelihood of a particular rate of return on an investment.

PROFITS (p. 40). The excess of *revenues* over *expenses*.

PRO FORMA STATEMENT (p. 673). A carefully formulated expression of predicted results.

PROMISSORY NOTE (p. 371). A written promise to repay *principal* plus *interest* at specific future dates.

PROPRIETORSHIP (p. 15). A separate organization with a single owner.

PROTECTIVE COVENANT (p. 379). See *covenant*.

PUBLIC ACCOUNTING (p. 4). The field of accounting in which practitioners render services to the general public on a fee basis. These accountants are licensed by individual states.

PURCHASE ALLOWANCES (p. 214). The reduction of the selling price received by the buyer; generally, the reduction is below a price previously agreed upon.

PURCHASE METHOD (p. 560). A way of accounting for the acquisition of one company by another; based on the market prices paid for the acquired company's *assets*.

PURCHASE RETURNS (p. 214). See *sales returns*. A customer calls these *purchase returns*.

RATE OF RETURN ON COMMON EQUITY (p. 446). Net income less preferred *dividends* divided by average common equity.

RATE OF RETURN ON STOCKHOLDERS' EQUITY (p. 688). Net income divided by average *stockholders' equity*.

REAL ACCOUNTS (p. 177). Those *accounts* not subject to periodic *closing*, frequently called *permanent accounts* or *balance sheet* accounts.

REAL INTEREST RATE (p. 380). See *effective interest rate*.

RECEIVABLES (p. 220). See *accounts receivable*.

RECOGNITION (p. 43). A test for determining whether *revenues* should be recorded in the financial statements of a given period. To be recognized, revenues must be earned and realized.

REDEMPTION PRICE (p. 445). The *call price*, which is typically 5% to 10% above the *par value* of the *bond* or *stock*.

REGISTERED INSTRUMENT (p. 379). *Bonds* that require the *interest* and maturity payments to be made to specific owners.

REINVESTED EARNINGS (p. 59). See *retained income*.

RELEVANCE (p. 713). The capability of information to make a difference to the decision maker.

RELIABILITY (p. 8). The quality of information that allows users to depend on it to represent the conditions or events that it purports to represent.

REPORT FORMAT (p. 136). A classified *balance sheet* with the *assets* at the top.

REPRESENTATIONAL FAITHFULNESS (p. 713). See *validity*.

RESERVE (p. 464). Has one of three meanings: (1) a restriction of dividend-declaring power as denoted by a specific subdivision of *retained income*, (2) an *offset* to an *asset*, or (3) an estimate of a definite *liability* of indefinite or uncertain amount.

RESERVE FOR DOUBTFUL ACCOUNTS (p. 223). See *allowance for doubtful accounts*.

RESERVE METHOD (p. 222). See *allowance method*.

RESIDUAL VALUE (p. 321). The amount received from disposal of a long-lived asset at the end of its useful life.

RESTRICTED RETAINED INCOME (p. 464). Any part of *retained income* that may not be reduced by *dividend* declarations.

RESULTS OF OPERATIONS (p. 59). See *income statement*.

RETAIL INVENTORY METHOD (p. 645). A procedure for obtaining an inventory valuation for control and for financial statement purposes.

RETAIL METHOD (p. 645). See *retail inventory method*.

RETAINED EARNINGS (p. 59). See *retained income*.

RETAINED INCOME (p. 40). Additional *owners' equity* generated by *profits*.

RETURN ON SALES (p. 681). Net income divided by sales.

RETURN ON STOCKHOLDERS' EQUITY (p. 688). See *rate of return on stockholders' equity*.

RETURN ON TOTAL ASSETS (p. 687). *Income* before *interest expense* divided by average total *assets*.

REVALUATION EQUITY (p. 728). That portion of *stockholders' equity* that shows all accumulated *holding gains* not otherwise shown in *retained income*.

REVENUE EXPENDITURE (p. 335). An *expenditure* with short-term effects expected to benefit only the current accounting year.

REVENUES (p. 40). Generally gross increases in *owners' equity* arising from gross increases in *assets* from the delivery of goods or services to customers.

REVERSING ENTRIES (p. 189). Entries that switch back all *debits* and *credits* made in a related preceding *adjusting entry*.

SALES ALLOWANCE (p. 214). Reductions of the selling price (the original price previously agreed upon).

SALES RETURNS (p. 214). Products returned by the customer.

SALVAGE VALUE (p. 321). See *residual value*.

SCRAP VALUE (p. 321). See *residual value*.

SECURITIES AND EXCHANGE COMMISSION (SEC) (p. 61). The federal agency designated by the U.S. Congress as holding the ultimate responsibility for authorizing the *generally accepted accounting principles* for companies whose stock is held by the general investing public.

SHAREHOLDERS' EQUITY (p. 17). See *stockholders' equity*.

SHORT PRESENTATION (p. 393). An item included in the body of a financial statement, but its amount (if any) is not shown on the face of the *balance sheet*. Used often for *contingent liabilities*.

SHORT-TERM INVESTMENT (p. 533). A temporary investment in *marketable securities* of otherwise idle cash.

SHORT-TERM LIQUIDITY (p. 673). An organization's ability to meet current payments as they become due.

SHRINKAGE (p. 639). See *inventory shrinkage*.

SIMPLE ENTRY (p. 90). An accounting entry that affects only two *accounts*. Contrast with *compound entry*.

SIMPLE INTEREST (p. 400). For any period, *interest* rate multiplied by an unchanging *principal* amount. Also see *compound interest*.

SINGLE-STEP INCOME STATEMENT (p. 137). One that groups all *revenue* together (sales plus *interest* and rent *revenues*) and then lists and deducts all *expenses* together without drawing any intermediate subtotals.

SINKING FUND (p. 380). Cash or securities segregated for meeting obligations on bonded debt.

SINKING FUND BONDS (p. 380). *Bonds* with *indentures* that require the issuer to make annual payments to a *sinking fund*.

SOLVENCY (p. 673). See *long-term solvency*.

SOLVENCY DETERMINATION (p. 134). Assessment of an *entity's* ability to meet its financial obligations as they become due.

SOURCE DOCUMENTS (p. 88). The supporting original records of any *transaction*, internal or external, that occurs in the *entity's* operation. They are memorandums of what happened.

SPECIAL JOURNALS (p. 648). *Journals* used for particular types of voluminous *transactions*. Four widely used special journals are for cash receipts, cash disbursements, credit purchases, and credit sales.

SPECIFIC CHARGE-OFF METHOD (p. 221). See *specific write-off method*.

SPECIFIC IDENTIFICATION (p. 265). This inventory method concentrates on the physical tracing of the particular items sold.

SPECIFIC PRICE INDEX (p. 729). An index used to approximate the *current costs* of particular *assets* or types of assets.

SPECIFIC WRITE-OFF METHOD (p. 221). This method of accounting for *bad debt* losses assumes all sales are fully collectible until proved otherwise.

STATED INTEREST RATE (p. 377). See *nominal interest rate*.

STATED VALUE (p. 17). A nominal value of a *stock certificate* that is usually far below the actual cash invested. See *par value*.

STATEMENT OF CASH FLOWS (p. 491). A required statement that reports the cash receipts and cash payments of an *entity* during a period.

STATEMENT OF EARNINGS (p. 59). See *income statement*.

STATEMENT OF FINANCIAL CONDITION (p. 6). A synonym for *balance sheet*.

STATEMENT OF FINANCIAL POSITION (p. 6). A substitute term for *balance sheet*.

STATEMENT OF INCOME (p. 46). See *income statement*.

STATEMENT OF OPERATIONS (p. 46). See *income statement*.

STATEMENT OF PROFIT AND LOSS (p. 46). See *income statement*.

STATEMENT OF RETAINED INCOME (p. 52). A statement that lists the beginning *balance* of *retained income*, followed by a description of any changes, and the ending *balance*.

STATEMENT OF REVENUES AND EXPENSES (p. 59). See *income statement*.

STOCK CERTIFICATE (p. 16). Formal evidence of ownership shares in a *corporation*.

STOCK DIVIDEND (p. 454). A distribution to stockholders of additional shares of any class of the distributing company's stock, without any payment to the company by the stockholders.

STOCKHOLDERS' EQUITY (p. 17). *Owners' equity* of a *corporation*. The excess of *assets* over *liabilities* of a corporation.

STOCK OPTION (p. 464). Special rights usually granted to executives to purchase a *corporation's* capital stock.

STOCK SPLIT (p. 451). Issuance of additional shares for no payments by stockholders, and under conditions indicating that the objective is to increase the number of outstanding shares for the purpose of reducing the unit market price, in order to bring the stock price down into a more popular range.

STRAIGHT-LINE DEPRECIATION (p. 322). A method that spreads the *depreciable value* evenly over the useful life of an *asset*.

SUBORDINATED DEBENTURE (p. 378). *Bonds* that are junior to the other general creditors in the exercise of claims against the total *assets*.

SUBSIDIARY (p. 540). A *corporation* owned or controlled by a parent company, through the ownership of more than 50% of the voting stock.

SUBSIDIARY LEDGER (p. 101). A supporting *ledger* that provides details for a specific *account* in the *general ledger*.

SUM-OF-THE-YEARS'-DIGITS DEPRECIATION (SYD) (p. 324). A popular form of *accelerated depreciation* where the sum of the digits is the total of the numbers representing the years of life.

T-ACCOUNT (p. 82). A *ledger account* that takes the form of the capital letter *T*. It is useful for discussion and learning, but too informal for using in actual books of account.

TANGIBLE ASSETS (p. 319). See *fixed assets*.

TAX ALLOCATION (p. 592). See *interperiod tax allocation*.

TAX CREDIT (p. 586). Direct reductions in a company's income taxes.

TEMPORARY ACCOUNTS (p. 177). See *nominal accounts*.

TEMPORARY DIFFERENCE (p. 589). A situation that arises whenever the book value of an asset for shareholder reporting differs from the book value for tax reporting.

TERMINAL VALUE (p. 321). See *residual value*.

TIME-SERIES COMPARISONS (p. 679). Comparison of a company's financial ratios with its own historical ratios.

TIMES INTEREST EARNED (p. 690). See *interest coverage*.

TOTAL ASSET TURNOVER (p. 685). Sales divided by average total *assets* available.

TRADE ACCOUNTS PAYABLE (p. 371). Obligations resulting from purchasing goods and services on credit.

TRADE DISCOUNTS (p. 215). Those discounts that are based on some larger selling price (list price) and apply a reduction thereto to arrive at the real selling price (invoice price).

TRADEMARKS (p. 341). Distinctive identifications of a manufactured product or of a service taking the form of a name, a sign, a slogan, a logo, or an emblem.

TRADE RECEIVABLES (p. 220). See *accounts receivable*.

TRADING ON THE EQUITY (p. 687). Using borrowed money at fixed *interest* rates with the objective of enhancing the *rate of return on common equity*.

TRANSACTION (p. 8). Any event that both affects the financial position of an *entity* and can be reliably recorded in money terms.

TREASURY STOCK (p. 441). A *corporation's* issued stock that has subsequently been repurchased by the company and not retired.

TRIAL BALANCE (p. 100). A list of all *accounts* with their *balances*.

TRUE INTEREST RATE (p. 380). See *effective interest rate*.

TRUST INDENTURE (p. 379). A contract whereby the issuing *corporation* of a *bond* promises a trustee that it will abide by stated provisions.

UNDERWRITERS (p. 380). A group of investment bankers that buys an entire *bond* or stock issue from a *corporation* and then sells the bonds to the general investment public.

UNEARNED INCOME (p. 126). See *unearned revenue*.

UNEARNED REVENUE (p. 125). *Revenue* received or recorded before it is earned.

UNEXPIRED COSTS (p. 48). Any *expenditures* benefiting the future; any *asset*, including prepaid *expenses*, normally appearing on a *balance sheet*.

UNIT DEPRECIATION (p. 323). A method based on units of service when physical wear and tear is the dominating influence on the useful life of the *asset*.

UNLIMITED LIABILITY (p. 444). Legal responsibility not limited by law or contract; personal *assets* can be seized to satisfy corporate debts.

UNREGISTERED INSTRUMENT (p. 379). *Bonds* generally issued by American governmental bodies and requiring *interest* to be paid to the individual who presents the *interest* coupons attached to the bond.

UNSUBORDINATED DEBENTURES (p. 378). *Bonds* unsecured by the pledge of specific property. The holders of such bonds have the same general priority as ordinary creditors, such as those reflected in *accounts payable*.

VALIDITY (p. 713). A correspondence between the accounting numbers and the resources or events those numbers purport to represent.

VERIFIABILITY (p. 102). See *objectivity*.

VOUCHER (p. 656). A form that verifies a *transaction* and authorizes the writing of a check. Sometimes called a *disbursement voucher*.

VOUCHER REGISTER (p. 656). A *special journal* that is a central part of a *voucher system*.

VOUCHER SYSTEM (p. 656). A system for controlling cash disbursements.

WEIGHTED-AVERAGE COST (p. 267). An average that is affected by the relative number of items and their unit prices rather than just their unit prices alone.

WORKING CAPITAL (p. 135). The excess of *current assets* over *current liabilities*.

WORKING CAPITAL RATIO (p. 135). See *current ratio*.

WORKING PAPER (p. 182). See *work sheet*.

WORK SHEET (p. 182). A columnar approach to moving from a *trial balance* to the finished financial statements. Also called *working paper*. In auditing, the term *working papers* has a broader meaning. It refers to all schedules, analyses, memoranda, and so on, prepared by an auditor while making an examination.

YIELD RATE (p. 380). See *effective interest rate*.

Index